The American Drug Scene

Readings in a Global Context

Seventh Edition

James A. Inciardi
University of Delaware

Karen McElrath
Fayetteville State University

New York   Oxford
OXFORD UNIVERSITY PRESS

Oxford University Press is a department of the University of Oxford.
It furthers the University's objective of excellence in research, scholarship,
and education by publishing worldwide.

Oxford   New York
Auckland   Cape Town   Dar es Salaam   Hong Kong   Karachi
Kuala Lumpur   Madrid   Melbourne   Mexico City   Nairobi
New Delhi   Shanghai   Taipei   Toronto

With offices in
Argentina   Austria   Brazil   Chile   Czech Republic   France   Greece
Guatemala   Hungary   Italy   Japan   Poland   Portugal   Singapore
South Korea   Switzerland   Thailand   Turkey   Ukraine   Vietnam

Published in the United States of America by
Oxford University Press
198 Madison Avenue, New York, NY 10016
http://www.oup.com

Library of Congress Cataloging-in-Publication Data

The American drug scene : readings in a global context / [edited by] James A. Inciardi,
University of Delaware, Karen McElrath, Fayetteville State University. -- Seventh edition.
        pages cm
    Summary: "Now in its seventh edition, The American Drug Scene, edited by
James A. Inciardi and Karen McElrath, is a collection of contemporary and classic articles
on the changing patterns, problems, perspectives, and policies of legal and illicit drug use.
Offering a unique focus on the social contexts in which drug usage, drug-related problems,
and drug policies occur, it presents theoretical and descriptive material drawn from both
ethnographic and quantitative sources"-- Provided by publisher.
    Includes bibliographical references and index.
    ISBN 978-0-19-936208-0 (paperback)
    1. Drug abuse--United States. I. Inciardi, James A. II. McElrath, Karen, 1959-
    HV5825.A696 2015
    362.29'120973--dc23
                                                            2014017178

Printing number: 9 8 7 6 5 4 3 2 1

Printed in the United States of America
on acid-free paper

The sixth and seventh editions of The American Drug Scene *are dedicated to Jim Inciardi, who passed away on November 23, 2009. He battled cancer with courage and dignity, and continued to work until a month before he died. Jim understood the true spirit of mentoring and many of us are grateful for his long-standing support. His many contributions to the drug field have shaped drug prevention and treatment initiatives, as well as policy and the work of other scholars. I remember him for his kindness, generosity, and great knowledge. A giant in the field, he will be missed tremendously by friends, coworkers, and most of all by Hilary, his spouse, friend, and coauthor.*

—Karen McElrath

CONTENTS

Note: New or revised articles/chapters are indicated with an asterisk.

The *American Drug Scene*, seventh edition, is a collection of both classic and contemporary essays and articles on the changing patterns, problems, perspectives, and policies related to both legal and illicit drug use in diverse settings. The articles and the section introductions illustrate the complex and changing nature of drug use, interventions, and policy. The majority of the thirty-nine articles are new.

This reader is organized into thirteen sections beginning with historical perspectives of drug use, images and portrayals of people who use drugs, and patterns of drug taking (Parts I through IV). Part V is entitled "Power, Privilege, and Drug Use" and here we attempt to deconstruct the perceptions around drug use among social groups. In Part VI we feature articles on subcultures, social networks, and drug scenes. People who use drugs often engage in particular practices and behaviors that are linked to drug taking; rituals and drug-use practices are the focus in Part VII.

Articles on drug markets are included in Part VIII, and the essays were selected to encourage readers to think more broadly about the concept of the drug market. In the United States and elsewhere, people who use drugs are increasingly subjected to surveillance, and Part IX includes readings on this topic. Drug prevention and treatment are the subject of Part X, and we devote Part XI to harm reduction initiatives. In Part XII, we address drug use and street crime, and the response by the criminal justice system. We include readings on sentencing reform as well as mass incarceration that is envisioned as the new Jim Crow. The final section (Part XIII) focuses on domestic and foreign drug policies.

One of the many strengths of *The American Drug Scene*, seventh edition, is the inclusion of readings and commentary that pertain to drug use or drug policy in other countries. As a behavior, drug use is a local phenomenon, but it is increasingly shaped by the global diffusion of information, supply, and response. The international dimension to this edition is intended to encourage readers to draw comparisons, and to think about drug use and policy beyond the geographic boundaries of the United States. We hope that readers find the material interesting, stimulating, and instructive.

New to the Seventh Edition

A new organization, reflecting a thematic focus

- New sections, including "Stages of Drug Use," "Power, Privilege, and Drug Use," "Social Control and Surveillance," "Drug Prevention and Treatment," and "Harm Reduction"
- New section introductions
- A revised general introduction
- Thirty-two new articles and one revised article
- A new focus on drug use and policies in countries outside of the U.S.

Acknowledgments

We thank Sherith Pankratz, Katy Albis, and the rest of the team at Oxford University Press for editorial support. We are grateful for the production assistance from Diane Kohnen and the team at S4Carlisle Publishing Services. We would also like to thank Elizabeth Bortka for her skillful copyediting. We also acknowledge the very helpful comments and suggestions from the following reviewers:

Doug Goldsmith, John Jay College of Criminal Justice

Andrea Leverentz, University of Massachusetts Boston

Catherine Marrone, Stony Brook University

Amanda Reiman, University of California, Berkeley

Judy Rosovsky, Johnson State College

James A. Inciardi (1939–2009)
University of Delaware
Karen McElrath
Fayetteville State University

James A. Inciardi, Ph.D. (1939–2009), was director of the Center for Drug and Alcohol Studies at the University of Delaware; professor in the Department of Sociology and Criminal Justice at Delaware; adjunct professor in the Department of Epidemiology and Public Health at the University of Miami School of Medicine; and a guest professor in the Department of Psychiatry at the Federal University of Rio Grande do Sul in Porto Alegre, Brazil. Jim was also a recipient of a Merit Award from the National Institutes of Health and the author or editor of more than 500 articles, chapters, and books in the areas of substance abuse, criminology, criminal justice, history, folklore, public policy, HIV/AIDS, medicine, and law.

Karen McElrath, Ph.D., is a professor in the Department of Criminal Justice at Fayetteville State University. Although her roots are in the United States, Karen spent seventeen years living in Ireland, where she worked in the School of Sociology, Social Policy, and Social Work at Queen's University, Belfast. While in Ireland, Karen learned about drug interventions and policies of several western European countries and that experience helped shape some of the changes that are reflected in this edition of *The American Drug Scene*. Karen's research has focused on people who use heroin, people who use MDMA, and more recently, people who use novel psychoactive substances. Her work attempts to highlight the voice of the user. Her current research interests include (1) methadone as social control, (2) transitions to and from prescription drug misuse, and (3) the role of Big Pharma in producing and maintaining illicit drug markets.

Ernest L. Abel is professor in the School of Medicine at Wayne State University.

Michelle Alexander is associate professor of law at Ohio State University.

Harry J. Anslinger (1892–1975) was the first US Commissioner of Narcotics and presided over the Federal Bureau of Narcotics from 1930 to 1962.

Edward G. Armstrong is an assistant professor in the Department of Sociology and Anthropology at St. Cloud State University.

Elizabeth M. Armstrong is associate professor of sociology and public affairs at Princeton University.

Masuma Bahora is a Ph.D. student in the Rollins School of Public Health, Emory University.

J. Ross Barnett is a professor in the Department of Geography at the University of Canterbury, New Zealand.

Monica J. Barratt is a research fellow at the National Drug Research Institute, Curtin University, Australia.

Howard S. Becker is an internationally renowned sociologist with major contributions to the study of deviance, field methods, and visual sociology.

Kirsten Bell is a research associate in the Department of Anthropology at the University of British Columbia.

Brian Bishop is associate professor in the School of Psychology and Speech Pathology at Curtin University, Australia.

Miriam W. Boeri is a lecturer in sociology at Bentley University.

J. Michael Bostwick is a professor in the Department of Psychiatry and Psychology, Mayo Clinic.

Stephen J. Bright is a psychologist and coordinator of Addiction Studies at Curtin University, Australia.

John J. Casey is president and managing partner at Evans Hagen and Company.

Courtney Ryley Cooper (1886–1940) was a journalist and author of such "true crime" classics as *Ten Thousand Public Enemies* (1935), *Here's to Crime* (1937), and *Designs in Scarlet* (1939).

David T. Courtwright is a distinguished professor in history at the University of North Florida.

Melissa DiThomas is a product manager at First Advantage.

Micheline Duterte is a research associate with the Institute for Scientific Analysis, San Francisco.

Kirk Elifson is professor emeritus in the Department of Sociology, Georgia State University.

Laura L. Finley is assistant professor in the Department of Sociology and Criminology at Barry University.

Laurence Armand French is a senior associate at Justiceworks, University of New Hampshire.

Mindy Thompson Fullilove is professor of clinical psychiatry at Columbia University.

Robert E. Fullilove is an associate dean for Community and Minority Affairs, and professor of clinical sociomedical sciences at Columbia University.

David Gibson is a research assistant and student at Kennesaw State University.

Kara Gotsch is the director of national programs for the National Coalition to Abolish the Death Penalty.

Lesley L. Green is vice president of social services for the Abyssinian Development Corporation in New York.

Peter Hakim is president emeritus of Inter-American Dialogue.

Laura Hanson is a Ph.D. student in the School of Social Policy, Sociology and Social Research, University of Kent, England.

Liam Harbry is the executive director of the DeKalb County Drug Court in Atlanta.

Julie Harris is a Ph.D. student in the School of Sociology, Social Policy and Social Work, Queen's University, Belfast.

James A. Inciardi. See "About the Editors."

Camille Jacinto is a research associate with the Institute for Scientific Analysis, San Francisco.

Curtis Jackson-Jacobs is a visiting assistant professor at the University of Illinois at Chicago.

Robert Kane is a senior lecturer in the School of Psychology and Speech Pathology at Curtin University, Australia.

Steven P. Kurtz is a professor and director of the Center for Applied Research on Substance Use and Health Disparities, Nova Southeastern University.

Jo Lindsay is professor of sociology and gender studies in the School of Political and Social Inquiry, Monash University, Australia.

Travis Linnemann is an assistant professor in the Department of Sociology and Criminal Justice at Old Dominion University.

Ali Marsh is a lecturer in the School of Psychology and Speech Pathology at Curtin University, Australia.

Karen McElrath. See "About the Editors."

Katherine McLean participated in the Behavioral Sciences Training Program, National Development and Research Institutes, and completed her Ph.D. in sociology in 2013.

Julien Mercille is a lecturer in the School of Geography, Planning, and Environmental Policy, University College Dublin, Ireland.

Heather Z. Mui is a research analyst at the Institute for Scientific Analysis, and a research assistant at Davis Y. Ja & Associates in San Francisco.

Sheigla Murphy is a senior scientist at the Institute for Scientific Analysis in San Francisco.

Jamie Pearce is professor in the School of GeoSciences, University of Edinburgh, Scotland.

Robert L. Peralta is associate professor is the Department of Sociology at the University of Akron.

Gretchen Peters conducts research in support of the US Department of Defense and is an affiliate instructor in the Terrorism, Transnational Crime, and Corruption Center at George Mason University.

Gary Potter is a senior lecturer in the Department of Social Sciences at London South Bank University, England.

Edward Preble (deceased 1982) was an anthropologist and ethnographer with Manhattan State Hospital and spent much of his career conducting street studies of the drug scenes in New York City.

Amanda Reiman is a lecturer in the School of Social Welfare, University of California, Berkeley.

Marsha Rosenbaum is director emerita of the Drug Policy Alliance in San Francisco.

Paloma Sales is a project director at the Institute for Scientific Analysis in San Francisco.

Amy Salmon is a clinical assistant professor in the School of Population and Public Health at the University of British Columbia.

Claire E. Sterk is the provost and executive vice president for academic affairs and Charles Howard Candler Professor of Public Health at Emory University.

Hilary L. Surratt is a professor in the Division of Applied Interdisciplinary Studies at Nova Southeastern University.

Angela Taylor is an associate professor in the Department of Criminal Justice at Fayetteville State University.

Matthew Taylor is a Ph.D. student in criminology at the University of Kent, England.

Lee Thompson is a senior lecturer in the Department of Public Health and General Practice, University of Otago, New Zealand.

Marie Claire Van Hout is a lecturer in the Department of Health Sciences, Health, Sport, and Exercise Science at Waterford Institute of Technology, Ireland.

Matthew D. Varga is an assistant professor of counselor education at the University of West Georgia.

Andrew Weil is a professor of medicine and public health, and founder and director of the Arizona Center for Integrative Medicine, University of Arizona.

L. Susan Williams is associate professor in the Department of Sociology, Anthropology, and Social Work at Kansas State University.

Conceptual Discussion of Drugs and Drug Use

The American drug scene has a long and enduring history. To begin with, the drinking of alcohol to excess is centuries old. In *The Life and Times of the Late Demon Rum*, the celebrated American social historian and biographer, J. C. Furnas, suggests that alcohol came to colonial America with the first English and Dutch settlers and that the drinking of "spirits" and "strong waters" was prevalent since the first days of the emerging American republic. Traditional beliefs held that rum, gin, and brandy were nutritious and healthful. Distilled spirits were viewed as foods that supplemented limited and monotonous diets; as medications that could cure colds, fevers, snakebites, and broken legs; and as means of relaxation that would relieve depression, reduce tension, and enable hardworking laborers to enjoy a moment of happy, frivolous camaraderie. Alcohol use was embedded in the social fabric of colonial America. Moreover, it was often used as a substitute for fresh water due to frequent contamination of the latter. By the early 1700s, most men and women of every social class drank alcoholic beverages in quantity, although intoxication was viewed less favorably. By the end of the eighteenth century, the daily per capita drinking of Americans was almost a half pint of hard liquor. Alcohol consumption began to decline somewhat in the early- to mid-1800s (in part due to the influence of temperance movements); however, consumption increased during the American Civil War.

The use of other drugs for the enhancement of pleasure and performance or for the alteration of mood also has a long history. Opium was a popular substance for thousands of years. It derives from the opium poppy (*Papaver somniferum* L.) and was known as the "plant of joy" some 4,000 years ago in

parts of Mesopotamia. In the early 1700s, Thomas Dover developed a form of medicinal opium that was sold as Dover's Powder. Introduced in England in 1709 and in the colonies several years later, it contained one ounce each of opium, ipecac (the dried roots of a tropical creeping plant), and licorice, combined with saltpeter, tartar, and wine. The attraction of Dover's Powder was in the euphoric and anesthetic properties of opium. The introduction of Dover's Powder in the American colonies apparently started a trend. By the latter part of the eighteenth century, medications containing opium were readily available in urban and rural areas. These medications were sold over the counter in grocery and general stores, at traveling medicine shows, and through the mail. In addition to Dover's Powder, they were marketed under such labels as Ayer's Cherry Pectoral, Mrs. Winslow's Soothing Syrup, McMunn's Elixir, Godfrey's Cordial, and Scott's Emulsion. Many of these remedies were seductively advertised as "painkillers," "cough mixtures," "soothing syrups," "consumption cures," and "women's friends." Others were promoted for the treatment of such varied ailments as diarrhea, dysentery, colds, fever, teething, cholera, rheumatism, pelvic disorders, athlete's foot, and even baldness. The drugs were produced not only from imported opium but also from white opium poppies that were being legally grown in the New England states, Florida and Louisiana, the West and Southwest, and the Confederate States of America during the Civil War.

For thousands of years, opium had been the only known product of *Papaver somniferum* L. (the botanical name for the opium poppy). In 1803, however, a young German pharmacist, Frederick Serturner, isolated the chief alkaloid of opium.

Serturner had hit upon morphine, which he named after Morpheus, the Greek god of dreams. The discovery had profound effects on both medicine and society, and to date, morphine is the single greatest pain reliever the world has ever known. Alexander Wood was a physician in Edinburgh (Scotland) who is often credited with inventing the hypodermic syringe in 1853. His wife later died as a result of accidental morphine overdose after self-injection. The use of morphine by injection in military medicine during the American Civil War and the Franco-Prussian War granted the procedure legitimacy and familiarity to both physicians and the public. Furthermore, hypodermic medication had its pragmatic aspects—it brought quick local relief, its dosage could be regulated, and it was effective when oral medication was impractical. The regimen, however, was used promiscuously, for many physicians were anxious to illustrate their ability to quell the pain suffered by their patients, who, in turn, expected instant relief from discomfort.

By the close of the nineteenth century, it was estimated that millions of Americans were addicted to over-the-counter medications. Although historical evidence is limited, women—particularly those from middle- and upper-income backgrounds—were believed to outnumber men among people who were addicted to opioids. Interestingly, England experienced a similar pattern, that is, patterns of addiction that were shaped by gender and social class. Indeed, in the late 1800s, it was far more socially acceptable for women to consume opioids than to drink alcohol.

The over-the-counter medicine industry expanded even further to include cocaine and heroin, beginning in the late-1800s. Coca products as well as cocaine were used as medicines and folk remedies to address a variety of ailments. Agitation had begun for controls over the manufacture and distribution of products containing cocaine, opium, and their various derivatives. One result was the passage of the Pure Food and Drug Act in 1906, which prohibited the interstate transportation of adulterated or misbranded food and drugs. The act brought about the decline of over-the-counter medications because the proportions of alcohol, opium, morphine, heroin, cocaine, and a number of other substances in each preparation now had to be indicated. As a result, most of the remedies lost their appeal.

The Pure Food and Drug Act merely imposed standards for quality, packaging, and labeling; it did not actually outlaw the use of cocaine and opiate drugs. Public Law No. 47, 63rd Congress (H.R. 1967), more popularly known as the Harrison Act, sponsored by New York Representative Francis Burton Harrison and passed in 1914, ultimately served that purpose. At the same time, the new legislation went a long way toward altering public and criminal justice responses to drug use in the United States for generations to come. The Harrison Act required all people who imported, manufactured, produced, compounded, sold, dispensed, or otherwise distributed cocaine and opiate drugs to register with the Treasury Department, pay special taxes, and keep records of all transactions. As such, it was a revenue code designed to exercise some measure of public control over drugs, rather than to penalize all the users of narcotics in the United States. In effect, however, criminalization is specifically what occurred. Although subcultures and criminal cultures of drug users already existed prior to the passage of the Harrison Act, the legislation served to expand their membership. Since then, US policy has viewed drug use as a social as well as a criminal problem.

Despite the change from legal to illegal status of several psychoactive drugs in the United States, various substances continue to be explored or used regularly by large numbers of people. Some of these drugs have been used by humans for hundreds if not thousands of years. Other substances have disappeared for the most part, although the cyclical nature of "drugs of choice" suggests that they might re-surface in the future. This edition of *The American Drug Scene* includes thirteen sections that address drug use, the social context of consumption, and the social and political response to individuals who are engaged in drug taking. Additionally, this edition includes several articles that address drug use in other regions of the world. Drug use is a global phenomenon in that it occurs to some extent and in some form in every part of the world. Moreover, we live in an increasingly globally connected world which has implications for the diffusion of drug use in terms of distribution, access, and users' experiences. The content in these additional articles makes for interesting comparisons with drug scenes and drug policy in the United States.

Before proceeding with this material, however, it is important that readers have some understanding of drug-related concepts—the meanings of which are often taken for granted and debated. As such, this introduction closes with a short glossary of concepts that we feel are most important. We also provide the federal schedules associated with the US Controlled Substances Act.

Selected Drug Groups and Categories

Drugs: any natural or artificial substances (aside from food) that by their chemical nature alter the functioning of the body.

Psychoactive drugs: drugs that alter perception and consciousness, including analgesics, depressants, stimulants, hallucinogens, and empathogens. The word "psychoactive" refers to "mind-altering."

"Hard drugs" and "soft drugs": Although these terms are used widely, their meanings are socially constructed. That is, the way that we perceive "hard" and "soft" drugs and the meanings we attach to these terms depends on the culture and era in which we live, and the cultural and historical discourse that takes prominence in societies. For example, substances that are often viewed as "hard drugs" in the United States (and elsewhere) are not necessarily more physically harmful than substances perceived to be "soft drugs."

Analgesics: drugs used for the relief of various degrees of pain without rendering the user unconscious. There are both narcotic and nonnarcotic varieties of analgesics.

Depressants: drugs that act on and lessen the activity of the central nervous system (CNS), diminishing or stopping vital functions.

Empathogens: drugs that increase feelings of social connectedness or empathy towards others. 3,4-Methylenedioxymethamphetamine (MDMA, Ecstasy) is an empathogen but one with stimulant properties.

Hallucinogens: drugs that act on the CNS, producing mood and perceptual changes varying from sensory illusions to hallucinations. Sometimes referred to as "psychedelics," hallucinogenic drugs include LSD, PCP, and psilocybin. Cannabis and marijuana can effect changes in mood, but they generally do not produce visual or auditory hallucinations.

Hypnotics: CNS depressant drugs that produce sleep. Barbiturates are hypnotics but in several developed nations, barbiturates have been replaced by benzodiazepines.

Narcotic: opioids (including synthetic opioids such as methadone) or morphine-like substances.

Sedatives: CNS depressant drugs that produce calm and relaxation. Alcohol and benzodiazepines are examples of sedative drugs, although benzodiazepines have both sedative and hypnotic properties.

Stimulants: drugs that stimulate the central nervous system and increase the activity of the brain and spinal cord. Caffeine, amphetamine (including methamphetamine), and cocaine are examples of CNS stimulant drugs. Several new synthetic stimulants have emerged in recent years, including mephedrone and MDPV ("bath salts").

Terms Relating to Consumption and Dependence

Detoxification: a process by which the toxins associated with physical dependence are cleared from the body during withdrawal. Detoxification is often overseen by medical professionals, although a number of individuals have engaged in self-detoxification. Detoxification is not drug treatment, but it can be viewed as an important step on the road to recovery.

Drug addiction: the definition of drug addiction has been debated for over 100 years. It is sometimes defined as an intense preoccupation with using a psychoactive substance. It generally involves psychological or physical cravings for a substance that are difficult to control.

Drug dependence: a condition with identifiable physical symptoms (withdrawal symptoms) that emerge when a drug is abruptly withdrawn. Drug dependence suggests tolerance and intense cravings for the drug. Alcohol, opioids, and benzodiazepines can produce drug dependence. Individuals who experience alcohol or benzodiazepine dependency and aim to undergo detoxification need to be monitored closely by health professionals to prevent fatality. The terms *addiction* and *dependence* are sometimes used interchangeably.

Drug use, abuse, and misuse: *drug use* is a broad term that refers to the consumption of psychoactive drugs, regardless of their legal status. However, it is often differentiated from alcohol use, even though alcohol is a psychoactive drug, because it alters the way we think and the way we perceive things. Conceptually, *drug abuse* is more contentious. In the United States, drug abuse often refers to drug use that creates health, social, or legal problems for individuals engaged in drug use. However, some commentators refer to all drug use as drug abuse. In contrast, the term *drug abuse* is rejected by some people who view it as too judgmental. The term is used less often in western Europe, where researchers and drug service/treatment professionals often prefer the term *problem drug use*. In the United States, *drug misuse* generally refers to the use of prescription drugs for purposes other than what they are intended. In several European countries, *drug misuse* refers to either drug use in general, or problem drug use. In summary, defining these terms is fraught with difficulty, and there is a lack of consensus about their meanings—particularly when we explore these concepts across cultures.

Poly-drug use: the use of two or more psychoactive substances. *Simultaneous poly-drug use* refers to the consumption of two or more psychoactive substances during the same drug episode, and an episode can extend for several hours.

Recreational drug use/recreational drugs: drug use as part of social leisure or pleasure, often described in contrast to problem drug use. These terms are also socially constructed and are more widely used in Europe, Australia, and New Zealand—less so in the United States.

Tolerance: a state of acquired resistance to some or all of the effects of a drug. Tolerance develops after the repeated use of certain drugs, resulting in a need to increase the dosage in order to experience the original effects of the drug. Not all psychoactive drugs produce tolerance.

Withdrawal: a series of reactions that result during the abrupt cessation of a drug on which the user's body is dependent.

Drug Reactions

Antagonism: a situation in which two drugs taken together have opposite effects on the body. An antagonistic reaction can be expressed mathematically as $1 + 1 = 0$; it typically occurs with certain mixtures of depressants and stimulants. Combining alcohol and MDMA can produce antagonism in that alcohol use has the potential to reduce the effects of MDMA. Additionally, both substances can dehydrate.

Potentiation: the ability of one drug to increase the activity of another drug when the two are taken simultaneously. Potentiation can be expressed mathematically as $a + b = A$. For example, aspirin (a) plus caffeine (b) increases the potency of the aspirin (A).

Synergism: similar to potentiation, a situation in which two or more drugs are taken together and the combined action dramatically increases the normal effects of each drug. A synergistic effect can be expressed mathematically as $1 + 1 = 5$; it typically occurs with mixtures of alcohol and benzodiazepine.

Routes of Drug Administration

Anal: absorbed through rectal tissues.

Cutaneous: absorbed through the skin.

Injecting: generally means injecting into a vein, but it can also refer to injecting more generally.

Insufflation (inhalation): drawn into the lungs through the nose or mouth, e.g., "snorting," "sniffing," "tooting," inhaling.

Intramuscular: injecting into the muscle. Anabolic steroids are often injected into a muscle rather than a vein.

Intravenous: injecting into the vein.

Oral: swallowed and absorbed through the stomach.

Subcutaneous: inserted under the skin.

Sublingual: absorbed through the tissues under the tongue.

Vaginal: absorbed through vaginal tissues.

Drug Schedules Under the Controlled Substances Act

The Comprehensive Drug Abuse and Control Act of 1970 brought together under one law most of the federal drug control legislation that had been enacted since the early part of the nineteenth century. Title II of the law, known as the Controlled Substances Act, categorized certain substances into five "schedules" and defined the offenses and penalties associated with the illegal manufacture, distribution, dispensation, and possession of any drug in each schedule.

Readers might wish to think critically about why some drugs are categorized as Schedule I and others are categorized elsewhere.

Schedule I includes drugs with a "high potential for abuse," with no currently accepted medical use in the United States. Moreover, Schedule I drugs lack an accepted level of safety when used under medical supervision. Schedule I includes approximately 150 substances, including heroin, lysergic acid diethylamide (LSD), marijuana (cannabis), peyote, and 3,4-methylenedioxymethamphetamine ("Ecstasy"). At the time of this writing (December 2013), the federal scheduling does not differentiate between marijuana used for medical and nonmedical purposes. Federal penalties for selling less than 50 kilograms of marijuana could result in a five-year prison sentence. The penalty is doubled when sold to a minor.

Schedule II includes drugs that are used for medical treatment in the United States but also have a "high potential for abuse." Schedule II drugs include several opioids (e.g., hydrocodone, morphine, methadone), certain amphetamines (Dexedrine, Adderall), methamphetamine, methylphenidate (Ritalin), and some precursors that have been used to produce methamphetamine.

Schedule III includes drugs that are classified as having a "potential for abuse" less than those in Schedules I and II, that are currently accepted for medical use in the United States, and that may lead to moderate or low physical dependence or high psychological dependence. Examples of Schedule III drugs include anabolic steroids, ketamine, and small amounts of some opioids.

Schedule IV includes drugs that are perceived to have a "low potential for abuse" and are currently accepted for medical use in the United States. If used inappropriately, these drugs could lead to limited physical or psychological dependence. Examples of Schedule IV drugs include a number of benzodiazepines, e.g., Valium, Xanax.

Schedule V includes a small number of drugs that have a potential for dependence lower that those listed in Schedule IV. Examples of Schedule V drugs are those that contain limited quantities of some opioids, such as dihydrocodeine and codeine cough syrup.

Reference

Furnas, J. C. 1965. *The Life and Times of the Late Demon Rum*. New York: Putnam.

Historical Perspectives and Images of Drug Use and Addiction

Historical contexts are always important for understanding contemporary issues. In the introductory section to this book, we provided a brief history of psychoactive drug use in the United States, and the three articles in Part I expand on those points. Additionally, prejudicial attitudes toward racial and ethnic minorities have influenced a number of drug control strategies.

The late David Musto was a historian and scientist who offered several historical accounts of drug use and described repressive policies that were aimed at minority groups (1973). For example, in the 1920s, some Mexican immigrants grew and used marijuana for relaxation and entertainment. During the same era, government discourse over marijuana began to fuel public fear about the drug. Politicians and news media began to allege that there were strong links between marijuana use and various forms of violence—and people of Mexican descent were often targeted because of these alleged links. Moreover, the economic depression of the 1930s added to these repressive views. Similar to immigrant groups in other eras, several people of Mexican descent in the United States worked in low-paying jobs and were blamed for taking jobs away from "real" Americans (Musto 1972).

Similar views were held about people of Chinese descent. Encouraged by the gold rush, some 30,000 Chinese immigrated from Hong Kong to San Francisco in 1852, and worked in mines and on railroads. These immigrants were "racially abused, cheated of their earnings and considered of little importance" (Booth 1997, 178–179). Opium dens surfaced in some Chinese communities in the United States and became portrayed as venues known for other acts of "immorality." Booth (1997, 195) noted the description by a physician in San Francisco who visited one such opium den, who mentioned the

> sickening sight of young white girls from sixteen to twenty years of age lying half-dressed on the floor or couches, smoking with their lovers. Men and women, Chinese and white people, mix in China-town smoking houses.

These views were not restricted to the United States. During the 1880s, several Canadians perceived opium smoking to be depraved and associated with persons of Chinese descent. The Royal Commission on Chinese Immigration (1885) focused on several issues pertaining to the Chinese community and also investigated whether Chinese communities in Canada were contributing to the corruption of whites, and white women in particular. Chan (2011) described the Asiatic Exclusion League that operated in Toronto in the early 1900s. The League voiced several concerns, including the corruption of white women by people of Chinese descent who were involved in the opium trade. Chan reports that in 1907, the Asiatic Exclusion League destroyed several homes and businesses

that were occupied by people of Chinese descent. The League then targeted the homes of people with Japanese ancestry. In Australia, the Royal Commission on Alleged Chinese Gambling and Immorality investigated opium smoking and dens. The evidence gathered included questions that focused on "race mixing" between Chinese and whites, such as "Did you ever find any young girls in bed with the Chinese?" (1892, n343). All of these illustrations reflect what Musto (1991, 41) described as an important historical theme in perceptions about drugs: "linkage between a drug and a feared or rejected group in society."

References

Booth, M. 1997. *Opium: A History*. London: Pocket Books.

Chan, A. 2011. *The Chinese in Toronto from 1878: From Outside to Inside the Circle*. Toronto: Dundurn Press.

Musto, D. F. 1972. "The History of the Marihuana Tax Act of 1937." *Archives of General Psychiatry* 26: 101–108.

———. 1973. *The American Disease: Origins of Narcotic Control*. New Haven, CT: Yale University Press.

Report of the Royal Commission on Alleged Chinese Gambling and Immorality. 1892. Sydney: Charles Potter, Government Printer.

Report of the Royal Commission on Chinese Immigration: Report and Evidence. 1885. Ottawa: Author.

I

The Evolution of Drug Taking and Drug Seeking in America

JAMES A. INCIARDI AND KAREN MCELRATH

If anything has been learned about drug taking in the United States, it is that patterns of psychoactive drug use are continually shifting and changing. Drugs of choice emerge, disappear, and sometimes re-emerge much later in different drug scenes. Some drugs are reinvented, revitalized, repackaged, recycled, and become permanent parts of the landscape. New psychoactive drugs emerge followed by concomitant media and political feeding frenzies and calls for a strengthening of the "War on Drugs." In the early days of America, the target was potent "patent medicines." Then came marijuana in the 1930s, followed by heroin in the inner cities in the 1950s, and LSD and marijuana in the 1960s. In the 1970s, there were amphetamines and other prescription drugs, as well as powder cocaine. The 1980s witnessed the beginning of the crack epidemic, which has endured but is now less visible. In the 1990s through the present, we have witnessed a resurgence of prescription drug misuse, and a host of new psychoactive drugs have surfaced during the past few years. And the beat goes on. All these phenomena are discussed at length in this opening chapter.

Although marijuana, opium, the coca leaf, and other organic substances with psychoactive properties have been known for thousands of years, their use on a large scale for the enhancement of pleasure and performance spans just over two hundred years. The misuse of drugs as such can be traced to a number of factors—advances in chemistry and medicine, the discovery of new intoxicants, and a variety of social and political changes—all of which combined to make drugs readily available for the relief of many ills, both physical and psychological.

Opium and Its Derivatives

The specific beginnings of drug misuse in the United States are probably buried in antiquity, but in great part were tied to the introduction of over-the-counter patent medicines during the early 1700s. In the introduction to this book, we described that opium was a common ingredient in these preparations, and by the close of that century, medications containing the narcotic were readily available throughout urban and rural America. They were sold in pharmacies, in grocery and general stores, at traveling medicine shows, and through the mail. Many of these remedies were seductively advertised as "painkillers," "cough mixtures," "soothing syrups," "consumption cures," and "women's friends" (Cook and Martin 1951). Others were promoted for the treatment of such varied ailments as diarrhea, dysentery, colds, fever, teething, cholera, rheumatism, pelvic disorders, athlete's foot, and even baldness and cancer.

The medical profession also fostered the use of opium. Dr. William Buchan's *Domestic Medicine,* for example, first published in Philadelphia in 1784 as a practical handbook on simple medicines for home use, recommended tincture of opium for the treatment of numerous common ailments, to be prepared as follows:

> Take of crude opium, two ounces; spirituous aromatic water, and mountain wine, of each ten ounces. Dissolve the opium, sliced, in the wine, with a gentle heat, frequently stirring it; afterward add the spirit and strain off the tincture. (Buchan 1784, 225–226)

Yet the mere appearance of patent medicines in America was only minimally related to the evolution of drug taking; other more potent social forces were of considerably greater significance. Remedies were initially shipped to the colonies from London, as were most of the medications of the period. They were available from physicians or over the counter from apothecaries, grocers, postmasters, and printers, but only in modest quantities. When trade with England was disrupted during the Revolutionary War, a patent medicine industry emerged in the United States. Expansions in the industry were also related to the growth of the American press. The manufacturers of the "medicines" were the first business entrepreneurs to seek national markets through widespread advertising. They were the first hucksters to use psychological lures to entice customers to buy their merchandise. They were the first manufacturers to help the local merchants who retailed their wares by going directly to consumers with a message about their products. In total national advertising, this segment of the drug industry ranked highest in expenditures. During the post–Civil War decades, some individual proprietors spent in excess of $500,000 each year for advertising. As to the number of different varieties of patent medicines that were available, an 1804 New York catalog listed some 90 brands of elixirs, an 1857 Boston periodical included almost 600, in 1858 one newspaper account totaled over 1,500 patent medicines. By 1905, the list had stretched to more than 28,000 (Young 1961).

While for the longest time opium had been the only known product of the oriental poppy, in 1803 a young German pharmacist, Frederick Serturner, isolated the chief alkaloid of opium (Jaffe and Martin 1975). Serturner had hit upon morphine, which he named after Morpheus, the Greek god of dreams. The discovery was to have profound effects on both medicine and society for morphine was, and still is, the greatest single pain reliever the world has known. Then the hypodermic syringe was invented, and the use of morphine by injection in military medicine during the Civil War and the Franco-Prussian War granted the procedure legitimacy and familiarity to both physicians and the public (see Bartholow 1891). Furthermore, hypodermic medication had its pragmatic aspects—it brought quick local relief, its dosage could be regulated, and it was effective when oral medication was impractical. The regimen, however, was used promiscuously, for many physicians were anxious to illustrate their ability to quell the pain suffered by their patients, who, in turn, expected instant relief from discomfort.

The use of morphine by needle had become so pervasive by the 1890s that technology soon responded with the production of inexpensive equipment for mass use. In the 1897 edition of the Sears, Roebuck & Co. catalog, for example, hypodermic kits, which included a syringe, two needles, two vials, and a carrying case, were advertised for $1.50, with extra needles available at 25¢ each or $2.75 per dozen.

As to the full volume of opium and morphine that was actually consumed during the nineteenth century, the picture is not altogether clear. Estimates of the number of individuals who were actually addicted to opium during the latter part of the nineteenth century tended to be compiled rather loosely, ranging as high as 3 million. Yet other, more rigorously collected, data for the period did indicate that the use of narcotic drugs was indeed pervasive. In 1888, for example, one examination of 10,000 prescriptions from Boston-area pharmacies found that some 15 percent contained opiates, and that was only in Boston. In 1900 it was estimated that in the small state of Vermont, 3.3 million doses of opium were sold each month (Terry and Pellens 1928).

Cocaine

Beyond opium and morphine, the patent medicine industry branched even further. Although chewing coca leaves for their mild stimulant effects had been a part of the Andean cultures of South America for perhaps a thousand years, for some obscure reason the practice had never become popular in either Europe or the United States. Moreover, the full potency of the coca leaf remained unknown until 1860 when cocaine was first isolated in its pure form. Yet little use was made of the new alkaloid until 1883, when Dr. Theodor Aschenbrandt secured a supply of the drug and issued it to Bavarian soldiers during maneuvers. Aschenbrandt, a German military physician, noted the beneficial effects of cocaine, particularly its ability to suppress fatigue.

Among those who read Aschenbrandt's account with fascination was a struggling young Viennese neurologist, Sigmund Freud. Suffering from chronic fatigue, depression, and various neurotic symptoms, Freud obtained a measure of cocaine and tried it himself. He also offered it to a colleague who was suffering from both a disease of the nervous system and morphine addiction and to a patient with a chronic and painful gastric disorder. Finding the initial results to be quite favorable in all three cases, Freud decided that cocaine was a "magical drug." In a letter to his fiancée, Martha Bernays, in 1884, Freud commented on his experiences with cocaine:

> If all goes well I will write an essay on it and I expect it will win its place in therapeutics by the side of morphine and superior to it. I have other hopes and intentions about it. I take very small doses of it regularly against depression and against indigestion, and with the most brilliant success. . . . In short it is only now that I feel that I am a doctor, since I have helped one patient and hope to help more. (Jones 1953, 81)

Freud then pressed the drug on his friends and colleagues, urging that they use it both for themselves and for their patients; he gave it to his sisters and his fiancée and continued to use it himself. By the close of the 1880s, however, Freud and the others who had praised cocaine as an all-purpose wonder drug began to withdraw their support for it in light of an increasing number of reports of compulsive use and undesirable side effects. Yet by 1890, the patent medicine industry in the United States had also discovered the benefits of the unregulated use of cocaine. The industry quickly added the drug to its reservoir of home remedies, touting it as helpful not only for everything from alcoholism to venereal disease, but as a cure for addiction to other patent medicines. Since the new tonics contained substantial amounts of cocaine, they did indeed make users feel better, at least initially, thus spiriting the patent medicine industry into its golden age of popularity.

Heroin

Research on the mysteries of opium during the nineteenth century led not only to Serturner's discovery of morphine in 1806, but to the discovery of more than two dozen other alkaloids, including codeine in 1831. Yet more important, in an 1874 issue of the *Journal of the Chemical Society,* British chemist C. R. A. Wright described a series of experiments he had carried out to determine the effect of combining various acids with morphine. Wright (1874) produced a series of new morphine-like compounds, including what became known in the scientific literature as diacetylmorphine.

Wright's work went for the most part unnoticed. However, some twenty-four years later pharmacologist Heinrich Dreser reported on a series of experiments he had conducted with diacetylmorphine for Friedrich Bayer and Company of Elberfeld, Germany. He noted that the drug was highly effective in the treatment of coughs, chest pains, and the discomforts associated with pneumonia and tuberculosis (Trebach 1982). Dreser's commentary received immediate notice for it had come at a time when antibiotics were still unknown, and pneumonia and tuberculosis were among the leading causes of death. He claimed that diacetylmorphine had a stronger sedative effect on respiration than either morphine or codeine, that therapeutic relief came quickly, and that the potential for a fatal overdose was almost nil. In response to such favorable reports, Bayer and Company began marketing diacetylmorphine under the trade name of Heroin—so named from the German *heroisch,* meaning heroic and powerful.

Although Bayer's heroin was promoted as a sedative for coughs and as a chest and lung medicine, it was advocated by some as a treatment for morphine addiction. This situation seems to have arisen from three somewhat related phenomena. The first was the belief that heroin was non-addicting. Indeed, a physician reported in the *New York Medical Journal* that individuals could use heroin for long periods of time without developing dependence on the drug (Manges 1900).

Second, commentators perceived that the drug had a greater potency than morphine so that small doses were required for the desired medical effects, thus reducing the potential for the rapid onset of addiction. And third, at the turn of the twentieth century, the medical community did not fully understand the dynamics of cross-dependence. Cross-dependence refers to the phenomenon that among certain pharmacologically related drugs, physical dependence on one will carry over to all the others. For a person who was suffering from the unpleasant effects of morphine withdrawal, the administration of heroin would reduce withdrawal effects. Thus, heroin was envisioned as a cure for morphine withdrawal, even though opioid dependence continued. Given the endorsement of the medical community, with little mention of its potential dangers, heroin quickly found its way into routine medical therapeutics and over-the-counter patent medicines.

Early Drug Control Measures

By the early twentieth century, the steady progress of medical science had provided physicians with a better understanding of the long-term effects of the drugs that they had been advocating. Sigmund Freud had already recognized his poor judgment in the claims he had made about cocaine, the addiction potential and misuse liability of morphine had been well established, and the dependence-producing properties of Bayer's heroin were being noticed. Yet these drugs—cocaine, morphine, and heroin— often combined with alcohol, were still readily available from the totally unregulated patent medicine industry. Not only were they unregulated, but many were highly potent as well. Birney's Catarrah Cure, for example, was 4 percent cocaine. Colonel Hoesteller's Bitters contained such a generous amount of C,H,OH (alcohol) in its formula "to preserve the medicine" that the fumes from just one tablespoonful fed through a gas burner could maintain a bright flame for almost five minutes.

In 1906 the Pure Food and Drug Act was passed, prohibiting the interstate transportation of adulterated or misbranded food and drugs. The act brought about the decline of the patent medicine industry because henceforth the proportions of alcohol, opium, morphine, heroin, cocaine, and a number of other substances in each preparation had to be indicated. Thus, because of the medical profession's emphasis on the negative effects of these ingredients, a number of the remedies lost their appeal. Moreover, it suddenly became difficult to market as a cure for morphine addiction a preparation that contained one or more other addicting drugs. The new legislation merely imposed standards for quality, packaging, and labeling; it did not actually outlaw the use of cocaine and opiate drugs. The Harrison Act, sponsored by New York Representative Francis Burton Harrison and passed in 1914, served to some extent in that behalf and at the same time substantially altered the nature of drug use in the United States.

The Harrison Act required all people who imported, manufactured, produced, compounded, sold, dispensed, or otherwise distributed cocaine and opiate drugs to register with the Treasury Department, pay special taxes, and keep records of all transactions. As such, it was a revenue code designed to exercise some measure of public control over drugs, rather than to penalize the estimated 200,000 users of cocaine and opiates in the United States. In effect, however, criminalization is exactly what occurred. Certain provisions of the Harrison Act permitted physicians to prescribe, dispense, or administer certain psychoactive drugs to their patients for "legitimate medical purposes" and "in the course of professional practice." But how these two phrases were interpreted by the courts ultimately defined the use of opiates and cocaine as criminal acts.

Many commentators on the history of drug use in the United States have argued that the Harrison Act forced people who were dependent on drugs to access substances through illicit markets, a transition that facilitated contact with dangerous individuals. However, such a cause-and-effect interpretation tends to be an oversimplification. Without question, at the beginning of the twentieth century, most individuals who used opiates and cocaine were members of legitimate society. In fact, the vast majority had first encountered these substances through their family physicians, local pharmacists, or grocers. In other words, their addiction had been medically induced during the course of treatment for some other perceived ailment.

Yet long before the Harrison Act had been passed, there were indications that this population of users had begun to shrink (Morgan 1974). Agitation had existed in both the medical and religious communities against the haphazard use of psychoactive drugs, defining much of it as a moral disease. For many, the sheer force of social stigma and pressure served to alter their use of drugs. Similarly, the decline of the patent medicine industry after the passage of the Pure Food and Drug Act was believed to have substantially reduced the number of opiate and cocaine users. Moreover, by 1912, most state governments had enacted legislative controls over the dispensing and selling of opiates. Thus, it is plausible to assert that the size of the drug-using population had started to decline years before the Harrison Act had become the subject of court interpretation. Then, too, the combined effects of stigma, social pressure, the Pure Food and Drug Act, and state controls had also served to create an underworld of drug users and illicit drugs. By 1914, a number of commentators had noted this change.

During the latter part of the decade, other observers were noting that although the medically induced "addict" was still prominent, a new population had recently emerged (see, for instance, McPherson and Cohen 1919). These new users were believed to have initiated drug use as the result of associations with criminals. Thus, it would appear that a newly defined "criminal class" of drug users resulted from federal and state legislation but also from drug initiation that was fueled through prior association with criminals.

Although accurate data on the incidence and prevalence of drug use have been available only recently, by the early 1920s, readers of the popular media were confronted, almost on a daily basis, with how drug use, particularly heroin use, had become a national epidemic. Estimates were placed as high as 5 million, with a number of explanations offered for the increased number of users. Some blamed it on the greed of drug traffickers, others on the inadequate personalities of the users. A few argued that it was a natural consequence of the Prohibition amendment.

Marijuana

By the 1930s, the national concern over the use of drugs was not focused solely on heroin, for another substance was considered by some to represent an even greater evil. One might expect that it was cocaine, since the drug's stimulant effects had been promoted in the United States well before the introduction of Bayer's heroin. But this was not the case. The new drug was marijuana, alternatively called the "devil drug," the "assassin of youth," and the "weed of madness."

Marijuana, historically referred to in the United States as cannabis or hashish, was introduced to the American public in essentially the same manner that opium, morphine, cocaine, and heroin were. A derivative of the Indian hemp plant *Cannabis sativa*, it appeared among the patent medicines hawked from the tailgates of medicine-show wagons and sold as a cure for depression, convulsions, hysteria, insanity, mental retardation, and impotence. Moreover, during the late 1800s, such well-known pharmaceutical companies as Parke-Davis and Squibb produced tincture of cannabis for family pharmacists to dispense. As a medicinal agent, however, the drug quickly fell into disfavor. Because of its insolubility, it could not be injected and oral consumption produced effects that were slow acting and generally ineffective. Moreover, its potency was variable, making it difficult to standardize the dosage. Yet as a recreational drug, marijuana had its devotees. By the middle of the 1880s, every major American city had its clandestine hashish clubs, catering to a rather well-to-do clientele (Sloman 1979).

At the beginning of the twentieth century, what was referred to in Mexico as marijuana (also marihuana) began to appear in New Orleans and a number of towns along the Texas-Mexico border. Having been used in parts of South and

Central America for quite some time, it was a substance less potent than the hashish that was first smoked in the underground clubs decades earlier. Whereas hashish is the resinous extract of the hemp plant, marijuana is composed of the plant's dried leaves, stems, and flowering tops.

By 1920, the use of marijuana was perceived by people in power to be affiliated with minority groups—African Americans in the South and people of Mexican descent in the Southwest. The social and political climate that resulted in the passage of the Harrison Act was still active, and the movement for national prohibition of alcohol was at its peak. Marijuana was viewed by many as an intoxicant among minority group members whose drug use was perceived to be a corrupting influence on white society. Moreover, marijuana was considered to be particularly dangerous because of its *alien* (spelled "Mexican") and un-American origins.

Through the early 1930s, state after state enacted anti-marijuana laws, usually instigated by lurid newspaper articles depicting the madness and horror attributed to the drug's use. Even the prestigious *New York Times*, with its claim of "All the News That's Fit to Print," helped to reinforce the growing body of beliefs surrounding marijuana use. In an article headlined "Mexican Family Goes Insane," and datelined Mexico City, July 6, 1927, the *New York Times* reported:

> A widow and her four children have been driven insane by eating the Marijuana plant, according to doctors, who say that there is no hope of saving the children's lives and that the mother will be insane for the rest of her life. The mother was without money to buy other food for the children, whose ages range from 3 to 15, so they gathered some herbs and vegetables growing in the yard for their dinner. Two hours after the mother and children had eaten the plants, they were stricken. Neighbors, hearing outbursts of crazed laughter, rushed to the house to find the entire family insane. Examination revealed that the narcotic marijuana was growing among the garden vegetables. (1927, 10)

A crusade against marijuana ensued, culminating on August 2, 1937, with the passage of the Marijuana Tax Act—a piece of legislation that classified the scraggly tramp of the plant world as a dangerous drug, and placed it under essentially the same controls as the Harrison Act had placed on opium and coca products.

The Postwar Heroin Epidemic

The crusade against marijuana during the 1930s had attributed to drug taking a level of wickedness that could only have been matched by the Victorian imagery of masturbation and its consequences. The 1940s all but ignored the drug problem, principally because if it was indeed a problem, it was an invisible one—hardly a topic that should divert attention away from the events of a world at war. Then came the 1950s, a time when the prevailing *image* of drug use was one of heroin addiction on the streets of the urban inner city. As the author and journalist Max Lerner (1957, 666) summarized in his work *America as a Civilization:*

> As a case in point we may take the known fact of the prevalence of reefer-and-dope addiction in Negro areas. This is essentially explained in terms of poverty, slum living, and broken families, yet it would be easy to show the lack of drug addiction among other ethnic groups where the same conditions apply.

Lerner believed that addiction among African Americans was due to the adjustment problems associated with their rapid movement from a depressed status to the improved standards and freedoms of the era. Yet Lerner's interpretation was hardly correct, and not only about "reefer addiction," but about the prevalence of drug use in other populations. He overlooked drug misuse among the wealthy and middle-class, and among whites.

In the popular media, a somewhat more detailed (and distorted) portrait of the problem was offered. *Time, Life, Newsweek,* and other major periodicals discussed how teenagers, jaded on marijuana, had found greater thrills in heroin.[1] For most, the pattern of initiation had been the same. They began with marijuana, the use of which had become a fad in the inner city. Then, enticed in schoolyards by brazen Mafia pushers dressed in dark suits, white ties, and wide-brimmed hats, their first dose of heroin was given free. By then, however, it was too late—their fate had been sealed because they were already addicted. Or as the saying went, "It's so good, don't even try it once!"

Hollywood offered a somewhat different image of the situation in the 1955 United Artists release of *The Man with the Golden Arm*. The film was controversial in its day, for the Otto Preminger production had touched on a topic that most Americans felt should remain in the inner city where it belonged. Cast in the role of a would-be professional musician, singer-actor Frank Sinatra was the hero of the story. Plagued by the evils of heroin addiction, he was unable to get his life together. Finally, however, through the help and understanding of his girlfriend Molly (portrayed by Kim Novak), he was saved from a life of pathetic degradation. As in the case of other media images of the drug scene, *The Man with the Golden Arm* offered only a contorted view, failing to probe even the most basic issues.

Within the scientific community, segments of the literature and research were equally curious. As might be expected, most explanations of drug addiction focused on heroin use in the inner city. Young addicts were believed to be either psychotic or neurotic casualties for whom drugs provided relief from anxiety and a means for withdrawing from the stress of daily struggle in the slums. *The Road to H* was among the more celebrated books of the period. The authors, Isidor Chein and colleagues (1964, 14), focused on addiction in New York City and concluded:

> The evidence indicated that all addicts suffer from deep-rooted personality disorders. Although psychiatric diagnoses are apt to vary, a particular set of symptoms seems to be common to most juvenile addicts. They are not able to enter into prolonged, close, friendly relations with either peers or adults; they have difficulties in assuming a masculine role; they are frequently overcome by a sense of futility, expectations of failure, and general depression; they are easily frustrated and made anxious, and they find frustrations and anxiety intolerable.

By focusing on such maladies as "weak ego functioning," "defective superego," and "inadequate masculine identification," Chein et al. suggested a psychological predisposition to drug use—in other words, an addiction-prone personality. Their work completely ignored how structural inequalities can contribute to drug use and the reaction to it, and instead argued that a series of predispositions could be traced to the addict's family experiences. If the youth received too much love or not enough, or if the parents were overwhelming in terms of their affection or indulgence, then the child would develop inadequately. As a result, the youth would probably be unable to withstand pain and discomfort, to cope with the complexities of life in the neighborhood and community, to assess reality correctly, and to feel competent around others. Chein and colleagues concluded that this type of youth would be more prone to trying drugs than others from more "normal" family backgrounds.

The prevailing portrait of addiction in the scientific community, then, was one of passive adaptation to stress. Drugs allowed the user to experience fulfillment and the satiation of physical and emotional needs. This general view became the basis of the drug treatment philosophies that emerged during this period.

LSD

The 1960s was a time characterized by civil rights movements, political assassinations, campus and antiwar protests, and inner-city riots. Among the more startling events of the decade was the drug revolution. The use of drugs seemed to have leaped from the more marginal zones of society to the very mainstream of community life. No longer were drugs limited to the inner cities, jazz scenes, and the underground bohemian subcultures. Rather, drug use had become suddenly and dramatically apparent among members of the adolescent and young adult populations of rural and urban middle-class America. By the close of the decade, several commentators referred to the United States as "the addicted society"; that through drugs, millions had become "seekers" of "instant enlightenment"; and that drug taking and drug seeking would persist in the social fabric of American life (Farber 1966; Fort 1969).

A variety of changes in the fabric of American life had occurred during those years, which undoubtedly had profound implications for social consciousness and behavior. Notably, the revolution in the technology and handling of drugs that had begun during the 1950s was of sufficient magnitude to justify the designation of the 1960s as "a new chemical age." Recently compounded psychotropic agents were enthusiastically introduced and effectively promoted, with the consequence of exposing the national consciousness to an impressive catalog of chemical temptations—sedatives, tranquilizers, stimulants, antidepressants, analgesics, and hallucinogens—which could offer fresh inspiration, as well as simple and immediate relief from fear, anxiety, tension, frustration, and boredom (Inciardi 1974). Concomitant with this emergence of a new chemical age, a new youth ethos had become manifest, one characterized by a widely celebrated generational disaffection, a prejudicial dependence on the self and the peer group for value orientation, a critical view of how the world was being run, and a mistrust of an "establishment" drug policy the "facts" and "warnings" of which ran counter to reported peer experiences.

Whatever the ultimate causes of the drug revolution of the 1960s might have been, America's younger generations, or, at least, noticeable segments of them, had embraced drugs. The drug scene had become the arena of "happening" America; "turning on" to drugs to relax and to share friendship and love seemed to have become commonplace. And the prophet—the "high priest" as he called himself—of the new chemical age was a psychology instructor at Harvard University's Center for Research in Human Personality, Dr. Timothy Leary.

The saga of Timothy Leary had its roots not at Harvard in the 1960s, but in Basel, Switzerland, just before the beginning of World War II. It was there, in 1938, that Dr. Albert Hofmann of Sandoz Research Laboratories first isolated a new chemical compound that he called D-lysergic acid diethylamide. Known now as LSD, it was cast aside in his laboratory, where, for five years, it remained unappreciated, its properties awaiting discovery. On April 16, 1943, after absorbing some LSD through the skin of his fingers, Hofmann began to hallucinate. In his diary he explained the effect:

> With closed eyes, multihued, metamorphizing, fantastic images overwhelmed me. . . . Sounds were transposed into visual sensations so that from each tone or noise a comparable colored picture was evoked, changing in form and color kaleidoscopically. (Manchester 1974, 1362)

Hofmann had experienced the first LSD "trip" and allegedly went on to consume LSD on hundreds of occasions during his lifetime.[2]

Dr. Humphrey Osmond of the New Jersey Neuropsychiatric Institute neologized a new drug category for LSD. He called it "psychedelic," meaning mind-expanding. But outside the scientific community, LSD was generally unknown—even at the start of the 1960s. This situation was quickly changed by Leary and his colleague at Harvard, Dr. Richard Alpert. Leary and Alpert began experimenting with the drug—on themselves and with colleagues, students, artists, writers, members of the clergy, and volunteer prisoners. Although their adventures with LSD had earned them dismissals from Harvard by 1963, LSD had achieved a popular reputation among several users. Leary predicted that hallucinogens would be used in schools to enhance the senses of the nation's youth, a message that shocked the political establishment as well as hundreds of thousands of mothers and fathers across the nation. On March 26, 1967, Leary addressed some 15,000 cheering youth in San Francisco:

> Turn on to the scene, tune in to what's happening; and drop out—of high school, college, grad school . . . follow me, the hard way. (Manchester 1974, 1366)

The hysteria over Leary, LSD, and the other psychedelic substances was threefold. First, the drug scene was especially frightening to mainstream society because it reflected a willful rejection of rationality, order, and predictability. Second, there was the stigmatized association of drug use with antiwar protests and antiestablishment long-haired, unwashed, radical "hippies." Third, there were the drug's psychic effects, the reported "bad trips" that seemed to border on mental illness. Particularly in the case of LSD, the rumors of how it could "blow one's mind" became legion. One story told of a youth, high on the drug, who took a swan dive in front of a truck moving at 70 miles per hour.

Another spoke of two "tripping" teenagers who stared directly into the sun until they were permanently blinded. A third described how LSD's effects on the chromosomes resulted in fetal abnormalities. The stories were probably untrue; however, LSD "flashbacks" appeared to affect a small percentage of people who had previously consumed LSD. Apparently, these individuals re-experienced the LSD-induced state, days, weeks, and sometimes months after the original "trip" without having taken the drug a second time. Flashbacks were not well understood by the scientific community.

Despite the lurid reports, as it turned out, LSD was not widely used on a regular basis beyond a few individuals and social groups that were fully dedicated to hallucinogenic experiences. In fact, the psychedelic substances had earned reputations of being unpredictable, and most people avoided them. By the close of the 1960s, all hallucinogenic drugs had been placed under strict legal control, and the number of regular users was believed to be minimal (National Commission on Marijuana and Drug Abuse 1973).

Amphetamines

Throughout the 1960s, heroin remained the most feared drug, and by the close of the decade, national estimates of the number of problem heroin users tended to exceed 500,000. Yet despite the hysteria about the rising tide of heroin addiction, LSD and the youth rebellion, Timothy Leary and the psychedelic age, and the growing awareness of drug use along the Main Streets of white America, no one really knew how many people were actually using drugs. In fact, the estimates of the incidence and prevalence of marijuana, heroin, psychedelic, and other drug use were, at best, only vague and impressionistic. Although the reliability of political polling had long since demonstrated that the social sciences indeed had the tools to measure the dimensions of the "drug problem," no one at any time throughout the 1960s had gone so far as to count drug users in a systematic way. Yet several indicators existed. Studies were suggesting that the annual production of barbiturate drugs exceeded 1 million pounds, the equivalent of twenty-four

half-grain doses for every man, woman, and child in the nation—enough to kill each person twice (Chambers, Brill, and Inciardi 1972). For amphetamines and amphetamine-like compounds, the manufacturing figures came to some fifty doses per U.S. resident each year, with half the production reaching the illicit marketplace (Griffith 1966).

The amphetamines were not new drugs, but their appearance on the street had been relatively recent. Having been synthesized in Germany during the 1880s, their first use among Americans had not come until World War II. Thousands of service personnel in all the military branches had been issued Benzedrine, Dexedrine, and a variety of other amphetamines to reduce fatigue and anxiety. After the war, amphetamine drugs became more readily available, and they were put to a wider assortment of uses—for students who were cramming for examinations, for truck drivers and others who needed to be alert for extended periods, in weight-control programs, and as nasal decongestants. In turn, the strong stimulant effect of amphetamines led to their popularity across different drug scenes.

As the 1970s began, the amphetamines were the first item on the government's agenda for drug reform, with Indiana senator Birch Bayh conducting hearings. There was a parade of witnesses, and the worst fears about the drugs were confirmed— or so it seemed (U.S. Senate Subcommittee 1972). Bayh and his committee heard negative portrayals of "speed freaks" who injected amphetamine and who stalked the city streets suffering from paranoid delusions and exhibiting episodes of violent behavior at the onset of their psychotic states. They heard, too, that numerous people were stoned on "uppers," "bennies," "pinks," "purple hearts," "black beauties," and "King Kong pills." By that time, systematic surveys of the general population had finally begun, with the first, conducted in New York, empirically documenting that amphetamine misuse was indeed widespread (Chambers 1970).

Almost immediately, new legislation was proposed by the Bayh committee and pushed through by the Senate. Tighter controls were placed on the prescription and legal distribution of amphetamines, and legitimate production was ultimately cut by 90 percent. In so doing, it was thought that the drug problem, at least in terms of the amphetamines, would be measurably solved. Meanwhile, the heroin epidemic continued, and a new drug—methaqualone—made its entrance.

Methaqualone (Quaalude)

Methaqualone was initially synthesized in India during the early 1950s as a possible antimalarial agent. When its *hypnotic* (sleep-producing) properties were discovered later in the decade, many hoped that methaqualone might be a safer alternative to the barbiturates.

Barbiturate drugs had been available for the better part of the century. As potent central nervous system depressants, they were the drugs of choice for inducing sleep. Depending on the dosage level, they were also in common use for anesthesia, sedation, and the treatment of tension, anxiety, and convulsions. However, the barbiturates had their problems. They were widely used for the "high" they could engender. Moreover, they produced addiction after chronic use, were life threatening on withdrawal, and could cause fatal overdoses—particularly when mixed with alcohol.

As an alternative to barbiturates, methaqualone was introduced in England in 1959 and in Germany and Japan in 1960. Despite extensive medical reports of misuse in these three countries, the drug was introduced in the United States under the trade names of Quaalude, Sopor, Parest, Somnafac, and later Mequin. Although methaqualone was a prescription drug, the federal drug establishment decided that since there was no evidence of the potential for misuse, it need not be monitored, and the number of times a prescription could be refilled need not be restricted. This decision, combined with an advertising campaign that emphasized that the drug was a "safe alternative to barbiturates," led to the assumption by the medical profession, the lay population, and the media that methaqualone was nonaddictive. Even the prestigious American Medical Association's *Drug Evaluations* stated as late as 1973 that no more than "long-term use of larger than therapeutic doses may result in psychic and physical dependence" (313).

The most effective advertising campaign was launched by William H. Rorer Pharmaceuticals. Given the success of the catchy double-a in its antacid Maalox, the company named its methaqualone product Quaalude. Its advertising emphasized that Quaalude was a nonbarbiturate. Free samples of Quaalude were shipped throughout the country, and physicians began overprescribing the drug.

Looking for a new and safe "high," users sought out methaqualone, and the drug quickly made its way to the street. Rather than a safe alternative to whatever they had been taking previously, street users actually had a drug with the same addiction liability and lethal potential as the barbiturates. What they experienced were a pleasant sense of well-being, an increased pain threshold, and a loss of muscle coordination. Similar to alcohol, the drug acted on the central cortex of the brain to release normal inhibitions. Also common was "luding out"—attaining an intoxicated state rapidly by mixing the drug with wine.

In early 1973, after reports of widespread misuse, acute reactions, and fatal overdoses, Birch Bayh convened more Senate hearings. The problems with methaqualone were fully aired, and rigid controls over the drug were put into force. Shortly thereafter, methaqualone misuse began to decline, but peaked again between 1978 and the early 1980s. In 1980, some four tons of the drug were produced legally in the United States, and it is estimated that another 100 million tons were smuggled in principally from Colombia. In 1982, when tight restrictions were placed on the importation of methaqualone powder from West Germany to Colombia, trafficking in the drug declined substantially. In 1984, all legal manufacturing of methaqualone was halted in the United States, and since that time, misuse of the drug has been, at best, modest.

The Return of Marijuana

A major purpose of the Marijuana Tax Act of the 1930s was to reduce the number of individuals who used the drug. Although data on the prevalence and incidence of marijuana use were very limited during the 1940s and 1950s, increases in its usage were apparent during the 1960s. Indeed, from 1960 through the end of the decade, the number of

Americans who had used marijuana at least once had increased from a few hundred thousand to an estimated 8 million. By the early 1970s, marijuana use had increased geometrically across all socioeconomic strata.

Given such pervasive use of marijuana and arrests that were affecting the careers and lives of so many otherwise law-abiding citizens, legislation was introduced that reduced the penalties for the simple possession of the drug first at the federal level and later by the states. In Alabama, judges were no longer required to impose the mandatory minimum sentence of five years for the possession of even one marijuana cigarette. Missouri statutes no longer included life sentences for second possession offenses, and in Georgia second-sale offenses to minors were no longer punishable by death.

Then there was the issue of decriminalization—the removal of criminal penalties for the possession of small amounts of marijuana for personal use. The movement toward decriminalization began in 1973 with Oregon, followed by Colorado, Alaska, Ohio, and California in 1975; Mississippi, North Carolina, and New York in 1977; and Nebraska in 1978. Given that there were an estimated 50 million users of marijuana in the United States by the close of the 1970s, many hoped that decriminalization, and perhaps even the legalization of marijuana use, would become a national affair, but the "movement" suddenly stalled for a variety of reasons. Principally, Congress failed to pass legislation that would have decriminalized marijuana under federal statutes. The issue had not been salient enough throughout the nation as a whole to result in concerted action in favor of decriminalization. The lobbying on behalf of marijuana law reform had not yet demonstrated the power and influence necessary for repeal. Perhaps most important, marijuana had been portrayed as a drug favored by youths.

By the close of the 1970s and the onset of the 1980s, evidence indicated that marijuana use in the United States had actually declined. In 1975, surveys showed that some 30 million people were users (Domestic Council Drug Abuse Task Force 1975). By the early 1980s, this figure had dropped to 20 million, with the most significant declines among people aged 25 and younger (Drug Abuse Policy Office 1984). Perhaps the younger generation had begun to realize that although marijuana was not the "devil drug," "assassin of youth," or the "weed of madness," as it had been called earlier, it was not a totally innocuous substance either. For example, between 1975 and 1988, the proportion of high school seniors in the United States who believed the regular use of marijuana to be harmful increased from 39 percent to almost 80 percent (Johnston, O'Malley, and Bachman 1985). Perhaps the change occurred because of the greater concern with health and physical fitness that became so much a part of U.S. culture during the 1980s or as an outgrowth of the antismoking messages that appeared daily in the media. Alternatively, perhaps the change in marijuana use was a methodological artefact—produced by surveys characterized by low validity because people were simply less inclined to admit to the behavior.

Phencyclidine (PCP)

The propaganda campaigns that have periodically emerged to target specific drugs as the root causes of outbreaks of violent crime targeted PCP at various times as a "killer drug" that could change the user into a diabolical monster and a member of the "living dead."

PCP, or more formally phencyclidine, a central nervous system excitant agent that has anesthetic, analgesic, and hallucinogenic properties, is not a particularly new drug. It was developed during the 1950s, and following studies on laboratory animals, it was recommended for clinical trials on humans in 1957 (National Clearinghouse for Drug Abuse Information 1973). Parke, Davis & Company marketed the drug under the trade name Sernyl. Originally, phencyclidine was used as an anesthetic agent in surgical procedures. Although it was found to be generally effective, the drug often produced a number of unpleasant side effects—extreme excitement, visual disturbances, and delirium. As a result, in 1967 the use of phencyclidine was restricted to "veterinary use only." Under the trade name Sernylan, it quickly became the most widely used animal tranquilizer.

The street use of PCP (also known as "horse tranquilizer," "elephant juice," "angel dust," "hog," "Tic," "supergrass," and "rocket fuel") occurred initially in the Haight-Ashbury underground community of San Francisco and other West and East Coast cities during 1967. It was first marketed as the PeaCe Pill; hence, the name PCP quickly became popular.

Characteristic of the hallucinogenic drug marketplace has been the mislabeling and promotion of one substance as some other more desirable psychedelic, and for a time PCP occupied a conspicuous position as such a substitute. Samples of mescaline (the hallucinogenic alkaloid found in the peyote cactus) sold in Milwaukee, for example, were invariably PCP (Reed and Kane 1970). During the late 1960s and early 1970s, tetrahydrocannabinol (THC), the active ingredient in marijuana, was frequently sought after in its pure form as a prestige "fad" drug. Yet THC has *never* been sold on the street because in its isolated form it is so unstable a compound that it quickly loses its potency and effect. In 1970, analyses of "street drugs" from the greater Philadelphia area revealed that PCP was a common THC substitute (Schnoll and Vogel 1971). In an experiment undertaken in 1971, samples of alleged LSD, THC, mescaline, and PCP were obtained from street suppliers in New York City's Greenwich Village. Laboratory analyses identified the THC and mescaline samples as PCP, and the PCP sample as LSD, with only the LSD sample having accurate labeling. In a second experiment conducted during early 1972 in Miami's Coconut Grove area, twenty-five individual samples of alleged THC were purchased from an equal number of street drug dealers. Laboratory analyses showed that twenty-two of the twenty-five products that were marketed as THC were instead found to be PCP. Of the three remaining: one was Darvon (a prescription painkiller), another was an oral contraceptive, and the last was a chocolate-covered peanut (Inciardi 1972). It was quickly learned that these apparent deceptions had been aimed at "plastic," or weekend, hippies and "heads"—those children of two cultures whose social schizophrenia placed them partially in the straight world and partially in the new underground, never fully being a part of either. In both the New York and Miami drug subcultures, however, and probably in most others, THC was simply accepted as another name of PCP, which perhaps explains why the latter drug was called "Tic" for more than a decade in many cities.

The stories describing PCP as a "killer drug" date to its first introduction to the street community. In 1969, for example, a New York City chief of detectives commented to the first author: "Let me tell you, this stuff is bad, real bad. One dose of it and we're talking about some serious *instant addiction*" (personal communication 1969).

Similarly, a number of news stories at approximately the same time described PCP as a synthetic drug so powerful that a person could become "high" simply by touching it—instantly absorbing it through the pores. These early reports ran counter to both medical and street experiences (Domino 1964), and the drug quickly became relegated to the lengthening catalog of street substances that received little public attention after their initial appearance. Most of those who used PCP during those early years were not found among the populations who were addicted to opiates or cocaine. Rather, they tended to be individuals who consumed multiple psychoactive substances that included long-term use of marijuana and/or hashish, combined with the experimental, social-recreational, or spree use of hallucinogens, sedatives, tranquilizers, and stimulants.

During 1978, the hysteria over PCP emerged once again, but this time in earnest. In one episode of the popular *60 Minutes* television series, CBS News commentator Mike Wallace described PCP as the nation's "number one" drug problem, reporting on bizarre incidents of brutal violence allegedly caused by the new "killer" drug. In these and other reports, violence was nearly always associated with PCP use, as was the drug's propensity to destroy the user's mind (U.S. Congress, Select Committee on Narcotics Abuse Control 1978).

Emerging research demonstrated that comments such as these were probably overstated. In 1978, when PCP was labeled by *60 Minutes* as the number one drug problem, responsible for more emergency room admissions than any other drug, estimates from the Drug Abuse Warning Network found that PCP accounted for only 3 percent of all reported drug emergencies. Furthermore, ethnographic studies of PCP users in Seattle, Miami, Philadelphia, and Chicago demonstrated that the characterizations of users' experiences were slanted and misleading (Feldman 1979). In particular, individuals who consumed PCP were typically aware of its potency, and except for the few who sought a heavily anesthetized state, most used it cautiously. Although some had adverse reactions to the drug, violence was rarely a factor. In fact, among the more than three hundred individuals who participated in the study, almost all were baffled by the connection of the drug with violent behavior. The only known episodes of violence occurred during "bad trips" when someone tried to restrain a user, and these episodes were extremely unusual. Furthermore, the few who exhibited aggressive behavior typically had already developed a reputation for violence that was independent of PCP use. Still, PCP is not a harmless drug. On the contrary, hallucinations, altered mood states, feelings of depersonalization, paranoia, suicidal impulses, and aggressive behavior have been reported, only not to the extent that some commentators have suggested.

In the 1980s, it appeared that PCP use had begun to decline in the United States—at least among youth. For example, among national samples of high school seniors who were surveyed annually, the proportions who had ever used PCP declined from 13 percent in 1979 to 5 percent in 1984 and to less than 1 percent by 1988 (Johnston et al. 1985). However, more reports were appearing in the mass media describing bizarre behavior by individuals under the influence of PCP, particularly in Washington, DC, and Los Angeles, locales where PCP use seemed to be concentrated. Yet despite the renewed media attention, all systematic attempts to study the alleged relationship between PCP use and violent behavior, continued to conclude that only a small minority of users committed bizarre acts while in a PCP-induced state.

Crack Cocaine

Use of heroin and cocaine persisted into the 1980s. Of greater concern, however, was the reportedly new drug called "crack"—referred to in the media as a cheap variety of street cocaine that could be smoked and was highly addictive. Contrary to popular belief, crack is not a new substance, having been first reported in the literature during the early 1970s (i.e., *The Gourmet Cokebook: A Complete Guide to Cocaine*, cited in Schatzman, Sabbadini, and Forti 1976). At that time, however, crack was known as "base" or "rock" (not to be confused with "rock cocaine"—a cocaine hydrochloride product for intranasal snorting) and seemed to be restricted to a few individuals who were avid cocaine devotees. Crack is processed from cocaine hydrochloride by adding ammonia or baking soda and water. The mixture is then heated in order to remove the hydrochloride. The result is a pebble-sized crystalline form of cocaine base. Crack gets its name from the fact that the residue of sodium bicarbonate often causes a crackling sound when the substance is inhaled.

The rediscovery of crack during the early 1980s seemed to occur simultaneously on the East and West Coasts. As a result of the Colombian government's attempts to reduce the amount of illicit cocaine production within its borders, it apparently, at least for a time, successfully restricted the amount of ether available for transforming coca paste into cocaine hydrochloride. The result was the diversion of coca paste from Colombia, through Central America and the Caribbean, into South Florida for conversion into cocaine. Spillage from shipments through the Caribbean corridor acquainted local island populations with the smoking of coca paste (basuco),[3] which developed the forerunner of crack cocaine in 1980 (Hall 1986). Known as "baking-soda base," "base-rock," "gravel," and "roxanne," the prototype was a smokable product composed of coca paste, baking soda, water, and rum. Individuals with roots in Jamaica, Trinidad, the Leeward Islands, and the Windward Islands are believed to have introduced the crack prototype to Caribbean inner-city populations in Miami and New York, where it was ultimately produced from cocaine hydrochloride rather than coca paste. In 1986, a Miami-based immigrant from Barbados recalled the diffusion of what he referred to as "baking-soda paste" that emerged on several Caribbean islands and later hit Miami (Inciardi 1987).

Apparently at about the same time, a Los Angeles basement chemist rediscovered the rock variety of baking-soda cocaine, and it was initially referred to as "cocaine rock." It was an immediate success, as was the East Coast type, and for a variety of reasons. First, it could be smoked rather than snorted. When cocaine is smoked, it is more rapidly absorbed and reportedly crosses the blood-brain barrier within six seconds—hence, an almost instantaneous high. Second, it was cheap. A gram of cocaine for snorting sold for $60 or more, depending in part on its purity and a host of other drug market factors. The same gram can be transformed into anywhere from five to thirty "rocks." For the user, this meant that individual "rocks" could be purchased for as little as $5, $10, or $20. For the seller, $60 worth of cocaine hydrochloride (purchased wholesale for $30) could generate as much as $150 when sold as rocks. Third, it was easily hidden and transportable, and when hawked in small glass vials, it could be readily scrutinized by potential buyers.

By mid-1986, national headlines were calling crack a glorified version of cocaine and the major street drug in the United States. Additionally, there was the belief that crack was responsible for rising rates of street crime. As the media blitzed the American people with lurid stories depicting the hazards of crack, Congress and the White House began drawing plans for a more concerted war on crack and other drugs. At the same time, crack use was reported in a host of countries, including Canada, England, Finland, Hong Kong, Spain, South Africa, Egypt, India, Mexico, Belize, and Brazil.

By the close of the 1980s, crack-cocaine seemed to have emerged as the major drug of concern in many parts of the United States. Although national surveys were indicating that at the end of the decade only 3 percent of high school students, just over 1 percent of college students, and 3 percent of young adults aged 19 to 29 had used crack in the past year (University of Michigan 1989), the drug appeared to have a devastating effect on the social fabric of the inner cities. In New York, Los Angeles, Miami, and numerous other cities, including the nation's capital, the crack trade had turned many urban street gangs into inner city–based trafficking organizations,

some with direct connections to high-level South American smugglers. In addition, crack distribution rivalries had touched off homicide epidemics that turned entire stretches of urban America into "dead zones"—anarchic badlands written off by police enforcement officials as too dangerous to patrol. Moreover, large numbers of individuals who became addicted to crack cocaine experienced major life changes that substantially reduced their quality of life. Even if drug treatment was accessible, several treatment programs were ill prepared to deal with clients who were addicted to crack.

By the close of the 1990s, crack had lost its appeal to the media, and many observers assumed that the drug had disappeared from the inner cities. Clinicians in drug treatment programs as well as researchers studying the drug problem realized that this was not at all the case. Rather, crack remained part of the inner-city landscape and had spread to non-urban locations. Additionally, the injection of crack cocaine has been reported in the United States and the United Kingdom since the mid-1990s.

"Club Drugs" and Novel Psychoactive Substances

As a concept, "club drugs" is very broad and often inadequately defined. It generally refers to a number of substances that are used in a particular social setting (i.e., clubs). These substances include MDMA (3,4-methylenedioxymethamphetamine, also known as Ecstasy), Rohypnol (flunitrazepam), GHB (gamma-hydroxybutyrate), and ketamine. Some commentators add LSD and other hallucinogens to the list of club drugs, and in its "Tips to Parents," the Federal Bureau of Investigation (n.d.) lists methamphetamine as a "club drug." Note that the pharmacological nature and effects of these substances can differ greatly, but that this drug classification relates to the social setting in which drugs are consumed. However, use of these substances is by no means restricted to club settings. Lee et al. (2011) review evidence that highlights the diversity of social settings and contexts that are affiliated with Ecstasy use. Moreover, other drugs, for example, marijuana and alcohol, are used for "recreational" purposes within club settings but are not generally categorized as "club drugs."

MDMA is related structurally to amphetamine and has hallucinogenic properties; however, it does not generally produce major visual or audio distortions that are associated with other hallucinogenic drugs. MDMA is perhaps best described as an empathogen; individuals who use MDMA generally experience feelings of empathy, euphoria, or improved social interactions. Although some individuals experience negative effects of the drug (e.g., sleeplessness, difficult "comedowns," short-term depression), several others learn to control or manage the drug experience to reduce the likelihood of adverse outcomes (Bahora, Sterk, and Elifson 2009). Still, the debate over MDMA continues with the voice of the user portrayed in ethnographic and other qualitative studies that highlight MDMA use as part of leisure and in pursuit of pleasure. In contrast, the medical literature tends to highlight the adverse effects of Ecstasy either through case reports of individuals who have attended hospital emergency rooms after ingesting MDMA (often in combination with other substances), or through studies that examine the use of MDMA and neurotoxicity, brain functioning, mood, and memory.

MDMA was first synthesized in 1912 by Merck, a German pharmaceutical company. Although some literature states that MDMA was originally intended as an appetite suppressant by German troops during World War I, a comprehensive review of the original Merck documents failed to find support for this claim. Rather, Merck chemists were interested in developing a vasoconstrictor (i.e., a clotting agent to reduce bleeding), and in doing so, they stumbled on MDMA (Freudenmann, Öxier, and Bernschneider-Reif 2006). The historical review also uncovered that the pharmaceutical company did not conduct MDMA experiments with humans until 1960.

The biochemist, Dr. Alexander Shulgin, self-experimented with MDMA in the 1970s and recorded his observations, which he described as euphoric. His experiences, in turn, appeared to have influenced a number of therapists, and by the early 1980s, several hundred professionals in the United States were advocating patients' use of MDMA during therapeutic sessions. The drug was perceived to invoke feelings of empathy and introspection that enhanced the nature of therapy. The use of MDMA in this context captured some media attention, which might have contributed to the drug's albeit slow rise in popularity in other settings. Research has described how MDMA was used during the 1970s and early 1980s in the United States but that this use was generally limited to a small number of people residing in selected regions of the country (Beck and Rosenbaum 1994). MDMA's street name, Ecstasy, was probably coined in the early 1980s, and the term was allegedly chosen as a marketing strategy (Eisner 1994); anecdotal evidence suggests that the drug was originally known as *Empathy*, but suppliers believed that a drug labeled as Ecstasy would yield more sales. In the 1980s, MDMA gained popularity in the Spanish resort Ibiza and thereafter spread to various parts of Europe. The MDMA market was well under way in the United States during the 1990s, and similar to Europe, it became associated with particular forms of music, as well as the dance and rave scene.

In curious fashion, MDMA became illegal in the United States in 1985—before the drug gained popularity in the country. In that year, the Drug Enforcement Administration (DEA) categorized it as a Schedule I substance. One year later and after reviewing the evidence, an administrative law judge classified MDMA as a Schedule III substance, arguing that the drug did not meet the criteria for Schedule I classification and that it had some potential for use in medicine. However, the decision was reversed by the DEA administrator who had initially recommended the most restrictive scheduling, and in 1988, the drug was returned to Schedule I classification.

For years, MDMA was marketed largely in tablet form with the pills embossed with a pressed mark or symbol. The marketing of MDMA pills with labels or logos is similar to earlier distribution strategies involving LSD and, in some locations, heroin. However, pills embossed with the same symbol are not necessarily of the same batch and can contain diverse assortments of chemicals and adulterants. Globally, the purity of MDMA tablets began to decline in several regions (e.g., the United States, Australia, western Europe), particularly between 2009 and 2011. The availability of MDMA also declined during this era, particularly in Europe and Australia. Reductions in availability and purity were due in part to international controls over some of the main precursors that have been used to manufacture MDMA (European Monitoring Centre for Drugs and Drug Addiction 2011). Pills were still sold as MDMA but were very likely to contain other psychoactive chemicals, some of which mirrored the effects of MDMA. By 2009, laboratory analyses of tablets sold as MDMA in the Netherlands found that over half of them contained mephedrone—a new synthetic stimulant with effects similar to the "bath salts" sold in the United States.

By 2012, the lengthy drought appeared to have ended—or so it seemed. In the United States, perceptions among several users suggest that higher purity MDMA was once again available—much more so compared to the previous decade. Media frenzy focused on "Molly," a substance that some users believe to be "pure" MDMA. Molly is often sold as crystal or powder, or in capsules containing such, but claims about MDMA purity levels cannot be ascertained without laboratory analyses. In various countries, pills and capsules that are sold as MDMA have contained paramethoxyamphetamine (PMA), a substance that can pose significant harm to health. PMA can mimic the effects of MDMA but is considerably more toxic in that a much smaller dose of PMA produces the same physiological effects (e.g., rise in body temperature) as a higher dose of MDMA. In the United Kingdom, PMA was implicated in twenty deaths during 2012, up from one during 2011 and zero from 2010 and earlier (UK Office for National Statistics 2013). Several years ago, the Dutch government created its Drugs Information and Monitoring System (DIMS), which conducts tests of alleged MDMA pills and other drugs to ascertain purity levels and the presence of adulterants. Individuals can drop off drugs for testing, but without fear of prosecution. DIMS utilizes mass media to distribute information about dangerous substances to would-be users. Although the process cannot protect all users from health harms, it is a progressive system that is supported by government funding.

The national Monitoring the Future surveys show relatively little change in *past-year* use of Ecstasy among twelfth graders (2006 to 2012, roughly 4 percent).[4] Similarly, results from a national survey show that approximately 4 percent of adults aged 18 to 25 reported using MDMA during the past year.[5] Many individuals "mature out" of Ecstasy use with age or abstain when the effects of the drug are perceived as minimal.

Unlike MDMA, GHB and Rohypnol depress or sedate the central nervous system. Although both substances were developed for medical use, the negative side effects far outweighed the medical benefit. GHB and Rohypnol can result in amnesia or loss of consciousness, but they also can produce mild euphoria. Prior to 2000, GHB was sold in health food stores and similar outlets when it became popular as an appetite suppressant and muscle builder among some bodybuilders. It is less clear why the drugs became available in club settings, where the associated dance, rhythm, and music appear to be inconsistent with the depressed-like state induced by GHB and Rohypnol. In some instances, these drugs have been used to ease the *comedown* from MDMA and as a sleep aid after a late night out. In some instances, the substances have been used in drug-facilitated rapes. GHB is also known as "liquid Ecstasy," a term that may encourage novices to consume it with the mistaken belief that it is MDMA. GHB was designated a Schedule I substance in 2000, prompted, in part, by the death of two young women who had consumed GHB (one form of GHB is listed as a Schedule III drug but is available only for selected medical conditions and under the supervision of a physician). Rohypnol was never legally available in the United States.

Ketamine was developed in the 1960s as an anesthetic and has been used for that purpose since then. Some research suggests that it may assist with clinical depression (Price, Nock, Charney, and Mathew 2009), although more studies are needed to ascertain its effectiveness for treating depression. It is available in powder or tablet form and can also be prepared for injection. Although often described as a club drug, its dissociative properties (e.g., the perception that the self has separated from the body) are not necessarily conducive to club settings. For example, use of ketamine can affect speech and can make it difficult to process loud music.

Novel psychoactive substances (NPS) refer to a range of drugs that often emerge as legal substances that mirror the effects of illegal drugs. They can be classified into different categories based on their primary effects: stimulants, depressants, empathogens, synthetic cannabinoids, and hallucinogens. They are available in different forms (e.g., tablets, pre-rolled joints, herbal mixtures, powders, and crystals) and can contain (1) plants found in nature (e.g., kratom, kava, and *Salvia divinorum*), (2) synthetic substances (e.g., 2-aminoindan, butylone, mephedrone, synthetic cannabinoids such as JWH-018), or (3) semi-synthetic substances that are derived from natural oils (e.g., DMAA). In Europe, several NPS were initially referred to as "legal highs" and were sold in pre-sealed packages that featured "hippy style," "new age," or other symbols. Many packages were labeled with nomenclature that reminds consumers of illegal street drugs or their effects, for example, "Snow Blow," "White Ice Resin," "Charlie," "Sub-Coca," and "X Pillz." Some two hundred new NPS have been identified in Europe since 2009.

Hundreds of different *products* containing NPS have been manufactured. Globally, the primary chemical groups have included piperazine derivatives, phenethylamines, tryptamines, and cathinone derivatives. The packaging of several products has included the warning that the substance is not intended for human consumption. This marketing strategy has allowed products to skirt food, medicinal, and drug controls in several countries. Some products contain psychoactive substances found in nature (e.g., kratom, *Salvia divinorum*, guarana, and maté) but have been sold in extract form and consumed in ways that differ from ritualistic practices of indigenous people. We have little information about the potential risk of using extracts through different routes of administration.

NPS is a global phenomenon. In 2012, forty-five countries reported seizures of synthetic cannabinoids and thirty-five countries reported seizures of synthetic cathinones, such as MDPV ("bath salts") and mephedrone (United Nations Office on Drugs and Crime 2013). Most seizures occurred in Europe, although demand for NPS also appears to be disproportionately higher in Europe. In the United States, the Drug Enforcement Administration utilized emergency scheduling to prohibit MDPV, mephedrone, and other synthetic cathinones. Legislative controls have also been introduced in other countries in an attempt to prohibit use of NPS. The effect of these controls on usage patterns and other drug markets is not well understood. Some consumers—especially experienced drug takers—are likely to move on to other substances when the drug of choice becomes more difficult to access. In some regions (the United Kingdom and Ireland), synthetic cathinones became available through illicit drug markets once legislative controls were introduced. This transition led to an increase in price and a decline in the perceived purity of the cathinone products—at least temporarily. Several governments will be closely watching the situation in New Zealand, following that country's passage of the Psychoactive Substances Act in 2013. The Act regulates the sale and importation of NPS by shifting responsibility to the product owner to demonstrate that products have low risk of harm (rather than "no risk" of harm). Products must be approved by government, and must contain a list of ingredients and meet other criteria before they can be sold. The New Zealand government implemented the Act after acknowledging that legislative bans were largely ineffective and created additional harms to users.

Misuse of Prescription Drugs

The misuse of prescription drugs is defined here as the nonmedical use of a prescribed drug. Nonmedical use implies that the prescribed drug is used for reasons other than what it was intended. In general, we are referring here to patterns of nonmedical use of prescribed drugs rather than, for example, the one-time use of diazepam (Valium) that was provided by one individual to another. However, the available data on prescription drug misuse make it difficult to differentiate between the reasons for misuse, for example, use for the purposes of pleasure, in an attempt to address pain or because of dependence (McCabe, Boyd, and Teter 2009).

By the close of the 1990s, data gathered through a variety of mechanisms clearly indicated that rates of prescription drug misuse were rising, particularly with regard to prescription opioids (Zacny et al. 2003). The National Survey of Drug Use and Health (NSDUH), for example, found that the number of new incidents of the misuse of prescription pain relievers (primarily products containing codeine, hydrocodone, and oxycodone) increased from 600,000 in 1990 to more than 2.4 million in 2004, marking it as the drug category with the largest number of new users in 2004 (Substance Abuse and Mental Health Services Administration 2005), and similar increases were reflected in data on admissions to drug treatment programs. By 2010, the misuse of a variety of prescription medications was deemed to be of epidemic proportions in the United States (Executive Office of the President 2011; Hernandez and Nelson 2010), and media reports and documentaries highlighted the role of "disgraced" physicians and "pain clinics" that catered to and profited from individuals who were addicted to opioid pain medication.

Adolescents and young adults seem particularly vulnerable to the misuse of prescription opioids. In fact, 2012 data from NSDUH showed that past year misuse of prescription pain relievers among persons aged 18 to 25 ranked second after marijuana use in overall prevalence. Moreover, the percentage of individuals who reported using prescription pain relievers in the past year (10.1 percent) was more than twice that of cocaine and MDMA combined (Substance Abuse and Mental Health Services Administration 2013).

Concomitant with the widespread misuse of prescription drugs is the government's interest in *diversion*—the transfer of a prescription drug from a lawful to an unlawful channel of distribution or use (Inciardi et al. 2009). Diversion, furthermore, can occur in many ways, including the illegal sale of prescriptions by physicians and what are referred to on the street as "loose" pharmacists; "doctor shopping" by individuals who visit numerous physicians to obtain multiple prescriptions; through social networks that include people with legitimate prescriptions who engage in transactions with individuals who seek the prescription drug; theft, forgery, or alteration of prescriptions by health care workers and patients; robberies and thefts from manufacturers, distributors, and pharmacies; and

thefts of institutional drug supplies. Moreover, diversion occurs through residential burglaries as well as cross-border smuggling at both the retail and wholesale levels. In addition, anecdotal reports suggest that diversion occurs through such other channels as "shorting" (undercounting) and pilferage by pharmacists and pharmacy employees; recycling of medications by pharmacists and pharmacy employees; thefts from medicine cabinets by friends, relatives, and service personnel in residential settings; and insurance fraud by patients, pharmacists, and street dealers. Furthermore, it would appear that prescription drug misuse among adolescents occurs through medicine cabinet thefts, medication trading at school, and thefts and robberies of medications from other students. Finally, some observers consider the Internet to be a significant source for illegal purchases of prescription drugs; however, the popularity of this source varies considerably across countries.

The contemporary history of the misuse of opioid pain medication can be traced to OxyContin, an extended-release formulation of the painkiller oxycodone. When OxyContin was introduced to the market in early 1996, it was hailed as a breakthrough in pain management. The medication was unique in that its time-release formula allowed patients to enjoy continuous, long-term relief from moderate to severe pain. The active ingredient in OxyContin is oxycodone, a drug that has been used for the treatment of pain for some one hundred years. Oxycodone is a semisynthetic narcotic analgesic that is most often prescribed for moderate to severe pain, chronic pain syndromes, and terminal cancers. When used correctly under a physician's supervision, it can be highly effective in the management of pain, and there are scores of oxycodone products on the market—in various strengths and forms. However, shortly after the introduction of OxyContin, the misuse of the drug was quick to emerge.

OxyContin misuse first surfaced in rural Maine during the late 1990s, soon after spreading down the East Coast and the Ohio Valley and then into rural Appalachia. Communities in western Virginia, eastern Kentucky, West Virginia, and southern Ohio were especially hard hit, and a number of factors that are characteristic of these areas seem to correlate with their apparent high rates of misuse. In northern Maine and rural Appalachia, for example, there are aspects of the culture that are markedly different from those in other parts of the country. Many of the communities are small and isolated, often situated in the mountains and valleys located a considerable distance from major towns and highways. As a result, many of the usual street drugs are less available. Instead, locals make do with resources already on hand, like prescription drugs. In addition, isolation affects heavily options for amenities and entertainment— a major contrast to the distractions of metropolitan areas.

Many adults in these rural areas tend to suffer from chronic illnesses and pain syndromes, born out of hard lives of manual labor in perilous professions—coal mining, logging, fishing, and other blue-collar industries—that often result in serious and debilitating injuries. As a result, a disproportionately high segment of the population lives on strong painkillers. The use of pain pills evolves into a kind of coping mechanism, and the practice of self-medication becomes a way of life for many. Thus, the use of opioid analgesics has become normalized and integrated into the local culture of several communities. Even more widely misused than OxyContin are hydrocodone, alprazolam, and carisoprodol. Hydrocodone (Vicodin, Lortab, Vicoprofen) is both a cough suppressant and an analgesic agent for the treatment of moderate to severe pain. Studies indicate that hydrocodone is nearly equivalent to morphine for pain relief. Approximately 143 million prescriptions containing hydrocodone were dispensed in the United States during 2012 (Drug Enforcement Administration 2013).

Several other prescription drugs are misused. Benzodiazepines (e.g., Xanax) can reduce panic and anxiety but are intended for short-term relief. In fact, repeat prescriptions of benzodiazepines are generally not medically advisable because of addiction potential and their inability to sustain reduced anxiety over the long term. Benzodiazepines are one of the few drugs that can lead to death following rapid withdrawal after long-term use. Fatal overdoses in which benzodiazepines are involved have increased since 1999 (Center for Substance Abuse Research 2013).

Other drugs having widespread misuse patterns include Adderall and methylphenidate. Adderall is an amphetamine that is used to treat attention-deficit hyperactivity disorder (ADHD), narcolepsy, and severe cases of depression. Methylphenidate (Ritalin, Concerta) is also used in the treatment of ADHD. It has a high potential for misuse and produces many of the same effects as cocaine or the amphetamines.

Notes

1. See for example: *Newsweek*, November 20, 1950, 57–58; January 29, 1951, 23–24; June 11, 1951, 26–27; June 25, 1951, 19–29; August 13, 1951, 50; September 17, 1951, 60; *Life*, June 11, 1951, 116, 119–22; *The Survey*, July 1951, 328–29; *Time*, February 26, 1951, 24; May 7, 1951, 82, 85; *Reader's Digest*, October 1951, 137–40.
2. Albert Hofmann died in 2008 at the age of 102.
3. Coca paste, also known as basuco, is an intermediate product in the transformation of the coca leaf into cocaine. An off-white doughy substance, it is typically mixed with either marijuana or tobacco and smoked in cigarette form.
4. Survey findings from the Monitoring the Future study can be viewed at http://www.monitoringthe future.org
5. Survey results from the National Survey on Drug Use and Health can be viewed at https://nsduh web.rti.org

References

American Medical Association, Department of Drugs. 1973. *AMA Drug Evaluations*. Acton, MA: Publishing Sciences Group.

Bahora, M., C. E. Sterk, and K. W. Elifson. 2009. "Understanding Recreational Ecstasy Use in the United States: A Qualitative Inquiry." *International Journal of Drug Policy* 20 (1): 62–69.

Bartholow, Roberts. 1891. *A Manual of Hypodermatic Medication*. 5th ed. Philadelphia: Lippincott.

Beck, Jerome, and Marsha Rosenbaum. 1994. *The Pursuit of Ecstasy: The MDMA Experience*. Albany: State University of New York Press.

Buchan, William. 1784. *Domestic Medicine: Or, A Treatise on the Prevention and Cure of Diseases by*

Regimen and Simple Medicines. Philadelphia: Crukshank, Bell, and Muir.

Center for Substance Abuse Research, University of Maryland. 2013. "Number of Unintentional Opioid Analgesic Deaths Continue to Increase; Benzodiazepine-Related Unintentional Deaths Now Surpass Cocaine." *CESAR FAX* 22 (April 22).

Chambers, Carl D. 1970. *An Assessment of Drug Use in the General Population*. Albany: New York State Narcotic Addiction Control Commission.

Chambers, Carl D., Leon Brill, and James A. Inciardi. 1972. "Toward Understanding and Managing Nonnarcotic Drug Abusers." *Federal Probation* 36 (March): 50–55.

Chein, Isidor, D. L. Gerard, R. S. Lee, and E. Rosenfeld. 1964. *The Road to H: Narcotics, Delinquency, and Social Policy*. New York: Basic Books.

Cook, Ernest Fullerton and Eric Wentworth Martin. 1951. *Remington's Practice of Pharmacy*. Easton, PA: Mack Publishing Co.

Domestic Council Drug Abuse Task Force. 1975. *White Paper on Drug Abuse*. Washington, DC: U.S. Government Printing Office.

Domino, E. F. 1964. "Neurobiology of Phencyclidine (Sernyl), a Drug with an Unusual Spectrum of Pharmacological Activity." *Internal Review of Neurobiology* 6: 303–347.

Drug Abuse Policy Office, Office of Policy Development. 1984. *National Strategy for Prevention of Drug Abuse and Drug Trafficking*. Washington, DC: U.S. Government Printing Office.

Drug Enforcement Administration. 2013. "Hydrocodone." Springfield, VA: Drug Enforcement Administration, Office of Diversion Control, Drug and Chemical Evaluation Section.

Eisner, Bruce. 1994. *Ecstasy: The MDMA Story*. 2nd ed. Berkeley, CA: Ronin.

European Monitoring Centre for Drugs and Drug Addiction. 2011. *Report on the Risk Assessment of Mephedrone in the Framework of the Council Decision on New Psychoactive Substances*, no. 9. Luxembourg: Publications Office of the European Union.

Executive Office of the President. 2011. *Epidemic: Responding to America's Prescription Drug Abuse Crisis*. Washington, DC: Author.

Farber, Leslie. 1966. "Ours Is the Addicted Society." *New York Times Magazine* (December 11): 43.

Federal Bureau of Investigation (n.d.). "Tips for Parents: The Truth About Club Drugs." Accessed November 1, 2013. http://www.fbi.gov/scams-safety/clubdrugs

Feldman, Harvey W. 1979. "PCP Use in Four Cities: An Overview." In *Angel Dust: An Ethnographic Study of PCP Users*, edited by H. W. Feldman, M. H. Agar, and G. M. Beschner, 29–51. Lexington, MA: Lexington Books.

Fort, Joel. 1969. *The Pleasure Seekers: The Drug Crisis, Youth, and Society*. New York: Grove Press.

Freudenmann, R. W., F. Öxier, and S. Bernschneider-Reif. 2006. "The Origin of MDMA (Ecstasy) Revisited: The True Story Reconstructed from the Original Documents." *Addiction* 101 (September): 1241–1245.

Griffith, John. 1966. "A Study of Illicit Amphetamine Drug Traffic in Oklahoma City." *American Journal of Psychiatry* 123 (5): 560–569.

Hall, James N. 1986. "Hurricane Crack." *Street Pharmacologist* 10 (September): 1–2.

Hernandez, S. H. and L. S. Nelson. 2010. "Prescription Drug Abuse: Insight into the Epidemic." *Clinical Pharmacology & Therapeutics* 88 (3): 307–317.

Inciardi, James A. 1972. "Analysis of Alleged THC Sold by Street Dealers." Unpublished data. Newark: University of Delaware.

Inciardi, James A. 1974. "Drugs, Drug-Taking and Drug-Seeking: Notations on the Dynamics of Myth, Change, and Reality." In *Drugs and the Criminal Justice System*, edited by James A. Inciardi and Carl D. Chambers, 203–222. Beverly Hills, CA: Sage.

Inciardi, James A. 1987. "Beyond Cocaine: Basuco, Crack, and other Coca Products." *Contemporary Drug Problems* 14 (Fall): 461–492.

Inciardi, James A., Hilary L. Surratt, Theodore J. Cicero, Steven P. Kurtz, Steven S. Martin, and Mark W. Parrino. 2009. "The 'Black Box' of Prescription Drug Diversion." *Journal of Addictive Diseases* 28 (4): 332–347.

Jaffe, J. H. and W. R. Martin. 1975. "Narcotic Analgesics and Antagonists." In *The Pharmacological Basis of Therapeutics*, 5th ed., edited by Louis S. Goodman, and Alfred Gilman. New York: Macmillan.

Johnston, Lloyd D., Patrick M. O'Malley, and Jerald G. Bachman. 1985. *Use of Licit and Illicit Drugs by*

America's High School Students, 1975–1984. Rockville, MD: National Institute on Drug Abuse.

Jones, Ernest. 1953. *The Life and Work of Sigmund Freud*, vol. 1. New York: Basic Books.

Lee, Juliet P., Robynn S. Battle, Brian Soller, and Naomi Brandes. 2011. "Thizzin'—Ecstasy Use Contexts and Emergent Social Meanings." *Addiction Research and Theory* 19 (6): 528–541.

Lerner, Max. 1957. *America as a Civilization: Life and Thought in the United States Today*. New York: Simon & Schuster.

Manchester, William. 1974. *The Glory and the Dream: A Narrative History of America, 1932–1972*. Boston: Little, Brown.

Manges, M. 1900. "A Second Report on the Therapeutics of Heroin." *New York Medical Journal* 71: 51–55.

McCabe, Sean E., Carol J. Boyd, and Christian J. Teter. 2009. "Subtypes of Nonmedical Prescription Drug Misuse." *Drug and Alcohol Dependence* 102: 63–70.

McPherson, George. E. and Joseph Cohen. 1919. "Survey of 100 Cases of Drug Addiction Entering Camp Upton, New York, via Draft, 1918." *Boston Medical and Surgical Journal* 180: 636–645.

Morgan, Howard W. 1974. *Yesterday's Addicts: American Society and Drug Abuse, 1865–1920*. Norman: University of Oklahoma Press.

National Clearinghouse for Drug Abuse Information. 1973. *Phencyclidine (PCP)*, NCDAI Pub. 18. Rockville, MD: Author.

National Commission on Marijuana and Drug Abuse. 1973. *Drug Abuse in America: Problem in Perspective*. Washington, DC: U.S. Government Printing Office.

New York Times. 1927. "Mexican Family Goes Insane." July 6, 10.

Office for National Statistics. 2013. *Deaths Related to Drug Poisoning in England and Wales, 2012*. London: Author.

Personal communication with the first author, December 7, 1969.

Price, R. B., M. K. Nock, D. S. Charney, and S. J. Mathew. 2009. "Effects of Intravenous Ketamine on Explicit and Implicit Measures of Suicidality in Treatment-Resistant Depression." *Biological Psychiatry* 66 (September): 522–526.

Reed, A. and A. W. Kane. 1970. "Phencyclidine (PCP)." *STASH Capsules* (December): 1–2.

Schatzman, M., A. Sabbadini, and L. Forti. 1976. "Coca and Cocaine." *Journal of Psychedelic Drugs* 8: 95–128.

Schnoll, S. H. and W. H. Vogel. 1971. "Analysis of 'Street Drugs.'" *New England Journal of Medicine* 284 (14): 791.

Sears, Roebuck & Co. 1968. *1897 Sears Roebuck Catalogue*, reprinted, p. 32. New York: Chelsea House.

Sloman, Larry. 1979. *Reefer Madness: A History of Marijuana in America*. Indianapolis: Bobbs-Merrill.

Substance Abuse and Mental Health Services Administration. 2005. *Results from the 2004 National Survey on Drug Use and Health: National Findings*. Office of Applied Studies, NSDUH Series H-28, DHHS Publication No. SMA 05-4062. Rockville, MD: Author.

Substance Abuse and Mental Health Services Administration. 2013. *Results from the 2012 National Survey on Drug Use and Health: Summary of National Findings*. NSDUH Series H-46, HHS Publication No. (SMA) 13-4795. Rockville, MD: Author.

Terry, Charles E. and Mildred Pellens. 1928. *The Opium Problem*. New York: Bureau of Social Hygiene.

Trebach, Arnold S. 1982. *The Heroin Solution*. New Haven, CT: Yale University.

United Kingdom Office for National Statistics. 2013. *Deaths Related to Drug Poisoning in England and Wales, 2012*. Newport, Wales: Author.

United Nations Office on Drugs and Crime. 2013. *The Challenge of New Psychoactive Substances*. Vienna: Author.

University of Michigan. 1989. News release. Ann Arbor: Author, February 28.

U.S. Congress, Select Committee on Narcotics Abuse Control. 1978. *Executive Summary: Hearings on Phencyclidine*. Washington, DC: U.S. Government Printing Office, August 8.

U.S. Senate Subcommittee to Investigate Juvenile Delinquency. 1972. Legislative Hearings on S. 674, "To Amend the Controlled Substances Act to Move Amphetamines and Certain Other Stimulant Substances from Schedule III of Such Act to Schedule II, and for Other Purposes," July 15 and 16, 1971. Washington, DC: US Government Printing Office.

Wright, C. R. A. 1874. "On the Action of Organic Acids and Their Anhydrides on the Natural Alkaloids." *Journal of the Chemical Society* 27: 1031–1043.

Young, James H. 1961. *The Toadstool Millionaires: A Social History of Patent Medicines in America Before Federal Regulation*. Princeton, NJ: Princeton University Press.

Zacny, James, George Bigelow, Peggy Compton, Kathleen Foley, Martin Iguchi, and Christine Sannerud. 2003. "College on Problems of Drug Dependence Taskforce on Prescription Opioid Non-medical Use and Abuse: Position Statement." *Drug and Alcohol Dependence* 69 (April): 215–232.

For Discussion

1. Why has marijuana remained so popular over the years?
2. What kind of *novel psychoactive substances* might emerge in the next ten years? What kinds of challenges will governments face in trying to control new substances?

2

The Hidden Epidemic

Opiate Addiction and Cocaine Use in the South, 1860–1920

DAVID T. COURTWRIGHT

Race and drug use have been examined by several scholars; however, historical data on this topic are difficult to access and interpret. In this article, David T. Courtwright uses a collection of historical information to explore different kinds of opiate and cocaine use among African Americans and whites. Courtwright's focus is on a region characterized by extreme inequality—the Southern states in the United States.

One of the many memorable characters in Harper Lee's novel, *To Kill a Mockingbird*, is an aged morphine addict, Mrs. Henry Lafayette Dubose. Mrs. Dubose was a cantankerous widow who lived in Maycomb, a small, fictitious Alabama town. She had been addicted many years before by her

Reprinted from David T. Courtwright, 1983, "The Hidden Epidemic: Opiate Addiction and Cocaine Use in the South, 1860–1920." In *Journal of Southern History* 49 (February): 57–72.

physician, who gave her morphine to ease her pain. Informed that she had only a short while to live, she struggled to quit taking the drug, for she was determined "to leave this world beholden to nothing and nobody."[1]

There were tens of thousands of real-life Mrs. Duboses scattered throughout the postbellum South. With the possible exception of the Chinese, southern whites had the highest addiction rate of any regional racial group in the country, and perhaps one of the highest in the world. At the same time southern blacks had a relatively low rate of addiction, at least with respect to opiates. Blacks, when they used drugs at all, tended to use cocaine. It has been alleged—and heatedly denied—that black cocaine use manifested itself in a major crime wave around the turn of the century. Even discounting these reports, it is apparent that the postbellum South had an unusually severe narcotic problem characterized by racial preferences for different drugs.

Documenting this pattern of drug use is difficult since users tended to conceal their practices for fear of social or legal reprisals. There are, nevertheless, a few sources of statistical data. The most important of these is a by-product of the 1914 Harrison Narcotic Act, which was designed to regulate the sale and distribution of narcotics, defined primarily as the opiates and cocaine. The fateful weakness of the Harrison Act was its failure to resolve the issue of maintenance; that is, could a physician legally supply an addict with drugs for the sole purpose of supporting his or her habit? After years of pressure from the Treasury Department the Supreme Court finally decided in March 1919 that physicians might not maintain addicted patients. Consequently many addicts, denied a legal source of opiates, were forced to turn to the black market. However, many municipalities, for both practical and humanitarian reasons, responded to this crisis by establishing narcotic clinics, which were designed to supply narcotics to, and in some instances to treat, addicted persons. But the federal government continued to pursue its antimaintenance policies, and within two years it had succeeded in closing nearly all the clinics.[2] Fortunately, however, their records survived, and in 1924

Table 2.1 Number of Opiate Addicts per Thousand Residents Attending Clinics in Eleven Southern Cities.

Atlanta, Georgia	2.567
Augusta, Georgia	.799
Macon, Georgia	.981
Paducah, Kentucky	1.415
New Orleans, Louisiana	.646
Shreveport, Louisiana	9.550
Shreveport, Louisiana (revised estimate)	4.809
Durham, North Carolina	1.658
Knoxville, Tennessee	2.364
Memphis, Tennessee	2.002
Houston, Texas	.882
Clarksburg, West Virginia	1.758
Average number of addicts per thousand for eleven cities using revised Shreveport estimate	1.530

Sources: Lawrence Kolb and A. G. Du Mez, 1924, "The Prevalence and Trend of Drug Addiction in the United States and Factors Influencing It," *Public Health Reports* 39, no. 21 (May 23): 1182; Charles E. Terry and Mildred Pellens, 1970, *The Opium Problem* (Montclair, NJ: Patterson Smith), 40–41, for the revised Shreveport figure.

two United States Public Health Service officials, Lawrence Kolb and Andrew G. Du Mez, tabulated the number of addicts attending clinics in thirty-four cities in twelve states. The data for eleven southern cities are set forth in Table 2.1; those for twenty-three northern and western cities in Table 2.2.

"In compiling the . . . figures from the reports," Kolb and Du Mez remarked, "the highest number of addicts recorded at any one time or in a certain year are given. . . . No reduction whatever was made in the totals for transients, although the reports show that many of the clinics treated addicts from distant as well as near-by places." The average rate for all thirty-four cities was .99, or almost precisely one addict per thousand residents. Of the cities listed, one in particular stands out: Shreveport's rate of 9.55 addicts per thousand persons was nearly 9.7 times as great as the overall average. Kolb and Du Mez attributed this to the relative longevity of Dr. Willis P. Butler's Shreveport clinic, which was

Table 2.2 Number of Opiate Addicts per Thousand Residents Attending Clinics in Twenty-Three Northern and Western Cities.

Los Angeles, California	.834
San Diego, California	2.397
Bridgeport, Connecticut	.550
Hartford, Connecticut	.761
Meriden, Connecticut	.067
New Haven, Connecticut	.492
Norwalk, Connecticut	.685
Waterbury, Connecticut	.938
Albany, New York	1.059
Binghamton, New York	.479
Buffalo, New York	.493
Corning, New York	1.391
Elmira, New York	.220
Hornell, New York	1.065
Middletown, New York	1.628
Oneonta, New York	3.195
Port Jervis, New York	1.671
Rochester, New York	.541
Saratoga Springs, New York	.910
Syracuse, New York	.536
Utica, New York	.266
Youngstown, Ohio	.491
Providence, Rhode Island	.737
Average number of addicts per thousand for twenty-three cities	.931

Source: Lawrence Kolb and A. G. Du Mez, 1924, "The Prevalence and Trend of Drug Addiction in the United States and Factors Influencing It," *Public Health Reports* 39, no. 21 (May 23): 1182.

not closed until 1923. As clinics in Houston, New Orleans, and other southern cities were closed, addicts made their way to Shreveport, where treatment was available and morphine could still be obtained for six cents a grain. Butler, who was also aware of the problem of transients, later went back through his records, dividing resident patients from nonresident patients. He found that, of 542 cases treated during 1920, 211 had resided in Caddo Parish a year prior to registration at the clinic, yielding a revised resident rate of approximately 4.8 addicts per thousand.[3]

There are other problems with the clinic data as well. There was, for one, a likelihood of underenumeration because many well-to-do addicts undoubtedly preferred anonymity to cheap drugs. On the other hand, as Kolb and Du Mez pointed out, these totals were also inflated by nonresidents who took advantage of the various maintenance programs. It is difficult to say whether these factors balanced out. But even if the clinic data cannot be used to determine the absolute number of addicts, they do indicate something about their regional distribution. The twenty-three northern and western cities averaged .93 addicts per thousand persons, while the eleven southern cities averaged 1.53 per thousand—a 64.5 percent higher rate. Even controlling for differences in city size, there is only a very slight possibility that the observed difference is due to chance.[4]

Two other, prototypical southern maintenance programs are also of interest. In August 1912, Jacksonville, Florida, passed an ordinance drafted by the city health officer, Charles Edward Terry, requiring that the Health Department be sent duplicate copies of prescriptions for medicines containing more than three grains of morphine or two grains of cocaine or their equivalents. The law also stipulated that the health officer might, upon acquiring "satisfactory evidence of habitual use," offer free prescriptions for narcotics to the addict, to be filled by a local druggist. The system was thus designed to supply narcotics to, as well as to keep track of, addicts. Table 2.3 represents a classification by drug, race, and sex of those persons registered during the first five months of operation.

Eliminating those who used cocaine alone, there were 383 opiate addicts altogether, a rate of approximately 5.5 per thousand persons. The following year Terry reported an even higher figure of 541 opiate addicts registered at his clinic (Table 2.4), although there is evidence that many of the new cases were transients.[5] But even if the lower 1912 figure is used it appears that the Jacksonville rate was at least five times that of the northern and western clinic average.

Finally, in 1913, the year after the Jacksonville program was formulated, Tennessee passed a law forbidding the refilling of narcotic prescriptions unless the person holding the prescription had

Table 2.3 1912 Jacksonville Registration/Maintenance Data.

	Percent of Users	White Males	White Females	Colored Males	Colored Females	Total
Morphine	38.85	54	114	15	26	209
Cocaine	28.81	30	23	50	52	155
Laudanum	18.59	14	44	11	31	100
Heroin	4.09	10	10	0	2	22
Gum opium	2.23	5	3	3	1	12
Cocaine and opiate combined	7.43	21	10	3	6	40
Totals	100.00	134	204	82	118	538

Source: City of Jacksonville, Florida, *Annual Report of the Board of Health for the Year 1912*, 26–27.

Table 2.4 1913 Jacksonville Registration/Maintenance Data.

	Percent of Users	White Males	White Females	Colored Males	Colored Females	Total
Morphine	32.92	94	142	20	36	292
Cocaine	39.00	102	109	58	77	346
Laudanum	12.18	23	30	11	44	108
Heroin	3.16	19	9	0	0	28
Gum opium	1.58	4	4	3	3	14
Cocaine and opiate combined	11.16	48	34	6	11	99
Totals	100.00	290	328	98	171	887

Source: City of Jacksonville, Florida, *Annual Report of the Board of Health for the Year 1913*, 57.

previously registered with the state as an addict. After a year of operation State Food and Drugs Commissioner Lucius P. Brown reported a total of 2,370 registrants, representing a rate of approximately 1.04 addicts per thousand persons. Brown seriously doubted, however, that all or even a majority of addicts had registered; his best guess was that there were "in the neighborhood of 5,000 addicts in Tennessee."[6] It would appear, then, that Tennessee also had an addiction rate in excess of the northern and western clinic average.

Further evidence for higher southern use is found in pharmacy records. A survey of the records of thirty-four Boston drugstores published in 1888 revealed that, of 10,200 prescriptions sampled, 1,481 or 14.5 percent contained some type of opiate.[7] Unfortunately, there was no comparable study of prescriptions for a major southern city. However, a sampling of the contents of two surviving record

books of New Orleans pharmacists dating from the 1870s and 1880s shows that fully 24.5 percent of these prescriptions contained opium or morphine—ten percentage points more than the Boston average.[8] While a limited, two-city comparison does not prove that an entire region had a higher rate of addiction, it at least corroborates the differences in clinic registration. Taken together, the statistical evidence indicates that the South suffered an inordinately high rate of opiate addiction in comparison to other regions of the continental United States.

The burden of addiction was not borne equally, however. Whites were overrepresented among opium and morphine addicts, blacks underrepresented. In 1885 Dr. James D. Roberts of the Eastern North Carolina Insane Asylum, after making a number of inquiries, reported that he knew "of but three well-authenticated cases of opium-eating in the negro."[9] In Jacksonville, nearly three-quarters of the opium and morphine addicts were white, even though whites made up slightly less than half of that city's population. Commissioner Brown noted that not over 10 percent of Tennessee's registrants were black, even though blacks made up roughly one-quarter of that state's population.[10] In Shreveport, 91.5 and in Houston, 95.5 of the clinic patients were white, remarkable statistics in view of the substantial black population in those areas.[11] The high overall southern rate of addiction, together with the relatively low number of black addicts, suggests that postbellum southern whites, as a group, suffered an exceedingly high rate of opiate addiction.

The key to understanding both the extent and racial distribution of southern addiction is nineteenth-century medical practice. Most American physicians were ill equipped to cure most diseases—diseases whose etiology they but dimly understood. The majority of their remedies were useless; some, like calomel, were positively dangerous. Yet at the same time doctors, who received a fee for their professional services, felt compelled to do something for the patient, even if it was only blind, symptomatic treatment. Opiates were thus extremely popular as a way of offering temporary relief for a wide variety of ailments; they were in fact used as a virtual panacea. In 1850, for example, a young New Orleans physician named John Bernard Vandergriff began compiling a list of prescriptions used to combat various diseases. His notes show that opiates were administered, often in conjunction with other drugs, to treat such diverse conditions as asthma, bronchitis, cholera, chlorosis, colic, diarrhea, dysentery, hemorrhoids, intermittent fever, and leukorrhea. They were also recommended as a general anodyne and "anti-emetic," and even as a treatment for distemper in horses.[12]

If the opiates were popular at mid-century, they were even more so after the 1860s and 1870s, when the spread of hypodermic medication gave doctors a powerful new technique for administering morphine, whose soothing, analgesic effects were almost immediately felt. As New Orleans surgeon Charles Schuppert put it, an injection of morphine "acted like a charm," alleviating the symptoms and lifting the spirits of the ill and injured.[13] The danger, however, was that patients, especially if

they suffered from some chronic, painful condition, might become physically dependent through repeated administrations of the drug. Physical dependence is the state in which discontinuation of an opiate will bring on a train of characteristic withdrawal symptoms: yawning, sneezing, sweating, severe cramps, diarrhea, vomiting, and others. Once the dependent patient learned to banish these withdrawal symptoms by merely taking another dose, then he or she became a full-blown addict, using opiates on a daily basis.[14]

Treatment by physicians, it should be added, was not the only cause of opiate addiction. Some addicts undoubtedly owed their plight to self-medication, either with patent medicines or home remedies containing opiates. The recipe book of Texas pioneer Anna G. McKenney, for example, lists several medications for cholera, diarrhea, and chills in which laudanum (tincture of opium) was an active ingredient.[15] It is unlikely, however, that the occasional swig of a narcotic nostrum or dose of a folk remedy created as many addicts as did the direct administration of opium or one of its alkaloids by physicians. Remarks in the medical literature,[16] as well as a number of statistical studies,[17] indicate that a majority of nineteenth-century and early-twentieth-century addicts could trace their condition back to narcotics provided by their doctors.

The simplest way to avoid addiction, then, was to stay healthy, stay away from patent medicines, and, above all, stay away from hypodermic-wielding physicians. Unfortunately, this was something that relatively few southerners could do. The postbellum South was an insalubrious place; diarrhea, dysentery, and malaria were all widespread, endemic diseases.[18] Opiates, which possess constipating as well as analgesic properties, were very commonly used to treat diarrheal disorders.[19] They were also commonly used to relieve the paroxysms of malaria.[20] Since diarrhea, dysentery, and malaria were often chronic, debilitating diseases, the administration of opiates every time the symptoms recurred could easily lead to physical dependence, thence to addiction. There was, by way of comparison, a similar problem in the English Fenland, the low-lying country in and around Cambridgeshire. The Fens were one of the most unhealthy areas in nineteenth-century

England, the residents allegedly "prone to the ague, 'painful rheumatisms,' and neuralgia." The presence of these endemic diseases was, according to Virginia Berridge, a leading scholar of Victorian drug use, one important reason why the region had an exceedingly high rate of opium consumption.[21]

The Civil War also contributed to southern addiction. Per capita, the South suffered more casualties than the North; there were therefore relatively more wounded or shell-shocked soldiers who were candidates for addiction during or after the conflict.[22] The Civil War also had an enormous psychological impact on the South; with the realization that a way of life was irretrievably lost came a lingering, pervasive depression, especially among the planter elite. One knowledgeable New York opium dealer thought he saw a connection between the South's increased opiate consumption and its postwar malaise. "Since the close of the war," he remarked in 1877, "men once wealthy, but impoverished by the rebellion, have taken to eating and drinking opium to drown their sorrows."[23] Women, too, he might have added; they had their own war-related troubles, and the opiates were especially attractive as a semirespectable substitute for alcohol.[24]

The Civil War also provides a clue as to why blacks had a relatively low rate of addiction; Confederate defeat was for most of them an occasion of rejoicing rather than profound depression. This was almost certainly not as important, however, as the fact that blacks generally lacked access to professional medical care. Because they were poor, because they were discriminated against, and because there were relatively few doctors of their own race, blacks could not avail themselves of physicians' services as often as did southern whites.[25] While this may have exacerbated their high rates of morbidity and mortality, it at least conferred an ironic benefit: freedom from iatrogenic, or physician-caused, opiate addiction.

Two other factors also help to explain the lower black rate of addiction, although these should be considered of secondary importance. First, blacks tended to be younger than whites. In 1890, for example, the median age of blacks was 18.1 years; whites, 22.5 years.[26] Stated another way, relatively more whites survived to middle age and beyond. This is significant because many of the

chronic diseases commonly treated with opiates (such as arthritis, rheumatism, or delirium tremens) were conditions observed primarily among older patients, Mrs. Dubose again serving as a prime example. Second, it is now known that southern blacks, for a variety of complex genetic reasons, suffered fewer and less severe cases of malaria.[27] Since malaria was one of the chronic diseases treated symptomatically with opiates, this also conferred a slight advantage on blacks, from the standpoint of avoiding addiction.

The low rate of opiate addiction among southern blacks, however, does not necessarily mean that they were entirely drug free. Although opiates were by all odds the leading drug of addiction during the nineteenth and early twentieth centuries, other drugs, notably cocaine, were also overused. In the mid-1880s many American physicians, encouraged by the glowing reports of Sigmund Freud and other cocaine enthusiasts, administered the drug for a wide variety of ailments; cocaine, like opium and morphine, became something of a panacea.[28] Within a few years, however, more conservative physicians launched a counterattack, warning their colleagues in articles and speeches of the danger of creating "cocainists."[29]

Just as these animadversions began to have an effect growing numbers of blacks were beginning to use cocaine for other, essentially nonmedical, reasons. It appears that blacks were introduced to cocaine sometime in the late 1880s or 1890s when New Orleans stevedores began taking the drug to help them endure long spells of loading and unloading steamboats, a task at which they labored for up to seventy hours at a stretch.[30] In this respect they resembled South American natives, who chewed coca leaves to increase their nervous energy, avoid drowsiness, and "bear cold, wet, great bodily exertion, and even want of food . . . with apparent ease and impunity."[31] Whether these stevedores took to cocaine on their own initiative, or whether they were introduced to the drug by their foremen, is not known. It is known, however, that the use of cocaine by black laborers soon spread from New Orleans to other parts of the South, to cotton plantations, railroad work camps, and levee construction sites.[32] "Well, the cocaine habit is might' bad," ran one work song, "It kill ev-ybody I know it to have had."[33] Other blacks sniffed cocaine, not as a stimulus to work, but as a form of dissipation.[34] Altogether, there were proportionately more black cocaine users than white. In Jacksonville, for example, area blacks had a rate of cocaine use almost twice that of white residents in 1912.[35] Southern police chiefs who responded to a national survey on drug use in 1908 and 1909 stated that there were relatively more black cocaine users than white, an opinion shared by their northern colleagues.[36] Prison statistics, although fragmentary, are consistent with the belief that cocaine was more popular among blacks than whites.[37]

Less clear are the behavioral implications of cocaine use by blacks. From 1900 to 1914 several white authorities claimed that blacks, crazed by cocaine, went on superhuman rampages of violence. "[M]any of the horrible crimes committed in the Southern States by the colored people can be traced directly to the cocaine habit," charged Colonel J. W. Watson of Georgia in 1903.[38] Others who sounded variations on this theme included New Orleans district attorney St. Clair Adams, Vicksburg municipal court judge Harris Dickson, New Jersey physician Edward Huntington Williams, and Dr. Hamilton Wright, a leading member of the United States Opium Commission.[39] Police officials were also concerned with cocaine's exciting effects. "When negroes get too much of it," wrote Louisville police chief Jacob H. Haager, "they are inclined to go on the war-path, and when in this condition they give a police officer who attempts to arrest them . . . a hard time."[40]

In recent years a number of authors have flatly denied these allegations. David F. Musto, a psychiatrist and historian, has argued that "These fantasies characterized white fear, not the reality of cocaine's effects. . . ."[41] Richard Ashley has also dismissed them as "fear-mongering fantasies," while Joël L. Phillips and Ronald D. Wynne conclude that "No reputable researchers have uncovered any statistical or other type of evidence to indicate that the use of cocaine resulted in a massive (black) crime wave."[42]

Why, then, did so many contemporaries make the link between blacks, cocaine, and crime? One possible explanation is that they had ulterior political motives. Hamilton Wright, for example, may

have used the cocaine stories in an effort to secure the support of Negrophobic southern congressmen for pending antinarcotic legislation. Similarly, Edward Williams was an antiprohibitionist who, by suggesting that when blacks were denied liquor they switched to cocaine, may have been attempting to persuade the public that alcohol was the lesser of two evils. Beyond discrediting the testimony of Drs. Williams and Wright, Musto has also suggested that, in general, the cocaine stories served as a further excuse to repress and disfranchise blacks and as a convenient explanation for crime waves.[43]

While there is much validity in these arguments, and while it is virtually certain that there was no massive wave of cocaine-related crime, there may be additional reasons why so many authorities made this association. One possibility is that they were simply repeating a legend, a legend based upon a few scattered incidents. It is not impossible to imagine that a "hitherto inoffensive, law-abiding negro," as Dr. Williams described him, chafing under accumulated slurs and outrages, might, under the influence of cocaine, vent his rage on a white person, especially a white policeman. Such an attack might represent genuine cocaine psychosis or simply relaxed inhibitions combined with long-standing grievances.[44]

Given the supercharged racial atmosphere of the South, it would take only a few such episodes to fashion a full-fledged cocaine "menace." The fear of cocaine-sniffing blacks was thus not unlike the fear of slave rebellion which swept the South after Nat Turner's short-lived foray; both were exaggerated reactions to isolated but potently symbolic deeds. A second likely explanation involves the background of black cocaine users, especially those who lived in cities. As New Orleans police inspector William J. O'Connor put it, they often belonged to the "immoral and lower" elements of the black community.[45] Some of them were, in other words, already involved in a range of criminal activities, and a white authority, aware that they also sniffed cocaine, could easily have inferred that cocaine caused the crimes: *post hoc, ergo propter hoc.*

Finally, there is a sense in which cocaine indirectly contributed to crimes against property. Regular cocaine use could be expensive, especially after restrictive state legislation increased its price; therefore, many impoverished black users would have had to resort to petty crime in order to obtain the drug. Once again an observer—particularly one who had heard other cocaine-crime stories—could well have drawn the inference that the action of the drug itself, rather than the lack of money to purchase it, had inspired the deed. A similar mistake was made during the early 1920s, when it was commonly believed that heroin, rather than the addicts' compulsion to obtain it, was a direct incentive to crime.[46] Thus, the widespread belief that cocaine caused blacks to commit crimes, which perhaps originated in one or two *bona fide* episodes, was sustained and expanded by a false sense of causation. The legend grew when Wright and Williams, both physicians with apparently impeccable credentials, used it to suit their own political ends.

Exaggerated fears of black cocaine rampages may also have had the effect of drawing attention from the real southern drug problem—opiates— and obscuring the majority of the real victims— white medical addicts. Opiate addicts were, in any event, ailing, secretive, and heavily tranquilized individuals, reluctant to come into the public eye. Their reluctance was due, in large measure, to unfavorable attitudes toward addicts. Prior to 1870 most Americans—including physicians—regarded opiate addiction as a vice, a bad habit indulged in by the weak-willed and the sinful. Even though they may have originally received the drug from a doctor, the addicts continued taking it, according to one Methodist minister, because "They learn to love the excitement which it produces. . . . "[47]

After 1870, however, a small but growing number of physicians, most of whom specialized in treating addicted and alcoholic patients, challenged this prevailing view. They argued that opiate addiction was a variety of a more general condition called *inebriety* and that inebriety was a functional disease triggered by an underlying mental disturbance. An individual who had, for example, either inherited or acquired a weakened, nervous constitution was thought to be more susceptible than a neurologically normal person. It followed that opiate addiction was not necessarily a vice but was more often a manifestation of a genuine disease. Advocates of this position, who established the American Association for the Cure of Inebriates in 1870 and began publishing a house organ called the *Quarterly Journal of Inebriety* in 1876, had considerable influence in both northern and southern medical circles.[48] It is doubtful, however, that they drastically changed the attitudes of most ordinary men and women, whose understanding of such matters was shaped less by specialized journals than by gossip, stereotypes, and the strictures of evangelical Protestantism. So, as a practical matter, most addicts continued to conceal their condition from relatives and neighbors, even as medical interpretations of their plight were beginning to change during the closing decades of the nineteenth century.

Thus, the spread of opiate addiction through the South after 1860 was, in many respects, a hidden epidemic. The roots of this epidemic were the presence of endemic infectious and parasitic diseases and the lingering trauma, physical and psychological, of the Civil War. The principal reason for the unbalanced racial distribution of opiate addiction was that blacks generally lacked access to professional medical care. The age distribution of blacks and their partial immunity to malarial diseases may also have played a role. The epilogue of this story is that blacks were not significantly afflicted by opiate addiction until they left the South and began settling in large numbers in the drug-ridden tenderloins and ghettos of northern cities.

Notes

1. Lee, 1960, *To Kill a Mockingbird* (Philadelphia: Lippincott), 94–105; quotation on 104.
2. For further details on the evolution of the anti-maintenance policy see David F. Musto, 1973, *The American Disease: Origins of Narcotic Control* (New Haven, CT: Yale University Press), 54–182.
3. Kolb and Du Mez, 1924, "The Prevalence and Trend of Drug Addiction in the United States and Factors Influencing It," *Public Health Reports* 39 (May 23): 1180–88 (quotation on 1182); Case 73790 (Houston), Treasury Department Files, hereinafter cited as TDF (accessed through the Freedom of Information Division of the Drug Enforcement Administration, Washington, DC); Charles E. Terry

and Mildred Pellens, 1970, *The Opium Problem* (Montclair, NJ: Patterson Smith), 40–41. Butler's description of the clinic, "How One American City Is Meeting the Public Health Problems of Narcotic Addiction," appears in *American Medicine* 28 (March 1922), 154–62.

4. Using the data in Tables 2.1 and 2.2 (including the revised Shreveport estimate), a regression of the addiction rate (*A*) on city population (*P*) and a dummy variable (*D*, where South = 1, North and West drug 0) yields
$$\hat{A} = 1.1435 - .16357 \times 10^{-5}P + .84083D$$
$$(n = 34)\ (t = -1.47)\ (t = 2.60)$$
The relationship between the addiction rate and city size is relatively weak, but the relationship between the addiction rate and the dummy variable, representing regional differences, is significant at $p < .01$.

5. Charles E. Terry, "Habit-Forming Drugs," in City of Jacksonville, Florida, *Annual Report of the Board of Health for the Year 1912* (n.p., n.d.), 24–29; ibid., 1913 (n.p., n.d.), 55–58; Terry, 1914, "Drug Addictions, a Public Health Problem," *American Journal of Public Health* 4 (January): 28–37; and Terry and Pellens, *Opium Problem*, 24–27 (quotation on 24). On the influx of transients see Kolb and Du Mez, "Prevalence and Trend," 1201; and Lawrence Kolb to Lawrence C. Kolb, December 12, 1932, Box 6, Lawrence Kolb Papers (History of Medicine Division, U.S. National Library of Medicine, Bethesda, MD).

6. Lucius P. Brown, 1915, "Enforcement of the Tennessee Anti-Narcotics Law," *American Journal of Public Health* 5 (April): 323–33; quotation on 331.

7. Virgil G. Eaton, 1888, "How the Opium-Habit Is Acquired," *Popular Science Monthly* 33 (September): 665.

8. Thirty of a hundred randomly selected entries in the prescription record book of George D. Feldner (Rudolph Matas Medical Library, cited hereinafter as RMML, Tulane University School of Medicine, New Orleans, LA) contained opiates; likewise nineteen of a hundred randomly selected entries in the prescription record book of Erich Brand (Historical Pharmacy Museum of New Orleans). The Feldner sample falls in the years 1886–1889; the Brand sample, 1877–1878. Both druggists were situated on Magazine Street. Levi Nutt, head of the Narcotic Division of the Prohibition Unit of the Bureau of Internal Revenue, also commented on the high southern rate in U. S. House of Representatives, 1921, *Exportation of Opium: Hearings Before a Subcommittee of the Committee on Ways and Means on H.R. 14500*, 66th Cong., 3rd Sess., 133.

9. Roberts, 1885, "Opium Habit in the Negro," *North Carolina Medical Journal* 16 (September): 206–207; quotation on 207.

10. Brown, "Enforcement of Tennessee Law," 330–31; see Tables 2.3 and 2.4 for Jacksonville.

11. Dan Waldorf, Martin Orlick, and Craig Reinarman, 1974, *Morphine Maintenance: The Shreveport Clinic, 1919–1923* (Washington, DC), 28; memorandum to L. G. Nutt, March 26, 1920, Houston file, Case 73790, TDF. Southern clinics, like much else in southern life, were segregated. New Orleans, for example, had separate entrances for white males, white females, and "colored" patients. M. W. Swords, 1920, "A Résumé of Facts and Deductions Obtained by the Operation of a Narcotic Dispensary," *American Medicine* 26 (January): 25–26. In spite of the segregated facilities, I have uncovered no evidence to suggest that blacks were denied access to the clinics. Since a major goal of these programs was to preempt the illicit traffic in narcotics, they necessarily catered to all groups. Had black addicts been excluded, they would have been forced to resort to crime to pay the peddlers' high prices—and this was something that both local police and public health officials earnestly wished to avoid.

12. John B. Vandergriff, 1850, "Pharmaceutical Preparations and Select Prescriptions" (MS; RMML), 77, 79, et passim.

13. Charles Schuppert, "Notes, Case Records and Observations, Charity Hospital Medical College" (MS, 1875–1879; RMML), 54.

14. For more on the addiction process see Alfred R. Lindesmith, *Addiction and Opiates* (Chicago, 1968), 23–155. It should be noted that the term "addiction" is used here for convenience and consistency; nineteenth-century addicts were called "opium eaters," "morphine eaters," "morphinists," and various other names.

15. "Mrs. McKenney's Cook Book," MS, n.d., 1830?–1860? (Texas History Research Library, The Alamo, San Antonio, TX), 77, 83, 88, 91.

16. Of the dozens of journal articles that attributed the bulk of opium and morphine addiction to

physicians, the following are typical: J. S. Weatherly, 1869, "Increase in the Habit of Opium Eating," Medical Association of the State of Alabama, *Transactions*, 67; H. S. Duncan, 1885, "The Morphia Habit—How Is It Most Usually Contracted, and What Is the Best Means to Diminish It?" *Nashville Journal of Medicine and Surgery* N.S., 35 (June): 247; Harry M. Nickerson, 1900, "The Relation of the Physician to the Drug Habit," *Journal of Medicine and Science* 6 (January): 50; and Brown, "Enforcement of Tennessee Law," 329.

17. Terry, "Drug Addictions," 32, concluded that physicians were responsible for about 55 percent of the cases of opiate addiction that he observed, the remainder being divided among self-medication on the advice of friends (21.6 percent), "dissipation" (21.2 percent), and "chronic incurable disease" (2.4 percent). These figures were based on a subsample of 213 users. See also Lyman F. Kebler, 1911, "The Present Status of Drug Addiction in the United States," *Monthly Cyclopaedia and Medical Bulletin* 4 (January): 15; and the manuscript case records on oversized sheets, Box 6, Kolb Papers. The latter were described by Kolb as "representing . . . addicts in various situations, from various walks of life, and in widely separated sections of the country, [and] may be considered fairly representative of the addict population as a whole." Kolb, 1925, "Types and Characteristics of Drug Addicts," *Mental Hygiene* 9 (April): 300. There are 230 decipherable cases altogether, including 174 opium and morphine, 40 heroin, 7 smoking opium, 7 cocaine only, and 2 veronal. Most of the case histories were taken in late 1923 or shortly thereafter. Of the 171 opium and morphine addicts whose backgrounds were known, 41.5 percent were designated as "physician," 25.1 percent as "self-medication," and 22.2 percent as "associates." Another category, 11.1 percent, consisted of those who were introduced to the drug by a physician but continued use on their own. Thus, physicians were directly or indirectly responsible for over half (52.6 percent) of all the opium and morphine cases in Kolb's sample.

18. William H. Deaderick and Loyd Thompson, 1916, *The Endemic Diseases of the Southern States* (Philadelphia and London: W. B. Saunders Co.), 21, 399; Joseph I. Waring, 1967, *A History of Medicine in South Carolina, 1825–1900* (Charleston), 177–79. The prevalence of diarrheal diseases in the South is also reflected in Samuel M. Bemiss, comp., "Record of Cases Attended at Charity Hospital, New Orleans, October 1868–February 1875" (MS; RMML). Note that "diarrhea" and "dysentery" signified in the nineteenth century practically any disease in which the chief symptom was a loose stool (diarrhea) or loose stool with blood and pus (dysentery). Other diseases in which diarrhea was a symptom, such as cholera, or in which diarrhea was sometimes present, such as typhoid fever, were also treated with opium and morphine.

19. Anon., "Notes on Dudley's Lectures Taken in 1830" (MS; RMML), 153; the second and sixth cases in Jacob E. Fitch, 1881, "Case Records, Charity Hospital, New Orleans" (MS; RMML); and W. B. Cheadle, 1894, "A Lecture on the Clinical Uses of Opium," *Clinical Journal* 4 (September 26), 350. Leslie C. Campbell, 1974, *Two Hundred Years of Pharmacy in Mississippi* (Jackson, MS), 78, notes that in 1907 paregoric "was being 'abused in Mississippi most grievously.'" This is significant, since paregoric is the form of opium commonly given for diarrhea.

20. John B. Beck, 1861, *Lectures on Materia Medica and Therapeutics . . .* 3rd ed., ed. by C. R. Gilman (New York: Samuel S. and William Wood), 368; and "Opium in Fevers," 1887, *Journal of the American Medical Association* 8 (March 5): 265. Kolb and Du Mez, "Prevalence and Trend," 1184, also mention hookworm as a factor, but I have found little evidence that this condition was routinely treated with opiates.

21. Berridge, 1977, "Fenland Opium Eating in the Nineteenth Century," *British Journal of Addiction to Alcohol and Other Drugs* 72 (September): 275–84; quotation on 275.

22. On the role of the war in fostering addiction see David T. Courtwright, 1978, "Opiate Addiction as a Consequence of the Civil War," *Civil War History* 24 (June): 101–11.

23. "Opium and Its Consumers," *New York Tribune*, July 10, 1877, 2. Gaines M. Foster, who has investigated the impact of the war on alcohol consumption, writes that drink may also have served as an escape for some embittered southerners, though the extent of this phenomenon is by no means clear. Personal correspondence.

24. T. J. Happel, 1895, "The Opium Curse and Its Prevention," *Medical and Surgical Reporter* 72 (May 25): 727–31; John S. Haller, Jr., and Robin M. Haller, 1974, *The Physician and Sexuality in Victorian America* (Urbana, Chicago, and London: University of Illinois Press), 302. Other reasons for the relatively large numbers of women addicts, both North and South, were the use of opiates to treat "female troubles," especially dysmenorrhea, and the propensity of male physicians to diagnose the ailments of their female patients as "nervous disorders" and then to treat them with the tranquilizing opiates. See also Fred H. Hubbard, 1881, *The Opium Habit and Alcoholism* (New York: A. S. Barnes & Co.), 17. W. P. Crumbacker to Hamilton Wright, September 3, 1908, Records of the United States International Opium Commission and Conference, Record Group 43 (National Archives, Washington, DC; hereinafter cited as USIOC Records); and Brown, "Enforcement of Tennessee Law," 332–33.

25. Horace W. Conrad, 1887, "The Health of the Negroes in the South: The Great Mortality Among Them; the Causes and Remedies," *Sanitarian* 18 (June): 505, 507; W. E. Burghardt Du Bois, ed., 1906, *The Health and Physique of the Negro American* (Atlanta: Atlanta University Press), 110; Herbert M. Morais, 1967, *The History of the Negro in Medicine* (New York: Publishers Company), 85–86; and Marshall S. Legan, 1973, "Disease and the Freedmen in Mississippi During Reconstruction," *Journal of the History of Medicine and Allied Sciences* 28 (July): 267.

26. U. S. Bureau of the Census, 1975, *Historical Statistics of the United States: Colonial Times to 1970* (2 pts., Washington), Part 1, Series A-146 and A-149, p. 19. The hypothesis that age differences might be associated with the unbalanced racial distribution of addicts was suggested to me by Gerald N. Grob.

27. Todd L. Savitt, 1978, *Medicine and Slavery: The Diseases and Health Care of Blacks in Antebellum Virginia* (Urbana, Chicago, and London: University of Illinois Press), 17–35.

28. Sigmund Freud, 1975, *Cocaine Papers*, ed. Robert Byck with notes by Anna Freud (New York: Stonehill), especially xvii–xxxix, 49–88, 121–50.

29. For example, J. B. Mattison, 1892, "Cocainism," *Medical Record* 42 (October 22): 474–77; 43 (January 14, 1893): 34–36.

30. "Negro Cocaine Fiends," 1902, *Medical News* 81 (November 8): 895; also abstracted as "The Cocaine Habit Among Negroes," 1902, *British Medical Journal* (November 29): Part 2, p. 1729. See also George E. Pettey, 1913, *The Narcotic Drug Diseases and Allied Ailments: Pathology, Pathogenesis, and Treatment* (Philadelphia: F. A. Davis Company), 426.

31. J. T. Whittaker, 1885, "Cocaine in the Treatment of the Opium Habit," *Medical News* 47 (August 8): 148. See also G. Archie Stockwell, 1877, "Erythroxylon Coca," *Boston Medical and Surgical Journal* 96 (April 5): 401.

32. "The Cocaine Habit Among Negroes," 1729; Harris Dickson to Hamilton Wright, December 7, 1909, USIOC Records.

33. Cited in Lawrence W. Levine, 1977, *Black Culture and Black Consciousness: Afro-American Folk Thought from Slavery to Freedom* (New York: Oxford University Press), 283. On the basis of his study of black music Levine believes that cocaine use was common among southern blacks, although he doubts that the drug provoked interracial violence as some have alleged. Personal correspondence. I am indebted to Eugene D. Genovese for calling my attention to Levine's work.

34. "Cocaine Alley," 1900, *American Druggist and Pharmaceutical Record* 37 (December 10): 337–38; "The Cocain Habit," 1900, *Journal of the American Medical Association* 36 (June 23): 330.

35. From Table 2.3, not counting combination opiate-cocaine users or the occasional cocaine users who failed to find their way into Terry's program. The following year the situation was reversed, but only, as has been already noted, after a large influx of outside users. It is my view that the original 1912 data best represent the Jacksonville situation.

36. Representative of the southern authorities were Colonel Swan in "Baltimore Notes" (MS, 1908), no pp.; and W. P. Ford of Norfolk, VA, to Hamilton Wright, June 18, 1909, USIOC Records. For the views of northern and midwestern police chiefs who wrote to Wright, see for example J. J. Donahue of Omaha, June 21, 1909; A. G. Miller of Des Moines, June 21, 1909; and Thomas A. McQuaide of Pittsburgh, June 29, 1909, ibid.

37. Two prison physicians, O. J. Bennet of the Western Penitentiary of Pennsylvania and Frank A. McGuire of the City Prison of New York, stated that blacks tended to use cocaine more than

whites. Bennet found that 7 of 682 inmates examined over a two-year period admitted the use of cocaine and that all were black. "My candid opinion of the matter," he was quoted as saying, "is that the use of . . . [cocaine] is increasing rapidly, especially among the black population." Thomas G. Simonton, 1903, "The Increase of the Use of Cocaine Among the Laity in Pittsburgh," *Philadelphia Medical Journal* 11 (March 28): 558; McGuire to Wright, August 4, 1908, USIOC Records. Years later blacks were still overrepresented among federal drug prisoners who used only cocaine; of eleven such cases listed in U. S. House of Representatives, 1928, *Establishment of Two Federal Narcotic Farms: Hearings Before the Committee on the Judiciary,* 70th Cong., 1st Sess. (Washington), 140–47, 151–60, four were black, six were white, and one was Mexican. There is one contrary article, E. M. Green, 1914, "Psychoses Among Negroes—A Comparative Study," *Journal of Nervous and Mental Disease* 41 (November): 702, to the effect that cocaine was a factor in only 2 of 2,119 black cases admitted to the Georgia State Sanitarium between January 1, 1909, and January 1, 1914. Green thought cocaine sufficiently expensive and disruptive of working ability that few blacks could afford its habitual use, hence few psychoses resulted. However, that was in the years 1909 to 1914, well after adverse legislation had driven up the price of the drug. Green's statistics, moreover, do not of themselves prove a low incidence of cocaine use among Georgia blacks; they prove only that cocaine-using blacks were not confined in Georgia sanitaria. Either cocaine psychosis was uncommon or, when it occurred, some other agency dealt with it. The latter would apply especially to incidents involving theft or violence, which would more likely terminate in prison, or at the end of a rope, than in an asylum. Note too that Green's analysis does not apply to occasional black cocaine use, which would not have been likely to produce psychoses.

38. "Cocaine Sniffers," 1903, *New York Tribune* (June 21): Pt. II, p. 11.

39. "Aaron Martin Sold 470 Ounces of Cocaine in Nine Months," New Orleans *Item,* n.d., n.p., clipping in USIOC Records; Charles W. Collins and John Day, 1909, "Dope, the New Vice: Part 1, the Eighth Deadly Sin," *Everyday Life* 4 (July): 4, 29;

Edward H. Williams, "Negro Cocaine 'Fiends' Are a New Southern Menace," 1914, *New York Times* (February 8, 1914): Sec. 5, p. 12; and Williams, 1914, "The Drug-Habit Menace in the South," *Medical Record* 85 (February 7): 247–49; Hamilton Wright, 1910, *Report on the International Opium Commission and on the Opium Problem as Seen Within the United States and Its Possessions (Senate Documents,* 61st Cong., 2nd Sess., No. 377, Serial 5657, Washington), 48–50; and U.S. House of Representatives, 1911, *Importation and Use of Opium: Hearings Before the Committee on Ways and Means on H. 25240–42 and 28971 . . . ,* 61st Cong., 3rd Sess., 83.

40. Jacob Haager to Hamilton Wright, July 9, 1909, USIOC Records. Other police chiefs who corresponded with Wright also stated that cocaine was an incentive to crime, without going into particulars. See J. J. Reagan of Lexington, KY, June 17, 1909; W. P. Ford of Norfolk, VA, June 18, 1909; and E. E. Creecy of St. Louis, June 21, 1909, ibid. It should be added that all these police officials were replying to a routine letter of inquiry and had no apparent motive for distortion. See also [Louis] Werner, "The Illegal Sale of Cocaine," in International Association of Chiefs of Police, 1909, *The Police Yearbook . . . Containing the Proceedings of the Sixteenth Annual Session* (Grand Rapids, MI), 84–86.

41. Musto, *American Disease,* 7.

42. Richard Ashley, 1975, *Cocaine: Its History, Uses and Effects* (New York), 67–72 (quotation on 68); Phillips and Wynne, 1980, *Cocaine: The Mystique and the Reality* (New York), 64–71 (quotation on 68).

43. Musto, *American Disease,* 7, 43–44, 254–55 n. 15, 256 n. 20; Joseph L. Zentner, 1977, "Cocaine and the Criminal Sanction," *Journal of Drug Issues* 7 (Spring): 97–98, follows Musto's argument closely.

44. The quotation by Dr. Williams is from his "Drug-Habit Menace in the South," 247. For specific incidents of violent crimes committed by blacks allegedly under the influence of cocaine see Werner, "Illegal Sale," 84–85; and "10 Killed, 35 Hurt in Race Riot Born of Cocaine 'Jag,'" 1913, *New York Herald* (September 29): 1. Significantly, whites were also sometimes observed to engage in violent or vengeful behavior under the influence of cocaine. For example, T. D. Crothers, 1910, "Cocainism," *Journal of Inebriety* 32 (Summer): 80; "Aaron Martin Sold 470 Ounces of Cocaine"; and Henry O. Whiteside, 1978, "The Drug Habit in Nineteenth-Century

Colorado," *Colorado Magazine* 55 (Winter): 64. See also Phillips and Wynne, *Cocaine*, 162–63.

45. O'Connor to Wright, June 22, 1909, USIOC Records. "As a rule," noted Acting Chief W. P. Ford of Norfolk, VA, "the lowest class of white's [*sic*] and negroes . . . [use it]; 'Sniffing' is (or was) mostly indulged by white and negro prostitutes, the latter being given to the practice, to a considerably greater extent than the former." Ford to Wright, June 18, 1909, ibid. See also Werner, "Illegal Sale," 84.

46. See, for example, *The Case Against Heroin*, 1924 (Foreign Policy Association Pamphlet No. 24, New York), 4.

47. J. Townley Crane, 1858, "Drugs as an Indulgence," *Methodist Quarterly Review* 40 (October): 562.

48. A[rnold] Jaffe, 1978, "Reform in American Medical Science: The Inebriety Movement and the Origins of the Psychological Disease Theory of Addiction, 1870–1920," *British Journal of Addiction to Alcohol and Other Drugs* 73 (June): 139–47. For further details, see Chapter 5 of David T. Courtwright, 1982, *Dark Paradise: Opiate Addiction in America Before 1940* (Cambridge, MA, and London: Harvard University Press).

For Discussion

1. Discuss how some of the findings are shaped by the intersection of social class *and* race.
2. Place or locale is important. Would some of the findings be different had the study been focused on states located in the northeastern region of the United States? Why or why not?

3

Marijuana

Assassin of Youth

HARRY J. ANSLINGER AND COURTNEY RYLEY COOPER

In the 1930s, Harry J. Anslinger was appointed commissioner of the Federal Bureau of Narcotics. This article is one of many that he wrote describing marijuana as a "Frankenstein" drug that was stalking American youth. As a result of Anslinger's crusade, on August 2, 1937, the Marijuana Tax Act was signed into law, classifying the scraggly tramp of the vegetable world as a narcotic and placing it under essentially the same controls as the Harrison Act had done with opium and coca products.

Reprinted from Harry J. Anslinger and Courtney Ryley Cooper, 1937, "Marijuana: Assassin of Youth." In *American Magazine*, July 1937.

The sprawled body of a young girl lay crushed on the sidewalk the other day after a plunge from the fifth story of a Chicago apartment house. Everyone called it suicide, but actually it was murder. The killer was a narcotic known to America as marijuana, and to history as hashish. It is a narcotic used in the form of cigarettes, comparatively new to the United States and as dangerous as a coiled rattlesnake.

How many murders, suicides, robberies, criminal assaults, holdups, burglaries, and deeds of maniacal insanity it causes each year, especially among the young, can be only conjectured. The sweeping march of its addiction has been so insidious that, in numerous communities, it thrives almost unmolested largely because of official ignorance of its effects.

Here indeed is the unknown quantity among narcotics. No one can predict its effect. No one knows, when he places a marijuana cigarette to his lips, whether he will become a philosopher, a joyous reveler in a musical heaven, a mad insensate, a calm philosopher, or a murderer.

That youth has been selected by the peddlers of this poison as an especially fertile field makes it a problem of serious concern to every man and woman in America.

There was the young girl, for instance, who leaped to her death. Her story is typical. Some time before, this girl, like others of her age who attend our high schools, had heard the whispering of a secret which has gone the rounds of American youth. It promised a new thrill, the smoking of a type of cigarette which contained a "real kick." According to the whispers, this cigarette could accomplish wonderful reactions and with no harmful aftereffects. So the adventurous girl and a group of her friends gathered in an apartment, thrilled with the idea of doing "something different" in which there was "no harm." Then a friend produced a few cigarettes of the loosely rolled "homemade" type. They were passed from one to another of the young people, each taking a few puffs.

The results were weird. Some of the party went into paroxysms of laughter; every remark, no matter how silly, seemed excruciatingly funny. Others of mediocre musical ability became almost expert; the piano dinned constantly. Still others found themselves discussing weighty problems of youth with remarkable clarity. As one youngster expressed it, he "could see through stone walls." The girl danced without fatigue, and the night of unexplainable exhilaration seemed to stretch out as though it were a year long. Time, conscience, or consequences became too trivial for consideration.

Other parties followed, in which inhibitions vanished, conventional barriers departed, all at the command of this strange cigarette with its ropy, resinous odor. Finally there came a gathering at a time when the girl was behind in her studies and greatly worried. With every puff of the smoke the feeling of despondency lessened. Everything was going to be all right—at last. The girl was "floating" now, a term given to marijuana intoxication. Suddenly, in the midst of laughter and dancing, she thought of her school problems. Instantly they were solved. Without hesitancy she walked to a window and leaped to her death. Thus can marijuana "solve" one's difficulties.

The cigarettes may have been sold by a hot tamale vendor or by a street peddler, or in a dance hall or over a lunch counter, or even from sources much nearer to the customer. The police of a Midwestern city recently accused a school janitor of having conspired with four other men, not only to peddle cigarettes to children, but even to furnish apartments where smoking parties might be held.

A Chicago mother, watching her daughter die as an indirect result of marijuana addiction, told officers that at least fifty of the girl's young friends were slaves to the narcotic. This means fifty unpredictables. They may cease its use; that is not so difficult as with some narcotics. They may continue addiction until they deteriorate mentally and become insane. Or they may turn to violent forms of crime, to suicide or to murder. Marijuana gives few warnings of what it intends to do to the human brain.

The menace of marijuana addiction is comparatively new to America. In 1931, the marijuana file of the United States Narcotic Bureau was less than two inches thick, while today the reports crowd many large cabinets. Marijuana is a weed of the Indian hemp family, known in Asia as *Cannabis indica* and in America as *Cannabis sativa*. Almost everyone who has spent much time in rural communities has seen it, for it is cultivated in practically every state. Growing plants by the thousands were destroyed by law enforcement officers last year in Texas, New York, New Jersey, Mississippi, Michigan, Maryland, Louisiana, Illinois, and the attack on the weed is only beginning.

It was an unprovoked crime some years ago which brought the first realization that the age-old drug had gained a foothold in America. An entire family was murdered by a youthful addict in Florida. When officers arrived at the home they found the youth staggering about in a human slaughterhouse. With an ax he had killed his father, his mother, two brothers, and a sister. He seemed to be in a daze.

"I've had a terrible dream," he said. "People tried to hack off my arms!"

"Who were they?" an officer asked.

"I don't know. Maybe one was my uncle. They slashed me with knives and I saw blood dripping from an ax."

He had no recollection of having committed the multiple crime. The officers knew him ordinarily as a sane, rather quiet young man; now he was pitifully crazed. They sought the reason. The boy said he had been in the habit of smoking something which youthful friends called "muggles," a childish name for marijuana.

Since that tragedy there has been a race between the spread of marijuana and its suppression. Unhappily, so far, marijuana has won by many lengths. The years 1935 and 1936 saw its most rapid growth in traffic. But at least we now know what we are facing. We know its history, its effects, and its potential victims. Perhaps with the spread of this knowledge the public may be aroused sufficiently to conquer the menace. Every parent owes it to his children to tell them of the terrible effects of marijuana to offset the enticing "private information" which these youths may have received. There must be constant enforcement and equally constant education against this enemy, which has a record of murder and terror running through the centuries.

The weed was known to the ancient Greeks and it is mentioned in Homer's *Odyssey*. Homer wrote that it made men forget their homes and turned them into swine. Ancient Egyptians used it.

In the year 1090, there was founded in Persia the religious and military order of the Assassins, whose history is one of cruelty, barbarity, and murder, and for good reason. The members were confirmed users of hashish, or marijuana, and it is from the Arabic "*hashshashin*" that we have the English word "assassin." Even the term "running amok" relates to the drug, for the expression has been used to describe natives of the Malay Peninsula who, under the influence of hashish, engage in violent and bloody deeds.

Marijuana was introduced into the United States from Mexico, and swept across America with incredible speed. It began with the whispering of vendors in the Southwest that marijuana would perform miracles for those who smoked it, giving them a feeling of physical strength and mental power, stimulation of the imagination, the ability to be "the life of the party." The peddlers preached also of the weed's capabilities as a "love potion." Youth, always adventurous, began to look into these claims and found some of them true, not knowing that this was only half the story. They were not told that addicts may often develop a delirious rage during which they are temporarily and violently insane; that this insanity may take the form of a desire for self-destruction or a persecution complex to be satisfied only by the commission of some heinous crime.

It would be well for law-enforcement officers everywhere to search for marijuana behind cases of criminal and sex assault. During the last year a young male addict was hanged in Baltimore for criminal assault on a ten-year-old girl. His defense was that he was temporarily insane from smoking marijuana. In Alamosa, Colorado, a degenerate brutally attacked a young girl while under the influence of the drug. In Chicago, two marijuana-smoking boys murdered a policeman.

In at least two dozen other comparatively recent cases of murder or degenerate sex attacks, many of them committed by youths, marijuana proved to be a contributing cause. Perhaps you remember the young desperado in Michigan who, a few months ago, caused a reign of terror by his career of burglaries and holdups, finally to be sent to prison for life after kidnapping a Michigan state policeman, killing him, then handcuffing him to the post of a rural mailbox. This young bandit was a marijuana fiend.

A sixteen-year-old boy was arrested in California for burglary. Under the influence of marijuana he had stolen a revolver and was on the way to stage a holdup when apprehended. Then there was the nineteen-year-old addict in Columbus, Ohio, who, when police responded to a disturbance complaint, opened fire upon an officer, wounding him three times, and was himself killed by the returning fire of the police. In Ohio a gang of seven young men, all less than twenty years old, had been caught after a series of thirty-eight holdups. An officer asked them where they got their incentive.

"We only work when we're high on 'tea'" one explained.

"On what?"

"On tea. Oh, there are lots of names for it. Some people call it 'mu' or 'muggles' or 'Mary Weaver' or 'moocah' or 'weed' or 'reefers'—there's a million names for it."

"All of which mean marijuana?"

"Sure. Us kids got on to it in high school three or four years ago; there must have been twenty-five or thirty of us who started smoking it. The stuff was cheaper then; you could buy a whole tobacco tin of it for fifty cents. Now these peddlers will charge you all they can get, depending on how shaky you are. Usually though, it's two cigarettes for a quarter."

This boy's casual story of procurement of the drug was typical of conditions in many cities in America. He told of buying the cigarettes in dance halls, from the owners of small hamburger joints, from peddlers who appeared near high schools at dismissal time. Then there were the "booth joints" or barbecue stands, where one might obtain a cigarette and a sandwich for a quarter, and there were the shabby apartments of women who provided not only the cigarettes but rooms in which girls and boys might smoke them.

"But after you get the habit," the boy added, "you don't bother much about finding a place to smoke. I've seen as many as three or four high school kids jam into a telephone booth and take a few drags."

The officer questioned him about the gang's crimes: "Remember that filling-station attendant you robbed—how you threatened to beat his brains out?"

The youth thought hard. "I've got a sort of hazy recollection," he answered. "I'm not trying to say I wasn't there, you understand. The trouble is, with all my gang, we can't remember exactly what we've done or said. When you get to 'floating,' it's hard to keep track of things."

From the other youthful members of the gang the officer could get little information. They confessed the robberies as one would vaguely remember bad dreams. "If I had killed somebody on one of those jobs, I'd never have known it," explained one youth. "Sometimes it was over before I realized that I'd even been out of my room."

Therein lies much of the cruelty of marijuana, especially in its attack upon youth. The young, immature brain is a thing of impulses, upon which the "unknown quantity" of the drug acts as an almost overpowering stimulant. There are numerous cases on record like that of an Atlanta boy who robbed his father's safe of thousands of dollars in jewelry and cash. Of high school age, this boy apparently had been headed for an honest, successful career. Gradually, however, his father noticed a change in him. Spells of shakiness and nervousness would be succeeded by periods when the boy would assume a grandiose manner and engage in excessive, senseless laughter, extravagant conversation, and wildly impulsive actions. When these actions finally resulted in robbery the father went at his son's problem in earnest—and found the cause of it a marijuana peddler who catered to school children. The peddler was arrested.

It is this useless destruction of youth which is so heartbreaking to all of us who labor in the field of narcotic suppression. No one can predict what may happen after the smoking of the weed. I am reminded of a Los Angeles case in which a boy of seventeen killed a policeman. They had been great friends. Patrolling his beat, the officer often stopped to talk to the young fellow, to advise him. But one day the boy surged toward the patrolman with a gun in his hand; there was a blaze of yellowish flame, and the officer fell dead.

"Why did you kill him?" the youth was asked.

"I don't know," he sobbed. "He was good to me. I was high on reefers. Suddenly I decided to shoot him."

In a small Ohio town, a few months ago, a fifteen-year-old boy was found wandering the streets, mentally deranged by marijuana. Officers learned that he had obtained the dope at a garage. "Are any other school kids getting cigarettes there?" he was asked.

"Sure. I know fifteen or twenty, maybe more. I'm only counting my friends."

The garage was raided. Three men were arrested and eighteen pounds of marijuana seized. "We'd been figuring on quitting the racket," one of the dopesters told the arresting officer. "These kids had us scared. After we'd gotten 'em on the weed, it looked like easy money for a while. Then they kept wanting more and more of it, and if we didn't have it for 'em, they'd get tough. Along toward the last, we were scared that one of 'em would get high and kill us all. There wasn't any fun in it."

Not long ago a fifteen-year-old girl ran away from her home in Muskegon, Michigan, to be arrested later in company with five young men in a Detroit marijuana den. A man and his wife ran the place. How many children had smoked there will never be known. There were sixty cigarettes on hand, enough fodder for sixty murders.

A newspaper in St. Louis reported after an investigation this year that it had discovered marijuana "dens," all frequented by children of high-school age. The same sort of story came from Missouri, Ohio, Louisiana, Colorado—in fact, from coast to coast.

In Birmingham, Alabama, a hot tamale salesman had pushed his cart about town for five years, and for a large part of that time he had been peddling marijuana cigarettes to students of a downtown high school. His stock of the weed, he said, came from Texas and consisted, when he was captured, of enough marijuana to manufacture hundreds of cigarettes.

In New Orleans, of 437 persons of varying ages arrested for a wide range of crimes, 125 were addicts. Of 37 murderers, 17 used marijuana, and of 193 convicted thieves, 34 were "on the weed."

One of the first places in which marijuana found a ready welcome was in a closely congested section of New York. Among those who first introduced it there were musicians, who had brought the habit northward with the surge of "hot" music demanding players of exceptional ability, especially in improvisation. Along the Mexican border and in seaport cities it had been known for some time that the musician who desired to get the "hottest" effects from his playing often turned to marijuana for aid.

One reason was that marijuana has a strangely exhilarating effect upon the musical sensibilities (Indian hemp has long been used as a component of "singing seed" for canary birds). Another reason was that strange quality of marijuana which makes a rubber band out of time, stretching it to unbelievable lengths. The musician who uses "reefers" finds that the musical beat seemingly comes to him quite slowly, thus allowing him to interpolate any number of improvised notes with comparative ease. While under the influence of marijuana, he does not realize that he is tapping the keys with a furious speed impossible for one in a normal state of mind; marijuana has stretched out the time of the music until a dozen notes may be crowded into the space normally occupied by one. Or, to quote a young musician arrested by Kansas City officers as a "muggles smoker":

> Of course I use it—I've got to. I can't play any more without it, and I know a hundred other musicians who are in the same fix. You see, when I'm "floating," I own my saxophone. I mean I can do anything with it. The notes seem to dance out of it—no effort at all. I don't have to worry about reading the music—I'm music-crazy. Where do I get the stuff? In almost any low-class dance hall or night spot in the United States.

Soon a song was written about the drug. Perhaps you remember:

> Have you seen
> That funny reefer man?
> He says he swam to China;
> Any time he takes a notion,
> He can walk across the ocean.

It sounded funny. Dancing girls and boys pondered about "reefers" and learned through the whispers of other boys and girls that these cigarettes could make one accomplish the impossible. Sadly enough, they can—in the imagination. The boy who plans a holdup, the youth who seizes a gun and prepares for a murder, the girl who decides suddenly to elope with a boy she did not even know a few hours ago, does so with the confident belief that this is a thoroughly logical action without the slightest possibility of disastrous consequences. Command a person "high" on "mu" or "muggles" or "Mary Jane" to crawl on the floor and bark like a dog, and he will do it without a thought of the idiocy of the action. Everything, no matter how insane, becomes plausible. The underworld calls marijuana "that stuff that makes you able to jump off the tops of skyscrapers."

Reports from various sections of the country indicate that the control and sale of marijuana has not yet passed into the hands of the big gangster syndicates. The supply is so vast and grows in so many places that gangsters perhaps have found it difficult to dominate the source. A big, hardy weed, with serrated, sword like leaves topped by bunchy small blooms supported upon a thick, stringy stalk, marijuana has been discovered in almost every state. New York police uprooted hundreds of plants growing in a vacant lot in Brooklyn. In New York State alone last year 200 tons of the growing weed were destroyed. Acres of it have been found in various communities. Patches have been revealed in back yards, behind signboards, in gardens. In many places in the West it grows wild. Wandering dopesters gather the tops from along the right of way of railroads.

An evidence of how large the traffic may be came to light last year near La Fitte, Louisiana. Neighbors of an Italian family had become amazed by wild stories told by the children of the family. They, it seemed, had suddenly become millionaires. They talked of owning inconceivable amounts of money, of automobiles they did not possess, of living in a palatial home. At last their absurd lies were reported to the police, who discovered that their parents were allowing them to smoke something that came from the tops of tall plants which their father grew on his farm. There was a raid, in which more than 500,000 marijuana plants were destroyed. This discovery led next day to another

raid on a farm at Bourg, Louisiana. Here a crop of some 2,000 plants was found to be growing between rows of vegetables. The eight persons arrested confessed that their main source of income from this crop was in sales to boys and girls of high-school age.

With possibilities for such tremendous crops, grown secretly, gangdom has been hampered in its efforts to corner the profits of what has now become an enormous business. It is to be hoped that the menace of marijuana can be wiped out before it falls into the vicious protectorate of powerful members of the underworld.

But to crush this traffic we must first squarely face the facts. Unfortunately, while every state except one has laws to cope with the traffic, the powerful right arm which could support these states has been all but impotent. I refer to the United States government. There has been no national law against the growing, sale, or possession of marijuana.

As this is written a bill to give the federal government control over marijuana has been introduced in Congress by Representative Robert L. Doughton of North Carolina, Chairman of the House Ways and Means Committee. It has the backing of Secretary of the Treasury Morgenthau, who has under his supervision the various agencies of the United States Treasury Department, including the Bureau of Narcotics, through which Uncle Sam fights the dope evil. It is a revenue bill, modeled after other narcotic laws which make use of the taxing power to bring about regulation and control.

The passage of such a law, however, should not be the signal for the public to lean back, fold its hands, and decide that all danger is over. America now faces a condition in which a new, although ancient, narcotic has come to live next door to us, a narcotic that does not have to be smuggled into the country. This means a job of unceasing watchfulness by every police department and by every public-spirited civic organization. It calls for campaigns of education in every school, so that children will not be deceived by the wiles of peddlers, but will know of the insanity, the disgrace, the horror which marijuana can bring to its victim. And, above all, every citizen should keep constantly before him the real picture of the "reefer man"—not some funny fellow who, should he take the notion, could walk across the ocean.

In Los Angeles, California, a youth was walking along a downtown street after inhaling a marijuana cigarette. For many addicts, merely a portion of a "reefer" is enough to induce intoxication. Suddenly, for no reason, he decided that someone had threatened to kill him and that his life at that very moment was in danger. Wildly he looked about him. The only person in sight was an aged bootblack. Drug crazed nerve centers conjured the innocent old shoe-shiner into a destroying monster. Mad with fright, the addict hurried to his room and got a gun. He killed the old man, and then, later, babbled his grief over what had been wanton, uncontrolled murder.

"I thought someone was after me," he said. "That's the only reason I did it. I had never seen the old fellow before. Something just told me to kill him!"

That's marijuana!

For Discussion

1. This article was published a few years after alcohol prohibition was repealed. Is it likely that the U.S. government will always keep some drugs illegal?

2. One of the authors of this article, Harry J. Anslinger, provided the following testimony to the U.S. Congress in 1937:

> There are 100,000 total marijuana smokers in the U.S., and most are Negroes, Hispanics, Filipinos and entertainers. Their Satanic music, jazz and swing, result from marijuana usage. This marijuana causes white women to seek sexual relations with Negroes, entertainers and any others.

Based on these statements and Anslinger's article in this section, what do you think were some of the main motives behind Anslinger's crusade against marijuana? Why do you think his views became so influential—greatly contributing to the passage of the Marijuana Tax Act in 1937?

Moral Panics and the Social Construction of Drug Use

In the introduction to this edited collection, we described that alcohol use was not perceived as a social problem in Colonial America. Although public intoxication was frowned upon during this era, the consumption of alcohol was an acceptable practice among people of all social classes and embedded into social life—in workplaces, during ceremonies and other public gatherings, and in homes. Later, the various temperance movements of the early to mid-1800s sought a collective abstinence. Temperance societies felt that alcohol consumption needed to be curtailed because it violated the moral order. In stark contrast to the previous century, many individuals who drank alcohol were portrayed as objects of disgrace. In other words, alcohol consumption became *constructed* as a social problem by *moral entrepreneurs*—individuals who attempt to create rules that reflect their moral beliefs (see Becker 1963).

Although Howard Becker (1963) introduced the important concept of moral entrepreneurs, scholars in England expanded on the idea of the social construction of deviance in part by outlining the role of the media. Jock Young (1971) allegedly proposed the phrase "moral panic," although his friend and colleague, Stanley Cohen, is generally given credit for its origins. Cohen's (1972) book, entitled *Folk Devils and Moral Panics: The Creation of the Mods and Rockers*, highlighted the amplified media reaction toward the behavior of two groups of working-class youth in Britain. Cohen suggested that moral entrepreneurs, law enforcement, and media collectively amplify a relatively minor social behavior that is perceived to threaten moral order. This reaction works to create discernible folk devils, and strategies are initiated to address the exaggerated threat.

Goode and Ben-Yehuda (1994) envisioned moral panic as a process—one that stems from unfavorable, if not hostile societal concern about particular behavior. This process assumes a general consensus that the behavior is risky, dangerous, or harmful, followed by an exaggerated reaction by institutions of power, for example, media, politicians, police, and schools. Some of these elements of the process have been contested. For example, sociologist and legal scholar David Garland (2008) suggested that moral panics can be characterized by strongly divided views rather than societal consensus. Since the work of Young (1971) and Cohen (1972), researchers from various disciplines have applied the moral panic perspective to dozens of topics. In a special issue of the *British Journal of Criminology*, Ben-Yehuda (2009) noted that the moral panic perspective has expanded to include, for example, a greater focus on the ways in which folk devils resist and how the condemners respond to this resistance. He also discussed the idea that moral panics might progress differently in multicultural societies characterized by competing moralities. The moral panic perspective has been critiqued in terms of its assumptions about public reaction. For example, Cornwell and Linders (2002) argued that the public are not necessarily a passive audience who believe all media images of danger and harm.

In the United States, the media have helped to socially construct and amplify several "drug problems." *Drug scares* are a type of moral panic that tend to focus not only on a particular drug, but also on particular groups of people who are perceived by those in power to be a threat to mainstream societal values and moral order (Reinarman 1999). In other words, drug scares "reinforce" social inequalities based on race, ethnicity, class, gender, and other power differentials. Hence, drug scares about methamphetamine use have incorporated discriminatory terms, for example, "redneck" and "white trash," to highlight the behaviors of white people from rural poor backgrounds (Armstrong 2007). Drug scares that focused on so-called crack babies tended to target African American women from low-income backgrounds.

Seven Ingredients of a Drug Scare

1. A kernel of truth
2. Media magnification
3. Politico-moral entrepreneurs
4. Professional interest groups
5. Historical context of conflict
6. Linking drug use to a "dangerous class"
7. Scapegoating drug use for public problems

Source: Reinarman, Craig, 1999, "The Social Impact of Drugs and the War on Drugs: The Social Construction of Drug Scares." In *The War on Drugs: Addicted to Failure, Recommendations of the Los Angeles Citizens' Commission on U.S. Drug Policy*, 58–79. Washington, DC: Institute for Policy Studies.

Reinarman and Levine (1997, 24) discussed how media present relevant news material during a drug scare. In their view, media engage in "routinization of caricature" in which "worst cases [are] framed as typical cases." Moreover, drug scares often serve to expand the reach of social control; hence, the "crack baby" scare contributed to public attitudes that favored criminal penalties for pregnant women who used crack cocaine. In turn, women in several US states faced arrest and prosecution for using crack cocaine while pregnant (although crimes were not enacted for the use of several other drugs, including alcohol while pregnant). Proponents of the drug scare perspective do not necessarily deny the existence of a particular behavior (e.g., drug use). Rather, they focus on how and why a behavior escalates into a major social problem, and they are concerned about the implications for the "folk devils," that is, people who lack power and privilege. The two chapters that follow explore moral panic relating to fetal alcohol syndrome and synthetic cannabis use.

References

Armstrong, E. G. 2007. "Moral Panic over Meth." *Contemporary Justice Review* 10 (4): 427–442.

Becker, H. S. 1963. *Outsiders: Studies in the Sociology of Deviance*. New York: Free Press of Glencoe.

Ben-Yehuda, N. 2009. "Foreword: Moral Panics—36 Years On." *British Journal of Criminology* 49: 1–3.

Cohen, S. 1972. *Folk Devils and Moral Panics: The Creation of the Mods and Rockers*. London: MacGibbon and Kee.

Cornwell, B., and A. Linders. 2002. "The Myth of Moral Panic: An Alternative Account of LSD Prohibition." *Deviant Behavior* 23: 307–330.

Garland, D. 2008. "On the Concept of Moral Panic." *Crime, Media, Culture* 4 (April): 9–30.

Goode, E., and N. Ben-Yehuda. 1994. *Moral Panics: The Social Construction of Deviance*. Oxford, England: Blackwell.

Reinarman, C. 1999. "The Social Impact of Drugs and the War on Drugs: The Social Construction of Drug Scares." In *The War on Drugs: Addicted to Failure, Recommendations of the Los Angeles Citizens' Commission on U.S. Drug Policy*, 58–79. Washington, DC: Institute for Policy Studies.

Reinarman, C., and H. G. Levine, eds. 1997. *Crack in America: Demon Drugs and Social Justice*. Berkeley: University of California Press.

Young, J. 1971. "The Role of the Police as Amplifiers of Deviancy." In *Images of Deviance*, edited by Stanley Cohen, 27–61. Harmondsworth: Penguin.

4

Fetal Alcohol Syndrome
The Origins of a Moral Panic

ELIZABETH M. ARMSTRONG AND ERNEST L. ABEL

In this article, Elizabeth M. Armstrong and Ernest L. Abel show how fetal alcohol syndrome escalated into a major social problem. The authors do not deny the existence of fetal alcohol syndrome; rather, they highlight how the portrayal of and response to the problem was characterized by moral panic.

Introduction

Fetal alcohol syndrome (FAS) is a pattern of anomalies occurring in children born to alcoholic women (Jones and Smith 1973). The main features of this pattern are pre- and/or postnatal growth retardation, characteristic facial abnormalities, and central nervous system dysfunction, including mental retardation (Stratton et al. 1996). Despite the pervasiveness of alcohol and drunkenness in human history (Abel 1997), FAS went largely unrecognized until 1973, when it was characterized as a "tragic disorder" by Jones and Smith, the Seattle physicians who discovered it (Jones and Smith 1973). By the 1990s, FAS had been transformed in the United States from an unrecognized condition to a moral panic characterized as a "major public health concern" (e.g., Stratton et al. 1996) and a "national health priority" (Egeland et al. 1998). In this paper, we trace this evolution, paying special attention to the ways in which this moral panic has inflated fear and anxiety about the syndrome beyond levels warranted by evidence of its prevalence or impact. To acknowledge that the current level of concern about FAS is exaggerated is not to suggest that the syndrome does not exist. One of us (E. L. A.) has spent his entire professional career researching and writing about FAS and continues to be actively engaged in its prevention.

Social Problems

Any activity people engage in is subject to someone's opprobrium. Activities can rise to the level of "social problems" when someone or some group attributes harms or dangers to those activities, calls upon governmental powers to put an end to those harms, and is able to convince others of that view. The likelihood of this occurring increases when the activity that is identified as a problem resonates with underlying societal concerns and anxieties and has endorsement by experts who give legitimacy to such claims (Blumer 1971; Stone 1989). Such legitimacy has the effect of attracting media attention which in turn can attract further support

Reprinted from Elizabeth M. Armstrong and Ernest L. Abel, 2000, "Fetal Alcohol Syndrome: The Origins of a Moral Panic," *Alcohol and Alcoholism* 35 (3): 276–282, by permission of Oxford University Press.

from the public and policy makers (Gerbner and Gross 1976; Best 1990).

In the USA alcohol has been a regularly targeted "social problem" since the beginning of the nineteenth century. During the colonial era when per capita alcohol consumption was four times higher than at present and drunkenness was commonplace (Gusfield 1963; Levine 1978, 1983), alcohol was hailed by Puritan clerics such as Cotton Mather as "the Good Creature of God" (Levine 1983). Two centuries later, the "Good Creature" had become symbolic of deep rifts in American society and was rechristened "demon rum." The first anti-drinking reform movement occurred in the 1830s–1850s when the poverty and disease of Irish immigrants was attributed to their liquor consumption. The next occurred in the 1880s–1910s, when problems of nascent industrialization, such as poverty, the disintegration of family life, rising crime, and mental illness, were attributed to the influence of saloons, which were also the gathering places of the second great wave of immigrants. The current anti-alcohol/drug crusade, which attributes rampant crime and the deterioration of inner cities to a breakdown in public morality abetted by alcohol and drug use, began in the 1970s as a reaction to the turbulent 1960s (Engs 1997) and intensified in the early 1980s, when the "war on drugs" was launched. In its wake, grassroots organizations such as Mothers Against Drunk Driving (MADD) emerged, and many states raised their legal drinking age and lowered their blood-alcohol level (BAL) criterion for impaired driving (Engs 1997). This new wave of morality was heralded in the media as America's "new temperance" (*Newsweek* 12/84; *Time* 5/85), the "sobering of America" (*Business Week* 2/85), and "America: New Abstinence" (*Fortune* 3/85) (quoted in Reinarman 1988).

Concurrent with the reinvigoration of the temperance mentality in American life was the emergence of a new social problem: the victimization of children (Best 1990). The problem of child neglect/abuse, reflected in the "battered child syndrome," was first described in the medical literature in 1962 (Kempe et al. 1962), and was broadened in the 1970s to encompass not only physical battering, but emotional, sexual and mental mistreatment as well. In the course of this evolution, child abuse and neglect became another symbol of America's moral decay (Best 1990). It was within this dual context of the new temperance zeitgeist and the concern about the victimization of children prevailing in America that FAS emerged as a social problem in the 1970s, evolved into a moral crusade by the 1980s with its disturbing images of children "wounded" (Greenfeld 1989) or "bruised before birth" (Steacy 1989), and became transmogrified into a moral panic characterized as "child abuse in the unborn fetus" (Apolo 1995) in the 1990s.

Breakdown in Public Morality

It is not unreasonable for people to become concerned about an issue which threatens social order, especially if the threat stems from a perceived deterioration in the values which people believe provide guidance for themselves, their children, and their society as a whole. It is probably not a coincidence that FAS entered the arenas of scientific and public awareness in the 1970s and gained such widespread acceptability and attention by the early 1980s, since the issue resonated with the renewed ideology of self control and personal responsibility associated with the conservative political climate that followed the turbulent 1960s (Reinarman 1988).

The early construction of drinking during pregnancy as a social problem shared many of the same ideologies as those underlying the crusade against drunk-driving, most notably a focus on individual, personal responsibility for "lifestyle choices" and a belief in the power of broad-based public education campaigns to change behavior (Reinarman 1988). However, in the case of FAS, much of the impetus behind the emerging crusade came from the biomedical community (Abel 1984). An example of moralizing about the "tragic disorder" of FAS and personal failing was an article in the *Journal of Dentistry for Children*, which described a despondent mother who consumed alcohol during her pregnancy allegedly lamenting "If only I had known," a regret, the author stated, that occurs "all too often" but need not if pregnant women would only learn that "life is not a beer commercial" (Waldman 1989, 435). Other biomedical experts voiced breast-beating recriminations. A common theme was that the dangers of drinking during pregnancy were well known in Biblical and Greco-Roman times (Abel 1984, 1997), implying that if we had only paid attention to the bitter lessons of the past, the modern "tragedy" might have been avoided. "Physicians, writers and theologians" had written about the effects of alcohol on the fetus "since Biblical times" intoned Hill and Tennyson (1980), who then chastized modern society with the inclusive moral lapse of failing "to heed the wisdom of our forefathers" (177). The authors concluded with a statement from a temperance tract dating to the 1860s that said it still "holds true today that parents are responsible for their children's infirmities, deafness, blindness and idiocy" (198).

The Crusade

Stirred by such moral rectitude, preventing FAS became an American crusade. The policy response rested on the unproven premise that any amount of drinking in pregnancy posed a threat to the fetus. In 1981, the Surgeon General of the United States advised "women who are pregnant (or considering pregnancy) not to drink alcoholic beverages and to be aware of the alcoholic content of foods and drugs" (Food and Drug Administration 1981). The Surgeon General's warning stands in stark contrast to the official advice offered in other countries. The British Royal College of Obstetricians and Gynaecologists, for example, issued guidelines in 1996 stating that "no adverse effects on pregnancy outcome have been proven with a consumption of less than 120 grams of alcohol per week" and recommending that "women should be careful about alcohol consumption in pregnancy and limit this to no more than one standard drink per day" (Royal College of Obstetricians and Gynaecologists 1996). Although these recommendations have been challenged by some (Guerri et al. 1999), they are typical of the European stance on prenatal drinking (EUROMAC 1992).

In the USA in the years following the Surgeon General's warning, several state and local governments mandated "point-of-purchase" warnings about drinking during pregnancy, and federal, state and local governments embarked on public education campaigns to alert all pregnant women to the potential dangers of drinking (Abel 1984). These campaigns culminated in 1988, when the USA became the first (and still the only) country to adopt legislation requiring an alcohol warning label on every can of beer and bottle of wine and spirits mentioning the potential dangers of drinking during pregnancy (Public Law 100–690, 27 USC 201–211). By the beginning of the following decade, the crusade had turned into a moral panic, when in 1990 Wyoming became the first state to charge a pregnant woman who was drunk with felony child abuse (Holmgren 1991).

Moral Panic

In essence, a moral panic is an exaggerated concern about some "social problem." Among the characteristics of every moral panic are the alleged breakdown in public morality described above, a heightened level of public concern, which is often feverish, exaggerated estimates of the numbers of people allegedly affected by the problem, a distortion of aetiology, and democratization of the condition's occurrence, such that no particular class, race, ethnic group, or any other socially constructed category is singled out as differentially affected (Goode and Ben-Yehuda 1994; Thompson 1998). The concept of moral panic originated in British sociology in the 1970s and has since been used to describe diverse social phenomena, ranging from Satanic ritual child abuse in the USA to child violence in the UK. Although some observers have critiqued the concept of moral panic and its overuse (Watney 1987), it has become an established category of explanation in both the professional sociological imagination and in lay thinking. The British media in particular have often resorted to the idea of moral panic to describe social turmoil over pornography, youth culture, mugging, and the AIDS epidemic. In the following sections, we demonstrate how the concept of moral panic is a useful way to understand the American response to FAS and the threat posed by drinking during pregnancy.

Feverish Public Concern

Much of the feverish concern over FAS originated and continues to be fanned in Seattle, Washington, where its discoverers first characterized it as a "tragic disorder" (Jones and Smith 1973) and suggested that doctors urge their pregnant alcoholic patients to consider aborting their pregnancies (Jones and Smith 1974). Although the abortion recommendation was immediately criticized as unwarranted and alarmist (Rosett 1974; Sturdevant 1974), Jones and Smith and their colleagues continued recommending that such women "be urged to terminate their pregnancies" (Smith et al. 1976). The fact that no prospective epidemiological study had as yet been conducted warranting such extreme measures did not deter this group, which maintained that such an "academic pursuit" should not get in the way of an "important human question" (Clarren and Smith 1978). As a result, the abortion recommendation continued to be reiterated until 1980 (e.g., Lindor et al. 1980), when the first prospective study showed that FAS was a rare outcome of maternal alcoholism during pregnancy (Sokol et al. 1980), an observation subsequently confirmed by numerous investigators (Plant 1985; Abel 1998a).

Concern was also fuelled by the Seattle group through a subtle broadening of the problem. The comment that no case of FAS had ever "been reported in a human being with a negative maternal history of ethanol use" (Clarren and Smith 1978) carried the implication that FAS could occur as a result of any amount of drinking. Although first described in 1973 as a condition related to maternal alcoholism, by 1978, the danger of FAS was now linked to any amount of drinking during pregnancy (Clarren and Smith 1978), and this in turn carried the implication that the problem was far greater than could be imagined: "FAS . . . resembles an iceberg with the bulk of the problem out of sight and of indeterminate extent" (Poskitt 1984). The emotional rhetoric in the biomedical literature was quickly picked up by the American mass media. Articles in newspapers and magazines introduced alleged cases with headlines such as "An Innocent Inherits the Anguish of Alcohol" (Dawson 1992),

"Pregnancy, Alcohol Can Be a Deadly Mix" (*Star-Tribune* 1992), "Drinking Devastating to Unborn" (King 1991), "Kids Pay for Prenatal Drinking" (Snider 1990), "Children Pay the Ultimate Price for a Drink" (Wilson 1998), "Prescription for Tragedy: Alcohol and Pregnancy Stack Deck against Baby" (*Seattle Times* 1996) and "The Tragic Inheritance" (Theroux 1989). The most trenchant description appeared in Michael Dorris's 1989 best-selling book *The Broken Cord*, an account of his experience raising an adopted son with FAS. The book brought the disorder to national attention and was made into a film for television.

Exaggerated Estimates

Describing FAS as a "tragic disorder" and a "major public health problem" implies that it claims thousands, if not tens or hundreds of thousands of victims, and is thereby endangering the national health. The estimates of its occurrence, however, rarely supported this notion. The Centers for Disease Control and Prevention (1995a) place the incidence of FAS in the general population at less than 1 case/1000 (0.67/1000), similar to that reported in most prospective studies (Abel 1998a). Predictably, Seattle researchers placed it much higher; their estimate of the combined prevalence of FAS and partial FAS (referring to the presence of only some of the features) is 9.1 cases/1000, or about 1 percent of all births in the USA (Sampson et al. 1997). This latter estimate is among the highest in the literature and is based on two carefully selected studies of women, many of whom were at high risk for various kinds of disorders.

Popular media reports of FAS have likewise exaggerated the extent to which the syndrome is increasing in frequency, with claims such as the "Rate of alcohol-injured newborns soars" (*Chicago Tribune* 1995) and "The percentage of babies born with health problems because their mothers drank alcohol during pregnancy [had] increased sixfold from 1979 through 1993" (*New York Times* 1995). However, since in 1979 FAS was still a new condition and most doctors did not recognize it, this "sixfold increase" is more likely to represent an increase in the identification and reporting of cases, and not in incidence. These media stories were based on a report issued by the Centers for Disease Control and Prevention (CDC 1995a) of the US Public Health Service. However, in the original report, the CDC noted that it had included not only diagnosed cases of FAS, but also any indication of excessive drinking, under the rubric of "noxious influences." Not only was the vagueness of this category not mentioned by the media, but neither was an accompanying report the CDC issued on the same day (CDC 1995b) stating that only a small portion of the medical records they examined that were coded for FAS actually met the criteria for a rigorous case definition; that is, there were many false positives for FAS. Three years later, the CDC further invalidated its earlier report when it recognized that "not all women who drink heavily will produce children with FAS" (CDC 1998). In other words, the "noxious influences" were not always "noxious." The earlier sixfold increase had in fact lacked validity.

Biomedical Entrepreneurship

As attention to and anxiety around FAS and drinking during pregnancy grew, the clinical symptoms of FAS multiplied (Armstrong 1998a). This process of "diagnosis expansion" (Armstrong 1998a) was closely related to another phenomenon: "expertise expansion" (Armstrong 1998a), in which physicians and researchers in a wide variety of subspecialties heralded with entrepreneurial zeal this "exciting new field" (Clarren and Smith 1978) and the "new opportunities for research." Between 1973 and 1984, 1.4 percent of all the articles in journals listed by *Index Medicus* dealt with alcohol and pregnancy compared to 0.9 percent for tobacco and pregnancy and 0.7 percent for narcotics and pregnancy (Abel and Welte 1986). Thirty-seven of these journals contained five or more articles specifically related to fetal alcohol research during this period (Abel 1990). An infusion of federal funding helped to support many new research initiatives. From 1990 to 1994 alone, the National Institute on Alcohol Abuse and Alcoholism (NIAAA) provided about 70 grants totalling between US\$9.8 million and US\$13.5 million annually (Stratton el al. 1996).

Subspecialists in virtually every field of medicine responded to the moral fervour and the new funding incentives with a predictable announcement of newly discovered clinical attributes of the syndrome. These new conditions were heralded as "a new feature associated with fetal alcohol syndrome" (Azouz et al. 1993), a new symptom "not previously . . . described in connection with fetal alcohol syndrome" (Adebahr and Erkrath 1984), an "underemphasized feature in FAS" (Crain et al. 1983), and "heretofore unreported symptoms" (Johnson 1979). Among these "new" symptoms were such isolated and rare anomalies as supernumerary mammillary bodies (Adebahr and Erkrath 1984), steep corneal curvature (Garber 1984), bilateral tibial exostoses (Azouz et al. 1993), tetraectrodactyly (Herrmann et al. 1980), clitoromegaly, hirsutism, and liver dysfunction (see Abel 1990). Other articles raised the spectre of cancer, with reports of an association between prenatal alcohol exposure and Hodgkin's disease and leukaemia, as well as a formidable litany of tumours in the brain, liver, kidney, and adrenals (see Abel 1990). More often than not, such reports were based on single isolated coincidences. The epidemiological evidence of an association between prenatal alcohol exposure and any of these conditions has never been demonstrated; most of the "new features" are so atypical they have only been seen in a single case of FAS and in fact are excluded from the most recent American diagnostic paradigm for FAS (Stratton et al. 1996).

Distortion of Aetiology

The amount of alcohol consumed during pregnancy that constitutes a danger to the unborn child was a critical issue in creating the moral panic over FAS, because the lower the amount, the greater the number of potential victims (the proverbial "tip of the iceberg"), and consequently the greater the national guilt for condoning such a moral lapse.

The biomedical research community which provided these estimates had a certain pragmatic interest in framing the issue in terms of low thresholds because the greater the national panic, the higher the research budgets to do something to combat this national health problem. It is therefore not surprising that the estimated thresholds were, and continue to be, routinely misrepresented through the obfuscation of citing average consumption over a particular time period, rather than disaggregating the specific kinds of drinking patterns that are associated with FAS. For instance, a woman who has one drink a day every day and a woman who binges once a week, consuming six or more drinks at once, both average seven drinks a week. Yet each of these drinking patterns represents potentially very different levels of alcohol exposure for the woman and her fetus. Since peak blood alcohol levels (BALs) reached per drinking episode are a crucial factor in FAS (Abel 1999), the "average drinks" measure distorts the relationship between alcohol and teratogenesis and muddies our perceptions of risky drinking. Only a handful of researchers, such as Jacobson et al. (1993) and Ernhart (1991), have been forthright enough to clarify this issue. For example, in evaluating children whose mothers drank during pregnancy, Jacobson et al. (1993) placed the threshold for alcohol-related cognitive damage to children at an average of one drink a day during pregnancy, but emphasized that the effects they had observed were due to much higher exposure than indicated by this "average." Since none of the mothers studied drank every day, they acknowledged that the average did not represent a typical drinking day. Instead, "the women who drank above this "average" threshold exposed their infants to a median of six drinks per occasion" (p. 181). Similarly, Ernhart (1991) noted that a woman in her study who consumed an average of one drink a day during the course of her pregnancy, confined her drinking to the first 3 months of her infant's gestation, when she drank a gallon of wine, and a half case of beer, every Friday and Saturday evening. After that she did not drink for 3 months. Nevertheless, because drinking was averaged over the longer period, the woman's drinking appeared to be very low.

This bias in the medical literature has been magnified in the popular press and in lay pregnancy manuals and public health educational materials. Although many researchers recognize the significance of binge drinking as a risk for FAS, the distinction between number of drinks per drinking episode and number of drinks per week or month has been largely glossed over in public discussions of FAS, which tend to present any type of alcohol consumption as dangerous.

Democratization

The essential criterion for any social problem is its universalization (Wagner 1997). As long as a problem is orphaned, especially if it is identified as a problem only within a minority race or social class, it has limited impact on society as a whole. Liberal-minded social scientists are especially wary of associating a stigmatized behaviour with race or class, because such associations perpetuate discrimination (Wagner 1997). By disassociating race or class from a stigmatized behaviour, the problem is more likely to gain public attention, because everyone now feels a vested interest in its elimination. The language of democratization therefore characterizes most social problems, e.g., child abuse, alcoholism, cocaine addiction, teenage pregnancy or domestic violence. Despite the fact that these are not "equal opportunity" disorders (Abel 1995; Wagner 1997), they are typically scaled up into the middle and affluent classes to draw greater attention to the problem at hand and to overcome any charges of racism, classism, elitism, or any other accusation of discrimination (Wagner 1997).

FAS has not been immune to democratization. When the disorder was first described in 1973, Jones and Smith and their co-workers took pains to emphasize its universalism by reporting that the eight unrelated children they had observed belonged to "three different ethnic groups . . ." (Jones and Smith 1973). However, FAS has never been an "equal opportunity birth defect" (Abel 1995); its inseparable handmaidens are poverty and smoking (Bingol et al. 1987; Abel 1995). What Jones and Smith and their colleagues did not emphasize was that the eight children, and virtually all the other children they and others subsequently examined, were seen in hospitals serving a predominantly lower socio-economic status population. Groups whose members suffer disproportionate poverty, such as Native Americans and African Americans, are especially prone to this disorder. In the Yukon and Northwestern areas of Canada, the rate for FAS and partial FAS has been estimated at 46/1000 for

Native children compared to 0.4/1000 for non-Native children, a thousand-fold difference (Asante and Nelms-Matzke 1985). In the USA, the rate of FAS among low income populations is 2.29/1000 compared to 0.26/1000, for middle- and high-income populations (Abel 1995). Despite the empirical evidence, grassroots organizations, such as the National Organization on Fetal Alcohol Syndrome (NOFAS), continue to espouse the view that FAS is a threat to *all* pregnancies. When NOFAS was founded, for instance, its executive director stated: "I think a lot of middle-class and upper-class women don't know that occasional use of alcohol during pregnancy is dangerous" (Information Access Company 1991).

While it is true that drinking occurs across all social categories in the USA, FAS is undeniably concentrated among disadvantaged groups. The very large socio-economic differences in FAS rates (Able 1995) are not due to differences in the number of alcoholic women among the poor compared to the middle classes. In fact, drinking is much more common among the middle and upper classes than among the poor (Abma and Mott 1990; Caetano 1994; Abel 1998a). Instead, the reason FAS occurs predominantly among poverty-stricken women is that they experience, or are characterized by, many more "permissive" factors, such as smoking and poor diet, that exacerbate the effects of alcohol (Abel and Hannigan 1995). Since FAS cannot be divorced from poverty, insisting that FAS "crosses all lines" perpetuates the problem by situating it solely within an alcohol context instead of the wider context of poverty.

Democratization disguises the extent to which moral panic about FAS may in fact spring from much deeper social unease about changing gender roles and about class and particularly race differences (Armstrong 1998a). Many legal commentators in the USA have noted that the recent rash of prosecutions of pregnant women for substance use and purported fetal harm are concentrated among poor and most often minority women (Roberts 1991; Gomez 1997). The moral panic over FAS likewise may reflect social divisions typically invisible in American society, particularly rifts over what constitutes a "good mother."

Implications

Although a debate exists about the extent to which the USA differs from other countries with regard to the incidence of FAS, there can be little doubt that the American response to drinking during pregnancy is exceptional. The USA remains the only country to legislate warning labels on alcoholic beverage containers; the American Surgeon General's warning about drinking during pregnancy is unique in the strength of its recommendations that women should abstain from alcohol altogether and should, moreover, be vigilant about the miniscule alcoholic content of food and drugs. In this respect, the moral panic over FAS echoes earlier periods of concern about alcohol in American history; to wit, the prolonged struggle over temperance in the nineteenth century and the prohibition of the manufacture, sale and consumption of all alcohol in the USA between 1919 and 1933.

However, the moral panic over FAS in the USA, unlike earlier periods of social preoccupation with alcohol, is driven as much by gender division as by class or socio-economic divisions. Although its sufferers appear to be concentrated among the poor, the public image of the condition as a universal one resonates with issues of social control and gender. As Armstrong (1998a) has noted in an earlier analysis, the diagnosis of FAS arose at a period of intense gender agitation in the USA, and thus reflects widespread social unease about the conflict between the traditional maternal role of women and their efforts to embrace more diverse roles in modern society.

Historically, moral entrepreneurs have mobilized moral rhetoric when they have felt social norms threatened by outsiders or newcomers to society; in other words, as response to social deviance. Moral panics may arise when social elites seek to preserve or defend their status in the social hierarchy (Gusfield 1963); alternatively, moral panics may serve to deflect political attention from intractable social problems, or inequality inherent in the social structure (Hall et al. 1978). As Plant (1997) has noted in the British context, the moral panic ignited by FAS in the USA served the further purpose of diverting attention from social inequality and displacing blame for poor pregnancy outcomes to individual mothers rather than social circumstances. Women, in their child-bearing and child-rearing roles, have always been held particularly responsible for the "future of society." The case of FAS illustrates that this is still true.

The moral panic ignited by concern over FAS, with its exaggerated claims, especially regarding the dangers of social and moderate drinking, and its universalization, has important implications. Reporting "averages" as if they represented a typical drinking day has led to a widespread perception among the American public that even one drink during pregnancy is dangerous. There have been countless reports of visibly pregnant women who were harassed by indignant strangers when seen to be drinking in public; likewise, there are accounts of morally righteous waiters and barstaff who have refused to serve visibly pregnant women alcoholic beverages. Even some American clinicians have fallen prey to this misunderstanding (Abel and Kruger 1998), which has caused some women to become so anxious that they have considered termination of their non-threatened pregnancies so as to avoid giving birth to a child with FAS (Armstrong 1998b; Lipson and Webster 1990; Koren 1991).

If we are to reduce the incidence of FAS, we must first accurately comprehend the problem at hand and abandon the rhetoric of moral panic. There is no epidemic of FAS births. Nor is "social" or "moderate" drinking among the almost 4 million pregnant women who give birth annually in the USA a risk factor for FAS. However, the risk is considerably greater for the relatively small number of women who abuse alcohol on a regular basis, and it is even greater for those women who have previously given birth to a child with FAS and continue to drink (Abel 1988).

While government has a moral duty to alert citizens to potential dangers (Abel 1998b), public education measures, such as warning labels, have no noticeable effect in reducing drinking during pregnancy (Hankin 1996), as evidenced by the fact that more, not fewer women, are now drinking during pregnancy than before the appearance of the labels (CDC 1997). Such broad-based prevention efforts are doomed to fail, because women who

give birth to children with FAS are not simply a variant of the general drinking population. A small proportion of women of child-bearing age, especially those who are most disadvantaged by poverty, bear the greatest burden of risk for FAS. If we are going to reduce the incidence of FAS, we need first to know who those women are, as well as what puts them at risk. If we hope to reduce the incidence of this birth defect, we must reconstruct the problem not as a moral panic, but as a moral imperative to find and help those women most at risk of adverse outcomes.

References

Abel, E. L. 1984. *Fetal Alcohol Syndrome and Fetal Alcohol Effects.* Plenum Press, New York.

_____. 1988. "Fetal Alcohol Syndrome in Families." *Neurotoxicology and Teratology* 10: 1–2.

_____. 1990. *Fetal Alcohol Syndrome: Medical Economics.* Oradell, New Jersey.

_____. 1995. "An Update on the Incidence of FAS: FAS Is Not an Equal Opportunity Birth Defect." *Neurotoxicology and Teratology* 17: 437–443.

_____. 1997. "Was the Fetal Alcohol Syndrome Recognized in the Ancient Near East?" *Alcohol and Alcoholism* 32: 3–7.

_____. 1998a. *Fetal Alcohol Abuse Syndrome.* Plenum Press, New York.

_____. 1998b. "Prevention of Alcohol-Abuse Related Birth Effects. I. Public Education Efforts." *Alcohol and Alcoholism* 33: 411–416.

_____. 1999. "What Really Causes FAS." *Teratology* 59: 4–6.

Abel, E. L. and J. L. Hannigan. 1995. "Maternal Risk Factors in Fetal Alcohol Syndrome: Provocative and Permissive Influences." *Neurotoxicology and Teratology* 17: 445–462.

Abel, E. L. and M. Kruger. 1998. "What Do Physicians Know and Say about Fetal Alcohol Syndrome: A Survey of Obstetricians, Pediatricians, and Family Medicine Physicians." *Alcoholism: Clinical and Experimental Research* 22: 1951–1954.

Abel, E. L. and J. W. Welte. 1986. "Publication Trends in Fetal Alcohol, Tobacco and Narcotic Effects." *Drug and Alcohol Dependence* 18: 107–114.

Abma, J. C. and Mott, F. L. 1990. "Is There a 'Bad Mother' Syndrome? An Analysis of Overlapping

High Risk Factors During Pregnancy." Paper presented at the Annual Meeting of the Population Association of America.

Adebahr, G. and K. K. Erkrath. 1984. "Uberzahlige Corpora mamillaria–Ein Befund bei Einme Fall mit Fetalem Alkohol–Syndrome [Super-Numerary Mammillary Bodies: A Finding in a Case of Fetal Alcohol Syndrome]." *Zeitschrift fur Rechtsmedizin* 92: 239–246.

Apolo, J. O. 1995. "Child Abuse in the Unborn Fetus." *International Pediatrics* 10: 214–217.

Armstrong, E. M. 1998a. "Diagnosing Moral Disorder: The Discovery and Evolution of Fetal Alcohol Syndrome." *Social Science and Medicine* 47: 2025–2042.

_____. 1998b. *Conceiving Risk, Bearing Responsibility: Ideas about Alcohol and Offspring in the Modern Era.* Doctoral dissertation, University of Pennsylvania, Philadelphia, PA.

Asante, K. O. and J. Nelms-Matzke. 1985. *Survey of Children with Chronic Handicaps and Fetal Alcohol Syndrome in the Yukon and Northwest B.C.* Department of Welfare, Ottawa.

Azouz, E. M., G. Kavianian, and V. M. der Kaloustian. 1993. "Fetal Alcohol Syndrome and Bilateral Tibial Exostoses." *Pediatric Radiology* 23: 615–616.

Best, J. 1990. *Threatened Children: Rhetoric and Concern about Child Victims.* University of Chicago Press, Chicago.

Bingol, N., C. Schuster, M. Fuchs, S. Iosub, G. Turner, R. K. Stone, and D. S. Gromisch. 1987. "The Influence of Socioeconomic Factors on the Occurrence of Fetal Alcohol Syndrome." *Advances in Alcohol and Substance Abuse* 6: 105–118.

Blumer, H. 1971. "Social Problems as Collective Behavior." *Social Problems* 18: 298–306.

Caetano, R. 1994. "Drinking and Alcohol-Related Problems among Minority Women." *Alcohol Health and Research World* 18: 233–241.

Centers for Disease Control and Prevention (CDC). 1995a. "Update: Trends in Fetal Alcohol Syndrome—United States 1979–1993." *Morbidity and Mortality Weekly Report* 44: 249–251.

_____. 1995b. "Use of International Classification of Diseases Coding to Identify Fetal Alcohol Syndrome—Indian Health Service Facilities 1981–1992." *Morbidity and Mortality Weekly Report* 44: 253–255, 261.

_____. 1997. "Alcohol Consumption among Pregnant and Childbearing-Aged Women—United States 1991 and 1995." *Morbidity and Mortality Weekly Report* 46: 346–350.

_____. 1998. "Identification of Children with Fetal Alcohol Syndrome and Opportunity for Referral of Their Mothers for Primary Prevention, Washington 1993–1997." *Morbidity and Mortality Weekly Report* 47: 861–864.

Chicago Tribune. 1995. "Rate of Alcohol-Injured Newborns Soars." April 7, N6.

Clarren, S. K. and D. W. Smith. 1978. "The Fetal Alcohol Syndrome." *New England Journal of Medicine* 299: 556.

Crain, L. S., N. E. Fitzmaurice, and C. Mondry. 1983. "Nail Dysplasia and Fetal Alcohol Syndrome." *American Journal of Diseases in Childhood* 137: 1069–1072.

Dawson, G. 1992. "An Innocent Inherits the Anguish of Alcohol." *Orlando Sentinel Tribune.* February 3, CI.

Dorris, M. 1989. *The Broken Cord.* Harper & Row, New York.

Egeland, G. M., K. A. Perham-Hester, B. D. Gessner, D. Ingle, J. E. Bernier, and J. P. Middaugh. 1998. "Fetal Alcohol Syndrome in Alaska 1977 through 1992: An Administrative Prevalence Derived from Multiple Data Sources." *American Journal of Public Health* 88: 781–786.

Engs, R. C. 1997. "Cycles of Social Reform: Is the Current Anti-Alcohol Movement Cresting?" *Journal of Studies on Alcohol* 58: 223–224.

Ernhart, C. B. 1991. "Clinical Correlations Between Ethanol Intake and Fetal Alcohol Syndrome." *Recent Developments in Alcoholism* 9: 127–150.

EUROMAC. 1992. "A European Concerted Action: Maternal Alcohol Consumption and Its Relation to the Outcome of Pregnancy and Child Development at 18 Months." *International Journal of Epidemiology* 21 (Suppl. l): S1–S87.

Food and Drug Administration (FDA). 1981. "Surgeon General's Advisory on Alcohol and Pregnancy." *FDA Drug Bulletin* 11: 9–10.

Garber, J. M. 1984. "Steep Corneal Curvature: A Fetal Alcohol Syndrome Landmark." *Journal of the American Optometric Association* 55, 595–598.

Gerbner, G. and L. Gross. 1976. "The Scarey World of TV's Heavy Viewer." *Psychology Today* 9: 41–45, 89.

Gomez, L. E. 1997. *Misconceiving Mothers: Legislators, Prosecutors and the Politics of Prenatal Drug Exposure*. Temple University Press, Philadelphia, PA.

Goode, E. and N. Ben-Yehuda. 1994. *Moral Panics: The Social Construction of Deviance*. Blackwell, Cambridge, MA.

Greenfeld, J. 1989. "Wounded before Birth: A Father Sadly Pursues His Adopted Son's Affliction." *Chicago Tribune*. July 23, CI.

Guerri, C., E. Riley, and K. Strömland, K. 1999. "Commentary on the Recommendations of the Royal College of Obstetricians and Gynaecologists Concerning Alcohol Consumption in Pregnancy." *Alcohol and Alcoholism* 34: 497–501.

Gusfield, J. 1963. *Symbolic Crusade: Status Politics and the American Temperance Movement*. Urbana, IL: University of Illinois Press.

Hall, S., C. Critcher, T. Jefferson, J. Clarke, and B. Roberts. 1978. *Policing the Crisis: Mugging, the State and Law and Order*. Macmillan, London.

Hankin, J. R. 1996. "Alcohol Warning Labels: Influence on Drinking." In *Fetal Alcohol Syndrome: From Mechanism to Prevention*, edited by E. L. Abel, 317–329. New York: CRC Press.

Herrmann, J., P. D. Pallister, and J. M. Opitz. 1980. "Tetraectrodactyly and Other Skeletal Manifestations in the Fetal Alcohol Syndrome." *European Journal of Pediatrics* 133: 221–226.

Hill, R. M. and L. M. Tennyson. 1980. "An Historical Review and Longitudinal Study of an Infant with the Fetal Alcohol Syndrome." In *Alcoholism: A Perspective*, edited by F. S. Messiha and G. S. Tyner, 177–201. Westbury, NY: P. J. D. Publications.

Holmgren, J. L. 1991. "Legal Accountability and Fetal Alcohol Syndrome: When Fixing the Blame Doesn't Fix the Problem." *South Dakota Law Review* 36: 81–103.

Information Access Company. 1991. "Group Forms to Battle Fetal Alcohol Syndrome." *Alcoholism and Drug Abuse Week* 3: 4.

Jacobson, J. L., S. W. Jacobson, R. J. Sokol, S. S. Martier, and J. W. Ager. 1993. "Teratogenic Effects of Alcohol on Infant Development." *Alcoholism: Clinical and Experimental Research* 17: 174–183.

Johnson, K. G. 1979. "Fetal Alcohol Syndrome: Rhinorrhea, Persistent Otitis Media, Choanal Stenosis, Hypoplastic Sphenoids and Ethnoid." *Rocky Mountain Medical Journal* 76: 64–65.

Jones, K. L. and D. W. Smith. 1973. "Recognition of the Fetal Alcohol Syndrome in Early Infancy." *Lancet* i: 999–1001.

————. 1974. "Offspring of Chronic Alcoholic Women." *Lancet* ii: 349.

Kempe, C. H., F. N. Silverman, B. F. Steele, W. Droegemueller, and H. K. Silver. 1962. "The Battered Child Syndrome." *Journal of the American Medical Association* 181: 17–24.

King, W. 1991. "Drinking Devastating to Unborn." *Seattle Times*. April 16, Bl.

Koren, G. 1991. "Drinking and Pregnancy." *Canadian Medical Association Journal* 145: 1552.

Levine, H. G. 1978. "The Discovery of Addiction: Changing Conception of Habitual Drunkenness in American History." *Journal of Studies on Alcohol* 39: 143–167.

————. 1983. "The Good Creature of God and the Demon Rum: Colonial and 19th Century American Ideas about Alcohol, Accidents and Crime." In *Alcohol and Disinhibition*, edited by R. Room and G. Collins. National Institute on Alcohol Abuse and Alcoholism, Washington, DC.

Lindor, E., A. M. McCarthy, and M. G. McRae. 1980. "Fetal Alcohol Syndrome: A Review and Case Presentation." *Journal of Obstetrics, Gynecology and Neonatal Nursing* 9: 222–228.

Lipson, A. H. and W. S. Webster. 1990. "Response to Letters Dealing with Warning Labels on Alcoholic Beverages." *Teratology* 41: 479–481.

New York Times. 1995. "Use of Alcohol Linked to Rise in Fetal Illness," April 7.

Plant, M. 1985. *Women, Drinking and Pregnancy*. Tavistock, London.

————. 1997. *Women and Alcohol: Contemporary and Historical Perspectives*. Free Association Books, London.

Poskitt, E. M. E. 1984. "Fetal Alcohol Syndrome." *Alcohol and Alcoholism* 19: 159–165.

Reinarman, C. 1988. "The Social Construction of an Alcohol Problem: The Case of Mothers Against Drunk Drivers and Social Control in the 1980s." *Theory and Society* 17: 91–120.

Roberts, D. E. 1991. "Punishing Drug Addicts Who Have Babies: Women of Color, Equality and the Right of Privacy." *Harvard Law Review* 104: 1419–1482.

Rosett, H. L. 1974. "Maternal Alcoholism and Intellectual Development of Offspring." *Lancet* 2: 218.

Royal College of Obstetricians and Gynaecologists. 1996. *Guideline No. 9: Alcohol Consumption in Pregnancy.* Royal College of Obstetricians and Gynaecologists, London.

Sampson, P. D., A. P. Streissguth, F. L. Brookstein, R. E. Little, S. K. Clarren, P. Dehaene, J. W. Hanson, and J. M. Graham. 1997. "Incidence of Fetal Alcohol Syndrome and Prevalence of Alcohol-Related Neurodevelopmental Disorder." *Teratology* 56: 317–326.

Seattle Times. 1996. "Prescription for Tragedy: Alcohol and Pregnancy Stack Deck Against Baby." January 14, A17.

Smith, D. W., K. L. Jones, and J. W. Hanson. 1976. "Perspectives on the Cause and Frequency of the Fetal Alcohol Syndrome." *Annals of the New York Academy of Sciences* 273: 138–139.

Snider, M. 1990. "Kids Pay for Prenatal Drinking." *USA Today.* December 10, ID.

Sokol, R. J., S. I. Miller, and G. Reed. 1980. "Alcohol Abuse during Pregnancy: An Epidemiologic Study." *Alcoholism: Clinical and Experimental Research* 4: 135–145.

Star-Tribune (Minneapolis, MN). 1992. "Pregnancy and Alcohol Can Be a Deadly Mix." April 26, A18.

Steacy, A. 1989. "Bruised before Birth: Alcoholic Mothers Damage Their Babies." *Maclean's* 102: 48.

Stone, D. A. 1989. "Causal Stories and the Formation of Policy Agendas." *Political Science Quarterly* 104: 280–300.

Stratton, K., C. Howe, and F. Battaglia, eds. 1996. *Fetal Alcohol Syndrome: Diagnosis, Epidemiology, Prevention and Treatment.* National Academy Press, Washington, DC.

Sturdevant, R. 1974. "Offspring of Chronic Alcoholic Women." *Lancet* 2: 349.

Theroux, P. 1989. "The Tragic Inheritance: A Father's Chronicle of Fetal Alcohol Syndrome." *The Washington Post.* July 19, D3.

Thompson, K. 1998. *Moral Panics.* Routledge, New York.

Wagner, D. 1997. "The Universalization of Social Problems: Some Radical Explanations." *Critical Sociology* 23: 3–23.

Waldman, H. B. 1989. "Fetal Alcohol Syndrome and the Realities of Our Time." *Journal of Dentistry for Children* 56: 435–437.

Watney, S. 1987. *Policing Desire: Pornography, AIDS and the Media.* Methuen, London.

Wilson, D. 1998. "Children Pay the Ultimate Price for a Drink." *Houston Chronicle.* August 11.

For Discussion

1. Prior to reading this article, what had you heard about fetal alcohol syndrome and how does that information compare to the material presented here by the authors?

2. Fetal alcohol syndrome focuses on the behaviors of women who are pregnant. The moral panic over crack-addicted babies also highlighted the behaviors of pregnant women. Why has male behavior not been similarly targeted? Should it be?

5

Kronic Hysteria

Exploring the Intersection Between Australian Synthetic Cannabis Legislation, the Media, and Drug-Related Harm

STEPHEN J. BRIGHT, BRIAN BISHOP, ROBERT KANE, ALI MARSH, MONICA J. BARRATT

The focus of this article is on synthetic cannabis, a novel psychoactive substance that emerged in various regions of the world beginning in 2004. Kronic is a brand of synthetic cannabis that gained popularity in Australia. Researchers Stephen J. Bright and his colleagues use a unique methodological approach to examine moral panic and policy response to synthetic cannabis use.

Synthetic cannabis refers to products containing a herbal mixture that is then sprayed with synthetic cannabinoid agonists (Dargan et al. 2011; Dresen et al. 2010; Schifano et al. 2009). Synthetic cannabis first emerged in Europe in 2004 with reports of a product called Spice producing effects that were very similar to cannabis, such as euphoria, increased sociability, relaxation, increased appetite, and sometimes anxiety and paranoia (Castellanos et al. 2011; Psychonaut Web Mapping Research Group 2009). These marked psychoactive effects were unlikely to have been produced by the largely inert herbal materials that Spice was purported to contain, which included: *Althaea officinalis* (Marshmallow), *Canavalia maritima* (Beach bean), *Leonotis leonurus* (Wild dagga), *Leonotis sibericus* (Siberian motherwort), *Nelumbo nucifera* (Pink lotus), *Nymphaea caerulea* (Blue lotus), *Pedicularis densiflora* (Indian warrior), *Rosa cania* (Dog rose),

Scutellaria nana (Dwarf skullcap), and *Zornia latifolia* (Maconha brava) (Psychonaut Web Mapping Research Group 2009).

An analysis of Spice (Auwärter et al. 2009; Lindigkeit et al. 2009) revealed that it contained a range of synthetic cannabinoid agonists. These chemicals included a homologue of CP 47,497, which within the Australian Criminal Code Act of 1995 is considered an analogue of delta-9-tetrahydrocannabinol (Δ^9-THC) based on the similarity of its structure to Δ^9-THC. As such, possession of this product was a breach of federal law. However, outside of federal jurisdictions (e.g., airports, border control and universities), in those Australian states without analogues clauses within their drug acts, products containing this chemical were legal.

JWH-018, or 1-pentyl-3-(1-naphthoyl) indole, is another synthetic cannabinoid agonist that was identified to be present in Spice (Auwärter et al.

Stephen J. Bright, Brian Bishop, Robert Kane, Ali Marsh, Monica J. Barratt, 2013, "Kronic Hysteria: Exploring the Intersection Between Australian Synthetic Cannabis Legislation, the Media, and Drug-Related Harm." In *International Journal of Drug Policy* 24: 231–237. Reprinted by permission of Elsevier via Copyright Clearance Center.

2009; Lindigkeit et al. 2009). JWH is an abbreviation for John W. Huffman, the individual who first synthesised these cannabinoid agonists. Later analyses have revealed a range of JWH's chemicals present in synthetic cannabis products including: JWH-019, JWH-022, JWH-073, JWH-122, JWH-250, and JWH-398 (de Jager et al. 2012; Fattore and Fratta 2011; Hastie 2011). These chemicals were structurally dissimilar from Δ^9-THC and other scheduled cannabinoid agonists, and thus were not considered analogues within the Australian Criminal Code Act of 1995. Consequently, prior to legislative changes in 2011, products containing these chemicals were legal to supply and possess in all Australian states and territories.

While anecdotal reports of synthetic cannabinoid use in Australia date back to 2005, it was in 2011 that synthetic cannabis emerged as a drug of concern in Australia. Kronic has been the most well-known brand of synthetic cannabis in Australia with various blends produced, including Skunk, Purple Haze, Tropical, Pineapple Express, and Black Label. In April 2011, radio and tabloid newspapers first began reporting on the use of Kronic at Western Australian (WA) mine sites as a means of evading drug testing (Macdonald 2011). Media interest swiftly grew, and by June the WA government moved to schedule seven synthetic cannabinoid agonists: JWH-018, JWH-073, JWH-122, JWH-200, JWH-250, CP47,497, and the C8 Homologue of CP 47,497 (*Misuse of Drugs [No. 2]* 2011).

Within days, new synthetic cannabis blends appeared that claimed to contain new unscheduled synthetic cannabinoid agonists. For example, Kronic released its "Black Label" blend specifically for its WA customers. This is consistent with the experience in the UK (Dargan et al. 2011) and the USA (Shanks et al. 2012) where analysis of synthetic cannabis blends available after bans found the presence of a range of new chemicals. de Jager et al. (2012) have reported that blends of Kronic purchased after bans in Australia contained chemicals previously unknown to them that were later revealed via mass spectra to be JWH-022 and AM2201.

Then in August 2011, the media reported on a Perth man with a pre-existing heart condition who had a heart attack. While this event is not something the media would normally report on, the man had allegedly been smoking Kronic Black Label prior to his death (Phillips 2011). In a response to this alleged first "Kronic-related death," the WA government scheduled 14 more cannabinoid agonists (*Poisons* 2011). Again, new blends appeared that claimed to contain new unscheduled chemicals.

Other Australian states followed WA's lead. South Australia outlawed 17 cannabinoid agonists (Trans-Tasman Mutual Recognition [South Australia] Variation Regulations 2011, South Australia). In addition to the seven cannabinoid agonists that WA banned, the New South Wales government banned AM-694 (*Drug Misuse and Trafficking Act* 1985). Tasmania outlawed four cannabinoid agonists (CP 47,497, JWH-018, JWH-073, and JWH-250), and also introduced an analogues clause into their *Misuse of Drugs Acts* (*Misuse of Drugs Order 2011 [S.R. 2011, No. 74]*). The Northern Territory banned 18 synthetic cannabinoid agonists (*Misuse of Drugs Amendment [Synthetic Cannabinoids] Regulations 2011 [No. 33 of 2011]*, Northern Territory), while the Queensland government has proposed banning a total of 22 cannabinoid agonists and redefining the definition of what is considered a dangerous drug (*Criminal and Other Legislation* 2011; *Drugs Misuse Amendment Regulation [No. 1]* 2011; *Drugs Misuse Amendment Regulation [No. 2]* 2011). The new definition states that a dangerous drug includes anything that is intended to "have a substantially similar pharmacological effect" to an illicit substance (*Criminal and Other Legislation* 2011).

The Australian Therapeutic Goods Agency (TGA 2011) received a request from the WA government to review the status of synthetic cannabinoid agonists, and subsequently scheduled eight cannabinoid agonists in July 2011. This made their possession a federal offence. Most Australian state drug acts refer to the Standard for the Uniform Scheduling of Medicines and Poisons (SUSMP) or Poisons Standard, which is the legislative instrument over which the TGA has authority. Consequently, products containing any of these eight cannabinoid agonists were by default illegal in states that had not specifically scheduled these chemicals.

It might be suggested that the Australian legislative response to synthetic cannabis has been reactive and piecemeal rather than evidence-based. Some have suggested that banning each chemical as it emerges is like a dog chasing its own tail (Fattore and Fratta 2011). Other commentators have described this approach to legislation as a merry-go-round—as one new drug gets discovered and banned, another one emerges purporting to be "legal" (Dargan et al. 2011; Evans-Brown, Bellis, and McVeigh 2011; Measham et al. 2010). So why has Australia's legislative response to synthetic cannabis not been evidence-based?

It is possible that media reports concerning synthetic cannabis created a moral panic that contributed to a legislative reaction. Early descriptions of moral panic, such as Cohen's (1972) analysis of "Mods" and "Rockers" in the UK, have noted that moral panic first involves a person, group, episode, or situation being framed by the media as a threat to society. Sometimes the moral panic quickly dissipates, while other moral panics reach critical mass with significant and long lasting repercussions, such as changes in policy. In this respect, Brosius and Weimann (1996) have suggested that the media sets the agenda for policy debate.

McArthur (1999, 151) has stated that the media "shape[s] not only the public profile of [drug] problems but also the political response to them." Forsyth (2012) has proposed that once media reports concerning the emergence of a new drug break in the mainstream press, they will draw on the "drug scare" narrative that constructs the new drug as dangerous and the need for urgent action. In turn, a media campaign against the drug develops that recruits politicians, researchers and the morally righteous. The subsequent moral panic leads to a perception that urgent legislative action is required and is likely to result in policy that is reactive rather than responsive.

Moral panic occurs within the context of the dominant discourses that exist within a society. For example, Cohen (1972) stated that "by thrusting certain moral directives into the universe of discourse" the media can create drug problems "suddenly and dramatically" (10). Dominant discourses are linguistic frameworks inherent to any given

culture that develop in symbiotic relationships with those institutions with power (Burr 2003). They constrain what can be rationally said, written, and thought about drugs. Each discourse provides specific subject positions that demarcate the narratives that are coherent within the discourse (Burr 2003). These narratives, such as the "drug scare narrative," are perceived by individuals within the culture from which the dominant discourse emanates to hold the most "truth" value. Nonetheless, there are competing dominant discourses with some being more privileged than others, and it is in the interest of any given institution to promote those discourses that maintain the institution's version of reality as "truth" since this provides the institution with power.

Bright, Marsh, Bishop, and Smith (2008) undertook an analysis of the dominant discourses within Australia that frame Alcohol and Other Drugs (AOD). They examined newspaper reports of AOD over a 12 month period, and then triangulated this analysis with a sample of newspaper reports from five years prior and a televised debate on AOD. Bright et al. (2008) determined that in Australia, six dominant discourses framed AOD-related issues: medical, moral, legal, political, economic, and glamour (see Table 5.1). Within medical discourse, for example, drug use is often pathologised such that drug users are sick. This limits the degree to which "recreational drug use" can be considered since any drug use is defined as inherently unhealthy. Within this discourse, experts are afforded a subject position that has significant authority and typically support the pathogenic narrative. Further, since medical discourse is paternal, the pathogenic narrative supports prohibition-based drug policy.

The methodology used by Bright et al. (2008) might not be appropriate for understanding the discourses that framed the emergence of synthetic cannabis in Australia given its rapid emergence and the subsequent constant flux. Rather, methodologies that have explored the rapid emergence of new drugs might have more utility. In this journal, Forsyth (2012) has recently described the phenomena of the "drug scare" using the UK experience with mephedrone as a case study. He proposed that media reports about the emergence of a new drug that are fuelled by "moral panic" are unhelpful

Table 5.1 Description of the Dominant AOD-Related Discourses in Australia, as Reported by Bright et al. (2008).

Discourse	Subject Positions	Narrative
Economic	Consumers and businesses	Alcohol and other drugs (AOD) are something that are made, bought, and sold, in the same way as any other product or service (e.g., bread or a taxi fare)
Medical	Patients and experts	Using AOD is like having a disease and health professionals can cure it
Moral	Irresponsible/ deviants and morally righteous	Using drugs is wrong because of the negative effect they have on a person's behaviour
Legal	Law breakers, law abiders and law enforcers	Using drugs is against the law and people who use them should be arrested
Political	Constituents and politicians	People cannot make the right decisions about drugs so we need to help them by making policies, thus protecting society
Glamour	Celebrities	Drugs are mysterious and that is why we like to hear about famous people who use them

since they might divert attention from other more significant public health concerns (e.g., alcohol, diabetes, cardiovascular disease, cancer, etc.), and also provide free advertising through creating increased public awareness of the drug. Through examining online media, Forsyth was able to demonstrate that interest in buying mephedrone increased following sensationalist media coverage.

The present study draws from Forsyth's (2012) methodology using Australian online media and self-reports from a sample of Australian synthetic cannabis users to understand how synthetic cannabis emerged as a drug of concern in 2011. In doing so, we aim to explore how the media, legislative change, and drug-related harm intersect. Discursive analysis was used to help disentangle this complex intersection. Such analysis is particularly useful here given the dynamic and rapid social

changes that occurred in 2011, since it allows for subjective interpretations of the available anecdotal evidence given limited empirical data.

Method

Drawing from Forsyth's (2012) methodology, *Google Trends* was first used to produce time-trend graphs detailing the number of stories being published online about synthetic cannabis and Kronic, and also the amount of traffic searching for these terms. *Google Trends* also generated links to media reports at key milestones. Forsyth has noted some limitations in using this application since *Google* is not the only search engine; however, it is the most widely used. Further, *Google Trends* are normalised so the graphs do not represent the absolute number of searches conducted or the number of media stories. Additionally, the media volume reported is dependent on the parameters that *Google* uses to determine if text is a "news story."

It is reasonable to assume that the ways in which the Australian online media was able to frame the emergence of synthetic cannabis was limited by the available dominant discourses. As such, the discourse and narratives were examined within the key reports generated by *Google Trends*. This examination was conducted by the first author (SB). It was iterative and involved consideration of the various subject positions that were available within the text, in addition to the way in which synthetic cannabis was constructed. As each discourse emerged, it was considered within the context of the institutions that support and maintain the discourse. Finally, the discourse was considered within the context of Bright et al.'s (2008) delineation of the dominant discourses available for AODs in Australia.

To ensure credibility (Lietz 2010), the data were triangulated with radio media. Two episodes of the Australian Broadcasting Commission's (ABC) Triple J show *Hack* that reported on synthetic cannabis were analysed. The first show, entitled "Cheating Workplace Drug Tests," aired on May 10 (Quartermaine et al. 2011). The second show was entitled "National Kronic Ban" and aired on July 7 (Tilley and Sawrey 2011). Purposeful sampling of media reports and social media was also conducted to reconstruct a timeline of the emergence of, and response to, synthetic cannabis. In addition, thick descriptions were provided of each text that used direct quotes to ensure that the analysis stayed true to the original text.

Rigour was ensured through an audit trail that documented the analysis and the reasoning that underpinned the emergent discourses (Morse 1994). Thoughtful consideration of the discursive researcher's (SB) standpoint and opinions was documented in the audit trail to ensure reflexivity. This can be summarised in the following disclosure statement:

> I dislike paternalism since I value freedom of choice and believe that drug users can rationally weigh up the pros and cons of drug use in the context of the available evidence regarding harm. I believe that drug policy is rarely developed in the context of the available evidence and is often reactive in nature.

By including this statement, we acknowledge that it is impossible for the researcher to be "objective" or "neutral" in the production of knowledge. Subjectivity, while once seen as negative or as bias to be eliminated, can be used as a fruitful path to greater understanding of the subject matter and our role in its construction. Instead, readers should

interpret our paper with knowledge of the discursive researcher's positioning as stated above.

Finally, two pieces of previously unpublished data were included in this paper from a study by the final author and colleagues (Barratt, Cakic, and Lenton forthcoming): (a) month and year of first use of synthetic cannabis, and (b) where synthetic cannabis users first reported hearing about the drug. A purposive sample of 316 Australian synthetic cannabis users answered these questions as part of an online survey. A description of the sample and the survey methodology has been published elsewhere (Barratt et al. forthcoming).

Findings and Discussion

Figs. 5.1 and 5.2 contain graphs produced using *Google Trend*. The lower line in each figure depicts the volume of media stories being published online that referred to Kronic and synthetic cannabis, respectively. The upper line in each figure indicates how many people were searching for "Kronic" and "synthetic cannabis." As can be seen in Figs. 5.1 and 5.2, the first online media stories about synthetic cannabis and Kronic began to emerge in March, with a sharp increase in the number of stories in May and June.

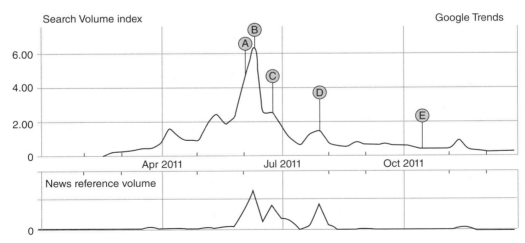

Figure 5.1

Google Trends data for "Kronic" in Australia for 2011. *Note.* The letters indicate the publication of key stories. The headlines for these are (A) "Roadtesting Kronic: Is Fake Grass Worth the Hype?" (B) "WA Becomes First State with Kronic Ban," (C) "NZ Importer Admits Kronic Contaminated," (D) "WA Police Query Banned Drug Kronic Link to Man's Death," and (E) "Tall Black Slapped with One-Year Ban for Kronic Use." The lower line represents the volume of stories being published about Kronic and the upper line represents the number of searches for Kronic.

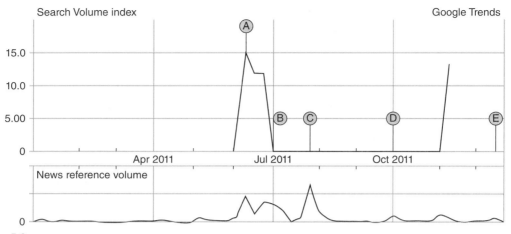

Figure 5.2

Google Trends data for "synthetic cannabis" in Australia for 2011. *Note.* The letters indicate the publication of key stories. Only story A was included in the analysis as the other stories were from New Zealand. The lower line represents the volume of stories being published about Kronic and the upper line represents the number of searches for Kronic.

The first key story concerning Kronic was from *The Age* on June 8 (indicated by "A" in Fig. 5.1) and was entitled "Roadtesting Kronic: Is Fake Grass Worth the Hype?" This "gonzo journalism" piece describes the author's experience of smoking Kronic and is framed within neo-liberal and economic discourse. For example, the author states that "so many people were having fun with [Kronic] that the anti-fun brigade had no choice but to swing into action" and compared the effects of Kronic to "two glasses of champagne." Bright et al. (2008) note that within the dominant Australian discursive landscape, only alcohol, tobacco, and caffeine can typically be framed within economic discourse, which means that this story is framed outside of the dominant discourses.

Similarly, the individuals who were interviewed as part of the first radio report on Kronic in May (Quartermaine et al. 2011) framed their use of Kronic outside of dominant discourses. Again, use of Kronic was framed within neo-liberal and economic discourse. For example, interviewees stated how they made an informed choice to use Kronic in which the harms associated with failing a drug test outweighed the unknown harms associated with using chemicals with little to no toxicology data. Further, they described responsible use of Kronic,

such as not using it before or during work, which also falls outside of the dominant discourses.

Such initial framing was possible without widespread concern regarding synthetic cannabis and is consistent with Forsyth's (2012, 198) observation that initial reports regarding a new drug are generally published in alternative publications such as music press (e.g., *Triple J Radio*) "or equivalent specialist sections of mainstream titles" (e.g., *The Age*). For example, in the UK a report preceding the moral panic regarding mephedrone appeared in the *Telegraph* by a prominent medical personality entitled "I Took Mephedrone and I Liked It" (Pemberton 2010). Despite being situated outside of the dominant discursive frameworks, such early stories increase the public's awareness and might provide an advertisement for the emergent drug. Indeed, as can be seen from the upper line in Fig. 5.1, the number of Australian's searching for Kronic on Google began increasing significantly around this time. It is interesting to note that "Kronic" was more searched than "synthetic cannabis," perhaps highlighting the effect that the media had on "branding" synthetic cannabis. This is similar to the way in which MDMA was branded as Ecstasy in the early 1980s, perhaps since the latter term created additional public interest and may have contributed to the moral panic that precipitated the prohibition of MDMA in the USA (Eisner 1989).

The increased awareness also provides an impetus for a "moral panic," with subsequent stories framed within the dominant discourses. The second key story concerning Kronic was published by the *Sydney Morning Herald* on 16 June and was entitled "WA becomes first state with Kronic ban" (see "B" in Fig. 5.1). Interestingly, the first and only relevant key story concerning synthetic cannabis was also about legislative change—this time the South Australian government's intention to ban synthetic cannabis (see "A" in Fig. 5.2). Both stories were framed within dominant discourses. Specifically, they were framed within legal, medical and moral discourse.

Within medical discourse synthetic cannabis was constructed as a pathogen with similar (or greater) dangers to cannabis. Such constructions were typically reinforced by experts attesting to these dangers. Within this discursive framework, primacy is given to those individuals assuming the subject position of expert. This subject position is highly regarded in contemporary society, and might be considered to have subsumed the role of the priest as the figure of authority. Like the priest, the information provided by a medical expert is not necessarily "true" despite it being perceived as holding the greatest "truth" value. Indeed, there are often little to no toxicity data for most emergent drugs. For example, Forsyth (2012) noted that it was the news of a mephedrone-related death that was later found to be false, which provided the impetus for the UK government to refer the matter to the Advisory Council on the Misuse of Drugs.

Similarly, the second ABC radio show that aired in July focused on the national legislative changes. Here, the federal secretary for health assumed the subject position of expert. From this position she was able to authoritatively declare that synthetic cannabis is "just not safe," causing hallucinations and heart palpitations. While there have been increasing reports of synthetic cannabis harms, a recent survey of 316 Australian community-based synthetic cannabis users found that while such effects were reported by around one third of the

sample, very few respondents reported that their symptoms were serious enough to seek help and many respondents did not report experiencing these harms (Barratt et al. forthcoming). Barratt et al.'s (forthcoming) survey results also indicate that a desire to use a legal recreational drug was one of the main reasons for first trying synthetic cannabis. Consistent with medical discourse, there was no available subject position for recreational drug users with the secretary stating that there "is no therapeutic reason to be using [synthetic cannabinoid agonists] and that is why they have been banned."

Within moral discourse, users assume the subject position of an irresponsible deviant. For example, the South Australian Attorney-General expressed a concern that "users are driving under the influence, posing a serious danger to themselves and others." Such constructions, alongside the pathogenic narrative available within medical discourse, indicate a need for urgent legislative intervention. In turn, these discourses provided a fertile environment for "moral panic."

This moral panic is likely to have contributed to the first wave of bans that occurred in June and July of 2011 since Australian governments had a moral imperative to take urgent legislative action. Such urgent action was naturally reactive and led to a number of bans placed on individual synthetic cannabinoid agonists. Although authorities may be well-intentioned as they prohibit emerging drugs like synthetic cannabinoid agonists, the unintended consequences of these policies may have increased harm to some users since the reporting of each scheduling decision creates increased awareness. Such increased awareness could lead to increased use of synthetic cannabis.

Indeed, as can seen be from the lower lines in Figs. 5.1 and 5.2, online media interest first increased in the lead-up to the first wave of bans in June and July. There was also an increase in the number of Australians searching for "Kronic" and "synthetic cannabis," as indicated by the lower lines in Figs. 5.1 and 5.2, which tracks in relative accordance with the increased volume in media. It is reasonable to assume that many of these individuals would not have previously been aware of synthetic cannabis. The first hit for a *Google* search for "Kronic to be banned" that we conducted in June was an Australian-based online Kronic shop, and Google advertisements at the end of many commercial online media reports were for online shops selling synthetic cannabis. Kronic could not have asked for better advertising. For example, Green (2011) reported on a man who "saw [Kronic] on the news and thought . . . holy smoke, I'm going to order this."

Barratt et al.'s (forthcoming) survey collected as-yet-unpublished data on the month that respondents first used synthetic cannabis. Reported in Fig. 5.3, these data appear to be indicative of two distinct cohorts of Australians who initiated synthetic cannabis use in 2011: (i) those whose initial use preceded media reporting, and (ii) those who initiated use at around the same time as reports about Kronic peaked in the media. A statistical analysis of the data indicated that those who used synthetic cannabis for the first time in 2011 or 2012, which was

when media interest began to heighten, were also significantly more likely to have reported to have heard about it through the media, whereas those who used synthetic cannabis for the first time before 2011 were significantly more likely to have heard about it through other means (e.g., social media, friends, vendors, etc.), $X^2(1, N = 273) = 15.7$, $p < 0.001$.

In the lead-up to the bans, people reportedly tried to stockpile Kronic (Rickard 2011), and Kronic manufacturers endeavoured to sell any remaining stock. Kronic distributors used social media, especially Facebook and Twitter, to engage their customers. These technologies provided a unique way of monitoring drug-related social interactions in real-time. For example, a post on the Kronic Facebook page from June reads:

we only found out about the ban today so just clearing out the last of our stock. It has to be gone

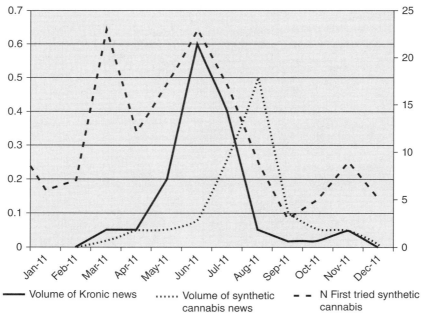

Figure 5.3

Month and year that participants from Barratt et al.'s (forthcoming) survey respondents who reported first trying synthetic cannabis in 2011 versus the volume of Kronic and synthetic cannabis media reports, as indicated by *Google Trends*. *Note*. As *Google Trends* does not provide raw data, the volume of media reports is only an approximation. Further, the data is normalised and does not represent the absolute number of media stories.

by 2mmorow close of business so we have 2 options . . . give heaps away for free or just dispose of it tomorrow. I know what we'd prefer!

Hundreds of Facebook users "liked" and commented on this and other posts. For example, "James" stated, "I want some, no money but I've already bought heaps from yas [sic] so give me it for free."

The announcement by the WA government to ban seven synthetic cannabinoid agonists also led to a "smoke em party" that was shut down by police as a matter of public safety. The party was moved to another venue, but then cancelled following further police intervention ("Kronic Party Plans" 2011).

The next key Kronic story according to *Google Trends* was published in *The Brisbane Times* on June 30. Entitled "NZ importer admits Kronic contaminated," this story describes the findings from an analysis of Kronic conducted by the New Zealand governments that found traces of a novel benzodiazepine. This story was primarily framed within medical discourse, with the incident constructed as a "contamination."

Just days after the WA government banned seven synthetic cannabinoid agonists, new products were released that claimed to circumvent the legislative changes. One such product was Kronic "Black Label." The final key Kronic-related story, which was published on August 5 in *The Australian,* described how a man who was "believed" to have been smoking Kronic "Black Label" was rushed to hospital after "suffering a suspected heart attack." He later died. Entitled "WA Police Query Banned Drug Kronic Link to Man's Death," this story was framed within medical and legal discourse. Again, the potential harms associated with Kronic indicated an urgent need for legislative intervention. In response to this death, the WA government banned an additional 14 cannabinoid agonists (*Poisons* 2011). Again, media interest and Internet traffic searching for "Kronic" and "synthetic cannabis" increased in the lead-up to these bans, as can be seen in Figs. 5.1 and 5.2.

Conclusions

By examining the emergence of synthetic cannabis as a drug of concern in Australia, the present paper aimed to help understand how the media, legislative change, and drug-related harm intersect. The notion of dominant discourses was proposed to be helpful in understanding this relationship since they will demarcate how the media constructs the emergence of a new drug, how policy makers are able to frame the debate, and in turn, people's drug using behaviour.

The pre-existing Australian dominant discourses, as outlined by Bright et al. (2008), appear to have led to the construction of synthetic cannabis as a dangerous pathogen. This construction may have contributed to a "moral panic." The moral panic appears to have been fuelled by experts highlighting the potential dangers of the new drug. Whilst such claims are presumably intended to reduce the likelihood of people using these substances, they might not be completely accurate given an absence of toxicological data and do not appear to be a deterrent. For example, Forsyth (2012) found that the most significant increases in interest in purchasing mephedrone occurred following each report of an alleged mephedrone-related death. A similar trend has been reported by Dasgupta, Mandl, and Brownstein (2009), who found that the number of overdoses from prescription opiates increased significantly two to six months after major stories concerning prescription opiates broke in the media.

Given the truth value of these expert statements within the dominant discourse, governments have a moral imperative to ban the new drug. This can lead to reactive policies that may have a negative impact on drug-related harm since: (i) further awareness is created which could increase harm as more individuals try synthetic cannabis, and (ii) once banned, newer, less-understood psychoactive products enter the market to replace the banned drug. Thus, while the availability of the newly illegal drug decreases following prohibition, other similar drugs with unknown health harms become more available in their place. Even if the new products do not contain new legal chemicals, and in fact contain recently scheduled chemicals, consumers are then at heightened risk of prosecution for possession of a product they believed to be legal. The possession of synthetic cannabinoid agonists could be treated more severely than the possession of cannabis in Australia since individuals charged with possession of synthetic cannabinoid agonists might not be eligible to participate in cannabis diversion schemes.

An alternative approach would have been to have regulated this market. Regulation would mandate the provision of accurate information, purity and strength. There is currently a disincentive for companies to provide information to potential users about the active ingredients or about safer ways to consume synthetic cannabis. To avoid litigation, most brands of synthetic cannabis state that they are "not for human consumption," misrepresent what they contain, or provide obscure instructions for use. For example, a packet of Kronic's Pineapple Express stated that it "contains a unique blend of all natural organic extracts" and it "emits a pleasant, relaxing smoke when burned." The lack of quality control is evident in the recall of this particular brand of Kronic due to it containing a novel benzodiazepine (Couch and Madhavaram 2012).

Restrictions on where and to whom synthetic cannabis could be sold would also be easier to manage in a regulated environment. Some (e.g., Evans-Brown et al. 2011; Hughes and Winstock forthcoming) suggest that emerging psychoactive substances be regulated as medicinal products as a pragmatic compromise to the current, arguably unsustainable, approach. We believe Australia should also consider alternative models of regulation, based on careful examination of the likely intended and unintended consequences. The recently regulatory scheme proposed by the New Zealand government provides an example of such alternative models (Office of the Associate Minister of Health 2012). It will be interesting to see how this new model affects the synthetic cannabis market and drug-related harm.

Evidence-based policy development must consider a psychoactive substance within the complex interrelationships between state and federal legislation, media reporting and dynamic webs of supply and demand. The unpredicted and unintended outcomes of drug policy typically result from inadequate consideration of these factors. For example, workplace drug testing is a well-intentioned policy that aims to reduce drug-related harm, but has had the unintended effect of producing a market for synthetic cannabis as a substitute for cannabis, which, until recently, was unable to be detected by workplace drug testing technologies.

However, it is unlikely that Australia's response to synthetic cannabis will consider alternative models of regulation. In May 2012, eight broad chemical groups were scheduled by the TGA: benzoylindoles, cyclohexylphenols, dibenzopyrans, naphthoylindoles, naphthylmethylindoles, naphthoylpyrroles, naphthylmethylindenes, and phenylacetylindoles (TGA 2012). In addition, they scheduled "synthetic cannabinomimetics," though no definition of this term has been provided. Only time will tell what effects (both intended and unintended) this latest legislative actions will have on drug-related harm.

References

Auwärter, V., S. Dresen, W. Weinmann, M. Müller, M. Pütz, and N. Ferreirós. 2009. "'Spice' and Other Herbal Blends: Harmless Incense or Cannabinoid Designer Drugs?" *Journal of Mass Spectrometry* 44: 832–837.

Barratt, M., V. Cakic, and S. Lenton. Forthcoming. "Patterns of Synthetic Cannabinoid Use in Australia." *Drug and Alcohol Review*, forthcoming.

Bright, S. J., A. Marsh, B. Bishop, and L. M. Smith. 2008. "What Can We Say about Substance Use? Dominant Discourses and Narratives Emergent from Australian Media." *Addiction Research and Theory* 16: 135–148.

Brosius, H. B., and G. Weimann. 1996. "Who Sets the Agenda? Agenda Setting as a Two Step Flow." *Communication Research* 23: 561–580.

Burr, V. 2003. *Social Constructionism.* 2nd ed. London: Routledge.

Castellanos, D., S. Singh, G. Thornton, M. Avila, and A. Moreno. 2011. "Synthetic Cannabinoid Use: A Case Series of Adolescents." *Journal of Adolescent Health* 49: 347–349.

Cohen, S. 1972. *Folk Devils and Moral Panics.* London: MacGibbon and Kee.

Couch, R. A. F., and H. Madhavaram. 2012. "Phenazepam and Cannabinomimetics Sold as Herbal Highs in New Zealand." *Drug Testing and Analysis* 4: 409–414.

Criminal and Other Legislation Amendment Bill, 2011. 2011. Queensland. From statute on Internet. <http://www.legislation.qld.gov.au/Bills/53PDF/2011/CriminalOLAB11.pdf> Accessed 01.08.11.

Criminal Code Act, 1995. 1995. Australia.

Dargan, P. I., S. Hudson J. Ramsey, and D. M. Wood. 2011. "The Impact of Changes in UK Classification of the Synthetic Cannabinoid Receptor Agonists in 'Spice.'" *International Journal of Drug Policy* 22: 274–277.

Dasgupta, N., K. D. Mandl, and J. S. Brownstein. 2009. "Breaking the News or Fueling the Epidemic? Temporal Association Between News Media Report Volume and Opioid-Related Mortality." *PLoS ONE* 4(11). http://dx.doi.org/10.1371/journal.pone.0007758

de Jager, A. D., J. V. Warner, M. Henman, W. Ferguson, and A. Hall. 2012. LC-MS/MS "Method for the Quantitation of Metabolites of Eight Commonly-Used Synthetic Cannabinoids in Human Urine—An Australian Perspective." *Journal of Chromatography B* 897: 22–31.

Drug Misuse and Trafficking Act 1985, New South Wales.

Drugs Misuse Amendment Regulation (No. 1). 2011. Queensland.

Drugs Misuse Amendment Regulation (No. 2). 2011. Queensland.

Dresen, S., N. Ferreirós, M. Pütz, F. Westphal, R. Zimmermann, and V. Auwärter. 2010. "Monitoring of Herbal Mixtures Potentially Containing Synthetic Cannabinoids As Psychoactive Compounds." *Journal of Mass Spectrometry* 45: 1186–1194.

Eisner, B. 1989. *Ecstasy: The MDMA Story.* Berkeley: Ronin.

Evans-Brown, M., M. A. Bellis, and J. McVeigh. 2011. "Should 'Legal Highs' Be Regulated As Medicinal Products?" *British Medical Journal* 342. http://dx.doi.org/10.1136/bmj.d1101

Fattore, L., and W. Fratta. 2011. "Beyond THC: The New Generation of Cannabinoid Designer Drugs." *Frontiers in Behavioral Neuroscience* 5, article 60.

Forsyth, A. J. M. 2012. "Virtually a Drug Scare: Mephedrone and the Impact of the Internet on Drug News Transmission." *International Journal of Drug Policy* 23: 198–209.

Green, S. 2011. "Kronic Made Me 'Bloody Useless.'" November 18. <http://cqnews.com.au/story/2011/11/18/kronic-made-me-bloody-useless>

Hastie, H. 2011. "WA 'Kronicles' Detection of Synthetic Cannabinoids." *Science Network Western Australia.* Archived at http://www.webcitation.otg/64bFcL2hQ. Accessed 01.08.12. http://www.sciencewa.net.au/3520-wa-kronicles-synthetic-cannabinoid-detection.html

Hughes, B., and A. R. Winstock. Forthcoming. "Controlling New Drugs under Marketing Regulations." *Addiction.*

Lietz, C. A. 2010. "Evaluating Qualitative Research for Social Work Practitioners." *Advances in Social Work* 11: 188–202.

Lindigkeit. R., A. Boehme, I. Eiserloh, M. Luebbecke, M. Wiggermann, L. Ernst, et al. 2009. "Spice: A Never Ending Story?" *Forensic Science International* 191: 58–63.

Macdonald, K. 2011. "Drug Invisible to Mine Site Tests." *The West Australian.* April 13. <http://au.news.yahoo.com/thewest/a/-/newshome/9184524/drug-invisible-to-mine-site-tests/> Accessed 01.08.12.

McArthur, M. 1999. "Pushing the Drug Debate: The Media's Role in Policy Reform." *Australian Journal of Social Issues* 34: 149–165.

Measham, F., K. Moore, R. Newcombe, and Z. Welch. 2010. "Tweaking, Bombing, Dabbing and Stockpiling: The Emergence of Mephedrone and the Perversity of Prohibition." *Drugs and Alcohol Today* 10 (1): 14–21. http://dx.doi.org/lo.5042/daat.2olo.0123

Misuse of Drugs (Amounts of Prohibited Drugs) Order (No. 2) 2011. 2011. Western Australia. Statute on Internet. <http://www.parliament.wa.gov.au/publications/tabledpapers.nsf/displaypaper/38l3677a4ad0d66loca4ff4e482578e8001dac50/$file/3677.pdf> Accessed 01.08.12.

Misuse of Drugs Order, 2011 (S.R. 2011, No. 74)—Reg 4. 2011. Tasmania.

Misuse of Drugs Amendment (Synthetic Cannabinoids) Regulations 2011 (No. 33 of 2011). 2011. Northern Territory.

Morse, J. 1994. "Designing Funded Qualitative Research." In *Handbook of Qualitative Research,* edited by N. K. Denzin and Y. S. Lincoln. Thousand Oaks, CA: Sage.

Office of the Associate Minister of Health. *Regulation of Psychoactive Substances.* 2012. <http://www.health.govt.nz/about-ministry/legislation-and-regulation/regulatory-impact-statements/new-regulatory-regime-psychoactive-substances> Accessed 31.07.12.

Pemberton, M. 2010. "I Took Mephedrone and I Liked It." (March). <http://www.telegraph.co.uk/health/7481469/I-took-mephedrone-and-I-liked-it.html> Accessed 28.11.12.

Phillips, Y. 2011. "Kronic Blamed for Death as Government Ban Widens." *Perth Now.* August 5. <http://www.perthnow.com.au/news/hillman-man-38-dies-after-smoking-kronic/story-e6frg12c-1226108817744> Accessed 31.07.12.

Poisons (Appendix A Amendment) Order (No. 2) 2011. 2011. Western Australia.

Psychonaut Web Mapping Research Group. *Spice Report.* 2009. <http://www.psychonautproject.eu/documents/reports/Spice.pdf> Accessed 01.08.12.

Quartermaine, C., T. Tilley, J. Barrington, and K. Kaitlyn (reporters). 2011. "Cheating Workplace Drug Tests." May 10. [Podcast radio programme]. Sydney: ABC Triple J Radio. <http://www.abc.net.au/triplej/hack/stories/s3212555.htm> Accessed 11.06.11.

Rickard, L. 2011. "Kronic Ban Sparks 'Fire-Sale' Fears." June 14. <http://www.watoday.com.au/wa-news/kronic-ban-sparks-firesale-fears-20110613-1g06a.html#ixzzleUgKuARZ>.

Schifano, F., O. Corazza, P. Deluca, Z. Davey, L. Di Furia, M. Farre, et al. 2009. "Psychoactive Drug or Mystical Incense? Overview of the Online Available Information on Spice Products." *International Journal of Culture and Mental Health* 2: 137–144.

Shanks. K. G., T. Dahn, G. Behonick, and A. Terrell. 2012. "Analysis of First and Second Generation Legal Highs for Synthetic Cannabinoids and Synthetic Stimulants by Ultra-Performance Liquid Chromatography and Time of Flight Mass Spectrometry." *Journal of Analytical Toxicology* 36: 360–371.

The Standard for the Uniform Scheduling of Medicines and Poisons (SUSMP) also known as the Poisons Standard 2011. 2011. Australia.

Therapeutic Goods Administration (TGA). 2011. "Reasons for Scheduling Delegate's Final Decisions." July. Canberra: Commonwealth of Australia.

Therapeutic Goods Administration (TGA). 2012. *Final Decisions and Reasons for Decisions by Delegates of the Secretary to the Department of Health and Ageing.* Canberra: Commonwealth of Australia.

Tilley, T., and K. Sawrey (reporters). 2011. "National Kronic Ban." July 7. [Podcast radio programme]. Sydney: ABC Triple J Radio. <http://www.abc.net.au/triplej/hack/stories/s3263955.htm> Accessed 11.06.11.

Trans-Tasman Mutual Recognition (South Australia) Variation Regulations 2011. 2011. South Australia.

For Discussion

1. What are some of the benefits and consequences of introducing legislative bans over psychoactive substances that emerged as legal substances?

2. In 2013, hospitals in Colorado and Georgia reported that several patients had presented to emergency rooms with adverse psychological effects that were linked to the consumption of synthetic marijuana. There are dozens of synthetic cannabinoids, and the testing of some patients revealed that they had consumed a new type of synthetic cannabinoid, one that had surfaced recently in parts of Japan and in Europe. What does this example tell us about the global diffusion of psychoactive drug use and drug products? Additionally, if people insist on using cannabis products, is it less harmful for them to consume marijuana or synthetic brands? Why?

The Onset of Drug Use

The terms "onset" and "initiation" of drug use generally refer to the first time that individuals use a particular psychoactive substance. That substance might be alcohol, tobacco, marijuana, heroin, or another drug. Onset might also refer to the first time that *any* drug is consumed. Initiation can be a pleasurable experience for some individuals and a frightening one for others. The overall experience at initiation can be shaped by several factors, including the pharmacological effects of the drug (e.g., stimulant, hallucinogen or the purity of the substance), the physical and mental health of individuals, the way that novices interpret their immediate social and physical surroundings, and their expectations of the drug's effects. Negative drug experiences at initiation can sometimes deter people from using again, but not always. For example, people who use MDMA or heroin sometimes feel nauseous or vomit during the initiation episode. This kind of sickness has been described as being different from "real illness," and certainly different from the nausea that can result during or after alcohol intoxication. Some users of MDMA have reported that nausea or vomiting leads to a "better high." Thus, although researchers might describe these outcomes in negative terms, users often attach a different meaning to this experience. The actions and reactions of others in the immediate setting also can influence a person's experience with a drug—and this point applies to both novices and more experienced users. Trusted friends and acquaintances can reassure an individual who is experiencing a difficult initiation episode or their reactions can serve to escalate panicky feelings that a novice might be experiencing.

In the United States, use of the first psychoactive drug tends to occur during adolescence or young adulthood. Much of the evidence suggests that individuals who use drugs initiate at younger ages compared to previous generations. Johnson and Gerstein (1998) found that only 2 percent of people born between 1930 and 1940 had used marijuana before the age of 21. In contrast, more than 50 percent of people born between 1956 and 1965 had used marijuana before the age of 21. In other words, the percentage who initiated marijuana use before the age of 21 differed considerably between these two birth cohorts. Johnson and Gerstein (1998) proposed a number of explanations that might account for the increase in initiation, including demographic changes that led to more interaction among young people (creating more opportunity to use substances and with fewer adult guardians relative to the population of young people). Their study also suggested a narrowing of the gender gap over time. That is, gender differences in marijuana initiation decreased over time.

Survey Data from Nationally Representative Samples in the U.S. Show That

- In 2011, 8.1% of students in grades 9–12 reported that they had tried marijuana before the age of 13 (*Youth Risk Behavior Survey*)
- In 2011, 23.1% of students in grades 9–12 reported using marijuana during the thirty days prior to the survey (*Youth Risk Behavior Survey*)
- In 2012, 5% of students in grade 8 reported that they initiated cigarette smoking before grade 6 (*Monitoring the Future Survey*)
- Among youth aged 12–17, females were more likely than males to report onset of cigarette smoking in the past year. This pattern has continued since 2002 (*National Survey on Drug Use and Health*)

Scholars have attempted to explain *why* people initiate drug use. One perspective is that throughout history and cross-culturally, people have sought to alter their levels of consciousness, and the use of psychoactive substances is one way of doing that. Anthropologists and historians have found considerable evidence of universal drug taking. Moreover, archaeological digs in various parts of the world have confirmed these claims. However, some individuals never initiate drug use, or if they do, their experimentation is so limited that they have more in common with non-users than users. Others consume several different types of drugs, but eventually desist entirely without ever developing major problems associated with drug use. And some individuals develop serious problems associated with drug use and onset at an early age is alleged to be a contributing factor for later drug-related problems. Thus, researchers try and identify the individual, environmental, and/or structural factors that contribute to initiation into drug use. These are sometimes referred to as "risk factors" because they are said to increase the likelihood of initiation. Dozens of "risk factors" relating to biological/genetic conditions or life circumstances have been highlighted in the literature. This body of work attempts to better understand the factors that contribute to initiation, so that prevention efforts can be implemented that might delay onset or perhaps deter people from engaging in drug use entirely.

Theoretical perspectives from various disciplines have attempted to explain why people initiate drug use, and theories about initiation often differ greatly from explanations about why some people *continue* to use drugs. The number of theoretical perspectives is vast. Indeed, one publication of the National Institute on Drug Abuse devoted 488 pages that outlined the major theoretical views. Early explanations of initiation considered substance use to be a moral weakness of individuals. Many contemporary theories draw from the fields of sociology/criminology (e.g., social learning, subcultural theory, social disorganization, social construction), psychology (e.g., cognitive-control, disordered personalities), and biology (e.g., neurobiological). Some scholars attempt to integrate theoretical concepts from two or more disciplines (e.g., psychosocial). Theories of initiation are important in part because they help to identify and explain "causal" links between individual/environmental factors and onset of drug use. However, theoretical perspectives are characterized by strengths as well as weaknesses. For example, peers and peer pressure are environmental or social network factors that are often said to contribute greatly to initiation into drug use. We know that most people do not initiate drug use on their own. Rather, initiation tends to occur in dyads or in groups of people who have common interests or lifestyles.

These social networks can provide access to drugs and opportunity to use them. That is, with the exception of alcohol and tobacco, most drugs are not readily available to most people. Potential initiates require knowledge of where and how to access drugs, particularly illegal substances. However, what does it mean to be pressured by peers? Does pressure take the form of coercion, or is it more subtle? We now know that most people are not coerced into initiating drug use. Moreover, some novices take an active as opposed to passive role in their initiation, even when drug-using peers attempt to deter them from initiating. Additionally, if peer pressure leads to initiation, then who pressured the peer who may have subsequently pressured others? Pressure from peers cannot fully explain onset, although in most instances, peers are present during initiation. In this section, we include three articles that address initiation, albeit in somewhat different contexts.

Reference

Johnson, R. A., and D. R. Gerstein. 1998. "Initiation of Use of Alcohol, Cigarettes, Marijuana, Cocaine, and Other Substances in US Birth Cohorts Since 1919." *American Journal of Public Health* 88: 27–33.

6

Why People Take Drugs

ANDREW WEIL

Andrew Weil, a graduate of Harvard Medical College, suggests that people of all cultures are born with the desire to periodically alter their consciousness. He suggests that this desire can be observed in young children, but because adults object to these actions, children learn through socialization to suppress or conceal their urges. According to Dr. Weil, the use of alcohol and other drugs is a natural expression of our innate desires to experience different states of consciousness.

The use of drugs to alter consciousness is nothing new. It has been a feature of human life in all places on the earth and in all ages of history, In fact, to my knowledge, the only people lacking a traditional intoxicant are the Eskimos, who had the misfortune to be unable to grow anything and had to wait for white men to bring them alcohol. Alcohol, of course, has always been the most commonly used drug, simply because it does not take much effort to discover that the consumption of fermented juices produces interesting variations from ordinary consciousness.

The ubiquity of drug use is so striking that it must represent a basic human appetite. Yet, many Americans seem to feel that the contemporary drug scene is something new, something qualitatively different from what has gone before. This attitude is peculiar, because all that is really happening is a change in drug preference. There is no evidence that a greater percentage of Americans are taking drugs, only that younger Americans are coming to prefer illegal drugs, like marijuana and hallucinogens, to alcohol. Therefore, people who insist that everyone is suddenly taking drugs must not see alcohol in the category of drugs. Evidence that this is precisely the case is abundant, and it provides another example of how emotional biases lead us to formulate unhelpful conceptions. Drug taking is bad. We drink alcohol. Therefore, alcohol is not a drug. It is, instead, a "pick-me-up," a "thirst quencher," a "social lubricant," "an indispensable accompaniment to fine food," and a variety of other euphemisms. Or, if it is a drug, at least it is not one of those bad drugs that the hippies use.

This attitude is quite prevalent in the adult population of America, and it is an unhelpful formulation for several reasons; in the first place, alcohol is very much a drug by any criterion and causes significant alterations of nervous functioning, regardless of what euphemistic guise it appears in. In fact, of all the drugs being used in our society, alcohol has the strongest claim to the label *drug,* in view of the prominence of its long-term physical effects. In addition, thinking of alcohol as something other than a drug leads us to frame wrong hypotheses about what is going on in America. We are spending much time, money, and intellectual energy trying to find out why people are taking drugs; but, in fact, what we are doing is trying to find out why some people are taking some drugs that we disapprove of. No useful answers can come out of that sort of inquiry; the question is improperly phrased.

Of course, many theories have been put forward. People are taking drugs to escape, to rebel against parents and other authorities, in response to tensions over foreign wars or domestic crises, in imitation of their elders, and so on and so on. No doubt, these considerations do operate on some level (for, instance, they may shape the forms of illegal drug use by young people), but they are totally inadequate to explain the universality of drug use by human beings. To come up with a valid explanation, we simply must suspend our value judgments about kinds of drugs and admit (however painful it might be) that the glass of beer on a hot afternoon and the bottle of wine with a fine meal are no different in kind from the joint of marijuana or the snort of cocaine; nor is the evening devoted to cocktails essentially different from the day devoted to mescaline. All are examples of the same phenomenon: the use of chemical agents to induce alterations in consciousness. What is the meaning of this universal phenomenon?

It is my belief that the desire to alter consciousness periodically is an innate, normal drive analogous to hunger or the sexual drive. Note that I do not say "desire to alter consciousness by means of chemical agents." Drugs are merely one means of satisfying this drive; there are many others, and I will discuss them in due course. In postulating an inborn drive of this sort, I am not advancing a proposition to be proved or disproved but simply a model to be tried out for usefulness in simplifying our understanding of our observations.

The model I propose is consistent with observable evidence. In particular, the omnipresence of the phenomenon argues that we are dealing not with something socially or culturally based, but rather with a biological characteristic of the species. Furthermore, the need for periods of nonordinary consciousness begins to be expressed at ages far too young for it to have much to do with

social conditioning. Anyone who watches very young children without revealing his presence will find them regularly practicing techniques that induce striking changes in mental states. Three- and four-year-olds, for example, commonly whirl themselves into vertiginous stupors. They hyperventilate and have other children squeeze them around the chest until they faint. They also choke each other to produce loss of consciousness.

To my knowledge these practices appear spontaneously among children of all societies, and I suspect they have done so throughout history as well. It is most interesting that children quickly learn to keep this sort of play out of sight of grownups, who instinctively try to stop them. The sight of a child being throttled into unconsciousness scares the parent, but the child seems to have a wonderful time; at least, he goes right off and does it again. Psychologists have paid remarkably little attention to these activities of all children. Some Freudians have noted them and called them "sexual equivalents," suggesting that they are somehow related to the experience of orgasm.

But merely labeling a phenomenon does not automatically increase our ability to describe, predict, or influence it; besides, our understanding of sexual experience is too primitive to help us much.

Growing children engage in extensive experimentation with mental states, usually in the direction of loss of waking consciousness. Many of them discover that the transition zone between waking and sleep offers many possibilities for unusual sensations, such as hallucinations and out-of-the-body experiences, and they look forward to this period each night. (And yet, falling asleep becomes suddenly frightening at a later age, possibly when the ego sense has developed more fully. We will return to this point in a moment.) It is only a matter of time before children find out that similar experiences may be obtained chemically; many of them learn it before the age of five. The most common route to this knowledge is the discovery that inhalation of the fumes of volatile solvents in household products induces experiences similar to those caused by whirling or fainting. An alternate route is introduction to general anesthesia in connection with a childhood operation—an experience that invariably becomes one of the most vivid early memories.

By the time most American children enter school, they have already explored a variety of altered states of consciousness and usually know that chemical substances are one doorway to this fascinating realm. They also know that it is a forbidden realm, in that grownups will always attempt to stop them from going there if they catch them at it. But, as I have said, the desire to repeat these experiences is not mere whim; it looks like a real drive arising from the neurophysiological structure of the human brain. What, then, happens to it as the child becomes more and more involved in the process of socialization? In most cases, it goes underground. Children learn very quickly that they must pursue anti-social behavior patterns if they wish to continue to alter consciousness regularly. Hence, the secret meetings in cloakrooms, garages, and playground corners where they can continue to whirl, choke each other, and, perhaps, sniff cleaning fluids or gasoline.

As the growing child's sense of self is reinforced more and more by parents, school, and society at large, the drive to alter consciousness may go underground in the individual as well. That is, its indulgence becomes a very private matter, much like masturbation. Furthermore, in view of the overwhelming social pressure against such indulgence and the strangeness of the experiences from the point of view of normal, ego-centered consciousness, many children become quite frightened of episodes of non-ordinary awareness and very unwilling to admit their occurrence. The development of this kind of fear may account for the change from looking forward to falling asleep to being afraid of it; in many cases, it leads to repression of memories of the experiences.

Yet, co-existing with these emotional attitudes is always the underlying need to satisfy an inner drive. In this regard, the Freudian analogy to sexual experience seems highly pertinent. Like the cyclic urge to relieve sexual tension (which probably begins to be felt at much lower ages than many think), the urge to suspend ordinary awareness arises spontaneously from within, builds to a peak, finds relief, and dissipates all in accordance with its own intrinsic rhythm. The form of the appearance and course of this desire is identical to that of sexual desire. And the pleasure, in both cases, arises from relief of accumulated tension. Both experiences are thus self-validating; their worth is obvious in their own terms, and it is not necessary to justify them by reference to anything else. In other words, episodes of sexual release and episodes of suspension of ordinary consciousness feel good; they satisfy an inner need. Why they should feel good is another sort of question, which I will try to answer toward the end of this chapter. In the meantime, it will be useful to keep in mind the analogy between sexual experience and the experience of altered consciousness (and the possibility that the former is a special case of the latter rather than the reverse).

Despite the accompaniment of fear and guilt, experiences of non-ordinary consciousness persist into adolescence and adult life, although awareness of them may diminish. If one takes the trouble to ask people if they have ever had strange experiences at the point of falling asleep, many adults will admit to hallucinations and feelings of being out of their bodies. Significantly, most will do this with a great sense of relief at being able to tell someone else about it and at learning that such experiences do not mark them as psychologically disturbed. One woman who listened to a lecture I gave came up to me afterward and said, "I never knew other people had things like that. You don't know how much better I feel." The fear and guilt that reveal themselves in statements of this sort doubtless develop at early ages and probably are the source of the very social attitudes that engender more fear and guilt in the next generation. The process is curiously circular and self-perpetuating.

There is one more step in the development of adult attitudes toward consciousness alteration. At some point (rather late, I suspect), children learn that social support exists for one method of doing it—namely, the use of alcohol—and that if they are patient, they will be allowed to try it. Until recently, most persons who reached adulthood in our society were content to drink alcohol if they wished to continue to have experiences of this sort by means of chemicals. Now, however, many young people are discovering that other chemicals may be preferable. After all, this is what drug users themselves say: that certain illegal substances give better highs than alcohol. This is a serious claim, worthy of serious consideration.

At this point, I would like to summarize the main ideas I have presented so far and then illustrate them with personal examples. We seem to be born with a drive to experience episodes of altered consciousness. This drive expresses itself at very early ages in children in activities designed to cause loss or major disturbance of ordinary awareness. To an outside, adult observer, these practices seem perverse and even dangerous, but in most cases adults have simply forgotten their own identical experiences as children. As children grow, they explore many ways of inducing similar changes in consciousness and usually discover chemical methods before they enter school. Overwhelming social pressures against public indulgence of this need force children to pursue antisocial, secretive behavior patterns in their explorations of consciousness. In addition, the development of a strong ego sense in this social context often leads to fear and guilt about the desire for periods of altered awareness. Consequently, many youngsters come to indulge this desire in private or to repress it. Finally, older children come to understand that social support is available for chemical satisfaction of this need by means of alcohol. Today's youth, in their continuing experimentation with methods of changing awareness, have come across a variety of other chemicals which they prefer to alcohol. Thus, use of illegal drugs is nothing more than a logical continuation of a developmental sequence going back to early childhood. It cannot be isolated as a unique phenomenon of adolescence, of contemporary America, of cities, or of any particular social or economic class.

I feel confident about this developmental scheme for two reasons. First, I have seen it clearly in the histories of many hundreds of drug users I have interviewed and known. Second, I have experienced it myself. I was an avid whirler and could spend hours collapsed on the ground with the world spinning around—this despite the obvious unpleasant side effects of nausea, dizziness, and sheer exhaustion (the only aspects of the experience visible to grownups). From my point of view, these effects were incidental to a state of consciousness that was extraordinarily fascinating—more interesting than any other state except the one I entered at the verge of sleep. I soon found out that my spinning made grownups upset; I learned to do it with other neighborhood children in out-of-the-way locations, and I kept it up until I was nine or ten. At about the age of four, like most members of my generation, I had my tonsils out, and the experience of ether anesthesia (administered by the old-fashioned

open-drop method) remains one of my strongest memories of early life. It was frightening, intensely interesting, and intimately bound up with my thoughts about death. Some years later, I discovered that a particular brand of cleaning fluid in the basement of my house gave me a similar experience, and I sniffed it many times, often in the company of others my age. I could not have explained what I was doing to anyone; the experience was interesting rather than pleasant, and I knew it was important to me to explore its territory.

Alcohol was not forbidden in my home; I was even allowed occasional sips of cocktails or after-dinner cordials. Because I never liked the taste of alcohol, I was unable to understand why grownups drank it so often. I never connected it with my own chemical experiences. I did not discover a real alcohol high until I was a senior in high school; then, at age sixteen, it suddenly became clear to me that alcohol was another method, apparently a powerful one, of entering that interesting realm of consciousness. Soon, I fell into a pattern of weekend drinking parties, at which everybody consumed alcohol in order to get drunk. These highs were enjoyable for a time, but once their novelty wore off, I indulged in them for purely social reasons. Before long, I began to find the objective, physical effects of alcohol unpleasant and hard to ignore. I hardly knew of the existence of illegal drugs and would not have considered trying them. To me, marijuana was a narcotic used by criminals, and I had no idea why anyone would take amphetamines or opiates.

In the summer of 1960, just before I entered Harvard College as a freshman, I read an article in the Philadelphia *Evening Bulletin* about the death of a student at a southern California college, supposedly from an overdose of mescaline. He had been taking it "to get inspiration for papers in a creative-writing course." A paragraph from a recent paper was quoted—a visionary description of "galaxies of exploding colors." Mescaline was identified as an experimental drug largely unknown, said to produce visions. My curiosity was aroused at once, and I resolved to devote my ingenuity to getting and trying mescaline.

At Harvard, excessive weekend consumption of alcohol by students and faculty was the rule rather than the exception, and I went along with the majority, even though the experience of being high on alcohol had long since ceased being interesting to me in my explorations of consciousness. Use of illegal drugs was non-existent except in a very submerged underground. I read everything I could find in scientific journals about mescaline, then came across Aldous Huxley's famous essay, *The Doors of Perception*. The little book convinced me that my intuitions about mescaline as something to be checked out were right. For example, I read:

> [Mescaline] changes the quality of consciousness more profoundly and yet is less toxic than any other substance in the pharmacologist's repertory.[1]

And:

> [I]t had always seemed to me possible that, through hypnosis, for example, or autohypnosis, by means of systematic meditation, or else by taking the appropriate drug, I might so change my ordinary mode of consciousness as to be able to know, from the inside, what the visionary, the medium, the mystic were talking about.[2]

Huxley made a convincing case that mescaline was the appropriate drug. Coincidentally, he appeared at the Massachusetts Institute of Technology that fall to give a series of Saturday lectures on visionary experience that were broadcast on the Harvard radio station. I listened carefully to Huxley's thesis that altered states of consciousness included the highest forms of human experience and that chemicals like mescaline were the most direct means of access.

> That humanity at large will ever be able to dispense with Artificial Paradises seems very unlikely. Most men and women lead lives at the worst so painful, at the best so monotonous, poor, and limited, that the urge to escape, the longing to transcend themselves, if only for a few moments, is and has always been one of the principal appetites of the soul. Art and religion, carnivals and saturnalia, dancing and listening to oratory—all these have served, in H. G. Wells' phrase, as Doors in the Wall. And for private, for everyday use, there have always been chemical intoxicants. All the vegetable sedatives and narcotics, all the euphorics that grow on trees, the hallucinogens that ripen in berries or can be squeezed from roots—all, without exception, have been known and systematically used by human beings from time immemorial. And to these

natural modifiers of consciousness, modern science has added its quota of synthetics.[3]

As a project for David Riesman's course on American society, I began to write a long study of psychoactive drugs and social attitudes toward them. An instructor in the course suggested that I look up a psychologist, Timothy Leary, who, he thought, was actually doing research with hallucinogens.

I first talked with Leary in his tiny office in the Center for Personality Research on Divinity Avenue. He spoke with sincerity, conviction, and enthusiasm about the potential of drugs like LSD, psilocybin, and mescaline. He envisioned a graduate seminar based on regular consumption of hallucinogens, alternating with intensive periods of analysis to identify and apply the insights gained while high. He predicted that within ten years everyone would be using the drugs: "from kindergarten children on up." And he did not anticipate strong opposition by society. I asked whether I could be a subject in his psilocybin studies. He said no, he was sorry, but he had promised the university administration not to use undergraduates. He encouraged me to try to get mescaline, which he thought would be possible.

It took two months and only moderate ingenuity to obtain legally a supply of mescaline from an American chemical firm. Then seven other undergraduates and I began taking mescaline and evaluating our experiences with great care. A dozen experiences I had with the drug in 1961 (in half-gram doses) were highly varied. Most were nothing more than intensifications of preexisting moods with prominent periods of euphoria. Only a small percentage of the time did the sensory changes (such as constant motion of boundary lines and surfaces or vivid imagery seen with the eyes closed) seem worth paying much attention to. In a few instances, great intellectual clarity developed at the peak of the experience, and insights were gained that have had lasting importance. After a dozen trips (we called them "sessions"), I was able to see that much of the mescaline experience was not really so wonderful: the prolonged wakefulness, for example, and the strong stimulation of the sympathetic nervous system with resultant dilated eyes, cold extremities, and stomach butterflies. Yet, its potential for showing one good ways of interpreting one's own mind seemed enormous. Why was that potential realized so irregularly?

During the year that our drug ring operated out of Claverly Hall, I had a chance to watch perhaps thirty mescaline experiences of other undergraduates, and, again, what was most striking was the variability of these sessions. All of the experiences were mostly pleasant, with no bad reactions, but no two were alike, even in the same person. What we were seeing was also being noted by Leary and Alpert in their continuing studies with psilocybin. They gave the drug to large numbers of intellectuals, artists, alcoholics, prisoners, addicts, and graduate students; reported that the vast majority of the experiences were positive; and pointed out the importance of "set" and "setting" in determining the subject's reaction. Set is a person's expectations of what a drug will do to him, considered in the context of his whole personality. Setting is the environment, both physical and social, in which a drug is taken. Leary and Alpert were the first investigators of the hallucinogens to insist on the importance of theses two variables. Without them, we are unable to explain simply why the drug varies so unpredictably in its psychic effects from person to person. With these variables, the observations become suddenly clear; hence, the usefulness of the concept of set and setting.

I will discuss this concept and its implications when I talk about marijuana. At this point, I will merely note that the combined effects of set and setting can easily overshadow the pharmacological effects of a drug, as stated in a pharmacology text. One can arrange set and setting so that a dose of an amphetamine will produce sedation or a dose of a barbiturate, stimulation. The first time I tried mescaline, my set included so much anxiety (a roomful of people sat around watching to see what would happen) that I felt nothing whatever for four hours after swallowing the dose and, thereafter, only strong physical effects. There were simply no psychic effects to speak of. This phenomenon has been reported often with marijuana (which I did not try until two years later) and is of great significance, for it argues that the *experience* associated with use of a drug may not be as causally related to the drug as it appears to be.

It is not my purpose here to recount my drug experiences. I write of them to indicate that the route to mescaline, for me and others, was a highly logical one traceable back to earliest childhood. My desire to try mescaline, once I had learned of its existence, was as natural as my desire to whirl myself into dizziness, hallucinate while falling asleep, sniff cleaning fluid, or get drunk in high school. I did not take mescaline because I went to Harvard, met Timothy Leary, rebelled against my parents, was motivated, or sought escape from reality. I took it because I was a normal American teenager whose curiosity had survived thirteen years of American education. And it is instructive to note that the way mescaline first came to my attention was through a scare story in a newspaper describing a fatal reaction to the drug (a most improbable event, as it turns out).

Now, when I say that people take drugs in response to an innate drive to alter consciousness, I do not make any judgment about the taking of drugs. The drive itself must not be equated with the forms of its expression. Clearly, much drug taking in our country is negative in the sense that it is ultimately destructive to the individual and, therefore, to society. But this obvious fact says nothing about the intrinsic goodness or badness of altered states of consciousness or the need to experience them. Given the negativity of much drug use, it seems to me there are two possibilities to consider: (1) altered states of consciousness are inherently undesirable (in which case, presumably, the drive to experience them should be thwarted); or (2) altered states of consciousness are neither desirable nor undesirable of themselves but can take bad forms (in which case the drive to experience them should be channeled in some "proper" direction). Do we have enough evidence to make an intelligent choice between these possibilities?

Primarily, we need more information about altered states of consciousness. Altered from what? is a good first question. The answer is: from ordinary waking consciousness, which is "normal" only in the strict sense of "statistically most frequent"; there is no connotation of "good," "worthwhile," or "healthy." Sleep and daydreaming are examples of altered states of consciousness, as are trance, hypnosis, meditation, general anesthesia, delirium, psychosis, mystic rapture, and the various chemical "highs." If we turn to psychology or medicine for an understanding of these states, we encounter a curious problem; Western scientists who study the mind tend to study the objective correlates of consciousness rather than consciousness itself. In fact, because consciousness is non-material, there has been great reluctance to accord it the reality of a laboratory phenomenon; psychologists, therefore, do not study consciousness directly, only indirectly, as by monitoring the physiological responses or brain waves of a person in a hypnotic trance or in meditation. Non-material things are considered inaccessible to direct investigation, if not altogether unreal. Consequently, there has been no serious attempt to study altered states of consciousness as such.

In the East, psychological science has taken a very different turn. Subjective states are considered more directly available for investigation than objective phenomena, which, after all, can only be perceived through our subjective states. Accordingly, an experiential science of consciousness has developed in the Orient, of which yoga is a magnificent example. It is a science as brilliantly articulated as Western conceptions of neurophysiology, but no attempt has been made to correlate it carefully with the physical realities of the nervous system as demonstrated by the West.

Therefore, Eastern science should be helpful in understanding altered states of consciousness, but it must always be checked against empirical knowledge of the objective nervous system. Now, one of the puzzling and unifying features of altered states of consciousness is their relative absence of physical correlates. For example, there are really no significant physiological differences between a hypnotized person and an unhypnotized person, or even any way of telling them apart, if the hypnotized subject is given appropriate suggestions for his behavior. As we shall see, the same holds true for the person high on marijuana—he is not readily distinguishable from one who is not high. Consequently, research as we know it in the West really cannot get much of a foothold in this area, and the scientific literature is dreadfully inadequate.

Nevertheless, I think it is possible to come to some useful conclusions about altered states of consciousness from what we can observe in ourselves and others. An immediate suggestion is that these states form some sort of continuum, in view of how much they have in common with each other. For example, trance, whether spontaneous or induced by a hypnotist, is simply an extension of the daydreaming state, in which awareness is focused and often directed inward rather than outward. Except for its voluntary and purposeful character, meditation is not easily distinguished from trance. Masters of meditation in Zen Buddhism warn their students to ignore *makyo*, sensory distortions that frequently resemble the visions of mystics or the hallucinations of schizophrenics. In other words, there is much cross-phenomenology among these states of consciousness, and, interestingly enough, being high on drugs has many of these same features, regardless of what drug induces the high.

The sense of physical lightness and timelessness so often reported by drug users is quite common in trance, meditation, and mystic rapture, for instance. Great ease of access to unconscious memories is also common in these states. Hypnotic subjects capable of sustaining deep trances can be "age regressed"—for example, made to reexperience their tenth birthday party. In deepest trances, awareness of present reality is obliterated, and the subject is amnesic for the experience when he returns to normal consciousness. In lighter trances, age-regressed subjects often have a sense of dual reality—the simultaneous experience of reliving the tenth birthday party, while also sitting with the hypnotist. Exactly the same experience is commonly reported by users of marijuana, who often find themselves spontaneously reliving unconscious memories as present realities; I have had this sense of dual reality myself on a number of occasions when I have been high on marijuana in settings that encouraged introspective reverie.

I want to underline the idea that these states form a continuum beginning in familiar territory. When we watch a movie and become oblivious to everything except the screen, we are in a light trance, in which the scope of our awareness has diminished but the intensity of it has increased. In the Oriental scientific literature, analogies are often drawn between consciousness and light: intensity increases, as scope decreases. In simple forms of concentration, like movie watching or daydreaming, we do not become aware of the power of focused awareness, but we are doing nothing qualitatively different from persons in states of much more intensely focused consciousness where unusual phenomena are the rule. For example, total anesthesia sufficient for major surgery can occur in deep trance; what appears to happen is that the scope of awareness diminishes so much that the pain arising from the body falls outside it. The conscious experience of this state is that "the pain is there, but it's happening to someone else." (Patients given morphine sometimes report the same experience.) I have myself seen a woman have a baby by Caesarean section with no medication; hypnosis alone was used to induce anesthesia, and she remained conscious, alert, in no discomfort throughout the operation.

I have also seen yogis demonstrate kinds of control of their involuntary nervous systems that my medical education led me to believe were impossible. One that I met could make his heart go into an irregular pattern of beating called fibrillation at will and stop it at will. Such men ascribe their successes in this area solely to powers of concentration developed during regular periods of meditation. There is no need, I think, to point out the tremendous implications of these observations. Because we are unable to modify consciously the operations of a major division of our nervous system (the autonomic system), we are prey to many kinds of illnesses we can do nothing much about (cardiovascular diseases, for example). The possibility that one can learn to influence directly such "involuntary" functions as heart rate, blood pressure, blood flow to internal organs, endocrine secretions, and perhaps even cellular processes by conscious use of the autonomic nervous system, is the most exciting frontier of modern medicine. If, by meditation, a man can learn to regulate blood flow to his skin (I have seen a yogi produce a ten-degree-Fahrenheit temperature difference between right and left hands within one minute of getting a signal; the warmer hand was engorged with blood and dark red, the cooler hand was pale), there is no reason why he could not also learn to shut off blood flow to a tumor in his body and thus kill it.

Another chief characteristic of all these states is a major change in the sense of ego, that is, in awareness of oneself as a distinct entity. Thus, when we catch ourselves daydreaming, we wonder where we were for the past few minutes. Now, it is most interesting that many systems of mind development and many religions encourage their adherents to learn to "forget" themselves in precisely this sense. For example, in Zen archery (an application of Zen technique that can be used as a spiritual exercise) the meditating archer obliterates the distinction between himself and the bow; hitting the bull's eye with the arrow then becomes no more difficult than reaching out and touching it, and the shot is always a bull's eye. D. T. Suzuki, who brought Zen to the attention of the West, has written of this process: "The archer ceases to be conscious of himself as the one who is engaged in hitting the bull's eye which confronts him."[4] In fact, the ability to forget oneself as the doer seems to be the essence of mastery of any skill. And since the observing ego is the center of normal waking consciousness, the essence of mastery of any skill is the ability to forsake this kind of consciousness at will.

Furthermore, mystics from all religious traditions testify that this same loss of sense of self is an essential aspect of the highest of human experiences—an assertion the Christian might associate with Jesus' words: "Whoever loses his life for my sake will gain it."[5] In higher forms of yogic or Buddhist meditation, the aim is to focus consciousness on a single object or thought and then to erase all notion of anyone doing the meditation. Patanjali, the ancient writer who first codified and recorded the principles of the much more ancient science of yoga, wrote of *samadhi* (the highest state of consciousness envisioned in yoga): "When alone, the object of contemplation remains and one's own form is annihilated, this is known as *samadhi*."[6] *Samadhi* is a real experience that has been attained by many.

It is noteworthy that most of the world's highest religious and philosophic thought originated in altered states of consciousness in individuals (Gautama, Paul, Mohammed, etc.). It is also noteworthy that creative genius has long been observed to correlate with psychosis, and that intuitive genius is often associated with daydreaming, meditation, dreaming, and other non-ordinary modes of consciousness.

What conclusions can we draw from all this information? At the least, it would seem, altered states of consciousness have great potential for strongly positive psychic development. They appear to be the ways to more effective and fuller use of the nervous system, to development of creative and intellectual faculties, and to attainment of certain kinds of thought that have been deemed exalted by all who have experienced them.

So there is much logic in our being born with a drive to experiment with other ways of experiencing our perceptions, in particular to get away periodically from ordinary ego-centered consciousness. It may even be a key factor in the present evolution of the human nervous system. But our immediate concern is the anxiety certain expressions of this drive are provoking in our own land, and we are trying to decide what to make of altered states of consciousness. Clearly, they are potentially valuable to us, not inherently undesirable, as in our first hypothesis. They are also not abnormal, in that they grade into states all of us have experienced. Therefore to attempt to thwart this drive would probably be impossible and might be dangerous. True, it exposes the organism to certain risks, but ultimately it can confer psychic superiority. To try to thwart its expression in individuals and in society might be psychologically crippling for people and evolutionarily suicidal for the species. I would not want to see us tamper with something so closely related to our curiosity, our creativity, our intuition, and our highest aspirations.

If the drive to alter consciousness is potentially valuable and the states of altered consciousness are potentially valuable, then something must be channeling that drive in wrong directions for it to have negative manifestations in our society. By the way, I do not equate all drug taking with negative manifestations of the drive to alter consciousness. Drug use becomes negative or abusive only when it poses a serious threat to health or to social or psychological functioning. Failure to distinguish drug use from drug abuse—another unhelpful conception arising from emotional bias—has become quite popular, especially in federal government propaganda. The National Institute of Mental Health continues to label every person who smokes marijuana an abuser of the drug, thus creating an insoluble marijuana problem of enormous proportions. Professional, legal and medical groups also contribute to this way of thinking; in fact, the American Medical Association has gone so far as to define drug abuse as any use of a "drug of abuse" without professional supervision—an illustration of the peculiar logic necessary to justify conceptions based on emotional rather than rational considerations.

Certainly, much drug use is undesirable, despite the claims of drug enthusiasts, although this problem seems to me much less disturbing than the loss to individuals and to society of the potential benefits of consciousness alteration in positive directions. But let us not get ahead of ourselves. Our inquiry in this chapter is directed to the question of why people take drugs. I have tried to demonstrate that people take drugs because they are means of satisfying an inner need for experiencing other modes of consciousness and that whether the drugs are legal or illegal is an unimportant consideration. To answer the question most succinctly: people take drugs because they work.

Or, at least, they seem to.

Notes

1. Aldous Huxley, *The Doors of Perception* (New York: Perennial Library, 1970), 9–10.
2. Aldous Huxley, *The Doors of Perception*, 14.
3. Aldous Huxley, *The Doors of Perception*, 62–63.
4. D. T. Suzuki, Introduction to *Zen in the Art of Archery* by Eugene Herrigel (New York: Vintage Books, 1971), 10.
5. Matthew 16:26; compare Luke 10:24.
6. Patanjali, *Yoga Aphorisms* III:3, quoted by James Hewitt in *A Practical Guide to Yoga* (New York: Funk and Wagnalls, 1968), 146. Further commentary on this aphorism may be found in *How to Know God: The Yoga Aphorisms of Patanjali,* translated by Swami Prabhavananda and Christopher Isherwood (New York: Signet Books, 1969), 122–123.

For Discussion

1. If drug use can result from the natural desire to alter one's consciousness, why do we punish drug offenders for something over which they have little control?
2. Think of ways in which set or setting negatively or positively affected the drug experience of someone you know.

7

Becoming a Marihuana User

HOWARD S. BECKER

In this classic piece written more than fifty years ago, Howard S. Becker argues that experiencing the positive effects of marijuana must be learned. According to Becker, the learning process includes three stages: (1) learning how to smoke so that the effects of marijuana are experienced, (2) learning to recognize the effects of being "high," and (3) learning to enjoy the positive effects of the drug. Following his analysis of interviews conducted with fifty people from diverse social backgrounds, Becker argues that the "sequence of changes" helps users experience the drug in a pleasurable way.

The use of marihuana is and has been the focus of a good deal of attention on the part of both scientists and laymen. One of the major problems students of the practice have addressed themselves to has been the identification of those individual psychological traits which differentiate marihuana users from nonusers and which are assumed to account for the use of the drug. That approach, common in the study of behavior categorized as deviant, is based on the premise that the presence of a given kind of behavior in an individual can best be explained as the result of some trait which predisposes or motivates him to engage in the behavior.[1]

This study is likewise concerned with accounting for the presence or absence of marihuana use in an individual's behavior. It starts, however, from a different premise: that the presence of a given kind of behavior is the result of a sequence of social experiences during which the person acquires a conception of the meaning of the behavior, and perceptions and judgments of objects and situations, all of which make the activity possible and desirable. Thus, the motivation or disposition to engage in the activity is built up in the course of learning to engage in it and does not antedate this learning process. For such a view it is not necessary to identify those "traits" which "cause" the behavior. Instead, the problem becomes one of describing the set of changes in the person's conception of the activity and of the experience it provides for him.[2]

This paper seeks to describe the sequence of changes in attitude and experience which lead to *the use of marihuana for pleasure*. Marihuana does not produce addiction, as do alcohol and the opiate drugs; there is no withdrawal sickness and no ineradicable craving for the drug.[3] The most frequent pattern of use might be termed "recreational." The drug is used occasionally for the pleasure the user finds in it, a relatively casual kind of behavior in comparison with that connected with the use of

Reprinted from H. S. Becker, 1953, "Becoming a Marihuana User," in *American Journal of Sociology* 59: 235–242. Copyright © 1953 by paper read at the meetings of the Midwest Sociological Society in Omaha, Nebraska, April 25, 1953.

addicting drugs. The term "use for pleasure" is meant to emphasize the noncompulsive and casual character of the behavior. It is also meant to eliminate from consideration here those few cases in which marihuana is used for its prestige value only, as a symbol that one is a certain kind of person, with no pleasure at all being derived from its use.

The analysis presented here is conceived of as demonstrating the greater explanatory usefulness of the kind of theory outlined above as opposed to the predispositional theories now current. This may be seen in two ways: (1) predispositional theories cannot account for that group of users (whose existence is admitted)[4] who do not exhibit the trait or traits considered to cause the behavior and (2) such theories cannot account for the great variability over time of a given individual's behavior with reference to the drug. The same person will at one stage be unable to use the drug for pleasure, at a later stage be able and willing to do so, and, still later, again be unable to use it in this way. These changes, difficult to explain from a predispositional or motivational theory, are readily understandable in terms of changes in the individual's conception of the drug as is the existence of "normal" users.

The study attempted to arrive at a general statement of the sequence of changes in individual attitude and experience which have always occurred when the individual has become willing and able to use marihuana for pleasure and which have not occurred or not been permanently maintained when this is not the case. This generalization is stated in universal terms in order that negative cases may be discovered and used to revise the explanatory hypothesis.[5]

Fifty interviews with marihuana users from a variety of social backgrounds and present positions in society constitute the data from which the generalization was constructed and against which it was tested.[6] The interviews focused on the history of the person's experience with the drug, seeking major changes in his attitude toward it and in his actual use of it and the reasons for these changes. The final generalization is a statement of that sequence of changes in attitude which occurred in every case known to me in which the person came to use marihuana for pleasure. Until a negative case is found, it may be considered as an explanation of all cases of marihuana use

for pleasure. In addition, changes from use to nonuse are shown to be related to similar changes in conception, and in each case it is possible to explain variations in the individual's behavior in these terms.

This paper covers only a portion of the natural history of an individual's use of marihuana,[7] starting with the person having arrived at the point of willingness to try marihuana. He knows that others use it to "get high," but he does not know what this means in concrete terms. He is curious about the experience, ignorant of what it may turn out to be, and afraid that it may be more than he has bargained for. The steps outlined below, if he undergoes them all and maintains the attitudes developed in them, leave him willing and able to use the drug for pleasure when the opportunity presents itself.

I

The novice does not ordinarily get high the first time he smokes marihuana, and several attempts are usually necessary to induce this state. One explanation of this may be that the drug is not smoked "properly," that is, in a way that insures sufficient dosage to produce real symptoms of intoxication. Most users agree that it cannot be smoked like tobacco if one is to get high:

> Take in a lot of air, you know, and . . . I don't know how to describe it, you don't smoke it like a cigarette, you draw in a lot of air and get it deep down in your system and then keep it there. Keep it there as long as you can.

Without the use of some such technique[8] the drug will produce no effects, and the user will be unable to get high:

> The trouble with people like that [who are not able to get high] is that they're just not smoking it right, that's all there is to it. Either they're not holding it down long enough, or they're getting too much air and not enough smoke, or the other way around or something like that. A lot of people just don't smoke it right, so naturally nothing's gonna happen.

If nothing happens, it is manifestly impossible for the user to develop a conception of the drug as an object which can be used for pleasure, and use will therefore not continue. The first step in the sequence of events that must occur if the person is to become a user is that he must learn to use the proper smoking technique in order that his use of the drug will produce some effects in terms of which his conception of it can change.

Such a change is, as might be expected, a result of the individual's participation in groups in which marihuana is used. In them the individual learns the proper way to smoke the drug. This may occur through direct teaching:

> I was smoking like I did an ordinary cigarette. He said, "No, don't do it like that." He said, "Suck it, you know, draw in and hold it in your lungs till you . . . for a period of time."
>
> I said, "Is there any limit of time to hold it?"
>
> He said, "No, just till you feel that you want to let it out, let it out." So I did that three or four times.

Many new users are ashamed to admit ignorance and, pretending to know already, must learn through the more indirect means of observation and imitation:

> I came on like I had turned on [smoked marihuana] many times before, you know. I didn't want to seem like a punk to this cat. See, like I didn't know the first thing about it—how to smoke it, or what was going to happen, or what. I just watched him like a hawk—I didn't take my eyes off him for a second, because I wanted to do everything just as he did it. I watched how he held it, how he smoked it, and everything. Then when he gave it to me I just came on cool, as though I knew exactly what the score was. I held it like he did and took a poke just the way he did.

No person continued marihuana use for pleasure without learning a technique that supplied sufficient dosage for the effects of the drug to appear. Only when this was learned was it possible for a conception of the drug as an object which could be used for pleasure to emerge. Without such a conception marihuana use was considered meaningless and did not continue.

II

Even after he learns the proper smoking technique, the new user may not get high and thus not form a conception of the drug as something which can be used for pleasure. A remark made by a user suggested the reason for this difficulty in getting high and pointed to the next necessary step on the road to being a user:

> I was told during an interview, "As a matter of fact I've seen a guy who was high out of his mind and didn't know it."
>
> I expressed disbelief: "How can that be, man?"
>
> The interviewee said, "Well, it's pretty strange, I'll grant you that, but I've seen it. This guy got on with me, claiming that he'd never got high, one of those guys, and he got completely stoned. And he kept insisting that he wasn't high. So I had to prove to him that he was."

What does this mean? It suggests that being high consists of two elements: the presence of symptoms caused by marihuana use and the recognition of these symptoms and their connection by the user with his use of the drug. It is not enough, that is, that the effects be present; they alone do not automatically provide the experience of being high. The user must be able to point them out to himself and consciously connect them with his having smoked marihuana before he can have this experience. Otherwise, regardless of the actual effects produced, he considers that the drug has had no effect on him: "I figured it either had no effect on me or other people were exaggerating its effect on them, you know. I thought it was probably psychological, see." Such persons believe that the whole thing is an illusion and that the wish to be high leads the user to deceive himself into believing that something is happening when, in fact, nothing is. They do not continue marihuana use, feeling that "it does nothing" for them.

Typically, however, the novice has faith (developed from his observation of users who do get high) that the drug actually will produce some new experience and continues to experiment with it until it does. His failure to get high worries him, and he is likely to ask more experienced users or provoke comments from them about it. In such conversations he is made aware of specific details of his experience which he may not have noticed or may have noticed but failed to identify as symptoms of being high:

> I didn't get high the first time . . . I don't think I held it in long enough. I probably let it out, you

know, you're a little afraid. The second time I wasn't sure, and he [smoking companion] told me, like I asked him for some of the symptoms or something, how would I know, you know. . . . So he told me to sit on a stool. I sat on—I think I sat on a bar stool—and he said, "Let your feet hang," and then when I got down my feet were real cold, you know.

And I started feeling it, you know. That was the first time. And then about a week after that, sometime pretty close to it, I really got on. That was the first time I got on a big laughing kick, you know. Then I really knew I was on.

One symptom of being high is an intense hunger. In the next case the novice becomes aware of this and gets high for the first time:

They were just laughing the hell out of me because like I was eating so much. I just scoffed [ate] so much food, and they were just laughing at me, you know. Sometimes I'd be looking at them, you know, wondering why they're laughing, you know, not knowing what I was doing. [Well, did they tell you why they were laughing eventually?] Yeah, yeah, I come back, "Hey, man, what's happening?" Like, you know, like I'd ask, "What's happening?" and all of a sudden I feel weird, you know. "Man, you're on, you know. You're on pot [high on marihuana]." I said, "No, am I?" Like I don't know what's happening.

The learning may occur in more indirect ways:

I heard little remarks that were made by other people. Somebody said, "My legs are rubbery," and I can't remember all the remarks that were made because I was very attentively listening for all these cues for what I was supposed to feel like.

The novice, then, eager to have this feeling, picks up from other users some concrete referents of the term "high" and applies these notions to his own experience. The new concepts make it possible for him to locate these symptoms among his own sensations and to point out to himself "something different" in his experience that he connects with drug use. It is only when he can do this that he is high. In the next case, the contrast between two successive experiences of a user makes clear the crucial importance of the awareness of the symptoms in being high and re-emphasizes the important role of

interaction with other users in acquiring the concepts that make this awareness possible:

[Did you get high the first time you turned on?] Yeah, sure. Although, come to think of it, I guess I really didn't. I mean, like that first time it was more or less of a mild drunk. I was happy, I guess, you know what I mean. But I didn't really know I was high, you know what I mean. It was only after the second time I got high that I realized I was high the first time. Then I knew that something different was happening.

[How did you know that?] How did I know? If what happened to me that night would of happened to you, you would've known, believe me. We played the first tune for almost two hours—one tune! Imagine, man! We got on the stand and played this one tune, we started at nine o'clock. When we got finished I looked at my watch, it's a quarter to eleven. Almost two hours on one tune. And it didn't seem like anything.

I mean, you know, it does that to you. It's like you have much more time or something. Anyway, when I saw that, man, it was too much. I knew I must really be high or something if anything like that could happen. See, and then they explained to me that that's what it did to you, you had a different sense of time and everything. So I realized that that's what it was. I knew then. Like the first time, I probably felt that way, you know, but I didn't know what's happening.

It is only when the novice becomes able to get high in this sense that he will continue to use marihuana for pleasure. In every case in which use continued, the user had acquired the necessary concepts with which to express to himself the fact that he was experiencing new sensations caused by the drug. That is, for use to continue, it is necessary not only to use the drug so as to produce effects but also to learn to perceive these effects when they occur. In this way marihuana acquires meaning for the user as an object which can be used for pleasure.

With increasing experience the user develops a greater appreciation of the drug's effects; he continues to learn to get high. He examines succeeding experiences closely, looking for new effects, making sure the old ones are still there. Out of this there grows a stable set of categories for experiencing the drug's effects whose presence enables the user to get high with ease.

The ability to perceive the drug's effects must be maintained if use is to continue; if it is lost, marihuana use ceases. Two kinds of evidence support this statement. First, people who become heavy users of alcohol, barbiturates, or opiates do not continue to smoke marihuana, largely because they lose the ability to distinguish between its effect and those of the other drugs.[9] They no longer know whether the marihuana gets them high. Second, in those few cases in which an individual uses marihuana in such quantities that he is always high, he is apt to get this same feeling that the drug has no effect on him, since the essential element of a noticeable difference between feeling high and feeling normal is missing. In such a situation, use is likely to be given up completely, but temporarily, in order that the user may once again be able to perceive the difference.

III

One more step is necessary if the user who has now learned to get high is to continue use. He must learn to enjoy the effects he has just learned to experience. Marihuana-produced sensations are not automatically or necessarily pleasurable. The taste for such experience is a socially acquired one, not different in kind from acquired tastes for oysters or dry martinis. The user feels dizzy, thirsty; his scalp tingles; he misjudges time and distances; and so on. Are these things pleasurable? He isn't sure. If he is to continue marihuana use, he must decide that they are. Otherwise, getting high, while a real enough experience, will be an unpleasant one he would rather avoid.

The effects of the drug, when first perceived, may be physically unpleasant or at least ambiguous:

> It started taking effect, and I didn't know what was happening, you know, what it was, and I was very sick. I walked around the room, walking around the room trying to get off, you know; it just scared me at first, you know. I wasn't used to that kind of feeling.

In addition, the novice's naive interpretation of what is happening to him may further confuse and frighten him, particularly if he decides, as many do, that he is going insane:

> I felt I was insane, you know. Everything people done to me just wigged me. I couldn't hold a conversation, and my mind would be wandering, and I was always thinking, oh, I don't know, weird things, like hearing music different.... I get the feeling that I can't talk to anyone. I'll goof completely.

Given these typically frightening and unpleasant first experiences, the beginner will not continue use unless he learns to redefine the sensations as pleasurable:

> It was offered to me, and I tried it. I'll tell you one thing. I never did enjoy it at all. I mean it was just nothing that I could enjoy. [Well, did you get high when you turned on?] Oh, yeah, I got definite feelings from it. But I didn't enjoy them. I mean I got plenty of reactions, but they were mostly reactions of fear. [You were frightened?] Yes. I didn't enjoy it. I couldn't seem to relax with it, you know. If you can't relax with a thing, you can't enjoy it, I don't think.

In other cases the first experiences were also definitely unpleasant, but the person did become a marihuana user. This occurred, however, only after a later experience enabled him to redefine the sensations as pleasurable:

> [This man's first experience was extremely unpleasant, involving distortion of spatial relationships and sounds, violent thirst, and panic produced by these symptoms.] After the first time I didn't turn on for about, I'd say, ten months to a year.... It wasn't a moral thing; it was because I'd gotten so frightened, bein' so high. An' I didn't want to go through that again, I mean, my reaction was, "Well, if this is what they call bein' high, I don't dig [like] it."... So I didn't turn on for a year almost, accounta that....
>
> Well, my friends started, an' consequently I started again. But I didn't have any more, I didn't have that same initial reaction, after I started turning on again.
>
> [In interaction with his friends he became able to find pleasure in the effects of the drug and eventually became a regular user.]

In no case will use continue without such a redefinition of the effects as enjoyable.

This redefinition occurs, typically, in interaction with more experienced users who, in a number of ways, teach the novice to find pleasure in this experience which is at first so frightening.[10] They may reassure him as to the temporary character of the unpleasant sensations and minimize their seriousness, at the same time calling attention to the more enjoyable aspects. An experienced user describes how he handles newcomers to marihuana use:

> Well, they get pretty high sometimes. The average person isn't ready for that, and it is a little frightening to them sometimes. I mean, they've been high on lush [alcohol], and they get higher that way than they've ever been before, and they don't know what's happening to them. Because they think they're going to keep going up, up, up till they lose their minds or begin doing weird things or something. You have to like reassure them, explain to them that they're not really flipping or anything, that they're gonna be all right. You have to just talk them out of being afraid. Keep talking to them, reassuring, telling them it's all right. And come on with your own story, you know: "The same thing happened to me. You'll get to like that after awhile." Keep coming on like that; pretty soon you talk them out of being scared. And besides they see you doing it and nothing horrible is happening to you, so that gives them more confidence.

The more experienced user may also teach the novice to regulate the amount he smokes more carefully, so as to avoid any severely uncomfortable symptoms while retaining the pleasant ones. Finally, he teaches the new user that he can "get to like it after awhile." He teaches him to regard those ambiguous experiences formerly defined as unpleasant as enjoyable. The older user in the following incident is a person whose tastes have shifted in this way, and his remarks have the effect of helping others to make a similar redefinition:

> A new user had her first experience of the effects of marihuana and became frightened and hysterical. She "felt like she was half in and half out of the room" and experienced a number of alarming physical symptoms. One of the more experienced users present said, "She's dragged because she's high like that. I'd give anything to get that high myself. I haven't been that high in years."

In short, what was once frightening and distasteful becomes, after a taste for it is built up, pleasant, desired, and sought after. Enjoyment is introduced by the favorable definition of the experience that one acquires from others. Without this, use will not continue, for marihuana will not be for the user an object he can use for pleasure.

In addition to being a necessary step in becoming a user, this represents an important condition for continued use. It is quite common for experienced users suddenly to have an unpleasant or frightening experience, which they cannot define as pleasurable, either because they have used a larger amount of marihuana than usual or because it turns out to be a higher-quality marihuana than they expected. The user has sensations which go beyond any conception he has of what being high is and is in much the same situation as the novice, uncomfortable and frightened. He may blame it on an overdose and simply be more careful in the future. But he may make this the occasion for a rethinking of his attitude toward the drug and decide that it no longer can give him pleasure. When this occurs and is not followed by a redefinition of the drug as capable of producing pleasure, use will cease.

The likelihood of such a redefinition occurring depends on the degree of the individual's participation with other users. Where this participation is intensive, the individual is quickly talked out of his feeling against marihuana use. In the next case, on the other hand, the experience was very disturbing, and the aftermath of the incident cut the person's participation with other users to almost zero. Use stopped for three years and began again only when a combination of circumstances, important among which was a resumption of ties with users, made possible a redefinition of the nature of the drug:

> It was too much, like I only made about four pokes, and I couldn't even get it out of my mouth, I was so high, and I got real flipped. In the basement, you know, I just couldn't stay in there anymore. My

heart was pounding real hard, you know, and I was going out of my mind; I thought I was losing my mind completely. So I cut out of this basement, and this other guy, he's out of his mind, told me, "Don't, don't leave me, man. Stay here." And I couldn't.

I walked outside, and it was five below zero, and I thought I was dying, and I had my coat open; I was sweating, I was perspiring. My whole insides were all . . ., and I walked about two blocks away, and I fainted behind a bush. I don't know how long I laid there. I woke up, and I was feeling the worst, I can't describe it at all, so I made it to a bowling alley, man, and I was trying to act normal, I was trying to shoot pool, you know, trying to act real normal and I couldn't and I couldn't stand up and I couldn't sit down, and I went up and laid down where some guys that spot pins lay down, and that didn't help me, and I went down to a doctor's office. I was going to go in there and tell the doctor to put me out of my misery . . . because my heart was pounding so hard, you know. . . . So then all weekend I started flipping, seeing things there and going through hell, you know, all kinds of abnormal things. . . . I just quit for a long time then.

[He went to a doctor who defined the symptoms for him as those of a nervous breakdown caused by "nerves" and "worries." Although he was no longer using marihuana, he had some recurrences of the symptoms which led him to suspect that "it was all his nerves."] So I just stopped worrying, you know; so it was about thirty-six months later I started making it again. I'd just take a few pokes, you know. [He first resumed use in the company of the same user-friend with whom he had been involved in the original incident.]

A person, then, cannot begin to use marihuana for pleasure, or continue its use for pleasure, unless he learns to define its effects as enjoyable, unless it becomes and remains an object which he conceives of as capable of producing pleasure.

IV

In summary, an individual will be able to use marihuana for pleasure only when he goes through a process of learning to conceive of it as an object which can be used in this way. No one becomes a user without (1) learning to smoke the drug in a way which will produce real effects; (2) learning to

recognize the effects and connect them with drug use (learning, in other words, to get high); and (3) learning to enjoy the sensations he perceives. In the course of this process he develops a disposition or motivation to use marihuana which was not and could not have been present when he began use, for it involves and depends on conceptions of the drug which could only grow out of the kind of actual experience detailed above. On completion of this process he is willing and able to use marihuana for pleasure.

He has learned, in short, to answer "Yes" to the question: "Is it fun?" The direction his further use of the drug takes depends on his being able to continue to answer "Yes" to this question and, in addition, on his being able to answer "Yes" to other questions which arise as he becomes aware of the implications of the fact that the society as a whole disapproves of the practice: "Is it expedient?" "Is it moral?"[11] Once he has acquired the ability to get enjoyment out of the drug, use will continue to be possible for him. Considerations of morality and expediency, occasioned by the reactions of society, may interfere and inhibit use, but use continues to be a possibility in terms of his conception of the drug. The act becomes impossible only when the ability to enjoy the experience of being high is lost, through a change in the user's conception of the drug occasioned by certain kinds of experience with it.

In comparing this theory with those which ascribe marihuana use to motives or predispositions rooted deep in individual behavior, the evidence makes it clear that marihuana use for pleasure can occur only when the process described above is undergone and cannot occur without it. This is apparently so without reference to the nature of the individual's personal makeup or psychic problems. Such theories assume that people have stable modes of response which predetermine the way they will act in relation to any particular situation or object and that, when they come in contact with the given object or situation, they act in the way in which their makeup predisposes them.

This analysis of the genesis of marihuana use shows that the individuals who come in contact with a given object may respond to it at first in a great variety of ways. If a stable form of new behavior toward the object is to emerge, a transformation of meanings must occur, in which the person develops a new conception of the nature of the object.[12] This happens in a series of communicative acts in which others point out new aspects of his experience to him, present him with new interpretations of events, and help him achieve a new conceptual organization of his world, without which the new behavior is not possible. Persons who do not achieve the proper kind of conceptualization are unable to engage in the given behavior and turn off in the direction of some other relationship to the object or activity.

This suggests that behavior of any kind might fruitfully be studied developmentally, in terms of changes in meanings and concepts, their organization and reorganization, and the way they channel behavior, making some acts possible while excluding others.

Notes

1. See, as examples of this approach, the following: Eli Marcovitz and Henry J. Meyers, 1944, "The Marihuana Addict in the Army," *War Medicine* 6 (December): 382–91; Herbert S. Gaskill, 1945, "Marihuana, an Intoxicant," *American Journal of Psychiatry* 102 (September): 202–4; Sol Charen and Luis Perelman, 1946, "Personality Studies of Marihuana Addicts," *American Journal of Psychiatry* 102 (March): 674–82.

2. This approach stems from George Herbert Mead's discussion of objects in *Mind, Self, and Society* (Chicago: University of Chicago Press, 1934), 277–80.

3. Cf. Roger Adams, 1942, "Marihuana," *Bulletin of the New York Academy of Medicine* 18 (November): 705–30.

4. Cf. Lawrence Kolb, 1938, "Marihuana," *Federal Probation* 2 (July): 22–25; and Walter Bromberg, 1939, "Marihuana: A Psychiatric Study," *Journal of the American Medical Association* 113 (July 1): 11.

5. The method used is that described by Alfred R. Lindesmith in his *Opiate Addictions* (Bloomington: Principia Press, 1947), chap. 1. I would like also to acknowledge the important role Lindesmith's work played in shaping my thinking about the genesis of marihuana use.

6. Most of the interviews were done by the author. I am grateful to Solomon Kobrin and Harold Finestone for allowing me to make use of interviews done by them.

7. I hope to discuss elsewhere other stages in this natural history.

8. A pharmacologist notes that this ritual is in fact an extremely efficient way of getting the drug into the blood stream (R. P. Walton, 1938, *Marihuana: America's New Drug Problem* [Philadelphia: J. B. Lippincott], p. 48).

9. "Smokers have repeatedly stated that the consumption of whiskey while smoking negates the potency of the drug. They find it very difficult to get high while drinking whiskey and because of that smokers will not drink while using the 'weed'" (cf. New York City Mayor's Committee on Marihuana, 1944, *The Marihuana Problem in the City of New York* [Lancaster, PA: Jacques Cattell Press], 13).

10. Charen and Perelman, "Personality Studies," 679.

11. Another paper will discuss the series of developments in attitude that occurs as the individual begins to take account of these matters and adjust his use to them.

12. Cf. Anselm Strauss, 1952, "The Development and Transformation of Monetary Meanings in the Child," *American Sociological Review* 17 (June), 275–86.

For Discussion

1. Do Becker's findings apply in contemporary society? Also, consider whether his findings apply to initiation into other drugs.

2. What may occur if novices initiate marijuana use with other novices? In these scenarios, how can the learning process occur?

8

Everybody's Doing It

Initiation to Prescription Drug Misuse

HEATHER Z. MUI, PALOMA SALES, AND SHEIGLA MURPHY

In this study, researchers at the Institute for Scientific Analysis in San Francisco investigated people's initiation into prescription drug misuse. The study focuses particularly on the nonmedical use of prescription opioids, stimulants, and central nervous system (CNS) depressants. Using an integrated theoretical framework, the authors find several factors that contribute to first use of prescription drug misuse.

Introduction

Young adults' nonmedical prescription drug use is a growing public health concern. Between 1992 and 2003, while the U.S. population grew 14%, the number of people misusing controlled prescription drugs increased 94% (Califano 2005). In 2011, there were 6.1 million persons aged 12 or older who used prescription psychotherapeutic drugs nonmedically in the past month (Substance Abuse and Mental Health Services Administration [SAMHSA] 2012). And the three largest national epidemiological studies on nonmedical prescription drug use—National Survey on Drug Use and Health (NSDUH), Monitoring the Future (MTF), and National Epidemiological Survey on Alcohol and Related Conditions (NESARC)—indicate that 18- to 25-year-olds continue to have the highest prevalence rate of nonmedical prescription drug use (Kroutil et al. 2006; McCabe, Boyd, and Teter 2009; SAMHSA 2005, 2006, 2007, 2008, 2009, 2010, 2011,

2012). Among young adults between 18 and 25 years of age, the rate of past-year nonmedical use of prescription-type drugs in 2011 was 5.0%, compared with 2.8 among adolescents aged 12 to 17 and 1.9 among adults 26 years of age and older (SAMHSA 2012).

In 2011, the number of new pain reliever users was 1.9 million, 1.2 million for tranquilizers, 670,000 for stimulants, and 159,000 for sedatives. Among recent initiates aged 12 to 49, the average age of first nonmedical use of any psychotherapeutics was 22.4 years. Specifically, the average age of initiation was 24.6 years for tranquilizers, 22.0 years for sedatives, 22.2 years for stimulants, and 21.8 years for pain relievers (SAMHSA 2012). Not only did the 18- to 25-year-old age group have the highest rate of nonmedical prescription drug use, but the average age of first nonmedical use of any and all psychotherapeutics falls within that age cohort as well. Interviewing 18- to 25-year-olds

Reprinted from Heather Z. Mui, Paloma Sales, and Sheigla Murphy, 2013, "Everybody's Doing It: Initiation to Prescription Drug Misuse," in *Journal of Drug Issues*, first published on August 14, 2013. Reprinted by permission of SAGE Publications via Copyright Clearance Center.

focused our approach and provided important insights into their nonmedical prescription drug initiation process.

Various factors contribute to an individual's decision to use prescription drugs nonmedically for the first time. In this article, we explore how the interplay of individual factors and social context impact initiation of nonmedical prescription drug use. The questions we explore include the following: Where and when were participants exposed to nonmedical prescription drug use? What were their beliefs, expectations, and perceived attractions for initiation? How did they access the drug(s)? Where were they and what was the nature of the social situation during their first experience? There are various forms of exposure to prescription drugs and their effects, which may either deter or motivate individuals' prescription drug misuse. Then there is the matter of access, the actual possession of the prescription pill that the individual is willing to try. And the final component is the physical and social environment in which an individual initiates nonmedical prescription drug use.

An individual's personal characteristics, experiences, and attributes interact with the external physical and social situation to shape the overall drug-using experience. Yet, most survey data collected on nonmedical prescription drug use convey the incidence and prevalence rates rather than understanding users' reasons for and implications of their behaviors. Studies that do focus on understanding nonmedical prescription drug use are scarce and limited, and often rely only on college student samples or focus on prescription opioids (Arria, Caldeira, Vincent, O'Grady, and Wish 2008; Daniulaityte, Carlson, and Kenne 2006; Daniulaityte, Falck, and Carlson 2012; Lankenau et al. 2012; McCabe, Teter, and Boyd 2006; Peralta and Steele 2010; Quintero 2009). Moreover, only a handful of recent studies have focused on the initiation of drugs, and those that do have mainly examined marijuana, heroin, methamphetamine, or Ecstasy. For first-time methamphetamine users, researchers found that for the most part, friends and sometimes partners introduced them to the drug, often in social situations (Brecht, O'Brien, von Mayrhauser, and Anglin 2004; Parsons, Kelly,

and Weiser 2007; Sheridan, Butler, and Wheeler 2009). Exposure to drugs and drug users opens the door to the idea of individuals using themselves, increasing the probability that they will use as well. Exposure, most commonly through friends, allowed many of our study participants to become acquainted with the idea of nonmedical prescription drug use.

Similarly, Vervaeke, van Deursen, and Korf's (2008) study on Ecstasy initiation found that Ecstasy-using friends played an important role in their participants' decisions to use the drug. Our findings indicate that friends were not only the most common point of exposure but also often played a part in our participants' decisions to use prescription drugs nonmedically. Sometimes participants' friends were already using while other times they initiated nonmedical use together. There were various descriptions of motivating factors, but the most common were curiosity, a friend's suggestion to try it, to get high, and everybody seemed to be doing it.

We also found that access to prescription drugs often came from friends and peers, as well as family and doctors. Our own findings and those from other studies indicate that teenagers and young adults believe prescription drug use is more "responsible," "controlled," or "safe" compared with street drug use (Friedman 2006; Manchikanti 2007). Prescription drugs are not only available on the streets or through introductions from friends or family, like street drugs, but also through legitimate prescriptions from doctors. In fact, similar to Lankenau and colleagues' (2012) study on the initiation into prescription opioid misuse among young injection drug users, some of our participants reported legitimate prescriptions as one of their main sources for prescription drugs used nonmedically. Many had a prescription of their own or had a friend or family member with one, which made prescription drugs easily accessible.

In Best, Manning, and Strang's (2007) heroin initiation study, they found that there was at least one other person present when their participants initiated heroin use, and it was usually in a group setting. Likewise, the majority of our interviewees tried prescription drugs nonmedically for the first time in a social setting. Some initiated nonmedical prescription drug use in their own homes with a friend, while others had their first experience in a college dorm, and still others at a party.

In sum, most studies of initiation of illegal drug use found that initiation was a social process, which was also true for our study sample. The most prominent and commonly referenced factor for initiation was the influence of friends and peers. They were not only sources of exposure and access but also key influencers in the initiation process and present during the time of initiation. Our study of nonmedical prescription drug use points to the magnitude of peer influence, along with other social actors such as family, doctors, and communities. Thus, the social context in which exposure, motivation, access, and setting contribute to the initiation of nonmedical prescription drug use warrants further in-depth examination.

Theoretical Model
Zinberg's Drug, Set, and Setting

We explore nonmedical prescription drug initiation using Zinberg's (1984) theoretical model of drug, set, and setting. According to Zinberg, drug, set, and setting determine the nature of one's drug experience. He defines "drug" as the drug's actual pharmacological properties and actions. "Set" refers to the individual's psychology, meaning the personal characteristics and personality attributes the user brings to the experience, which includes the user's past experiences, mood, motivations, and expectations (Jansen 1997; McElrath and McEvoy 2002; Zinberg 1984). "Setting" is the physical and social environment in which drug use occurs. The physical setting is the place, people, and things present during the time of use. And the social component encompasses the immediate social situation and "the set of other people present" (Jansen 1997), the broader beliefs and values of the social group, which establishes the social and cultural milieu at that particular place and time (Moore 1993; Zinberg 1984).

The "drug" in question is prescription drugs used in a nonmedical manner. However, in this analysis, rather than examining the actual drug effects, we focus on how set and setting, the individual and environmental factors, interact in the process of initiating nonmedical prescription drug use. Zinberg emphasizes that an individual is not isolated from the society in which she or he lives; both personal characteristics and social context must be considered in understanding drug use initiation. People experience different events throughout their lives that shape their decisions and behaviors. These experiences build on existing beliefs, attitudes, and expectations, expanding one's set. Thus, one's set is dependent on the varying events in the life of an individual, and these experiences are dictated by the social milieu. As Zinberg (1984) notes, "Both individual personality structure and social setting must be included in any coherent explanation of the way in which the social learning process makes controlled intoxicant use possible" (177). Thus, set and setting provide the analytic structure with which to consider the interconnected factors that lead to the initiation of nonmedical prescription drug use.

Akers' Social Learning Theory

We incorporate Social Learning Theory (Akers 1985) to further our understanding of nonmedical prescription drug use initiation as a social learning process. Social Learning Theory describes how behaviors are learned within a social context through four major components: differential association, imitation, definitions, and differential reinforcement (Akers 1985, 2009; Ford 2008; Peralta and Steele 2010). The most relevant component to our study is differential association, which states that the values, attitudes, techniques, and motives of deviant behavior are learned through interactions with others, such as family, friends, and peers (Peralta and Steele 2010). The differential association, the frequent interactions with the behavior, impacts one's values and attitudes, and builds on one's experiences, contributing to an individual's overall set regarding that behavior. And the probability that someone will engage in a deviant behavior increases when they associate with others who model such conduct, which may lead to the imitation of these actions and the adaptation of desirable and justifiable definitions for the behavior (Akers 2009). Differential association explains the normalization of deviant behavior, in this case, nonmedical prescription drug use. The more one associates with those who model such behavior, the more common and normal the behavior seems. More exposure to a behavior increases the chances of an individual learning and accepting the behavior as ordinary, normal, and conventional.

The social process of nonmedical prescription drug use can be understood with the combined framework of Zinberg's set and setting and Akers' Social Learning Theory. Both theories acknowledge the interaction of individual characteristics and sociocultural milieux. These theories provide a framework for understanding the impact of social context on individuals' constructions of nonmedical prescription drug use, cost-benefit analysis of use, and the social circumstances that facilitate the decisions and actions to initiate nonmedical prescription drug use.

Method

Between September 2008 and February 2012, we recruited and interviewed 120 individuals between 18 and 25 years of age who had used prescription drugs nonmedically at least 12 times in the 6 months prior to the interview. We define "nonmedical prescription drug use" as follows: Prescription drugs, whether they were prescribed or not, used to get high, for the experience it caused, for self-medication, to enhance school/work performance, or to modify the effects of other drug or alcohol use. The study focused on the nonmedical use of pharmaceutical opioids, stimulants, and central nervous system (CNS) depressants because based on the research done by ourselves, other investigators, and the National Institute on Drug Abuse (NIDA), these are the three most popular categories of prescription drugs among nonmedical prescription drug users. For purposes of this study, opioids included OxyContin (oxycodone), Percocet (acetaminophen and oxycodone), Vicodin (acetaminophen and hydrocodone), Dilaudid (hydromorphone), Darvocet (acetaminophen and propoxyphene), codeine, morphine, and methadone. Stimulants reported were Adderall (amphetamine and dextroamphetamine), Dexedrine (dextroamphetamine), and Ritalin and Concerta

(methylphenidate). CNS depressants included barbiturates and benzodiazepines, such as Xanax (alprazolam), Valium (diazepam), Klonopin (clonazepam), Ativan (lorazepam), and Soma (aspirin and carisoprodol). To be eligible, the individual had to be between the ages of 18 and 25, and had used prescription drugs nonmedically at least 12 times in the 6 months prior to the interview. We chose the criteria of 12 or more use episodes because we wanted to include new initiates, regular users, and bingers.

Our recruitment strategy included the use of key informants (Spradley 1979), and snowball or chain referral sampling methods (Biernacki and Waldorf 1981; Watters and Biernacki 1989), proven techniques for accessing hard-to-reach populations. Key informants vouch for the authenticity of the research project and the staff's commitment to respectful treatment and confidentiality. Key informants were participants in previous studies, selected according to quality of knowledge, level of involvement with nonmedical prescription drug users, and contact with different communities throughout San Francisco. These informants were asked to refer people they knew to be nonmedical prescription drug users to project staff for screening, eligibility, and enrollment into the study sample. Then, employing the chain referral sampling method, we asked study participants, following the completion of the interview, to refer up to, but no more than three friends who were nonmedical prescription drug users, to ensure penetration into numerous social worlds.

After screening potential participants and upon receiving IRB approval, we obtained informed consent from those deemed eligible before beginning each interview. Eligibility criteria for initial recruits was very broad (age, number of times used) becoming more precise with subsequent interviews employing Targeted Sampling (Charmaz 2006) as categories filled and we refined our emerging codes. Trained interviewers then proceeded to conduct recorded in-depth interviews and administer a questionnaire with participants at our offices in San Francisco, each lasting 2 to 3 hours. Our questions ranged from early life histories, school, employment, and personal relationships to medical histories, other drug use, current life, and the impact of nonmedical prescription drug use on health, lifestyle, and social relationships. More specifically, we inquired about their feelings, thoughts, expectations, and surroundings at the time they were first exposed to drugs and the first time they initiated drug use of each subsequent drug used, including prescription drugs. For their time, participants were provided a 50 dollar honorarium.

The recorded qualitative portions of the interviews were then transcribed, coded, and analyzed. We analyzed the qualitative data collected using a grounded theory methodology (Charmaz 1983; Glaser and Strauss 1967; Kuzel 1992; Strauss and Corbin 1990) to uncover emerging themes, utilizing QSR's Nvivo, a qualitative data analysis software, to facilitate these analyses. Although we had some pre-determined categories—based on our own and others' prior studies—we wanted to address that Grounded Theory methods gave us the flexibility to adjust our lines of inquiry to explore more in-depth any emerging themes. From the data, many themes emerged, including exposure to prescription drugs, medical prescription, access to prescription drugs, and initiation to prescription drugs, which became the codes in the code list used in our analyses.

Findings

To date, nonmedical prescription drug use remains quite popular, especially among the 18- to 25-year-old age group. Interviewees expressed different motives and manners of initiation. They each brought their own set of beliefs, expectations, and attitudes to the experience, and were in varying physical and social settings at the time of initiation. But there were commonalities in thought, expectations, and settings, and it was most often the interaction of set and setting that had led to nonmedical prescription drug initiation. Set and setting were heavily influenced by peers and social learning, through observations and discussions around nonmedical prescription drug use.

Table 8.1 presents some of the general characteristics of our study sample. We had chosen to interview 60 (50%) men and 60 (50%) women to

Table 8.1 General Characteristics of Nonmedical Prescription Drug Users (N = 120).

Gender	
Male	50%
Female	50%
Age (at time of interview)	
M, in years (SD)	21.3 (2.0)
Median, in years	21
Range, in years	18–25
Age of ªRx initiation	
M, in years (SD)	16.1 (2.8)
Median, in years	16
Range, in years	5–24
Ethnicity	
White	69.2%
Latino	10.8%
Middle Eastern	0.8%
Asian	13.3%
Mixed ethnicity	10.0%
Latino	1.7%
African American	4.2%
Native American	1.7%
Pacific Islander	1.7%
Education	
Some high school	6.7%
High school graduates	13.3%
Some college	64.2%
Associate degree	0.8%
Bachelor's degree	12.5%
Master's degree	0.8%
Doctorate	0.8%
Education status (in 12 months prior)	
Not attending	26.7%
Attending	73.3%
Full-time	61.7%
Part-time	10.8%
Full- and part-time	0.8%
Employment status (in 12 months prior)	
Unemployed	29.2%
Employed	70.8%
Full-time	23.3%
Part-time	45.8%
Full- and part-time	1.7%

ªRx = nonmedical prescription drug use.

explore nonmedical prescription drug use among men and women of different racial and ethnic groups and social classes. The median age was 21. The majority of the sample had at least some college education, with 61.7% attending school full-time and 70.8% employed during the 12 months prior to the interview.

The interviewees were all active nonmedical prescription drug users. Nonmedical prescription drug use among our sample ranged from 1 to 14 different prescription drugs with a median of five different types used in the 6 months prior to the interview. The most prevalent prescription drug used was Vicodin, with 112 of the 120 interviewees reporting use of the drug in the 6 months prior to the interview. The next most prevalent prescription drug was Xanax (70 interviewees) followed by Adderall and oxycodone (57 each), Valium (49), Percocet (47), codeine (45), Klonopin (42), morphine (32), Soma (31), Ativan (21), Ritalin (13), and Dilaudid (12). While a few only used one prescription drug, most used several different varieties, often due to availability and access, and still others also used other drugs and alcohol in the 6 months prior to the interview. In fact, the majority of participants had reported trying other drugs and alcohol before initiating nonmedical prescription drug use, but a few did report prescription drugs to have been the first drug they ever used. The median age of nonmedical prescription drug initiation was 16, with a range of 5 to 24 years old. Many of our interviewees (35.0%) began regular nonmedical use of prescription drugs, defined as at least once a month, shortly after initiation, another 16.6% began using regularly within a year after initiation, while 48.4% began 1 to 7 years after their initiation. Of our 120 participants, 64 (53.3%) had initiated nonmedical prescription drug use with an opioid, 28 (23.3%) with a CNS depressant, and 22 (18.3%) a stimulant.

Our findings revealed a common trajectory for initiation characterized by exposure to nonmedical drug use, motivation to use, access to prescription drugs, and finally, the opportunity or setting to initiate use. Exposure to nonmedical prescription drug use normalized the behavior, impacting the individual's set, allaying fears about deviant aspects of nonmedical prescription drug use. Exposure led to an assessment of personal costs and benefits and motivations for use. Once the normalizing effects of exposure, coupled with assessed motivation for use, were part of the set, access to prescription drugs was the next step toward the decision to initiate use. For most, prescription drugs were readily available, in the family's medicine cabinet, student health centers, or from friends. The final step was the proper setting in which to initiate use, not just the physical setting but also the social setting in which interviewees felt safe or ready to initiate use. In the following, we explore exposure, motivation, access, and setting within the context of set and setting and Social Learning Theory to better understand the initiation process of prescription drug misuse.

Exposure: Everybody's Doing It

Deviant behavior is learned through observation and consideration, followed by imitation. We learn by observing and examining others in given social contexts, then processing and giving meaning to that information. When we study others, our perception of their behaviors may be positive, negative, or neutral, but we are nonetheless processing what our observations are relaying to our brain in making sense of them. Our participants' exposure to nonmedical prescription drug use contributed to their set by expanding their understandings about and constructions of meaning around nonmedical prescription drug use.

Participants were exposed to prescription drugs at different stages in their life and in various social situations. The three main modes in which participants recalled being exposed to prescription drugs were through parents, friends or peers, and doctors' prescriptions. Family and peers are the most direct social influencers to an individual, and have been considered the two most important social influences through childhood and adolescence (Kandel 1996; Tang and Orwin 2009). This is the time when many of our participants first became aware of the nonmedical use of prescription drugs.

As interviewees reflected on their childhoods, some remembered seeing their parents taking pills or finding their parents' pills in the house. Even when parents tried to hide their drugs and drug use from them, as children, participants were very observant and aware of their parents' actions. They knew that their mother and/or father had these substances and were using them. As was the case with a 20-year-old White female, who at 13 years of age initiated nonmedical prescription drug use:

> I didn't realize like, my dad was on heroin 'cause I always saw him taking other opiates. I like knew that he did it but I didn't know it was like serious . . . Like before school I could go in his room, walk past him, he'd be passed out, I'd grab like an eighth of weed, grab like a gram of coke, grab a few pills and go to school and like just do it during the day and like he would never notice. But then it was like three of us were doing that so he started to notice and then he got a safe but he had [methadone] on him which is like an opiate whatever and we never—we were just foolish it's like it gets us high, whatever . . . like you have no concept. So we would take his methadone and like snort lines with it which you're not supposed to do at all . . . we were like oh this is heroin, this is like synthetic heroin and it did have that effect it was like stronger than Oxycontin pretty much and we did it and um, and he would, he would absolutely lose his mind when there was no—and all his stuff is gone, he's like what the hell, what's going on? He's like in serious withdrawals and we didn't even connect it. We're just like oh he does this for fun but like it wasn't the case at all.

She lived with her father, who used drugs in the house, sometimes to the point where he would pass out, leaving his drugs available to the participant. She told us she and her siblings thought he was doing the drugs for fun. The participant saw her father's drug-using behavior and imitated it.

Another interviewee learned about nonmedical prescription drug use from his mother. He was initially exposed to prescription drugs through a legitimate prescription of his own, but his mother would ask him for the drugs to use nonmedically:

> Uh, believe it or not um, 'cause my mom used to always go crazy over Vicodin. She be like I need some Vikes, I need some Vikes. You got some drugs for me? And she called it drugs because like you know when I used to get prescribed my Vicodin and stuff like 'cause I caught a couple injuries skatin' a few of 'em broke my ankle one time, fucked up my elbow and I had to go get some uh, pills so like my mom would always like take a third of 'em like I'm a need these. (24-year-old male of mixed ethnicity; Age of Nonmedical Prescription Drug Initiation [AI]: 14)

Nonmedical prescription drug use was even more apparent and common place for others. A 21-year-old White male noticed his parents used prescription drugs quite often and freely:

> Vicodin? I mean my parents like I said take pills for everything . . . It's a pretty common drug. Even in high school people were talking about it, people know what it is, people can get it, probably stealing it from their parents or something. (AI: 14)

Vicodin was also a hot topic among his peers in high school. His attitude, his set, toward nonmedical prescription drug use was that it was normal because the behavior was so widespread in his social world. His parents were modeling nonmedical prescription drug use, and his peers were talking about using as well. As a matter of fact, peers and/or friends was the most frequent response to the question, "how were you first exposed to prescription drug use?" Peers and friends were important in shaping many participants' perceptions and expectations of drugs. When everybody around is talking about doing something and it seems everybody is in fact doing it, one might want to do it as well, such as the following 19-year-old White female, who first tried prescription drugs nonmedically at age 18:

> Yeah um, just from what my friends had told me that I met here because they had all done a lot of drugs in high school and so like they were like oh you have to try this, you have to try this it's so great and I'd be like alright.

Similarly, another participant, a 22-year-old Pacific Islander male, experienced persistent exposure to prescription drug misuse from his roommate. In fact, he regularly drove and made transactions for her. The continued exposure and contact, the differential association, with prescription drug use accompanied by his perception of his friend feeling and still looking good while using informed his set. His opinion of nonmedical prescription drug use was positive, and eventually led to his initiation at age 21:

> Um, the person that I lived with she takes [prescription drugs] every day and she would literally like she has the car, wake me up in the morning, drive me [to] the Tenderloin, make me get out and get her some pills. She'd give me the money or whatever but after doing it 20, 30, 40 times you're like oh, I want some pills too . . . you're taking them all I see how you feel, you look great, you know what I'm saying? . . . That's how it really started for me.

Although the majority of our interviewees were exposed to drugs through family or friends, another major source of exposure was a legitimate prescription. Opioids were commonly prescribed to participants after wisdom teeth extraction. One participant had initially used for the pain as prescribed, but his use became recreational when he felt the additional effects and enjoyed the feeling of being high:

> [O]ne month in March I got my wisdom teeth out and then like a week later I got um, toe surgery on two of my toes and so I was on bed rest for like two weeks or something with like three uh, refilled prescriptions of Percocets and so that's—I wasn't railing (snorting) them or something I was just popping them like you were supposed to . . . It's pretty much how I found out that you can get really high off prescription pills. (19-year-old male of mixed ethnicity; AI: 17)

And in a few cases, the neighborhood or school was identified as the initial exposure to prescription drugs:

> INT: Okay, so where'd you get the idea of using Soma for fun?
> 081: Uh, 'cause like in Chinatown when I was little I used to hang out there and you'll see the older guys like probably like two, three years older they always at the playground called Chinese playground and then they always take it and then I would always see them and one of my friends hung out with them and he started taking it and that—I thought it was (unclear) back then and then I tried it once. (20-year-old Asian male; AI: 16)

Exposure alone did not always lead to prescription drug use but was a necessary step to initiation. For our study sample, who are active nonmedical prescription drug users, exposure contributed to their overall set, shaping their expectations and decisions to initiate nonmedical prescription drug use, but they also needed to feel a motivation to initiate use.

Motivation

Exposure taught our participants about nonmedical prescription drug use, but what were the reasons or factors behind their decisions to initiate? To answer this, we asked participants about their motivations to use prescription drugs nonmedically for the first time. Tang and Orwin (2009) found that the most consistent predictors of marijuana initiation for youth were experience with alcohol and/or cigarettes, and marijuana offers. In our sample, the initiation of prescription drugs often occurred after experiences with alcohol, cigarettes, and/or marijuana, and sometimes even other illicit drugs, not because it was a natural progression in their drug use but because there was a desire to get high and experiment coupled with the opportunity that offers of prescription drugs presented. After experimenting with marijuana, a 22-year-old White male was open to trying other drugs, including prescriptions, which he did at the age of 15. In fact, he said he "would be down to try pretty much anything." Like many other participants, his decision to initiate nonmedical prescription drug use was influenced by his prior drug use experience. The positive experience he had with marijuana in addition to his desire to get high were part of his set when deciding to use prescription drugs nonmedically.

The more offers and suggestions to use prescription drugs, the more opportunities there are to consider and want to try pills. A majority of the young adults we interviewed reported being with someone who offered it to them or suggested they try the prescription drug, so they did:

> My friend that got into a couple of car accidents, she like, she got [prescription drugs] and like abused them so much and she kept going back to

the doctor to get more and more . . . she was like, "Holy crap this is coolest feeling! You have to try it!" So then I did and like after that like others were introduced and just . . . (19-year-old White male; AI: 17)

Other reported motives for use included curiosity, to get high, because others were doing it, or a combination of these factors. Many explicitly stated curiosity as their main motivation to initiate use:

> Just curious . . . I was like, couldn't hurt. I heard good things about it, plus my roommate, he enjoyed it so much I was like it can't be that bad but uh it was just pure curiosity. (25-year-old White male; AI: 24)

For many, it seemed like everybody around them was using prescription drugs: their parents, siblings, neighbors, celebrities, classmates, and/or friends. It seemed that everyone in their immediate social network was engaging in nonmedical prescription drug use, and they wanted to know how it felt and to share in the experience. Such was the case with an 18-year-old Asian male, whose friends all used Somas:

> All my other friends were doing it so I thought it was okay. They said it was okay, it seemed like it was okay. They say it doesn't mess with your mind . . . it relaxes your muscles so I thought it was okay to take it you know so I started . . . it was safe . . . I never seen any of my friends OD, overdose on it or anything . . . (AI: 16)

Others felt overwhelmed by the pressure to achieve academically and wanted to keep up with other students whom they believed were using prescription drugs. They were motivated to initiate use for performance enhancement, and used a prescription stimulant as their first nonmedical prescription drug. White, Becker-Blease, and Grace-Bishop (2006) found the motives for stimulant use included to improve attention (69%), study habits (54%), grades (20%), and reducing hyperactivity (9%), with an additional 65% using for "partying." Other researchers have found additional motives such as to increase alertness, concentration, to get high, curiosity and experimentation, weight control, and athletic endurance (Barrett et al. 2005; Boyd et al.

2006; Low and Gendaszek 2002; Teter et al. 2005; Weiner 2000). Several of our participants also mentioned the motivations found by other investigators to have played a part in their initiations. One particular participant felt overwhelmed and unmotivated to write a paper, so he used Ritalin to focus. He knew about the drug because other people were using it, and he had access to his brother's prescription:

> [U]sing Ritalin in college . . . pretty much exclusively to write papers . . . I knew for some time that other people had been doing it. And I think my brother had a prescription. He had, like, a legitimate prescription for Ritalin, and I got some from him . . . And I just tried it one time because I was feeling really overwhelmed and unmotivated to write a paper. (22-year-old White male; AI: 18)

Still others may have been self-medicating. Many researchers have suggested that use may be an effort to self-medicate psychiatric symptoms (Chilcoat and Breslau 1998; Dowling, Storr, and Chilcoat 2006; Khantzian 1997). A few of our participants were prescribed several medications at young ages for different diagnoses or symptoms, from depression to attention deficit hyperactivity disorder (ADHD) to bipolar, and felt like "guinea pigs." To feel normal or not to feel, they would use prescription drugs to help them function, sleep, forget, or to modify the effects of other drugs. Once exposed and motivated, our participants were mentally prepared to initiate nonmedical prescription drug use. However, to initiate use, the prescription drug had to be available. Access was another necessary component of initiation. For all of our participants, access to prescription drugs when they first used them nonmedically was easy and uncomplicated.

Access: The Power of Prescription

Over the years, prescription drugs have become increasingly more available to young adults in North America. The United States consumes 80% of the global supply of opioids and two thirds of the world's illegal drugs (Califano 2007; Kuehn 2007; Manchikanti 2007). The NSDUH found that between 1992 and 2002, the U.S. population increased by 13% while prescriptions written for controlled drugs increased 154.3% (Califano 2005). Not surprisingly, the majority of our interviewees had a legitimate prescription of their own, or knew a family member or friend with a prescription. A 22-year-old Middle Eastern female articulated just how powerful prescriptions can be:

And then as far as drug use opening up more— I would say pills came after pot because it was just, you know, everyone's taken a pill in their life. So they're not scared of that so I wasn't necessarily scared of taking pills. And I think the first kind of pills it was definitely like a Vicodin kind of thing 'cause everyone kind of had access to Vicodin. If someone got surgery or something, you know Vicodin was more apparent. So Vicodin, Valium, Percocet, Klonopin, SOMAs, Norcos, Xanax didn't come about until later and when it did, it's just crazy . . . (AI: 15)

Prescription drugs are prescribed by doctors for medical purposes, so most interviewees felt they were safe and socially acceptable to use. Other studies' findings have indicated that patients who take opioids for pain can progress from therapeutic use to misuse or dependence (Brands et al. 2004; Ives et al. 2006; Potter et al. 2004). When a 25-year-old female of mixed ethnicity had her wisdom teeth removed at age 16, she recovered quickly and had some pills left over, so when her friend suggested taking it for fun, they did:

I was prescribed Percocet when I had my wisdom teeth removed but at that time I was in so much pain that I don't think I— oh, okay I do remember sort of after the fact still having a few and then it hadn't occurred to me to use it recreationally but then other people were like, "ooh, you have this? You should you know have fun with it." . . . I remember being at a friend's house and her mom was where ever and we were drinking beer and I was taking it when I was drinking . . . It was fun.

Several participants referenced student health centers as places for easy prescription drug access. Interviewees reported that once someone discovered that a sore throat could result in a Vicodin prescription, "everybody" started going to the health center claiming to be sick to get prescription drugs:

[W]hen you're going to [college], you get a free like health care kind of plan—well you pay for it but like um, you get to go to the health center for free and see doctors and what not. In like December and January, you know one kid gets sick and then it just sweeps the entire building and everybody is sick . . . And one girl went in and got a bottle of Vicodin for having a sore throat and we were just like well—what the hell? And then more and more people started going in and everyone was getting like liquid Codeine and Vicodin just like [snaps] easy. You know like they wouldn't—"Oh you have a sore throat? Like here, get 2,500s." And it started from that. Like I took—the first thing I ever tried was Vicodin. (21-year-old White male; AI: 18)

And if participants did not have their own prescription, they often had friends or family who did. Similar to our findings, McCabe and Boyd (2005), who studied prescription drug use among undergraduate students, identified three different categories of prescription drug sources: peers, family, and other sources. They found that peers often shared their legitimately prescribed drugs. This was echoed by our own participants:

I had a friend in college that had a lot of Vicodin and Norcos that he would just give me . . . He was prescribed them and he would just give 'em to me whenever I wanted. So I woke up with a hangover someday I'd just walk over there and he'd give me like 5 or something for free and then—you know can't beat that, you know? (21-year-old White male; AI: 19)

Family was the other major prescription drug source in McCabe and Boyd's (2005) study, which was also where a number of our interviewees obtained the prescription drug they first used nonmedically, mainly from parents. Parents were not only a source of exposure, but also for access. Again, some participants were exposed to prescription drugs in their homes as children or adolescents by their parents. This provided a source of prescription drugs for participants to use recreationally. In fact, the family medicine cabinet was a common place where participants accessed their parents' medications:

> Valiums and Xanax . . . They were in my mom's medicine cabinet. (24-year-old female of mixed ethnicity; AI: 15)

Other times, parents used pills openly. One participant mentioned that her mom trusted her with handling her prescriptions. When her mother switched prescriptions, she asked the interviewee to get rid of the remaining pills. She kept them for herself and later used the prescription drugs recreationally:

> My mom got into a car accident . . . I visited her for three weeks and I guess I was 16, 15. And, she gave me her pills to give 'em to her whenever she was in pain. And, I didn't take them then, I'm not that horrible . . . But, she decided that the OxyContin was too strong so she told me to throw 'em out and got Percocets instead so I kept the OxyContin. (18-year-old Latina female; AI: 16)

Access to prescription drugs was rather trouble-free for all of our interviewees. Rarely did our participants have to actively seek out prescription drugs for their initial use. However, three interviewees did report buying them. They knew someone who had a prescription and was selling or had a friend who knew somebody selling pills. But for most, there were numerous opportunities or offers from friends in social settings. We found that the drug was often suggested and supplied by others at no financial cost within the setting in which nonmedical prescription drug initiation took place, similar to the findings of Sheridan et al.'s (2009) methamphetamine initiation study and Daniulaityte et al.'s (2006) prescription opioid study. Once participants' set toward nonmedical prescription drug use was favorable and they had access to prescription drugs, all they needed was to be in an appropriate setting in which to initiate use.

Setting

Setting is not simply the physical location where the drug use occurs, but includes other dimensions, such as the people present and their social relationships and activities, which establish the social context. As Zinberg (1984) explained, an individual is not infinitely adaptive, but rather functions within a range of experiences, determined and structured by the physical and social environment that is one's setting. Initiation occurred when the individual felt comfortable doing so, usually with people they trusted, who had an open attitude toward nonmedical prescription drug use. A trusted place where initiation often occurred was at a friend's house or with a friend in the participant's home:

> [F]irst time I tried Adderall was when one of my friends ended up coming over to my house and we were kinda just doing homework or whatever um, and we ended up getting like I don't know kind of restless and tired and then that's when she you know kinda brought the whole Adderall thing up and then kinda explained what it was. And in a way like I don't know it's kind of weird because it's like coming from the whole meth thing, like in a way it kind of is like the same little substances but it's like I don't know but in a way it's not even I don't know it's like different like I, I know like with meth it's like yeah during that time or whatever. But then it was like Adderall I'm looking at it more as like a positive thing like helping me through school even though you get kind of the same um, feelings or whatever you do with meth 'cause that's kind of what it is in a way. But it's like I don't know to me it's like different it feels different. (24-year-old African American female; AI: 23)

The combination of her set and setting influenced her decision to use. Although she believed Adderall to produce the same feelings as meth, her motivation and attitude about using the prescription pill was different. Factors such as her previous experience with meth, along with her trust in her friend, her positive feeling about the benefits for school work, and being in her own home were contributing components of her set and setting and ultimately her decision to initiate.

School settings often played a part in the initiation process. It was at school that some participants were exposed to prescription drugs, where friends and peers accessed prescription drugs, or the place where first use occurred, especially in college. College was not just an institution of higher academic learning but also the time and place for participants to explore, grow, and find their identity and niche in society. This was especially important during their dorm experience, where interviewees adapted to a new social milieu. In the dorms, some learned new behaviors, such as nonmedical prescription drug use, as some participants shared:

> [W]hen I came to college, all of a sudden I saw all these people around me always having pills. So it was when I moved here that I saw really saw those . . . 'cause I lived in the dorms freshman year so—yeah obviously it was on campus. (21-year-old Latina female; AI: 18)

The deviant behavior of nonmedical prescription drug use became normalized in college settings as part of a social learning process. It seemed everybody used prescription pills and they were readily available; thus, the behavior was seen as a normal and popular activity. Prescription drug use was fairly common in the dorms and at social gatherings and those who used seemed to enjoy the effects. The curiosity and desire to be engaged in this component of peer bonding and belonging became increasingly attractive for some:

> It was my freshman year at the (academy) and it was in the dorms and I had met this group of people . . . from Alaska. And in Alaska, Oxycontin is extremely, extremely common that's like what all the people end up doing up here I don't know like certain towns it's like a meth town or a coke town or whatever up in (Alaskan city) specially Oxycontin is the drug of choice for everyone. So I met this group of people and this guy (name) . . . had been free-basing Oxycontin up in the dorm room and I had become friends with them 'cause they were all in my classes and stuff like that we hang out up there and at first they didn't even want me to touch the stuff like they didn't want me to do it with them and that was fine with me. But then I started getting curious. I was like come on what's one hit gonna do or what not? And like I don't snort or eat the pills, I smoke them. (21-year-old White female; AI: 16)

The dorms were a very social experience, an environment conducive for much interaction and imitation. And although the majority of our participants attended college full-time (61.7%), some may not have lived in dorms and there were others who did not attend college. Other settings for social encounters included parties and get-togethers, where active social roles were played and nonmedical prescription drug use initiated:

> I was at this party with some friends and then my other friend had these pills [Somas] like had 20 of them and then like he said take one and then I took it with soda and then it started hitting me but like the effect wasn't that strong so I took like two more and took it all at once. I started feeling relaxed but then I was just sitting there like I didn't really feel like moving but it was a good feeling though. Yeah, that's how I got started. (19-year-old Asian male; AI: 17)

Usually when someone goes to a party, he or she wants to have a good time. In these instances, as was the case with many interviewees, they associated the party setting with doing drugs and fun times, further contributing to the initiation process, as described by the following 24-year-old White female, who recalled her experience at age 17:

> 110: Xanax um, you know people would have at parties and we would take it when we're drinking so that was the first prescription drug that I was like around . . . I think the first time that I took the—that I took Xanax I member I was at a party um, this kid's parents were away maybe like 20 people were there everyone was sleeping over and we got like a lot of sushi and a lot of sake and we're taking shots of sake and I think like right before we sat down to eat I took a Xanax so I did my Xanax and they were taking like—
> INT: Only you took it or did everyone—
> 110: A lot of people, a lot of people.

A lot of people were doing it, so her perception of nonmedical prescription drug use was that it was probably not that bad, since it seemed to be a popular behavior that often accompanied drinking and having fun. An important factor that led to her initiation as well as that of many others was that everybody around her was doing it. However, there were also a few participants who used alone, usually in their own homes. They wanted to keep their use private and/or were more comfortable getting high on their own. But for most, nonmedical prescription drug use was a social experience. For our interviewees, initiation was a social process of learned behavior. They learned, through exposure to and interactions with nonmedical prescription drug users, how prescription drugs can be used in different ways and for different reasons. The behavior was first modeled and normalized by the people around them and then imitated by our interviewees. Drug-using peers reinforced the behavior, strengthening interviewees' sense of greater rewards than punishment for nonmedical prescription drug use. Interviewees' set and setting, through social learning, along with access, intertwined to facilitate their initiation of nonmedical prescription drug use.

Discussion

During the course of their interviews, young adult nonmedical prescription drug users relayed their thoughts and feelings about their first experience using prescription drugs nonmedically and described the social contexts in which they initiated use. We have examined the social processes of initiation using Zinberg's theory of drug, set and setting, emphasizing the set and setting, along with Akers' Social Learning Theory, which further illuminates the social component of initiation and the ways in which deviant behavior is learned. The set refers to participants' thoughts, motivations, and expectations that are shaped by prior drug exposures and experiences. Social Learning Theory explicates the role of socialization to and normalization of nonmedical prescription drug use, particularly through peer influence, as a social learning process that shapes set and setting.

We learned from our participants' accounts that initiation of nonmedical prescription drug use followed a trajectory of exposure, motivation, access, and setting. Many reported being exposed through friends, family, doctors, or within their communities. Initial exposure to prescription drugs informed their set about the perceived safety of using the drugs, since they are prescribed by doctors and used by parents, grandparents, siblings, and friends, even as children. Exposure to nonmedical use of prescription drugs awakened curiosity in some about possible alternative uses of the drugs. Some saw a benefit of using stimulants to enhance academic performance. Others became aware of the possibility of using prescription drugs to party and get high, and still others were exposed to widespread peer use and wanted to fit in with their friends. Once they had assessed the benefits of using nonmedically and felt motivated to use, then gaining access to the drugs was the next step. Most seized the opportunity to use nonmedically when pills were offered or prescribed to them, while others actively sought the drug, either from their parents' medicine cabinets, a friend, or purchasing from an acquaintance. Finally, the majority seemed to initiate use at social gatherings, be it in the college dorms, parties, or small gatherings. The settings were usually comfortable spaces, both physically and socially.

Nonmedical prescription drug use initiation was a social process, similar to findings in other drug initiation studies. However, unlike other drugs, prescription drugs were perceived to be safer than street drugs because they were used medically. As a participant noted, everybody had probably taken prescription drugs at some time in their life, thus further normalizing use. And for our study sample, there were no indications of gender differences in the initiation process. The median age of initiation for both males and females was 16, and there were no significant differences in the type of prescription drug used nonmedically for the first time. Regardless of gender and type of prescription drug participants initiated with, the initiation process involved the merging of exposure, motivation, access, and setting.

Understanding the initiation process of nonmedical prescription drug use can inform prevention and intervention strategies to address the increasing numbers of nonmedical prescription drug users. And although the data is retrospective, and subject to problems of recall, it is still important because it reveals participants' current set with which he or she describes and interprets past experiences. Their current understandings of what led to their own initiations of nonmedical prescription drug use are valuable for the design of efficacious intervention and prevention measures for problematic prescription drug misuse.

However, we do recognize the limitations of our study. We acknowledge that our sample is not representative of the general population, and findings cannot be generalized. Our study sample includes people from a specific age cohort in the San Francisco Bay Area, who had used prescription drugs nonmedically at least 12 times in the 6 months prior to their interview. The majority of our participants were attending college at the time of interview, and the ethnic breakdown does not properly represent that of the San Francisco Bay Area. In addition, this article focuses on prescription drugs as a whole, and disaggregating the different categories may provide deeper insights into the initiation process of each type of prescription drug to better inform and educate the public, medical professionals, and interventionists. Thus, we believe future research should focus on understanding initiation for each of the different categories of misused prescription drugs (opioids, stimulants, and CNS depressants) independently, particularly stimulants, for which there are limited data. Furthermore, there is a fine line between medical and nonmedical use of prescription drugs, and this complicates the kinds of prevention messages that are appropriate for specific populations. Further research is necessary to help determine the best approaches to address the problem.

Declaration of Conflicting Interests

The author(s) declared no potential conflicts of interest with respect to the research, authorship, and/or publication of this article.

Funding

The author(s) received no financial support for the research, authorship, and/or publication of this article.

References

Akers, R. L. 1985. *Deviant Behavior: A Social Learning Approach*. Belmont, CA: Wadsworth.

_____. 2009. *Social Learning and Social Structure: A General Theory of Crime and Deviance*. New Brunswick, NJ: Transaction Publishers.

Arria, A. M., K. M. Caldeira, K. B. Vincent, K. E. O'Grady, and E. D. Wish. 2008. "Perceived Harmfulness Predicts Nonmedical Use of Prescription Drugs among College Students: Interaction with Sensation-Seeking." *Prevention Science* 9: 191–201.

Barrett, S. P., C. Darredeau, L. E. Bordy, and R. O. Pihl. 2005. "Characteristics of Methylphenidate Misuse in a University Student Sample." *Canadian Journal of Psychiatry* 50: 457–461.

Best, D., V. Manning, and J. Strang. 2007. "Retrospective Recall of Heroin Initiation and the Impact on Peer Networks." *Addiction Research & Theory* 15: 397–410.

Biernacki, P. and D. Waldorf. 1981. "Snowball Sampling: Problems, Techniques and Chain-Referral Sampling." *Sociological Methods & Research* 10: 141–163.

Boyd, C. J., S. E. McCabe, J. A. Cranford, and A. Young. 2006. "Adolescents' Motivations to Abuse Prescription Medications." *Pediatrics* 118: 2472–2480.

Brands, B., J. Blake, B. Sproule, D. Gourlay, and U. Busto. 2004. "Prescription Opioid Abuse in Patients Presenting for Methadone Maintenance Treatment." *Drug and Alcohol Dependence* 73: 199–207.

Brecht, M. L., A. O'Brien, C. von Mayrhauser, and M. D. Anglin. 2004. "Methamphetamine Use Behaviors and Gender Differences." *Addictive Behaviors* 29: 89–106.

Califano, J. A. 2005. *Under the Counter: The Diversion and Abuse of Controlled Prescription Drugs in the U.S.* New York, NY: The National Center on Addiction and Substance Abuse at Columbia University (CASA).

_____. 2007. *High Society: How Substance Abuse Ravages American and What To Do about It*. New York, NY: Perseus Publishing.

Charmaz, K. 1983. "The Grounded Theory Method: An Explication and Interpretation." In *Contemporary Field Research*, edited by R. Emerson, 109–126. Boston, MA: Little-Brown.

_____. 2006. *Constructing Grounded Theory: A Practical Guide Through Qualitative Analysis*. Thousand Oaks, CA: SAGE.

Chilcoat, H. D. and N. Breslau. 1998. "Investigations of Causal Pathways Between PTSD and Drug Use Disorders." *Addictive Behaviors* 23: 827–840.

Daniulaityte, R., R. G. Carlson, and D. R. Kenne. 2006. "Initiation to Pharmaceutical Opioids and Patterns of Misuse: Preliminary Qualitative Findings Obtained by the Ohio Substance Abuse Monitoring Network." *Journal of Drug Issues* 36: 787–809.

Daniulaityte, R., R. Falck, and R. G. Carlson. 2012. "'I'm Not Afraid of Those Ones Just 'Cause They've Been Prescribed': Perceptions of Risk among Illicit Users of Pharmaceutical Opioids." *International Journal of Drug Policy* 23: 374–384.

Dowling, K., C. Storr, and H. D. Chilcoat. 2006. "Potential Influences on Initiation and Persistence of Extramedical Prescription Pain Reliever Use in the US Population." *The Clinical Journal of Pain* 22: 776–783.

Ford, J. 2008. "Social Learning Theory and Nonmedical Prescription Drug Use among Adolescents." *Sociological Spectrum* 28: 299–316.

Friedman, R. A. 2006. "The Changing Face of Teenage Drug Abuse: The Trend Toward Prescription Drugs." *The New England Journal of Medicine* 354: 1448–1450.

Glaser, B. and A. Strauss. 1967. *The Discovery of Grounded Theory*. Chicago, IL: Aldine.

Ives, T. J., P. R. Chelminski, C. A. Hammett-Stabler, R. M. Malone, J. S. Perhac, N. M. Potisek, and M. P. Pignone. 2006. "Predictors of Opioid Misuse in Patients with Chronic Pain: A Prospective Cohort Study." *BMC Health Services Research* 6: 46.

Jansen, K. L. R. 1997. "Adverse Psychological Effects Associated with the Use of Ecstasy (MDMA) and Their Treatment." In *Ecstasy Reconsidered*, edited by N. Saunders, 112–128. London, England: Neal's Yard.

Kandel, D. B. 1996. "The Parental and Peer Contexts of Adolescent Deviance: An Algebra of Interpersonal Influences." *Journal of Drug Issues* 26: 289–315.

Khantzian, E. J. 1997. "The Self-Medication Hypothesis of Substance Use Disorders: A Reconsideration and Recent Applications." *Harvard Review of Psychiatry* 4: 231–244.

Kroutil, L. A., D. L. V. Brunt, M. A. Herman-Stahl, D. C. Heller, R. M. Bray, and M. A. Penne. 2006. "Nonmedical Use of Prescription Stimulants in the United States." *Drug and Alcohol Dependence* 84: 135–143.

Kuehn, B. M. 2007. "Opioid Prescriptions Soar: Increase in Legitimate Use as Well as Abuse." *The Journal of the American Medical Association* 297: 249–251.

Kuzel, A. 1992. "Sampling in Qualitative Inquiry." In *Doing Qualitative Research*, edited by B. Crabtree and W. Miller, 31–45. Newbury Park, CA: Sage.

Lankenau, S. E., M. Teti, K. Silva, J. J. Bloom, A. Harocopos, and M. Treese. 2012. "Initiation of Prescription Opioid Misuse amongst Young Injection Drug Users." *International Journal of Drug Policy* 23: 37–44.

Low, K. G. and A. E. Gendaszek. 2002. "Illicit Use of Psychostimulants among College Students: A Preliminary Study." *Psychology, Health & Medicine* 7: 283–287.

Manchikanti, L. 2007. "National Drug Control Policy and Prescription Drug Abuse: Facts and Fallacies." *Pain Physician* 10: 399–424.

McCabe, S. E. and C. J. Boyd. 2005. "Sources of Prescription Drugs for Illicit Use." *Addictive Behaviors* 30: 1342–1350.

McCabe, S. E., C. J. Boyd, and C. J. Teter. 2009. "Subtypes of Nonmedical Prescription Drug Misuse." *Drug and Alcohol Dependence* 102: 63–70.

McCabe, S. E., C. J. Teter, and C. J. Boyd. 2006. "Medical Use, Illicit Use, and Diversion of Abusable Prescription Drugs." *Journal of American College Health* 54: 269–278.

McElrath, K., and K. McEvoy. 2002. "Negative Experiences on Ecstasy: The Role of Drug, Set and Setting." *Journal of Psychoactive Drugs* 34: 199–208.

Moore, D. 1993. "Beyond Zinberg's 'Social Setting': A Processural View of Illicit Drug Use." *Drug and Alcohol Review* 12: 413–421.

Parsons, J. T., B. C. Kelly, and J. D. Weiser. 2007. "Initiation into Methamphetamine Use for Young Gay and Bisexual Men." *Drug and Alcohol Dependence* 90: 135–144.

Peralta, R. L. and J. L. Steele. 2010. "Nonmedical Prescription Drug Use among US College Students at a Midwest University: A Partial Test of Social Learning Theory." *Substance Use & Misuse* 45: 865–887.

Potter, J. S., G. Hennessy, J. A. Borrow, S. F. Greenfield, and R. D. Weiss. 2004. "Substance Use Histories in Patients Seeking Treatment for Controlled-Release Oxycodone Dependence." *Drug and Alcohol Dependence* 76: 213–215.

Quintero, G. 2009. "Rx for a Party: A Qualitative Analysis of Recreational Pharmaceutical Use in a Collegiate Setting." *Journal of American College Health* 58: 64–70.

Sheridan, J., R. Butler, and A. Wheeler. 2009. "Initiation into Methamphetamine Use: Qualitative Findings from an Exploration of First Time Use among a Group of New Zealand Users." *Journal of Psychoactive Drugs* 41: 11–17.

Spradley, J. 1979. *The Ethnographic Interview.* New York, NY: Holt, Rinehart and Winston.

Strauss, A. and J. Corbin. 1990. *Basics of Qualitative Research.* Newbury Park, CA: Sage.

Substance Abuse and Mental Health Services Administration. 2005. *Results from the 2004 National Survey on Drug Use and Health: National Findings* (Office of Applied Studies, NSDUH Series H-28, DHHS Publication No. SMA 05–4062). Rockville, MD: Author.

———. 2006. *Results from the 2005 National Survey on Drug Use and Health: National Findings* (Office of Applied Studies, NSDUH Series H-30, DHHS Publication No. SMA 06–4194). Rockville, MD: Author.

———. 2007. *Results from the 2006 National Survey on Drug Use and Health: National Findings* (Office of Applied Studies, NSDUH Series H-32, DHHS Publication No. SMA 07–4293). Rockville, MD: Author.

———. 2008. *Results from the 2007 National Survey on Drug Use and Health: National Findings* (Office of Applied Studies, NSDUH Series H-34, DHHS Publication No. SMA 08–4343). Rockville, MD: Author.

———. 2009. *Results from the 2008 National Survey on Drug Use and Health: National Findings* (Office of Applied Studies, NSDUH Series H-36, HHS Publication No. SMA 09–4434). Rockville, MD: Author.

———. 2010. *Results from the 2009 National Survey on Drug Use and Health: Volume I. Summary of National Findings* (Office of Applied Studies, NSDUH Series H-38A, HHS Publication No. SMA 10-4856 Findings). Rockville, MD: Author.

———. 2011. *Results from the 2010 National Survey on Drug Use and Health: Summary of National Findings* (NSDUH Series H-41, HHS Publication No. SMA 11-4658). Rockville, MD: Author.

———. 2012. *Results from the 2011 National Survey on Drug Use and Health: Summary of National Findings* (NSDUH Series H-44, HHS Publication No. SMA 12-4713). Rockville, MD: Author.

Tang, Z., and Orwin, R. 2009. "Marijuana Initiation among American Youth and Its Risks as Dynamic Processes: Prospective Findings from a National Longitudinal Study." *Substance Use & Misuse* 44: 195–211.

Teter, C. J., S. E. McCabe, J. A. Cranford, C. J. Boyd, and S. K. Guthrie. 2005. "Prevalence and Motives for Illicit Use of Prescription Stimulants in an Undergraduate Student Sample." *Journal of American College Health* 53: 253–262.

Vervaeke, H., L. van Deursen, and D. Korf. 2008. "The Role of Peers in the Initiation and Continuation of Ecstasy Use." *Substance Use & Misuse* 43: 633–646.

Watters, J., and P. Biernacki. 1989. "Targeted Sampling: Options for the Study of Hidden Populations." *Social Problems* 36: 416–430.

Weiner, A. L. 2000. "Emerging Drugs of Abuse in Connecticut." *Connecticut Medicine* 64: 19–23.

White, B. P., K. A. Becker-Blease, and K. Grace-Bishop. 2006. "Stimulant Medication Use, Misuse, and Abuse in an Undergraduate and Graduate Student Sample." *Journal of American College Health* 54: 261–268.

Zinberg, N. E. 1984. "*Drug, Set, and Setting: The Basis for Controlled Intoxicant Use.*" New Haven, CT: Yale University Press.

For Discussion

1. The authors note that at times "there is a fine line between medical and non-medical use of prescription drugs." What did the authors mean by this statement? Additionally, how does the "fine line" complicate matters for researchers who wish to collect survey data on non-medical use of prescribed drugs?

2. Think about the college that you now attend. Are prescription drugs readily available from non-medical sources? Do the reasons for using these substances differ from what Mui and colleagues found in this article? How so?

IV

Stages of Drug Use

Some individuals initiate drug use but never use again. Other individuals are perhaps best described as *experimenters*, who initiate and then infrequently "dip" in and out of drug use, depending on the social circumstances. In general, they do not proactively seek out drugs to use, but they might consume substances occasionally when the opportunity is presented and when the social setting is conducive for using.

A third group consists of individuals who regularly engage in drug use as part of recreation or leisure. They might use drugs during weekends and on special occasions (e.g., birthday celebrations), but they tend to avoid using drugs at other times. They generally do not perceive their drug use as being problematic for their work, health, or social relationships. Still, they might "binge" and participate in other behavior that could pose risk to themselves or to others (e.g., polydrug use, driving under the influence). A subset of this group becomes more involved in drug use and drug seeking. Although they are still quite able to function—in

school, on the job, or as a parent or spouse—their proficiency in some areas begins to decline markedly. Personal and social functioning tends to be inversely related to the amount of time in which they are involved in drug consumption. At this stage, the effects of a drug do something *for* them. For example, some individuals use drugs to deal with an unbearable work or family situation. Others use drugs to enhance performance, bolster their self-esteem, or because of stress, anxiety, depression, or trauma.

Problem drug use occurs when drugs become the significant part of individuals' lives. Daily routines become focused on or around drug seeking and drug use so that these routines take precedence over other life activities. Usage seriously affects social functioning in the domains of relationships, work, or educational pursuits. Physical and emotional health also are affected in negative ways. Problem drug use can last for years, even decades, although some individuals manage recovery extremely well. The life course theoretical perspective emphasizes the importance of trajectories, transitions, and turning points (Hser, Longshore, and Anglin 2007) for understanding problem drug use, recovery, and relapse.

These stages are not necessarily sequential. For example, people who are engaged in problem drug use have not necessarily progressed from the recreational phase, and recreational users may have skipped the experimental stage. Moreover, it is incorrect to assume that problem drug use is always linked to particular drugs, for example, heroin, cocaine, or alcohol. In a Scottish study, Shewan and Dalgarno (2005) conducted interviews with 126 individuals who had been using heroin for several years. Over the course of the longitudinal study, only six of the 126 respondents had received drug treatment. The respondents had few long-term health or social problems, and their educational and occupational experiences were similar to those found in the wider population. The authors discussed the findings in the context of "controlled heroin use," and the study caused considerable stir among Scottish politicians and media. Similarly, Waldorf, Reinarman, and Murphy (1991) based their study on life history interviews with people involved in "heavy" cocaine use. Many of their respondents were employed, had good relationships with family members, and functioned relatively well. In fact, these social ties with mainstream society were critical for keeping "many heavy users from falling into the abyss of abuse, and what helps pull back those who do fall, is precisely this *stake in conventional life*" (italics in original, p. 10). Our intention here is not to downplay the major problems experienced by a subset of people who use drugs. Rather, we wish to highlight that controlled use is possible for some individuals (see also, Zinberg 1984) and that members of this group are part of a very hidden population who rarely come to the attention of treatment providers or police. As a result, we know considerably less about long-term users of heroin or cocaine who control or manage their drug use in a systematic way.

The gateway perspective assumes a sequential pattern of drug taking that can result in problem drug use. This perspective assumes that drug taking tends to be sequential, beginning with tobacco or alcohol, and progressing to marijuana use. The idea is that particular substances can increase curiosity to try other substances, or can link individuals to new social networks where other kinds of drug use are accepted. Proponents of the gateway perspective argue that this sequence increases the likelihood that individuals will become regular users of "hard" drugs or become addicted or dependent on other psychoactive substances. Some politicians, school officials, and policymakers believe that the gateway perspective is factual and the idea has also received support among some researchers. However, the perspective has been widely criticized. For example, Joel Best, author of *More Damned Lies and Statistics: How Numbers Confuse Public Issues* (2004), argues that scholars who promote the gateway perspective tend to ignore the rules around causality. Gateway proponents suggest, for example, that several people who use heroin previously have used marijuana. That point does not imply that marijuana use "causes" or contributes to heroin use. Indeed, millions of people have used marijuana, but very few of them have also used heroin. In other words, although most people who use heroin probably have used marijuana, that assumption does not imply that most people who use marijuana go on to use heroin.

There are other problems with the gateway perspective. First, people who are addicted to cocaine or dependent on heroin may have skipped some of the earlier pathways that the gateway perspective assumes. That is, cocaine may be the first psychoactive substance that is consumed. Or individuals might commence drug taking with alcohol, later become addicted to painkillers, but never smoke marijuana. Second, most studies that have tested the gateway perspective have focused exclusively on samples of adolescents and young people. We know considerably less about the sequence and patterns of drug taking when individuals reach their 30s and 40s. Third, large numbers of people have experimented with cocaine, MDMA, and a host of other substances, but without becoming regular users. Fourth, the gateway argument rests heavily on the social construction of "hard" and "soft" drugs. It assumes that "soft" drugs, such as alcohol and tobacco, lead to the use of more harmful substances. However, the meanings of "soft" and "hard" drugs are socially constructed. For example, are the social and physical effects of hallucinogenic drugs or cocaine potentially more harmful than the effects of alcohol?

Findings from an international study highlighted the importance of culture and cultural differences when investigating gateway effects. Degenhardt and colleagues (2010) used data collected in 17 countries as part of the World Health Organization's World Mental Health survey, to examine the gateway effect in a cross-cultural context. They identified *different* kinds of drug sequences that appeared to be linked to the prevalence of particular drugs in a given country. The authors of this international study concluded that substances are often consumed in different orders, depending on the country. Their findings also suggested that early initiation of any drug use and the number of different drugs that are used had a greater effect on subsequent drug dependence than did the sequence of drug taking. Cross-cultural comparisons revealed other interesting findings. For example, links between marijuana/cannabis use and subsequent use of other drugs were much more prevalent in the United States than in the Netherlands. In Japan and Nigeria, respondents were more likely to use other illicit substances before consuming alcohol or tobacco. The articles in this section address stages of drug use, but in very different contexts.

References

Best, J. 2004. "More Damned Lies and Statistics: How Numbers Confuse Public Issues." Berkeley: University of California Press.

Degenhardt, L., L. Dierkerb, W. T. Chiu, M. E. Medina-Mora, Y. Neumark, N. Sampson, J. Alonso, M. Angermeyer, J. C. Anthony, R. Bruffaerts, G. de Girolamo, R. de Graaf, O. Gureje, A. N. Karam, S. Kostyuchenko, S. Leep, J.-P. Lépine, D. Levinson, Y. Nakamura, J. Posada-Villa, D. Stein, J. E. Wells, and R. C. Kessler. 2010. "Evaluating the Drug Use 'Gateway' Theory Using Cross-National Data: Consistency and Associations of the Order of Initiation of Drug Use Among Participants in the WHO World Mental Health Surveys." *Drug and Alcohol Dependence* 108: 84–97.

Hser, Y-I., D. Longshore, and M. D. Anglin. 2007. "The Life Course Perspective on Drug Use: A Conceptual Framework for Understanding Drug Use Trajectories." *Evaluation Review* 31: 515–547.

Shewan, D. and Dalgarno, P. (2005). "Evidence for Controlled Heroin Use? Low Levels of Negative Health and Social Outcomes among Non-Treatment Heroin Users in Glasgow (Scotland). *British Journal of Health Psychology* 10: 33–48.

Waldorf, D., C. Reinarman, and S. Murphy. 1991. *Cocaine Changes: The Experiences of Using and Quitting*. Philadelphia: Temple University Press.

Zinberg, N. D. 1984. *Drug, Set, and Setting: The Basis for Controlled Intoxicant Use*. New Haven, Connecticut: Yale University Press.

9

Cannabis as a Substitute for Alcohol and Other Drugs

AMANDA REIMAN

In this study, Amanda Reiman focuses on the behavior of substitution. Using anonymized survey data collected from medical marijuana patients in Berkeley, Reiman describes how medical cannabis is sometimes used as a substitute for other drugs. She discusses these findings in the context of harm reduction.

Background

It has been observed that those who use large amounts of cannabis frequently use other drugs as well, especially alcohol. This can create a potential synergistic effect, resulting in increased harms.[1-4] Economic research has looked at the substitution and complementarity of particular substances by modelling the effects of price fluctuation on use, although the limits of such research have been noted.[5] When considering youth, Pacula has found cannabis and alcohol to be complements. As beer prices rose, cannabis use declined.[6] This could potentially be because the introduction of alcohol into an adolescent environment increases the likelihood of other substances being brought into that environment; once the presence of alcohol decreases, the presence of other substances might decrease as well. Among adults, amphetamine has been found to be a substitute for those whose drug of choice is alcohol, and alcohol as a substitute for those who cannot obtain MDMA and cocaine.[7,8] This research suggests that through various patterns, individuals are making personal decisions about alcohol and drug substitution.

For the purposes of this study, substitution was operationalized as the conscious choice to use one drug (legal or illicit) instead of, or in conjunction with, another due to issues such as: perceived safety; level of addiction potential; effectiveness in relieving symptoms; access and level of acceptance. The substitution of cannabis for alcohol and other drugs has been observed among individuals using cannabis for medical purposes. Medical cannabis patients are regular cannabis users with a stable supply, and their access to cannabis is not granted under a standardized prescription system, yet still legitimized by a doctor's recommendation (self-medication). This, in addition to the legal protection given to patients in California, increases the freedom of choice regarding the use of cannabis as a substitute among this population. A survey of 11 medical cannabis doctors in California found that all doctors had seen patients who were using cannabis as a substitute for alcohol. Furthermore, one said that over half of her patients reported preferring cannabis to alcohol, and another reported that 90% of his patients reduced their alcohol use after beginning the use of medical cannabis.[4] The dual use of

Reprinted from Amanda Reiman, 2009, "Cannabis as a Substitute for Alcohol and Other Drugs," in *Harm Reduction Journal*, 6: 35 doi:10.1186/1477-7517-6-35. © 2009 Reiman; licensee BioMed Central Ltd.

alcohol and cannabis has been observed in several research studies on medical cannabis patients. First, previous alcohol abuse was reported in 59 of 100 medical cannabis users in a University of California, San Francisco study. Furthermore, 16 of 100 subjects reported previous alcohol dependence.[9]

Beyond the population of medical cannabis patients, substituting cannabis or other drugs for alcohol has been described as a radical alcohol treatment protocol. If alcohol negatively affects a person's level of functioning, cannabis or another drug might be an alternative for the user. Charlton has suggested that the radical approach of substitution with substances such as benzodiazepine might be used to address heavy alcohol use in the British Isles by incorporating the idea of self-medication into his discussion by his assertion that "the drug-substitution strategy is based on the assumption that most people use lifestyle [recreational] drugs rationally for self-medication purposes" (457). It is posited that people might substitute a safer drug with less negative side-effects if it were socially acceptable and available.[10]

The first cannabis substitution study was a single subject study conducted by Tod Mikuriya in 1970, in which a female (age 49) who was an alcoholic was instructed to substitute cannabis for alcohol. The subject was also administered Antabuse to assist in her abstention from alcohol. The subject reported increased ego strength, useful behaviour, ability to control cannabis intake, euphoria and tranquilization. In addition, there were improvements in concentration, disposition, physical health, ability to revisit social situations and ability to appropriately express anger.[11] The issue was revisited in 2001 with a study of 104 medical cannabis patients in California who used cannabis in an effort to stop the use of other drugs, in particular alcohol. For example, participants may have been previous alcoholics who have replaced their alcohol use with a daily regimen of cannabis. Demographic data were collected as well as information on family alcohol history and alcohol and cannabis usage patterns. The authors included both descriptive statistics and excerpts from interviews. With respect to family alcohol history, 55% of participants reported having one or two alcoholic parents. Most of the participants (90%) listed alcohol as their primary

drug of choice, although a few participants had also had addiction issues with heroin, cocaine, amphetamine and other drugs. One interesting finding in this study is that 45% of patients reported using cannabis to relieve pain that they suffered as a result of an alcohol related injury.[12]

Cannabis substitution has also been discussed as part of a harm reduction framework. A record review of 92 medical cannabis patients who used marijuana as a substitute for alcohol was conducted with the goal of describing these patients and determining the reported efficacy of treatment. Fifty-three percent of participants reported being raised by at least one alcoholic/addict parent. Concerning reported health problems, 64% of the sample identified alcoholism or cirrhosis of the liver as their presenting problem. Thirty-six percent identified themselves as alcohol abusers but listed another health problem as their primary concern. As in Mikuriya's 2001 study, 21% of the sample reported having been injured in an alcohol related incident. When addressing the efficacy of cannabis as a substitute for alcohol, all participants reported cannabis substitution as very effective (50%) or effective (50%). Ten percent of the patients reported being abstinent from alcohol for more than a year and attributed their success to cannabis. Twenty-one percent of patients had a return of alcoholic symptoms when they stopped using cannabis. Reasons for stopping the cannabis use ranged from entering the armed forces to being arrested for using cannabis.[13]

Previous alcohol use, treatment, and substitution were also documented in a sample of 130 medical cannabis patients in the San Francisco Bay Area. Twenty four had reported previous alcohol treatment. Half of the sample reported using cannabis as a substitute for alcohol, 47% for illicit drugs and 74% using it as a substitute for prescription drugs. The most common reason reported for using cannabis as a substitute was fewer side effects from cannabis and better symptom management from cannabis.[14]

The personal health practice of substitution among medical cannabis patients can provide information concerning non-traditional and alternative means used by individuals to personally address their health issues without official involvement in the health care system. Furthermore, examining substitution among this population might translate into the development of more effective, client-centred treatment practices within the field of addiction.

Methods

The survey sample for this study consisted of 350 medical cannabis patients between the ages of 18 and 81 from the San Francisco Bay Area, California. Participants are members of Berkeley Patients Group (BPG), a medical cannabis dispensing collective in Berkeley, CA. The sample was 68.4% male (N = 238), 66.2% White (N = 231) and 14.6% Multiracial (N = 51). The mean age was 39.43.

A survey was created by the researcher, with portions adapted from a patient survey administered by Dr. Frank Lucido at his medical practice in Berkeley, CA. The survey had five sections: demographic information, medical information, cannabis use pattern, alcohol and drug use and service utilization. Participants were asked the quantity and frequency of alcohol, tobacco and drug (prescription and illicit) use as well as current and past alcohol and/or drug treatment. Participants were also asked about whether they use cannabis as a substitute for alcohol, illicit drugs or prescription drugs and why to investigate medical cannabis as a treatment for alcohol and/or drug dependence.

The survey data were collected by the researcher at BPG. The researcher approached patients as they came into BPG and asked if they would like to participate in an anonymous survey being conducted by BPG. If patients were not able to fill out the survey, it was administered by the researcher. The survey included an explanation of the study and the right to refuse to participate or to stop the survey at any time. Data collection occurred for the most part during the hours of 1–5 pm and took place during the week and on weekends. Data were analyzed in SPSS, and frequencies were calculated.

There are several limitations of this study. First, due to the close proximity to the campus of the University of California, Berkeley, there might be an over-representation of college students in this sample. This might affect data on employment status, age, marital status, income and to a lesser extent, gender and race. Secondly, although data were collected in the middle of the day regularly for several months, it is possible that some patients might come to BPG at times when data collection was not occurring. Furthermore, patients who are extremely ill might not be able to stay and fill out a survey. The sample itself prevents the generalization of these results to the greater population of cannabis users, as medical cannabis patients might differ in substantial ways from the general population, especially concerning areas of substance using behaviour, and patients from Berkeley Patients Group may not represent the greater population of medical cannabis patients. Furthermore, there are not formal measures of alcohol drug related problems on the survey, making it impossible to explore the behavioural implications of cannabis substitution. Finally, although the survey was anonymous, the legal status of medical cannabis might prevent some patients from filling out surveys and some participants from being completely forthcoming with information. Furthermore, although the practice of substitution was described to participants in the survey, the data do rely on self report and the participant's own reality concerning their substitution behaviour.

Results

Alcohol, Tobacco and Other Drug Use

Fifty-three percent of the sample reported that they currently drink alcohol. The average number of drinking days per week was 2.63 (N = 180). The average number of drinks on drinking days was 2.88 (N = 163). One quarter of the sample currently smoke tobacco. The average number of cigarettes smoked per day is 9.54 (N = 80). Eleven percent of the sample reported using a drug other than cannabis, a prescription or over the counter drug in the past 30 days. Cocaine, MDMA and Vicodin were reported most frequently (N = 5), followed by LSD (N = 4), mushrooms and Xanax (N = 3).

Treatment

One quarter of the sample reported growing up in an alcoholic or abusive household, 16.4% reported previous alcohol or substance abuse treatment, and 2.4% are currently in a 12 Step or some other type of substance abuse or alcohol dependence program.

Substitution

As shown in Table 9.1, 40% of the sample reported using cannabis as a substitute for alcohol,

Table 9.1 Percent of Sample Reporting Using Cannabis as a Substitute.

	N	%
Alcohol substitute	134	40
Illicit drug substitute	87	26
Prescription drug substitute	219	65.8

Table 9.2 Reasons for Using Cannabis as a Substitute.

	N	%
Less adverse side effects	197	65
Less withdrawal potential	103	34
Ability to obtain cannabis	54	17.8
Greater social acceptance	36	11.9
Better symptom management	174	57.4
Other reason	37	12.2

26% reported using it as a substitute for illicit drugs, and 65.8% use it as a substitute for prescription drugs. Referring to Table 9.2, 65% reported using cannabis as a substitute because it has less adverse side effects than alcohol, illicit or prescription drugs, 34% use it as a substitute because it has less withdrawal potential, 17.8% use it as a substitute because its easier to obtain cannabis than alcohol, illicit or prescription drugs, 11.9% use it as a substitute because cannabis has greater social acceptance, 57.4% use it as a substitute because cannabis provides better symptom management, and 12.2% use it as a substitute for some other reason.

Discussion

Research has suggested that medical cannabis patients might use more alcohol than nonpatients, and might have a higher instance of alcohol abuse than the general population [3,9]. Drinking patterns among the BPG sample were average, with 53.4% of the sample being current drinkers, the mean number of drinking days per week being 2.63 and the mean number of drinks on occasion being 2.88. When looking at the national rate of alcohol use, 55% of the U.S. population 18+ is a current drinker, compared to 53% of the BPG sample. The national data report 7.8% of the 18+ national sample have used an illicit drug in the past month, compared to 11% of the BPG sample.[15] The study of 100 patients from San

Francisco found a much higher rate of tobacco smoking (78% vs. 24.9% of the BPG sample) [9].

When considering previous alcohol and/or substance abuse treatment, 16.4% of the BPG sample reported previous treatment for alcohol or substance abuse; this was the same percentage found in Reiman's sample of 130 medical cannabis patients.[14] Mikuriya found in 2001 and 2004 that 55% and 53% of patients respectively reported having one or two alcoholic parents.[12,13] One quarter of this sample reported growing up in an alcoholic or abusive household.

As previously discussed, research on medical cannabis patients has alluded to the use of cannabis as a substitute for alcohol, illicit or prescription drugs [9–13]. This phenomenon was also reflected in the data on substitution from the BPG sample, as 40% of participants reported using cannabis as a substitute for alcohol, 26% as a substitute for illicit drugs and 65.8% as a substitute for prescription drugs. These substitution rates were very similar to those found by Reiman.[14] Additionally, three patients noted during the survey that they used cannabis to quit smoking tobacco.

Eighty-five percent of the BPG sample reported that cannabis has much less adverse side effects than their prescription medications. Additionally, the top two reasons listed by participants as reasons for substituting cannabis for one of the substances previously mentioned were less adverse side effects from cannabis (65%) and better symptom management from cannabis (57.4%).

Conclusion

The substitution of one psychoactive substance for another with the goal of reducing negative outcomes can be included within the framework of harm reduction. Medical cannabis patients have been engaging in substitution by using cannabis as an alternative to alcohol, prescription and illicit drugs. This brings up two important points. First, self determination, the right of an individual to decide which treatment or substance is most effective and least harmful for them. If an individual finds less harm in cannabis than in the drug prescribed by their doctor, do they have a right to choose? Secondly, the recognition that substitution might be a viable alternative to abstinence for those who are not able, or do not wish to stop using psychoactive substances completely. Due to a potential conflict between the use of medical cannabis and philosophies of recovery programs such as Alcoholics Anonymous, some dispensaries offer harm reduction based recovery groups aimed at those in recovery who use medical cannabis. Mikuriya has suggested the development of 12 Step groups tailored towards those who want to take advantage of the cost free, fellowship driven nature of 12 Step programs, but wish to use cannabis actively during recovery.[13] The lack of drug and alcohol related problem measures utilized in this study calls for a further investigation into the relationship of such problems and the use of cannabis as a substitute. To that end, more research needs to be done on the possibilities for substitution that lie in the field of addiction, and on the individuals who have already successfully incorporated substitution into their health care regime.

Notes

1. Looby, A. and M. Earleywine. 2007. "Negative Consequences Associated with Dependence in Daily Cannabis Users." *Substance Abuse Treatment, Prevention and Policy* 2: 3–10.

2. Midanik, L., T. Tam, and C. Weisner. 2007. "Concurrent and Simultaneous Drug and Alcohol Use: Results of the 2000 National Alcohol Survey." *Drug and Alcohol Dependence* 90: 72–80.

3. Ogborne, A., R. Smart, and E. Adlaf. 2000. "Self-Reported Medical Use of Marijuana: A Survey of the General Population." *Canadian Medical Association Journal* 162: 1685–1686.

4. Mikuriya. T. 2007. "Medical Marijuana in California, 1996–2006." *O'Shaughnessy's: Journal of the California Cannabis Research Medical Group* (Winter/Spring): 2, 8–10.

5. Williams, J., R. Pacula, F. Chaloupka, and H. Wechsler. 2006. "Limits of Current Economic Analyses of the Demand for Illicit Drugs." *Substance Use and Misuse* 41: 607–609.

6. Pacula, R. 1998. "Does Increasing the Beer Tax Reduce Marijuana Consumption?" *Journal of Health Economics* 17: 557–585.

7. Sumnall, H., E. Tyler, G. Wagstaff, and J. Cole. 2004. "A Behavioural Economic Analysis of Alcohol, Amphetamine, Cocaine, and Ecstasy Purchases by Polysubstance Misusers." *Drug and Alcohol Dependence* 76: 93–99.

8. Petry, N. 2001. "A Behavioral Economic Analysis of Polydrug Abuse in Alcoholics: Asymmetrical Substitution of Alcohol and Cocaine." *Drug and Alcohol Dependence* 62: 31–39.

9. Harris, D. 2000. "Self-Reported Marijuana Effects and Characteristics of 100 San Francisco Medical Marijuana Club Members." *Journal of Addictive Diseases* 19: 89–103.

10. Charlton, B. G. 2005. "Diazepam with Your Dinner, Sir? The Lifestyle Drug-Substitution Strategy: A Radical Alcohol Policy." *Qualitative Journal of Medicine* 98: 457–459.

11. Mikuriya, T. 1970. "Cannabis as a Treatment for Alcoholism." *Psychedelic Review* 11: 71–73.

12. Mikuriya, T. and J. Mandel. 2001. "Cannabis Substitution: Harm Reduction Treatment for Alcoholism and Drug Dependence." Retrieved October 13, 2005. http://mikuriyamedical.com/about/cw_cansub.html

13. Mikuriya, T. 2004. "Cannabis as a Substitute for Alcohol: A Harm-Reduction Approach." *Journal of Cannabis Therapeutics* 4: 79–93.

14. Reiman, A. 2000. "Patient Profiles: Medical Cannabis Patients and Health Care Utilization Patterns." *Complementary Health Practice Review* 12: 31–50.

15. Substance Abuse and Mental Health Services Administration. 2007. *Results from the 2006 National Survey on Drug Use and Health: National Findings*. Office of Applied Studies, NSDUH Series H-32, DHHS Publication No. SMA 07-4293. Rockville, MD.

For Discussion

1. The study sample included 350 medical cannabis patients whose ages ranged from 18 to 81. What kinds of drug use patterns might differ between the youngest and oldest age groups?

2. The availability and effectiveness of medical marijuana have been hotly debated. What information/findings in this study would be beneficial to supporters of medical marijuana? Similarly, what information/findings would bolster the arguments of opponents?

10

A Qualitative Exploration of Trajectories among Suburban Users of Methamphetamine

MIRIAM WILLIAMS BOERI, LIAM HARBRY, DAVID GIBSON

In this next article, Miriam Williams Boeri, Liam Harbry, and David Gibson examine methamphetamine use among individuals who reside in suburban areas—an extremely under-researched population. The authors utilize a qualitative design that includes interviews with forty-eight individuals. Boeri and her colleagues discuss initiation into methamphetamine as well as the "turning points" that led some individuals to problem drug use.

The goal of this exploratory study was to gain an understanding of the trajectories of methamphetamine use among a suburban sample of users. Methamphetamine users living in the suburbs comprise a hidden population of hard-to-reach individuals. We know very little about the mechanisms of initiation or patterns of methamphetamine use among this under-researched population. Methamphetamine studies have focused on users among urban populations and rural areas (Halkitis, Parsons, and Wilton 2003; Haight et al. 2005; Kushel et al. 2005; Worth and Rawstone 2005). Suburban-focused research on methamphetamine use is almost nonexistent. We know that drug use patterns change by setting of use, particularly the setting of initiation (Boeri 2004; Faupel 1991). Therefore, we expected that drug use trajectories of suburban users would differ from trajectory patterns found among urban and rural users. In this study, we explored the trajectories of methamphetamine use in suburbs, including the influence of environmental factors, social roles, and associated use patterns. This is not a comparison study between use of methamphetamine in urban, rural, and suburban areas; however, some similarities and differences are noted. The specific research focus addressed in this article is to examine the patterns of onset, progression, cessation, and relapse of methamphetamine use in suburban neighborhoods in order to increase our understanding of prevention, intervention, and treatment.

Methamphetamine is a stimulant that affects the central nervous system and releases dopamine neurotransmitters to the brain while inhibiting their uptake. This process produces a pleasurable experience along with increased activity and decreased appetite. Methamphetamine, which is similar to the chemical structure of amphetamine, can be smoked, snorted, injected, or orally consumed. According to the National Institute on Drug Abuse (NIDA) (2005), methamphetamine use can damage nerve terminals and cause the body temperature to

Reprinted from Miriam Williams Boeri, Liam Harbry, and David Gibson, 2009, "A Qualitative Exploration of Trajectories among Suburban Users of Methamphetamine." In *Journal of Ethnographic and Qualitative Research* 3: 139–151. Reprinted by permission of JEQR.

become dangerously elevated. Short-term effects of methamphetamine include increased wakefulness, increased physical activity, and decreased appetite. Long-term effects of methamphetamine include addiction, violent behavior, anxiety, confusion, insomnia, paranoia, auditory hallucinations, mood disturbances, and delusions.

Research on methamphetamine use suggests a long history of use in the United States (Anglin et al. 2002; Miller 2001). Epidemiological data show a dramatic increase in treatment for methamphetamine users, and all indicators continue to show a steady increase in methamphetamine use and associated health problems (Hser et al. 2003). Treatment studies show that methamphetamine users typically have more severe problems than other drug users entering treatment and need more effective strategies for treatment as a result (Substance Abuse and Mental Health Services Administration [SAMHSA] 2006). Further behavioral concerns include the association of methamphetamine use with risky sexual behaviors, injection use, and HIV transmission (Jones and Urbina 2004). Users typically rely on methamphetamine for both recreational and functional purposes (Haight et al. 2005; Halkitis et al. 2003; Kushel et al. 2005; Lende et al. 2007; Worth and Rawstone 2005).

Our qualitative study specifically focused on the trajectories of methamphetamine use among suburban users. The Diagnostic Statistical Manual of Mental Disorders (DSM-IV) delineates developmental stages of drug use, abuse, and dependence (American Psychiatric Association 1994). The sociological perspective distinguishes phases in a drug career of initiation, continuation, escalation, remittance, and relapse (Abadinsky 1997). This article provides a better understanding of the social contexts and cultural processes that influence transition from one phase to another by identifying patterns in drug trajectories. Greater knowledge in this field can develop better prevention, intervention, and treatment programs for suburban methamphetamine users.

Method

A qualitative approach in drug research facilitates access to hidden, hard-to-reach populations and identifies the complexity of drug use patterns among new using networks (Biernacki 1986; Bourgois 1995). Qualitative research can provide insights about the diversity of drug users and the various social contexts of specific drug use (Lofland et al. 2006; Nichter et al. 2004; Pierce 1999). We examined the processes associated with initiating methamphetamine, the progression in use, discontinuation, and relapse for different types of methamphetamine users living in the suburbs.

We used ethnographic fieldwork and in-depth interviews of both current and former users of methamphetamine to collect our data. We defined former use as using methamphetamine for at least 6 consecutive months, but not in the past month. We defined current use as using methamphetamine for at least 6 consecutive months, including the past month. The Kennesaw State University Institutional Review Board approved the study methods. A Certificate of Confidentiality obtained from the National Institute of Drug Abuse protected all information from court subpoena. All research team members completed the Collaborative Institute Training Initiative (CITI) online course for investigators conducting social behavioral research with human subjects. This research was supported by NIDA grant 1R15DA021164-01A1 (Miriam Boeri, PI). The views presented in this article are those of the authors and do not represent those of the funding agency.

Data Collection

Each interview consisted of three interrelated parts: (1) the life history matrix, (2) the drug history matrix, and (3) an audio-recorded in-depth interview guided by a semi-structured instrument. The life history matrix helped the participant focus on retrospective life events, develop rapport with the interviewer, and establish an additional validating strategy. The interviewer accomplished these tasks by asking the participant specific questions regarding social roles throughout the life course. A drug use matrix facilitated the investigation of transitions in drug career phases. The drug history matrix determined the first use of each drug, past 30-day use, past 6-month use, and routes of administration.

The major themes addressed in each interview were the context of drug use, interaction with others, social roles, and progression of drug use over time. In addition, interviews explored reasons for initiating, continuing use, cessation, and relapse. As is often the case in qualitative interviews, the interview developed a path of its own, directed by the unique experiences of each participant. Because the voices of the drug users were the center of the analysis, rich textual detail provided supporting evidence of the patterns that emerged. The interview process, including matrices and recorded interview, lasted on average 1 to 2 hours.

We recruited participants in this purposive sample using a combination of targeted, snowball, and theoretical sampling methods (Strauss and Corbin 1998; Watters and Biernacki 1989). Targeted sampling involved focused recruitment efforts to identify different types of users in the ethnographic fieldwork. Using snowball sampling, we asked participants and interested inquirers to refer other potential participants to the study. We limited snowball sampling to ensure that not too many participants were recruited from one network. Theoretical sampling involved targeting further recruitment efforts based on analysis of the collected data, particularly after preliminary analysis of the first interviews. We established contact with methamphetamine users in this study by talking with people at public sites, such as coffee houses, bars, clubs, grocery stores, malls, or other areas. After a brief discussion about the research study, we left a card or flier with a contact telephone number. If the setting allowed, we developed trust and rapport in the field and immediately conducted interviews or arranged to meet again. Usually, users who heard about the study contacted us through people we met in the field.

Once we located potential participants, we discussed the study time commitment, how the interview would be conducted, anonymity and confidentiality issues, and reimbursements. We obtained oral consent, since written consent could have jeopardized participant anonymity. We conducted interviews in a safe place agreed upon by the participant and interviewer. Sites used for interviewing included a library study room, the participant's home, and the interviewer's car. We offered participants $25 cash or a $25 gift certificate at the end of the interview.

Data Analysis

We transcribed all recorded in-depth interviews. A member of the research team then reviewed each transcript to ensure the deletion of all identifying material and the accuracy of transcribed words. Data analysis began with initial coding of the first interviews using the constant comparison analysis for qualitative data (Charmaz 2001; Strauss and Corbin 1998). During the first stage of open coding, the team of three researchers each coded the same five transcripts using trajectory phases already known from research on drug trajectories, adding codes for any new concepts found in the data. Coders made use of memos—thoughts or new ideas written in the margins. The research team discussed the coding process at weekly meetings to promote reliability between coders. The team then organized the codes into the main themes and subthemes or categories. At least two coders coded each interview transcript and added new codes as needed. Transcripts ranged from 12 to 50 pages, single-spaced. We then entered the transcripts and coding themes into the qualitative data analysis program, NVivo, for easier data management. The NVivo program calls these codes or categories "nodes." NVivo organized nodes into a node "tree" or listed them alone as a "free node." At the time of the analysis for this article, a total of 10 main tree nodes and 23 free nodes were entered into NVivo.

For this article, we analyzed only the data coded in NVivo for trajectory-related nodes. For the preliminary analysis, we entered 21 of the transcripts into NVivo and all coded data at the tree nodes: (a) initiation, (b) access, (c) turning points, (d) treatment, and (e) relapse. This decision produced 57 pages of quotes related to trajectories. We employed the trajectory nodes to hand-code the remaining 27 transcripts analyzed for this article. We entered the data collected on the drug matrices into a data set using the statistical software program SPSS. We used the statistical data for descriptive purposes in this article.

We utilized a modified version of analytical induction to develop the codes (Lofland et al. 2006). We started with findings on trajectories already established in the literature and refined the patterns in the trajectory to fit emerging findings over the course of the analysis. For example, specific drug trajectories start with initiation, but users initiate drags for both functional and recreational reasons. During our analysis, we focused on the functional themes discussed by Lende et al. (2007)—to increase productivity, to function normally, and to enhance functional activities. We refined these themes to include a more complex description of the analysis of the data, which we more thoroughly discuss in the results section.

We followed an iterative model of triangulation to establish validity. The iterative model of triangulating data throughout the study—comparing information collected from various data sources, and addressing issues of validity and reliability as the study progresses—has been shown to provide greater confidence in understanding complex information (Nichter et al. 2004; Rhodes and Moore 2001). We collected data from many sources, used multiple methods, and increased the clarity or the lens through which we analyzed the data. The iterative model followed processes similar to grounded theory analysis (Strauss and Corbin 1998). We clarified, validated, or refuted inconsistencies found between data sources in further data collection.

Ongoing data analysis included triangulation of the life history matrices, drug history matrices, and in-depth interviews. We clarified emerging results during the ongoing in-depth interviews, not necessarily to find congruence, but instead to inform the continuing data collection and analyses. For example, when we heard of a new way to produce methamphetamine, we asked about it in our next interviews; we addressed inconsistencies between the data by continuously refining the interview questions.

Results

This article provides the preliminary qualitative analysis and findings on a sample of 48 methamphetamine users. We did not choose transcripts in any specific manner. We included both former (N = 32) and current users (N = 16). Table 10.1 depicts the sample demographics. The sample is not meant to be representative; however, our sample does reflect research showing that methamphetamine users are predominantly White males (SAMHSA 2006).

Table 10.1 Suburban Methamphetamine Users: Sample Demographics (N = 48).

Demographic Characteristics	N	%
Gender		
Male	38	79.2
Female	10	20.8
Race		
White	41	85.4
African American	15	10.4
Latino	12	14.2
Use status		
Former user	32	66.7
Current user	16	33.3
Age: Mean (range)	34.9 (19 – 56)	
Age: First use of methamphetamine	22.5 (11 – 54)	

We categorized the trajectory phases of methamphetamine use explored in this study by initiation, progression, turning points in controlled to uncontrolled use, cessation of use, and relapse. We further developed each of these phases to examine the complex differences we found between users. While many quotes were used to develop the patterns found, we selected those that we felt best illustrated the pattern by the majority of participants described. We repeated quotes verbatim, with the exception of omitted ums, ahs, and other terms used casually in conversation, but not needed in print.

Initiation

Suburban methamphetamine users learned about methamphetamine at work, from parents, or from a dealer who sold them other drugs. Friends, neighbors, partners, and co-workers on the job typically introduce suburban users to methamphetamine. Introduction by friends, neighbors, and partners was common, but being initiated to methamphetamine at work appeared to be a distinctive suburban pattern. For example, a 41-year-old White male explained:

> We were working, and I guess working overtime, and I was really exhausted, really tired and

[a supervisor at work] said: "Here, I got something to make you feel better." So, therefore, we went into his office and I was, like, I did it with him, and he showed me how he did it. He rolled up a dollar bill, and I was like, "Well shit," and I tried it and I liked it.

Another unexpected finding was the number of youth who reported that their parents' use of methamphetamine or other drugs influenced their use. A 19-year-old White male explained how he was introduced to methamphetamine:

My dad was selling it. Well he wasn't selling it, he was holding it for some guy and he was like the guy's bodyguard, too. He had it in the basement when I lived in the city, and he moved down here and he still had a car up there, and I found it in the car one day. That's how I first tried it.

Participants reported that a drug dealer or drug user to whom they went for another drug introduced them to methamphetamine:

The first time I was introduced to it I didn't have any cocaine to go with my heroin and someone asked me if I wanted to try some of their speed. And I asked them about it and they told me about it and I went ahead and said: "Yeah, sure, I'll try it."

Typically, the users we interviewed started using methamphetamine for functional or recreational purposes. Lende et al. (2007) identified three categories of functional use of methamphetamine: (1) enhanced function, (2) increased productivity, and (3) functioning normally. While we found similar purposes, we added or modified this list as new categories emerged from the analysis of the users' perspectives. For example, users in our sample talked about "maintaining" use in ways that appeared to be consistent with what Lende et al. (2007) termed "functioning normally." We employed the term "maintaining" as an NVivo code.

The functional purpose for using methamphetamine appeared to be similar to reasons why doctors prescribe amphetamine-type medications for children diagnosed with attention deficient disorder—to focus. Lende et al. (2007) described the enhancing function as being more focused on the task. We found that subjects in our sample used methamphetamine for enhancement purposes.

However, other than increased focus, they also mentioned increased quality of work. A 34-year-old woman who worked as an artist explained:

But, normally, you can focus so clearly. Like, I used to like to do my artwork and carve—especially by hand, but even with a drill and what not. But by hand, it's like I would just have an exact, I could just make the most intricate carvings, and keep my mind as to different tricks to use to get different textures and different techniques. I was very—just on point. Very tactful, and I felt that was a result of the drug.

Participants mentioned that the quality of their work improved when they first began using methamphetamine, although with continued use and after consecutive days of using, called binges, the quality decreased.

Increased productivity refers to getting more accomplished in terms of quantity rather than quality (Lende et al. 2007). Those who mentioned starting methamphetamine for purposes of functioning stated that use enhanced work because they worked more hours. One 50-year-old White male who used while running his own business to support his family was asked why he used methamphetamine as a middle-class family man. He responded: "You know, to work the long hours, plus to try to enjoy it. It worked for a while, but then I'd start screwing up." Others confirmed that productivity did not continue once methamphetamine use pattern became chronic.

The middle-aged users we interviewed said they started using methamphetamine to have the energy to maintain the "normal" suburban lifestyle. For example, one married man explained:

It just made me want to work harder mainly. It made me more motivated. It made my mind work, you know, faster. The effects of it were you could get more hours out of the day sort of thing when you're trying to maintain a family and a job. You could still get home in the evenings and still have enough strength.

A 35-year-old female echoed this explanation "to maintain" from a woman's point of view:

'Cause it would give me energy. Yeah, I'd get up and clean the whole house up, and cook, have a big dinner ready, and felt happy. That's the devil in methamphetamine because it makes you happy. And you don't know why, and you don't really care. Personally, I never associated it with being high. At that point I was not doing enough to get the high, high feeling. Just enough to, wow, I feel great. I feel good; let's paint the house.

As revealed in interviews with both males and females, maintaining while on methamphetamine was specifically conducive to a suburban lifestyle, whether that meant having energy for work and family life at home, or staying at home to perform housework and sustain a good attitude.

In contrast, the young adults in our sample stated a common reason to start methamphetamine was for recreational purposes, "to have fun." Others reported that along with having fun, using methamphetamine helped them "to fit in" with their social group: "When you started doing drugs it made you fit in. You can talk better to people and fit in with anybody, well probably most of the drug users." This social aspect of methamphetamine use especially appealed to young adults who were denied access to desired social groups, such as the football team or cheerleading squad, and to those who felt awkward or socially inept. Methamphetamine use seemed advantageous for its energy and social bonding effects.

In addition, participants indicated that they initially used methamphetamine to escape the pain typically related to emotional stress or psychological depression. Even when participants said they started using methamphetamine for fun, upon further inquiry they often cited other purposes for use. For example, one middle-aged man reflected on his reason to start methamphetamine use:

> I mean you want to believe you're doing it for recreation, but to look back on my life, I'm doing it because of the psychological pain and emotional pain. I mean, if my life was healthy or a normal thing, I never would be doing it to begin with.

Since methamphetamine affects dopamine neurotransmitters, the user feels euphoria while on the drug, but previous feelings of depression return and may increase when methamphetamine use ceases. This increased sadness often motivates the person to use again.

Turning Points from Controlled to Uncontrolled Use

The turning point from controlled to uncontrolled use was linked to the goal of maintaining a "normal" successful suburban lifestyle. We categorized these turning points as (a) dealing with family or work difficulties, (b) experiencing emotional or psychological difficulties, and (c) having easier access to the drug. While in some cases these categories appeared to be extensions of the purposes for initiation of methamphetamine, in other cases participants indicated a progression from one purpose for initial use to a different reason for using methamphetamine in an uncontrolled manner.

Difficulties with family and/or work indicated an increased use for the participants in our sample. Keeping up with an increased workload or working with others who used methamphetamine (thereby working harder or longer hours) was a reason to increase use. One 28-year-old male explained: "It seemed like all my co-workers did drugs. Using meth felt like you were getting more done, being more productive." Another middle-aged, working-class male who worked with methamphetamine-using colleagues explained: "It's like, by God, I had to use it just to stay up with them." A 41-year-old male who had started his own business said it was difficult to stay afloat without using methamphetamine:

> I was falling behind in my bills. I wanted to work. I wanted to keep up. I was running my company and I was, you know, I had left [another company] to start my own construction business. It was really hard. Life's hard when you work for yourself. The day doesn't stop at 5 o'clock.

Participants expressed similar issues regarding the need for methamphetamine to avoid losing their suburban lifestyle, especially young adults who were starting families and middle-aged adults who ran into economic difficulties.

Others cited family issues and family-related difficulties as reasons to increase their use. One 37-year-old housewife explained why she used methamphetamine:

> I wasn't miserable anymore. We always had financial problems. We never had enough money because I was depressed a lot, I think. But then along came Ice [methamphetamine] and no more

depression and no more pills, no more feeling sleepy and then feeling better tomorrow. You feel better now.

Psychological turmoil was a turning point to increased use for methamphetamine users of all ages and from all walks of life. The woman above had family-related financial difficulties. Loss of a relationship was one of the most cited reasons to increase methamphetamine use. A 53-year-old male explained: "You know, it seemed like during the bad times maybe the usage would pick up. Like after a relationship split up, or divorce, or something like that. It usually had to do with that."

The death or illness of a loved one was also a reason to increase methamphetamine use. A young male explained: "When I first found out my wife had cancer, I used it for an escape, because she's really the love of my life." In addition, participants reported having been molested or abused as children or young adults. The experience left them with re-occurring emotional pain. Avoiding or forgetting emotional pain was cited as a reason to increase methamphetamine use. For example, a 35-year-old female revealed: "I had a rough childhood and some of the things that's in my childhood I wanted to forget about, because I was molested by my stepfather."

A third turning point for increasing use of methamphetamine was obtaining easier access to the drug. In this case, the user had started dealing the drug or had a partner who was dealing. A middle-aged male recounted that the first time his methamphetamine use increased was when he was a teenager: "I was 17 going into 18. I started doing it frequently. It was always accessible. Somebody always had it. And I started dealing actually." A 22-year-old male explained that dealing started with merely buying enough to pay for his habit: "You know, it'd go from just middle-manning a half gram to going and picking up a half an eight ball. And you know, distributing it amongst three or four people, but keeping the leftovers."

Two other turning points merit mentioning in this section: (a) the progression from another drug to methamphetamine and (b) the progression into injection use. While our current data are insufficient to identify these as turning points from controlled to uncontrolled use, they are nevertheless turning points in the user's drug career. Using another drug, even temporarily, affects the progression of methamphetamine use, and injecting a drug for the first time marks a significant change that affects all areas of the user's life.

Some methamphetamine users in our sample were already using another drug in an uncontrolled manner and started using methamphetamine either to stop the other drug or because it was available. So while this progression cannot be called a turning point into uncontrolled methamphetamine use, it appears to be a turning point in an uncontrolled use from one drug to another. Most often the drug the user was trying to control was cocaine or crack. For example, one African American male explained that he switched to methamphetamine so that he could stop using crack, a drug that did not allow him to function at work:

> I would smoke [crack] all night long and then just go to work for 2 and 3 days. I just got really tired of it 'cause I couldn't really function on the job. I was a mechanical engineer at a textile plant and I couldn't function right. And I was so anxious to get off work every day at 3 o'clock, you know, so I could go home and do my crack.

Injection can also be considered a progression in the methamphetamine use trajectory. A middle-aged White male said he injected methamphetamine to stop his crack cocaine use: "I injected it and you know—go really, really high one time. I guess because I injected a whole bunch. I was always chasing the big high." This participant indicated that injection was the ultimate high in drug use, and once experienced, it was hard to return to other routes of administration.

Cessation

The diverse routes to cessation of methamphetamine found in our sample include (a) stopping cold turkey, (b) slowly decreasing use, (c) replacing drug-use role with another social role, (d) entering a formal or informal treatment program, and (e) substituting another drug for methamphetamine.

Stopping use of methamphetamine without any help or formal treatment plan is often called "cold turkey," a phrase borrowed from the heroin addiction literature. While this cessation was often linked to another reason to stop, such as having a new social role or loss of finances, a few participants, primarily younger users, appeared to have successfully decided that they would discontinue use. These participants looked in the mirror and said they did not like what they saw—a junkie. One of our coders called this the "looking glass effect." Other participants attributed willpower to their success at stopping use. One 21-year-old female reported:

> I'm a very strong-minded person because I just stopped cold turkey and most people cannot do that. I just decided it was stupid for me to be not only ruining my health, but ultimately it was going to ruin my life and I knew that. I knew it the whole time, and I finally just got to a point where all of the chaos from it was time to end.

Participants indicated they stopped using because they did not like what they had become, how they looked, or what they did, but could not explain how that could be accomplished for anyone who lacked willpower.

A few participants mentioned slowing down their usage. A former user who was a father slowed down his use until he eventually stopped without treatment. This trajectory of eventual cessation was envisioned by current users as well, as with the middle-aged male whose goal was cessation:

> It's getting to the point where I know I got to put the brakes on. But yet at the same time I know that even though I'm slowing down, just doing it here and there, it's not going to work, because eventually, I'm going to get tired of that and just bust loose again. So what I got to do is just try to take care of these issues and get these dealt with and leave my last use farther and farther behind down the road and just turn in another direction, and just change my playmates and playground. That's what I got to do.

As implied by the participant above, slowing down use was often linked to a change in social roles.

Users who had ceased use reported substitution of the drug role with a social role that was more important to them. Often this was a family role, such as the husband and parent role, as indicated by this 26-year-old male: "My wife gave me a talk. She was about to leave, you know, and I really just, I had my son then and I didn't want to lose my family." Others indicated that they replaced their drug addict role with a drug counselor role. A 36-year-old male who had been using methamphetamine since he was a teenager shared the following insight:

> And then once I realized by helping other people it kept me focused on my recovery as well, as I could see they're looking at me and they're seeing me stay sober and clean and it gives them hope. If I wasn't staying clean and I'm trying to tell these other people how long I been clean and how I done it, well if I go back out and I get high then that just destroyed the whole theory that we can do recovery.

While this participant went to a treatment program, it appears that his role as a drug counselor was the major influence on his current cessation status.

Participants also cited entering and staying in a treatment program as a route to ceasing use of methamphetamine. Treatment for methamphetamine users included various types of residential programs, outpatient counseling, and a 12-step program, such as Alcoholics Anonymous (AA), Narcotics Anonymous (NA), or Crystal Methamphetamine Anonymous (CMA). While all these groups adhere to a 12-step program, CMA focuses on methamphetamine dependence in particular. Participants often did not have a CMA group available, or they preferred a specific AA or NA group in their area. Most of the residential and outpatient programs incorporated a 12-step component in the treatment plan, but some participants went to a 12-step group without any other formal treatment.

From the perspectives of the participants, residential treatment ranged from a very effective to a meaningless mechanism for collecting their insurance money only. Here we focused on those who attributed their ceased use of methamphetamine to the treatment program. For example, one 26-year-old Latino male explained how he was able to stop using methamphetamine:

> I was homeless. It was a residential treatment for homeless men. It was 12-step based transitional housing. My probation officer pretty much told me I needed to go get a drug test and needed to go do something about this. I went to them and they talked to me and they were talking about, "You seem like you need to come in here. We're going to give you a bed." And I really was sick and tired of all the crap that came along with using drugs.

As noted in this participant's response, the criminal justice system was involved in his eventual cessation by its demand that he stop using drugs. We found other participants in our sample who attributed their success in stopping to requirements imposed by the law. The emerging Drug Court concept, a diversion program for criminal offenders who are also drug users, appeared to influence the younger adults in one suburban area to stop use. For example, a 22-year-old male recounted what happened when he was arrested: "They put me in the Drug Court, and I started the Drug Court rehab." He attributed his eventual cessation to the strict requirements of the Drug Court program.

Participants described outpatient programs that helped them to stop methamphetamine, albeit not for permanent duration. For example, the young man mentioned above had previously been in a number of treatment programs before being assigned to Drug Court by the judge, including an outpatient program:

It was a 90-day outpatient program. Real lax; they didn't require NA or AA. You just went there like three nights a week and talked for like an hour and a half. They claimed they would do two random drug tests over the 90 days. The only thing I ever got was the initial drug screen when I went in, but I stayed clean for actually all those 90 days. No, no, I take that back. I stayed clean for about the first forty-five.

Participants generally reported multiple attempts in drug treatment before achieving success, and having an extended period without drug use appeared to convince users that they could eventually and permanently cease use.

For the participants in our sample, "clean" often involved some experience with a 12-step program. The 12-step program may be a "phase" in the users' lives or they may believe that they will need 12-step for life. Cessation can occur in both cases, but most of the participants we interviewed claimed to need 12-step for life. While the 12-step program does not specify one particular religion, all adherents must have a spiritual belief in a "higher power" that helps them resist drug use. This belief, along with the support of the group and a specific group sponsor, provides a foundation for addiction recovery. For example, one 42-year-old woman who had been using methamphetamine for many years and lost her five children due to drug use described her recent healing through a 12-step program:

And there is a 12-steps to freedom, which is a Christian 12-step program. I knew that higher power had to be higher than me or the drugs, because I always had to be the super-mom. There could be nothing stronger than me. I had to be the tops. I had to be the best. I had to look the best. I had to act the best. I wanted people to see, you know, my checkerboard pattern in my front lawn, all the crosswalks washed.

You know, there was nothing stronger than me until I realized that when my prayers were answered and I was accepted into rehab, I knew that there had to be something stronger than me or the drugs. And I let that be faith.

Participants who could not stop using methamphetamine, even when they lost important social roles such as being a parent or a spouse, mentioned they obtained strength in faith typically found through attending 12-step programs.

Those participants who at the time of the interview were in a 12-step program believed they would participate forever. For example, when asked if he was willing to go to the 12-step group for life, one 36-year-old male replied: "I have to be. I have to go after my recovery like I went after them drugs every day. I done drugs every day, so you know, if I'm going to recover I got to go." Participants indicated that other types of cessation routes did not work as well as the 12-step programs, since 12-step helped them to stay away from all drugs including alcohol. For example, one young man explained: "I know, it's a lifelong thing now that I have to commit my life to. I can't drink. I can't smoke pot. I can't be around them kind of people." Participants in a 12-step program said they had tried to use other drugs such as alcohol or marijuana moderately, but this use eventually led them back to using methamphetamine.

Not all participants agreed, however, and some chose a controversial route to cessation of methamphetamine—the substitution of another drug. Most often the drug used was marijuana, preferred for its calming effect. When asked if he used marijuana during his recovery, one 23-year-old former user of methamphetamine responded: "Yes. Absolutely! Absolutely! In a lot of ways that was my sanity."

Others cited a traumatic experience, such as an accident or health problem, that prompted them to cease use. Typically, the younger the user, the more affected they were by the health consequences they saw in other drug users, such as a 19-year-old female who decided to stop use after seeing another user almost die:

> Apparently somebody had taken him to the hospital 'cause he was dying. He was hooked up to all these tubes and stuff like that, and it like screwed my head up real bad. And that's when I knew I needed to get help. And I went to my parents' house and I was like: "I need help."

Those who stopped using due to health reasons, or because of how the drug affected the health of their friends, were young adults. We do not know if they eventually will return to drug use, as did many of the older adults who said they had stopped previously in their lives and started drugs again later.

The participants indicated several influences on their ultimate cessation of methamphetamine, and it was difficult to disentangle the major impact. For example, one 34-year-old woman cited financial reasons and health difficulties, as well as substituting illegal drugs with a legal drug, as her route to cessation of all drugs, including methamphetamine:

> Part of the thing is I need my heart medicine. My heart medicine was costing me just under five grand for one medication. But the methadone clinic I go to, they get me all eight of my medications through a grant, and I pay for the price of my methadone, all my heart medicine and everything. That's what was costing me just under five grand a month for just one medication. And now I get all eight of them and that including my methadone. So seven of them and then my methadone for $12 a day, $84 a week, under the agreement that I have clean methadone-only drug screens.

This participant's health status and financial difficulties led her to use a legal substitute drug, albeit one that was illegal if sold on the streets, to help her to stay clean for the first time in her life.

Relapse

While the treatment successes we report are inspiring as well as educational, we know from statistics that many of the participants are likely to relapse, defined as using again after at least 3 months of consciously ceasing use. Reasons for relapsing after cessation of use typically involved a social trauma in the users' lives, with use of methamphetamine seen as an escape from psychological pain or emotional suffering. Other users returned to methamphetamine as a reward for good behavior, often believing they could control their use. Some relapse was due to peer influence or for functional reasons, such as to stay awake and have energy for work or study. Some who substituted another drug for methamphetamine often found that use of that drug led back to methamphetamine use.

A psychological or emotional difficulty appeared to be the main reason former users returned to methamphetamine. Often this difficulty resulted from a loss within a family or relationship. For example, one 26-year-old male was trying to keep his young family together when his wife went to the hospital with a difficult pregnancy and lost the baby. Alone in the hospital, seeing his deceased baby and not knowing if his wife would pull through, he said he felt hopeless:

> I was so alone at the time, you know what I mean? I was sitting there in the hospital and, I don't know, even when there's people around, nobody was asking me how I was doing, how I was handling it, "Are you okay?" And, you know, I really felt like I didn't have, like there was just no more for me to do, you know? And at that time, I'd actually been sober, I think about 3 months. And (long pause) I just, I just decided, you know, screw it. I'm gonna throw in the towel and just go get high. You know what I mean?

As the above participant suggested, loss can be so painful that only methamphetamine can take it away. This was also the case with a 41-year-old male who described his relapses when a serial killer murdered his mother: "I wanted to kill the guy. I think I had just gotten clean. And then I relapsed right after that." Difficulty in a relationship often triggered the return to methamphetamine, as in the example of a young man who reported:

> I found out the wife was sleeping with somebody while I was in jail and, you know, this guy was spanking my kids, and I don't even know who this guy is. And, I don't know, I really slipped up, I was real low. I didn't feel good about myself at all. So I just kept using for those few weeks.

Relationship problems appeared to be a cause of relapse regardless of age, but males expressed this motivation more than females in our sample.

Participants indicated that another common route to relapse was being around other people who use the drug, such as friends or work colleagues. For example, a young man reported relapsing when offered the drug while at work:

> I came across somebody who was actually at my job. I was working at a little pallet place. And he asked me if I liked to get messed up. And I was like: "No, not really." He was like: "Are you sure?" He's like: " 'Cause I got some Ice [methamphetamine]." I was like: "Yeah, let's go." I mean, just instantly.

Others relapsed by first using other drugs, including alcohol, which eventually led back to methamphetamine. This route back to use was also linked to social environment, as described by a young man fresh from a successful treatment program who started to associate with people who drank alcohol:

> I started drinking and smoking pot first. I thought I was cured pretty much. I had all this going on, you know. I'm normal. So I started drinking and smoking, being at parties, people using meth, and eventually I couldn't say no to it no more.

Others relapsed when they used methamphetamine again for functional reasons, typically for energy to work, as one 42-year-old described: "[I] entirely planned on moving into the house, never touching drugs again, but just needed the energy to move into the house." Another former user who relapsed for a few weeks reported a temporary functional use of methamphetamine:

> I intended on doing it very slowly and just doing it to boost me while I was at work. That was the sole

intention of me doing it. I didn't do it to stay up. I didn't do it to socialize. It was strictly for energy. And I did that for 3 weeks and ran out and had no desire to contact that person again. So I just haven't done it since.

Akin to this young female, younger users mentioned intentional use of methamphetamine for work and studying.

Only time will reveal if participants' intentional temporary use might lead back to sustained use in the future. Much appeared to depend on the type of user and their understanding of their drug use patterns. For example, one 41-year-old male who currently used methamphetamine after a recent relapse reported: "If I drink, though, I immediately go to get some crack or some meth. Two beers, I'm gone." In contrast, a 38-year-old male who had ceased using methamphetamine in the last year after more than 20 years of use said he stopped using methamphetamine by substituting it with alcohol. He reported that he never had a desire to use methamphetamine again, but without the opportunity to have a few beers, he might be tempted. Clearly, treatment and relapse prevention cannot be conceptualized in a one-size-fits-all model.

Discussion and Implications

Research about drug prevention and treatment emphasizes the importance of matching the client with treatment (Farabee et al. 2004). Our findings call for more targeted treatment for methamphetamine users living in suburbs. We know that methamphetamine in urban areas is often related to recreational use at clubs and in gay leisure environments (Halkitis et al. 2003; Worth and Rawstone 2005). Homelessness, unemployment, and poverty are associated with methamphetamine use in both urban and rural areas (Haight et al. 2005; Kushel et al. 2005), with implications that methamphetamine is used to self-medicate or deal with stress. Lende et al. (2007) suggested that functional purposes include recreational and self-medicating motivations, as well as being able to function normally while using methamphetamine. Our study about methamphetamine users living in the suburbs revealed a wide range of users by socioeconomic status. Targeting methamphetamine prevention and treatment in the suburbs, then, requires a greater understanding of why people use. First, prevention programs should focus on functional versus recreational purposes for initiating use of methamphetamine. Second, treatment plans should address the functional reasons for use. Third, treatment providers should acknowledge different triggers for relapse, as well as tools for combating these triggers. Finally, treatment plans and relapse prevention education should take into account the users' life experiences, including social and psychological issues.

Our findings show that while some suburban methamphetamine users indicated use patterns similar to those of urban and rural users, there were patterns specific to suburban use. First, many suburban users initiated use and returned to use for the functional purpose of maintaining a "suburban" family lifestyle. The pressure of keeping the family and home up to the standard expected in suburban neighborhoods appeared to be particularly stressful for young men and women who were just starting families in a difficult economic environment. Loss of job or other financial problems can also trigger a turning point into uncontrolled use or a relapse. Second, use of methamphetamine appeared to be prevalent in suburban areas where we least expect it, such as in family-oriented neighborhoods and work environments not generally known for methamphetamine use. We suggest that more educational and prevention programs be targeted toward these areas. Finally, treatment was successful in many cases; however, other routes to cessation of use should also be explored, such as establishing criteria for a focused plan toward eventual cessation, or exploring a substitution drug program for methamphetamine users similar to methadone maintenance. While methadone has been shown to be highly successful for heroin and other opiate drug abusers, little research exists about legal substitute drugs for methamphetamine. Through this qualitative inquiry into suburban settings, we have a better understanding of the diverse trajectories in methamphetamine use that can help us develop and implement more focused treatment, intervention, and prevention programs.

Limitations and Future Research

The major limitation of this study is that it cannot be generalized beyond the research sample. However, as an exploratory qualitative study, it does not require a probability sample. The goal was to gain a better understanding of methamphetamine use patterns among a suburban sample of methamphetamine users, and this targeted convenience sample was sufficient to achieve this goal. We presented preliminary analysis of the first 48 interviews. We plan to explore the emerging trajectory patterns found here as we collect and analyze the remaining sample data. Additionally, these preliminary findings provide insight into the complex process of methamphetamine use trajectories that can be used in future large-scale studies. The patterns of suburban methamphetamine use we discussed can be examined more fully in quantitative data collection methods, such as questionnaire surveys. The findings also call for more research about middle-aged and middle-class users, as well as the need for treatment focused on this emerging population of methamphetamine users.

References

Abadinsky, H. 1997. *Drug Abuse: An Introduction.* Chicago: Nelson Hall.

American Psychiatric Association. 1994. *Diagnostic and Statistical Manual of Mental Disorder (DSM-IV).* Washington, DC: Author.

Anglin, M., C. Burke, B. Perrochet, E. Stamper, and S. Dawud-Noursi. 2002. "History of the Methamphetamine Problem." *Journal of Psychoactive Drugs* 32: 37–141.

Biernacki, P. 1986. *Pathways from Heroin Addiction: Recovery Without Treatment.* Philadelphia: Temple University Press.

Boeri, M. 2004. " 'Hell, I'm an Addict but I Ain't No Junkie': An Ethnographic Analysis of Aging Heroin Users." *Human Organization* 63: 236–245.

Bourgois, P. 1995. *In Search of Respect: Selling Crack in El Barrio.* New York: Cambridge University Press.

Charmaz, K. 2001. "Grounded Theory." In *Contemporary Field Research: Perspectives and Formulations,* edited by R. Emerson, 335–352. Prospect Heights, IL: Waveland.

Farabee, D., Y. Hser, M. Anglin, and D. Huang. 2004. "Recidivism among an Early Cohort of California's Proposition 36 Offenders." *Criminology and Public Policy* 3: 563–584.

Faupel, C. 1991. *Shooting Dope: Career Patterns of Hard-Core Heroin Users.* Gainesville, FL: University of Florida Press.

Haight, W., T. Jacobsen, J. Black, L. Kingery, K. Sheridan, and C. Mulder. 2005. "'In These Bleak Days': Parent Methamphetamine Abuse and Child Welfare in the Rural Midwest." *Children and Youth Services Review* 27: 949–971.

Halkitis, P., J. Parsons, and L. Wilton. 2003. "An Exploratory Study of Contextual and Situational Factors Related to Methamphetamine Use among Gay and Bisexual Men in New York City." *Journal of Drug Issues* 33: 413–432.

Hser, Y., D. Huang, C. Chou, C. Teruya, and M. Anglin. 2003. "Longitudinal Patterns of Treatment Utilization and Outcomes among Methamphetamine Abusers: A Growth Curve Modeling Approach." *Journal of Drug Issues* 33: 921–938.

Jones, K. and A. Urbin. 2004. "Crystal Methamphetamine, Its Analogues, and HIV Infection: Medical and Psychiatric Aspects of a New Epidemic." *Clinical Infectious Diseases* 38: 890–894. [PubMed: 14999636]

Kushel, M., J. Hahn, J. Evans, D. Bangsberg, and A. Moss. 2005. "Revolving Doors: Imprisonment among the Homeless and Marginally Housed Population." *American Journal of Public Health* 95: 1747–1752. [PubMed: 16186453]

Lende, D., T. Leonard, C. Sterk, and K. Elifson. 2007. "Functional Methamphetamine Use: The Insider's Perspective." *Addiction Research and Theory* 15: 465–477.

Lofland, J., D. Snow, L. Anderson, and L. Lofland. 2006. *Analyzing Social Settings: A Guide to Qualitative Observation and Analysis.* Belmont: CA: Thomson Wadsworth.

Miller, M. 2001. "History and Epidemiology of Amphetamine Abuse in the United States." In *The American Drug Scene*, 3rd edition, edited by J. Inciardi, and K. McElrath, 216–228. Los Angeles: Roxbury Publishing Company.

National Institute on Drug Abuse (NIDA). 2005. "NIDA InfoFacts: Methamphetamine." Retrieved May 22, 2008, from <www.nida.nih.gov/infofacts/methamphetamine.html>

Nichter, M., G. Quintero, M. Nichter, J. Mock, and S. Shakib. 2004. "Qualitative Research: Contributions to the Study of Drug Use, Drug Abuse and Drug Use(r)-Related Interventions." *Substance Use and Misuse* 39: 1907–1969. [PubMed: 15587954]

Pierce, T. 1999. "Gen-X Junkie: Ethnographic Research with Young White Heroin Users in Washington, DC." *Substance Use and Misuse* 34: 2095–2114. [PubMed: 10573306]

Rhodes, T. and D. Moore. 2001. "On the Qualitative in Drug Research: Part One." *Addiction Research and Theory* 9: 279–297.

Strauss, A. and J. Corbin. 1998. *Basics of Qualitative Research: Techniques and Procedures for Developing Grounded Theory.* Thousand Oaks, CA: Sage.

Substance Abuse and Mental Health Services Administration (SAMHSA). 2006. *Trends in Methamphetamine/Amphetamine Admissions to Treatment 1993–2003: The DASIS Report*, 9. Retrieved May 22, 2008, from http://www.oas.samhsa.gov/2k6/methTx/methTX.htm

Watters, J. and P. Biernacki. 1989. "Targeted Sampling: Options for the Study of Hidden Populations." *Social Problems* 36: 416–430.

Worth, H. and P. Rawstone. 2005. "Crystallizing the HIV Epidemic: Methamphetamine, Unsafe Sex and Gay Diseases of the Will." *Archives of Sexual Behavior* 34: 483–486. [PubMed: 16211470]

For Discussion

1. How might the consequences of methamphetamine differ by place of residence, that is, across urban, suburban, and rural domains?
2. Boeri and her colleagues described that some individuals substituted another drug for methamphetamine. Compare this kind of substitution with the substitution described by Amanda Reiman in the previous article.

Power, Privilege, and Drug Use: Race, Ethnicity, Social Class, Gender, and Sexual Identity

Race and Ethnicity

One of the editors of this volume (Karen McElrath) often asks her students about their definitions of race; the majority of students tend to define it by some kind of biological marker, namely "skin color." In fact, variations of "skin color" are found in all social groups, and genetic differences between social groups are extremely miniscule. In the United States, however, race is an important *social construct*. That is, *we* created the concept of race and racial categories and distributed unequal privilege across the categories. Thus, although genetic differences between racial groups are diminutive, the implications of "belonging" to or identifying with a racial group are powerful and can shape life chances.

Policymakers and academics conduct research and estimate patterns of drug use for racial and ethnic groups. Surveys based on national probability samples are considered by many policymakers to be the "gold standard" of research that examines *prevalence* of drug use among social groups. Some surveys are administered at various points in time and provide information on trends in drug use over time. One limitation of these surveys focuses on the way that race is measured, that is, problems with the questions and response categories that are intended to describe the race of respondents. Too often, response categories include "white," "black," and "other" or some variation of these three categories. For instance, the National Survey on Drug Use and Health (NSDUH) is designed to capture information on the use of tobacco, alcohol, and a host of illicit drugs among people aged 12 and older in the United States, excluding a number of social groups, for example, people in jail, prison, and other institutions; people who lack accommodation (homeless); and some university students. In 2012, the NSDUH used the following categories of race: White, Black or African American, American Indian or Alaska Native, Native Hawaiian/other Pacific Islander, Asian, and the elusive category, "other." These response categories are similar to those used in the US Census. Writing in the *New York Times*, Kenneth Prewitt (2013) commented:

> Remarkably, a discredited relic of 18th-century science, the "five races of mankind," lives on in the 21st century. Today, the census calls these five races white, black, American Indian or Alaska Native, Asian, and Native Hawaiian or other Pacific Islander.

Prewitt notes the limitations of these categories. For instance, black immigrants from countries in Africa are grouped in the same category as African Americans, even though these individuals probably have very different life experiences. Moreover, "whites" include vastly different groups of people, including recent immigrants from eastern Europe combined with "descendants of New England pilgrims" (Prewitt 2013).

Survey measures of *ethnicity* also present problems. For example, although the NSDUH and other national surveys attempt to measure Hispanic ethnicity, people of Cuban, Mexican, and Puerto Rican descent are often "lumped" together, even though there are considerable cultural differences and life experiences across these groups. Creators of some official data confuse race and ethnicity by using such response categories as "white," "black," or "Hispanic." This kind of format assumes that these categories are

mutually exclusive, that is, that all individuals fall neatly into one category only. They do not. Students who are interested in this issue are strongly encouraged to read the interesting discussion by Wendy Roth (2013), *Creating a "Latino" Race.*

Surveys of sensitive behaviors such as drug use have other limitations, and these have been described elsewhere. In particular, a number of people are unwilling to disclose information about their drug use to survey researchers. This response is a rational one; drug use is highly stigmatized by mainstream society and despite assurances of confidentiality, many individuals avoid disclosure for fear of the social and legal consequences. Thus, although survey estimates of drug use by race and ethnicity have limitations, they are perceived to be an important tool by policymakers.

Results from nationally representative surveys show a complex picture of the association between race, ethnicity, and drug use. According to data collected in the 2012 Monitoring the Future survey, Hispanic students in eighth grade showed higher rates of any illicit drug use during the past year compared to white or African American students in eighth grade (Office of National Drug Control Policy 2012). However, the Office of National Drug Control Policy also claims that past year use of illicit drugs was approximately the same for race/ethnic groups among students in the twelfth grade. Our interpretation of the same data (Johnston et al. 2012) is that past year use among white twelfth-grade students was higher than among other twelfth grade students for drugs such as alcohol, cigarettes, marijuana, inhalants, hallucinogens, cocaine, crack, OxyContin, and tranquilizers (significance tests not reported). The use of anabolic steroids in the past year appeared to be slightly higher for African-Americans than for other groups. Despite these collective findings, arrest rates for drug possession are considerably higher for blacks compared to whites.

Studies of a nationally representative sample of university students in the United States found that non-medical use of prescription stimulants and opioids was higher among whites than other race groups (McCabe et al. 2005; 2005). Data analyzed from the National Survey of Workplace Health and

Safety found no differences in drug use across "racial" categories (i.e., white, black, Hispanic, other) when controlling for other variables (Frone 2006). Adding to the difficulties of interpreting survey data, a Chicago study found that African Americans were more likely than whites to underreport drug use in surveys (e.g., Fendrich and Johnson 2005), except when controlling for social class. Misrepresentation in self-report studies might result from African American perceptions that they have more to lose by self-disclosing illicit drug use, and those concerns are realistic. African Americans in possession of illicit drugs are overrepresented in arrest data, which has implications for case processing at various stages of the criminal justice system.

Social Class

Contrary to stereotypical assumptions, there is no causal link between poverty and psychoactive drug use. Rather, drug use occurs among people regardless of their social class backgrounds. However, there are some fundamental differences in the nature of drug use among social classes. First, drug use and drug transactions are often less visible among people from middle- and upper-income backgrounds. Their privilege is likely to provide them with greater means to conceal drug use. They are less often defined as "suspect." Their status often protects them from the gaze of agents of formal social control, communities, and publicly funded drug treatment. Moreover, individuals from middle- and upper-income backgrounds are more likely to be shielded from the stigma associated with "drug user" identities (Granfield and Cloud 1996). Stigma can negatively affect recovery and can create further social exclusion. Additionally, people who are from middle- and upper-income backgrounds and who use drugs are less visible to researchers. Thus, research findings pertain largely to individuals from lower-income backgrounds.

Second, poverty can contribute to marginalization, and people who are marginalized by mainstream society appear to be at greater risk for a host of physical and mental health problems, including drug use. Income is a key resource that can help alleviate some health issues and other problems;

thus, poverty makes it more difficult to access good-quality interventions that might address drug use. Lack of secure accommodation often results from poverty; homelessness can further exacerbate problem drug use. The assumption that social marginalization can increase the likelihood of problem drug use has been discussed for decades. The now extensive misuse of prescription drugs in the United States has somewhat altered the nature of that link. That is, prescription drug misuse has had a profound effect on large numbers of people from all social backgrounds, and in many ways, this kind of problem drug use contributes to marginalization—rather than the other way around. A third point is that drug use can vary when social class intersects with race and ethnicity. Consider the following: Is a white person from a poor background likely to have similar drug experiences as a white person from a middle-class background? Do African Americans from middle-class backgrounds face the same drug-related stigma as African Americans from low-income backgrounds? These questions are important because they focus on the intersection between social class and race, and the implications of those intersections.

Gender

Researchers who investigate drug use/misuse often confuse "gender" and "sex," by substituting the latter with the former. "Sex" refers to the biological differences that distinguish males and females, for example, differences that relate to hormones, genitalia, and chromosomes. In contrast, gender is socially constructed. In other words, notions of masculinity and femininity can change over time, and vary across cultures; behaviors perceived as feminine in one culture can be perceived as masculine in another. The meanings of femininity and masculinity are created by and perpetuated during social interaction. Moreover, social institutions (e.g., family, religion, schools) reinforce the construction of gender by socializing us to behave in ways that are consistent with our biological sex. Although the distinction between biological sex and gender has been debated, feminist scholars tend to be critical of mainstream scholars who often use biological sex as a measure of gender. Additionally, national surveys and other indicators of drug use generally rely on a very narrow measure of gender: female and male. More often than not, gender identities that depart from these two categories (e.g., variations of transgender) are not included.

While acknowledging these limitations, most indicators of drug use from the 1970s showed that men were more likely (1) to use illicit drugs than women, (2) to use more frequently than women, and (3) to develop more drug-related problems than women. In the 1980s and 1990s, the "gender" gap began to narrow with higher percentages of girls and women using drugs that were previously consumed largely by men and boys. In particular, women's use of amphetamines and benzodiazepines appeared to be increasing. More contemporary data from developed nations usually show that although males are more likely than females to report illicit drug use, the gender gap has continued to narrow. For some drug categories, however, use among females exceeds that of males. For example, school-based surveys from Europe show that girls are more likely than boys to self-report use of tranquilizers and sedatives (EMCDDA 2005). Additionally, some studies in England have reported that women are on par with men in terms of their patterns of recreational drug use, and their active role in drug taking for the pursuit of pleasure—at least during their 20s (Measham, Williams, and Aldridge 2011).

Problem drug use is often associated with other life problems in areas such as physical health, family relationships, employment, and housing. Women experiencing problem drug use often face additional problems compared to their male counterparts. In particular, large numbers of women who experience drug problems have been victimized by child sexual abuse, domestic violence, and the trauma associated with these crimes. Additionally, increasing numbers of women in the United States have been arrested and incarcerated for drug offenses. The impact on children has been substantial because women are more likely than men to be primary carers for children.

Sexual Identities

Alison Ritter and her colleagues in Australia (2012) identified several inconsistencies in terms of how researchers have defined and measured sexual identities in studies of drug use. They noted that some measures draw on people's self-identifications, whereas other measures focus on same-sex attraction or behaviors. Still, their review of several studies that were conducted largely in the United States found that use of tobacco, alcohol, and illicit drugs is often higher among lesbian, gay, bisexual, and transgender (LGBT) individuals compared to heterosexual populations. In another review of eighteen studies published between 1994 to 2006, Marshal et al. (2008) found that LGBT youth were significantly more likely to engage in substance use compared to heterosexual youth (Marshal et al. 2008). A study of participants in the Manhattan club scene found that women who reported their sexual orientation as being lesbian or bisexual had higher rates of drug use than women who were described as heterosexual (Parsons, Kelly, and Wells 2006). Stigma, discrimination, abuse, and stress associated with identity disclosure might explain these differences; however, research based on strong methodologies is needed to identify explanations so that appropriate interventions can be developed for LGBT populations.

References

European Monitoring Centre for Drugs and Drug Addiction (EMCDDA). 2005. *Differences in Patterns of Drug Use Between Women and Men.* Lisbon: Author.

Fendrich, M. and T. P. Johnson. 2005. "Race/Ethnicity Differences in the Validity of Self-Reported Drug Use: Results from a Household Survey." *Journal of Urban Health* 82: 67–81.

Frone, M. R. 2006. "Prevalence and Distribution of Illicit Drug Use in the Workforce and in the Workplace: Findings and Implications from a U.S. National Survey." *Journal of Applied Psychology* 91: 856–869.

Granfield, R. and W. Cloud. 1996. "The Elephant That No One Sees: Natural Recovery Among Middle-Class Addicts." *Journal of Drug Issues* 26: 45–61.

Johnston, L. D., P. M. O'Malley, J. G. Bachman, and J. E. Schulenberg. 2012. *Demographic Subgroup Trends for Various Licit and Illicit Drugs, 1975–2011,* Occasional Paper Series 77. Ann Arbor: Institute for Social Research, University of Michigan.

Marshal, M. P., M. S. Friedman, R. Stall, K. M. King, J. Miles, M. L. Gold, O. G. Bukstein, and J. Q. Morse. 2008. "Sexual Orientation and Adolescent Substance Use: A Meta-Analysis and Methodological Review." *Addiction* 103: 546–556.

McCabe, S. E., J. R. Knight, C. J. Teter, and H. Wechsler. 2005. "Non-medical Use of Prescription Stimulants among Us College Students: Prevalence and Correlates from a National Survey." *Addiction* 100: 96–106.

McCabe, S. E., C. J. Teter, C. J. Boyd, J. R. Knight, H. Wechsler. 2005. Nonmedical Use of Prescription Opioids among U.S. College Students: Prevalence and Correlates from a National Survey." *Addictive Behaviors* 30: 789–805.

Measham, F., L. Williams, and J. Aldridge. 2011. "Marriage, Mortgage, Motherhood: What Longitudinal Studies Can Tell Us about Gender, Drug 'Careers' and the Normalisation of Adult 'Recreational' Drug Use." *International Journal of Drug Policy* 22: 420–427.

Office of National Drug Control Policy. 2012. *2012 Monitoring the Future Study: Highlights.* Washington, DC: Author.

Parsons, J. T., B. C. Kelly, and B. E. Wells. 2006. "Differences in Club Drug Use Between Heterosexual and Lesbian/Bisexual Females." *Addictive Behaviors* 31: 2344–2349.

Prewitt, K. 2013. "Fix the Census' Archaic Racial Categories." *New York Times*, August 21. Available at: http://www.nytimes.com/2013/08/22/opinion/fix-the-census-archaic-racial-categories.html?_r=0

Ritter, A., F. Matthew-Simmons, and N. Carragher. 2012. *Prevalence of and Interventions for Mental Health and Alcohol and Other Drug Problems amongst the Gay, Lesbian, Bisexual and Transgender Community: A Review of the Literature.* Sydney: National Drug and Alcohol Research Centre.

Roth, W. D. 2013. "Creating a 'Latino' Race." *The Society Pages*, March 13. Available at: http://thesocietypages.org/papers/creating-a-latino-race/

11

Hard Drugs in a Soft Context
Managing Trouble and Crack Use on a College Campus

CURTIS JACKSON-JACOBS

Most studies of crack cocaine use have focused on samples that include largely African Americans. Similarly, media portrayals also point to links between African Americans and crack cocaine use. In this article, Curtis Jackson-Jacobs uses qualitative data collected at several points in time to examine the use of crack cocaine among white, middle-class college students.

Crack cocaine inspired fear in many Americans in the 1980s. As for many "drug scares" before it and since, the drug of the moment was felt to be the most dangerous ever (Musto 1973; Reinarman and Levine 1997a; Jenkins 1999). Crack started to become relatively available in several cities across the country in 1984 (Grogger and Willis 2000) and was quickly blamed for widespread addiction, urban street crime, and rampant gang violence. The first sources of information about the new drug were lurid news reports (e.g., four articles printed in *Newsweek*, June 16, 1986) and frenzied political speeches (e.g., Reagan and Reagan [1986] 1989), introducing crack as an addictive menace of "epidemic" proportion. Americans overwhelmingly came to believe drugs were the most pressing threat to their society by 1989 (Reinarman and Levine 1997b).

Crack, or "rock," was a marketing innovation, quickly adopted by urban street-corner sellers (Jacobs 1996a). It is a smokeable form of cocaine, often sold in pea-sized units costing $20 or less. Unlike powder cocaine, traditionally popular among the rich, crack produces a considerably more powerful high in smaller doses, and appears more conducive to patterns of binge use (Morgan and Zimmer 1997). Crime and addiction were attributed to the more powerful pharmacological effects of the rock form of cocaine.

Strict laws and sentencing guidelines were imposed in response to the perceived tide of lawlessness, disorder, and inhumane violence thought to be riding a wave of crack addiction (*Federal Sentencing Guidelines Manual* 1995). American jails and prisons filled with unprecedented numbers of young minority males (*Correctional Populations in the United States, 1997* 2000). A pervasive cultural stereotype of the users, colloquially dubbed "crackheads," quickly spread, conjuring images of crazed criminal men with superhuman strength and wasting women prostituting in abject degradation.

Journalistic stories in the 1980s and sociological studies in the 1990s depicted images of distinctively "ghetto" and "street" users. Crime, violence, and exploitation were at the core of these accounts

Reprinted from Curtis Jackson-Jacobs, 2004, "Hard Drugs in a Soft Context: Managing Trouble and Crack Use on a College Campus," in *Sociological Quarterly* 45: 835–856. Reprinted by permission of John Wiley and Sons via Copyright Clearance Center.

of the worlds of crack use. Poverty, minority status, and desperation characterized the users.

In this paper I present an ethnographic case study of a network of four regular crack users on a major university campus. The environment in which I did my fieldwork is perhaps as socially distant from the sites of previous crack research as one can get in America. As young, upper-middle-class, mostly white college students, the subjects of this research were at the other end of the social-inequality spectrum, commanding economic, social, and cultural resources.

The result was that I found users whose experiences of crack use were equally distant from those reported in other research. Unlike the users described elsewhere, those described here did not commit crime, were not afraid of victimization by criminals or the law, and did not face the same risks of suffering negative social esteem. Of these "troubles" (Emerson and Messinger 1977) potentially related to participating in crack use, only becoming stigmatized was a real concern. In contrast to street users' frequent troubles in the course of interaction with others, these college-student users were able to manage the moral, practical, and social demands of daily life with considerable success.

The point of this article is twofold. First, I present an alternative to the dominant images of crack use in the most impoverished conditions in American society. Second, by way of a comparison of the social conditions of crack use across a variety of settings, I argue that features of the environments of use critically shape the organization of crack-related troubles, including criminality, victimization, legal sanction, and stigmatization.

The focus of the paper is purposely comparative with data from other sources. In reviewing previous findings and then in presenting my own, I highlight variations in how users experience trouble. Two conditions increase the probability of successfully avoiding crack-related trouble: (1) using in secure contexts and (2) bounding crack use from conventional life. By comparing users' experiences across settings, I discuss how these conditions are differentially distributed across social worlds, especially with regard to economic resources and "conventional ties" (Becker 1955). The emphasis here is on

making the link between class and crack-related trouble by examining particularly consequential qualities of daily life.

Sociological Understandings of Crack Use

The best known and most powerful sociological studies of marijuana and heroin use have countered popular beliefs that the effects of drug use are due to properties of the drugs alone (Becker 1953, 1955, 1963; Winick 1961; Ray 1964; Coleman 1978; Zinberg 1984). The role of social rituals, patterns of interaction, and users' understandings of drugs have often been developed by researchers who found that there are users who "get away with it."

Historically, the sociology of drug use has profited from the study of variation in outcomes. Reversing this trend, sociologists who have studied crack users have focused on the people who get into the most trouble without developing explanations of how this outcome varies. Members of their samples have been involved in precisely the types of destructive activities that were originally used to demonize crack in the media.

Sociologists have studied crack users in a strikingly narrow range of contexts. Researchers have focused nearly universally on the poorest, most desperate users they can find, especially those involved in dealing, prostitution, and violence.[1] As Katz points out, although ethnographers often "debunk" prevailing stereotypes, ethnographers of crack users have portrayed the inside of crack houses as places where "humanity is tortured and degraded," even more so than posed by popular claims (1997, 395). Indeed, such places do exist. By portraying only the most shocking settings, though, researchers have done little to convey the diversity of experiences people have using rock cocaine. Such selective attention risks reinforcing simple stereotypes at the expense of understanding the wide variation in how crack is used and how it affects its users.

As the media did in the 1980s, sociologists in the 1990s presented numerous striking and disturbing images of crack users in the context of the ghetto and the barrio. Bourgois (1995) described the sexual degradation and conquest of crack-addicted teenage girls, the violence endemic to the crack market, and the trickery and cheating done by addicts and dealers. Inciardi, Lockwood, and Pottieger (1993), Ratner (1993), and Williams (1992) portrayed the dismal activities of crack prostitutes and the exploitation and violence pervading their lives. The users generally had a weak hold on mainstream economic and social networks before using crack and experienced arrest, victimization, and increased poverty after using (important, but rare, exceptions are discussed below).

There are two reasons why it is important to continue to study users who do not get in trouble. First, although we would expect, given past experience, that any new drug will be used without destroying all of its users, there is a powerful, recurrent, countervailing argument. Historically, each time a new drug inspires "moral panic" (Goode 1994), the panic is sustained by the belief that the new drug is "the worst ever," representing a level of inevitable destructiveness never previously known (Jenkins 1999; cf. Best 1999). Thus, popular understandings continually seek to abolish, for the present drug, the relevance of previous sociological explanation.[2] As new drugs emerge, so do new demands for critical investigation and tests to see if the limits of social explanations have been reached.

Second, interactionist theories of the consequences of drug use, though outlined in a few powerful statements, are, as yet, rather underspecified in important ways. The perspective gains most of its leverage by suggesting a few questions we can profitably ask, in any situation, and in doing so expect to find valuable insights: What troubles do users get into through social interaction? Who gets labeled and how? Who confers negative social esteem and how? How do some people avoid stigma?

In asking these questions, researchers come to some repeated findings, including that people with power escape sanction more often. Yet the analytic thrust of the interactionist perspective eschews simple conclusions that, for example, class has a universal and direct effect on the process of "getting in trouble." Instead, the mandate is to develop a nuanced understanding of the relationship between trouble, the everyday experiences of users, and macrolevel traits through continued qualification by additional results in new contexts. The following

comparative analysis attempts to draw the contemporary sociology of drug use back to these historically fruitful concerns.

A Grounded Typology of Modes of Crack Using

Only two kinds of users—indicating two modes of crack using—are portrayed in the imagery of sociological or popular accounts. These are, first, the menacing, violent, irrational street criminals willing to commit crime to fuel their addiction and, second, the pitiful, degraded, destitute addicts whose humanity and dignity have been devoured by an all-consuming drug. From the current literature, sociological and journalistic, however, at least two other classifications of users and modes of using can be established. These are described in the following paragraphs, and to that, below, I add a fifth type drawn from my own observation.

I present here a comparative description based on two levels of causal conditions that shape the user's experience of trouble (see Table 11.1). The social-organizational conditions I identify are, first, the security of the user's social world and, second, the degree to which spheres of the user's social life are bounded from one another. I suggest that each of these has a causal impact on the kinds of troubles the user is likely to encounter and also that features of the typical subjective experience of crack use under these varying conditions have additional effects. These features, corresponding to the organizational conditions, are, first, the user's orientation to crack and related troubles and, second, the perceptual horizons of crack use with respect to social identity and relationships.

"Street Predators" and "Street Victims"

The biographies of "street predators" and "street victims," and their corresponding modes of use, illustrate the ways in which local troubles common to many residents become intensified in the course of crack use.

The social, economic, and physical environments of "street" use are dramatically insecure in a variety of ways quite apart from, though seriously compounded by, dynamics of the crack market. Spheres of family life, friendship, residence, and

Table 11.1 Modes of Crack Using, Their Features, and Troubles.

| Mode of Crack Using | Social-Organizational Features of the Context | | Users' Experience of Crack | | Most Prescient Troubles |
	Secure/Insecure Context	Boundedness of Spheres of Life	Orientation to Crack Use	Horizons of Crack Use in Life	
Street predators	Insecure	Unbounded	Hardness	Expansive	Arrest
			High living	Consuming	Victimization
					Addiction
					Homelessness
Street victims	Insecure	Unbounded	Despair	Expansive	Arrest
			Downward trajectory	Consuming	Victimization
					Addiction
					Homelessness
					Stigma
Stable users	Insecure	Partially bounded	Leisure	Limited to domestic life	Financial
					Employment
					Relational trouble
			Relational rewards		
Sneaky dabblers	Insecure	Bounded	Thrill	Leisure time	Financial trouble
			"Street wisdom"	Street associates	Addiction
Campus smokers	Secure	Bounded	Leisure	Leisure time	Anxiety
			Social ritual	Close associates	Stigma

drug use often run into one another, so that trouble in one foreshadows trouble in another. In addition to these sources of vulnerability, "street" users characteristically orient to both crack use and its associated trouble in ways that appear destructive and frequently use crack in ways such that it expands to infuse virtually all aspects of social life and identity.

Users in the ghetto face a number of dangers, more or less regardless of how they understand the drug. Predatory violence and criminal sanctions are common concerns (Jacobs 1996a, 1996b). Buying or using crack in the ghetto puts users in the physical and interactional proximity of violent and property criminals. In this sense they are at risk of victimization. In another sense, the more users become entrenched in cycles of heavy drug use and avoiding conventional responsibilities, the more they are at risk of losing conventional relationships and needing to turn to crime for money (Inciardi, Horowitz, and Pottieger 1993).

The blurring of spheres of social life in poor American communities serves to magnify trouble. Each loss of a conventional relationship compounds trouble; work, friendships, and residence are themselves structured by and dependent on social networks. The precarious housing situation of poor crack users is especially revealing. They often follow a downward trajectory, moving from residences of families, to residences of friends, to the streets (Anderson 1990, 86–87). The high degree of visibility in urban communities, where much of social life goes on literally on "the streets" (Anderson 1990), the lack of residential mobility, and the social and physical proximity of work and residential life all contribute to public stigma and social exclusion.

Women especially seem vulnerable, finding few options when they lose their apartments. They must often choose between living in exploitative relationships or dangerous drug houses (Fullilove, Lown, and Fullilove 1992, 280, 281; Maher et al. 1996; Maher 1997). Users are vulnerable to being labeled "crack-heads" (Furst et al. 1999), especially women who turn to prostitution on public streets in the same communities where they have lived and grown up (Fullilove, Lown, and Fullilove 1992). In the absence of economic security and sharp boundaries between professional, criminal, and private life, maintaining family relationships and holding employment are often difficult for the crack users described by sociologists (Hamid 1992; Murdoch 1999).

Beyond these structural threats, the impoverished users depicted in published research are more vulnerable as a result of how they understand crack and the troubles of daily life. The most alarming portraits of crack users represent those who have begun using in the midst of either criminal or downward social trajectories in their lives, incorporating crack as an additional element in this experience.

Two characteristic ways of orienting to crack are represented in the imagery of "street predators" and "street victims." Criminality, among committed predators such as burglars (Cromwell, Olson, and Avary 1991; Wright and Decker 1994) and armed robbers (Jacobs 2000), provides the economic and spiritual means to do "high living." "Street predators" tend to live in cycles that alternate between crime and heavy partying, making money and then spending enormous amounts of it and their time on drugs, alcohol, and sex.

They disregard trouble before using crack and continue to do so through their orientation to crack as integral to "open-ended pursuit of illicit street action" (Jacobs 2000; see also Wright and Decker 1994). Rational calculations of the likelihood of arrest, for example, are ignored in favor of a commitment to being "hard" (Katz 1988). "Keeping the party going" focuses attention on grandiose action, often to the point of obliterating concern for sanctions or mundane, conventional responsibilities.[3] The users conjure within themselves an intoxicated compulsion to continue both crime and bingeing, the one fueling the other, while conventional life recedes from the foreground of experience.

More common are those users whose image is one that appears more pitiful than menacing.

To "street victims," like the "predators," the experiential horizons of crack use are often all-consuming. These more or less nonviolent, compulsive users come to focus much of their lives and activities on using crack, treating it as a means of psychological escape from acknowledging a general downward social and economic trajectory in life, while ignoring the troubles of victimization, stigmatization, and arrest that pervade their lives.

Their crack use itself does not so much "cause" a decline into desperation but represents a medium for exaggerating and compounding their existing problems. When many of America's most desperate, impoverished users begin, they are already entrenched in numerous types of trouble (Williams 1992; Inciardi, Lockwood, and Pottieger 1993; Bourgois 1995, 319; Murphy and Rosenbaum 1997), balancing precariously between worlds of a marginally "reputable" existence (Matza 1971) and a downward trajectory into abject hopelessness. When they begin using, crack becomes another thread woven into the dense fabric of psychological, social, and economic hardships pervading daily life. Crack use is part and parcel of all-encompassing trouble, on which users may turn their backs and say "let come what may."

"Stable Users"

A third type of user has gone virtually unnoticed. These users compartmentalize their crack use to a greater degree than the previous two, allowing it to pervade only certain areas of social life. A few researchers have described middle-income, middle-aged men with stable employment in the inner city and no commitment to crime as a way of life who use crack in order to develop more or less exploitative relationships with female users (Hamid 1992; Maher et al. 1996; Maher 1997).

For the men described, the seductions of crack use and women go hand in hand. Crack is not the defining concern itself but is interwoven with easy access to women, which, in itself, is not likely to lead to many of the troubles often associated with worlds of crack use.

Characteristically, these users begin to use in the midst of relatively stable social and economic trajectories and actively seek to maintain the centrality of conventional pursuits to their lives. As indicated in scattered reports, they are protected both by their social insulation from some of the everyday troubles of poverty and by their inclination to bound and distinguish their identities as crack users from their conventional lives. At the margins of predatory worlds, they may risk experiencing some of the same troubles as those more severely entrenched in street life, though these concerns do not appear especially prescient. Instead, the troubles intimated by researchers tend to be confined within the boundaries of the crack-related transactions: financial and romantic relational.

"Sneaky Dabblers"

Nonghetto residents who travel to the ghetto to buy crack also share the risks of physical proximity to criminals and addicts to some degree. However, they are markedly more successful at managing their housing, employment, and personal relationships. First, especially among upper-middle-class suburbanites and urbanites, they participate only fleetingly in predatory contexts, have the social and economic means to bound their use, and, largely because they live far from crack markets, remain invisible to people they relate to outside of crack worlds. Further, such users typically understand episodes of crack use as something of a "sneaky thrill" (Katz 1988, ch. 2) and try to keep their use "within limits." They cut back or discontinue when they see crack impinging on their conventional lives (Waldorf, Reinarman, and Murphy 1991; Reinarman et al. 1997).

We see from sparse accounts, usually journalistic, the seductive, sneaky appeal of crack use to middle-class and upper-class urban and suburban residents. They are oriented to conventional life; however, encounters with the "street" are central to their crack-using experience. The exotic thrill of participating in brief episodes of ghetto life gives emotional flavor to those who travel across class lines.

A Harvard economist at the time, Glen Loury explained about his own crack habit, "Nobody at the Kennedy School could have known about this other world, and nobody in that world . . . could have imagined the sophistication and power of the society of which I was a part" (Shatz 2002). He described "moving back and forth between these worlds" as "a rush." For users like this, the appeal of the societal balancing act, in which alternately experiencing the unfamiliar exoticism of the ghetto and bringing their street "wisdom" (Goffman 1963, 29) back to upper-class society, provides the distinctive thrill of using crack. The commitment in this mode of use is to flirt with the streets, while maintaining fidelity to the conventions of mainstream American social life.

"Campus Users"

To these four types I add a description of the social world of a new variant, the "campus users" I studied. The characterization is not meant to suggest that the type is strictly limited to campuses. More research into the diversity of crack use may well reveal a similar mode of using in other contexts. Alternatively, research on other college students may reveal their crack use to be organized differently. What is most important is not that these people were "college students" but that: They used crack in a social world comparatively quite safe from violence and financial or legal trouble; important spheres of their lives such as housing, work, leisure, and family were loosely coupled relative to other social worlds; they used crack only in highly ritualized ways; and they understood crack use as something that should be subordinate to conventional activities. The logic of this comparative analysis suggests that under similar circumstances—whether on campus or not—we should find other users who do not get into trouble.

Methods

All of the observation for this research was conducted in a Midwestern American college town with a population around 200,000.[4] Around the time of my research, the town was labeled one of the most crime-free and best cities in which to live and raise a family by national magazines like *Money* and *Parenting*.

After moving out of their dormitory, the primary participants moved into and around a 15-square block student neighborhood that I call "Midtown." In neither the town nor the Midtown neighborhood did I note media or other attention to drug problems, much less concern about crack.

I met the primary participants in this study in the fall of 1996. All were living on the same dormitory floor on the campus of a well-respected public university. Jon, Martin, and Mark were white, and Casey was Korean American. They all came from upper-middle-class families, their parents working in professional positions, some requiring graduate or professional degrees. Over the years I knew them, they all went to school and worked jobs at least part time, even as they used crack and other drugs. Before that year all had used drugs of some kind, including marijuana, hallucinogens, and narcotics, but only Jon had used crack. Jon had used crack throughout high school, traveling with suburban friends to buy it in the inner city of the adjacent large urban center.

Jon and Casey were out-of-state students and did not come to school with any friends. Mark and Martin had moved from other cities in the state. Mark was in his second year of college, having already lived on the floor the previous year, making new friends during that time. During the fall I met them, they were in the process of forming new friendship groups, largely organized by their common residence.

Between fall 1996 and fall 1997, I hung out with the group and a wider circle of dozens of friends and acquaintances on campus. During the fall of 1997, I asked if I could watch them whenever they smoked, which they permitted. I began to take field notes on their activities and interview them about their experiences with crack and family and social life generally. During the binges lasting several hours, I would sit outside their circle and take jottings and do homework alternately. By doing homework (sometimes only pretending to do homework), I was able to write without making them visibly uncomfortable.

I kept up taking notes for the duration of a one-semester fieldwork course and for a short time the following semester. In total my systematic observation continued for six months, although I had known and interacted with the users for a year prior to that time. My friendships with and observations of the group continued until I moved away from Midtown at the end of 1998. After that I kept speaking with Casey by phone for 2 years and have continued to speak with Jon.

Around the time I left Midtown, Mark had started to "lose control" of his drug use. He reportedly took out and squandered loans, lost his job, dropped out of school, and wrote bad checks. His mother arrived there and took him back to his hometown. Since that time I have been unable to locate him, though Jon had heard he relocated to another university in the same state. Casey transferred to a college in his home state at the beginning of 1999 and continued attending until I lost track of him in 2000. By May 2001 both Jon and Martin had graduated from the university with "B" average grades or better. Martin continued his studies toward a Ph.D. Jon has since worked in various service jobs while moving around the United States and then back to his hometown. In the past four years we have gotten together several times. He developed what he and I both considered to be a serious heroin problem during this time, though he is working to keep it under control through treatment. Now seven years since we first met, he tells me he continues to use rock occasionally without any detriment to his life that he can identify.

Sample-Size Considerations

By the end of my observation, I had seen at least 20 male and female college students smoking crack. Yet my data focus only on Jon, Martin, Casey, and Mark, except incidentally. A brief justification for the study of only four participants in this case is in order.

First, my reasons for focusing on these four: The primary participants in this study were the only ones who smoked crack regularly for very long. Many of the others only smoked once or only once every few months. While I can attest to their presence in the setting, I did not gather the data to provide a detailed analysis of the numerous occasional users.

The core group developed a particular culture, body of local knowledge, and set of practices together not shared to the same degree by the nonregular smokers. By focusing in detail over an extended period of time, I was able to gather varied and in-depth data on four persistent users. The methodological decision was to seek deep understanding of a few participants rather than thinner data on a larger sample. My goal was to use a portrait of these students' experience to contribute to a developing understanding of varieties of using crack.

Although data on four participants have only a suggestive quality, they can be nonetheless highly instructive. The sample and the data lend themselves to some purposes, not others. The logic is to use a "strategic research site," albeit one that I have "come upon serendipitously" (Merton 1987, 10–24, 11), to illustrate generalizable causal principles by analyzing variation between this and previously studied sites (Glaser and Straus 1967).[5] Using this method, the warrant is not that it characterizes a general phenomenon, such as "crack smoking on campus." Instead, the point is to discover new theory by looking at one group in depth with appreciation of local contexts and meanings and through comparison with other samples.

The sample gains particular value because it is unusual with respect to the current literature and is "hidden." There are no observational studies of noncompulsive, white, middle-class, or college-student crack users. Furthermore, it will be difficult to locate such users with typical fieldwork strategies. Previous fieldworkers have capitalized on desperate and poor users' inability to hide their use, seeking out such users by approaching them in the ghetto (e.g., Inciardi, Lockwood, and Pottieger 1993; Bourgois 1995) or through institutional means (e.g., Boyd and Mieczkowski 1990; Fullilove, Lown, and Fullilove 1992). Users with social resources are hard to find precisely because, as I argue here, they are better able to hide their use from anyone but their fellow users.

Features of Campus Life: Social-Organizational Dimensions

Two social-organizational features of social life among the campus users are brought into relief when compared with reports from other contexts. First, they used crack in a context that afforded them economic, social, and physical security. They had grown up with the typical economic, social,

and cultural rewards of upper-middle-class suburban life in America. Neither crime nor victimization had been especially relevant to their youthful cultures, nor did they become relevant to life on campus. There was no ghetto near Midtown. Street crime was not a visible feature of Midtown life.

Second, they were able to bound their lives as crack users from their other roles and relationships. As I describe below, they were also geographically removed from their families and experienced little pressure to show up at school regularly and sober. They successfully maintained the boundaries of their identities as crack users to such a degree that they could often even deceive certain friends and roommates about their use.

How they understood crack also helped them to maintain their conventional lives. First, they oriented to crack as a social object to be used in leisure rituals. Before ever using crack together they had used drugs only in similar groups, especially among circles of marijuana-smoking friends. Social and ritual drug use were widespread among students, while the kinds of paranoid and predatory relationships found in poor urban neighborhoods were completely absent.

Second, the perceptual horizons of crack use stopped at the edge of the circle of users. In contrast to users in other reports, the place of crack in these users' lives grew out of the context of developing friendships as a shared interest and social ritual (see Jackson-Jacobs 2001). Crack was, for them, something to be controlled and placed secondary to other concerns, namely their conventional relationships and activities. They overwhelmingly used it in their "spare time," organizing consumption not to interfere with conventional pursuits, not the other way around, as observed among hard-core users.

The Social Worlds of the Crack Users

The relationship between resources and trouble is not as simple as might be assumed. Campus life—not simply upper-middle-class status—at once provided social resources to these men and a locus for bounding identity as crack users, and it provided them with the understandings of crack, trouble, and social life that motivated them to actively maintain conventional identities. On the one hand, their conventional identities were central concerns, things to be managed vigilantly. They wanted to avoid being identified as crack users by their roommates, at school, at work, or by their families. On the other hand, related aspects of these same relationships served as resources, allowing them to hide their drug use. They were able to move residences often to manage their use, were able to miss school without drawing attention, were largely free from parental supervision, and almost never interacted with street criminals.

Residential Mobility

Like many students, the small group of crack users and their larger group of friends moved often, affording them control over their crack use. In the town there was a virtually uniform term for apartment leases. All Midtown landlords required one-year leases beginning and ending on August 15. Despite the one-year imposition on apartment leases, many of these men moved more often than once per year. They did this by subleasing apartments to and from conventional acquaintances and friends.

As many college students in areas like Midtown do, they organized groups of friends to rent large apartments. For the crack smokers the ease of mobility allowed them to shape their drug use. At times they moved in with roommates who did not use crack in order to cut back. At other times they moved in with other users in order to get high more often.

At one point Jon and Mark moved into an apartment together, where they frequently had company over to use various drugs. Attracted to the steady source of clientele, a cocaine dealer soon began spending several hours each day in the house. When Jon decided that he could not stand to live where a cocaine dealer spent so much time, he looked for another place to live. It was too crazy, he told me once; he had to get out of there.

Martin, who had been spending a lot of time at this house, also hoped to cut down on his use. The two moved into another house together. They had five women roommates who did not use crack but smoked marijuana from time to time and drank alcohol on weekends. Jon signed his lease over to their regular dealer, Paul, while Martin simply stopped paying rent at his old apartment.

Moving residences to get away from drugs was, compared to the residential troubles described in other studies of crack users, quite simple. As nice-looking white college students looking for housing in a student neighborhood, they did not face the type of discrimination frequently experienced by black renters, especially poor black renters (Massey and Denton 1993; Yinger 1995). Also, they had access to financial resources from parents, providing them with the cash to put down damage deposits and rent at any time. The combination of race, financial resources, and type of neighborhood is especially important in light of findings that African Americans are less likely to move out of neighborhoods that they describe as "undesirable" than are whites (South and Deanne 1993).

Furthermore, this type of movement would be very difficult and costly for many members of the middle-class, especially homeowners, who cannot move on a moment's notice. Additionally, moving around middle-class neighborhoods frequently, among middle-aged adults, would be suspicious and damaging to financial credit.

Residential mobility among the group provided some control of the crack-using experience. Migrating from apartment to apartment might have raised suspicion in typical suburban and city environments. And it is often unmanageable for many ghetto residents, especially unemployed women (Maher et al. 1996; Maher 1997). For the men I knew, though, moving in order to control crack use was seen as nothing more than typical migration through friendship circles, at the same time depending on student status and access to social networks.

Roommates

For several months during my observation, Martin lived with Casey and two other male roommates. A coworker of the two roommates, Ray, who coincidentally was also a crack user, slept on the couch without paying rent. The other two never used crack, although one of them, Lonnie, did use powder cocaine a few times. Martin and his three roommates signed a joint lease, which he defaulted on by moving out. When Martin moved out to live with Jon, he quit paying his share of the rent.

His roommates called his mother to complain. Lonnie told me, "I called Martin's mom and told her that he had money to spend on crack but not on rent. I said he was worthless and the product of worthless parents." Martin confirmed that his roommates had called his mother and been confrontational, but he did not know exactly what they said. He said, though, that he wished he hadn't told them about his crack use and that they were unfairly trying to use this against him. Especially important, Martin said, was the possibility that they would use this information against him when suing for unpaid rent—the only serious reference to legal trouble related to crack I heard in Midtown.

Having moved out of this house, Martin and Jon began to share a room in a house with five female college-student roommates. Although Martin and Jon were friends with their roommates, they did not at first tell any of the five that they smoked crack in their room. Two of them eventually did find out (see "Coming Out," below), but Jon and Martin continued to try to deceive them while high and to keep the others in the dark completely.

They kept their roommates from learning of their crack use by assigning a "door man." His job was specifically to watch out for roommates. The door man was instructed in how to deal with a knock.

Jon said on one occasion, "Hey, Martin, you be the door man, okay?"

"What do you want me to do?" Martin asked.

"Tell them we're naked."

This role was often crucial in delaying entry when a roommate did knock; during the delay everyone else had time to hide the paraphernalia.

Inciardi, Lockwood, and Pottieger (1993) also described the role of door man, but in the context of "crack houses." He was someone "who lets people in, checks for weapons, and watches for police" (Inciardi, Lockwood, and Pottieger 1993, 154). Looking at the door man as a security guard gives us a way to see what the users feel threatened by in a specific context. In inner-city "crack houses" violence and arrest are pressing threats from the outside world.

For the Midtown smokers, however, violence and arrest were not real concerns. Their environment posed little threat to their life or liberty.

Instead, they feared losing their social standing and relationships. Roommates' gazes, not predators' violence, were the most prescient sources of trouble. We see in these interactions not only the physical security of life on campus but the success these men had at bounding crack use from relationships: even among friends and close acquaintances, only a select group were let in on the secret.

Parents

All of the men claimed to keep close ties with their parents. The special problems of concealing crack use from them were primarily dealt with on the phone. I observed all of the central members speaking on the telephone with their parents on occasion. All of their parents lived in different cities, so they never feared a surprise visit.

Mark would almost never answer his phone when he was high on cocaine or crack. When it rang, he asked someone else to pick it up and ask who was calling. If no one would do this, he was so afraid it might be his mother and she would know he was on drugs that he allowed the phone to ring until the caller hung up. When someone did answer for him, even before the caller was announced, he would wave his arms, shake his head, and mouth the words, "I don't want to talk to my mom." Martin and Casey used similar strategies.

While the other three went to the extreme of not answering potential calls from parents, Jon said, "when they call, actually, I become instantly sober." He would talk to them, but, he continued, "I try to answer in short, direct statements and don't try to keep them on the phone for too long."

Their dealings with parents show how fearful these men could be in some situations. Although they hid their drugs from roommates, they would often "pass" as sober just minutes after smoking. Over the phone with their parents, though, they would not take this risk.

It seemed to me that, in fact, these men could speak just fine on the telephone when they were high on crack. The invasion of the family world into the crack circle inspired an immediate shame. These brief collisions of the worlds of parental supervision and campus freedom opened a window into a tension these men experienced in their drug lives. While they were, for the most part, free to use drugs in their campus life, they were at rare times compelled to bear the constraints of conventional family life.

Work

Being identified as a crack user at work poses some of the same problems as detection by parents and roommates: "It's the stigma of it. That people will do anything to get it," Jon explained. But, in addition to negative social esteem, he expected that the stigma generally associated with crack users would present practical concerns for his employer: "It's kind of implicit that I would be stealing to buy crack." Their strategies for avoiding roommates and parents were inapplicable to work. Hiding from employers may lead employees to be fired for missing work. Crack smokers cannot just say to their employers, as they might to their roommates or parents, "I can't deal with you right now."

Jon and Martin were able to maintain both their jobs and school activities despite using crack several times a month, often very soon before going to work. Jon explained that they would decide to "stop [using crack] at least three hours early for work, which might mean to finish as quickly as possible." Usually smoking together, they had a pact that they would smoke whatever was left well before going to work. Doing this was hazardous, though, as they were sometimes "coming down" and "strung out" at work; symptoms include diarrhea, talking nonsense, "fiending"[6] for another hit, minor hallucinations, and various other acute health problems. This, they believed, could result in a noticeable change from their sober behavior. On the few occasions that he was noticed, Jon claimed to be hung over or sick, more legitimate excuses for withdrawn and sickly behavior than claiming to be fiending for crack. The group orientation to maintaining conventional identities, in this case as "good employees," was a basis for concerted and individual efforts to bound their crack-using identity.

School

Whereas the main responsibility of conventional American adult worlds, besides family, is to maintain employment, for college students it is to go to school. This responsibility was fairly easy for my sample to maintain despite their crack use. All that these crack users really felt obligated to do was pass their courses in order to make progress toward graduation and to satisfy their parents.

Oftentimes after a night or more of heavy smoking, these men would miss class. And, unlike a full-time job, no one cared much. At worst they lost some credit for class participation. Furthermore, when they felt motivated, it was no problem for them to sit quietly through classes while under the influence of crack without being detected, especially in large lectures.

The schedule of "work" required of college students also made it easy for them to manage crack use and homework. Many college students spend days in a row binge drinking (Clapp, Shillington, and Segars 2000), playing video games, seeking out sex partners (Maticka-Tyndale, Herold, and Mewhinney 1998), or wasting time without doing homework. Like more conventionally idle students, these crack smokers could simply cram schoolwork in large doses during their days-long hiatuses from crack use (Vacha and McBride 1993).

Strangers

One window into the kind of trouble most relevant to their life on campus, their intense anxiety about being stigmatized, came when these users purchased legal paraphernalia at stores. In order to "cook up" crack from powder cocaine and smoke it, they had to buy certain household items before a binge. Although they interacted only with strangers in the store, they showed reluctance to buy the necessary items.

All the supplies needed to produce and smoke crack, other than the cocaine, are legal to buy: spoons, candles, baking soda, copper scouring pads, metal sockets, lighters, etc. Many of the crack smokers claimed that although legal, some items are known by the general public to be primarily used for crack. Baking soda and Chore-Boy brand scouring pads (specifically the copper ones that come in bright orange boxes), according to several of the smokers, are easily recognized by "most people" as crack paraphernalia. Jon spoke once of a convenience store in his hometown that "put a sign up next to the Chore Boy that said 'crack pipe screens,' because that's all people buy it for." Martin, Mark, and Casey also agreed that making crack screens "is the only reason people buy Chore-Boy."

Several times Jon gave money to one of the others and asked him to purchase the Chore-Boy. I pointed out that there was nothing illegal about it. "Yeah," Jon said and laughed one evening. "But I don't want people to see me buy it. I mean, cause they'll know what it's for."

Jake, another student who smoked rock with them on several occasions, recounted a story to me and to the group members that seemed to confirm their fears. Jake was buying Chore Boy and baking soda, he explained, when a woman behind him in line made a chilling statement. Out loud she said, "I know what that's for. You're going to smoke crack with that." The only negative consequence that came of this episode was that Jake was verbally "outed." Nonetheless, this was enough to mortify him and was accepted as a serious, noteworthy event in itself by the rest of the group. Being verbally identified was terrifying, regardless of any secondary consequences that could imaginably follow.

Jake's story illustrated both the product and the process of fear. His story confirmed to the group that their anxieties were well founded. His statement, and Jon's, show just how deeply these men feared being "outed," even by strangers. That this fear was felt so intensely illustrates how bounded their identities as crack users were and how strictly they wanted to maintain that boundary. Not only people who could "do something" about it (Erikson 1962) but people who might simply interpret their behavior as deviant were felt to seriously threaten their identities.

Neither Jon nor any of the others ever showed any apprehension about buying the cocaine. The transaction was always conducted in a private home with a well-known and trusted dealer. When buying the cocaine, because of the privacy of the transaction, they were confident that no one outside the cocaine community would know what they were doing. In buying the screen material, though, they

perceived that they were at risk of detection by people in the store. Although they couldn't be arrested, their concern was that some anonymous other in the community would recognize them as crack users.

Sources of Vulnerability and Trouble
Stigma

Visibility to others is a constituent part of the boundedness of crack use, or any potentially discrediting activity, in social life. In daily life impoverished users are highly visible. They buy and often use in public, and their poverty and heavy use lead them to appear identifiably as addicts (Jacobs 1996a), increasing the likelihood of arrest and stigmatization. Many of the ways in which Jon, Martin, Casey, and Mark remained "invisible" were due to features of campus life independent of conventionally defined social resources.

As college-student drug users, they were tied to networks of powder cocaine users. They bought cocaine from friends who were dealers involved in these networks. The purchases were made in private residences from otherwise law-abiding dealers who sold only to conventional users. Not only using but also purchasing crack remained tied to their friendships.

Jon, Martin, Casey, and Mark were intensely aware that their being discovered as crack users could lead to their being deeply stigmatized. Their understanding that using crack was a disreputable activity was treated as common sense; it was rarely spoken of and was acted on collectively without discussion. Furthermore, it was understood, crack was the most discreditable drug one could use. Even among people who were allowed to know about some of their drug use, crack was not revealed, or was revealed only after progressive disclosure of other drug use.

In Midtown arrest and violence were not relevant to using crack, at least from their perspective. Instead they feared, to varying degrees according to the particular relationship, becoming stigmatized, being found out, or losing conventional status as students, family members, or roommates. Unlike the most self-destructive users, these college students placed avoiding trouble at the forefront of their crack-using experience. Though they were only likely to experience one specific trouble, stigmatization, they focused their attention heavily on avoiding it.

Only once did I hear an open discussion about whether using crack was or was not a potentially discrediting activity (Goffman 1963). Martin asked Jon whether other people, referring to their peers, thought of crack as less respectable than other drugs. Jon seemed shocked that Martin even asked, nearly laughing, and said, "Yeah, man. Crack is like the worst thing you can do. It's not respected at all." This understanding is consistent with the finding that college students associate crack, unlike other drugs, specifically with ghetto users (Alden and Maggard 2000). The intensity of the potential stigma these users associated with crack, though, was rarely verbalized. Instead it was displayed in their various practices of hiding crack use and managing their identities as crack users.

Coming Out

Although all of these men felt intense pressure to hide their behavior, some came out and admitted their crack use to others at work or to roommates. Drug use was only admitted to others who, because they themselves used some form of drugs or indicated tolerance, seemed unlikely to confer negative esteem or otherwise sanction them. Furthermore, they admitted crack use only after first gauging responses to the admission of using less stigmatized drugs.

At Jon's work he had come out with several coworkers through "casual drug conversation." Despite his vigilant secrecy around some employees, and all the managers, Jon was willing to own up to his habit with certain individuals. He told me that "basically, the conversation always starts about marijuana smoking," which he explained was not a stigmatized behavior. "That leads to, 'have you ever tried this?' At first you don't admit it, but say 'I've got a friend who does it,' or 'I've seen people doing this.'" If the other went along and talked about a similar experience, Jon told the employee that he smoked crack. In this way he found several other users who then smoked crack with him.

When Jon and Martin lived with five non-crack-using women, they at first kept their use completely hidden. After some time, though, two of the roommates were let in on the secret, as explained to me by Martin: "Most of them suspect something, but usually just [that we use] coke. Elaine and Karen know. I don't think anyone else does. . . . We told Elaine. And Karen heard us talk about it when we were drunk." These roommates all used both marijuana and alcohol. Only after using marijuana and drinking together did Jon and Martin let their guard down. Additionally, they were satisfied to allow their roommates to believe they used cocaine, rather than crack, evidencing their belief that crack is the most discrediting drug of all.

Coming out about their crack use proceeded along a path of progressive disclosure about other drug use, either in "casual drug conversation" or mutual activity. The progression of disclosure from alcohol, to marijuana, sometimes to other drugs, and then to crack engenders the secrecy in which crack use was shrouded. Although knowledge of their crack use was off limits to some, these users felt that the negative esteem accorded crack varied among those they knew. Despite this, though, they felt that of any drug involvement to be revealed, crack was potentially the most discrediting. Unlike for other drugs, these users felt that there were no images or stereotypes of crack users except for those of addicted ghetto users involved in thievery or other crime. They only revealed crack use to those they believed were "wise" enough to look beyond such stereotypes.

Experiences of Trouble

None of the men became seriously involved in street crime or were criminally victimized in Midtown, except in the rare instances I describe below. They were not around nor did they interact with anyone who they thought might victimize them. Nor did they feel they were likely to be arrested. Unlike users described elsewhere, these men bought and used cocaine privately in the company of friends, They did not buy on street corners, in crack houses, or from strangers, especially likely ways to get caught.[7]

So far I have described how Jon, Martin, Casey, and Mark stayed out of trouble and, in fact, hardly ever thought of any trouble besides stigma. Yet these data offer two suggestive, but limited, contrasts within. First is Mark's experience of "losing control" of both his drug use and social life. Second are Jon and his hometown friends' descriptions of concerns and experiences using crack in an urban ghetto when Jon was not living in Midtown. Each shows that the troubles associated with crack both are shaped by and shape contexts of use.

After I left the field, Mark experienced what might be considered "serious" loss of social standing. After using for two years, he dropped out of school and lost his job. He inherited $3,000, took out a loan of the same size, and sold much of his property, spending all in under a year. Finally, after exhausting his supply of legal economic resources, he began writing bad checks. After a year out of school, his mother realized something was wrong and took him back home.

Mark did not commit serious crime but instead turned to a form of misdemeanor, low-level white-collar crime, one that in its illegality was identical to a legal counterpart behavior: writing bad checks. Mark's experience shows that this group was not immune from trouble or addiction. Nonetheless, in the midst of "losing control" of his use, Mark's troubles were shaped by his social standing. The most serious consequences turned out to be those that he had feared most. He was thought to be a "crack-head," was considered a failure in social life by his friends, and was "found out" by his mother. Mark's trouble coincided precisely, and was itself constituted by, a progressive failure to maintain a boundary between his crack use and his work, school, and family life. The process of getting into social trouble, Mark's case illustrates, is a process of a breakdown of the boundaries between crack use and conventional activities.

Jon and his high school friends' experience, using in urban slums before he moved to Midtown and on his trips home, points to the critical importance of the immediate contexts of use. They suffered many of the same troubles as the users who lived in these places. Back home, they told me, they would drive from their affluent suburban neighborhood to the most impoverished ghettos of the city to buy rock. Part of the lore of this circle of friends was the violent experiences they had when buying crack in the ghetto.

Jon or his friends reported that on separate occasions they were: punched in the face; dragged in an alley and choked in a robbery attempt; confronted with racial threats; arrested while buying on a public street; beaten by police; forced to make an undercover buy to avoid arrest; and pursued in a high-speed car chase by a dealer who thought they were buying with a fake twenty-dollar bill. Such stories were of exotic interest to the rest of the Midtown group who had no such experiences.

While Mark's case shows that troubles emerge when the boundaries between crack using and conventional identities break down, Jon's experience shows that troubles depend also on the environment of use. Although the drug, the user, and the user's understandings were held constant, Jon experienced serious trouble only in the dangerous context of the ghetto. Furthermore, he experienced the kinds of trouble endemic to interacting with the street economy. Though victimization and arrest were pressing concerns, becoming stigmatized, the fear on campus, was not relevant.[8]

Conclusion

The users Americans feared in the 1980s are precisely the ones documented in sociological field research: poor minority addicts from urban ghettos. Among these users, in these places, we see not just the effects of crack but, more specifically, the effects of crack on people who live in some of the most impoverished conditions in America. The "social pathologies" sociologists find in the ghetto, including violence, crime, and addiction, are largely due to the concentration of face-to-face interactions among those who experience the worst of America's structural inequalities (Wilson 1987; Massey and Denton 1993). These structurally distributed troubles infuse the lives of crack users, blurring the results of research on the effects of crack with the effects of marginality.

In the ghetto there are users who do not use compulsively (Ratner 1993, p. viii) and who may not get into serious trouble. Research has yet to document their lives. That no one has recognized or tried to account for nondestructive crack use should trouble sociologists, especially given the tremendous social costs associated with the societal reaction it has received. Professional sociology appears to have contributed to what Best calls the "Iron Quadrangle" that institutionalizes perspectives on social problems (1999, 63–69): mass media, activists, government, and experts (including, in this case, sociologists and anthropologists) all perceived some advantage in treating crack as universally devastating.

The experiences of the men I observed were only colored by a faint shadow of the stigma and other troubles that met the "street" users widely reported elsewhere. Nestled in the world of postadolescence and preadulthood, this group of crack smokers shared an experience of both social security and the resources to bound spheres of social life. These cushy, lax conditions made it possible to manage crack use alongside conventional pursuits.

The practical necessities and moral constraints placed on crack users have a great deal to do with whether and how they experience negative outcomes. Variation in these constraints across context, not simply conventionally defined class dimensions, should be a topic of sociological research. For those in urban slums it may be necessary to buy crack in public, thus risking arrest or the dreaded label "crack-head." Poor smokers, if they lose an apartment or a job, may not have the financial resources to regain a stable lifestyle. Middle-class adults are in constant contact with their families and their colleagues. If they are not careful about the hours or company they keep, their use may be discovered.

The causal arguments developed here also suggest lines of inquiry in the study of drug use, stigma, and trouble more generally. We can locate "hardness" and "softness" in particular social worlds and biographies, not only in particular kinds of drugs and personalities. Socially, economically, and physically insecure communities present endemic threats. Harder or softer contexts present variable future implications for the relationship between one trouble and potential future troubles in other spheres of social life. Where individuals and social groups cannot or do not keep typical, local problems from spreading across these boundaries, their suffering becomes intensified and diversified.

Moreover, different people understand their potentially discrediting activities, conventional life, and the prospects of trouble differently. Not only are some individuals more vulnerable, but they orient to threats differently. More or less troubled trajectories in life shape how people experience their criminal or deviant activities. For individuals successfully navigating conventional institutions, including university life, serious trouble is likely to be seen as both realistically avoidable and to be avoided. In social worlds permeated by serious suffering, in contrast, members appear more often to see trouble as unavoidable and to adopt perspectives that embrace or disregard it.

Acknowledgments

I benefited from several critical readings by Jack Katz; substantial guidance from Mitchell Duneier, Robert Emerson, Gail Kligman, Sally Jackson, Scott Jacobs, and Mel Pollner; and comments from Craig Reinarman, Jonathan Courtney, and reviewers at *TSQ*.

Notes

1. Nearly 20 years after crack rose to American national consciousness, there have yet to be depictions of users that do not horrify and outrage the reader. It is not the case, as might be suspected, that such users do not exist. In crack houses Ratner notes that "study researchers also encountered many individuals whose crack use was not compulsive" (1993, viii), though their words and images are absent from published reports. Waldorf, Reinarman, and Murphy (1991; see also Reinarman et al. 1997) recruited 53 middle-class crack users who did not suffer serious trouble for an interview study, though by interviewing alone they were not able to take readers into nondestructive worlds of crack use. By comparing the samples in ethnographic studies with the reported characteristics of users in the general population, it becomes clear that something is missing from the sociology of crack use. Most ethnographic studies suggest that crack is largely confined to older black users, usually male (Hamid 1992; Maher et al. 1996; Maher 1997; Furst et al. 1999). The suggestion is confirmed by national surveys. In 1998, the year I completed my observation, one in eight black males (12.5 percent) ages 30–49 reported having tried crack, in contrast to less than one in thirty (3.3 percent) white men of the same age group. However, contrary to popular imagery, crack use is very unpopular among *young* black males. Among men ages 18 to 22—the

sex and approximate age of my sample—only 1 percent of blacks but 4.4 percent of whites reported having used crack. For the older generation, black men are about four times as likely to have used crack. Among young males, whites are more than four times as likely to have used crack. (Numbers are based on my own analysis of data from the 1998 National Household Survey on Drug and Alcohol Abuse, United States Department of Health and Human Services [1998].)

2. See Best (1999) for a similar argument that the popular understandings developed by experts, government, media, and activists during moral panics deny systematic, and by implication sociologically explainable, causes of "random violence."

3. Although the data for his analysis generally predate the advent of crack, Katz (1988) describes more or less the same orientations to trouble and openness to any kind of "illicit action," including crime and drug use, defining serious offenders' experience of everyday life.

4. In order to protect confidentiality, potentially identifying details about the location, the participants, and some specific indications of my relationship to the research participants have been excluded or obscured (e.g., the exact local population, names, parents' exact occupations).

5. Other justifications for generalizing from case studies are entrenched in the logic of ethnography. One is that they may illustrate the impact of larger processes in concrete social interactions, represented by the "extended case method" (Burawoy 1991). Another is that some particular feature of social life can be seen most clearly in rare samples or events. The latter logic suggests that, for instance, general qualities of urban life are dramatized in the lives of sidewalk magazine vendors (Duneier 1999) or that a culture can be understood especially clearly as it copes with the sudden destruction of natural disaster (Erikson 1976).

6. "Fiending" is the feeling of intense craving for another hit. They describe it as almost overwhelming; all one can think about is another hit. Like low-status "fiends," the users would sometimes scour the carpet looking for a rock that might have fallen.

7. Only Jon had frequented a crack house in Midtown. He disliked the environment so much,

though, that he quickly stopped going. He had also tried to purchase on the street from homeless men, but each time bought a fake product (see Jackson-Jacobs 2001).

8. Though stigmatization could have conceivably resulted if anyone found out Jon was arrested, he did not think this was a real concern. His charges were misdemeanors, thus not likely to come to anyone's attention.

References

Alden, Helena, and Scott Maggard. 2000. "Perceptions of Social Class and Drug Use." Abstract of paper presented to the Southern Sociological Society. Indexed in Sociological Abstracts.

Anderson, Elijah. 1990. *Streetwise: Race, Class, and Change in an Urban Community.* Chicago: University of Chicago Press.

Becker, Howard. 1953. "Becoming a Marihuana User." *American Journal of Sociology* 59: 235–242.

———. 1955. "Marihuana Use and Social Control." *Social Problems* 3: 35–44.

———. 1963. *Outsiders.* Glencoe, IL: Free Press.

Best, Joel. 1999. *Random Violence: How We Talk about New Crimes and New Victims.* Berkeley and Los Angeles: University of California Press.

Bourgois, Philippe. 1995. *In Search of Respect: Selling Crack in el Barrio.* Cambridge, UK: Cambridge University Press.

Boyd, Carol, and Thomas Mieczkowski. 1990. "Drug Use, Health, Family and Social Support in 100 Drug Program In-Patients." *Addictive Behaviors* 15: 481–485.

Burawoy, Michael. 1991. *Ethnography Unbound: Power and Resistance in the Modern Metropolis.* Berkeley and Los Angeles: University of California Press.

Clapp, John, Audrey Shillington, and Lance Segars. 2000. "Deconstructing Contexts of Binge Drinking among College Students." *American Journal of Drug and Alcohol Abuse* 26: 139–154.

Coleman, James. 1978. "The Dynamics of Narcotic Abstinence: An Interactionist Approach." *The Sociological Quarterly* 19: 555–564.

Correctional Populations in the United States, 1997. 2000. Washington, DC: Department of Justice.

Cromwell, Paul, James Olson, and D'Aunn Wester Avary. 1991. *Breaking and Entering: An Ethnographic Analysis.* Newbury Park, CA: Sage.

Duneier, Mitchell. 1999. *Sidewalk*. New York: Farrar, Straus and Giroux.

Emerson, Robert, and Sheldon Messinger. 1977. "The Micro-politics of Trouble." *Social Problems* 25: 121–134.

Erikson, Kai. 1962. "Notes on the Sociology of Deviance." *Social Problems* 9: 307–314.

———. 1976. *Everything in Its Path: Destruction of Community in the Buffalo Creek Flood*. New York: Simon and Schuster.

Federal Sentencing Guidelines Manual 1995. 1995. Washington, DC: United States Sentencing Commission.

Fullilove, Mindy, E. Anne Lown, and Robert Fullilove. 1992. "Crack 'Hos and Skeezers: Traumatic Experiences of Women Crack Users." *Journal of Sex Research* 29: 275–287.

Furst, Terry, Bruce Johnson, Eloise Dunlap, and Richard Curlis. 1999. "The Stigmatized Image of the 'Crack Head': A Sociocultural Exploration of a Barrier to Cocaine Smoking among a Cohort of Youth in New York City." *Deviant Behavior* 20: 153–181.

Glaser, Barney, and Anselm Strauss. 1967. *The Discovery of Grounded Theory: Strategies for Qualitative Research*. New York: Aldine de Gruyter.

Goffman, Erving. 1963. *Stigma: Notes on the Management of Spoiled Identity*. New York: Simon and Schuster.

Goode, Erich, and Nachman Ben-Yehuda. 1994. *Moral Panics: The Social Construction of Deviance*. Cambridge, MA: Blackwell.

Grogger, Jeffrey, and Michael Willis. 2000. "The Emergence of Crack Cocaine and the Rise in Urban Crime Rates." *The Review of Economics and Statistics* 82: 519–529.

Hamid, Ansley. 1992. "Drugs and Patterns of Opportunity in the Inner City: Tie Case of Middle-Aged, Middle-Income Cocaine Smokers." In *Drugs, Crime, and Social Isolation: Barriers to Economic Opportunity,* edited by Adele Harrell and George Peterson, 209–240. Washington, DC: Urban Institute Press.

Inciardi, James, Ruth Horowitz, and Anne Pottieger. 1993. *Street Kids, Street Drugs, Street Crime: An Examination of Drug Use and Serious Delinquency in Miami*. Belmont, CA: Wadsworth Publishing Company.

Inciardi, James, Dorothy Lockwood, and Anne E. Pottieger. 1993. *Women and Crack-Cocaine*. New York: Macmillan Publishing Company.

Jackson-Jacobs, Curtis. 2001. "Refining Rock: Practical and Social Features of Self-Control among a Group of College-Student Crack Users." *Contemporary Drug Problems* 28: 597–624.

Jacobs, Bruce. 1996a. *Dealing Crack: The Social World of Streetcorner Selling*. Boston, MA: Northeastern University Press.

———. 1996b. "Crack Dealers and Restrictive Deterrence: Identifying Narcs." *Criminology* 34: 409–431.

———. 2000. *Robbing Drug Dealers: Violence beyond the Law*. New York: Aldine de Gruyter.

Jenkins, Philip. 1999. *Synthetic Panics: The Symbolic Politics of Designer Drugs*. New York: New York University Press.

Katz, Jack. 1988. *Seductions of Crime*. New York: Basic Books.

———. 1997. "Ethnography's Warrants." *Sociological Methods and Research* 25: 391–423.

Maher, Lisa. 1997. *Sexed Work: Gender, Race and Resistance in a Brooklyn Drug Market*. Cambridge, UK: Oxford University Press.

Maher, Lisa, Eloise Dunlap, Bruce Jacobs, and Ansley Hamid. 1996. "Gender, Power, and Alternative Living Arrangements in the Inner-City Crack Culture." *Journal of Research in Crime and Delinquency* 33: 181–205.

Massey, Douglas, and Nancy Denton. 1993. *American Apartheid: Segregation and the Making of the Underclass*. Cambridge, MA: Harvard University Press.

Maticka-Tyndale, Eleanor, Edward Herold, and Dawn Mewhinncy. 1998. "Casual Sex on Spring Break: Intentions and Behaviors of Canadian College Students." *Journal of Sex Research* 35: 254–264.

Matza, David. 1971. "Poverty and Disrepute." In *Contemporary Social Problems*, edited by Robert Merton and Robert Nisbet, 601–656. New York: Harcourt, Brace and Jovanovich.

Merton, Robert. 1987. "Three Fragments from a Sociologist's Notebooks: Establishing the Phenomenon, Specified Ignorance, and Strategic Research Materials." *Annual Review of Sociology* 13: 1–28.

Morgan, John, and Lynn Zimmer. "The Social Pharmacology of Smokeable Cocaine: Not All It's

Cracked Up to Be." In *Crack in America*, edited by Craig Reinarman and Harry Levine, 131–170. Berkeley and Los Angeles: University of California Press.

Murdoch, R. Owen. 1999. "Working and 'Drugging' in the City: Economics and Substance Use in a Sample of Working Addicts." *Substance: Use and Misuse* 34: 2115–2133.

Murphy, Sheigla, and Marsha Rosenbaum. "Two Women Who Used Cocaine Too Much: Class, Race, Gender, Crack, and Coke." In *Crack in America*, edited by Craig Reinarman and Harry Levine, 98–112. Berkeley and Los Angeles: University of California Press.

Musto, David. 1973. *The American Disease: Origins of Narcotic Control*. New Haven, CT: Yale University Press.

Ratner, Mitchell, ed. 1993. *Crack Pipe as Pimp: An Ethnographic Investigation of Sex-for-Crack Exchanges*. Lexington, MA: Lexington Books.

Ray, Marsh. 1964. "The Cycle of Abstinence and Relapse among Heroin Addicts." In *The Other Side: Perspectives on Deviance*, edited by Howard Becker, 163–177. New York: The Free Press.

Reagan, Ronald, and Nancy Reagan. 1989. "Address to the Nation on the Campaign against Drug Abuse [September 14, 1986]." In *Public Papers of the Presidents of the United States 1986*, 1178–1182. Washington, DC: United States Government Printing Office.

Reinarman, Craig, and Harry Levine. 1997a. "Crack in Context: America's Latest Demon Drug." In *Crack in America*, edited by Craig Reinarman and Harry Levine, 1–17. Berkeley and Los Angeles: University of California Press.

———. 1997b. "The Crack Attack: Politics and Media in the Crack Scare." In *Crack in America*, edited by Craig Reinarman and Harry Levine, 18–52. Berkeley and Los Angeles: University of California Press.

Reinarman, Craig, Dan Waldorf, Sheigla B. Murphy, and Harry G. Levine. 1997. "The Contingent Call of the Pipe: Bingeing and Addiction among Heavy Cocaine Smokers." In *Crack in America*, edited by Craig Reinarman and Harry Levine, 77–97. Berkeley and Los Angeles: University of California Press.

Shatz, Adam. 2002. "About Face," *New York Times Magazine*, January 20.

South, Scott, and Glenn Deanne. 1993. "Race and Residential Mobility: Individual Determinants and Structural Constraints." *Social Forces* 72: 147–167.

United States Department of Health and Human Services, Substance Abuse and Mental Health Services Administration, Office of Applied Studies. 1998. *National Household Survey on Drug Abuse*. Ann Arbor, MI: Inter-university Consortium for Political and Social Research. Distributed by Research Triangle Institute, Research Triangle Park, NC.

Vacha, Edward, and Michael McBride. 1993. "Cramming: A Barrier to Success, a Way to Beat the System or an Effective Learning Strategy." *College Student Journal* 27: 2–11.

Waldorf, Dan, Craig Reinarman, and Sheigla B. Murphy. 1991. *Cocaine Changes: The Experience of Using and Quitting*. Philadelphia: Temple University Press.

Williams, Terry. 1992. *Crackhouse: Notes from the End of the Line*. New York: Addison-Wesley.

Wilson, William Julius. 1987. *The Truly Disadvantaged: The Inner City, the Underclass, and Public Policy*. Chicago: University of Chicago Press.

Winick, Charles. 1961. "Physician Narcotic Addicts." *Social Problems* 9: 174–186.

Wright, Richard, and Scott Decker. 1994. *Burglars on the Job: Street Life and Residential Break-ins*. Boston, MA: Northeastern University Press.

Yinger, John. 1995. *Closed Doors, Opportunities Lost: The Continuing Costs of Housing Discrimination*. New York: Russell Sage Foundation.

Zinberg, Norman, 1984. *Drug, Set, and Setting: The Basis for Controlled Intoxicant Use*. New Haven, CT: Yale University Press.

For Discussion

1. Why has research uncovered so little about the use of crack cocaine among white, middle-class college students?
2. Can friendships between researchers and respondents help or hinder a study? Why?

12

Pain, Physical Dependence and Pseudoaddiction

Redefining Addiction for "Nice" People?

KIRSTEN BELL AND AMY SALMON

Prescription opioid misuse is a major problem in the United States and elsewhere. However, pain medication should be available to individuals experiencing major pain. Using a critical analysis, Kristin Bell and Amy Salmon use peer-reviewed literature written by and for physicians to explore discourse surrounding pain relief and pain management. They find that much of this discourse serves to further marginalize and stigmatize people identified as "addicts."

It's a fine line between pleasure and pain
You've done it once you can do it again
Whatever you done don't try to explain
It's a fine, fine line between pleasure and pain
—*Divinyls*

Introduction: Reframing Pain Management as a Human Right

Since the 1980s health care professionals have been aware of widespread shortfalls in the treatment of cancer and non-cancer pain (Brennan, Carr, and Cousins 2007; Elliott and Elliot 1992; Sun et al. 2007; Weissman, Gutman, and Dahl 1991). In an effort to respond to these deficiencies, and in light of emerging evidence that opioid analgesics provide an effective form of relief for certain types of intractable pain (Katz et al. 2007; Nicholson and Passik 2007; Portenoy 1996; WHO 1986), the past two decades have seen an increase in the medical use of opioids to treat both cancer and chronic pain (Højsted and Sjøgren 2007).

However, in spite of growing concern with standards of care for pain treatment and widespread support for improved pain control, the undertreatment of pain continues to be a serious public health issue (Bhamb et al. 2007; Brennan et al. 2007; Cheattle and Gallagher 2006; Fishman 2007; Frantsve and Kerns 2007; Gilson and Joranson 2002; Glajchen 2001; Green, Wheeler, and LaPorte 2003; Rich 2000). Three factors are generally emphasised in the academic and clinical literature as responsible for the continuing undertreatment of pain. First, many physicians lack *technical competence* in effective pain management because they are inadequately trained in this area (Brennan et al. 2007). Second, clinicians and researchers have identified *attitudinal barriers* which exist among practitioners, who are sometimes viewed as unduly concerned with the potential dangers of prescribing opiate medications (e.g., morphine, oxycodone, codeine and fentanyl) for pain—a fear termed "opiophobia" by some commentators

Reprinted from Kristen Bell and Amy Salmon, 2009, "Pain, Physical Dependence and Pseudoaddiction: Redefining Addiction for 'Nice' People?" in *International Journal of Drug Policy* 20: 170–178. Reprinted by permission of Elsevier via Copyright Clearance Center.

(Brennan et al. 2007; Elliott and Elliot 1992; Rich 2000; Sees and Clark 1993).

A third key barrier is the *criminal-legal and regulatory restrictions* governing physicians' abilities to prescribe opiate medications (Brennan et al. 2007; IASP/EFIC 2004). Specifically, the US-led "war on drugs," bolstered by international conventions and agencies concerned with the control of narcotic drugs, has created an environment in which access to opiate drugs of all types is lightly controlled and highly surveilled in their manufacture, import and circulation (Brewley-Taylor 2005). Consequently, physicians in many countries are required to register and receive an exemption to laws governing the traffic of narcotics by a government regulatory agency in order to prescribe opiate drugs, and records of physicians' prescriptions of these medications are closely and uniquely monitored by the state (Brennan et al. 2007). Indeed, there have been a number of highly publicised cases whereby physicians treating patients for pain (including terminally ill cancer patients) have been arrested and jailed for violating laws pertaining to the "appropriate" prescription of pain medications (see Brennan et al. 2007 for a discussion). These encroachments on physicians' abilities to prescribe opiates have been of considerable concern to many members of the profession (Fishman 2005a 2005b), and may be at least partially related to an increasing level of physician interest in rights-based discourses (see Fishman 2007).

Building on established standards of care for pain treatment and widespread support for improved pain control, a group of pain clinicians and researchers have recently begun to frame access to pain management through the lexicon of human rights (Brennan et al. 2007; Fishman 2007). A declaration by the International Association on the Study of Pain (IASP), the European Federation of IASP Chapters (EFIC), and the World Health Organization emphasises the legitimacy of pain as an urgent public health issue, its negative impact on quality of life, and the social and economic costs for individuals and societies when pain is undertreated. It also calls on government and international agencies to support the view that "the relief of pain should be a human right," and to improve access to pain relief in medical settings (IASP/EFIC 2004).

However, the pain management movement as a whole relies on a very rigid distinction between the "legitimate" use of "medication" to ease pain and the "illegitimate" use of "drugs" by "junkies" (see Schuster 1989). As criminologist Neil Boyd notes, in the current criminal-legal relevancies of the war on drugs, "the taking of *medication* is socially acceptable; the taking of *drugs* is not" (cited in Boyd 2004, 67; emphasis ours). Because opiate analgesics are both "useful medications" and "abusable drugs," "maintaining the line between the proper use and harmful misuse of [such] psychoactive substances requires careful discursive and practical management" (Keane 2008, 5).

In this paper, we explore the discursive and practical management of the line between the "proper" and "improper" use of pain medications. Accordingly, the key questions we focus on are: what is the relationship between pain management and addiction and how are physicians entreated to respond to it in practice? How are "addicts" constructed in pain management discourses and what implications does this have for their access to pain relief? To this end, we argue that recent efforts to frame access to opiate analgesics as a critical tool in optimising pain relief have rested on problematic assumptions about who has pain and who needs drugs, which explicitly reify the marginalisation of people labelled "drug addicts."

Methodology

In this paper, we critically examine the discourses on pain management and addiction exemplified in published academic and clinical literature. It is important to note at the outset that there is no unitary theoretical framework or methodology for critical discourse analysis (Antaki et al. 2003; McGregor 2003; van Dijk 1999). Rather, "Discourse analysis is best seen as an umbrella term covering a wide range of different approaches and traditions" (Martin and Stenner 2004, p. 399). Our approach draws on Michel Foucault's (1980, 1991, 1994 2002) theorisation of the conceptual terrains (or "discourses") through which knowledge is formed and produced. For Foucault, discourses are fundamentally linked to the exercise of power: discourse is both constituted by and ensures the reproduction of social systems through forms of selection, exclusion and domination which are normalised and naturalised in language (Hook 2001; Young 1981). Hence, we have chosen to examine discourses on pain management and addiction through micro-level texts, linking them with macro-level discursive practices. Following Acevedo (2007), it is not our intention to prove or disprove the veracity of discourses regarding pain management and addiction produced in these texts. Instead our interest lies in determining how these discourses actually create, define or construct "addiction" and, by implication, "addicts."

Key literature for our analysis was found through inputting the word "addiction" into the search engines of highly regarded pain management journals, including: the *Journal of Pain and Symptom Management,* the *Clinical Journal of Pain,* the *Journal of Pain,* the *European Journal of Pain, Pain Medicine* and *Pain.* Additional references were found through citation chasing. While recognising that a variety of healthcare professionals are involved in pain management, and a variety of texts would lend themselves to a critical discourse analysis on this topic, we have chosen to focus on published, peer-reviewed literature written by and for physicians, as it is physicians who are generally perceived to have primary responsibility for mediating patients' access to prescription pain medications (see IASP/EFIC 2004).

An Addict by Any Other Name: De-linking Dependence and Addiction

One of the salient challenges identified in the literature on overcoming opiophobia among clinicians and ensuring improved access to pharmacological treatment for pain has been the perceived need to separate clinically and discursively the spectre of "addiction" from the "natural" consequences of "proper" use of opioid medications by "legitimate" patients. To illustrate, specialists in pain medicine emphasise "the important difference between the *natural physiological dependence* that develops to opioid analgesics and the *pathological psychological dependence* that characterises addiction" (Rich 2000, 64; emphasis ours; see also Adams et al. 2004; American Pain Society 2007; Cohen et al. 2002;

Heit 2001; Højsted and Sjøgren 2007; Kirsch et al. 2002; Nicholson and Passik 2007; Portenoy 1996; Savage 2002; Sees and Clark 1993). This distinction is underscored in the following statement by a former director of the National Institute on Drug Use: "The confusion between the use of *narcotics by street addicts* [and the use of opioid analgesics by people with chronic pain] influences the attitudes and behaviour of dispensing practitioners, patients, and their families, as well as government policy-makers who regulate the availability of these drags" (Rich 2000, 64; emphasis ours). In this respect, the behaviour of the "illegitimate" drug user or "street addict" is seen not only as conceptually and behaviourally separate from that of the "legitimate" (prescribed) drug user, but is, in fact, viewed as an impediment to achieving optimal pain management of "real" pain patients.

To achieve this distinction between the deserving pain patient and the undeserving addict, definitions of addiction in the field of pain management separate the physical and psychological components of the DSM-IV definitions of "substance use disorders" and "dependence" (see American Pain Society 2007). To further consolidate a conceptual separation between dependence and addiction, pain researchers have argued that while physical dependence does develop with the use of medically prescribed opioids, it is not generally accompanied by other features of substance "abuse." This has led to growing physician calls to replace the word "dependence" with "addiction" in the DSM-V, so that patients requiring pain medication will no longer be "made to suffer" because clinicians, misled by the DSM-IV, confuse their tolerance and withdrawal symptoms with addiction (O'Brien, Volkow, and Li 2006, 764). Implicit in this critique is the reality that an "addict" identity is a legitimate source of suffering which supersedes any other claim to "suffering" (such as chronic pain) an individual so identified might advance. By contrast, those with a physiological dependence risk suffering not by virtue of their biology, medical condition, or behaviour, but in being mistaken for an "addict." This suffering on the basis of a "spoiled identity" (Goffman 1962) is thus seen as illegitimate only when it is misattributed.

Physical Dependence and Chronic Pain: Deconstructing or Stigmatising Addiction?

The experiences of clinicians and researchers working in the pain management field would appear to pose a challenge to mainstream understandings of addiction, where compulsive efforts on the part of the individual to get high and avoid withdrawal are often deemed a critical and defining constituent. As Room (2003, 227) notes, "in thinking about heroin, the classic image of the 'monkey on the back,' the need for the drug arising out of the fear of going into withdrawal, has often been seen as all that needs to be known to understand addiction." However, instead of challenging the paradigm of addiction itself, the general tendency evident in the literature has been to merely pull apart the physiological and psychological components of this concept. In this way, not only does the hegemonic paradigm of addiction remain intact, but it also becomes a method of destigmatising pain patients in and through justifications for withholding or providing sub-optimal pain management to those labelled as "real addicts." For example, Gilson and Joranson (2002, p. S94) note, "misuse of terminology relating to pain and addiction has the potential to mislabel pain patients as 'addicts' and, thus, to interfere with their pain treatment." That an attribution of "addiction" may also interfere with the pain treatment of those so labelled is not of apparent concern.

Much of the discourse on access to pain relief explicitly restigmatises and marginalises addiction and "addicts." For example, Passik (2001, 360) asserts, "because 6–15% of the U.S. population abuses drugs, the history of pain management is marked by the undertreatment of the other 85–94% of the population." The implications of Passik's analysis are that the 6–15% of the population who "abuse" drugs must either have their pain adequately (if incidentally) controlled by the drugs they take, or, more likely, are not in a position to advance legitimate claims for access to medical treatment for pain because they "abuse" drugs. Indeed, US Senator Susan Collins has stated, "It is tragically ironic that, while our streets are awash with prescription medications, the undertreatment of pain in *legitimate* patients remains a national problem" (in Katz et al.

2007; emphasis ours). The outcome is clear: the bid to legitimise of the claims of one population to pain medication comes at the price of delegitimising and restigmatising another.

Although definitive evidence to support the claim is lacking, the hegemonic position in the literature is that chronic pain patients with a history of problematic substance use are at higher risk for addiction to opioid analgesics than other groups (Cohen et al. 2002; Michna et al. 2004; Nicholson and Passik 2007; Portenoy 1996; Weaver and Schnoll 2002). Nevertheless, a number of clinicians and researchers have argued that it is unnecessary and inhumane to exclude chronic pain patients with histories of addiction from receiving opioid medications (see Cohen et al. 2002; Dunbar and Katz 1996; Gilson and Joranson 2002; Passik 2001; Weaver and Schnoll 2002). As Passik (2001, 360) notes, "A blanket contraindication like this would represent nothing more than a blatant commitment to the undertreatment of these patients [with a history of addiction]."

However, most clinicians agree that *differential treatment* of current, former or "at risk" addicts is warranted, suggesting that these patients should be carefully monitored to ensure that addiction does not (re)occur as a consequence of treatment with opiates. Measures commonly suggested in this literature for surveilling opiate use include: requiring regular urine drug screens, increasing the frequency of office visits, providing only a very limited supply of medication at any one time, regular pill or patch counts, witnessed dosing (usually at a pharmacy or medical clinic), use of an opioid agreement, and adjuvant psychotherapy or required attendance at Alcoholics or Narcotics Anonymous (Cohen et al. 2002; Kirsh et al. 2002; Lipman 2005; Nicholson and Passik 2007; Passik 2001).

Pain, Addiction and Undertreatment: The Emergence of "Pseudoaddiction"

The need to separate out the "legitimate" pain patient from the "drug-seeking addict" becomes further apparent in the concept of "pseudoaddiction." According to the American Pain Society (2007):

> Pseudoaddiction is a term which has been used to describe patient behaviors that may occur when

pain is undertreated. Patients with unrelieved pain may become focused on obtaining medications, may "clock watch," and may otherwise seem inappropriately "drug seeking." Even such behaviors as illicit drug use and deception can occur in the patient's efforts to obtain relief. *Pseudoaddiction can be distinguished from true addiction in that the behaviors resolve when pain is effectively treated* (emphasis ours).

Weissman and Haddox (1989) first introduced the term pseudoaddiction to describe the behaviours of a 17-year-old man with acute leukaemia who began to exhibit progressively escalating pain behaviour and assertively requesting additional medication for its relief. Medical staff were unconvinced of his claims and suspected that he had become "addicted" to his pain medication; however, Weissman and Haddox (1989) argued that this patient manifested an "iatrogenic syndrome" caused by inadequate pain management, whereby a patient starts to develop abnormal behaviours that appear very similar to "idiopathic opioid psychological dependence." Although it is often expanded well beyond its original use (Weissman 1994), the concept of "pseudoaddiction" has been widely taken up in the pain management literature and has become a standard way of explaining "aberrant behaviours" which look like, but should not be interpreted as, "addiction" in the context of both chronic and cancer pain management (see American Pain Society 2007; Cohen et al. 2002; Elander, Lusher, Bevan, Telfer, and Burton 2004; Heit 2001; Kirsch et al. 2002; Nicholson and Passik 2007; Passik and Kirsch 2007; Passik et al. 2000; Savage 2002; Ziegler 2007).

Pseudoaddiction is a phenomenon that is difficult to empirically demonstrate (Nicholson and Passik 2007, 1003). Indeed, it can only be diagnosed ex post facto. In other words, the defining features of pseudoaddiction as an iatrogenic syndrome can only be recognised when pain is adequately relieved and the "pseudoaddictive" behaviours disappear. Thus, according to the American Pain Society (2007), "Addiction in the course of opioid therapy for pain can best be assessed after the pain has been brought under adequate control, though this is not always possible." Nicholson and Passik (2007, 1032) similarly note, "Adequate pain relief

eliminates the abnormal behaviour, and this differentiates pseudoaddiction from true addiction" (see also Heit 2001; Højsted and Sjøgren 2007; Savage 2002; Sees and Clark 1993; Weissman and Haddox 1989). The possibility of "pseudoaddiction" is seen to create a dilemma for the clinician, who must ask him or herself: "Is the observed behaviour due to inadequate pain control or is it a manifestation of addiction?" (Dunbar and Katz 1996, 268).

This creates a significant problem for physicians who need to make decisions about whether to prescribe opiate drugs for pain, because those decisions are typically made in the context of interactions with patients claiming to have *current*, *unrelieved* and *chronic* pain. The physician encountering such pain complaints faces a quandary: one can only determine whether a patient is an "addict" or a "pseudoaddict" if medication to relieve pain is provided and effective. However, medication is only to be provided (and thus can only have a chance to be effective) if the physician believes that the patient is not an addict, but a pseudoaddict. Consequently, when trying to decide whether a patient is an "addict" or a "pseudoaddict" (and therefore whether to provide medication or not), the clinician must discern the *intent* of the drug-seeking behaviours (Kirsch et al. 2002) and ascertain whether patients are being "truthful" about their subjective claims of pain (Passik and Kirsch 2007).

Clinicians' values and assumptions about who is likely to abuse pain medications inform decisions to treat or not treat a pain complaint. There is evidence of endemic undertreatment of pain in certain populations, such as sickle cell disease patients of African or Caribbean origin (see Elander, Lusher, Bevan, and Telfer 2003; Elander et al. 2004) and prisoners with cancer (Lin and Mathew 2005). Researchers in these contexts observe that undertreatment of pain in these populations occurs primarily due to prejudicial and racist stereotypes suggesting high levels of substance abuse amongst these groups. Work with HIV/AIDS patients (Passik et al. 2000; Kirsch et al. 2002) also demonstrates a heightened risk for undertreatment of pain in this population. This suggests that the label of "pseudoaddiction" may be more readily applied to pain patients who are white, middle class, and do not have a history of problematic substance use than to patients from less privileged backgrounds who have (or are believed to have) such a history.

To further complicate matters, although pain is largely assessed via subjective reports only, clinicians are often warned not to trust the patients' self-reports of pain. To illustrate, Passik and Kirsch (2007, 443) advise clinicians that "The self-deceiving addicted pain patient's self-report will not help the pain physician; they will inevitably tell a pseudoaddiction tale when queried about why they are out of their medication early." This advice crystallises the moral underpinnings of the concept of pseudoaddiction and the ways in which the clinician is set up as an arbiter of the moral order. In this context the clinician's goal is to assess whether the drug-seeking patient is experiencing "real" pain, or is craving "unauthorised pleasure" (Keane 2008, 5).

The problem of pleasure is also highlighted in discourses on Ritalin—which exhibit a number of intriguing parallels with opiate analgesics. According to Keane (2008, 5):

> The issue of pleasure is vital to this management [of the unstable identity of psychoactive drugs], as medical use of psychoactive drugs is justified because it does not produce euphoria or a high, but rather returns the subject to a state of normality . . . it is the unearned and artificially produced pleasure of the drug user that attracts intense social disapprobation. Therefore in the context of prescribing psychoactive medications to improve health, it is crucial that the corporeal, artificial and excessive pleasures of drug use do not contaminate the therapeutic project.

The desired state of normality that the "proper" use of Ritalin produces is that of a disciplined, self-regulating and *productive* child—in contrast to the hedonistic, undisciplined, irrational and pleasure-seeking speed user (Keane 2008). Although one might argue that seeking relief of pain is inherently a pleasurable-seeking aspiration, from a hegemonic standpoint, the "proper" use of opiate analgesics by "good" pain patients should similarly be guided by a desire to return to a state of normality that heightens productivity, rather than hedonistic impulse.

It is worth underscoring here that one of the central arguments for viewing pain management as a human right is the elaboration of the economic costs chronic pain entails—particularly in relation to worker productivity losses (see Brennan et al. 2007; IASP/EFIC 2004). Thus, access to pain relief often becomes explicitly tied to evidence of the pain patient's worth as a "productive citizen" (see Meekosha 1999; Meekosha and Dowse 1997; Meekosha and Jakubowicz 1996). For example, according to Sees and Clark (1993, 260), "the patient who is prescribed long-term opioids for pain control may be better able to fulfil major role obligations at work, school, or home than before the opioids were taken" (Sees and Clark 1993, 260). Indeed, in the case of S. K. detailed below, decisions to provide access to opioid medication appear to be tied to the fact that "S. K. worked hard and achieved recognition in his field. Opioid treatment of his pain allowed him to fulfil the responsibilities of his position in a public relations firm" (Cohen et al. 2002, p. S. 105).

Addiction as Aberrance: The Rebirth of an Old Trope

If clinicians are asked to be moral gatekeepers when it comes to differentiating between legitimate and illegitimate pain patients, they are also required to be legal gatekeepers. According to Rich (2000), physicians and state medical licensing boards have allowed themselves to be conscripted into the war on drugs. Indeed, physician checklists designed to distinguish "drug-seeking" behaviours stemming from undertreatment versus those stemming from an underlying addiction often hinge on distinctions that seem more appropriate to a legal than medical setting. To illustrate, the influential checklist provided in Table 12.1 was developed by Portenoy (1994), but has been reproduced, with minor variation many times since (e.g., Kirsch et al. 2002; Nicholson and Passik 2007).

Here, "behaviours less indicative of aberrancy" are equated with pseudoaddiction, and are to be seen as evidence that the patient is being undertreated for their pain. On the other side, "behaviours more indicative of aberrancy" are equated with addiction, and are seen as evidence that the

Table 12.1 Examples of Behaviours Indicative of Aberrancy.

Behaviours Less Indicative of Aberrancy	Behaviours More Indicative of Aberrancy
Drug hoarding during periods of reduced symptoms	Prescription forgery
Acquisition of similar drugs from other medical sources	Concurrent abuse of related illicit drugs
Aggressive complaining about the need for higher doses	Recurrent prescription losses
Unapproved use of the drug to treat other symptoms	Selling prescription drugs
Unsanctioned dose escalation one or two times	Multiple unsanctioned dose escalations
Reporting psychic effects not intended by the clinician	Stealing or borrowing another patient's drugs
Requesting specific drugs	Obtaining prescription drugs from non-medical sources

patient is seeking drugs for illegitimate purposes. The purpose—and consequence—of such checklists is to aid the clinician in it deciding who needs and deserves drugs for pain and who does not. A close reading of the criteria in Table 12.1 also reveals an increasing commitment to viewing "real" addiction as manifested through unsanctioned and illegal behaviours (see also Katz et al. 2007). Seen in this way, it becomes difficult for the clinician to see the "addict" as anything less than a criminal, while great effort is undertaken to ensure that the "pain patient" is viewed by the clinician as anything but an "addict."

An example of the application of such checklists to treatment decisions based on understandings of "aberrancy" which conflate addiction and unsanctioned and criminal behaviours can be found in Cohen and colleagues' (2002) case study documenting the case of "S. K.," a 49-year-old male advertising executive with insulin-dependent diabetes, lower back pain, diabetic neuropathy, and a distant history of problematic oral amphetamine, cocaine and alcohol use. After discussing the risks of addiction with S. K. and his spouse, his physician prescribed him long- and short-acting oxycodone, with the admonishment that a set number of pills were to be dispensed monthly and a warning that his prescription would not be refilled early if he consumed the medication more rapidly than prescribed. S. K. was subsequently found stealing prescription pads and tearfully explained, "I did not want to get high, I just needed more medicine and I thought Dr. Blank would get angry with me if I asked for more. I did a stupid thing" (Cohen et al. 2002, p. PS 100). However, his explanation that he

needed more medication to treat the pain and did not feel that he could legitimately ask for it was ultimately dismissed.

In the S. K. case study, the distinctions drawn between addiction and pseudoaddiction are not medical but legal. Specifically, it is the illegality of S. K.'s behaviours which made him an "addict" rather than a "pseudoaddict." This conflation of addiction with unsanctioned and criminal behaviours conflicts with emerging public policy responses which view addiction primarily as a health problem mediated by the social and economic conditions of people's lives (Small 2007; Fischer et al. 2005). Such responses have also become salient in clinical research on problematic substance use, with findings offering increased support for positions that people with addictions require treatment and support, not criminalisation and punishment (Drucker 2001; Grabowski et al. 2004; Guttinger et al. 2003; Miller et al. 2004; Shearer et al. 2003). In fact, calls for access to opiate substitution therapy as both a harm reduction and treatment measure are increasingly being framed as both a public health and human rights issue (see, for example, Canadian HIV/AIDS Legal Network 2007).

Asserting One Human Right and Negating Another? Human Rights Discourses on Pain and Their Implications for "Addicts"

Clearly, while calling for access to pain relief as a human right, many pain researchers and clinicians arguing for access to opioid analgesic treatment for "addicts" have asserted that the realisation these "rights" ought to occur only when patients are subjected to increased and considerable surveillance.

The extension of this human right to "addicts" therefore implicitly invokes discourses similar to those which would also argue for the withholding of these rights, such as: "addicts" are not to be trusted, "addicts" do not seek the right kind of treatment unless they are forced to by others, "addicts" use drugs for the "wrong" reasons, and "addicts" require discipline and surveillance from people in positions of authority "for their own good." In this way, the "addict" becomes separated discursively, clinically and administratively from the "pain patient," and the contradictions underwriting such rights-based discourses remain invisible: the claims of "addicts" are deemed illegitimate, requiring a punitive response, while the claims of the pain patient are lauded a major human rights concern requiring an urgent and compassionate response.

According to Brewley-Taylor (2005), such internal contradictions are a key feature of United Nations drug policy more broadly, as the UN's overarching position on human rights is at odds with the rigidly prohibitive ethos of the UN's drug control system and the well-established harms of this ethos—to both drug users and non-users. However, the key drug control organ, the International Narcotics Control Board (INCP), is careful to frame its prohibitionist position within the lexicon of human rights, stating:

> Protecting the wellbeing of the individual and society is the purpose of prohibiting *the non-medical use of drugs,* which is certainly not an attempt to limit human rights. ... The prevention of drug abuse problems by means of national and international control and demand reduction activities can be regarded as a basic human right of the individual and society. (in Brewley-Taylor 2005, 424; emphasis ours)

In this respect it mirrors almost word for word the arguments of pain management advocates.

Harm reduction advocates have stressed the benefits of a human rights approach to addressing drug use (see Canadian HIV/AIDS Legal Network 2007; Ezard 2001; Hathaway 2001; Hunt 2004; Miller 2001) in relation to the human rights abuses frequently suffered by people who use illicit drugs

(Barrett 2008; Barrett et al. 2008; Jürgens 2008) and the human right to use drugs (Hunt 2004; Van Ree 1999). However, the use of human rights discourses in pain management advocacy supports Keane's (2003, 227–228) comment that:

> While human rights are highly effective tools for argument in some contexts, it is not clear that their mobilisation in the field of drugs will be politically efficacious. In fact, they may work to reinforce a universal model of the "normal" sovereign individual that pathologises and marginalises drug users.

Citing Johnson, Keane (2003, 230) points out that rights often come in contradictory pairs. Thus, the "rights" of drug users invariably become pitted against the "rights" of other groups, such as the presumed "rights" of non-drug users to be protected from societal consequences of illicit drug use. This is precisely what occurs in moves to frame pain relief as a human right, as rights of "legitimate" pain patients are framed in binary opposition to rights of "drug-seeking addicts." Therein, the rights of the former formally preclude the rights of the latter.

Conclusions and Implications: Toward a New Understanding of the "Addict" in Pain

Our aim in this paper has been to illustrate the ways in which discourses on pain management and the right to pain relief implicitly serve to further stigmatise people labelled as "addicts." Current criminal-legal and regulatory sanctions surrounding the use of opioids have created an environment in which pain management clinicians and researchers are virtually *required* to frame their "good" pain patients in opposition to "street addicts"—and resulting discourses on pain management create a situation in which so-called "addicts" are demonised and made directly responsible for the "suffering" of people in pain. This framework is likely to undermine recognition of the pain issues that people labelled as "addicts" experience, because their pain is automatically delegitimised.

While the undertreatment of pain is a recognised issue amongst pain researchers, we argue that the concept of "pseudoaddiction" is problematic because it ultimately relies on a clinical judgment that attempts to separate out "bad" drug-seeking addicts from "good" undertreated pain patients in the face of behaviours that are *virtually indistinguishable*. Moreover, as we have shown, in this context, addiction becomes conflated with illegal behaviours—a view that has been highly contested in the substance use field. Thus, even when attempts are made to treat pain issues in people with a history of addiction, the overarching climate is one of suspicion, framed by the assumption that "addicts" are not to be trusted and require discipline and surveillance.

Clearly, assumptions about whose pain is legitimate are as much moral as clinical, and are impacted by judgments about the patient's value as a citizen and contributing member of society. The rhetoric of "productive citizenship" frames Cohen et al.'s (2002, p. S105) assertion that "Pain sufferers . . . live in social context in which they have responsibilities and privileges." However, many people labelled "addicts" live in social contexts where they are seen to have a responsibility to manage pain "legitimately," but are provided with none of the privileges or resources that enable them to fulfil this "responsibility." Ultimately, efforts to secure access to pain relief as a "human right" are necessary and urgent, as are efforts to advance social, political, and economic justice for the marginalised and the disenfranchised. However, if access to pain relief is to be a human right, it is a right that must, by definition, extend to all humans—including so-called "drug addicts."

Acknowledgments

We would like to thank Paul Cohen, Bernadette Pauly and the two anonymous UDP reviewers for their useful feedback on the manuscript. We would also like to acknowledge the role played by the VANDU (Vancouver Area Network of Drug Users) women's group in informing the ways we think about the issues explored in the paper.

References

Acevedo, B. 2007. "Creating the Cannabis User: A Post-structuralist Analysis of the Re-classification of Cannabis in the United Kingdom (2004–2005)." *International Journal of Drug Policy* 18 (3): 177–186.

Adams, L. L., R. J. Gatchel, R. C. Robinson, P. Polatin. N. Gajraj, M. Deschner, et al. 2004. "Development of a Self-report Screening Instrument for Assessing Potential Opioid Medication Misuse in Chronic Pain Patients." *Journal of Pain & Symptom Management* 27 (5): 440–159.

American Pain Society. 2007. *Definitions Related to the Use of Opioids for the Treatment of Pain.* Accessed January 21, 2008. http://www.ampainsoc.org/advocacy/opioids2.hlm

Antaki, C., M. G. Billig, D. Edwards, and J. A. Potter. 2003. "Discourse Analysis Means Doing Analysis: A Critique of Six Analytic Shortcomings." *Discourse Analysis Online* 1 (1).

Barrett. D. 2008. *"Unique in International Relations"? A Comparison of the International Narcotics Control Board and the UN Human Rights Treaty Bodies.* London: International Harm Reduction Association.

Barrett, D., R. Lines, R. Scheifer, R. Elliot, and D. Bewley-Taylor. 2008. *Recalibrating the Regime: The Need for a Human Rights–Based Approach to International Drug Policy.* London: Beckley Foundation Drug Policy Program and International Harm Reduction Association.

Bhamb, B., D. Brown, J. Hariharan, J. Anderson, S. Balousek, and M. F. Fleming. 2007. "Survey of Select Practice Behaviors by Primary Care Physicians on the Use of Opioids for Chronic Pain." *Journal of Pain* 8 (7): 573–582.

Boyd, S. 2004. *From Witches to Crack Moms: Women, Drug Law, and Policy.* Durham: Carolina Academic Press.

Brennan, F., D. B. Carr, and M. Cousins. 2007. "Pain Management: A Fundamental Human Right." *Anesthesia & Analgesia* 105 (1): 205–221.

Brewley-Taylor, D. R. 2005. "Emerging Contradictions Between the United Nations Drug Control System and the Core Values of the United Nations." *International Journal of Drug Policy* 16: 423–431.

Canadian and HIV/AIDS Legal Network. 2007. *Dependent on Rights: Assessing Treatment of Drug Dependence from a Human Rights Perspective.* Toronto: Canadian HIV/AIDS Legal Network.

Cheatle, M. D. and R. M. Gallagher. 2006. "Chronic Pain and Comorbid Mood and Substance Use Disorders: A Biopsychosocial Treatment Approach." *Current Psychiatry Reports* 8 (5): 371–376.

Cohen, M. J. M., S. Jasser, P. D. Herron, and C. G. Margolis. 2002. "Ethical Perspectives: Opioid Treatment of Chronic Pain in the Context of Addiction." *Clinical Journal of Pain* 18 (4): S99–S107.

Drucker, E. 2001. "Injectable Heroin Substitution Treatment for Opioid Dependency." *The Lancet* 358: 1385.

Dunbar, S. A. and N. P. Katz. 1996. "Chronic Opioid Therapy for Nonmalignant Pain in Patients with a History of Substance Abuse: A Report of 20 Cases." *Journal of Pain & Symptom Management* 11 (3): 163–171.

Elander, J., J. Lusher, D. Bevan, and P. Telfer. 2003. "Pain Management and Symptoms of Substance Dependence among Patients with Sickle Cell Disease." *Social Science & Medicine* 57: 1683–1696.

Elander, J., J. Lusher, D. Bevan, P. Telfer, and B. Burton. 2004. "Understanding the Causes of Problematic Pain Management in Sickle Cell Disease: Evidence That Pseudoaddiction Plays a More Important Role Than Genuine Analgesic Dependence." *Journal of Pain & Symptom Management* 27 (2): 156–169.

Elliott, T. E. and B. A. Elliot. 1992. "Physician Attitudes and Beliefs about Use of Morphine for Cancer Pain." *Journal of Pain and Symptom Management* 7 (3): 141–148.

Ezard, N. 2001. "Public Health, Human Rights and the Harm Reduction Paradigm: From Risk Reduction to Vulnerability Reduction." *The International Journal of Drug Policy* 12: 207–219.

Fishman, S. M. 2005a. "From Balanced Pain Care to Drug Trafficking: The Case of Dr. William Hurwitz and the DEA." *Pain Medicine* 6 (2): 162–164.

———. 2005b. "The Politics of Pain and Its Impact on Pain Medicine." *Pain Medicine* 6 (3): 199–200.

———. 2007. "Recognizing Pain Management as a Human Right: A First Step." *International Anesthesia Society* 105 (1): 8–9.

Fischer, B., J. Rehm, S. Brissette, S. Brochu, J. Bruneau, N. El-Guebaly, et al. 2005. "Illicit Opioid Use in Canada: Comparing Social, Health, and Drug Use Characteristics of Untreated Users in Five Cities (OPICAN study)." *Journal of Urban Health: Bulletin of the New York Academy of Medicine* 82: 250–266.

Foucault, M. 1980. *Power/Knowledge*. New York: Pantheon Books.

———. 1991. *The Order of Things*. New York: Vintage Books.

———. 1994. *The Birth of the Clinic*. New York: Vintage Books.

———. 2002. *The Archaeology of Knowledge*. New York: Routledge Books.

Frantsve, L. M. and R. D. Kerns. 2007. "Patient-Provider Interactions in the Management of Chronic Pain: Current Findings within the Context of Shared Medical Decision Making." *Pain Medicine* 8 (1): 25–35.

Gilson, A. M. and D. E. Joranson. 2002. "U.S. Policies Relevant to the Prescribing of Opioid Analgesics for the Treatment of Pain in Patients with Addictive Disease." *The Clinical Journal of Pain* 18: S91–S98.

Glajchen, M. 2001. "Chronic Pain: Treatment Barriers and Strategies for Clinical Practice." *Journal of the American Board of Family Practice* 14 (3): 211–218.

Goffman, E. 1962. *Stigma: Notes on a Spoiled Identity*. New Jersey: Prentice-Hall.

Grabowski, J., H. Rhoades, A. Stotts, K. Cowan, C. Kopecky, A. Dougherty, et al. 2004. "Agonist-like or Antagonist-like Treatment for Cocaine Dependence with Methadone for Heroin Dependence: Two Double-blind Randomized Clinical Trials." *Neuropsychopharmacology* 29: 969–981.

Green, C. R., J. R. Wheeler, and F. LaPorte. 2003. "Clinical Decision Making in Pain Management: Contributions of Physician and Patient Characteristics to Variations in Practice." *Journal of Pain* 4 (1): 29–39.

Guttinger, F., P. Gschwend, B. Schulte, J. Rehm, and A. Uchtenhagen. 2003. "Evaluating Long-Term Effects of Heroin-Assisted Treatment: The Results of a 6-Year Follow-up." *European Addiction Research* 9: 73–79.

Hathaway, A. D. 2001. "Shortcomings of Harm Reduction: Towards a Morally Invested Drug Reform Strategy." *The International Journal of Drug Policy* 12: 125–137.

Heit, H. A. 2001. "The Truth about Pain Management: The Difference between a Pain Patient and an Addicted Patient." *European Journal of Pain* 5 (Suppl. A): 27–29.

Højsted, J. and P. Sjøgren. 2007. "Addiction to Opioids in Chronic Pain Patients: A Literature Review." *European Journal of Pain* 11: 490–518.

Hook, D. 2001. "Discourse, Knowledge, Materiality, History: Foucault and Discourse Analysis." *Theory & Psychology* 11: 521–547.

IASP/EFIC. 2004. *Global Day against Pain: IASP & EFIC's Declaration Supporting the Relief of Pain Should Be a Human Right.* Geneva: International Association for the Study of Pain/European Federation of IASP Chapters.

Jürgens, R. 2008. *Nothing about Us without Us: Greater, Meaningful Involvement of People Who Use Illegal Drugs. A Public Health, Ethical, and Human Rights Imperative* (International edition). Toronto: Canadian HIV/AIDS Legal Network, International HIV/AIDS Alliance, Open Society Institute.

Katz, N. P., E. H. Adams, H. Chilcoat, R. D. Colucci, S. D. Comer, P. Goliber, et al. 2007. "Challenges in the Development of Prescription Opioid Abuse: Deterrent Formulations." *Clinical Journal of Pain* 23 (8): 648–660.

Keane, H. 2003. "Critiques of Harm Reduction, Morality and the Promise of Human Rights." *International Journal of Drug Policy* 14: 227–232.

Keane, H. 2008. "Pleasure and Discipline in the Uses of Ritalin." *International Journal of Drug Policy* 19 (5): 401–409.

Kirsch, K. L., L. A. Whilcomb, D. Donaghy, and S. D. Passik. 2002. "Abuse and Addiction Issues in Medically Ill Patients with Pain: Attempts at Clarification of Terms and Empirical Study." *Clinical Journal of Pain* 18: S52–S60.

Lin, J. T. and P. Mathew, P. 2005. "Cancer Pain Management in Prisons: A Survey of Primary Care Practitioners and Inmates." *Journal of Pain & Symptom Management* 29 (5): 466–473.

Lipman, A. G. 2005. "Pain as a Human Right: The 2004 Global Day against Pain." *Journal of Pain & Palliative Care Pharmacotherapy* 19 (3): 85–100.

Martin, A., and P. Stenner. 2004. "Talking about Drug Use: What Are We (and Our Participants) Doing in Qualitative Research?" *International Journal of Drug Policy* 15 (5): 395–405.

McGregor, S. L. T. 2003. "Critical Discourse Analysis: A Primer." *Kappa Omicron Nu Forum* 15 (1).

Meekosha, H. 1999. "Disability, Political Activism, and Identity Making: A Critical Feminist Perspective on the Rise of Disability Movements in Australia, the USA, and the UK." *Disability Studies Quarterly* 19: 4.

Meekosha, H., and L. Dowse. 1997. "Enabling Citizenship: Gender, Disability, and Citizenship." *Feminist Review* (Autumn): 49–72.

Meekosha, H. and A. Jakubowicz. 1996. "Disability, Participation, and Representation in Social Justice." In *Disability and the Dilemmas of Education and Justice*, edited by C. Christensen and F. Rizvi, 79–95. Buckingham: Open University Press.

Michna, E., E. L. Ross, W. L. Hynes, S. S. Nedeljkovic, S. Soumekh, D. Janfaza et al. 2004. "Predicting Aberrant Drug Behavior in Patients Treated for Chronic Pain: Importance of Abuse History." *Journal of Pain & Symptom Management* 28 (3): 250–258.

Miller, P. G. 2001. "A Critical Review of the Harm Minimization Philosophy in Australia." *Critical Public Health* 11 (2): 167–178.

Miller, C. L., M. T. Schechter, E. Wood, P. M. Spittal, K. Li, N. Laliberte, et al. 2004. "The Potential Health and Economic Impact of Implementing a Medical Prescribed Heroin Program among Canadian Injection Drug Users." *International Journal of Drug Policy* 15: 259–263.

Nicholson, B. and S. D. Passik. 2007. "Management of Chronic Noncancer Pain in the Primary Care Setting." *Southern Medical Journal* 100 (10): 1028–1036.

O'Brien, C. P., N. Volkow, and T.-K. Li. 2006. "What's in a Word? Addiction versus Dependence in DSM-V." *American Journal of Psychiatry* 163 (5): 764–765.

Passik, S. D. 2001. "Responding Rationally to Recent Reports of Abuse/Diversion of Oxycontin." *Journal of Pain & Symptom Management* 21 (5): 359–360.

Passik, S. D., K. L. Kirsh, M. V. McDonald, S. Ahn, S. M. Russak, L. Martin, et al. 2000. "A Pilot Survey of Aberrant Drug-Taking Attitudes and Behaviours in Samples of Cancer and AIDS Patients." *Journal of Pain and Symptom Management* 19 (4): 274–286.

Passik, S. D. and K. L. Kirsch, K. L. 2007. "Commentary on Jun and Reidenberg's 'Physician's Being Deceived': Aberrant Drug-Taking Behaviors: What Pain Physicians Can Know (or Should Know)." *Pain Medicine* 8 (5): 442–443.

Portenoy, R. K. 1994. "Opioid Therapy for Chronic Non-malignant Pain: Current Status." In *Progress* in *Pain Research and Management: Vol. 1. Pharma-cological Approaches to the Treatment of Chronic Pain: New Concepts and Critical Issues*, edited by H. L. Fields and J. C. Liebeskind, 247–287. Seattle: IASP Publications.

Portenoy, R. K. 1996. "Opioid Therapy for Chronic Nonmalignant Pain: A Review of the Critical Issues." *Journal of Pain & Symptom Management* 11 (4): 203–217.

Rich, B. A. 2000. "An Ethical Analysis of the Barriers to Effective Pain Management." *Cambridge Quarterly of Healthcare Ethics* 9: 54–70.

Room, R. 2003. "The Cultural Framing of Addiction." *Janus Head* 6 (2): 221–234.

Savage, S. R. 2002. "Assessment for Addiction in Pain-Treatment Settings." *The Clinical Journal of Pain* 18: S28–S38.

Schuster, C. R. 1989. "Does Treatment of Cancer Pain with Narcotics Produce Junkies?" In *Advances in Pain Research and Therapy*, edited by C. S. Hill Jr. and W. S. Fields. New York: Raven Press.

Sees, K. L., and H. W. Clark. 1993. "Opioid Use in the Treatment of Chronic Pain: Assessment of Addiction." *Journal of Pain & Symptom Management* 8 (5): 257–264.

Shearer, J., A. Wodak, Richard P. Mattick, I. Van Beek, and J. Lewis. 2003. "Pilot Randomized Double Blind Placebo-Controlled Study of Dexamphetamine for Cocaine Dependence." *Addiction* 98: 1127–1141.

Small, D. 2007. "Fools Rush in Where Angels Fear to Tread: Playing God with Vancouver's Supervised Injection Facility in the Political Borderland." *International Journal of Drug Policy* 18 (1): 18–26.

Sun, V. C.-Y., T. Borneman, B. Ferrell, B. Piper, M. Koczywas, and K. Choi. 2007. "Overcoming Barriers to Cancer Pain Management: An Institutional Change Model." *Journal of Pain and Symptom Management* 34 (4): 359–369.

Van Dijk, T. A. 1999. "Critical Discourse Analysis and Conversation Analysis." *Discourse & Society* 10 (4): 439–450.

Van Ree, E. 1999. "Drugs as a Human Right." *International Journal of Drug Policy* 10: 89–98.

Weaver, M. and S. Schnoll. 2002. "Abuse Liability in Opioid Therapy for Pain Treatment in Patients with an Addiction History." *Clinical Journal of Pain* 18: S61–S69.

Weissman, D. E. 1994. "Understanding Pseudoaddiction." *Journal of Pain & Symptom Management* 9 (2): 74.

Weissman, D. E., M. Gutman, and J. L. Dahl. 1991. "Physician Cancer Pain Education: A Report from the Wisconsin Cancer Pain Initiative." *Journal of Pain and Symptom Management* 6 (7): 445–448.

Weissman, D. E., and J. D. Haddox. 1989. "Opioid Pseudoaddiction: An Iatrogenic Syndrome." *Pain* 36: 363–366.

WHO. 1986. *Cancer Pain Relief*. Geneva: World Health Organization.

Young, R., ed. 1981. *Untying the Text: A Post-structural Anthology*. Boston, MA: Routledge & Kegan Paul.

Ziegler, S. J. 2007. "Pain, Patients and Prosecution: Who Is Deceiving Whom?" *Pain Medicine* 8 (5): 445–446.

For Discussion

1. What happens when regulations make it more difficult for people to access pain medication from physicians? What are the different kinds of responses available to individuals?

2. How might some physicians contribute to the problem of prescription opioid misuse in the United States? What about the role of the pharmaceutical industry?

13

"With Scenes of Blood and Pain"

Crime Control and the Punitive Imagination of the Meth Project

TRAVIS LINNEMANN, LAURA HANSON, AND L. SUSAN WILLIAMS

In this article, Travis Linnemann, Laura Hanson, and L. Susan Williams critically analyze images and text that have been used by a methamphetamine intervention program. The authors' main focus is on twenty-nine advertisements featured on the website of *The Meth Project*. The authors find that the ads portray images that are "sexualized, racialized and gendered caricatures of young meth users." Linnemann and colleagues also deconstruct the claim of a methamphetamine "epidemic" in the United States.

Introduction

Late in 2011, a public service advertisement (PSA) meant to warn young adults of the dangers of binge drinking, stirred considerable public contempt. Produced by the state of Pennsylvania's Liquor Control Board, the advertisement featured an image of a woman's tangled legs on a bathroom floor, underwear around her ankles and the caption "she didn't want to do it, but she couldn't say no" (Stebner 2011). Critics claimed the underlying warning—drink too much and be raped—placed the onus of sexual assault on victims, rather than the social conditions encouraging binge drinking and violence. Even though the Liquor Control Board defended the PSA and its broader anti-drinking campaign, it eventually relented to public pressure and removed it from circulation.

Reaching at least as far back as the ill-famed 1930s film *Reefer Madness*, "fear appeals" like Pennsylvania's are in no way new. Though well

worn, the distinct ideological and technological logics employed by the campaigns offer insight into the shape and direction of contemporary crime control and the constitution of victim, offender and other. The tactic, what we call *pedagogical policing* (Linnemann and Wall 2013), intends to deter, in fact, scare citizens into avoiding risky behaviours. Built on fear, sophisticated advertising techniques and free market rationalities, campaigns like Pennsylvania's mark an important intersection of late-modern consumer culture and crime control (Greer et al. 2007).

While some might see the disparate images featured in the campaign as perpetuating broad social inequalities, others view attempts to shame particular behaviours and stigmatize certain identities as perfectly sound and common sense acts of deterrence (see Kohm 2009). Despite ongoing contention and a rather large body of contradictory evidence (see Witte and Allen 2000), fear appeals remain

Reprinted from Travis Linnemann, Laura Hanson, and L. Susan Williams, 2013, "'With Scenes of Blood and Pain': Crime Control and the Punitive Imagination of the Meth Project," in *British Journal of Criminology* 53: 605–623, by permission of Oxford University Press.

popular among policy makers and the public alike, particularly in political climates favouring inexpensive, privatized public services (O'Malley and Palmer 1996). Oddly, however, advocates of these sorts of projects claim to reduce crime and champion the vulnerable, by imagining, producing and circulating markedly disparate images of crime and victimization. In the case of Pennsylvania's anti-drinking campaign, the advertisement seemed to promote victim blaming and in many ways make light of brutal images of gendered violence.

In order to advance the critique of this sort of project, we take aim at another pedagogical policing programme and the social anxieties surrounding the illicit drug methamphetamine (meth). Like Pennsylvania's campaign, the Montana Meth Project (MMP) and its later iteration The Meth Project (TMP) achieved notoriety because of the jarring tactics used to deter teen meth use. Characterizing itself as a "research-based marketing campaign that realistically and graphically communicates the risks of methamphetamine," TMP expands the fear-driven logics of *Reefer Madness* with graphic images of teen meth users as pimps and prostitutes, who prey on family, friends and strangers. By pairing shocking images with indifferent warnings like, "15 Bucks for Sex Isn't Normal. But on Meth It Is," the project advances a crude "see what happens if you use meth" causality (Linnemann and Wall 2013).

As such, we argue fear appeals like TMP's are problematic, not only because they prove only marginally effective, but also because they support disparate social imaginaries of crime and victimization. Flowing from and reinforcing broader class, race and gender insecurities, these structures of ideological penal policies and practices or "imaginary penalties" (see Carlen 2008a) become fixed and commonsense realities that inform policy and obscure alternatives for harm reduction and meaningful social change. Though critical of the campaign and the supposed "meth epidemic" it mobilized against, we in no way dismiss the grim realities of meth addiction. Rather, we take issue with the unequal social relations the programme and its materials emerge from and help reproduce. We argue, TMP's advertisements are deeply sexualized, racialized and gendered caricatures of young

meth users, organized around a system of binary representation (see Young 1996), pitting the sexual vulnerabilities of young women against the violent predation of young men.

Importantly, then, in addition to helping to fashion "imaginary" social relations, we contend TMP structures a particular way of seeing the world or *visuality* (see Mirzoeff 2006). We contend this particular way of seeing agitates white middle-class social anxieties, through a "meth epidemic" unfairly imagined as uniquely "white" and "rural." Following Michelle Brown (2009), we see the visuality conjured by TMP's punitive imagination, as one of the many ways everyday actors participate in punishment from the privileged position of spectator. Largely removed from the interworkings of criminal justice, Brown (2009) argues, "penal spectators" access punishment through cultural practices that "although largely unacknowledged, massively extends throughout our social foundations" (Brown 2009, 4). Eliciting penal spectatorship and following self-justifying drug war discourses, we argue TMP battles an epidemic it helps to create and sustain. In doing so, the project fashions a particular vision of meth-induced criminality and vulnerability that obscures alternate avenues to harm reduction and the more pervasive ills of the neo-liberal order.

An Imaginary Epidemic

The war on drugs is the heart of contemporary criminal justice and the American carceral landscape. Yet, despite the drug war's apparent intractability, critics hardly agree on the causes of its rise (Lynch 2012). Some argue that, by playing upon fear of crime and mobilizing the political power of crime victims, the state achieves its broader goals of ordering territories and populations and effectively governs "through" its wars on crime, drugs and terror (see Simon 2007). Others view harsh drug laws as instrumental and effective means for excluding and managing the inner-city poor in the post-welfare state (see Wacquant 2009). From a slightly different vantage still, it is argued that so-called "colour blind" drug laws offer a circuitous, yet no less effective, method of ensuring America's racial-caste system, thus making the war on drugs part and parcel of a "New Jim Crow" (see Alexander 2010). For Dimitri Bogazianos (2012), crack cocaine—a drug distinctly linked to inner-city ghettos and people of colour—is the "lethal core" of the entire drug war project and the engine of profound transformations in social relations and everyday life. He argues that, because of the spectacular rise in lethal violence associated with crack, the drug continues to shape perceptions of urban life, even as violence drops and the "crack epidemic" all but disappears. As an enduring and vital area of social experience, crack helps fashion an overlapping system of values or "criminological structures of feeling"[1] favouring criminal justice over social justice and helps to explain the collective impulse to "punish away" the significant moral and material changes witnessed with the rise of mass imprisonment (Bogazianos 2012, 8).

Focusing its methamphetamine intervention efforts first in Montana, we see TMP helping to fashion distinct structures of feeling (Williams 1977) in an oft-overlooked corner of the war on drugs—the supposed "white" and "rural" landscapes of America. Describing how in the wider cultural imagination urban spaces have long animated the poor as "contemptible yet threatening figures of debased humanity," John Hartigan provocatively warns that "monsters and cities go hand in hand" (Hartigan 2005, 33–5). If true, then, in many ways, Hartigan helps imagine the rural as a tedious refuge from the monstrous danger of the city. This uncomplicated relationship between the country and the city helps to explain the public and governmental interest in methamphetamine, for, in it, and perhaps for the first time in the era of mass imprisonment, the rural United States has a plausible danger, threat and boogeyman (Linnemann 2013). Given the remarkably effective criminalization of black and brown bodies and the inner-city "ghettos" they are said to inhabit, it seems that oft-neglected corners of rural America offer ripe territories to expand carceral landscapes. Just as capital must develop new markets to ensure continued accumulation, the American carceral state—in many ways a capitalist enterprise—must locate new spaces (markets) and bodies (materials) to ensure its survival. Thus, we argue this nascent corner of the drug war provides an instance in which drug-control practices do not fall *solely* on the inner-city poor and racial minorities (Simon 2007, 18–20). Entwined with the public's punitive desire to look, the media-savvy techniques employed by the project also provide a tremendous example of neoliberal crime governance "from below" or from other than the sovereign "from above" and a method of policing social boundaries, by means other than outright repression (see Lea and Stenson 2007). Viewing TMP as an important site of cultural production, our critique highlights the faintly shifting nature of the American carceral state its war on drugs. Indeed, as Jock Young argues, the state and its endless wars are bolstered by, if not reliant on, taken-for-granted "facts" advanced by projects like the TMP. Young argues that:

> The war against crime, drugs, terrorism, demands facts, numbers, quantitative incomes and outcomes it does not demand debates as to the very nature of these battles, it does not want to question definition, rather it wants "hard" facts and "concrete" evidence. (Young 2011, 22)

Therefore, before turning to our main critique, it is important to consider, first, the "hard facts" and "concrete evidence" regarding methamphetamine in the United States, advanced by The Meth Project Foundation. According to the website, billionaire Thomas M. Siebel established the foundation in 2005, "in response to the growing Meth epidemic in the U.S." This is an important point of contention, as the punitive logics of anti-meth projects discussed in this paper rest on catastrophic visions of epidemic and emergency. As we will argue, while it is important to take the sufferings of drug use seriously, to describe meth in terms of a "growing epidemic" is problematic at best (Weisheit and White 2009, 10).

Once described as "the worst drug ever to hit America" by drug czar Barry McCaffery, methamphetamine is remarkably resilient (*The Economist* 1999). Not unlike Appalachian "moonshiners" and more recently "Hillbilly Heroin" users (see Tunnell 2004), meth is distinctively one of the only illicit substances commonly associated with poor rural whites. Dubbed "white man's crack," "poor man's cocaine" and "redneck coke," the drug appears in popular culture as the "white trash" equivalent to crack cocaine (Gillespie 2005). Consequently, poor whites in small rural towns, said to be the main producers and consumers of meth, are seen in many of the same ways as the inner-city minorities blamed for the so-called crack epidemic. Also like crack, the anxieties swirling around meth seem to outpace its actual use. At the time of this writing, the state's own estimates placed the number of meth users at around 439,000 or about 0.2 percent of the US population—estimates that have not exceeded 0.3 percent for the last decade (SAMHSA 2012). Despite being used by a very small share of the population, news media accounts still portray the issue as "a matter of life and meth" with unsubstantiated claims that "an estimated 12 million Americans have tried meth and 1.5 million are regular users" (Hendricks 2012, 1).

As the largest and highest-profile anti-meth group, TMP is an important site of cultural production, where the popular understandings of meth's social harms are imagined, "pronounced" (see Loader 1997) and circulated. In this regard, it is important to take an inventory of TMP's claims concerning methamphetamine and its alleged social and corporeal corrosiveness. So, for instance, on its website, TMP defines "Meth in the U.S." with a number of dubious claims.[2] According to the website:

> According to the U.S. Department of Justice, methamphetamine is one of the greatest drug threats to the nation. In 2011, the agency reported Meth is at its highest levels of availability, purity, and lowest cost since 2005 due to increased supply from Mexico and growing rates of small-scale domestic production.
>
> Methamphetamine's effects cost the U.S. between $16.2 and $48.3 billion per year. Meth is one of the most addictive substances known and its use imposes a significant disproportionate burden on individuals and society in money spent on treatment, healthcare, and foster care services, as well as the costs of crime and lost productivity.

Though meth appears in the DOJ's "drug threat assessment," the ambiguous problem statement offers little context as to what actually constitutes "one of the greatest drug threats to the nation."

Similarly, TMP claims the drug has not been more available, pure or cheap since 2005—a familiar warning made of other drugs like marijuana. We can only assume the statement is referring to a DEA programme called STRIDE (System to Retrieve Information from Drug Evidence) that collects this sort of data. While STRIDE might support this claim, TMP fails to include the important disclaimer that the estimates are "not a representative sample of drugs available in the United States" (DOJ 2011). Omission of this important caveat bolsters the project's assertions and helps guide public imagination along TMP's preferred path of emergency and epidemic. The statement also makes the offhand claim that meth is "one of the most addictive substances known" and, again, the state's own data offer a different picture. For instance, roughly 3 percent of those who have "ever tried" meth reported continued use in the last 30 days, while rates for marijuana and cocaine are much higher, at 34.7 and 9.5 percent, respectively (SAMSHA 2012). If methamphetamine were "one of the most addictive substances known," it would certainly lead to many more instances of continued use. Lastly, the problem statement cites a recent RAND study estimating the "economic costs of meth use in the US" (Nicosia et al. 2009). Gathering data from seven separate domains the study—actually "sponsored" by TMP and the National Institute on Drug Abuse—arrives at cavernous estimates ranging from 16.2 on the low end to 48.3 billion dollars per year on the high end (Nicosia et al. 2009). Indeed, for many uncritical readers, imprecise estimates of "billions" of dollars lost to meth use may be reason enough to support authoritarian drug-control practices.

To be clear, according to the National Survey on Drug Use and Health (NSDUH), the estimated number of regular meth users (0.2 percent) is particularly small, especially compared to cocaine (1.4 percent), prescription drugs (6.1 percent) and marijuana (18.1 percent). And, while we do not suggest these data are infallible, they do offer compelling contradictions to descriptions of meth as "one of the greatest drug threats to the nation." However, like the imprecise estimates of the "monetary costs" of meth abuse, TMP's forceful presentation helps animate meth's dangers—even if imaginary.

From inception, TMP has been championed by firebrands like former drug czar John Walters, who called it an "extraordinary example of the results we can achieve when we combine the power of advertising with the dedication and expertise of the leaders of this community" (The Meth Project, 2007). However, like other scare and fear appeal campaigns, independent empirical evaluations have directly challenged the programme's claims of effectiveness (see Anderson 2010). In fact, at least one study found evidence that the advertisements may actually increase the acceptability of meth use and decrease the perceived dangers of using drugs among teens (Erceg-Hurn 2008). The stubborn faith in the campaign, despite mounting contradictory evidence, reminds of the much-maligned Drug Abuse Resistance and Education (D.A.R.E.) programme, founded by the equally maligned LAPD Chief, Daryl Gates. Now entering its 30th year, D.A.R.E. carries on in stubborn indifference to considerable evidence to its ineffectual and perhaps harmful outcomes (Lilienfeld 2007). Like D.A.R.E., TMP's entire *raison d'être* rests on a collection of imprecise assumptions about meth use and a misplaced faith in pedagogical policing. Yet, we are not so much concerned with refuting the project's claims of effectiveness; rather we are concerned with how the images themselves may perpetuate or exacerbate long-standing social inequalities. With graphic fear appeals as its centrepiece, the organization advances a very narrow and, as we argue, imaginary view of the causes and consequences of meth use and the lives entangled with addiction. Despite all this, TMP's national profile grows, with at least eight states having established their own "Meth Projects."

"With Scenes of Blood and Pain": Methamphetamine and the Visualities of Disgust

As Jeff Ferrell (2012) recently remarked, "our whole damn world is awash in images, and images of images, and more so every day." Circulating in the cultural ether, images like those here help structure and are in fact inseparable from "the real" circumstances of crime and punishment (Greer et al. 2008). Indeed, as Manderson (1995) has written, many of the everyday realities of drug use and the drug war are meted out at the level of image and symbol:

> The images which we associate with drug use have taken on a profound emotional significance partly because of the kinds of things they have come to symbolize and partly because this symbolism is fraught with ambiguity. The "war against drugs" is a civil war, fought out on the level of the symbol. At stake is the social meaning to be attributed to images as tangible as the needle, as incorporeal as consciousness and as all-consuming as sex. (Manderson 1995, 800)

Like Manderson (1995), we recognize how TMP's "gritty" advertisements help fashion a visceral emotionality "as tangible as the needle." Fostering a keen sense of the visual, attuned to meaning, affect, situation and the power of the image, allows our analysis and critique to take aim at the very point at which "commons sense knowledge" is constructed, negotiated and transgressed (see Hayward and Presdee 2010). Not simply a staid representation of a particular point in time and space, the social force of the image is a product of the viewer's subjectivity and broader ideological structures of the culture from which it emerged (Schonberg and Bourgois 2002). Therefore, rather than viewing TMP's advertisements and their particular aesthetic as an approximation or artistic interpretation of social life, we view the advertisement as dynamic, forceful social productions and attend to what they do in the real (Carney 2010).

Shortly after the MMP's launch, the editorial "With Scenes of Blood and Pain, Ads Battle Methamphetamine in Montana" appeared in the *New York Times* (Zernike 2006). The article, describing how MMP advertisements had "blanketed" radio, television, newspapers and billboards to become the "biggest advertiser in the state," quoted Siebel touting "state officials want to make it a national template for halting a problem that has cursed mainly largely poor rural states" (Zernike 2006). In addition to reproducing meth's "largely poor and rural" trope, the piece highlighted the "blood and pain" that would soon make MMP famous. As one of the teens interviewed for the piece described, the advertisements are "like a car wreck, you can't take your eyes off it. . . . It's totally gross, totally graphic, you know it's going to be bad, but all you can do is watch it go down" (Zernike 2006). This observation is crucial, as it reveals the project's foundational logic—to shock, scare and disgust young viewers.

To be sure, these "totally gross, totally graphic" images of meth-fuelled crime and victimization are no accident. From its earliest days, prominent directors and cinematographers responsible for the acclaimed films *American History X*, *Black Swan*, *21 Grams* and *The Dark Knight* trilogy have each taken lead roles in the project.[3] Like their associated films, these artists deliver a dark, "hard hitting," "gritty," "unflinching" aesthetic, that, according to Siebel, is intended to "stigmatize use, making meth use socially unacceptable" (Siebel and Mange 2009). Like Pennsylvania's anti-drinking advertisement, to "stigmatize use," TMP has imbued familiar "Reefer Madness" fear appeals, with a grotesque and often sexually sadistic aesthetic. Of course, the advertisements could take any form but, by taking this one, they fashion a particular visuality ordering "how we see, how we are able, allowed, or made to see" the "realities" of meth use (Foster 1998, quoted in Mirzoeff 2006, 55).

While clearly crafting a narrow vision of methamphetamine, to resonate with public consciousness beyond knee-jerk visceral response, the advertisements count on a public eager to engage with scenes of crime, victimization and punishment from a distance—as spectator. Whether prison tour or PSA campaign, penal spectatorship allows the public to witness and consume the pain of others, without direct participation in the visceral realities of crime, victimization and punishment. This is an important consideration, as the project's images forcefully impose the underlying pedagogical mantra, "see what happens if you do meth," in all of its bloody and horrifying detail. Accessing, contemplating and judging the lives of others through highly stylized advertisements, the project harnesses the "peculiar energy" bound up in the enduring human fixation on the traumatic and grotesque (Brown 2009, 23). That is, "much like passing the scene of an accident," the project's advertisements—featuring brutal

scenes of victimization, violence and corporeal decay—rely on the "remarkable amount of collective enthusiasm and energy in this looking, an inability in fact to turn away" (Brown 2009, 23). Indeed, as one teen described, "like a car wreck, you can't take your eyes off," shocking images of "blood and pain" are a defining feature of penal spectatorship and TMP's advertisements.

Admittedly, TMP hopes to increase its effectiveness with overtly "disgusting" images of corporeal decay and sexual victimization, described here as *visualities of disgust*. For TMP, this means coupling graphic warnings of the drug's supposed somatic effects, with scenes of drug-fuelled crime and victimization. Arguing "fear" and "disgust" together is a more effective deterrent than "fear" alone, marketing researchers recently attempted to quantify and thus legitimize the logics of disgust (Morales et al. 2012). Not unlike the RAND study discussed earlier, TMP published the research findings to legitimize its work. From a TMP press release:

> [A]ccording to the study, the Meth Project ads and others that incorporated an element of "disgust," such as rotting teeth, skin sores or infections, did compel viewers to "undertake distancing behaviors," such as deciding not to use illegal drugs. (The Meth Project 2012a)

Clearly, TMP intends to provoke the rational self-interest of penal spectators with its reminder "see what happens if you use meth" (Linnemann and Wall 2013). Again, this is not a major departure from projects intending to shock and shame onlookers (Kohm 2009). However, the particular criminological aesthetics (Young 1996) and visualities (Mirzoeff 2006) developed and employed by the project provoke social insecurities along very specific race, class and gender lines. It is important to recall that these images are products of the imaginations of elite film-industry creatives, advertising executives and the project's billionaire founder. As such, the project's overstated warnings of "epidemics" entwined with the human desire "to look" shape and guide the actively lived and felt experiences of methamphetamine and particularly the social imaginaries of life in the supposed "white" and "rural" geographies of the United States.

Method

To confront the complexities of TMP imagery, we take basic inventory of *context*, *format* and *content* (Valverde 2006). Emerging from the broader war on drugs, TMP's presentation or format is such that its products, at least on their surface, appear state-sanctioned. The whole programme, from professional websites, prominently placed billboards and the immediately recognizable logo "Meth: Not Even Once," mimics iconic projects like "Just Say No" and D.A.R.E. It matters less that TMP is a private endeavour because its format is such that only the most critical viewer would question its origin and legitimacy.

The focus of our analysis is 29 static advertisements, featured on the project's website at the time of this writing, intended for print and the Internet. Treating each advertisement as a single case, we reviewed the ads, noting basic stylistic elements and presentation. Attempting to ignore textual information and focus only on the image sharpened our analysis to the particular aesthetics of each advertisement. The first consensus reached was that almost every advertisement featured a subject or character that a meth user or the drug itself was acting on—the message imparting "what meth does to you." So, for instance, the "15 bucks" advertisement features the scene of what appears to be a young white woman in a physical struggle with a white man. The gaunt skin and blank stare of the young woman do not evoke terror, but a subjectivity more akin to a lamb led to slaughter. Perhaps playing off the supposed blue-collar appeal of "poor man's cocaine," the man's clothing suggests he is working-class. In this sense, staged emotionality, dark imagery and distinct race and class cues help to imagine meth crimes as a white working-class phenomenon. Though aesthetically stunning, the advertisement is even more powerful and grim when coupled with the caption "15 Bucks for Sex Isn't Normal. But on Meth It Is." Viewed through its text, ambiguity falls away and the *photographic message* (Barthes 1977) and its *preferred reading* (Hall et al. 1980) are clear—the sex work rape of a young woman, undoubtedly born of meth addiction. Victim of both meth and attacker, the young woman's blank stare communicates a hardened emotionality, where a 15-dollar sex work transaction is "normal" recourse to meth addiction. For vulnerable young women, as the caption warns, meth use makes the unknowable terror of rape knowable.

We followed this convention to develop four conceptual themes instructing what "meth does to you" (see Table 13.1). On a cursory level, we found the advertisements feature women and young girls more than men and boys and, in keeping with meth's racialization, all advertisements display what appear to be white bodies.

It is important to acknowledge that, while we focused on finding the most obvious "message" or the preferred reading of each advertisement, we in no way suggest that these complex productions advance a single message. Concerned with spectators' engagement with the images, while also aware of the difficulty in locating a singular meaning, we developed a process to explore the advertisements' pedagogical instructions further. One hundred and seven students from three different undergraduate "crime, media, society" courses responded to the format of TMP's website and ten advertisements selected at random. First, volunteers were shown a screen shot image (taken that day) of the project's

Table 13.1 Advertisement Themes.

Instruction	Female Subject	Male Subject	Location Only
Sexual insecurities	4	1	2
Corporeal decay, death	8	4	1
Emotional and relational harm	4	1	1
Criminality and addiction	0	3	0
Total	16	9	4

website and asked to respond to the following open-ended question: "Based on the information on the website, who produces The Meth Project?". Ninety-eight of 107 volunteers believed the website was an official state project, with the rest reporting that a private entity produced the website. This is an important starting point for the analysis, as the presentation and appearance of TMP as an official state project certainly speak to the affective force of its images.

Next, volunteers responded to ten advertisements for content and theme. Focusing on the main character or subject of the advertisement, we simply asked volunteers, "What is the race of this person?" and "What is the sex of this person?". Resoundingly, volunteers confirmed our previous assertions of the advertisements' overt racialization. With 107 responses for each of the ten images (1,070) nearly all (1,059) believed the advertisements featured "white" people, with just 11 responding with "Hispanic" or "Latino." In fact, in all but two of the ten images, respondents were in total agreement with the whiteness of the subject. The perceived sex of the subjects was even clearer, with all 1,070 responses in agreement with our reading and each other.

Next, volunteers identified the "message" of each advertisement, by responding to the question "According to the advertisement meth use leads to?" Volunteers were provided with a document with our themes and asked to mark any they felt appropriately represented the advertisement. We also encouraged volunteers to write in a description if they believed an image conveyed a message not represented by our themes. Tallied by theme, we used the category with the most responses as an approximation of consensus. For each of the ten advertisements, volunteers most often selected the theme in agreement with our analysis and none wrote in an alternate reading (see Table 13.2). While certainly not "proof" of audience reception, we view the volunteers' reading as some support for our themes. Additionally, the process demonstrated the consistent theme of instant addiction, characterized by the tag line "Meth: Not Even Once," and refocused our attentions to this important aspect of the campaign.

A Crude Pedagogy

Playing upon meth's distinct constructions, we see the project helping to fashion disparate criminological structures of feeling in a number of ways. As such, the crude pedagogy undergirding the project exaggerates already starkly gendered distinctions in criminal offending, victimization and the drug's effects on bodies and families. Perhaps most importantly, we argue the project polices cultural boundaries between hegemonic white identities (see Webster 2008) and polluted "white trash" meth users (Linnemann and Wall 2013).

Table 13.2 Volunteer Readings of TMP Advertisements.

Ad	Race	Sex	Sexual Vulnerabilities	Corporeal Decay	Relational Harm	Criminality	Addiction
15 bucks	107 white	107 female	107	16	4	4	40
Hook-up	107 white	107 female	96	68	4	4	80
Lipstick	107 white	107 female	1	107	0	0	56
Hallucinations	102 white	107 female	24	107	8	0	76
Sister	101 white	107 female	96	0	102	12	40
Beating	107 white	107 female	0	44	44	106	40
Prostitute	107 white	107 female	58	0	103	66	40
Junkie	107 white	107 female	0	0	106	3	56
Death	107 white	107 female	0	107	98	12	39
Bugs	107 white	107 female	0	107	1	2	43

Sexual Insecurities

Many of the advertisements seem to excite a punitive fascination with women and girls who transgress mainstream social conventions (Chesney-Lind and Eliason 2006). Like the "15 bucks" ad described earlier, many warn meth users will become victims of sexual crime or be forced into sex work. Importantly, almost all feature young women, as if to suggest that meth use does not lead young men to sex work or sexual victimization. Built firmly on seedy vulnerabilities, the project imagines a brutal subjectivity where young women exist only by "virtue of things being done to them" (Waiton 2009, 372). However, the few ads that do play upon the sexual vulnerabilities and insecurities of young men do so from a different vantage altogether. For instance, the ad "Hook-up," featuring a sickly young man and text "Actually, Doing Meth Won't Make It Easier to Hook Up," suggests his sexual virility, not safety, will suffer. Even advertisements that do not feature a character powerfully manipulate sexual insecurities. One such advertisement, "Bathroom" showing a filthy public restroom and the text "No One Thinks They'll Lose Their Virginity Here. Meth Will Change That," imagines a horrible turn in adolescent development where meth use begets sex work or rape in public space.

Another piece, entitled "Girlfriend," features both a young man and a woman, with the caption "My Girlfriend Would Do Anything For Me, so I Made Her Sell Her Body." This advertisement clearly advances notions of subordination of women and girls to their meth-using male counterparts. Turned out by opportunistic boyfriends, as the logic goes, the drug invariably transforms young women into sex workers. Reproduction of these normative practices contributes to highly gendered binary logics of representation, where women are simply victims and men are virulent predators—one visible, the other invisible. In this way, the advertisements follow the logic of gender dualism (see Spelman 1988), where long-standing "white discourses on womanhood" offer the privilege and protection of whiteness, while simultaneously structuring dependency and subservience to criminal men (Miller 2002, 448). Thus, the project's underlying logic "see

what happens if you use meth" reinforces a dualistic logic, warning young women that their transgressive behaviour begets further abuse by and subordination to the men in their lives.

Importantly, TMP's gendered imaginaries seem to compliment a growing collection of meth-specific policies that promise to befall women more harshly than men. For instance, at least one state (Kansas) has developed meth-specific "child endangerment" laws to punish those who expose children to meth or meth-making materials. While "aggravated child endangerment," a felony, carries an underlying prison sentence and untold collateral consequences, it treats "child endangerment" involving all other drugs (crack, heroin, etc.) as misdemeanours and substantially less serious by definition (Linnemann 2013). Even though the statute is not sex-specific, it is not a huge conceptual leap to assume the law will punish women disproportionately. Indeed, some evidence already suggests that the ongoing "meth panic" has driven the noticeable increase in the number of women incarcerated in federal prisons (Bush-Baskette and Smith 2012). Subordinating women and girls to meth-fuelled "mad men" (Linnemann 2010), TMP's intervention materials hardly challenge the broader binary systems of value (Young 1996, 1).

Corporeal Insecurities

In terms of corporeal insecurities, the advertisements again follow disparate, particularly gendered, cultural logics. For instance, the advertisement "Lipstick" displaying a close-up image of a young girl's disfigured mouth, replete with sores, horribly rotten teeth and the caption "You'll Never Worry about Lipstick on Your Teeth Again," powerfully links meth's physical decay to the decay of conventional feminine beauty.

Unsurprisingly, advertisements of this sort featuring young men are unrelated to beauty and rather describe users digging at skin, chasing illusory "meth bugs" or warn of overdose or death.

It is important to recall the campaign does not direct its warnings of "meth bugs" and "meth mouth" at the bodies of an anonymous population, but specifically at the bodies of young white users.

Therefore, we argue that, given meth's construction as a "white trash" drug, the project forcefully warns of the decay of white privilege and the precariousness of white social position (see Webster 2008). While whites are often viewed as raceless or in race-neutral terms, the scars, marks, sores, inseparable from popular of notions of methamphetamine abuse buttressed by the project, imagine and define a stained, polluted form of whiteness. As a powerful racializing practice, the images captivate the "voyeuristic middle-class self" (Hartigan 2005, 35) to entwine and encode notions of "white trash" into the social imaginary and fashion a racial hierarchy from relative homogeneity.

What's more, because unsightly teeth are often seen as a marker of low or working-class status (Murakawa 2011), we see the project's prominent use of the "meth mouth" trope reinforcing disparate class distinctions. Indeed, as one critic wrote, if you could represent all the anxieties swirling around the drug with a single image, it would be of a meth user "whose gums are pus-streaked and whose rotting teeth—what teeth he still has—are blackened and broken" (Shafer 2005). Importantly, Murakawa (2011) draws attention to the intellectual dishonesty of failing to consider other conditions, such as poor nutrition, limited access to health care and the other drugs that might also contribute to "meth mouth." Despite these obvious contradictions, "meth mouth" endures as a unique diagnosis, cultural pejorative and forceful racializing practice. Therefore, in addition to meth-induced crime and victimization, when viewed through the dominant white racial frame (see Daniels 2012), TMP warns of the perils of dishonouring white bodies and thus white privilege. In this way, claims made by the project police gender, race and class lines simultaneously, "naming" (Loader and Mulcahy 2001) subjects that have dishonoured and transgressed middle-class white sensibilities.

Emotional and Relational Insecurities

Several advertisements reflect the campaign's recent direction to include family in its warnings rather than only users. As Siebel explains:

> [The] first campaign focused on the impact Meth has on the individual—the user. . . . For this next phase, we listened closely to our target audience—the teenagers in the state most affected by this epidemic—and used their input to drive our strategy. They wanted us to show the collateral damage that occurs to users' families and friends. (Montana Meth Project 2007)

So, for instance, an advertisement featuring a young girl's graduation picture with the caption "Before Meth I Had a Sister, Now I Have a RUN-AWAY," instructs children, parents, family and friends of the emotional anguish entwined with the drug.

Given meth's association with white users and rural geographies, the new focus seems intended to agitate concerns for the American "heartland" and "traditional" family. In other words, a "white" drug that leads sons and daughters down the road to violent criminality, prostitution and rape strikes at the heart of the American dream itself—however mythical. Take, for example, the recent case of Jody Ockert, who, from her small Kansas town, drew the attention of the US media under headlines like "Grandmother Accused of Selling Meth while Babysitting" (The Associated Press 2011). Ockert, 36, allegedly sold meth to undercover narcotics officers in her home, while also caring for her two-year-old granddaughter. Of course, the woman's apparent indifference towards her innocent granddaughter is easy for the public to revile. However, it is perhaps Ockert's age which begs spectators to ponder meth's effects on families. The narrative cobbled together by the stained sexuality of a child-neglecting, meth-dealing "36-year-old grandmother" characterizes meth's assault on the American family and traditional morality—provoking visceral passions and the most punitive imaginaries.

Like the "Prostitute" advertisement that somehow evokes a middle-class aesthetic with modest wallpaper and a simple school photo, TMP cautions of an "epidemic" that quite literally reaches into the living rooms of working-class families and drags their children off to horrible ends.

Criminality and Addiction

Featuring conspicuous violence, the project also draws on and reinforces the spectre of volatile and menacing "tweakers" (Ayers and Jewkes 2012). For example, the advertisement "Beating," showing two boys rifling through the pockets of a man lying on a dirty floor and with the caption "Beating an Old Man for Money Isn't Normal, but on Meth It Is," warns yet again that the drug makes unpredictable violence a certainty. However, the state's own data seem to refute this assumption, showing arrestees positive for meth (4.7 percent) much less than other drugs like marijuana (43.3 percent) and cocaine (25.1 percent) and very rarely implicated in violent crimes (less than 2 percent; ONDCP 2011). More importantly and unsurprisingly, none of these advertisements includes a woman or girl under the drug's violent spell. It seems, in the project's punitive imagination, only men are capable of violence, thereby relegating women and girls to relational difficulties, wrecked beauty and sexual victimization.

Lastly, as reminded by the volunteers' readings of the advertisements, each advances the logics of instant addiction characterized by the trademarked motto "Meth: Not Even Once." Remarkably similar to Nancy Reagan's famous slogan "Just Say No," "Not Even Once" imparts with clarity that meth's ruin ensues after just the first use. Thus, with allusions to the "crack epidemic," TMP instructs an anxious public of the gravity of this latest drug epidemic. With warnings of the fragile sexualities of young women and the violent potentials of young men, TMP's crude instructions agitate broader social and cultural anxieties about the state of "traditional" American family life and the precariousness of white social position, serving only to widen existing social fissures and intra-class contempt.

Conclusion

What began as a privately funded project in one sparsely populated US state is now a nationally visible campaign, with an annual budget of more than 30 million dollars (Siebel Foundation 2012). Despite volumes of research critical of fear appeals (Stainback and Rogers 1983; Struckman-Johnson et al. 1990; NIDA 1997; Witte and Allen 2000) of "meth epidemics" in general (Weisheit and White 2009) and its advertisements specifically

(Erceg-Hurn 2008; Anderson 2010), TMP still proudly advertises its role in "significant declines in teen Meth use in several states" (The Meth Project, 2012b). In this way, TMP's claims are similar to the "voodoo criminology" (Young 2004), used to justify the contentious practices of broken windows policing. Indifferent or perhaps unable to challenge broader social structures that foster addiction, violence and social exclusion, its punitive display does make useful political fodder.

With risk and insecurity at the centre of its strategies, what Carlen (2008b) calls "risk-crazed governance," TMP thus demonstrates a commitment to a "civil and political order structured around the problem of violent crime" (Simon 2007, 3). Mobilizing cultural fascinations with meth to stir the insecurities of penal spectators, the project is perhaps even more explicitly part of a specialized regime that *governs through meth* (Linnemann 2013). The project's "disgusting" visualities powerfully reveal the entwinements of penal spectatorship and non-state crime control. It is also important to recall that this marriage of penal spectatorship and crime control is the product not of academics or crime control practitioners, but of the advertising and film industries. Carrying the undeniable influences of both fields, the advertisements can be seen as part Hollywood drama and part marketing campaign. In this sense, the actual deterrent effects of the programme are secondary to its ability to capture the attention of the voyeuristic public. To accomplish its goals, the project need not meaningfully reduce meth use; it just has to appear to—or claim to (Hope 2004; 2008).

Our concern is not necessarily whether the project fails to accomplish its mission of eradicating methamphetamine use, or even that it apparently bolsters claims of its own effectiveness in order to legitimize its efforts—indeed, criminal justice is littered with such programmes. Rather, we take issue with the binary logics that the images advance and the myth of a runaway "meth epidemic" that the project presupposes. With the help of film-industry elites, the campaign provides a cultural reference point for what meth "does" and what a meth user "is" (see Valier and Lippens

2004). Influencing the ways in which people imagine their relationship with others and indeed their own existence (see Taylor 2004), the campaign buttresses punitive criminological structures of feeling, framing the drug as a white, working-class and rural plague.

Utterly dependent on its imaginary vision of the world, TMP and programmes like it view all oppositional and contradictory knowledge as a challenge and thus a threat to its existence (see Carlen 2008a). From a problem statement rife with inconsistencies and exaggerations to its patented visualities of disgust, the project "says a lot"—and it speaks loudly. However, what is equally important is what the project does not say about the "gritty" realities of methamphetamine in the United States. As Hallsworth and Young (2008) have written, "just as there can be no photograph without a negative," what is currently "said" about methamphetamine in the United States—largely constituted by TMP—cannot, indeed will not, exist apart from what is left *unsaid* (Hallsworth and Young 2008: 132). That is, TMP, its advertisements and the everyday politics of crime and punishment are structured and animated by silence. Accordingly, we can see how the whole project—expertly crafted advertisements, self-congratulatory evaluations, press releases—influences how we are to view the problems associated with methamphetamine and obfuscates possible remedies that differ from the dominant authoritarian practices. Moving towards both "propaganda and myth" (Ayers and Jewkes 2012: 10), the project's punitive imagination of methamphetamine as criminal transgression differs little from the ideas and cultural logics that have helped to build the largest prison population on the planet and in recorded history. Therefore, in many ways, what is "imagined" and "said" by the project helps ineffective and harmful penal practices and the carceral state to stand beyond reproach—unquestioned.

Expanding the drug war's fear and discord to the supposed white landscapes of rural America, projects like TMP cast a "deep fog" on the vicissitudes of security and police projects, fundamental to maintenance of the bourgeois social order (Rigakos 2011, 63). As such, projects built on steady warnings of the other, both external and from within (whites versus white trash), serve as a method for policing social boundaries and for intensifying and harnessing competition in the economic and social realms (Hall and Winlow 2005, 108). We can thus view TMP as a pacification project, which, at the broadest level, expands the deliberate political strategy of endless war to new spaces and cultural territories and at the interpersonal level instructs citizens of the boundaries of acceptable moral and legal behaviour (Rigakos 2011). That the class interests of the project's billionaire funder are in line with maintenance of these broader authoritarian and neo-liberal doctrines is not lost on us—nor is it coincidence.

Images can be powerful, haunting things. Indeed, the image-centred and market-based techniques harnessed by the punitive imagination of TMP "move us to feel and act, in unforeseen and sometimes surprising ways" (Valier 2004, 4). As we have argued, the project agitates long-standing social insecurities and drowns out alternate remedies for the problems of drug use and victimization and the ills of late-capitalist order itself. And, while we offer no explicit policy suggestions to counter its punitive imagination, we hope that, by challenging TMP's pronouncements, we open up space for a different view of very real human suffering. After all, with millions behind bars and millions more under the thumb of its vast correctional fields, the American carceral state does "blood and pain" quite well; it has, however, failed to master a comparable degree of restraint and compassion.

Notes

1. As Loader and Walker note, Raymond Williams's "structures of feeling," Charles Taylor's "social imaginaries," and Pierre Bourdieu's notion of "habitus" all bear "close and suggestive comparison" with each other (Loader and Walker 2007, 44).
2. Please see http://foundation.methproject.org/About-Us/index.php.
3. *Tony Kaye* (American History X), *Darren Aronofsky* (Requiem for a Dream, Black Swan), *Alejandro González Iñárritu* (21 Grams) *and Wally Pfister* (The Dark Knight).

References

Alexander, M. 2010. *The New Jim Crow: Mass Incarceration in the Age of Colorblindness*. The New Press.

Anderson, D. 2010. "Does Information Matter? The Effect of the Meth Project on Meth Use among Youths." *Journal of Health Economics* 29: 732–42.

Ayers, T. and Y. Jewkes. 2012. "The Haunting Spectacle of Crystal Meth: A Media-Created Mythology?" *Crime, Media, Culture* 8 (3): 1–18.

Barthes, R. 1977. *Image–Music–Text*. Fontana.

Bogazianos, D. 2012. *5 Grams: Crack Cocaine, Rap Music, and the War on Drugs*. NYU Press.

Brown, M. 2009. *The Culture of Punishment: Prison, Society, and Spectacle*. New York University Press.

Bush-Baskette, S. R., and V. C. Smith. 2012. "Is Meth the New Crack for Women in the War on Drugs? Factors Affecting Sentencing Outcomes for Women and Parallels Between Meth and Crack." *Feminist Criminology* 7 (1): 48–69.

Carlen, P. 2008a. *Imaginary Penalities*. Willan.

———. 2008b. "Imaginary Penalities and Risk-Crazed Governance." In *Imaginary Penalties*, edited by P. Carlen. Willan.

Carney, P. 2010. "Crime, Punishment and the Force of the Photographic Spectacle." In *Framing Crime: Cultural Criminology and the Image*, edited by K. Hayward and M. Presdee, 17–35. Routledge.

Chesney-Lind, M. and M. Eliason. 2006. "From Invisible to Incorrigible: The Demonization of Marginalized Women and Girls." *Crime, Media, Culture* 2: 29–47.

Daniels, J. 2012. "Intervention: Reality TV, Whiteness, and Narratives of Addiction." *Critical Perspectives* 33 (35): 37.

Department of Justice. 2011. Resource Center, Statistics and Facts, STRIDE Data. Retrieved from http://www.justice.gov/dea/resource-center/stride-data.shtml

Economist, The. 1999. "High in the Heartland." February 4.

Erceg-Hurn, D. M. 2008. "Drugs, Money, and Graphic Ads: A Critical Review of the Montana Meth Project." *Prevention Science* 9 (4): 256–263.

Ferrell, J. 2012. "Crime and the Visual: Critical Criminology and the Photodocumentary Tradition." *Critical Criminologist* 21: 1.

Gillespie, N. 2005. "Meth Still Driving People Nuts: Newsweek, on the Media, and Me." *Reason* (October 26).

Greer, C., J. Ferrell, and Y. Jewkes. 2007. "It's the Image that Matters: Style, Substance and Critical Scholarship." *Crime, Media, Culture* 3: 5–8.

———. 2008. "Investigating the Crisis of the Present." *Crime, Media, Culture* 4 (1): 5–8.

Hall, S. and Winlow, S. 2005. "Radgies, Gangstas, and Mugs: Imaginary Criminal Identities in the Twilight of the Pseudo-Pacification Process." *Social Justice* 32: 100–12.

Hall, S., D. Hobson, A. Lowe, and P. Willis. 1980. *Culture, Media, Language*. Hutchinson.

Hallsworth, S. and T. Young. 2008. "Crime and Silence: 'Death and Life Are in the Power of the Tongue' (Proverbs 18:21)." *Theoretical Criminology* 12: 131–52.

Hartigan, J. 2005. *Odd Tribes: Toward a Cultural Analysis of White People*. Duke University Press.

Hayward, K. and Presdee, M. 2010. *Framing Crime: Cultural Criminology and the Image*. Routledge.

Hendricks, M. 2012. "A Matter of Life and Meth: Drug Has Tragic Consequences." *The Kansas City Star* (July 21).

Hope, T. 2004. "Pretend It Works: Evidence and Governance in the Evaluation of the Reducing Burglary Initiative." *Criminal Justice* 4: 287–308.

———. 2008. "The First Casualty: Evidence and Governance in a War Against Crime." In *Imaginary Penalities*, edited by P. Carlen. Willan.

Kohm, S. 2009. "Naming, Shaming and Criminal Justice: Mass-Mediated Humiliation as Entertainment and Punishment." *Crime, Media, Culture* 5: 88–105.

Lea, J. and K. Stenson. 2007. "Security, Sovereignty and Non-State Governance from Below." *Canadian Journal of Law and Society* 22: 9–27.

Lilienfeld, S. 2007. "Psychological Treatments that Cause Harm." *Perspectives on Psychological Science* 2: 53–70.

Linnemann, T. 2010. "Mad Men, Meth Moms, Moral Panic: Gendering Meth Crimes in the Midwest." *Critical Criminology* 18: 95–110.

———. 2013. "Governing through Meth: Local Politics, Drug Control and the Drift toward Securitization." *Crime, Media, Culture*. doi:10.1177/1741659012454125

Linnemann, T. and Wall, T. 2013. "'This Is Your Face on Meth': The Punitive Spectacle of 'White Trash' in the Rural War on Drugs." *Theoretical Criminology*. doi:10.1177/1362480612468934

Loader, I. 1997. "Policing and the Social: Questions of Symbolic Power." *British Journal of Sociology* 48: 1–18.

Loader, I. and A. Mulcahy. 2001. "The Power of Legitimate Naming: Part I—Chief Constables as Social Commentators in Post-War England." *British Journal of Criminology* 41: 41–55.

Loader, I. and N. Walker. 2007. *Civilizing Security*. Cambridge University Press.

Lynch, M. 2012. "Theorizing the Role of the 'War on Drugs' in US Punishment." *Theoretical Criminology* 16: 175–99.

Manderson, D. 1995. "Metamorphoses: Clashing Symbols in the Social Construction of Drugs."*Journal of Drug Issues* 25: 799–816.

Miller, J. 2002. "The Strengths and Limits of 'Doing Gender' for Understanding Street Crime." *Theoretical Criminology* 6: 433–60.

Mirzoeff, N. 2006. "On Visuality." *Journal of Visual Culture* 5: 53–78.

Montana Meth Project. 2007. "Montana Meth Project Kicks Off New Campaign with Ads by Critically Acclaimed Director Darren Aronofsky: Next Wave of Meth Prevention Campaign Will Continue to Saturate Television, Radio, and Print Outlets throughout the State." March 7. http://foundation.methproject.org/documents/MMP%20Wave%20III%20Campaign%20Release-FINAL.pdf

Morales, A., E. Wu, and G. Fitzsimons. 2012. "How Disgust Enhances the Effectiveness of Fear Appeals." *Journal of Marketing Research* 49: 383–93.

Murakawa, N. 2011. "TOOTHLESS: The Methamphetamine 'Epidemic,' 'Meth Mouth,' and the Racial Construction of Drug Scares." *Du Bois Review: Social Science Research on Race* 8 (1): 219–88.

National Institute on Drug Abuse (NIDA) 1997. *Drug Abuse Prevention: What Works*. National Institutes of Health.

Nicosia, N., R. Pacula, B. Kilmer, R. Lunberg, and J. Chiesa. 2009. *The Economic Costs of Methamphetamine Use in the United States, 2005*. RAND.

O'Mally, P. and D. Palmer. 1996. "Post-Keynesian Policing." *Economy and Society* 25 (2): 137–155.

Office of National Drug Control Policy (ONDCP) 2011. *ADAM II: 2010 Annual Report*. Office of National Drug Control Policy.

Rigakos, G. 2011. "'To Extend the Scope of Productive Labour': Pacification as a Police Project." In *Anti-Security*, edited by M. Neocleous and G. Rigakos. Red Quill Books.

Schonberg, J. and P. Bourgois. 2002. "The Politics of Photographic Aesthetics: Critically Documenting the HIV Epidemic among Heroin Injectors in Russia and the United States." *The International Journal of Drug Policy* 13 (5): 387–392.

Shafer, J. 2005. "The Meth Mouth Myth: Our Latest Moral Panic." *Slate* (August 9). Accessed November 26, 2012. http://www.slate.com/articles/news_and_politics/press_box/2005/08/the_methmouth_myth.html

Siebel, T. and S. Mange. 2009. "The Montana Meth Project: 'Unselling' a Dangerous Drug." *Stanford Law & Policy Review* 20: 405–16.

Siebel Foundation 2012. *2011 Siebel Foundation Annual Report*. Siebel.

Simon, J. 2007. *Governing through Crime: How the War on Crime Transformed American Democracy and Created a Culture of Fear*. Oxford University Press.

Spelman, E. 1988. *Inessential Woman: Problems of Exclusion in Feminist Thought*. Beacon Press.

Stainback, R. and R. Rogers. 1983. "Identifying Effective Components of Alcohol Abuse Prevention Programs: Effects of Fear Appeals, Message Style and Source Expertise." *International Journal of Addictions* 18: 393–405.

Stebner, B. 2011. "'She Couldn't Say No': The Shocking State Date-Rape Ad Pulled amid Anger over Suggestions that Drunken Victims Are to Blame." *Mail Online* (December 9). www.dailymail.co.uk/news/article-2071890/She-say-Pennsylvania-Liquor-Control-Board-pulls-controversial-ad-blames-date-rape-victims-victims-friends-receiving-hundreds-complaints.html

Struckman-Johnson, C., R. Gilliland, D. Struckman-Johnson, and T. North. 1990. "The Effects of Fear of AIDS and Gender on Responses to Fear-Arousing

Condom Advertisements." *Journal of Applied Social Psychology* 20: 1396–410.

Substance Abuse and Mental Health Services Administration (SAMHSA). 2012. *Results from the 2011 National Survey on Drug Use and Health: Summary of National Findings*. NSDUH Series H-44, HHS Administration, 2012.

Taylor, C. 2004. *Modern Social Imaginaries*. Duke University Press.

The Associated Press 2011. "Report: Grandmother Sold Meth while Baby-Sitting." November 3. http://6lawrence.com/news/crime-fire-courts/report-grandmother-sold-meth-while-baby-sitting/

The Meth Project. 2007. *The Meth Project Newsletter* (Summer). Palo Alto, CA.

The Meth Project. 2012a. "New Research Cites Meth Project Ads as Effective." Press Releases. Retrieved from: http://colorado.methproject.org/News/articles/press_03072012.php

The Meth Project. 2012b. "Results: Impact." Retrieved from:. http://montana.methproject.org/Results/index.php.

Tunnell, K. D. 2004. "Cultural Constructions of the Hillbilly Heroin and Crime Problem." In *Cultural Criminology Unleashed*, edited by J. Ferrell, K. Hayward, W. Morrison and M. Presdee, 133–42. Cavendish.

Valier, C. 2004. "Introduction: The Power to Punish and the Power of the Image." *Punishment and Society* 6: 251–4.

Valier, C. and R. Lippens. 2004. "Moving Images, Ethics and Justice." *Punishment & Society* 6: 319–33.

Valverde, M. 2006. *Law and Order: Images, Meanings, Myths*. Rutgers University Press.

Wacquant, L. 2009. *Punishing the Poor: The Neoliberal Government of Social Insecurity*. Duke University Press.

Waiton, S. 2009. "Policing After the Crisis: Crime, Safety and the Vulnerable Public." *Punishment & Society* 11: 359–76.

Webster, C. 2008. "Marginalized White Ethnicity, Race and Crime." *Theoretical Criminology* 12 (3): 298–312.

Weisheit, R. and W. L. White. 2009. *Methamphetamine: Its History, Pharmacology, and Treatment*. Hazelden Publishing & Educational Services.

Williams, R. 1977. *Marxism and Literature*. Oxford University Press.

Witte, K. and M. Allen. 2000. "A Meta-Analysis of Fear Appeals: Implications for Effective Public Health Campaigns." *Health Education & Behavior* 27: 591–615.

Young, A. 1996. *Imagining Crime: Textual Outlaws and, Criminal Conversations*. Sage.

Young, J. 2004. "Voodoo Criminology and the Numbers Game." In *Cultural Criminology Unleashed*, edited by J. Ferrell, K. Hayward, W. Morrison and M. Presdee, 13–29. Cavendish.

———. 2011. *The Criminological Imagination*. Polity.

Zernike, K. 2006. "With Scenes of Blood and Pain, Ads Battle Methamphetamine in Montana." *The New York Times* (February 26).

For Discussion

1. Check out the latest ads from *The Meth Project* (http://www.methproject.org) and discuss the caricatures of the individuals featured in the ads. The particular state projects can be found here: http://www.methproject.org/about.

2. Is it appropriate to use drug prevention material that is designed to frighten people in hopes of deterring them from using substances? Why or why not?

"Alcohol Allows You to Not Be Yourself"

Toward a Structured Understanding of Alcohol Use
and Gender Difference among Gay, Lesbian, and Heterosexual Youth

ROBERT L. PERALTA

Using qualitative interviews with a diverse sample of college students, Robert L. Peralta examines how the use and effects of alcohol allow individuals to engage in and also justify behaviors
that violate traditional gender norms. Peralta introduces the concept of "gender blunder,"
that is, the accidental and sometimes intentional behavior that departs from "acceptable"
gender norms. The effects of alcohol and the meaning ascribed to them served to reproduce
the social construction of gender.

Introduction

When norm violations occur (e.g., gender norm
violations), a common response is to excuse or justify such violations. The accounts literature as referenced by Scott and Lyman (1981) fundamentally
distinguishes between excuses (e.g., "it was wrong,
but it wasn't my fault") and justifications (e.g.,
"I did it, but it wasn't wrong"). Scott and Lyman's
distinction enables us to understand how excuses
and justifications are used to deflect deviant labels.
Social rituals, such as alcohol use, can serve to relax
the justification and discrediting of action (Montemurro and McClure 2005). Research on alcohol use
as an excuse or the deviance disavowal phenomenon (Leonard 2002; Scully and Marolla 1984) suggests that alcohol use often serves as a resource for
the neutralization of norm violations (Montemurro
and McClure 2005). The time out or excuse value of

alcohol use is thought to have meaning for the
management or maintenance of self-identity, to
retain a rationale of the self, and to excuse deviant
or undesirable behavior (Luckenbill 1977; McCaghy
1968; Rhodes and Cusick 2002; Tryggvesson 2004).

MacAndrew and Edgerton's (1969) classic
study on drunken comportment empirically demonstrated how many societies establish alcohol use
as a time-out period. The time-out period allows
social space for otherwise unacceptable behavior to
occur. In other words, intoxication can provide a
context of freedom from responsibility. More
recently, Cohen and Lederman (1998) report that
alcohol is used to deny responsibility for engaging
in sexual practices deemed socially unacceptable.
Cohen and Lederman's (1998) findings, however,
are limited in that they refer only to women's deviance situated in casual heterosexual encounters.

Reprinted from Robert L. Peralta, 2008, "'Alcohol Allows You To Not Be Yourself': Toward a Structured
Understanding of Alcohol Use and Gender Difference among Gay, Lesbian, and Heterosexual Youth," in *Journal
of Drug Issues* 38: 373–399. Reprinted by permission of SAGE Publications via Copyright Clearance Center.

While alcohol use has been associated with masculinity construction (West 2001), little research has examined the meaning of alcohol for women who construct alternative gender expressions. Moreover, few studies have explained how alcohol use might be used to excuse gender-violating behavior. As an exception, Parks (1999) studied the social meaning of alcohol for lesbians. Parks, in part, concluded that alcohol use among lesbians and the social contexts in which drinking took place (e.g., gay bars) served to provide an escape from heterosexism and homophobia; public alcohol use also facilitated new social networks and identities.[1]

Little research has examined alcohol use in conjunction with the doing of "gender difference" (West and Fenstermaker 1995). Similarly, little qualitative research in particular has examined women's social drinking and the contexts in which women drink (see Montemurro and McClure 2005). Most research on women and alcohol use has focused on alcoholism, problem drinking, or drinking in response to a male partner's drinking (Jersild 2001; National Institute on Alcohol and Alcoholism 1999; Wiseman 1991). Likewise, until recently, little research has been conducted on alcohol use among gay individuals. This may be due in part to the difficulties of operationalizing what it means to be "gay" and the difficulties associated with research on hidden populations (Benoit et al. 2005).

The recent research on gay and lesbian populations appears to suggest those who have had same-sex partners have similar or higher prevalence rates of alcohol use compared to their heterosexual counterparts (Amadio 2006; Eisenberg and Wechsler 2003; Finlon 2002; Hughes 2003; Hughes et al. 2006; Hughes and Wilsnack 1994; Parks and Hughes 2005; Stall et al. 2001; Trocki 2005). Nevertheless, the prevalence rate of alcohol use among "gay" or homosexual populations has been constructed as a problem related to the stress of being marginalized, a product of heterosexism, and a tension reliever used to reduce feelings of low self-worth (Stall and Willey 1988; Tori 1989). Alternatively, Caceres and Cortinas (1996) interpret the higher prevalence rate of alcohol use as a social resource and as a disinhibitor. Caceres and Cortinas note that alcohol use may

allow the exploration of identities rendered taboo outside the gay bar. These researchers suggest alcohol becomes a tool to negotiate sexual intimacy and to celebrate sexual differences in a safe public space. The point of alcohol use, the authors state, is "to decrease the normal agency of the people involved," thereby creating a context where norm violations are more likely to occur (Caceras and Cortinas 1996, 56). Examining alcohol use in relation to the social construction of gender expands the existing literature in terms of what social construction theory can add to the existing literature on gender in relation to drinking behavior. Below I review the alcohol use and gender literature and discuss the ways in which these literatures converge.

The Situated Structure and Action of Gender, Difference, and Alcohol Use

A dominant theme in the research literature conceptualizes gender as socially constructed (Anderson 2002; Goffman 1976; Kane and Schippers 1996; Lucal 1999; Orcutt 1975; West and Zimmerman 1987; Vander Ven 2005) and suggests that the social use of alcohol may symbolically express gender, particularly masculinity (Peralta 2005). While this conceptualization includes the recognition that femininity is subordinated to masculinity, the meaning of gendered behavior is also contextually bound in terms of where and when particular demonstrations of gender are appropriate. Men and women engage in the "doing" of gender (e.g., choice of alcoholic beverage, hairstyles, clothing, emotional expression, and displays of sexuality) appropriate to the social situation, with consequences at both the individual and group level (West and Zimmerman 1987). Despite the potential fluidity implied by the social construction of gender, entrenched cultural and normative beliefs for men and women result in inflexible expectations for the performance of gendered behavior. Failure to do gender appropriately can result in threats to identity, embarrassment, stigma, and other negative sanctions (e.g., ostracism) (Miller et al. 2003; Connell and Messerschmidt 2005).

Gender relations are maintained through the creation and reproduction of gendered practices (Connell and Messerschmidt 2005). Operating within patriarchal social institutions, where femininity is devalued and masculinity exalted, men and women are expected to function within the confines of that system. The denigration of femininity and alternative forms of masculinity serves to ascend hegemonic masculinity. Conformity in many respects means to abide by a social structure where gender has been dichotomized (Lorber 1994). In this day to day operation, men and women engage in the doing of gender displays and practices (e.g., gendered hairstyles and clothing) (West and Zimmerman 1987). Conforming to societal expectations is the linchpin of regularly occurring gendered behavior. Interaction is moderated by gendered social structure (Garfinkel 1967; Martin and Collinson 2000). Individuals are accountable to their assigned sex and subject to condemnation for violations of gender performance depending on the situated context. Those who violate gender and sexuality norms are likely to be labeled deviant. Thus, social structure itself appears to be gendered, the performance of gender is situated, and gendered behavior reproduces structure.

Divergent gender practices have been described as forms of gender difference (Messerschmidt 1993) or gender deviance (Cromwell 1999; Garfinkle 1967), and those who engage in gender difference have been referred to as transgenderists (Dozier 2005). Messerschmidt (1993) extended West and Fenstermaker's (1995) and Connell's (1987) theories on gender to signify doing gender in different situations and with different degrees of salience. Structured action theory (SAT) (Messerschmidt 1993, 1999) advanced sociological research on gender and gender norm violation by arguing that gender is a mechanism through which situated social action reproduces social structure. That is, normative beliefs for men and women require all participants to present, monitor, interpret, and reproduce gender displays, which are structured by specific social sites, contexts, and situations.

Empirical documentation of the social processes of resistance, challenge, conflict, and change related to alternative gender constructions reveal the nature of social construction (Collins et al. 1995). Substantial resistance can be illustrated by the popularity of women's studies, "queer theory"

courses, and active student organizations such as gay, lesbian, and transgendered student groups. Studying examples of gender norm violation or gender resistance in the context of alcohol use enables us to understand the fluidity of gender and the contextual basis upon which gender is dependent. Researchers have examined how gender difference is met with resistance (Leblanc 1999) while others have noted the difficulties of successfully challenging the gender hierarchy (Hollander 2002). Examining accidental or purposeful "gender crossing" in the context of alcohol use demonstrates how the social construction of gender operates and illuminates the structural forces that facilitate the use of alcohol.

This paper contributes to the empirical literature on alcohol use and the social construction of gender in three important ways. First, this investigation seeks to understand how contexts where alcohol use is taking place allow women and men to engage in inappropriate displays of gender or ignore the gender difference of others. Second, this study examines how the alcohol excuse is experienced when purposeful or accidental gender difference occurs. Thirdly, the accounts literature is expanded to address the relevance of situational contexts (e.g., alcohol use) in gender construction. In this paper, I examine instances of doing gender difference as these practices relate to alcohol use. Because I focus on inappropriate gender displays, I also explore the ways in which doing gender difference is disavowed and thus a form of deviant behavior.

The Current Study

In this paper, three questions are explored. First, does alcohol use motivate women and men and/or those they interact with to engage in or ignore inappropriate displays of gender? Second, how does alcohol use excuse inappropriate gender displays (e.g., gender difference)? Finally, how are accounts used in situated contexts to assuage guilt and shame associated with gender difference? The social practice of inappropriate gender displays or gender difference is defined here as engaging in nontraditional gender practices. That is, how are alcohol use accounts used to excuse men doing femininity (e.g., paying attention to appearance, wearing jewelry, sitting "lady-like") and women doing masculinity (e.g., being assertive, restraining emotional expression, disregarding others). I broaden the study of gender by examining gender norm violations among college students.[2] In the analysis, I address the social construction of gender as it occurs in the context of alcohol use. Relying on SAT as my analytic framework and using Scott and Lyman's (1981) concept of accounts as a heuristic tool, I explore students' experiences and beliefs regarding alcohol use as an excuse for gender norm violations. I ask: What accounts do men and women provide to excuse or justify behavior that diverges from typical or expected gender displays (Goffman 1976; Scott and Lyman 1981)? The University Office of Human Research granted ethical approval for the project. Data were collected between 1997 and 2001.

Method

Sample Characteristics

Seventy-eight one-on-one in-depth interviews lasting on average 1.5 hours were conducted in the office of the primary investigator with an all-volunteer purposive sample. Informed consent was given for participation and all respondents were assured confidentiality. Participants were from a medium-sized public university in the mid-Atlantic region of the United States. College class ranking ranged from freshmen to senior status. Thirty-two percent (N = 24) reported being freshmen at the time of the interview. Participants lived both on and off campus. Seventy-one percent (N=55) of the sample were European American (EA) and 26% (N=20) were African American (AA). Two respondents were Hispanic men and one respondent self-described as Asian and was male. Fifty-three percent (N=41) were male, and 47% were female (N=37). Seventy-two percent (N=56) self-identified as heterosexual, 22% (N=17) self-identified as homosexual, and the remaining 6% (N=5) self-identified as bisexual. The mean age was 20 years old (SD = 2.75). Fifteen percent (N=11) of the sample reported being a member of a fraternity or sorority. The majority of participants (50%) were in the College of Arts and Sciences at the time of the

study. Thirty percent had undeclared majors and the remainder were either in the College of Engineering, Business, or Fine Arts.

Sample Recruitment and Eligibility

Undergraduate attendance at the target university was the only eligibility criterion for this study. The majority of participants responded to announcements in sociology and criminology courses and to 10 notices posted in campus areas frequented by students. To prevent a response from a narrow or specific grouping of participants (e.g., heavy drinkers or abstainers), announcements and notices utilized general and nonspecific language. Flyers and announcements called for participation in a study on experiences with alcohol use among college students. In addition to this statement about the topic of the study, contact information of the principal investigator, a confidentiality statement, and the stamp of approval from the Institutional Review Board were included.

Twenty-one percent of the sample (N = 16, all EA, all heterosexual) were recruited from the Dean of Students Office. These participants were undergoing disciplinary procedures for alcohol-related violations at the time of the study.[3] Participants were informed of the study with the same flyer described above and were asked if they would be interested in participating in the study. Minority participants were purposely oversampled to give representation to those who have been traditionally excluded from research. Difficulty recruiting minority participants (AA and gay/lesbian students) prompted the use of $10 stipends to encourage their participation.

Instrument

A semi-structured open-ended interview guide consisting of 12 guiding questions was developed and pilot tested by the author. Many questions were presented in projective form to reduce the response effect on threatening questions (see Sudman and Bradburn 1982). Demographic questions were asked in addition to questions regarding drinking quantity, frequency, attitudes toward drinking, reasons for drinking, expectations of alcohol use, and the consequences of drinking. Some of the questions specific to the study were (a) what does drinking and getting drunk mean to you? (b) what have been your experiences with alcohol? (c) what are your expectations of people who get drunk? and (d) what goes through your mind when you see someone drinking or getting drunk? Respondents were asked if they perceived gender differences for each question.

Analysis

The paper uses in-depth interviews to gain a nuanced understanding of young people's attitudes and beliefs about gender norms, gender norm violations, and alcohol use. Qualitative methods, grounded theory in particular, provide the tools necessary to address the study of gender difference in the context of alcohol use. Grounded theory allows respondents to inform the development of theory (see Lincoln and Guba 1985). The data presented here are based on over 100 hours of interview data. All interviews were taped and transcribed verbatim with participant consent. Themes were inductively generated from the data using a line-by-line open coding method (Strauss and Corbin 1990). An initial content analysis was conducted for patterns of responses emerging from the data. After this initial analysis, a more thorough examination of the transcripts was conducted for emergent themes. I utilized a constant-relational approach to gender (Emirbayer 1997), thus not abandoning the central tenets of gender. My analytic goals were to examine the relationship between gender norm violation and alcohol use and to generate concepts and hypotheses directly from the data (Glaser 1995; Glaser and Strauss 1967). It was necessary to read through all interview data several times with a focus on accounts of activities that reflected gender construction. In qualitative research, reliability refers to the stability of responses to multiple coders of data sets (Creswell 2007). The author and a research assistant compared and agreed upon the names of codes, the passages coded, and the way in which passages were coded. Only agreed-upon codes were used in the final analysis. Once coding and analysis were complete, I selected representative accounts from the data to illustrate each theme. These accounts were used as illustrations of themes

stemming from the analytic framework used in organizing data coding and analysis.

Findings

The data in this study suggest that participants perceive that the expression of gender can be interrupted or impaired due to the "physiological" effect of alcohol on the body. Although the use of alcohol can justify behavior that aligns with prevailing gender norms (Peralta and Cruz 2006), alcohol use also appears to excuse behavior that deviates from societal expectations. If women or men begin to exhibit gender practices that do not correspond with their assigned gender, the use of alcohol appears to provide an effective and legitimate excuse for gender deviation.

At the onset of the study, I did not expect deviance to be defined by gender norm violations. Participants describe how alcohol use functioned as an excuse for bad or embarrassing behaviors, which I refer to as gender norm violations or doing gender difference. It was striking that many of the behaviors discussed were deviant in that they violated gender norms. Early on and throughout the study, this type of deviance was described by participants in virtually every interview, albeit in varying degrees. Collectively, these gender deviations came to be interpreted as a significant emergent theme. Grounded in these data, I found that alcohol use provided a context where differential constructions of gender took place. For the purposes of this paper, this theme is explored separately for men and women. Thus the findings section is divided into two sections: (a) purposefully doing gender differently among women in the situated context of alcohol use and (b) purposeful gender difference and accidental gender blunders among men in the situated context of alcohol use. Table 14.1 below corresponds with sections 1 and 2 described above. This table displays the number of participants who used alcohol as an excuse for gender difference while in college and the number of participants who recalled receiving at least one alcohol-related excuse from peers during college for a gender norm violation. The table is meant to provide data on the distribution of themes and is not meant to be generalized beyond those interviewed.

Table 14.1 Percent of Men and Women Using Alcohol-Related Excuses for Expressing Gender Difference and Percent of Men and Women Receiving Alcohol-Related Excuses for Experiencing Gender Difference.

	Yes % (N)	No % (N)	Total % (N)
Men using alcohol-related excuses for expressing gender difference	68.3 (28)	31.7 (13)	100 (41)
Women using alcohol-related excuses for expressing gender difference	83.8 (31)	16.2 (6)	100 (37)
Men receiving an alcohol-related excuse when experiencing gender difference	73.2 (30)	26.8 (11)	100 (41)
Women receiving an alcohol-related excuse when experiencing gender difference	75.7 (28)	24.3 (9)	100 (37)

While previous research suggests that alcohol is used to express traditional or emphasized gender practices, I focus on the management of stigma associated with deviating from one's assigned gender whether the behavior in question was purposeful or not. Below, accounts are used to illustrate how the use of alcohol allows individuals to successfully excuse gendered behaviors deemed deviant. Participants provided many examples of using alcohol as an excuse for deviant behavior. Students report that their excuses (e.g., "I wouldn't have done it if I weren't drunk") were often tied to alcohol use. Moreover, participants described how alcohol excuses were used by their friends and peers for behaviors considered bad, wrong or immoral. Given the expectation that alcohol can excuse bad behavior, it became clear that participants used alcohol not only to facilitate positive social interaction but to test the boundaries of gender norms. I address the gendered aspects of the alcohol-related contextual basis of sexuality and gender difference in the analysis that follows.

Purposefully Doing Gender Differently among Women in the Situated Context of Alcohol Use

The gender performance of women under the influence of alcohol looked and felt different compared to men according to participants interviewed. Consider Jenny's (EA and heterosexual) statements, which support the purposeful deviant gender expressions engaged in by women while under the influence of alcohol:

> ... (Alcohol) allows you not to be yourself. It is very common, we use it to have an excuse for things that we do ... like hooking up with a guy or saying something very mean to your friends or

doing something very wrong ... I mean girls are so much more outgoing when drinking. I do things that I wouldn't do sober, like going up to boys to say, "Hi, my name is. ..."

This account demonstrates the license alcohol gives young women to take risks, be more bold, assertive and in some cases, more aggressive in their social interaction and pursuit of romantic partners. Alcohol use appeared to offer some protection against shame and stigma for women engaging in gender difference. Given that women know their behavior is accountable to other women and men, women construct their actions as acceptable in relation to the situated context in which the behavior took place, one which involved alcohol use. Take the next account from a EA heterosexual woman as an example of how young women alter the traditional mode of doing femininity in order to suit their needs as individuals instead of as girls or women.

> JULIA: It is about being more open when people drink, like being able to talk to people you wouldn't talk to. I think that women are much more self-conscious than guys are and so drinking gets rid of that. You don't care what you look like...., (because) you are drunk.

Above, Julia expressed how strict female specific appearance norms are momentarily suspended when drinking. Another EA heterosexual female student said, "[Y]ou don't go into the bathroom and like put your makeup on when you're drunk. You don't even think about it." These statements represent the preoccupation with appearance and beauty in everyday femininity performance. Julia states that women in general, when drinking, no longer need to worry about some forms of gender-appropriate behavior. In the specific social situation of the co-ed party scene, these women are challenging a feminine identity that requires attention to appearance. Alcohol use allows the culturally appropriate display of femininity to be suspended. Thus, drinking can be understood as an alluring reprieve from one labor-intensive component of doing femininity.

Alcohol use allowed women to ignore the judgment of others. Tina, an AA heterosexual female, felt she was able to be freer in what she said when drinking. She states, "the liquor makes you a little more free to say whatever you want." Jen and Susan (EA, heterosexual) illustrated this point as well.

> JEN: I think it (alcohol) opens you up a little more. . . . you're not as worried about what people are thinking.
> SUSAN: It's just a sense of false confidence that you get—like you're more open to talk to just anyone. . . . I don't care . . . what I'm saying. When I am sober . . . I'm more cautious. There is this sense that a girl should be either passive or quiet and when they are drunk . . . they can be loud . . . more outgoing and not care what people think.

Women constructed an inappropriately assertive, active, and outspoken gender in the situationally specific context of public alcohol use. According to these participants, these inappropriate gender displays rarely occurred in mixed gender settings, especially when alcohol was not present. EA gay women also expressed how alcohol use provided the context to escape negative labeling. In one example, sexual behavior became less constrained as described by Liz. Sex became more "enjoyable" with her partner after imbibing alcohol. In her words, sexual "inhibitions" were momentarily dismissed.

> LIZ: We have the best sex when we're drunk. We are much freer when we are drunk. It is easier to do a lot of things when you're drunk . . . than like say sober sex. We can do or say things that might sound pushy or weird if you weren't, um, drunk. When we are sober

we think, "oh that was a dumb thing to say" but I can say "oh, I was drunk!" I'm not big on public displays of affection and neither is my girlfriend but after drinking, that changes. If we are in public and drunk, we do stuff that we think would be inappropriate otherwise.

Above, Liz makes the distinction between sober sex and the bodily empowerment of drunken sex, which includes conspicuous displays of assertiveness. Bodily empowerment displays are typically reserved for men, but not in the situated context of public alcohol use. She also mentions the fear of sounding pushy, which is eliminated in the situated context of alcohol use. Cindy, an EA lesbian, discusses how alcohol is used to explain sexual promiscuity. Alcohol is needed because women are not supposed to be interested in sex in the same way men are. Cindy discusses how her use of alcohol is used as an excuse to hook up with other women. Without the excuse, Cindy would face the labels of "slut" or "whore," whereas men would be considered "studs" or "players." Cindy states:

> So I am flirting with Tina and she was sitting on my lap . . . we ended up hooking up . . . we did it another night too and I didn't want to do it if I was sober because I couldn't go back to Jane (Cindy's partner) and because me and Jane believe that the truth is more important. I told her "I was drunk both times" and that "it was no big deal." But I wanted it to happen both times.

The account above is interesting because it reveals how the double standard of sexuality that exists for women in heterosexual space also exists, in this case, for women in the lesbian community. The unequal gendered structural arrangements can be ignored in certain situated contexts. The risk of gender assessment found in the broader culture is suspended during alcohol use. The suspension power of alcohol use affords protection against the potential discrediting of their gendered feminine identities. Liz, in a complementary illustration, points out that one of her friends becomes very sexual after using alcohol. Liz (EA, homosexual) says:

> My friend . . . would get all drunk and when everybody was drunk she would say, "Okay, who wants

to fuck me?' And she would come home with like a random guy. If she wants to have sex with guys, it's not like, "you are gay, and you shouldn't be having sex with guys." Drinking helped her do that in my opinion.

Liz discussed how her friend embodied sexual aggression, which was presumptively a form of masculine behavior. Again, the situational construction of gender in this example took place in the context of alcohol use and thus facilitated this form of construction. Many men discussed how forward women can be in initiating contact when drinking or drunk. Men expressed surprise at this forward behavior. Anthony, an EA heterosexual observes, "Yeah, (women) will be more flirtatious. They will be willing to initiate the first touch." Adrian, an AA heterosexual male, expresses his dismay at the forward behavior of an intoxicated young woman. He states:

> I went to a party and this girl grabbed my privates, right? And she was like, "Yo dude, what is up?" I was like, "look man, you need to go ahead and chill out." And I thought about it and I was like, "No, I can't do it [reciprocate the sexual advancement].

The quote above demonstrates how a deviant gender display was constructed, yet the sex category of the person engaging in the deviant construction was defined as female. Alcohol use was understood to be the cause of the deviant gender display. If gender violating behaviors did not sit well with peers, alcohol excuses were employed to contextualize gender norm violations. Individuals who privately feared that their own behavior violated their assigned gender also used alcohol as an excuse to explain away potential embarrassment. This conclusion is in part drawn from the fact that many participants freely reported using alcohol for the purpose of losing control. One female student said, "Using alcohol means losing your inhibitions." Thus, a major benefit stemming from the use of alcohol rests in its ability to absolve behavior considered in some way nonconforming, offensive, immoral or otherwise deviant. And, as mentioned before, many of these deviant actions centered on gender norm violations. Women in

this study reported using alcohol to behave in socially unacceptable ways, which included masculine behaviors. For example, the issue of women being assertive, making sexual advancements, or otherwise being forward when drinking was frequently raised by male and female respondents alike. While drinking, especially in their pursuit of romantic or sexual contacts, women (according to self-reports of their own behavior and male and female respondent observations of other women) became more aggressive. Women interviewed were more likely to discuss "trying to get what they wanted" while under the influence of alcohol.

Men and women reported that assertiveness among women was possible because alcohol was involved. The alcohol excuse exempted these women from acquiring one of the many labels reserved for women who exert desire, power, and/or control. Descriptions of sober women exhibiting and pursuing desired outcomes included "slut," "bitch," "whore," "tramp," and "hoochie." Interestingly, in doing these alternative gender expressions, women reported feeling as if their appeal and self-esteem were enhanced during and after this proactive stance. This result corroborates findings by Sheehan and Ridge (2001), which suggests that young women find alcohol use both meaningful and positive in terms of improving self-esteem.

Taken together, these accounts resonate with the accounts literature. Excuses, a type of account, minimize or absolve responsibility when behavior is challenged. The common belief that individual-level factors (i.e., biological, psychological) explain much of human behavior, such as the presumed individual effect alcohol has on the body, is appealing as an excuse when social norms are broken. Thus, the context of alcohol use allows situational defiance of emphasized femininity without changing women's overall gender identity. Further examples of how this robust conviction works to suspend gender norms follow. The section below will elaborate on how alcohol is used to do gender differently, whether purposefully or accidentally, for heterosexual and gay men.

Purposeful Gender Difference and Accidental Gender Blunders among Men in the Situated Context of Alcohol Use

Men interviewed described the social practice of gender construction in the situated context of alcohol use. In this context, the practice of gender that was not in accordance with their gender identity was purposeful for some heterosexual men, and for gay men in particular. Alcohol use served as an account to counteract the negative labeling associated with gender difference. For others, I introduce the concept of "gender blunder," which refers to accidental gender norm violations that reveal the fluidity of gender and the necessary situational characteristics that produce them. I use quotation marks because it was unclear whether or not gender deviations were always accidental. Accidentally acting "like a fag" or unknowingly being "too butch"[4] are terms participants used and are terms for which I interpret to be gender blunders. When a behavior that is expressive of the opposite gender is exhibited yet unintended, a gender blunder has been committed; this is often considered a shameful act in need of explanation. Alcohol use provided a socially acceptable explanation that worked to neutralize gender blunders according to actors and audiences. The following accounts illustrate what gender blunders are, how they take place in student's lived reality, and how accounts of alcohol use provide the context necessary to permit gender difference.

Sammy, an EA heterosexual, discusses the behaviors he can do while drinking that are outside the realm of his masculine identity-appropriate practices. Sammy shares his thoughts on poetry and what the writing of poetry means. In Sammy's description, writing poetry is an activity normally reserved for women, that his poetry writing was "girl" behavior.

> I got really drunk and I said "give me a pad and paper" (to my friends). I started writing poetry! I went on and on for like three hours writing poetry. It was ridiculous. It was all about God and all this stuff. The next morning . . . I felt like an idiot (laughter).

Sammy explains he would not normally engage in such behavior unless he was drunk. Whether it was through poetry or frank discussion, male participants discussed the difficulty of expressing emotion when not relying on alcohol. These gender indiscretions were to a degree absolved via alcohol use, thus maintaining male gender identity and the overall gender order. Steve (EA, heterosexual) further illustrates this theme:

> During this year, some girl denied me and I got upset. She was like (in a feminine voice) "Oh, I don't want a relationship with you." I really liked the girl. . . . I was pretty drunk and I got upset and I just left and I went back to the dorms and cried. . . . I would have been all right if I wasn't drunk.

Steve said he would have been all right if he hadn't been drinking. To cry due to disappointment is not an appropriate male bodily display and is thus a deviant gender construction. Steve displayed feminine qualities through his bodily display of crying. Steve's alcohol use excused his gender blunder.[5] Thus, situationally, Steve is able to cry, express feminine practice, and maintain his masculine identity. Below, an EA heterosexual male makes a similar statement about emotion and the context-appropriate expression of emotion:

> ALEX: When it is just me and my friends hanging out, and we get really liquored up, we've gotten into really deep conversation. We have cried on each other's shoulders. . . . we don't have to act tough.

Because of the cultural expectation for disinhibition to take place after alcohol use, respondents' expected accidental gender violations or gender blunders to be more likely. Todd, a heterosexual AA, expresses this theme in discussing an exchange between him and an inebriated male friend:

> He was talking to me about how hard it is having guys hit on your younger sister. . . . he said something to me and he started crying and (he said) "It is so hard and no one understands but you." I was (thinking) how embarrassing is that? I seen him cry! (Men) don't cry. If you cry, that is something you keep to yourself. But he was drunk, so I can understand.

To cry is to be soft. To be soft is not masculine, it is feminine, and feminine traits among men are not acceptable unless alcohol is involved. Through alcohol, men were able to express their emotions, which would otherwise be bottled up and difficult to share given existing gender norms. The situation structured the action accordingly. Alcohol allows men to vent, and, in some cases, cry. When discussing the heavy use of alcohol in particular, by implication, respondents assume that the ability to control behavior is all but lost. Participants reify the disinhibition qualities assumed to be psychopharmacologically associated with alcohol. An EA heterosexual male, for example, stated, "When you are drinking, you really don't have any responsibility. Your only responsibility is to have fun." However, when control is lost, appropriate gender performance can become a precarious task. Because respondents assumed that self-control becomes more difficult, the act of doing gender becomes less precise, and mistakes become more probable. For those who fear straying too far from socially prescribed gender norms, acting too feminine or too masculine can be a mistake or blunder. For example, an EA heterosexual male said, "Alcohol gives you like a get out of jail free card. You can dance and sing and fuck up and it won't matter because you are drunk. That is what I do."

Men discussed how the use of alcohol created a context where variations of masculinity that include behaviors considered nonmasculine, effeminate, or homosexual in nature were performed. On the extreme end, purposefully doing gender differently took the form of homosexual contact for men who identified as heterosexual. How this takes place behaviorally largely stems from the meanings and cultural significance of alcohol use and its power to excuse. Consider the following quotes that refer to homosexual activity:

> SAM (AA, heterosexual): When people do things when they are drunk, they meant to do it. So they can have the opportunity to do things that they otherwise couldn't do cause it is morally or ethically incorrect. They have an excuse. And most of the time people accept it.
>
> ADAM (EA, heterosexual): There are straight people that use alcohol as an excuse (or) as

an outlet because they think that it is wrong at some level (to be gay). I think they do (engage in homosexual activity) and they can say "oh I was drunk so it's okay. . ." They can say "I was really drunk and I didn't know what I was doing."

Both Sam and Adam discuss the fluidity of sexuality when alcohol is involved. Drunkenness permits inappropriate gender practices without jeopardizing one's gender identity. Participants in the study raised the condition of "beer goggles" induced by alcohol, which blurred the distinction between appropriate sex partners and inappropriate sex partners. The blurring effect caused by "beer goggles" to an extent was supposed to excuse normative infractions involving sexual behavior. Below, James (EA and homosexual), shares a specific alcohol-related sexual experience with men understood to be heterosexual.

> JAMES: When I was like 18 and just finally coming to terms with being gay, I had friends that let me hang with them. I had dealt with guys in high school calling me fag. So I had these friends who liked me for me so it was nice finally to have people accept me. Well these friends had a few guy friends that didn't like me much because I was gay. One night we had this knock-out party, we all got . . . drunk. Well these guys suddenly wanted me to perform oral sex with them and I refused of course. Then they wanted to do it to me so I let them. Anyway, they did it after calling me faggot. These guys went down on me and performed oral sex on me . . . I was not shocked at all. I believe they were covering up their true feelings with alcohol use and the like. I believe men do it to cover it up.

The experience described above reveals how situated behavior occurs. Situationally, these men were not acting like males, yet their overall identity as men remained intact because of the alcohol excuse. Below, David recounts high school experiences with homosexuality among individuals identified as heterosexual.

> DAVID (EA, heterosexual): I eventually had sex with two of my high school friends when

they were drunk. It was a one or two time experience for them and the first for me. One in the mall at Hooters . . . (we were) just drinking . . . another at a gay bar . . . he felt safe (at a gay bar) from not being seen. Another straight guy was at a major work function. After the weekend convention, we had a big party. In the hotel bar, I remember being with some higher-up person at the table and someone else. But I remember we played footsy or something and he got a room at the hotel. We went and we had sex in his room. I later found out from a friend at the call center where I worked that he was married and his wife was pregnant. Obviously he was very drunk and didn't know we were being obvious. I was fired three weeks later.[6]

We see from the experience described above how specific circumstances allow for the construction of gender via practices understood to be feminine or masculine. Victor, an EA heterosexual, shares a similar alcohol related sexual encounter. In this case, instead of the partner being male, Victor's partner was not a desirable or normative sexual partner due to her appearance. Victor states:

VICTOR: I had sex with someone, like a rather big girl. I was drunk and I didn't have like unprotected sex but the bottom line is I had sex with her. I just like totally gave in.
INTERVIEWER: Is that something you regretted?
VICTOR: Oh my God, yeah . . . really bad. But I was drunk, so it was an accident.

Victor uses the alcohol excuse to distance himself from sexual behavior with women deemed inappropriate. Masculine men practice sexual acts with appropriate targets, which do not include other men or undesirable women. Much like the accounts from homosexual respondents discussed above, alcohol was used as an excuse.

Alcohol is used as an excuse only for those who need an excuse. It is used as an excuse for those who resist nonconformity, for those who fear marginalization, or for those who have taken expected gendered performance to an extreme (e.g., date rape). Young gay men who are first experiencing the difficult process of coming out reported using alcohol

to nullify the stigma of being different. Relying upon alcohol as a way to excuse deviant sexual activity was a common theme expressed by young gay male participants struggling to come out. Take the following account for example. Hector, an EA homosexual, talks about the drinking scene, which sounds similar to the drinking scenes of heterosexual EA men. The underlying reasons for drinking, however, are different. Hector states:

HECTOR: [H]aving one or two drinks helped me to loosen up . . . it helps (me be more) comfortable in a situation and open up a little bit more. . . .
INTERVIEWER: Have you been progressing with your coming out; are you getting more comfortable?
HECTOR: Oh yeah, definitely. I can actually go to a club sober now.

Internalized homophobia and the resulting self-loathing stemming from conflict between desire and cultural sexual standards make alcohol a powerful device to experiment with gender practices. Hector suggests that he could not enter the gay bar sober during his initial coming out period; Hector needed to be drunk. Situated intoxication thus permitted Hector to engage in constructing nonhegemonic masculinities. Gender difference here means choosing to be a patron at a local gay bar as a way to pursue his sexual interests. As Hector's gay identity progressed, the role of alcohol was less likely to be used as a way to do gender differently, but rather as a way to socialize with his peers.

Caceres and Cortinas (1996) report that the gay bar provides a social setting where gender and sexuality, as social categories, are reconstructed via alcohol use. That is to say, alcohol use was a catalyst of sorts used to disrupt the normative gender and sexual social order within a specific social space—the gay bar. Thus, for individuals who identify as gay, and are comfortable doing so, gender blunder is not necessarily an appropriate description. Gay participants who had come to embrace their sexuality reported celebrating the opportunity to break free from gender norms in settings afforded by spaces such as gay bars. For these gay men and women, the ritual use of alcohol is not necessarily about celebrating the 21st birthday or the completion of a difficult week of exams. Instead, alcohol use among gay women and men is centered on the opportunity to be hyper-masculine, hyper-feminine, or whatever form of gender construction is needed, as dictated by the intersection between the immediate circumstance, situated context, and individual goals of the person in question. Alcohol can still be blamed for deviant behavior should the person in question be eventually asked to explain his or her actions to friends and or peers (i.e., informal agents of social control). "The alcohol made me do it" excuse thus appears to be acceptable, as illustrated by the accounts documented here and the research literature in general (Caceres and Cortinas 1996).

Conclusion

Using accounts theory as a heuristic tool, this data-driven piece supports SAT. Participants report the use of alcohol situated men and women to engage in gender difference. Through deviant gender constructions situated in the context of alcohol use, the fluidity of gender is exposed, while the alcohol excuse at the same time maintains gender identity. Because there is no evidence to suggest alcohol in and of itself alters behaviors considered to be naturally male or female, I conclude that because gender is a social construct, and the use of alcohol has cultural and social meaning, gender displays and practices become more varied in alcohol use contexts. Participants in the study were inclined to attribute the psychopharmacological properties of alcohol to explain the expression of traditional or nontraditional gendered behaviors. This serves to reproduce and reinforce the status quo of gendered structure. Public alcohol use facilitated the construction of gender regardless of whether gender displays coincided with assigned gender. What was important in gender practices and displays was the situated context in which participants found themselves. The use of alcohol aids not only in the doing of masculinity,[7] but also excuses gender performances not in accordance with proscribed gender practices for both men and women.

This research is important because it (a) implicates alcohol as a tool used in the reproduction of gender, (b) adds to our knowledge on the fluidity and social construction of gender, (c) illuminates how gender is used as a tool for achieving a desired goal (i.e., situated social action), and (d) exemplifies how both men and women use alcohol-related excuses to meet normative expectations (i.e., reproducing social structure). Finally, this analysis contributes to the accounts literature by virtue of its focus on excuses for constructing gender difference. It is important, however, to recognize the limitations of this study. This data collection procedure, which produced the subsample of participants recruited by the Dean of Student's Office, may have biased the sample. It is important to note that the accounts of drinking provided by these participants did not differ from the rest of the sample (e.g., differences in underage drinking or alcohol-related violence). Next, these data were reliant upon participants' memories of alcohol use. It is possible that participants did not accurately report events. However, the manner in which participants constructed their drinking stories is telling of gender dynamics in general and is telling of the meaning of alcohol in particular (see Orbuch 1997, for a discussion on the importance of accounts in deriving meaning from social behavior). Finally, because these data were collected between 1997 and 2001, drinking cultures may have shifted since this study was conducted (see Day, Gough, and McFadden 2003). It is important, however, to recognize that the purpose of this study was not to purport a fixed and unchanging gendered reaction to alcohol, but to provide a snapshot of the significance of gender in drinking cultures and to illustrate the fluidity of gender in situated contexts. With these limitations in mind, I now review the findings and discuss their implications.

Women commonly report using alcohol purposefully as an excuse to engage in behaviors not associated with their prescribed and traditional gender role. Women violated the expected role of passivity, especially when actively pursuing sexual or romantic partners. Public alcohol use absolved women from the consequences of norm violation. Women stated that feelings of low self-worth and low self-confidence were boosted in the context of alcohol use. Women felt good about themselves when engaging in more active instead of passive behaviors. Gay men used alcohol to purposefully celebrate difference. For gay participants, alcohol was used to escape from a perceived heterosexist society and from confining gender norms that did not fit their marginalized ways of doing gender. Alcohol was also used as a means to escape the pain associated with deviant status. Alcohol use provided the excuse to be different and facilitated the ability to be different in the accepting space of the gay bar. The gay bar is a social space, centered on alcohol, where gender-based norms can be left at the doorstep and the construction of gender can take on alternative forms. Bars are thus locations where the boundaries of gender are redrawn, recreated, and reinvented because of the time-out period afforded by alcohol use. Participants also provided evidence of how men use alcohol to construct gender in ways not afforded by their gender identity. These constructions involve emotional expression, poetry writing, dancing, and sexual encounters with inappropriate partners. Importantly, alcohol use simultaneously allowed for gender difference and the structure of gender to remain in place (Lucal 1999) through its power to excuse gender norm violations.

While participants accepted the excuse of drunkenness for gender blunders, they simultaneously believed that a drinking person has control of the body and mind. This discrepancy reveals that the mysterious psychopharmacological nature of alcohol is invoked only when convenient. For participants, the notion that gender is an active accomplishment is a foreign concept. Many believe the expression of gender is entirely a natural extension of human behavior uninfluenced by social structure, social control, or social norms. These accounts reveal that self-control is not entirely lost when heavy drinking occurs. Thus gender, in the face of heavy alcohol use, is being actively and purposefully constructed. What is more, while all participants agree that alcohol should never be accepted as an excuse for improper behavior in general, this collective stance quickly disappears as evidenced by their frequent use of alcohol-related excuses in individual interaction, both as recipient and invokers of alcohol-related excuses.

Notes

1. Research of this kind has not examined the social setting of the college campus. Nor has prior research explored how individuals who self-describe as heterosexual use alcohol to blur the constructed dichotomous identities of straight, gay, masculine, or feminine. In other words, prior research has not explored situated actions that reproduce gendered social structure.

2. College students happen to be an ideal group to study gendered social structure and the role of alcohol use. First, colleges and universities are replete with examples of gender segregation, emphasized femininity, and hegemonic masculinity (Anderson 2002; Bemiller 2005) despite the reputation of colleges and universities have for pursuing gender equality and diversity (Davies and Guppy 1997). Pressures to conform to norms while in college are formidable. Students learn to actively avoid behaviors understood to be deviant in order to avoid marginalization. Researchers have found traditional forms of deviance (i.e., theft, vandalism, and violence) are excused away via alcohol use (Corbin, et al. 2001; Norris, Nurius, and Dimeff 1996). Secondly, college and university students are routinely found to be among the heaviest of drinkers relative to other social groups according to nationally representative surveys (Gfroerer, Greenblatt, and Wright 1997).

3. It is important to note that drinking accounts provided by this group of participants did not differ from those who were not drawn from the Dean of Students Office. The described experiences of both groups could have easily placed any of these participants into the university's judiciary system. Infractions against university policy included underage drinking and destruction of university property.

4. The term "butch" refers in a rough sense to hypermasculinity; to exhibit characteristics traditionally thought of as masculine.

5. The specific context largely determines the extent to which alcohol is able to facilitate alternative gender performances.

6. This account and the others from lesbian, gay, and bisexual (LGB) participants interviewed were more sexually explicit compared to the accounts told by their heterosexual counterparts. I do not know why this was the case. Perhaps the LGB

participants interviewed were more open about sexuality in general. Nevertheless, the accounts expressed here reflect differences in the sharing of sexual details by sexuality.

7. The doing of alcohol and the doing of masculinity are discussed elsewhere (Peralta 2002). Essentially, previous research suggests that particularly heavy and frequent drinking and the particular types of alcohol used are fraught with masculine symbolism. Heavy alcohol use among men in masculine oriented occupations and settings: police, college fraternities, and military (Obst, Davey, and Sheehan 2001; Wechsler and Kuo 2003; Bray, Fairbank and Marsden 1999) has been found to be common.

References

Amadio, D. M. 2006. "Internalized Heterosexism, Alcohol Use, and Alcohol-Related Problems among Lesbians and Gay Men." *Addictive Behaviors* 31: 1153–1162.

Anderson, E. 2002. "Openly Gay Athletes: Contesting Hegemonic Masculinity in a Homophobic Environment." *Gender and Society* 16: 860–877.

Bemiller, M. 2005. "Men Who Cheer." *Sociological Focus* 38: 205–222.

Benoit, C., M. Jansson, A. Millar, and R. Phillips. 2005. "Community-Academic Research on Hard-to-Reach Populations: Benefits and Challenges." *Qualitative Health Research* 15: 263–282.

Bray, R. M., J. A. Fairbank, and M. E. Marsden. 1999. "Stress and Substance Abuse among Military Women and Men." *American Journal of Drug and Alcohol Abuse* 25: 239–256.

Caceres, C. F., and J. I. Cortinas. 1996. "Fantasy Island: An Ethnography of Alcohol and Gender Roles in a Latino Gay Bar." *Journal of Drug Issues* 26: 245–260.

Cohen, D., and L. Lederman. 1998. "Navigating the Freedom of College Life: Students Talk about Alcohol, Gender, and Sex." In *Women and AIDS: Negotiating Safer Practices, Care, and Representation*, edited by N. Roth and L. Fuller, 101–126. New York: Haworth Press.

Collins, P. H., L. A. Maldonado, D. Y. Takagi, B. Thorne, L. Weber, and H. Winant. 1995. "Symposium: On West and Fenstermaker's 'Doing Difference.'" *Gender and Society* 9: 491–513.

Connell, R. W. 1987. *Gender and Power.* Stanford, CA: Stanford University Press.

Connell, R., and J. W. Messerschmidt. 2005. "Hegemonic Masculinity: Rethinking the Concept." *Gender and Society* 19: 829–859.

Corbin, W., J. A. Bernat, K. S. Calhoun, L. D. McNair, and K. L. Seals. 2001. "The Role of Alcohol Expectancies and Alcohol Consumption among Sexually Victimized and Nonvictimized College Women." *Journal of Interpersonal Violence* 16: 297–311.

Creswell, J. W. 2006. *Qualitative Inquiry and Research Design: Choosing among Five Approaches.* London, UK: Sage.

Cromwell, J. 1999. *Transmen and FTMs: Identities, Bodies, Genders and Sexualities.* Urbana: University of Illinois Press.

Davies, S., and N. Guppy. 1997. "Fields of Study, College Selectivity, and Student Inequalities in Higher Education." *Social Forces* 75: 1417–38.

Day, K., B. Gough, and M. McFadden. 2003. "Women Who Drink and Fight: A Discourse Analysis of Working-Class Women's Talk." *Feminism and Psychology* 13: 141–158.

Dozier, R. 2005. "Beards, Breasts, and Bodies: Doing Sex in a Gendered World." *Gender and Society* 19: 297–316.

Eisenberg, M., and H. Wechsler. 2002. "Substance Use Behaviors among College Students with Same-Sex and Opposite-Sex Experience: Results from a National Study." *Addictive Behaviors* 28: 899–913.

Emirbayer, M. 1997. "Manifesto for a Relational Sociology." *American Journal of Sociology* 103: 281–317.

Finlon, C. 2002. "Substance Abuse in Lesbian, Gay, Bisexual, and Transgender Communities." *Journal of Gay and Lesbian Social Services* 14: 109–116.

Garfinkel, H. 1967. *Studies in Ethnomethodology.* Englewood Cliffs, NJ: Prentice Hall.

Gfroerer, J. C., J. C. Greenblatt, and D. A. Wright. 1997. "Substance Use in the U.S. College-Age Population: Differences According to Educational Status and Living Arrangement." *American Journal of Public Health* 87: 62–65.

Glaser, B. G., ed. 1995. *Grounded Theory 1984–1994: A Reader.* Sociology Press.

Glaser, B. G., and A. Strauss. 1967. *The Discovery of Grounded Theory: Strategies for Qualitative Research.* Chicago, IL: Aldine.

Goffman, E. 1976. "Gender Display." *Studies in the Anthropology of Visual Communication* 3: 69–77.

Hollander, J. A. 2002. "Resisting Vulnerability: The Social Reconstruction of Gender in Interaction." *Social Problems* 49: 474–496.

Hughes, T. L. 2003. "Lesbians' Drinking Patterns: Beyond the Data." *Substance Use and Misuse* 38: 1739–1758.

Hughes, T. L., and S. C. Wilsnack. 1994. "Research on Lesbians and Alcohol: Gaps and Implications." *Alcohol Health and Research World* 18: 202–205.

Hughes, T. L., S. C. Wilsnack, L. A. Szalacha, T. Johnson, W. B. Bostwick, and R. Seymour. 2006. "Age and Racial/Ethnic Differences in Drinking and Drinking-Related Problems in a Community Sample of Lesbians." *Journal of Studies on Alcohol* 67: 579–590.

Jersild, D. 2001. *Happy Hours: Alcohol in a Woman's Life.* New York: Cliff Street Books.

Kane, E. W., and M. Schippers. 1995. "Men's and Women's Beliefs about Gender and Sexuality." *Gender and Society* 10: 650–665.

Leblanc, L. 1999. *Pretty in Pink: Girls' Resistance in a Boys' Subculture.* New Brunswick, NY: Rutgers.

Leonard, K. E. 2001. "Alcohol's Role in Domestic Violence: A Contributing Cause or an Excuse?" *Acta-Psychiatric Scandinavia* 106 (supplement 412): 9–14.

Lincoln, Y. S., and E. G. Guba. 1985. *Naturalistic Inquiry.* Beverly Hills, CA: Sage.

Lorber, J. 1994. *Paradoxes of Gender.* New Haven, CT: Yale University Press.

Lucal, B. 1998. "What It Means to Be Gendered Me: Life on the Boundaries of a Dichotomous Gender System." *Gender and Society* 13: 781–797.

Lukenbill, D. F. 1977. "Criminal Homicide as a Situated Transaction." *Social Problems* 25: 176–186.

MacAndrew, C., and R. B. Edgerton. 1969. *Drunken Comportment: A Social Explanation.* Los Angeles, CA: University of California.

Martin, P. Y., and D. L. Collinson. 1998. "Gender and Sexuality in Organizations." In *Revisioning Gender*, edited by M. M. Ferree, J. Lober, and B. B. Hess, 285–310. Walnut Creek: Rowman and Littlefield Publishers.

McCaghy, C. H. 1967. "Drinking and Deviance Disavowal: The Case of Child Molesters." *Social Problems* 16: 43–49.

Messerschmidt, J. W. 1993. *Masculinities and Crime: Critique and Reconceptualization of Theory.* Lanham, MD: Rowman and Littlefield.

Messerschmidt, J. W. 1999. "Making Bodies Matter: Adolescent Masculinities, the Body, and Varieties of Violence." *Theoretical Criminology* 3: 197–220.

Miller, K. E., J. H. Hoffman, G. M. Barnes, M. P. Farrell, D. Sabo, and M. J. Melnick. 2001. "Jocks, Gender, Race, and Adolescent Problem Drinking." *Journal of Drug Education* 33: 445–462.

Montemurro, B., and B. McClure. 2005. "Changing Gender Norms for Alcohol Consumption: Social Drinking and Lowered Inhibitions at Bachelorette Parties." *Sex Roles* 52: 279–288.

National Institute on Alcohol Abuse and Alcoholism. 1999. *Are Women More Vulnerable to Alcohol's Effects?* Rockville, MD.

Norris, J., P. S. Nurius, and L. A. Dimeff. 1995. "Through Her Eyes: Factors Affecting Women's Perceptions of and Resistance to Acquaintance Sexual Aggression Threat." *Psychology of Women Quarterly* 20: 132–145.

Obst, P. L., J. D. Davey, and M. C. Sheehan. 1998. "Does Joining the Police Service Drive You to Drink? A Longitudinal Study of the Drinking Habits of Police Recruits." *Drugs: Education Prevention and Policy* 8: 347–357.

Orbuch, T. L. 1995. "People's Accounts Count: The Sociology of Accounts." *Annual Review of Sociology* 23: 455–478.

Orcutt, J. D. 1975. "Deviance as Situated Phenomenon: Variations in the Social Interpretation of Marijuana and Alcohol Use." *Social Problems* 22: 346–356.

Parks, A. C. 1999. "Lesbian Social Drinking: The Role of Alcohol in Growing Up and Living as Lesbian." *Contemporary Drug Problems* 26: 75–82.

Parks, A. C., and T. L. Hughes. 2005. "Alcohol Use and Alcohol-Related Problems in Self-Identified Lesbians: An Historical Cohort." *Journal of Lesbian Studies* 9: 31–44.

Peralta, R. L. 1998. "Alcohol Use and the Fear of Weight Gain in College: Reconciling Two Social Norms." *Gender Issues* 20: 23–42.

Peralta, R. L. 2005. "Race and the Culture of College Drinking: An Analysis of White Privilege on a College Campus." In *Cocktails & Dreams: An*

Interpretive Perspective on Substance Use, edited by W. R. Palacios, 127–141. Upper Saddle River, NJ: Prentice Hall.

Peralta, R. L., and J. M. Cruz. 2005. "Conferring Meaning onto Alcohol-Related Violence: An Analysis of Alcohol Use and Gender in a Sample of College Youth." *The Journal of Men's Studies* 141: 109–125.

Rhodes, T., and L. Cusick. 2002. "Accounting for Unprotected Sex: Stories of Agency and Accountability." *Social Science and Medicine* 55: 211–226.

Scott, M. B., and S. M. Lyman. 1981. "Accounts." In *Social Psychology through Symbolic Interaction*, 2nd ed., edited by G. P. Stone and H. A. Farberman, 343–61. New York: John Wiley.

Scully, D., and J. Marolla. 1984. "Convicted Rapists' Vocabulary of Motive: Excuses and Justifications." *Social Problems* 31: 530–544.

Sheehan, M., and D. Ridge. 2001. "'You Become Really Close. . . . You Talk about the Silly Things You Did, and We Laugh': The Role of Binge Drinking in Female Secondary Student's Lives." *Substance Use and Misuse* 36: 347–372.

Stall, R., J. P. Paul, G. Greenwood, L. M. Pollack, E. Bein, and G. M. Crosby. 2001. "Alcohol Use, Drug Use and Alcohol-Related Problems among Men Who Have Sex with Men: The Urban Men's Health Study." *Addiction* 96: 1589–1601.

Stall, R., and J. Willey. 1987. "A Comparison of Alcohol and Drug Use Patterns of Homosexual and Heterosexual Men: The San Francisco Men's Health Study." *Drug and Alcohol Dependence* 22: 63–73.

Strauss, A., and J. Corbin. 1990. *Basics of Qualitative Research: Grounded Theory Procedures and Techniques*. Newbury Park, CA: Sage.

Sudman, S., and N. M. Bradburn. 1981. *Asking Questions: A Practical Guide to Questionnaire Design*. San Francisco: Jossey-Bass.

Tori, C. 1987. "Homosexuality and Illegal Residency Status in Relation to Substance Abuse and Personality Traits among Mexican Nationals." *Journal of Clinical Psychology* 45: 814–821.

Trocki, K. F. 2005. "Use of Heavier Drinking Contexts among Heterosexuals, Homosexuals, and Bisexuals: Results from a National Household Probability Survey." *Journal of Studies on Alcohol* 66: 105–110.

Tryggvesson, K. 2001. "The Ambiguous Excuse: Attributing Violence to Intoxication: Young Swedes about the Excuse Value of Alcohol." *Contemporary Drug Problems* 31: 231–261.

Vander Ven, T. 2001. "The Community Construction of the Underage Drinker." *Deviant Behavior* 26: 63–83.

Wechsler, H., and M. Kuo. 2002. "Watering Down the Dinks: The Moderating Effect of College Demographics on Alcohol Use of High-Risk Groups." *American Journal of Public Health* 93: 1929–1932.

West, C., and S. Fenstermaker. 1994. "Doing Difference." *Gender and Society* 9: 8–37.

West, C., and D. H. Zimmerman. 1987. "Doing Gender." *Gender and Society* 1: 125–151.

West, L. A. 2001. "Negotiating Masculinities in American Drinking Subcultures." *The Journal of Men's Studies* 9: 371–392.

Wiseman, J. P. 1991. *The Other Half: Wives of Alcoholics and Their Social Psychological Situation*. Aldine de Gruyter: New York.

For Discussion

1. Think about how society expects us to conform to gender norms and consider how these norms influence, and at times, restrict our behaviors. Is it important to be free of these societal expectations?

2. In the endnotes, Peralta explains the importance of examining this topic with a sample of college students. What if the study had used a sample of bar patrons as opposed to college students? What do you think the findings would show in terms of gender norms in bar settings? Might the findings differ from those reported by Peralta?

Subcultures, Social Networks, and Drug Scenes

Albert Cohen (1955) suggested that society was comprised of several sub-groups and used the term "subculture" to refer to cultures within cultures. According to Cohen, the *delinquent subculture* was a reaction to middle-class norms and mainstream visions of social status. He argued that working-class youth had difficulties achieving status in the middle-class world; thus, they reacted against the middle-class way of life and created their own value system. The delinquent subculture comprised a means for interacting with other youth who were similarly placed. It also promoted alternative kinds of status that group members could achieve. Cohen's work was very influential and contributed to further scholarly interest in subcultural theory.

More recently, the relevance of subcultural theories for explaining drug use has been debated among scholars. Similar to Cohen's study, much of the earlier work on subcultures assumed that they could be delineated by social class, and considerable research focused on male youth from working-class or low-income backgrounds. This emphasis has been critiqued by some scholars, because it ignores drug use among youth from upper- and middle-class backgrounds. Moreover, Blackman (2004) argued that working-class youth represent a heterogeneous group; that is, there is not necessarily a shared value system that unites youth from working-class backgrounds. Friendship networks are not the same as subcultures and not all working-class youth belong to or identify with the latter. According to Blackman, the concept of subculture fails to acknowledge that values and beliefs among working-class youth can vary across and within geographic areas. Australian anthropologist David Moore (2004) suggested that researchers in the United States have assumed that subcultures maintain distinct boundaries and are largely detached and isolated from mainstream society. Moore's study described two groups of individuals who used drugs: the *Players* and the *Bohemians*. However, Moore concluded that neither group could be characterized as a subculture. Players shared the same ethnicity, but individual Players maintained different hairstyles, music taste, and fashion interests. Although their patterns of drug use differed, most Players engaged in "playing the game," that is, accessing, selling, and using drugs in the context of unethical business practices in an illicit market. Patterns of drug use also differed among Bohemians as did their music interests and sexual identities. However, they often shared housing and maintained friendships with other Bohemians. Moore did not deny the existence of subcultures but argued that the concept assumes that groups of drug takers share similar beliefs and customs that are important for group identity. Instead, Moore found that individual members of the two social groups were quite different in terms of their drug use patterns and other lifestyle interests. Moore's study led him to conclude that *drug scenes* are perhaps better descriptors than drug subcultures; a particular drug scene might include members of various subcultures (2004, 201).

Other scholars continue to assert that subcultures are important for the study of drug use. For instance, Golub, Johnson, and Dunlap (2005) noted different kinds of drug subcultures; some subcultures include individuals who use drugs primarily for recreation, whereas other drug subcultures are comprised of individuals whose drug use and drug seeking tend to dominate their lives. Importantly, Golub et al. (2005) also note that the focus and membership of drug subcultures can change over time, and that individuals can identify with more than one drug subculture.

In the mid-1980s, a dance/club scene emerged on the Mediterranean island of Ibiza that incorporated a unique music genre. Allegedly, DJs from England were visiting the island and consumed MDMA during a night out in a local club. The experience of MDMA in the context of the DJs' innovative music encouraged the group to re-create the scene in London. Referred to as acid house, the music was a collective sound of various music genres that had roots in Chicago and Detroit. Shortly thereafter, the "rave scene" emerged from acid house phenomena and techno music parties. Raves tended to be unlicensed events lasting all night or over the course of several days, and were held in fields, abandoned factories and warehouses, and other secluded venues. In the late-1980s and early-1990s, the rave scene seemed to expand into a "movement" that was shaped by collective identity and solidarity among its members: friends, acquaintances and strangers. However, solidarity varied by locale. In Belfast (Northern Ireland), the second editor of this book was involved in a study that was based on interview data collected from current and former users of MDMA. In that study, individuals from middle-class backgrounds who used MDMA at raves, often made disparaging remarks about their working-class peers who also participated in the rave scene. That finding suggests that solidarity depended on the social class backgrounds of participants in the rave scene.

Still, characteristics of raves held in various countries suggest the presence of subcultural attributes. For instance, the behavior at raves was often guided by informal norms and the scene was characterized by symbolic logos and in some locales, unique fashion and accessories. In many ways, rave participants shared an anti-establishment ideology. Although not all rave participants engaged in drug use, MDMA in particular became strongly associated with raves because for most participants, the pharmacological effects of MDMA were enhanced by the music featured at raves and vice-versa.

By the 2000s, raves began to dissipate in the United States, western Europe and elsewhere, replaced by the electronic dance music (EDM) scene. Unlike raves, EDM caters to various groups of people, including "mainstream" youth. Moreover, EDM has entered the pop charts, and whereas raves were part of the underground, EDM concerts are bolstered by corporate funding and are advertised publicly. Venues have expanded to include everyday clubs, and solidarity is rarely found in the collective. Although early raves were characterized by subcultural properties, EDM is more appropriately described as a scene or collection of scenes.

Social Networks

Most of us have strong as well as weak social ties with other individuals. These links represent our social networks. Social networks are important to the study of drug use because several individuals use drugs with and certainly access drugs from other people. The study of social networks has been particularly important for the prevention of blood-borne viruses (e.g., hepatitis B and C virus, HIV) among people who inject psychoactive drugs. Injecting environments can include individuals from different social networks who are loosely or strongly tied to several others. The diverse social linkages among network members can contribute to or reduce the transmission of blood-borne viruses. Social networks are also important for diffusing knowledge about ways to prevent transmission (Heckathorn et al. 1999). Social linkages can contribute to, mediate, or reduce the likelihood of drug use and particular injecting practices. The two articles in this section focus on drug use among individuals who might be characterized as belonging to particular subcultures, social networks, or scenes.

References

Blackman, S. 2004. *"Chilling Out": The Cultural Politics of Substance Consumption, Youth and Drug Policy*. Maidenhead: McGraw Hill—Open University Press.

Cohen, A. 1955. *Delinquent Boys: The Culture of the Gang*. New York: Free Press.

Golub, A., B. D. Johnson, and E. Dunlap. 2005. "Subcultural Evolution and Illicit Drug Use." *Addiction Research and Theory* 13: 217–229.

Heckathorn, D. D., R. S. Broadhead, D. L. Anthony, and D. L. Weakliem. 1999. "AIDS and Social Networks: HIV Prevention Through Network Mobilization." *Sociological Focus* 32: 159–179.

Moore, D. 2004. "Beyond 'Subculture' in the Ethnography of Illicit Drug Use." *Contemporary Drug Problems* 31: 181–212.

15

Adderall Abuse on College Campuses

A Comprehensive Literature Review

MATTHEW D. VARGA

This article summarizes several issues that relate to the misuse of Adderall—a prescribed stimulant—among college and university students. Matthew D. Varga discusses the factors that might contribute to misuse of Adderall, the implications of misuse for students, the challenges for university administrators, and interventions that might assist students who misuse Adderall.

In 2007, Major League Baseball found itself in a whirlwind of accusations, congressional hearings, skeptical records, and questionable credibility at a time when steroid use was *technically* (emphasis added) not a violation of Major League Baseball policy. However, that did not stop fans or the media from lashing out, criticizing, and boycotting the sport. Players such as Sammy Sosa, Mark McGuire, and Barry Bonds—previously considered among the greatest players in the history of baseball—suddenly found their careers and successes scrutinized for cheating. Barry Bonds, Mark McGuire, and Sammy Sosa became the poster boys for society's anger at cheating for personal gain, unfair competition, and the use of performance enhancing chemicals.

Unfortunately, as common as this story may be in other professional athletics, it is becoming increasingly common in not only high school athletics (Dodge and Jaccard 2006), but also high school academics (Wroble, Gray, and Rodrigo 2002).

Indeed, high school students' use of anabolic steroids reportedly increased 126% between 1991 and 2003 according to The National Center on Addiction and Substance Abuse (CASA 2005). CASA revealed that approximately 1.7 million high school students admitted self-medicating with prescription steroids in 2003 (CASA 2005). The actual cause for this increase is little more than speculation, but one study explained high school students' motives as improving physical appearance, bettering athletic abilities, and impersonating adults (Kindlundh, Isacson, Berglund, and Nyberg 1999). The serious health consequences that accompany anabolic steroids deter very few users. In fact, the passion to achieve their dreams and outdo competitors is so great, anabolic steroid users may intentionally risk their life obtaining personal goals despite steroid use being widely condemned by society (Wichstrom and Pedersen 2001).

One of the most commonly known performance enhancers is anabolic steroids. Recently,

Reprinted from Matthew D. Varga, 2012, "Adderall Abuse on College Campuses: A Comprehensive Literature Review," in *Journal of Evidence-Based Social Work* 9: 293–313. Reprinted by permission of Taylor & Francis via Copyright Clearance Center.

another variation of performance enhancers has become introduced onto campuses across the country and has gone relatively unnoticed by teachers, professors, administrators, and others. However, most high school and college students are quite aware of this world, so much so that campus cultures begin to morph into a microcosm that expects the abuse of prescription stimulants. Middle schools, high schools, and especially colleges are encountering students who abuse prescription narcotic stimulants such as Adderall, Ritalin, and others, in hopes of achieving higher grades, getting "high," or other effects (Moline and Frankenberger 2001).

Students may be exposed to prescription stimulants as early as middle school and continue using into college, resulting in nonpatients becoming exposed to the drugs and the effects. As more students are introduced to these stimulants and acknowledge perceived benefits, the harmful and additive attributes may go unnoticed compared to the benefits students possibly experience. The consequence of this behavior is a gross misperception of a drug capable of assisting attentiveness and concentration that improve academic performance. This becomes even more dangerous when accounting for the current student generation's academic ambitions. Prescription stimulant use is spreading across college campuses and instead of condemnation it is implicitly being praised and validated by parents and students who view these drugs as a means of academic assistance by increasing attentiveness and concentration (Babcock and Byrne 2000; Hall et al. 2005; McCabe, Teter, and Boyd 2006; Teter et al. 2005; White et al. 2005).

The following personal experience involves working with a small group of student athletes and is an example of how some students misperceive the benefits of prescription stimulants as a miracle drug. One night the author was reviewing a student athlete's upcoming academic week, which included reading three books and studying for an exam, an essay, and a quiz. This student athlete broke down crying in fear of failing and losing NCAA eligibility. The author and student reviewed the assignments and broke them down into daily tasks. The author then asked the student how she felt about her upcoming week. She responded, "I feel better; besides, I will get Adderall from my friend and just pump it

out." The response was incredibly carefree, and the only concern she had was completing her assignments and maintaining eligibility. Unfortunately, this mindset is common among a majority of college students striving for success, both academically and professionally (Babcock and Byrne 2000; Cavagnero 2006; Comos and DeBard 2004).

A whole host of prescription stimulants has increasingly found its way onto college campuses, and they are being used in ways and by persons for which they were not necessarily intended. These drugs include methylphenidate (e.g., Ritalin, Concerta), dextroamphetamine (e.g., Dexdrine), Sibutramine hydrochloride monohydrate (e.g., Meridia), and amphetamine-dextroamphetamine, also known as Adderall (CASA 2005). The Controlled Substances Act classifies the aforementioned drugs as schedule II drugs due to the high potential of addiction, medical/non-medical abuse, and for patients and nonpatients to self-medicate, use for recreation, or sell to non-patients is high (CASA 2005). For example, 2.3 million middle and high school students are reputed to self-medicate with Adderall and Ritalin, an increase of 212% from 1992 to 2003 (CASA 2005).

While widely used in the past to treat asthma and other respiratory problems including obesity and specific neurological disorders, stimulant medications are becoming the primary treatment for mental disorders such as Attention Deficit Disorder and Attention Hyperactivity Disorder despite medical concerns about stimulants' abusive and addictive potential. The effects of these drugs can produce a pleasurable effect, similar to cocaine, speed, and Ecstasy. Hard drugs such as these and said prescription stimulants replicate the natural brain chemicals effecting neurotransmitters called norepinephrine and dopamine, which assists patients with Attention Deficit Hyperactivity Disorder (ADHD) focus and concentrate comparable to students without the disorder. However, for those who do not suffer from ADHD the additional chemicals overload the brain with artificial chemicals producing a sense of pleasure resembling the effects of cocaine and speed, subsequently increasing the possibility of chemical dependence and addiction. Therefore, stimulant use is primarily reserved as a treatment for a few disorders, including narcolepsy, ADHD, and, in some cases, depression (United States Drug Enforcement Administration 2005).

Despite the limited mental health disorders that suggest stimulants as a treatment, the diagnoses of these disorders, specifically Attention Deficit Disorder and ADHD, have significantly increased over the past 10 to 15 years and show little signs of slowing down (Howe and Strauss 2000); consequently, written prescriptions for stimulants have also increased during the same time. The aforementioned prescriptions for stimulants increased 368.5% from 1992 to 2002 (Drug Enforcement Agency 2002). An increase in Adderall production naturally followed increased demand requiring a production jump of approximately 9,008,000% over 10 years. It is the most widely prescribed stimulant, second only to Ritalin with 12,881,000 prescriptions from 1992 to 2002 (Drug Enforcement Agency 2002).

The dramatic increase in Adderall and Ritalin is suggestive of widespread use of these prescription medications, but we have only limited and speculative information about the extent of their use and/or abuse on campus. Various independent studies have assessed the levels of stimulant abuse on campuses. Surprisingly, the studies suggest comparable percentages of students self-reporting their illicit use; averaging the respective percentages, approximately 20% represent a campus subpopulation who abuse prescription stimulants, specifically Adderall and/or Ritalin (Babcock and Byrne 2000; Hall et al. 2005; McCabe et al. 2006; White et al. 2005). According to the 2004 National Survey on Drug Use and Health (NSDUH), young adults between the ages of 18 and 25 years self-reported the highest incidence of illicit prescription use (14.8%). Additionally, the 2004 Monitoring the Future (MTF) national survey revealed that the prevalence of non-medical use of several prescription drug classes was at its highest rate in 15 years; additionally, college students self-reported higher rates of Ritalin abuse than their non-collegiate peers: 4.7% to 1.6% respectively (Johnston et al. 2005). Interestingly, White college males reported a slightly higher rate of illegal use than White college females (16.1% to 13.4%).

While the studies of collegiate abuse found similar levels (20% of surveyed students) of reported use (Babcock and Byrne 2000; Hall et al. 2005; McCabe et al. 2006; White et al. 2005), additional findings from White et al. (2005) reported that 90% of the students denoting such use indicated they were not ADHD. Babcock and Byrne (2000) found that 40% of said students admitted to snorting the medication to increase the drug's intensity. Thus, while the evidence of abuse and illicit use remains limited and rests largely on self-reports, it is highly suggestive of extensive prescription stimulant abuse across campuses.

Purpose

The purpose of the author in this article is to examine stimulant abuse on college campus, review potential implications for failing to address the problem, and explore possibilities confronting the abusive behavior. The article consists of three sections: (a) factors contributing to illicit use, self-medication, and recreational use of controlled prescription stimulants as drawn from the literature; (b) discussion of potential consequences for those students abusing stimulants, and possible implications confronting higher education institutions; (c) finally, recommendations for educating, combating, and assisting students who illicitly use prescription stimulants.

Contributing Factors

Not all of today's students abuse stimulants; in fact the literature has shown approximately 20% of students self-report abusing Adderall and/or Ritalin on a college campus (Babcock and Byrne 2000; Hall et al. 2005; McCabe et al. 2006; White et al. 2005). However, it is unclear how many students are actually using, and not reporting it. Although, it can be speculated from those who self report using the stimulants and other variables within the literature that many factors may contribute to students abusing stimulants, but all of these factors cannot possibly be known. Further, students may be exposed to similar factors but only a few may demonstrate abusive habits. As a result, factors thought to contribute to Adderall abuse are generalized and based on the existing literature.

There are four main factors contributing to Adderall abuse: (a) pressure to succeed;

(b) socio-cultural expectations; (c) collegiate life-style; (d) and accessibility to prescription stimulants. Today, students are pressured to succeed more than in previous years (Howe and Strauss 2000). The origin of the pressure lies with increased parental expectations and their excessive educational involvement (Bishop 2003; Kadison and Digeronimo 2004; Taylor, Pogrebin, and Dodge 2002), competing within peer groups or maintaining unspoken standards (Bishop 2003; Taylor et al. 2002), meeting college admission requirements (Bishop 2003; Chronicle of Higher Education 2005; Farrell 2006; Kohn 2003), and/or personal academic expectations (Bishop 2003; Howe and Strauss 2000; Kadison and Digeronimo 2004; Sax 2003). There are socio-cultural factors contributing to students using Adderall such as growing up with multiple friends on prescription stimulants. Thirdly, the college lifestyle may contribute to some students' illicit use. A stimulant medication could assist with staying up late, social gatherings, and battling exhaustion from participating in multiple clubs and organizations (Brooks 2001; Dworkin 2005; Labig, Zantow, and Peterson 2005; Law 2007; Quintero, Peterson, and Young 2006). Finally, students have increased accessibility to stimulant drugs since more students are now on college campuses with peers legitimately receiving prescriptions for various mental disorders (CASA 2005; Kadison and Digeronimo 2004).

Pressure for Success

The desire for success is a strictly personal quest and can originate from a metaphysical or existential motivator. Additionally, defining what a student perceives as successful cannot be determined since it is very individualistic. However, external pressures that force students to use prescription stimulants can be determined. These include parental pressures, pressures regarding college admissions during high school, and the pressure coping with the collegiate lifestyle; additionally, there are personal pressures a student may have for him/herself.

Parental Pressures

More likely to have graduated college themselves, today's parents are more likely to understand the significance of grades, in addition to other necessities required for college (Howe and Strauss 2000). Parents are cognizant to the fact that colleges expect high grades, extracurricular activities, and various other requirements for admission. Parents of today's student are not ignorant to the hardships their son or daughter confronts during their academic pursuit. In fact, the pressure they place on students can be so great that students are forced to find additional methods, such as prescription drug abuse, to meet parental expectations.

Typically, the student's well-being is the primary motive for parents' ambitious expectations of their children; however, Kadison and Digeronimo (2004) argue another perspective. Parents are deemed "good parents" by society if their child is successful. Therefore, high expectations, providing multiple opportunities, and becoming aggressively involved in their students educational lives are means to ensure they are viewed as "good parents." As a result, some parents may continually raise expectations in academics, athletics, and community and social involvement to validate their parental worth and hope it benefits their children for the future (Kadison and Digeronimo 2004).

Whatever the motive for parents to place standards on their son or daughter one thing is certain: students experience intense pressure to succeed in school from their parents and failure is not an option. In support, Bishop (2003) reports 55% of students "work really hard in school" to please their parents and 44% do it in response to parental pressures (2). A quote from a teacher reinforces this idea of insurmountable pressure:

> I've seen increasing expectations, anxiety, and downright disappointment from parents . . . who expect their 17- or 18-year-old kids to have attained some rarefied state of perfection . . . at some parent conferences, I find myself defending bright, talented students whose mothers or fathers act as if they have a defective product on their hands. (Howe and Strauss 2000, 162)

Parents raise their academic expectations as the student progresses through school, and each new grade usually means harder coursework without lower expectations (Kadison and Digeronimo 2004).

Regardless of course load or difficulty level, parents expect students to earn high academic accomplishments consistently while maintaining extracurricular activities and a social life (Kadison and Digeronimo 2004). The parents unable to accept a mediocre or satisfactory performance may disprove of this level of performance with the best of intentions; but the pressure can have detrimental consequences. College students may feel "forced to cope" by abusing performance enhancing drugs like Adderall, or other drugs, to deal with the resulting stress and anxiety (Kadison and Digeronimo 2004).

High School Pressures

One college student averred, "In high school, it wasn't too difficult for the best students to rise to the top and for even average students to get exceptional grades"; however, she reported, once she began college her parents continued to expect the same academic success as she had had in high school, or even more (Kadison and Digeronimo 2004, 36). Such expectations increase the pressure to surpass previous academic performances. Satisfactory performance may be viewed as unacceptable by parents and students, since society is seen as becoming much more competitive (Bishop 2003; *Chronicle of Higher Education* 2005; Debard 2004; Farrell 2006; Howe and Strauss 2000; Kadison and Digeronimo 2004; Sax 2003; Taylor et al. 2002), requiring the student to be "better than" just to remain in competition.

This is no easy task in a generation of approximately 100 million (Howe and Strauss 2000) youth. Students are applying to colleges in record numbers and most admissions offices are receiving between an 8% (University of Michigan in 2006) and 41% (College of Holy Cross in 2006) increase in applicants (Farrell 2006). Kadison and Digeronimo (2004) explain the impact this has on students: "With record numbers of high school seniors applying for a finite number of spaces at public and private colleges and universities across the country, the institutes of higher learning have become far more selective than in the past" (35). Students quickly learn that good is not good enough; and that using prescription stimulants is sometimes interpreted as one means to get the edge on the competition.

High school is usually the birthplace of academic competition (Bishop 2003; Debard 2004; Howe and Strauss 2000; Kadison and Digeronimo 2004; Kohn 2003; Woodruff and Ziomek 2004). Students tend to view academic achievement in high school as the means to college acceptance. Bishop (2003) argues that 79% of students work hard just to earn the grades needed to get into college. The *Chronicle of Higher Education* (2005) interviewed six experts regarding the admissions' process as it stands today. Robin C. Brown, Vice President for Enrollment at Willamette University and Vice President for Admission, Counseling, and Enrollment Practices at the National Association for College Admission Counseling, captured the situation aptly, stating:

> Then there are the population increases that will continue to stretch our resources and prevent institutions from admitting qualified students. The increasing lack of predictability about who will be admitted, particularly to the most selective colleges, has added to the flood of applications into a system already overwhelmed; the proliferation of early-decision and early-action programs has increased confusion for students in a process already wrought with mystery. Changing admissions and standardized testing requirements add to the anxiety. Finally, management-enrollment practices that rely on offering some students discounted tuition add to the unpredictability about who will be admitted and, equally as important, may force institutions to admit students who are not the best fit. (Chronicle of Higher Education 2005, 24)

High achieving students tacitly compete to earn the best grade, be the most involved, do the most community service, have the highest ACT or SAT score, or whatever else is perceived as necessary to guarantee admission into their top college (Kohn 2003). Kohn (2003) explained the impact of this intense competition during a speech to high school students, but Luthar and Becker (2002) subsequently corroborated it with empirical research:

> They were joining clubs without enthusiasm because they thought the membership would look impressive. They were ignoring—or perhaps, by now, even forgetting—what they enjoyed doing . . . grimly

trying to squeeze out another few points on the GPA or the SAT, in the process of losing sleep, losing friends, losing perspective. Many of them may have been desperately unhappy, filled with anxiety and self-doubt. Some of them may have had eating disorders, substance abuse problems, even suicidal thoughts. They might have gone into therapy except they had no spare time. None of this was a secret to these students, but what few realized was that the process wouldn't end once they finally got to college. This straining toward the future, this poisonous assumption that the value of everything is solely a function of its contribution to something that may come later—it would start all over again in September of their first year away from home. (14–15)

Kohn (2003) points out students are facing this pressure throughout high school and for the next four to six years of their lives. Their inability to adjust to these pressures forces some students to abuse amphetamines like Adderall and Ritalin to cope with the growing expectations. Luthar and D'Avanzo (1999) linked self-reported maladjustment, by affluent White teens to substance use, which suggests that affluent teens used substances to self-medicate. Interestingly enough, substance abuse among affluent White suburban students is greater than that of their inner-city counterparts, 59% to 38%, respectively.

Collegiate Pressures

After arriving at college, a new set of pressures and expectations befall students, especially for those who experienced little trouble earning as in high school. Most students entering college know only themselves and their abilities in relation to high school performance. For the students who were academically successful in high school and had little difficultly in rising to the top of their class, college success is often viewed as a guarantee, until the first B or C is earned. Students who were tops in their high school class may now find themselves in the middle, surrounded by other students that were successful in high school (Kadison and Digeronimo 2004).

Previously perceived as the smartest, brightest, and most successful, these students may struggle with the reality of earning lesser grades. In order to redeem their self-identity as a top academic achiever, formerly successful students may increasingly focus on achieving the best grade to prove to themselves and parents that they are still as good as they were (Kadison and Digeronimo 2004). A drastic concern for grades among college students today has not gone unnoticed by faculty. One faculty member explains, "I received an e-mail from a student saying that if she fails this course, she's going to kill herself" (Kadison and Digeronimo 2004, 36). It is not the objective stress of failing a grade or earning a B; instead, it is the subjective stress of over-generalizing the life consequences of a lesser grade. In response, some students vow to work harder. Kadison and Digeronimo (2004) provide an example of a student who became overwhelmed and challenged his self-identity after he received a C on the first term paper. He obsessed over earning high marks and:

> Gave up his morning job, barely grabbed a snack during the day, stopped "unnecessary" socializing, and stayed up to the wee hours of the morning studying. Ted thought he was doing a good thing . . . By studying too much and too long, Ted was soon studying less and less efficiently. This increased his need to study more, setting up a dangerous cycle. (39)

Grade-obsessed students, such as Ted, are less likely to admit their failures and more likely to search for other means of achieving their goal. Adderall becomes a perfect solution for assisting these students reaffirm their self-identity (Kadison and Digeronimo 2004). Ted entered a cycle of studying and giving up all other activities, which caused his studying to become less efficient. Since Adderall assists college students to focus intensely on their work and indirectly improve efficiency, the cycle can be broken subsequently allowing time for other activities (Kadison and Digeronimo 2004).

Socio-Cultural Factors

Overall, pressure to succeed contributes to Adderall abuse; however, sociocultural acceptance of its abuse poses a greater, potentially more dangerous threat (Quintero et al. 2006). College students typically perceive recreational prescription drug use, including the use of Ritalin and Adderall, as acceptable compared to the use of other drugs, such as cocaine and heroin. In a study of such perceptions, Quintero et al. (2006) found:

> [Prescription drug use] involves a form of comparative reasoning that creates a juxtaposition between "soft" and "hard" drugs. The former allow for pleasure and performance if used wisely while the latter are associated with greater social and physical risks, including loss of control, role failure, and addiction. (914)

This comparative reasoning incorporates perceptions of prescribed drugs as safe since the medications are intentionally designed for a specific purpose, and individuals, their families, and friends have used prescription drugs such as Adderall all of their lives (Quintero et al. 2006). It has been suggested by Quintero et al. (2006) that in terms of physical risks, "college students consider prescription drugs safer to use than other drugs because pharmaceuticals are subjected to extensive laboratory testing, are manufactured in clean laboratories by professionals, and produce a standard dose dependent effect" (915). In addition, the fact that potential side effects of Adderall are listed on the label significantly contributes to the perception of a more predictable experience. Most interestingly, they found that students considered peers to be one of the most reliable sources of information about using Adderall. One student explains this dangerous thinking:

> I'm pretty informed. I take pharmacy classes. And then the other thing too with prescription drugs is my peers. There are some drugs that I haven't learned about in class or something. I don't know the effects. But then I hear about it from my peers because either someone tried it, or someone's doing it, or someone has it. Books are a reliable source of information but in terms of really knowing about something, in my opinion, you can only learn so much from a book. But the amount of information you can get from people you interact with is kind of interesting because you hear a lot of stuff from people, especially regarding what's out there, what's the latest thing or something. I'd say

my peers are the best source of information. One of them is bound to know something about it. (Quintero et al. 2006, 921)

This is extremely frightening considering that the number of students for whom Adderall has been prescribed has increased significantly over the past 10 years (CASA 2005). More students possess knowledge about the effects and can offer that information to non-users, potentially transforming them into new abusers of prescription stimulants.

An additional factor contributing to students' recreational misuse of Adderall is related to the real and perceived legal consequences for using such drugs (Quintero et al. 2006). More often than not students believe that using prescribed drugs is not illegal or that legal sanctions can be easily avoided if caught with the medications. Students can claim it belonged to a friend, a defense with no viability if they are caught possessing drugs such as cocaine.

Media advertisements for prescription stimulants reinforce drugs such as Adderall as safe for academic, recreational, and self-medication purposes. They are government approved and legal, easily leading to the belief that the drug is manageable, controllable, non-addictive, and more appropriate than "hard drugs" (Quintero et al. 2006). In addition to governmental approval, the simple fact that doctors prescribe Adderall contributes to the perception of security and harmlessness; after all, doctors seek to promote health.

A final contributing factor to Adderall abuse is parental behaviors and negligence in their own use of controlled prescription medicine. Baby-boomer parents are the highest consumers of prescription drugs (CASA 2005), which provides a dangerous example to adolescents (McCabe et al. 2006). Parental behaviors perceived as acceptable, appropriate, and safe may contribute to students' assumptions that prescription drugs are not harmful (CASA 2005).

Collegiate Lifestyle

The lifestyle of college students serves as a contributing factor to Adderall abuse. Features commonly associated with college life, such as staying up all night partying, studying through the night, and having rigorous academic and extracurricular schedules, provide incentives for using stimulants to students suffering from exhaustion (Babcock and Byrne 2000; Law 2007). Students may abuse Adderall to cope with juggling multiple extracurricular activities while maintaining academic standards (Kadison and Digeronimo 2004). Adderall becomes, for them, an ideal way of ensuring academic success and assisting them through a structured day of classes, extracurricular activities, and sometimes work (Brooks 2001). Brooks (2001) interviewed students regarding their daily lives and the pressure associated with them. One student explained his day as "crew practice at dawn, classes in the morning, resident-advisor duty, lunch, study groups, classes in the afternoon, tutoring disadvantaged kids in Trenton, a cappella practice, dinner, study, science lab, prayer session, hit the StairMaster, study a few more hours" (40). Law (2007) suggests days such as these have been known to cause exhaustion and burnout, and a central nervous stimulant becomes a viable option for treating the exhaustion and persevering through the day. A student interviewed by Quintero et al. (2006) reiterated this point. He shared, "I found myself starving for energy and just needing to be focused and I tried [Adderall] and it actually helped me concentrate and be alert for an extended amount of time. And I found that I could study more efficiently with it than I could without it" (914).

Testimonials such as this are common for today's ambitious, overly extended college students. Students must value and take advantage of every moment to study. Eventually, students suffer from stress and struggle to make time for studying. Therefore, students may resort to obtaining and consuming prescription medicine, illicitly or illegally, to increase their efficiency, focus, energy, and alertness (Babcock and Byrne 2000).

In contrast, other students use Adderall experimentally and recreationally, considering college is a time for drug experimenting, pushing the limits, and discovering one's self (Quintero et al. 2006). Armed with the perception that Adderall is acceptable and safe, it may be seen as a "good" drug to experiment with. Quintero et al. (2006) reported that several of their interviewees "consciously recognized this period of their life as a time for drug use and suggested that this practice would have to diminish in the future as they completed their studies and entered a new life phase" (922). Given the perceptions of acceptability and low risk, users' knowledge and experiences, and willingness to experiment, Adderall and other controlled stimulants may be particularly valued as a means of engaging in this culturally acceptable behavior (Quintero et al. 2006).

Accessibility

The fourth and final factor contributing to Adderall misuse is the ease of accessibility (Babcock and Byrne 2000; CASA 2005; Hall et al. 2005; McCabe et al. 2006; Quintero et al. 2006; Teter et al. 2005). Adderall is available to students from various sources. The increase in students coming to college with this medication allows for ready access, as is the ability to obtain a prescription for it from campus health centers, family physicians and parents, and to purchase the medication from other students (CASA 2005).

Attention Deficit Disorder (ADD) ranks third among child afflictions and the numbers of children diagnosed with ADD has grown dramatically over the years (Howe and Strauss 2000). Due to the difficulty and subjectivity of diagnosing the condition, it is unclear just how large the number is or how sharp this increase has been. However, information regarding Ritalin and Adderall production shows it has increased dramatically over the past 10 years (CASA 2005), which could be an indicator of the increase in ADD or at least its diagnosis. A possible explanation for this increase is the simplified diagnosis process being used by doctors, thus allowing students to present false symptoms in order to obtain a prescription (Hall et al. 2005). ABC News (2006) reported, "Some kids say it's easy to get a prescription after a brief consultation with a doctor. One [college] student said all she had to do was fill out a true-false questionnaire of 5–10 questions. [She reported she] 'Marked all 10 of them true and was prescribed'" (CASA 2005, 60).

The Diagnostic and Statistic Manual of Mental Disorders (DSM–IV) defines the symptoms and diagnostic procedure for identifying ADD (American Psychological Association 1994), and prescribes that an ADD/ADHD symptoms checklist be followed by a complete medical history and family testimonials, among other methods, to confirm the diagnosis (CASA 2005). However, the entire process is rarely completed and students have access to diagnostic criteria (Quintero et al. 2006), which provides them with the means to say what is necessary to secure a prescription from the doctor (CASA 2005). A CASA (2005) interviewee described the process succinctly, stating:

> Obviously, doctors don't like to give you controlled substances easily; but if you're aggressive and persistent enough . . . and can talk a good enough game, I don't know how they could not give it to you. I mean they're in the health field and they're caring people and they're trying to take care of their patients' individual needs. (CASA 2005, 55)

His statement suggests a willingness to manipulate a health professional to obtain the prescription that is reminiscent of drug addicts, and there is not much a doctor can do to prevent patients faking symptoms if they answer the questionnaire correctly (CASA 2005). The symptoms checklist, as defined by DSM–IV, includes (a) trouble starting tasks; (b) procrastination on assignments or other tasks; (c) frequent loss or misplacing of items such as ID card, keys, etc.; (d) poor time management skills; (e) forgetfulness; (f) trouble comprehending readings; (g) saying or acting without thinking; (h) feeling as if they are on the go or acting often as if driven by a motor; (i) often avoiding, disliking, or reluctant to engage in tasks that require sustained mental effort; (j) difficulty in waiting their turn; (k) interrupts or intrudes on others (American Psychiatric Association 1994). The questionnaire could arguably define most college students, so they may not even have to lie to answer the questions correctly gaining access to Adderall or other prescription stimulants.

The lack of regulation provides students other avenues to acquire prescription stimulants, such as "doctor shopping." The practice of "doctor shopping" entails visiting various doctors in hopes of obtaining multiple prescriptions for the medication (CASA 2005). Students are then able to fill the prescriptions at various pharmacies. The only preventive measure to this behavior is insurance companies since they regulate prescriptions and will only cover controlled substances every 30 days. In other words, if Adderall is filled the 1st of the month and covered by the insurance company, the insurance company will not pay to have that same medicine filled until the 31st. This does serve as a deterrent for some, but students can easily avoid this by visiting other pharmacies, claim they do not have insurance, and pay full retail cost for the medicine.

However, getting these drugs can be even easier. A student at Florida State University explains, "it's so easy to get now, especially at college . . . I usually get it from friends that have prescriptions" (Emerick 2006, 8). A fellow classmate elaborated "[Adderall] really is so easy to get whenever you need it . . . Usually anyone with a prescription will sell it to you" (Emerick 2006, 10). Students are widely reported to be willing to sell their prescriptions to others for a price (CASA 2005; Emerick 2006). Stealing roommates' medication, asking parents with prescribing powers or doctors who are friends of the family, lying to new doctors that they have previously held prescriptions, and getting drugs from extended family members are other common means of acquisition (CASA 2005). The Internet also provides access to online pharmacies that illegally dispense legitimate and counterfeit prescription stimulants (CASA 2005). And students have shared yet other methods they have used including forging prescriptions or claiming to have lost a prescription (CASA 2005).

Discussion

Adderall abuse is a convoluted problem with an eclectic group of factors contributing to the epidemic of its use on college campuses. Students start using Adderall and Ritalin for any number of reasons. Some students engage in abusive behavior to manage the academic pressures and family stressors. Others become involved for recreational purposes, or to avoid the use of "hard" drugs. For whatever reasons, students are engaging in abusive behaviors on college campuses and there are few signs of its slowing down. On the contrary, it appears to be increasing. Thus for higher education, the use and abuse of stimulants has serious implications.

Effects of Prolonged Use

Illicit use of Adderall on college campuses combined with its high potential for leading to addiction poses a serious situation for college personnel concerned with the health and welfare of students. Use may start innocently enough, but illicit use increases gradually as does the need to increase the supply. A teenager interviewed by *ABC News* explained the journey he took: "It all started with Ritalin and Adderall. I started taking them every day [to get high] and pretty soon it didn't work anymore and I needed something more. I needed a bigger, faster boost" (CASA 2005, 16). The path to addiction does not exclude harder drugs. In fact, Adderall abusers are 20 times more likely to use cocaine and heroin once the body builds a tolerance for Adderall (CASA 2005). Addiction and increased drug use on college campuses is an important, likely implication of Adderall abuse, particularly since college is viewed as a "time off" period where experimentation with drugs is deemed appropriate. A focus group participant for CASA (2005) explained how the addiction began: "I realized that taking drugs was fun so I wanted to experiment. Before that I was against it, but this [Adderall] was a pill from a doctor that helped you take tests better … There couldn't be anything bad about it" (16). A teenage girl interviewed by *New York Magazine* explained, "You swallow Adderall to study, and snort it for fun" (CASA 2005, 18). The potential for addiction alone underlies the need to address Adderall abuse on college campuses before more students fall victim.

The long- and short-term effects of stimulant drugs are known to always increase with continual use. Short-term side effects include gastrointestinal problems, blurred vision, increased body temperature, increased blood pressure, increased heart rate, reduced circulation, irritability, and insomnia (CASA 2005). As usage continues or becomes excessive, more long-term side effects begin evolving. Long-term and excessive use of Adderall may result in hallucinations, psychotic episodes, cardiac arrest, a comatose state, or even death (CASA 2005). Intense mood changes and physical and mental cravings are common symptoms long-term users can also experience. Furthermore, drug tolerance increases with continual use, resulting in heightened physiological dependency, which intensifies the impact of withdrawal symptoms when usage ceases. Individuals entering withdrawal can experience violent mood swings, extreme fatigue, and uncontrollable cravings (CASA 2005).

Addiction and recreational use are certainly important implications of cavalier attitudes regarding Adderall and Ritalin abuse. Moreover, students are placing their lives, and the lives of those they share their medication with, in danger. Death is a possible outcome of self-medication. Less severe but no less serious side effects include comas, cardiac arrest, high blood pressure, and others. The long-term effects of this drug are still unknown, since it is relatively new to the market, but students could be damaging their brains or bodies. These realities and possibilities raise questions of liability for higher education institutions. Despite the moral obligation to ensure the health, safety, and overall well-being of students, higher education institutions *do* (emphasis added) have a legal obligation to address Adderall and other drug abuse on campuses. In fact, two pieces of litigation require colleges and universities to intervene.

Post-secondary schools are required to enforce the Drug-Free Schools and Campuses regulations, which require institutions to adopt and implement "a program to prevent unlawful possession, use, or distribution of illicit drugs and alcohol by students and employees" (Office of National Drug Control Policy 2004, 29). Failure to comply with the regulations can lead to forfeit of financial assistance under any federal program. Furthermore, if an institution fails to enforce or abide by their written plan, the Secretary of Education not only has the power to cease financial assistance, but also can demand repayment of funds provided to assist with implementing the drug campaigns (Office of National Drug Control Policy 2004, 29). This potential financial loss is in addition to any potential civil suit.

In addition, Congress passed the Illicit Drug Anti-Proliferation Act, sometimes referred to as the "Rave" Act, "which prohibits individuals from knowingly opening, leasing, renting, or maintaining any place for the purpose of using, distributing, or manufacturing any controlled substance" (Office of National Drug Control Policy 2004, 30). Adderall abuse on college campuses may well fall within the province of this legislation. Students abusing drugs during social events on campus place the institution in an interesting situation if punitive actions are not pursued. For example, if a fraternity advisor is aware of drug use at a fraternity party located on campus, then the advisor could be liable in his or her personal capacity and also as an agent of the university.

Similar to liability concerns, another potential implication might be hypothesized. Students are abusing Adderall to increase their abilities to outperform peers and secure admission into graduate school or employment. In any other situation, the question of whether or not that is cheating would arise. Academic dishonor in higher education is already at an all-time high (Taylor et al. 2002). Violators are typically expelled and do not receive a degree when the institution was aware of the cheating. It is also highly likely that high school students would not be admitted to college if cheating were on their transcripts. Grade inflation and increasing standardized test scores have led colleges to increase their standards for admission, causing students to do more to meet those standards (Cavagnero 2006). Interestingly, Adderall production and ADD diagnoses have increased alongside grade inflation and increasing test scores. Students using Adderall may increase their chance of acceptance over sober students. This may also be true for college seniors seeking admission into graduate school, which has also steadily increased its admission standards (Cavagnero 2006). It raises questions about cheating and the affect of Adderall abuse on others. First, an illicit user of Adderall admitted into college can directly affect another student unable to gain admission due to a finite number of spaces. Second, the ranking system of some standardized tests (e.g., LSAT) determines whether a score is decent (Cavagnero 2006). Adderall abusers could skew the percentages and directly affect other students earning lesser scores. Students illicitly using Adderall to study and take tests not only have an unfair advantage over others, but the standards literally increase, placing other students at an apparent disadvantage (Cavagnero 2006). The irony of the situation is non-users may be cheated out of a career or graduate school because they refuse to engage in illegal behavior.

When abusers of Adderall achieve goals with the help of prescription medications, colleges and universities indirectly validate the benefits perceived by the student and condone cheating as well as illegal drug abuse. The integrity of an education system that rewards cheaters and indirectly penalizes honest students is questionable. Students charged with cheating usually receive sanctions ranging from probation, to suspension, to expulsion for violating the academic integrity of the institution. It is for this purpose schools have honor codes, value statements, and judicial reviews. Is it possible to maintain academic and institutional integrity if 20% of the student population is illegally using prescription stimulants to enhance their personal agenda?

Recommendations

Correcting students' dangerous and careless behavior may prove difficult for various reasons. Since Adderall abuse is self-reported, the actual extent of the problem on a campus cannot be accurately known; therefore, populations cannot be targeted to attempt to reduce the problem. Moreover, the secretive nature and number of legitimate prescriptions on campus almost ensure accessibility; thus, a constant supply makes Adderall increasingly easy to acquire. Colleges and universities cannot singlehandedly stop or prevent students from abusing Adderall, especially since students may engage in this behavior while in middle school. However, schools can take steps to protect the institution and non-users. The first step to addressing any problem is to recognize its existence and determine the level of severity.

Colleges should assess the campus culture; identifying rate of abuse, level of acceptance, and factors that contribute to use in order to develop an effective campaign against Adderall abuse. After assessing the situation, institutions can begin educating students, faculty, and staff on the dangers, signs, and symptoms of Adderall abuse. In addition, through assessing the drug abuse epidemic, other contributing aspects of the campus culture may be revealed, such as a competitive environment and campus pressures, as well as needs for mental health and counseling services and for self-help groups. Students may feel more inclined to seek help if there is a place for it.

In order to address student drug abuse, the perceptions held by the students should become the focal point. Students perceive the drugs as a safe alternative to cocaine and harder drugs, which is not necessarily true. Educating students on the fallacies of their perceptions is one method of prevention. Secondly, students need to be preparing for the pressures of collegiate work prior to their arrival. Furthermore, a majority of institutions have first-year orientations, which could be an ideal place to inform students on the rigors and differences of college. Incorporating a seminar on drug abuse, college expectations, and study habits might help to prevent some use. Additionally, a concomitant result would be an identifiable strategy for institutional protection against liability since each student is mandated to attend the seminar. Teaching students stress management and proper study and time management skills may also help prevent the use of Adderall. These methods will at least provide students with the tools necessary to succeed independently and be academically successful without stimulants.

A third precautionary measure could involve students entering college with prescription stimulants. Although it is unlawful to ask students to disclose prescription medications they may be taking, providing a seminar on the legal consequences of sharing, selling, trading, or stealing prescription medications may make students reluctant to openly share their medication. Allowing the DEA to speak on this matter might add authority to the seriousness of the legal consequences. Most students fail to realize it is a serious and illegal offense to sell, trade, steal, or consume any prescription drug not prescribed for them, let alone a schedule II drug. Increasing this

awareness may affect those students who are using the drug for achievement and recreational purposes.

Faculty and staff encounter students continually throughout the day. Their engagement and relationships with students should serve as a primary focal point for helping to communicate to students the dangers of abusing prescription stimulants. Educating faculty and staff on symptomatic behaviors of Adderall abuse could provide help to those students. In addition, establishing preventative measures in residence halls and libraries would also confront the problem by addressing the most common places of transaction. Increased training for residence hall staff to better assist students addicted to, or abusing, Adderall, and educating library staff on suspicious behavior or mannerisms related to the sale of prescription stimulants might enable them to provide assistance and supervision.

On average, parents are extremely close to their son and daughter and serve as the primary source of academic pressure. Informing parents on the consequences of the pressure may be helpful to students. However, this is an extremely difficult task. Despite the level of difficulty, parents must understand the problems their love can cause. Encouraging parents to listen to students and the problems they are facing, providing methods for parents to be supportive while their son or daughter transitions to college, and educating parents on the symptoms and signs of Adderall abuse will give them information they may not have. More often than not, parents know when something is wrong, potentially even before the student realizes it. This presents parents with a valuable opportunity to recognize substance abuse symptoms and alert college administrators or private physicians to intervene. Finally, alerting parents to the difficulties associated with student life can provide parents with a student perspective of college life.

An additional recommendation will not only address Adderall abuse, but also bring recognition and finances. Research institutions have the luxury of discovering knowledge and new methods for current and future problems. It would be beneficial if some of these institutions would undertake research projects to develop new understandings of prescription drug abuse and addiction or augment current treatments for ADD/ADHD to phase out stimulates.

Longitudinal research on college students and Adderall abuse is currently lacking in the literature. Establishing a research team to address this gap could provide invaluable information to institutions and the health profession across the country. Finally, validating the accuracy, effectiveness, and flaws of current ADD/ADHD testing methods would provide rich data that could prevent false or improper diagnoses.

Finally, medical and pharmacy school curricula should be reviewed to include prescription abuse and diversion awareness classes. The doctors prescribing stimulants and pharmacists who fill prescriptions should receive thorough and continual training on prescription drug abuse. Focusing on the severity of the problem and their contribution to it is a start in controlling access. Adequate training for medical professionals could reduce actions such as "doctor shopping" or other means that are used to manipulate inexperienced doctors.

These recommendations will not solve the problem, but may increase awareness and slow the illicit use of Adderall on college campuses. The implementation of Federal programs and legislation can address problems such as accessibility, doctor shopping, and acquiring multiple prescriptions more effectively. Legislation such as the Rave Act and the Drug-Free Schools and Campuses Regulations are a start. Nevertheless, the problem needs to address the source—students—which complicates the problem considering that increased pressure, competition, and societal pressures are contributing to Adderall abuse. Educating students on the dangers of recreational use is likely to be more effective than attempting to reduce competition, pressures, and a drive for achievement. Eventually, cooperation with middle and high schools may be possible, but as of now, higher education institutions must protect the academic integrity of the institution as well as the health of the student. It will take society as a whole to address the problem of stimulant abuse similar to steroids, hard drugs, and smoking. Colleges and universities can only address the problems on campuses. Society holds the key to challenging the mentality behind its use.

References

ABC News. 2006. "Teen Prescription Drug Abuse on the Rise." March 14. Retrieved from http://abcnews.go.com/nightline/print?id=1726349

American Psychiatric Association. 1994. *Diagnostic and Statistic Manual of Mental Disorders*, 4th ed. Washington, DC: Author.

Babcock, Q. and T. Byrne. 2000. "Student Perceptions of Methylphenidate Abuse at a Public Liberal Arts College." *Journal of American College Health* 49: 143–145.

Bishop, J. 2003. "Nerd Harassment and Grade Inflation: Are College Admissions Policies Partly Responsible?" Retrieved from http://digitalcommons.ilr.cornell.edu/cgi/viewcontent.cgi?article=1112&context=cahrswp

Brooks, D. 2001. "The Organization Kid." *The Atlantic Monthly* (April): 40–54.

Cavagnero, C. 2006. "Adderall as a Study Drug Cheats Everyone." (October 12). Retrieved from Lexis-Nexis Academic: http://web.lexis-nexis.com/universe/

Chronicle of Higher Education. 2005. "Admissions Today: 6 Experts Speak Out." *Chronicle of Higher Education* 51 (February 25): B15.

Comos, M. and R. DeBard. 2004. "A Generational Approach to Understanding Students." *New Directions for Student Services, 2004* 106: 5–16. doi: 10.1002/ss.121

Debard, R. 2004. "Millennials Coming to College." *New Directions for Student Services* 106 (Summer): 33–45. doi: 10.1002/ss.123

Dodge, T. and J. Jaccard. 2006. "The Effect of High School Sports Participation on the Use of Performance-Enhancing Substances in Young Adulthood." *Journal of Adolescent Health* 39: 367–373.

Drug Enforcement Agency. 2002. *Yearly Aggregate Production Quotas (1990–2000)*. Washington, DC: Office of Public Affairs, Drug Enforcement Administration.

Dworkin, J. 2005. "Risk Taking as Developmentally Appropriate Experimentation for College Students." *Journal of Adolescent Research* 20: 219–240.

Emerick, J. 2006. "Unprescribed Adderall Gives Aid in Focus and Concentration, with Risk." April 24. Retrieved from http://web.lexis-nexis.com/universe

Farrell, E. 2006. "College Searches Gone Wild: An Unprecedented Surge in Applications Catches Admissions Off-Guard." *The Chronicle of Higher Education* 52 (March 31): A39.

Hall, K., M. Irwin, K. Bowman, W., Frankenberger, and D. Jewett. 2005. "Illicit Use of Prescribed Stimulant Medication among College Students." *Journal of American College Health* 53: 167–174.

Howe, N. and W. Strauss. 2000. *Millennials Rising: The Next Great Generation.* New York, NY: Vintage Books.

Johnston, L., P. O'Malley, J. Bachman, and J. Schulenberg. 2005. *Monitoring the Future: National Results on Adolescent Drug Use.* Bethesda, MD: National Institute on Drug Abuse.

Kadison, R. and T. Digeronimo. 2004. *College of the Overwhelmed: The Campus Mental Health Crisis and What to Do about It.* San Francisco, CA: Jossey-Bass.

Kindlundh, A., D. Isacson, L. Berglund, and F. Nyberg. 1999. "Factors Associated with Adolescent Use of Doping Agents: Anabolic-Androgenic Steroids." *Addiction* 94: 543–553.

Kohn A. 2003. "How Not to Get into College." *Independent School* 62: 12–22.

Labig, C., K. Zantow, and T. Peterson. 2005. "Factors Affecting Students' Medicine-Taking Habits." *Journal of American College Health* 54: 177–183.

Law, D. 2007. "Exhaustion on University Students and the Effect of Coursework Involvement." *Journal of American Health* 55: 239–245.

Luthar, S. and B. Becker. 2002. "Privileged but Pressured? A Study of Affluent Youth." *Child Development* 73: 1593.

Luthar, S. and K. D'Avanzo. 1999. "Contextual Factors in Substance Use: A Study of Suburban and Inner-City Adolescents." *Development and Psychopathology* 11: 845–867.

McCabe, S., C. Teter, and C. Boyd. 2006. "Medical Use, Illicit Use, and Diversion of Abusable Prescription Drugs." *Journal of American College Health* 54: 269–278.

Moline, S., and W. Frankenberger. 2001. "Use of Stimulant Medication for Treatment of Attention-Deficit/ Hyperactivity Disorder: A Survey of Middle and High School Students' Attitudes." *Psychology in Schools* 38: 569–585.

National Center on Addiction and Substance Abuse (CASA). 2005. "Under the Counter: The Diversion and Abuse of Controlled Prescription Drugs in the U.S." July. Retrieved from http://www.casacolumbia .org/absolutenm/articlefiles/380-under_the_ counter_-_diversion.pdf

Office of National Drug Control Policy. 2004. *The Challenge in Higher Education: Confronting and Reducing Substance Abuse on Campus.* Washington, DC: Author.

Quintero, G., J. Peterson, and B. Young. 2006. "An Exploratory Study of Socio-cultural Factors Contributing to Prescription Drug Misuse among College Students." *Journal of Drug Issues* 36 (4): 903–932.

Sax, L. 2003. "Our Incoming Students: What Are They Like?" *About Campus* 8 (3): 15–20.

Taylor, L., M. Pogrebin, and M. Dodge. 2002. "Advanced Placement–Advanced Pressures: Academic Dishonesty among Elite High School Students." *Educational Studies* 33: 403–421.

Teter, C., S. McCabe, B. Cranford, and S. Guthrie. 2005. "Prevalence and Motives for Illicit Use of Prescription Stimulants in an Undergraduate Student Sample." *Journal of American College Health* 53: 253–262.

United States Drug Enforcement Administration. 2005. *Drug Abuse.* Washington, DC: Author.

White, B., K. Becker-Blease, and K. Grace-Bishop. 2005. "Stimulant Medication Use, Misuse, and Abuse in an Undergraduate and Graduate Student Sample." *Journal of American College Health* 54: 261–268.

Wichstrom, L. and W. Pedersen. 2001. "Use of Anabolic-Androgenic Steroids in Adolescence: Winning, Looking Good or Being Bad?" *Journal of Studies on Alcohol* (January): 5–13.

Woodruff, D. and R. Ziomek. 2004. *High School Grade Inflation from 1991 to 2003.* March. Retrieved from http://www.act.org/research/reports/pdf/ACT_ RR2004-4.pdf

Wroble, R., M. Gray, and J. Rodrigo. 2002. *Anabolic Steroids and Pre-adolescent Athletes: Prevalence, Knowledge, and Attitudes.* Fall. Retrieved from http://www.thesportjournal.org/2002journal/ Vol5-No3/anabolic-steroids.asp

For Discussion

1. The author cites information from the Drug Enforcement Administration that suggests that Adderall and Ritalin were the most commonly prescribed stimulants in the United States over a ten-year period. Millions of prescriptions are written annually. Compared to the United States, prescription stimulants are far less common in a number of other countries. Discuss cultural factors that characterize the United States that might have contributed to the increase in prescription stimulant misuse among college students.

2. Surveys from various universities have shown mixed results in terms of the percentage of students who consume Adderall and Ritalin. Self-reported use is high at some colleges and very low in others. What factors might explain the vast differences in self-reported use across colleges and universities in the United States?

16

Taking Care of Business

The Heroin Addict's Life on the Street

EDWARD PREBLE AND JOHN J. CASEY

"Taking Care of Business," one of the classic papers in the drug field, begins with a brief history of heroin use and distribution in New York City from World War I through the late 1960s. Preble and Casey dispel the widely held belief that individuals use heroin as an escape. Rather, they argue, heroin allows individuals to experience purposeful lives.

Introduction

This report is a description of the life and activities of lower-class heroin users in New York City in the context of their street environment. It is concerned exclusively with the heroin users living in slum areas, who comprise at least 80 percent of the city's heroin-using population. They are predominantly Negro and Puerto Rican, with some Irish, Italian, and Jewish.

Reprinted from Edward Preble and John J. Casey, "Taking Care of Business—The Heroin User's Life on the Street," *Substance Use & Misuse*, Vol. 4, No. 1, copyright © 1969, Informa Healthcare. Reproduced with permission of Informa Healthcare.

It is often said that the use of heroin provides an escape for the user from his psychological problems and from the responsibilities of social and personal relationships—in short, an escape from life. Clinical descriptions of heroin addicts emphasize the passive, dependent, withdrawn, generally inadequate features of their personality structure and social adjustment. Most sociological studies of heroin users make the same point. Thus, Chein et al. (1964) reported that street-gang members are not likely to become heroin users, because they are resourceful, aggressive, well-integrated boys who are "reality-oriented" in their street environment. They held that it is the passive, anxious, inadequate boy, who cannot adapt to street life, who is likely to use heroin. Similarly, Cloward and Ohlin (1960) referred to heroin users as "retreatists" and "double failures" who cannot qualify for either legitimate or illegitimate careers. Unaggressive "mamma's boys" is the usual stereotype these days for the heroin addict, both for the students of narcotic use and the public at large. Experienced researchers and workers in the narcotics field know that there is no such thing as "the heroin addict" or "the addict personality." However, most attempts to generalize—the goal of all scientific investigation—result in some version of the escape theory.

The description which follows of the activities of lower-class heroin users in their adaptation to the social and economic institutions and practices connected with the use of heroin contradicts this widely held belief. Their behavior is anything but an escape from life. They are actively engaged in meaningful activities and relationships seven days a week. The brief moments of euphoria after each administration of a small amount of heroin constitute a small fraction of their daily lives. The rest of the time they are aggressively pursuing a career that is exacting, challenging, adventurous, and rewarding. They are always on the move and must be alert, flexible, and resourceful. The surest way to identify heroin users in a slum neighborhood is to observe the way people walk. The heroin user walks with a fast, purposeful stride, as if he is late for an important appointment—indeed, he is. He is hustling (robbing or stealing), trying to sell stolen goods, avoiding the police, looking for a heroin dealer with a good bag (the street retail unit of heroin), coming back from copping (buying heroin), looking for a safe place to take the drug, or looking for someone who beat (cheated) him—among other things. He is, in short, *taking care of business*, a phrase which is so common with heroin users that they use it in response to words of greeting, such as "how you doing?" and "what's happening?" *Taking care of biz* is the common abbreviation. *Ripping and running* is an older phrase which also refers to their busy lives. For them, if not for their middle-and upper-class counterparts (a small minority of opiate addicts), the quest for heroin is the quest for a meaningful life, not an escape from life. And the meaning does not lie, primarily, in the effects of the drug on their minds and bodies; it lies in the gratification of accomplishing a series of challenging, exciting tasks, every day of the week.

Much of the life of the heroin user on the street centers around the economic institutions of heroin distribution. Therefore, this report features a description of the marketing processes for heroin, from importation to street sales. The cost of heroin today is so high and the quality so poor that the street user must become totally involved in an economic career. A description of typical economic careers of heroin users will be presented. Preceding these two sections is a brief historical account of heroin use in New York City from World War I to the present, in which it will be seen that patterns of heroin use have changed at a pace and in a direction in correspondence with the social changes of the past fifty years. Theories and explanations about heroin use, based upon observations of fifty, twenty-five, or even five years ago, are inadequate to account for the phenomenon today. It is hoped that this contemporary account of the social setting for heroin use will provide useful data for the modifications of theory and practice which should accompany any dynamic social process.

Methodology

The data on which this report is based have come from interviews with patients at the Manhattan State Hospital Drug Addiction Unit and from participant observation and interviews with individuals and groups in four lower-class communities in New York City—East Harlem, Lower East Side, Yorkville, Claremont (Bronx). The communities represent the neighborhoods of approximately 85 percent of the addict patients at Manhattan State Hospital. The anthropologist's role and approach to the heroin-using study of informants was in the tradition of Bronislaw Malinowski (1922) and William F. Whyte (1955), which, in Whyte's words, consists of "the observation of interpersonal events." Another dimension was added with the modified use of research techniques, introduced by Abraham Kardiner and his collaborators (1939) in their psychosocial studies of primitive and modern cultures. The main feature of this methodology is the life-history interview with individual subjects. Initial and subsequent contacts with the research informants occurred, in all cases, with their voluntary consent and cooperation. The anthropologist had the advantage of twelve years experience of street work and research in the study neighborhoods, and was able to enlist the assistance of longtime acquaintances for this special project. Four major ethnic groups were represented among the approximately 150 informants: Irish, Italian, Negro, and Puerto Rican.

History of Heroin Use in New York City

The recent history of heroin use in the city can be broken down into six time periods: (1) between World War I and World War II, (2) during World War II, (3) 1947 to 1951, (4) 1951 to 1957, (5) 1957 to 1961, and (6) 1961 to the present.

1. Between World War I and World War II

Prior to World War II the use of heroin was limited, for the most part, to people in the *life*—show people, entertainers, and musicians; racketeers and gangsters; thieves and pickpockets; prostitutes and pimps. The major ethnic groups represented among these users were Italian, Irish, Jewish, and Negro (mostly those associated with the entertainment life). There were also heroin users among the Chinese, who had a history of opium use. The distribution of heroin by those who controlled the market was limited mostly to these people, and there was little knowledge or publicity about it.

2. During World War II

World War II interrupted the trade routes and distributorships for illicit heroin supplies, which resulted in a five-year hiatus in heroin use.

3. 1947 to 1951

When World War II ended, there was a greatly expanded market for heroin in the increased population among Negroes from the South and among migrating Puerto Ricans who came to New York during the war in response to a manpower shortage. In 1940, the Negro population in New York City was 450,000; in 1960, it was over 1 million. In 1940, the Puerto Rican population was 70,000; in 1960, it was over 600,000. As with all new immigrants in New York, they worked at the lowest economic levels, settled in slum neighborhoods, and were the victims of unemployment, poverty, and discrimination. From 1947 to 1951, the use of heroin spread among lower-class Negro and Puerto Rican people and among other lower-class, slum-dwelling people, mainly the Irish and Italians. The increased rate of use was gradual, but steady, and did not attract much attention. Most of the users were young adults in their twenties and thirties. They were more or less circumspect in their drug consumption, which they were able to be because of the relatively low cost and high quality of the heroin.

During this period, heroin was sold in number-five capsules (the smallest capsules used for pharmaceutical products). These *caps* could be bought for about one dollar apiece, and two to six persons could get high on the contents of one capsule. Commonly, four persons would contribute one quarter each and *get down on a cap*. There was social cohesion, identification, and ritual among the users of this period. Sometimes as many as twenty people would get together and, in a party atmosphere, share the powder contents of several capsules which were emptied upon a mirror and divided into columns by means of a razor blade, one column for each participant. The mirror was passed from person to person and each one would inhale his share through the nose by means of a tapered, rolled-up dollar bill which served as a straw, and was called a *quill*. A twenty, fifty, or hundred dollar bill was used on special occasions when someone wanted to make a show of his affluence. Since heroin was so inexpensive during this time, no addict had to worry about getting his fix; someone was always willing to loan him a dollar or share a part of his drug. The social relationships among these addicts were similar to those found in a neighborhood bar, where there is a friendly mutual concern for the welfare of the regular patrons. The most important economic factor in these early post-war days of heroin use was that heroin users were able to work even at a low-paying job and still support a habit, and many of them did. Relatively little crime was committed in the interest of getting money to buy heroin. A habit could be maintained for a few dollars a day, at little social or economic cost to the community.

4. 1951 to 1957

Around 1951, heroin use started to become popular among younger people on the streets, especially among street-gang members who were tired of gang fighting and were looking for a new high. As heroin use had become more common in the latter days of the previous period, the more streetwise teenagers learned about it and prevailed upon the experienced users to introduce them to it. Contrary to popular reports, experimentation with heroin by youths usually began at their initiative and not through proselytism. The stereotype of the dope *pusher* giving out free samples of narcotics to teenagers in school yards and candy stores, in order to addict them, is one of the most misleading myths about drug use. Also, contrary to professional reports about this development, it was not the weak, withdrawn, unadaptive street boy who first started using heroin, but rather the tough, sophisticated, and respected boy, typically a street-gang leader. Later, others followed his example, either through indoctrination or emulation. By 1955, heroin use

among teenagers on the street had become widespread, resulting, among other things, in the dissolution of fighting gangs. Now the hip boy on the street was not the swaggering, leather-jacketed gang member, but the boy nodding on the corner, enjoying his heroin high. He was the new hero model.

As heroin use spread among the young from 1951, the price of heroin began to rise in response to the greater demand, and the greater risks involved in selling to youths. Those who started using heroin as teenagers seldom had work experience or skills and resorted to crime in order to support their heroin use. They were less circumspect in their drug-using and criminal activity, and soon became a problem to the community, especially to those who were engaged in non-narcotic illegal activities, such as bookmaking, loan-sharking, and policy (the gambling game popular among working-class people in which a correct selection of three numbers pays off at 50 to 1). The activities and behavior of young drug users brought attention and notoriety to the neighborhood, which jeopardized racketeer operations. It was not uncommon for a local racketeer to inform the parents of a young heroin user about his activities, hoping that they would take action.

5. 1957 to 1961

In 1957, the criminal organization, or *syndicate*, which had been mainly responsible for heroin distribution (according to law-enforcement agencies and government investigation committees), officially withdrew from the market. This resulted from two conditions: the passage of stricter federal laws that included provision for conspiracy convictions, and the related fact that illegal drug use was receiving increased attention from the public and officials, especially as a result of the increased involvement of youth with heroin. The risks had become too great, and the syndicate did not want to endanger the larger and more important sources of revenue, such as gambling and loan-sharking. However, the instruction to get out of narcotics was more honored in the breach than in the observance by certain syndicate members. Those who stayed involved in narcotics operated independently.

Some made it their primary operation, while others would make only one or two big transactions a year when they needed to recoup quickly from an unexpected financial loss in some other operation. Dealing irregularly in narcotics for this purpose became known as a *fall-back*—a quick and sure way to make money. The syndicate also stayed involved indirectly through loan-shark agreements. In these transactions, large sums of money were lent to narcotic dealers for a period of one month at a fixed rate of return. No questions were asked regarding its use. By this means, the syndicate avoided some of the undesirable aspects of narcotic distribution and still participated in the profits. The official withdrawal of the syndicate from narcotics created opportunities for independent operators, which resulted in a relatively free market.

6. 1961 to the Present

The next major development in the history of heroin use in the city occurred in November 1961, when there was a critical shortage of heroin. Known as a *panic*, this development, whatever its cause, had a profound effect on the course of heroin use in the city. The panic lasted only for a few weeks. During this time, the demand for the meager supplies of heroin was so great that those who had supplies were able to double and triple their prices and further adulterate the quality, thus realizing sometimes as much as ten times their usual profit. By the time heroin became available again in good supply, the dealers had learned that inferior heroin at inflated prices could find a ready market. Since that time, the cost of heroin on the street has continued to climb, through increased prices, further adulteration, and *short counts* (misrepresentation of aggregate weight in a given unit). A few minor panics—about two a year—help bolster the market. Today, an average heroin habit costs the user about $20 a day, as compared to $2 twenty years ago. This fact is responsible for a major social disorder in the city today. It has also had important effects on the personal, social, and family relationships of the heroin users themselves. There is no longer social cohesion among addicts. The competition and struggle necessary to support a habit has turned each one into an independent operator who looks out only for himself. Usually, addicts today will associate in pairs (partners), but only for practical purposes: in a criminal effort which requires two people (as when one acts as lookout, while the other commits a burglary), to share in the price of a bag of heroin, to assist in case of an overdose of drugs, to share the use of one set of works (the paraphernalia used to inject heroin). There is no longer a subculture of addicts, based on social cohesion and emotional identification, but rather a loose association of individuals and parallel couples. Heroin users commonly say, "I have no friends, only associates."

The economic pressures on heroin users today are so great that they prey on each other, as well as on their families and on society at large. An addict with money or drugs in his possession runs a good risk of being *taken off* (robbed) by other addicts. An addict who has been robbed or cheated by another addict usually takes his loss philosophically, summed up by the expression, "That's the name of the game." Referring to a fellow addict who had cheated him, one victim said, "He beat me today, I'll beat him tomorrow." Another addict who specializes in robbing other addicts said, "I beat them every chance I get, which is all the time." Sociability, even among partners, extends no farther than that suggested by the following excerpt: "You might be hanging out with a fellow for a long time, copping together and working as crime partners. You might beat him for a purpose. You might beat him, because maybe you bought a bag together and you know it's not going to do both any good, so you beat him for it. But then you try to go and get some money and straighten him out; make it up to him." Another informant summed up the attitude between partners this way: "I'm looking out for myself—I might be sick tomorrow; anyway, he's got something working for him that I don't know about." Sometimes, a distinction is made between a hustling partner and a crime partner (*crimey*), where it is suggested that the latter is more dependable; however, as one informant put it, "There are larceny-minded crimeys." The causes of these changes in the relationships of heroin users to each other, to family members, and to other members of the community are to be found in the economic practices of heroin distribution.

The Distribution of Heroin in New York City

Heroin contracted for in Europe at $5,000 per kilo (2.2 pounds) will be sold in $5 bags on the street for about one million dollars, after having passed through at least six levels of distribution. The following description of the distribution and marketing of heroin, from the time it arrives in New York until it reaches the hands of the heroin user in the street, is a consensus derived from informants in the hospital and in the street representing different ethnic and racial groups from different parts of the city. There are many variations to the account given here at all levels of the marketing process. For example, as in the marketing of any product, a quantity purchase can be made at a lower price; and a dealer who makes a rapid turnover of the product for a wholesaler will receive higher benefits for his work. All the way down the line, the *good customer* is the key to a successful operation. He is one who buys regularly, does a good volume of business, does not ask for credit or try to buy short (offer less than the established price), and can be trusted. The following account does not include all the many variations, but can be taken as a paradigm.

Opium produced in Turkey, India, and Iran is processed into heroin in Lebanon, France, and Italy, and prepared for shipment to the East Coast of the United States. A United States importer, through a courier, can buy a kilogram of 80-percent heroin in Europe for $5,000. The quality is represented to him in terms of how many cuts it will hold (that is, how many times it can be adulterated). In earlier days, when the marketing of heroin was a more controlled operation, the word of the European seller was accepted. Now, it is customary for the importer to test it, either by means of scientific instruments, or through a reliable tester—an addict who makes experimental cuts, uses the drug, and reports on its quality. The importer, who usually never sees the heroin, sells down the line to a highly trusted customer through intermediaries. If it is a syndicate operation, he would only sell to high level, coded men, known as *captains*. These men are major distributors, referred to as *kilo connections* and, generally, as *the people*.

Major Distribution

The *kilo connection* pays $20,000 for the original kilogram (kilo, kee), and gives it a one and one cut (known as *hitting it*); that is, he makes two kilos out of one by adding the common adulterants of milk sugar, mannite (a product from the ash tree, used as a mild laxative), and quinine. The proportions of ingredients used for the cutting vary with the preferences of the cutter. One may use 5 parts milk sugar, 2 parts quinine, and 1 part mannite; while another may use 2 parts milk sugar, 3 parts quinine, and 1 part mannite. All three of these products are quickly soluble with heroin. A match lit under the cooker (bottle cap) will heat and dissolve the mixture into a clear liquid in a few seconds. The milk sugar contributes the bulk, the mannite inflates the volume—described as *fluffing* it up—and the quinine heightens the sensation of the *rush* when, upon injection into the vein, the mixture first registers on the nervous system. In the cutting procedure, the substance to be cut is placed under a fine sieve, often made from a woman's nylon stocking stretched over a coat hanger. The adulterants are sifted on top of it, then the new mixture is sifted through several more times. After the cut, the kilo connection sells down the line in kilos, half kilos, and quarter kilos, depending upon the resources of his customers. He will get approximately $10,000 per half kilo for the now adulterated heroin.

The customer of the kilo connection is known as *the connection* in its original sense, meaning that he knows *the people*, even though he is not one of them. He may also be called an *ounce man*. He is a highly trusted customer. (One common variation here is that the kilo connection may sell to a third line man, known, if a syndicate operation, as a *soldier* or *button man*. He, in turn, will make a one and one cut and sell to the connection.) Assuming that the connection buys directly from a kilo connection, he will probably give the heroin a one and one cut (make two units of each one), divide the total aggregate into ounces, and sell down the line at $700 per ounce. In addition to the adulteration, the aggregate weight of the product is reduced. Known as a *short count*, this procedure occurs at every succeeding level of distribution. At this stage, however, it is called a *good ounce*, despite the adulteration and reduced weight.

The next man is known as a *dealer in weight*, and is probably the most important figure in the line of distribution. He stands midway between the top and the bottom, and is the first one coming down the line who takes substantial risk of being apprehended by law-enforcement officers. He is also the first one who may be a heroin user himself, but usually he is not. He is commonly referred to as one who is *into something* and is respected as a big dealer who has put himself in jeopardy by, as the sayings go, *carrying a felony with him* and *doing the time*; that is, if he gets caught, he can expect a long jail sentence. It is said of him that "he let his name go," or "his name gets kicked around," meaning that his identity is known to people in the street. This man usually specializes in cut ounces. He may give a two and one cut (make three units of each one) to the good ounce from the connection and sell the resulting quantity for $500 per ounce. The aggregate weight is again reduced, and now the unit is called a *piece*, instead of an ounce. Sometimes, it is called a *street ounce* or a *vig ounce* (*vig* is an abbreviation for *vigorish*, which is the term used to designate the high interest on loans charged by loan sharks). In previous years, twenty-five to thirty level teaspoons were supposed to constitute an ounce; today, it is sixteen to twenty.

The next customer is known as a *street dealer*. He buys the *piece* for $500, gives it a one and one cut and makes *bundles*, which consist of twenty-five $5 bags each. He can usually get seven bundles from each piece, and he sells each bundle for $80. He may also package the heroin in *half-bundles* (ten $5 bags each), which sell for $40, or he may package in *half-loads* (fifteen $3 bags), which sell for $30 each. This man may or may not be a heroin user.

The next distributor is known as a *juggler*, who is the seller from whom the average street addict buys. He is always a user. He buys bundles for $80 each and sells the twenty-five bags at about $5 each, making just enough profit to support his own habit, day by day. He may or may not make a small cut, known as *tapping the bags*. He is referred to as someone who is "always high and always short"; that is, he always has enough heroin for his own use and is always looking for a few dollars to get enough capital to cop again. The following actual account is typical of a juggler's transactions: he has $25 and

needs $5 more to buy a half-load. He meets a user he knows who has $5 and would like to buy two $3 bags; he is short $1. The juggler tells him he needs only $5 to cop, and that, if he can have his $5, he will buy a half load and give him his two $3 bags—$1, in effect, for the use of the money. When the juggler returns, he gives the person his two bags. In the example here, the person had to wait about two hours for the juggler's return, and it was raining. For taking the risk of getting beat for his money by the juggler, for the long wait and the discomfort of the weather, the juggler was expected to go to the *cooker* with him (share the use of some of the heroin), with the juggler putting in two bags to the other person's one bag and sharing equally in the total. The juggler had his fix and now has eleven bags left. He sells three bags for $9. From the eight bags he has left he uses two himself to get straight—not to get high, but enough to keep from getting sick so that he can finish his business. Now, he sells four bags for $12 and has three left. He needs only $7 more to cop again, so he is willing to sell the last three bags for the reduced price, and he can begin a similar cycle all over again. He may do this three or four times a day. The juggler leads a precarious life, both financially and in the risks he takes of getting robbed by fellow addicts or arrested. Most arrests for heroin sales are of the juggler. Financially, he is always struggling to stay in the black. If business is a little slow, he may start to get sick or impatient and use some of the heroin he needs to sell, in order to recoup. If he does this, he is in the red and temporarily out of business. A juggler is considered to be doing well if he has enough money left over after a transaction for cab fare to where he buys the heroin. One informant defined a juggler as a "non-hustling dope fiend who is always messing the money up."

Other Specialists

There are ancillary services provided by other specialists in the heroin-marketing process. They are known as: (1) lieutenants, (2) testers, (3) drop-men, (4) salesmen, (5) steerers, (6) taste faces, and (7) accommodators.

   1. *Lieutenant*: Very often, a connection or weight dealer will have in his employ a

trusted associate who handles the details of transactions with the street-level dealers. He arranges for deliveries, collects the money, and acts as an enforcer, if things go wrong. He may work for a salary or a commission, or both. Sometimes, he will be given some *weight* (part of a kilo) to sell on his own as a bonus.

2. *Tester*: Heroin dealers down the line are likely to keep a trusted addict around to test the quality of the drug for them. In return for this service, he gets all the heroin he needs and pocket money.

3. *Drop-man*: This person, often a young, dependable non-user, is used by sellers to make deliveries, He works for cash and may make as much as $500 for a drop [on] behalf of a top-level seller. He may also handle the transfer of money in a transaction. He is usually a tough, intelligent, trusted street youth who is ambitious to work his way up in the criminal hierarchy.

4. *Salesman*: Sometimes, the type of person used as a drop-man will be used as a street salesman of heroin for a fairly big dealer. The use of this kind of salesman is growing, because of the unreliability of addict jugglers and the desirability of having a tough person who can be trusted and not be easily robbed and cheated by addicts. Sometimes, these boys are about 16 to 18 years old and may be going to school. Being young, they usually do not have a police record, and they attract less attention from the police. One informant summed up their attributes this way: "The police won't pay much attention to a kid, but if they do get busted (arrested) they don't talk; they want to be men . . . they (the dealers) trust a guy that don't use it, because they know the guy ain't going to beat him. They got a little gang, and nobody is going to get their stuff, because they're going to gang up on the guy. In that case, they can use a gun in a hurry. The kids that sell the stuff, they don't use it. They buy clothes or whatever they want with the money." They often sell on consignment, starting with a small advance (usually a bundle) and working up to more if they are successful.

5. *Steerer*: The steerer is one who in racetrack parlance would be known as a *tout*, or in a sidewalk sales operation as a *shill*. He is one who tries to persuade users to buy a certain dealer's bag. He may work off and on by appointment with a particular dealer (always a small street dealer or juggler) in return for his daily supply of drugs. Or he may hear that a certain dealer has a good bag and, on a speculative basis, steer customers to him and then go to him later and ask to be taken care of for the service. This is known as *cracking* on a dealer. One of his more subtle selling techniques is to affect an exaggerated-looking high, and, when asked by a user where he got such a good bag, refer him to the dealer. Usually, he is a person who stays in the block all day and is supposed to know what is going on; he is, as they say, *always on the set*.

6. *Taste face*: This is a derogatory term given to one who supports his habit by renting out works—loaning the paraphernalia for injecting heroin—in return for a little money or a share of the heroin. Possession of works (hypodermic needle, eyedropper fitted with a baby's pacifier nipple, and bottle cap) is a criminal offense, and users do not want to run the extra risk of carrying them; thus, they are willing to pay something for the service. Although they perform a useful service, these people are held in contempt by other users. Taste refers to the small amount of heroin he is given (known as a *G shot*) and face is a term applied to anyone on the street who is known as a *creep*, *flunky*, or *nobody*.

7. *Accommodator*: The accommodator is a user who buys at a low level—usually from a juggler—for someone new to the neighborhood who has no connections. These purchases are for small amounts bought by users from other parts of the city or the suburbs. The accommodator receives a little part of the heroin or money for his services. Sometimes, he will also cheat the buyer by misrepresenting the price or the amount, or just by

not coming back. However, he has to be somewhat reliable, in order to support his habit regularly in this way. Many selling arrests by undercover narcotics police are of these low-level accommodators.

The Street Bag of Heroin

The amount of heroin in the street bag is very small. A generous estimate of the aggregate weight of a $5 bag is ninety milligrams, including the adulterants. Assuming, as in the above account, that the original kilo of 80-percent heroin is adulterated twenty-four times by the time it reaches the street, the amount of heroin would be about three milligrams. There is considerable fluctuation in the amount of heroin in the retail unit, running the range from one to fifteen milligrams, which depends mainly upon the supply available in the market. The important point is that, no matter how small the amount, heroin users are never discouraged in their efforts to get it. The consensus figure of three milligrams is a good approximation for an average over a one-year period. This is the average analgesic dosage that is used in those countries, such as England, where heroin can be prescribed in medical practice. It is a minimal amount, being considered safe for someone who does not use opiates. It is equivalent to about ten milligrams of either morphine or methadone.

In controlled experiments with opiate addicts, as much as sixty milligrams of morphine have been administered four times a day (Martin, personal communication 1967). Each dosage is equivalent to about twenty milligrams of heroin, which is seven times the amount in the average street bag. In another experiment, it was found that the average heroin addict "recognized" heroin at a minimum level of about fifteen milligrams—five times the amount in the street bag (Sharoff, personal communication 1967). The average dosage of methadone used in opiate-maintenance treatment is one hundred milligrams—about ten times the amount in the street bag. One informant said of the effects of a street bag today: "All it does is turn your stomach over so that you can go out and hustle, and you had better do it fast." Heroin users who are sent to jail report that they are surprised when they do not

experience serious withdrawal symptoms after the abrupt cessation of heroin use. Physicians working in the withdrawal wards of narcotic treatment centers refer to the abstinence syndrome among most of their patients today as "subclinical."

The amount of heroin in the street unit has resulted in an institution known as *chasing the bag*. In a community with a high incidence of heroin use, there will be two, three, or four competing bags on the street; that is, bags which have come down through different distributorship lines. Because of the low quality of the heroin, users want to get the best one available on a given day. The number of times it has been cut and the ingredients that were used to cut it are the main considerations. The dealer who has the best bag on the street at a given time will sell his merchandise fast and do a big volume of business, A dealer with a good bag who works hard can sell forty to fifty bundles a day. A good bag dealer can sell seventy-five to one hundred bags a day. By keeping the quality relatively high—for example by giving a one and a half cut to a quantity represented as being able to hold two cuts—he makes less profit on each unit. However, this loss can be offset by the greater volume and the reduced price he gets from his wholesaler, as a result of buying more often and in large quantities. Those with inferior bags on the street do not have a rapid turnover, but they know that sooner or later they can sell their stock, since the demand tends to exceed the supply. There are also other factors operating in their favor. Some users are not known to the dealer of the best bag and cannot buy from him except through the mediation of someone else. This service costs the prospective buyer something and he has to weigh that consideration against the better bag. Usually, however, if he is sure that one bag is much better than another one, he will find the price to pay for the service to get it; the quality of the bag, not the money, is always the primary consideration.

Another condition favorable to the dealers of inferior bags is that a user who hustles for his drugs is too busy to be around all the time waiting for a particular bag to come on the street. He is usually pressed for time and has to take what is available. If the dealer of the good bag is out recopping, the user cannot afford to wait for what may be a long time. The dealer of an inferior bag, whose heroin moves more slowly is reliable; that is, he is always around and can be depended upon. Even in extreme cases, where a bag is so bad that the dealer builds up a surplus because of slow business, he knows that sooner or later a temporary shortage of heroin—even for a few days—will ensure his selling out. Heroin does not spoil and can be easily stored for an indefinite period.

Sometimes, the dealer of an exceptionally good bag will be approached by his competitors, and they will make a deal, whereby he agrees to leave the street on the condition that they buy their bundles from him. In such a deal, those buying the good bundles will *tap the bags* (adulterate them a little more) and put them on the street at the same price. This is one of the many variations in marketing heroin.

It is common practice for a new dealer to come on the street with a good bag and keep it that way, until he has most of the customers. Then, he will start to adulterate the heroin, knowing that his reputation will carry him for a few days; by that time, he has made a good extra profit. When he starts losing customers in large number, he can build the bag up again. Users are constantly experimenting with the products of different dealers, comparing notes with other users, and attempting to buy the best bag that is around. As one informant put it: "You keep searching. If the guy is weak and you buy from him and it's nothing, then you go to Joe or Tom. Like you get a bag over here now, you run over there about in an hour and get another bag from the other guy, and get another from this other guy after a while. You just go in a circle to see. You run in different directions." One informant said, "There are no longer dope addicts on the street, only hope addicts." A report on the street that a heroin user died of an overdose of heroin results in a customer rush on his dealer for the same bag.

Economic Careers of Heroin Users

The nature of the economic careers of heroin users on the street is epitomized in the following quote from a research informant: "I believe in work to a certain extent, if it benefits my profit; but I do believe there is more money made otherwise." Another informant, in referring to a fellow user, said: "He just got no heart to be pulling no scores. He can't steal, he don't know how to steal. You can't be an addict that way. I don't know how he's going to make it."

Virtually all heroin users in slum neighborhoods regularly commit crime, in order to support their heroin use. In addition to the crimes involving violation of the narcotic laws, which are described above, heroin users engage in almost all types of crime for gain, both against property and the person. Because of the greatly inflated price of heroin and because of its poor quality, it is impossible for a heroin user to support even a modest habit for less than $20 a day. Since the typical street user is uneducated, unskilled, and often from a minority racial group, he cannot earn enough money in the legitimate labor market to finance his drug use; he must engage in criminal activity. It is a conservative estimate that heroin users in New York City steal $1 million a day in money, goods, and property. About 70 percent of the inmates in New York City Department of Correction institutions are heroin users whose crimes were directly or indirectly connected with their heroin use.

As with non-addict criminals, addict criminate tend to specialize in certain activities, depending upon their personalities, skills, and experience. One of the myths derived from the passivity stereotype of the heroin user is that the heroin user avoids crimes of violence, such as robbery, which involve personal confrontation. This no longer seems to be the case. A 1966 New York City Police Department study of the arrests of admitted narcotic (primarily heroin) addicts for selected felonies, other than violations of narcotic laws, showed that 15.1 percent of the arrests were for robbery ([City of] New York Police Department 1966). This compared with 12.9 percent robbery arrests of all arrests (addict and non-addict) during the same year. Murder arrests among the addicts amounted to 1 percent of the selected felonies, as compared to 1.4 percent of all arrests in the same categories. The biggest differences between addict arrests and all arrests in the seventeen felony categories selected for study were in the categories of burglary and felonious assault.

Among the addicts, 40.9 percent were burglary arrests, compared to 19.7 percent of all arrests; felonious assault constituted 5.6 percent among the addicts, compared to 27.9 percent of all arrests. What these figures reveal is not that heroin users avoid crimes of violence, as compared to non-addicts, but that they avoid crimes not involving financial gain, such as felonious assault. Where financial gain is involved, as in robbery, the risk of violence is taken by heroin users in a higher percentage of cases than with non-addicts. These statistics confirm the observations and opinions of street informants, both addict and non-addict. The high percentage of burglaries committed by heroin users is often cited as evidence that, in comparison with non-addict criminals, they prefer nonviolent crime. What is overlooked here is that burglary, especially of residences, always involves the risk of personal confrontation and violence. Of the 1745 burglary arrests of admitted addicts in 1966, 975 (51 percent) were residence burglaries.

Analysis of the data from the informants for this study showed the following, with regard to principal criminal occupations, not including those connected with narcotic-laws offenses: burglar—22.7 percent, *flatfooted hustler*—12.2 percent, shoplifter—12.1 percent, robber—9.0 percent. *Flatfooted hustler* is a term used on the street for one who will commit almost any kind of crime for money, depending upon the opportunities. As one self-described flatfooted hustler put it: "I'm capable of doing most things—jostling (picking pockets), boosting (shop-lifting), con games, burglary, mugging, or stick-ups; wherever I see the opportunity, that's where I'm at." The main advantage of crimes against the person is that the yield is usually money, which does not have to be sold at a discount, as does stolen property. It is easily concealed and can be exchanged directly for heroin. In the case of stolen goods and property, the person has to carry the proceeds of, say, a burglary around with him, as he looks for a direct buyer or a fence. . . . This exposes him to extra risk of apprehension. When he does find a buyer, he can only expect to get from 10 percent to 50 percent of the value, the average being about 30 percent, depending upon the item—the more expensive the item, the higher the discount.

The distribution and sales of goods and property stolen by heroin users has become a major economic institution in low-income neighborhoods. Most of the consumers are otherwise ordinary, legitimate members of the community. Housewives will wait on the stoop for specialists in stealing meat (known as *cattle rustlers*) to come by, so that they can get a ham or roast at a 60-percent discount. Owners of small grocery stores buy cartons of cigarettes stolen from the neighborhood supermarket. The owner of an automobile places an order with a heroin user for tires, and the next day he has the tires—with the wheels. During the Easter holidays, there is a great demand for clothes, with slum streets looking like the streets of the Garment District.

It has often been noted that retail stores in a slum neighborhood have higher prices than those in more affluent neighborhoods, and this has been attributed to discrimination and profiteering at the expense of poor people with little consumer education and knowledge. Although such charges have some foundation, another major cause of higher prices is the high rate of pilferage by heroin users and others from such stores, the cost of which is passed on to the consumer. One chain store operation which locates exclusively in low-income neighborhoods in New York City is reportedly in bankruptcy due to a 10 percent pilferage rate. This rate compares to about 2 percent citywide.

One economic institution that has resulted directly from the increased criminal activity among heroin users is the *grocery fence*. He is a small, local businessman, such as a candy store owner, bar owner, or beauty parlor owner, who has enough cash to buy stolen goods and property on a small scale and has a place to store them. He then sells the items to his regular customers, both for good will and a profit. He provides a service for the user in providing him with a fast outlet for his goods.

The heroin user is an important figure in the economic life of the slums. In order to support a $20-a-day habit, he has to steal goods and property worth from $50 to $100. Usually, he steals outside his neighborhood, not out of community loyalty, but because the opportunities are better in the wealthier neighborhoods; and he brings his merchandise back to the neighborhood for sale at high discounts. This results, to some extent, in a redistribution of real income from the richer to the poorer neighborhoods. Although non-addict residents in the slums may deplore the presence of heroin users, they appreciate and compete for their services as discount salesmen. The user, in turn, experiences satisfaction in being able to make this contribution to the neighborhood.

The type of criminal activity he engages in, and his success at it, determine, to a large extent, the addict's status among fellow addicts and in the community at large. The appellation of *real hustling dope fiend* (a successful burglar, robber, con man, etc.) is a mark of respect and status. Conversely, *non-hustling dope fiend* is a term of denigration applied to users who stay in the neighborhood begging for money or small tastes of heroin, renting out works, or doing small-time juggling. There are also middle-status occupations, such as *stealing copper*, where the person specializes in salvaging metal and fixtures from vacant tenement buildings and selling to the local junkman. About the only kinds of illegal activity not open to the heroin user are those connected with organized crime, such as gambling and loan sharking. Users are not considered reliable enough for work in these fields. They may be used as a lookout for a dice game or policy operation, but that is about as close as they can get to organized criminal operations.

Respite from the arduous life they lead comes to heroin users when they go to jail, to a hospital or, for some, when they take short-time employment at resort hotels in the mountains. In the present study, it was found that 43 percent of the subjects were in some type of incarceration at any given period of time. In jail they rest, get on a healthy diet, have their medical and dental needs cared for, and engage in relaxed socialization which centers around the facts and folklore of the heroin user's life on the street.

If a user has been making good money on the street, he eventually builds up a tolerance to heroin which gets to the point where he can no longer finance the habit. He may then enter a hospital for detoxification. If he stays the medically recommended period of time—usually three weeks—he can qualify for Department of Welfare assistance, which eases the economic pressures on him when he resumes his heroin-using life on the street. More often than not, however, he will leave the hospital when his tolerance has been significantly lowered, which occurs in about a week.

Some users solve the problems of too much physical and economic pressure which build up periodically by getting temporary employment out of the city, usually in the mountain resort hotels. There are employment agencies in the Bowery and similar districts which specialize in hiring drifters, alcoholics, and drug addicts for temporary work. In the summer, there is a demand for menial laborers in the kitchens and on the grounds of resort hotels. The agencies are so eager to get help during the vacation season that they go to the street to solicit workers. Some of them provide a cheap suitcase and clothes for those who need them. One informant reported about a particular agency man this way: "He'll grab you out of the street. He'll say, 'Do you want a job, son? I'll get you a good job. You want to work up in the country and get fat? You'll eat good food and everything.'" The agency charges the worker a substantial fee, which is taken out of his first check, and makes extra money by providing private transportation at a price higher than the bus fare. The heroin user usually works through one pay period and returns to the city somewhat more healthy, with a low heroin tolerance, and with a few dollars in his pocket.

It can be seen from the account in this section that the street heroin user is an active, busy person, preoccupied primarily with the economic necessities of maintaining his real income—heroin. A research subject expressed the more mundane gratifications of his life this way:

> When I'm on the way home with the bag safely in my pocket, and I haven't been caught stealing all day, and I didn't get beat, and the cops didn't get me—I feel like a working man coming home; he's worked hard, but he knows he done something, even though I know it's not true.

Conclusions

Heroin use today by lower-class, primarily minority-group, persons does not provide for them a euphoric escape from the psychological and social problems which derive from ghetto life. On the contrary, it provides a motivation and rationale for the pursuit of a meaningful life, albeit a socially deviant one. The activities these individuals engage in, and the relationships they have in the course of their quest for heroin, are far more important than the minimal analgesic and euphoric effects of the small amount of heroin available to them. If they can be said to be addicted, it is not so much to heroin as to the entire career of a heroin user. The heroin user is, in a way, like the compulsively hard-working business executive, whose ostensible goal is the acquisition of money, but whose real satisfaction is in meeting the inordinate challenge he creates for himself. He, too, is driven by a need to find meaning in life which, because of certain deficits and impairments, he cannot find in the normal course of living. A big difference, of course, is that with the street user, the genesis of the deficits and impairments is, to a disproportional degree, in the social conditions of his life.

In the four communities where this research was conducted, the average median family income is $3,500, somewhat less than that of family Welfare Department recipients. Other average population characteristics for the four communities include: public welfare recipients—four times the city rate; unemployment—two times the city rate; substandard housing—two times the city rate; no schooling—two times the city rate; median school years completed—eight years. Neither these few statistics nor an exhaustive list could portray the desperation and hopelessness of life in the slums of New York. In one short block where one of the authors worked, there was an average of one violent death a month over a period of three years—by fire, accident, homicide, and suicide. In Puerto Rican neighborhoods, sidewalk *recordatorios* (temporary shrines at the scenes of tragic deaths) are a regular feature.

Given the social conditions of the slums and their effects on family and individual development, the odds are strongly against the development of a legitimate, non-deviant career that is challenging and rewarding. The most common legitimate career is a menial job, with no future except in the periodic, statutory raises in the minimum-wage

level. If anyone can be called passive in the slums, it is not the heroin user, but the one who submits to and accepts these conditions.

The career of a heroin user serves a dual purpose for the slum inhabitant; it enables him to escape, not from purposeful activity, but from the monotony of an existence severely limited by social constraints, and, at the same time, it provides a way for him to gain revenge on society for the injustices and deprivation he has experienced. His exploitation of society is carried out with emotional impunity on the grounds, for the most part illusory, that he is *sick* (needs heroin to relieve physical distress), and any action is justified in the interest of keeping himself well. He is free to act out directly his hostility and, at the same time, find gratification, both in the use of the drug and in the sense of accomplishment he gets from performing the many acts necessary to support his heroin use. Commenting on the value of narcotic-maintenance programs, where addicts are maintained legally and at no cost on a high level of opiate administration, one informant said:

> The guy feels that all the fun is out of it. You don't have to outslick the cop and other people. This is a sort of vengeance. This gives you a thrill. It's hiding from them. Where you can go in the drugstore and get a shot, you get high, but it's the same sort of monotony. You are not getting away with anything. The thing is to hide and outslick someone. Drugs is a hell of a game; it gives you a million things to talk about.

This informant was not a newcomer to the use of heroin, but a 30-year-old veteran of fifteen years of heroin use on the street. *Soldiers of fortune* is the way another informant summed up the lives of heroin users.

Not all, but certainly a large majority of, heroin users are in the category, which is the subject of this paper. It is their activities which constitute the social problem which New York City and other urban centers face today. The ultimate solution to the problem, as with all the problems which result from social injustice, lies in the creation of legitimate opportunities for a meaningful life for those who want it. While waiting for the ultimate solution, reparative measures must be taken. There are

four major approaches to the treatment and rehabilitation of heroin users: (1) drug treatment (opiate
substitutes or antagonists), (2) psychotherapy,
(3) existentialist-oriented group self-help (Synanon
prototype), (4) educational and vocational training
and placement.

To the extent that the observations and conclusions reported in this paper are valid, a treatment
and rehabilitation program emphasizing educational and vocational training is indicated for the
large majority of heroin users. At the Manhattan
State Hospital Drug Addiction Unit, an intensive
educational and vocational program, supported by
psychological and social treatment methods, has
been created in an effort to prepare the patient for a
legitimate career which has a future and is rewarding and satisfying. The three-year program is divided into three parts: (1) eight months of education,
vocational training, and therapy in the hospital;
(2) one month in the night hospital, while working
or taking further training in the community during
the day; (3) twenty-seven months of aftercare,
which includes, where needed, further education

and training, vocational placement, and psychological and social counseling. With this opportunity
for a comprehensive social reparation, those who
have not been too severely damaged by society have
a second chance for a legitimate, meaningful life.

References

Chein, Isidor, et al. 1964. *The Road to H: Narcotics,
Delinquency, and Social Policy*. New York: Basic
Books, Inc.

City of New York, Police Department. 1966. *Statistical
Report: Narcotics*.

Cloward, Richard A., and Lloyd E. Ohlin. 1960. *Delinquency and Opportunity*. Glencoe, IL: The Free
Press.

Kardiner, Abraham, et al. 1939. *The Individual and His
Society*. New York: Columbia University Press.

Malinowski, Bronislaw. 1922. *Argonauts of the Western
Pacific*. London: Routledge and Kegan Paul Ltd.

Martin, W. R. 1967. Personal Communication.

Sharoff, Robert. 1967. Personal Communication.

Whyte, W. F. 1955. *Street Corner Society*. Chicago: The
University of Chicago Press.

For Discussion

1. The authors argue that the daily activities of people who use heroin create purposeful
lives, particularly when legitimate educational and work opportunities are structurally
limited. However, some people who use heroin are employed in culturally defined prestigious occupations, such as physicians who often derive a sense of purpose from their
work. How might these types of individuals take care of business?
2. How might women who use heroin take care of business?

VII

Rituals and Drug-Use Practices

In 2013, National Public Radio featured a story about a branch of the União do Vegetal (UDV) church in Santa Fe that combines elements of Christianity with indigenous rituals (Burnett 2013). One ritual involves the collective consumption of huasca tea, also known as ayahuasca. The plant is grown in the Amazon region, and the tea is made from the stem of the ayahuasca vine but is usually combined with other plants. *Ayahuasca* is a term from Quechua, an ancient language still spoken by large numbers of people in parts of South America. Ayahuasca has been used as part of ritual and ceremony among indigenous groups for centuries. The combination substance produces hallucinogenic effects but also heightens emotions and intro-spection. The tea has been incorporated into the spiritual practices of the UDV and other non-mainstream churches in Brazil, where the practice is not criminalized. Burnett (2013) highlights the twice-monthly consumption of ayahuasca among UDV church members in Santa Fe and describes their desire to maintain a "low profile." The plant that is often added to the ayahuasca base contains a natural form of dimethyltryptamine (DMT), which is a Schedule I substance in the United States (there are also synthetic variations of DMT). The UDV won the right for its members to consume the psychoactive substance for spiritual purposes after the Supreme Court ruled in their favor. Referring to the development of a similar church in Canada, Tupper (2008, 299) noted that:

> These cases epitomize the struggle between groups seeking the legitimation of the sacramental use of ayahuasca and governments in liberal democratic states endeavouring to uphold both religious free-dom and punitive drug laws.

Hundreds of psychoactive substances are found in nature and have been used by indigenous people from all parts of the world. For instance, *Tabernanthe iboga* is a shrub found in some rainforest regions. The shrub's roots contain *ibogaine*, a substance that anecdotally has been claimed to reduce cravings associated with heroin dependence. The Chontal Indians of Mexico were known to use the dried leaves of *Calea zacatechichi* to induce dreaming. The use of water lilies has been documented in ancient Mayan and Egyptian cultures, and the coca plant continues to be used as medicine, and to relieve sickness and fatigue at high altitudes. Remnants of mescal beans have been discovered through archeological digs near the Rio Grande, and peyote has been commonly used by the Kiowa-Apache and other indigenous people dating back some 7,000 years. Plants, herbs, barks, seeds, and flowers have been used for thousands of years in various parts of the world. Used in ceremonies and for spiritual enlightenment and healing, there is little evidence that this kind of psychoactive substance use creates addiction or serious drug-related problems.

Psychoactive drugs often feature in *contemporary society* during rites of passage (e.g., 21st birthdays, graduations), celebratory occasions (e.g., weddings, promotions, parenthood), and other culturally important events (e.g., funerals). In several countries, alcohol use in particular is embedded into the cultural fabric to mark celebration as well as loss. However, the role of drug use in contemporary industrialized nations goes beyond that of cultural ritual. For many individuals, drug use is a major component of leisure and recreation, and it can occur frequently and excessively and without the customary boundaries that appear to control drug use among indigenous people.

This section of the book includes an important article that addresses drug use as cultural ritual. Two other articles focus on "drug-use practices," which refer to a range of behaviors that are associated with the consumption of drugs during a drug episode. In many instances, drug-use practices are not rituals but become routine and sometimes ritualized behaviors. These ritualized behaviors are perceived to alter the effects of drugs or are otherwise deemed to be important for the overall drug experience. For example, some individuals engage in "preloading," that is, the consumption of substances immediately prior to using the main drug of interest. In a US study,

Kelly (2009) describes preloading as an intentional behavior that involves the use of substances such as health supplements and antidepressants in order to minimize the negative effects of ecstasy. In contrast, researchers in the United Kingdom describe preloading as the consumption of alcohol in a residential setting prior to attending a club or bar (Measham, Moore, and Østergaard 2011). Preloading with alcohol and other drugs also occurs prior to attending concerts, festivals, and related events. Although conceptual definitions of preloading might differ across studies, the behavior is an example of a drug-use practice that is believed by users to shape the drug experience.

Other practices are perceived to affect drug outcomes associated with injecting. People who inject drugs might engage in booting/flushing (pulling the plunger back so that blood is intentionally drawn up into the syringe and then re-injected), or frontloading (using a syringe to measure the amount of drug, and then inserting the mixture into a syringe that will be used by another person). Jean-Paul Grund (1993) provides an excellent ethnographic account of injecting practices in Rotterdam. Certain drug-use practices can increase the likelihood of (health) harm to the individual, whereas other practices can reduce or minimize the harm to one's health.

References

Burnett, J. 2013. "Controversy Brews Over Church's Hallucinogenic Tea Ritual." National Public Radio, April 25.

Grund, J.-P. 1993. "Drug Use as a Social Ritual: Functionality, Symbolism and Determinants of Self-Regulation." Rotterdam: Instituut voor Verslavingsonderzoek. Available at: http://www .drugtext.org/pdf/grund01.pdf

Kelly, B. C. 2009. "Mediating MDMA-Related Harm: Preloading and Post-Loading Among Ecstasy-Using Youth." *Journal of Psychoactive Drugs* 41: 19–26.

Measham, F., K. Moore, and J. Østergaard. 2011. *Emerging Drug Trends in Lancashire: Night Time Economy Surveys, Phase One Report.* Lancaster (England): Lancashire Drug and Alcohol Action Team and Lancaster University.

Tupper, K. W. 2008. "The Globalization of Ayahuasca: Harm Reduction or Benefit Maximization?" *International Journal of Drug Policy* 19: 297–303.

17

Psychoactive Agents and Native American Spirituality

Past and Present

LAURENCE ARMAND FRENCH

In this next article, Laurence Armand French carefully weaves historical information with contemporary data to illustrate the role of drug use as ritual among Native Americans. Rituals are regulated by informal social control that has guided Native American cultures for hundreds of years. US drug policy is created by people who hold power in mainstream society, and important Native American cultural traditions that involve psychoactive substances have been marginalized by US drug laws and policies.

Introduction

Alcohol and other psychoactive agents have played a role among Native Americans since aboriginal times—long before Euro-American contact and influence. The major difference between aboriginal use and current substance-related disorders is that substance use in the past was closely linked to social customs and rituals. Alcohol—notably fermented corn—was an integral component of many aboriginal groups including the Incans, while the coca leaf has long been a tradition among South American Indians—a tradition that continues to the present day (Brodzinsky 2005). Tribes in Mexico and the southwest United States continue to use fermented cactus wine in their rituals. Tobacco has long been associated with the sacred pipe, purification sweats and vision quests. Peyote also plays a special sacred role within both aboriginal and contemporary Native American rituals. However, 150 years of strictly enforced prohibitions

against traditional rituals, including the use of psychoactive agents, has resulted in the current problem of high substance abuse in Indian Country. This article traces the cultural and policy implications of this phenomenon.

Cultural Conflict and Marginality

Many blame the Europeans for the introduction of alcohol (perhaps the most significant social ill associated with psycho-cultural marginality), but this is not really the case since alcohol and other psychoactive agents played a role among American Indians in aboriginal times prior to Euro-American contact and influence. The major difference between aboriginal use and what transpired following the Euro-American influence was that, under the dictates of the "harmony ethos," substance use was highly regulated and related to social customs and rituals (Weber 1930; French 1994). Another significant distinction was the potency of the psychoactive

Reprinted from Laurence Armand French, 2008, "Psychoactive Agents and Native American Spirituality: Past and Present." In *Contemporary Justice Review* 11: 155–163. Reprinted by permission of Taylor & Francis via Copyright Clearance Center.

agent in these rituals. A brief review of these contravening worldviews is necessary in order to better understand the emergence of pathological substance abuse among Native American groups.

Pre-Columbian North America aboriginal groups subscribed to a basic worldview that dictated intra-group cooperation. Evidence suggests that a sense of balance also prevailed in inter-group conflicts with excesses held in check. Vast trading routes indicate a fluid intra-continental interaction between the various tribes prior to European contact and the advent of the horse. The normative structure supportive of this cooperative lifestyle is termed the "harmony ethos." A common theme prevailed across tribal groups despite variations in their creation myths—one that promoted respect for *Mother Earth* and *Father Sky*. Here, Mother Earth was the land, water and living creatures, while Father Sky represented the wind, weather, sun, stars and moon—all that affected or interacted with the land.

Generally speaking, the aboriginal harmony ethos consisted of a complex social code governing individual freedom *vis-à-vis* the demands of the extended family and clan. Respect for, and cooperation with, nature was imperative for their existence. Accordingly, animals and plants were thanked for providing sustenance to the group. Elements of the harmony ethos have survived to the present and are reflected in tribal traditionalism such as the sweat, vision quest and sun dance. Many of these traditional tenets differ markedly from the values inherent in Western cultures (i.e., those promoted by European-American norms). Psychocultural marginality—a loss of one's cultural identity—is likely when American Indians and Alaskan Natives (called "First Nations" and "the Inuit," respectively, in Canada) are denied access to their traditional cultural values and norms. Moreover, many Native Americans are not resocialised adequately, and hence do not subscribe fully to either their traditional culture or the larger Western-based North American society. Hence, the combination of cultural alienation and personal disorganisation (anomie) places these marginalised individuals at high risk of self-mediation and escapism and substance abuse (French 1994).

This was not always the case. In aboriginal times, psychoactive substances played a significant role in many Native American groups. Clearly, the effects of cultural genocide did much to destroy Native American traditionalism, greatly contributing to Indian marginality. Policies of forced removal and placement in concentration camps and boarding schools for the purpose of resocialisation met with mixed success. These policies did much to reduce the Native American population and clear up desired lands for white settlers, but with a great price for the surviving tribal members. The late Rueben Snake, the noted Winnebago-Sioux chair of the Federal Task Force on Alcohol and Drug Abuse, articulated the sad results of these policies in Indian Country:

> The steamrolling effect of the "civilized society" upon Indian people has wreaked a havoc which extends far beyond that of loss of material possessions. The American Indian and Alaska Native are caught in a world wherein they are trying to find out who they are and where they are, and where they fit in. The land which was once their "mother," giving them food and clothing, was taken. Their spiritual strengths were decried as pagan, and familial ties were broken. Their own forms of education, i.e., that of legends, how to live, how to respect themselves and others, were torn asunder by the "white society's" reading, writing and arithmetic. No culture could, or can be, expected to be thrust into a world different from its own and adapt without problems of cultural shock. Also, the Indian people were not even given citizenship until 1924. An 1832 federal Indian law prohibiting the sale of liquor to Indian people remained in effect until 1953 and could have been instrumental in the formation of "hidden group," "drink until it's gone" and "quick" drinking patterns that Native American people exhibit. The Indian people of today are proud of their heritage and are fighting to maximize its influence upon their lives in a dominant white world. Many have succeeded. Many have not. (Snake 1976)

Aboriginal Culturally Endorsed Substance Use

The New World had a number of indigenous psychoactive plants, in addition to corn, that had psychoactive properties. For the most part, it appears that the use of these psychoactive agents as linked to socially prescribed customs and rites. One of the most pervasive psychoactive agents used by Native Americans is the coca leaf. It continues to be used by the Indians of Peru (Martin 1970; Mortimer 1901).

> The plant from which cocaine is extracted has been cultivated in South America for thousands of years, and a large part of the population of Bolivia and Peru, smaller numbers in Columbia, and a few people in Argentina and Brazil now chew its leaf every day. One student of the coca leaf has gone so far as to write of the Peruvian Indians, "Never in the life of a people has a drug had such importance." A sixteenth-century Spanish administrator of the conquered Inca Empire said, "If there were no coca, there would be no Peru." The magical leaf that . . . "satisfies the hungry, gives new strength to the weary and exhausted and makes the unhappy forget their sorrows" became perhaps even more important when the Spanish conquest made its consumption more widespread. Since then it has been alternately extolled and condemned, and it remains a topic of controversy today. (Grinspoon and Bakalar 1976, 9)

Part of the current controversy revolves around the United States' targeting of cocaine in its worldwide War on Drugs effort (Andrews and Solomon 1975; Ashley 1975). The United States has embarked on massive eradication programmes in South America in order to wipe out the major source of the cocaine market, often at the expense of indigenous tribes. Nonetheless, native tribes in Columbia and Peru continue to raise and use coca as they have for centuries. Indeed, the Nasa tribe in southwestern Columbia recently began selling a coca-based drink called "*Coca-Sek*," while the newly elected Indian president of Bolivia, Evo Morales, has made the decriminalization of coca a major campaign promise—both situations seriously challenge the United States' massive eradication programme in the area.

Fermented corn beer was perhaps the most common aboriginal substance used during the pre-Columbian era among North American native groups. We know today that alcohol was an integral

component of Incan rites, including human sacrifices. Directly across the Mexican border in southern Arizona, the Tohono O'odham (formerly known as the "Papago") traditionally made fermented wine by boiling the fruit of the saguaro cactus. This drinking ritual was most prominent during their fall festival, *Wihgita*, which occurred in what is now August. Apparently, social license was allowed at this time resulting in a communal bout-drinking ritual, much like the Christian (Catholic) celebrations preceding Lent. Sanctioned aboriginal communal drinking bouts later gave way to social collective binge drunks commonly known throughout Indian country as *Forty Niners*. The sacred role of corn is illustrated by its significance for the aboriginal Cherokee.

> In former times the annual thanksgiving ceremony of the Green Corn dance, preliminary to eating the first new corn, was the most solemn tribal function, a propitiation and expiation for the sins of the past year, an amnesty for public criminals, and a prayer for happiness and prosperity for the year to come. Only those who had properly prepared themselves by prayer, fasting and purification were allowed to take part in this ceremony, and no one dared to taste the new corn until then. Seven ears from the last year's crop were always put carefully aside, in order to *attract the corn* until the new crop was ripened and it was time for the dance, when they were eaten with the rest. In eating the first new corn after the Green Corn dance, care was observed not to blow upon it to cool it, for fear of causing a wind storm to beat down the standing crop in the field. (Mooney 1891, 424)

The indication here is that corn and other sources of fermented beers and wines were held in high regard by the aboriginal Native Americans and therefore would hardly be used outside of prescribed rituals. Custom also prohibited their abuse according the dictates of their adaptation of the harmony ethos. Studies of the Wari Empire of the Central Andes, notably Peru, indicate ancient breweries over a thousand years old. Unlike the *chicha* of fermented corn used today by Peruvian Indians, this earlier form was made from molle using local grains and fruits including the berries of the pepper tree. Moreover, it appears that the preparation of this ceremonial drink was made by high-status female noblewomen (Jennings and Craig 2001; Borzo 2004).

Tobacco was another psychoactive agent long associated with aboriginal customs and rituals. With its use dictated by customs and rituals rooted within their versions of the harmony ethos, tobacco abuse was not widespread during pre-Columbian times. Indeed, lung disease was most likely to occur among those who had prolonged exposure to unvented or poorly vented pit fires—the most common source of both cooking and heat. The role of tobacco during these times, according to the traditional ways of the three largest tribes today (Athapaskan, Sioux and Cherokee), was used sparingly due to its spiritual significance. Within the harmony ethos adaptations of these three linguistic groups, tobacco represented man's spiritual link with Father Sky. James Mooney, the noted ethnographer wrote about the use of tobacco among the early Cherokee in his 1891, Bureau of American Ethnology publication on the *Sacred Formulas of the Cherokee*:

> Tobacco was used as a sacred incense or as the guarantee of a solemn oath in nearly every important function—in binding the warrior to take up the hatchet against the enemy, in ratifying the treaty of peace, in confirming sales or other engagements, in seeking omens for the hunter, in driving away witches or evil spirits, and in regular medical practice. It was either smoked in the pipe or sprinkled upon the fire, never rolled into cigarettes, as among the tribes of the Southwest, neither was it ever smoked for the mere pleasure of the sensation. Of late white neighbors have taught the Indians to chew it, but the habit is not aboriginal. It is called *tsalu,* a name which has lost its meaning in the Cherokee language, but is explained from the cognate Tuscarora, in which *charhu,* "tobacco," can still be analyzed as "fire to hold in the mouth," showing that the use is as old as the knowledge of the plant. The tobacco originally in use among the Cherokee, Iroquois, and the eastern tribes was not the common tobacco of commerce (*Nicotiana tabacum*), which has been introduced from the West Indies, but the *Nicotiana rustica*, or wild tobacco, now distinguished by the Cherokee as *tsalagayun'li*, "old tobacco," and by the Iroquois as "real tobacco." (Mooney 1891, 423)

The most common tobacco ritual practiced by Native Americans today, notably within the Pan-Indian movement, involves aboriginal adaptations of the Sioux sacred pipe sacrament. According to the aboriginal Siouan adaptation of the harmony ethos, the sacred pipe, with the bowl of pipestone, stem of wood and adorned with 12 eagle feathers, shell fragments and colored beads sewed into a buckskin wrap, is symbolic of the universe (Mother Earth and Father Sky). The bowl represents both Manka (Mother Earth) and man's blood, while the red beads represents the west, blue the north, green the east and yellow the south. The north/south direction represents the red road or good way where north signifies purity and south the source of life. On the other hand, the east/west direction represents the blue or black road, the path of error and destruction.

The sacred pipe was the most significant and common of their seven sacred rituals in that it provided a form of communion and purification so that the four virtues of bravery, fortitude, generosity and wisdom could be maintained and reinforced on a regular basis. Specifically, the bowl represents Mother Earth and all the Grandmothers (female ancestors) as well as all the two-leggeds (American Indians) who are red. It also is symbolic of the red road (good way) provided to the inhabitants of Mother Earth by Father Sky (the Great Spirit or Waken-Tanka). The wooden stem represents all that grows upon Earth, while the shell, leather and feathers decorations represent respectively those things of the water, the land and the sky. The 12 feathers of the sacred pipe are taken from Wanbli Galeshka (the spotted eagle), which itself represents Wakan-Tanka. The sacred tobacco mix is offered up to Wakan-Tanka and placed into the bowl in a ritual that involves pointing the pipe bowl first to the heavens, then to the west, north, east, south and finally down toward Mother Earth. When not in use, the sacred pipe is wrapped in buckskin and kept by the medicine man (keeper of the sacred pipe). The smoke itself is the medium of spiritual communication with Wakan-Tanka.

Like their Cherokee counterparts, the aboriginal Sioux did not use tobacco casually (Brown 1953; French 1997). Indeed, tobacco from the eastern tribes was a valued commodity as was the pipestone from the western quarries. According to Wilbert, shamans of the Warao Indians of Venezuela use tobacco as their primary vehicle for communication with their gods:

> Tobacco may be one of several vehicles for ecstasy; it may be taken in combination with other plants, as we have seen, to induce narcotic trance states; or it may represent the sole psychoactive agent employed by shamans to transport themselves into the realm of the supernatural, as is the case among the Warao of the Orinoco Delta in Venezuela. (Wilbert 1972, 57)

Wilbert noted that the Warao priests-shamans smoked enormous cigars, having done so since first contact with Europeans. Like their counterparts in North America, the Warao believed that the smoke from their cigars allowed for communication with the supernatural, providing a celestial bridge with the Great Spirit (*Bahana*). Smoke communication with the spirits was used for both good and evil purposes. Accordingly, tobacco use among the traditional Warao was restricted to certain rituals and used only by the priest-shaman: "In the old days, ordinary mortals hesitated to smoke for fear of precipitating an undesirable encounter with tobacco-craving spirits" (Wilbert 1972, 60).

Peyote, like fermented alcohol (corn or cacti) and tobacco, held a special sacred role within aboriginal cultures. However, peyote and other plant hallucinogens used during aboriginal times fall within the broad class of illicit drugs within contemporary American society and their use among Native Americans has resulted in considerable litigation until the passage of Public Law 103–344 by Congress on 25 January 1994, which amended the American Indian Religious Freedom Act to provide for the traditional use of peyote by Indians for religious and other purposes. This Act was signed by President Clinton on 6 October 1994 (French 1994; Public Law 103–344).

Peyote is a small, spineless round cactus with psychedelic properties, containing more than fifty alkaloids—most notably mescaline. It grows naturally in the deserts of southwestern United States (especially south Texas) and northwestern Mexico. It was called *peyote* by the Aztec, hence its current name. "Dry Whisky," "Divine herb," "Devil's Root" and "Medicine of the Gods" are other terms used to describe peyote. This *cactaceae* plant species was first documented by Hernandez in 1651, who called it *Peyote zacatecensis*. It was given its current name, *Lophophora williamsii*, by John Coulter in 1894. Hernandez noted that it appeared to have a sweetish and hot taste and, when ground up, was used to alleviate joint pain. He also noted its hallucinogenic properties and its use in sacred rituals by medicine men to foresee and predict things. It was also used by warriors, providing them with courage to fight and the ability to abate thirst, hunger and fear.

Aboriginal use of peyote among Native Americans extends from the Yanomamma Indians of Venezuela to the Plains Indians of the United States. Today an estimated 250,000 members of the Native American Church in the United States and Canada legally use peyote during religious ceremonies. Schultes noted that while the spread of the peyote sacred rituals from Mexico is unknown, several routes at different periods were likely.

> Raids into the Mescalero country may have been the principal method of acquainting Plains Indians with the plant and its cult. Slow and gradual diffusion northward almost certainly took place as well. At any rate, the cult was well established among the Kiowas and Comanche between 1880 and 1885 and was being spread with missionary zeal. By the late 1920s, the cult had been forced, by the strong hostility and outright untruthful propaganda of many organized Christian missionary groups, to incorporate itself into the Native-American Church—a legally constituted religious sect due the protection and respect enjoyed by any other religious group. In 1920 there were some 13,300 adherents in about thirty tribes. At present, an estimated 250,000 Indians in tribes as far north as Saskatchewan, Canada, practice this religion, which advocates brotherly love, high moral principle, abstention from alcohol and other admirable teachings. There is still disagreement about the reasons peyote use spread so fast, edging out other well-established

Indian "nativistic" movements, such as the famous Ghost Dance. (Schultes 1972, 13)

The use of peyote among the Huichol Indians of Mexico illustrates a ritual similar to the Siouan Sun Dance, considered to be the ultimate rite-of-passage for adult males. Those who have completed four Sun Dances are considered to have "counted coup" on life, having obtained the critical dimension of wisdom and are now considered respected elders (grandfathers) among their people. This status and ritual is also popular among pan-Indian groups in the United States and Canada. The Huichol Indian rite-of-passage for its respected elders, *Peyoteros*, is the peyote quest or pilgrimage. Furst described the significance of this ritual as such:

> The pilgrimage helps one attain whatever one desires—health, children, rain, protection from lightning and sorcerers, or diving intervention against the ever-troublesome *vecinos* ("neighbors," Mestizos), who encroach illegally on the Huichol lands with their cattle and sometimes employ force to drive the Indians from their farms. Above all, one goes to attain visions of great beauty, to hear the voices of the spirits, the divine ancestors, and to receive their guidance. (Furst 1972, 151)

Other psychoactive agents were used during aboriginal times, including the Cherokee's "black drink." Mooney hinted that the concoction drunk at the new-year purification rite was a root the Cherokee called *unaste' tstiyu*, or the Virginia or black snakeroots (*Aristolochia serpentarid*). It produces stimulation while inducing vomiting and sweating—the elements required for internal cleansing (Mooney 1891). Schultes later noted that the *snake plant* (a member of the morning glory family) was used for its hallucinogenic properties among Mexican Indian groups. The Aztecs used hallucinogenic mushrooms, known as *teonanacatl* ("god's flesh"), in their sacred rituals, as did the aboriginal Indians of western Mexico. Along the current Mexican/United States border, aboriginal Indians used the seeds of the *Sophora secundiflora* shrub for thousands of years prior to European contact. These tribes participated in what is known as the "mescal," or "Red Bean," cult. Archeological evidence also indicates pre-Columbian use of the morning glory, whose seeds have an hallucinogenic

property (Schultes 1972, 31, 32). Indeed, dozens of plants, mushrooms and tree barks were used for their psychoactive properties by aboriginal groups in the Americas, mainly in conjunction with sacred rituals. There is little evidence that psychoactive agents were abused by these native populations. However, the use of tobacco and peyote is increasingly being introduced into contemporary healing ceremonies among Native American groups as tribes exercise more autonomy over their lives under the auspices of Indian self-determination.

The Indian Self-Determination and Education Assistance Act (Public Law 93-638) of 1975 was greatly influenced by work being done by the American Indian Policy Review Commission, which included the work of Ruben Snake, cited earlier in this article. The Congressional findings leading to passage of PL 93-638 include the following:

> SEC. 2. (a) (that) the prolong Federal domination of Indian service programs has served to retard rather than enhance the progress of Indian people and their communities by depriving Indians of the full opportunity to develop leadership skills crucial to the realization of self-government, and has denied to the Indian people an effective voice in the planning and implementation of programs for the benefit of Indians which are responsive to the true needs of Indian communities. . . .
>
> SEC. 3. (a) The Congress hereby recognizes the obligation of the United States to respond to the strong expression of the Indian people for self-determination by assuring maximum Indian participation in the direction of educational as well as other Federal services to Indian communities so as to render such services more responsive to the needs and desires of those communities.
>
> (b) The Congress declares its commitment to the maintenance of the Federal Government's unique and continuing relationship with and responsibility to the Indian people through the establishment of a meaningful Indian self-determination policy which will permit an orderly transition from Federal domination of programs for and services to Indians to effective and meaningful participation by the Indian people in the planning, conduct, and administration of those programs and services.
>
> (c) The Congress declares that a major national goal of the United States is to provide the quantity and quality of educational services and

opportunities which will permit Indian children to compete and excel in the life areas of their choice, and to achieve the measure of self-determination essential to their social and economic well-being. . . .

An expansion of Indian self-determination extended to child abuse following disclosure of rampant child sex abuse by white Bureau of Indian Affairs (BIA) teachers. Congressional findings of chronic child abuse in Indian Country, especially those abuses committed by non-Indian BIA teachers, provided a new impetus for tribal control of education. It also expanded child protection laws to include Indian Country. In 1990, the American government, for the first time, established an Indian child protection statute: Title IV of Public Law 101–630 (Miscellaneous Indian Legislation). Title IV provided the Indian Child Protection and Family Violence Prevention Act, which requires that reports of abused Indian children are made to the appropriate authorities in an effort to prevent further abuses; authorizes such actions as are necessary to ensure effective child protection in Indian Country; establishes the Indian Child Abuse Prevention and Treatment Grant Program to provide funds for the establishment on Indian reservations of treatment programmes for victims of child sexual abuse; provides for the treatment and prevention of incidents of family violence; and authorizes other actions necessary to ensure effective child protection on Indian reservations.

Tribal-Centric Clinical Models

The incentive toward tribal-centric treatment programmes grew out of the Indian self-determination process with passage of Public Law 99-570, the Anti-Drug Abuse Act of 1986. It was responsible for the establishment of Indian Health Service (HIS)-funded Regional Youth Treatment Centers (RYCT), which represents the major substance abuse prevention initiative in Indian Country among federally recognised tribes in the United States. HIS-funded Regional Youth Treatment Centers serve enrolled tribal youth aged 12–19. Currently this initiative serves over 400 American Indian/Native Alaskan substance abuse programmes operating in nearly 300 communities within Indian Country. Moreover, over a thousand native healers

serve these programmes. Tribal substance abuse counselors/healers receive training similar to that prescribed by the National Certification Reciprocity Consortium (NCRC), including the Twelve Core Functions of Counseling and Professional Ethics. A major difference is that these counselors/healers must be knowledgeable in Native American cultural ways. IHS provides specialty certification in five areas: Dual Diagnosis Counselor Specialist (substance abuse counseling and medical/mental health); Adolescent Specific Counselor; Senior/Elder Specific Counselor; Female-Specific Counselor; and Prevention Specialist (French 2003).

Some of the problems with these programmes include mistrust among Native Americans of interventions presented to them by outsiders, language barriers and the geographic isolation of tribes in Indian Country. Tribal leaders suggest that for these programmes to be more effective they need to incorporate native cultural beliefs into the healing process as well as making better use of tribal leaders and community members in the prevention programmes. Nonetheless, treatment successes do occur in Indian Country, but often are not recognised because these methods involve traditional methods applied outside the federally recognised IHS venue (Coyhis 2000; French 2004; Jilck 1994; Vicks et al. 1998). The greatest successes are where traditional healers are afforded greater recognition and given the opportunity to operate in the open. This includes the Native American Church and its use of peyote in healing rituals.

References

Andrews, G. and D. Solomon, eds. 1975. *The Coca Leaf and Cocaine Papers*. New York: Harcourt Brace Jovanovich.

Ashley, R. 1975. *Cocaine: Its History, Uses and Effects*. New York: St. Martin's Press.

Borzo, G. 2004. "Ancient Brewery Discovered on Mountaintop in Peru." *The Field Museum*. July 27. http://www.eurekalert.org/pub_releases/2004-07/fm-abd072704.php

Brodzinsky, S. 2005. "Columbia Sells Coca-Leaf Soda." *Christian Science Monitor* (December 22): 1.

Brown, J. E. 1953. *The Sacred Pipe: Black Elk's Account of the Seven Rites of the Oglala Sioux*. Norman, OK: University of Oklahoma Press.

Coyhis, D. 2000. "Culturally Specific Addiction Recovery for Native Americans." In *Bridges to Recovery*, edited by J. Kristen, 26–32. New York: Free Press.

French, L. A. 1994. "Indian Marginality." In *The Winds of Injustice: American Indians and the US Government*. New York: Garland, 143–178.

———. 1997. *Counseling American Indians*. Lanham, MD: University Presses of America.

———. 2003. *Native American Justice*. Chicago, IL: Burnham (Lexington Books).

———. 2004. "Alcohol and Other Drug Addictions among Native Americans: The Movement toward Tribal-centric Treatment Programs." *Alcohol Treatment Quarterly* 22 (1): 81–91.

Furst, P. T. 1972. "To Find Our Life: Peyote among the Huichol Indians of Mexico." In *Flesh of the Gods: The Ritual Use of Hallucinogen*. New York: Praeger, 151.

Grinspoon, L. and J. B. Bakalar. 1976. *Cocaine: A Drug and Its Social Evolution*. New York: Basic Books.

Jennings, J. and N. Craig. 2001. "Politywide Analysis and Imperial Political Economy: The Relationship between Valley Political Complexity and Administrative Centers in the Wari Empire of the Central Andes." *Journal of Anthropological Archaeology* 20: 479–502.

Jilck, W. G. 1994. "Traditional Healing in the Prevention and Treatment of Alcohol and Drug Abuse." *Transcultural Psychiatric Research Review* 31: 219–256.

Martin, R. T. 1970. "The Role of Coca in the History, Religion and Medicine of South American Indians." *Economic Botany* 24: 422–438.

Mooney, J. 1891. *The Sacred Formulas of the Cherokees*. Washington, DC: US Government Printing Office (Seventh Annual Report of the Bureau of Ethnology to the Secretary of the Smithsonian Institute, 1885–1886).

Mortimer, W. G. 1901. *Peru: History of Coca*. New York: J. H. Vail.

Public Law 93-638. 1975. "Indian Self-Determination and Educational Assistance Act." *US Statutes at Large* 88 (January 4): 2203–2214.

Public Law 99-570. 1986. *The Indian Alcohol and Substance Abuse Prevention Act of 1986, Part III: Indian Youth Programs*. October 27. 99th Congress, 2nd Session, Section 4210, 100 Stat. 3207-143-146 (H.R. 5484).

Public Law 101-630. 1990. *Indian Child Protection and Family Violence Prevention Act, Title IV*. November 28. 25 USC 3210.

Public Law 103-344. 1994. *American Indian Religious Freedom Act, Amendments of 1994*. January 25. 103rd Congress, Second Session, H.R. 4230-3.

Schultes, R. E. 1972. "An Overview of Hallucinogens in the Western Hemisphere." In *Flesh of the Gods: The Ritual Use of Hallucinogen*, edited by P. T. Furst, 10–15. New York: Praeger.

Snake, R. 1976. "Snyder Act of 1921." In *Report of Alcohol and Drug Abuse (Task Force Eleven: Alcohol and Drug Abuse): First Report to the American Indian Policy Review Commission*. Washington, DC: US Government Printing Office, 31-32.

Vicks, Sr., R., L. M. Smith, and C. I. R. Herrera. 1998. "The Healing Circle: An Alternative Path to Alcoholism Recovery." *Counseling and Values* 42 (2): 133–141.

Weber, M. 1930. *The Protestant Ethic and the Spirit of Capitalism*, translated by T. Parsons. New York: Charles Scribner's Sons.

Wilbert, J. 1972. "Tobacco and Shamanistic Ecstasy among the Warao Indians of Venezuela." In *Flesh of the Gods: The Ritual Use of Hallucinogen* edited by P. T. Furst, 53–60. New York: Praeger.

For Discussion

1. What are some of the informal social controls that regulated traditional rituals among Native Americans? Compare drug use as ritual with drug use for recreation and pleasure.

2. The author argues that "150 years of strictly enforced prohibitions against traditional rituals, including the use of psychoactive agents, has resulted in the current problem of high substance abuse in Indian Country." Why are these traditional rituals perceived as so threatening to mainstream US society?

18

Poly-Drug Use among Ecstasy Users

Separate, Synergistic, and Indiscriminate Patterns

MIRIAM W. BOERI, CLAIRE E. STERK, MASUMA BAHORA, AND KIRK W. ELIFSON

Poly-drug use generally refers to the use of two or more psychoactive substances during the same drug episode or within a much longer time frame (e.g., 30 days, 6 months). Although researchers and other writers often refer to poly-drug use, the concept is generally undefined or measured too broadly. In this study, Boeri and her colleagues identify several poly-drug combinations among young people who use MDMA. Importantly, they differentiate between the different kinds of poly-drug use and the meaning that poly-drug use holds for individuals.

Introduction

Ecstasy, also known as MDMA (3, 4-methylene-dyoxymethamphetamine), is a popular "designer" drug, especially among young adults (Johnston et al. 2005; National Institute on Drug Abuse [NIDA] 2005; Substance Abuse and Mental Health Services Administration [SAMHSA] 2005). According to the DSM IV-TR, Ecstasy is classified as a hallucinogen (American Psychiatric Association [APA] 2000), but it also produces alerting effects similar to those of stimulants such as (meth)amphetamine. Its popularity partly is driven by effects such as an increased ability to produce a strong sense of comfort and empathy to others (Cohen 1998; Elk 1996; Hastings 1994; Millman and Beeder 1994; Schwartz and Miller 1997). Initial research on Ecstasy use tended to focus on its use at raves and clubs, thereby resulting in its label as a club drug (Allaste and Lagerspetz 2002; Bellis, Hughes, and Lowey 2002; Diemel and Blanken 1999; Gross et al. 2002;

Hammersley et al. 1999; Hitzler 2002; Hunt et al. 2005; Measham, Parker, and Aldridge 1998; Pedersen and Skrondal 1999; Riley et al. 2001; Ter Bogt et al. 2002). However, Ecstasy use no longer primarily is limited to raves and clubs, but instead is used in a wide variety of settings (see, for example, Boeri, Sterk, and Elifson 2004; Galaif and Newcomb 1999; Soar, Turner, and Parrott 2006).

In this paper we focus on the various forms of poly-drug use and the reasons for combining multiple drugs among Ecstasy users. We note that poly-drug use is not unique to Ecstasy users (Feilgelman, Gorman, and Lee 1998; Grant and Harford 1990; Martins, Mazzotti, and Chilcoat 2005; SAMHSA 2005). Findings from studies among Ecstasy users reveal that poly-drug use is widespread; in other words, few individuals use only Ecstasy (Copeland, Dillon, and Gascoigne 2006; Hansen, Maycock, and Lower 2001; Martins et al. 2005; Schensul, Convey, and Burkholder 2005; Sneed, Morisky,

Reprinted from Miriam W. Boeri, Claire E. Sterk, Masuma Bahora, and Kirk W. Elifson, 2008, "Poly-Drug Use among Ecstasy Users: Separate, Synergistic, and Indiscriminate Patterns." In *Journal of Drug Issues* 38: 517–541. Reprinted by permission of SAGE Publications via Copyright Clearance Center.

Rotheram-Borus, Lee, and Ebin 2004; Soar et al. 2006; Sterk, Elifson, and Theall 2000). Research also shows that it is more common among drug users to add Ecstasy to an already existing repertoire as opposed to adding other drugs to a primary Ecstasy use pattern (Forsyth 1996; Hammersley et al. 1999; Reid, Elifson, and Sterk 2007; Schifano et al. 1998; Solowij, Hall, and Lee 1992; Sterk et al. 2000). Additional research suggests that Ecstasy use can serve as a strategy to enhance a high from other drugs (e.g., alcohol, cocaine or heroin) or to come down from a high on other drugs (e.g., methamphetamine, cocaine or heroin). Again other research reveals the use of other drugs to enhance the Ecstasy high or to soften coming down off Ecstasy (Brecht and von Mayrhauser 2002; Gahlinger 2004; Hammersley et al. 1999; McElrath and McEvoy 2002; Riley et al. 2001; Schifano et al. 2003; Sneed et al. 2004; Sterk et al. 2000; Uys and Niesink 2005; Wu et al. 2006). Poly-drug use appears to be more complex than the typical definition of multiple drug use by a particular user within a certain time period. Nevertheless, researchers often limit themselves to listing all drugs used within a given time period without elaborating on the exact nature of combined or poly-drug use (Boys, Lenton, and Norcross 1997; Forsyth 1996; Grob 2000; Hansen et al. 2001; Pedersen and Skrondal 1999; Reid et al. 2007; Schifano et al. 1998; Solowij et al. 1992).

Frequently, in Ecstasy studies as well as those on other drugs, poly-drug use is defined as having consumed more than one drug during a specific time period. The selected time period may range from a person's lifetime (Hammersley et al. 1999; Montgomery, Fisk, Newcombe, and Murphy 2005; Scholey et al. 2004; Sneed et al. 2004; Wu et al. 2006) to the past six months, 90 or 30 days, week, or one or two days prior to data collection (Carlson et al. 2005; Copeland et al. 2006; Degenhardt 2005; Hansen et al. 2001; Hunt et al. 2005; Isralowitz and Rawson 2006; Montgomery et al. 2005; Sterk et al. 2000). Such definitions of poly-drug use often ignore relevant dimensions such as the frequency of use and the differences between combined or sequential use. Users may report having taken multiple drugs while referring to the actual highs on each drug as independent events. Others may refer

to connected events in which the use of multiple drugs is part of the same experience, as a time-bound event of "getting high" (Schensul et al. 2005; Sterk et al. 2000). The latter may include simultaneous use (e.g., a speedball consisting of heroin and cocaine) as well as sequential use (e.g., alcohol or marijuana use that follows smoking crack cocaine). A central feature of the time-bound event is the user's intent to experience the synergistic effects of the drugs used. Despite the prevalence of the use of more than one drug, the drug use/addiction field has not agreed on a shared conceptualization of poly-drug use.

In addition to the conceptual challenges associated with defining poly-drug use, certain methodological questions arise. Poly-drug use that involves independent experiences within a certain time period is easier to measure in close-ended questions than poly-drug use that involves synergistic experiences. Moreover, quantitative measures have limited capability to capture the complexities involved with poly-drug use. For instance, the details around the reasons for poly-drug use, including the meaning attached to such use, are missed in quantitative measures. A qualitative or mixed-design approach may be more suitable for inquiries into poly-drug use. We apply such an approach in our inquiry into poly-drug use among young adult Ecstasy users with the goal to gain an understanding of their perspective. Based on the findings, we distinguish between separate, synergistic, and indiscriminate poly-drug use, including the use of licit and illicit drugs.

Methods

The findings presented in this paper are part of a larger study among young adult Ecstasy users and HIV risk. For the purposes of this paper, we focus on 94 Ecstasy users who participated in a survey and an in-depth qualitative interview between September 2002 and August 2006 in Atlanta, Georgia. To be eligible, the study participants had to have used Ecstasy at least four times in the past 90 days (on separate occasions), not be in a drug treatment or other institutional setting, and not be intoxicated or otherwise cognitively impaired at the time of the interview. The use criterion for our study is more stringent than that frequently used in most previous studies (Allaste and Lagerspetz 2002; Gross et al. 2002; Hammersley et al. 1999; Hitzler 2002; Riley et al. 2001; Van de Wingaart et al. 1999) because we aimed to focus on participants with extensive experience in Ecstasy use as well as experimental and other types of users.

Initial participant recruitment involved the community identification (CID) process, a mapping method to record epidemiological indicators of the prevalence of Ecstasy use (e.g., from emergency rooms, law enforcement, and drug treatment), expert opinions (e.g., local political leaders and public health officials), and ethnographic information from local researchers (Tashima, Crain, O'Reilly, and Sterk-Elifson 1996). As the CID process progressed, including its ethnographic mapping and targeted sampling (Sterk 1999; Sterk-Elifson 1996; Watters and Biernacki 1989), the recruitment became more targeted. The use of the CID process also allowed us to become familiar with the social ecology of the Ecstasy scene, including the different types of users, the various social settings of use, and the associated behaviors and interaction patterns. The CID process is especially effective when studying "hidden" populations of which the parameters are unknown.

The field team consisted of five women, three of whom were White, one African American and one Asian American, and five men, whose racial/ethnic background was African American (n = 2), White (n = 2), and Latino (n = 2). They all engaged in recruitment as well as interviewing. Using a short form, potential respondents were screened either in the setting where they were recruited, such as at clubs, raves, and near college dorms or off-campus student housing, or at public settings such as parks. Passive recruitment, involving the posting of flyers in local clubs and venues, colleges and universities, coffee shops, and on the street in targeted areas of the city with heavier concentrations of young adults, was also utilized. Potential respondents, who called the project phone line listed on the flyers, initially were screened over the phone using the same short form. Once a potential respondent was identified as eligible, the field team member first described the study and time required to participate. The two most common reasons for

ineligibility were not having used Ecstasy at least four times in the past 90 days or not being between 18 and 25 years.

Interviews were scheduled with interested individuals who passed the screening. The interviews took place at a mutually convenient location such as one of the project offices, the respondent's home, a local restaurant or coffee shop, community centers, or the interviewer's car. Additional information was provided on the nature of the study, the time required, and the informed consent and other confidentiality procedures. The consent form and procedures were approved by the Emory University and Georgia State University Institutional Review Boards. The respondents and the interviewers each retained a copy of the signed consent form.

The survey interview covered domains such as demographics, drug use history and patterns, drug treatment experiences, health history, criminal justice involvement, and issues around HIV testing and risk and protective behaviors. The average time needed to complete the survey was two hours (range from one to three and a half hours). Respondents were reimbursed $25 for their participation. The in-depth interviews were organized around an interview guide that listed topics derived from the literature and our own past research. Among these topics were initial and subsequent use, the impact of the social context, reasons for use, being high, craving, and withdrawal. The topics were not addressed in any particular order, and the respondent was allowed to guide the conversations. If a topic did not arise at all, the interviewer would probe. As is common in such qualitative interviews, not all topics were addressed in all interviews. New topics raised by a respondent were introduced in the ongoing data collection. The average length of the qualitative interview was 90 minutes (range from one to two and a half hours). The study respondents were reimbursed $15 for participating in the open-ended interview.

The quantitative data analysis was limited to descriptive statistics. The qualitative data analysis was guided by a modified grounded theory approach (Charmaz 2001; Glaser and Strauss 1967; Sterk et al. 2000; Strauss and Corbin 1998). The in-depth interviews were transcribed and the text was imported into a qualitative data management program. The data were then coded for general themes related to Ecstasy use. Following the analytical induction method, we analyzed the narratives so that emerging theory fit the details of the majority of cases. A preliminary examination of the data focused on initial and continued Ecstasy use, including when, where, and with whom. Poly-drug use emerged as a broader and more relevant category after initial analysis of ten interviews. Subsequent analyses involved frequent discussions on the emerging categories of analysis and a comprehensive manual search for poly-drug use related statements in the interview transcripts. The data were then recoded for sub-themes within each of the newly emerging categories related to poly-drug use. Each transcript was coded by at least two project staff. We identified themes as described by the experiences recounted by our respondents (Malterud 2001). For example, the three main themes that organize our findings were arrived at by a process of first searching for patterns in frequency, setting, and types of poly-drug use, but it became clear that the meaning of poly-drug use was the most salient issue for the majority of respondents. The use of quantitative and qualitative data allowed for triangulation (Caudle 1994; Creswell 1994; Denzin 1970; Hunt, Joe-Laidler, and Evans 2002; Lempert and Monsa 1994; Lincoln and Guba 1985; Lofland, Snow, Anderson, and Lofland 2006; Nichter et al. 2004; Rhineberger, Hartmann, and Van Valey 2005; Van Maanen 1988). We used triangulation to validate our findings by looking for congruence between the quantitative and the qualitative data as well as to aggregate the findings.

Findings

Upon describing selected demographic characteristics of the study participants, we present a series of descriptive quantitative findings on their Ecstasy use and their poly-drug use. Next we move into the qualitative findings as we distinguish between experiences of separate, synergistic, and indiscriminate poly-drug use from the perspective of the users.

Study Sample

As shown in Table 18.1, the majority of the study participants were male (71.3%), with slightly over one

Table 18.1 Sample Demographics (N = 94).

	%
Gender	
Male	71.3
Female	28.7
Age	
18	19.1
19	21.3
20	14.9
21	11.7
22	6.4
23	7.4
24	9.6
25	9.6
Ethnic/racial background	
African American	33.0
White	51.1
Other	15.9
Education	
Less than high school	20.2
High school diploma/GED	43.6
Some college	33.0
College degree	3.2
Sexual orientation	
Heterosexual	77.7
Homosexual/Lesbian/Gay	11.7
Bisexual	10.6
Relationship status	
Single (not in relationship)	43.6
Married or living with partner	14.9
Steady relationship (not living together)	24.5
Casual relationship	17.1
Self-ranked socio-economic status	
Less than middle class	38.3
Middle class	39.4
Upper-middle class	19.1
Higher than upper-middle class	3.2
Employment status	
Full-time (35 hours/week or more)	24.5
Part-time (less than 35 hours/week)	23.4
Unemployed	27.7
In school or training only	12.8
Other (odd jobs, seasonal work, etc.)	11.7

half (53.3%) being between 18 and 20 years. The study participants' median age was 21 years (range 18–25). The majority reported having completed high school or the equivalent thereof (43.6%) or some college education (36.2%). Approximately one-half of the study respondents self-identified as White (51.1%), with another one third (33.0%) self-identifying as African American. Approximately three-fourths (77.7%) of the study participants identified themselves as heterosexual. In terms of their current relationship status, approximately two-fifths (43.6%) were single.

Given that income information among young adults may not accurately reflect their socio-economic status, the study participants were asked to self-rank their status. Most viewed themselves as middle class or below (77.7%). Regarding their employment status, about one fourth (24.5%) were employed full time with another one fourth (23.4%) being employed part time.

Current Ecstasy Use

The median number of years that that study participants had been using Ecstasy was 2.6 years, with a range between less then one to 11 years. When asked about the number of days Ecstasy was used in the past 90 days, the median number was 9 days, with a range between 4 and 88 days (data not shown). Approximately one fourth (27.7%) of the study participants indicated that Ecstasy was their drug of choice. In terms of the settings where they used Ecstasy during the past 90 days, use at raves, parties, or clubs was mentioned most frequently (85.1%), followed by use at a friend's place with a party going on (58.5%), and at home without a party going on (54.3%). Three fourths (74.5%) of the study participants reported ever having taken a booster dose of Ecstasy, with the most common reason being to make the high last longer (40.4%).

Poly-Drug Use

Table 2 shows the use of drugs other than Ecstasy during the past 90 days. Alcohol use during the past 90 days was reported by all respondents and cigarette smoking/nicotine use by almost four fifths (79.8%). In terms of illicit drugs, marijuana was the most commonly reported illegal drug used (85.1%) in addition to Ecstasy. Substantial

Table 18.2 Favorite Drugs Used With Ecstasy (n = 94).

Drugs used in past 90 days	(%)
Alcohol	100.0
Tobacco/nicotine	79.8
Hallucinogens	38.3
Marijuana	85.1
GHB	12.8
Ketamine	18.1
Amphetamine	18.1
Methamphetamine	40.4
Cocaine	34.0
Crack	8.5
Heroin	12.8
Unprescribed opiates	25.5
Other unprescribed pills	30.9
Favorite drug to use with Ecstasy	
Alcohol	9.6
Tobacco	4.3
Marijuana	45.7
Methamphetamine	10.6
Hallucinogen	8.5
Heroin	4.3
Cocaine	2.1
GHB	1.1
Ketamine	1.1
Rohypnol	1.1
Other (nitrous, Adderall)	2.1
None	9.6
Preferred drug to use to come down	
Alcohol	5.3
Tobacco	5.3
Marijuana	48.9
Methamphetamine	5.3
Heroin	4.3
Cocaine	2.1
Amphetamine	1.1
GHB	1.1
Rohypnol	1.1
Unprescribed opiates	3.2
Other unprescribed pills	3.2
None	19.2

proportions of the study respondents reported using methamphetamine (40.4%), hallucinogens/LSD (38.3%), and powder cocaine (34.0%). Unprescribed pills (30.9%) and unprescribed opiates (25.5%) also were commonly mentioned.

When asked about their favorite drug to use with Ecstasy, almost one in ten (9.6%) study participants preferred no other drug to use as part of the Ecstasy high. In contrast, the majority indicated a preference for using another drug with Ecstasy. Almost one half of the study participants (45.7%) preferred using marijuana while taking Ecstasy, followed by methamphetamine (10.6%), and alcohol (9.6%) next. In terms of their favorite other drugs to aid in coming down from an Ecstasy high, only one fifth (19.2%) of the study participants indicated not having such a drug. Almost one half (48.9%) reported marijuana as their preferred drug used to come down from Ecstasy. Others mentioned alcohol, tobacco, and methamphetamine (5.3% for each).

Qualitative Findings

Based on narratives from the study participants three forms of poly-drug use were identified. The thematic categories were developed through a process of coding the data, paying attention to meanings and experiences described by the respondents, and interpreting the emerging classifications in team discussions as we gained further insight into poly-drug use among Ecstasy users. The three primary categories include: (1) separate poly-drug use, (2) synergistic poly-drug use, including enhancing a high and/or coming down from one, and (3) indiscriminate poly-drug use.

Separate Poly-Drug Use

This form of poly-drug use refers to the use of multiple drugs as separate and unrelated experiences. The study participants viewed their Ecstasy use as independent from their other drug use. For each of the drugs they used, they purposefully sought the effect of each on separate occasions. A number of the study respondents described that they made decisions on what drug to use based on its anticipated effect. For example, stimulants such as methamphetamine or cocaine were used when facing a demanding task that required long hours of work

and alertness. Other drugs, such as marijuana, hallucinogens, and prescription drugs, were chosen because these allowed them to relax. Several study participants mentioned that their Ecstasy use did not serve a functional purpose whereas that of other drugs might. A 19-year-old woman elaborated on her Ecstasy and methamphetamine use:

> Ecstasy, I feel like I can do that maybe once a month or maybe even less than that because it's fun but it's an intense experience. And doing meth is really intense, but it's something you can do every day too, it's a very functional drug . . . You can't eat Ecstasy and go to school and go to work . . . On meth, you can go to work and still act normal and you got more energy but you can still act more normal.

A number of study participants explained that daily use of Ecstasy was uncommon and that its use tended to be concentrated to specific events, including the weekend. A 19-year-old male reflected on his use patterns, and he explained that he may use marijuana but not Ecstasy during the week. His Ecstasy use is limited to the weekend:

> I have my reality during the week. My school, my responsibilities . . . But on the weekends I have my alternate universe where I go to and I have fun. . . . I go off, I leave all my worries behind on Friday and Saturday, sometimes into Sunday. . . . But those are the days I use. And those are the days I get so bent that I can't function. Now during the week, yeah I might smoke some pot or something, calm down, but I don't get to the point where I can't function. . . . I keep myself, for the majority, sober during the week.

Among other study participants, the drug they would use depended on the social environment, including the setting and the people present. Ecstasy use was acceptable while at a rave or party, but not in other settings or when with friends who do not use drugs. A 21-year-old female who used marijuana frequently and methamphetamine episodically explained that the environment influenced when she used Ecstasy:

> I enjoy doing Ecstasy but it's not something that I would want to do all the time. I couldn't imagine doing it everyday. . . . I couldn't even imagine doing it every weekend. It's something I can do

every once in awhile and enjoy it. Like, maybe once a month if that, you know, and I can enjoy doing it. . . . I like to do it when I'm going most of the time to a rave. Or if I'm going to be around my friends who give light shows who also roll . . . I could be at a house at, like, at an Ecstasy party and be just fine. I could sit on the couch with glow sticks and techno in the background and just everyone else around me rolling and be fine too.

Frequently, as a study participant became experienced with a variety of drugs, a drug of choice would emerge, though this drug was not necessarily the drug used most frequently. For a majority of the study participants, marijuana was the drug of choice, with Ecstasy being preferred episodically at special occasions. For example, a 24-year-old female who started using Ecstasy at a rave when she was 19 recalled using Ecstasy every weekend. Over time, though, her Ecstasy use has become less frequent, having replaced it with alcohol and marijuana use. She explained that Ecstasy use is not conducive to adulthood responsibilities:

> You get to the point where you realize that, okay, I have to have my life, and I need to be responsible. A lot of times when you do Ecstasy, you are so out of it . . . wasted the whole day . . . You realize you have to be responsible for your life. Whereas when you are taking Ecstasy a lot, you get to the point where you just want to do it all the time. Was I addicted? Well, I wasn't doing it every day all the time or taking it all night and the next day and the next day after that, but I definitely enjoyed it too much for a responsible person.

She began preferring alcohol and marijuana for those days that she could not "afford" an Ecstasy high and coming down. She noted that her hard drug use was carefully planned so that it would not interfere with her responsibilities. Later in the interview, however, she also hinted at the fact that she might be cutting down on her Ecstasy use and shifting to alcohol and marijuana because that is what her current boyfriend uses.

Synergistic Experience and Poly-Drug Use

The study participants provided numerous scenarios of poly-drug use that was part of the same event.

The main reason for this use pattern was to achieve the synergistic effect of the combined drugs, including those while coming down off a high. Many study participants described how alcohol enhanced the Ecstasy high and softened coming down off it. One user described this as follows:

> Alcohol really does boost it. Like an hour after you take your pill or something, and you're starting to come down a little bit, you take a shot of vodka—that really boosts your roll. You roll a lot harder for that few minutes. You roll a lot harder while you're drunk.

Another user shared the following about her motivation to drink alcohol when using Ecstasy:

> [Alcohol] doesn't make [Ecstasy] last longer, but it makes it more exciting. Well, like with alcohol, you can drink a lot of alcohol to where you can't get drunk. It's like if you drink and you get to the point where you get drunk, you're not going to get any drunker. You're just drinking. But with X it takes you to the next level. . . .
>
> You won't be feeling all drunk and falling around out there. You'll be more high, more like, up, more aware of things. With alcohol, you get drunk and I'll just got to sleep for a little bit, but with X I don't go to sleep.

Similarly, combined Ecstasy and nicotine use was a favorite combination. For some, Ecstasy was perceived as enhancing the smoking experience. As one user said: "A cigarette has like 10 times the power it would normally have, you know, the nicotine hitting you . . . more of an upper." One woman explained that Ecstasy made her smoking smoother, or as she puts it: "it makes you breathe easier."

For others, nicotine added to the Ecstasy high. They expressed that the cigarettes added a buzz to the Ecstasy high, specifically when they smoked menthol cigarettes. Several study respondents began smoking (again) once they started taking Ecstasy. An 18-year-old male who also uses methamphetamine said:

> I had quit smoking for three months up until that night, and then I rolled (used Ecstasy) and then I smoked three packs of cigarettes. Then that's when I started back smoking . . . smoking is like

the greatest thing in the world when you're on X . . . Just 'cause of the way it makes you feel. And plus the, you know, cigarettes kinda give you a buzz anyways.

Marijuana was the most popular drug to use while on Ecstasy and while coming down from Ecstasy. One young female said that marijuana would ruin the peak of Ecstasy but helps when coming down; therefore, she used marijuana after the Ecstasy peak. A 19-year old male talked about his reasons for combining Ecstasy and marijuana:

Rolls and weed go well together. It's just—mellows you out that one little bit more. . . . You can just chill and just enjoy the nice sensations of tingling in your body. Sit back, watch a movie, whatever . . . Weed just helps the comedown. It helps me go to sleep. I have a lot of trouble sleeping coming down from a pill.

And if I'm awake for too long . . . I've just got a headache and I don't feel like dealing with anybody. I will not be able to sleep.

I'll just lay there all night. And so I'll smoke [marijuana] and it'll help me fall asleep.

Another common pattern was taking Ecstasy with a hallucinogen. One 19-year-old male described his experience of taking LSD and Ecstasy as "amazing . . . it's called a candy flip when you mix the two together. It's a more intense mind kind of thing, and the visuals last longer and you come up and down from like rolling one minute and then you're tripping . . . it lasts longer, too."

One 21-year-old male explained that he had learned on the Internet how to combine Ecstasy with mushrooms in a particular sequential order to achieve a specific effect:

I had read on the internet that if you take mushrooms and Ecstasy together, if you do it in the right order—like if you take Ecstasy first and establish a really great mood, you know, and then you take the mushrooms—when you start tripping, you're not really rolling anymore, but you've got all the positive stuff from when you're rolling. So that means, like, as you start coming down from the shrooms, you're not worried about dying and stuff like that. Because whenever I came down from mushrooms I was always worried about dying for some reason.

But when I did it with rolls, it was just the perfect, great trip. The best mushroom trip I ever had.

A combination that according to the respondents seemed to have gained popularity was Ecstasy with methamphetamine. For some, like the following male user, it enhanced their interactions with others:

Crystal meth. Incredible! All it does is just keeps you up and have energy so you want to move—you want to be more active. I mean, any kind of roll in general I'll still want to get up, walk around, talk to people. But it's hard a lot of times without any type of other amphetamine to get myself to dance while I'm rolling. Just 'cause, you know, you're just so— my body feels kind of heavy, but my mind's racing. So that combination is great.

A 20-year-old female said Ecstasy and methamphetamine were her favorite drugs to use together. She explained the combined effects of "X and meth . . . the meth will make it last longer. The meth with make you feel better . . . It will increase how the Ecstasy feels. It will give you a little bit more energy to go along with it. You get more zoned out."

Again others explained that methamphetamine can help overcome a negative Ecstasy high. A 23-year-old female described this effect: "I know when you're having a bad roll you snort meth and it gets you out of it. When I was telling you when I did the Sand Dollars and was throwing up, I snorted a line of meth and it got me out of it. My stomach felt better . . . it just kills the roll out."

Synergetic effects between Ecstasy and heroin were achieved by some users by crushing the Ecstasy pill into powder and mixing it with heroin. Among others, it was more common to take an Ecstasy pill and to follow it up with a heroin injection. A 21-year-old male injection drug user described this as follows:

Well more than a couple of times, but only if we had a whole lot, because it [Ecstasy] doesn't last long enough. It's like something that you'll do. You'll like eat what you're going to take to get high and then shoot one [heroin dose] before you feel the effects of the pills that you've just eaten. So, you know, you don't ever come down, and you get blown up immediately.

A number of participants explained their preference for mixing Ecstasy and prescription pills, which often were illegally acquired. A young White male combined Ecstasy and OxyContin:

Because the Oxy will leave, it'll like go away and you can't feel it and then it'll come back and hit you, like, 10 times harder, and then it—if you do it on a roll—you can just like sit there and like feel it, you can tell it's coming and then it comes and then you're—then it's game over. . . It's like a train hitting you.

It appears that those participants who were already on a prescription medication for depression did not like to combine these pills with Ecstasy. More than one Ecstasy user mentioned that their prescribed antidepressants did not work for them when they used Ecstasy. A 21-year-old White male who lived in the suburbs explained:

I took Ecstasy a couple of times while I was on antidepressants and did not feel a thing. And all my friends were completely blown out of their minds, and they were, like, man, what's your problem? How come you're not feeling anything? And I got kind of pissed off 'cause I wasted my money, and I got to reading up on that and figured out what the problem was. And, you know, I came to a conclusion, well, Ecstasy makes me happy, and I'm taking antidepressants and I'm still depressed. And it makes me more depressed that I can't take a drug that I really like. So I stopped taking antidepressants.

Several study participants referred to using various prescription pills in combination with marijuana at different times during the Ecstasy high in order to moderate the effects or ease the comedown. For example, one 19-year-old male explained the combination of amphetamines, Ecstasy, and marijuana as building blocks, each with a specific purpose at a specific time:

I'll take two or three Adderall, something like that. And for some reason when I've already got the amphetamines in my system it makes my roll kick in more quickly. And it'll also keep me awake. Most rolls these days are . . . smacky rolls . . . and unless I take something speedy along with it, I'll be doing

that sitting on the stairs all night long . . . I'll smoke weed, definitely. Usually I'll bring, like, a little bit with me into the (rave) and smoke while I'm there, have some in the car, smoke on the way home. If I have enough money, I'll eat another roll when I get home and just sit there and smoke and just hang out for the rest of the night talking with friends. I see 'em kind of as like building blocks almost. Like with the amphetamines, I see that as like a base layer. Alright, there's no real good feeling off of that. All that it's gonna do is keep me awake and give me energy. And then I add the Ecstasy to that and it's, like, alright, so I've got the awake energy part already. Now it's time for the feel-good effect. And so I just see 'em as kind of working as separate things but together at the same time. Weed just helps the comedown. It helps me go to sleep.

There are many forms of synergistic experience poly-drug use among the study participants. Nevertheless, like with separate experience poly-drug users, the combination of drugs taken is planned to achieve a desired outcome.

Indiscriminate Poly-Drug Use

A number of the study participants described using multiple drugs either as independent experiences or to achieve some combined effect. Yet, in most cases what drugs they took tended to be driven by availability. Some referred to this type of poly-drug users as garbage heads. A 23-year-old male explained that "I would mix all sorts of different drugs and it didn't matter if they were uppers or downers or narcotics because you just want to get messed up, and they don't counteract it or whatever. You just get totally messed up."

He, as did other study participants, would use Ecstasy when it became available but would not go out of his way to find it. A 20-year-old female described how indiscriminate use caused her to end up in the emergency room:

I've gone to the hospital for a night because of it [Ecstasy] . . . I did X, I did speed first and then had some Ecstasy and then to come down I did some heroin. But that was before I actually started coming down so I got really scattered all over the place. I started running around and eventually I just blacked out.

Another 22-year-old male on spring break described a poly-drug use experience based on whatever was easily accessible:

> I would do all kinds of drugs, you know, I'd be eating pills—first I'd eat a couple pills, and may do some coke, may eat a Xanax, drink some alcohol . . . and I'd eat another one, 'cause, you know, I had tons of them. I didn't—I wasn't worrying about it. . . I just ate Ecstasy too, you know, to have a good time.

We identify the "garbage head" experiences as indiscriminate poly-drug use. One of the difficulties of identifying this type of use is that indiscriminate use is not necessarily a characteristic of a type of user. An indiscriminate experience does not signify that the user never cares what he or she is taking. At times, indiscriminate use may be followed by intentional separate use, such as when the user has to counterbalance the effects of using multiple drugs indiscriminately in order to function in a social role. Such was the case with one 19-year-old college student who had used crack, heroin, and cocaine as they became available, but then "I had a paper due the next day, so I went out and bought some crystal meth to do the paper."

Discussion

The objectives of the present analysis were to describe poly-drug use among young adult Ecstasy users from their perspective. We limited the time period to the past 90 days. Others have explored lifetime or shorter term poly-drug use. For the purposes of this paper, however, we were primarily interested in gaining an understanding of poly-drug use within a time period for which the users would have to be able to recollect their drug intake, while also being long enough to allow for the identification of patterns. Recent research on poly-drug use calls for refining the definition of poly-drug use in order to capture variations of experiences (Schensul et al. 2005), motivations for poly-drug use (Hansen et al. 2001), and environmental effects (Schifano et al. 2003). By exploring forms of poly-drug use and providing insights on the motivations and settings of poly-drug use from the perspective

of active young adult Ecstasy users, the findings presented here suggest areas for further research aimed at identifying risk and protective behaviors and strategies for risk reduction. Based on the qualitative analyses, we defined three distinct types of poly-drug experiences: the separate, synergistic, and indiscriminate consumption of multiple drugs. In terms of ways to disentangle intentional and unintentional poly-drug use, the findings suggest that separate and synergistic use tend to be intentional. Indiscriminate use, on the other hand, is unintentional or unplanned. In addition, the latter tends to be associated with more risk-taking and negative outcomes, including overdosing.

Ecstasy is different from many other drugs in that its users tend not to take it on a daily basis. In addition, it often tends not to be the drug of choice but one of a series of drugs taken by a user. Among the study participants in our sample, Ecstasy was the drug of choice for only one in four. Alcohol and nicotine were used both as part of separate and synergistic poly-drug use. The quantitative and qualitative data support this finding.

Marijuana was the other illicit drug most frequently used among the study participants. For some, their marijuana use was independent of their Ecstasy use. More common, however, was the use of marijuana to enhance an Ecstasy high, including coming down from a high. Through the quantitative data, we were able to identify this pattern. Yet, it was via the examination of qualitative data which helped us understand the complexities of this form of poly-drug use. We would not have been able to detect the separate and synergistic poly-drug use pattern from only the quantitative data. In addition, the qualitative data provided insight into the reasons for the synergistic use and the users' perceptions of its advantages. The same is true for the use of other illicit drugs. Also common among more than one half of the Ecstasy users in this sample was the use of prescription drugs. For some this involved medications that actually were prescribed to them. We especially note that even though Ecstasy and SSRIs (a type of antidepressant) tend to have a similar impact on the brain, some users experienced that their prescription antidepressants were preventing them from experiencing an Ecstasy high. Unfortunately, they would give up their prescription medications in order to get high on Ecstasy as opposed to taking the opposite choice of giving up Ecstasy.

Independent of the licit or illicit status of the drugs, all were described as being used in the context of separate experiences as well as synergistic experiences. From a prevention and risk reduction perspective, it is important to be aware of this and to incorporate it into health education messages, formal and informal risk reduction programs, and social and health services, including drug treatment.

The study has a number of limitations, including the small sample size. In addition, unique cultural or geographic characteristics of the sample may limit the generalizability of the findings to a wider population. On the other hand, researchers have demonstrated the external validity of purposive samples of Ecstasy users compared to national population studies (Topp, Barker, and Degenhardt 2004). Furthermore, the study's cross-sectional design has its limitations. A longitudinal design would allow for an exploration over time and, in the case of a quantitative study, causal inferences. The data were based on self-reports, which may be affected by recall, social desirability, or additional types of bias. Nonetheless, researchers have found that drug use reports tend to be valid and reliable (Magura et al. 1987; Needle et al. 1995; Weatherby et al. 1994). The limitations of qualitative research methods also serve as its strengths. For example, the open-ended unstructured format of the interviews allowed the respondents to determine the flow of the interview and to introduce new topics. Interviewers using close-ended questions typically only receive answers to questions included in a survey and that fit the answer categories. Furthermore, the use of a mixed design allows for data triangulation.

In conclusion, the sample of young adult Ecstasy users in our study highlights the importance of recognizing that poly-drug use is a common phenomenon. Researchers often separate licit from illicit drugs, thereby resulting in findings that are incomplete. In addition, it is common to sample based on the use of a specific drug without considering the impact of poly-drug use. For example, a user may fit the eligibility criteria in terms of frequency of use for a research project on one drug but when asked about the primary drug of choice indicate another drug. Similarly, drug treatment programs often are designed around the treatment of one drug, thereby ignoring the prevalence of poly-drug use. Finally, we add to the literature a clearer distinction between the types of poly-drug experiences, as well as the motivations for the various types of use and the influence of the setting. We hope that the findings presented in this paper will result in future research that takes a mixed-methods approach and that it will yield comprehensive risk reduction programs and drug treatment services that recognize the prevalence of poly-drug use, including its variations.

References

Allaste, A. and M. Lagerspetz. 2002. "Recreational Drug Use in Estonia: The Context of Club Culture." *Contemporary Drug Problems* 29 (1): 183–200.

American Psychiatric Association. 2000. Diagnostic and Statistical Manual of Mental Disorders. Washington, DC: American Psychiatric Association.

Beilis, A. B., K. Hughes, and H. Lowey. 2002. "Healthy Nightclubs and Recreational Substance Use: From a Harm Minimisation to a Healthy Settings Approach." *Addictive Behaviors* 27 (6): 1025–1035.

Boeri, M., C. Sterk, and K. Elifson. 2004. "Rolling beyond Raves: Ecstasy Use outside the Rave Setting." *Journal of Drug Issues* 34 (4): 831–860.

Boys, A., S. Lenton, and K. Norcross. 1997. "Polydrug Use at Raves by a Western Australian Sample." *Drug and Alcohol Review* 16 (3): 227–234.

Brecht, M. and C. V. Von Mayrhauser. 2002. "Differences between Ecstasy-Using and Nonusing, Methamphetamine Users." *Journal of Psychoactive Drugs* 3 (2): 215–223.

Carlson, R. G., J. Wang, R. S. Falck, and H. A. Siegal. 2005. "Drug Use Practices among MDMA/Ecstasy Users in Ohio: A Latent Class Analysis." *Drug and Alcohol Dependence* 79 (2): 167–179.

Caudle, S. 1994. "Using Qualitative Approaches." In *Handbook of Practical Program Evaluation*, edited by J. S. Wholey, H. P. Hatry, and K. E. Newcomer, 69–95. San Francisco: Jossey-Bass.

Charmaz, K. 2001. "Grounded Theory." In *Contemporary Field Research: Perspectives and Formulations*, edited by R. M. Emerson, 335–352. Prospect Heights, IL: Waveland Press.

Cohen, R. S. 1998. *The Love Drug: Marching to the Beat of Ecstasy*. Binghamton, NY: Haworth Press.

Copeland, J., P. Dillon, and M. Gascoigne. 2006. "Ecstasy and the Concomitant Use of Pharmaceuticals." *Addictive Behaviors* 31 (2): 367–370.

Creswell, J. W. 1994. *Research Design: Qualitative and Quantitative Approaches*. Thousand Oaks, CA: Sage.

Degenhardt, L. 2005. "Drug Use and Risk Behaviour among Regular Ecstasy Users: Does Sexuality Make a Difference?" *Culture, Health, and Sexuality* 7 (6): 599–614.

Denzin, N. 1970. *The Research Act*. Chicago: Aldine.

Diemel, S. and P. Blanken. 1999. "Tracking New Trends in Drug Use." *Journal of Drug Issues* 29 (3): 529–548.

Elk, C. 1996. "MDMA (Ecstasy): Useful Information for Health Professionals Involved in Drug Education Programs." *Journal of Drug Education* 26 (4): 349–356.

Feilgelman, W., B. S. Gorman, and J. A. Lee. 1998. "Binge Drinkers, Illicit Drug Users, and Poly-Drug Users: An Epidemiological Study of American Collegians." *Journal of Alcohol and Drug Education* 44 (1): 47–69.

Forsyth, A. J. 1996. "Are Raves Drug Supermarkets?" *The International Journal of Drug Policy* 7 (2) 105–110.

Gahlinger, P. M. 2004. "Club Drugs: MDMA, Gamma-hydroxybutyrate (GHB), Rohypnol, and Ketamine." *American Family Physician* 69 (11): 2619–2626.

Galaif, E. R. and M. D. Newcomb. 1999. "Predictors of Polydrug Use among Four Ethnic Groups: A 12-Year Longitudinal Study." *Addictive Behaviors* 24 (5): 607–631.

Glaser, B. G. and A. Strauss. 1967. *Discovery of Grounded Theory*. New York: Aldine.

Grant, B. and T. Harford. 1990. "Concurrent and Simultaneous Use of Alcohol with Sedatives and with Tranquilizers: Results of a National Survey." *Journal of Substance Abuse* 2 (1): 1–14.

Grob, C. 2000. "Deconstructing Ecstasy: The Politics of MDMA Research." *Addiction Research* 8: 549–588.

Gross, S., S. P. Barrett, J. S. Shestowsky, and R. O. Pihl. 2002. "Ecstasy Drug Consumption Patterns: A Canadian Rave Population Study." *Canadian Journal of Psychiatry* 47 (6): 546–551.

Hammersley, R., J. Ditton, I. Smith, and E. Short. 1999. "Patterns of Ecstasy Use by Drug Users." *British Journal of Criminology* 39 (4): 625–647.

Hansen, D., B. Maycock, and T. Lower. 2001. " 'Weddings, Parties, Anything . . .': A Qualitative Analysis of Ecstasy Use in Perth, Western Australia." *International Journal of Drug Policy* 12 (2): 181–199.

Hastings, A. 1994. "Some Observations on MDMA Experiences Induced Through Posthypnotic Suggestion." *Journal of Psychoactive Drugs* 26 (1): 77–83.

Hitzler, R. 2002. "Pill Kick: The Pursuit of Ecstasy at Techno-Events." *Journal of Drug Issues* 32 (2): 459–466.

Hunt, G., K. Evans, E. Wu, A. Reyes. 2005. "Asian American Youth, the Dance Scene, and Club Drugs." *Journal of Drug Issues* 35 (4): 695–731.

Hunt, G., K. Joe-Laidler, and K. Evans. 2002. "The Meaning and Gendered Culture of Getting High: Gang Girls and Drug Issues." *Contemporary Drug Issues* 29 (2): 375–415.

Isralowitz, R. and R. Rawson. 2006. "Gender Differences in Prevalence of Drug Use among High Risk Adolescents in Israel." *Addictive Behaviors* 31 (2): 355–358.

Johnston, L. D., P. O'Malley, J. Bachman, and J. Schuleberg. 2005. *Monitoring the Future: National Survey Results on Drug Use, 1975–2004*. National Institute on Drug Abuse: Bethesda, MD: National Institutes of Health.

Lempert, R. and K. Monsa. 1994. "Cultural Differences and Discrimination: Samoans before a Public Housing Eviction Board." *American Sociological Review* 59 (6): 890–910.

Lincoln, Y. and E. Guba. 1985. *Natural Inquiry.* Beverly Hills, CA: Sage.

Lofland, J., D. Snow, L. Anderson, and L. H. Lofland. 2006. *Analyzing Social Settings: A Guide to Qualitative Observation and Analysis.* Belmont: Thomson Wadsworth.

Magura, S., D. Goldsmith, C. Casriel, P. J. Goldstein, and D. S. Lipton. 1987. "The Validity of Methadone Clients' Self-Reported Drug Use." *International Journal of the Addictions* 22 (8): 727–749.

Malterud, K. 2001. "Qualitative Research: Standards, Challenges, and Guidelines." *Lancet* 358: 483–488.

Martins, S., G. Mazzotti, and G. Chilcoat. 2005. "Trends in Ecstasy Use in the United States from 1995 to 2001: Comparison with Marijuana Users and Association with Other Drug Use." *Experimental and Clinical Psychopharmacology* 13 (3): 244–252.

McElrath, K. and K. McEvoy. 2002. "Heroin as Evil: Ecstasy Users' Perceptions about Heroin." *Drugs: Education, Prevention, and Policy* 8 (2): 177–189.

Measham, F., H. Parker, and J. Aldridge. 1998. "The Teenage Transition: From Adolescent Recreational Drug Use to the Young Adult Dance Culture in Britain in the Mid-1990s." *Journal of Drug Issues* 28 (1): 9–25.

Millman, R. and A. Beeder. 1994. "The new Psychedelic Culture: LSD, Ecstasy, 'Rave' Parties and the Grateful Dead." *Psychiatric Annals* 24 (3): 148–150.

Montgomery, C., J. E. Fisk, R. Newcombe, and P. N. Murphy. 2005. "The Differential Effects of Ecstasy/Polydrug Use on Executive Components: Shifting, Inhibition, Updating and Access to Semantic Memory." *Psychopharmacology* 182: 262–267.

National Institute on Drug Abuse (NIDA). 2005. *Epidemiological Trends in Drug Abuse.* Community Epidemiology Work Group (NIH Publication No. 06-5281A). Bethesda, MD: Department of Health and Human Services.

Needle, R., D. Fisher, N. Weatherby, D. Chitwood, B. Brown, H. Cesari, R. Booth, M. Williams, J. Watters, M. Anderson, and M. Braunstein. 1995. "Reliability of Self-Reported HIV Risk Behaviors of Drug Users." *Psychology of Addictive Behaviors* 9 (4): 242–250.

Nichter, M., G. Quintero, M. Nichter, J. Mock, and S. Shakib. 2004. "Qualitative Research: Contributions to the Study of Drug Use, Drug Abuse and Drug Use(r)-Related Interventions." *Substance Use and Misuse* 39: 1907–1969.

Pedersen, W., and A. Skrondal. 1999. "Ecstasy and New Patterns of Drug Use: A Normal Population Study." *Addiction* 94: 1695–1706.

Reid, L., K. Elifson, and C. Sterk. 2007. "Ecstasy and Gateway Drugs: Initiating the Use of Ecstasy and Other Drugs." *Annals of Epidemiology* 17 (1): 74–80.

Rhineberger, G., D. J. Hartmann, and T. L. Van Valey. 2005. "Triangulated Research Designs: A Justification?" *Journal of Applied Sociology/Sociological Practice* 22 (1)/7 (1): 56–66.

Riley, S., C. James, D. Gregory, H. Dingle, and M. Cadger. 2001. "Patterns of Recreational Drug Use at Dance Events in Edinburgh, Scotland." *Addiction* 96: 1035–1047.

Schensul, J., M. Convey, and G. Burkholder. 2005. "Challenges in Measuring Concurrency, Agency and Intentionality in Polydrug Research." *Addictive Behaviors* 30: 571–574.

Schifano, F., A. Oyefeso, J. Corkery, R. Cobain, R. Jambert-Gray, G. Martinotti, and A. Hamid Ghodse. 2003. "Death Rates from Ecstasy (MDMA, MDA) and Polydrug Use in England and Wales 1996–2002." *Human Psychopharmacological Clinical Experience* 18: 519–528.

Schifano, F., L. Di Furia, G. Forza, N. Mimicuci, and R. Bricolo. 1998. "MDMA ('Ecstasy') Consumption in the Context of Polydrug Abuse: A Report on 150 Patients." *Drug and Alcohol Dependence* 52 (1): 85–90.

Scholey, A. B., A. C. Parrott, T. Buchanan, T. M. Heffernan, J. Ling, and J. Rodgers. 2004. "Increased Intensity of Ecstasy and Polydrug Usage in the More Experienced Recreational Ecstasy/MDMA Users: A WWW Study." *Addictive Behaviors* 29 (4): 743–752.

Schwartz, R. H. and N. S. Miller. 1997. "MDMA (Ecstasy) and the Raves: A Review." *Pediatrics* 100 (4): 705–708.

Sneed, C., D. Morisky, M. J. Rotheram-Borus, S. Lee, and V. Ebin. 2004. "Indices of Lifetime Polydrug

Use among Adolescents." *Journal of Adolescence* 27 (3): 239–249.

Soar, K., J. D. Turner, and A. C. Parrott. 2006. "Problematic versus Non-problematic Ecstasy/MDMA Use: The Influence of Drug Usage Patterns and Pre-existing Psychiatric Factors." *Journal of Psychopharmacology* 20 (3): 417–424.

Solowij, N., W. Hall, and N. Lee. 1992. "Recreational MDMA Use in Sydney: A Profile of 'Ecstasy' Users and Their Experiences with the Drug." *British Journal of Addiction* 87 (8): 1161–1172.

Sterk, C. 1999. *Fast Lives: Women Who Use Crack Cocaine.* Philadelphia: Temple University Press.

Sterk, C., K. Elifson, and K. Theall. 2000. "Women and Drug Treatment Experiences: A Generational Comparison of Mothers and Daughters." *Journal of Drug Issues* 30 (4): 839–862.

Sterk-Elifson, C. 1996. "Just for Fun? Cocaine Use among Middle-Class Women." *Journal of Drug Issues* 26: 63–76.

Strauss, A. and J. Corbin. 1998. *Basics of Qualitative Research: Techniques and Procedures for Developing Grounded Theory*, 2nd ed. Thousand Oaks: Sage.

Substance Abuse and Mental Health Services Administration. 2005. *Results from the National Survey on Drug Use and Health: National Findings.* (NIH Publication No. SMA 05-4062). Rockville, MD.

Tashima, N., C. Crain, K. O'Reilly, and C. Sterk-Elifson. 1996. "The Community Identification Process: A Discovery Model." *Qualitative Health Research* 6: 23–48.

Ter Bogt, T., R. Engels, B. Hibbel, F. Van Wel, and S. Verhagen. 2002. "'Dancestasy': Dance and MDMA use in Dutch Youth Culture." *Contemporary Drug Problems* 29 (1): 157–181.

Topp, L., B. Barker, and L. Degenhardt. 2004. "The External Validity of Results Derived from Ecstasy Users Recruited Using Purposive Sampling Strategies." *Drug and Alcohol Dependence* 73 (1): 33–40.

Uys, J. R. Niesink. 2005. "Pharmacological Aspects of the Combined Use of 3,4 Methylenedioxymethamphetamine (MDMA, Ecstasy) and Gamma-Hydroxybutyric Acid (GHB): A Review of the Literature." *Drug and Alcohol Review* 24 (4): 359–368.

Van de Wijngaart, G., R. Braam, D. De Bruin, M. Fris, M. J. M. Maalaste, and H. T. Verbraeck. 1999. "Ecstasy Use at Large-Scale Dance Events in the Netherlands." *Journal of Drug Issues* 29 (3): 679–702.

Van Maanen, J. 1988. *Tales of the Field: On Writing Ethnography.* Chicago: University of Chicago Press.

Watters, J. and P. Biernacki. 1989. "Targeted Sampling: Options for the Study of Hidden Populations." *Social Problems* 36 (4): 416–430.

Weatherby, N., R. Needle, H. Cesari, R. Booth, C. McCoy, J. Watters, M. Williams, and D. Chitwood. 1994. "Validity and Self-Reported Drug Use among Injection Drug Users and Crack Cocaine Users Recruited through Street Outreach." *Evaluation and Program Planning* 17 (4): 347–355.

Wu, Z. H., C. E. Holzer III, C. R. Breitkopf, J. J. Grady, and A. B. Berenson. 2006. "Patterns and Perceptions of Ecstasy Use among Young, Low-Income Women." *Addictive Behaviors* 31 (4): 676–685.

For Discussion

1. Poly-drug combinations that include alcohol during the drug episode can pose health risks (e.g., enhanced dehydration, pronounced effects on the central nervous system) for individuals. Yet cultural norms surrounding alcohol mean that several people do not consider alcohol to be a drug. What kind of peer interventions might help reduce the consumption of alcohol and other drugs during the same drug episode?

2. Some respondents in this study consumed poly-drug combinations for the purpose of enhancing the "high." Why are some drug takers not satisfied with the psychoactive effects of one drug?

19

Peer Injecting

Implications for Injecting Order and Blood-Borne Viruses among Men and Women Who Inject Heroin

KAREN MCELRATH AND JULIE HARRIS

A large body of research has highlighted injecting practices that can contribute to the transmission of blood-borne viruses, such as HIV and hepatitis C. Compared with other injecting practices, considerably less is known about peer injecting, that is, receiving or giving injections, and the social context in which it occurs. In this article, Karen McElrath and Julie Harris explore peer injecting and injecting order at initiation into injecting drug use and during subsequent injections. The results suggest gendered similarities as well as differences in terms of peer injecting, the order of injection, and micro-risk contexts for blood-borne viruses.

Introduction

Considerable research has described behaviours among injecting drug users (IDUs) that can pose risk for hepatitis C and HIV infection. These behaviours include the loaning and borrowing of injecting equipment (Chitwood et a1. 2000; Hagan et al. 2001; De et al. 2007), frontloading and backloading (Grund et al. 1991; Jose et al. 1993; Stark et al. 1996), booting/flushing and other needle/syringe rituals (Pates et al. 2001; McElrath 2006; Paintsil et al. 2010). IDU often occurs within dyads or small groups, micro-environments that can heighten the risk for blood-borne viruses because of a greater likelihood of blood-to-blood among dyad or group members. In this article, we focus on another injecting practice in which IDUs often engage, i.e. peer injecting, which we define as receiving injections from or giving injections to another IDU.

Peer Injecting

The injecting process is generally more complicated than other routes of administering drugs; thus, individuals are usually taught how to inject by more experienced injectors. Indeed, the first injection is rarely self-administered, which means that the process is facilitated by others and therefore occurs within a socially interactive context (Bryant and Treloar 2007; Frajzyngier et al. 2007; Harocopos et al. 2009; Rhodes et al. 2011). While there is a growing body of research into first injection, scholars have noted that this literature is largely epidemiological (Sánchez et al. 2006).

Following initiation into IDU or the early stage of the injecting career, many individuals begin to self-inject. However, some individuals never learn how to self-inject or never feel comfortable injecting themselves. Others cannot self-inject because of withdrawal symptoms, venous or other health problems (Carlson 2000; Wood et al. 2003; Fairbairn et al. 2010) and may consistently or periodically rely on other individuals to inject them. Thus, receiving injections from others can occur among IDU initiates, novices as well as long-term users. This practice has been described as "injection assistance" (Robertson et al. 2010), "assisted injection/injecting" (Wand et al. 2009; Fairbairn et al. 2010; Lloyd-Smith et al. 2010), "requiring help injecting" (Wood et al. 2003; O'Connell et al. 2005), "receiving help injecting" (Robertson et al. 2010) and "peer injecting" (Wright et al. 2007). The extent of receiving injections is not well known; however, two studies found that approximately one-quarter of IDUs reported seeking assistance with injecting (Robertson et al. 2010) or providing assistance with injections during the 6-month period prior to interview (Fairbairn et al. 2006). A third study found that 41.3% of IDUs had required help with injecting during the past 6 months (O'Connell et al. 2005). The measures used in these studies were likely to capture receiving and giving injections, as well as other kinds of injecting assistance.

Receiving help with injecting has been found to contribute to the transmission of hepatitis C virus (HCV) (Wand et al. 2009) and HIV (O'Connell et al. 2005). The practice can increase the likelihood of blood-to-blood contact not only through contaminated injecting equipment but also through physical contact during the giving and receiving of injections (Carruthers 2003). Some injectors have reported accidental "sharing" of syringes while receiving injections (Fairbairn et al. 2010), and peer injectors have been found to be significantly more likely than other IDUs to loan needles/syringes, binge inject and attend shooting galleries (Fairbairn et al. 2006), and behaviours that have been identified as factors that contribute to blood-borne viruses (Shah et al. 1996; Miller et al. 2006).

Receiving injections from other IDUs can occur in different contexts and appear to vary in terms of the social distance between the recipient and provider of injections. For example, the recipient and the peer injector may be loosely connected through injecting networks, whereby recipients of injection offer money or drugs in exchange for being injected. These providers of injections have been described as "hit doctors"[1] (Fairbairn et al. 2010) or "injection doctors" (Carlson 2000) who are sought out because they are perceived to have injecting expertise (Carlson 2000; Robertson et al. 2010). The social role of hit doctor can be embedded within drug scenes and attached to particular settings, e.g., shooting galleries (Friedman et al. 2002), and hit doctors are used extensively in some locales. For example, a respondent in Carlson's (2000) ethnographic study reported injecting between 8 and 15 people daily in exchange for cash and a place to inject. Khan et al. (2009) identified 34 urban and rural injecting locations in Sargodha, Pakistan, where two or three street injectors provided daily injections to 15–16 people. The heavy reliance on street injectors in that study was linked to wider drug market factors, e.g., high-purity heroin, drug trafficking routes, as well as individual factors, e.g., relative inexperience with injecting among the majority of the sample.

Alternatively, the recipient and provider of injections can be friends who are members of the same social network whereby the peer injector may or may not be reimbursed with cash or drugs. In other contexts, the two individuals are partners or significant others who have an intimate relationship that was established prior to injection initiation or during the injecting career. Studies have described the importance of gender and gendered dynamics that characterise initiation into IDU. For example, some research has found that females and males are likely to be injected by males at initiation (Kermode et al. 2007). Although earlier research found that women tend to be first injected by a (male) sex partner (Crofts et al. 1996; Sherman et al. 2002), the relationship between female initiates and peer injectors has been found to differ across geographic areas (Tompkins et al. 2005), with an increasing number of reports highlighting women's role in initiating other women into IDU (Doherty et al. 2000; Bryant and Treloar 2007).

Other research has focused on gender and receiving injections among IDUs with relatively long injecting histories. For example, studies have shown that females are significantly more likely than males to require help with injecting or to engage in assisted injecting (Wood et al. 2003; O'Connell et al. 2005; Wand et al. 2009; Robertson et al. 2010). These gender differences might result from unequal power relationships that can characterise the social context of injecting, venous differences between men and women (Kral et al. 1999), frequency of receiving or giving injections (Wand et al. 2009) and/or disparate knowledge of the injecting process (Treloar et al. 2003; Wood et al. 2003). Although the previous research tends to suggest that females are more likely than males to require help with injecting, findings from a social epidemiological study suggest that males and females were equally likely to *provide* injections during the 6 months prior to the interview (Fairbairn et al. 2006).

Peer Injecting and the Order of Injecting

The setting that characterises peer injecting involves a minimum of two people, and the person who injects another IDU might also self-inject in the same setting. This kind of peer injecting suggests that injecting is ordered, i.e. one injection follows and precedes another. Peer injectors who inject first can pass on blood particles to the recipient of injection who is injected second. If the peer injector injects second, the blood spill from the recipient of injection can be passed on to the peer injector. Thus, the order of injecting in these settings can further escalate the risk for transmission of blood-borne viruses. This risk is intensified when the same injecting equipment (e.g., needle, syringe, filter, cooker, water and tourniquet) is used, but can also occur through other blood-to-blood contact that occurs during injections that are given or received by another.

Research that focuses on the order of injecting suggests a complex picture whereby injecting order appears to vary over the injecting career and across injecting settings. At initiation, women IDUs have been reported of being injected by an IDU after she/he self-injects (Tompkins et al. 2005), although the same injecting order might also occur among male initiates. As IDUs progress through an injecting career, the order of injecting appears to be affected by multiple factors and can change depending on the social context as well as the

"capital" that IDUs bring to the scene (Crisp et al. 1997, 1998). In general, Crisp et al. (1997) found that the first injection was reserved for the individual who possessed or owned the needle/syringe, particularly when they also had purchased the drugs (see also Tompkins et al. 2005). In a few instances, individual factors (e.g., assertiveness, aggressiveness, knowing and sharing whether a group member was HIV antibody positive) affected injecting order even when individuals did not possess needles/syringes or purchase the drugs. The authors found that gender had no consistent effect on the order of injecting; females injected first in some settings (males being chivalrous) and second in other settings (females as subordinate). Both contexts are linked to traditional gender norms and gender role expectations. Crisp et al. (1997, 283) did not report extensively on the link between peer injecting and order of injecting but noted that that majority of the 32 respondents reported that peer injectors tended to inject first. A second qualitative study was conducted in England and focused on the experiences of 45 female IDUs in contact with drug or health services (Tompkins et al. 2005 2006). Those authors suggested that injecting order also is affected by a range of situational and contextual factors, including the severity of withdrawal, the level of intoxication of the injector, inexperience of the person being injected and the nature of social and sexual relationships among the persons present.

Aims of the Study

Peer injecting appears to be a relatively common practice at initiation and at various stages of the injecting career. When peer injectors self-inject within the same setting, the practice is likely to necessitate a particular injecting order that can escalate risk for blood-borne viruses. The purpose of this study is to explore the context of receiving injections from other IDUs at initiation and during subsequent stages of the injecting career. We also address the order of injecting as it relates to IDUs who are peer injected. We focus on the experiences of male and female IDUs in order to explore the role of gender differences and gendered dynamics as they relate to these practices.

Background

The available public health and police indicators suggest that problem heroin use and injecting began to surface in Northern Ireland during the mid-1990s to late 1990s, relatively later than other western European countries. Although data are not widely available from earlier decades, indicators suggest that individuals experiencing heroin dependence rarely came to the attention of medical professionals or treatment services during the 1970s and 1980s (Murray 1994). The large-scale presence of police and British army, frequent stops and searches and some of the most sophisticated surveillance systems in Europe would have probably uncovered a heroin market that had once existed (McElrath 2004). Problem heroin use and IDU began to surface during the mid-1990s to late 1990s, coinciding with the progress towards peace in Northern Ireland (McElrath 2004). In 2001, the number of *problem heroin users* was estimated to be 828 (95% CI: 695–1018) (McElrath 2002). Hay et al. (2006) found an estimated 1395 opiate users (including problem heroin users) in Northern Ireland during 2004, but substantially lower prevalence rates compared to England, Scotland and the south of Ireland. Pharmacy-based needle/syringe exchange schemes were introduced in Northern Ireland during 2001, and substitute prescribing (methadone and high-dose buprenorphine) became available in 2004.

The study site was the Eastern Health and Social Services Board (EHSSB) area, a geographic area that includes Belfast, the largest city in Northern Ireland. Near the time of the study, EHSSB claimed the largest estimated number of opiate users in Northern Ireland (1.68 per 1000 people aged 15–64 years) (Hay et al. 2006), as well as the largest number of individuals registered by medical professionals in the region's register of "addicts" (Department of Health, Social Services and Public Safety 2011). Qualitative research into IDU in Northern Ireland previously found that IDU respondents in this health board area had injected more frequently, were more likely to inject stimulants, had longer histories of injecting, knew substantially more IDUs with hepatitis C infection and were less likely to be engaged with treatment services compared to IDUs in other health and social service board areas (McElrath and Jordan 2005).

Method

Data presented in this article are a subset from a larger study that focuses on gender, risk environments and transitions to injecting among 54 adult men and women (Harris, forthcoming). All respondents had injected illicit drugs (namely heroin), or had smoked or sniffed heroin within 4 weeks prior to the interview. Data were collected between 2008 and 2010, primarily within the Belfast region. In this article, we focus on the subset of respondents who had received injections from another IDU ($N = 41$), either during initiation or subsequently during the injecting career.

Multiple recruitment strategies were used in an attempt to include a range of respondents with diverse drug histories and different sociodemographic backgrounds. Sample characteristics were monitored frequently and targeted sampling was introduced when particular types of respondents appeared to be under-represented. The study was advertised in hostels, three pharmacy-based needle/syringe exchange schemes and *via* professional and personal contacts. Snowballing sampling was also utilised and attracted the highest number of respondents with 15 chains established. Drug outreach workers also helped with recruitment, which resulted in the participation of five other respondents.

Data were collected through semi-structured interviews that focused on initiation into heroin use and injecting, patterns of use, transitions in and out of injecting and social contexts of use. Interviews were digitally recorded, lasted between 60 and 150 minutes and were conducted by the second author. Interviews were conducted in private settings, including university offices, drug outreach premises and in a local hostel. Considerable time was taken to establish rapport with respondents before, during and after each interview. Experiences were shared and interviewer's self-disclosure was utilised when necessary. Each participant was reimbursed £20 as an acknowledgement of their time and travel expenses to/from the interview, and the second author transcribed the interview data.

Ethical approval was obtained from four bodies: (1) Research Ethics Committee, School of Sociology, Social Policy and Social Work, Queen's University, (2) Research Governance, Queen's University, (3) the Belfast Health Trust, and (4) the Office for Research Ethics for Northern Ireland. Strict ethical protocols were followed. Respondents were provided with information about the study and time was taken to fully explain the purposes of the research. Written consent was obtained prior to the interview and assurances were provided in regard to anonymity and confidentiality.

Analysis

The analytical approach commenced with several reads of the interview transcripts, noting emerging themes and categories, and developing coding schemes. Preliminary patterns relating to peer injecting and order of injecting were analysed, followed by a system of corroboration and comparison with other cases. The thematic framework was refined by searching the interview data for variations in peer injecting experience. Segments of text were tagged and integrated under the core themes and then refined further into sub-themes, e.g., gender and gendered contexts. We explored dominant patterns, socio-environmental conditions where patterns remained as well as outliers.

Member validation was provided to respondents who were provided the opportunity to read their interview transcript and review selected analytical findings. This form of validation appeared to further enhance rapport and, in turn, helped to improve the credibility and validity of the research by ensuring that the findings presented a relevant and acceptable interpretation of the respondents' experiences (Karnieli-Miller et al. 2009).

Results

Approximately three-quarters of the sample ($N = 41$) reported receiving injections from another IDU.[2] This sub-sample included 14 females and 27 males, whose ages ranged from 20 to 54 years (mean = 33; median = 31). The average age of initiation into IDU was 20 years, with a range of 15 to 33 years. The duration of injecting spanned from 1 month to 25 years.

Initiation

The majority of male and female respondents were injected by males at initiation, and females were more likely than males to be injected by a partner (females = 50%; males = 11%). Nine male and female respondents were first injected by females, and respondents' reports suggested that female peer injectors had considerable experience with injecting and were well-connected to drug networks. Both males and females recalled their lack of injecting knowledge at initiation:

> She [partner] had called round to my house and she got me quite a wee bit of it [heroin] and she done the business. She prepared it and everything and then she injected me with it. So that was basically my first time and then she had given me the rest of it of what she had got for me but I wasn't aware of getting needles or anything and all the rest of it [other injecting equipment, the injecting process], so I didn't really know what to do with the rest of the stuff then. (Male, late 20s)

Three respondents were first injected by male or female family members whose injecting histories tended to normalise injecting for these respondents. A female recalled being injected first by her mother who reportedly tried to "help" when her daughter experienced trauma:

> Well I was 16 years of age and I got pregnant at 15 and then I lost the baby at 16 and my Mum was an addict so the best way for my Ma to try and help me was to give me an injection of heroin. (Female, mid-20s)

In contrast with previous research that highlighted the role of "dominant [male] partners" (Tompkins et al. 2005, 27) or persuasion by others to initiate IDU (Frajzyngier et al. 2007), we found little evidence of respondents being coerced or persuaded into injection, even when they had smoked heroin for lengthy periods of time. Indeed, respondents recalled how some peer injectors were reluctant to inject them (see also Rhodes et al. 2011) and several females as well as males noted how they talked to other IDUs into injecting them. Reluctance on the part of the peer injector appeared to be influenced by peers' interest in trying to protect would-be initiatives from stigmatised identities and the health risks associated with injecting. However, most male and female respondents were proactive, demonstrating agency in their quest to be injected:

> She didn't really want me to do it, but I talked her into doing it. (Male, early 40s)
>
> I eventually talked someone into it. No one wanted to do it for me [and] I didn't know how to inject myself at the time. But I eventually talked someone into doing it, who I think to this day, the person still feels guilt-ridden about it. But again it was my choice at the end of it. (Female, early 30s)

Only one respondent in this study described an initiation scenario that might be described as being influenced by coercion or persuasion from others. He recalled how he was encouraged to inject by his female partner and another male who was present at the scene:

> It [injecting] came from basically pressure from the person [partner] who I was with, they wanted me to inject and I didn't want to inject. I was quite happy to smoke it. There was three of us and she [partner] was like, "Come on and inject it" and he was like, "Yeah, come on and we'll try it." And I was like, "Nah man, I don't want to" and then the next thing was that it was there and it was happening and that's how it sort of happened. (Male, early 30s)

The majority of respondents (28 out of 41) reported injecting before the peer injector at initiation. Of the 14 females who were injected by another IDU at initiation, approximately half (8 out of 14) reported that they were injected first, that is, before the peer injector. In contrast, three-quarters of males (20 out of 27) reported being injected first during initiation. These results suggest that the relationship between the initiate and the peer injector helped shape injecting order. Specifically, female initiates tended to inject second when the peer injector was a partner, largely because of their intimate relationship with the peer injectors.

Continuation of Peer Injecting

The majority of respondents (31 out of 41) continued to be injected by another IDU as they progressed through the injecting career. In general,

however, respondents tended to vacillate between self-injecting and receiving injections from others. Although the majority of female respondents (11 out of 14) reported self-injecting within 6 months of initiation, they also received injections from other IDUs:

> You see trying to rely on other people to get the drugs as well and then relying on other people to do it? I learnt pretty quickly how to inject myself. But in saying that there, my veins now . . . I've been doing it [injecting] for about ten years now and my veins are bolluxed [damaged, ruined] now. Absolutely bolluxed. (Female, early 30s)

A number of males also continued to receive injections from another IDU; however, all but one male learned to self-inject within 6 months of initiation. Moreover, approximately one-third of males self-injected during the second injection episode, whereas only 2 of 14 females reported self-injecting during the next injecting session.

Following initiation, respondents noted that they continued to rely on males (partners, acquaintances or friends) to inject them; however, some respondents relied on or preferred female peer injectors. Respondents recalled using more than one peer injector during the same setting:

> We were all in a squat and it was just when I got out of prison. We all shot in there and we had two spoons there. I got [male friend] to do me. She [female friend] couldn't find a vein. She used to do everybody . . . and was just looking for a vein but couldn't find one. She was going mental [and] was going at it for about an hour. [Male friend eventually] found the vein. (Female, early 30s)

Similar to previous research findings, data from this study suggest that withdrawal symptoms and venous problems were the primary reasons for most subsequent peer injections. This pattern held for both male and female respondents:

> Nah, they [male friends/acquaintances] had their hit first. They always had to get their gear into them first. You had to wait. You were the second person because you didn't know how to bang up [inject]. You were standing there with your needle waiting for them to hit you up. (Male, early 30s)

I used to keep mine [drugs] in a wee tin pencil case and a couple of needles and citric and your wee things of water. I would keep it all in the thing . . . But all the time somebody would have to hit me up, 'cause I've never went myself [never self-injected]. Well I've went myself when I started you know when my veins, you could see them. But my veins only lasted about six months. That was it, they were gone. Where as well I didn't know what I was doing it, I was just sticking it everywhere so I was. Didn't know where I was going and once I actually put it in here [points to arm]. Then after that I started getting afraid to hit up, so then I was asking other people to do it for me and it was flipping going in my wrists, everywhere. I've still got the scars [shows scars on wrists and arms]. (Female, late 30s)

Although most respondents reported being careful about their choice of peer injector, respondents who were experiencing withdrawal or in the company of less experienced peer injectors often were less selective. In some instances, claims about cautiousness were not substantiated by partners who were present during some interviews:

R1: I'm very meticulous about the people who inject me. I wouldn't just let anybody do it. (Male, early 30s)

R2: Well that's not really true. If you were sick it would be whoever. (Female partner, early 30s)

R1: No, if I was sick I would go to a certain person who I know would do it for me.

R2: That would be for the last ten years because you haven't been able to inject yourself. [He's] always had to buy two bags.

R1: One for them [the peer injector] and one for me . . . I would get the stuff [heroin] and I would make a phone call to the two or three people who I knew, that I could trust and go to them. One of them was like a heroin addict then, so the chances of him saying no to you were slim to none. So I had three trusted people who I know I could phone and at least one of them would definitely say, "Yes, come on round." . . My veins are in good condition because other people do it for me. They take

more care, whereas if you're doing it yourself you could hurt yourself more.

The data show that injecting order fluctuated among males and females during subsequent peer injections. That is, when asked about injecting order during subsequent peer injections, most respondents (21 out of 31) reported that they "sometimes" were the first to be injected during these episodes. Injecting order was influenced by multiple micro- and macrolevel factors, including the availability of heroin:

They [male friends/acquaintances] just wanted the hit first. I mean in [place in NI], there would maybe be times [. . .] when you would have to wait three days [for heroin]. Four days for some of it, you know? Even waiting longer than that and when you're waiting that length of time, whenever you do get some, you don't want to be bothered doing somebody else you know? You want to do your own first. (Male, mid-40s)

Both male and female respondents demonstrated some degree of power and control over the injecting order. Their degree of influence depended on their relationship with other IDUs in the setting, as well as which party bought or owned the drugs. These factors often took precedent over an injector's withdrawal symptoms:

He [partner] just couldn't wait [withdrawal] and I'm going like, "Now hold on a second, I don't want to bring this to account, but I bought it. It's my money and I want to hit up first before you get so out of it and you miss." And I said "No, if I buy it then I get to hit up first," and I always did buy it. (Female, late 30s)

Females who were injected by partners recalled "going second," because partners were experiencing withdrawal symptoms. A few female respondents questioned male partners' justifications for insisting on injecting first:

I: So it was really to stop him from withdrawal?

R: Yeah, something to stop him shaking so that he would be steady with me. That's what he said and I could sort of understand, and it was true some of the time, but it wasn't true all of the time. He just couldn't wait. (Female, late 30s)

The majority of females and about half the males reported paying an IDU to inject them, and payment was nearly always made with drugs as opposed to cash. Males were more likely than females to report *never* having to provide cash or drugs in exchange for being injected. A female respondent who reported always being injected by other IDUs described an exchange:

> You would have had to give them a bit in the needle, yeah. They would have been like, "What are you going to give me out of it?" And I would have just put a bit of powder out and went, "Right, there. And that's all I've got." But money? No. (Female, early 30s)

At times, however, peer injectors had considerable access to drugs and did not expect compensation for peer injecting. This pattern was observed primarily among same-sex friendships:

> I: Did you have to give anything to the person injecting you?
> R: Aye, like sort them out. Yeah, I would have had to give them about half a bag [of heroin], depending on who it was. Just say they had their own [heroin] . . . Just say I used to go round to my mate [female friend] but she sold it as well so she didn't mind, know what I mean? I would usually have given [female friend] a pipe or whatever, but she didn't care about a hit cause she had her own [heroin]. Or else I would have put a bit of crack into her thing, and then she would have a snowball, you know mixing it? And we would have done it that way.
> I: So it just depended on who you were with?
> R: Yeah.

Although payment for being injected by an IDU was the norm in this sample, a few respondents reported that they never or rarely paid for this service with either drugs or money. A female reported that nearly all her injections were provided by other IDUs, and that her peer injectors were always male who rarely asked for compensation. She described her relationships with the peer injectors:

> The first time it was my ex-partner. Second time it was my present boyfriend, and the other two times it was men that I'd known for years but they had already come on to me anyway. I knew that they wanted to be lovers with me on previous occasions but it never happened but they did end up injecting me. (Female, late 30s)

She continued by describing the negotiation over clean needles/syringes during her quest to be injected by a male IDU. In the excerpt below, she demonstrates control over the exchange with the male peer injector:

> Like if they said to me, "Give us that needle after you," and I says, "Nah, this is a clean needle. You have hepatitis and I haven't. I'll only give you a run [bit of heroin]." Or, "I'll give you £20 or I'll give you a bag." [They'd say] "Right, well then go on and give me a bag if you won't give me a needle." I could have four or five needles but I wasn't going to be telling them that.

Some respondents recalled the difficulties with coordination and dexterity among peer injectors who self-injected first, and then began to experience the effects of heroin before they injected the respondent. In these scenarios, peer injectors sometimes made several attempts to inject the other person, missing veins during the attempts. A female reported that male IDUs always injected before her, "They had to have it. They needed it." The interviewer asked whether the male peer injectors ever missed a vein, while attempting to inject her:

> Oh god yeah. You could even see somebody standing and they'd be gouching [nodding off as a result of heroin use; intoxication]. Their eyes would be closed and then somebody would come over and take over and even [my partner] at times, he'd be standing and you'd think his legs were going to buckle underneath him. And then there'd be arguments around hep C, and me going, "Make sure you use separate equipment." And him saying, "But I didn't use that spoon." And I'm going, "Well, that's the only spoon that shape 'cause I stole it out of [restaurant] and you've just used it and you're using it with me again." (Female, late 30s)

Previous research has also highlighted "gouching" among peer injectors who attempt to administer injections to women (Tompkins et al. 2005). In this study, this experience intensified risk scenarios, particularly when respondents used more than one peer injector:

I: Would the person that was injecting have gone first?

R: Aye, and I hated it because they were always like, "Eeow," gouching and they sticking the needle everywhere in my arm and I'm sitting going, "Fuck sake, I'm busting for a hit." And I had to say to them, "Would you open your eyes fuck's sake?" They were just like really gouching out and I couldn't do it [inject] myself, so it was so frustrating, so it was.

I: Did that vary in terms of who you were with? Like if you were with [female friend] would she have done you first?

R: Aye, most of the time she would have done me first because she would have went [injected] into her groin . . . But she would usually been always really gouched out on gear [heroin]. I was never really one for gouching. I was always up, if you know what I mean. I think that was because of the crack. I never ever felt gouched out, you know? (Female, late 20s)

Discussion

The findings highlight the layers of risk associated with the peer injecting environment. These layers of risk begin during initiation into IDU when respondents were administered an injection by an IDU who also self-injected. Although the majority of respondents reported that they injected first at initiation, 13 other respondents recalled injecting second, which likely entails greater exposure to blood from the peer injector. Peer injecting commenced because male and female initiates lacked knowledge about the injecting process. Although the majority of respondents learned to self-inject within 6 months of initiating IDU, a few individuals never felt confident with injecting, preferring other IDUs to provide injections for them. For other respondents, peer injecting did not necessarily continue immediately after initiation; rather, it re-surfaced when respondents developed venous problems or experienced withdrawal symptoms that prevented self-injection.

Additional layers of risk were introduced because recipients of injecting utilised several different peer injectors over the injecting career; similar to the various levels of skill among professional phlebotomists, some peer injectors were perceived as better than others. A few respondents recalled being exposed to more than one peer injector in the same injecting setting. In these contexts, peer injectors' incapability to administer injections appeared to be affected by the pharmaceutical effects of heroin. Respondents spoke of peer injectors' several attempts to administer injections. The physical scarring left by some attempts was likely preceded by the presence of blood at the injecting sites. These findings suggest that although peer injectors can introduce risk to injecting settings, they also can be disproportionately exposed to it. Risk environments were also created by peer injectors who experienced withdrawal symptoms prior to injecting, and insisted on self-injecting prior to peer injecting. Observing a peer injector undergo "dope sickness" created anxiety for respondents who wished to inject first due to their own withdrawal effects or concerns over safety.

Gender and Peer Injecting

We found similarities as well as gender differences at initiation. Most males and females actively sought out IDUs to first inject them, despite the initial reluctance of other IDUs. Additionally, most males and females were most likely to be peer injected by a male IDU; however, roughly half of all females were first injected by a male partner, whereas only three males (approximately 10% of male respondents) were injected by a female partner. Injecting order tended to favour male respondents; however, heterosexual partners who were peer injectors tended to inject first regardless of whether the recipient was male or female. The relatively small number of study participants prevented us from further investigating this pattern among male/female dyads.

Both male and female recipients of injection were affected by the well-being of the peer injector and considered whether peer injectors experiencing withdrawal were more capable than peer injectors who were intoxicated. Additionally, men and women recalled the difficulties associated with frequent attempts to locate peer injectors, and relied on more than one IDU to inject them. However, females were more likely than males to provide drugs in exchange for being peer injected, particularly as they progressed through the injecting career. Although some scholars might view this finding as evidence of a gendered power imbalance, we view it as an example of female injectors' attempt to assert control over their injecting episodes. We suggest that these exchanges tended to influence women's place in the injecting order. Compensating the peer injector meant that women could better justify their choice to inject first, thus diminishing some risk associated with the injecting environment.

Bryant et al. (2010, 185) found that a number of female IDUs in their study could not be described as "passive participants," in relation to their drug lifestyle roles. Rather, the authors noted that several females in partnerships with male IDUs were integrated with IDU networks, and solely or jointly involved in drug purchase and preparation for injection. A few females in this study behaved passively or assumed stereotypical gender roles, e.g., expecting to inject second, preferring a male peer injector. However, our findings are more consistent with those of Bryant et al. (2010). As discussed above, several other females proactively asserted themselves with regards to the informal rules around injecting order. Additionally, many females voiced knowledge about some safer injecting practices and this knowledge was considered as they negotiated with peer injectors. Most males and females in this study continued to or subsequently relied on peer injectors not because they lacked knowledge about injecting but because they developed venous problems, and women tended to experience venous problems more quickly than men.

The findings from this study add further weight to the assumption that injecting risk is influenced greatly by social networks and the social context in which it occurs. Harm reduction and prevention efforts that target the behaviours of individual IDUs are unlikely to be effective because they often ignore the role of structural factors and social network influences that contribute to individual behaviours (Neaigus et al. 1994; Rhodes 2002). Reducing risk around peer injecting requires peer interventions that can be integrated with trusted street outreach workers.

Notes

1. According to Fairbairn et al. (2010), "hit doctors" were initially described in the literature by Murphy and Waldorf (1991) in their study of San Francisco shooting galleries.
2. The remainder had either always self-injected or had never transitioned from smoking heroin to injecting.

References

Bryant, J., L. Brener, P. Hull, and C. Treloar. 2010. "Needle Sharing in Regular Sexual Relationships: An Examination Of Serodiscordance, Drug Using Practices, and the Gendered Character of Injecting." *Drug and Alcohol Dependence* 107: 182–187.

Bryant, J. and C. Treloar. 2007. "The Gendered Context of Initiation to Injecting Drug Use: Evidence for Women as Active Initiates." *Drug and Alcohol Review* 26: 287–293.

Carlson, R. 2000. "Shooting Galleries, Dope Houses, and Injection Doctors: Examining the Social Ecology of HIV Risk Behaviors among Drug Injectors in Dayton, Ohio." *Human Organization* 59: 325–333.

Carruthers, S. J. 2003. "The Ins and Outs of Injecting in Western Australia." *Journal of Substance Use* 8: 11–18.

Chitwood, D. D., J. Sanchez, M. Comerford, J. B. Page, D. C. McBride, and K. R. Kitner. 2000. "First Injection and Current Risk Factors for HIV among New and Long-Term Injection Drug Users." *AIDS Care* 12: 313–320.

Crisp, B. R., J. G. Barber, and R. Gilbertson. 1997. "The Etiquette of Needle Sharing." *Contemporary Drug Problems* 24: 273–291.

———. 1998. "The Relative Importance of Factors Which Influence Order of Injecting with a Shared Needle and Syringe." *AIDS Care* 10: 713–721.

Crofts, N., R. Louie, D. Rosenthal, and D. Jolley. 1996. "The First Hit: Circumstances Surrounding Initiation into Injecting." *Addiction* 91: 1187–1196.

De, P., J. Cox, J. Boivin, R. W. Platt, and A. M. Jolly. 2007. "The Importance of Social Networks in Their Association to Drug Equipment Sharing among Injection Drug Users: A Review." *Addiction* 102: 1730–1739.

Department of Health, Social Services and Public Safety. 2011. *Statistics from the Northern Ireland Drug Addicts Index, 2010*. Belfast: Author.

Doherty, M. C., R. S. Garfein, E. Monterroso, C. Latkin, and D. Vlahov. 2000. "Gender Differences in the Initiation of Injection Drug Use among Young Adults." *Journal of Urban Health* 77: 296–414.

Fairbairn, N., W. Small, N. Van Borek, E. Wood, and T. Kerr. 2010. "Social Structural Factors That Shape Assisted Injecting Practices among Injection Drug Users in Vancouver, Canada: A Qualitative Study." *Harm Reduction Journal* 7: 20.

Fairbairn, N., E. Wood, W. Small, J. Stolz, K. Li, T. Kerr. 2006. "Risk Profile of Individuals Who Provide Assistance with Illicit Drug Injections." *Drug and Alcohol Dependence* 82: 41–46.

Frajzyngier, V., A. Neaigus, V. A. Gyarmathy, M. Miller, and S. R. Friedman. 2007. "Gender Differences in Injection Behaviours at the First Injection Episode." *Drug and Alcohol Dependence* 89: 145–152.

Friedman, S. R., S. Y. Kang, S. Deren, R. Robles, H. M. Colón, J. Andia, D. Oliver-Velez, and A. Finlinson. 2002. "Drug-Scene Roles and HIV Risk among Puerto Rican Injection Drug Users in East Harlem, New York and Bayamón, Puerto Rico." *Journal of Psychoactive Drugs* 34: 363–369.

Grund, J. P., C. D. Kaplan, N. F. Adriaans, and P. Blanken. 1991. "Drug Sharing and HIV Transmission Risks: The Practice of Frontloading in the Dutch Injecting Drug User Population." *Journal of Psychoactive Drugs* 23: 1–10.

Hagan, H., H. Theide, N. S. Weiss, N. S. G. Hopkins, J. S. Duchin, and E. R. Alexander. 2001. "Sharing of Drug Preparation Equipment as a Risk Factor for Hepatitis C." *American Journal of Public Health* 91: 42–46.

Harocopos, A., L. A. Goldsamt, P. Kobrak, J. J. Jost, and M. C. Clatts. 2009. "New Injectors and the Social Context of Injection Initiation." *International Journal of Drug Policy* 20: 317–323.

Harris, J. (Forthcoming). *Initiations and Transitions into Injecting Drug Use: The Social and Gendered Context of Risk*. Ph.D. thesis. Belfast: Queen's University.

Hay, G., K. Higgins, M. Gannon, and C. Carroll. 2006. *Estimating the Prevalence of Problem Opiate and Problem Cocaine Use in Northern Ireland*. Glasgow: Centre for Drug Misuse Research, University of Glasgow.

Jose, B., S. R. Friedman, A. Neaigus, R. Curtis, J. P. Grund, M. F. Goldstein, T. P. Ward, and D. C. Des Jarlais. 1993. "Syringe-Mediated Drug-Sharing (Backloading): A New Risk Factor for HIV among Injecting Drug Users." *AIDS* 7: 1653–1660.

Kamieli-Miller, O., R. Strier, and L. Pessach. 2009. "Power Relations in Qualitative Research." *Qualitative Health Research* 19: 279–289.

Kermode, M., V. Longleng, B. C. Singh, J. Hocking, B. Langkham, and N. Crofts. 2007. "My First Time: Initiation into Injecting Drug Use in Manipur and Nagaland, Northeast India." *Harm Reduction Journal* 4: 19.

Khan, A. A., A. B. Awan, S. U. Qureshi, A. Razaque, and S. T. Zafar. 2009. "Large Sharing Networks and Unusual Injection Practices Explain the Rapid Rise in HIV among IDUs in Sargodha, Pakistan." *Harm Reduction Journal* 6: 13.

Kral, A. H., R. N. Bluthenthal, E. A. Erringer, J. Lorvick, and B. R. Edlin. 1999. "Risk Factors among IDUs Who Give Injections to or Receive Injections from Other Drug Users." *Addiction* 94: 675–683.

Lloyd-Smith, E., B. S. Rachlis, D. Tobin, D. Stone, K. Li, W. Small, E. Wood, and T. Kerr. 2010. "Assisted Injection in Outdoor Venues: An Observational Study of Risks and Implications for Service Delivery and Harm Reduction Programming." *Harm Reduction Journal* 7: 6.

McElrath, K. 2002. *Prevalence of Problem Heroin Use in Northern Ireland*. Belfast: Department of Health, Social Services and Public Safety.

McElrath, K. 2004. "Drug Use and Drug Markets in the Context of Political Conflict: The Case of Northern Ireland." *Addiction Research and Theory* 12: 577–590.

McElrath, K. 2006. "Booting and Flushing: Needle Rituals and Risk for Bloodborne Viruses." *Journal of Substance Use* 11: 177–189.

McElrath, K. and M. Jordan, M. 2005. *Drug Use and Risk Behaviours among Injecting Drug Users.* Belfast: Department of Health, Social Services and Public Safety.

Miller, C. L., T. Kerr, J. C. Frankish, P. M. Spittal, K. Li, M. T. Schechter, and E. Wood. 2006. "Binge Drug Use Independently Predicts HIV Seroconversion among Injection Drug Users: Implications for Public Health Strategies." *Substance Use and Misuse* 41: 199–210.

Murphy, S. and D. Waldorf. 1991. "Kickin' Down to the Street Doc: Shooting Galleries in the San Francisco Bay Area." *Contemporary Drug Problems* 18: 9–29.

Murray, M. 1994. "Use of Illegal Drugs in Northern Ireland." In *Heroin Addiction and Drug Policy: The British System,* edited by J. Strang and M. Gossop, 134–147. Oxford: Oxford University Press.

Neaigus, A., S. R. Friedman, R. Curtis, D. C. Des Jarlais, R. T. Furst, B. Jose, B. Stepherson, M. Sufian, T. Ward, and J. W. Wright. 1994. "The Relevance of Drug Injectors' Social and Risk Networks for Understanding and Preventing HIV Infection." *Social Science and Medicine* 38: 67–78.

O'Connell, J. M., T. Kerr, K. Li, M. W. Tyndall, R. S. Hogg, J. S. Montaner, and E. Wood. 2005. "Requiring Help Injecting Independently Predicts HIV Infection among Injection Drug Users." *Journal of Acquired Immune Deficiency Syndromes* 40: 83–88.

Paintsil, E., H. He, C. Peters, B. D. Lindenbach, and R. Heimer. 2010. "Survival of Hepatitis C Virus in Syringes: Implication for Transmission among Injection Drug Users." *Journal of Infectious Diseases* 202: 984–990.

Pates, R. M., A. J. McBride, N. Ball, and K. Arnold. 2001. "Towards an Holistic Understanding of Injecting Drug Use: An Overview of Needle Fixation." *Addiction Research and Theory* 9: 3–17.

Rhodes, T. 2002. "The 'Risk Environment': A Framework for Understanding and Reducing Drug Related Harm." *International Journal of Drug Policy* 13: 85–94.

Rhodes, T., S. Bivol, O. Scutelniciuc, N. Hunt, S. Bernays, and J. Busza. 2011. "Narrating the Social Relations of Initiating Injecting Drug Use: Transitions in Self and Society." *International Journal of Drug Policy* 22: 445–454.

Robertson, A. M., A. Y. Vera, M. Gallardo, R. A. Pollini, T. L. Patterson, P. Case, L. Nguyen, and S. A. Strathdee. 2010. "Correlates of Seeking Injection Assistance among Injection Drug Users in Tijuana, Mexico." *American Journal of Addiction* 19: 357–363.

Sánchez, J., D. D. Chitwood, and D. J. Koo. 2006. "Risk Factors Associated with the Transition from Heroin Sniffing to Heroin Injection: A Street Addict Role Perspective." *Journal of Urban Health* 83: 896–910.

Shah, S. M., P. Shapshak, J. E. Rivers, R. V. Stewart, N. L. Weatherby, K. Q. Xin, J. B. Page, D. D. Chitwood, D. C. Mash, D. Vlahov, and C. B. McCoy. 1996. "Detection of HIV-1 DNA in Needle/Syringes, Paraphernalia, and Washes from Shooting Galleries in Miami: A Preliminary Laboratory Report." *Journal of Acquired Immune Deficiency Syndromes and Human Retrovirology* 11: 301–306.

Sherman, S. G., L. Smith, G. Laney, and S. A. Strathdee. 2002. "Social Influences on the Transition to Injection Drug Use Among Young Heroin Sniffers: A Qualitative Analysis." *International Journal of Drug Policy* 13: 113–120.

Stark, K., R. Müller, U. Bienzle, and I. Guggenmoos-Holzmann. 1996. "Frontloading: A Risk Factor for HIV and Hepatitis C Virus Infection among Injecting Drug Users in Berlin." *AIDS* 10: 311–317.

Tompkins, C., L. Sheard, N. Wright, N. Howes, and L. Jones. 2005. *Women and the Peer Injecting of Illicit Drugs: A Focus On the Implications for Practice.* Leeds/Mansfield: Leeds North East Primary Care Trust and Nottingham County Drug and Alcohol Action Team.

Tompkins, C. N. E., L. Sheard, N. M. J. Wright, N. Howes, and L. Jones. 2006. "Exchange, Deceit and Harm: The Consequences for Women of Receiving Injections from Other Drug Users." *Drugs: Education, Prevention and Policy* 13: 281–297.

Treloar, C., J. Abelson, J. Crawford, S. Kippax, J. Howard, I. van Beek, J. Copeland, and A. M. Weatherall. 2003. *Risk For Hepatitis C: Transition and Initiation to Injecting Drug Use Among Youth in a Range of Injecting Drug User Networks.* Sydney: National Centre in HIV Social Research, University of New South Wales.

Wand, H., D. Spiegelman, M. Law, M. Jalaludin, J. Kaldor, and L. Maher. 2009. "Estimating Population Attributable Risk for Hepatitis C Seroconversion in Injecting Drug Users in Australia: Implications for Prevention Policy and Planning." *Addiction* 104: 2049–2056.

Wood, E., P. Spittal, T. Kerr, and W. Small. 2003. "Requiring Help Injecting as a Risk Factor for HIV Infection in the Vancouver Epidemic: Implications for HIV Prevention." *Canadian Journal of Public Health* 94: 355–359.

Wright, N. M. J., C. N. E. Tompkins, and L. Sheard. 2007. "Is Peer Injecting a Form of Intimate Partner Abuse? A Qualitative Study of the Experiences of Women Drug Users." *Health and Social Care in the Community* 15: 417–425.

For Discussion

1. If peers are important for injecting other individuals, how can peers be used to distribute information on reducing harm associated with injecting?

2. Other kinds of illicit drugs (e.g., marijuana, cocaine) are also used in group settings or dyads. These settings can also be characterized by a particular order of who uses first. What do these kinds of social contexts tell us about power distribution in groups that collectively use illicit drugs? Additionally, what kinds of power shape decisions about "who uses first"?

VIII

Drug Markets

In October 2013, Ross Ulbricht was indicted in the United States for drug trafficking and for conspiracy to commit murder. He was the alleged owner and operator of Silk Road, believed to be one of the most profitable online markets for the sale and purchase of psychoactive substances until it was shut down by United States federal agents following a sting operation. The sophistication of Silk Road's operations differed greatly from online "pharmacies." The former was part of the Deep Web, or the hidden Internet comprised of several websites that cannot be located via Google or other search engines (Barratt 2013). Silk Road facilitated the purchase and sale of thousands of illegal psychoactive substances over a span of a few years. It required the use of specialized software (Tor) and a uniform currency known as Bitcoins, which buyers purchased and were then used in drug transactions. The encrypted nature of the software and the currency made it very difficult for buyers and sellers to be identified and tracked during or after drug transactions because of the difficulties linking transactions to specific Internet protocol addresses (Barratt, Lenton, and Allen 2012). Several different psychoactive substances were sold regularly on Silk Road, including cannabis/marijuana, heroin, cocaine, and some prescription drugs (Christin 2013). The price of drugs was reportedly lower on Silk Road compared to traditional drug markets. Researcher Monica Barratt (Australia) noted, for example, that MDMA advertised by a Silk Road seller in the Netherlands was about one-fifth the price of MDMA sold via street-level drug markets in Australia. Individuals who purchased drugs on Silk Road were said to be motivated by the anonymous nature of the site, the higher purity of the drugs, and concerns about their personal safety when negotiating transactions in traditional street-based drug markets (Barratt 2013; Van Hout and Bingham 2013).

In an eight-month period during 2011–2012, a computer guru at Carnegie-Mellon University concluded that Silk Road sellers collectively earned about $1.2 million per month—sales that generated an estimated $92,000 in commission fees for the site's operators. Although 43.83 percent of Silk Road sellers were allegedly based in the United States (and a reported 10.15 percent in the United Kingdom), the site helped to facilitate thousands of international drug transactions.

Silk Road was one of several online venues where illegal drugs are bought and sold to an international market. Although federal agents in the United States shut down Silk Road and seized some of the profits via the Bitcoin currency, similar online drug markets are believed to continue doing business on the Deep Web. Moreover, online chat about the launch of Silk Road 2 commenced within a month after Ulbricht's arrest.

Several other suppliers of psychoactive drugs operate through traditional Internet websites and can be located via common search engines. Some of these sites advertise as pharmacies and sell prescription drugs, but without the comprehensive practices that regulate traditional pharmacies. Other sites sell non-prescription psychoactive drugs that are portrayed as legal substances. These substances have been referred to as "legal highs," "research chemicals," or more recently, "novel psychoactive substances." Products are often sold in pre-sealed packages that feature "hippy style," "new age," or other symbols. Many packages are labeled with nomenclature that reminds consumers of illegal street drugs or their effects, for example, "Snow Blow," "White Ice Resin," and "X Pillz." Consumers purchase products which are then delivered to private residences or other venues. Many individuals perceive the products to be safe, or safer than drugs that are available through traditional drug markets. Online buyers sometimes perceive that their identities are shielded, which protects them from the potential stigma associated with street suppliers. The common feature of online drug markets is that they are not regulated; thus, the contents of products are unknown. Second, consumers have no recourse when products do not produce the desired effects. Moreover, the products cannot generally be traced to distributors; online drug markets might have a registered domain in one country but distribute the drugs from another.

Although online drug markets appear to have flourished in recent years, some if not most consumers avoid them entirely, preferring to source drugs through traditional means. Other than markets found on the hidden web, online purchases can be linked directly to bank accounts or credit cards and a number of individuals fear that their identities will be compromised. Other concerns are that products will not arrive, will be confiscated, or that buyers' identities will become known when the products are delivered. Moreover, online markets cannot provide an *immediate* supply of drugs; hence, they are limited in their ability to respond to spontaneous interest in consuming drugs.

This introduction to Part VIII commenced with a discussion of drug transactions that occur online because we want readers to consider "drug markets" more broadly. In other words, images about drug markets are sometimes restricted to drug suppliers whose work takes place in "open air drug markets," usually in urban settings. Clearly, open air drug markets operate in hundreds of locations in various countries, and the violence and other social problems that are associated with these markets have been widely documented in the United States. We know that interventions that involve police *and* local communities have shown promising results in terms of reducing crime associated with open air drug markets—much more so than interventions led by police alone (Kennedy and Wong 2012). However, open air drug markets are visible—to residents, police, media, and to researchers, and it is this visibility that shapes our images about drug markets. Sellers who operate within open air drug markets are commonly referred to as "retailers," "lower level dealers," or "street level dealers" (Desroches 2007, 828), and hold positions or roles that are relatively low on the hierarchal distribution chain. Considerably less is known about the roles held by individuals who are involved in distributing drugs at higher levels. In a review of studies from various countries, Desroches (2007) concluded that individuals involved in higher level positions perform different kinds of roles, including smuggling, distributing via wholesale, manufacturing, and growing psychoactive substances. They tend to operate informally in small groups, pursue entrepreneurial objectives, and prefer to avoid violence (Desroches 2007).

Importantly, many people who use drugs rarely have direct contact with street dealers. Instead, they rely on friends or acquaintances to access drugs for them. Although they might provide cash for drugs, it is others who engage in the risk of arrest through negotiating access to supplies, and transporting drugs from one place to another. Friends and acquaintances who provide this service are not generally viewed as "real" dealers by the users who rely on them.

The links between drug markets, drug takers, and law enforcement are complex and change regularly. For example, drug markets are influenced by changes in users' preferences for particular drugs, and users' preferences are affected by market-level factors, for example, major fluctuations in the price and purity of drugs. Supply-side interventions (e.g., control of precursors used to manufacture some drugs; large-scale drug seizures) can impact on markets and, in turn, can affect users. In this section, we include three readings that highlight different aspects of drug markets.

References

Barratt, M. J. 2013. "The Road Less Travelled. Silk Road: Drug Dealing Evolved." *Whack* 30: 16–19.

Barratt, M. J., S. Lenton, and M. Allen. 2013. "Hidden Content Regulation, Public Drug Websites and the Growth in Hidden Internet Services." *Drugs: Education, Prevention and Policy* 20: 231–237.

Christin, N. 2013. *Traveling the Silk Road: A Measurement Analysis of a Large Anonymous Online Marketplace.* Paper presented at the International World Wide Web Conference, May 13–17. Rio de Janeiro.

Desroches, F. 2007. "Research on Upper Level Drug Trafficking: A Review." *Journal of Drug Issues* 37: 827–844.

Kennedy, D. M. and S.-L. Wong. 2012. *The High Point Drug Market Intervention Strategy*, updated version. Washington, DC: U.S. Department of Justice, Office of Community-Oriented Policing Services.

Van Hout, M. C. and T. Bingham. 2013. "'Surfing the Silk Road': A Study of Users' Experiences." *International Journal of Drug Policy*, early access http://dx.doi.org/10.1016/j.drugpo.2013.08.011.

20

From "Social Supply" to "Real Dealing"

Drift, Friendship, and Trust in Drug-Dealing Careers

MATTHEW TAYLOR AND GARY R. POTTER

Media-perpetuated myths about "evil drug pushers" have long been dispelled. Still, some people who use drugs view "dealers" very differently from friends who supply drugs. The authors of this article—Matthew Taylor and Gary R. Potter—discuss a drug market that is loosely structured where transactions rarely involve violence. They focus on the ways in which dealers "drift" between social supply of drugs to "real" dealing.

Introduction

There is a persistent popular image of drug dealers as evil criminals peddling in and preying on the misery of addiction in the pursuit of profit (Coomber 2006, 2010). Such individuals—whether operating as low-level drug pushers or high-level "Mr. Bigs"—are seen, in this popular view, to operate in drug markets structured along an organized-crime version of the pyramid model of commodity markets (see, for example, Potter 2010, 35–40) "controlled by heinous, evil individuals or groups that rule with a rod of iron" in which "[v]iolence, mistrust and fear are seen as [the] primary characteristics" (Coomber 2010, 10).

Academic studies are, however, increasingly challenging this perception. Although it is said that there is a shortage of empirical research into drug distribution (Pearson 2007), there is an increasingly large number of studies on drug markets, with one review focusing (only) on upper level trafficking citing nearly 300 studies (Dorn, Levi, and King 2005). The problem is that there is great variation in drug markets. As Bean (2008) points out, drug trafficking involves "large-scale operations, which can and often do cross national boundaries, as well as the small-scale syndicates which distribute drugs at a local level" (140). Potter (2009) makes the point that "[d]rug trafficking occurs globally, but markets are ultimately local" (51), going on to argue that drug distribution at the lower level of the market varies by drug type, by "socio-geographical location of the market" and by "attitudes toward the drug, or sociocultural aspects of the market" (68). The popular idea of "homogenisation of the drug dealer and the drug market is neither accurate nor helpful" (Coomber 2010, 10).

This article looks at drug distribution at the lower end of the market. It reports on a group of dealers operating in the small, predominantly middle-class city of "Rivertown," England. It focuses on

Reprinted from Matthew Taylor and Gary R. Potter, 2013, "From 'Social Supply' to 'Real Dealing': Drift, Friendship, and Trust in Drug-Dealing Careers," in *Journal of Drug Issues* 43 (October): 392–406, first published on February 8, 2013. Reprinted by permission of SAGE Publications via Copyright Clearance Center.

those involved in the retail (and some wholesale) supply of cannabis, MDMA, cocaine, ketamine, and other synthetic drugs. We hope to offer a detailed understanding of the drug dealers operating within this sociocultural scene, with particular focus on the structure and mechanics of the drug market and the motivation, initiation, career progression, and supplier-customer relationships of those who operate within it.

We reveal a group of drug dealers who do not fit the stereotypical image of violent, dishonest members of organized-crime outfits, rather a market populated by individuals who "drifted" into dealing (Murphy, Waldorf, and Reinarman 1990) from a friendship-based "social supply" market for whom friendship and trust remain key to relationships with suppliers and customers. Our suppliers have thousands or even tens of thousands of pounds in weekly turnover, undoubtedly making the participants "real" dealers (cf. Parker 2000). However, the market still retains closer resemblance to the markets of "social supply" (discussed below) than the violent underworld of drug-trafficking-as-organized-crime portrayed by some literature (Bean 2008; Brownstein 1996) and by the media. This may be because the dealers depicted here started out as social suppliers, drifting into real dealing as opportunities presented themselves, but maintaining many of the characteristics—and customers—from their previous roles.

Retail-Level Drug Distribution and "Social Supply"

A good starting point for understanding drug markets is the recognition that the distribution of drugs largely follows the same economic principles as the sale of any other product (Bean 2008; Brownstein 1996; Pearson and Hobbs 2001; Potter 2009). Therefore, as with other commodity markets, we can recognize "layers" or vertical stratification within drug markets. Pearson and Hobbs (2001), for example, divide domestic (UK) drug markets into four such layers (although recognizing that such a model is an oversimplification of what is often a very complicated reality): *importation* (assuming production takes place overseas; see Potter 2010), *wholesale* distribution, the *middle market*, and *retail*-level dealing.

Drug markets can and do vary widely in characteristics. Each market has its own "cultural norms, roles, behaviours and economic aspects," and market types vary depending on a number of variables (Ritter 2005, 6), including drug(s) sold, market level, market type (e.g., "open" or "closed"; Home Office 1998; Hough and Natarajan 2000), location and method of transaction (e.g., private house, public space, delivery, or collection; Curtis and Wendel 2000), the socio-economic background of those who sell (and those who buy) the drugs (Bean 2008; Coomber and Turnbull 2007), and the cultural context of the market and the drug-using scene it supplies (Potter 2009). The result is horizontal stratification, meaning any one drug may be distributed through multiple market "types" even at the same market level (Adler 1993; Coomber and Turnbull 2007).

Although the literature recognizes a degree of hierarchy within the structure of drug markets, recent research argues that hierarchical or central *control* is rarely present in the UK context, with markets usually "highly competitive" rather than monopolized (Coomber 2006, 125). Even in the United States, where the monopolization of retail markets has been observed, it remains generally uncommon and small scale (Reuter 2000). Pearson and Hobbs (2001) offer a similar picture, dismissing the theory of top-down control, instead suggesting that most dealers are independent traders with no fixed obligations to buy exclusively from any one supplier. Reuter (2000) states that rather than being fixed to one supplier as is often assumed, dealers may aim to maximize supply options to militate against risks of disruption to supply. In terms of organization, although most studies do not rule out the possibility of there being some highly organized markets, *disorganization* is the common feature (Adler 1993; Coomber 2006; Dorn, Karim, and South 1992; Pearson 2007; Pearson and Hobbs 2001).

Much recent research has focused specifically on the lower levels of drug markets, suggesting that the retail end of the market is a lot more complicated than Pearson and Hobbs' (2001) model may suggest. In particular, much has been made of the concept of "social supply" of drugs and how much end-use or retail-level distribution (at least for "soft" drugs) may take a form that is very different from traditional views of drug markets, conducted by people who are *not* best understood as being drug dealers.

Social supply blurs the distinction between end users and retail dealers, a level of distribution that is seen as below that of retail dealing (Pearson 2007) while remaining above the level of the end consumer (Potter 2009). There is no single accepted definition of social supply, with academics offering a number of (at times contrasting) classification criteria, although the term is mainly used to describe the "non-commercial" supply of soft drugs between "friends" (Potter 2009). It has been suggested that social supply acts as a buffer that protects buyers from the "real" market of drug supply (Parker 2000). UK and European research shows that cannabis users generally obtain their supply through social networks rather than from "established drugs markets," illustrating the importance and scale of social supply within that market (Coomber and Turnbull 2007, 828; see also Duffy, Schafer, Coomber, O'Connell, and Turnbull 2008; Parker 2000; Stevenson 2008; Werse 2008).

Social supply at the bottom end of the drug market is inextricably linked to friendship, with transactions often seen as an "act of friendship and trust" (Parker 2000, 28). Small drug transactions and gifting or sharing drugs within certain groups can be recognized as a cultural norm and part of friendship building: It can, for example, be likened to the social bonds that are built as a result of cigarette sharing in some groups of teenage girls (Coomber and Turnbull 2007). However, there are a number of further advantages that can be gained from "friendship" for dealers and customers. For the customer, it helps ensure the product received is of good quality and quantity, and reduces the risk of being sold adulterated drugs. For the dealer, trust is an important issue and selling to friends can be a form of risk management, reducing the chances of being reported to the police and also of theft of goods (Potter 2009; Werse 2008). Werse (2008) further illustrates the importance of friendship by outlining that trust is an important factor in an otherwise unregulated market, so for dealers and customers, friendship and the trust it entails are mutually beneficial.

Users will often avoid contact with those they class as "real dealers," choosing to buy only from friends or "friends of friends" (Parker 2000; Stevenson 2008). Real dealers are assumed to be those who profit from drugs or sell drugs for a living rather than just helping friends. In Stevenson's (2008) study, "real dealers" were perceived by cannabis users as those who were unknown (beyond the dealing transaction) to their customers and who supplied drugs to strangers with the intention of making profit, or those who supplied drugs as their sole or major economic activity. Similarly, other UK and American studies have found drug users unwilling to describe their "friends" (who supply their drugs) as "dealers," again with real dealers perceived as the profit-driven "stranger" or nonfriend (e.g., Jacinto, Duterte, Sales, and Murphy 2008; Parker 2000).

Suppliers themselves in some cases avoid using the deviant "dealer" label: They often claim they are simply helping out friends or doing favors. Jacinto et al.'s (2008) U.S. study found 76% of their sample of Ecstasy sellers did not accept the label "dealer" (419). However, this self-definition must be considered in a critical light: Jacinto et al. found that some suppliers with Ecstasy-dealing revenues as high as US$25,000 per week still rejected the dealer label, suggesting that label avoidance may be seen as a "technique of neutralisation" (Sykes and Matza 1957; see also Potter 2009).

Legally speaking, there is little or no difference between social supply and other approaches to distributing drugs as the law in many jurisdictions is worded in terms of *supply*, with factors such as profit and motivation irrelevant to defining the offense (although they may be relevant to sentencing; Duffy et al. 2008; Home Affairs Select Committee 2002; Potter 2009; Stevenson 2008). However, there is a widespread perception that social supply *should* be seen as being different to "real" dealing, with some commentators suggesting it should be separately defined by law (Coomber and Turnbull 2007; Duffy et al. 2008; Hough et al. 2003; Police Foundation 2000; RSA 2007; cf. Potter 2009).

A key aim of our research was to identify how individuals became involved in "real" drug dealing, as opposed to "mere" social supply, and how their careers developed over time. Within existing research, there are a number of possible entry paths (to "real" dealing) outlined. Jacinto et al. (2008, 420) identified three main paths of entry: "drifting into dealing," "extension of an existing product line," and "profit driven move." Although these categories are not exclusive and were taken from an Ecstasy-only study, they offer a useful starting point for our analysis.

"Drifting into dealing" reflects broader ideas of how young people "drift" into delinquency through a series of gradual escalations of deviant behavior where each individual step may seem relatively innocuous and may be barely noticeable (Matza 1964). When applied to drug dealing, "drift" describes those sellers who do not make a clear or explicit choice to become a drug dealer, but rather become involved in drug supply "in such small steps they are hardly noticed by the individuals involved" (Coomber 2006, 162). These small steps follow an easy process of progression especially within social groups where the use and (social) supply of soft drugs is largely normalized, thus removing the psychological barriers to deviancy that may be associated with "real" dealing, or the supply of harder drugs. Variations on this theme of drift exist in the literature: Potter (2010, 190), for example, describes how cannabis growers, originally motivated by the desire to cover their own consumption, may sell their excess crop and embark on the "slippery slope" from not-for-profit cultivation to cannabis dealer.

Although described by Jacinto et al. (2008) as drift, it should be noted that the process may in fact be quite rapid as the extension of credit to dealers by their own suppliers can allow fast expansion in a relatively short period of time. "Social supply" is often a key part of this process as individuals will often drift from "user" to "social supplier" and then onto greater involvement in drug distribution. Suppliers who drift often fail to notice (or at least fail to be concerned about) this progression as each step of increased sales is commonly accompanied by increased use of techniques of neutralization to resist the label of deviancy. Suppliers who drift into dealing are the least likely to perceive themselves as

"real dealers," and often fail to see the risks associated with being caught due to their self-perception of their activities as being nondeviant (Jacinto et al. 2008; Murphy et al. 1990).

"Extension of an existing product line" is where a supplier diversifies or changes his product range. Although this does not describe the initial route into drug dealing, it shows why suppliers may start to deal in a certain (new) substance. This is relevant to the current research as many of the sellers interviewed are multicommodity suppliers. There are a number of reasons why suppliers will diversify into new substances. Similar to the "criminal diversifier" (Dorn et al. 1992, see below), dealers extending their product lines may already be well connected. Suppliers often have extensive networks of buyers and sellers known to them: extending to new products can be an easy route to increased profit with minimal extra effort (Murphy et al. 1990). For our dealers, diversification into mephedrone or other synthetics was reported also as a response to a drought in the Ecstasy market.

"Profit-driven choice" is a wide category that covers those who entered into drug distribution seeking profits, the presumed motivation behind dealing in the stereotypical understanding of the drug dealer. One important subcategory here is the "criminal diversifier": a criminally involved individual who starts to supply drugs as a sideline to or change from their existing criminal career. Dorn et al. (1992) suggest that those already involved in the distribution of stolen goods are already criminally connected, allowing an easy transition to drugs distribution: Their criminal networks may include potential suppliers and potential customers. As a result, the criminal diversifier will often enter the market at a higher level than those who drift into dealing from social supply (Dorn et al. 1992; Murphy et al. 1990).

As Jacinto et al.'s (2008) breakdown suggests, profit is not always the sole motivating factor for suppliers (Dorn et al. 2005; Potter 2009, 2010). Some studies have found dealers becoming involved in supply for the lifestyle and material goods the money can generate, whereas others have found sellers simply trying to pay the bills to live a normal life (Adler 1993; Murphy et al. 1990; Potter 2010; Weisheit 1991, 1992).

Suppliers may deal drugs as a service to help out friends as is found in "social supply" or in the "trading charities" described by Dorn et al. (1992), where individuals may distribute drugs at minimal profit in line with ideological beliefs. Students may supply as a means to pay their education and living costs, whereas many young people may be motivated by the status and social standing conferred by being a supplier of drugs to their friends (Parker 2000; Potter 2009). An individual's motivations often change over time and will differ significantly depending on the market type (i.e., drugs supplied) and level of the seller. In the literature, it seems not uncommon for those whose initiation into drug supply was not primarily motivated by profit to drift toward profit-oriented dealing.

Elsewhere in the literature on—and inherent in the popular view of—the drug dealer, we encounter the idea that violence is a key feature of drug markets (Bean 2008; Coomber 2006). Violence is seen as an essential element in enforcing deals, debts, and quality of product and in expanding and protecting markets. However, studies offer competing views on how much violence actually exists in drug markets. Bean (2008), acknowledging that different market types may have different levels of violence, states that drugs supply is a "world where violence is an essential part of the lifestyle" (169). In the UK context, O'Mahoney's (1997) insider exposé fits this picture, outlining widespread violence and intimidation in wholesale MDMA and cocaine markets. However, although violent markets undoubtedly do exist, violence is by no means a feature of all drug markets. Pearson and Hobbs (2001, 2003) claim violence tends to be overstated in research and public opinion. They suggest that violence tends to be avoided by dealers as it is bad for business and many suppliers run their trade on the "business principles" of "cooperation and harmony" to avoid the unwanted police attention that the use of violence is likely to entail (Pearson and Hobbs 2003, 341). However, they do acknowledge that all levels of distribution hold the *potential* for violence, stating that violence should be seen as the "result of market dysfunction and instability" rather than as part of a working drug market (Pearson and Hobbs 2001, 42).

Coomber (2006) adds to this debate by suggesting that levels of violence depend on a number of factors, including the "class, gender, culture and personal dispositions" of the sellers involved (132). He suggests that violent markets tended to arise from macho, already violent subcultures hosting drugs distribution rather than involvement in drug supply causing individuals to take up violent behavior, a view supported by Sommers and Baskin (1997). Some drugs are more associated with market violence than others, with cocaine often assumed to have a more common association to violence than cannabis or MDMA (Bean 2008; Coomber 2006). Overall, although violence is found at different levels in different markets, it is clearly not always central. It seems equally clear that violence should be largely absent from the sort of distribution labelled "social supply."

It is around the borderline area between "social supply" and the "real dealer" that this study focuses. Although the research draws on suppliers who are undoubtedly "real dealers," the concept of social supply is still core to understanding the way they run their enterprises, their relationships with their customers, and their initiation into drug dealing.

Method

Data were collected primarily through interviews with 13 drug dealers living in and around "Rivertown." Interview data were supplemented with further qualitative data collected through participant observation in the form of informal conversation and social contact with the research participants, including the witnessing of drug transactions. Most participants were already known to the researcher (Taylor) through social networks based around the local dance-music scene (e.g., nightclubs, "raves," and parties) and other local drug-using social networks. Other participants were recruited through referral from the original contacts.

As well as geographical location, respondents had to meet the criteria of having bought drugs in quantities with a retail value in excess of £1,000 per week (on average) regularly (i.e., for sustained periods or recurring shorter periods totalling *at least* 6 months) across the 18 months prior to the research commencing. The reason for this financial threshold was to focus on those clearly involved in "real" dealing.

We followed the ethical procedures of London South Bank University (which in turn require compliance with the ethical guidelines of the British Society of Criminology) and ethical clearance was granted before fieldwork commenced. Interview participants were offered assurances over confidentiality, anonymity, and the safe storage of data. No names were recorded during the interview process and participants were asked not to refer to names at any point while on tape—where they did, these were anonymised in the transcription process.

Interviews were semistructured, with participants encouraged to supply lengthy in-depth responses to questions focussing on initiation into dealing, career progression, and the mechanics and structures of the markets they operated in. In particular, respondents were asked to comment in detail on the nature of their relationships with their customers *and* their own suppliers, giving some insight into a wider drug-dealing population.

Some methodological limitations must be taken into account. Our sample size is small and drawn from short chain referrals from a single initial contact (Taylor). Such sampling problems may generate a degree of bias as each participant is known to others and may share common characteristics (Salganik and Heckathorn 2004). However, although this places limits on the generalizability of our findings, the focus on a small number of individuals operating in the same broad network allows for a greater depth of understanding of drug dealing in this particular cultural scene. This depth was further enhanced by the researchers' preexisting relationships with many respondents, allowing for more reliable findings as interview responses could be compared with concurrent and previous observations.

Having said this, one important methodological issue is how the identity of the researcher may have affected the research process. Although the researcher cannot be classed as an "insider" as he did not distribute drugs, neither can he be classed as an "outsider" as many of the respondents were members of his own social network. Being from the same background in some aspects highly aided the research, not only in terms of access but also in terms of cultural understanding; it allowed free-flowing conversation with a level of intimacy and trust unattainable by an outside researcher. This semi-insider status also removes the issues of "culture clash" (Adler 1993). However, there are disadvantages: It is possible that this shared culture resulted in the overlooking of cultural norms that an outside researcher may have identified as significant; it may also mean the research undertaken did not have the level of "analytical distance" considered necessary by some (Akhtar and South 2000).

In our opinion, the advantages of researcher–participant friendships in this study outweigh the limitations. Nevertheless, there are clear limits to the generalizability of our findings, and we present this study as an insight into a particular lower level drug market that is most useful when considered alongside other research into other drug markets in other social and cultural contexts.

Findings

Sample Description and Drugs Dealt

All participants were male and aged between 21 and 31 years old. Eleven were White British, one Asian, and one Afro-Caribbean/White mixed race, largely reflecting the predominantly White population of "Rivertown." Respondents had varying levels of education: All had General Certificates of Secondary Education (GCSE), 9 had A levels, and 4 had reached university level, although 1 had dropped out. At the time of interview, 9 of the 13 were in employment.

Participants distributed cannabis, ketamine, cocaine, or MDMA (Ecstasy) as their main products, with some selling two or more of these products side by side. The weekly retail value of drugs distributed ranged from £1,000 to £35,000. Overall, the most prevalent drug dealt was premium herbal cannabis (often known generically, albeit erroneously, as "skunk") with weekly amounts handled ranging from 126 g to 5 kg. Ketamine was sold regularly by three of the sample, with amounts purchased ranging from 50 to 250 g. Cocaine was regularly sold by two of the interviewees in amounts ranging from 14 g to 6 oz (168 g) per week. MDMA was supplied regularly by two respondents who bought between 1 and 9 oz per transaction; in addition, five of the sample had sold MDMA occasionally as a sideline to their main product. Synthetic dance drugs and hallucinogens such as mephedrone, LSD (lysergic acid diethylamide) and 2C-B were sold as occasional sidelines.

Market Structure

The pyramid model was observed to the extent that suppliers generally bought in wholesale amounts then sold on in smaller quantities. Market tiers were evident: Two participants talked about moving up the distribution levels in their supply careers, and it was common for participants to describe things in terms of "the level above" when talking about their suppliers. However, the pyramid structure was not straightforward. Individual dealers tended to sell in wholesale and retail quantities and at times changed places within the distribution structure. For example, Dom bought around 4 to 5 kg of cannabis weekly from a number of suppliers, buying different quantities of different quality "skunk" and hash (cannabis resin). He distributed the bulk of this in kilo and half-kilo divisions, but he also sold in "bars" (9 oz; 252 g), "half bars" (4.5 oz; 126 g), ounces (28 g), and at times divisions as small as "eighths" (⅛th oz; 3.5 g). As such, he acted as wholesaler and retailer simultaneously. Dom also often "middled" a product (Adler 1993), buying multiple kilos of cannabis and selling it on at a set profit without breaking it down, thus disrupting the pyramid structure further by adding intralevel distribution at the middle-market level (cf. Pearson and Hobbs 2001). The overlap between wholesale, retail, and social supply is further illustrated by Paul:

> I had it down to four or five people, well four people who would really take all the big bits, and that's where the key profit was . . . and then the little bit that was left over would just be between social circles . . . you know, literally mates doing mates' rates.

None of the suppliers interviewed operated under any form of centralized, organized, or hierarchical control, nor were they involved in organized crime or market monopolization. Most dealers had multiple supply options for each drug they sold and no one was fixed to any one supplier in terms of obligation to buy. Rather, "supply option maximisation" was common (Reuter 2000). These findings fit with other recent research on UK drug distribution, supporting the argument that top-down controlled markets are in reality rare (at least in "soft" drug markets), contrary to public belief (Coomber 2006, 2010; Pearson and Hobbs 2001). Interestingly though, one of the more experienced sellers in the sample had observed a situation where a dealer *was* pressured into continuing to sell drugs by his supplier. This may, of course, be a reflection of the personality of that particular supplier or that particular relationship or may be evidence that top-down control can occur within this type of market, albeit as the rare exception rather than the norm.

In terms of organizational structure within the market, there were apparent differences between drug types. The wholesale "skunk" market seemed to be the most structured with cannabis often arriving to the dealers on a fixed weekly or fortnightly credit cycle. This was the norm for eight of the interviewees, who bought a similar quantity each time and generally (but by no means exclusively) stuck to one main supplier:

> I pick up once every 2 weeks, works like clockwork, it's always a Thursday . . . I either get a bar, which is nine ounces, or half a kilo. (John)

This fast turnover and extensive use of credit was not found to the same extent with any of the other substances dealt. The wholesale cannabis suppliers interviewed were generally well organized in comparison with other sellers: Many were able to give a breakdown of their weekly sales and profit margins in seconds. This was the market that seemingly contained the most business-minded individuals, and the only market where not all the sellers interviewed used the drug that they sold. Business mind-set and low personal drug consumption are outlined as important factors to successful distribution at all market levels (e.g., Adler 1993; Murphy et al. 1990). These characteristics were less evident among those in our sample who primarily dealt substances other than cannabis.

The chemical markets (MDMA, ketamine, LSD, and other substances) had fairly similar characteristics to each other and appeared irregular and disorganized in comparison with the cannabis market, with some suppliers occasionally adding these products to their existing range as and when they were either cheap or readily available, rather than maintaining a constant supply:

> The mephedrone, we bought that in a kilo . . . only bought that once as it kind of ticked over. (Baz)

MDMA was the most commonly distributed drug in this category with five respondents selling it at times. One supplier sold MDMA as his main product, but to a wide base of occasional customers (both retail and wholesale) rather than the regular customer base found in the other markets. Interestingly, at the time of the interviews, the MDMA market was perceived (by our respondents and by experts cited in national media) to be at a point of instability and shortage (e.g., BBC News 2010, January 19): Wholesale prices had (reportedly) increased as much as 300% and the shortage left some suppliers looking for new drugs to sell, with mephedrone reported as a popular alternative.

The ketamine market seemed even more unstructured and disorganized. One experienced ketamine dealer sourced ketamine from multiple suppliers from three different cities up to 3-hr drive away from "Rivertown" just to maintain a constant supply:

> I have multiple [suppliers], not really got off the same person for more than a couple of months I don't think. It fluctuates so much . . . People have other issues to deal with so they can't always bring it in, so I have to find someone else who is. (Fred)

Ketamine seems to be an "addictive" substance for some users (Morgan, Muetzelfeldt, and Curran 2009), and those who sold it at retail level at least partly relied on a base of daily and weekly customers, as well as semiregular customers who would appear when their normal supply was not available. The personal organization of participants involved in ketamine supply was lower than in other markets observed, possibly due to all those interviewed having high levels of personal consumption.

Ketamine fails to feature in any of the reviewed literature on drug markers and clearly needs further research attention.

Motivation, Initiation, and Career Progression

For the dealers in our study, initiation into drug dealing followed similar routes to those described elsewhere and discussed earlier. Eleven of the sample entered supply in a manner that fitted the notion of "drifting into dealing," moving up from a background of social supply. Two of our dealers entered through a more explicit "profit-driven move," although both of these also had a background in social supply within their own friendship circles. The significant factor here is that *all* the participants had social supply backgrounds.

Most participants *started* dealing to help friends out or to acquire free or subsidized drugs for their personal use. Although most participants still talked about helping out friends and maintaining personal use as part of their current motivation to supply drugs, it seemed to have become a secondary motive to profit. All the suppliers interviewed admitted they had become increasingly interested in profit:

> I don't smoke anymore, the only reason I do it is for profit. (John)
>
> I suppose I have been getting a bit more greedy, kind of expecting more in a way, because I got used to a bit more income. I started to spend more and become more flippant with money, in which case you get used to it and the demand for it becomes more . . . you kind of feel you need to, so the bigger the score the better. (Fred)

Individual suppliers would use their profit in different ways. Some saved their weekly profits and had built up substantial savings or possessions. For example, Dom used his £13,000 profits saved between September 2008 and February 2009 to buy a sound system and a new truck. Marley put a £30,000 deposit down on a house as well as buying a small boat. Other sellers spent their profits as they earned them and enjoyed the hedonistic lifestyle it allowed:

> Going and staying in five star hotels with girls, taking girls to very nice restaurants . . . going to

Amsterdam . . . not having to think twice about money, getting taxis to college, taxis home from college, taxis everywhere . . . money never being an issue, never having a thought about money, never eating at home, always eating out. (Paul)

Meanwhile, others spent their profits on normal things such as rent and paying their bills: John commented that he was "opposed to working eight hours a day" for the "very small wage available," and used his profits to retake his A-level exams, something he could not have done without his dealing activities. Gerard saved his profits:

I found that I save really . . . I thought well I'm going to make money and save it for a time when I'm maybe not doing it.

Profit levels varied between suppliers with a mean of £475 per "average" week, but seven respondents reported regular weekly profits of more than £1,000. These profit levels illustrate that the suppliers in this sample undoubtedly constitute "real dealers" rather than social suppliers: For most, drug profits were their primary source of income. However, profit was not the only motivating factor. Ten participants stated they enjoyed supplying, mainly due to the social aspect of seeing and spending time with friends and meeting new people. Drug supply is clearly a very sociable activity for this group, giving dealers the chances to maintain and extend their friendship groups. This demonstrates how sociability can remain a core element of drug dealing even when profit becomes the primary motive.

Dealer-Customer Relations: Friendship, Trust, and Violence

Overall, friendship was an extremely important aspect of drug supply and all respondents sold almost exclusively to friends, friendly acquaintances or friends-of-friends. As such, markets were closed in nature: None of the suppliers sold to strangers; new customers would be gained through a process of introduction by trusted friends:

It's really sociable actually. I met a lot of people through it, friends I've kept as well not just associates. (Fred)

They're my friends; they're people I see on a regular basis anyway. (Baz)

Pretty much most of my mates, are good mates I have sold drugs to, cos we all kind of grew up together. (Paul)

Friendship ties operated upwards to wholesale suppliers as well as downwards to customers: Without these close friendship ties, it seems that this market would be unable to operate as the credit offered by suppliers was based on trust and recommendation. Although the suppliers interviewed distributed significant amounts of drugs each week, the markets clearly exhibited the values of trust and friendship found in the social supply markets discussed earlier. These friendly markets are a vast contrast to studies into drug markets characterized by dishonesty, mistrust, and violence (e.g., Akhtar and South 2000; O'Mahoney 1997; Reuter 2000).

Friendship, it seems, serves at least two purposes. First, as outlined in the previous section, the social aspect of drug dealing is a major attraction even to those operating on a relatively large scale. Second, friendship reinforces the trust sought by those involved in drug dealing as some insurance against the risks of legal repercussions and against the risks of advancing credit.

Markets dependent on a concept of friendship should, presumably, show minimal levels of violence. In our study, the incidence of violence is summed up by this quote:

It's uncommon . . . completely uncommon for violence to be used . . . I don't remember anyone getting beaten up or having anything done to them as the result of being late with money. (James)

Only one of the sellers interviewed had ever resorted to violence in relation to drug dealing and this was a one-off occurrence resulting from an argument over money rather than a specific attempt at debt collection. For other sellers, drug-related violence was either totally unheard of or extremely rare.

One other respondent, a cannabis kilo-dealer, answered our questions about the role of violence differently, stating that it was "not common, but present" in the market. He was aware that violence had been used to collect debts by one of his customers and, in the past, by one of his suppliers. These two examples show that the market observed is not totally free of violence. Most of the sample had interaction with 15 to 50 drug contacts on a weekly basis, with some suppliers having dealing careers spanning up to 15 years. All were asked about violence in relation to the wider market they were involved in rather than just their personal experiences. Despite this, there were only the two indications of violence throughout the study, illustrating its rare and unusual nature.

Instead of violence, dealers had other mechanisms used to minimize the possibility of debt default and other sources of conflict. Most, as we have seen, dealt only with friends or highly trusted and recommended individuals, and the use of credit was highly dependent on this trust.

> If you are going to lend someone £4,000 worth of drugs, then you kind of trust them in the first place. (Paul)
> I wouldn't give someone an amount [of drugs] worth a large amount of money unless they had the cash for it, unless they were very, very well trusted and had always been able to get it back straight away. (James)

At the level of wholesale supply, those who fell behind on repaying debts were generally perceived to be having trouble getting the cash together rather than deliberately trying to avoid payment. As such, it was not uncommon for suppliers either to credit debtors extra drugs to allow them to work off the debt, or to borrow money themselves to cover their own resultant short-fall. Here, a multikilo cannabis buyer talks about borrowing money to cover his customer's debt:

> If they couldn't get it . . . I have mates I can go to who do similar sorts of things in different lines I can sort of borrow money off . . . It was generally a problem with timings rather than people not wanting to pay. (Paul)

It seemed that if debts really needed to be dealt with, every effort would be made for them to be resolved in an amicable manner with pressure in the form of regular communication being the primary tactic used:

> I let them know how disappointed I am and try and do the old guilt trip, rather than threatening them. (Fred)
> Usually the person feels very sorry about it and pays you back as soon as they can. (Zac)

However, continued failure to pay would in some cases lead to consequences. Some suppliers would tell their debtors that their own supplier was unhappy and if the debt was not settled quickly, he (the higher level supplier) may become involved. Five of our cannabis suppliers suggested that although it had never happened, they were aware that they had support from the level "above" them, who would issue threats or potentially collect debts on their behalf:

> Not me personally, I wouldn't do anything to them, I would say that the people who were up the chain might become involved. (Gerard)
> It wasn't a direct threat in a way where I tell them what's going to happen. I just basically let them know that . . . I had ticked [credited] the weed just like they had ticked it off me . . . and my dealer would come down and I'm not sure of the consequences. (Kinkle)

We can see from this that threats of violence were available as a last resort but we must emphasize that not one supplier interviewed had taken this route of debt enforcement. Interestingly, one supplier, Baz was robbed of £10,000 by a customer and chose not to take any action. It was suggested that Baz had the option to gain support from his own supplier but chose not to, and paid off the debt at his own expense, illustrating Topalli, Wright, and Fornango's (2002) contention that drug dealers are often the victims of violence rather than the perpetrators, and the more general observation made earlier that violence is something to be avoided. In another example of a supplier avoiding violence at their own expense, Gerard mentioned that he was aware of his own supplier leaving large debts owed:

> I know people above me . . . who I know have lost out on money because they don't think it's worth going down that route . . . Anyone who sells drugs,

obviously is clever enough, would know that there is no point getting violence involved, because the last thing you want is for anything to be obvious . . . you know.

This is an example of a drug supplier avoiding using violence as it compromises the interests of business security (Pearson and Hobbs 2001, 2003). However, it was not only good business sense that limited the recourse to violence but also a personal moral code and a recognition of friendship ties which encouraged suppliers to remain patient with debtors.

Overall, for the smaller retail suppliers in the sample, violence is an aspect that never features in their markets, which may be due in part to the relatively small amounts of potential debt resulting from such dealing relationships, and is undoubtedly linked to the personal friendships between suppliers and customers. With the larger suppliers, in markets with a fast credit turnaround, there was the potential for violence, but this was almost entirely held in check by the strong friendship ties within the group.

Discussion and Conclusion

Our research involved only a small number of drug dealers, so there is a clear limit to the generalizability of our findings. Nevertheless, when we consider our findings alongside existing research, it is possible to offer some general comments on retail-level drug markets and the grey area between social supply and real dealing. Some general observations can be made about market structures and organization. As our findings depict, the pyramid structure, where evident, was certainly not hierarchically *controlled*, nor linked to organized crime. However, the larger cannabis suppliers interviewed did operate on a credit system with suppliers and customers, and had potential support from their suppliers in collecting debts from customers, if necessary. This support is partly a result of the use of credit in this market: Money was owed up the supply chain, and missing money had a knock-on effect on higher level suppliers; therefore, it was in the interest of the participants' suppliers to help them retrieve the cash. Having said this, we should reemphasize that violence was extremely rare in the markets observed.

There was variation, in terms of market structure and mechanics, between different drugs distributed. The cannabis market, as demonstrated by the credit cycles and apparent interlevel support, exhibited a structure and regularity that was absent in the markets for other drugs featured. We can only speculate here, but this may be a reflection of how established a particular drug market is: There are more users of cannabis than of the other drugs, and mephedrone, 2C-B, and even ketamine can all still be considered as "new" drugs.

Generally, the market studied here does not fit the stereotypical violent, organized crime image often associated with drug distribution. The high levels of friendship, the lack of violence and the absence of a hierarchically organized market are perhaps partly due to suppliers having drifted in to "real" dealing from a background of "social supply." In this process, our suppliers maintained some of the associated values of social supply (i.e., the "between friends" aspect) while moving away from others (i.e., the "non-commercial" element).

It has been suggested that social supply offers retail customers a buffer from the dangers of the real market (Coomber and Turnbull 2007; Pearson 2007; Potter 2009). However, this research suggests that no such buffer is necessary between users and some "real" dealers, or perhaps that these dealers themselves act as a buffer protecting their customers from the next level up the supply chain (although our dealers' relationships with their own suppliers were not dissimilar to their relationships with their customers). This market could possibly be described as "social dealing" as although profits are achieved, and are a central motivating factor, other areas still retain similarity to the social supply markets depicted elsewhere (e.g., Coomber and Turnbull 2007; Duffy et al. 2008; Parker 2000). It is important to remember that although the suppliers interviewed no longer fit the full definition of "social supply," they were still closely linked to it: For example, many of their customers themselves acted as social suppliers, and our dealers often acted as social suppliers to their friends. Our dealers backgrounds in and close ties with the social supply market perhaps also play a role in maintaining some of its characteristics.

An important point to take here in terms of possible suggestions for future research, debate, and policy developments pertaining to social supply is that while social supply may be seen as distinct from real dealing, it seems to be an important stage in *becoming* a real dealer, at least for a number of those involved in the retail distribution of "softer" drugs (our dealers avoided the "hardest" drugs such as heroin and crack-cocaine). Specifically, we recommend further research is carried out on other, preferably larger and more varied samples (i.e., drawn from multiple or more diverse distribution networks) to see whether our findings are replicated, and if so, for what sorts of drug markets and under what conditions.

References

Adler, P. A. 1993. *Wheeling and Dealing: An Ethnography of Upper-Level Drug Dealing and Smuggling Community*, 2nd ed. New York, NY: Columbia University Press.

Akhtar, S. and N. South. 2000. "Hidden from Heroin History: Heroin Use and Dealing Within an English Asian Community." In *Illegal Drug Markets: From Research to Prevention Policy* (Crime Prevention Studies, vol. 11), edited by M. Hough and M. Natarajan. New York, NY: Criminal Justice Press.

BBC News. 2010. "Why Ecstasy Is Vanishing from UK Nightclubs." January 19. Retrieved from http://news.bbc.co.uk/1/hi/england/london/8468372.stm

Bean, P. 2008. *Drugs and Crime*, 3rd ed. Cullompton, England: Willan.

Brownstein, H. 1996. *The Rise and Fall of a Violent Crime Wave: Crack Cocaine and the Social Construction of a Crime Problem*. New York, NY: Criminal Justice Press.

Coomber, R. 2006. *Pusher Myths: Re-Situating the Drug Dealer*. London, England: Free Association Books.

———. 2010. "Reconceptualising Drug Markets and Drug Dealers: The Need for Change." *Drugs and Alcohol Today* 10: 10–13.

Coomber, R., and P. Turnbull. 2007. "Areas of Drug Transactions: Adolescent Cannabis Transactions in England." *Journal of Drug Issues* 37: 845–866.

Curtis, R. and T. Wendel. 2000. "Towards the Development of a Typology of Illegal Drugs Markets." In *Illegal Drug Markets: from Research to Prevention Policy* (Crime Prevention Studies, vol. 11), edited by M. Hough and M. Natarajan. New York, NY: Criminal Justice Press.

Dorn, N., M. Karim, and N. South. 1992. *Traffickers: Drug Markets and Law Enforcement*. London, England: Routledge.

Dorn, N., M. Levi, and L. King, L. 2005. *Literature Review on Upper Level Drug Trafficking* (Home Office online report 22/05). London, England: Home Office. Retrieved from http://www.ivac.ehu.es/p278-content/es/contenidos/informacion/ivckei_isabel_german/es_igerman/adjuntos/rdsolr2205.pdf

Duffy, M., N. Schafer, R. Coomber, L. O'Connell, and P. Turnbull. 2008. *Cannabis Supply and Young People: "It's a Social Thing."* York, England: Joseph Rowntree Foundation.

Home Affairs Select Committee. 2002. *The Government's Drug Policy: Is It Working?* London, England: Home Office.

Home Office. 1998. *Tackling Drugs to Build a Better Britain: The Government's Ten Year Strategy for Tackling Drug Misuse*. London, England: HMSO.

Hough, M. and M. Natarajan. 2000. "Introduction." In *Illegal Drug Markets: From Research to Prevention Policy* (Crime Prevention Studies, vol. 11), edited by M. Hough and M. Natarajan. New York, NY: Criminal Justice Press.

Hough, M., H. Warburton, B. Few, T. May, L.-H. Man, J. Witton, and P. Turnbull. 2003. *A Growing Market: The Domestic Cultivation of Cannabis*. York, England: Joseph Rowntree Foundation.

Jacinto, C., M. Duterte, P. Sales, and S. Murphy. 2008. "I'm Not a Real Dealer: The Identity Process of Ecstasy Sellers." *Journal of Drug Issues* 38: 419–444.

Matza, D. 1964. *Delinquency and Drift*. New York, NY: John Wiley.

Morgan, C. J. A., H. Muetzelfeldt, and V. Curran. 2009. "Consequences of Chronic Ketamine Self-Administration Upon Neurocognitive Function and Psychological Wellbeing: A 1-Year Longitudinal Study." *Addiction* 105: 121–133.

Murphy, S., D. Waldorf, and C. Reinarman. 1990. "Drifting into Dealing: Becoming a Cocaine Seller." *Qualitative Sociology* 13: 321–343.

O'Mahoney, B. 1997. *So This Is Ecstasy?* London, England: Mainstream Publishing.

Parker, H. 2000. "How Young Britons Obtain Their Drugs: Drugs Transactions at the Point of Consumption." In *Illegal Drug Markets: From Research to Prevention Policy* (Crime Prevention Studies, vol. 11), edited by M. Hough and M. Natarajan. New York, NY: Criminal Justice Press.

Pearson, G. 2007. "Drug Markets and Dealing: From 'Street Dealer' to 'Mr Big.'" In *Drugs in Britain: Supply, Consumption and Control*, edited by M. Simpson, T. Shildrick, and R. MacDonald. Basingstoke, UK: Palgrave.

Pearson, G. and D. Hobbs. 2001. *Middle Market Drug Distribution* (Home Office Research Study 224). London, England: Home Office.

———. 2003. "King Pin? A Case Study of a Middle Market Drug Broker." *Howard Journal of Criminal Justice* 42: 335–347.

Police Foundation. 2000. *Drugs and the Law: Report of the Independent Inquiry into the Misuse of Drugs Act 1971.* London, England: Author.

Potter, G. R. 2009. "Exploring Retail-Level Drug Distribution: Social Supply, 'Real' Dealers and the User/ Dealer Interface." In *Old and New Policies, Theories, Research Methods and Drug Users Across Europe*, edited by Z. Demetrovics, J. Fountain, and L. Kraus. Lengerich, Germany: Pabst Science Publishers.

———. 2010. *Weed, Need and Greed: A Study of Domestic Cannabis Cultivation.* London, England: Free Association Press.

Reuter, P. 2000. "Epilogue: Connecting Drug Policy and Research On Drug Markets." In *Illegal Drug Markets: From Research to Prevention Policy* (Crime Prevention Studies, vol. 11), edited by M. Hough and M. Natarajan. New York, NY: Criminal Justice Press.

Ritter, A. 2005. *A Review of Approaches to Studying Illicit Drugs Markets* (DPMP Monograph 8). Melbourne, Victoria, Australia: Turning Point Alcohol and Drug Centre.

Royal Society for the Encouragement of Arts, Manufactures and Commerce. 2007. *Drugs-Facing Facts: The Report of the RSA Commission On Illegal Drugs, Communities and Public Policy.* London, England: Author.

Salganik, M. J. and D. D. Heckathorn. 2004. "Sampling and Estimation in Hidden Populations Using Respondent-Driven Sampling." *Sociological Methodology* 34: 193–239.

Sommers, I. and D. Baskin. 1997. "Situational or Generalized Violence in Drug Dealing Networks." *Journal of Drug Issues*: 833–849.

Stevenson, C. 2008. "Cannabis Supply in Northern Ireland: Perspectives from Users." In *Cannabis in Europe: Dynamics in Perception, Policy and Markets*, edited by D. J. Korf. Lengerich, Germany: Pabst Science Publishers.

Sykes, G. and D. Matza. 1957. "Techniques of Neutralisation: A Theory of Delinquency." *American Sociological Review* 22: 664–670.

Topalli, V., R. Wright, and R. Fornango. 2002. "Drug Dealers, Robbery and Retaliation: Vulnerability, Deterrence and the Contagion of Violence." *British Journal of Criminology* 42: 337–351.

Weisheit, R. 1991. "The Intangible Rewards from Crime: The Case of Domestic Marijuana Cultivation." *Crime & Delinquency* 37: 506–527.

———. 1992. *Domestic Marijuana: A Neglected Industry.* New York, NY: Greenwood Press.

Werse, B. 2008. "Retails Markets for Cannabis: Users, Sharers, Go Betweens and Stash Dealers." In *Cannabis in Europe: Dynamics in Perception, Policy and Markets*, edited by D. J. Korf. Lengerich, Germany: Pabst Science Publishers.

For Discussion

1. What are the legal implications of social supply? Should criminal laws treat social supply differently than "real" dealing? Why or why not?

2. The authors discuss the researcher role in terms of insider/outsider status. How might insider and outsider roles shape the research findings, particularly for those studies that focus on sensitive topics such as illicit drug use?

21

A Preference for Mephedrone

Drug Markets, Drugs of Choice, and the Emerging "Legal High" Scene

KAREN MCELRATH AND MARIE CLAIRE VAN HOUT

In the mid- to late 2000s, mephedrone emerged as novel psychoactive substance in western Europe, Australia, and other countries. Around the same time, its chemical cousin—MDPV ("bath salts")—surfaced in the United States. In this article, Karen McElrath and Marie Claire Van Hout use data collected from interviews with people who consumed mephedrone to explore why mephedrone became a drug of choice within a relatively short period of time.

The findings suggest the importance of macro-level drug market factors that shaped people's preferences for mephedrone. Additionally, respondents' preferences were guided by pharmacological properties that helped them conceal the effects of mephedrone in public and semi-public spaces.

Introduction

New psychoactive substances continue to emerge in various countries, and have gained popularity within various drug scenes. In some regions, these substances have surfaced initially as legal psychoactive products, later to be prohibited by law. Known in several European countries as "legal highs," these substances produce psychoactive effects similar to illegal stimulants, depressants or hallucinogens. "Legal high" products are available in different forms (e.g., tablets, pre-rolled joints, herbal mixtures, powders, crystals) and can contain (1) plants found in nature (e.g., kratom, kava, *Salvia divinorum*),[1] (2) synthetic substances (e.g., 2-aminoindan, butylone, mephedrone, synthetic cannabinoids such as JWH-018), or (3) semisynthetic substances that are derived from natural oils (e.g., DMAA). Often sold in pre-sealed packages that feature "hippy style," "new age," or other symbols, many packages are labeled with nomenclature that reminds consumers of illegal street drugs or their effects (e.g., Snow Blow, Tijuana, Ice Gold, Charleeze, Sub-Coca, and X Pillz).

Hundreds of legal high products have been identified in Europe (Hillebrand, Olszewski, and Sedefov 2010; Long 2010; Schmidt 2009), although they can differ in terms of potency, form (e.g., powder or crystal) and additives. Several products contain synthetic stimulants, consistent with the popularity of "amphetamine-type stimulants" (ATS) with an estimated 30–40 million users worldwide (United Nations Office on Drugs and

Crime 2010). Mephedrone (4-methylmethcathinone) is a synthetic stimulant designed in part to mirror the effects of cathinone, a compound found in the Khat plant. Mephedrone produces stimulant-like properties (e.g., increased energy, talkativeness, insomnia), as well as feelings of empathy and euphoria. Anecdotal evidence suggests the availability of synthetic cathinones in Israel in 2004 (Power 2009) and mephedrone in selected European regions in 2008 (e.g., Amsterdam, parts of Sweden), with mephedrone-focused discussions appearing on internet forums beginning in 2007 (Psychonaut WebMapping Research Group 2009). During 2009 and 2010, mephedrone was situated in drug scenes across Britain (Carhart-Harris, King, and Nutt, in press; Measham, Moore, Newcombe, and Welch 2010; Winstock, Mitcheson, Ramsey, and Marsden, in press) and North/South Ireland (McElrath and O'Neill 2011; Van Hout and Brennan 2011), and available for sale through various sources including dealers (Dargan, Albert, and Wood 2010; McElrath and O'Neill 2011; Newcombe 2009; Winstock et al., in press), street-based headshops[2] (Van Hout and Brennan 2011), and online shops[3] (Dargan et al. 2010; European Monitoring Centre for Drugs and Drug Addiction 2010). In April 2010, the UK banned mephedrone and other cathinone derivatives, and under the Misuse of Drugs Act (1971) specified criminal penalties for possession and supply of the drug. Mephedrone and related cathinones were banned in the Republic of Ireland one month later.

The potential health implications of mephedrone are unknown because the substance has not been subjected to rigorous testing. Analyses of legal high products have found that ingredients, potential side effects and drug interactions are at times misrepresented or are omitted altogether (Brandt et al. 2010; Pillay and Kelly 2010; Schmidt et al. 2011; Wolowich, Perkins, and Clenki 2006). Moreover, mephedrone is often consumed with other psychoactive substances, particularly alcohol (Carhart-Harris et al., in press; Winstock et al., in press; McElrath and O'Neill 2011). Adverse biochemical interactions between alcohol and other drugs are well documented (Cone et al. 2003; National Institute on Alcohol Abuse and Alcoholism

2007; Therapeutic Research Center 2008); thus, simultaneous polysubstance use that involves mephedrone has the potential for adversely affecting users' health.

Users' Experiences with Mephedrone

Although population-based surveys of mephedrone use are lacking, an emerging body of work has focused on users' experiences with mephedrone. Some studies have examined the use of mephedrone prior to the introduction of legislative controls (e.g., Dargan et al. 2010; Newcombe 2009; Van Hout and Brennan 2011; Winstock, Mitcheson, Deluca, Davey, Corazza, and Schifano 2011). For example, an online survey of UK readers of a leading dance/music magazine found that 41.3% of respondents reported lifetime use of mephedrone, and approximately one-third had used the substance during the past month (Winstock et al. 2011). A lower rate of lifetime prevalence was reported by Dargan et al. (2010) in their Scottish survey of 1006 individuals enrolled in schools, colleges, and universities. Their pre-ban survey data revealed that 20.3% of the respondents reported ever using mephedrone (the survey response rate was not reported); of this group, 23.4% reported using mephedrone on one occasion only. Daily use (4.4%) occurred among respondents aged 21 or younger. Winstock et al. (in press) conducted telephone interviews with 100 individuals who had participated in an online survey in 2009. Data collection ended in April 2010, just prior to the introduction of the UK ban on mephedrone. The authors found that the incidence of negative drug outcomes was relatively low in comparison to users' reports of the positive effects of the drug. However, 29.5% reported a minimum of three symptoms that suggested stimulant dependence. In an Australian study, Matthews and Bruno (2010) found that 21% of "regular Ecstasy users" had also used mephedrone. Those authors observed considerable variation of lifetime prevalence rates (mephedrone) across Australian cities.

In the UK, a pre-ban study of data collected through 100 telephone interviews found that nearly half the sample (47%) planned to use mephedrone during the month following the interview, i.e., after the ban (Winstock et al., in press). Two months after the ban, an online survey of 150 mephedrone users found that 63% had continued to use the substance despite its illegal status (Winstock, Mitcheson, and Marsden, 2010). A second online survey was conducted during the four-month period that followed the UK ban (Carhart-Harris et al., in press). All of the 1,506 respondents reported lifetime use of mephedrone. The majority (84%) of the sample resided in the UK, and 64% of the UK respondents reported that their use of mephedrone had declined since the ban. Moreover, 58% indicated that they would not "try to get hold of mephedrone now that it is illegal." A qualitative study from Northern Ireland explored sources of mephedrone supply during the ten-week period following the UK ban (McElrath and O'Neill 2011). Those authors described a developing illicit market, with users reporting increased reliance on dealers, higher prices, and changes to product labelling.

Studies have found that few people progress to daily use of mephedrone (Dargan et al. 2010; Newcombe 2009), dosage and frequency of use increase over time (Newcombe 2009), and intranasal or oral ingestion are common routes of administering the substance (Carhart-Harris, in press; Matthews and Bruno 2010; Van Hout and Brennan 2011; Winstock et al. 2011). Research has highlighted both positive (Brunt, Poortman, Niesink, and van den Brink, in press; McElrath and O'Neill 2011; Van Hout and Brennan 2011) and negative psychoactive effects of mephedrone (Carhart-Harris, in press).

To summarize the literature: (1) most studies have used data collected from users residing in the UK, Ireland, or Australia, (2) mephedrone availability in these regions appeared to surface relatively quickly, and (3) the available evidence suggests that several individuals continued to use mephedrone after legislative controls were introduced, at least during the two- to four-month period that followed the ban. The studies are limited in terms of their sample characteristics, i.e., the disproportionate number of respondents who are experienced drug takers. We know considerably less about mephedrone use among novice drug takers, including their patterns of use and source of supply pre- and post-ban.

Purpose of the Study

Scholars in England have suggested that although the (former) legal status of mephedrone contributed to the drug's popularity, the declining availability and purity of illicit drugs represented the more salient motivator that shaped people's preferences for mephedrone (Measham et al. 2010). Those authors observed that the rising popularity of mephedrone coincided with the availability of lower purity Ecstasy and cocaine. Similar observations were noted in Australia where "regular Ecstasy users"—many of whom had used mephedrone—reported that Ecstasy was more difficult to obtain and of lower purity compared to the year earlier (Matthews and Bruno 2010). Other research has shown that changes in local and regional drug markets can affect users' behaviors. For example, a decline in the availability of heroin contributed to an increase in cocaine injections among problem heroin users (Maher et al. 2007), and heroin form and purity can influence users' preferred routes of administration (Valdez, et al. 2011), which in turn has implications for the spread of blood-borne viruses. Also, the expansion of drug markets to include different and more potent forms of methamphetamine (i.e., crystal) has been linked with more extensive health problems among users (Topp et al. 2002). We continue this line of inquiry by examining the role of localized drug markets in shaping people's preferences for mephedrone. We also explore perceptions of positive and negative effects of the drug, preferred routes of administration, and attitudes concerning the (once) legal status of mephedrone. We explore these issues by drawing on data collected in two jurisdictions (Republic of Ireland, Northern Ireland) where legislative controls differed at the time of data collection.

Methods

The study sites included (1) a town and surrounding area located in the southeast of the Republic of Ireland, and (2) an urban area (Belfast) and small town in Northern Ireland. Although the two jurisdictions share a land border, the study sites were in many ways separated by social and geographic distance (i.e., approximately five to six hour driving time by car). Semi-structured interviews were conducted in April/May (Republic of Ireland) and May/June 2010 (Northern Ireland) with individuals aged 18 or older who had used mephedrone since January 2010. Interviews in the Republic of Ireland were conducted four weeks prior to the ban on mephedrone in that country; interviews in Northern Ireland were conducted during the ten-week period following the wider UK ban on mephedrone. Our intention was to conduct interviews during the pre-ban periods in both regions. However, legislative controls were introduced quickly and with relatively short notice. As a result, the interviews commenced when mephedrone was legal in one jurisdiction (Republic of Ireland) and illegal in another (Northern Ireland), although the data collection period in the regions overlapped by one month.

Interviews lasted between one and two hours and focused on the social context of first and last use, perceived effects and experiences, preferred social settings for use, access to mephedrone and related issues (some of these issues are addressed in other articles). The interview questions were asked in conversational tone and without judgment. Four interviewers were used, including the authors and two Privileged Access Interviewers (PAI). Prior to the study, the PAIs had established contact and developed excellent rapport with a number of individuals who had used mephedrone. They had previous experience with basic research skills and were trained by the authors in terms of the interview guide and ethical protocol. Interviews were conducted face-to-face, with the exception of one respondent who was interviewed by telephone. Interview settings included university offices, private residences of respondents or their acquaintances, and to a lesser extent, semi-public spaces such as cars parked in retail area car parks. Respondents were recruited largely through personal contacts of the authors and PAIs, social networking sites, local blogs, and chain referral. We monitored the sample carefully to encourage diversity in terms of gender and age. Respondents in the Republic of Ireland received compensation of 20 Euro (USD 27) for their participation in an interview[4]; Northern Ireland respondents did not receive financial reimbursement. The final sample included 22 respondents from the Republic of Ireland and 23 individuals from Northern Ireland ($N = 45$).

The majority of interviews were digitally or tape recorded, and detailed notes were taken in lieu of audio recordings for some interviews. All interview data were transcribed by one of the four interviewers. The study was granted ethical approval from the Research Ethics Committee, School of Sociology, Social Policy and Social Work, Queen's University, Belfast (Northern Ireland).

The analytical strategy commenced with several reads of the interview data within the respective study sites. The authors noted emerging themes and categories, and developed coding schemes. Preliminary patterns in the data were analyzed, followed by a system of corroboration and comparison with other cases. "Outliers" were analyzed under the conditions in which outliers might be explained. As patterns and outliers emerged, periodic briefing sessions were held between the authors, and between author and respective PAI. At times, the PAIs helped clarify ambiguities in the data and assisted with interpretation.

Results

A comparison of sample characteristics across the two cohorts suggests differences in terms of female representation (Northern Ireland = 52%, 12/23; Republic of Ireland = 36%, 8/22). Additionally, respondents' ages ranged from 19–51 (Northern Ireland) and 18–35 (Republic of Ireland). The Northern Ireland sample also included proportionately fewer respondents in the 20–29 age category sample (57%, 13/23) compared to the Republic of Ireland sample (91%, 20/22). In sum, the Republic of Ireland sample included respondents who were younger and disproportionately male, compared to the Northern Ireland sample. The cohorts were similar in terms of employment, with nearly all respondents employed in full- or part-time work.

The vast majority of respondents in both samples had a history of drug taking prior to consuming mephedrone. This history included lifetime use of cannabis, amphetamine, cocaine, Ecstasy, hallucinogens, ketamine and poppers. The majority of respondents had initiated illicit drug use during adolescence, although two respondents from Northern Ireland were aged 30 or older before initiation into any drug use at all. Several respondents had consumed mephedrone with illicit substances (e.g., simultaneous use with cocaine or Ecstasy, and cannabis or benzodiazepine to ease the comedown), and approximately one-fourth of the sample had done so during the most recent mephedrone experience. All of the Northern Ireland respondents had consumed alcohol during their most recent use of mephedrone, although the amount and timing of alcohol varied across respondents. Respondents from the Republic of Ireland were substantially less likely to combine alcohol and mephedrone. We acknowledge that respondents' subjective reports of mephedrone experiences might have been affected by their intake of other psychoactive substances.

Most respondents had last used mephedrone within the two-week period prior to the interview (including Northern Ireland respondents who had used mephedrone pre- and post-ban). Respondents had first used mephedrone between May 2009 and January 2010, although many recalled hearing about mephedrone prior to initiation. Stories about mephedrone experiences began to emerge in the summer of 2009, and circulated quickly within and across social networks. Northern Ireland respondents tended to rely exclusively on the reports or experiences of friends who had tried mephedrone:

> [Before initiation] I had heard of it through friends, even before it hit the media. Some had tried it, some hadn't tried it. Got the low down on it and they were telling me it was good. (NI 19, male, age 28)
>
> My mates had all been talking about it [mephedrone] before I tried it like. It was peer pressure. They just recommended I take it, and I'd be blew out of it in ten minutes. None of them had any bad reports about it. (NI 22, male, age 24)

In contrast, respondents from the Republic of Ireland placed greater trust not only in friends, but additionally in headshop staff, online discussion forums, and to a lesser extent, media reports:

> I've friends all over Ireland that run headshops so having access to the products isn't a problem, especially now as there's more headshops in [town] than there are post offices. (ROI 16, male, age 25)
>
> [Heard about it through] discussion with friends and advice from headshop staff. (ROI 9, male, age 31)
>
> . . . through word of mouth from other users or by happening across an online discussion about a

new product on some clubbing forums. (ROI 11, male, age 27)

Mephedrone information provided by headshop staff and discussion forums were considered trustworthy among respondents in the Republic of Ireland, who perceived these sources to be concerned with optimizing safety and reducing harm for consumers. In contrast, only two of the 23 Northern Ireland respondents had purchased pre-ban supplies of mephedrone from street-based headshops, opting instead to access mephedrone from dealers, friends, and to a lesser extent online shops ($N = 4$).

Preferences for Mephedrone

Respondents from both study sites tended to report positive experiences with mephedrone. The beneficial effects of mephedrone included a "heightened sense of absolutely everything," extremely pleasurable conversation (although subsequently nonsensical to some respondents), enhanced interaction with others, and overall emotional euphoria. Additionally, perceptions about positive effects were shaped by comparisons with other psychoactive substances, namely Ecstasy and cocaine. We used prompts to generate these contrasts but also noted that respondents made further comparisons as the interviews progressed.

Slightly more than half of the Northern Ireland sample and the majority of respondents from the Republic of Ireland noted their preference for mephedrone over Ecstasy and cocaine. These preferences were influenced by macro-level factors associated with localized drug markets. First, respondents reported either limited availability of Ecstasy or poor quality Ecstasy and cocaine that had characterized local drug markets for several months. We observed this pattern in both study sites:

> M1 [mephedrone] is very good—better than normal coke that you'd get around here anyway . . . (ROI 17, male, age 19)
>
> I'd prefer illegal drugs with the exception of mephedrone which is better than the poor quality Ecstasy around these days, and the absolute shit coke that there is around. (ROI 13, male, age 22)
>
> It was a Friday night—the day before my birthday. There was no coke about, and the dealer said,

"But I've got plant food—it's not the same as coke, don't take as much." So it was new to me—never did it, and I didn't want to do it in public the next night [her birthday] 'cause I wasn't sure what I'd be like. So I thought, "I'll try this alone." Went home, had a few vodkas, went up to my room and took it. (N 15, female, age 28)

The legal status of mephedrone meant that it was cheaper than Ecstasy and cocaine, and the lower cost of mephedrone emerged as a second drug market factor that contributed to respondents' preferences for the drug. Respondents also reported that mephedrone was easy to obtain:

Everyone seems to be taking mephedrone. It's better than MDMA and it's cheaper. It's like a proper drug for less money. My reason would probably be mainly financial. (ROI 9, male, age 31)

Meph was legal and that was a bit of a novelty. It wasn't that I thought it was safe—but you could buy it in bulk, legally. It was easy to get, and it was cheap. I mean used to be £10–15 a gram [USD 16–23]. (N I3, female, age 19)

The consistency of mephedrone effects was identified as a third drug market factor that shaped people's preferences for mephedrone. Consistency of effects was described by respondents in terms of the perceived quality and potency of the substance. That is, the effects of one batch of mephedrone (or one mephedrone outcome) were believed to be largely similar to the effects of another. These perceptions were noted by respondents from the Republic of Ireland and by Northern Ireland respondents who recalled mephedrone experiences prior to the introduction of legislative controls. As stated earlier, respondents were seasoned drug takers who were accustomed to purchasing other drugs from the illicit market. These previous transactions were sometimes characterized as "poor value for money," resulted in financial loss and at times "spoiled" drug-related leisure time. Psychoactive substances that produced consistent and desired effects were perceived to be advantageous and contributed to preferences for mephedrone:

Mephedrone does what it's supposed to do. Es [MDMA] can be rubbish [poor quality] now, and

I've heard the coke is no good here. (N I9, male, early 40s)

I suppose the appeal of mephedrone is the fact that you know it's going to be a good buzz. You might spend €100 [USD 155] on a bag of coke and get nothing off it. (ROI, 7, male, age 33)

In addition to the role of macro-level drug market factors, we observed that some respondents preferred mephedrone because of the pharmacological properties that allowed them to maintain physical control of the drug experience. This physical control was deemed to be important in the presence of other drug takers, as well as in public or semi-public spaces where respondents might come into contact with "normals":

Mephedrone gives the effect of a good Ecstasy pill *without the messiness* [emphasis added] and good coke without the edginess. (ROI 6, female, age 25)

Es became so unpopular. . . . I mean, just the effect they had on some people. Next day we'd think, "God, he was a real mess last night." With mephedrone, it's not like that. There's no holy show of yourself. (NI1, female, age 23)

And pills [Ecstasy]—you definitely can't control your face. (NI 20, female, age 25)

It's easier to normalize yourself on meph [mephedrone] rather than pills [Ecstasy]. On pills, it's harder to snap yourself out of it. You sort of just have to ride with it like. (NI 21, female, age 28)

Negative Effects and Route of Administering Mephedrone

The negative effects of mephedrone were not necessarily framed as such, but were more often viewed as necessary stages of an overall positive drug outcome. Still, some respondents in both cohorts reported weight loss, temporary bouts of insomnia, blurred vision, facial numbness, offensive bodily smells that emerged through their pores or skin, and infections. A few respondents developed paranoia that they associated with using mephedrone. Over time, they had managed paranoia through particular coping mechanisms:

We got such a ritual—if she's paranoid, I'd pull her out of the hole and I'll talk. If I'm paranoid, she'll pull me out. (NI 1, female, age 23)

Pain in the nasal passages was perhaps the most consistently reported negative effect associated with mephedrone use, and this effect was linked directly to route of administering the substance. Respondents from both cohorts tended to prefer intranasal use of mephedrone, referred to as "bumping" or sniffing (i.e., snorted from lines or off a key or coin). This route of administration was characterized by "burning" sensations in the nasal passages and at times contributed to severe nose bleeds. Respondents in the Republic of Ireland reported "bumping" mephedrone only. In contrast, some Northern Ireland respondents reported a preference for "bombing" mephedrone (i.e., wrapped in cigarette paper and swallowed, or mixed with water and swallowed). However, the majority of respondents in both cohorts believed that the intranasal route incurred greater speed of effect:

It burns a lot, but it's kind of like "no pain, no gain." The buzz is your reward for going up the nose. [The pain] maybe lasts ten seconds or so. My friend bombed it but it wasn't as intense [the effects] she said . . . up the nose, the vein at the top of your head pops out. (NI 1, female, age 23)

Other respondents disputed the claim that intranasal use resulted in a more powerful effect:

See a snort and a bomb? The hit is just as good. Don't know why people snort it—waste of money. We bomb it and it lasts for 3–4 hours. Snorting—doesn't last nearly as long. There's a big difference in bombing and sniffing. (N I9, male, early 40s)

And bombing mephedrone was viewed by some Northern Ireland respondents as a harm reduction strategy:

When you're bombing it, it takes longer to hit you [feel the effects] but the actual effects are no different. None at all like. People say the effect is better if you snort it. The truth is, they're not. It's just quicker. Anything's quicker if you snort it. But if it's that sore on your nose and it burns that much, you should know not to do it. Like earlier XXX's [friend's] nose was that fucked from it [snorting mephedrone] that she couldn't talk. (NI 16, male, age 31)

I only drink it when I'm really at the bottom of the fucking barrel like—when I literally can't get

anymore up my nose 'cause it's jammed. And then you end up sweating it and it's coming out of your pores. (NI 22, male, age 24)

In general, respondents consumed ½ to two grams of mephedrone during each drug episode, although some respondents recalled mephedrone binges, ingesting larger amounts of the substance over a span of two or more days. In general, mephedrone doses were gauged in which small amounts of the drug were ingested at different times over the course of a mephedrone episode, which often extended to several hours. Respondents from the Republic of Ireland described "gauging" doses with repeated intranasal dosage guided by personal tolerance that was grounded in prior drug taking experiences:

Take meph [mephedrone] just like coke . . . bit by bit . . . don't blow the head off yourself too quickly. (ROI 7, male, age 33)

I take a small portion at first and if I don't feel any effects after about ten minutes, I take and extra dose until the buzz/sickness sets in. Then I stop. (ROI 2, female, age 27)

I'm quite careful when taking drugs and always wait to feel the effect of what I've taken first. (ROI 18, male, age 26)

Change in Legal Status

Respondents from both jurisdictions observed little concern over the changing legal status of mephedrone. Respondents from the Republic of Ireland were aware that the ban on mephedrone was imminent, and most respondents reported that they would not be deterred by forthcoming legislative controls in the region:

I expect M1 [mephedrone] to become available on the street fairly fast. It's too popular to just disappear. I'll certainly be buying it anyway. (ROI 12, male, age 24)

Yes, I will purchase M1 when it pops up illegally as will anyone who has ever tried it, I imagine. (ROI 11, male, age 27)

The data suggest that all respondents from the Republic of Ireland intended to purchase mephedrone if the substance were to become available through the illicit market. These decisions were grounded in respondents' previous access to and negotiations with the illegal market. That is, most respondents had accessed other illegal drugs and these skills minimized anxieties about subsequent illicit transactions:

> I guess I will buy them after the ban. I have been buying illegal drugs for years, so I don't see why not. (ROI 21, female, age 23)

Data from the Northern Ireland cohort suggest a similar trend, with 21 of 23 respondents using mephedrone after the legislative ban in that region (McElrath and O'Neill 2011). Respondents from Northern Ireland recalled when mephedrone was legal, although none reported that the legal status directly contributed to their use:

> About a year ago, I just remember these ones [friends] talking about this plant food stuff. But then someone said it was only £15 (USD 24 a gram and then the wee lights up in my eyes. To me, it was immaterial that it was legal. (N16, male, age 31)

> I just enjoy it [mephedrone]. It was legal but that had no bearing on me. I've taken illegal things before, so I didn't start using this because it was legal. And really, I just like the effects [of mephedrone]. When it was legal, it was easier to get . . . (NI, female, age 23)

The majority of respondents from both jurisdictions did *not* equate the legal status of a substance with safety. However, many voiced concern about adulterated mephedrone once legislative controls were introduced. Respondents appeared to be more concerned about the non-regulated illicit market than they were about the non-regulated market when mephedrone was legal:

> I also recognize that it is an industry which needs to be regulated rather than banned outright as this [change] will push these substances onto the black market where regulation is nonexistent. (ROI 22, male, age 30)

The era of legal mephedrone was characterized by supplies that were branded, labeled and contained in pre-sealed packages, even when sold by street dealers. This packaging encouraged trust by willing buyers and gave the appearance of a market that was far more regulated than the illicit drug market to which respondents were accustomed.

Limitations of the Study

Both cohorts were comprised of adults who had extensive histories of illicit drug taking. These histories helped negate fears regarding mephedrone consumption. We acknowledge, however, that our findings might have been different had we interviewed people who were novice drug takers. Unfortunately, we were unable to recruit these individuals into the study. A second limitation concerns the characteristics of our samples, which differed in terms of gender and age representation. Still, the findings suggest several cohort similarities in terms of how drug market factors contributed to people's preferences for mephedrone, as well as similarities regarding the timing of initiation and dosage. A final limitation concerns the potential effect of concurrent polydrug use, which might have contributed to respondents' experiences of mephedrone. Some respondents had consumed one or more psychoactive substances during mephedrone episodes, although we also noted that these patterns fluctuated depending in part on the availability of other drugs. The relative frequency of mephedrone consumption made it difficult for us to ascertain the influence of other drugs on mephedrone outcomes. Additionally, the majority of Northern Ireland respondents consumed alcohol with mephedrone, although the timing and amount of alcohol intake varied considerably across respondents.

Discussion

This research was based on interview data collected from adults who had experience with mephedrone between 2009 and 2010. The same interview guide was administered to two samples of individuals, residing in separate jurisdictions. The cross-border study is intended to contribute to the emerging literature on this new party drug, in terms of illustrating (1) positive and negative mephedrone outcomes, (2) route of administration, (3) the role of drug market factors in shaping user preferences, and (4) perceptions surrounding the changing legal status of mephedrone. The main findings of this cross-border study are discussed below.

First, the data suggest that macro-level drug market factors contributed greatly to consumer preferences for mephedrone. In comparison to the subjective purity of Ecstasy and cocaine, mephedrone was viewed more favorably. This finding supports Measham et al. (2010), who argued that the declining availability and purity of illicit drugs was the primary motivator for using mephedrone. The declining purity of MDMA has been linked to international controls over some of the main precursors that have been used to manufacture Ecstasy (European Monitoring Centre for Dings and Drug Addiction 2011). Brunt et al. (in press) reported results from laboratory analyses of approximately 12,000 tablets sold as MDMA in the Netherlands. The authors found that MDMA purity levels began to decline in mid-2008 and by 2009, upwards of 54% of tablets sold as MDMA contained mephedrone. Although the Netherlands once was one of the leading sites for MDMA manufacture, production has since spread to other countries (European Monitoring Centre for Drugs and Drugs Addiction 2010) where international controls might have less impact. In the present study, the reliability of mephedrone effects coupled with competitive pricing emerged as additional drug market factors that contributed to respondents' preferences for mephedrone. Taken together, these findings suggest the presence of drug displacement patterns between illicit and licit substances (Measham et al. 2010) that are fuelled largely by the interplay among wider drug market factors. We are less clear about the relative importance of these factors in regions characterized by higher purity cocaine and better quality Ecstasy. Future research in these geographic regions would help clarify the relationship.

Second, although drug market variables emerged as primary reasons for using mephedrone, the data also suggest the importance of "feeling in control" of the drug experience. Compared to the effects of Ecstasy, respondents felt better able to conceal the physical effects of mephedrone while still enjoying the psychoactive changes. Informal social control worked to regulate expected behaviors, even among people under the influence of psychoactive substances.

Third, the data reveal differences in the preferred route of administering mephedrone as well as the combined use of alcohol. Specifically, some respondents in Northern Ireland chose to bomb mephedrone, whereas all respondents from the Republic of Ireland reported a preference for sniffing. We observed that respondents who preferred to bomb mephedrone were either older (i.e., over 30 years), believed bombing to be less harmful than sniffing, or were unable to sniff mephedrone because of the temporary damage to intranasal passages. Compared to oral ingestion, intranasal route of administering mephedrone has been linked to higher consumptive patterns as well as greater frequency of use (Winstock et al. 2011). Some investigators have speculated that the intranasal route may contribute to a greater potential for negative effects of mephedrone (Brunt et al., in press). Taken together, these findings suggest that bombing mephedrone may represent an important harm reduction strategy. The results also indicate that respondents from Northern Ireland were far more likely to combine alcohol with mephedrone, compared to study participants from the Republic of Ireland. This finding is consistent with survey data from the general population, which show that Northern residents consume nearly double the alcohol intake of Southern residents (Ward et al. 2009). These differences may be due to established social norms around drinking, and the reduced price of alcohol in Northern Ireland. The frequent use of alcohol with mephedrone is of concern because the interaction and synergistic effects of the combined substances have not been researched thoroughly.

Fourth, although few respondents perceived that the (previous) legal status of mephedrone implied safety, respondents in the Republic of Ireland tended to view "unregulated" mephedrone as safer when sold through street-based headshops. Further, they often failed to recognize that psychoactive products purchased from headshops also were "unregulated." Product labels indicating "not for human consumption" did not deter nor heighten perceptions of drug-related risk. In the Republic of Ireland, the pre-ban insular presence of networks among consumers, headshop staff and online discussion forums appeared to support and reinforce continued use of mephedrone and reduce perceived harm. In contrast, most of the Northern Ireland respondents tended to avoid headshops.

Previous analysis of the Northern Ireland data found that those respondents tended to distance themselves from headshops in order to conceal their "drug user" identities (McElrath and O'Neill 2011). The political conflict in Northern Ireland was characterized by strong yet informal social control mechanisms that served to regulate deviant behavior within particular communities. Those wider societal controls operated to a much lesser extent in the Republic of Ireland, and we suggest that this explanation might account for the difference in preferred supply sources across the two regions.

The vast majority of Northern Ireland respondents continued to use mephedrone after the ban and respondents from the Republic of Ireland noted an interest in continued use of mephedrone following legislative controls. These results suggest that laws prohibiting the distribution and possession of psychoactive substances that were once legal may be ineffective among seasoned drug takers who have experienced positive effects of the substance. However, research is needed to investigate the role of prohibition among individuals who have consumed mephedrone but are less experienced with drug use.

Postscript

Previous analysis of the Northern Ireland data (McElrath and O'Neill 2011) described an emerging but fluctuating illicit mephedrone market in the immediate months following the ban on the substance. During the 12-month post-ban period, the authors learned from the PAIs and other contacts that mephedrone has been readily available through illicit markets in their respective regions. Although street prices have increased since the introduction of legislative controls, illicit mephedrone is still cheaper than cocaine. In Northern Ireland, the relative ease by which mephedrone entered the illicit drug market was perhaps influenced by its pre-ban availability through dealers, some of whom were selling illicit drugs.[5] In the Republic of Ireland, additional research is needed that investigates the shift from headshop to dealer supplies of mephedrone, and the experiences of buyers who changed their source of supply. The illicit mephedrone market in that region may have taken longer to establish, given the greater reliance on headshops during the pre-ban period.

Beginning in August 2010, the PAIs and street contacts described users' perceptions about the availability of better quality Ecstasy tablets in both jurisdictions. Although these reports have suggested a fluctuating Ecstasy market during the past ten months, we find the timing of this pattern (in line with the recent bans on mephedrone) to be intriguing and we speculate about the wider competitive nature of illicit drug markets more generally. In the context of international controls over some MDMA precursors (International Narcotics Control Board 2011), it is possible that users' perceptions are incorrect, and that current batches of MDMA in the regions may be marketed as Ecstasy, but are in fact produced from chemicals that share similar psychoactive properties to MDMA. Regardless of what is perceived by some users to be better quality Ecstasy, we suggest the possibility that preferences for mephedrone will continue as long as the relative consistency of mephedrone purity and price remain stable in an otherwise changing drug market.

Research and anecdotal evidence suggests the global diffusion of mephedrone to areas outside Europe, including the United States (Associated Press 2011a; Freeman 2011), Canada (Associated Press 2011b), and Australia (Matthews and Bruno 2010). This diffusion is aided in part by the internet as a source of information, shared drug-taking experiences and sales distribution (Griffiths, Sedefov, Gallegos, and Lopez. 2010). The popularity of mephedrone in some countries may well be curtailed by new emerging psychoactive substances that are viewed by consumers as being more beneficial in producing mind-altering experiences. Longitudinal data of a qualitative nature are perhaps best suited to monitor the relationship between localized drug markets and changing drugs of choice.

Notes

1. Kratom, kava, and salvia divinorum have long been used by indigenous people as part of ritual and ceremony.
2. Street-based headshops are specialty shops and stores that sell drug paraphernalia, counterculture reading and art, and more recently, legal high products.
3. Online shops include a) web-based headshops that sell a range of products described in note 2

above, and b) online businesses that sell psycho-active substances only and may focus exclusively on one type of psychoactive substance, (e.g., mephedrone.) During a three-day period in March 2010, the European Monitoring Centre for Drugs and Drug Addiction (2011) identified 77 websites that sold mephedrone.

4. Van Hout paid respondents from her personal funds.

5. We thank the anonymous reviewer for suggesting this possibility.

References

Associated Press. 2011a. "Poison Control Says Bath Salts Are Being Abused in Minnesota." Retrieved February 5, 2011, from http://www.twincities.com/health/ci_17216238?nclick_check=1

Associated Press. 2011b. "Bath Salt Abuse Brings 'Horrible Trip,' MD Warns." January 24. Retrieved February 5, 2011, from http://www.cbc.ca/news/technology/bath-salt-abuse-brings-horrible-trip-md-warns-1.1105604

Brandt, S. D., H. R. Sumnall, F. Measham, and J. Cole. 2010. "Analyses of Second-Generation 'Legal Highs' in the UK: Initial Findings." *Drug Testing and Analysis* 2: 377–382.

Brunt, T. M., A. Poortman, R. J. M. Nieskink, and W. van den Brink. Forthcoming. "Instability of the Ecstasy Market and a New Kid on the Block: Mephedrone." *Journal of Psychopharmacology*.

Carhart-Harris, R. L., L. A. King, and D. J. Nutt. Forthcoming. "A Web-Based Survey on Mephedrone." *Drug and Alcohol Dependence*.

Cone, E. J., R. V. Fant, J. M. Rohay, Y. H. Caplan, M. Ballina, R. F. Reder, D. Spyker, and J. D. Haddox. 2003. "Oxycodone Involvement in Drug Abuse Deaths: A DAWN-Based Classification Scheme Applied to an Oxycodone Postmortem Database Containing over 1000 Cases." *Journal of Analytical Toxicology* 27: 57–67.

Dargan, P. I., S. Albert, and D. M. Wood. 2010. "Mephedrone Use and Associated Adverse Effects in School and College/University Students before the UK Legislation Change." *Quarterly Journal of Medicine* 103: 875–879.

European Monitoring Centre for Drugs and Drug Addiction. 2010. *Annual Report 2010: The State of the Drugs Problem in Europe.* Retrieved May 23, 2011, from http://www.emcdda.europa.eu/publications/annual-report/2010

———. 2011. *Report on the Risk Assessment of Mephedrone in the Framework of the Council Decision on New Psychoactive Substance.* Risk assessments, Number 9. Luxembourg: Publications Office of the European Union.

Freeman, D. W. 2011. "Bath Salts Drugs Should Be Banned, Senator Says: Why?" *CBS News*, Health Blog, February 1. Retrieved February 5 from http://www.cbsnews.com/news/bath-salts-drugs-should-be-banned-senator-says-why/

Griffiths, P., R. Sedefov, A. Gallegos, and D. Lopez. 2010. "How Globalization and Market Innovation Challenge How We Think About and Respond to Drug Use; 'Spice': A Case Study." *Addiction* 105: 951–953.

Hillebrand, J., D. Olszewski., and R. Sedefov. 2010. "Legal Highs on the Internet." *Substance Use and Misuse* 45: 330–340.

International Narcotics Control Board. 2011. *Precursors and Chemicals Frequently Used in the Illicit Manufacture of Narcotic Drugs and Psychotropic Substances, 2010.* New York: United Nations.

Long, J. 2010. *Headshop Drugs across Europe: Data from the EMCDDA.* Paper presented at the National Regional Drugs Task Force "Legal Highs" Conference, January 26, Mullingar, Ireland.

Maher, L., J. Li, B. Jalaludin, H. Wand, R. Jayasuriya, D. Dixon, and J. M. Kaldor. 2007. "Impact of a Reduction in Heroin Availability on Patterns of Drug Use, Risk Behaviour and Incidence of Hepatitis C Virus Infection in Injecting Drug Users in New South Wales, Australia." *Drug and Alcohol Dependence* 89: 244–250.

Matthews, A. J. and R. Bruno. 2010. "Mephedrone Use among Regular Ecstasy Consumers in Australia." *EDRS Drug Trends Bulletin,* December. Sydney: National Drug and Alcohol Research Centre, University of New South Wales. Retrieved February 5, 2011, from http://www.med.unsw.edu.au/Ndarcweb.nsf/resources/BulletinsEDRS2010/$file/EDRS+December+2010.pdf

McElrath, K. and C. O'Neill. 2011. "Experiences with Mephedrone Pre- and Post-legislative Controls: Perceptions of Safety and Sources of Supply." *International Journal of Drug Policy* 22: 120–127.

Measham, F., K. Moore, R. Newcombe, and Z. Welch. 2010. "Tweaking, Bombing, Dabbing and Stockpiling: The

Emergence of Mephedrone and the Perversity of Prohibition." *Drug and Alcohol Today* 10: 14–21.

National Institute on Alcohol Abuse and Alcoholism. 2007. *Harmful Interactions: Mixing Alcohol with Medicines*. Bethesda, MD: National Institutes of Health.

Newcombe, R. 2009. *Mephedrone: The Use of Mephedrone (M-Cat, Meow) in Middlesborough*. Manchester (England): Lifeline Publications.

Pillay, D. and B. D. Kelly. 2010. "Recreational Drugs and Health Information Provided in Head Shops." *The Psychiatrist* 34: 100–102.

Power, M. 2009. "Mephedrone: The Future of Drug Dealing." *DrugLink* 25 (March/April): 6–7, 9.

Psychonaut WebMapping Research Group. 2009. *Mephedrone Report*. Retrieved January 25, 2011, from http://www.psychonautproject.eu/documents/reports/Mephedrone.pdf

Schmidt, M. 2009. "Legal Highs in the UK: Overview and the Results of a User Survey." Paper presented at the Psychonaut Conference, September 18, Ancona, Italy. Retrieved January 11, 2011, from http://www.psychonautproject.eu/documents/presentations/SchmidtMPsychonautConference2009.pdf

Schmidt, M. M., A. Sharma, F. Schifano, and C. Feinmann, C. 2011. "'Legal highs' on the Net: Evaluation of UK-Based Websites, Products and Product Information." *Forensic Science International* 206: 92–97.

Therapeutic Research Center. 2008. "Alcohol-Related Drug Interactions." *Pharmacist's Letter/Prescriber's Letter*. Stockton, CA: Author.

Topp, L., L. Degenhardt, S. Kaye, and S. Darke. 2002. "The Emergence of Potent Forms of Methamphetamine in Sydney, Australia: A Case Study of the IDRS as a Strategic Early Warning System." *Drug and Alcohol Review* 21: 341–348.

United Nations Office on Drugs and Crime. 2010. *World Drug Report 2010*. Vienna: Author.

Valdez, A., A. Neaigus, C. Kaplan, and A. Cepeda. 2011. "High Rates of Transitions to Injecting Drug Use among Mexican American Non-injecting Heroin Users in San Antonio, Texas (Never and Former Injectors)." *Drug and Alcohol Dependence* 114: 233–236.

Van Hout, M. C. and R. Brennan. 2011. "Plantfood for Thought: A Qualitative Study of Mephedrone Use in Ireland." *Drugs: Education, Prevention, and Policy*. Advanced online. Retrieved June 25, 2011, from http://informahealthcare.com/doi/abs/10.3109/09687637.2010.537713

Ward, M., H. McGee, K. Morgan, E. Van Lente, R. Layte, M. M. Barry, D. Watson, and I. Perry. 2009. *One Island—One Lifestyle? Health and Lifestyles in the Republic of Ireland and Northern Ireland*. Dublin: Department of Health and Children.

Winstock, A. R., L. R. Mitcheson, P. Deluca, Z. Davey, O. Corazza, and F. Schifano. 2011. "Mephedrone, New Kid for the Chop?" *Addiction* 106: 154–161.

Winstock, A., L. Mitcheson, and J. Marsden. 2010. "Mephedrone: Still Available and Twice the Price." *Lancet* 376: 1537.

Winstock, A., L. Mitcheson, J. Ramsey, S. Davies, M. Puchnarewicz, and J. Marsden. 2011. "Mephedrone: Use, Subjective Effects and Health Risks." *Addiction* 106 (11): 1991–1996.

Wolowich, W. R., A. M. Perkins, and J. J. Clenki. 2006. "Analysis of the Psychoactive *Terpenoid salvinorin*: A Content in Five *Salvia divinorum* Herbal Products." *Pharmacotherapy* 26: 1268–1272.

For Discussion

1. These findings suggest that limited availability of a popular psychoactive substance (e.g., MDMA) can contribute to the demand for another substance, for example, mephedrone. Consider this conclusion in light of Andrew Weil's arguments in Part III of this book.

2. Several novel psychoactive substances (NPS) have emerged in recent years and gained popularity in a number of drug scenes across the globe. Governments then seek to criminalize NPS and attach penalties for their possession and supply. How do you think users respond after certain drugs are criminalized? That is, do individuals abstain, substitute with other drugs, or access the preferred drug on the illicit market?

22

Step by Step

A Situational Analysis of Drug Business Disputes

ANGELA TAYLOR

Previous research has examined violent acts that are associated with illicit drug markets. Angela Taylor expands upon that research in this next article. Using interview data with a hard-to-reach population (male sellers), she analyzes fifty-three conflicts that are linked to illicit drug transactions. Taylor compares nonviolent and violent outcomes and examines the sequence of events leading up to these outcomes.

Introduction

Violence and drug selling share a strong connection. The connection is implicit in arguments for drug legalization which cite, among other potential benefits, reduced violence from the elimination of illegal trafficking (Cussen and Block 2000). It is also implicit in arguments linking changes in the nature of the crack market as one of various reasons for New York City's decline in crime (Blumstein and Wallman 2006; Johnson, Golub, and Dunlap 2000). Research has examined various proposed casual pathways to what Goldstein (1985) has called systemic violence—violence linked to the use and distribution of drugs. Drug sellers are often part of a broader social environment featuring widespread proviolence norms, which lessen the restraints against violence (Anderson 1999; Bourgois 1995; Ousey and Lee 2007). Drug sellers themselves have an increased propensity to engage in violence (Chaiken and Chaiken 1982; Fagan and Chin 1990). Substance use, an endemic feature of drug settings,

may also serve to heighten violence (White and Gorman 2000; Kuhns 2005). Drug sellers are often armed with guns, which makes homicide a likely occurrence (Blumstein 1995; Zimring and Hawkins 1997). Finally, the potential for violent disputes is heightened by various contextual features of the selling environment, including type of selling organization; position of individuals in drug hierarchy; level of market activity; market stability; and location of drug sales (Curtis and Wendel 2007; Korf et al. 2008; Ousey and Lee 2007; Reuter 2009; Taylor and Brownstein 2003).

Some argue that, given the illicit nature of drug selling, violence is a necessary aspect. Drug selling is a complex economic activity that lies outside of the law. When conflicts occur, they obviously cannot be resolved through legal means. As a result, violence is used to resolve disputes and impose social control (Goldstein 1985). Types of disputes that might lead to violence in drug-selling settings include struggles over territory, punishment of

Reprinted from Angela Taylor, 2012, "Step by Step: A Situational Analysis of Drug Business Disputes," in *Journal of Drug Issues* 42: 279–297. Reprinted by permission of SAGE Publications via Copyright Clearance Center.

errant workers, and conflicts with customers (Goldstein 1989). An especially important source of conflict in drug settings is the robbery of drug sellers (Jacobs 2000; Topalli, Wright, and Fornango 2002). These can often result in violent retaliation, and thus amplify the level of violence present.

Given the importance of systemic violence as a source of drug-related violence, it is surprising that there has been little research which examines these conflicts specifically as a form of social control, that is, as dispute resolution. Moreover, although much attention is paid to extraordinary forms of violence that can occur, there is relatively less information about the ordinary everyday assaults that are perhaps more typical of selling environments. Finally, until recently, there has been almost no direct research focus on the phenomenon of nonviolent outcomes of drug business disputes (although see Jacques and Wright 2008, for an elegant theoretical treatment of the issue). This is surprising as such outcomes are likely more common than media stereotypes of drug selling would allow researchers to presume (Coomber and Maher 2006).

Theoretical and empirical examination of nonviolent drug-related dispute outcomes is an important part of assessing the role of systematic drug violence in contributing to general levels of community violence. Uncovering the dynamics of violent and nonviolent drug business disputes can improve our understanding of the nature of conflict in drug market settings. The results of this work may also help improve the abilities of law enforcement and other entities to control these events, specifically by pinpointing the degree of flexibility available to guide efforts at control and prevention. Applying situation-based perspectives to the study of such events is a potentially useful approach for completing this task.

Exploring the Violent Situation

Situational theories or perspectives are focused on understanding and explaining crime situations or events (Birkbeck and LaFree 1993). Here, the focus is on violent events. Toch (1969) defines a violent event as "an interaction which begins when one person approaches another with some purpose in mind and ends in an act of aggression" (35). Situation-based theories regard violence as an interpersonal process where the outcome is determined by elements within the interaction itself as well as those that exist alongside it, including weapons, and the actions of the parties to the conflict as well as the actions and thoughts of the individuals.

These theories serve as a distinct contrast to traditional theoretical approaches to violence. Most research on violence is directed either toward explaining variations in its prevalence among social entities (gender, racial/ethnic, economic groups; see Kruttschnitt 1994; Luckenbill and Doyle 1989; Sampson 1987) or elucidating the relationship between violent behavior and antecedent factors, whether personality factors (Megargee 1982) or external circumstances, such as childhood exposure to violence (Widom 1989). Although this research has generated important findings, it runs up against a key puzzle: People with a high propensity to engage in violence are not violent under all circumstances. A person who is violent in one condition may, in another situation, refrain from violence. Thus, the situation is an important factor in generating a particular outcome. Theories of violence that limit attention to antecedent personal factors are less useful in accounting for the emergence of violence in particular instances. This inability to account for varying outcomes given a common set of conditions is likely because dispositional theories of violence mainly address factors that are quite distant from the actual act, and thus do little to illuminate the processes leading to the production of the act itself.

Situational approaches direct our attention to the generation of specific violent acts, thus improving our understanding of violent behavior overall. In addition, they also provide a closer fit with some of the information that we know about violence, such as the fact that it is not randomly distributed in time or place, even in locations that have a high potential for violence.

Initial empirical work in the application of situational theories to violent situations has looked at how these events unfold. The germinal work here is an article done by Luckenbill (1977) which posited violence as a "situated transaction," defined as "the chain of interaction between two or more individuals that lasts the time they are in each other's physical presence" (177). He analyzed written criminal justice records of criminal homicides as staged character contests where there is mutual consent by both parties to use violence as a means of defending positive social identities. Research involving situational theories has expanded to address a wide variety of topics: the role played by accounts in event escalation (Felson 1984), retaliatory factors in assault events (Felson and Steadman 1983), impression management concerns in violent incidents (Felson 1982), gun conflicts among adolescent males (Wilkinson 2003), and violent confrontations by Black males in bar settings (Oliver 1994), among others.

Although research done from the situational perspective has provided us with useful information on violence, there are a few areas where an expanded focus is needed. Much of the event-based research focuses on conflicts that are characterized by identity concerns. That is, one person takes personal offense at the actions or comments of another and it evolves (or devolves) into violence. There is less attention given to studying other types of violent interaction, for instance, assaults that are not strictly over identity concerns. As a result, there is less knowledge about such events, and about whether they proceed in a manner similar to that found in Luckenbill's character contests.

Second, there is comparatively little empirical attention paid to situations that could end in violence but do not. This is surprising, as it is likely that nonviolent outcomes to conflict are a common result. It strains credulity to assume that every dispute faced by a male, minority, lower class, inner-city dweller, say, a drug seller for instance, is doomed to end in aggression. It can be challenging for researchers to conceptualize a nonviolent outcome given that the focus is necessarily on something that is absent (specifically, an aggressive act). Nevertheless, failure to examine situations that result in nonviolent outcomes is an unnecessary hindrance to the goal of establishing robust causal links between situational features and violence (Sampson and Lauritsen 1994). Specifically, a more complete assessment of the influence of various situational features on violence requires the comparison of such features between violent and nonviolent event outcomes.

Turning to the empirical literature, one finds few studies that even elicit accounts of nonviolent events, much less conduct detailed analyses of such events. In one early study, Felson (1984) compared verbal aggression events with physical aggressive ones in exploring the role played by accounts in violent conflict. An account is defined as an excuse/justification for a deviant or untoward act (e.g., "I'm sorry about bumping into you"). His chief finding was that accounts were less likely to be present in instances of physical violence. This led him to conclude that when an account is given, a dispute is less likely to come to physical violence. Other research has proceeded by comparing events similar to violent ones that might have been violent but did not end up that way.

Athens (1997) explored the role of restraining judgments in the avoidance of violence. He asked violent prisoners to describe a situation in which they almost, but did not, attack another person. He found that in those instances, the prisoners formed restraining judgments which kept them from violent action. These judgments were fear of failure, fear of damaging a relationship, consideration of others' desires, change in actions of the opponent, and fear of law enforcement. An issue not addressed in this work is whether and how specific attributes of the situation influenced the formation of these restraining judgments.

Phillips (2003) used a case-control method to compare violent conflicts (termed *violent vengeance*) with similar conflicts that did not end violently. Testing a model of Black's theory of self-help, Phillips found that two concepts—relational distance and functional independence were significantly associated with whether an event became violent. Specifically, when there was a personal connection tie between the disputants, a nonviolent result was likely. This was also the case when the parties depended on each other for support. However, being of equal status and being confined in the same space, and coming from different cultures did not distinguish between violent and nonviolent events. Other factors that were associated with violent outcomes/nonviolent outcomes were presence of a gun, size difference, and the use of drugs/alcohol.

Third parties, outside persons linked to one or both of the main disputants, also play a role in how an event unfolds. Phillips and Cooney (2005) examined the nature and influence of third parties on the ability to distinguish violent from violent outcomes. They looked at both personal and institutional third-party parties, and whether they were linked to one side in the conflict (partisan ties), both sides (crosscutting ties), or neither side (distant ties). Partisan ties were more associated with violent conflicts, whereas distant ties (those third parties that were not connected to either side) were associated with nonviolent outcomes. The presence of crosscutting ties was associated with acts of mediation during a dispute.

Jacques and Wright's (2008) *resource exchange-social control* typology is an attempt to apply a general conceptual framework to encompass all activities in drug settings, both violent and nonviolent. Actions taken in the drug market can be viewed as either resource exchange or social control. Resource exchange describes how goods and services are traded. The process can take one of three forms: predatory (i.e., one side takes), altruistic (i.e., one side gives), or mutual (i.e., give and take). Social control is about imposing order among interactions, and includes addressing claims of wrongdoing. Actions here can take violent forms (retaliation) or nonviolent ones (fraud, deception, or mediation). As the goal of the authors is to construct and apply a theoretical framework, there is less focus on exploring how specific elements of disputes lead to a particular outcomes.

Wilkinson's (2003) research on the construction of violent events among adolescent males provides a basis for conceptualizing nonviolent event outcomes that is useful for the present study. In one type, conflict is settled before violence occurs. Such interactions featured a mutual agreement to end hostilities. The wish not to jeopardize the relationship is a prime reason given for ending the event. Another type of nonviolent outcome is compliance before violence; simply, one party gives into the demands of the other, and the event ends. Violence does not occur because it is not needed. Finally,

there are times when a conflict is forced to end. Called "forced endings" or "disrupted violence," an outside force acts to interfere with the continuation of the conflict interaction. Maybe the police are on their way, or someone interrupts the scene, causing parties to stop. These cases are more likely than any other to be restarted at a later date. In addition, Wilkinson found that certain reasons for disputes, such as robbery or self-defense, are more likely to be linked to a violent outcome.

Research findings on nonviolent event outcomes point to a leading role for certain situational attributes. Nonviolent events are likely to occur among individuals who have a social bond, such as friends or relatives. Third parties can thwart events, by serving as mediators, by presenting a deterrent show of force, or by directly intervening before violence occurs. An explanatory account by the offending party lessens the potential for violence, as does compliance with the original demand. Fears about negative consequences, such as criminal justice involvement or injuring the other party, can also lead to nonviolent outcomes. Finally, at least according to Wilkinson's work, disputes are more likely to end nonviolently if the conflict does not involve self-defense or robbery.

These findings have important implications for understanding drug business disputes and their aftermath. Specifically, what drives a nonviolent outcome to a drug business dispute? Is it the nature of the offense? The actions of the individuals involved? The operation of intervening factors? Some combination of these? It is possible that certain conflicts are inherently resistant to a nonviolent resolution, at least not without some external intervention. Thus, for a nonviolent result to emerge (e.g., via mutual agreement), some degree of flexibility is needed to allow the individual to make choices to forego aggression. If this is the case, what is the basis for that flexibility? What types of conflict conditions allow individuals to refrain from violence by their own efforts, and which ones make this option impossible?

One way to attempt to answer these questions is to deconstruct these conflicts, that is, to break them apart and explore their progression, step-by-step, from start to finish. Examining disputes in this way allows one to distinguish the effects of factors present at the start of a conflict with those that operate during the interaction. As a result, we can observe whether and how the configuration of elements in a dispute leads to the development of a particular dispute outcome, either violent or nonviolent.

Using this analytical approach, the present study analyzes dispute accounts provided by a sample of New York City drug sellers. These conflicts are analyzed as sequences of influence tactics performed by the participants. A concept drawn from impression management theory, an influence tactic is a behavior designed to get some party to act or to refrain from acting (Felson 1984). Behaviors typically displayed in conflict, such as requests for compliance, threats, and physical attacks, can be viewed as influence tactics, as they are often used to influence individuals to act.

For the sequence analysis, actions reported during drug business disputes were mapped in their order of occurrence. This allowed comparison of the nature and pattern of dispute actions for both violent and nonviolent conflicts. Along with the sequence analysis, there was a qualitative comparative examination of how two types of influence tactics, compliance and resolution efforts, operated within the broader context of both violent and nonviolent disputes.

The sequence analysis combined with the comparative examination was used to address the following research questions: What types of influence tactics are present in drug business disputes? What are the steps taken by the main dispute participants, from the initial confrontation to the final result? Does this process look different in violent versus nonviolent events? Finally, what additional contextual elements help distinguish between drug business disputes that are violent and those that are nonviolent?

Method

The data used in this study were drawn from a 1998 exploratory study on drug markets and violence funded by the National Consortium of Violence Research and conducted at the National Development and Research Institutes, Inc. Recruitment and interviewing of respondents began in February 1998 and was completed in May 1998. Participants were recruited via targeted sampling. Potential respondents were screened for then-active involvement in drug selling and for involvement in violence within the past year. Respondents were paid US$45.00 for their participation. A total of 28 male sellers were interviewed for the study; however, 1 person failed to complete the interview, leading to a final interview sample of 27 African American and Hispanic males. They were adults between the ages of 19 and 55 years, involved in drug and nondrug crime, the latter mainly small-time property offending (e.g., shoplifting). As drug sellers, these men mostly sold crack cocaine, and tended to be either employees connected to a drug organization (12 men), or freelancers who brought drugs on their own and sold them on an ad hoc basis (15 men).

Tape-recorded interviews were conducted with the men, using a semistructured questionnaire. The first part of the instrument queried the sellers about their families, jobs, involvement in drug selling, and involvement in other crimes. In the second portion of the questionnaire, a timeline was constructed using as anchors key dates of personal interest to the respondent (birthday, holidays). Using the timeline as a memory guide, each man was asked to recall any violent events experienced, as either a target or a perpetrator, during the 2 years prior to the interview. A 2-year time period was chosen to maximize the number of violent events obtained. Respondents were encouraged to recall up to 10 events occurring inside and outside the drug market setting. They were also asked whether they had encountered any near violent incidents, that is, conflict situations that could have become violent, but did not. The decision was made to let the respondent self-define what constituted a near violent event. If he asked for guidance, he was prompted with examples from the list of violent events that he provided. For instance, if he mentioned a territorial conflict that was violent, he was asked whether there was a similar situation that ended without violence.

Out of the initial list of events, a subsample of three events was chosen for deeper examination: one drug business violent, one nondrug business violent, and one nonviolent, which could be drug business or not. The sellers provided a narrative for each incident, containing information such as the reason for the dispute, the nature of the opponent, the presence of fellow combatants on each side, the existence and actions of third parties, and other key features. The objective here was to obtain a detailed, step-by-step picture of each dispute, from beginning to end. Fifty-three detailed descriptions of drug business conflicts were obtained.

It is possible that respondents could have described events that happened before or after the reference period (i.e., telescoping). The likelihood of this was reduced by using the timeline containing significant personal events to help target the respondent's memory of conflicts. This makes it more likely that events happened during the time frame discussed. To obtain the most accurate information possible, the respondents were questioned closely to assess whether their accounts had internal consistency. Contradictory or unclear responses were pointed out to and resolved with the respondent to obtain the most accurate recollection possible.

Admittedly, it was impossible to obtain independent verification of the conflicts that the men discussed. This is difficult to avoid problem in criminological research on topics like violence.

Because of the near impossibility of observing violent events or of obtaining accounts of violence from multiple sources, researchers are left to rely on self-reports of individuals to obtain information about this behavior. Furthermore, self-reports are the only way to uncover how individuals perceive their actions and those of others during conflict. An examination of those perceptions is an important component of the present study.

Sequence Analysis

Drug business disputes were analyzed by looking at the sequence of actions, or influence tactics that occurred during the event. A concept drawn from impression management theory, an influence tactic is a behavior designed to get some party to act or to refrain from acting (Felson 1984). They can range from relatively benign interactions (requests, minor complaints) to more serious engagement (threats, insults) to violence. The current analysis partially replicates research by Felson and Steadman (1983), which examined the role of influence tactics in robbery and assaults.

The original codes were altered for use in this study (the codes for influence tactics are in Table 22.1). This research addresses nonviolent dispute outcomes, an issue not explored in the 1983 article; thus, new codes were needed to capture actions occurring in those types of events. These new actions include attempts by the main protagonists

Table 22.1 Codes for Influence Tactics.

A—Influence attempt: actions in which one party tries to get another party to act or to "refrain" from acting (e.g., "you have to leave the [selling] spot"). Has to be made without insults or threats.

B—Noncompliance: "refusing to comply (with an influence attempt); includes excuses and justifications given for not complying." ("I don't have it right now"; "I didn't do it.")

C—Explicit identity attack: actions that cast the other party in a negative light. Examples: insults, rejections, accusations, complaints, and physical violations that involve no harm. For example, "you're trying to rob me"; pushing or grabbing.

D—Threat: verbal threats of harm, as well as some physical acts (such as brandishing a weapon). For example, "you'd better give me my money or else"; with guns, they should be pulled out, not pointed at a person.

E—Evasive action: "leaving the scene, fleeing, pleas for help, apologizing," focuses more on trying to leave an event.

F—Mediation: A third party acts to "reconcile the conflicted parties."

G—Instigation: A third party acts to incite the combatants (asking other people to help on one's behalf, giving a weapon to one of the combatants, urging others on); this is coded whether it occurs prior to the interaction or during it.

H—Physical attack: physical attacks that either lead to or have high potential for leading to physical harm.

I—Resolution effort: some action taken by combatants themselves to resolve the conflict (e.g., doing the count over).

J—Compliance: When one principal gives into the other's demand, whether violence has taken place or not. Also used when someone promises to give in, whether it happens or not (e.g., promises to pay money that later on do not materialize).

to resolve the conflict, as well as indicators of compliance in response to specific demands.

The sequences were created as follows. Each dispute narrative was divided into a series of steps (Step 1, Step 2, etc.), numbered from first to last (e.g., a dealer asking a customer for money owed would be Step 1). Each step was assigned two codes. The first code marked the type of influence tactic that occurred, whether it was an influence attempt, noncompliance, explicit identity attack, and so on. This code was assigned according to the most prominent interpretation of the action.[1] The second code identified the person(s) who performed the activity—see Table 22.2 for the five categories used.

The code "I" was assigned to the person who either initiated the complaint or began the interaction (initiator). The person who is asked to respond to the complaint was given a code of "R," for responder. Third-party participants were assigned a code indicating a connection to the initiator, the responder or to neither side. An influence tactic could be assigned to more than one person. For instance, if there was a fight involving a responder and his friends, it would be coded as "HRZ" (H = *physical attack,* R = *respondent makes the attack,* and Z = *respondent's friends joined in the attack*).

Each dispute event was coded from the first interaction between the parties involved up to the point where interaction ended. Note this allows an action type to be recorded more than once. When there was an argument, with no additional information on turn taking by the participants, the event was coded as a single exchange of identity attacks.

Table 22.2 Codes for Participants.

I—Initiator: This person(s) initiates the interaction, usually by expressing a complaint or making a request.

R—Responder: This person responds to the complaint, request, and so on.

Y—Initiator's friends: Third parties who are friends of the initiator.

Z—Responder's friends: Third parties who are friends of the responder.

OTH—Other third parties: These are third parties unconnected to either side (e.g., police or bystanders).

Most of the dispute interactions occurred in a single setting, and had a limited time span, mostly minutes or (rarely) hours. However, there were two disputes that spanned multiple days. In those instances, each separate interaction was coded, and then all interactions combined to create a grand sequence of the entire dispute.[2]

In the next step, the order of influence tactics was established separately for the violent and nonviolent disputes. This was done by calculating the mean position of each influence tactic among all sequences examined, and then ordering the tactics based on their mean values. For this process, all sequences, which varied in the total number of steps present, were standardized by assigning the value of "1" for the completed sequence. Next, each step was given a positional value as a proportion of 1, calculated based on the total number of steps in the sequence. For instance, if a sequence has five steps, Step 1 would receive a value of .200; Step 2, .400; Step 3, .600; Step 4, .800; and Step 5, 1.00. The mean positional value for each influence tactic was determined by grouping all steps featuring a particular influence tactic (e.g., all "threats" occurring among the violent disputes), summing the individual positional values and then dividing by the total. Finally, the influence tactics were listed in order of their mean positional values. The end result was two lists portraying the typical ordering of influence tactics used within violent and nonviolent events.

Once the sequences were derived, they were first used to determine whether violent and nonviolent disputes differed in the nature and order of influence tactics present. Then, after comparing the order of influence tactics, a qualitative comparative analysis was performed to examine the role of two influence tactics, compliance and resolution efforts, in both violent versus nonviolent disputes.

Findings

Out of the 53 drug business conflicts, 18 were nonviolent and 35 were violent. Disputes fell into the following categories, derived according to the primary theme of the conflict:

Territory. The disputes here involve situations where someone is either defending a drug-selling area, or seeking to redefine its boundaries. There were eight events in this category: In five, there was violence, whereas three ended nonviolently.

Debt. The second category of reasons involves conflicts over debts. Simply, one party owed either money or drugs and had not provided repayment. The money was owed chiefly to a dealer or supplier. Of the 16 events in this category, 12 had violent outcomes and 4 had nonviolent ones.

Theft and deceit. This group of concerned deceptive practices where one party attempts (or is perceived to be attempting) to acquire undeserved goods through stealth and or deceit. There are 14 events in this category, all ending in violence.

Insult. Here, the conflict was due to one party insulting the other, with the insult having some relationship to involvement in drugs. There are three events in this category, all ending in nonviolent outcomes.

Other. This category contains events with motives that are unique relative to the remainder of this sample (e.g., threats to snitch, disagreement over nature of drug partnership). Of the 12 events in this category, 8 ended nonviolently and 4 were violent.

Comparing Violent and Nonviolent Dispute Sequences

The average number of steps in the violent dispute sequences was about 5 (4.52).[3] This is slightly shorter than the number of steps present in non-violent events. The difference may be due to the presence of a few incidents where violence occurred rather quickly in the interaction. The number of steps present in violent events ranged from 1 (where violence was the initial step) to 8 (a few disputes that spanned a few days). The violent events exhibit the following general pattern[4]: They start with influence attempts, move through threats, noncompliance and explicit identity attacks, then onto evasive actions and finally physical attack. Described in another way, these conflicts start out with a request for something (e.g., money owed), and then move through verbal threats and rejections of the initial claim. These then lead to the use of insults, by either one or both sides, followed by attempts by either or both parties to leave

the interaction, with physical violence occurring at the end.

Within the general pattern, there is much variation in the sequences of these conflicts. For a few events, violence happens very early, usually after a brief exchange consisting of an influence attempt coupled with a rejection/noncompliance. In several instances, violence followed within one or two steps of rejection by the other side. An exchange of insults ended in violence in a few other cases. Finally, with the multiday disputes, the initial interaction ended, with violence occurring almost immediately upon the next meeting.

The average number of sequence steps for nonviolent disputes was 5.8. These disputes had as few as 2 and as many as 10 steps. The events with the longest steps included two disputes that were mediated close to the point of violence, and one where a respondent was asked by multiple parties to leave a selling area, which he did after some initial reluctance. The general pattern of influence tactics for nonviolent disputes (see Table 22.3) starts with influence attempts and identity attacks, move through noncompliance and threats, and end with compliance and resolution efforts. To summarize, the nonviolent disputes start out with a request. From there, the situation advances to verbal insults, rejection of claims, and threats. As the dispute moves into the end stages, tactics shift toward compliance (responding positively to the initial claim), and/or resolution efforts (where the conflict or the issues surrounding the conflict are resolved).

The order of influence tactics for nonviolent and violent disputes reflects the stage model of

Table 22.3 Order and Type of Influence Tactics in Dispute Events (N = 53).

Order of Influence Tactics	Violent Dispute Tactics (n = 35)	Nonviolent Dispute Tactics (n = 18)
1st	Influence attempts	Influence attempts
2nd	Threats	Explicit identity attacks
3rd	Noncompliance	Noncompliance
4th	Explicit identity attacks	Threats
5th	Evasive action	Compliance
6th	Physical attack	Resolution efforts

disputes as posited by Luckenbill (1977) and the order of influence tactics found by Felson and Steadman (1983). However, apart from the general patterns outlined above, both violent and nonviolent dispute sequences showed much diversity in the configuration of individual event sequences, indicating the varied processes by which disputes evolve. For both types of outcomes, however, compliance, resolution, and mediation all occur later in the dispute. This highlights an important point: The main distinction between violent and nonviolent events is the presence of successful avoidance tactics, consisting of either giving into the initial demand or resolving a problematic issue. This point is explored in greater depth below.

Making Room for Compliance

Compliance efforts are defined by the giving into a request or the promise to do so. A few nonviolent outcomes occurred when a request by one person is acceded to by another. Simply, if you do what people ask, there is no violence. For instance, there were territorial disputes where one dealer agreed to leave another's selling territory when asked to do so. In one case, Rick agrees to leave, even in the face of insults by the other party:

> Rick: I came to an agreement that he was there first and the customers all know him. And, you know, he's been there like 20 something years. And I just, I came out there. So I gave him respect. I told him so where you would like me to go, you know? Or where can I, where can I so that it doesn't bother you? And, you know, tell me on the other side, whatever. So I did it like that. That's all.

Mike is faced with repeated requests to leave, which he finally does.

> Mike: . . . Even though I had to step and go down the block, which was okay. He didn't put me completely out, but still got some of his customers, you know.

In another example, Bob challenges a person who lied about giving him money to tell the truth about it. Once the other party did so, this restored Bob's good name, thus lessening his desire to do violence. In fact, according to Bob, it was likely the only way to avoid violence. As he said, if the person had lied, he would have been hurt.

> Bob: Then again even if he woulda said that he did give it to me and I know he didn't, then I woulda whupped his ass and they would did whatever . . .

One example of promised compliance occurred during a debt dispute. Briefly, James confronted someone who owed him a couple hundred dollars for past credit given to purchase drugs. After some back and forth, the man promised to repay the money (although it is not clear that this will happen).

Agreeing to comply with a demand is linked to concerns about the risk of noncompliance. As Rick said,

> RICK: Because, um, I was in the wrong neighborhood at the wrong place at the wrong time. I mean, I was in his neighborhood. So I didn't have no wins.
> INTERVIEWER: You didn't have any . . .
> RICK: I didn't have no wins in this neighborhood.
> INTERVIEWER: Wins?
> RICK: 'Cause, you know, I couldn't win in this neighborhood. 'Cause he has the whole block. He has like 20 guys working for him. And they were all out there. So I, I figured the best way to handle this is without, just verbally. Just talking.

Being outnumbered (and out-powered) made it a good idea for him to leave the selling spot. These situations are also less highly charged, so that compliance, or the promise to do so, is easily given and accepted. However, disputes may vary in the level of flexibility available for the offender to respond with an ameliorative gesture. Conflicts that are highly serious or which have certain types of constraints make compliance difficult. This can set the stage for violence.

This dynamic is present for some of the disputes that ended in violence. Among these were a few examples of attempts at compliance, or actions that could potentially be interpreted in that manner. Lucky approaches an individual who owes him money and promises to repay it. When Lucky goes to collect the money, the person does not have it, and Lucky breaks his arm in response. This incident starkly demonstrates the risks of noncompliance. There are other, similar violent events where the promise to comply is more likely an evasive tactic, designed to put off a presumed inevitable attack. In this example, a man who owes money to a group of dealers insisted that he had to wait for the bank to deposit the money later on that day. Fred talks about his frustration that this tactic caused:

> *Fred:* I guess the things that he was saying, you know, when the addict was lying and the guy, you know that had been calling his bank account and he was you know, talking to him and making sense and the addict was constantly still lying, yeah, it was making my temper change, you know, I was getting more upset. And I was thinking about picking up something and beating him with it. You know, 'cause I was just getting more upset because the addict was lying, you know, I was like, well, "this is what got you in this situation now, you lying, you playing games and you still doing it, what's wrong with you," this is what I'm thinking in my mind. Yeah, so I was getting more upset.

How do these disputes differ from those where violence did not occur? Simply, promises to comply that are not backed by behavior or that are undermined by additional facts are disbelieved and rejected. This rejection allows the offended party to use violence, as either an additional influence tactic or as payback; that is, punishment.

Promised compliance to avoid punishment is especially likely when the dispute centers on suspicions of theft or snitching. In one case, Joe was confronted by a dealer whose money he stole. During the confrontation, he said that he would pay the man back. The dealer disregarded this and went on to stab Joe. In another event, a man who originally said he would snitch to the police about a group of rival dealers tries to take it back, but is beaten up anyway:

> JAMES KIRK: And when we pulled him in, like, one of them threatened him. I think it was Cabeza, one of them threatened him, like, to kill him, if he would snitch.
> INTERVIEWER: And what did he say?

JAMES KIRK: Who?
INTERVIEWER: The snitch?
JAMES KIRK: The snitch? He said he wasn't gonna snitch, but you can't trust that. You can't trust nobody like that, nobody.

In these two instances, the gravity of the offense (theft, snitching) combined with the high level of emotion in the situation militated against acceptance of these offers at compliance. As a result, an attack occurs, one which is likely as much about punishing an offender as it is about getting money (protection) restored. The point is this: If I cannot get relief, I can at least get payback. In this way, what might be deemed false compliance has the same effect as noncompliance, which, as we have seen, can be linked to violence.

Resolution Efforts

Resolution efforts refers to situations where individuals take active steps to resolve a disagreement that has escalated, or otherwise act to restore positive relations between those in conflict. Resolution efforts mostly occur in incidents where there are misunderstandings or insults, although in one instance the original conflict was over a physical attack.

In some cases, the parties in conflict themselves took steps to reduce the chances that the dispute would evolve into something more severe. In one example, an insult between subordinates was deemed not important enough for a dealer to jeopardize his relationship with a good friend, a rival dealer.

> *Malik:* It was just gonna be a talk, it was a lot of shit talking 'cause we all grew up together and we know each other, so it's like, you can't tell me nothin', I can't tell you nothin', but down the line we squashed it.

In another dispute, an argument that threatened to get out of hand ended when one party said he was being misunderstood, and the other individual, his friend, decided to accept the account.

> *John Brown:* Then he started saying "it's not nothing about that, it's not nothing about that." So what you saying is, fuck it, forget you ah, forget, forget. We both stress—let's go get a bag of smoke. Alright, come on.

In other instances, a resolution effort can simply be solving the issue at the heart of a conflict. A dispute over the amount of crack proceeds was resolved by simply recounting. Although the challenged dealer was still angry, he had no reason to act on it as the main issue had been settled.

In two cases, resolution efforts are preceded by mediation; that is, there was third-party intervention into an escalating conflict. In each situation, the third parties helped individuals to redefine the situation as to make violence unnecessary or undesirable. Mediation worked in part because the participants were open to the reinterpretation. In one instance, the reminder of close relationships among friends of the main combatants helped the respondent to establish empathy with his opponent.

Bob: Yeah, they . . . yeah they told me . . . I don't know what you thinkin' about but don't, don't do nothin' to him man 'cause his family, he loved his family and his mother you know what I'm sayin'? They like, you know, somethin' happen to him they know we friends. They wouldn't understand it, so the best thing for me to do is just forget about it.

In Bob's newfound understanding, he saw violence as an act to be avoided.

In the other instance, it appears that mediation worked due to an underlying unwillingness to engage in violence. Here, Fred and his friends were asked to fight on behalf of someone who was an addict, and also had a negative reputation, in this case for disrupting selling spots.

Fred: And also the brother that got jumped is a crack addict. He's also an addict. Interviewer: And do you think that had anything to do with this situation?

Fred: Maybe it did, because maybe he was standing around there harassing customers, or begging, or whatever, they don't know, you know, as far as why did they jump him, you know what I mean.

This, combined with the disputed ownership of the selling spot, perhaps weakened the desire to engage in violence. Thus, the impulse to commit or avoid violence is affected by the specific issues of the dispute. Simply put, if the stakes are not important, the need to fight lessens.

Among the events that ended violently, there were few attempts at mediation prior to physical attack. In the one case, mediation efforts were disregarded by the main combatant, who was highly angered at the time of the incident:

MALIK: No, my people was trying to break it up.
INTERVIEWER: Okay, and what types of things were they saying?
MALIK: You don't need this, you just got home, yo, let it, let it ride, you know how to take care of the business, just leave it alone.
INTERVIEWER: And what were, did that influence you in any way?
MALIK: No, just made me madder.
INTERVIEWER: What did you think about that, why did that make you madder?
MALIK: They were trying to make me don't do something I wanted to do right then and there at that time.
(The respondent, Malik, earlier admitted to wanting to challenge his opponent.)
MALIK: They say he was a violent person, so at that time, been going to him for a long time, I was making a reputation for myself.
INTERVIEWER: For what?
MALIK: Drug game, I was moving up in the drug games, I was a dealer, I was a . . . how you say, a manager, like somewhat enforcer, so I was just moving up, making a name for myself on the streets in the drug game, so they told me about him. I knew him from school, but I couldn't see him as that type of person, so I just challenged him, like gonna take it to him, see how tough he is. I was known for shooting my gun, and hitting and just taking care of my business, so I like . . . 'cause I knew I was gonna take him, too, so I wanted to take his reputation.

This reinforces the point that he was on a path, at the start of the interaction, to engage in violence whatever else happened. This demonstrates that for some disputes, the impulse to do violence can override earnest attempts at de-escalation.

This example brings into sharp relief the point that the ability to avoid violence via resolution efforts depends partly on the inclinations of the participants involved. Social relationships have an important influence on the desire to use violence. The hesitation by two people to disrupt a valued relationship leads them to grab onto ways of resolving any disagreements they may have. Alternately, a positive relationship can make mediation attempts more successful. Apart from any social connections, resolution attempts also work when the desirability for violence is not high in the first place. In these circumstances, individuals are more easily dissuaded from violence. Both tendencies are likely to be stronger where the seriousness of the original offense is low. However, once seriousness exceeds a certain level, resolution efforts may not work to prevent violence.

Discussion

An analysis examining drug business disputes as sequences of influence tactics produced findings on the progression of conflict, and it can vary for events of different outcomes. Both violent and nonviolent drug business disputes show patterns similar to Luckenbill's stage model. Generally, these events show a progression of influence tactics, starting from minor ones (influence attempts/requests) and, based on the responses to the initial claim, proceeding to those of increased intensity (threats). The event concludes with either violence or some nonviolent alternative. However, the main difference between the two event outcomes is the presence and operation of violence-avoiding tactics, such as compliance and resolution efforts. The specific elements of this distinction are revealed in a comparative examination of compliance and resolution efforts occurring within nonviolent and violent disputes. Compliance associated with nonviolent outcomes is offered when there is a risk of continued noncompliance, and is accepted when there is enough flexibility for it to be seen as credible. Repeated or serious instances of inadequate or false compliance make it difficult for the offended party to accept last-ditch attempts at placation, and thus are linked to violence. Resolution efforts work when parties have a vested interest in not fighting, generally due to a valued social relationship. Resolution can also occur when mediation by trusted others leads participants to reinterpret an event so that violence becomes unnecessary, or when the main problem at the heart of the dispute is solved. Thus, looking at the progression of events helps to show that the overall context of a dispute influences whether certain actions occur, and how, as a result, particular outcomes emerge.

Limitations

The conflicts discussed here reflect the experiences of a small number of drug sellers from an urban setting. The sellers themselves were not chosen at random but were targeted based on their selling activity and involvement in violence. Furthermore, the conflicts that they described, and the ones that were analyzed in this study, were not a random sample of their dispute experiences. Thus, it would be hazardous to generalize these findings to other drug business disputes. Furthermore, drug sellers who operate in different locations (suburban or rural areas, for instance) or situational contexts (where guns are less prevalent) may experience different types of events than those provided by the men in this sample. Thus, their disputes could be driven by different factors from those found in this study.

Another limitation is the use of an all-male sample. The gendered nature of drug selling is well established (Dunlap, Johnson, and Manwar 1994; Fagan 1994; Hutton 2005; Maher and Hudson 2007; Sommers, Baskin, and Fagan 1996). Thus, gender cannot be discounted as an important element of drug business disputes. Specifically, expressions of masculinity specific to inner-city environments (Mullins 2006; Wilkinson 2003) may have played a role in the type and nature of the influence tactics used by the men in this study. Men who sell drugs in non-inner-city settings may experience pressures to display different types of masculine images. Accordingly, the processes by which their business disputes unfold and conclude may differ from those seen here. The same may be said for female drug sellers. Given the precarious position of women in drug environments (Hutton 2005), a sequence examination of their disputes may reveal different configurations of influence tactics (in particular, compliance and resolution efforts).

Research Implications

These findings have empirical and theoretical implications for research on violent situations in general, and situations in drug business environments in particular. Regarding empirical implications, the study results provide distinctive contributions to the larger research literature on drug selling and violence. Few studies have focused on assaults in research on drug selling and violence. Previous studies have largely focused on homicide or robbery (Jacobs 2000; Riley 1998). The violent events in this sample consisted almost exclusively of assaults. In addition, the sample includes drug conflicts with nonviolent outcomes, a little-studied research topic. Attention to processes underlying drug business assaults (and avoided assaults) is beneficial, as it provides a picture of behavior that is more common than is robbery or homicide. Thus, it better reflects the garden-variety experience of violence in drug selling. This is an important corrective to the general tendency in criminology to focus on activity that is at the serious end of the crime spectrum.

On a theoretical note, the findings echo those from past research on situations and violence. Elements of the situation, such as the reasons for conflict, the actions taken by the parties during the conflict, and the involvement of third parties all play an important role in leading a dispute toward or away from a violent end. Clearly, a comprehensive examination of violence (and its absence) requires attention not only to the dispositions of persons but also to the settings and contexts within which they act.

This work fits into a small but growing body of research that focuses on drug business violence as disputes (see Jacques and Wright 2008, 2011, and Jacques 2010, for work in a similar vein). Violence in drug-selling environments can be viewed as one pole in a continuum of social control efforts, with nonviolent outcomes sitting at the opposite end. Exploring conflicts and the myriad ways they can be resolved without violence fits with an emerging effort to fully use Black's (1998) theory of social control to explain aspects of drug market activity (e.g., Jacques 2010; Jacques and Wright 2008). For example, Black's hypothesis on the influence of relational distance on violence is supported by the findings of this study. A violent end to a drug dispute was less likely when the two parties were friends on otherwise good terms. Alternatively, when the parties lacked a social bond, violence was more often the result. Dispute resolution was also linked to the social location of third parties, another important idea from Black. Echoing findings of Phillips and Cooney (2005), successful third-party mediation in this sample is associated with crosscutting ties, where the third parties were linked to both sides. Partisan third parties, those linked to one side of the dispute, was a strong feature of the violent conflicts. Finally, the violent attacks linked to failure to compliance may be viewed as a form of discipline (Black 1998), although this idea requires more development.

The sample examined in this study is small, and does not permit detailed examination of the full range of conflict resolution strategies suggested by Black's model. For instance, there is evidence that toleration (one do-nothing approach) is a common option that dealers use when faced with conflict. Topalli et al. (2002) have found that victims of robbery in drug settings decide to forgo violent vengeance, either for fear of physical harm or because it would be, as one put it, "bad for business" (348). Jacques and Wright (2011) have explored the business-related consequences of specific types of dispute resolution in greater depth. They theorize that the type of strategy chosen to address conflict affects the level of drug market activity. Violent retaliation (in the form of physical attack) can have costs in terms of reduced business (scaring away customers, for instance); negotiation, alternately, can preserve business (after a short-term falloff) by maintaining ties between the disputing parties. Other nonviolent strategies, avoidance and toleration, can dampen or heighten market activity, respectively. Future work should continue examination of the impact of these informal controls, in conjunction with other situational elements, on how drug sellers manage their business activities and the resulting consequences of those efforts.

Policy Implications

The policy implications of these findings are a little more complicated. One task of this research was to look at contextual factors in conflicts. How can this knowledge be helpful in policy making? One way would be to direct attention to factors that can be usefully addressed in reducing violence in drug market settings. It can also expand thinking about what should be the appropriate target of crime prevention. For instance, it may be worthwhile for law enforcement to attend to crimes occurring to drug sellers that, left unaddressed, can generate violence as retaliation. This follows the suggestions made by Topalli et al. (2002) in their work on dealers and robbery. They assert that the failure to see criminals as crime victims sets up the potential for violent retaliation by pushing victims to engage in self-help. One could argue that if there were legal options to handle victimization, this would provide less of a reason to resolve the problem on the street. Of course, this is a more potent argument when the issue is violent crimes, such as robbery or rape, which have the potential for more serious consequences. However, it must be noted that even nonviolent offenses (e.g., theft) have the potential to lead to violent retaliation.

The study findings can be useful in other criminal justice-based prevention efforts. For instance, law enforcement can take actions to manipulate the environment to avoid some types of intractable conflict. As mentioned above, there are strong links between forms of drug-selling organizations and violence. Following suggestions made by Curtis and Wendel (2007), antidrug efforts by police can be geared toward shifting the configuration of drug markets from forms linked to conflict (such as street-based selling) to those that are comparably peaceful (such as delivery services). Such a shift may decrease the number and type of disputes, thus reducing the level of violence. This is not an unrealistic idea. Recent work (Mazarolle, Soole, and Rombouts 2006; Rengert, Ratcliffe, and Chakravorty 2006) has shown that problem-oriented policing strategies are more effective than traditional arrest-based enforcement for addressing drug markets and associated crime. Thus, it seems reasonable to assume that such efforts may be able to reduce dispute-related violence associated with those environments. At the very least, the findings from this study help to make drug business disputes more comprehensible by reinforcing two points: They follow predictable patterns, and nonviolent outcomes are not an entirely unexpected result.

Notes

1. This was done for simplicity. Acts can obviously have multiple goals (e.g., hitting someone can also be viewed as an attack on a person's identity), but it seemed prudent to choose the one that was most salient given the overall context of the incident.

2. For example, take an event where two people got into an argument, only to have it broken up by a mediator, with the two people departing the scene. The first interaction, say, a request for money owed, would be coded as "Step 1, influence attempt, initiator (AI)." If the response was a denial of having money, the code would be "Step 2, noncompliance, by the responder (BR)." An exchange of insults would be coded as "Step 3, identity attack by the initiator (CI)" and "Step 4, identity attack by the responder (CI)." If at this point, a bystander intervened in the argument, it would be coded as "Step 5, bystander mediation (FOTH)." If after the intervention, the responder walked away, this would be coded as the "Step 6, departure by the responder (ER)."

3. Because a key focus is on factors affecting whether a first blow is drawn, for the violent disputes, the current discussion addresses only those steps occurring up to the point of the first attack. For the nonviolent disputes, all steps until the end of the interaction were included. This means that for some of the violent events, influence tactics were coded, but not used directly in the analyses described below. This also creates a bit of an imbalance, as in some situations, it was impossible to say that that the dispute itself truly ended in nonviolence. However, this does not detract from the primary objective, which is to examine whether the interaction proceeded and concluded without violence occurring, and identify the factors contributing to the variation in outcome.

4. The general sequences were obtained by narrowing the focus to those cases where a tactic occurred for more than one event.

References

Anderson, E. 1999. *The Code of the Streets*. Chicago, IL: University of Chicago Press.

Athens, L. 1997. *Violent Criminal Acts and Actors Revisited*. Urbana: University of Illinois Press.

Birkbeck, C. and G. LaFree. 1993. "The Situational Analysis of Crime and Deviance." *Annual Review of Sociology* 19: 113–137.

Black, D. 1998. *The Social Structure of Right and Wrong*, rev. ed. San Diego, CA: Academic Press.

Blumstein, A. 1995. "Youth Violence, Guns, and the Illicit-Drug Industry." *Journal of Criminal Law and Criminology* 86: 10–36.

Blumstein, A. and J. Wallman. 2006. *The Crime Drop in America*. New York, NY: Cambridge University Press.

Bourgois, P. 1995. *In Search of Respect*. Cambridge, UK: Cambridge University Press.

Chaiken, J. and M. Chaiken. 1982. *Varieties of Criminal Behavior*. Santa Monica, CA: Rand.

Coomber, R. and L. Maher. 2006. "Street-Level Drug Market Activity in Sydney's Primary Heroin Markets: Organization, Adulteration Practices, Pricing, Marketing and Violence." *Journal of Drug Issues* 36: 719–754.

Curtis, R. and T. Wendel. 2007. " 'You're Always Training the Dog': Strategic Interventions to Reconfigure Drug Markets." *Journal of Drug Issues* 37: 867–892.

Cussen, M. and W. Block. 2000. "Legalize Drugs Now! An Analysis of the Benefits of Legalized Drugs." *American Journal of Economics and Sociology* 59: 525–536.

Dunlap, E., B. D. Johnson, and A. Manwar. 1994. "A Successful Female Crack Dealer: Case Study of a Deviant Career." *Deviant Behavior* 15: 1–25.

Fagan, J. 1994. "Women and Drugs Revisited: Female Participation in the Cocaine Economy." *Journal of Drug Issues* 24: 179–225.

Fagan, J. and K. Chin. 1990. "Violence as Regulation and Social Control in the Distribution of Crack." In *Drugs and Violence: Causes, Correlates, and Consequences*, vol. 103, edited by M. de la Rosa and E. Y. Lambert, 8–43. Rockville, MD: National Institute on Drug Abuse.

Felson, R. B. 1982. "Impression Management and the Escalation of Aggression and Violence." *Social Psychology Quarterly* 45: 245–254.

Felson, R. B. 1984. "Patterns of Aggressive Social Interaction." In *Social Psychology of Aggression: from Individual Behavior to Social Interaction*, edited by A. Mummendey, 107–126. Berlin Heidelberg, Germany: Springer-Verlag.

Felson, R. B. and H. S. Steadman. 1983. "Situations and Processes Leading to Criminal Violence." *Criminology* 21: 59–74.

Goldstein, P. J. 1985. "The Drugs/Violence Nexus: A Tripartite Conceptual Framework." *Journal of Drug Issues* 15: 493–506.

Goldstein, P. J. 1989. "Crack and Homicide in New York City, 1988: A Conceptually Based Event Analysis." *Contemporary Drug Problems* 16: 651–687.

Hutton, F. 2005. "Risky Business: Gender, Drug Dealing and Risk." *Addiction Research & Theory* 13: 545–554.

Jacobs, B. A. 2000. *Robbing Drug Dealers: Violence Beyond the Law*. New York, NY: Aldine de Gruyter.

Jacques, S. 2010. "The Necessary Conditions for Retaliation: Toward a Theory of Non-violent and Violent Forms in Drug Markets." *Justice Quarterly* 27: 186–205.

Jacques, S. and R. Wright. 2008. "The Relevance of Peace to Studies of Drug Market Violence." *Criminology* 46: 221–253.

Jacques, S. and R. Wright. 2011. "Informal Control and Illicit Drug Trade." *Criminology* 49: 729–765.

Johnson, B. D., A. Golub, and E. Dunlap. 2000. "The Rise and Decline of Hard Drugs, Drug Markets, and Violence in Inner-City New York." In *The Crime Drop in America*, edited by A. Blumstein and J. Wallman, 145–200. New York, NY: Cambridge University Press.

Korf, D. J., S. Brochu, A. Benschop, L. D. Harrison, and P. G. Erickson. 2008. "Teen Drug Sellers: An International Study of Segregated Drug Markets and Related Violence." *Contemporary Drug Problems* 35: 153–176.

Kruttschnitt, C. 1994. "Gender Differences in Violence." In *Understanding and Preventing Violence*, vol. 3., Social Influences, edited by A. J. Reiss Jr. and J. A. Roth, 293–370. Washington, DC: National Academy Press.

Kuhns, J. B. 2005. "The Dynamic Nature of the Drug Use/Serious Violence Relationship: A Multi-Causal Approach." *Violence and Victims* 20: 433–454.

Luckenbill, D. F. 1977. "Criminal Homicide as Situated Transaction." *Social Problems* 25: 176–186.

Luckenbill, D. F. and D. P. Doyle. 1989. "Subcultural Position and Violence: Developing a Cultural Explanation." *Criminology* 27: 419–436.

Maher, L. and S. L. Hudson. 2007. "Women in the Drug Economy: A Metasynthesis of the Qualitative Literature." *Journal of Drug Issues* 37: 805–826.

Mazarolle, L., D. W. Soole, and S. Rombouts. 2006. "Street-Level Drug Enforcement: A Meta-Analytical Review." *Journal of Experimental Criminology* 2: 409–435.

Megargee, E. I. 1982. "Psychological Determinants and Correlates of Violence." In *Violent Crime, Violent Criminals*, edited by N. A. Weiner and M. E. Wolfgang, 81–170). Beverley Hills, CA: SAGE.

Mullins, C. W. 2006. *Holding Your Square: Masculinities, Street Life & Violence*. Portland, OR: Willan.

Oliver, W. 1994. *The Violent Social World of Black Men*. Boston, MA: Lexington Books.

Ousey, G. C. and M. R. Lee. 2007. "Homicide Trends and Illicit Drug Markets: Exploring Differences across Time. *Justice Quarterly* 24: 48–79.

Phillips, S. 2003. "The Social Structure of Vengeance: A Test of Black's Model." *Criminology* 41: 673–708.

Phillips, S. and M. Cooney. 2005. "Aiding Peace and Abetting Violence: Third Parties and the Management of Conflict." *American Sociological Review* 70: 334–354.

Rengert, G. F., J. H. Ratcliffe, and S. Chakravorty. 2006. *Policing Drug Markets: Geographic Approaches to Crime Reduction*. Monsey, NY: Criminal Justice Press.

Reuter, P. 2009. "Systemic Violence in Drug Markets." *Crime, Law and Social Change* 52: 275–284.

Riley, K. J. 1998. "Homicide and Drugs: A Tale of Six Cities." *Homicide Studies* 2: 176–205.

Sampson, R. J. 1987. "Urban Black Violence: The Effect of Male Joblessness and Family Disruption." *American Journal of Sociology* 93: 348–382.

Sampson, R. J. and J. L. Lauritsen. 1994. "Violent Victimization and Offending: Individual, Situational and Community-Level Risk Factors." In *Understanding and Preventing Violence*, vol. 3, Social Influences, edited by A. J. Reiss Jr. and J. A. Roth, 1–114. Washington, DC: National Academy Press.

Sommers, I., D. Baskin, and J. Fagan. 1996. "The Structural Relationship Between Drug Use, Drug Dealing, and Other Income Support Activities Among Women Drug Sellers." *Journal of Drug Issues* 26: 975–1006.

Taylor, B. and H. H. Brownstein. 2003. "Toward the Operationalization of Drug Market Stability: An Illustration Using Arrestee Data from Crack Cocaine Markets in Four Urban Communities." *Journal of Drug Issues* 33: 73–98.

Toch, H. 1969. *Violent Men: An Inquiry into the Psychology of Violence*. Chicago, IL: Aldine.

Topalli, V., R. Wright, and R. Fornango. 2002. "Drug Dealers, Robbery and Retaliation: Vulnerability, Deterrence and the Contagion of Violence." *British Journal of Criminology* 42: 337–351.

White, H. R. and D. M. Gorman. 2000. "Dynamics of the Drug-Crime Relationship." In *The Nature of Crime: Continuity and Change*, vol. 1 of *Criminal Justice 2000*, edited by G. LaFree, 152–218. Washington, DC: United States Department of Justice.

Widom, C. S. 1989. "The Intergenerational Transmission of Violence." In *Pathways to Criminal Violence*, edited by N. A. Weiner and M. E. Wolfgang, 137–201. Newbury Park, CA: SAGE.

Wilkinson, D. L. 2003. *Guns, Violence, and Identity Among African American and Latino Youth*. New York, NY: LFB Scholarly Publishing.

Zimring, F. E. and G. Hawkins. 1997. *Crime Is Not the Problem: Lethal Violence in America*. New York, NY: Oxford.

For Discussion

1. Consider the difficulties in recruiting active drug sellers for a research project. What kinds of strategies would help or hinder recruitment?

2. Discuss the role of third parties in terms of their contribution to violent and nonviolent outcomes in drug disputes.

Social Control and Surveillance

"Social control" refers to a range of mechanisms that attempt to regulate behavior by imposing sanctions for persons who violate dominant social and legal norms. Our behaviors are influenced greatly by *informal social control*, which includes an array of interpersonal reactions by significant others who show disapproval when we violate social norms. Informal social control occurs in public spaces, workplaces, families, neighborhoods, and other social networks, including peer groups. It can take multiple forms, including verbal or nonverbal signs of disapproval, shaming, coercion, ostracism, and exclusion. *Formal social control* is generally influenced by the power elite, codified into laws or regulations and practiced by social institutions, including criminal justice, social welfare, and educational and health systems. Michel Foucault (1977) introduced the concept of *carceral society*, where beginning in the late 1700s,

all kinds of conditions, statuses, and behaviors (e.g., insanity, childhood, employment, criminality, disabilities, poverty) that departed from dominant social norms came under the control of the state and its agents.

Power is a key theoretical concept of social control. In particular, agents of formal social control (e.g., police, gatekeepers of homeless shelters, welfare investigators, immigration officials) have been allocated power to apply rules or laws that aim to regulate and monitor individuals whose behaviors are perceived as threatening to the social order. Surveillance is a tool of social control that aims to monitor people and their behaviors. Although technological advances have expanded the reach of surveillance into our daily lives, formal social control systems often use surveillance to focus on behaviors among people who lack power, that is, individuals who are marginalized or disenfranchised.

For example, John Gilliom (2001) argues that extensive surveillance of welfare recipients represents the main technique by which power elites exercise political domination over the poor. Monahan (2009, 291) describes that monitoring by the State is conducted because welfare recipients are assumed to be deviant and thus require "paternalistic supervision" by authorities.

In his book, *Visions of Social Control*, Stanley Cohen (1985) discussed the expansion of state-initiated social control in post-industrial societies. In the nineteenth and early twentieth centuries, formal social control strategies were characterized by exclusion, that is, the separation of the deviant class from mainstream society. Later, reform movements sought more community-based sanctions (e.g., regular and intensive probation with and without electronic monitoring), strategies that Cohen referred to as inclusionary practices. This change had unintended consequences, namely that the State expanded its reach by widening the net. In other words, the traditional social control apparatus (e.g., prison industry) remained, but it was supplemented by community-based sanctions.

Surveillance is used regularly to monitor the "criminal class." Hence, criminal records and DNA profiles are accessible to the global law enforcement community and thousands of people in various countries are controlled through electronic monitoring (most recently via Global Positioning Satellite). Offender management systems have been developed in the federal and state prison systems and camera surveillance has emerged as a primary tool for crime prevention.

Drug testing is yet another surveillance tool that is used to monitor the "criminal class." It is commonly used to identify recent use of particular drugs among parolees, probationers, jail detainees, and prisoners. The reach of this social control mechanism extends to several other populations, including the US military, professional and collegiate athletes in the United States, federal employees, and other workers. In the United States, an estimated 30–40 million job applicants and employees were tested for drugs in 2007 (Walsh 2008). Few people object to drug testing of employees who work in occupations where public safety is a critical aspect of their jobs, for example, airline pilots and other transport workers. However, drug testing in other job sectors is a contentious issue.

Drug testing has been widely implemented against people who lack power and privilege, for example, staff employees at universities (but not faculty), pregnant women from minority backgrounds, and people who are homeless and seek access to shelters. It is used extensively in drug treatment settings. And despite claims that drug testing can be used to help individuals who experience drug problems, the results are very often used as tools of exclusion from shelters, treatment facilities, community-based punishment schemes, and work environments. The irony is that drug testing cannot reveal the extent or nature of drug problems. Rather, drug testing is primarily conducted via urinalysis, which can only detect very recent use of particular substances. Urinalysis is prone to different kinds of errors and these errors have the potential to favor some individuals and harm others (false negatives and false positives). The results also require people to record the information and make decisions based on test results. Those processes are also subject to error. In 2013, the policy of drug testing thousands of probationers in Harris County, Texas (Houston area), was suspended after judges learned that the method of recording drug test results was prone to human error. In some cases, a technician provided the wrong identification numbers that incorrectly altered the drug screening results from negative to positive. Some probationers who were affected by the errors experienced further loss of liberties. In Massachusetts, a chemist in a state laboratory was accused of falsifying and tampering with evidence that included thousands of drug test results. Subsequently, state prosecutors dismissed hundreds of cases that relied on the tainted evidence. By 2013, over 300 people were released from prison because their convictions were based on the drug test evidence produced by the state lab. Compensation to the victims is expected to cost the State $30 million.

Social control is a fundamental part of society. We cannot eliminate it and clearly, various aspects of social control are important for social order. However, social control is fueled by power imbalances whereby those in positions of power can identify, track, control, and punish behaviour. The concept of power also features in stigma theory, because stigma derives from unequal power relations. Stigma can be practiced by individuals, and within peer groups, communities, and social institutions. The articles in this section offer material for debate over drug testing, highlight contradictory practices in schools, and discuss how social control has the potential to stigmatize and marginalize particular groups.

References

Cohen, S. 1985. *Visions of Social Control: Crime, Punishment and Classification.* Cambridge: Polity Press.

Foucault, M. 1977. *Discipline and Punish: The Birth of the Prison,* translated by Alan Sheridan. London: Penguin Books.

Gilliom, J. 2001. *Overseers of the Poor: Surveillance, Resistance, and the Limits of Privacy.* Chicago: University of Chicago Press.

Monahan, T. 2009. "Dreams of Control at a Distance: Gender, Surveillance, and Social Control." *Cultural Studies ↔ Critical Methodologies* 9: 286–305.

Walsh, J. M. 2008. "New Technology and New Initiatives in US Workplace Testing." *Forensic Science International* 174: 120–124.

23

Drug Testing Promotes Workplace Safety

MELISSA DITHOMAS

In this article, Melissa DiThomas argues that workplace drug testing has several benefits for organizations, including reductions in employee turnover and absenteeism as well as increases in worker productivity. She uses survey data collected from employers to support her arguments. DiThomas notes that employers often test for five kinds of psychoactive substances, but she suggests that some organizations might move to a nine-panel screen.

An effective drug testing program promotes a safe, productive workplace in addition to a multitude of other benefits, according to a recent industry poll. This article explores the many advantages of employee drug testing, and illustrates how a program's effectiveness is directly impacted by quickly evolving industry trends and federal testing legislation.

How Effective Is Drug Testing?

Employment drug testing is a powerful risk tool that provides far-reaching organizational benefits. In addition to promoting a safer, more productive workplace, it can help decrease employee turnover and absenteeism, reduce employer risk and lower workers' compensation incidence rates, according to Drug Testing Efficacy 2011, a recent poll conducted by the Society for Human Resource Management (SHRM) and the Drug and Alcohol Testing Industry Association (DATIA). The poll, one of the most comprehensive and current surveys regarding drug testing available today, questioned employers ranging from 500 to 2,500 employees, most of which were publicly owned for-profit organizations. The following key points were discovered:

- What percentage of organizations conducted pre-employment drug testing in 2011? More than one-half of organizations (57 percent) indicated they conduct drug testing on *all job candidates*. More than one-quarter (29 percent) of the organizations do not have a pre-employment drug testing program.
- **Is there a connection between drug testing programs and absenteeism?** Yes. In organizations with high employee absenteeism rates (more than 15 percent), the implementation of a drug testing program appears to have an impact. Nine percent of organizations reported high absenteeism rates (>15 percent) prior to a drug testing program, whereas only 4 percent of organizations reported high absenteeism rates after the implementation of a drug testing program, a decrease of approximately 50 percent.
- **Are workers' compensation incidence rates affected by drug testing programs?** Yes. In

Reprinted from Melissa DiThomas, 2012, "Drug Testing Promotes Workplace Safety." In *Occupational Health and Safety*, October 1.

organizations with high workers' compensation incidence rates (>6 percent), the implementation of a drug testing program appears to have an impact. Fourteen percent of organizations reported high workers' compensation incidence rates prior to a drug testing program, whereas only 6 percent of organizations reported similar rates of workers' compensation after the implementation of a drug testing program, a decrease of approximately 50 percent.

- **Do drug testing programs improve employee productivity rates?** Nearly one-fifth (19 percent) of organizations experienced an increase in productivity after the implementation of a drug testing program.
- How much of an impact do drug testing programs have on employee turnover rates? Sixteen percent of organizations saw a decrease in employee turnover rates after the implementation of drug testing programs.
- **Do multinational organizations apply similar drug testing protocols/policies in the United States and globally?** Nearly three-quarters (72 percent) of organizations with multinational operations indicated that all, almost all or some of the same protocols/policies are applied while conducting drug tests outside the United States.

Maintain Program Efficacy by Understanding Trends and Federal Programs

Just as there are many types of drug testing programs, ranging from those regulated by the U.S. Department of Transportation (DOT) to privately developed and managed programs, there are also many testing options available today. However, in order to create the most appropriate and effective testing program, you must first understand what's happening in the industry.

The drug testing industry was born 30 years ago, after the launch of federal drug testing requirements in the 1980s. A lot has changed in 30 years. The types of drugs being abused are quickly evolving and so are the abusers.

- While marijuana is still the number one most abused drug globally, prescription drugs

have moved into second place, overshadowing cocaine. Technology has played a big role in these changes. For example, the street distributor has morphed into the Internet distributor, making it easier than ever to access prescription medication without ever visiting a doctor.

- The use of pill mills, which are clinics, doctors or pharmacies that are prescribing large amounts of prescription medication for non-medical use, are also becoming prominent in the U.S., prompting abusers to travel across state lines to access these mills.

In lock-step with these trends, new federal legislation and program guidelines are also appearing. For example, in addition to standard illicit drugs, prescription medication and designer drugs must now be considered for testing. Just two years ago in October 2010, the DOT expanded its standard test panel to include Ecstasy as part of the amphetamines drug panel and also lowered cutoff levels of testing for amphetamines and cocaine. The result was as expected; such that DOT regulated programs are seeing an increase in positives for both categories.

Now, the U.S. government is enhancing its program even further. A breakthrough this year has been the approval by the Department of Health and Human Services (DHHS) of the recommendations made by the Drug Test Advisory Board (DTAB), which include testing for synthetic opiates such as hydrocodone and oxycodone, also known as Vicodin or Oxycontin by their brand names. Additionally, DTAB recommended using oral fluid testing as an alternative testing method. The process for the DOT to implement these recommendations could still take years, but this is a big first step in modifying the federal drug testing program and provides guidance on potential drugs you can test for within your own program.

Designer drugs such as synthetic marijuana and synthetic amphetamines are also on the federal government's radar. Known as K2/Spice and Bath Salts, these drugs are manufactured and marketed in such a way as to avoid legal roadblocks to distribution, which makes testing for them difficult and expensive. President Obama signed the Synthetic Drug Abuse Prevention Act of 2012 into law on July 9, 2012, as part of S. 3187, the Food and Drug Administration Safety and Innovation Act. The legislation bans synthetic compounds commonly found in synthetic marijuana ("K2" or "Spice"), synthetic stimulants ("Bath Salts"), and hallucinogens, by placing them under Schedule I of the Controlled Substances Act.

Table 23.1 Drugs and Testing Panels.

	Drug Name	Description
DOT5/9/panel	Amphetamines (amphetamines, methamphetamines)	Methamphetamine is a highly addictive drug with potent central nervous system stimulant properties. Effective 10/1/2012 Ecstasy is now part of the DOT Amphetamines panel.
DOT5/9/panel	Marijuana	Marijuana is the most commonly abused illicit drug in the United States.
DOT5/9/panel	Cocaine	Cocaine is a powerfully addictive stimulant that directly affects the brain. It can be administered by a doctor for legitimate medical uses, such as local anesthesia for some eye, ear, and throat surgeries.
DOT5/9/panel	Opiates (codeine, morphine, heroin)	Codeine, morphine and heroin. Heroin is an illegal, highly addictive drug. It is both the most abused and the most rapidly acting of the opiates. Today, heroin is an illicit substance having no medical utility in the United States.
DOT5/9/panel	Phencyclidine (PCP)	Originally designed as a human anesthetic and later produced only as a veterinary anesthetic, PCP is no longer produced or used for legitimate purposes.
DOT	Specimen validity testing	Checking to see if specimen is consistent with human urine. Checks for pH, specific gravity, and oxidizing adulterants.
9 panel	Barbiturates	Barbiturates produce a wide spectrum of central nervous system depression, from mild sedation to coma, and have been used as sedatives, hypnotics, anesthetics, and anticonvulsants.
9 panel	Benzodiazepines	The benzodiazepine family of depressants is used therapeutically to produce sedation, induce sleep, relieve anxiety and muscle spasms, and to prevent seizures. In general, benzodiazepines act as hypnotics in high doses, anxiolytics in moderate doses, and sedatives in low doses.
9 panel	Methadone	Although chemically unlike morphine or heroin, methadone produces many of the same effects. Introduced into the United States in 1947 as an analgesic (Dolophinel), it is primarily used today for the treatment of narcotic addiction.
9 panel	Propoxyphene	Propoxyphene is used to relieve mild to moderate pain.
Add on	Ecstasy	MDMA (3,4-methylenedioxymethamphetamine) is a synthetic, psychoactive drug chemically similar to the stimulant methamphetamine and the hallucinogen mescaline.
Add on	Hydrocodone/ hydromorphone	Expanded opiate/synthetic. Hydrocodone is an orally active analgesic and antitussive Schedule II narcotic that is marketed in multi-ingredient Schedule III products. Hydrocodone has an analgesic potency similar to or greater than that of oral morphine.
Add on	Oxycodone/ oxymorphone	Expanded opiate/synthetic. OxyContin is a prescription painkiller used for moderate to high pain relief associated with injuries, bursitis, dislocations, fractures, neuralgia, arthritis, lower back pain, and pain associated with cancer. OxyContin contains oxycodone, the medication's active ingredient, in a timed-release tablet. Oxycodone products have been illicitly abused for the past 30 years.
Add on	Meperidine	Currently it is used for pre-anesthesia and the relief of moderate to severe pain, particularly in obstetrics and post-operative situations. Meperidine is available in tablets, syrups, and injectable forms under generic and brand name (Demerol, Mepergan, etc.) Schedule II preparations.

Sources: http://www.usdoi.gov/dea/concern/concern.htm

This new law will make it easier for law enforcement agencies to take action against the manufacturers, importers and sellers of these products. While this represents progress in the battle against synthetic drugs, authorities must still continue to monitor and update the list of prohibited substances as manufacturers modify the composition of the drugs to circumvent legislation. Some employers have begun testing for these types of drugs in reasonable cause situations.

While the DOT and most non-regulated employers test a standard five-panel, these changes in prescription and designer drug abuse are creating a legitimate opportunity for employers to expand that panel to include additional drugs. For example, First Advantage, a large third party administrator, notes that its manufacturing customers are moving to a nine-panel test with an additional two drugs—hydrocodone and oxycodone.

Table 23.1 lists common drugs and testing panels included in employer drug testing programs.

Conclusion

An effective drug testing program promotes a safe, productive workplace. By monitoring industry trends, you can maintain your program effectiveness by understanding which drugs are being abused and modifying your testing panel based on that information. Likewise, laws and regulations will help dictate what can be tested and how that testing should be conducted.

It is always recommended that employers retain internal or external legal counsel specializing in drug testing to review drug and alcohol testing laws in the states where their applicants and employees reside, and states where they have physical locations. An organization such as DATIA is also a great resource to help you stay updated on drug testing industry trends and legislation. Visit the website www.datia.org to learn more about DATIA and membership opportunities.

For Discussion

1. Workplace drug testing can screen for different kinds of drugs. Should drug testing also screen for alcohol? Why or why not? Additionally, employers as well as the criminal justice system spend considerable amounts of money on drug testing. Do the benefits of workplace safety outweigh the costs?

2. The author cites survey data which showed that slightly more than half of employers who participated in the research reported that all job candidates underwent drug testing prior to being hired. At some universities in the United States, non-academic staff members are required to undergo pre-employment drug testing, however, faculty members are exempt from this requirement. How do you think universities justify these different practices? Are they fair?

24

Drug Testing in the Workplace

Summary Conclusions of the Independent Inquiry into Drug Testing at Work

This next article pertains to workplace drug testing in the United Kingdom. The article is a summary of a full report conducted by an independent panel in the United Kingdom. The report's conclusions differ from the arguments in favor of drug testing that were outlined by DiThomas in the previous article. Collectively, the two articles summarize the key aspects of the debate over workplace drug testing.

What role, if any, does drug and alcohol testing have in the workplace in modern Britain? In what circumstances, if any, should an employer discipline or dismiss staff for using drugs and alcohol? Does business have a legitimate involvement in what people do in their own time? The report from the Independent Inquiry on Drug Testing at Work (IIDTW) sets out and considers the arguments on drug testing at work, and concludes with a set of detailed recommendations. Over an 18-month period, the IIDTW considered written and oral evidence from employers and employees, providers of drug testing services, trade unions and business organisations, insurers and police officers, occupational health physicians and health and safety specialists, natural and social scientists, lawyers, philosophers and other experts in drug testing policy. This was an independent inquiry, facilitated by DrugScope and funded by the Joseph Rowntree Foundation and the Network of European Foundations.

Key Findings

- The evidence on the links between drug use and accidents at work, absenteeism, low productivity and poor performance was inconclusive. Most employers who had drug tested employees told the IIDTW that levels of positive results were very low.

- There is a lack of evidence for a strong link between drug use and accidents in safety-critical industries, such as transport, engineering, quarrying and mining. Clearly, however, drug- and alcohol-induced intoxication will be a source of risk in such environments.

- However, other factors may have a greater impact on safety, productivity and performance, including bad working conditions, sleeping and health problems, excessive workloads and work-related stress.

Reprinted from *Drug Testing in the Workplace: The Report of the Independent Inquiry into Drug Testing at Work*, published in 2004 by the Joseph Rowntree Foundation. Reproduced by permission of the Joseph Rowntree Foundation.

- Evidence considered by the IIDTW suggests that alcohol is probably a greater cause for concern in the workplace than illicit drugs.
- There is no clear evidence that drug testing at work has a significant deterrent effect.
- Drug testing is not a measure of current intoxication and will reveal information about drug use that can have no impact on safety, productivity or performance. Someone may test positive after taking a drug days, weeks or months before.
- People are not generally required to organise their lives to maximise their productivity at work, and employers do not have a direct law enforcement function. Empowering employers to investigate private behaviour actively—in the absence of legitimate safety or performance concerns—is in conflict with liberal-democratic values.
- The IIDTW found that the legal position on drug testing at work is confused. Employers could be open to legal challenge if they invade the privacy of employees unnecessarily, particularly under the Human Rights Act 1998 and the Data Protection Act 1998.
- Drug testing services in the UK are being provided by a very disparate group of companies and individuals. Many of them are very responsible. But the picture is mixed, with evidence that some of these companies may be making what appear to be inflated claims about the extent and impact of alcohol and drug problems in the workplace and the effectiveness of their own products.
- Remarkably little is known about the extent of drug testing at work in the UK. Perhaps the most reliable information comes from a small survey conducted by the IIDTW which found that 4 percent of employers who responded were conducting drug tests, and a further 9 percent were "likely" to introduce drug tests in the next year.
- Many employers and experts who gave evidence to the IIDTW highlighted the costs of drug testing at work. These include not only financial costs but also the potentially divisive nature of testing and the costs of

excluding otherwise responsible and capable people from employment.

Key Recommendations

- Employers have a legitimate interest in drug and alcohol use amongst their employees in a restricted set of circumstances only. These circumstances are:
  i. where employees are engaging in illegal activities in the workplace;
  ii. where employees are actually intoxicated in work hours;
  iii. where drug or alcohol use is (otherwise) having a demonstrable impact on employees' performance that goes beyond a threshold of acceptability;
  iv. where the nature of the work is such that any responsible employer would be expected to take all reasonable steps to minimise the risk of accident; and
  v. where the nature of the work is such that the public is entitled to expect a higher than average standard of behaviour from employees and/or there is a risk of vulnerability to corruption (for example, in the police or prison service).
- There is a need for continued research, monitoring and analysis of the impact and development of drug testing at work.
- The system of accreditation for providers of drug testing services is unsatisfactory. Laboratories that are not currently accredited should be given three years either to bring themselves up to the standards for accreditation of the UK Accreditation Service (UKAS) or form an equivalent self-regulatory system. If they fail to do so, then a legal requirement should be introduced.
- The government should produce clear and definitive guidance on drug testing at work, and particularly on the legal issues.
- If staff have drug or alcohol problems then this is a health and welfare issue as well as a disciplinary matter and should not be an automatic trigger for dismissal. Wherever possible, employees in safety-critical functions

should be redeployed in other roles and provided with help and support.

- Drug and alcohol policy should not be something that is imposed on employees by managers. Drug testing should only ever be introduced following proper consultation with staff and their representatives and should be even-handed.
- For the majority of businesses, investment in management training and systems is likely to have more impact on safety, performance and productivity than the introduction of drug testing at work. There is a wealth of evidence that good and open management is the most effective method of improving workplace performance and tackling drug and alcohol problems amongst staff.

The Inquiry

The IIDTW was set up in 2002 and has since considered written and oral evidence over an 18-month period. It was facilitated by DrugScope and supported by the Joseph Rowntree Foundation and the Network of European Foundations. It arose out of concerns about the lack of any independent assessment of the arguments for and against—and the lack of reliable evidence about—drug testing at work, and at a time when there was concern that this practice was growing in the UK.

The IIDTW conducted its inquiry under the supervision of an independent chair in Ruth Evans—formerly Director of the National Consumer Council and Chair of the Independent Inquiry into Paediatric Cardiac Services at the Royal Brompton and Harefield Hospitals—and an independent director, Yolande Burgin. The evidence was considered by the Chair and Director along with 16 distinguished commissioners, including leaders from the voluntary and community sector, social policy specialists, clinicians, academics, lawyers, trade unionists and representatives from employers groups.

Background

The term "drug testing" refers to the analysis of biological material to detect drugs or their metabolites in the body. Urine tests are most common in the UK, but saliva, sweat and hair can be tested. For alcohol, breath tests are most common. Drug testing at work takes a variety of forms, including pre-employment testing, random testing of employees and post-accident testing.

The use of drug testing has expanded in the criminal justice system and in sports, and there has been recent public and media discussion of the potential for expanding drug testing in both the police service and schools. Work-related drug testing is more widespread in the UK than ever before, and could increase significantly in the future, partly as a consequence of the marketing of drug testing services to employers.

The issue of drug testing is complex and has scientific, ethical, economic, legal and social dimensions.

However, the questions that it raises are not simply technical ones for the relevant experts. They include questions about the rapidly changing nature of work and leisure in the modern world; the balance between the interests of employers and the individual privacy of employees; and the relationship between substance misuse and workplace stress. The expansion of drug testing at work could have a profound impact on all employees and potential employees in modern Britain, and there is a danger that this practice could become increasingly routine in the absence of a full and proper public debate.

The Science

Drug tests can detect if a drug has been used in a given time period, but, generally, do not directly measure the effects of drugs and alcohol in terms of intoxication or impairment. They may reveal that drugs were used weeks or months previously, and cannot distinguish one-off users from people with serious dependency problems. There is a problem of "false positives," with some legally available drugs capable of producing a positive test for illicit substances. Drug testing is not infallible. But the science is already sufficiently sophisticated to enable employers to find out a great deal of information about drug use among staff and prospective staff. Tests may also reveal other information, such as the use of prescription drugs to treat medical conditions.

The Law

The legal position on drug testing at work is confused. There is no direct legislation and important legal questions hinge on interpretation of a range of provisions in health and safety, employment, human rights and data protection law. The main principles behind the current legal and self-regulatory provisions appear to be as follows:

- that people are entitled to a private life;
- that employers are required to look to the safety of the public;
- that people are entitled to dignity;
- that people are entitled to proper quality standards for evidence used against them in court or disciplinary proceedings.

These are emerging issues for jurisprudence and there has, to date, been little case law on drug testing arising from the Human Rights Act 1998 and the Data Protection Act 1998. Some of the issues have been clarified to some degree with the publication by the Information Commissioner of the consultation draft of Part 4 of the Employment Practices Data Protection Code in November 2003 (Information Commissioner, 2003). The Information Commissioner is responsible for the implementation of the Data Protection Act. According to the Commissioner's draft Code, the legitimacy of drug testing will depend on showing that there are health and safety concerns and on providing evidence of real (not assumed) impairment of performance.

Trends and Trajectories

A MORI poll was conducted on behalf of the IIDTW in 2003. Over 200 companies were surveyed, of which 4 percent conducted drug tests and a further 9 percent said that they were likely to introduce tests in the next year. In addition, 78 percent said that they would be more likely to test if they believed that drug or alcohol use was affecting performance or productivity. Overall numbers might seem comparatively low on the MORI findings, but this is highly misleading. If 4 percent of businesses are drug testing this will affect hundreds of thousands of employees. If the 9 percent of businesses who told MORI that they were likely to introduce testing in the next year do so, then this trebles the proportion of UK businesses testing over a 12-month period.

The IIDTW was not able to establish the extent of drug testing at work or the overall trends to its own satisfaction, with other surveys producing different figures to the MORI poll, largely reflecting the differences in their respective samples.

A major expansion of drug testing at work, while far from inevitable, is now a genuine possibility. The North American experience shows how rapidly drug testing at work can expand, with testing in the US developing into a multi-billion dollar industry since the 1980s. There is evidence that increasing numbers of British employers are identifying drug and alcohol use as a problem for them. There is a lack of evidence to suggest that drug and alcohol use is in fact having a serious and widespread effect on the workplace in modern Britain. There is a need for continued monitoring of trends and trajectories.

Health and Safety

Overall, the IIDTW was unable to find conclusive evidence for a link between drug use and accidents at work, except for alcohol. A literature review by the Health and Safety Executive reports that "five studies have found some association between drug use and work place accidents, whereas seven others found little or no evidence" (Beswick et al. 2002). The relationship between drug use and workplace accident is far from clear-cut. Nor is there conclusive evidence that drug testing is a deterrent to drug and alcohol consumption or that it reduces accident rates.

The IIDTW was satisfied, however, that drug and alcohol testing can have an important role in safety-critical environments. First, it is apparent from what we know about the psychological effects of various drugs, that intoxication impairs performance and it is a reasonable supposition that testing can deter and detect drug use in some circumstances. Second, even if the deterrent effect is fairly marginal, the IIDTW was made acutely aware that in some occupations a single mistake could have disastrous consequences in terms of injury and death. Third, the IIDTW was advised that it is difficult—if not impossible—to prove a deterrent effect anyway. And, finally, while some of the evidence presented to the IIDTW suggested that drug testing in safety-critical industries is more about maintaining public confidence than having a demonstrable impact on behaviour, the confidence of the public is an entirely valid consideration in its own right.

Performance Issues

Organisations cannot require staff or prospective staff to organise their lives in such a way that they maximise their productivity at work. Sociable drinking, late nights and childcare responsibilities, for example, can all impact on performance at work. The private activities of employees are a legitimate concern only if they impact on performance to a degree that exceeds a certain threshold for acceptable performance.

Employers have an interest in staff performance, but there is little or no conclusive evidence on the effectiveness or otherwise of drug and alcohol testing as a means of enhancing performance. Even if drug testing is beneficial in terms of performance, the benefits will need to be weighed against costs, including the impact on staff morale and workplace relationships and the potential recruitment and human resource cost of excluding illicit drug users from jobs that they are otherwise well-qualified to perform.

Employment and the Criminal Law

Employers will rightly be concerned if they find that staff are breaking the law by using or supplying drugs at work, and could face criminal proceedings for turning a blind eye. But employers do not have a law enforcement role in our society. Nobody would suggest that employers should be given powers to look at the bank accounts of job applicants or acquire stop and search powers to investigate their staff. For similar reasons, employers should not be granted drug testing powers simply as a means of investigating the private activities of employees.

The possible illegality of otherwise private activities is a legitimate concern in some occupations where the public is entitled to expect exemplary standards of probity and honesty, particularly with respect to professionals directly involved in administering the criminal law, such as police and prison officers.

Conclusion

Drug testing can have an important role in safety-critical and other occupations where the public is entitled to expect the highest standards of safety and probity. Aside from this, there is no justification for drug testing simply as a way of policing the private behaviour of the workforce, nor is it an appropriate tool for dealing with most performance issues. Even where drug testing does have a role it should be approached with caution, and implemented in a fair, transparent and inclusive way. The IIDTW concludes that good all-round management is the most effective method for achieving higher productivity, enhanced safety, low absentee rates, low staff turnover and a reliable and responsible workforce. For most businesses, investment in management training and systems will have more impact on safety, performance and productivity than drug testing at work.

References

All-Party Parliamentary Drug Misuse Group. 2003. *Drug Testing On Trial.* July.

Beswick, J. et al. 2002. *Review of the Literature On Illegal Drugs in the Work Place.* Health and Safety Laboratory, Sheffield: Crown.

Chartered Management Institute. 2003. *Managing the Effects of Drugs and Alcohol in the Workplace.* London: CMI.

Coomber, R. 2003. *Literature Review on Behalf of the Independent Inquiry on Drug Testing at Work.* University of Plymouth (available at www.drugscope .org.uk).

European Monitoring Centre for Drugs and Drug Addiction (EMCDDA). 1997. *Drug Demand Reduction in the Workplace: Final Report.* Lisbon: EMCDDA.

Francis, P., N. Hanley, and D. Wray. 2003. *Literature Review on Behalf of the Independent Inquiry on Drug Testing at Work* (available on request), University of Northumbria.

Hanson, M. 1999. "Overview on Drug and Alcohol Testing in the Workplace." *Bulletin on Narcotics* 45, no. 2.

Information Commissioner. 2003. *Part 4 of the Employment Practices Data Protection Code* (draft). Available at http://ico.org.uk/Global/~/media/ documents/library/Data_Protection/Detailed_ specialist_guides/the_employment_practices_ code.ashx

International Labour Organization. 2003. *Management of Alcohol and Drug Related Issues in the Workplace*. Available at www.ilo.org

MacDonald, S. 1995. "The Role of Drugs in Workplace Industries: Is Testing Appropriate?," *Journal of Drug Issues* 25/4: 703–722.

Smith, A., E. Wadsworth, S. Moss, and S. Simpson. 2004. *The Scale and Impact of Illegal Drug Use by Workers*. London: Health and Safety Executive.

Verstraete, A. G. and A. Pierce. 2001. "Workplace Drug Testing in Europe," *Forensic Science International*. 121: 2–6.

For Discussion

1. Discuss the possibility that workplace drug testing in the United States is consistent with the goals of the US War on Drugs. For example, why is that workplace drug testing is embraced by several employers in the United States, whereas the practice is used far less often in other industrialized nations?

2. In this article, the authors cite evidence from a MORI poll of organizations in the United Kingdom. Compare those results to the findings from the survey of US employers, as described by DiThomas in the previous article.

25

Our Drugs Are Better Than Yours

Schools and Their Hypocrisy Regarding Drug Use

LAURA L. FINLEY

Laura L. Finley discusses the important issue of contradictory drug policies in schools. Adderall and Ritalin are prescribed for ADD/ADHD to large numbers of school pupils in the United States. Finley shows how this prescribing pattern is influenced by parents, physicians, and educators. She uses illustrations to show that punishments are light for students who distribute these drugs to classmates. In contrast, several schools operate under a zero-tolerance policy when it comes to marijuana use. Some schools utilize drug testing or strip searches, and punishments are severe. Finley argues that the contradiction is based on a good/bad drug dichotomy.

Reprinted from Laura L. Finley, "Our Drugs Are Better Than Yours: Schools and Their Hypocrisy Regarding Drug Use." In *Contemporary Justice Review* 10 (2007): 365–381. Reprinted by permission of Taylor & Francis via Copyright Clearance Center.

American society tends to create ADD-like symptoms in all of us. We live in an ADD-ogenic culture.

(HALLOWELL and RATEY)

It is remarkable that the "Just Say No" campaign against stimulants has faded away into the "Just Say Yes" campaign for stimulants.

(BREGGIN, p. 104)

Introduction

Schools have long been asked to intervene in social problems, either real or constructed (Caulfield 2000; Finley 2003). Schools have been used to prevent unwanted pregnancies and to garner support for wars, among other things. It is no surprise, then, that we find schools playing a major role in the war on drugs. They have done this in a number of ways—through curricula, through special programs like Drug Awareness and Resistance Education (D.A.R.E.), through drug testing of students, and even by asking students to tip off school officials about classmates' drug use. While such programs target all types of illicit drugs, marijuana tends to receive the bulk of the attention. This does make sense; although marijuana use among juveniles dropped 11% between 2001 to 2003, the largest decline in juvenile drug use in more than 10 years, it remains the most commonly used illicit drug among all age groups (Curley 2005). Although research shows tremendous increases in the use and abuse of prescription drugs, these drugs are often not considered, and are certainly not the focus of school anti-drug efforts.

In contrast to the decrease in marijuana use, the amount of prescription drugs being prescribed for teens has grown tremendously. Current estimates suggest that 15–20% of boys in the U.S. are taking methylphenidate, or Ritalin (Mercogliano 2003). Additionally, there seems to be no lower age limit for those to whom these drugs can be prescribed. A 2003 study found that Ritalin prescriptions for two-to four-year-olds increased 300% between 1991 and 1995 (Mercogliano 2003). The FDA has found that since 1994 more than 3000 prescriptions for Ritalin have been written for children under one (Steinberg 2000)! Many of these students take their prescription drugs, or at least one dose of them, while at school. In 1996, the International Narcotics Control Board estimated that 20% or more of children in American schools were taking some form of stimulant during school hours (Breggin 1998). The DEA has maintained that some schools have a greater stock of methylphenidate than do pharmacies (Breggin 1998). As Eberstadt (1999) asserts, it seems schools are now stressing not three but four R's—Reading, Writing, 'Rithmatic, and Ritalin.

Not all prescription drugs used by teens are physician-prescribed, however. According to the Federal Substance Abuse and Mental Health Services Administration, prescription drugs are second only to marijuana on the list of substances most abused by people aged 12–24 (Birhanemaskel 2005). The National Survey of American Attitudes on Substance Abuse found that between April 2004 and June 2005, 86% of students surveyed knew a friend or classmate who had abused prescription drugs (Eberstadt 2005). According to *Girl Life*, 14% of high school seniors have used prescription drugs for non-medicinal purposes, 20% of U.S. teens have abused the pain reliever Vicodin, and 10% have abused Ritalin and/or Adderall (Monarch Avalon 2005).

One might argue that there are tremendous differences between teen use of illegal drugs like marijuana and teen use of legally prescribed medication. While certainly there are important differences, there are a number of striking similarities. Exploring these similarities and differences is important for our understanding of the disparity in the way the two types of drugs are treated in a school setting and the consequences of such disparate treatment. Allow me to assert at the very beginning: the responses of the authorities to prescription drugs in a school setting are dramatically different from their responses to student use of marijuana. In short, any use of marijuana in or around school is treated severely. In fact, even if a student pretends to be using marijuana, s/he faces suspension or worse. When two 10-year-old girls in

Florida pretended a baggie of parsley was pot, they were arrested, suspended, and forced to attend drug awareness classes (*Girls Arrested* 2005).

In order to catch students using illegal substances, schools might drug test those involved in sports or other extracurricular activities; estimates suggest that 18–20% of schools conduct some form of drug testing (Finley and Finley 2005). Schools might also search students' lockers, belongings, or vehicles parked on school grounds, sometimes with grounds for suspicion but often randomly. A Georgia school has instituted a pay-for-information program, giving students up to $100 for "narcing out" others for using drugs or carrying weapons (*Georgia High School* 2005). At other schools, snitching on peers is expected but not rewarded financially. In November 2004, middle school students in Jefferson County, Colorado, were asked to make a list of peers they thought might be using drugs (*Students Asked* 2004). In 2000, the American Civil Liberties Union filed suit on behalf of a group of Maryland teens and their parents, maintaining that the students were told they must submit to a drug test or face expulsion, based solely on the allegations of other student (ACLU 2000). On rare occasions, schools might even strip-search a student in a quest to find contraband. Zero tolerance laws in most states require that students be suspended or expelled if they are caught with illegal substances.

However, while school authorities are busily telling students in as many ways as possible that illegal drugs are bad and they should "Just Say No," they pass out prescription drugs. Until recently all but four states allowed teachers and counselors to recommend to a parent or guardian to put their child on medication (Hyman and Snook 1999; Mercogliano 2003). Dr. Lawrence Diller, in his book *Running on Ritalin,* describes one school where the school secretary doles out pills from a tray labeled with the names and pictures of 14 students. The school has approximately 350 students. Another school of similar size passes out pills in shifts since there are too many students receiving them to do it all at once (Diller 1998).

This form of drug trafficking, if you will, is clearly not an exact science. A study published in

Health and Healthcare in Schools found that almost half of the 649 school nurses responding to inquiries on these matters observed major errors in the administration of prescription medications at school, the most common being that unlicensed personnel pass them out ("Study Finds" 2001). Nurses passed out prescription drugs in only 25% of the schools from which nurses responded, with some schools relying on paraprofessionals, teachers, parents, and even students to administer prescribed substances ("Study Finds" 2001).

Many teachers encourage the distribution of these drugs in schools, asserting that it makes their teaching easier: unruly students are now manageable. According to one teacher:

> I have thirty-two kids in my class. We used to have a teaching aide, so one of us could spend extra time with the "difficult" kids. But when there are this many, all I can do is try to get the really tough ones into a special-education class—or get them checked for ADD. (Diller 1998, 13)

Arianna Huffington (2000) describes a case where parents stopped their child's prescription drugs—he had been on Ritalin and Paxil at different times since he was two—because they were concerned about the side effects they were seeing. School officials called Child Protective Services and the parents were charged with neglect.

In most instances these students are indeed more manageable, but what about the message it sends students? Your drugs are bad—but our drugs are good? As Finley and Finley (2005) ask, "Ritalin is an amphetamine, but a good one?" (28). DeGrandpre (1999) quotes a psychologist as saying, "There is something odd, if not downright ironic, about the picture of millions of American school children filing out of "drug awareness" classes to line up in the school nurses' office for their midday dose of amphetamine" (180).

Not only is such doublespeak a problem in and of itself, it impacts on students' trust in educators and, ultimately, the social environment in which they are expected to learn (Finley and Finley 2005; Hyman and Snook 1999). As Webber (2001) explains, "These forms of monitoring and control do chip away at the confidence students may have and the trust they may feel for one another. Specifically, these disciplinary procedures act as subtle forms of fear-based indoctrination" (194).

The Similarities

Easy Access

It probably comes as no surprise that many types of illegal drugs are easy for students to obtain. Roughly 60% of juveniles who use drugs use marijuana exclusively, partly because of easy access to sources. Students report that marijuana is easier to obtain than beer or cigarettes (Califano 2002). In the 2003 National Survey of American Attitudes on Substance Abuse, 20% of teens reported that they could buy marijuana within an hour, and almost 40% said they could do so within a day (Califano 2003). While recent studies indicate decreasing trends in use among juveniles, more than half of the teenagers surveyed said they could obtain marijuana easily if they wanted to (Califano 2003). More than half of the juveniles who use marijuana get it for free or share with someone else, with the vast majority of teens obtaining the drug from a friend. The International Narcotics Control Board maintains that access to drugs is even easier online than in the street market (*Want Pot?* 2005). A quick Google search on the internet reveals many sites offering marijuana and paraphernalia.

Adderall and Ritalin are also very easy to obtain. One way to get these drugs is to have them prescribed for you. Many have suggested that doctors in the U.S. are too quick to diagnose child or teen depression and ADD/ADHD, and consequently prescribe drugs too frequently (Casey 2007). While estimates of the number of children and adolescents with ADD or ADHD vary, many suggest that 9–10% of boys and about 3% of girls have this disorder. However, diagnosis is notoriously vague: most doctors use a simple checklist of behaviors and one, often short, visit to make their diagnosis (Breggin 1998).

Arthur Caplan, director for the Center for Bioethics at the University of Pennsylvania, says: "There's either a strange plague of hyperactivity in the U.S., or we've got a lot of folks prescribing Ritalin as a psychopharmacological nanny" (Breggin 1998, 119). Upon learning that some doctors will prescribe Ritalin after just a 15-minute evaluation of a child, one Drug Enforcement Agency officer commented, "I wouldn't accept dope from an informer I'd only talked to for fifteen minutes!" (Diller 1998, 14). Some physicians and clinics have come to be known as "Ritalin mills" because they prescribe the drug so frequently and easily. A 1995 study found that two providers out of the 1309 in Virginia had prescribed over one quarter of the Ritalin in the state (Diller 1998). In Michigan, 5% of the providers were prescribing 50% of the Ritalin (Diller 1998). An investigation of 10 pediatricians found that more than a quarter of the children diagnosed with ADD did not meet the diagnostic criteria (Diller 1998).

Students say they can easily obtain prescription drugs without a prescription, so over-prescription and marketing are not the only issues. Students can purchase such drugs from classmates or friends, or borrow (or take) them from family members. Ritalin has become so common as a street drug it has been given the street names "Vitamin R," "R-ball," and the "smart drug" (Breggin 1998). Timothy Chernyaev, a 15-year-old having behavioral issues with friends and family, simply called a friend who had a prescription and asked to "borrow" some pills. The decision to make the phone call was not difficult—he previously had dabbled with other prescription drugs, including Adderall, as had every kid he knew (Amsden 2004). One student who tried Xanax, Valium, Oxycontin, and Adderall said, "At the time, it felt like I knew more kids who were doing it than who weren't" (Birhanemaskel 2005, B1). Teens in New York City generally make $3–$10 per pill for Adderall and Ritalin (Amsden 2004). Like marijuana, it is easy to buy Ritalin online without a prescription—having access to a credit card is enough (Eberstadt 1999).

Undercover narcotics officers have said Ritalin is even easier to obtain on playgrounds than on the streets (Diller 1997). Sometimes adults "get in on the action" too: in one case in Nashville, Tennessee, a drug-addicted middle-school teacher was convicted of stealing the schools' stock of student Ritalin. She was the second teacher from that school caught stealing from the vault (DeGrandpre 1999).

Why Teens Use the Drugs

Teens struggling with daily life may turn to, or be turned on to, a number of substances to alleviate their pain. Some will self-medicate with alcohol or marijuana. One doctor has estimated that 30% of her teen patients had used pot or alcohol after a depressive episode (Chua-Eoan 1999). Teens also use marijuana to appear "cool" and to alleviate anxiety in social situations such as parties. Similarly, teens use Ritalin and other forms of methylphenidate to be cool. Students who are not so popular suddenly become so when they provide the Ritalin for a party (Beal 1998). Students in high schools and colleges are having "pharming" parties, where they shift responsibility for bringing the prescription drugs (*Youth Trade* 2005). Kids also use marijuana and prescription drugs out of boredom. In the case of both marijuana and prescription drugs, use is greatest amongst teens with more spending money (Califano 2003).

One young woman, an honor roll student, reported that she started taking prescription drugs because she constantly felt self-conscious about her body while in school. She thought that taking stimulant medication would help her lose weight and, consequently, fit in better (Monarch Avalon 2005). Another young lady who abused prescription drugs explained, "[W]hen everyone in high school found out I had pills, suddenly I was cool" (Monarch Avalon 2005, 68).

Parents are the biggest influence on whether a child will use marijuana. According to the U.S. Department of Health and Human Services (2004), parental lifetime use and last-year-use of marijuana increases threefold the risk that their child will use marijuana. This research also found that if parents see little risk in marijuana use, their children will tend to hold a similar point of view. In fact, some research has suggested it is not unusual for parents and other adults to drink or smoke with their children. A supplement to the 1995 Monitoring the Future survey found that 60.5% of high school seniors drank beer or wine in the presence of people over the age of 30, while 32.7% smoked marijuana with people of that age range. Rates were higher for use of other illegal narcotics with adults over 30, at 40.5% (Males 1999).

Likewise, parents are an important influence on the likelihood that a child will misuse prescription drugs. Parents may encourage their child's rush to medicate by their own pill-taking. "It's very common that it's the parent who first introduces the child to the drug. The parents are often in similar environments, often relying on substances to wake up, to get through the day," said Tessa Kleeman, coordinator of the independent school program at the Freedom Institute, a Manhattan outpatient rehabilitation facility (Amsden 2004). Kimberly Mitchell-Sellwood, an addictions specialist in San Diego, concurs. She maintains that girls are more likely to use prescription drugs that are not prescribed for them than illicit drugs, because they see their moms supplied with prescriptions (Monarch Avalon 2005).

Attitudes about the Drugs

Teens generally see marijuana use as no big deal. Anti-drug programs like D.A.R.E. tend to be ineffective because most teens know someone who smokes some pot on the weekends but is not the stereotypical "pothead loser." Consequently, they dismiss the fear-based tactics used in such educational interventions. Recent research demonstrates that scare tactics do not work. The Safety First website features a poll in which 43% of teens said their decision not to use drugs was "not at all" related to what they learned in classes or at school, with an additional 16.6% saying that school had little effect on their decision ("Teens and Drugs," n.d.). A National Institute of Health panel of 13 experts concluded that scare tactics are not effective in preventing teen violence either, and indeed are more likely to alienate teens who most need help (*CBC News* 2004). Such scare tactics are also likely to reduce adults' credibility with teens on the topic of drugs, enabling them to dismiss legitimate information as overblown rhetoric about the danger of marijuana (Finley and Finley 2005; Szalavitz 2005).

Many students who misuse Ritalin or Adderall see little wrong with their actions, claiming that such drugs are like any stimulant such as caffeine or Red Bull (*Adderall Used* 2005). A drug researcher at a nationally known treatment facility in Center City, Minnesota, maintained, "Pills are more seductive to kids because they see them as cleaner, safer and less illegal" (Birhanemaskel 2005). Lawrence Diller (1998) wrote that teens "think that since their younger brother takes it under a doctor's prescription, it must be safe" (42). Carol Falkowski, Director of Research Communications at the Hazelden Foundation in Minnesota, explained:

> We live in a world where 5 million school-age children take a prescription drug for behavior disorders, so kids learn at an early age that pills change moods. There are pills all around as they grow up, so they don't see them as inherently dangerous. (Monarch Avalon 1005, 68)

Students claim it is normal and natural to want to escape life (Amsden 2004). Many teens, however, recognize the potential dangers and dislike the side effects of drugs—sleepless nights, chills, racing heart, and weight loss—but continue using them because of the pay-off. One student explained that Adderall helped him balance school, sports, and a social life, arguing that it even helped him think more deeply (*Adderall Used* 2005). Kids say they are more appealing because they don't have the telltale smell of marijuana (Birhanemaskel 2005). Girls in particular hold this view, and thus they are less likely than boys to use marijuana or other illicit drugs but are just as likely to use prescription drugs (Birhanemaskel 2005).

A Drug Culture

Another similarity—perhaps the most important similarity—between the use of marijuana and the use of prescription drugs is their broader, cultural roots. There can be little argument that the U.S. has a drug culture; we medicate ourselves for virtually anything and everything. The 1980s punk rock band the Dead Kennedys summed it up in their song "Drug Me," which explains why people use drugs of all types: "I don't want to think. Don't make me care. I wanna melt in with the group. I need the balls to leap out of my shell" (Finley and Finley 2005, 28). It should come as no surprise, then, that prescription drug sales have gone up almost 400% since 1990, for almost half of all Americans regularly take at least one prescription drug (Birhanemaskel 2005). The average person is now

prescribed 12 drugs per year, and one in six people takes three or more drugs per day (Critser 2005).

While other countries prescribe Ritalin, and some have seen dramatic increases in its use, the U.S. still produces and uses approximately 90% of the Ritalin sold in the world (Diller 1998). We are "generation Rx," as Critser (2005) maintains, glued to video games like "Narc" which allow players to arrest dealers and then sample their wares. The game is designed so that players believe that the consumption of small quantities of drugs improves play (*Drug Use* 2005).

However, research has shown that fewer parents are discussing drugs with their kids. More than one in 10 parents say they have never had a conversation about drugs with their child, according to a new survey by the Partnership for a Drug-Free America. That is double the rate of just six years ago (*Study: Fewer Parents* 2005).

The Differences
The Drugs' Effects

Adderall and Ritalin have been created to serve as high-powered stimulants. The federal government has classified Ritalin as a Schedule II drug, which means there is a significant chance it will be abused (Diller 1998). As such, it sits in the company of morphine, opium, and barbiturates, as well as cocaine and other stimulants (Breggin 1998). After escalating rates of abuse among its people, the Swedish government withdrew Ritalin from the marketplace altogether (Breggin 1998). People have been known to use Adderall when they are trying to stop using cocaine, because it gives a similar rush with a less intense come-down phase (Amsden 2004).

In research into various stimulants, heroin, morphine, amphetamines, and a placebo were injected into healthy volunteers who were unaware of which substance they received; those who got the amphetamine overwhelmingly defined it as the most pleasurable (Diller 1998). Research with monkeys has found they will self-administer doses of drugs repeatedly, ignoring food, sex, and sleep; however, they did not prefer cocaine over Ritalin (DeGrandpre 1999). However, if a child displays characteristics such as hyperactivity, impulsivity, and inattention while taking Ritalin, which are the logical effects of a stimulant, it is typically viewed as evidence that a higher dose is needed (Breggin 1998).

Moreover, other research has called attention to the possible long-term effects on users' cognitive and intellectual processes, producing what is often referred to as "zombie-like behavior" (Breggin 1998). One study found that children who had taken Ritalin gave more rote answers to open-ended questions, while parents and doctors have anecdotally pointed to the narrowed thinking which Ritalin produces (Diller 1998). Other studies report that children and teens display enthusiasm for almost nothing (Breggin 1998). DeGrandpre (1999) quotes one journalist as saying:

> Americans would be horrified to learn that 2 million children across the nation are being given cocaine by their parents and doctors to make them behave better in school. It's also close to the truth that it takes a chemist to tell the difference. (176)

Clearly, there are dangers associated with the use of Ritalin, Adderall, and the like, as we have indicated, even when prescribed by a physician. However, many young people are not using these drugs as designed. The DEA has reported that rates of Ritalin abuse increased 13% between 1992 and 1995 (DeGrandpre 1999). Between 1991 and 1995, the number of children aged 10–14 admitted to emergency rooms for Ritalin abuse increased from 25 to over 400—a level approximately the same as this age group's admittance for cocaine-related overdoses (DeGrandpre 1999). Between 1990 and 2000, 186 deaths attributed to methylphenidate were reported to the FDA's MedWatch program. Since this is a voluntary reporting program, experts say it probably captures only 10–20% of the actual incidence of the problem (*Info for Parents* 2002).

Ritalin is among the top 10 drugs involved in drug thefts (Breggin 1998). Police in Vancouver, Canada, have stated that Ritalin addicts commit 60–70% of the city's property crime (*Ritalin*, n.d.).

Interestingly, while claims that marijuana is a "gateway drug" are commonly offered as an argument that it should remain illegal, few are aware of the studies suggesting that methylphenidate is a gateway drug (Breggin 1998).

There is little evidence to suggest that the use of marijuana carries with it major long-term effects. According to Zimmer and Morgan (1997), "A few researchers have reported subtle marijuana effects persisting up to twenty-four hours. However, in dozens of studies measuring psychomotor ability and intellectual performance, researchers have found that all marijuana effects disappear within a few hours" (120). Surveys conducted in 1969 and 1978 compared marijuana-using college seniors with non-using peers. They found the two groups to be non-distinguishable with respect to grades, other measures of academic performance, athletic activity, career plans, and feelings of alienation (Sullum 2003). In a recent rendition of the 1920s *Reefer Madness*, researchers in January 2006 announced that some kids, who are genetically vulnerable from the outset and who smoke marijuana more than once a week, are at a somewhat greater risk for psychosis (Goldberg 2006). However, as Szalavitz (2005) points out, the results do not prove that marijuana causes schizophrenia, merely that the two are correlated. Further, the positive correlation between the two variables tends to disappear when researchers control for other relevant variables such as a childhood history of disturbed behavior.

ADD Drugs Encouraged in School?

Adderall and Ritalin are often prescribed for students who are struggling in school. Parents may push teenage children to submit to such medication, believing it will help them achieve greater success in school. They may hear other parents describe how Ritalin was effective for their child, or may unknowingly push their child to drug use by stressing grades, college admittance, and other concerns associated with school, buying into the cut-throat ethic of a capitalist culture. In particular, the abuse of prescription drugs has increased at highly competitive private schools, where parents and students feel intense pressure for academic success (Breggin 1998). Diller (1998) explains that middle- and upper-class families increasingly perceive anything below average as of grave concern. One doctor commented that parents "talk about underperformance as if it's a disorder, which really goes to the heart of the issue: Are we still treating disorders here? Or are we offering performance enhancement?" (Amsden 2004, para. 11).

Dr. Sidney Wolfe, director of the Public Citizens Health Research Group, said, "We are moving into an era where any quirk of a personality is fair game for a drug. On one hand, we are telling kids to just say no to drugs, but on the other hand, their pediatricians are saying, 'Take this. You'll feel good'" (Chua-Eoan 1999).

Parents may initially resist medicating their children, but many succumb to enticing ads. Breggin (1998) reports how a physician offered families an "Evaluation/Treatment Fun Package" to Las Vegas, which included free accommodation, coupons for meals, and discounts for shows if they got their children evaluated for ADD/ADHD at his medical clinic. Parents are often misinformed, or under-informed, by doctors who never mention that these drugs are stimulants (Breggin 1998). Some doctors have told parents that kids with ADHD who are not medicated are destined to be criminals, insidiously insinuating that every "good" parent would medicate her or his child immediately (Breggin 1998). In contrast, no-one is marketing marijuana to parents as an academic performance enhancer.

Educators may also be an impetus. Teachers want compliant, well-behaved students in their classrooms and principals want to minimize management problems overall. Surveys show that about 85% of educators have attended at least one workshop on attention deficit disorder/attention deficit hyperactivity disorder, where they heard about the wonders of medication to ease its effects (Breggin 1998). The U.S. Department of Education (DOE) has published information for teachers about ADD/ADHD which includes extensive information about treating it with drugs (Breggin 1998). The DOE encourages educators to act as the "frontline" in diagnoses (Breggin 1998). A recent study found that over 50% of diagnoses of ADD/ADHD were initially made by teachers and that doctors seemed more or less to rubber-stamp such diagnoses. As early as 1970, the House of Representatives Subcommittee on Government Operations held hearings on "Federal Involvement in the Use of Behavior Modification Drugs on Grammar School

Children." Testifying at those hearings, the noted author and educator John Holt explained that lack of attention in school is considered a disorder:

> [I]t makes it difficult to run our schools as we do, like maximum security prisons, for the comfort and convenience of the teachers and administrators who work in them. The energy of children is "bad" because it is a nuisance to the exhausted and overburdened adults who do not want to or know how to and are not able to keep up with it. (Breggin 1998, 181)

Breggin (1998) tells of a principal in New York informing a mother that his school would not be able to handle her daughter unless she was put on Ritalin.

Teaching about the Drugs

Despite the fact that prescription drugs are in many ways worse than marijuana, they are treated quite differently in schools. Schools address the horrors of becoming a pothead in health classes but include virtually nothing in the curriculum to prevent prescription drug use and abuse. Analyses of the health textbooks used in schools and by local social service agencies in developing drug intervention strategies found coverage of prescription drugs to be sorely lacking (Weller 2005).

In addition to differences in school texts regarding the use of prescription drugs versus marijuana, the responses of school and other officials to students found using or selling marijuana on school grounds differ tremendously from official responses to students found using prescription drugs illicitly. The following sections describe and critique several of the response modes school officials employ to prevent students from using marijuana, or to make corrections when students have been detected using it.

School Responses
Drug Testing

Drug testing is one of the many ways in which schools have tried to deter and address the use of marijuana and illegal drugs. Conducted under the guise of helping kids, this paternalistic measure is not only ineffective but also alienating to many students, especially those supposed to be "helped." The federal government has devoted a lot of money to "helping children make right choices," as President Bush claimed when he designated $23 million to support drug testing (Curley 2005). Of course, the grant money is available only for testing for illicit drugs—hence a student abusing prescription drugs remains under the school's radar.

We see schools constantly looking to innovate in measures to crack down on illicit drugs. The Palm Beach County district in Florida trained administrators to use a portable drug test for use when they have reason to suspect a student is using illegal drugs. Similar to the tests used at airports, the drug test involves a piece of sticky material that is rubbed on a student's body or possessions, then sprayed with chemicals. If it turns a certain color, this is an indication that marijuana, heroin, ecstasy, or other drugs may be present. Advocates of the test maintain that it is non-intrusive, and a pilot program is being funded by a grant from the National Institute of Justice (*Florida County* 2004). The Broward County school district, in the author's home county, is considering using the same test, arguing that it is not punitive (*Florida Schools* 2004). No such innovations can be found that test for prescription drugs.

Most studies place the percentage of schools with drug testing policies at approximately 18–20% (Mayer 2003). While few schools randomly test their entire student body, the Bush administration has offered support for such a practice (Lorenz 2004). The Drug and Alcohol Testing Industry Association (DATIA) found a 10% increase in the number of schools implementing student drug testing after the 2002 *Earls* decision declared that drug testing for students involved in an extracurricular activity was constitutional (Keynes 2003).

Although the public often believes that such drug testing ensures that athletes are not using performance-enhancing substances, most schools are not searching for steroids but other forms of illegal drugs. Some schools have proposed making student access to certain rights and privileges contingent on a negative drug test. Illinois has considered requiring teens wishing to obtain a driving license to pass a drug test (*Drug Tests* 2004).

Advocates of such testing claim that drug testing acts as a deterrent. Drug Czar John Walters has touted drug testing as the most effective deterrent. (*ONDCP* 2005). However, research reveals that drug testing is not effective as a deterrent. The largest study of drug testing ever conducted—involving 76,000 students nation-wide—found drug use to be as prevalent in schools utilizing testing as in those that did not (Mayer 2003). Another study found athletes in schools with testing programs to hold negative attitudes about testing and more positive attitudes about drug use than students in schools without drug testing (Greenwood 2003).

One of the major problems with the tests schools use is that they are quite inaccurate. For one, they are terribly easy to cheat on; students can procure a sample from someone else or use some form of masking agent. Some states are seeking to get around this issue by making it a Class Four felony to use, sell, or make products that alter drug test results (*Cheating on Drug Tests* 2004).

Most schools use cheap immunoassay urine tests, costing between $20 and $40 per sample. More accurate tests, such as those used by the National College Athletic Association, are available; however, these are far more costly at about $200 per sample (Hawkins 1999). The cheap tests typically screen for one substance at a time. Hence schools must be satisfied with a very limited result or the cost of additional tests. In addition, the less expensive tests get it wrong 5–50% of the time (Hawkins 1999). According to an ACLU guide for educators entitled *Making Sense of Drug Testing*, drug tests may cost more than a school spends on all its drug education, prevention, and counseling programs (*Drug Policy Alliance* 2004).

In addition, tests have been known to produce false positives when a legally prescribed or over-the-counter medication is misidentified or cross-reacts with the test. In some instances Nyquil has been misidentified as an opiate or amphetamine (Greenwood 2003), ibuprofen as marijuana (Tunnell 2004), and Robitussin and diet pills as amphetamines (Greenwood 2003). Conversely, since the tests we are talking about are not very robust, admitted drug users often test negative. One person who admitted using marijuana tested negative nine times.

Clearly there are concerns about how drug testing impinges upon a student's privacy. For example, students are required to disclose any medications they are taking to prevent misidentifications. It is obviously mortifying for some students if their principal, faculty, and even peers are made aware that they are taking Prozac (Finley and Finley 2005). Always ready to respond in a Panopticon mode, some schools are looking at building on-site testing facilities so samples can be done "in-house" (Hawkins 1999).

Schools vary in the degree to which their policies involve punitive consequences. In some districts, kids testing positive might not be allowed to participate in sports; in others they might be suspended or expelled. One district in Pennsylvania seeks to suspend, or to transfer to an alternative school, any kid who tests positive, as well as any kid who refuses to be tested (PA *Schools* 2004).

While the process of providing a urine sample is by nature humiliating, some schools, recognizing the ease with which students can cheat on such tests, are devising more invasive means of securing samples. Amy Valdez said she was stripped to her underwear prior to urinating on demand so that the tester could ensure she was not hiding someone else's urine. "I felt like I was on display. It was devastating" (Hawkins 1999, 72).

Whatever the method, such testing sends a mixed message to students. Group-based, suspicionless testing presumes that students are guilty of using drugs. Schools could easily utilize only suspicion-based testing. Justice O'Connor noted this in the *Vernonia* case, where athletes suspected of drug use were allegedly singing and dancing at inappropriate times and bragging about their drug use. She dissented with the majority in this case, arguing that collective suspicion runs counter to the spirit of the Fourth Amendment (Finley and Finley 2005).

Although the above sections have highlighted the myriad ways in which drug testing is an ineffective means to address teen drug use of any sort, plans are in the works to test for prescription drugs as well. The drug-prevention program notMYkid, founded in Arizona in 1999, is expanding to 24 new cities with a program for seventh-grade students that will feature drug testing. It is no wonder that notMYkid co-founder Steve Moak is an investor in the drug test company (*Prevention Group* 2006). NotMYkid has passed out free drug test kits to parents that test for 12 different drugs, including prescriptions drugs (PR Newsire Association 2006).

Strip Searches

Many people labor under the misconception that schools are not allowed to strip-search students when looking for drugs. While strip-searches do not happen with great frequency, virtually any time a school claims they are strip-searching for illicit drugs, courts will rule the search constitutional (Finley and Finley 2005). However, we do not see such searches for prescription drugs.

One of the most heinous examples was the search of special-ed student Brian Cornfield. A teacher's assistant felt his genitals when they appeared to be especially large one day. A rumor had been spread that the student was "crotching" drugs. Despite Cornfield's mother's request that the school wait until she arrived, school officials made Brian strip down to his underwear and hold his genitals out for inspection. Although the search revealed nothing, the 7th Circuit Court dubbed the search "justified at its inception" (Finley and Finley 2005).

Sadly, research has demonstrated that special education students are more likely to be searched. Minorities are more likely to be searched as well, despite the fact that rates of use of most drugs by minorities are comparable with those of white students. Caucasian students are far more likely to use (or abuse) prescription drugs, yet they are not subject to the same invasive searches as minority counterparts.

The success rates of strip searches, like those of drug tests, are not terribly encouraging. Philadelphia administrators estimated a 13% success rate in drug-related strip searches, and close to 50% success in weapons-related strip searches (Hyman and Snook 1999). Requiring students to remove articles of clothing, regardless of the reason, can be as damaging emotionally as events that cause some people to suffer post-traumatic stress disorder (Hyman and Snook 1999). Students become depressed, moody, and/or rebellious.

Responses to ADD Drugs in Schools

Schools typically bar students from carrying prescription drugs on their person or keeping them in their lockers, but enforcement is notoriously sparse. According to Diller (1998), most teenagers who take a dose of Ritalin while at school ignore such regulations while parents and school officials often look the other way. While it is a violation of federal law to possess controlled substances without a prescription, aside from the widespread attention given to radio personality Rush Limbaugh for possessing prescription painkillers, prosecutions are rare (Birhanemaskel 2005). For example, Kansas City passed a law barring children from sharing prescription drugs, yet exempts those authorized by school officials or emergency personnel (Wiese 2005). The law will do little to address the abuse of prescription drugs because students are free to share their legitimately prescribed substance with others who seek them.

The North Carolina parents of a 14-year-old girl were disturbed to discover that she had distributed her Ritalin to fellow students on the school bus, and more disturbed to discover that no-one from the school called the home to say that the bottle had not been checked in with the school nurse when it was supposed to be. In fact, even though the girl had been sharing and not taking the medication, a teacher reported her behavior much improved on the drug (DeGrandpre 1999)!

Obviously, schools are not providing the oversight needed for the successful administration of ADD drugs. In hospitals it is standard practice to lock up Ritalin, as would be required with any other medication. But school officials tend to handle Ritalin and similar drugs far less formally. In one Pittsburgh school, the nurse said Ritalin was generally kept in a shoe box in an unlocked desk in the office (DeGrandpre 1999). When punishments are meted out to students for prescription drug infractions, they tend to be far less severe than those for students found possessing, taking, or selling marijuana. When students admitted using, selling, and distributing Ritalin in Dallas, Texas, they were given a three-day suspension and made to take summer school classes (DeGrandpre 1999)— a marked difference from the zero-tolerance expulsion policies so common for students caught with illegal drugs.

Conclusion

In the U.S. generally and more specifically in schools, students are sent mixed messages about drugs. U.S. culture has a tendency to label drugs as either "good" or "bad" rather than acknowledging that chemical substances can be both, depending on the context of their use (DeGrandpre 1999; Sullum 2003). The U.S. drug culture makes it increasingly difficult to see the distinctions between so-called "good" and "bad" drugs. While on the one hand we vilify illegal drugs that are meant only to make you feel good, like marijuana, on the other hand legal drugs such as SSRIs are marketed as making people feel good (Breggin 1994). These mixed messages have

> a normalizing effect on kids' overall views of drugs and drug-taking. Despite all the "just say no" slogans, the "just do it" manner in which children are now prescribed psychotropic drugs, from Prozac to Ritalin, greatly undermines the anti-drug rhetoric of saying no. (DeGrandpre 1999, 180)

Students are left in the dark about what to say yes to.

Perhaps it would be useful to consider whether the school environment asks children and teens to do something unnatural—to stay seated and exercise utmost self-control for seven straight hours. Small wonder that many students wish to escape this docilizing environment, some by electing to use marijuana to expand stifled consciousness. The mundane routine of a day in most schools in most parts of our country stands in stark contrast to the highly stimulating world in which we live (DeGrandpre 1999; Diller 1998). When some students fail to submit to the routine, educators choose to define and medicate them as non-conformists. Ultimately, the responses to both marijuana use and ADD in schools are about greater control. Perhaps Daniel L. Zeidner, a New York pediatrician, best summed up how we should address this issue:

> It has become increasingly apparent to me, and perhaps to other pediatricians, that a new syndrome exists among adults who teach our school-aged

children: Teacher Deficit Disorder, or TDD. I have observed that this diagnosis should be made on the teacher when the following classic signs and symptoms exist among one or more of his/her students: students who fidget in class, constantly moving their fingers or legs, who do not pay attention, who frequently daydream, who do not complete their homework or classwork, and who frequently get out of their seats. When students exhibit these manifestations, the teacher should be diagnosed with TDD and, of course, should be medicated immediately with amphetamine or other drugs that should speed him/her up, thus making him/her . . . more dynamic and interesting to his/her students. (quoted in Diller 1998, 64)

References

Adderall used to boost school performance. 2005. May 9. Retrieved May 11, 2005, from http://www.drugfree.org/join-together/drugs/adderall-used-to-boost-school

American Civil Liberties Union. 2000. *Students and Parents Challenge "Rumor Mill" Drug Testing at Maryland High School.* May 2. Retrieved November 19, 2001, from https://www.aclu.org/drug-law-reform/students-and-parents-challenge-rumor-mill-drug-testing-maryland-high-school

Amsden, D. 2004. "Pop, Snort, Parachute." *New York Metro.* Retrieved March 6, 2005, from http://www.newyorkmetro.com/nymetro/news/culture/features/9945

Beal, E. 1998. *Ritalin: Its Use and Abuse.* New York: Rosen Publishing Group.

Birhanemaskel, M. 2005. "Addiction." *Rocky Mountain News.* March 23, B1.

Breggin, P. 1994. *Talking Back to Prozac.* New York: St. Martin's Press.

Breggin, P. 1998. *Talking Back to Ritalin.* Monroe, Maine: Common Courage Press, 104.

Califano, J. 2002. *National Survey on Drug Use and Health, 2002 Results.* Retrieved March 1, 2006, from http://www.samhsa.gov/data/nhsda/overview/2k2Overview.htm

Califano, J. 2003. *National Survey on Drug Use and Health, 2003 Results.* Retrieved March 1, 2006, from http://www.samhsa.gov/data/NSDUH/2003SummNatFindDetTables/Index.aspx

Casey, B. 2007. "Bipolar Illness Soars as a Diagnosis for the Young." *The New York Times*, September 4. Retrieved September 5, 2007, from http://www.nytimes.com/2007/09/04/health/04psych.html?_r=1&oref=slogin

Caulfield, S. 2000. "Creating Peaceable Schools." *Annals of the American Academy of Political and Social Science* 567 (January): 170–185.

"Cheating on Drug Tests in Illinois May Become a Felony." 2004. March 15. Retrieved March 17, 2004, from https://www.drugfree.org/join-together/government/cheating-on-drug-tests-in-may

Chua-Eoan, H. 1999. "Escaping from the Darkness." *Time.* May 31. Retrieved May 10, 2005 from http://content.time.com/time/magazine/article/0,9171,991077,00.html

Copeland, L. 2005. "Students Paid for Tattling on Peers." USA Today. Retrieved March 31, 2014, from http://usatoday30.usatoday.com/news/nation/2005-04-17-students-snitch_x.htm

Critser, G. 2005. *Generation Rx.* Boston, MA: Houghton Mifflin.

Curley, B. 2005. "Survey Finds Little Change in U.S. Drug Use." August 9. Retrieved August 10, 2005, from http://www.drugfree.org/join-together/drugs/survey-finds-little-change-in

DeGrandpre, R. 1999. *Ritalin Nation.* New York: W. W. Norton & Co.

Diller, L. 1998. *Running on Ritalin.* New York: Bantam.

"Drug Policy Alliance and ACLU Publish Student Drug Testing Booklet." (2004, January 30). Retrieved February 1, 2005, from http://www.drugpolicy.org/docUploads/drug_testing_booklet.pdf

"Drug Tests for Teen License." 2004. February 14. Retrieved February 20, 2004, from https://www.drugfree.org/join-together/drugs/drug-tests-for-teen-licenses

"Drug Use a Key Part of 'Narc' Video Game." 2005. March 17. Retrieved March 21, 2005, from http://www.drugfree.org/join-together/legal/drug-use-a-key-part-of-narc

Eberstadt, M. 1999. "Stop Drugging So Many Children." *Policy Review.* April-May.

Eberstadt, M. 2005. September 25. "A Prescribed Threat: Among the Harshest Critics of the Child Wonderdrug Regimen? Think Rock Icons." *Los Angeles Times*, 5.

Finley, L. 2003. "Militarism Goes to School." *Essays in Education*.

Finley, L. and Finley, P. 2005. *Piss Off! How Drug Testing and Other Privacy Violations Are Alienating America's Youth*. Monroe, MN: Common Courage Press.

"Florida County Evaluates Portable Drug Test for Students." 2004. March 10. Retrieved March 11, 2004, from http://www.drugfree.org/join-together/other/florida-county-evaluates-drug

"Florida Schools May Use Spray to Detect Drug Use." 2004. July 2. Retrieved July 3, 2004, from http://www.drugfree.org/join-together/other/fla-schools-may-use-spray-to

"Girls Arrested for Pretending Parsley Was Pot." 2005. December 1. Retrieved December 3, 2005, from http://www.drugfree.org/join-together/drugs/girls-arrested-for-pretending

Goldberg, C. 2006. January 26. "Studies Link Psychosis, Teenage Marijuana Use." *The Boston Globe*, Al.

Greenwood, M. 2003. April 1. "False Positives." *PRIMEDIA Business Magazines & Media, Inc*. Retrieved March 2, 2006 from LexisNexis academic database.

Hallowell, M., and J. Ratey. n.d.. *Pseudo ADD*. PBS. Retrieved November 5, 2007 from www.pbs.org/wgbh/pages/frontline/shows/medicating

Hawkins, D. 1999. May 31. "Trial by Vial." *U.S. News and World Report*, 126, 70–73.

Holguin, James. 2004. "Teen 'Scare Tactics' Not Working." *CBS News*. October 15. Retrieved March 5, 2006, from http://www.cbsnews.com/news/teen-scare-tactics-not-working/

Huffington, A. 2000. May 21. "P Is for Prozac." *Salon*. Retrieved September 12, 2005, from http://www.salon.com/news/feature/2000/03/21/prozac/index.html

Hyman, I., and P. Snook. 1999. *Dangerous Schools*. San Francisco, CA: Jossey Bass.

"Info for Parents Who Are Pressured to Diagnose and Drug Their Children for ADD or ADHD." 2002. Retrieved February 5, 2006, from http://www.ritalindeath.com

Keynes, A. 2003. "More Schools Test for Drugs After Court Ruling." *Inside School Safety*, 7(9), 5.

Lorenz, B. 2004. June 4. "'Drug Czar' Backs Random Testing at Pewaukee High School." *GMToday Online*. Retrieved March 6, 2005, from http://www.gmtoday.com/news/local_stories/2004/june_04/06042004_03.asp

Males, M. 1999. *Framing Youth: 10 Myths About the Next Generation*. Monroe, ME: Common Courage Press.

Mayer, P. 2003. May. "Student Drug Testing Not Effective at Detecting Drug Use." *University of Michigan News and Information Source*. Retrieved June 12, 2003, from http://ns.umich.edu/Releases/2003/May03/r051903.html

Mercogliano, C. 2003. *Teaching the Restless*. Boston, MA: Beacon.

Monarch Avalon. 2005. October. "Prescription for Trouble." *Girl's Life* 12 (2): 68.

"ONDCP, Ed. Dept. Award $7.2 Million for Student Drug Testing." 2005. October 21. Retrieved March 5, 2006, from http://www.drugfree.org/join-together/funding/ondcp-education-dept-award-72

"PA Schools Would Punish Students Who Refuse Drug Test." 2004. February 11. Retrieved February 12, 2004, from http://www.jointogether.org

PR Newswire Association. 2006. February 15. "Notmykid Unveils Project 7th Grade." Retrieved May 10, 2005 from http://www.prnewswire.com/news-releases/notmykid-unveils-project-7th-grade—national-25-city-education-program-on-teen-drug-use-and-the-need-to-address-the-escalating-abuse-of-prescription-drugs-55337347.html

"Prevention Group Focuses on Prescription Drugs, Testing." 2006. February 16. Retrieved February 17, 2006, from http://www.drugfree.org/join-together/drugs/prevention-group-focuses-on

"Ritalin: the Drug Time Bomb in Our Schools." 2002. Retrieved February 5, 2006, from http://www.sntp.net/ritalin/time_bomb.htm

Steinberg, M. 2000. May 24. "Ritalin: The New Violence." *Executive Intelligence Review*. Retrieved May 10, 2005, from http://members.tripod.com/american_almanac/ritalin1.htm

"Students Asked to List Peers Suspected of Drug Use." 2004. July 2. Retrieved July 5, 2004, from http://www.drugfree.org/join-together/drugs/students-asked-to-list-peers

"Study: Fewer Parents Talk to Kids About Drugs." 2005. February 22. Retrieved February 23, 2005, from https://www.drugfree.org/join-together/other/study-fewer-parents-talk-to

"Study Finds More Children, More Medications, More Errors." 2001. January. *Health and Healthcare in Schools*, 1. Retrieved March 5, 2006, from http://www.healthinschools.org/static/ejournal/january_print.aspx

Sullum, J. 2003. *Saying Yes.* New York: Jeremy P. Tarcher/Putnam.

Szalavitz, M. 2005. September 19. "The Return of Reefer Madness." *Salon.com.* Retrieved October 21, 2005 from http://www.salon.com/2005/09/19/reefer_madness/

"Teens and Drugs." n.d. *Safety First.* Retrieved February 21, 2006, from http://www.drugpolicy.org/docUploads/safetyfirst.pdf

Tunnell, K. 2004. *Pissing on Demand.* New York: New York University Press.

United States Department of Health and Human Services, Office of Applied Studies. 2004. January 2. "Parental Influences On Adolescent Marijuana Use and the Baby Boom Generation." Retrieved from http://www.samhsa.gov/data/NHSDA/BabyBoom/highlights.htm

"Want Pot? Go Online." 2005. July 8. Retrieved July 10, 2005, from https://www.drugfree.org/join-together/drugs/want-pot-go-online

Webber, J., ed. 2001. *Failure to Hold: the Politics of School Violence.* Lanham, MD: Rowman & Littlefield.

Weller, R. 2005. *Prescription Drug Education: An Analysis of Prescription Drug Information in Health Textbooks and State Health Curricular Frameworks.* Abstract for American Alliance for Health, Recreation, and Physical Education conference. Retrieved from http://aahperd.confex.com/aahperd/2005/finalprogram/session_26152.htm

Wiese, K. 2005. August 27. "Law Bans Children from Sharing Prescription Drugs at School." *Kansas City Star.*

"Youth Trade Drugs at 'Pharming' Parties." 2005. July 26. Retrieved July 28, 2005, from http://www.drugfree.org/join-together/drugs/youth-trade-drugs-at-pharming

Zimmer, L., and J. Morgan, J. 1997. *Marijuana myths, marijuana facts: A review of the scientific evidence.* New York: Drug Policy Alliance.

For Discussion

1. What are the long-term implications for students who attend schools that operate under a zero-tolerance policy with regards to drug use?
2. How can we address what appears to be a disproportionate number of young people in the US who are prescribed drugs for ADD/ADHD?

Drug Prevention
and Treatment

Drug prevention is broadly classified into three main areas: primary, secondary, and tertiary prevention. *Primary prevention* is aimed at individuals who have not used or who have limited experience with drugs (including alcohol, nicotine, and tobacco). Primary prevention initiatives are often directed at children and adolescents in an effort to deter them from initiating substance use. Although primary prevention research has made several advances over the last two decades, the United Nations Office on Drugs and Crime (2013) has highlighted the limitations of the global evidence base. First, the majority of studies have addressed the effectiveness of primary prevention in "false" environments (such as schools) so that less is known about the effects of prevention initiatives in "real world" settings where initiation opportunities become available for youth. Second, most

studies have been conducted in North America, Europe, and Australia; thus, prevention efforts and their effects in other nations are not well understood. Third, more information is needed about the *collective* program components that are most important in preventing the onset of drug use.

Project D.A.R.E. (Drug Abuse Resistance Education) is an example of a school-based primary prevention program, aimed at children and adolescents. D.A.R.E. has its roots in the United States but has now extended to several other countries. The program is believed to be operating in the majority of school districts in the United States, despite a wealth of evidence that has questioned the effectiveness of the program and in some instances has found that it is counterproductive. In general, the extent of subsequent self-reported drug use is about the same for program participants as it is for non-participants.

The D.A.R.E. curriculum is organized and distributed by D.A.R.E. America, which also oversees the training provided to thousands of police officers who deliver the program in schools. A detailed analysis by Shepard (2001) estimated that the costs to operate D.A.R.E. ranged from $1 billion to $1.3 billion annually. The program is funded by local, state, and federal taxes and to a lesser extent, by private donors. After several years of studies that pointed to the program's ineffectiveness, some school districts have replaced D.A.R.E. with other alternatives (e.g., a focus on life education, social skills, and resilience). However, additional schools have added the D.A.R.E. curriculum. Despite weak evidence for its impact on self-reported drug use, D.A.R.E. has continued its popularity in part due to the perception that it fosters good relationships between children and police (Birkeland, Murphy-Graham, and Weiss 2005), its focus on abstinence (which is appealing to parents, school administrators, and politicians), and the support from powerful spokespersons (e.g., President Obama's official proclamation of National D.A.R.E Day).

Secondary prevention is intended for individuals who are using psychoactive substances but who have not experienced continuous problems associated with drug misuse. Secondary prevention strategies (sometimes referred to as "early intervention") aim to reduce drug misuse before it develops into addiction, dependence, or other drug-related problems. For example, secondary prevention in the workplace might involve counseling for employees whose recent drug tests have indicated recent use. Considerably fewer studies have focused on secondary compared to primary drug prevention. DeMatteo and colleagues (2006) suggested that secondary prevention might be more suitable than drug treatment for those drug court participants who have low levels of drug use. *Tertiary prevention* strategies are aimed at people who experience problem drug misuse. These strategies might encourage individuals to abstain from or reduce problem drug use, or they may focus on reducing the harms associated with problem drug use. Treatment initiatives (discussed below) and relapse prevention are examples of tertiary prevention. Relapse prevention is a critical component of aftercare programs whereby individuals in recovery are taught the skills needed to avoid and manage relapse.

Treatment

Treatment is an intervention that is intended to help people who are experiencing problems with substance use. The nature of drug treatment and the way it is delivered depend greatly on the way in which drug use and addiction are perceived by treatment providers. Treatment initiatives that require the end-goal of abstinence at times incorporate punitive measures that are designed to control treatment clients and impose punishments (e.g., terminate clients' involvement in the treatment program) when clients do not comply with program rules and regulations. Other treatment ideologies view addiction as a health issue that affects the individual and the wider community. These initiatives employ the principles of harm reduction. That is, treatment providers help clients work toward the goal of reducing the harms associated with problem substance use, including reducing the frequency of drug use.

According to findings from the 2012 (US) National Survey on Drug Use and Health, an estimated 20.6 million individuals aged 12 and older did not receive treatment in the past year even though they met diagnostic criteria for alcohol or drug dependence (SAMHSA, 2013). Of this figure, only 1.1 million individuals self-reported that they needed drug/alcohol treatment during the past year, although most of them made no effort to engage with treatment. These figures suggest that either the diagnostic criteria overstated the need for treatment, or that vast numbers of individuals who are in need of treatment do not recognize or acknowledge the need.

Treatment modalities refer to the ways that we classify the different types of drug treatment. In general, modalities include residential treatment, drug-free day programs or outpatient programs, and medication-assisted addiction therapies (also referred to as opioid prescribing, opioid replacement, opioid pharmacotherapy, substitute prescribing, and a host of other terms, all of which have been contested). These modalities can incorporate behavioral therapies, counseling, or other interventions. Self-help groups are not generally categorized as a treatment modality, but we include them in the discussion below because they can be instrumental for recovery. Detoxification is not a treatment modality but is an important *stage* of the treatment process for drugs (e.g., alcohol, opioids, benzodiazepines) that produce physical dependence.

Residential treatment. The word "residential" implies overnight stays in a venue that is located away from one's home. Dozens of private residential facilities operate in the United States and elsewhere. Costs of private residential treatment in the United States often exceed $20,000 for a 30-day stay; thus, they tend to cater to people from middle- and upper-income backgrounds. Public or not-for-profit residential programs are funded by the government and, to a lesser extent, private donations. The high demand for non-private residential programs has resulted in lengthy waiting lists that often extends to six months or a year; people have fatally overdosed while waiting for a residential bed. Moreover, the effectiveness of residential treatment tends to decline unless good aftercare programs are available once the residential component has ended. Aftercare is part of a "continuum of care" approach but can be difficult to access when clients live in non-urban or remote areas of a state. Moreover, residential treatment is often not possible for parents who are the sole carers of children.

Residential therapeutic communities. The therapeutic community, or TC, is a total treatment environment in which the primary clinical staff members are typically individuals in recovery from problem substance use. These staff members often were rehabilitated in therapeutic communities. The treatment perspective of the TC is that problem drug use is a disorder of the whole person—that the problem is the person and not the drug, that addiction is a symptom and not the essence of the disorder. The TC view of recovery focuses on changing the negative patterns of behavior, emotions, and attitudes that are believed to predispose drug use. As such, the overall goal is a responsible, drug-free lifestyle. Recovery through the TC process depends on positive and negative pressures to change, and this change is brought about through a self-help process in which relationships of mutual responsibility are developed among program residents.

In addition to individual and group counseling, the TC process has a system of explicit rewards that reinforce the value of achievement. As such, privileges are earned and TCs have their own specific rules and regulations that guide the behavior of residents and the management of facilities. Violation of the cardinal rules (e.g., drug use while participating in a TC) typically results in immediate expulsion from a TC. Therapeutic communities have been available in some states for decades and have played a positive role in several prisons.

Drug-free outpatient treatment. Drug-free outpatient treatment or day programs encompass a variety of nonresidential programs that do not generally allow clients to participate in methadone or other pharmacotherapeutic maintenance while engaging with the drug-free program. Most of these programs are based on a mental health perspective, and the primary services include individual and group therapy, while some offer family therapy and relapse-prevention support. Some outpatient programs are intensive and require treatment clients to engage daily with program staff members. In other outpatient programs, clients and staff meet a few times per month or less. An increasing number of drug-free outpatient programs include case management services as adjuncts to counseling. A case management approach is designed to assist clients in obtaining needed services (e.g., medical and dental treatment, accommodation) in a timely and coordinated manner. The key components of the approach are assessing, planning, linking, monitoring, and advocating for clients within the existing nexus of treatment and social services. Evaluating the effectiveness of drug-free outpatient treatment is difficult because programs vary widely—from drop-in "rap" centers to highly structured arrangements that offer counseling or psychotherapy as the treatment mainstay. Although outpatient treatment has been moderately successful in reducing daily drug use and criminal activity, the approach appears to be less appropriate for individuals who experience major problems with drug addiction.

Medication-assisted addiction therapies. Methadone was synthesized during World War II by German chemists when supply lines for morphine were interrupted. Although chemically unlike morphine or heroin, it produces many of the same effects. Methadone was introduced in the United States in 1947, and since the 1960s the drug has been used as an important pharmacological treatment for heroin dependence (known as methadone maintenance). Methadone has unique properties in that it can be administered orally, once per day, and helps to reduce cravings for and withdrawal symptoms associated with heroin dependence. In the 1960s, Vincent Dole, Marie Nyswander, and Mary Jeanne Kreek envisioned methadone maintenance to be an important part of treatment for heroin dependence but also believed that treatment should include psychosocial interventions, depending on the needs of the clients. More recently, high-dose buprenorphine (Subutex in some western European countries; Suboxone in the United States) also has been recognized as an effective intervention for opioid dependence. In some countries (e.g., United Kingdom), methadone or high-dose burprenorphine prescriptions are available at no financial cost to the patient. In contrast, clients on methadone or Suboxone maintenance in the United States pay as much as $400 to $500 per month, depending on health insurance and their eligibility for social welfare (i.e., Medicaid).

Self-help/12-step groups. Self-help groups that incorporate 12-step principles are composed of individuals who meet regularly to stabilize and facilitate their recovery from problem substance use. The best known is Alcoholics Anonymous (AA), in which sobriety is based on fellowship and adhering to the "12 Steps" of recovery. The 12 steps stress faith, confession of wrongdoing, and passivity in the hands of a "higher power," and move group members from a statement of powerlessness over drugs and alcohol to a resolution that they will carry the message of help to others and will practice the principles learned in all affairs. In addition to AA, other popular self-help groups are Narcotics Anonymous (NA) and Cocaine Anonymous (CA), both of which follow the 12-step model. All of these organizations operate as standalone fellowship programs but are also used as adjuncts to other modalities. Although few evaluation studies of self-help groups have been carried out, the weight of clinical and observational data suggest that they can be crucial to facilitating recovery.

In conclusion, treatment is best viewed as a process that can span several years. Indeed, some individuals engage in cyclical patterns that involve drug use, treatment, abstinence, relapse, and additional treatment attempts. Some of the most successful treatment initiatives incorporate holistic approaches that attempt to address addiction as well as other lifestyle problems, for example, housing, employment, education and training, and relationships with significant others and family. Finally, some individuals who experience drug dependence or addiction eventually abstain from drug use without ever engaging with treatment services. This process is referred to as "natural recovery" (Waldorf 1983), and although difficult, it is certainly possible. The chapters in this section address drug prevention, 12-step programs (i.e., Narcotics Anonymous), methadone maintenance, and issues affecting women who experience drug problems.

References

Birkeland, S., E. Murphy-Graham, and C. Weiss. 2005. "Good Reasons for Ignoring Good Evaluation: The Case of the Drug Abuse Resistance Education (D.A.R.E.) Program." *Evaluation and Program Planning* 28: 247–256.

DeMatteo, D. S., D. B. Marlowe, and D. S. Festinger. 2006. "Secondary Prevention Services for Clients Who Are Low Risk in Drug Court: A Conceptual Model." *Crime and Delinquency* 52: 114–134.

Dole, V. P., & Nyswander, M. E. (1980). Methadone maintenance: A theoretical perspective. In D. J. Lettieri, M. Sayers, & H. W. Pearson (Eds.), Theories on drug abuse: Selected contemporary perspectives (pp. 256–261). NIDA Research Monograph 30. Washington, DC: U. S. Government Printing Office. Retrieved from http://archives.drugabuse.gov/pdf/monographs/download30.html

Shepard, E. M. 2001. *The Economic Costs of D.A.R.E.* Research Paper Number 22. Syracuse, NY: LaMoyne College, Institute of Industrial Relations.

Substance Abuse and Mental Health Services Administration (SAMHSA). 2013. *Results from the 2012 National Survey on Drug Use and Health: Summary of National Findings*, NSDUH Series H-46, HHS Publication No. (SMA) 13-4795. Rockville, MD: Author.

United Nations Office on Drugs and Crime. 2013. *International Standards on Drug Use Prevention.* Vienna: Author.

Waldorf, D. 1983. "Natural Recovery from Opiate Addiction: Some Social-Psychological Processes of Untreated Recovery." *Journal of Drug Issues* 83: 237–280.

26

Safety First

A Reality-Based Approach to Teens and Drugs

MARSHA ROSENBAUM

Drug Abuse Resistance Education (D.A.R.E.) has been embraced by the majority of public schools, despite evidence that questions its effectiveness. Marsha Rosenbaum presents an alternative to D.A.R.E.—one that focuses on a "safety first" approach when addressing drug education with teenagers.

Understanding Teenage Drug Use

The 2010 Monitoring the Future survey states that more than 48 percent of high school seniors have tried illegal drugs at some point in their lifetime; 38 percent used a drug during the past year; and nearly 23.8 percent profess to have used drugs in the past month. The numbers are even higher for alcohol: 72.5 percent have tried alcohol (itself a potent drug in every regard); 65 percent have used it within the year; and 41 percent (almost twice the statistic for marijuana) of those surveyed imbibed "once a month or more."[3] The Centers for Disease Control and Prevention's (CDC) 2009 Youth Risk Behavior Survey found that 21 percent of high school students reported taking "more than a few sips" of alcohol before the age of 13.[4]

In order to understand teenage drug use, it is imperative to recognize the context in which today's teens have grown up. Alcohol, tobacco, caffeine, over-the-counter and prescription drugs are everywhere. Though we urge our young people to be "drug-free," Americans are constantly bombarded with messages encouraging us to imbibe and medicate with a variety of substances. We use alcohol to celebrate ("Let's drink to that!"), to recreate ("I can't wait to kick back and have a cold one!") and even to medicate ("I really need a drink!"). We use caffeine to boost our energy, prescription and over-the-counter drugs to modify our moods, lift us out of depression and help us work, study and sleep.

Drugs are an integral part of American life. In fact, eight out of ten adults in the U.S. use at least one medication every week, and half take a prescription drug.[5] One in two adults in this country use alcohol regularly; and more than 104 million Americans over the age of 12 have tried marijuana at some time in their lives—a fact not lost on their children.[6]

Today's teenagers have witnessed first-hand the increasing, sometimes forced "Ritalinization" of their fellow students.[7] Stimulants such as Adderal, an amphetamine product, have become a drug of choice on many college campuses. We see prime-time network commercials for drugs to manage such ailments as "Generalized Anxiety

Reprinted from Marsha Rosenbaum, 2012, *Safety First: A Reality-Based Approach to Teens and Drugs*. New York: Drug Policy Alliance.

Disorder," and teenagers see increasing numbers of their parents using anti-depressants to cope with life's problems.

While "peer pressure" is often blamed for teenage drug use, the 2008–2009 State of Our Nation's Youth survey found that, contrary to popular belief, most are not pressured to use drugs. Instead, teenage drug use seems to mirror modern American drug-taking tendencies.[8] Some psychologists argue that given the nature of our culture, teenage experimentation with legal and illegal mind-altering substances should not be considered abnormal or deviant behavior.[9]

Problems with Current Prevention Strategies

Americans have been trying to prevent teenage drug use for more than a century—from the nineteenth-century temperance campaigns against alcohol to Nancy Reagan's "Just Say No." A variety of methods, from scare tactics to resistance techniques to zero-tolerance policies and random drug testing (not to mention more than 750,000 arrests in 2009 for marijuana possession alone), have been used to try to persuade, coax and force young people to abstain.

The effectiveness of these conventional approaches, however, has been compromised by:

- the unwillingness to distinguish between drug use and abuse by proclaiming "all use is abuse";
- the use of misinformation as a scare tactic; and
- the failure to provide comprehensive information that would help users to reduce the harms that can result from drug use.

Use Versus Abuse

In the effort to stop teenage experimentation, prevention messages often pretend there is no difference between use and abuse. Some use the terms interchangeably; others emphasize an exaggerated definition that categorizes any use of illegal drugs as abuse.

This hypocritical message is often dismissed by teens who see that adults routinely make distinctions between use and abuse. Young people rapidly learn

this difference, too, as most observe their parents and other adults using alcohol without abusing it. They know there is a big difference between having a glass of wine with dinner and having a bottle of wine with breakfast. Many also know that their parents have tried an illegal drug (likely marijuana) at some point in their lives without abusing it or continuing to use it.

Few things are more frightening to a parent than a teenager whose use of alcohol and/or other drugs gets out of hand. Yet virtually all studies have found that the vast majority of students who try legal and/or illegal drugs do not become drug abusers.[10]

Of course, any substance use involves risk. But we need to talk about alcohol and other drugs in a sophisticated manner and distinguish between *use* and *abuse*. If not, we lose credibility. Furthermore, by acknowledging distinctions, we can more effectively recognize problems if and when they occur.

Scare Tactics and Misinformation: Marijuana As a Case in Point

A common belief held by many educators, policymakers and parents is that if young people believe drug use is risky, they will abstain.[11] In this effort, marijuana (the most popular illegal drug among U.S. teens) is consistently mischaracterized by prevention programs, books, ads and websites, including those managed by the federal government. Exaggerated claims of marijuana's dangers are routinely published, and although the old *Reefer Madness*–style messages have been replaced with assertions of scientific evidence, the most serious of these allegations falter when critically evaluated.

In my workshops parents regularly question claims they have heard about marijuana:

- Is it true that marijuana is significantly more potent and dangerous today than in the past?
- Is today's marijuana really more addictive than ever before?
- Does marijuana really cause users to seek out "harder" drugs?
- Is it true that smoking marijuana causes lung cancer?

To separate myth from fact, (the late) Professor Lynn Zimmer of Queens College of the City University of New York and Dr. John P. Morgan of the City University of New York Medical School carefully examined the published, peer-reviewed scientific evidence relevant to the most popular claims about marijuana in their book, *Marijuana Myths, Marijuana Facts: A Review of the Scientific Evidence*. Professor Mitch Earleywine of the State University of New York at Albany also took a critical look at the research in *Understanding Marijuana: A New Look at the Scientific Evidence*. Each found that claims of marijuana's risks had been exaggerated, even in some instances fabricated.[12] Their findings are not uncommon, as these same conclusions have been reached by numerous official commissions, including the La Guardia Commission in 1944, the National Commission on Marijuana and Drug Abuse in 1972, the National Academy of Sciences in 1982 and the federally chartered Institute of Medicine in 1999. Using these resources, as well as many others, here's how I've tried, ever so briefly, to answer parents' questions:

Potency

Many people believe that the marijuana available today is significantly more potent than in decades past. The drug czar says so; growers marketing their product say so; and adolescents trying to distinguish themselves from their parents' generation say so.[13] As marijuana-growing techniques have become more advanced and refined, there has been a corresponding increase in the plant's average psychoactive potency, otherwise known as its THC (delta-9 tetrahydrocannabinol) content level.

As a result, the federally funded University of Mississippi's Marijuana Potency Project estimates that average THC levels have increased since 1988 from approximately 3.7 percent to over 8 percent. However, the National Drug Intelligence Center reports that "most of the marijuana available in the domestic drug markets is lower potency, commercial grade marijuana,"[14] and the Drug Enforcement Administration affirms that of the thousands of pounds of marijuana seized by law enforcement annually, fewer than 2 percent of samples test positive for extremely high (above 20 percent) THC levels.[15]

In short, it appears that marijuana now is, on average, somewhat stronger than in the past, though variation has always been the norm. Does this mean that the marijuana available today is a qualitatively different drug than that smoked by 40- and 50-something-year-olds when they were teenagers? Not really. Essentially, marijuana is the same plant now as it was then, with any increased strength akin to the difference between beer (at 6 percent alcohol), and wine (at 10–14 percent alcohol), or between a cup of tea and an espresso.

Furthermore, even with higher potency, no studies demonstrate that increased THC content is associated with greater harm to the user or any risk of fatal overdose.[16] In fact, among those who report experiencing the effects of unusually strong marijuana, many complain of dysphoria and subsequently avoid it altogether. Others adjust their use accordingly, consuming very small amounts to achieve the desired effect.[17]

Addiction

Although marijuana lacks the severe physical dependence associated with drugs such as alcohol and heroin, a minority of users find it psychologically difficult to moderate their use or quit. The vast majority of those who experience difficulty with marijuana also have pre-existing mental health problems that can be exacerbated by cannabis.[18] According to the National Academy of Sciences, 9 percent of marijuana users exhibit symptoms of dependence, as defined by the American Psychiatric Association's DSM-IV criteria.[19]

Those who argue that marijuana is addictive often point to increasing numbers of individuals entering treatment for cannabis. While some of these individuals are in rehab because they (or their families) believed their marijuana use was adversely impacting their lives, most were arrested for possession and referred to treatment by the courts as a requirement of their probation.

Over the past decade, voluntary admissions for cannabis have actually dropped, while criminal justice referrals to drug treatment have risen dramatically. According to current state and national statistics, almost 60 percent of all individuals in treatment for marijuana are "legally coerced" into treatment.[20]

The Gateway Theory

The "gateway" theory suggests that marijuana use inevitably leads to the use of harder drugs, such as cocaine and heroin.[21] However, population data compiled by the National Survey on Drug Use and Health and others demonstrate that the vast majority of marijuana users do not progress to more dangerous drugs.[22] The gateway theory has also been refuted by the Institute of Medicine and in a study published in the prestigious *American Journal of Public Health.*[23]

The overwhelming majority of marijuana users never try any other illicit substance.[24] Furthermore, those populations who report using marijuana in early adulthood typically report voluntarily ceasing their cannabis use by the time they reach age 30.[25] Consequently, for most who use it, marijuana is a "terminus" rather than a "gateway."

Recent research also reveals that the vast majority of teens who try marijuana do not go on to become dependent or even use it on a regular basis.[26]

Lung Cancer

Although inhaling cannabis can irritate the pulmonary system, research has yet to demonstrate that smoking marijuana, even long term, causes diseases of the lung, upper aero digestive tract, or mouth.[27]

Most recently, in the largest study of its kind ever conducted, National Institute on Drug Abuse researcher Dr. Donald Tashkin and his colleagues at the University of California at Los Angeles compared 1,212 head, lung or neck cancer patients to 1,040 demographically matched individuals without cancer and reported, "Contrary to our expectations, we found no positive associations between marijuana use and lung or [upper aero digestive tract] cancers . . . even among subjects who reported smoking more than 22,000 joints over their lifetime."[28]

No drug, including marijuana, is completely safe.

Yet the consistent mischaracterization of marijuana may be the Achilles' heel of current drug prevention approaches because programs and messages too often contain exaggerations and misinformation that contradict young people's own observations and experience. As a result, teens become cynical and lose confidence in what we, as parents and teachers, tell them. We've got to tell the truth, because if we don't, teenagers will not consider us credible sources of information. Although they know we have their best interests at heart, they also know we'll say just about anything—whether or not it's true—to get them to abstain.

Just Say No or Say Nothing at All?

Most drug education programs are aimed solely at preventing drug use. After instructions to abstain, the lesson ends. There is no information on how to avoid problems or prevent abuse for those who do experiment. Abstinence is treated as the sole measure of success, and the only acceptable teaching option.

While the abstinence-only mandate is well-intended, this approach is clearly not enough. It is unrealistic to believe that at a time in their lives when they are most prone to risk-taking, teenagers—who find it exciting to push the envelope—will completely refrain from trying alcohol and/or other drugs.[29] The abstinence-only mandate puts adults in the unenviable position of having nothing to say to the young people we need most to reach—those who insist on saying "maybe," or "sometimes" or even "yes" to drugs.[30]

Teenagers will make their own choices about alcohol and other drugs, just as we did. Like us, their mistakes are sometimes foolish. To help prevent drug abuse and drug problems among teenagers who do experiment, we need a fallback strategy that includes comprehensive education, and one that puts safety first.

Safety First: A Reality-Based Approach

Surveys tell us that despite our admonitions and advice to abstain, large numbers of teenagers will occasionally experiment with intoxicating substances, and some will use alcohol and/or other drugs more regularly. This does not mean they are bad kids or we are neglectful parents. The reality is that drug use is a part of teenage culture in America today. In all likelihood, our young people will come out of this phase unharmed.

Keeping teenagers safe should be our highest priority. To protect them, a reality-based approach enables teenagers to make responsible decisions by:

- providing honest, science-based information;
- encouraging moderation if youthful experimentation persists;
- promoting an understanding of the legal and social consequences of drug use; and
- prioritizing safety through personal responsibility and knowledge.

Honest, Science-Based Education

Young people are capable of rational thinking. Although their decision-making skills will improve as they mature, teenagers are learning responsibility, and do not want to destroy their lives or their health.[31] In fact, in our workshops with students, they consistently request the "real" facts about drugs so they can make responsible decisions—and the vast majority actually do. According to the 2009 National Survey on Drug Use and Health, although experimentation is widespread, 90 percent of 12- to 17-year-olds choose to refrain from regular use.[32]

Effective drug education should be based on sound science and acknowledge teenagers' ability to understand, analyze and evaluate. The subject of drugs can be integrated into a variety of high school courses and curricula, including physiology and biology (how drugs affect the body), psychology (how drugs affect the mind), chemistry (what's contained in drugs), social studies (who uses which drugs, and why) and history and civics (how drugs have been handled by various governments).

Rodney Skager, Professor Emeritus, University of California at Los Angeles and Chair of the California Statewide Task Force for Effective Drug Education, suggests that through family experience, peer exposure and the media, teenagers often know more about alcohol and other drugs than we assume. Therefore, students should be included in the development of drug education programs, and classes should utilize interaction and student participation rather than rote lecturing. If drug education is to be credible, formal curricula should incorporate the observations and experiences of young people themselves.[33]

Teens clamor for honest, comprehensive drug education, and it is especially apparent when they leave home and go to college. According to Professor Craig Reinarman at the University of California at Santa Cruz:

> Students seem to hunger for information about licit and illicit drugs that doesn't strike them as moralistic propaganda. I've taught a large lecture course called "Drugs and Society" for over twenty years and each year I have to turn away dozens of students because the class fills up so quickly.
>
> I always start by asking them, "How many of you had drug education in high school?" and nearly all of them raise their hands. Then I ask, "How many of you felt it was truthful and valuable?" Out of 120 students, perhaps three hands go up.[34]

The Importance of Moderation

The vast majority of teenage drug use (with the exception of nicotine) does not lead to dependence or abusive habits.[35]

Teens who do use alcohol, marijuana and/or other drugs must understand there is a huge difference between use and abuse, and between occasional and daily use.

They should know how to recognize irresponsible behavior when it comes to place, time, dose levels and frequency of use. If young people continue, despite our admonitions, to use alcohol and/or other drugs, they must control their use by practicing moderation and limiting use. It is impossible to do well academically or meet one's responsibilities at work while intoxicated. It is never appropriate to use alcohol and/or other drugs at school, at work, while participating in sports, while driving or engaging in any serious activity.

Understanding Consequences

Young people must understand the consequences of violating school rules and local and state laws against the use, possession and sale of alcohol and other drugs—whether or not they agree with such policies.

With increasing methods of detection such as school-based drug testing and zero-tolerance policies, illegality is a risk in and of itself which extends beyond the physical effects of drug use. There are real, lasting consequences of using drugs and being caught, including expulsion from school, a criminal record and social stigma. The Higher Education Act—now being challenged by many organizations, including Students for Sensible Drug Policy (www.ssdp.org)—has resulted in the denial of college loans for more than 200,000 U.S. students convicted of any drug offense. This law was scaled back in 2006, but the penalty still applies to students who are convicted while they are enrolled in school.[36]

Fortunately, zero-tolerance policies—which have contributed to a high school drop-out rate of 30 percent in this country—have come under serious attack. The American Psychological Association concluded in 2008 that such policies "run counter to our best knowledge of child development" and have created "unintended consequences for students, families, and communities."[37] Support is now growing for "restorative practices" that attempt to bring students closer to their communities and schools rather than suspending and expelling those who are troublesome or truant.[38]

Young people need to know that if they are caught in possession of drugs, they will find themselves at the mercy of the juvenile and criminal justice systems.

More than half a million Americans, almost a quarter of our total incarcerated population, are behind bars today for drug law violations. As soon as teenagers turn eighteen they are prosecuted as adults and run the risk of serving long mandatory sentences, even for something they believe to be a minor offense.

Put Safety First

Alcohol as a Case in Point

Motor vehicle accidents continue to be the number one cause of untimely death among young people,

according to the National Highway Safety Administration. Each year, nearly 2,400 American teenagers die in car accidents involving alcohol and far more are seriously injured.[40]

In suburban communities, where so many young people drive, the teenage practice of having a "designated driver" has become commonplace. In these same communities, there are some parents who have strongly encouraged their teens to abstain, assessed reality and reluctantly provided their homes as safe, non-driving spaces to gather.

Others see these practices as "enabling." They hope to stop alcohol use completely by passing laws that make it a crime to be a teenaged designated driver, as well as "social host" ordinances that impose civil or criminal penalties on parents whose homes are used for parties—with or without their knowledge and/or consent.

What worries me is how young people respond to the proliferation of such ordinances. When asked in particular about social host laws, the response is not, "Okay then, I'm going to stop drinking." Too many teens say they will just move the party to the street, the local park, the beach or some other public place. And they'll drive there.

These are hot-button issues to be sure, with reasonable and well-meaning people coming down on all sides of the debate.

Sober gatherings should, of course, be promoted in every way possible, and parents should devise strategies for minimizing the harm that can result from the use of alcohol. To involve the criminal justice system in parental decisions, however, is not the answer, and will certainly reduce, not improve, teen safety.

Safe Sex as a Model

A useful model for envisioning safety-oriented drug abuse prevention is the modern, comprehensive sex education approach.

In the mid-1980s, when scientists discovered that the use of condoms could prevent the spread of HIV and other sexually transmitted diseases, as well as teen pregnancies, parents, teachers and policy makers took action. They introduced reality-based sex education curricula throughout the country. This approach strongly encouraged abstinence, and provided the facts along with accurate "safe sex" information.

According to the Centers for Disease Control and Prevention (CDC), this approach has resulted not just in the increased use of condoms among sexually active teenagers, but has also served to decrease overall rates of sexual activity.[41]

This effective, comprehensive prevention strategy presents a strong case and provides a model for restructuring our drug education and abuse prevention efforts.

What's a Parent to Do?

Today's parents get more advice, too often in excruciating detail, about how to raise their children, than any generation in history. Yet they're open and listening because they're concerned about their teens' safety and well-being, and worried that the world has become a much more dangerous place. They want to know what to do, and are looking for solutions.

There are no easy answers, but for parents who have requested specifics, here are the steps I suggest:

Step 1: Listen

The first step is to "get real" about drug use by listening to what teens have to tell us about their lives and their feelings. This will guide us toward intelligent, thoughtful action.

A useful venue is the dinner table. As much as possible, families should eat together once a day so they can "catch up," talk and otherwise connect.[42]

There are many other natural openings for conversation, such as drug use in movies, television and music. If we can remain as non-judgmental as possible, teenagers will seek our opinions and guidance. Let them know they can talk freely. Our greatest challenge is to listen and try to help without excessive admonishment. If we become indignant and punitive, teenagers will stop talking to us. It's that simple.

Remember that advice is most likely to be heard when it is requested. Realize that teens bring their own experiences to the table, some of which you may not want to hear. But breathe deeply and be grateful when they share these experiences because this means you have established trust.

Step 2: Learn

Parents and teachers need to take responsibility for learning about the physiological, psychological and sociological effects of alcohol and other drugs. This involves reading and asking questions.

Familiarize yourself with teenage culture through print and electronic media, especially the Internet. Watch MTV. Learn about the array of drugs available to young people, but be sure your sources are scientifically grounded and balanced. Any source that fails to describe both risks and benefits should be considered suspect.

The Drug Policy Alliance website, www.drugpolicy.org/safetyfirst, contains balanced information with facts about the effects of today's most prevalent drugs.

For an all-around resource that covers nearly every popular drug, you and your teen should read *From Chocolate to Morphine: Everything You Need to Know about Mind-Altering Drugs*, by renowned health expert, Andrew Weil, MD, and former high school teacher, Winifred Rosen (Boston: Houghton-Mifflin, 2004).

For information about marijuana in particular, read *Understanding Marijuana: A New Look at the Scientific Evidence* by Mitch Earleywine, Ph.D. (New York: Oxford University Press, 2002) and/or *Marijuana Myths, Marijuana Facts: A Review of the Scientific Evidence* by Lynn Zimmer, Ph.D. and John P. Morgan, MD (New York: The Lindesmith Center, 1997).

Step 3: Act

Drug abuse prevention is not a curriculum package or a "magic bullet," so make some plans.

It is important to keep teens engaged and busy, not just during the school day, but from 3 to 6 p.m., when the use of drugs by bored, unsupervised teens is highest. Extracurricular programs such as sports, arts, drama and other creative activities should be available to all secondary school students, at low or no cost to parents. Become an advocate for such programs in your community and teens' school.

Prevention is fundamentally about caring, connected relationships and an open exchange of information. There are no easy answers, just thoughtful conversations.

When it comes to opening the ongoing "drug talk," some parents don't know where to begin. Many have started with my "Dear Johnny" letter or other resources listed above. Teens often respond better to these "just say know" approaches than to the one-sided messages they've been hearing all their lives.

Many parents today have experimented with drugs. The question, "What should I tell my child about my own past drug use?" comes up in each and every workshop I facilitate—from California to Utah to Connecticut. Many parents are uneasy about revealing their own experience, fearing such admissions might open the door to their own teen's experimentation.

There is no one simple resolution to this difficult dilemma. While you do not need to rehash every detail, it can be very helpful to share your own experiences with your teen because it makes you a more credible confidant.

Honesty is usually the best policy in the long run. Just as parents often know or eventually find out when their child is lying, teenagers have a knack for seeing through adults' evasions, half-truths and hypocrisy. Besides, if you don't tell, you can rest assured that eventually one of your siblings or close friends will delight in recounting your "youthful indiscretions" to your eager child.

Trusting relationships are key in preventing and countering drug use. While it is tempting to cut through difficult conversations and utilize detection technologies such as urine testing, think hard before you demand that your child submit to a drug test. Random, suspicionless school-based drug testing—which has been opposed by the California State Parent Teacher Association (PTA)—has been shown to be ineffective and often counterproductive (see www.drugpolicy.org/safetyfirst).

Regarding in-home test kits, researchers at Children's Hospital in Boston, who studied home drug testing products, warn that most people are not appropriately educated about the limitations and technical challenges of drug tests (including collection procedures, the potential for misinterpretation and false positive/negative results). They also note unanticipated consequences and the negative effect on parent-child relationships of collecting a urine sample to ascertain drug use.[43]

The reality is that a trusting, open relationship with a parent or other respected adult can be the most powerful element in deterring abusive patterns. And trust, once lost, can be hard to regain.

Perhaps most important, teenagers need to know that the important adults in their lives are concerned primarily with their safety; that they have someone to turn to when they need help. If they find themselves in a compromising or uncomfortable situation, they need to know we will come to their aid immediately.

Step 4: Lead

PTA leaders and other parent groups often request "Safety First" speakers for their meetings.

A few years ago I addressed the National PTA convention, showing parent leaders how they could facilitate a drug education workshop at their own school. I told the attendees that outside "experts" are not necessary. Parent workshops, after all, are fundamentally about opening a discussion to share science-based information and to connect with others in the community. Training resources and information about such workshops (such as our DVD, *Safety First: The Workshop*) are available at www.drugpolicy.org.

I understand that it is difficult to get parents to come out for evening meetings, but one parent at a middle school in Torrance, California, had a brilliant idea. She was so committed to the importance of parent drug education that she convinced several teachers to offer extra credit to students whose parents attended the workshop. A record 272 parents packed the auditorium that night!

In general, it is important for parents to get to know each other and work together to promote safety-oriented strategies. The emphasis on safety does not mean we are giving teens permission to use drugs. It simply affirms that their welfare is our top priority.

Step 5: Help

It is important to know what to do if you believe a teenager (or anyone else) is having a negative reaction to alcohol and/or other drugs.

For instance, do not allow a person who has consumed too much alcohol and is passed-out to lay on their back. Many people in this situation have choked on their own vomit and asphyxiated.

In an acute situation, if you fear something is seriously wrong—such as when a person is unconscious or having trouble breathing—do not hesitate to phone 911 immediately. The lives of many young people could have been saved if paramedics had been called—or called sooner.

Don't take a chance. If you share nothing else you have read here, please convey this information to your own teen, who may one day need to assist a friend.

Even when it's not an emergency, there is little more disturbing to a parent than a teenager who is obviously intoxicated, stoned or high. Many parents want to know how to identify problem use, what to do about it and when to seek professional help.

I highly recommend the work of psychologist Stanton Peele, Ph.D., who lays out criteria for deciding whether your child needs treatment, the treatment options and your role as a parent, in his book, *Addiction Proof Your Child*. For parents concerned that their teen may have a marijuana problem, I also recommend Timmen Cermak's book, *Marijuana: What's a Parent to Believe?*[44]

Keep in mind there is no "one size fits all" method for dealing with troubled teens that have alcohol and/or other drug problems. Remember that many of today's well-meaning programs are still unevaluated and inflexible. Be especially leery of boot camp–style programs that can do more harm than good, such as those studied by journalist Maia Szalavitz in her book, *Help At Any Cost: How the Troubled-Teen Industry Cons Parents and Hurts Kids*.[45]

In the end, the healthiest kids, whether or not they experiment with drugs, have parents who are present, loving and involved. Carla Niño, past president of the California State PTA (the largest state PTA in America, with one million members, and second-largest parent organization in the world), gives the following advice:

> Trust your instincts, which are to love your kids enough to give them the space to explore and grow, to forgive their mistakes and to accept them for who they are. Kids go through tough times, sometimes seemingly prolonged. Those who make it do so because they're embraced and loved by their families.

Notes

1. Office of National Drug Control Policy, 2010, *The White House National Drug Control Strategy: FY 2011 Budget Summary* (Washington, DC: U.S. Government Printing Office, March), http://www.whitehouse.gov/sites/default/files/ondcp/policy-and-research/fy11budget.pdf

2. Marsha Rosenbaum, "A Mother's Advice," 1998, *San Francisco Chronicle*, sec. A, September 7, http://www.erowid.org/psychoactives/families/families_article2.shtml

3. Johnston, L. D., P. M. O'Malley, J. G. Bachman, and J. E. Schulenberg, 2011, *Monitoring the Future: National Results on Adolescent Drug Use: Overview of Key Findings, 2010.* (Ann Arbor: Institute for Social Research, University of Michigan), http://www.monitoringthefuture.org/pubs/monographs/mtf-overview2010.pdf

4. Centers for Disease Control and Prevention, 2009, "Drank Alcohol for the First Time Before Age 13 Years (Other Than a Few Sips)," *High School Youth Risk Behavior Survey, 2009.* (Atlanta, GA: Centers for Disease Control and Prevention)

5. Slone Epidemiology Center at Boston University, 2006, *Patterns of Medication Use in the United States 2006*, Slone Survey, http://www.bu.edu/slone/files/2012/11/SloneSurveyReport2006.pdf

6. Substance Abuse and Mental Health Services Administration (SAMHSA), 2009, *Results from the 2009 National Survey on Drug Use and Health: National Findings*, NSDUH Series H-30, DHHS Publication No. SMA 06-4194 (Rockville, MD: Office of Applied Studies), http://oas.samhsa.gov/NSDUH/2k9NSDUH/2k9ResultsP.pdf

7. Brad Knickerbocker, 1999, "Using Drugs to Rein in Boys," *The Christian Science Monitor*, May 19, http://www.csmonitor.com/1999/0519/p1s2.html

8. Peter D. Hart Associates, 2008, *The State of Our Nation's Youth: 2008–2009* (Alexandria, VA: Horatio Alger Association of Distinguished Americans); for an excellent discussion of the role of drugs in American culture, see Craig Reinarman and Harry G. Levine, 1997, "The Cultural Contradictions of Punitive Prohibition" in *Crack in America: Demon Drugs and Social Justice*, eds. Craig Reinarman and Harry G. Levine, 334–44 (Berkeley: University of California Press).

9. Michael D. Newcomb and Peter M. Bentler, 1988, *Consequences of Adolescent Drug Use: Impact on*

the *Lives of Young Adults* (Newbury Park, CA: Sage); Jonathan Shedler and Jack Block, 1990, "Adolescent Drug Use and Psychological Health: A Longitudinal Inquiry," *American Psychologist* 45, no. 5 (May): 612–30.

10. United States General Accounting Office, 1993, *Drug Use Among Youth: No Simple Answers to Guide Prevention*, Report to the Chairman, Subcommittee on Children, Family, Drugs, and Alcoholism, Committee on Labor and Human Resources, U.S. Senate (Washington, DC: U.S. Government Printing Office, December), http://archive.gao.gov/t2pbat4/150661.pdf (hereafter cited as *Drug Use Among Youth*); D. F. Duncan, 1991, "Problems Associated with Three Commonly Used Drugs: A Survey of Rural Secondary School Students," *Psychology of Addictive Behavior* 5 (2): 93–6.

11. J. G. Bachman, L. D. Johnston, and P. M. O'Malley, 1990, "Explaining the Recent Decline in Cocaine Use Among Young Adults: Further Evidence That Perceived Risks and Disapproval Lead to Reduced Drug Use," *Journal of Health and Human Social Behavior* 31 (2): 173–84.

12. Lynn Zimmer, Ph.D. and John P. Morgan, MD, 1997, *Marijuana Myths, Marijuana Facts: A Review of the Scientific Evidence* (New York: The Lindesmith Center), (hereafter cited as Zimmer and Morgan); Mitch Earleywine, 2005, *Understanding Marijuana: A New Look at the Scientific Evidence* (New York: Oxford University Press).

13. Maggie Fox, "U.S. Marijuana Even Stronger Than Before: Report," *Reuters*, April 25, 2007; Katherine Seligman, "Connoisseurs of Cannabis," *San Francisco Chronicle*, April 22, 2007.

14. University of Mississippi Marijuana Potency Monitoring Project, Report 95, January 9, 2007, University, MS: Author.
National Drug Intelligence Center, "Marijuana," *National Drug Threat Assessment 2007* (October 2006), http://www.justice.gov/archive/ndic/pubs21/21137/21137p.pdf

15. National Drug Intelligence Center, 2008, *National Drug Threat Assessment, 2008* ed. (Washington, DC: U.S Department of Justice), http://www.justice.gov/archive/ndic/pubs25/25921/25921p.pdf

16. Mitch Earleywine, 2005, *Understanding Marijuana: A New Look at the Scientific Evidence* (New York: Oxford University Press).

17. Ronald I. Herning, William D. Hooker, and Reese T. Jones, 1986, "Tetrahydrocannabinol Content and Differences in Marijuana Smoking Behavior," *Psychopharmacology* 90, no. 2 (September): 160–2; D. I. Abrams and others, 2007, "Vaporization as a Smokeless Cannabis Delivery System: A Pilot Study," *Clinical Pharmacology & Therapeutics*, April 11, http://www.nature.com/clpt/journal/vaop/ncurrent/full/6100200a.html.

18. F. M. Tims and others, 2002, "Characteristics and Problems of 600 Adolescent Cannabis Abusers in Outpatient Treatment," *Addiction* 97, no. 1 (December): 46–57.

19. Janet Elizabeth Joy, John A. Benson, and Stanley J.Watson, eds., 1999, *Marijuana and Medicine: Assessing the Science Base* (Washington, DC: National Academies Press) (hereafter cited as Joy, Benson, and Watson).

20. U.S. Dept. of Health and Human Services, Substance Abuse and Mental Health Services Administration (SAMHSA), Office of Applied Studies, 2010, *Treatment Episode Data Set—Admissions (TEDS-A)*. Prepared by Synectics for Management Decisions, Incorporated. ICPSR03024-v10. Ann Arbor, MI: Inter-university Consortium for Political and Social Research; U.S. Dept. of Health and Human Services, SAMHSA, Office of Applied Studies, 2011, *Treatment Episode Data Set—Admissions (TEDS-A)*. Prepared by Synectics for Management Decisions, Incorporated. ICPSR27241-v3. Ann Arbor, MI: Inter-university Consortium for Political and Social Research.

21. Denise B. Kandel, 1975, "Stages in Adolescent Involvement in Drug Use," *Science* 190, no. 4217 (November): 912–4; S. G. Gabany and P. Plummer, 1990, "The Marijuana Perception Inventory: The Effects of Substance Abuse Instruction," *Journal of Drug Education* 20 (3): 235–45.

22. Zimmer and Morgan; Joel H. Brown and Jordan E. Horowitz, 1993, "Deviance and Deviants: Why Adolescent Substance Use Prevention Programs Do Not Work," *Evaluation Review* 17, no. 5 (October): 529–55; SAMHSA; Andrew R. Morral, Daniel F. McCaffrey, and Susan M. Paddock,

2002, "Reassessing the Marijuana Gateway Effect," *Addiction* 97, no. 12 (December), 1493–1504.

23. Joy, Benson, and Watson; A. Golub and B. D. Johnson, 2001, "Variation in Youthful Risks of Progression from Alcohol/Tobacco to Marijuana and to Hard Drugs Across Generations," *American Journal of Public Health* 91, no. 2 (February): 225–32.

24. Advisory Council on the Misuse of Drugs, 2002, *The Classification of Cannabis under the Misuse of Drugs Act 1971* (London: Home Office Government Printing Office).

25. Denise B. Kandel and Kazuo Yamaguchi, 1984, "Patterns of Drug Use from Adolescence to Young Adulthood: III. Predictors of Progression," *American Journal of Public Health* 74, no. 7 (July): 673–81; Jerald G. Bachman and others, 1992, *Changes in Drug Use during the Post-High School Years. Monitoring the Future Occasional Paper No. 35* (Ann Arbor, MI: Institute for Social Research); Joy, Benson, and Watson.

26. SAMHSA; Ralph E. Tarter and others, 2006, "Predictors of Marijuana Use in Adolescents Before and After Licit Drug Use: Examination of the Gateway Hypothesis," *The American Journal of Psychiatry* 163, no. 12 (December): 2134–40.

27. S. Sidney and others, 1997, "Marijuana Use and Cancer Incidence," *Cancer Causes and Control* 8, no. 5 (September): 722–8; Daniel E. Ford and others, "Marijuana Use Is Not Associated With Head, Neck or Lung Cancer in Adults Younger Than 55 Years: Results of a Case Cohort Study," in *National Institute on Drug Abuse Workshop on Clinical Consequences of Marijuana* (Rockville, MD: National Institute of Health, 2001), http://archives.drugabuse.gov/meetings/marijuanaabstracts.html#Ford; Mia Hashibe and others, 2005, "Epidemiologic Review of Marijuana Use and Cancer Risk," *Alcohol* 35, no. 3 (April): 265–75; W. Hall, M. Christie, and D. Currow, 2005, "Cannabinoids and Cancer: Causation, Remediation, and Palliation," *Lancet Oncology* 6, no. 1 (January): 35–42; R. Mehra and others, 2006, "The Association Between Marijuana Smoking and Lung Cancer: A Systematic Review," *Archives of Internal Medicine* 166, no. 13 (July): 1359–67; Mia Hashibe and others, 2006, "Marijuana Use and the Risk of Lung and Upper Aerodigestive Tract Cancers: Results of a Population-Based Case-Control Study," *Cancer Epidemiology Biomarkers & Prevention* 15, no. 10 (October): 1829–34 (hereafter cited as Hashibe and others); Karin A. Rosenblatt and others, 2004, "Marijuana Use and Risk of Oral Squamous Cell Carcinoma," *Cancer Research* 64, no. 11 (June 1): 4049–54; Carrie D. Llewellyn and others, 2004, "An Analysis of Risk Factors for Oral Cancer in Young People: A Case-Control Study," *Oral Oncology* 40, no. 3 (March): 304–13.

28. Marc Kaufman, 2006, "Study Finds No Cancer-Marijuana Connection," *The Washington Post*, May 26; Hashibe and others; Angela Zimm, 2007, "Study: Marijuana Halts Growth of Lung Cancer Tumors," *Bloomberg News Wire*, April 18.

29. *Drug Use Among Youth*; for an excellent discussion of teenagers and risk, see Lynn Ponton, 1997, *The Romancing of Risk: Why Teenagers Do the Things They Do* (New York: Basic Books) and C. L. Ching, 1981, "The Goal of Abstinence: Implications for Drug Education," *Journal of Drug Education* 11 (1): 13–18.

30. G. Botvin and K. Resnicow, 1993, "School-Based Prevention Programs: Why Do Effects Decay?" *Preventive Medicine* 22, no. 4 (July): 484–90.

31. David Moshman, 1999, *Adolescent Psychological Development: Rationality, Morality and Identity* (Mahwah, NJ: Lawrence Erlbaum Associates); M. J. Quadrel, B. Fischhoff, and W. Davis, 1993, "Adolescent (In)vulnerability," *American Psychologist* 48, no. 2 (February): 102–16.

32. SAMHSA, 2009, *Results from the 2009 National Survey on Drug Use and Health: National Findings*, NSDUH Series H-30, DHHS Publication No. SMA 06-4194 (Rockville, MD: Office of Applied Studies), http://oas.samhsa.gov/NSDUH/2k9NSDUH/2k9ResultsP.pdf

33. C. E. Martin, D. F. Duncan, and E. M. Zunich, 1983, "Students' Motives for Discontinuing Illicit Drug Taking," *Health Values: Achieving High Level Wellness* 7 (5): 8–11; Gregory Austin, Ph.D. and Rodney Skager, Ph.D., 2006, *11th Biennial California Student Survey: Drug, Alcohol and Tobacco Use; 2005–2006* (Sacramento, CA: California Attorney General's Office, Fall), see http://www.adp.ca.gov/prevention/pdf/11th_CSS_Final_Report.pdf online. For an excellent discussion

of peer education, see J. Cohen, 1993, "Achieving a Reduction in Drug-Related Harm through Education," in *Psychoactive Drugs and Harm Reduction: From Faith to Science*, eds. Nick Heather and others (London: Whurr Publishers Limited).

34. Craig Reinarman, Ph.D., 2001, personal communication, August.

35. Thomas Nicholson, 1992, "The Primary Prevention of Illicit Drug Problems: An Argument for Decriminalization and Legalization," *The Journal of Primary Prevention* 12, no. 4 (June): 275–88; C. Winick, 1991, "Social Behavior, Public Policy, and Nonharmful Drug Use," *The Milbank Quarterly* 69 (3): 437–59; Erich Goode, 2004, *Drugs in American Society*, 6th ed. (New York: McGraw-Hill).

36. Students for Sensible Drug Policy, 2006, *Harmful Drug Law Hits Home: How Many College Students in Each State Lost Financial Aid Due to Drug Convictions?* (Washington, DC: Students for Sensible Drug Policy), http://ssdp.org/assets/2013/05/State-By-State-Impact-of-the-Aid-Elimination-Penalty.pdf

37. Cecil R. Reynolds, Ph.D. and others, 2008, *Are Zero Tolerance Policies Effective in the Schools? An Evidentiary Review and Recommendations; A Report to the American Psychological Association Zero Tolerance Task Force* (Washington, DC: American Psychological Association), http://www.apa.org/pubs/info/reports/zero-tolerance.pdf

38. Ted Wachtel, *SaferSanerSchools: Restoring Community in a Disconnected World* (Bethlehem, PA: International Institute for Restorative Practices), http://www.iirp.edu/article_detail.php?article_id=NTEw

39. Mitch Earleywine, Ph.D., 2006, "Marijuana Drug Safety," lecture at State University of New York, Albany, February 13.

40. National Highway Traffic Safety Administration, 2009, "Young Drivers," *Traffic Safety Facts*, DOT HS 811 400. http://www-nrd.nhtsa.dot.gov/Pubs/811400.pdf

41. Centers for Disease Control and Prevention, 2011, *Trends in the Prevalence of Sexual Behaviors, National Youth Risk Behavior Survey: 1991–2009.* http://www.cdc.gov/healthyyouth/yrbs/pdf/us_sexual_trend_yrbs.pdf

42. Lisa Richardson, 2006, "Dishing out Dinner as the Anti-Drug," *Los Angeles Times*, sec. B, September 26, 2006.

43. Sharon Levy, Shari Van Hook, and John Knight, 2004, "A Review of Internet-Based Home Drug-Testing Products for Parents," *Pediatrics* 113, no. 4 (April): 720–6, http://pediatrics.aappublications.org/cgi/reprint/113/4/720

44. Stanton Peele, 2007, *Addiction Proof Your Child.* (New York: Three Rivers Press); Timmen Cermak, MD, 2003, *Marijuana: What's a Parent to Believe?* (Center City, MN: Hazelden).

45. Maia Szalavitz, 2006, *Help at Any Cost: How the Troubled-Teen Industry Cons Parents and Hurts Kids* (New York: Penguin Group).

For Discussion

1. D.A.R.E. programs utilize police officers to deliver a number of programs, and these officers are cast as role models. What types of role models, if any, should we utilize in a reality-based educational approach?

2. Were drug education programs offered in your school? If so, what messages did these programs try and convey? Did these programs alter your behavior? Why or why not?

27

Gender-Specific Issues in the Treatment of Drug-Involved Women

HILARY L. SURRATT

In this article, Hilary Surratt notes the increasing numbers of women who are incarcerated for drug offenses, with little opportunity for engaging in quality drug treatment while in prison. Treatment needs often differ for women and men, and Surratt describes how women can benefit from treatment programs that acknowledge these needs. The author presents data collected from women who were enrolled in a residential drug treatment program that allows participants' children to be present.

Substance abuse and dependence are significant problems in the United States, affecting some twenty million individuals (SAMHSA 2005; Uziel-Miller and Lyons 2000; Uziel-Miller et al. 1998; Wright 2004), almost one-third of whom are women (Wright 2004). Compared with men, substance-dependent women tend to differ in terms of precursors and pathways to addiction, the addictive process itself, and patterns of related comorbid conditions (CASA 2006; McMahon et al. 2002). Overall, research has documented consistent gender differences in biological responses to drugs of abuse, with women typically showing greater increases in brain and metabolic activity after exposure, as well as greater and longer-lasting feelings of physical and mental well-being associated with substance use (Fallon et al. 2005; McCance-Katz et al. 2005). As a result, women tend to progress to addiction more quickly than men, have higher severities of negative consequences related to substance abuse, and often have more difficulties achieving abstinence from drugs than their male counterparts (CASA 2006; Zilberman and Blume 2005).

Substance abuse and its associated harms are increasingly affecting the lives of greater numbers of women (CASA 2006). These harms include not only a range of physical and mental health problems, but also social marginalization, separations from children and other family members, homelessness, and arrest and incarceration, to name but a few. The growing number of women involved with the criminal justice system is in many ways a reflection of increasing rates of substance abuse among women, as well as the enactment of tougher drug laws and mandatory sentencing policies as part of the nation's continuing "war on drugs" (Inciardi 2002). At mid-year 2005, for example, 106,174 women were incarcerated in state or federal prisons nationwide, and over 950,000 female offenders were on probation across the country (Glaze and Palla 2005; Harrison and Beck 2006), and many of these were serving sentences for drug-related offenses.

Possession and sale of illicit drugs and other drug-related offenses have contributed significantly to the continuing increases in the female correctional population (Inciardi 2002; Wilsnack et al. 1997). Across the nation, moreover, women are more likely than men to be serving sentences for drug-related offenses and to have committed their crimes under the influence of drugs, but less likely to be incarcerated for violent crimes (Conly 1998). In fact, a nationwide survey of women inmates found that nearly 45 percent were serving time for drug or drug-related charges, up from 15 percent in 1979 (Greenfield and Snell 1999). Nearly half reported committing their crimes under the influence of drugs or alcohol and approximately 6 in 10 had used illegal drugs in the month before the offense (Mumola and Beck 1997). More recently, studies have indicated even higher levels of drug-involvement among female offenders than male offenders. In a national survey Peugh and Belenko (1999) documented that 79 percent of male and female prisoners in state correctional institutions had histories of substance abuse problems, but females were more likely to have used drugs in the month before their crimes and more likely to have committed their offenses under the influence of drugs. Going further, Staton-Tindall and colleagues (2003) found that 85 percent of female inmates interviewed in Kentucky prisons had used multiple substances in the 30 days prior to their incarceration, a prevalence well beyond that observed for male inmates.

Despite the overwhelming need for treatment among women in criminal justice populations, researchers have estimated that only about 13 percent receive treatment while incarcerated (Blanchard 1999; Sheridan 1996). Among the chief reasons for the paucity of institutionally based treatment programs is a lack of funding for treatment space and severe shortages of treatment personnel. One approach to providing substance abuse treatment for offenders has been the creation of "drug courts"— special courts that are given the responsibility for handling criminal cases among drug-involved offenders. Drug courts leverage the coercive power of the criminal justice system to impose judicial supervision, substance abuse treatment, drug testing, and case management of drug-involved offenders (Inciardi, McBride, and Rivers 1996). The primary procedure has been to require the offender, by legislative mandate or court order, to attend substance abuse programs as a form of legal leverage to ensure participation (Shearer, Myers, and Ogan 2001). Drug courts currently operate in all 50 states, and the successful completion of the treatment regimen assigned by the court can result in dismissal of criminal charges, reduced sentences, or lesser penalties for the offender. And with the proliferation of drug courts throughout the United States, treatment populations in many communities are becoming more and more dominated by drug court referrals.

Treatment Needs of Drug-Involved Women

Historically, treatment programs for drug abuse have been developed for male clients, because men represented the majority of drug abusers and because policymakers have been concerned with reducing violent crimes more commonly associated with men's involvement with drugs. As such, many treatment programs fail to address women's most common needs (Ashley, Marsden, and Brady 2003). Numerous studies have documented a variety of gender-specific issues and barriers to treatment that confront women drug abusers, including pregnancy and childcare responsibilities, partner violence and abuse, histories of other trauma, resistance from family and friends, stigma associated with women's alcohol and drug use, poverty and financial need, conflict between traditional and changing gender roles, and low social support (Grella 1996; Klee, Jackson, and Lewis 2002; Pottieger and Tressell 2000; Uziel-Miller and Lyons 2000; Wechsberg, Craddock, and Hubbard 1998; Whiteside-Mansell, Crone, and Conners 1999; Wobie et al. 1997). In fact, an analysis of the national Drug Abuse Treatment Outcome Study data found that women entering substance abuse treatment tend to be younger, less educated, and more often unemployed than their male counterparts, with significantly higher levels of emotional and psychological distress, more depression and anxiety, poorer physical health, more physical and sexual abuse histories, and burdened by more child-related responsibilities (Uziel-Miller and Lyons 2000; Wechsberg, Craddock, and Hubbard 1998; Wobie et al. 1997). In addition, because substance abuse among pregnant or parenting women is often viewed as more deviant and stigmatizing than drug or alcohol abuse by men, women's sense of shame and guilt related to their drug use may also be heightened (Klee, Jackson, and Lewis 2002; Whiteside-Mansell, Crone, and Conners 1999). As such, drug abuse is rarely a woman's sole problem, and is likely just one of a myriad of adverse circumstances that profoundly affect the lives of women.

In response to the findings that the antecedents and consequences of substance abuse differ markedly for women and men, the number of specialized treatment programs for drug-abusing women has begun to increase. In this regard, an analysis of national treatment program data by Grella (1999) found that approximately 19 percent of the programs surveyed could be classified as "women only" programs. More recent analyses indicate that 19 percent of community treatment programs offer special therapeutic regimens for pregnant women, and 28 percent include gender-specific programming for other groups of women (Ashley, Marsden, and Brady 2003). And within the criminal justice system, 49 state departments of correction indicate that they have initiatives designed specifically for women, primarily in the areas of parenting, drug abuse treatment, victimization, and life skills (National Institute of Corrections 1998).

Typically, treatment adaptations for gender-appropriate programs include establishing programs staffed by women, changing the nature of staff-client interactions to a more supportive, less confrontational tone, including gender-specific issues in the programming content, and creating safe treatment environments (Kaplan and Sasser 1996). Although the recognition of differences in treatment needs and the implementation of specialized programs have expanded, until recently detailed descriptions of the services provided under the auspices of such programs and data on the effectiveness of these treatment approaches for women were generally absent from the literature. A recent comprehensive review of nearly 40 published studies

reported consistent positive associations between specialized treatment programming for women and length of stay in treatment, treatment completion, decreased substance use, and reduced mental health symptoms (Ashley, Marsden, and Brady 2003). These data suggest that the provision of gender-specific treatment is more successful at reducing traditional barriers to treatment entry and retention for women, and a key component of this success may be the increased availability of ancillary services and tangible support in other areas of importance to women.

One of the most consistent and well-documented findings in the scientific literature on drug abuse relates to gender differences in parenting and childcare concerns. Drug-dependent women are far more likely to be parents and to be living with their children than are their male counterparts (CASA 2006; McMahon et al. 2002), and concern about the effects of drug use on their children is one of the primary motivations for women to seek treatment (Klee, Jackson, and Lewis 2002). Though often situated within a context of extreme poverty and disadvantage, women drug users nevertheless express high levels of commitment to their children and value motherhood as a personally meaningful role (Kearney, Murphy, and Rosenbaum 1994; Sterk 1999; Surratt 2003). For many women, children function as a powerful motivating force toward abstinence from drugs, and pregnancy and motherhood are often looked upon as opportunities for a "new beginning," a chance to become a "good mother," and to promote positive, healthy lifestyle change (Kissin et al. 2004; Klee, Jackson, and Lewis 2002; Lesser, Koniak-Griffin, and Anderson 1999; Murphy and Rosenbaum 1999).

Within this context, a particularly important recent development in substance abuse treatment has been the creation and implementation of programs designed to serve parenting women and their children. Historically, there was a strong belief within traditional residential substance abuse treatment programs for women that having children present would be a deterrent to recovery (Dudley-Grant, Williams, and Hunt 2000). It was believed that women needed time away from maternal responsibilities to focus solely on recovery-related issues, and children were alleged to act as barriers to drug-involved women in admitting and confronting their addiction. The problem was that many women could not enter or complete substance abuse treatment because of child-care responsibilities, and as a result concern about childcare and children's well-being have acted in some cases as deterrents to women's help-seeking behavior (McMahon et al. 2002; Wilke, Kamata, and Cash 2005).

Ultimately recognizing this dilemma, providers have recently established a larger number of residential treatment programs that accommodate women and their young children. Although there is a growing body of literature describing such model substance abuse treatment programs for parenting women, there is little published research on the treatment processes and outcomes related to participation in these programs (Conners et al. 2001). The most consistent findings from this research have been that women will remain in residential treatment longer and are more likely to complete treatment goals if they are permitted to have their children with them (Greenfield et al. 2004; Uziel-Miller et al. 1998; Wobie et al. 1997). A recent analysis of national data on women entering drug abuse treatment between 1995 and 2001 confirmed these findings, noting that women who brought children into treatment remained in the facility almost twice as long as those who did not (Chen et al. 2004). As such, it appears that enabling parenting women to remain together with their children during residential treatment is an important key to achieving the extended period of stay needed to accomplish treatment objectives (Chen et al. 2004). As retention is a major challenge in many treatment programs, these findings are particularly important indicators of women's potential for success in treatment. Treatment research has consistently found strong associations between length of stay in treatment and post-treatment outcomes including decreased drug use, decreased criminal activity, and increased employment (Anglin and Hser 1991; De Leon 1994; Inciardi, Martin, and Butzin 2004; NIDA 2006).

Although these findings indicate that specialized programs for parenting women are generally effective in reducing drug use and promoting at least short-term abstinence, the processes of engagement and participation through which this occurs are not well understood. This has led some to refer to treatment as a "black box" (Simpson 2001), with little understanding of how and why treatment does and does not work. In this regard, Reisinger and colleagues (2003) have suggested that traditional approaches to substance abuse treatment research, which often focus on discrete outcome measures such as treatment completion, do not fully capture the experiences and engagement of individuals in these programs.

New Approaches to Studying Women in Substance Abuse Treatment

Within the context of these remarks, the balance of this chapter reports the findings of a qualitative study that examined the motivations and experiences of women as they participated in a residential drug abuse treatment program together with their children. The data were collected in 2003 as part of a larger research initiative focusing on identity development among drug-involved women. The sample of women in the specialized treatment program was drawn from "The Village," one of the oldest and largest residential drug abuse treatment facilities in the State of Florida. The Village operates several substance abuse treatment programs in South Florida for adults and adolescents, including the Families in Transition (FIT) program—a 24-hour residential substance abuse treatment program for women and their children under twelve years of age. At any given time, there are nearly 50 women in various phases of the Families in Transition program with their children, and the typical length of stay in primary treatment is approximately six months.

Semi-structured, in-depth interviews were conducted with twelve women in the women and children's substance abuse treatment program. These were organized by an interview guide, containing broad questions about key topic areas: the women's experiences of residency in substance abuse treatment, histories of drug use, previous treatment experiences, experiences of mothering, views of addiction, and views of self in the past, present, and future. Interviews lasted between 60 and 90 minutes, and were audio-recorded for the purposes of transcription. Attempts were made to interview each woman on two occasions, with initial interviews occurring early in each woman's treatment experience, typically within four weeks after admission into the program. The second interview occurred two to three months later, after substantial exposure to primary treatment in the women and children's program. The second interview focused on significant events occurring since the first contact, and the women's experiences in treatment.

Four primary steps were taken to analyze the textual data elicited in the in-depth interviews. These included: (1) initial verbatim transcription and verification of interview audiotapes; (2) a series of four focused readings of these transcripts; (3) the construction and application of a detailed coding scheme based on analyses of the transcripts; and (4) the construction of an interpretive summary for each participant based on specific patterns of coding and a final reading of the full narrative. The word-processing files generated by transcription were converted into files compatible with the qualitative software package N6, which is designed to aid in the storage, coding, retrieval, and analysis of text (Weitzman and Miles 1995).

Analyses of the qualitative interviews revealed that the women universally attributed their motivation for and engagement with the treatment program to the presence of their children, as well as their desire to be responsible caregivers. As a group, the women displayed high levels of acceptance of treatment practices and participated actively in the components of the treatment program. Over time, women in the parental treatment program began to see the tangible benefits of participation in recovery-related activities as they progressed to increased visitations with their children, and ultimately co-residence. As this occurred, women began to interweave recovery and motherhood in their personal narratives, and a sense of personal accomplishment emerged. In this sense, engagement with their children afforded a sense of greater commitment to recovery, and many attributed personal change and development to their participation in this specialized program. In this regard, recovery was empowering for women in this specialized treatment context, supporting their emerging abilities to make positive change and to pursue valued commitments.

Themes surrounding the importance of motherhood were apparent in the narratives of virtually all of the women participating in family-centered treatment. Vanessa, a 37-year-old African American woman, had been a cocaine user for some 16 years when she entered the women and children's residential treatment program. Although Vanessa's initiation into crack cocaine use took place only a year prior to our interview, she recalled a rapid deterioration in her life at that point that she connected to her chronic and compulsive drug use. Although she had participated in treatment for cocaine use on several occasions, this was her first experience in a specialized women and children's facility. Through her interactions with this unique treatment community, she had developed a sense of herself as a recovering addict, but at the same time built a stronger sense of herself as a mother:

> I'm definitely an addict. But I'm workin' on that. I have to learn how to get some. . . . I'm learnin' how to get some control over myself. I did things in my addiction that, I mean, I ignored my kids. I never would do anything to just actually just hurt them, you know, physically or anything like that. But mentally I know I hurt them. I know they're, they're hurt. They do know that somethin' was wrong with mommy. They know mommy wasn't mommy anymore. Um, but they, they really sweet kids. They, they very intelligent kids. All I can do is move on with them, just hold on to them. Ask the Lord to guide me in how to raise them. And they, they precious. They very smart, like I say. They um, they love mommy. They uh, they support mommy. They know that I'm sick. That I'm gettin' well.

Clearly Vanessa viewed recovery as supporting her ability to mother, and in fact she attributed her successful participation in treatment to the structure of the program and the opportunity to maintain and strengthen ties with her children. Growing up for the most part without guardianship due to her mother's heavy drug use and long periods of absence from the family, Vanessa appeared to view recovery as important in its own right, but also as a mechanism for achieving meaningful reconciliation with her children. She vividly described the deprivation of her own childhood, culminating in her first pregnancy at age 13. Her youth and lack of parental role models afforded her a limited understanding of the possibilities for mothering at that time, yet she expressed a strong commitment to altering her own path as a mother:

> My mom was a addict. I remember always wantin' my momma. I remember lovin' my mom. And I'd go lookin' for her. I used to walk around looking for her 'cause I knew where she'd be hangin' out. I stopped lookin' for her 'cause I started findin' her. And then when I found her I couldn't stand how I'd find her so I stopped looking for her. And my brother, my oldest brother, he took care of all of us. We stayed in the house, we stayed there by our-self. You know, my brother always told us not to let nobody know what was goin' on or else, you know, HRS [Health and Rehabilitative Services] would take us. We never said anything but eventually it came out. We lived for, I maybe was five and I was eight goin' on nine when they found out. My oldest brother, he'd been going to jail since he was ten. Tryin' to take care of us. He been gettin' shot at. He was almost killed and he wasn't but, maybe but eleven years old. Tryin' to break into somebody's house to get money to feed us. Now it's strange that I'm not angry at my mom anymore about me. I've learned that in order for me to recover I have to accept the responsibilities for all my actions. But I, I still sometime think about my brother and I get angry at her. 'Cause he never had a life. It's like, she took his life away from him. I definitely don't ever want to be to a point where I make my kid do somethin' that can get his life taken away from him so I can use. I never meant to, to be the way I am. That's the same way my mom was. She got high. Just didn't care. I want to be, I see myself working. Holding down a job. And I plan to live somewhere along this, somewhere along by this water with my kids. As long as I, I'm able to provide for us, I'm happy. As long as we be together. Long as I can teach them things and they can teach me things. When I was usin', I, I didn't have time for any of it. But now I'm gonna make sure I be there to their

schools. To do the things that I need to do to help my kids grow into responsible adults. 'Cause I want them to be able to take of them, and not have to be like me.

For many women, it was precisely the felt connection with their children that initiated and maintained their very participation in treatment, and their commitment to motherhood and "good" mothering that supported their recovery from addiction. This consistently emerged as a central feature of the narratives of women most committed to recovery. Kristen, a 22-year-old mother, placed considerable emphasis on this point:

> The first two weeks I was here, I didn't want to be here. I didn't think I had a problem. Once I found out I did, I was like shit! Now what am I gonna do? Well I started, you know, really listening intensely, and I was like ok, I'm gonna do this for K, my daughter. I came in because of my daughter. And I knew that I had to stay because of her. And I didn't want it for me, I wanted it for her and figured I'll do it for her. But you learn in here, you have to want it for yourself. I mean, whatever keeps you in here, wonderful. Like she's the reason I stayed in here and that worked. That's what I needed to get by to this point where I can have it for myself and I want it. And it was just gradually throughout, you know. The classes back-to-back every day, and the counselors and everything that I've heard. And I started wanting a better life for me. That way I could give her a better life. So it's been really a big factor because part of me recovering is getting better so I can be with her.

Here, Kristen assesses her future in recovery in terms of its impact on her goal of raising her child. In this way, her focus was not on recovery as an end in itself, but on what sobriety allowed her to achieve in other areas of her life—in this case the opportunity to re-claim her daughter and to contribute positively to her development.

The centrality and importance of motherhood remained a highly salient goal, even among women who were grappling with extreme poverty, health issues, and prior incidents of abuse and victimization in their childhood and adult lives. Theresa's story was a particularly poignant illustration of the violence endemic to many women's lives. A 19-year-old African American woman, she came to the women and children's program with a substantial history of cocaine use in spite of her young age, and continued to struggle with the extensive trauma she had undergone in her adolescence:

> I have a really bad anger problem. Maybe 'cause of the things that happened when I was a child. I felt not wanted. I felt left out. It's somethin' that grew inside of me, like anger just grew inside of me. My father passed when I was twelve. My mother wasn't there. You know, and after my father passed like my grandmother didn't really care no more. And I had these anger tantrums. I would act out and stuff. So I guess they couldn't take it anymore. Um, and they kicked me out the house but it was okay. So I got introduced to the street. At the age of twelve I got kicked out the house. I was strippin' in the strip club at fourteen. That's how I made my money. The reason that I used drugs was to hide up, all those hurtin' feelings that's inside me. But when I came down off the drug, it ain't do nothin' but make it worse. And that's why I wanted the drug more and more and more. And I have to relive that, that incident that happened and it's, it's kinda hard but it has helped me a lot. Because at the age of sixteen I was raped by five boys. And when I got raped, I had to take care of myself. It made me feel like I was nothin'. That I, I didn't matter to nobody.

In spite of this traumatic personal history, Theresa displayed remarkable resilience as she organized much of her narrative around the topic of mothering, and her goal of being a "normal mother." Eight months pregnant when she entered treatment, her newborn had been removed from her care immediately after birth, as was her 15-month-old daughter. She had little opportunity to develop an attachment to her youngest daughter, and had had little meaningful contact with her 15-month-old due to her drug using activities over the prior year. Yet the very fact of their young ages afforded Theresa the hope that she could raise her own children and become the mother she would like to be. Since entering the treatment program

she had been granted supervised visitation by the court, which positioned her children as highly salient, visible symbols of her recovery:

> The most important thing to me today is gaining custody of my kids back. That's, that's, that's my number one goal that I have to achieve. And I can't stand the fact that somebody else will raise them. Because my, my biological mother is an addict herself. And I'm not . . . She chose drugs over me. And I'm not gonna choose drugs over my kids. But by me bein' in the program now, this is my first treatment center. It has really taught me how to deal with life on life's terms without the use of drugs. And in order for me to be right for my kids I have to get right for myself first, you know. It's, it's the first thing is stayin' clean. Because if I'm not clean, I'm not gonna be able to take care of my kids the way a normal mother would.

Through her continued participation in the specialized treatment regimen, Theresa began to speak of structuring her life around meaningful participation in recovery-related activities, and emphasized the role of sobriety in achieving her family-related goals. Her words regarding motherhood suggested that the valued goal of becoming a "good mother" was achievable through a process of learning and engagement afforded by the family-centered program activities:

> My momma was never there for me. And I don't, I don't want to use drugs no more because I don't want my children to look at me how I look at my mom. Because the way I used to look at my mom was like ugh, you ain't my momma, you just had me, you know. And I'm learnin a lot. I wanna, I'm only nineteen years old. I wanna learn how to be a parent to my, to my child. I wanna learn how to raise my children. You know, that's why I go to parenting classes. For me to get off drugs, to get my life back in order, and to become a mother again, those are my goals. To raise my children I have a chance, you know. Because addicts, drug use, it only leads to jail, or institution, or death. You know? And either way it goes, you don't have a mother. And I'm not dead. I'm in a institution but I still have a chance to be with my child, another chance at life for me and my children. I'm gonna try to be the

best mother that I can be. And if I'm in active addiction, I'm not gonna be able to do that.

As suggested in the presentation of individual women's narratives, virtually all of the participants in the women and children's treatment program developed strong commitments to recovery that were uniquely connected to their goals of providing stable and responsible care for their children. The tremendous value of this connection was evident over time, as none of the participants in the women and children's treatment program declined in their commitment to recovery. The findings of this research suggest that women's connections to their children in the specialized treatment program reinforced recovery as meaningful in tangible, concrete ways. In particular, recovery became personally meaningful as it supported a desired path to motherhood.

Discussion

Taken together, these findings clearly demonstrate that substance-abusing women are a highly marginalized and vulnerable population. Frequently situated in a complex of adverse and chaotic social environments, their lives are marked by both intimate partner and community-level violence, poverty, homelessness, disease, and mental illness (Baseman, Ross, and Williams 1999; Davis 2000; Falck et al. 2001; Gilbert et al. 2001; Kettinger, Nair, and Schuler 2000). Chronic drug-using women often inhabit a world of economic deprivation and indigence, where the shifting and precarious nature of their financial resources, health, safety, and fragile social ties often engenders criminal involvement and perpetuates drug-using careers (Boyd 1999; Inciardi 1995). Many of these concerns are magnified even further for women from socioeconomically disadvantaged backgrounds or minority communities. These factors had a substantial impact on the participants in the present study, as many experienced periods of homelessness and very few had histories of stable employment. As such, drug abuse is rarely a woman's sole life problem, but is likely one of a myriad of adverse life events that profoundly affect the lives of women—and for those who are mothers, their children as well.

Nevertheless, research on women drug users has traditionally focused on their lack of parenting abilities and failure to be responsible or responsive caregivers (Blume 1991; Hans 1995; Kumpfer and Bayes 1995; Tarter et al. 1993). In spite of these portrayals, women drug users express high levels of commitment to their children and value motherhood as a personally meaningful role (Kearney, Murphy, and Rosenbaum 1994; Sterk 1999). For many women, becoming a "good mother" is a motivator for abstinence and recovery, and this was the case in this study as well. The women were overwhelmingly concerned not only with avoiding the removal of their children from their care, but also with making positive contributions to their development.

Cultural expectations for mothering emphasize unconditional love, nurturing, and self-sacrifice for one's children (Boyd 1999). While these idealized notions of motherhood may obscure the realities of daily life for many mothers, drug-using mothers are stigmatized by visible shortfalls in these expectations, and they often express guilt for failure to meet personal expectations as well (Baker and Carson 1999; Carter 2002; Lewis, Klee, and Jackson 1995; Murphy and Rosenbaum 1999; Sharpe 2005). Specialized treatment programs for pregnant and parenting women are designed in part to build women's parenting skills and to support women's confidence in their ability to mother, and thus have demonstrated increased retention in treatment and improved outcomes (Clark 2001; Conners et al. 2001; Grella 1999; Kissin et al. 2004; Surratt 2005). The qualitative research described above extends our understanding of family-centered approaches to substance abuse treatment for women by documenting the beneficial synergy between commitments to children and commitments to recovery that support women's meaningful engagement with treatment.

Implications for Future Research

As drug abuse continues to touch the lives of increasing numbers of women, expanded research in formal treatment settings and self-help venues is needed in order to understand women's experiences in these programs and the ways that their participation supports or impedes positive treatment outcomes. Process-oriented research has the potential to unpack the "black box" of treatment, and ultimately to improve the delivery of treatment services to women and their families by refining or redesigning the structure of programs and the meanings of participation in these regimens. One such fundamental redesign in drug abuse treatment has been the creation and expansion of women and children's residential programs. Clearly the structure and design of the parental treatment program described above impacted individual women's experiences of treatment. Participants in this program very clearly understood the paths to recovery and motherhood as intertwined, and each goal was seen to support the other. In fact, most attributed their active engagement in treatment to their children, and this fundamental engagement allowed them to remain in treatment long enough to achieve their treatment goals.

As a final point, it is important to note that while the family-centered treatment program was designed to incorporate children into the facility, this modification did not entail a transformation in the underlying structure of treatment practices or the philosophy of treatment promoted by the program. Rather, the treatment program continued to regard successful recovery as accomplished only for oneself, and the treatment regimen failed to optimize time for interaction between women and their children. It is often the case with women's treatment programs that, in spite of gender-specific modifications to a program's content and design, the fundamental philosophical orientation of the program remains unchanged (Grella 1996, 1999). In other words, the basic assumptions about the nature and process of treatment persist, unaltered by new patterns of staffing or the expanded purview of treatment to address gender-specific topics related to substance abuse. The inherent contradictions in the women and children's treatment program described above were difficult for many women to understand. Clearly, women's sense of connection to their children was a powerful part of the recovery process in treatment, yet the institutional emphasis on recovery as an individual process often failed to consider or build upon the value of this social

connectedness. As such, future research in women and children's programs should examine whether and how children are meaningfully integrated into the treatment community as potentially important participants, and the impact of these factors on women's treatment outcomes. From a social policy perspective, in-depth explorations of such programs could lead to improved programming and structured services for drug-involved women and their children.

References

Anglin, M. D., and Y. I. Hser. 1991. "Criminal Justice and the Drug Abusing Offender: Policy Issues of Coerced Treatment." *Behavioral Sciences and Law* 9 (3): 243–267.

Ashley, O. S., M. E. Marsden, and T. M. Brady. 2003. "Effectiveness of Substance Abuse Treatment Programming for Women: A Review." *The American Journal of Drug and Alcohol Abuse* 29 (1): 19–53.

Baker, P. L., and A. Carson. 1999. "I Take Care of My Kids: Mothering Practices of Substance-Abusing Women." *Gender and Society* 13 (3): 347–363.

Baseman, J., M. Ross, and M. Williams. 1999. "Sale of Sex for Drugs and Drugs for Sex: An Economic Context of Sexual Risk Behaviors for STDs." *Sexually Transmitted Diseases* 26 (8): 444–449.

Blanchard, C. 1999. "Drugs, Crime, Prison and Treatment." *Spectrum: The Journal of State Government* 72 (1): 26–28.

Blume, S. B. 1991. "Children of Alcoholic and Drug Dependent Parents." In *Alcohol and Drugs Are Women's Issues*, edited by P. Roth, 166–172. Metuchen, NJ: Women's Action Alliance.

Boyd, S. C. 1999. *Mothers and Illicit Drugs: Transcending the Myths*. Ontario, Canada: University of Toronto Press.

Carter, C. S. 2002. "Perinatal Care for Women Who Are Addicted: Implications for Empowerment." *Health and Social Work* 27 (3): 166–174.

CASA (The National Center on Addiction and Substance Abuse at Columbia University). 2006. *Women under the Influence*. Baltimore, MD: Johns Hopkins University Press.

Chen, X., K. Burgdorf, K. Dowell, T. Roberts, A. Porowski, and J. M. Herrell. 2004. "Factors Associated with Retention of Drug Abusing

Women in Long-Term Residential Treatment." *Evaluation and Program Planning* 27 (2): 205–212.

Clark, H. W. 2001. "Residential Substance Abuse Treatment for Pregnant and Postpartum Women and Their Children: Treatment Policy Implications." *Child Welfare* 80 (2): 179–198.

Conly, C. 1998. *The Women's Prison Association: Supporting Women Offenders and Their Families.* Washington, DC: National Institute of Justice.

Conners, N. A., R. H. Bradley, L. Whiteside-Mansell, and C. C. Crone. 2001. "A Comprehensive Substance Abuse Treatment Program for Women and Their Children: An Initial Evaluation." *Journal of Substance Abuse Treatment* 21 (2): 67–75.

Davis, N. J. 2000. "From Victims to Survivors: Working with Recovering Street Prostitutes." In *Sex for Sale: Prostitution, Pornography, and the Sex Industry*, edited by R. Weitzer, 139–158. New York: Routledge.

De Leon, G. 1994. "Therapeutic Communities." In *Textbook of Substance Abuse Treatment*, edited by M. Galanter and H. D. Kleber, 391–414. Washington, DC: Psychiatric Press.

Dudley-Grant, G, R., I. Williams, and K. Hunt. 2000. "Substance Abusing Women with Children in Treatment: A Virgin Islands Residential Model." *Interamerican Journal of Psychology* 34 (1): 17–28.

Falck, R. S., J. Wang, R. G. Carlson, and H. A. Siegal. 2001. "The Epidemiology of Physical Attack and Rape among Crack-Using Women." *Violence and Victims* 16 (1): 79–89.

Fallon, J. H., D. B. Keator, J. Mbogori, D. Taylor, and S. G. Potkin. 2005. "Gender: A Major Determinant of Brain Response to Nicotine." *International Journal of Neuropsychopharmacology* 8 (1): 17–26.

Gilbert, L., N. El-Bassel, V. Rajah, A. Foleno, and V. Frye. 2001. "Linking Drug-Related Activities with Experiences of Partner Violence: A Focus Group Study of Women in Methadone Treatment." *Violence and Victims* 16 (5): 517–536.

Glaze, L. E., and S. Palla. 2005. *Probation and Parole in the United States, 2004.* Bureau of Justice Statistics Bulletin. November. NCJ 210676. US Department of Justice, Office of Justice Programs.

Greenfeld, L. A., and T. L. Snell. 1999. *Women Offenders.* Bureau of Justice Statistics Bulletin. December. NCJ 175688. US Department of Justice, Office of Justice Programs.

Greenfield, L., K. Burgdorf, X. Chen, A. Porowski, T. Roberts, and J. Herrell. 2004. "Effectiveness of Long-Term Residential Substance Abuse Treatment for Women: Findings from Three National Studies." *The American Journal of Drug and Alcohol Abuse* 30 (3): 537–550.

Grella, C. E. 1996. "Background and Overview of Mental Health and Substance Abuse Treatment Systems: Meeting the Needs of Women Who Are Pregnant or Parenting." *Journal of Psychoactive Drugs* 28 (4): 319–343.

———. 1999. "Women in Residential Drug Treatment: Differences by Program Type and Pregnancy." *Journal of Health Care for the Poor and Underserved* 10 (2): 216–229.

Hans, S. 1995. "Diagnosis in Etiologic and Epidemiologic Studies." In *NIDA Technical Review: Methodological Issues: Etiology and Consequences of Drug Abuse among Women*, edited by C. Jones and M. De La Rosa. Rockville, MD: National Institute on Drug Abuse.

Harrison, P. M., and A. J. Beck. 2006. *Prison and Jail Inmates at Midyear 2005.* Bureau of Justice Statistics Bulletin. May. NCJ 213133. US Department of Justice, Office of Justice Programs.

Inciardi, J. A. 1995. "Crack, Crack House Sex, and HIV Risk." *Archives of Sexual Behavior* 24 (3): 249–269.

———. 2002. *The War on Drugs III: The Continuing Saga of the Mysteries and Miseries of Intoxication, Addiction, Crime, and Public Policy.* Boston, MA: Allyn and Bacon.

Inciardi, J. A., S. S. Martin, and C. A. Butzin. 2004. "Five-Year Outcomes of Therapeutic Community Treatment of Drug-Involved Offenders after Release from Prison." *Crime and Delinquency* 50 (1): 88–107.

Inciardi, J. A., D. C. McBride, and J. E. Rivers. 1996. *Drug Control and the Courts.* Thousand Oaks, CA: Sage Publications.

Kaplan, M. S. and J. E. Sasser. 1996. "Women Behind Bars: Trends and Policy Issues." *Journal of Sociology and Social Welfare* 23 (4): 43–56.

Kearney, M., S. Murphy, and M. Rosenbaum. 1994. "Mothering on Crack: A Grounded Theory Analysis." *Social Science and Medicine* 38 (2): 351–361.

Kettinger, L. A., P. Nair, and M. E. Schuler. 2000. "Exposure to Environmental Risk Factors and Parenting Attitudes among Substance Abusing Women." *American Journal of Drug and Alcohol Abuse* 26 (1): 1–11.

Kissin, W. B., D. S. Svikis, P. Moylan, N. A. Haug, and M. L. Stitzer. 2004. "Identifying Pregnant Women at Risk for Early Attrition from Substance Abuse Treatment." *Journal of Substance Abuse Treatment* 27 (1): 31–38.

Klee, H., M. Jackson, and S. Lewis. 2002. *Drug Misuse and Motherhood*. London: Routledge.

Kumpfer, K. L., and J. Bayes. 1995. "Child Abuse and Drugs." In *The Encyclopedia of Drugs and Alcohol*, vol. 1, 217–222. New York: Simon and Schuster.

Lesser, J., D., Koniak-Griffin, and N. L. R. Anderson. 1999. "Depressed Adolescent Mothers' Perceptions of Their Own Maternal Role." *Issues in Mental Health Nursing* 20 (2): 131–149.

Lewis, S., H. Klee, and M. Jackson. 1995. "Illicit Drug Users' Experiences of Pregnancy: An Exploratory Study." *Journal of Reproductive and Infant Psychology* 13: 219–227.

McCance-Katz, E. F., C. L. Hart, B. Boyarsky, T. Kosten, and P. Jatlow. 2005. "Gender Effects Following Repeated Administration of Cocaine and Alcohol in Humans." *Substance Use and Misuse* 40 (4): 511–528.

McMahon, T. J., J. D. Winkel, N. E. Suchman, and S. S. Luthar. 2002. "Drug Dependence, Parenting Responsibilities, and Treatment History: Why Doesn't Mom Go for Help?" *Drug and Alcohol Dependence* 65 (2): 105–114.

Mumola, C. J., and A. J. Beck. 1997. *Prisoners in 1996*. Bureau of Justice Statistics Bulletin. June. NCJ 164619. US Department of Justice, Office of Justice Programs.

Murphy, S., and M. Rosenbaum. 1999. *Pregnant Women on Drugs: Combating Stereotypes and Stigma*. New Brunswick, NJ: Rutgers University Press.

National Institute of Corrections. 1998. *Current Issues in the Operation of Women's Prisons*. Longmont, CO: U.S. Department of Justice.

National Institute on Drug Abuse. 2006. *Principles of Drug Abuse Treatment for Criminal Justice Populations: A Research Based Guide*. NIH Publication No. 06–5316, Rockville, MD.

Peugh, J., and S. Belenko. 1999. Substance-Involved Women Inmates: Challenges to Providing Effective Treatment. *The Prison Journal* 79 (1): 23–44.

Pottieger, A. E., and P. A. Tressell. 2000. Social Relationships of Crime-Involved Women Cocaine Users. *Journal of Psychoactive Drugs* 32 (4): 445–460.

Reisinger, H. S., T. Bush, M. A. Colom, M. Agar, and R. Battjes. 2003. Navigation and Engagement: How Does One Measure Success? *Journal of Drug Issues* 33 (4): 778–800.

Sharpe, T. T. 2005. *Behind the Eight Ball: Sex for Crack Cocaine Exchange and Poor Black Women*. Binghamton, NY: Haworth Press.

Shearer, R. A., L. B. Myers, and G. D. Ogan. 2001. "Treatment Resistance and Ethnicity among Female Offenders in Substance Abuse Treatment Programs." *The Prison Journal* 81 (1): 55–72.

Sheridan, M. J. 1996. "Comparison of Life Experiences and Personal Functioning of Men and Women in Prison." *Families in Society: The Journal of Contemporary Human Services* 77 (7): 423–434.

Simpson, D. D. 2001. "Modeling Treatment Process and Outcomes." *Addiction* 96 (2): 207–211.

Staton-Tindall, M., C. Leukefeld, and J. M. Webster. 2003. "Substance Use, Health, and Mental Health: Problems and Service Utilization among Incarcerated Women." *International Journal of Offender Therapy and Comparative Criminology* 47 (2): 224–239.

Sterk, C. E. 1999. *Fast Lives: Women Who Use Crack Cocaine*. Philadelphia: Temple University Press.

Substance Abuse and Mental Health Services Administration, and Office of Applied Studies (SAMHSA). 2005. *Substance Use During Pregnancy: 2002 and 2003 Update*. The NSDUH Report. Available at http://www.oas.samhsa.gov/2k5/pregnancy/pregnancy.pdf

Surratt, H. L. 2003. "Parenting Attitudes of Drug-Involved Women Inmates." *The Prison Journal* 83 (2): 206.

———. 2005. *Constructing the Self as Addict: Narratives of Recovery and Resistance among Women in*

Drug Abuse Treatment. Doctoral Dissertation, City University of New York.

Tarter, R., T. Blackson, C. Martin, R. Loeber, and H. Moss. 1993. "Characteristics and Correlates of Child Discipline Practices in Substance Abuse and Normal Families." *American Journal on Addictions* 21 (1): 18–25.

Uziel-Miller, N. D., and J. S. Lyons. 2000. "Specialized Substance Abuse Treatment for Women and Their Children: An Analysis of Program Design." *Journal of Substance Abuse Treatment* 19 (4): 355–367.

Uziel-Miller, N. D., J. S. Lyons, C. Kissiel, and S. Love. 1998. "Treatment Needs and Initial Outcomes of a Residential Recovery Program for African-American Women and Their Children." *American Journal an Addictions* 7 (1): 43–50.

Wechsberg, W. M., S. G. Craddock, and R. L. Hubbard. 1998. "How Are Women Who Enter Substance Abuse Treatment Different Than Men? A Gender Comparison from the Drug Abuse Treatment Outcome Study (DATOS)." *Drugs and Society* 13 (1/2): 97–115.

Weitzman, E. A., and M. B. Miles. 1995. *Computer Programs for Qualitative Data Analysis: A Software Sourcebook.* Thousand Oaks, CA: Sage Publications.

Whiteside-Mansell, L., C. C. Crone, and N. A. Conners. 1999. "The Development and Evaluation of an Alcohol and Drug Prevention and Treatment Program for Women and Children: The AR-CARES Program." *Journal of Substance Abuse Treatment* 16 (3): 265–275.

Wilke, D. J., A. Kamata, and S. J. Cash. 2005. "Modeling Treatment Motivation in Substance-Abusing Women with Children." *Child Abuse and Neglect* 29 (11): 1313–1323.

Wilsnack, S. C., N. D. Vogeltanz, A. D. Klassen, and T. R. Harris. 1997. "Childhood Sexual Abuse and Women's Substance Abuse: National Survey Findings." *Journal of Studies on Alcohol* 58 (3): 264–271.

Wobie, K., F. D. Eyler, M. Conlon, L. Clarke, and M. Behnke. 1997. "Women and Children in Residential Treatment: Outcomes for Mothers and Their Infants." *Journal of Drug Issues* 27 (3): 585–606.

Wright, D. 2004. *State Estimates of Substance Use from the 2002 National Survey of Drug Use and Health: Findings.* DHHS Publication No. SMA 04-3907, NSDUH Series H-23. Rockville, MD: Substance Abuse and Mental Health Services Administration, Office of Applied Studies.

Zilberman, M, L., and S. B. Blume. 2005. Drugs and Women. *In Substance Abuse: A Comprehensive Textbook*, 4th edition, edited by J. H. Lowinson, P. Ruiz, R. B. Millman, and J. G. Langrod, 1064–1075. Philadelphia: Lippincott, Williams and Wilkins.

For Discussion

1. Are mothers who use drugs treated differently by society, in comparison to fathers who use drugs? If so, why?

2. Should state and federal prisons be required to offer treatment programs that are similar to the one described in this article? Why or why not?

28

Remembering the Lizard

Reconstructing Sexuality in the Rooms of Narcotics Anonymous

LESLEY L. GREEN, MINDY THOMPSON FULLILOVE, AND ROBERT E. FULLILOVE

At times, drug transactions involve sex-for-drug exchanges and these behaviors were highlighted during the wave of crack cocaine use in the 1980s and 1990s. In this article, Lesley L. Green, Mindy Thompson Fullilove, and Robert E. Fullilove discuss how people who participated in a 12-step program often "reconstructed" their sexualities and sexual behaviors as part of the recovery process.

Addiction is associated with the development of a set of behaviors and thought patterns that enable the addicted person to acquire drugs without regard to the harm such acquisition might cause to self or others. The preoccupation with using drugs can lead to neglect of family and friends, the drive for money to pay for drugs is often associated with stealing from loved ones, and the social nature of getting high privileges relationships with people who are getting high. Commercial sex work and sex outside of marital relationships are likely to accompany addiction to many substances, partly related to obtaining money for drugs and partly due to a freeing of inhibitions that follows the general erosion of concern for others (Kandall 1998).

The crack cocaine epidemic was accompanied by distinct new patterns of sexual behavior related to the binge nature of crack use (Fullilove et al 1993; Fullilove, Lown, and Fullilove 1992; Inciardi, Lockwood, and Pottieger 1993; Lown et al. 1993; Ratner 1993). Crack binges could be sustained for days at a time, limited more by the money available to the user than by any intrinsic limit set by the drug. Bartering sex for drugs enabled the user to continue drug consumption after cash had been dissipated. In the peculiar evolution of this barter economy, sexual services were sold for quite low prices, undercutting the much higher fees of those engaged in more traditional forms of commercial sex work. Ethnographic descriptions of these sexual activities often identified practices that were at odds with cultural norms, often influenced by the extreme power imbalance that was created between user and dealer by the user's insatiable desire for the drug (Bowser 1989; Fullilove et al. 1992; Ratner 1993).

The exchange of sex for drugs was linked to increases in STDs and AIDS as early as 1988 (Edlin et al. 1994; Fullilove et al. 1990; Goldsmith 1988; Schwarcz et al 1992). Unintended pregnancies were another consequence of this sexual behavior and contributed to a massive increase in the number of children in foster care (Wachtler 1990). Crack users were embedded in poor neighborhoods (Lillie-Blanton, Anthony, and Schuster 1993), and the sexual practices associated with crack use permeated the larger culture of these areas. This had broad effects on commercial sex work, gender power relations, and family stability, to a name a few place-based institutions that were challenged by the crack culture.

Despite the importance of the crack epidemic, the public health system of the U.S. provided very little prevention or treatment funding (Garcia-Soto et al. 1998; Reinerman and Levin 1997; Watkins, Fullilove, and Fullilove 1998). In the absence of targeted intervention strategies, addicted people had to rely on their own resources for recovery. One such resource was the 12-step fellowship program Narcotics Anonymous, which developed new tactics to meet the needs of those with crack addiction. A crucial part of the evolving program was the elaboration of a discourse around the particular ways in which sex and sexuality were part of the period of active drug-taking.

Relationship repair has always been a primary focus of Narcotics Anonymous (NA; Green, Fullilove, and Fullilove 1998; Peteet 1993). Men and women attending NA meetings learn through personal narratives how others in recovery make amends and develop new relationships that support their newfound sobriety (Green 2002; Steigerwald and Stone 1999). Many of the personal narratives told during NA meetings illustrate how difficult it can be for a person to develop or reestablish positive relationships once he or she enters recovery. Many men and women enter the rooms of NA with little or no knowledge of what it means to be involved in a mutually supportive relationship, romantically or platonically. NA deepened and expanded this work to help with recovery in the crack era.

This article focuses on the reconstruction of sexuality by men and women as described in personal narratives told at NA meetings. Twelve-step fellowship is based on the premise that "A meeting happens when two or more addicts gather to help each other stay clean." This slogan is crucial to investigating NA meetings from the perspective of

place. While meetings might be held in well-established locations, the essence of the meeting is not the setting but the sharing that goes on or, we might say, that "takes place." In that sense, what "takes place" is what constitutes both the place as setting and the place as actor in the drama of recovery.

Barker (1968) coined the concept of *standing patterns of behavior* to refer to places that are constituted by people engaged in the pursuit of a specific activity. He proposed the following:

> A standing pattern of behavior is a discrete behavior entity with univocal temporal-spatial coordinates; a basketball game, a worship service, or a piano lesson has, in each case, a precise and delimited position in time and space. Furthermore, a standing pattern of behavior is not a characteristic of the particular individuals involved; it is an extra-individual behavior phenomenon; it has unique characteristics that persist when the participants change. (18)

This paper uses narratives collected at 12-step meetings to explore the manner in which participation in such a standing pattern of behavior influenced sexuality.

Methods

Setting

The data presented here were collected between December 1998 and May 1999. The participants in this study were men and women participating in recovery at Lincoln Recovery Center, a freestanding outpatient drug treatment center that offers a wide variety of services to its clients. Lincoln Recovery Center is located in the South Bronx, a deprived inner-city community characterized by severe physical, social, and economic disintegration, which has triggered high rates of violent crime, substance abuse, and AIDS (Wallace 1988; Wallace and Fullilove 1991; Wallace and Wallace 1998).

The majority of Lincoln Recovery Center's clients suffered from crack cocaine addiction. Many were in treatment because the courts had remanded them there or because they had had their children taken away by the Administration for Children's Services (ACS) and had to complete a program of treatment in order to have them returned. Lincoln Recovery Center's clients were predominately African American (55%) and Hispanic American (45%; N. Smalls, personal communication, April 30, 2002). Clients described themselves as "hard core," meaning that they were victims of a particularly severe addiction, most often to crack cocaine.

Data Collection

Data presented here were originally collected during a qualitative study on the spiritual awakening process as it is described in 12-step fellowship meetings. Specifically, 95 12-step fellowship meetings were attended by the research team. Team members attended only those meetings that they were eligible to attend. Some NA meetings are open to people who do not have substance abuse problems, and others are not. One member of our team was in recovery and thus able to attend closed meetings. Each meeting lasted approximately one half hour, and attendance ranged from 15 to 45 people. Brief notes were made of all speech segments that contained a story. Immediately after the meeting, these notes were elaborated to document each story as completely as possible.

Two types of narratives were collected: main narratives (those related by the meeting speaker) and additional comments, which were offered by meeting attendees. Ninety-five main narratives were collected, each told by a different speaker. The 300 additional comments made by meeting attendees may have been given by the same individuals in some instances. Thus, the data set consists of approximately 400 stories, identified by date and gender of speaker.

Due to NA's tradition of anonymity, no data were collected about individual meeting attendees. Stories were stripped of remarks that might identify the speaker. Meeting attendees were predominately African American and Hispanic American, and mixed meetings were attended by equal numbers of men and women. Some attendees disclosed their age during meetings, but others did not. The range

of ages reported was 18 to 60. These procedures were approved by the New York State Psychiatric Institute Institutional Review Board.

Team members made observations of the meetings and jotted brief notes of each presentation that occurred during meetings. Immediately after the meetings, we prepared detailed field notes. Stories and interchanges were reconstructed as accurately as possible and entered into Atlas.ti (Muhr 1997), a qualitative data management software. As stated above, no information that could link remarks to a specific speaker was recorded.

Although both partial and complete narratives are presented here, it is useful to know that all the narratives generally followed the same format. The storyteller began by introducing herself or himself and explaining how he or she came to NA. The individual proceeded to tell his or her story, recounting the worst phases of the addiction and giving minute details about the process of "hitting bottom," a state of profound despair that is associated with the birth of readiness to stop using drugs. The final component of the story involved the addicted individual relating where she or he was in recovery from addiction and giving advice to those with less recovery time.

At the end of every meeting, members were given an opportunity to confess any "burning desires," that is, desires to use drugs, use people, hurt oneself, or hurt others. Members often confessed wanting to use drugs or to engage in activities that might lead to use. More often than not, these confessions were made by newcomers and resulted in members giving individuals explicit advice about what to do with their burning desire. Many confessions involved newcomers who were experiencing highly emotional situations that they felt ill-equipped to handle.

Analysis

We used an iterative process throughout the analysis phase of the project. The unit of analysis was the NA story, described above. Once the story had been entered into Atlas.ti (Muhr 1997), we identified and applied a series of codes. The coded material was then examined to compare and contrast stories. For purposes of this paper, we selected codes related to sexuality, relationships, and the process of meetings and examined the coded material for themes. We compared drafts of the paper to the raw data to assess the accuracy and fairness of the report. These steps of coding, ascertainment of themes, and writing were repeated until we felt that a reasonable representation of the data had been made.

Results

What Takes Place in NA Meetings

"Using" is a central concept that emerged in these narratives of drug use, but the concept also embraces the sexuality that accompanied the drug use. People described themselves as using drugs, using people to get drugs, and using sex. In this volatile mix, relationships were based on utility and self-interest. The following story is a classic narrative of a using relationship:

> One of the addiction counselors was attracted to me, he called me at my grandmother's house where I was staying and talked me into moving in with him. He thought he could save me. He treated me well, bought me clothes, food, but I couldn't see him as anything more than another trick, someone to feed my drug habit. I stayed with him until the day he said he wanted to try crack with me. He had 10 years clean. I felt that if he started smoking he wasn't going to give me any more drugs and that knowing what crack had done to me I couldn't let him get started so when he asked me for some I gave him toilet paper in a vial, I knew once I did this that I had to leave. I robbed him that night of some money and even though we had gone shopping that day for clothes and shoes for me, I left the house in slippers, headed to Hunts Point and stayed there for 5 years.

The woman's view of her lover as "another trick"—a way to get drugs, rather than a real person—is the central problem. Seen in the perspective of that time, sex for drugs and robbing were necessary to support her drug use, and hence justified. In fact, the woman was more than generous in her treatment of her trick, because she left before he relapsed.

Recovery involves both giving up the "right" to use others and reassuming responsibility for one's actions. The result is a wish for new kinds of relationships and the skills to enact those new desires. The woman in the following story offers an insight into this shift:

> The basic [NA] text does not tell us not to get into relationships in the first year. It tells us not to make any major decisions in the first year and that relationships can be disruptive to your recovery. Know your motives because they tell us "the men with the men and the women with the women," but we do have people in recovery who like members of the same sex and this could be a dangerous area when picking a sponsor. Step work is the backbone of this program and if you truly want to recover you must do step work and make some changes in all areas of your life, including your relationships. Through doing some work I found out that using is not only about drugs. When I first came here I would still sleep with my baby's father and get money from him to do my hair and stuff and I realized that was just a form of using and that I didn't have to do those things anymore. So I got some information and supported myself.

Twelve-step fellowship meetings are expected to provide a safe place of recovery where addicted people feel totally free to express themselves. Though the content of the meetings varies, each meeting is an occasion for "sharing and caring" among addicted people. Individuals in recovery are encouraged to trust others and to be open about their addiction and their character flaws.

In general, the meetings we attended opened with the following traditional activities: the Serenity Prayer, Who Is An Addict?, What Is the Narcotics Anonymous Program?, Why Are We Here?, How It Works (the 12 Steps), and a recitation of the 12 Traditions (Narcotics Anonymous 1988). After opening remarks, a speaker was introduced who gave the main address of the meeting. After the address, participants could make comments. As noted above, prior to the end of the meeting the question of burning issues was raised. This was a time to respond to pressing needs of participants. When that was done, the meeting was closed with the Serenity Prayer.

People who spoke at NA meetings would introduce themselves by saying, "My name is [first name] and I am a grateful recovering addict." Others in the room would respond, "Hi, [first name]." The famous and fundamental anonymity was not faceless or nameless or cold. In fact, the proceedings we observed were intimate, passionate, and connected. Within this dynamic setting, the frank and open conversation used some specific strategies to foster recovery.

A turning point for most participants took place when they were willing not only to face the exact nature of their addiction but also to reveal their "dark side" to fellow NA members, a process often referred to as "housecleaning." The recovering individual is encouraged to thoroughly and honestly take a personal moral inventory, admitting to himself or herself, to his or her Higher Power, and to at least one other NA member the exact nature of his or her wrongs. Ultimately, he or she is expected to make amends with all persons harmed by his or her addiction. Five distinct processes—listening for solidarity, hearing one's own story, sharing, trying new behaviors, and doing homework—act together to help those in recovery through this painful process.

Listening for solidarity. The first process is that of listening. Newcomers are encouraged to listen and not speak. While listening, newcomers learn that others have been through similar experiences. Hearing the stories of others helps the addicted person see that others experienced similar humiliations during active addiction and provides a blueprint for corrective behavior. An NA member may learn to be a better friend, spouse, and/or son or daughter by listening to the stories of others. Given the severity of negative life events experienced by most addicts, this becomes an important motivation for staying in the rooms of NA. One man recognized a need to hear that he was not alone in his suffering:

> When I came into this process I needed to hear the war stories because if I had heard people who had expensive cars or telling stories meant to sound like they were having a good time, I probably wouldn't have stayed.

Listening creates a sense of solidarity with the group. This is an essential first step, because it is the step of unconditional love. Without the sense of acceptance that accompanies being in the presence of people who really know about the "life" of drug addiction, it would be much more difficult for the individual to face the negative parts of addiction. Getting high is one way of managing the pain that accompanies knowing what happened. Unconditional love, such as that offered by NA, is a powerful alternative that can enable people to tolerate self-awareness: The message of the speaker's story is that "I've been there, too; you're not alone."

Hearing one's own story. At the same time, the more experienced members try to pierce the denial of newcomers so that they can begin to hear the wrong and harm in the classic story of using. The teaching story is used to accomplish this task and does so by foregrounding the harm in a manner that defamiliarizes the story and allows it to be experienced in all its hateful aspects. Thus, the addict is slowly alienated from using.

In the teaching story, the narrative is constantly interrupted to allow for a running commentary. This commentary interrupts the rhythm of the story to insert a new, and unexpected, analysis. In the following example, the storyteller is able to reflect on many aspects of his behavior while using drugs. He decodes each action, allowing us an insider view of his world. He is also stating the group's shared understanding of the process, as captured in his comment, "An addict always tries to take everything for themselves." This is a particularly vivid teaching story, but it is not at all unique. We have inserted spaces at each of the interpretive points.

> I went to the projects looking for the local lizard. My plans were to get the drugs, the woman and go clubbing. Of course this is not how it turned out, because once you get started using all bets are off. In the Basic Text it says, "We were living like animals," and that's what I mean when I say I went to the local lizard.
>
> This woman was skinny with sunken cheeks, hair half permed and I don't know when was the last time she had washed. Yet that's where I went to look for drugs.

366 PART X: DRUG PREVENTION AND TREATMENT

When I called her over and she asked me what I wanted all I said was the rock [crack] and when she asked me how much, all I did was show her the $100s and she rushed me to her house where she proceeded to throw everyone she had in there out. Because immediately upon seeing all the money she started calling me her man. An addict always tries to take everything for themselves. Because of the disease, their main objective is to use drugs and people.

I sent the woman out with $50 and she came right back with the drugs only because I had allowed her to see the other money. I used for a couple of hours, after the first hit the Lizard started looking like Pam Grier and I turned into Denzel Washington and every time this illusion began fading I would proceed to use again. After a couple of hours and a couple of $100s, I decided to leave the house and go to the store to get some beer. The girl was frantic not wanting me to leave with the drugs and the money, so I told her I would return. I was so high I was just looking to use one drug to come down from another. As I was heading to the store to get the beer I felt a pain in my arm. I didn't pay any mind to it but the next thing I knew I felt a pain like I was being stabbed and I fell to the ground, fracturing my jaw, blood coming out of my mouth. I couldn't move, my lungs had collapsed. I tried to move my arm to take out the drugs from my pockets and the money, I was lying in a pool of blood one eye was lying inside of blood the other was the only one I could see out of, after I removed the drugs from my pockets I passed out.

I saw a white light and I felt like that was it for me and I asked God for help (the emergency God we always turn to in times of trouble).

Then I heard the beeping of the hospital machines and realized I was alive. The first thing I saw was an Indian doctor who asked me did I know where I was. I told him in a bed, and all I could ask was when I could go home. The doctor told me I was in serious condition. I had been in a coma for about 7 days. This was my bottom and I knew God had saved me for a reason.

When I was released I went back to my room and packed up and moved to a shelter. I went back to the treatment center with the attitude anything I could do to stay clean I would. I had finally surrendered.

When I returned to the treatment facility my counselor told me he was aware of what had happened to me and welcomed me back. He said the important thing was that I came back. I couldn't even lift my head to meet my counselor's eyes, I felt so ashamed. All he asked me was what was I willing to do. And I answered "whatever." That's what I did. I took the suggestions, I attended meetings, I read my basic text and I internalized the steps and traditions into my life, I stuck with the winners and I stay in the basics to remind myself that I'm only one step away from being right back where I came from.

I am grateful to my God for a new life and for people in the rooms for helping me stay clean. This is an indispensable program if you want to live, you must be honest with yourself and God in order to get the serenity you strive for in your life.

When sober, men and women look back on these experiences with shame and horror. Having sex with the lizard or being the lizard—the dehumanized, unwashed, drug-crazed, objectified or objectifying man or woman—is inconceivable to the sober mind, as are many things that happen during active addiction.

At some point, as the alienation proceeds, the addict will be able to *hear* his own story. This is a particular kind of hearing, in which the listener comes in contact with the anguish caused by addiction. As this message sinks in, using and getting high become less desirable. The link between hearing one's story and accepting the anti-high message is clear in the following passage:

There was this bus driver who sat in the front and when he would ask me to sit in the front I thought he wanted me sexually and all it took was for me to see his uniform and figure he made money so I kept coming to the meeting to sit next to this man, until one day I heard my story and I heard if you don't pick it up you can't get high . . .

Thus, the recovering person makes a cognitive shift from the logic of using to the logic of sobriety, which we might conceptualize in the following way: logic of using = "I got high and I did [unacceptable behavior], therefore I better get high again"; logic of sobriety = "I got high and I did [unacceptable behavior], therefore I should stop getting high." Over time, people investigate every area of life, searching all the ways in which they are using others. Payment of educational loans, as in this story, is an example of shifting to the logic of sobriety:

> I owed $12,000 dollars to Higher Education and my sponsor told me in order to really live this program you have to be a responsible individual so today I only owe $3,000 and I'm working on the balance. I feel good about it.

Sharing. When people had some weeks or months of sobriety under their belts, they were expected to begin to share their own stories. One participant described this as "digging deep inside yourself, exposing all your demons, sharing your demons with someone else, asking God to remove them, making amends with friends and family members, and practicing how not to let your demons back into your life." The pain of digging into memories and the fear of revelation created an internal confrontation between denial and revelation. One person said,

> My disease did not want me to reveal that I had been in jail for attempted homicide, and that I had sex with other men. My sponsor told me to sit across from an empty chair and speak to God and tell him the exact nature of my wrongs. I did and felt God there with me and a great weight lifted from my shoulders. I felt relieved that I no longer had anything to hide.

As people shared they got feedback from others. During feedback at the end of one meeting, two people responded to the message with the following comments:

> I understand where you are coming from. At first I asked, "Why do you have to tell God, He already knows." Yet when I did confess my wrongs to God I felt so much better. Revealing things to another human being is necessary so that you don't stifle yourself in your recovery. Sharing with another person and with God is a form of freeing yourself.

> I found sharing myself with my sponsor to be a moving experience. We found that we had similar stories, which helped my sponsor guide me more effectively.

Trying new behaviors. Although honesty was expected in NA meetings, there was a general understanding that a certain amount of clean time was needed before most addicted individuals could actually be honest. Most came to the rooms of NA attempting to put on a façade of self-control and independence. This façade was quickly shattered by either relapse or the unconditional love experienced in the fellowship. Both men and women related stories of having to make decisions to open their lives to others in the rooms and get the help they needed in order to stay sober. The following quote illustrates the importance of allowing others to help in the recovery process.

> For the first 8 to 9 months of my recovery I would attend meetings but wouldn't get to know anyone. I finally started opening up. I got some good people in my life, and I'm thankful for that.

The NA room is thus a location for practicing new behaviors, such as asking for support. It is also a place to practice restraint, to resist using others.

Homework. A final tactic practiced in the rooms was assigning homework. The following interchange offers an insight into this process.

> I had a little difficulty with the God concept. I called my sponsor and asked him "What does this mean, that I pray and God will remove all my character defects?" My sponsor told me "No, being aware of your character defects and not giving into them on a daily basis and asking God to guide you is how you practice the 6th step." In other words God doesn't make your character defects just disappear, you have to work at it. This is why they say the 6th and 7th steps are action steps.

This same man went on to give the following example of how he practiced steps 6 and 7 on a daily basis.

> Every time I want to release frustration I go play basketball, yet I sometimes forget that there are a lot of different personalities out on that court and

that I am not in control, so when I get angry I start cursing out the other ballplayers which sometimes leads to confrontations which could and mostly does lead to fights. I didn't like backing down and sometimes I would get into people's faces, people that were suppose to be my friends. After doing these things I would feel really lousy, and would have to get humble admit I was wrong and apologize. You see after you have been living the program and you are aware of the things you aren't suppose to do, when you act out they do not sit well with you. After getting into arguments with others, I would call my sponsor and most of the time get the answers I needed and have a chance to talk out my feelings. Being humble is being highly spiritual. Being humble is a gift in recovery, it means you are on the right road and when you practice spiritual principles the rewards you get are great.

Sex in the Context of "Living Life on Life's Terms"

Everything that takes place in the rooms is designed to shift the addict away from the addiction scenario, in which using others is the order of the day. During the period of active addiction, sexuality can become a tool for the acquisition of drugs and a source of immediate gratification. At the extreme, sexuality might itself be seen as an impediment to using. One man described that he had stopped having women in his life, not even tricks, "because I couldn't give anyone anything, not even my mother if she asked. It was all about my using."

Recovery always included a reorganization of sex and relationships, accepting the need to "live life on life's terms." Responsibility, kindness, humility, and openness were all key features of this sober state. Restructuring sexual relationships depended on the accumulation of listening and sharing in the rooms. One man, expressing his gratitude for recovery, shared that he was glad to be "awake on a Saturday morning and not having to suck on something to suck on something else." Fieldnotes recorded this story as well:

> All night I dreamed about sex and drugs, continuously I could see myself just getting high and having sex. Through my dreams I realized that sex

is like a drug to me. It's another form of my addiction and I must talk about it to expose my disease. Sex and drugs went hand-in-hand for me, and today I don't want to return to that cycle. I'm going to make another meeting after this.

Homework and working the steps were also crucial parts of renegotiating the sexual self in the process of recovery. This lengthy but illuminating story was recorded in fieldnotes:

> I felt like I had arrived home when I got here. I lived in abandoned buildings. I found a boyfriend who took care of me in these abandoned buildings, and proceeded to prostitute myself until I was performing oral sex for as little as 50 cents. All I knew was that I had to use. I even let somebody shit on me for money for crack. My disease told me if I stopped smoking I would die.... Nothing stopped me from using. At the end I looked so bad truck drivers wouldn't stop for me. I didn't eat except from garbage cans because I couldn't spend money on anything but crack. The bones were sticking out of my neck and people started thinking I was a man. I used that to my advantage. I put socks in my groin area to act like I was a man and prostituted myself to gay men for anal sex.
>
> When I left detox this was the first meeting I made. I sat up front and listened. Listening is a gift. It wasn't easy because my sick thinking was always working on me. I got a sponsor and a God of my understanding. In the beginning I only thought of getting with the men, but after being in the process for a little while, I noticed that the other women weren't doing this and I didn't have to either. I got some women in my life who gave me unconditional love and taught me how to wash everyday. I had a problem with hygiene: After so many years of not washing, I was comfortable that way. The women taught me how to be a lady, how to maintain good hygiene habits, and how to be loving and caring without sex.

In this story, the massive addiction-related alterations in sexuality, from participation in underpriced sex work to loss of gendered appearance, are slowly reworked in the context of meetings. Listening, alienation from her "sick thinking" (the logic of addiction), and relationships of unconditional love gave this woman space to revalue her self and reacquire fundamental skills like self-cleaning. Pretending to be a man in order to get money for drugs and learning to be a "lady" while sober are markers of the change in her perception of sexuality, which was overidentified as a tool for the acquisition of drugs but took on more complex meanings during recovery.

As suggested by this story, the reconstructed sexuality is based on interdependence and a search for goodness. The illusions described in the lizard story are replaced by the reality of quite ordinary people, who have to pay bills and would like some pleasure. One participant said,

> I came to this meeting because my girlfriend has been guiding me in my recovery. Now I feel I want to make meetings by myself. I want to go out with a girl that still uses, because the sex is outrageous, but now I have a taste of what life is like without using. I want a drug free life. I may need additional therapy besides the rooms, but I'm going to continue making meetings.

The reconstruction of sexuality, however, is not a one-step process. The tensions of real relationships can be a trigger for relapse. One woman commented,

> I'm on medication and ever since I started taking this medication I've been having these drug dreams that I'm shooting up. I've been drinking but not using cocaine for 5 years but because of a relationship with a married man, I went back to using. I have 22 days clean and I want to use something else.

In 12-step fellowship, people, places, and things that trigger relapse are given enormous attention. Whether it's the joy of uninhibited cheap sex or the pain of an unfulfilling relationship, sexuality is profoundly linked to relapse triggers, and this is especially true of crack addiction because the use culture involves a great deal of sexual activity. Sex in the context of "living life on life's terms" involves a gradual acceptance of both the pain and ordinariness of sober life. One person related the following:

> I'm grateful to be in the fellowship again and I no longer have any more reservations. When I came to recovery I tried to recover from the waist up and

I would pick up women who were still using to use them sexually. But this time I rode those feelings out and I feel that I understand that it's all about using for me. A drug, something, someone and I don't want to use today.

Discussion

Every day, and all around the world, ordinary spaces of all kinds are transformed into the "rooms" of NA. Barker's (1968) classic work on ecological psychology includes such gatherings under the rubric of standing patterns of behavior. Like a baseball game, a 12-step meeting has rules and players. It intersects with many other standing patterns of behavior that exist in society: it is not church, though it is spiritual; it is about drugs, though it does not endorse their excessive use. In the ecology of all such rule-bound gatherings, the rooms take a unique place.

In particular, we find that the rooms assume enormous importance in structuring the lives of people in recovery. This is not the kind of authority that Barker refers to when describing the power of the principal's office to run a school. Rather, the power of the rooms lies, we hypothesize, in the existential and spiritual domain. It is the ability to alter the logic of engagement with activities that go on outside of the rooms that gives NA meetings their power. People, places, and things are judged by a new logic: "If I do/go/see _____, will I start using again? If yes, I won't do/go/see _____. If no, I will do/go/see _____." The shift to this new logic is, in turn, powered by the ability to experience the consequences of addiction. Remembering that under the influence of drugs one had sex with a "lizard" generates the motivation to stay sober. Recognizing the harms done to others supports the shift to engaging in new kinds of relationships, free of "using."

In the crack use culture, using sex to get drugs or, conversely, using desperate people for low-cost pleasure were the order of the day. In the rooms, recovering people learned a new sexuality. It is important to underscore that the rooms we observed were not concerned with sexuality as particular acts or particular partnerings. People affected by the sexuality of crack use culture in the Bronx have seen—and often done—everything. The recovery culture used that experience as the basis for new kinds of decisions that had to do with the nature of interpersonal connection rather than the "who" and the "what."

At the heart of the process of reconstructing sexuality was learning to discern the difference between sex as using and sex as not using. In general, the former consisted of intense but illusory pleasure, while the latter, however pleasant, was linked to real life. Thus, sex as not using was responsible to self and others. It was obvious from the many stories of struggle that this responsible sex was a difficult goal to attain, in no small part because it was sex in the context of a relationship to another human being. When the pain of the relationship was intolerable, the allure of drugs became greater. It was possible to flip back to the older logic, "That was yucky, I better get high." On the other hand, being free of the lizard inspired intense emotions, perhaps best captured in the phrase, "My name is _____ and I am a grateful recovering addict."

The rooms of NA, by creating the setting for a tightly scripted discourse on addiction, not only structure what transpires during the meeting but also organize the recovering person's lifeworld. Participation in the standing behavior pattern of NA influences the choice of all other people, places, and things. A remarkable corollary of this is that people can recover from addiction in neighborhoods like the South Bronx, where drug use is ubiquitous and the use culture permeates every aspect of daily life.

This analysis extends our understanding of sexuality and place by suggesting that the settings that rule the logic of sex will have the greatest influence on sexuality in all settings. Other behaviors may be similarly influenced. Although the stream of behavior is shaped by the succession of places in which the person finds himself, it may be very important to understand the deeper logic that determines entry into any particular behavior setting.

References

Barker, R. G. 1968. *Ecological Psychology: Concepts and Methods for Studying the Environment of Human Behavior.* Stanford, CA: Stanford University Press.

Bowser, B. 1989. "Crack and AIDS: An Ethnographic Impression." *Journal of the National Medical Association* 81: 540–543.

Edlin, B. R., K. L. Irwin, S. Faruque, C. B. McCoy, C. Word, et al. 1994. "Intersecting Epidemics: Crack Cocaine Use and HIV Infection Among Inner-City Young Adults." *New England Journal of Medicine* 331: 1422–1427.

Fullilove, M. T., R. E. Fullilove, M. Smith, K. Winkler, C. Michael, P. Panzer, et al. 1993. "Violence, Trauma and Post-Traumatic Stress Disorder Among Women Drug Users." *Journal of Traumatic Stress* 6: 105–115.

Fullilove, M. T., A. Lown, and R. E. Fullilove. 1992. "Crack 'Hos and Skeezers: Traumatic Experiences of Women Crack Users." *The Journal of Sex Research* 29: 275–287.

Fullilove, R. E., M. T. Fullilove, B. P. Bowser, and S. A. Gross. 1990. "Risk of Sexually Transmitted Disease Among Black Adolescent Crack Users in Oakland and San Francisco, Calilfornia." *Journal of the American Medical Association* 26: 851–855.

Garcia-Soto, M., K. Haynes-Sanstad, R. E. Fullilove, and M. T. Fullilove. 1998. "The Peculiar Epidemic, Part I: Social Response to AIDS in Alameda County." *Environment & Planning A* 30: 731–746.

Goldsmith, M. F. 1988. "Sex Tied to Drugs = STD Spread." *Journal of the American Medical Association* 260: 2009.

Green, L. L. 2002. *Archetypes of Spiritual Awakening: The 12-Step Journey of Redemption.* Unpublished doctoral dissertation, Columbia University, Teachers College.

Green, L. L., M. T. Fullilove, and R. E. Fullilove. 1998. "Stories of Spiritual Awakening: The Nature of Spirituality in Recovery." *Journal of Substance Abuse Treatment* 15: 325–331.

Inciardi, A., D. Lockwood, and A. Pottieger. 1993. *Women and Crack-Cocaine.* New York: Macmillan Publishing Company.

Kandall, S. 1998. "Women and Addiction in the United States, 1920-Present." In *Drug Addiction Research and the Health of Women*, edited by C. L. Wetherington and A. B. Roman, 53–79. Rockville, MD: National Institute on Drug Abuse.

Lillie-Blanton, M., J. C. Anthony, and C. R. Schuster. 1993. "Probing the Meaning of Racial/Ethnic

Group Comparisons in Crack Cocaine Smoking." *Journal of the American Medical Association* 271: 755–760.

Lown, A., K. Winkler, R. Fullilove, and M. Fullilove. 1993. "Tossin' and Tweakin': Women's Consciousness in the Crack Culture." In *Women and AIDS: Psychological Perspectives*, edited by C. Squire, 91–105. London: Sage.

Muhr, T. 1997. *Atlas.ti* (Version 4.1 for Windows 95 and Windows NT) [Computer software]. Berlin, Germany: Scientific Software Development.

Narcotics Anonymous. 1988. *NA: Narcotics Anonymous* [Blue Book]. Van Nies, CA: World Service Office.

Peteet, J. 1993. "A Closer Look at the Role of a Spiritual Approach in Addictions Treatment." *Journal of Substance Abuse Treatment* 10: 263–267.

Ratner, M., ed. 1993. Crack Pipe as Pimp: An Ethnographic Investigation of Sex-for-Crack Exchanges. New York: Lexington Books.

Reinarman, C. and H. Levine, eds. 1997. *Crack in America: Demon Drugs and Social Justice*. London: University of California Press.

Schwarcz, S. K., G. A. Bolan, M. Fullilove, J. McCright, R. Fullilove, R. Kohn, et al. 1992. "Crack Cocaine and the Exchange of Sex for Money or Drugs: Risk Factors for Gonorrhea Among Black Adolescents in San Francisco." *Sexually Transmitted Diseases* 19: 7–13.

Steigerwald, F., and D. Stone. 1999. "Cognitive Restructuring and the 12-Step Program of Alcoholics Anonymous." *Journal of Substance Abuse Treatment* 16: 321–327.

Wachtler, S. 1990. *The State of the Judiciary 1990*. New York: State of New York Unified Court System.

Wallace, R. 1988. "A Synergism of Plagues: 'Planned Shrinkage' Contagious Housing Destruction, and AIDS in the Bronx." *Environmental Research* 47: 1–33.

Wallace, R., and M. T. Fullilove. 1991. "AIDS Deaths in the Bronx 1983–1988: Spatiotemporal Analysis from a Sociogeographic Perspective." *Environmental Planning A* 23: 1701–1723.

Wallace, R., and D. Wallace. 1998. *A Plague on Your Houses: How New York Was Burned Down and the National Pubic Health Crumbled*. New York: Verso Books.

Watkins, B., R. Fullilove, and M. Fullilove. 1998. "Arms Against Illness: Crack Cocaine and Drug Policy in the United States." *Health and Human Rights* 2: 193–208.

For Discussion

1. Some individuals have suggested that women are more likely to benefit from 12-step programs that are gender-specific, that is, that some programs should cater to women only. Do you agree with this suggestion? Why or why not? Additionally, could sexuality be "reconstructed" in a group comprised of women only?

2. What kinds of sexual behaviors are altered while under the influence of alcohol? Is it important for people who engage in alcohol-influenced sexual behavior to have the opportunity to reconstruct their sexualities and sexual behaviors?

29

Methadone as Social Control

Institutionalized Stigma and the Prospect of Recovery

JULIE HARRIS AND KAREN MCELRATH

Utilizing an integrated theoretical framework of social control and stigma, Julie Harris and Karen McElrath focused on the experiences of methadone maintenance from the perspective of clients. The authors found linkages between social control and institutional stigma that serve to reinforce "addict" identities, expose undeserving customers to the public gaze, and encourage clients to be passive recipients of treatment.

Methadone maintenance treatment (MMT) is widely recognized as an intervention for treating opioid dependence (primarily heroin dependence). Researchers have described MMT in terms of its effectiveness for reducing heroin and/or other drug use (Fareed et al. 2009; Simoens et al. 2005; Teesson et al. 2006), risk behaviors associated with HIV (Corsi, Lehman, and Booth 2009; Gowing, Farrell, and Bomemann 2008; Hartel and Schoenbaum 1998), crime (Lind et al. 2005; Sheerin et al. 2004), and fatal overdose involving heroin (Fugelstad et al. 2007).

Despite a vast research base into MMT, scholars have suggested that MMT outcome studies are limited because of methodological problems associated with program attrition, sample bias, and measures (Fischer et al. 2005). For example, client retention in MMT is one outcome variable that has been used to gauge the effectiveness of MMT. Retention is deemed to be important because it reduces the likelihood of relapse into heroin use,

and in turn, heroin overdose and injecting behaviors associated with blood-borne viruses. However, clients who have left treatment during the early stages of MMT are often excluded from retention studies (Fischer et al.). This omission can artificially boost the overall retention rate, i.e., making it appear higher than the true value had early program leavers been included in the calculation. This form of sample selection bias is important, particularly because dropping out of MMT has tended to occur more frequently within the first few months of treatment (Farré et al. 2002). In some studies, upwards of 40% to 60% of MMT clients were shown to leave treatment within 12 to 14 months (Kellogg et al. 2006; Liu et al. 2009; Nosyk et al. 2010). In their review of the literature, Fischer et al. concluded that "patient retention . . . is the exception rather than the rule" (3).

Compared to the large number of MMT outcome evaluation studies, less emphasis has been placed on MMT from the perspective of clients,

---

although this line of inquiry is expanding. Scholars have identified important links between client satisfaction and retention in MMT (Villafranca et al. 2006), and have linked client satisfaction at 3 and 12 months (Kelly et al. 2010). Why do so many MMT clients leave treatment early, and what factors contribute to it? Although individual-level factors have been found to be associated with MMT dropout (Mancino et al. 2010), many investigators have found that structural factors create the conditions for leaving MMT prematurely (Bao et al. 2009; Harris et al. 2006; Porter 1999; Reisinger et al. 2009).

MMT clients have voiced concerns about daily collections of methadone (Holt 2007), supervised consumption for stable clients (Stone and Fletcher 2003), limited methadone collection times (Anstice, Strike, and Brands 2009), lack of privacy in pharmacy settings (Anstice et al.; Fraser et al. 2007; Matheson 1998; Stone and Fletcher), lengthy wait times for collections (Fraser and Valentine 2008) and the control of methadone over daily lifestyles (Reisinger et al. 2009). Dole and Nyswander (1980) highlighted structural and interpersonal factors, and noted the importance of mutual respect between treatment staff and MMT clients. They suggested that, without this respect,

> an adversary relationship develops between patients and staff, reinforced by arbitrary rules and the indifference of persons in authority. Patients held in contempt by the staff continue to act like addicts. . . . Understandably, methadone maintenance programs today have little appeal to the communities or to the majority of heroin addicts on the street. (261)

More than 30 years ago, Newman (1976) observed that the rigid structure of MMT programs deviated substantially from the way that MMT was originally envisioned. In practice, MMT provision is highly regulated, characterized by intensive social control (Des Jarlais et al. 1995), and yet still is considered to be a dominant modality for treating heroin dependence.

In this article, we link the theoretical concepts of social control and stigma to examine client experiences with MMT. We draw from the work of Cohen (1985), who described the societal shifts that

incorporate the disciplining and regulating of deviance. He viewed social control as the "organized responses" to deviance (3) that are deemed necessary to establish order, define moral boundaries, and monitor deviants in a panoptic world. Social control is fueled by power imbalances whereby those in positions of power can identify, track, control, and punish behavior; hence, power is a critical element of social control. The concept of power also features in stigma theory, because stigma derives from unequal power relations (Gilmore and Somerville 1994); thus, social control and stigma are inherently linked through the concept of power. Link and Phelan (2006, 528) suggested that stigma is best understood as a multistage social process that begins with human differences that are labeled and stereotyped. Labelers (those with power) impose "them/us" distinctions, and discrimination and loss of status are experienced by the individuals who are labeled (those without power). Once in place, stigma can spread and create additional power imbalances (Parker and Aggleton 2003).

Stigma can be practiced by individuals, and within peer groups, communities, and agencies (Mill et al. 2010; Yang et al. 2007). In the fields of mental health and HIV/AIDS, scholars have found that stigma negatively affects treatment entry, relationships with health care providers, and treatment retention (Link and Phelan 2006; Varas-Díaz, Serrano-García, and Toro-Alfonso 2005). Drawing from the literature on mental illness, institutional stigma (macro level) is differentiated from internalized stigma (micro level). The former refers to the "rules, policies and procedures of private and public entities in positions of power that restrict the rights and opportunities of people with mental illness" (Livingston and Boyd 2010, 2151). Institutional stigma creates the conditions for people to internalize the stigma they experience (Campbell and Deacon 2006). In turn, "they believe they are devalued members of society" (Livingston and Boyd, 2151). Not all individuals will internalize the institutional stigma that they experience; internalized stigma occurs when individuals "accept the social meaning" of the stigma (Lloyd 2010, 43). In this article, we analyze data from four studies to explore how MMT clients experience the mechanisms of social control under MMT provision. We also examine the nature of institutionalized stigma in MMT delivery, and the ways in which this macrolevel stigma reinforces spoiled identities. We link these issues to the prospects of recovery among MMT clients, and question whether the provision of MMT is consistent with the wider philosophy of contemporary treatment and harm reduction.

The Setting

The study sites included Northern Ireland (North) and the Republic of Ireland (South). The regions are divided by a land border, with separate governmental jurisdiction over health, education, social welfare, and other services. The availability of MMT provision in the North commenced in 2004, after several years of policy that proscribed any form of pharmacological-based maintenance for opioid dependence. Referrals to one of 13 specialist addiction treatment services are primarily made by a general practitioner (GP). The substitute prescribing scheme (MMT or high-dose buprenorphine) operates within these specialized services and under the context of shared care.

On 31 March 2010, 466 individuals were being prescribed methadone or high-dose buprenorphine in Northern Ireland (Department of Health, Social Services and Public Safety 2010). Of this figure, 52% were in MMT in receipt of dosages that ranged from 5mg to 160mg per day (mean dosage = 66.6mg per day). Mechanisms of surveillance include the Addicts Index and the Northern Ireland Drugs Misuse Database (DMD). The Addicts Index is updated annually, and includes the names of individuals who have been officially identified as "addicts" by GPs and other health professionals, who are required by law to report patients whom they believe or reasonably suspect to be addicted to one of several opioids or cocaine. This information is supplied in writing to the Chief Medical Officer. These data also include patients who are referred to specialized addiction services; thus, MMT clients are included in the Addicts Index. The DMD includes information provided by statutory and voluntary agencies, and reflects individuals presenting for drug treatment. One major difference between the two surveillance systems is that individuals

presenting for treatment are required to provide consent before their details can be included in the DMD database.

MMT has been officially available in the South of Ireland (largely Dublin) since 1992, although several changes in its provision have been implemented since then. The Methadone Treatment Protocol was implemented in 1998 and encompassed systematic procedures for prescribing methadone and for managing patients in receipt of methadone treatment (Butler 2002). The Protocol sought to expand the number of people in methadone maintenance by encouraging community-based treatment in the context of primary care. General practitioners are required to complete at least one course of training (minimum 3 hours) if they intend to prescribe methadone. The level of addiction training and experience with treating MMT clients are the main factors that determine MMT caseload within primary care settings. A total of 259 GPs worked with the Methadone Treatment Protocol in 2008 (Health Service Executive 2011), although only a small number had sufficient training to initiate methadone treatment in primary care settings. In 2008 two thirds of methadone clients were treated in clinics and one third were treated in community-based settings (Health Service Executive).

From the mid-1990s, the rapid diffusion of heroin extended beyond the geographic boundaries of Dublin; however, methadone provision was very limited in these nonurban areas. Although the availability of MMT has expanded to some areas outside Dublin city, the waiting time for treatment is extensive in some locales. Surveillance and tracking of MMT clients are conducted through the Central Treatment List, which included 10,213 MMT clients in 2008 (EMCDDA 2010). In both jurisdictions, methadone is dispensed largely through community-based pharmacies, and most MMT clients undergo some degree of supervised consumption. Fixed durations of MMT provision are not specified in either region.

Methods

In this article, we pool data from four studies that we conducted in one of two regions (Northern Ireland

and the Republic of Ireland). Although our original studies did not focus exclusively on clients' experiences with substitute prescribing, in each of the studies we interviewed individuals who were dependent on heroin, a proportion of whom had participated in a methadone maintenance program. Two of the studies were conducted in Northern Ireland (Harris 2011; McElrath and Jordan 2005), and the remaining two were conducted in the Republic of Ireland (McElrath 2008; 2009). We followed strict ethical protocol in each study, and ethical approval was granted by the Research Ethics Committee, School of Sociology, Social Policy and Social Work, Queen's University, Belfast. Harris received additional ethical approval from the Research Ethics Committee, Northern Ireland, and was cosponsored by Queen's University, Belfast and the Belfast Health Trust. Respondents who were interviewed by Harris provided written informed consent prior to data collection, and participants in the three other studies gave verbal informed consent. Respondents provided implicit consent for the interview data to be used in various articles. Direct and indirect identifiers that emerged during interviews were omitted during transcription. Digital and tape recordings were kept in secure storage in a university office. We transcribed interviews for the study with which we were affiliated, a strategy that reinforced confidentiality. Additionally, we protected typed transcripts through individual passwords. We did not have access to the full transcripts that were generated in the original studies in which we were not directly involved. We reimbursed all respondents for their time and travel expenses. We briefly describe the studies below, and provide sample characteristics in Table 29.1.

Study A (heroin use and injecting drug use, Northern Ireland). Harris (2011) focused on risk environments and their influence on route of administering heroin, initiation and transitions to and from injecting, and patterns of heroin use among 54 adult men and women who had used heroin within the 4-week period prior to the interview. Data were collected between 2008 and 2010. A total of 44% of study participants were maintained on methadone at the time of the interview.

Study B (injecting drug use, Northern Ireland). McElrath and Jordan (2005) examined patterns of injecting, risk behaviors associated with injecting drug use, and experiences with drug services where relevant. The authors collected data over a 10-month period, ending in September 2004. In total, 90 adult men and women were interviewed by McElrath or by a privileged access interviewer. A total of 40% of the respondents were in contact with some treatment service at the time of the interview.

Study C (problem drug use, Republic of Ireland). McElrath (2009) explored drug service needs and experiences with drug treatment among adults experiencing problems with drug misuse—namely heroin, cocaine, and/or benzodiazepine. The study site was North County Dublin, and data were collected in 2008 and 2009. McElrath interviewed 10 individuals who were on methadone maintenance at the time of the study, and 25 individuals who were regular users of heroin, cocaine, and/or benzodiazepines and were not in contact with treatment services.

Study D (drug misuse, Republic of Ireland). McElrath (2008) analyzed people's experiences with drug treatment and related services, and

Table 29.1 Sample Characteristics of the Four Studies.

Study	N	Heroin	MMT	MMT[a]	Average Age	Women
Heroin/IDU—NI[b]	54	100%	44%	44%	32	33%
IDU—NI	90	97%	24%	24%	31	30%
Problem drug use—ROI[c]	35	80%	36%	36%	28	46%
Drug misuse—ROI	36	39%	64%	64%	25	29%

[a]Percentage maintained on methadone among individuals dependent on heroin.
[b]Injecting drug use, Northern Ireland.
[c]Republic of Ireland.

identified gaps in service delivery. The study site was a large town on the east coast of Ireland and outside the Dublin metropolitan area; data were collected in 2008. McElrath interviewed 36 adult men and women, of whom 39% had used heroin (primarily through smoking), and 25% had current or previous experience with methadone maintenance in the area.

Our choice of the four study sites was based on two reasons. First, although we were principal investigators (PI) for the studies, we did not hold joint responsibility for any one study. As PIs, we conducted and transcribed interviews and analyzed the data; thus, we knew the data well. Second, we discussed and shared emerging findings over the previous several years, and we began to observe several similarities across the study sites in terms of how people experienced methadone maintenance.

Analytical Approach

The methodological strategy of pooling qualitative data from multiple studies has several advantages. For example, the approach makes efficient use of data, allows for checks on construct validity across research settings and time periods, and reflects a degree of triangulation (Hammersley and Atkinson 1995). Our strategy evolved over a 3-year period, commencing with our discussions of the social worlds of people who use heroin. We were involved in separate studies but often shared preliminary research findings pertaining to the experiences of respondents, including their stories about treatment services. As we shared and processed these experiences, we noted that respondents' social worlds were often shaped by intensive surveillance consistent with a social control framework. We began with a broad notion of social control and borrowed from the work of Cohen (1985) and his descriptions of surveillance of the deviant in a panoptic world. We remained open to other interpretations after several reads of the interview transcripts, noting themes and comparing data across these themes.

We identified emerging themes that pertained to different settings of MMT provision, interactions between MMT clients and service providers, and other experiences of MMT clients within the context of service delivery. The concept of

institutionalized stigma surfaced in clients' stories about their experiences. We defined and examined outliers or deviant cases, and explored the conditions under which outliers might be explained. In general, the analytical approach involved largely inductive but also deductive reasoning.

A limitation of the analysis concerns the use of secondary data. None of the original studies focused specifically on experiences with methadone maintenance. This point raises the issue of data saturation. The sample sizes in the original studies were determined by funding agencies, although data saturation with regard to the original concepts was reached before final interviews were completed in those studies. Some of the themes we discuss in the present article emerged relatively quickly in the four original studies. However, had the original studies focused specifically on experiences with MMT, we would have likely recruited larger numbers of MMT clients to ensure that saturation relating to methadone experiences had been reached.

Results

Addict Identity as Master Status

Individuals who held power over methadone provision often framed client identities around the master status of "addict." Furthermore, MMT clients were treated as addicts regardless of their stage of recovery. The saliency of this identity was manifested through (a) rules and regulations that equated addicts with deviants and criminals, (b) contractual power differentials, (c) labels that incorporated a clean/dirty dichotomy, and (d) clients' lack of input into treatment decisions.

The addict as criminal. Stereotypical views about heroin addicts were closely tied to assumptions of deviance and crime. The majority of MMT clients in both jurisdictions visited on a daily basis pharmacies where methadone consumption was supervised by the pharmacy staff. Within these settings, clients from both jurisdictions were aware that they were watched closely and assumed to be deviant:

> One time I was buying toothpaste—toothpaste, like. She [counter staff] thought I was trying to steal it. Why would I steal toothpaste? And if somebody was stealing toothpaste, why would

they steal it from the chemist where they get their methadone? I know it's hard on the chemist too. Maybe they get ripped off [robbed] sometimes. But see being treated like that? Everyone needs to go through that to see what it's like.

They would literally watch you and follow you to the door, like you've just been caught shoplifting. That's how you would feel, which I think is just damn right rude. Now they've been told and told and told from [consultant psychiatrist], apparently, to stop.

Alleged fears that MMT clients would engage in shoplifting were reflected in rules and regulations that were imposed on clients in selected pharmacies. These additional regulations were particularly evident in the Republic of Ireland, where MMT clients from the two study sites reported that they were not permitted to enter the dispensing pharmacy with friends or adult relatives. A few MMT clients perceived that pharmacy staff assumed that clients' social networks were comprised only of other addicts, and that shoplifting could be curtailed by prohibiting groups of addicts in the pharmacy at any one time. These experiences were described by MMT clients in the South of Ireland:

Loads of pharmacists in town told meth [methadone] clients that they can't bring friends [with them into the pharmacy]. You can't bring friends unless they are buying something. What about other people picking up prescriptions for drugs? How come they bring friends?

The policy created difficulties when two or more clients happened to arrive at a pharmacy at the same time:

You see, we sign this contract, and we're not supposed to go in with other people. One time in [town], there were four of us who got there together. He [the pharmacist] said to me, "You're last in, you go out [and wait until the others have left the pharmacy]." I had my baby with me and it was raining, and then there was loads of us standing outside in the rain, and me with the baby. Now he [pharmacist] did apologize when he saw the baby.

It doesn't take a genius to know why you're in there. You had to sit in a chair. She had to call my name before I could go to the counter. You'd swear I had leprosy. And you couldn't go in if someone else was in there getting their methadone. There was like a screen, and you could see the top of their head [someone else taking the methadone]. I'd wait outside 'til they finished.

Contractual power differentials. The continuation of MMT depended in part on how clients behaved. Some clients in the South were provided with a contract, but were not asked to sign them. The contracts listed various client behaviors that could result in penalties. Clients in the North were required to be punctual for appointments with key workers and prescribing doctors, and a 24-hour notice was required to change the time or date of appointments. Although the contract was signed by the client, the prescriber, the dispenser, and the key worker, the behaviors outlined in these contracts related to the client only. Our review of the contractual language suggests an emphasis on controlling client behavior through rules that reinforce addict and deviant identities. Clients in the North faced "possible discharge" or the withholding of methadone for "consistent tardiness," for missing two consecutive appointments, and for "inappropriate" behavior in pharmacies. Clients in the South reported similar rules that regulated clients' behavior in these settings:

Respondent (R): I think they [pharmacy staff] just need to treat people better from the start. They look at us like dogs, [as if we are] robbing and all. You see that paper [list of rules; contract] they give us when we start? We're not supposed to even look around the room.
Interviewer (I): What room? The whole pharmacy?
R: Yeah, we're just supposed to look straight ahead, not look around at all. And we have to sit there.

"Clean/dirty" dichotomy. Speech associated with heroin dependency includes references to "clean" and "dirty," and these words equate with good and bad behavior.[1] Individuals are "clean" when in recovery, or when they have abstained from using heroin even for a brief time. MMT clients who are clean are often rewarded by treatment services. For example, they might be entitled to reduced visits to the clinic, and might be granted

unsupervised methadone consumption in the form of take-home doses. The "unclean" clients undergo more regular surveillance in the form of supervised consumption, daily collections of methadone, frequent meetings with drug workers, and the dreaded urinalysis testing for psychoactive substances other than methadone. If former addicts are clean, then by comparison, addicts are "unclean" or "less clean." This dichotomy and the associated system of reward and punishment serve to reinforce the distinction between good and bad behavior, and amplify the addict identity.

The tool of urinalysis is justified as a means to determine treatment compliance and to prevent overdose. The results of urinalysis are also dichotomized, whereby urines are either clean (no evidence of recent use of psychoactive substances) or dirty (recent consumption of psychoactive substances other than methadone), and dirty often reflects use of heroin. The psychoactive effects of methadone and its associated dependence are deemed by service providers to be acceptable in the name of treatment. Methadone clients are clean, whereas heroin use is considered to be dirty. Yet the effects of methadone have the potential to socially and physically incapacitate MMT clients (Bourgois 2000). Nevertheless, consistent "cleanliness" is likely to be rewarded (although not praised), whereas clients who provide "dirty" urines are subjected to warnings, reprimands, and sometimes punishment.

Prior to 2008, MMT clients in the North were subjected to program dismissal when three consistent urine samples showed dirty results. A change in policy in 2008 meant that clients who consistently (e.g., three times) provided dirty urines are referred to an "enhanced clinic" where they no longer have contact with their key worker; rather, use of heroin and other nonprescribed substances is monitored by a consultant psychiatrist. Similar procedures were in place in one study site in the South of Ireland, where one participant noted, "Stablized people go on Wednesday. That's me. One dirty urine, and they could put me back to Thursday." The dirty are separated from the clean, and this segregation is justified in terms of preventing the dirty from influencing the clean. The dirty are believed to have the power to influence the relapse of the clean.

As a mechanism of social control, urinalysis represents a powerful and intrusive form of surveillance. Clients in both jurisdictions reported procedures whereby urine samples were required under the watchful scrutiny of staff. Collecting and handling urine samples were heavily regulated under the assumption that addicts are deviant. For example, procedures were in place to deter clients from substituting their own urine with another's clean urine, or to prevent urine dilution with toilet water. Surveillance of urine sample provision differed across services located in the North. In particular, the regulations of one clinic were described as punitive:

> [Addiction service] is far better. Just the way they get on [do things; provide the service]. They're not all having a go at you 'cause you're giving dirty samples and all. They don't stand over you and watch you go to the toilet like in [other addiction service]. They let you go in privacy and stuff like.

Recovery from drug dependence is a process. However, as a means of social control, the clean/dirty distinction served to dichotomize recovery and reinforced spoiled identities. In turn, the dichotomy restricted opportunities for developing client identities that incorporated incremental steps of the self in recovery.

Lack of input in treatment decisions. MMT clients in all four studies recalled feelings of powerlessness over treatment decisions that were determined by service providers. Some of these decisions were based around methadone dosage, although we found only limited evidence of inadequate dosages. The majority of MMT clients from Study A reported satisfaction with their methadone dosage at the time of interview. However, some respondents recalled difficulties in negotiating a suitable level of dosage, i.e., a level that would "hold" them, diminish cravings and the effects of withdrawal. Northern clients raised concerns about the power of addiction services to define the amount of methadone needed for stabilization. Clients resisted the uniform dosage policy—the "one size, fits all" approach after several months or years on MMT.

Indeed, one respondent (the only study participant who had initiated an extant complaints procedure) had been very proactive in challenging the dominant discourse relating to suitable methadone dosages. He reported that his current dosage exceeded 150mg:

> They [addiction service] were saying that 120[mg] was the limit and that they weren't gonna put me up any higher. Eventually I ended up putting in a complaint to the Health Board, and eventually I got a test done on how the methadone was metabolized by my blood plasma. I researched it myself and found that there's cases where some people— their metabolism can affect the methadone. They metabolize it at different rates. But then I actually got moved up [dosage increased] . . . it more or less takes me through until about 8.00 in the morning, and then I feel a bit rough for about an hour, which is an awful lot better compared to what I was.

In Study D (Republic of Ireland), some respondents perceived their current methadone dosage to be too low. A woman respondent indicated that her current daily dosage of methadone (i.e., 50mg) was insufficient, and had reported this problem to addiction services on several occasions. At the time of interview, her dosage level still had not been increased. As a result, she was "topping up" with heroin periodically to avoid withdrawal and cravings. In the same locale, adjustments to dosage levels and withholding methadone altogether were at times used as punishment: "I was three minutes late one time—three minutes, and they took me down five mg [decreased the methadone dosage level]." Another client reported, "Some chemists in town—if you're late, they'll pour methadone down the sink. Pour it down, I swear. There's you—using heroin again." Dosage penalties were also recalled by MMT clients in the North:

> When they see people who are still using heroin and using their methadone it's not just because they want to get extra stoned [intoxicated]. Maybe there's an underlying reason why . . . the methadone isn't holding them enough so they need extra doses. With [addiction service], if you're caught using [heroin], it seems to be that you're given a warning, and then given another warning, and

then you're struck off [forced to leave treatment]. I've heard cases of that happening. One thing that I'll say for [consultant psychiatrist] is that he was always fair. If you were using he wouldn't condone it, but he would think that it was better maybe using once or twice and being on the methadone, once or twice in a week, as opposed to maybe using once or twice a day every day, so harm reduction.

In these instances, dosage penalties (and threats of dosage penalties) were perceived as mechanisms of social control that were used to encourage clients to conform to the rules of the clinic and pharmacy. Although proper dosing is important for preventing overdose, insufficient dose levels can contribute to relapse into heroin use.

The lack of client input in treatment decisions also was revealed through clients' concerns over progress. In the Republic of Ireland, clients' preferences for reducing methadone dosage levels over time did not appear to be an option at the two study sites (Study C and Study D). Two men from Study D were interested in having their methadone dosage level reduced gradually, in hopes of eventually coming off methadone completely. One client reported being depressed because he believed that his goal was ignored by addiction services: "I'm afraid of methadone. The years are flying by and I'm still on it. They won't let me come down [reduce dosage]."

Similar concerns were voiced by respondents in Study C. Despite abstaining from injecting drug use for several years, MMT clients were unable to see the progress they had made because they saw themselves as still being opioid dependent. They reported that gradual detoxification from methadone was rarely mentioned as an option for them: "Do you know anybody who's been on methadone for a few years? Got off the methadone and not on heroin again? People can't get off methadone, and if they do it's right back to the heroin." Other clients voiced similar concerns: "I think of all the people who have used heroin. Loads of them, and I only know a few people who got off it. I know people who've been on methadone for years. That scares me."

Some respondents in the North voiced their concerns over what they perceived to be a blanket policy to retain people on methadone with no option of reducing. One respondent reported,

> Methadone's a cure but methadone isn't a longterm cure. Methadone is there to cure you in the short term, but they're doing it wrong here. They're putting people on methadone for years and years and years. . . . If you go and say to them, "Could you put my methadone up?" they say to you, "You don't need it to go up." But see if you go in and say to them, "Could you start to take me down off my methadone?" they turn around and tell you that you need to go up. But if you go in and say that you need to go up they'll say you don't. . . . [Addiction service] is a load of shit, to be honest with you.

Over time, a few respondents were able to negotiate low dosages of methadone, which they believed kept the withdrawal symptoms and cravings at bay. These individuals envisioned a time when they would not be using heroin or methadone. Although methadone prevented withdrawal symptoms, they feared long-term use of the treatment more than heroin itself (see Bourgois 2000). Overall, treatment was determined largely if not solely by addiction staff, with limited input from clients. For the most part, MMT clients were passive recipients of treatment, and this provision reinforced power imbalances between service providers and clients. We suggest that encouraging client passivity in treatment serves to reduce the likelihood of self-empowerment in recovery.

Undeserving Customers

Several clients perceived that they were treated as undeserving customers in pharmacies and clinics. This theme was reflected by (a) limited privacy and lengthy wait times, and (b) poor facilities.

Limited privacy in pharmacy settings. In the context of methadone provision, pharmacy settings are important because MMT clients come into contact with "normals" (Goffman 1963) within these venues (Lloyd 2010); thus, addict identities become visible to the public gaze. Clients' perceptions of the gaze were heightened because they were placed well down the list of preferred pharmacy customers. The public wait was described as "embarrassing" or "agonizing":

> Sometimes I have to wait half an hour to get my meth. She has to serve everyone first, even people who come in after me. I'm waiting there, and people looking at me like I've got two heads. She's getting paid for helping us, but you feel like you have to kiss her toes.

In the present study, space restrictions within pharmacies might have been one factor that contributed to settings that were devoid of privacy. For instance, some MMT clients reported regular consumption of methadone behind temporary screens that had been set up for that purpose. A few others reported that consumption occurred within photo booths that were located inside pharmacies. For other respondents, however, methadone was consumed in the presence of other customers. In both the North and South of Ireland, lack of privacy was of great concern to clients because they perceived this setting to be characterized by a stigmatizing public gaze:

> You can ask to go in there [separate and private room], but you have to make a point of it. I ask [for privacy], as there's members of my old work and others [present] . . . there's always people standing there, and I get really embarrassed.
>
> Private? It's not really that private. They walk out with the cup [of methadone] like. And plenty of time there's some people in there—especially at lunch hour. Walks out with the cup, and says, "C'mon [client]." And I go into the room—not really a room; that's where they take the photos. And everyone knows what's in the cup.

Very few clients complained directly to the pharmacist or other service provider about the difficulties they (clients) had experienced in the pharmacy setting. MMT clients lacked a voice ("Who'd believe a junkie?"), and often feared that methadone provision would be discontinued if they voiced complaints. This perceived threat was enough to encourage clients to "keep their heads down," mind their manners, and avoid "rocking the boat."

Several clients attempted to minimize the stigma associated with the public gaze of the addict. For example, some arranged for early morning visits to pharmacies, when fewer customers were present. Other clients reported waiting outside the pharmacy until other customers had left, or had occasionally purchased a pharmacy item so as to appear like "normal" customers while waiting for others to be served. MMT clients residing in small towns, villages, or particular housing estates appeared to be more affected by the local public gaze. This finding pertained to MMT clients in both jurisdictions:

> I would be nervous going in there. There's a few reasons. Your ordinary people come and get their prescriptions. Could be your mom's mate, someone down the lane, someone in the UDA [Ulster Defence Association, a loyalist paramilitary group in the North of Ireland].
>
> It might be packed with people. Maybe your next-door neighbor. You got to get a cup of water and your methadone, and drink it. There's a wee [small] private area, but people [other customers] know what's going on back there.

To some extent, Belfast respondents voiced less concern about the public gaze in pharmacies. The urban environment might have provided the perception of anonymity within the Belfast pharmacies. Some clients negotiated a change to another pharmacy, in hopes of minimizing this stigma. A change in pharmacy was often beneficial for clients, and finding the right pharmacist appeared to increase clients' self-esteem on the slow road to recovery:

> Gentleman like [pharmacist]. He's stood by me, looked after me when I was down in the dumps and all. Gives you time, know what I mean? He would talk to you and you can go round the shop with him. "Have you twenty minutes?" [And he says] "I have, aye." I mean, we've talked so much and he knows when there's something wrong with me like. . . . So if there is anything wrong I would go and talk away to him.

Poor facilities. The physical appearance of clinics differed across the two regions. In particular, our observations of some clinics in the South of Ireland showed very grim, depressing, and near-dilapidated external facades that were characterized by barbwire and high barricaded walls, surrounded by litter-strewn entrances. In the North, the majority of facilities appeared similar to doctors' offices and other "respectable" health centers. At the time of the studies, the interior design of most northern clinics suggested a somewhat welcome atmosphere, with organized reading material available in waiting rooms, simple but fairly new décor, and the appearance of cleanliness. In contrast, the two southern study sites were characterized as being more "clinical" and less welcoming in appearance. In one southern site, toilet facilities were described by MMT clients as particularly demeaning. One respondent reported, "There's one toilet and there's urine all around the toilet bowl. It's disgusting." A woman client had accessed addiction services at the same site:

> I hate going to the toilet there. There's urine everywhere, and can you get something from someone else's piss? Can you get AIDS? I try and clean up the urine before I go, and then I wash my hands like mad.

MMT clients in this locale perceived that treatment staff thought them undeserving of clean toilets. Rather, the assumption was that "dirty" toilets are appropriate for "dirty" people. None of the respondents in Study D had ever complained to treatment staff about the condition of the restrooms. MMT clients were voiceless under the powerful constraints of treatment and those who held power over it.

Barriers to Reintegration

If one objective of drug treatment is to encourage and perhaps facilitate reintegration into mainstream society, then clearly, participating in meaningful employment is part of this process. However, the conditions under which MMT is provided can act as barriers to finding suitable employment and staying employed. Some respondents in Study D were searching for meaningful work, yet were conscious of the need to collect methadone frequently, and perceived that this lifestyle routine could affect relationships with employers. In this locale, seeking employment was deferred for another day. A man participant from the North reported similar difficulties:

> It's too much hassle. I got a phone call, says would I like to have a job. I was interested. It started at 8.00 in the morning and finished around 5.30. How could I get the [methadone] script

[prescription]? I needed to be in town at 9.00 or 9.30 [pharmacy opening hours], or else be back by 4.30 or 5.00 [closing hours]. I need to find work that allows me to get my script.

Although some MMT clients in the North (Study A) reported that they had worked while being dependent on heroin, none were searching for work at the time of interview. We attributed this finding to the regulations and routines of MMT:

I was working when I was on the heroin, when I had a pretty big habit. I was able to hold a job—no problem—whereas on the methadone at the minute, there's no way that I feel like I could hold down a job. I'm waking up in the morning feeling rough. Three days a week I have supervised consumption. Four days a week I have it [methadone doses] home with me. So there's not gonna be very many employers who go, "That's okay. Sure, come in an hour or two after you get your methadone," you know?

In one of the four study sites (Study C), nearly all of the MMT clients who participated in an interview worked in part- or full-time employment, consistent with county-wide data claiming the highest rate of labor force participation in 2006 (Central Statistics Office 2006). MMT clients in that study noted the difficulty associated with collecting methadone during working hours. A man reported,

The woman [counter staff] there looks down on you—all the time. Well, she's not there all the time. But when I see her, I go, "Oh God—here it comes." I was working, every day. See that chemist? It's always packed. I had [a] half hour for my lunch break, and it would take me half an hour to get my methadone . . . loads of times she'd keep me waiting 'til everyone had gone. And me getting back to work late. You'd have to sit there 'til everyone was away. Then they'd get your methadone. I'd be late for work after lunch, like. And they [coworkers] don't know I'm taking methadone.

Some respondents in Study C disclosed their MMT involvement to their employers or a trusted coworker. Others tended to carefully guard their treatment participation for fear of losing their jobs or being treated differently at work. Strategies to avoid potential stigma were incorporated into daily lifestyles. Indeed, some respondents described how they saw but never took possession of the business card that contained information about the study, used in an effort to recruit participants. They voiced apprehension that their drug use history might be disclosed if another party observed the card in their possession. A woman respondent and MMT client worked in a financial institution at the time of interview. Distancing herself from a drug user identity was paramount to her self-image and how she perceived others might view her: "I got the card, but I couldn't carry it with me. Thought maybe work might find out. Didn't want to leave the card at work."

A respondent in Study C had held the same job for several years, but had never disclosed his MMT involvement to his employer. He had long ago negotiated take-home methadone doses so that his work routine would not be affected. The respondent attributed meaningful employment to his involvement in MMT: "I've been with them for eight years, and it's the longest time that I've had a job. And that's due to the methadone."

Discussion

Methadone provision in both jurisdictions was characterized by social control and institutional stigma, which served to reinforce spoiled identities, expose "undeserving customers" to the public gaze, and create barriers to reintegration. We observed more similarities than differences across the study sites, but noted the contrasts in terms of the physical structure of the clinics (facilities in the North were more likely to resemble mainstream health centers) and pharmacy regulations that prevented MMT clients being accompanied by friends during pharmacy visits (southern sites). We conclude that social control is multifaceted and layered within and across the contexts in which MMT is provided. The layers of social control derive from the official registers or lists of MMT clients. In the official quest to identify and track MMT clients, informed and voluntary consent to be part of these lists is deemed to be unnecessary. The layers of social control expand from the official registers to the settings of clinics and pharmacies, and extend further to regulations and surveillance within these settings. In the clinics, for example, social control features in drug testing through urinalysis, dosage decisions, clean/dirty distinctions, and sanctions over missed appointments. Layers of social control within pharmacies are reflected in the wait experienced by "undeserving customers," the watchful gaze of pharmacy staff, and the rules that govern client behavior (e.g., contractual obligations).

These layers of social control are tied closely with institutional stigma. The label of addict emerged as a salient identity among MMT clients, and was imposed by service providers. Moreover, addicts were interpreted to be untrustworthy and part of a "dangerous class." Opsal (2011) described the social control of parolees with "felon" identities. Respondents in her study "lived under a system of surveillance that bounded their behavior" (142). She noted for example, the practices of regular drug testing, frequent meetings with agents of social control (i.e., parole officers), rules that prevented association with other felons, and the power over the body (i.e., parole officers had discretion over recommendations for parole revocation). These methods of regulating felon behavior are strikingly similar to the experiences of MMT clients in the present study, where spoiled identities equated addicts with criminals. Frequent exposure to institutional stigma across various settings served to reinforce spoiled identities of MMT clients.

MMT is most often utilized among people presenting with heroin dependence, and heroin is often viewed as the least-acceptable drug, even among individuals who are "heavy" users of other illicit drugs (McElrath and McEvoy 2001). In a previous study, Radcliffe and Stevens (2008) found that individuals whose addiction was associated with drugs other than heroin dropped out of treatment in an attempt to disassociate themselves from "junkies." Similar to people's assumptions about HIV (Miles et al. 2011; Worthington and Myers 2003), heroin dependence is perceived to be linked to lifestyle rituals that are associated with deviance, e.g., injecting drug use (Simmonds and Coomber 2009), and conditions that are presumed to be dangerous, e.g., blood-borne viruses. Moreover, heroin dependence is perceived to be intertwined with criminal activity

(Radcliffe and Stevens); hence, MMT provision is situated between the ideologies of medicalization and criminalization (Vigilant 2004).

We recognize that various drug treatment modalities can be stigmatizing (Luoma et al. 2007), but we suggest that in comparison to other interventions, MMT is characterized more by social control and institutional stigma that reinforce and perhaps create spoiled identities. We believe that this difference has its roots in how heroin dependence is perceived and stereotyped, and how these perceptions are connected to individuals who experience heroin dependence. Moreover, clients involved with other types of drug treatment are generally not exposed to the public gaze in pharmacies. Still, it would be useful to compare social control mechanisms across a diverse range of modalities that are designed to treat individuals with heroin dependence.

Perceptions about MMT clients are in some ways consistent with statutory MMT protocols (e.g., drug testing, supervised consumption of methadone, contracts) that permit and sometimes require some of the rules and regulations that characterized provision in these jurisdictions. Institutional stigma is reflected in some of these protocols; thus, "stigma plays a key role in producing and reproducing relations of power and control" (Parker and Aggleton 2003, 16). The implication of these findings is that institutional stigma has the potential to discredit and negate self-recovery, particularly when individuals internalize the stigma. (Re)developing nonaddict identities is important for recovery (Biernacki 1986), and positive self-identities are likely to surface in the absence of institutionalized and internalized stigma. Institutionalized stigma disempowers MMT clients, whereas recovery requires empowerment. Internalized stigma can contribute to leaving treatment prematurely (Lloyd 2010), which has been linked to increased likelihood of mortality (Fugelstad et al. 2007; Magura and Rosenblum 2001). Moreover, when individuals are devalued by the treatment process itself, how can recovery be achieved?

MMT might be the most regulated and controlled intervention that operates under the guise of treatment. By comparison, Fischer et al. (2005) noted that patients being treated for diabetes and

AIDS are not "penalized by the treatment provider for not complying with the prescribed treatment" (3). We compare the social control of MMT with long-term use of benzodiazepine, prescribed by physicians. Benzodiazepine dependence is well-documented in Ireland. Intended for short-term relief for anxiety, repeat prescriptions in the country have been described as commonplace (Department of Health and Children 2002). However, patients in receipt of repeat prescriptions do not consume the medication in the presence of specialist providers, and are not required to submit to urinalysis testing. These controls are not in place, despite benzodiazepines being implicated in overdoses when combined with alcohol (Koski, Ojanperä, and Vuori 2002; Tanaka 2002), and being diverted to illicit markets (Fountain et al. 1996; Inciardi et al. 2009). This contradiction in pharmacological delivery must be explained by the spoiled identities of heroin "addicts" who remain, even after several years, on MMT.

Under the current service provision in North and South Ireland, methadone maintenance is best viewed as an intervention rather than a treatment modality. The pharmacological potential of methadone is undermined by clients' experiences of MMT provision, which is inconsistent with contemporary visions of treatment and harm reduction. MMT provision is characterized by highly regulated social control mechanisms and institutional stigma that (a) reduce the likelihood of developing trusting relationships between providers and clients, (b) reinforce spoiled identities of clients, and (c) view clients as passive recipients of treatment. Unlike individuals who seek other health provision, MMT clients are not treated as patients (Vigilant 2001), but as suspects. MMT is more about controlling behavior than treating disease (Bourgois 2000; Saris 2008), and the control of clients' behavior is justified because of stereotypical assumptions that addicts are a deviant and to some extent dangerous class.

Suggestions for Change

We suggest that social control and institutional stigma create the conditions for poor outcomes with MMT. So how can stigma-free MMT be provided in the context of multifaceted social control? First, there is an urgent need to reframe MMT provision so that clients are viewed as customers (Fraser and Valentine 2008) or consumers (Reisinger et al. 2009) in the various contexts of service delivery. This ideological change represents an important step for reducing social control and institutional stigma. In regions where service users are not organized collectively, MMT programs can develop autonomous groups of service users and commit to dialogue for resolving complaints. Patterson, Backmund, Hirsch, and Yim (2007) argued that interventions designed to reduce stigma must consider macro-level changes. They offered the example of hospital advisory groups consisting of service users who could contribute to the development of antistigma interventions. They also suggested that advisory members should be compensated for their work. Broadening the voice of MMT clients to directly influence MMT programs has the potential for improving service delivery, boost retention, and benefit recovery. Although the Irish and British governments have recently called for service user involvement in the provision of health care, it remains to be seen whether the voice of the service user will have substantive impact.

Second, although relocating drug treatment services to mainstream health centers might reduce the stigma of treatment (Radcliffe and Stevens 2008), some general practitioners have voiced resistance about treating patients with drug problems (Matheson et al. 2003), which could result in the displacement of institutional stigma from clinics to physicians' offices. Instead, White (2010, 46) recommended that MMT clinics alter their "institutional identities" and be referred to as "addiction recovery centers" that are reflected by "strong cultures of recovery." Service users should be encouraged to develop a stake in ownership by participating in meaningful program aspects. These centers should actively involve individuals who were once heroin dependent but have since gained employment, education, training, or other meaningful life change. It is important that MMT clients know and learn from empowered others who also have experienced heroin dependence. Additionally, "clean" and "dirty" discourses should be avoided, and replaced with language that does not demonize or create hierarchies of MMT clients.

Third, there is an urgent need to rectify the institutional stigma that occurs in pharmacies. This issue represents significant challenges, because methadone is often dispensed in private pharmacies that lie outside the gaze of auditing. We suggest that antistigma training be required of pharmacists and counter staff, and that regular feedback meetings be held between pharmacists and collective groups of service users. Finally, we do not necessarily oppose the use of contracts, but believe that contracts should be balanced and power differentials eliminated by including specific responsibilities for prescribers, dispensers, treatment staff, and customers. Contracts should include the importance of privacy and confidentiality, and how these issues will be protected. Feedback from clients should be collected on a regular basis, and without threats to methadone availability or provision.

Note

1. Clean and dirty discourse was first raised by a drug outreach worker in discussions with the second author. We acknowledge Michele Jordan's insights here.

References

Anstice, S., C. J. Strike, and B. Brands. 2009. "Supervised Methadone Consumption: Client Issues and Stigma." *Substance Use and Misuse* 44: 794–808. doi:10.1080/10826080802483936

Bao, Y.-P., Z. M. Liu, D. H. Epstein, C. Du, J. Shi, and L. Lu. 2009. "A Meta-Analysis of Retention in Methadone Maintenance by Dose and Dosing Strategy." *American Journal of Drug and Alcohol Abuse* 35: 28–33. doi: 10.1080/00952990802342899

Biemacki, P. 1986. *Pathways from Heroin Addiction: Recovery Without Treatment*. Philadelphia: Temple University Press.

Bourgois, P. 2000. "Disciplining Addictions: The Bio-Politics of Methadone and Heroin in the United States." *Culture, Medicine and Psychiatry* 24: 165–195. doi:10.1023/A:1005574918294

Butler, S. 2002. "The Making of the Methadone Protocol: The Irish System?" *Drugs: Education, Prevention and Policy* 9: 311–324. doi: 10.1080/09687630210148465

Campbell, C. and H. Deacon. 2006. "Unravelling the Contexts of Stigma: From Internalization to Resistance to Change." *Journal of Community and Applied Social Psychology* 16: 411–417. doi: 10.1002/casp.901

Central Statistics Office. 2006. *Persons, Males and Females, Aged 15 Years and Over in Each Province, County and City, Classified by Labor Force, Employment Status and Labor Force Participation Rate*. Retrieved from http://census.cso.ie/census/ReportFolders/ReportFolders.aspx

Cohen, S. 1985. *Visions of Social Control: Crime, Punishment and Classification*. Cambridge: Polity.

Corsi, K. F., W. K. Lehman, and R. E. Booth. 2009. "The Effect of Methadone Maintenance On Positive Outcomes for Opiate Injection Drug Users." *Journal of Substance Abuse Treatment* 37: 120–126. doi: 10.1016/j.jsat.2008.11.004

Department of Health and Children. 2002. *Benzodiazepines: Good Practice Guidelines for Clinicians*. Dublin: Author. Retrieved from http://www.dohc.ie/publications/benzodiazepines_good_practice_guidelines.html

Department of Health, Social Services and Public Safety. 2010. *Statistics from the Northern Ireland Substitute Prescribing Database: 31 March 2010*. Belfast: Author. Retrieved from http://www.dhsspsni.gov.uk/substitute_prescribing_report_2009-10.pdf

Des Jarlais, D. C., D. Paone, S. R. Friedman, N. Peyser, and R. G. Newman. 1995. "Regulating Controversial Programs for Unpopular People: Methadone Maintenance and Syringe Exchange Programs." *American Journal of Public Health* 85: 1577–1584. Retrieved from http://www.ncbi.nlm.nih.gov/pmc/articles/PMC1615684

Dole, V. P. and M. E. Nyswander. 1980. "Methadone Maintenance: A Theoretical Perspective." In *Theories on Drug Abuse: Selected Contemporary Perspectives*, edited by D. J. Lettieri, M. Sayers, and H. W. Pearson, 256–261. NIDA Research Monograph 30. Washington, DC: U. S. Government Printing Office. Retrieved from http://archives.drugabuse.gov/pdf/monographs/download30.html

European Monitoring Centre for Drugs and Drug Addiction (EMCDDA). 2010. "Estimated Number of Clients in Methadone Treatment and of

All Clients Receiving any Opioid Substitution Treatment (OST), Table HSR-3." *Statistical Bulletin 2010*. Lisbon: Author. Retrieved from http://www.emcdda.europa.eu/stats10/hsrtab3b

Fareed, A., J. Casarella, R. Amar, S. Vayalapalli, and K. Drexler. 2009. "Benefits of Retention in Methadone Maintenance and Chronic Medical Conditions as Risk Factors for Premature Death Among Older Heroin Addicts." *Journal of Psychiatric Practice* 15: 227–234. doi: 10.1097/01. pra .0000351884.83377.e2

Farré, M., A. Mas, M. Torrens, V. Moreno, and J. Cami. 2002. "Retention Rate and Illicit Opioid Use During Methadone Maintenance Interventions: A Meta-analysis." *Drug and Alcohol Dependence* 65: 283–290. doi:10.1016/S0376- 8716(0)00171-5

Fischer, B., J. Rehm, G. Kim, and M. Kirst. 2005. "Eyes Wide Shut? A Conceptual and Empirical Critique of Methadone Maintenance Treatment." *European Addiction Research* 11: 1–14. doi:10.1159/000081410

Fountain, J., P. Griffiths, M. Farrell, M. Gossop, and J. Strang. 1996. *A Qualitative Study of Patterns of Prescription Drug Use amongst Chronic Drug Users*. London: Department of Health.

Fraser, S. and K. Valentine. 2008. *Substance and Substitution: Methadone Subjects in Liberal Societies*. New York: Palgrave Macmillan.

Fraser, S., K. Valentine, C. Treloar, and K. Macmillan. 2007. *Methadone Maintenance Treatment in New South Wales and Victoria: Takeaways, Diversion and Other Key Issues*. Sydney, NSW, Australia: National Centre in HIV Social Research. Retrieved from http://www.crr.unsw.edu.au/media/File/Methadonemaintenance.pdf

Fugelstad, A., M. Stenbacka, A. Leifman, M. Nylander, and I. Thiblin. 2007. "Methadone Maintenance Treatment: The Balance Between Life-Saving Treatment and Fatal Poisonings." *Addiction* 102: 406–412. doi: 10.1111/j.1360-0443.2006.01714.x

Gilmore, N. and M. A. Somerville. 1994. "Stigmatization, Scapegoating and Discrimination in Sexually Transmitted Diseases: Overcoming 'Them' and 'Us.'" *Social Science and Medicine* 39: 1339–1358. doi:10.1016/0277-9536(94)90365-4

Goffman, E. 1963. *Stigma: Notes on the Management of Spoiled Identity*. Englewood Cliffs, NJ: Prentice-Hall.

Gowing, L., M. Farrell, and R. Bornemann. 2008. "Substitution Treatment of Injecting Opioid Users for Prevention of HIV Infection." *Cochrane Database of Systematic Reviews* Issue 2, Art. No. CD004145.

Hammersley, M. and P. Atkinson. 1995. *Ethnography: Principles in Practice*, 2nd ed. London: Routledge.

Harris, J. 2011. "Risk and Enabling Environments: Influences on Initiations into Injecting Drug Use and Heroin Use, Transitions to and from Injecting Drug Use and Patterns of Use." Doctoral dissertation, in progress, Queen's University, Belfast.

Harris, K. A., J. H. Arnsten, H. Joseph, J. Hecht, I. Marion, P. Juliana, and M. N. Gourevitch. 2006. "A 5-Year Evaluation of a Methadone Medical Maintenance Program." *Journal of Substance Abuse Treatment* 31: 433–438. doi:10.1016/j.jsat.2006.05.018

Hartel, D. M. and E. E. Schoenbaum. 1998. "Methadone Treatment Protects Against HIV Infection: Two Decades of Experience in the Bronx, New York City." *Public Health Reports* 113: 107–115. Retrieved from http://www.ncbi.nlm.nih.gov/pmc/articles/PMC1307733

Health Service Executive. 2011. *The Introduction of the Opioid Treatment Protocol*. Dublin, Ireland: Author. Retrieved from fhttp://www.drugs.ie/resourcesfiles/reports/Opioid_Treatment_Protocol.pdf

Holt, M. 2007. "Agency and Dependency Within Treatment: Drug Treatment Clients Negotiating Methadone and Antidepressants." *Social Science and Medicine* 64: 1937–1947. doi:10.1016/j.socscimed.2007.01.011

Inciardi, J. A., H. L. Surratt, T. J. Cicero, and R. A. Beard. 2009. "Prescription Opioid Abuse and Diversion in an Urban Community: The Results of an Ultrarapid Assessment." *Pain Medicine* 10: 537–548. doi: 10.1111/j.1526-4637. 2009.00603.x

Kellogg, S., D. Melia, E. Khuri, A. Lin, A. Ho, and M. J. Kreek. 2006. "Adolescent and Young Adult Heroin Patients: Drug Use and Success in Methadone Maintenance Treatment." *Journal of Addictive Disease* 25: 15–25. doi:10/1300/J069v25n03_03

Kelly, S. M., K. E. O'Grady, B. S. Brown, S. G. Mitchell, and R. P. Schwartz. 2010. "The Role of Patient Satisfaction in Methadone Treatment." *American*

Journal of Drug and Alcohol Abuse 36: 150–154. doi:10.3109/009 52991003736371

Koski, A., I. Ojanperä, and E. Vuori. 2002. "Alcohol and Benzodiazepines in Fatal Poisonings." *Alcoholism: Clinical and Experimental Research* 26: 956–959. doi: 10.1111/j. 153 0-0277 .2002.tb02627.x

Lind, B., S. Chen, D. Weatherburn, and R. Mattick. 2005. "The Effectiveness of Methadone Maintenance Treatment in Controlling Crime: An Australian Aggregate-Level Analysis." *British Journal of Criminology* 45: 201–211. doi:10.1093/bjc/azh085

Link, B. G. and J. C. Phelan. 2006. "Stigma and Its Public Health Implications." *Lancet* 367: 528–529. doi:10.1016/S0140- 6736(06)68184-1

Liu, E. Liang, T., Shen, L., Zhong, H., Wag, B., Wu, Z., and R. Detels. 2009. "Correlates of Methadone Client Retention: A Prospective Cohort Study in Guizhou Province, China." *International Journal of Drug Policy* 20: 304–308. doi:10.1016/j.drugpo.2008.09.004

Livingston, J. D. and Boyd, J. E. 2010. "Correlates and Consequences of Internalized Stigma for People Living with Mental Illness: A Systematic Review and Meta-analysis." *Social Science and Medicine* 71: 2150–2161. doi:10.1016/j. socscimed.2010.09.030

Lloyd, C. 2010. *Sinning and Sinned Against: The Stigmatisation of Problem Drug Users.* London: UK Drug Policy Commission. Retrieved from www.ukdpc.org.uk/resources/ Stigma_Expert_Commentary_final.pdf

Luoma, J. B., M. P. Twohig, T. Waltz, S. C. Hayes, N. Roget, M. Padilla, and G. Fisher. 2007. "An Investigation of Stigma in Individuals Receiving Treatment for Substance Abuse." *Addictive Behaviors* 32: 1331–1346. doi:10.1016/j. addbeh.2006.09.008

Magura, S. and A. Rosenblum. 2001. "Leaving Methadone Treatment: Lessons Learned, Lessons Forgotten, Lessons Ignored." *Mount Sinai Journal of Medicine* 68: 62–74. Retrieved from http://www.ncbi.nlm.nih.gov/pubmed/11135508

Mancino, M., G. Curran, X. Han, E. Allee, K. Humphreys, and B. M. Booth. 2010. "Predictors of Attrition from a National Sample of Methadone Maintenance Patients." *American Journal of Drug and Alcohol Abuse* 36: 155–160. doi:10.3109/00952991003736389

Matheson, C. 1998. "Privacy and Stigma in the Pharmacy: Illicit Drug Users' Perspectives and Implications for Pharmacy Practice." *Pharmaceutical Journal* 260: 639–641.

Matheson, C., J. Pitcairn, C. M. Bond, E. van Teijlingen, and M. Ryan. 2003. "General Practice Management of Illicit Drug Users in Scotland: A National Survey." *Addiction* 98: 119–126. doi:10.1046/j.1360-0443 .2003.00263.x

McElrath, K. 2008. *Drug Misuse and Drug Service Provision in Dundalk: Improving the Community's Response.* Dundalk (County Louth, Ireland): Drugs Advisory Group.

McElrath, K. 2009. *Drug Use in Fingal and Associated Need for Support Services.* Swords (Fingal, Ireland): North Dublin City and County Regional Drugs Task Force.

McElrath, K. and M. Jordan, M. 2005. *Drug Use and Risk Behaviours Among Injecting Drug Users.* Belfast: Department of Health, Social Services and Public Safety. Retrieved from http://www .dhsspsni.gov.uk/index/stats_research/stats-public-health/stats-drug-alcohol.htm#dacurpubs

McElrath, K. and K. McEvoy. 2001. "Heroin as Evil: Ecstasy Users' Perceptions about Heroin." *Drugs: Education, Prevention and Policy* 8: 177–189. Retrieved from www.drugsandalcohol.ie/6876/1/McElrath_4060_Heroin_as_Evil.pdf

Miles, M. S., M. R. Isler, B. B. Banks, S. Sengupta, and G. Corbie-Smith. 2011. "Silent Endurance and Profound Loneliness: Socioemotional Suffering in African Americans Living with HIV in the Rural South." *Qualitative Health Research* 21: 489–501. doi:10.1177/ 1049732310387935

Mill, J. E., N. Edwards, R. C. Jackson, L. MacLean, and J. Chaw-Kent. 2010. "Stigmatization as a Social Control Mechanism for Persons Living with HIV and AIDS." *Qualitative Health Research* 20: 1469–1483. doi:10.1177/ 1049732310375436

Newman, R. G. 1976. "Methadone Maintenance: It Ain't What It Used to Be." *British Journal of Addiction* 71: 183–186. doi:10.1111/j.1360-0443.1976 .tb00077.x

Nosyk, B., D. C. Marsh, H. Sun, M. T. Schecter, and A. H. Anis. 2009. "Trends in Methadone Maintenance Treatment Participation, Retention, and Compliance to Dosing Guidelines in British

Columbia, Canada: 1996–2006." *Journal of Substance Abuse Treatment* 39: 22–31. doi:10.1016/j.jsat.2010.03.008

Opsal, T. D. 2011. "Women Disrupting a Marginalized Identity: Subverting the Parolee Identity Through Narrative." *Journal of Contemporary Ethnography* 40: 135–167. doi:10.1177/0891241610384995

Parker, R. and P. Aggleton, P. 2003. "HIV and AIDS-Related Stigma and Discrimination: A Conceptual Framework and Implications for Action." *Social Science & Medicine* 57: 13–24. doi:10.1016/S0277-9536(02)00304-0

Patterson, B. L., Backmund, M., Hirsch, G., and Yim, C. 2007. "The Depiction of Stigmatization in Research About Hepatitis C." *International Journal of Drug Policy* 18: 364–373. doi:10.10 16/j.drugpo.2007.02.004

Porter, J. 1999. "The Street/Treatment Barrier: Treatment Experiences of Puerto Rican Injection Drug Users." *Substance Use and Misuse* 34: 1951–1975. doi:10.3109/10826089909039434

Radcliffe, P. and A. Stevens. 2008. "Are Drug Treatment Services Only for 'Thieving Junkie Scumbags'? Drug Users and the Management of Stigmatised Identities." *Social Science and Medicine* 67: 1065–1073. doi:10.1016/j.socs- cimed.2008.06.004

Reisinger, H. S., R. P. Schwartz, S. G. Mitchell, J. A. Peterson, S. M. Kelly, K. E. O'Grady, and M. H. Agar. 2009. "Premature Discharge from Methadone Treatment: Patient Perspectives." *Journal of Psychoactive Drugs* 41: 285–296. Retrieved from http://www.tandfonline.com/doi/abs/10.1080/02791072.2009.10400539

Saris, A. J. 2008. "An Uncertain Dominion: Irish Psychiatry, Methadone and the Treatment of Opiate Abuse." *Culture, Medicine and Psychiatry* 32: 259–277. doi:10.1007/s11013-008-9089-z

Sheerin, I., T. Green, D. Sellman, S. Adamson, and D. Deering. 2004. "Reduction in Crime by Drug Users On a Methadone Maintenance Therapy Programme in New Zealand." *New Zealand Medical Journal* 117: U795. Retrieved from http://www.nzma.org.nz/journal/117-1190/795/

Simmonds, L. and R. Coomber. 2009. "Injecting Drug Users: A Stigmatised and Stigmatising Population." *International Journal of Drug Policy* 20: 121–130. doi:10.1016/j.drugpo. 2007.09.002

Simoens, S., C. Matheson, C. Bond, K. Inkster, and A. Ludbrook. 2005. "The Effectiveness of Community Maintenance with Methadone or Buprenorphine for Treating Opiate Dependence." *British Journal of General Practice* 55: 139–146. Retrieved from http://www.ncbi.nlm.nih.gov/pmc/articles/PMC1463190/

Stone, E. and K. Fletcher. 2003. "User Views on Supervised Methadone Consumption." *Addiction Biology* 8: 45–48. doi:10.1080/1355621031000069873

Tanaka, E. 2002. "Toxicological Interactions Between Alcohol and Benzodiazepines." *Clinical Toxicology* 40: 69–75. doi:10.1081/CLT-120002887

Teesson, M., J. Ross, S. Darke, M. Lynskey, R. Ali, A. Ritter, and R. Cooke. 2006. "One Year Outcomes for Heroin Dependence: Findings from the Australian Treatment Outcome Study (ATOS)." *Drug and Alcohol Dependence* 83: 174–180. doi:10.1016/j.drugalcdep.2005.11.009

Varas-Díaz, N., I. Serrano-García, and J. Toro-Alfonso. 2005. "AIDS-Related Stigma and Social Interaction: Puerto Ricans Living with HIV/AIDS." *Qualitative Health Research* 15: 169–187. doi:10.1177/1049732304272059

Vigilant, L. G. 2001. *"Liquid Handcuffs": The Phenomenology of Recovery on Methadone Maintenance.* (Doctoral dissertation, Boston College). Retrieved from WorldCat database (OCLC: 48134549).

———. 2004. "The Stigma Paradox in Methadone Maintenance: Naïve and Positive Consequences of a 'Treatment Punishment' Approach to Opiate Addiction." *Humanity and Society* 28: 403–418.

Villafranca, S. W., J. D. McKellar, J. A. Trafton, and K. Humphreys. 2006. "Predictors of Retention in Methadone Programs: A Signal Detection Analysis." *Drug and Alcohol Dependence* 83: 218–224. doi:10.1016/j.drugalcdep.2005.11.020

White, W. L. 2010. *Long-Term Strategies to Reduce the Stigma Attached to Addiction, Treatment, and Recovery Within the City of Philadelphia (with Particular Reference to Medication-Assisted Treatment/Recovery).* Retrieved from http://www.dev.facesandvoicesofrecovery.org/pdf/White/StigmaMedicationTreatment.pdf

Worthington, C. and T. Myers, T. 2003. "Factors Underlying Anxiety in HIV Testing: Risk Perceptions, Stigma, and the Patient-Provider Power Dynamic."

Qualitative Health Research 13: 636–655. doi: 10.1177/1049732303013005004

Yang, L. H., A. Kleinman, B. G. Link, J. C. Phelan, S. Lee, and B. Good. 2007. "Culture and Stigma: Adding Moral Experience to Stigma Theory." *Social Science & Medicine* 64: 1524–1535. doi: 10.1016/j.socscimed.2006.11.013

For Discussion

1. Locate the nearest methadone clinic in your area and request a copy of their program rules. Think about how the program rules attempt to regulate client behaviors. How might these rules help or hinder recovery among methadone clients?
2. What kinds of stigma exist on college campuses that might hinder students who are in recovery? How can we reduce stigma?

Harm Reduction

Simply stated, harm reduction is an *ideology* with the overall goal of reducing the harms associated with drug use. These harms include social, legal, health, and economic harms that affect individuals in the first instance, but also communities. Harm reduction principles are often contrasted with abstinence models or zero tolerance perspectives, which focus on total desistance from drug use.

Harm reduction has a long history and gained considerable interest during the early to mid-1980s when injecting drug use was linked to the epidemics of hepatitis, HIV, and AIDS in some countries. As blood-borne viruses, HIV and hepatitis B and C are spread primarily through blood-to-blood contact; thus, certain injecting practices can facilitate transmission. Access to new needles/syringes was greatly restricted during the early to mid-1980s; hence, many people engaged in the practices of loaning and borrowing needles or syringes that had been previously used by them or others. In other words, structural barriers that limited access to new needles contributed to the spread

of blood-borne viruses among people who injected drugs. Needle/syringe exchange schemes appeared to be the appropriate intervention because the schemes allow for the distribution of new needles/syringes and encourage individuals to return their used "works." Hence, the service reflects the principle of *reducing health harms* among people who inject drugs and among members of their social networks. Additionally, schemes that encourage people to return their used injecting equipment are believed to reduce harm to communities that might result from discarded needles in public or outdoor places.

Needle/syringe exchange schemes were established in the Netherlands in 1984 (led by a group of people who were actively injecting), in Canada and New Zealand in the late 1980s, and in several other western European countries by the mid-1990s. By 2012, needle/syringe provision was available to some extent in eighty-six countries or territories (Stoicescu 2012). Elsewhere, needle/syringe programs have been slow to develop, largely because of perceptions about costs or because government officials reject the principles of harm reduction and assert that the distribution of injecting equipment serves to endorse illicit drug use. The United States is one country where exchange schemes have been widely opposed by the federal government, largely due to its zero tolerance drug policies.[1] Activists such as Dave Purchase in Tacoma, and Jon Stuen-Parker in New Haven began to distribute injecting equipment in the 1980s, even though the actions violated state and local laws that prohibited drug paraphernalia. A handful of legal needle/syringe exchange programs were implemented in the United States during the late 1980s. Elsewhere in the country, access to new needles/syringes was greatly restricted and community activists, outreach workers, and, at times, drug ethnographers worked to share information about the importance of cleaning used works. Beginning in 1988, the US government banned the use of federal funds to support needle/syringe programs. The ban was in place until 2009 when President Barak Obama lifted it, paving the way for state and local governments to use federal funds to provide new and free needles/syringes to people who inject drugs. However, the ban on federal funding for exchange schemes was reinstated by the US Congress in 2011.

Needle/syringe exchanges in several western European countries have expanded provision to include the distribution of other kinds of injecting equipment. These changes have been informed by evidence. For example, the spread of blood-borne viruses (e.g., HIV, hepatitis C) can occur through injecting equipment other than needles/syringes. "Cookers" and spoons are often used to prepare heroin for injection; thus, they can be a source of contamination. Filters, water, and at times tourniquets are other "tools" that are used during the injection process, and these too can be contaminated with bits of blood to which others can be exposed. Thus, in addition to supplying new needles/syringes, exchange schemes in the United Kingdom also provide cookers (used to prepare drugs for injecting), filters, and other items that are intended to reduce harms to health. More recently, outreach workers and ethnographers described the "accidental sharing" of needles/syringes that occurs when

people who inject with others cannot recall later, the particular needle that they used for injection. In response, several schemes now offer color-coded needles/syringes in an attempt to reduce health harms associated with accidental sharing.

The ideology of harm reduction is reflected in other interventions that are designed to reduce health harms among people who inject drugs. By 2010, approximately ninety drug consumption rooms had been established in Europe (i.e., Switzerland, Spain, Germany, Luxembourg, Norway, and the Netherlands), Australia, and Canada (Hedrich, Kerr, and Dubois-Arber 2010). These programs allow individuals to inject drugs in settings that are supervised by healthcare professionals who promote safer and cleaner injections. Some drug consumption rooms also oversee individuals who use crack cocaine on site. Drug consumption rooms are believed to reduce unsafe injecting practices and reduce injecting in public places. Similar to needle/syringe exchange programs, they also provide referrals to other services, for example, drug treatment (Hedrich, Kerr, and Dubois-Arber 2010).

Naloxone for overdose prevention is another strategy that falls within the realm of harm reduction. Fatal overdoses from opioid drugs generally result from respiratory depression. Naloxone is an injectable opioid that has the potential to quickly reverse the respiratory depression associated with opioid overdose. For several years, health professionals and emergency response teams have relied on naloxone as an overdose prevention strategy. Although naloxone is injectable, it can also be administered intranasally with an atomizer that is attached to a syringe. In response to a large number of opioid overdoses in Wilkes County, North Carolina, a non-for-profit organization (Project Lazarus) encouraged doctors to prescribe naloxone to patients receiving opioid pain medication. Moreover, spurred by state legislation that now prohibits the prosecution of people with naloxone kits (once designated as drugs and drug paraphernalia), the North Carolina Harm Reduction Coalition has trained several individuals to administer naloxone to individuals who have overdosed. The Food and Drug Administration and the National Institute on Drug Abuse have provided federal funds to a

Kentucky company in its effort to develop a single-dose naloxone nasal spray that would be used in lieu of injectable naloxone or the atomizer. The spray is likely to be available over-the-counter by 2015. Even in injectable form, however, naloxone has prevented thousands of fatal overdoses. In the United States, nearly 17,000 people died of fatal overdose from prescription opioids in 2010 (Jones, Mack, and Paulozzi 2010), and heroin overdoses continue to increase.

Harm reduction interventions can focus on other kinds of drug use. For example, national guidelines in the United Kingdom suggest that although abstaining from cigarette smoking is the preferred public health advice, cutting down on the number of cigarettes is the second option, particularly for smokers who find it very difficult to quit. Other harm reduction initiatives include the use of electronic cigarettes or Snus, a product that is marketed in Sweden but differs from traditional chewed tobacco. For marijuana use, harm reduction initiatives have encouraged individuals to avoid deep inhalations and holding the breath after inhalation. These practices are said to increase the possibility of lung damage (although they also are perceived to enhance the psychoactive effects). Alternatively, some individuals avoid smoking entirely and consume marijuana that is mixed with baked desserts. Harm reduction strategies have also been implemented for people who consume MDMA (e.g., monitoring water intake and avoiding alcohol to prevent dehydration; tablet/powder testing), and the non-profit organization DanceSafe has actively promoted harm reduction within club venues and music festivals in the United States and Canada.

Harm reduction initiatives tend to be rejected by individuals and US policymakers who promote abstinence-only interventions through an ideology of zero tolerance. They tend to argue that harm reduction initiatives are counterproductive; that is, that they encourage drug use. Proponents of harm reduction are concerned primarily with the context and consequences of drug use, and less focused on consumption. Still, harm reduction advocates do not oppose (or promote) abstinence for individuals who seek that goal. Critics of the harm reduction ideology have also focused on the issue of harm. For example, to what extent do harm reduction strategies create additional or different risks for the individual and to public health more generally? And how should harm be defined? Clearly the debate will continue for the immediate future. However, harm reduction has become more than an ideology. It represents a large and important social and global movement that has impacted greatly on drug policy in some countries and has been embraced by the United Nations as a key initiative for addressing drug use. The readings in this section highlight the principles of harm reduction in real-world settings.

Note

1. Campbell and Shaw (2008) describe the contemporary history of the US government's opposition to harm reduction and how one federal agency attempted to circumvent the abstinence-only doctrine.

References

Campbell, N. D. and S. J. Shaw. 2008. "Incitements to Discourse: Illicit Drugs, Harm Reduction, and the Production of Ethnographic Subjects." *Cultural Anthropology* 23: 688–717.

Hedrich, D., T. Kerr, and F. Dubois-Arber. 2010. "Drug Consumption Facilities in Europe and Beyond." In *Harm Reduction: Evidence, Impacts and Challenges*, 305–331. Lisbon: European Monitoring Centre for Drugs and Drug Addiction.

Jones, C. M., K. A. Mack, and L. J. Paulozzi. 2013. "Pharmaceutical Overdose Deaths, United States, 2010." *Journal of the American Medical Association* 309: 657–659.

Stoicescu, C., editor. 2012. *The Global State of Harm Reduction: Towards an Integrated Response.* London: Harm Reduction International.

30

Needle Exchange and the Geography of Survival in the South Bronx

KATHERINE McLEAN

This ethnographic study focuses on extremely marginalized individuals for whom a needle/syringe exchange service provided considerable benefit. Katherine McLean offers an in-depth account of an exchange in New York City, where 75 percent of clients were homeless or lacked secure accommodation at the first visit to the exchange. McLean discusses how the exchange was utilized for multiple purposes, in addition to its primary service.

Background

Needle exchange has long been promoted as an essential, life-saving technology, which reduces the mortality of injection drug users (IDUs) through the prevention of HIV transmission and accidental overdose. Indeed, the historic slogan "clean needles save lives" is not mere rhetoric; an embarrassing wealth of studies worldwide have linked needle exchange to a drop in reported syringe sharing among users, as well as continued reductions in the prevalence of HIV infection (among IDUs) in cities hosting needle exchange programmes (NEPs) (Des Jarlais et al. 2005; Hurley, Jolley, and Kaldor 1997). Emerging research has further shown NEP-based naloxone distribution programmes to predict a decline in overdose fatalities among participants (Piper et al. 2007). Yet, while evaluation efforts have traditionally focused upon the effectiveness of needle exchange as a public health tool, its virtues arguably extend beyond matters of biological life and death.

In order to fully appreciate the benefits—and gauge the potential—of needle exchange, it may be necessary to define its role in promoting its users' survival more broadly. This is particularly the case in New York City, where stand-alone NEPs (as opposed to pharmacy-based exchanges) represent the major mode of sterile syringe access for illicit drug users (Rudolph et al. 2010). In New York City, stand-alone NEPs may assume several different service models, conducting exchange from a project storefront, during outreach excursions through local streets or single-room occupancy hotels, or via peer-delivery at user-negotiated sites; many organisations in fact offer multiple modes of syringe delivery. While different NEPs may vary in the types of ancillary goods and services provided, previous research has suggested that users may seek and receive more than just sterile injection equipment (Ruefli and Rogers 2004). In addition to other health-related goods like condoms or hygiene kits that may be available at different NEPs, all programmes arguably provide opportunities for meaningful social interactions (with staff, volunteers, and other participants), and many also offer a permanent enclosed physical space to rest in (Ruefli and Rogers 2004). This paper is specifically concerned with a New York City NEP abiding by the latter, "drop-in" model, where participants are, at minimum, allowed to sit and/or sleep for the entire duration of opening hours. The value of the drop-in model may seem modest at first, yet its significance deepens when set against a social backdrop of endemic local homelessness in a gentrifying city.

Previous studies of homelessness among needle exchange participants in the United States have revealed upwards of 50 percent to be unstably housed, with HIV-positive individuals reporting rates up to 60 percent (Song et al. 2000); furthermore, NEPs tend to be concentrated in poor neighbourhoods boasting booming drug sales and an entrenched homeless population—areas historically condemned as social service "dumping grounds," whose residents lack the clout to resist further socio-spatial stigmatisation (Strike, Myers, and Millson 2004; Takahashi 1997; Williams and Ouellet 2010). Nevertheless, users' right to occupy even these spaces is threatened, as gentrification in once working class neighbourhoods continues to push the urban periphery outward or invade once "abandoned" inner cities (Staples 2004; Smith 2010). While new community opposition may hinder the development of social service facilities in progressively gentrifying areas, the obvious hardships of homelessness are increasingly exacerbated by the movement towards its *de facto* criminalisation through the creative expansion of trespassing, disorderly conduct, and loitering laws, a trend that may particularly chafe against active drug users (Ehrenreich 2009; NCH 2004). While many municipal housing services are simply overwhelmed by the growing population facing or currently suffering from homelessness, their policies may also explicitly exclude present or past substance users from receiving assistance; in New York City, public housing, city-operated shelters, and single-room occupancy hotels all abide by an official policy of abstinence, while "Housing First" programmes for active substance users are severely overwhelmed by demand (Bosman 2010; Fernandez 2007). At the same time, injection drug users may not be able to risk remaining on the street in locales that prohibit the possession of injecting equipment (in law or reality). While Seattle's "Stay Out of Drug Areas" ordinance represents an especially severe example of the ways in which drug users are now spatially marginalised in the US, known drug users *legally* carrying injection paraphernalia are routinely harassed, if not arrested by police (Bluthenthal et al. 2001; England 2008).

In helping homeless/drug users inhabit ever more hostile urban terrains, contemporary NEPs arguably take their place in the "geography of survival" theorised by Don Mitchell and Nik Heynen. The authors poignantly characterise the geography of survival as "the spaces and spatial relations that structure not only how people may live, but especially *whether* they may live. For very poor people, such as the homeless, the geography of survival is knitted together into a network of public and private spaces and social services" (Mitchell and Heynen 2009, 611). Placed within a wider neoliberal cityscape, the brutal geography discussed by Mitchell and Heynen, and mapped in this study, is one forged by the wits of its inhabitants, yet constrained overall by laws targeting not only the homeless, but also substance users. In the United States, needle exchange and other harm reduction programmes are perhaps the only institutions that openly solicit the presence of active, unrepentant drug users, while not necessarily allowing on-site drug use. (Interestingly, drug treatment programmes also have a place in users' geographies of survival, serving functions that are hardly straightforward or sanctioned by their overseers, as this paper will discuss.) However, by virtue of locations in peripheral and/or impoverished communities, NEPs may serve a more diverse participant population than their mandates may immediately suggest. To the dismay of some workers and service users, harm reduction programmes have long been supplementing needle exchange and substance abuse services with HIV/AIDS prevention, testing, and care targeting the "general" population, an expansion that may itself be necessitated for organisational survival in a barren funding landscape

(Lune 2002). Yet, as observed in this paper, NEPs also accommodate individuals whose interests stray far from HIV/AIDS, while participants who do exchange injection equipment may employ NEP drop-ins for a much vaster range of reasons. In this way, an institution designed as a relatively limited public health tool has become reimagined by its users as a general welfare centre, occupying a paramount space in their personal geographies of survival.

Using ethnography and interviewing at an NEP in the South Bronx neighbourhood of New York City, this research describes the "off-label" uses of needle exchange within a population of generally poor and largely homeless service users who were all trying to make ends meet. By "off-label," I mean to refer to the exploitation of needle exchange towards ends that were not formally sanctioned, or seen as reflecting its official raison d'être as a public health, and specifically HIV prevention, programme. Of course, this definition is specific to a context in which needle exchange has been progressively redefined from above as a public health technology first and foremost (McLean 2011; Smith 2011). In contrasting participants' *de facto* uses of needle exchange with the official mission upheld by some employees, this paper also documents the strain arising from NEPs' "flexible" position within the local geography of survival. NEPs in New York State are not currently intended (nor adequately funded) to function as sites of general public assistance or recreation, and tension inevitably underwrites many interactions between needy service users and an underpaid staff, who may hold differing conceptions of the relevant "harms" in harm reduction (NYSDOHAI 2009). However, with no reprieve anticipated from harsh laws and frigid job markets, this paper also considers how this and other drop-in-oriented NEPs might provide a vital service within neighbourhoods characterised by "urban desertification" or inadequate housing and limited social services (Wallace 1990). As of writing, at least half of New York City's 13 stand-alone syringe exchange programmes housed an area wherein participants could simply "be," indefinitely, over the course of opening hours; while many offered services that extended beyond the provision of injection equipment, I have chosen to refer to my study site, and similar facilities, as NEPs (as opposed to the more general label of "harm reduction programmes"), a term which reflects both their legal status and also distinct streams of public health funding in New York. The drop-in model described herein may in fact represent a dying industry, as harm reduction contracts in New York (deriving largely from the state AIDS Institute) stipulate ever more medicalised models, and "syringe services" are integrated into federally funded substance use treatment programmes; however, the uses of needle exchange observed herein point to the need for a (re)expanded definition of harm reduction in the United States that addresses the social inequalities shaping already constricted geographies of survival.

Methods

This paper is based upon twelve months of participant observation at a community-based needle exchange in the South Bronx (hereafter, referred to as "Bronx Harm Reduction"), from July 2010 through June 2011; it also draws on 30 semi-structured interviews with service users and staff, which were conducted as part of a larger study of risk and its construction in harm reduction. Positioning myself as a "researcher-volunteer," I spent an average of 20 h each week observing, assisting, and interacting with staff and participants at Bronx Harm Reduction, in a variety of spaces and situations; the main drop-in centre, support and educational groups, meals and parties, staff meetings and trainings, and administrative offices. In this particular organisation, two unisex bathrooms also served as venues for (brief) sociality. As a volunteer, I helped staff with relatively mundane tasks such as food service, cleaning, reception, and simple clerical work, assistance that facilitated the development of rapport; at the same time, my status as a researcher, and not a staff member, was consistently disclosed to employees and participants alike.

Given my anomalous appearance, it is likely that some participants initially perceived me as a figure of authority or official surveillance in the drop-in, an image I attempted to counter by allowing service users to first approach, and interrogate, me. Upon first meeting, many participants asked if I was a social worker, while others guessed me to be a visiting representative of the New York City Department of Health, or the Centres for Disease Control. Such labels stuck even after multiple corrections, while my self-identification as "researcher" was often questioned or amicably mocked by participants and staff alike. Several service users teased me about being an undercover journalist seeking to capture the "real story" of drug addiction, while one man joked that I was little more than a "spy" or "busybody"—terms that I myself sometimes used in describing my research method. In trying to be reflexive about the disciplinary effects of my presence, I generally engaged in non-directive conversations with participants, which allowed them to control the disclosure of personal information. Prior to the onset of both research and volunteering, this study was approved by the City University of New York (CUNY) Graduate Centre Institutional Review Board.

Where much of this paper derives from informal conversations with staff and service users in the above contexts, I also cite formal interviews with 19 staff members and 11 programme participants; this numeric imbalance in interview subjects reflects the research aims of the larger study, which focused on the "work" of harm reduction. Interview subjects were recruited via flyers posted throughout the agency, and brief announcements at one staff meeting, and one Participant Advisory Board Meeting. All staff members, peer workers, volunteers, and participants who were able to converse in English were eligible for inclusion as interview subjects. It should be noted that this linguistic requirement, reflecting my own lack of Spanish language skills, excluded a unique demographic from interviewing. Mostly representing recent arrivals from Puerto Rico, participants who spoke only Spanish were more likely to be homeless, and may have mobilised larger or more diverse geographies of survival, as compared to English-speaking participants at Bronx Harm Reduction. All interviews were digitally recorded, and ranged in duration from 8 min to 2.5 h; service users were given a 2-ride transit ticket (worth $4.50) in exchange for their interviews, while employees were not offered any incentive. Interviews focused on the construction and negotiation of risk messages in harm reduction, but subjects were also asked to comment on what service users "got out of" coming to Bronx Harm Reduction; they were further asked to define and describe the purpose of harm reduction, in their own words and opinion. Often eliciting individuals' beliefs about the normative uses of needle exchange, these interviews also reflected subjects' mixed feelings around its *de facto* functions for its users. Data analysis was inductive and iterative, with four major categories ultimately emerging to characterise participants' off-label uses of Bronx Harm Reduction.

Site Background

One of the three local NEPs, Bronx Harm Reduction occupies several floors of a converted warehouse in the South Bronx, inhabiting a quiet side street, yet minutes away from several major thoroughfares. While staff members often refer to needle exchange as the "heart" of the organisation, Bronx Harm Reduction offers an extensive, and expanding, roster of services related to drug use and HIV/AIDS. At the time of writing, HIV-positive participants were able to access case management, mental health care, medical escort services, and housing placement assistance; all participants were allowed to attend educational and support groups, obtain sterile injecting equipment, and receive free HIV testing and medical/social service referrals. A small onsite primary care clinic, offering limited medical services to all participants, was also poised to open in the near future. Perhaps Bronx Harm Reduction's most distinctive feature, the multi-floor drop-in represented another space open to all individuals, and might be framed as a service in itself.

During this study, Bronx Harm Reduction was engaged in an ongoing total-facility renovation, which drastically altered the appearance and atmosphere in its main "public" spaces. Overall, the physical transition might be summarised as a move from a quirky, hodge-podge décor to a cleaner, more clinical, and streamlined aesthetic. This makeover was particularly noticeable in the main drop-in space, which was repainted a serene blue from a shocking green, and outfitted with two flat-screen televisions and two dozen padded chairs. The only space continuously open to all participants, the primary drop-in was typically the busiest, and noisiest, area in the building, adjacent to the needle exchange and a large group meeting room; it is also the first room one enters at Bronx Harm Reduction, and as a result, the drop-in often had the feel of a hospital emergency room. A participant bathroom was also situated on the first floor, boasting three stalls, a double sink, and a large shower for sign-up. During regular business hours, a second floor drop-in space was also accessible by participants, and offered a somewhat more relaxing, or less frenetic environment. Three vinyl couches were open to individuals who wanted to sleep, or establish a more elaborate camp, while another flat-panel television pegged to the "History Channel" was turned to an audible volume for most parts of the day. The second floor public space also contained a smaller group meeting room, and a tiny kitchen, from which lunch was served each day at noon.

As of 2010, Bronx Harm Reduction estimated its current participant population at around 3000 individuals, including over 750 people living with HIV/AIDS. On average, around 200 participants signed in to the drop-in daily. Across all service users, approximately 60 percent reported past or present injection drug use, while 75 percent were homeless or unstably housed at intake; nearly all participants were currently unemployed, and receiving less than $10,000 in official annual income. Located in an area of intense migration from Puerto Rico and Latin America, Bronx Harm Reduction further claimed a participant population that was two-thirds Latino/a, nearly half of whom were monolingual Spanish; the remaining 33 percent of participants were largely African-American. As in most local NEPs, participants were majority male, at 72 percent, with a mean age of 45. While showing a more balanced gender breakdown, Bronx Harm Reduction's 33 staff members closely mirrored the ethnic composition of its service users. As a relatively young, white female, I was often the most conspicuous feature of the drop-in.

In locating Bronx Harm Reduction within its users' geographies of survival, the unique landscape of the South Bronx must also be briefly described. Situated in the poorest Congressional District in the U.S., the South Bronx featured the highest levels of unemployment in New York City (13.4 percent), and the lowest median household income ($20,000) as of 2009 (Calahan 2009; Fiscal Policy Institute 2009). Borough-wide, Bronx residents represent about 1 in 4 people with newly diagnosed HIV in New York City, but account for more than 1 in 3 deaths: as of 2008, nearly 8000 people in the South Bronx specifically were living with HIV/AIDS (Project Samaritan 2009). These dire statistics may be perhaps summarized in others relating to the neighbourhood's status as a "social service ghetto" (Dear and Wolch 1987). Within Bronx Harm Reduction's 1.1 square mile zip code alone, at least six drug treatment programmes—including five opioid maintenance programmes—operated at the time of this study. While a new general intake centre for the New York City Department of Homeless Services was still under construction as of March 2011, the South Bronx is presently home to several public and private shelters, and at least 10 single-room occupancy hotels—transitional housing sites reserved for individuals living with AIDS or symptomatic HIV who are eligible for subsidised shelter from the New York City HIV/AIDS Service Administration (HASA).

Results

In the following paragraphs, I describe the ways in which various individuals (e.g., housed and homeless, HIV-positive and HIV-negative, active and former substance users) used Bronx Harm Reduction to survive during my twelve months of research. Participant observation and interviews revealed four latent functional aspects of needle exchange, which are elaborated below: Obtaining Basic Necessities, Hustling/Income, Safe Space, and Sociality. Other organisations and spaces situated within participants' local geographies of survival are addressed in a subsequent section. After depicting the "multiple logics" of needle exchange, and other social service organisations, for their users, I consider employee's reactions to the flexible exploitation of their agency. The final discussion ponders the implications of these user-end functions of needle exchange for the philosophy and practice of harm reduction in the United States, which is simultaneously being moulded from the "top-down," by funding streams.

Obtaining Basic Necessities

Perhaps the most legible latent function of the Bronx Harm Reduction needle exchange was the provision of basic sustenance to a sizable population of hungry and often homeless individuals. By "sustenance," I mean to refer not only to food and drink, but to the basic tools of survival more generally, including toiletries, clothing, and blankets. This usage of needle exchange may appear unremarkable at first, until one considers the ways in which these mundane resources structured participants' relationships to and time at Bronx Harm Reduction, while attracting a diverse group of service users.

The importance of food in particular was manifest in both daily and monthly patterns of attendance that followed meal schedules. Asked what initially brought her to, and kept her at Bronx Harm Reduction, one participant exclaimed, chuckling, "Free food!" On a daily basis, the drop-in population would spike without fail around 11:30 AM and 4:30 PM, when sign-up sheets for lunch and dinner were respectively made available. Similarly, festive dinners and parties for major and minor holidays alike drew participants rarely or never seen on a regular basis; indeed, infrequent visitors called in advance of Thanksgiving, Christmas and Easter to confirm the dates and times of special dinners. Consisting largely of microwavable meals, the quality of everyday lunch and dinner was often disparaged, and sometimes denounced as an indignation. Service users of greater means often held out for the "outside" food ordered for participants in certain support groups or service programmes; indeed, take-out pizza or fast food often served as a carrot promised to potential attendees at bimonthly community meetings.

As implied above, the material goods to be gained by attending Bronx Harm Reduction served as explicit tools of organisational recruitment in a neighbourhood hosting three "competing" needle exchanges. At the time of writing, Bronx Harm Reduction was commonly ranked second in terms of food provision by participants who patronised several programmes. Indeed, many participants made no secret of attending a nearby exchange for its superior, "home-made" lunch, only wandering over to Bronx Harm Reduction in the late afternoon, for dinner. This second-place status was a source of light-hearted irritation to some staff members, who sought to attract individuals by offering other goods, often branded with the organisational logo: t-shirts, backpacks, sleeping bags, and coats. Participants in special training programmes, such as the CDC-funded "Safety Counts," were promised weekly "grab bags" typically containing soap, sweets, and sometimes soup; while some would joke about the predictable contents of the bags ("My weekly soap!"), others bore out each meeting impatiently, declaring openly that they only came for their grab bag. The ability to offer such resources was a point of organisational pride—and perhaps organisational survival in a time of drastic budget cuts to publicly funded programmes like needle exchange. At one observed community meeting, a peer worker fretted that Bronx Harm Reduction's "puny" hygiene kits containing a small shampoo, soap, toothpaste, and razor were insufficient, and in fact embarrassing, by comparison to those offered by other organisations. Where participants relied upon this particular exchange for certain tangible goods, Bronx Harm Reduction also relied upon participants to show up, and justify revenue. While the agency's funding contracts did not stipulate any quotas for daily or yearly attendance, Bronx Harm Reduction's baseline funding was based upon the volume of individuals served each period. In light of local "competition," and rumours of dwindling turnout, some workers at Bronx Harm Reduction realised the need to attract potential "patrons" using unique lures.

Hustling/Income

While Bronx Harm Reduction provided the above necessities gratis to its users, it also served as an informal marketplace in which participants could buy, sell, and exchange a wider array of products among themselves. In general, participants used

Bronx Harm Reduction to generate income in ways that traversed the spectrum of legitimacy. In this setting, "income" might be considered to encompass not only money, but also "Metrocards," i.e. New York City mass transit passes. As in many social service organisations, Metrocards were the ubiquitous currency paid for user participation in meetings, support groups, and other odd events at Bronx Harm Reduction. Consequently, the pursuit of Metrocards or "carfare" might represent the most iconic hustle at Bronx Harm Reduction, which was (for the most part) amiably tolerated by staff. It was not unusual to see staff and participants joking about occasions on which participants had "gotten over" by taking more than one Metrocard; in fact, such anecdotes were told repeatedly, like old family stories, while the "shifty request" and "adamant refusal" of extra Metrocards played like a scripted interaction between service users and staff. Likewise, the inquiry "What group is this?" was frequently met with the laughing response "The Metrocard group!" Where some participants obviously employed their carfare for transportation to and from the organisation, many commanded an impressive wad of unused Metrocards that simply accumulated within their wallet or pockets, openly fretting when their stock was "running low." It should be noted that this study also participated in the local carfare economy, offering service users a packaged $4.50 (2 ride) Metrocard as an interview incentive—resaleable at local bodegas for three dollars.

Bronx Harm Reduction also offered its users opportunities to make real money through a handful of short- and long-term jobs, whose salary ranged from $10 per day to $100 per week. All such positions were fiercely coveted, despite limited pay, often tedious work, and strict supervision. Part-time "peer" positions, garnishing the highest income, were officially held for a year, and came with lengthy application processes; the opening of one such job during the study period attracted dozens of applications, from both regular and infrequent visitors to the exchange. Less desirable day-to-day jobs in maintenance or food service were generally filled on a first-come, first-served basis, while one individual might informally claim a position for weeks or months at a time. Though

less competitive than peer positions, such positions had the advantage of being "off the books"—and thus did not threaten individuals receiving cash benefits from public assistance. Many service users voiced an interest in permanent full-time (i.e., non-"peer") work in any area of Bronx Harm Reduction, yet no such positions were made available during this research.

Populated by individuals boasting limited money and oftentimes, recreational drug habits, Bronx Harm Reduction also served as an ideal site for more entrepreneurial participants looking to engage in less-than-legal sales. While several participants were terminated and/or arrested for selling illegal drugs on-site, individuals were also observed selling cigarettes, clothing, jewellery, electronics, and medicines during the study period. Noting that they offered lower prices to individuals who lacked the time, or simply felt uncomfortable patronising regular stores, some "salesmen" saw themselves as providing an essential service to the drop-in community. With the exception of illicit drug sales, staff typically turned a blind eye to these transactions, and occasionally succumbed to a good deal—particularly after New York State raised the cigarette tax in July 2010, resulting in a $10-plus price tag per pack.

Safe Space

When asked simply "what participants got out of" coming to Bronx Harm Reduction, nearly every staff member and service user noted the organisation's *de facto* service as a "safe space." with varying degrees of approbation. In using this term, most individuals meant to refer to the use of the drop-in as a proxy home for participants lacking stable shelter. Indeed, short of providing an overnight bed, Bronx Harm Reduction mimicked many of the amenities of permanent housing for twelve hours each day. Participants were allowed to sleep, undisturbed, in chairs, on couches, and even during support groups (so long as they did not snore). A spacious shower and washer/dryer were available on a sign-up basis, and rarely lacked for users; the popularity of these facilities sometimes resulted in conflict between service users, and further, between staff members, particularly when "non-participants" from the community attempted to access them. Given the large number of homeless participants who visited the drop-in daily, competition extended beyond shower and laundry time to locker space, and in fact, wall outlets—for charging cell phones. Irrespective of their housing status, many service users chose to receive mail at Bronx Harm Reduction, while listing the organisation's main phone line as their primary contact.

Though the dangers from which Bronx Harm Reduction protected its users often remained implicit in its "safe space" labelling, they were readily apparent in group discussions and participant observation in the drop-in. The most commonly reported danger faced by housed and unhoused participants alike at Bronx Harm Reduction was police harassment. Many participants complained of being detained, questioned and searched by police regularly, for no legitimate reason; the rationale for this harassment typically proposed by participants referenced their status as often homeless, largely minority, past and present drug users. Some perhaps accurately attributed their targeting by police as consequent to their affiliation with Bronx Harm Reduction—an organisation visited by local police officers with some regularity. While a recent amendment to New York City's criminal code legalised the possession of syringes by needle exchange participants, it was not uncommon for users to report detention for syringe possession nevertheless. On multiple occasions over the study period, police vans were seen parked within a block of the drop-in, prompting staff members to dissuade participants from standing in front of the building— an act understood to be boldly courting arrest.

While thus shielding participants from treatment as criminals, the drop-in further likely protected its users from victimisation by criminals. Individuals living on the street were obviously at a loss to reliably keep their belongings from thieves, particularly those whose alertness was compromised by legal and illegal substances. Overall, the individuals who appeared most vulnerable—to police harassment, muggings, or "getting punched in the face," as one participant put it—were those maintained on relatively high doses of methadone, who were allowed to "nod" at Bronx Harm

Reduction, for the most part, unperturbed. With a significant portion of service users enrolled within local methadone maintenance programmes, this study in many ways illuminates needle exchange and methadone maintenance as complementary programmes in unintended ways. Many studies have noted that NEPs boast high rates of participant referral to substance use treatment programmes like methadone maintenance, thus (in theory) advancing such individuals' struggle towards long-term drug abstinence (Hagan et al. 2000; Riley et al. 2002). Yet, for many homeless, methadone-maintained participants, Bronx Harm Reduction remained ensconced in their geographies of survival, whether or not they continued to use illegal drugs.

Sociality

Perhaps the most moving latent function of Bronx Harm Reduction was its use as a site to reestablish or maintain social contact. Feelings of isolation and loneliness were problems that appeared to unite service users presenting with vastly different housing, medical and substance use concerns. For participants living on the streets (or within shelters that were scarcely better), the drop-in provided an opportunity to interact with others in what might be termed a "normal," non-judgmental context (see also Macneil and Pauly 2011). In the words of one staff member, the drop-in gave such individuals "the chance to become human again." While this statement may read as pejorative to those described, its author meant rather to convey the dehumanising conditions, and treatment, experienced by many homeless participants. Indeed, describing his initial enrollment within Bronx Harm Reduction, one participant admitted, "I wasn't sure whether I was an animal or a human anymore." By "validating the humanity" of those who feared it lost, Bronx Harm Reduction allowed such individuals to re-develop basic social skills requiring a fundamental level of trust in themselves and others.

At the same time, many participants who were housed and financially stable used Bronx Harm Reduction as a means of fending off the loneliness that came with having their own apartment. Living off public assistance and occasional part-time work, such service users reported that they came to the drop-in simply because they had nothing to do at home. Many housed participants received their apartments with the assistance of the New York City HIV/AIDS Service Administration (HASA), and had relatively limited choice regarding neighbourhood. In the end, individuals thus housed were often forced to accept apartments in places far removed from friends and family. Coming to Bronx Harm Reduction to "make a group," volunteer some hours, or just watch TV in the drop-in provided such participants with some temporal structure necessary to avoid a sense of aimlessness or depression. The inception of Saturday drop-in hours during the study period was heralded as an obvious boon for homeless participants, who otherwise might suffer two straight days on the street; yet, housed participants also celebrated the Saturday programme as a too-short antidote to an otherwise too-long weekend. Such service users sometimes described extended networks of social survival, weaving beyond the South Bronx, to include other New York City social service organisations offering free classes, trainings, or weekly dinners. The situation of these individuals might be seen as pointing to enduring holes in the local geography of survival, which failed to provide full-time, permanent employment opportunities. Peer educator positions at Bronx Harm Reduction and similar organisations appeared to be the most accessible line of paid work for participants; however, these jobs too were maddeningly scarce, and stipulated lengthy application processes that rejected candidates experienced as arbitrary or "political." Of course, the persistent absence of work in the South Bronx may also be understood as highlighting the perfect, inescapable continuity of this geography, which guaranteed little beyond mere survival.

Mapping the Larger Geography of Survival

Participants described broader geographies of survival that, for the most part, remained within the boundaries of the South Bronx, and within the purview of harm reduction or HIV/AIDS services. Such geographies were both spatially and temporally patterned, as participants cited daily, weekly, or seasonal schedules of attendance at different organisations and spaces. The spatial and temporal

constraints fixing these geographies were clearly related, as individuals bemoaned not only the cost of moving around the vast city, but also the time required to reach other potentially fruitful services in the often far-flung, peripheral neighbourhoods that tended to host them. Given otherwise baroque schedules of appointments with clinics, public assistance workers, and shelters, leaving the neighbourhood seemed a near impossibility for some participants. Obviously, such "formal" institutions comprised vital links within many participants' survival networks, granting health care, income, food, and a bed to sleep in. Yet, following the discussion above, this section will again concentrate on the off-label exploitation of different community organisations.

Fulfilling a multiplicity of participants' needs, the two other needle exchange/drop-in centres in the neighbourhood appeared to assume comparable importance to Bronx Harm Reduction in the individuals' geographies of survival. Located less than 10 min away in either direction, these programmes may be seen as giving rise to a "participant stream" that flowed over the course of a day or week. As mentioned previously, another local needle exchange was famous for its hot, homemade lunches, resulting in a massive queue of individuals each day at noon; accordingly, some service users strategically spent their morning at this programme, hoping to avoid the line, while others would attend Bronx Harm Reduction for their "first lunch," only wandering over to their second once the crowd had subsided. Likewise, the third local drop-in was known to distribute grocery store gift cards every other Tuesday, thus drawing a biweekly turnout of informed individuals.

Despite the service similarities between these three organisations, participants often described them as representing very different, discrete, and almost insular communities. For individuals who had been officially "terminated" or unofficially alienated from one programme, refuge might be sought at either or both alternatives; indeed, on several occasions, participants who felt persecuted by staff, or unfairly passed over for peer positions at Bronx Harm Reduction threatened to "take [their] talents elsewhere." At the same time, some service users seemed to relish the relative independence of each programme, describing each as comprising a unique social circle, which they visited according to the time, the day, their needs, or moods. Taken together, these drop-in centres formed a web of social obligations that kept such participants comfortably busy, out of their apartments, and/or off the streets.

Apart from such "low-threshold" organisations, which offered little in the way of formal structure or participation requirements, service users also mobilised more regulated and rule-bound institutions towards creative ends. Despite attending Bronx Harm Reduction, a site ostensibly aimed at active drug users, many individuals were simultaneously enrolled in outpatient drug treatment programmes, which formally prohibited or discourage illicit drug use. While enrollment might accurately reflect an individual's desire to achieve or maintain abstinence, such programmes also met a multiplicity of user needs. For example, individuals receiving methadone were also allotted monthly transportation cheques, which represented a crucial source of income for participants struggling to pay mounting bills. In fact, this seemingly modest financial incentive, intended to promote treatment adherence, was experienced by some participants as a form of treatment compulsion, binding them to a regimen they might yearn to stop. Discussing his dependence on monthly carfare cheques, one individual exclaimed that he would immediately detox from methadone if he were otherwise able to pay his monthly electricity bill. Detox programmes, which sent daily pick-up vans to Bronx Harm Reduction, were employed by participants not only looking to cease or reduce their habits, but by those simply seeking a warm place to sleep, particularly in the winter. For individuals lacking insurance, or simply wary of committing to any treatment programme, the emergency room at the neighbourhood hospital was also an option of last resort on a cold winter night.

Staff and Peer Reactions

Full-time employees and peer workers expressed conflicting feelings about the *de facto* uses of Bronx Harm Reduction, whose public health mandate was always billed first and foremost. While not obeying strict divisions, staff members' approbation of

needle exchange as a broad tool for survival often followed from individuals' position and time at the organisation/in harm reduction. In general, staff members who had spent most or all of their working lives in the field of harm reduction (sometimes at Bronx Harm Reduction alone) expressed greater tolerance for participants who used the needle exchange towards diverse ends. Often former users of illegal drugs, needle exchange, and Bronx Harm Reduction themselves, such individuals often identified with drop-in users, while citing homelessness, isolation, and lack of income as major risks for and of drug use. One staff member, who obtained his first job at Bronx Harm Reduction, went so far as to say that he was happy to give participants whatever he could, stating that he'd "rather they hustle me than hustle on the street." By contrast, staff members relatively new to the field of harm reduction, and occupying administrative or supervisory positions, viewed such an attitude as irresponsible and potentially harmful to the organisation—and its users. Viewing the organisation's provision of basic social services to be indicative of mission slippage, such staff members believed the "real work" of risk reduction was thus threatened. For these individuals, harm reduction was a term exclusive to programmes directly addressing individual HIV risk behaviours—like needle sharing, or unsafe sex. Overall, staff dissonance surrounding the off-label uses of Bronx Harm Reduction, particularly by non-drug users, or non-participants, exacerbated existing interpersonal tensions; they also revealed a range of understandings about what "harm reduction" should or could involve, and consequently, what the real harms of drug use were. It should be said that the many needs presented by participants were obviously overwhelming to a limited staff of modestly paid employees. Where many staff members wished to offer as many possible life-saving services to participants, the organisation was not sufficiently funded or staffed to serve such a wide mandate. This tension was encapsulated in the presence of two contradictory signs in food service areas, one reading "Feed people first. They might be homeless on the streets" and the other stating in bold capitals "THIS IS NOT A SOUP KITCHEN."

Conclusion

Upon seeing the drop-in for the first time, one visitor to Bronx Harm Reduction asked, perplexed, "What is everyone waiting for?" Given many participants' long-term "careers" at the organisation, this question seemed particularly poignant. Seen in the worst light, the needle exchange drop-in may appear as a crowded waiting room where there is no end in sight. Indeed, for participants who were not HIV-positive, and thus ineligible for housing assistance from the New York City HIV/AIDS Service Administration, there were few prospects for improvement. In accepting its role as a way station for socially displaced individuals, Bronx Harm Reduction implicitly defined its diverse users as lives worthy of intervention; at the same time, the organisation did little to openly challenge the politics of abandonment that led them there (see also Evans 2010). This is not to blame this, or any other NEPs in New York City, which are simply not authorised or paid to address the social, political, and economic factors underlying and following substance use. Instead, NEPs and other harm reduction-oriented organisations are charged with providing services and disseminating information that frame HIV as the major risk attendant to drug use. Ultimately, harm reduction programmes are encouraged to empower their users as subjects of public health interventions—not to advance their basic rights as citizens and city residents. Evoking Sonia Fleury's notion of "inverted citizenship," these individuals are extended limited health and social assistance in the absence of real civil or political rights (cited by Biehl 2001, 136).

In describing the geographies of survival mobilised by the participants of Bronx Harm Reduction, this paper does not seek to show how individuals "scam the system," but rather endeavours to discuss how their behaviour illuminates its enduring gaps. As theorised by Mitchell and Heynen, geographies of survival reflect individual attempts to live in the face of economic and social policies that may condemn them to death—from exposure, hunger, and other socially generated pathologies, such as drug addiction and HIV. A strategy developed largely in response to the American "War on Drugs," needle exchange has become an important tool of survival for street-based substance users, who require not only clean works, but a respite from a society that harshly punishes and stigmatises certain types of drug use. As this paper has shown, the non-judgmental philosophy and service environment that characterise needle exchange attracts many non-users in need of basic amenities as well. Such unlikely service users speak to not only the relatively inviting atmosphere of NEPs, which at this point demand little of their participants, but also to the dearth of options faced by many long-time poor individuals in a country that lacks a comprehensive and adequate system of public assistance. In New York, for example, single adults are eligible for merely two years of severely limited welfare benefits—for which over 40 percent of applicants were denied in 2007, the last year of data available (FPWA 2009). In the absence of a public system of social protection, Bronx Harm Reduction, and other NEPs, have become important threads within a social safety net that is being woven from the ground up.

While clearly unsatisfactory as a long-term solution to the economic and political circumstances that drive a diversity of individuals through its doors, Bronx Harm Reduction is a necessary site of triage in a community crippled by poverty, unemployment, homelessness, and drug use. Of course, NEPs cannot alone be expected to alleviate the brutalities of late capitalism and welfare revanchism, but this study may be used to argue for a (re)expanded mission for harm reduction in the United States, in the face of constant moves to narrow its mandate and reduce its budget. In New York State specifically, a diminishing amount of public health funding increasingly demands of its needle exchange contractors the implementation of clinical models of care, a more stringent focus upon medical outcomes, and the deployment of a more professional, or credentialed staff. Funded to address the physical, and yet forced to deal with the social harms that precede and derive from drug use, organisations like Bronx Harm Reduction experience a never-ending strain on their finances and staff energies, while participants remain frustrated with the disproportionate attention to their biomedical needs. And yet, the unofficial, or "off-label," uses of needle exchange described in this study need not remain so: with the necessary political, economic and legal support, need exchange programmes may be able to offer their users a comprehensive and nutritious food service, free short-term or low-cost long-term housing, and a vastly expanded number of satisfying, fair wage jobs. Without the threat of lost contracts or political reproach, needle exchange and other harm reduction programmes in the US may begin to espouse (or revert to) a more radical politics of social justice for not only drug users, but the largely disenfranchised communities from which they come (Roe 2005). In short, harm reduction may actively engage the politics of abandonment that create and constrain its users' geographies of survival.

References

Biehl. J. 2001. "Vita: Life in a Zone of Social Abandonment." *Social Text* 68: 131–149.

Bluthenthal, R. N., J. Lorvick, A. H. Kral, E. A. Erringer, and J. G. Kahn. 2001. "Collateral Damage in the War On Drugs: HIV Risk Behaviors Among Injection Drug Users." *International Journal of Drug Policy* 10 (1): 25–38.

Bosman, J. 2010. "Number of People Living on New York Streets Soars." *The New York Times*, March 19, A1.

Calahan, S. 2009. "Grumble in the Bronx." *The New York Post*, December 20. Retrieved from http://www.nypost.com/p/news/local/bronx/grumble_in_the_bronx_ooRk5bNRgnmZXsinzCzJrN

Dear, M. and J. Wolch. 1987. *Landscapes of Despair: From Deinstitutionalization to Homelessness.* Princeton, NJ: Princeton University Press.

Des Jarlais, D., et al. 2005. "Reductions in Hepatitis C Virus and HIV Infections among Injecting Drug Users in New York City, 1990–2001." *AIDS* 19 (3): 520–525.

Ehrenreich, B. 2009. "Is It Now a Crime to Be Poor?" *The New York Times*, August 8, WK9.

England, M. 2008. "Stay Out of Drug Areas: Drugs, Othering and Regulation of Public Space in Seattle, Washington." *Space and Polity* 12 (2): 197–213.

Evans, J. 2010. "Exploring the (Bio)Political Dimensions of Voluntarism and Care in the City: The Case of a 'Low Barrier' Emergency Shelter." *Health & Place* 17 (1): 24–32.

Fernandez, M. 2007. "Barred from Public Housing, Even to See Family." *The New York Times*, October 1, A1.

Fiscal Policy Institute. 2009. *New York City in the Great Recession: Divergent Fates by Neighborhood and Race and Ethnicity, 2009.* Retrieved from http://www.fiscalpolicy.org/FPI_Neighborhood-Unemployment_NYC.pdf

FPWA (Federation of Protestant Welfare Agencies). 2009. *The State of New York's Social Safety Net for Today's Hard Times.* Retrieved from http://www.fpwa.org/binary-data/FPWA_BINARY/file/000/000/127-3.pdf

Hagan, H., J. P. McGough, H. Thiede, S. Hopkins, J. Duchin, and E. R. Alexander. 2000. "Reduced Injection Frequency and Increased Entry and Retention in Drug Treatment Associated with Needle Exchange Participation, in Seattle Drug Injectors." *Journal of Substance Abuse Treatment* 19 (3): 247–252.

Hurley, S. F., Jolley. D. J., and J. M. Kaldor. 1997. "Effectiveness of Needle-Exchange Programmes for Prevention of HIV Infection." *The Lancet* 349 (9068): 1797–1800.

Lune, H. 2002. "Weathering the Storm: Nonprofit Organization Survival Strategies in a Hostile Climate." *Nonprofit and Voluntary Sector Quarterly* 31: 463–483.

Macneil, J. and B. Pauly. 2011. "Needle Exchange as a Safe Haven in an Unsafe World." *Drug and Alcohol Review* 30 (1): 26–32.

McLean, K. 2011. "The Biopolitics of Needle Exchange in the United States." *Critical Public Health* 21 (1): 71–79.

Mitchell, D. and N. Heynen. 2009. "The Geography of Survival and the Right to the City: Speculations On Surveillance, Legal Innovation, and the Criminalization of Intervention." *Urban Geography* 30 (6): 611–632.

NCH (National Coalition for the Homeless). 2004. *Illegal to Be Homeless, 2004 Report.* Retrieved from http://www.nationalhomeless.org/publications/crimreport/introduction.html

NYSDOHAI (New York State Department of Health AIDS Institute). 2009. *Policies And Procedures. Syringe Exchange Programs.* January. Retrieved from http://www.health.ny.gov/diseases/aids/harm_reduction/needles_syringes/syringe_exchange/docs/policies_and_procedures.pdf

Piper, T. M., S. Rudenstine, S. Stancliff, S. Sherman, V. Nandi, A. Clean, and S. Galea. 2007. "Overdose Prevention for Injection Drug Users: Lessons Learned from Naloxone Training and Distribution Programs in New York City." *Harm Reduction Journal* 4 (3) doi: 10.1186/1477-7517-4-3

Project Samaritan. 2009. *Annual Report. 2009.* Retrieved from http://www.projectsamaritan.org/pdf/PSI_AnnualReport0809.pdf

Riley. E. D., M. Safaeian, S. A. Strathdee, P. Beilenson, and D. Vlahov. 2002. "Drug Treatment Referrals and Entry Among Participants of a Needle Exchange Program." *Substance Use and Misuse* 37 (14): 1869–1886.

Roe, G. 2005. "Harm Reduction as Paradigm: Is Better Than Bad Good Enough? The Origins of Harm Reduction." *Critical Public Health* 15 (3): 243–250.

Rudolph, A. E., N. D. Crawford, D. C. Ompad, E. O. Benjamin, R. J. Stern, and C. M. Fuller. 2010. "Comparison of Injecting Drug Users Accessing Syringes from Pharmacies, Syringe Exchange Programs, and Other Syringe Sources to Inform Targeted HIV Prevention and Intervention Strategies." *Journal of the American Pharmacists Association* 50 (2): 140–147.

Ruefli. T. and S. J. Rogers. 2004. "How Do Drug Users Define Their Progress in Harm Reduction Programs? Qualitative Research to Generate User-Developed Outcomes." *Harm Reduction Journal* 1: 8. doi: 10.1186/1477-7517-1-8

Smith, C. B. R. 2010. "Socio-Spatial Stigmatization and the Contested Space of Addiction Treatment: Remapping Strategies of Opposition to the Disorder of Drugs." *Social Science & Medicine* 70 (6): 859–866.

———. 2011. "Harm Reduction as Anarchist Practice: A User's Guide to Capitalism and Addiction in North America." *Critical Public Health* doi: 10.1080/09581596.2011.611487

Song. J. Y., M. Safaeian, S. A. Strathdee, D. Vlahov, and D. D. Celentano. 2000. "The Prevalence of Homelessness Among Injection Drug Users with and Without HIV Infection." *Journal of Urban Health* 77 (4): 678–687.

Staples, B. 2004. "Editorial Observer: How Needle Exchange Programs Fight the AIDS Epidemic." *The New York Times.* October 25. Retrieved from http://www.nytimes.com/2004/10/25/opinion/25mon4.html

Strike, C. J., T. Myers, and M. Millson. 2004. "Finding a Place for Needle Exchange Programs." *Critical Public Health* 14 (3): 261–275.

Takahashi, L. 1997. "The Socio-Spatial Stigmatization of Homelessness and HIV/AIDS: Toward an Explanation of the NIMBY Syndrome." *Social Science & Medicine* 45 (6): 903–914.

Wallace. R. 1990. "Urban Desertification, Public Health and Public Order: 'Planned Shrinkage,' Violent Death, Substance Abuse and AIDS in the Bronx." *Social Science & Medicine* 31 (7): 801–813.

Williams, C. T. and L. J. Ouellet. 2010. "Misdirected Opposition: Evidence Opposing 'Not in My Back Yard' Arguments Against Syringe Exchange Programs." *International Journal of Drug Policy* 21: 437–439.

For Discussion

1. The author served in the exchange for approximately 20 hours per week, as a "researcher-volunteer." Discuss the author's level of commitment in conducting the research.
2. Why is it that a needle/syringe exchange service that assists this kind of clientele faces so much opposition in some communities?

31

Maximising the Highs and Minimising the Lows

Harm Reduction Guidance within Ecstasy Distribution Networks

CAMILLE JACINTO, MICHELINE DUTERTE, PALOMA SALES, AND SHEIGLA MURPHY

Similar to several other psychoactive drugs, MDMA can produce pleasurable as well as negative effects. This next article is based on interviews conducted with a hidden population of 120 MDMA sellers in the San Francisco area. Camille Jacinto, Micheline Duterte, Paloma Sales, and Sheigla Murphy discuss how sellers take on an additional role—one that involves guidance to customers about how to enhance the MDMA experience and how to minimize the negative effects of the drug. The authors suggest that MDMA sellers in this study represent an important source of harm reduction information.

Background

Study results have shown that peers influence the nature of Ecstasy use within social networks (Beck and Rosenbaum 1994; Carlson et al. 2004; Gourley 2004; Hansen et al. 2001; Schensul et al. 2005). Research findings also reveal that friends are one of the most common and important sources of information about Ecstasy's effects (Falck et al. 2004; Gamma et al. 2005; Murphy et al. 2006). Little is known about how users build and share knowledge concerning Ecstasy's highs and lows. Some study findings indicate that users exchange advice and information regarding controlled Ecstasy use (Southgate and Hopwood 2001; Hansen et al. 2001). Few investigators, however, have examined the role of Ecstasy sellers in the dissemination of information among peer networks. Although sellers may not be traditionally viewed as agents of harm reduction guidance, our own research findings highlight their involvement in spreading knowledge regarding safer Ecstasy use. In this paper we examine how San Francisco Bay Area Ecstasy sellers formulated methods to maximise the pleasurable effects of their own Ecstasy experiences while attempting to minimise harms. We discuss how interviewees described their sources of information and disseminated knowledge to members of their social networks.

According to Becker's (1963) work on subcultural drug use, individuals learn how to experience drugs within a social context. Zinberg (1984) elaborated on this idea, positing that users' drug experiences are influenced by three major factors: drug (pharmacological properties of the drug), set (user's state of mind entering the use episode, along with personality factors), and setting (atmosphere in which the use episode occurs, including physical setting and surrounding people). New drug users build knowledge about drug related pleasure by

Reprinted from Camille Jacinto, Micheline Duterte, Paloma Sales, and Sheigla Murphy, 2008, "Maximising the Highs and Minimising the Lows: Harm Reduction Guidance within Ecstasy Distribution Networks." In *International Journal of Drug Policy* 19: 393–400. Reprinted by permission of Elsevier via Copyright Clearance Center.

observing and learning from more experienced users (Becker 1963; Gourley 2004). Transmission of information occurs because Ecstasy use is most often a social activity. Hunt and colleagues asserted, "The meanings [users] give drugs and the potential risks are all socially embedded and socially determined" (2007, 87). New Ecstasy users engage with more experienced users, who both support their use and advise them regarding what they should expect. They report they learned to overcome the drug's potentially negative side effects and find pleasure in its use (Gourley 2004). The social network is instrumental in influencing how an individual formulates methods to maximise Ecstasy's pleasurable effects while minimising risk.

Recent studies have examined how Ecstasy users balance pleasure with risk (Copeland et al. 2006; Gourley 2004; Hinchcliff 2001; Hunt et al. 2007; Rodgers et al. 2006; White et al. 2006). Hitchcliff's (2001) study of women Ecstasy users in the United Kingdom found women experienced positive changes in attitude that overshadowed Ecstasy's perceived potential risks. Hitchcliff explains, "Their active construction of use allowed for a balance between pleasure and pain" (2001, 464). Other research findings also indicate that users created social settings in which they could achieve optimal drug using experiences while decreasing potential problems (Hunt et al. 2007).

Our study participants developed various strategies attempting to maximise the highs and minimise the lows of Ecstasy intoxication. In this paper we examine the role of pleasure in interviewees' perceived harm reduction practices. Participants did not regularly use the phrase harm reduction; for the purposes of this paper, harm reduction denotes practices described by our participants as ways to "keep safe," "protect [their] health," and "replenish the body." The empathogenic qualities of the Ecstasy high and the social bonding it produces formed closer friendships between buyers and sellers who used the drug together. Ecstasy using networks are unique because close friendships between sellers and buyers allowed for sharing of Ecstasy-related information. We found participants' social networks shaped both their perceptions of pleasurable Ecstasy experiences and harm reduction.

Methods

We conducted an exploratory study of Ecstasy sellers in the San Francisco Bay Area (2003–2006) funded by the National Institute on Drug Abuse. The first phase of the project consisted of key informant interviews and field observations in three types of settings identified by our own and other investigators' work in this area as the main settings where Ecstasy was used and sold: (1) raves or public dance parties; (2) clubs; (3) private settings. During the second phase of the research, employing ethnographic sampling techniques, we recruited 120 participants who had sold five or more doses five or more times in the six months prior to the interview. We extended the study to relatively low-level dealers in hopes of garnering information from both initiates and experienced distributors.

We began recruitment by developing initial relationships with key informants from Ecstasy social scenes and hired these individuals as Community Consultants. Then using chain referral sampling we expanded our contacts with the help of Community Consultants and by asking interviewees to refer project staff to fellow sellers (Biernacki and Waldorf 1981; Watters and Biernacki 1989). In order to include a wide range of dealers, we employed a modified maximum variation sampling technique which allowed us to not only capture variation, but also to identify commonalities within a spectrum of cases. To maximise variation in sales levels, we recruited individuals who sold higher quantities of Ecstasy pills per transaction and asked participants to refer their own dealers. Concerning theoretical sampling, as themes emerged we recruited participants to help us understand the properties and dimensions of emerging concepts. For example, when the theme of friendship-based buyer-seller relationships appeared, we began to recruit sellers who sold in more public settings. We thought drug sellers who sold in public, such as in raves or clubs, might also sell to individuals who they would not consider to be friends and would help us to better understand the role of setting in buyer-sell relationships. We continued to let our theoretical exploration guide our recruitment efforts until we reached theoretical saturation regarding emergent themes.

The interview process began with staff's initial contact with potential participants. When the interviewee met inclusion criteria an interview appointment was scheduled as soon as possible. Since it was not feasible to conduct interviews in the midst of a party atmosphere, we interviewed participants in their homes, at other locations of their choice or at our field offices. After acquainting the participant with the nature of the study and completing informed consent procedures, we began with the tape-recorded, depth interview followed by the questionnaire.

In our qualitative data analysis, we used the grounded theory method (Charmaz 1983; Glaser and Strauss 1967; Kuzel 1992; Strauss and Corbin 1990). This method is employed in an effort to both discover new theory and reconstruct existing theory where it is applicable (Buroway et al. 1991). We began initial coding with the first completed interviews. In the coding we noted patterns that seemed salient due to their recurring nature. Through coding the data for salient dimensions, constellations of basic social, social-psychological and structural processes were discovered. The code list was derived directly from the interview texts and consisted of subject areas that, by virtue of the time the interviewee spent discussing them and/or their recurrent nature, seemed important. While reviewing the depth interview data, we generated relevant codes and linked descriptive themes regarding Ecstasy sellers' use of harm reduction and pleasure enhancing strategies as well as the exchange of information between sellers and buyers. Due to the recurring nature of these and other themes, we would then revise the interview guide to further explore these topics.

Results

Description of the Sample

These findings are based on 120 participants, 91 (76%) men, 28 (23%) women, and 1 (1%) transgender between the ages of 19 and 53 years with a median age of 27. Seventy-five (62%) of the interviewees were white, 12 (10%) African-American, 11 (9%) of mixed ethnicity, 10 (8%) Latino, 9 (8%) Asian, 2 (2%) Middle Eastern, and 1 (1%) Native American. The Ecstasy sellers we interviewed were predominantly white, male, middle to upper-middle class, and in their twenties.

Many interviewees described themselves as members of dance or art communities in which Ecstasy use was commonplace. These participants often sold within such networks to friends and acquaintances. In fact, the majority of sellers (98%) were also users and sometimes used Ecstasy with their customers. On average, interviewees sold ecstasy from 3 to 365 days out of the year, with a median of 49 days a year. In a typical week, interviewees sold between 2 and 2500 hits of Ecstasy with a median of 15 hits per week. While some viewed their Ecstasy sales as an important financial endeavour, most sellers also felt they provided a service to their friends (Jacinto et al. 2008). Eighty-nine percent of those who sold in private settings sold to their friends. Of those who sold at raves, 85 percent sold to their friends along with 78 percent of those who sold at clubs. Participants regarded trust as important in their relationships with their customers and dealers. These friendship-based relationships were a key factor in the exchange of quality Ecstasy and potentially useful information about how to maximise the highs and minimise the lows.

Sources of Ecstasy Information

Our interviewees obtained Ecstasy-related health information from various sources. Most participants reported that learning from their own Ecstasy experiences and those of their friends was the most valuable way to build knowledge about the drug. They believed that their own Ecstasy use episodes best informed them about how to manage possible negative outcomes and enhance the Ecstasy high. As noted by this 30-year-old man, sellers found it difficult to trust outside sources.

> You know the information that is out there is, like I said, very *Reefer Madness . . .* I haven't had a lot of experience with seeing a lot of the research that's been done on Ecstasy use. The information I like that pretty much is, you know, like as far as taking vitamin C and hydration and all that stuff is just from experience kind of. So I mean that's where I would get my information from. It's just my own personal experiences.

Peers were also trusted sources of information as sellers observed them as active agents in Ecstasy using social worlds. As with Becker's (1964) research, our participants learned how to use drugs from more experienced users. Even when sellers were not present to witness their friends' use episodes, peers still provided anecdotal information that helped build participants' overall knowledge. Interviewees perceived information from their peers as one of the most trusted resources of Ecstasy information, as illustrated in the following quote from a 27-year-old man:

> Humans are definitely the most valuable [source of information] because it's from experience. Like when I'm reading it, I can never fully trust it as much as if it's somebody that I know and love or trust that has experienced this stuff. So I think one-on-one is the primary source for education.

Similar to Gamma's (2005) findings, participants described other sources of Ecstasy information, such as television and the Internet; however, trust in these types of sources varied. Regardless of what resources they had available to them, the majority of our sample felt unsure about the real health effects, short and long term, of Ecstasy use. They relied mostly on friends and their own personal experiences to formulate harm reduction strategies as well as methods to maximise the pleasurable aspects of the drug experience. Although their Ecstasy knowledge may have been more experiential than scientifically based, participants perceived particular methods as successful and worthy of sharing with customers.

Maximising the Highs

When asked about the various effects of their Ecstasy use, many of our participants' responses conveyed the drug's positive impact. Some said the high made them euphoric and they had lots of energy while others said it made them feel relaxed. Ecstasy allowed some interviewees to feel more open and bond with others; many regarded this type of experience as both pleasurable and therapeutic. Participants practised various strategies to maximise the pleasure of the Ecstasy high. One of the more common practices mentioned was taking the drug on an empty stomach, which they believed enabled them to metabolise the drug more quickly and to "come on" faster.

Interviewees reported using other drugs in combination with Ecstasy to intensify the positive effects. For example, some interviewees liked to smoke marijuana upon peaking to enhance the high or as they were coming down to prolong the experience. Additionally, a few participants mentioned using GHB to extend the high or Viagra to heighten sexual feelings with Ecstasy. Reportedly "candy flipping" (taking LSD with Ecstasy) or "hippie flipping" (taking mushrooms with Ecstasy) also intensified the Ecstasy high.

Another method to maximise the high was to utilize various props or toys to enhance tactile and visual stimulation. One participant commented, "I knew all the little tricks and gadgets to kind of boost you." A popular technique was to use Vicks VapoRub (a mentholated salve used to alleviate cough and congestion) by applying it under the nose or in a mask worn over the mouth and nose to intensify the multi-sensory experience. Similar practices included applying lotion, exchanging massages, sucking on candies, and watching or performing light shows.

Interviewees also explained how various routes of administration influenced Ecstasy highs. While most had tried snorting, it had a much less positive reputation than other routes of administration. Sellers in our sample relayed rumors of using Ecstasy as a suppository supposedly producing the best high, though few had attempted that route of administration. Some participants dissolved the Ecstasy tab under the tongue, which was believed to make them feel the drug faster.

Interviewees' other recommendations to increase pleasure reflect the relevance of set and setting (Zinberg 1984). Several sellers discussed the importance of being in a positive state of mind prior to use, which was also seen in Panagopoulos and Ricciardelli's (2005) work where their participants suggested entering a use episode in a positive emotional state to achieve a better Ecstasy experience (also see Shewan et al. 2000). In Gourley's (2004) and Hunt's (2007) studies, both samples described the environment, their mental state, and being around close friends as allowing them to get the most out of their Ecstasy experiences. Similarly, our interviewees emphasised the importance of taking Ecstasy in comfortable surroundings that included being with trusted friends, as evident in the following quote from a 26-year-old woman:

> I tell people if they're nervous to make sure they're only around people they trust and around music that they like and um, I think I would tell anybody that, yeah that's how you achieve the maximum benefit, is by being in a great setting.

Another interviewee, a 19-year-old Middle Eastern man, spoke about how a rave setting, in particular, can maximise the high. His thoughts typify comments we heard about using Ecstasy at raves.

> The way I feel about E is that at rave parties or where everyone is a lot more aware of drug-induced feelings, there's a whole ambiance where . . . people are going to be there to make it feel the best it can, you know? They're gonna wrap things around you that they know will feel cool when you're on Ecstasy, and the music is almost—I feel in a way it's almost made for it. It's made for these kinds of drugs and just the whole ambiance, and the people is sort of what makes it an ideal place to do it.

While Ecstasy's inherent properties may have contributed to pleasurable use episodes, participants stressed the relevance of a positive setting, whether at a rave or at an intimate house party, in creating the optimal drug experience. Even though they regarded the Ecstasy high as a positive experience, they were still aware of possible negative outcomes.

Minimising the Lows

Despite the positive appeal of the Ecstasy high, our participants experienced some negative effects from Ecstasy use. For our interviewees, the most troublesome consequence of Ecstasy use was the comedown and hangover that followed the next day or two days later, or what some interviewees called "the day after the day after." Ecstasy hangovers were described from mildly debilitating—feeling tired and a little cranky—to serious depression lasting several weeks or even months. This finding is consistent with other studies that indicate depressive symptomatology is a common problem among heavy Ecstasy users (Curran and Travill 1997; Hinchcliff 2001; Lieb et al. 2002; MacInnes et al. 2001; Parrot and Lasky 1998; Soar

et al. 2006; Verheyden et al. 2003). One 28-year-old woman shared her experiences with depressive mood.

> For the first like 12 hours or 10 hours, 7 sometimes, 4 hours, yeah, sure it's great, it's wonderful, everything is great. And then afterwards I just get, like, the depression builds along with it . . . it feels like a chemical imbalance. I can feel, mentally, I can rationalize everything that's going well in my life and how happy I really am, but I just can't—my body just doesn't buy into it and for like a week, 5 days I'm just knocked out with depression. I don't want to get up. I'm totally apathetic about everything. I don't want to eat. I'm just like, eh, miserable.

In order to avoid depressive symptoms and other side effects, such as exhaustion and body aches, participants constructed strategies to reduce negative effects of the drug. One of the most common ways thought to counteract depression was to take 5-hydroxytryptophan (5-HTP), a serotonin precursor. Researchers have found that taking 5-HTP, also known as "Nature's Prozac," may aid in attenuating brain neurotoxicity and serotonin depletion (Birdsall 1998; Erowid 2001; Sprague et al. 1994; Weir 2000), although Sprague and colleagues' (1994) research was conducted with rats who were administered high doses of 5-HTP via injections. While the following participant's success with ingesting 5-HTP after taking Ecstasy may have been psychosomatic, this 33-year-old man believed that this strategy reduced his potential depressed mood.

> Well I know that [Ecstasy] depletes the serotonin in your brain so I know sometimes that it does afterwards make you feel depressed . . . so what I'll do sometimes I'll take, um, 5-HTP for a week afterwards . . . I'll take it the week after, everyday a couple times a day maybe a few times a day actually. And it'll help as far as change my mood and it'll help with the serotonin.

Some participants used other methods to lessen physical side effects, which included fatigue, lethargy, and body aches, rather than depressed mood. They restored their health by drinking water or electrolyte drinks when dehydrated, and eating a power bar or drinking juice. Other people made sure to stretch muscles to release tension and cramping, especially after dancing for long periods of time. Similar to other studies (Allott and Redman 2006; Baggott 2002; Measham et al. 2001), participants also practised "preloading," which is taking vitamins, such as B, C and potassium, or antioxidants, such as menthlysulfonylmethane (MSM), before taking Ecstasy. Some also made sure to get plenty of rest and to eat healthy, protein-rich foods in the days before and after an Ecstasy use period.

Participants developed various methods of diminishing the negative effects of Ecstasy that they believed were successful. Some methods had the added benefit of also maximising the high—in essence performing "double duty." In the following section we describe some of our participants' double duty strategies that simultaneously maximised the highs and minimised the lows of the Ecstasy experience.

Double Duty Strategies

An overall pleasurable Ecstasy experience can be characterized as feeling the maximum effects of the drug high while curtailing the negative health effects, both during the use episode and in the days following. Some sellers recognized that minimising lows helped to induce a better Ecstasy high and shared this information with their customers. For example, one belief was the importance, especially for novices, of starting with small doses of Ecstasy. This technique allowed new users to ease into the experience and not become overwhelmed when feeling the initial effects of the drug. One 41-year-old Latino said,

> My advice to anybody that I know might be trying it or that I'm giving it to, take a half a hit or quarter hit to whatever you feel comfortable with and then if you feel good about it continue taking the rest of the pill.

Another common piece of advice we heard from our participants was to avoid drinking alcohol. This suggestion worked to both maximise the pleasurable effects and minimise the hangover, as explained in the following quote from a 23-year-old man:

> I tell 'em try not to drink too much alcohol 'cause that will overpower it in some cases and they won't get their full effect and their money's worth out of

it . . . I was like, "Well, you know, you're not gonna feel it right away, it's kind of a waste of your money at the bar. But tomorrow you're probably gonna feel like shit because you're drinking more than you can actually really handle, so you'll wake probably feeling like shit tomorrow."

Many interviewees found that using the drug too often decreased Ecstasy's positive returns and exacerbated their hangovers. Participants' reports are consistent with other research findings regarding drug tolerance (Cottler et al. 2001; Parrott 2005; Verheyden et al. 2003). After using weekly for a few months, they no longer felt the euphoric effects and instead experienced only physical exhaustion and depressive symptoms in the days following use. Some interviewees did not take Ecstasy excessively to ensure their ability to achieve maximum highs while avoiding negative effects. One 39-year-old man said,

> The more you do [Ecstasy], the less effect it has. You know when I was doing it like weekly or every couple weeks, I was definitely getting diminished returns and that's one of the things that made me want to stop doing it so often.

Some interviewees attributed negative outcomes to using adulterated Ecstasy. Procuring Ecstasy from trusted dealers was an important strategy for achieving the best high while avoiding a bad experience due to the unexpected effects from different substances. Similar to other studies' findings, most sellers in our study avoided these problems by obtaining the drug from a consistent, trusted source (Carlson et al. 2004; Hansen et al. 2001; Measham et al. 2001). Procuring Ecstasy from a reliable source contributed to a positive set when beginning a use episode, enabling users to relax and enjoy their experience, trusting they were avoiding harmful adulterants.

Study participants engaging in double duty strategies reflect the interconnected nature of pleasure enhancement and harm reduction, both in their own use and in their advice to customers. Their ultimate enjoyment of the drug's effects hinged upon their ability to decrease any negative outcomes. They realized their customers' desire for the same type of experience and distributed information on how to maximise the high while minimising the lows. This finding is particularly remarkable because Ecstasy sellers in our study were more than just a source of Ecstasy. They provided a complete Ecstasy experience, which included advice on how to maximise the highs and minimise the lows. Sometimes sellers were present when their customers/friends used Ecstasy, acting as guides to ensure a safe and pleasurable experience.

Sellers as Guides

Members of Ecstasy using networks regularly looked after each other while using the drug. Many sellers were part of dance communities where the norm was to share Ecstasy information among friends and strangers. The user-seller communities in which they belonged fostered trusted communication. Similar to Southgate and Hopwood's (2001) "network nannies" and participants in Hansen and colleagues' (2001) study, some interviewees felt that it was important to be a designated caretaker for their Ecstasy using friends. The network nanny's role was to enhance the experience of new users, provide support, monitor physical and psychological effects of the drug, and, in crisis, help with "trouble-shooting." Our findings demonstrate that 16 percent (n = 19) of sellers in our sample took on a similar role. These individuals advised customers about maximising the Ecstasy highs and minimising the lows, while monitoring their friends during their drug using episodes. Our interviewees described roles similar to network nannies such as "guide" and "trip sitter." One interviewee, who was often a caretaker to many of her friends and customers, explained the responsibilities of a guide.

> I've been people's guides you know on their first times doing various [drugs]. I've actually had a bunch of people request that I be their first person around them which, you know, it's a huge honour, it's a huge responsibility and you know you got to treat them with care and monitor where they're at . . . and providing a safe and comfortable environment for them and trying to enhance the experience as much as possible, having fun things around and toys and music . . . try to make it as fun as possible, be there to listen if they need to talk, emotionally supportive is huge.

Another interviewee stressed the importance of having a trip sitter during one's first Ecstasy experience. He said that having a knowledgeable and seasoned user monitor novices is important for their physical and emotional safety. One 24-year-old male interviewee was conscientious about distributing a potentially dangerous drug and acted as a trip sitter for his friends.

> A lot of times people would be like, "Okay we're going out tonight, [name] can you hook some E up for us please?" I'm like, "I'll hook it up." And I'm going out with the people that are taking it and because they're taking it, it's like automatically I'm not going to take it. 'Cause I'm going to be the mentally stable one tonight. Cause I'm a person that when I'm out with my friends and I know like I sold them E, it's like I have that conscience that I need to look out for them. Yeah, like, okay, I sold this person the E, if anything they're not going to get in trouble when they're on it, not with me at least.

Additionally, a few sellers exhibited concern for their customers by refusing to sell to friends who they believed were abusing Ecstasy. One participant saw himself as a "drug dealer with a conscience."

Guides and trip sitters served as sources of Ecstasy as well as support during their customers' use episodes. In addition to selling a product, Ecstasy sellers also provided information. The guides and trip sitters offered a complete experience—a total package of quality drugs, pleasure enhancement, and harm reduction. Not all of the study participants regarded themselves as altruistic; instead some expressed their desire to engage in the business of Ecstasy dealing with no questions asked, no advice given. These participants were profit-motivated, expecting their customers to know about the drug they were purchasing. Still, the majority of the sample were at least willing to share what they had learned about maximising the pleasurable effects of the drug while maintaining health-consciousness.

Conclusion

The sharing of Ecstasy use and health strategies between sellers and buyers was an important aspect of their communities. Participants conveyed the belief that they were selling and using a distinctive drug that could produce a range of pleasurable and harmful effects. Ecstasy's unique psychopharmacology, particularly its empathogenic qualities, lends itself to social bonding between Ecstasy users, and as we discovered, between buyers and sellers since they often used together. Furthermore, sellers aided in creating a pleasurable set and setting in which customers could take the drug by providing information and guidance regarding Ecstasy use. Many perceived Ecstasy to have therapeutic value and took pride in giving their friends positive drug experiences, seeing themselves as providing a service. Similar to Southgate and Hopwood's (2001) and Hansen and colleagues' (2001) studies, our findings demonstrate that lay experts in Ecstasy using social networks engaged in folk pharmacology. Our findings are important because Ecstasy sellers, in particular, distributed harm reduction strategies among their networks.

Relying upon their own experiences and those of their friends and customers, some sellers became lay experts on the drug's potential benefits and pitfalls. As members of social worlds where Ecstasy use was customary, having such knowledge about the drug was expected. However, participants' knowledge of harm reduction techniques may not have always been accurate as it was rarely based on scientific research. The exchange of inaccurate information may endanger users rather than benefit them, which is troubling. It is noteworthy that study participants were only Ecstasy experts insofar as they were experienced drug users and sellers. While some of their knowledge was impressive, given they were not scientists in the field, they lacked complete medical knowledge about Ecstasy and proven harm reduction strategies. If armed with the most science-based and up-to-date information, these sellers could be effective educators.

Although drug sellers are not traditionally seen as peer educators, our findings suggest that sellers are important points of intervention for the dissemination of harm reduction information as friendship networks are a primary link in creating awareness of safer Ecstasy use. Participants reported that their friends were the most trusted sources of information. Findings from our study indicate that targeting sellers with information can be an effective pathway for the propagation of lifesaving information to

users. Translations of research findings should be accessible to Ecstasy user/sellers so that the information they pass on is more than anecdotal. Harm reduction agencies may be interested in Ecstasy sellers taking the role of distributors of valuable information. While drug sellers are not traditionally thought of as dispensers of health-conscious advice, the guides in our sample revealed that they had an interest in protecting their customers', or, more often, their friends', well-being.

There were some limitations of our study in regards to this paper's topics. One limitation is that the theme of maximising the Ecstasy high was not one of our original foci. This theme emerged too late in the course of the study to shape the focus of data collection, and specific data analyses became difficult. For example, while we gathered data from all interviewees regarding their levels of Ecstasy sales, we did not investigate harm reduction guidance in every interview due to its later emergence. Therefore, we were not able to analyze the differences regarding sales level's effect on the likelihood of sharing harm reduction and drug enhancing practices since relevant questions on this topic were not asked consistently in early interviews. Additionally, it would have been beneficial to examine systematically under what conditions or circumstances maximising Ecstasy highs took precedence over health concerns. Future studies should investigate further the Ecstasy high and the connection between maximising pleasure and minimising negative outcomes. Second, we did not ask all participants if they had served as guides for other users, as this notion arose in some early interviews, which caused us to probe for information concerning caretaking practices in later interviews. The concept of caretaking practices among both users and sellers would benefit from further exploration.

Harm reduction has been a continually growing movement. Among our study participants the construction of strategies to enhance drug highs while possibly reducing the harms was particularly noteworthy. Traditionally, harm reduction proponents have advocated minimising drug-related harms. We found that harm reduction may also encompass increasing pleasure, which is the first step in examining an alternative approach to harm reduction. Future research should explore whether or not pleasurable Ecstasy use may be safer than other use practices. The promotion of pleasurable drug use may be controversial, but in the context of harm reduction, novel methods of reaching users deserve to be explored. When supplied with timely and accurate information, perhaps user/sellers may teach us a different way of practising harm reduction by incorporating understandings of pleasure within harm reduction models.

References

Allott, K. and J. Redman. 2006. "Patterns of Use and Harm Reduction Practices of Ecstasy Users in Australia." *Drug and Alcohol Dependence* 82: 168–176. [PubMed: 16226850]

Baggot, M. 2002. "Preventing Problems in Ecstasy Users: Reduce Use to Reduce Harm." *Journal of Psychoactive Drugs* 34: 145–162. [PubMed: 12691205]

Beck, J. and M. Rosenbaum. 1994. *Pursuit of Ecstasy: The MDMA Experience*. Albany: State University of New York Press.

Becker, H. 1963. *Outsiders: Studies in the Sociology of Deviance*. New York: Free Press.

Biernacki, P. and D. Waldorf. 1981. "Snowball Sampling: Problems, Techniques and Chain-Referral Sampling." *Sociological Methods and Research* 10 (2): 141–163.

Birdsall, T. 1998. "5-Hydrotryptophan: a Clinically-Effective Serotonin Precursor." *Alternative Medicine Review* 3 (4): 271–280. [PubMed: 9727088]

Buroway, M., A. Burton, A. Ferguson, K. Fox, J. Gamson, N. Gartrell, L. Hurst, C. Kurzman, L. Salziner, J. Schiffman, and S. Ui. 1991. *Ethnography Unbound: Power and Resistance in the Modern Metropolis*. Berkeley and Los Angeles, CA: University of California Press.

Carlson, R. G., R. A. Falck, J. A. McCaughan, and H. A. Siegal. 2004. "MDMA/Ecstasy Use Among Young People in Ohio: Perceived Risk and Barriers to Intervention." *Journal of Psychoactive Drugs* 36 (2): 181–189. [PubMed: 15369199]

Charmaz, K. 1983. "The Grounded Theory Method: An Explication and Interpretation." In *Contemporary Field Research*, edited by R. Emerson, 109–126. Boston: Little-Brown.

Copeland, J., P. Dillon, and M. Gascoigne. 2006. "Ecstasy and the Concomitant Use of Pharmaceuticals." *Addictive Behaviors* 31: 367–370. [PubMed: 15961251]

Cottler, L. B., S. B. Womack, and W. M. Compton. 2001. "Ecstasy Abuse and Dependence: Applicability and Reliability of DSM-IV Criteria Among Adolescents and Young Adults." *Human Psychopharmacology* 16: 599–606. [PubMed: 12404539]

Curran, H.V. and R. A. Travill. 1997. "Mood and Cognitive Effects of +/-3,4-Methylenedioxymethamphetamine (MDMA, 'Ecstasy'): Week-End 'High' Followed by Midweek Low." *Addiction* 92 (7): 821–831. [PubMed: 9293041]

Erowid. 2001. "Do Antioxidants Protect Against MDMA Hangover, Tolerance and Neurotoxicity?" *Erowid Extracts* 2 (December): 6–11. Retrieved from http://www.erowid.org/chemicals/mdma/mdma_article3.shtml

Falck, R.S., R. G. Carlson, J. Wang, and H. A. Siegal. 2004. "Sources of Information About MDMA (3,4-Methylenedioxymethamphetamine): Perceived Accuracy, Importance, and Implications for Prevention Among Young Adult Users." *Drug and Alcohol Dependence* 74 (1): 45–54. [PubMed: 15072806]

Gamma, A., L. Jerome, M. E. Liechti, and H. R. Lumnall. 2005. "Is Ecstasy Perceived to Be Safe? A Critical Survey." *Drug and Alcohol Dependence* 77 (2): 185–193. [PubMed: 15664720]

Glaser, B., A. Strauss. 1967. *The Discovery of Grounded Theory*. Chicago: Aldine.

Gourley, M. 2004. "A Subcultural Study of Recreational Ecstasy Use." *Journal of Sociology* 40 (1): 59–73.

Gouzoulis, E., U. von Bardeleben, A. Rupp, K. A. Kovar, and L. Hermle. 1993. "Neuroendocrine and Cardiovascular Effects of MDE in Healthy Volunteers." *Neuropsychopharmacology* 8 (3): 1987–1993.

Hansen, D., B. Maycock, and T. Lower. 2001. "'Weddings, Parties, Anything ..': A Qualitative Analysis of Ecstasy Use in Perth, Western Australia." *International Journal of Drug Policy* 12: 181–199. [PubMed: 11399420]

Hinchcliff S. 2001. "The Meaning of Ecstasy Use and Clubbing to Women in the Late 1990s." *International Journal of Drug Policy* 12: 455–468.

Hunt, G.P., K. Evans, and F. Kares. 2007. "Drug Use and Meanings of Risk and Pleasure." *Journal of Youth Studies* 10 (1): 73–96.

Jacinto, C., M. Duterte, P. Sales, and S. Murphy. 2008 forthcoming. "'I'm Not a Real Dealer': The Identity Process of Ecstasy Sellers." *Journal of Drug Issues*.

Kuzel, A. 1992. "Sampling in Qualitative Inquiry." In *Doing Qualitative Research*, edited by B. F. Crabtree and W. L. Miller, 31–45. Newbury Park, CA: Sage.

Lieb, R., C. G. Schuetz, H. Pfister, K. von Sydow, and H. Wittchen. 2002. "Mental Disorders in Ecstasy Users: A Prospective Longitudinal Investigation." *Drug and Alcohol Dependence* 68: 195–207. [PubMed: 12234649]

MacInnes, N., S. L. Handley, and G. F. A. Harding. 2001. "Former Chronic Methylenedioxymethamphetamine (MDMA or Ecstasy) Users Report Mild Depressive Symptoms." *Journal of Psychopharmacology* 15 (3): 181–186. [PubMed: 11565625]

Measham, F., J. Aldridge, and H. Parker. 2001. "Dancing on Drugs: Risks, Health and Hedonism in the British Club Scene." London: Free Association Books.

Morton J. 2005. "Ecstasy: Pharmacology and Neurotoxicity." *Current Opinion in Pharmacology* 5: 79–86. [PubMed: 15661630]

Murphy, P. N., M. Wareing, and J. E. Fisk. 2006. "Users' Perceptions of the Risks and Effects of Taking Ecstasy (MDMA): A Questionnaire Study." *Journal of Psychopharmacology* 20 (3): 447–455. [PubMed: 16574719]

Parrott, A. C. 2005. "Chronic Tolerance to Recreational MDMA (3,4-Methylenedioxymethamphetamine)." *Journal of Psychopharmacology* 19 (1): 75–87.

Parrott, A. C. and J. Lasky. "Ecstasy (MDMA) Effects Upon Mood and Cognition: Before, During and After a Saturday Night Dance." *Psychopharmacology* 139: 261–269. [PubMed: 9784083]

Rodgers, J., T. Buchanan, C. Pearson, A. C. Parrott, J. Ling, T. Heffeman, and A. B. Scholey. 2006. "Differential Experiences of the Psychobiological Sequelae of Ecstasy Use: Quantitative and Qualitative Data from an Internet Study." *Journal of Psychopharmacology* 20 (3): 437–146. [PubMed: 16174668]

Schensul, J. J., S. Diamond, W. Disch, R. Bermudez, and J. Eiserman. 2005. "The Diffusion of Ecstasy Through Urban Youth Networks." *Journal of Ethnicity in Substance Abuse* 4 (2): 39–71. [PubMed: 16275634]

Shewan, D., P. Dalgarno, and G. Reith. 2000. "Perceived Risk and Risk Reduction among Ecstasy Users: The Role of Drug, Set and Setting." *International Journal of Drug Policy* 10: 431–453.

Soar, K., J. J. D. Turner, and A. C. Parrott. 2006. "Problematic Versus Non-Problematic Ecstasy/MDMA Use: the Influence of Drug Usage Patterns and Pre-Existing Psychiatric Factors." *Journal of Psychopharmacology* 20 (3): 417–424. [PubMed: 16574716]

Southgate, E. and M. Hopwood. 2001. "The Role of Folk Pharmacology and Lay Experts in Harm Reduction: Sydney Gay Drug Using Networks." *International Journal of Drug Policy* 12: 321–335.

Sprague, J. E., X. Huang, A. Kanthasamy, and D. E. Nichols. 1994. "Attenuation of 3,4 Methylenedioxymethamphetamine (MDMA) Induced Neurotoxicity with the Serotonin Precursors Tryptophan and 5-Hydroxytryptophan." *Life Science* 55 (15): 1193–1198.

Strauss, A. and J. Corbin. 1990. *Basics of Qualitative Research*. Newbury Park, CA: Sage Publications.

Verheyden, S. L., J. Hadfield, T. Calin, and H. V. Curran. 2002. "Sub-Acute Effects of MDMA (3, 4-Methylenedioxyinethamphetamine, "Ecstasy") on Mood: Evidence of Gender Differences." *Psychopharmacology* 161: 23–31. [PubMed: 11967627]

Verheyden, S. L., R. Maidment, and H. V. Curran. 2003. "Quitting Ecstasy: An Investigation of Why People Stop Taking the Drug and Their Subsequent Mental Health." *Journal of Psychopharmacology* 17 (4): 371–378. [PubMed: 14870948]

Watters, J. and P. Biernacki. 1989. "Targeted Sampling: Options for the Study of Hidden Populations." *Social Problems* 36 (4): 416–430.

Weir, E. 2000. "Raves: A Review of the Culture, the Drugs and the Prevention of Harm." *Canadian Medical Association Journal* 162 (13): 1843–1848. [PubMed: 10906922]

White, B., L. Degenhardt, C. Breen, R. Bruno, J. Newman, and P. Proudfoot. 2006. "Risk and Benefit Perception of Party Drug Use." *Addictive Behaviors* 31: 137–142. [PubMed: 15907371]

Zinberg, N. E. 1984. *Drug, Set and Setting: The Basis for Controlled Intoxicant Use*. New Haven, CT: Yale University Press.

For Discussion

1. What are some of the benefits of using "community consultants" in this study? Are there any drawbacks to this strategy?
2. What kinds of harm reduction advice should sellers be sharing with customers?

Drugs, Street Crime, and Criminal Justice

For generations, while commentators on the US drug scene have sensationalized the crimes committed by users of heroin, cocaine, and other drugs, researchers and clinicians addressed a related series of questions. Is criminal behavior antecedent to addiction, or does criminality emerge subsequent to addiction? More specifically, is crime the result of or a response to a special set of life circumstances brought about by the addiction to psychoactive substances? Or conversely, is addiction per se a deviant tendency that is characteristic of individuals who are already prone to offensive behavior? Moreover, and assuming that criminality may indeed be a pre-addiction phenomenon, does the onset of the chronic use of drugs bring about a change in the nature, intensity, and frequency of deviant and criminal acts? What kinds of crimes are committed by people who are addicted to drugs? Does the use of certain psychoactive

substances contribute to violent acts of aggression? Or do drug-related crimes tend to be motivated by profit? Or is it both?

As early as the 1920s, researchers conducted studies which sought to unravel these very questions. For example, Edouard Sandoz (1922) at the Municipal Court of Boston and Lawrence Kolb at the U.S. Public Health Service investigated the drug-crime relationship among hundreds of people who were dependent on heroin. They focused on criminal justice and treatment populations and described different types of profiles. They argued that some individuals were habitual criminals and likely always had been. Others were simply violators of the Harrison Act, having been arrested for no more than the illegal possession of drugs. Moreover, they found little evidence of violence or aggression among individuals in both groups. Rather, the analyses by Sandoz, Kolb, and others found that the effects of drug use tended to predispose people to serious criminal transgressions; however, "addicts" were essentially law-abiding citizens who were forced to steal to adequately support their drug habits. Additionally, "addicts" were not necessarily criminals but were forced to associate with an underworld element that tended to maintain control over the distribution of illicit drugs. The Federal Bureau of Narcotics and other law enforcement groups were fixed on the notion of criminality. They argued that on the basis of their own observations, the vast majority of people dependent on heroin were members of criminal groups. To support this view, the Bureau of Narcotics pointed to several studies that suggested that most addicts were already criminals before they began using heroin. Addicts, the Bureau emphasized, represented a destructive force and the background of their addiction was irrelevant because they were members of a highly subversive and antisocial group. Having been charged with the enforcement of laws that prohibited the possession, sale, and distribution of narcotics (namely heroin), there were incidents when Bureau agents were confronted with individuals who posed danger to them. Indeed, some agents had been wounded or killed during arrest situations. However, the Bureau was incorrect in assuming that the drug-crime link was the same for all drug users. Additionally, the early work by Sandoz, Kolb, and others was limited because they focused on people in treatment or people who had been arrested or prosecuted.

By the middle of the twentieth century, some clinicians and social scientists emphasized a medical model of drug addiction, in contrast to the criminal view held by law enforcement. The medical model, first proposed by physicians in the late nineteenth century, held that addiction was a chronic and relapsing disease. The addict, it was argued, should be dealt with as a patient suffering from a physiological or medical disorder. At the same time, numerous proponents of the view sought to mitigate "addict" criminality by putting forth the "enslavement theory of addiction." The idea here was that the monopolistic controls over the heroin black market forced "sick" and otherwise "law-abiding" drug users into lives of crime to support their habits.

In retrospect, from the 1920s through the close of the 1960s, hundreds of studies were conducted on the relationship between crime and addiction. Invariably, some findings supported the medical model of addiction while others affirmed the criminal model. Given these repeated contradictions, something had to be wrong—and indeed something was. The theories, hypotheses, conclusions, and other findings generated by almost the entire spectrum of research were actually of little value, for major biases and deficiencies were built into the very nature of their research designs. Data-gathering enterprises on criminal activity were for the most part restricted to arrest histories, and there can be little argument about the inadequacy of official criminal statistics as measures of the incidence and prevalence of offense behavior. Those studies that did manage to go beyond arrest figures to probe self-reported criminal activity were invariably limited to either individuals who were incarcerated or in treatment settings. During this time, the few studies that did manage to locate active heroin users in the street community typically examined drug-taking behaviors to the exclusion of drug-seeking behaviors. Given the many methodological difficulties, it was impossible to draw valid conclusions about the nature of drug-related crime—about its magnitude, shape, scope, or direction. Equally important was that the conclusions drawn from dozens of studies failed to consider a number of important features of the drug scene: (1) that the pharmacological effects of different drugs had important implications for the drug-crime relationship; (2) that the nature and patterns of drug use were constantly shifting and changing; (3) that the purity, potency, and availability of drugs were dynamic, rather than static; (4) that both drug-related crime and drug-using criminals were undergoing continuous metamorphosis; and (5) that external factors (e.g., structural inequalities) might explain both drug use and crime. It was not until the 1970s that stronger methodologies were used to address these issues in order to generate a better understanding of the drugs-crime connection in US drug scenes.

Beginning in the 1980s, researchers began to explore other domains of the drugs-crime relationship. For example, Paul Goldstein (1985) delineated among psychopharmacological, economic-compulsive, and systemic violence associated with drug use and drug markets. Others have explored the relationship with a focus on masculinities (Collison 1996; Contreras 2009), traumatic life events (Hammersley 2011), and other factors. On a wider scale, the expansion of "narco-terrorism" in some countries (e.g., Mexico) is linked in part to domestic and foreign policies that have been implemented by governments.

Drugs and the Criminal Justice System

The criminal justice system is shaped by key decision makers: lawmakers, police, prosecutors, judges, juries, prison staff, probation workers, and parole boards. Additionally, each stage of the system can potentially impact on the other parts. The criminal justice system primarily targets street crime (as opposed to corporate, white-collar or state crime), and individuals who are processed by the system tend to lack societal power and privilege. In the United States and elsewhere, racial and several ethnic minorities are disproportionately arrested, prosecuted, and convicted, relative to their numbers in the general population. Discretionary practices by agents of social control (e.g., police decisions to arrest) contribute to these disparities in the criminal justice system. Several extra-legal factors can influence discretion, including the perception that behavior among youth in particular challenges authority (at times misinterpreted as disrespectful behavior), "criminal images" that are fuelled by stereotypical assumptions (e.g., equating crime with being black), attributes of the victim if there is one, and so on.

In 2012, an estimated 400,000 people—African American and Latino—were stopped and frisked by New York City police who found no evidence of drugs or crime on their persons. A considerably lower proportion of whites were subjected to this public or semi-public police tactic. A national US study by the American Civil Liberties Union (2013) noted 8.2 million arrests for marijuana between 2001 and 2010. The majority of the arrests—88%—were for marijuana possession. The data also showed that blacks were 3.73 times more likely than whites to be arrested for marijuana, a finding that is inconsistent with what we know about race differences in marijuana use. The *New York Times* highlighted the findings—but only after it asked researchers at Stanford University to review that the nationwide data were consistent with the conclusions drawn by ACLU. A similar study was conducted in England and Wales and also published in 2013 (Eastwood, Shiner, and Bear 2013). That study found that blacks were roughly six times more likely than whites to be stopped and searched by police. People of Asian backgrounds were 2.5 times as likely to be stopped and persons of "mixed race" were twice as likely as white individuals to be stopped and frisked. Moreover, black people in London were five times more likely than whites to be charged for possession of cannabis. Criminal justice policies can create further disparities in subsequent stages of the system. For example, beginning in the late 1980s, US sentencing guidelines required mandatory minimum sentences that disproportionately affected African Americans and people from poor or working-class backgrounds. That is, the sale of 500 grams of powder cocaine netted the same sentence as the sale of 5 grams of crack cocaine. This policy continued for nearly twenty years. Collectively, criminal justice policies have produced prison populations comprised of large numbers of people who have been convicted of drug offenses, and similar patterns have emerged in other countries. The vast numbers of people who have been convicted for drug offenses in the United States are a major factor that has led to the epidemic of mass incarceration. The articles in this section focus on the links between drugs and crime, and drugs and criminal justice.

References

American Civil Liberties Union. 2013. *The War on Marijuana in Black and White*. New York: Author.

Collison, M. 1996. "In Search of the High Life: Drugs, Crime, Masculinities and Consumption." *British Journal of Criminology* 36: 428–444.

Contreras, R. 2009. "'Damn, Yo—Who's That Girl?':
An Ethnographic Analysis of Masculinity in Drug
Robberies." *Journal of Contemporary Ethnography*
38: 465–492.

Eastwood, N., M. Shiner, and D. Bear. 2013. *The Num-
bers in Black and White: Ethnic Disparities in the
Policing and Prosecution of Drug Offences in
England and Wales*. London: Release.

Goldstein, P. J. 1985. "The Drugs/Violence Nexus: A
Tripartite Conceptual Framework." *Journal of Drug
Issues* 39: 143–174.

Hammersley, R. 2011. "Pathways Through Drugs and
Crime: Desistance, Trauma and Resilience." *Journal of Criminal Justice* 39: 268–272.

Kolb, L. (1962). "Drug Addiction: A Medical Problem." Springfield, IL: Charles Thomas.

Sandoz, C. E. (1922). "Report on Morphinism to the
Municipal Court of Boston." *Journal of Criminal
Law & Criminology*, 13: 10–55.

32

Sex Work and Drug Use in a Subculture of Violence

HILARY L. SURRATT, JAMES A. INCIARDI, STEVEN P. KURTZ, AND MARION C. KILEY

Hilary L. Surratt and her colleagues use the "subculture of violence" perspective to examine childhood trauma and adult victimization among females engaged in sex work and who also consume drugs. They draw on data collected from 325 women who participated in focus groups. Most of the women had consumed crack cocaine in the 30 days prior to the interview. The authors found that the women had high rates of victimization during childhood and adulthood and that violence was perceived as normative.

The concept of a *culture of violence*, with origins in the fields of both sociology and anthropology, has been used to explain high rates of homicide and other violent behaviors in certain cultures and segments of society. The concept expresses the notion that cultural values and social conditions rather than simply individual biological or psychological factors are significant causes of violent behavior. For example, the culture of violence thesis has been used to explain the higher rates of violent crime in urban inner-city areas (Gottesman and Brown 1999) as well as the propensity among males in the American South to use violence to settle disputes (Lundsgaarde 1977; Montell 1986; Nisbett and Cohen 1996). In anthropological writings, the culture of violence concept has been considered when comparing the values, attitudes, and behaviors characteristic of generally peaceful cultures, such as the Limbu of Nepal, with those of violent societies like the Yanomano of Brazil or the Bena Bena of New Guinea (Langness 1974; Northrup 1985).

In the criminology and delinquency literature, a *subculture of violence thesis* has been introduced for the purpose of explaining social-structural causes of violence in urban areas. The general model of such a subculture is one characterized by "dense concentrations of socioeconomically disadvantaged persons with few legitimate avenues of social mobility, lucrative illegal markets for forbidden goods and services, a value system that rewards only survival and material success, and private enforcement of the informal rules of the game" (Gottesman and Brown 1999, 297). In this context, the subculture of violence thesis emphasizes Durkheim's (1893) idea of *anomie* rather than normative socialization. According to Merton (1968), furthermore, inner-city minority nihilism is sourced in the disparity between the cultural ideal of equal opportunity and real structural inequalities. Cloward and Ohlin (1960) emphasized that the form that deviant or criminal behavior takes in response to these anomic conditions—criminal, violent, or retreatist (drug addiction)—depends on the opportunity structures for illegitimate activity. Also, socialization remains an aspect of concern here because the exposure of generations of children to violent life experiences refashions inner-city norms to favor violence over nonviolence (Clark 1992; Shaw and McKay 1931). This rendering of the subculture of violence concept has been used to analyze juvenile gang violence (Clark 1992; Kennedy and Baron 1993; Thompson and Lozes 1976; Walker, Schmidt, and Lunghofer 1993), adolescent delinquency (Bernburg and Thorlindsson 1999), violence committed by black women against black men (Ray and Smith 1991), as well as generalized violence in urban inner-city neighborhoods (Baron and Hartnagel 1998; Clarke 1998).

Perhaps the best known elucidation of the subculture of violence thesis appeared in the work of Wolfgang and Ferracuti (1967), which concluded that young, lower socioeconomic class African Americans possessed a value system in which violence was an acceptable and "normal" part of everyday life in the inner city. In recent years, however, Wolfgang and Ferracuti's point of view has been widely criticized because of its stereotyping of young African American males and its failure to address the social-structural sources of the values in question, including the differential treatment of blacks and whites by criminal justice agencies and the media (Madriz 1999). Despite these limitations, the subculture of violence thesis can be a useful approach for understanding the extent to which certain types of violence are socially situated rather than for focusing exclusively on individual factors.

Within this context, it has been well documented that women sex workers who walk the boulevards and back streets of urban centers are typically at high risk for assault, rape, and other forms of physical violence—including murder—from a variety of individuals, including muggers, serial predators, drug dealers, pimps, police, "dates" ("johns" or customers), and even passersby (Carmen and Moody 1985; Dalla 2002; Inciardi 1993; Inciardi and Surratt 2001; Maher 1997; Miller 1986; Teets 1997). Furthermore, street sex workers are embedded in the same violent social spaces where street violence and other subcultures of violence exist. As such, it would appear that to a considerable extent, street sex workers ply their trade in a subculture of violence.

The violence experienced by sex workers has been attributed to a number of enduring social problems, including gender inequality and discrimination against women as well as the attempts by many men to exercise sexual control over women (Weitzer 2000). Class and racial discrimination are also issues, because a great majority of street sex workers are indigent minority women, many of whom lack the social and work skills that offer alternative options. In addition, many street-based sex workers are also embedded in a complex of social situations that are independently associated with violent victimization, including homelessness (Davis 2000; Wenzel, Leake, and Gelberg 2001) and drug abuse (Baseman, Ross, and Williams 1999; Davis 2000; Falck et al. 2001; Gilbert et al. 2001). As such, the sex worker milieu can be an extremely violent one. Furthermore, numerous studies have documented that although sex workers are victimized by a variety of different types of perpetrators, most of the violence they experience comes from their own customers, or dates (Church et al. 2001; Coston and Ross 1998; Davis 2000; Farley and Barkan 1998; Hoigard and Finstad 1986; Inciardi, Lockwood, and Pottieger 1993; Maher 1997; Silbert and Pines 1983; Sterk and Elifson 1990).

The impetus for this analysis of sex work and violent encounters was initially an outgrowth of field work in Miami, Florida, undertaken for the purpose of developing a culturally appropriate HIV and hepatitis prevention-intervention strategy that met the specific needs of street-based, drug-involved, women sex workers. In 1999 and 2000, a number of pilot interviews were conducted with police and public health officials, HIV/AIDS prevention groups, and commercial sex workers in an effort to obtain preliminary data and materials that would inform both logistical and substantive issues related to the implementation of such an intervention program. In addition, focus groups were conducted during the same period with 53 active and former sex workers. These women ranged in age from 21 to 46 years; 60% were African American, 30% were White, and 10% were Latina; and they had a mean of 6 years of sex work and 11-year careers in illicit drug use.

Importantly, most of the women consistently reported in the focus groups that they began their dates in the evening when they were "straight" (i.e., not "high"), and after they were paid for sex, they would immediately buy drugs and get high. As this initial high wore off, they would go back to the streets to find more dates and more drugs. As they did so, they became more intoxicated, their thinking became more impaired, and they "quit thinking and caring," which put them at additional risk not only for HIV and hepatitis infections but also for sexual and physical violence. In fact, the overwhelming majority of the women recalled occasions when they had been assaulted and/or raped by their dates. Only one woman mentioned ever seeking help or counseling, primarily because most were unaware that rape crisis counseling services were available. Others feared that they would be "blamed because of what we do."

Because the sex worker focus group participants regularly encountered physical and sexual violence and considered it to be a "hazard of doing business on the street," the prevention-intervention program that was developed as a result of the field research included strategies for assessing a potential "bad date" and ways of averting potentially dangerous situations. As such, it is not only an HIV/hepatitis prevention program but also a violence prevention initiative for women on the street. The research grant to test the efficacy and effectiveness of the model was funded by the National Institute on Drug Abuse (NIDA) at the close of 2000. The target population includes active, drug-using, female sex workers who are randomly assigned to either a standard public health intervention or the sex worker focused intervention noted above (see Inciardi and Surratt 2002). This article uses interview and focus group data drawn from a sample of the first 325 women recruited in Miami, Florida, during 2001 and 2002 to examine women's experiences of violent victimization, and it discusses sex work as constituting a subculture of violence.

Methods

The target population of *active, drug-using, female sex workers* is defined in this article as women ages 16 to 49 who have (a) traded sex for money or drugs at least 3 times a week in the past 30 days, and (b) used heroin and/or cocaine 3 or more times a week in the past 30 days. Although it has been argued in the literature that "sex work" and "sex exchange" are behaviorally different phenomena (Cohen and Alexander 1995), prior research in Miami combined with information from key informants suggests that these distinctions are less clear in the neighborhoods and "strolls" (locations where sex workers walk the streets soliciting customers) where study participants are recruited. It would appear that among drug-involved sex workers in Miami, virtually all drift back and forth between commercial solicitation on the streets and sex-for-drugs exchanges in automobiles, empty lots and backyards, crack houses, shooting galleries, and stroll motels, as well as behind fences, along the sidewalks of darkened streets, and in the many back alleys that are a characteristic part of the downtown Miami geography. Although most sex workers prefer commercial solicitation along the stroll, they also resort to sex-for-drugs exchanges when they have an immediate need for drugs, money is scarce, and paying dates are few in number.

Participants in the study were located and recruited through traditional targeted sampling strategies (Watters and Biernacki 1989), which are especially useful for studying drug-involved women in the sex industry. Because it is impossible to achieve a random sample of active sex workers, a purposive, targeted sampling plan was constructed that would best reflect what is typical of the larger population. Such a strategy has been used successfully in recent years in studies of injection and other out-of-treatment drug users (Braunstein 1993; Carlson, Wang, Siegal, Falck, and Guo 1994; Coyle, Boruch, and Turner 1991). Targeted sampling has been referred to as a purposeful, systematic method by which specified populations within geographical districts are identified, and detailed plans are designed to recruit adequate numbers of cases within each of the target areas (Watters and Biernacki 1989). Several elements are necessary for this approach, including the systematic mapping of the geographical areas in which the target population is clustered, the examination of official *indicator data* (such as police arrest reports), information from professional and indigenous informants, and direct observations of various neighborhoods for signs of sexual solicitation. Periodic updates of these are necessary should the locations of the strolls temporarily shift as the result of urban renewal or police activity.

Because the authors of this article have been conducting street studies in Miami for a number of years, numerous contacts have been built up with drug users and dealers, sex workers, police officers, HIV prevention specialists, and treatment professionals. A number of these informants were contacted prior to the onset of the research to elicit information about where the highest concentrations of active sex workers might be found. In addition, through focus groups with current and former sex workers, the downtown Miami strolls most heavily traveled in the sex industry were specifically described, identified, and subsequently located.

The field office for this study is located just east of Miami's well-known Biscayne Boulevard, a more than 15-mile-long major thoroughfare extending from the Broward County line into downtown Miami. An 80-block stretch at the lower end of "the Boulevard" is a major sex worker stroll. To the east are several gated, barricaded, and somewhat gentrified neighborhoods fronting Miami's Biscayne Bay, and to the west are mainly African American and Haitian residential areas long steeped in poverty. Numerous services for the homeless are found along the southern end of the Boulevard strip as it enters downtown Miami. Despite more than a decade of gradual revitalization, the Boulevard stroll continues its long-held reputation for prostitution, sex trading, drug dealing, fencing operations, and the widespread availability of cheap motels that cater not only to locals but also to those who participate in Miami's sexual tourism industry. Some 90% of the women in the sample who specified a particular neighborhood for their sex work indicated areas within the boundaries of eight zip codes hugging the main stroll. Almost half concentrated their work within three zip codes centered directly along Biscayne Boulevard.

A distinctive feature of this project is the use of active sex workers as client recruiters for sampling purposes. The effectiveness of indigenous client recruiters in drug abuse and HIV prevention research

has been well documented (Inciardi, Surratt, and McCoy 1997; Latkin 1998; Levy and Fox 1998; Wiebel 1990, 1993). Because active sex workers do the recruiting of study participants, and because of their membership in the target population, they know of many locations on and off the Boulevard stroll—such as motels, bars, convenience stores, crack houses and shooting galleries, laundromats, and secluded empty lots—where potential participants can be found. In addition, sex worker recruiters have familiarity with drug user networks, "copping areas," and drug markets; they typically approach potential clients with culturally appropriate language, dress, and methods; and their "insider status" helps to build the trust and confidence necessary for successful outreach and recruitment.

All contacts in the street represent prescreening interviews. Those meeting project eligibility requirements are scheduled for appointments at the project intervention center, where they are prescreened by project staff members. After eligibility is confirmed, informed consent is obtained and urine testing is conducted for cocaine and opiates. Interviews are conducted using a standardized data collection instrument based primarily on the NIDA Risk Behavior Assessment, the Childhood Trauma Questionnaire (short form), and the Georgia State University Prostitution Inventory (Bernstein et al. 1994; Dowling-Guyer et al. 1994; Elifson 1990; Needle et al. 1995; Weatherby et al. 1994). This interview process takes approximately one hour to complete. After the baseline interview is completed, the client is randomly assigned to one of two alternative HIV and hepatitis prevention interventions, either the sex-worker-focused intervention noted earlier or the NIDA Standard Intervention (Wechsberg et al. 1997). The NIDA Standard Intervention is delivered in two sessions and includes individual pretest counseling covering such topics as HIV disease, transmission routes, risky behaviors, risks associated with crack or cocaine use, unsafe sexual practices, rehearsal of condom use, disinfection of injection equipment, and rehearsal of needle/syringe cleaning. Testing for HIV and hepatitis A, B, and C is provided on a voluntary basis in both interventions, and the clients receive relevant risk reduction literature and service referrals as well as a hygiene kit containing a variety of risk reduction materials. Participants receive their HIV and hepatitis test results three weeks hence, and follow-up assessments and HIV prevention booster sessions are conducted at 3, 6, and 12 months post-Baseline.

Focus group participants were drawn from the larger sample of women enrolled in the study and therefore met all of the eligibility requirements for participation in the project, including active drug use and sex work in the month prior to interview. Six focus groups were conducted in total with an average of four participants per group. All groups were facilitated by a senior researcher experienced in the conduct of qualitative fieldwork. To protect confidentiality, participants were not personally acquainted with one another and names were not used during the groups. Focus groups lasted between 60 and 90 minutes and were audio recorded with the participants' permission for the purposes of transcription.

Results

Recruitment began in March 2001, and through mid-2002, 325 eligible clients had been enrolled into the study. Table 32.1 presents information on the demographic characteristics of the study participants. Their mean age is 38.1 years (SD 8.1), and some 24.6% are age 45 or older. In terms of race/ethnicity, the majority (60.3%) is African American, followed by White (23.4%) and Latina (12.9%). The living situation of the clients is typically unstable, with 44.7% reporting that they consider themselves to be homeless. Although most women reporting homelessness were staying in shelters or on the streets, some staying in the homes of other individuals on a nightly or weekly basis also considered themselves to be homeless because of the often precarious nature of the arrangement. Not surprisingly, less than half of the sample completed their high school education, and few had legal employment or income. The majority received less than $1,000 per month, primarily from sex work, a spouse or family members, and public assistance programs.

The drug-use histories of the clients (see Table 32.2) are substantial, with most beginning

Table 32.1 Demographic Characteristics of 325 Drug-Involved, Female Sex Workers in Miami, Florida.

Age	
18–24	7.4%
25–34	23.7%
35–44	44.3%
45+	24.6%
Mean age (SD)	38.1 (8.1)
Race/ethnicity	
African American	60.3%
White/Anglo	23.4%
Latina	12.9%
Other	23.4%
Level of education	
Less than high school	51.7%
High school graduate	30.1%
At least some college	18.1%
Percent homeless	44.7%
Sources of income	
Prostitution	100.0%
Spouse, family, friends	22.8%
Public assistance	16.9%
Other illegal activity	8.6%
Paid job	4.3%

alcohol and marijuana use at a mean age of 15.0 (SD 4.7) and 15.5 (SD 4.3), respectively, followed by powder cocaine at 20.3 (SD 6.1), heroin at 23.4 (SD 7.5), and crack cocaine at 25.7 (SD 8.0) years of age. On average, the clients' illegal drug-using careers span some 22.3 (SD 8.6) years. Reports of past-month drug use indicate that alcohol and crack cocaine are the most widely used substances (75.4% and 74.4%, respectively) by this sample, followed by marijuana (57.8%), powder cocaine (38.4%), and heroin (19.4%). The current use of drugs by injection was reported by 13.8% of the women. The sex work careers of the clients are similarly lengthy, spanning an average of 15.8 years (SD 9.2) and a mean of 792.2 (SD 1,997.3) sexual partners. Past-month sexual activity included a mean of 35.9 (SD 62.1) vaginal sexual contacts and

Table 32.2 Drug-Use Characteristics of 325 Female Sex Workers in Miami, Florida.

% Ever used	
Alcohol	95.7%
Marijuana	92.9%
Cocaine	77.5%
Crack cocaine	81.5%
Heroin	34.5%
Mean age at first use (SD)	
Alcohol	15.0 (4.7)
Marijuana	15.5 (4.3)
Cocaine	20.3 (6.1)
Crack cocaine	25.7 (8.0)
Heroin	23.4 (7.5)
% Currently using (last 30 days)	
Alcohol	75.4%
Marijuana	57.8%
Cocaine	38.4%
Crack cocaine	74.4%
Heroin	19.4%
% Currently injecting drugs	13.8%

Table 32.3 Childhood Trauma Histories of 325 Drug-Involved, Female Sex Workers in Miami, Florida.

% Physically abused	
None	55.1%
Low	13.8%
Moderate	7.1%
Severe	24.0%
% Sexually abused	
None	49.5%
Low	4.3%
Moderate	12.6%
Severe	33.5%
% Emotionally abused	
None	38.2%
Low	18.2%
Moderate	13.5%
Severe	30.2%
% Physically neglected	
None	54.8%
Low	18.5%
Moderate	11.4%
Severe	15.4%
% Emotionally neglected	
None	41.5%
Low	27.1%
Moderate	10.8%
Severe	20.6%

24.4 (*SD* 56.1) oral sexual contacts. A substantial proportion (26.8%) also engaged in less traditional forms of sex trading in the past month, including anal sex, bondage, sadism, "threesomes," and "golden showers" (sexual acts involving urination).

The substantial level of drug use and sex work engaged in by these women is often associated with violent encounters in their daily lives. In fact, the subculture of violence thesis might suggest that interpersonal conflict and violence have permeated the lives and experiences of these women from an early age. Interesting in this regard are the historical self-reports of trauma experienced by the women as children and adolescents. As indicated by Table 32.3, the prevalence of childhood abuse and neglect in this sample is extremely elevated. 44.9% reported a history of childhood physical abuse, 50.5% reported sexual abuse, and 61.8% reported emotional abuse. Neglect was also common, with 58.5% and 45.2%, respectively, indicating some

level of emotional or physical neglect in childhood. Because the data on childhood trauma experiences were collected on a 5-point Likert-type scale ranging from *never* to *very often*, this allowed the women's experiences to be rated and classified by severity. The severity scores on each of the items within the individual subscales (*physical abuse, sexual abuse, emotional abuse, emotional neglect, and physical neglect*) were then summed and recoded into four severity ratings based on criteria from the authors of the childhood trauma scale. Table 32.3 presents the prevalence of each of these categories, ranging from no history to severe

Table 32.4 Recent Violent Victimizations of 325 Drug-Involved, Female Sex Workers in Miami, Florida.

	Past Month	Past Year
Encountered violent date	20.9%	41.5%
Ripped off	16.6%	28.9%
Beaten	10.8%	24.9%
Threatened with weapon	5.5%	13.8%
Raped	4.0%	12.9%

Table 32.5 Childhood Trauma and Past Year Violent Victimizations among 325 Drug-Involved, Female Sex Workers in Miami, Florida.

	Physical Abuse	Level of Childhood Sexual Abuse	Emotional Abuse
Times encountered violent date	.118*	.124*	.128*
Times ripped off	.152**	.112*	.155**
Times beaten	.138*	.078	.126*
Times threatened with weapon	.121*	.122*	.132*
Times raped	.122*	.176**	.146*

*Spearman correlation coefficients significant at $p < .05$. **Spearman correlation coefficients significant at $p < .01$.

history. Among those reporting some history of abuse, *severe* trauma is the most frequent classification, regardless of the type of abuse considered.

Of interest in regard to the subculture of violence thesis, reports of childhood abuse are consistently related to current violent encounters. Tables 32.4 and 32.5 present data on the clients' recent violent victimizations and the associations among childhood and adult victimizations. Of the clients, 41.5% had some violent encounter while engaging in sex work in the past year. Most frequently, clients reported that these incidents involved being "ripped off" (forcibly taking back money paid for sex) by a customer or date (28.9%), being beaten by a date (24.9%), being threatened with a weapon by a date (13.8%), and being raped by a date (12.9%). The women themselves often took extreme measures to escape from violent dates, with 15.4% indicating that they had jumped from cars and 23.7% running away from dates.

Importantly for the subculture of violence thesis, current violent victimization is modestly but consistently correlated with childhood victimization. Table 32.5 presents these relationships in detail. Spearman correlation coefficients were computed because they are most appropriate for the analysis of the ordinal-level abuse history data in this study. Interestingly, the severity of abuse history, be it sexual, physical, or emotional, is consistently associated with more incidents of violence of all types in the past year, with a single exception. On the other hand, the severity of neglect history demonstrates a less consistent pattern of association with current violence (data not shown). These data lend support to the thesis that violence and victimization may be considered as normative occurrences by developing individuals situated in subcultures of violence.

To contextualize the findings from the interview data, a series of six focus groups was conducted with 24 female sex workers during mid- and late 2002. One of the many areas addressed in these sessions concerned sex workers' expectations of violence. A major theme expressed by the women participating in these groups was that the violent victimizations they experience are inevitable. One woman indicated:

Prostitution, drugs, and violence go hand in hand; it's all in one palm, OK? And because the prostitute is out there to get drugs and because she has an addiction and—whether it be violence from the date or violence from the dope boy, either way we're looking at it, there's still violence involved.

Or, as another woman reported:

I think people who have been abused, like from childhood, sexual, or physical . . . I think they become codependent [on it]. Like my first boyfriend . . . I was like codependent on him, even though he was violent, a drug dealer, a drug addict, and you know, I was used to that kind of lifestyle anyway cause that's what I had in my parents home. Violence and drugs.

And still another stated:

It's like there are two worlds, there's a good world and then there's a violent world and it's like alls we know is violence, alls we know is violent men.

These comments, along with many others, suggest that violence is a routine occurrence permeating many aspects of these women's lives and is normative to such a degree that many consider it to be an unavoidable cost of doing business on the street.

Discussion

The interview data collected on this cohort of drug-involved, female sex workers have documented that these women's historical and current life experiences are replete with episodes of victimization and violence. The prevalence of both physical and sexual victimization in childhood and adulthood is extremely elevated in comparison with national estimates. In fact, a recent National Violence Against Women survey sponsored by the National Institute of Justice and the Centers for Disease Control and Prevention placed the percentage of women experiencing rape or physical assault in the past 12 months at 0.3% and 1.9%, respectively (Tjaden and Thoennes 1998). In this analysis of drug-involved sex workers, the rates of date violence alone are some 43 and 13 times higher, supporting the contention that female sex workers are enmeshed in a social milieu wherein violence is commonplace and victimization is expected.

Numerous remarks and insights from focus group participants also lend plausibility to the idea put forth in this article that street-level sex work operates as a subculture of violence. Although the analysis is limited by the absence of systematic measures of subcultural attitudes about violence (Messner 1983), behavioral data demonstrate that violent victimization is concentrated among drug-using female sex workers, is perpetrated primarily by men who solicit their sexual services, and is both expected and inevitable. These encounters also serve to extend and deepen the patterns of violence and abuse that were experienced by many women in childhood.

The marginalization of the women sex workers is further extended by the fact that nearly 45% of those in the sample are homeless, the majority have limited education, and very few possess any sort of social or professional ties with the larger community. As such, negotiating the system and network of existing community resources in search of help can be extremely difficult. This fact is evidenced by the women's scant reports of accessing any type of community health or counseling service in the past three months. In spite of the elevated incidence of rape reported by this sample of women, only one (0.3%) indicated that she contacted a rape crisis center for assistance.

The policy and research implications of these findings are several. First, because drug-involved, women sex workers are so marginalized, some type of advocacy is warranted—advocacy in terms of promoting a safer work environment, providing access to mental and physical health care, and extending unbiased treatment by the police and other criminal justice organizations. Organizations such as COYOTE, PONY, and the National Task Force on Prostitution have been established for these very purposes, but their resources are minimal and their presence is limited to but a few places in the United States.

Second, mechanisms need to be established that serve to provide sex workers with alternatives to the street. Virtually all of the women encountered in this project indicated that prostitution is not a chosen career. Rather, for most it is *survival sex*, and for almost all it is the result of a drug habit combined with the lack of other skills or resources. Or as one sex worker indicated:

When you need *the cracks* [crack cocaine] and you need money for other things 'cause your rent money *went on the boards* [was used to buy crack], you got to survive, and you know, to do that, the pussy works!

The creation of alternatives to the street for this population, however, is not an easy task. Long-term substance abuse treatment that includes strategies for empowerment and the development of positive self-images is only the beginning. In addition, there is the need for vocational education and the introduction to networks that will enable women to use their newly developed skills rather than their sexuality to support themselves.

Third, because these data clearly document that the risk for violent victimization may exacerbate the potential for acquisition of HIV or some other sexually transmitted infection, existing HIV/AIDS prevention programs for sex workers need to immediately incorporate strategies for violence prevention as well.

In addition, studies designed to better understand the precursors and determinants of the violence aimed at women sex workers are needed at multiple sites to better identify mechanisms of violence avoidance.

Fourth, and finally, one of the more daunting and perhaps most difficult of tasks is outreach to the dates of female sex workers. This is a population also in need of empowerment to provide them with alternatives to battering and other violence in their interactions with women. Working with male dates may serve to reduce not only street violence but also other violence against women. Yet members of this population are unwilling to be identified. As such, perhaps the most immediate need is the development of effective strategies for outreach, earning trust, and designing and implementing appropriate interventions for this hard-to-reach population.

References

Baron, S. W. and T. F. Hartnagel. 1998. "Street Youth and Criminal Violence." *Journal of Research in Crime and Delinquency* 35 (2): 166–192.

Baseman, J., M. Ross, and M. Williams. 1999. "Sale of Sex for Drugs and Drugs for Sex: An Economic Context of Sexual Risk Behaviors for STDs." *Sexually Transmitted Diseases* 26 (8): 444–449.

Bernburg, J. G. and T. Torlindsson. 1999. "Adolescent Violence, Social Control, and the Subculture of Delinquency: Factors Related to Violent Behavior and Nonviolent Delinquency." *Youth and Society* 30 (4): 445–460.

Bernstein, D. P., L. Fink, L. Handelsman, J. Foote, M. Lovejoy, K. Wenzel, et al. 1994. "Initial Reliability and Validity of a New Retrospective Measure of Child Abuse and Neglect." *American Journal of Psychiatry* 151 (8): 1132–1136.

Braunstein, M. S. 1993. "Sampling a Hidden Population: Noninstitutionalized Drug Users." *AIDS Education and Prevention* 5 (2): 131–139.

Carlson, R. G., J. Wang, H. A. Siegal, R. S. Falck, and J. Guo. 1994. "An Ethnographic Approach to Targeted Sampling: Problems and Solutions in AIDS Prevention Research Among Injection Drug and Crack-Cocaine Users." *Human Organization* 53: 279–386.

Carmen, A. and H. Moody. 1985. *Working Women: The Subterranean World of Street Prostitution.* New York: Harper & Row.

Church, S., M. Henderson, M. Barnard, and G. Hart. 2001. "Violence by Clients Towards Female Prostitutes in Different Work Settings: Questionnaire Survey." *British Medical Journal* 322: 524–525.

Clark, C. M. 1992. "Deviant Adolescent Subcultures: Assessment Strategies and Clinical Interventions." *Adolescence* 27 (106): 283–293.

Clarke, J. W. 1998. *The Lineaments of Wrath: Race, Violent Crime, and American Culture.* Tucson: University of Arizona Press.

Cloward, R. and L. Ohlin. 1960. *Delinquency and Opportunity: A Theory of Delinquent Gangs.* Glencoe, IL: Free Press.

Cohen, J. B. and P. Alexander. 1995. "Female Sex Workers: Scapegoats in the AIDS Epidemic." In *Women at Risk, Issues in the Primary Prevention of AIDS*, edited by A. O'Leary and L. S. Jemmott. New York: Plenum.

Coston, C. T. M. and L. E. Ross. 1998. "Criminal Victimization of Prostitutes: Empirical Support for the Lifestyle/Exposure Model." *Journal of Crime and Justice* 21 (1): 53–70.

Coyle, S. L., R. F. Boruch, and C. F. Turner, eds. 1991. *Evaluating AIDS Prevention Programs*, exp. ed. Washington, DC: National Academy Press.

Dalla, R. 2002. "Night Moves: A Qualitative Investigation of Street-Level Sex Work." *Psychology of Women Quarterly* 26: 63–73.

Davis, N. J. 2000. "From Victims to Survivors: Working with Recovering Street Prostitutes." In *Sex for Sale: Prostitution, Pornography, and the Sex Industry*, edited by R. Weitzer, 139–158. New York: Routledge.

Dowling-Guyer, S., M. Johnson, D. Fisher, R. Needle, J. Watters, M. Andersen, et al. 1994. "Reliability of Drug-Users' Self-Reported HIV Risk Behavior and Validity of Self-Reported Recent Drug Use." *Assessment* 1: 383–392.

Durkheim, E. 1893. *The Division of Labour in Society*. Paris: P.U.F.

Elifson, K. 1990. *The Georgia State Prostitution Inventory*. Unpublished questionnaire.

Falck, R. S., J. Wang, R. G. Carlson, and H. A. Siegal. 2001. "The Epidemiology of Physical Attack and Rape Among Crack-Using Women." *Violence and Victims* 16 (1): 79–89.

Farley, M. and H. Barkan. 1998. "Prostitution, Violence and Posttraumatic Stress Disorder." *Women and Health* 27 (3): 37–49.

Gilbert, L., N. El-Bassel, V. Rajah, A. Foleno, and V. Frye. 2001. "Linking Drug-Related Activities with Experiences of Partner Violence: A Focus Group Study of Women in Methadone Treatment." *Violence and Victims* 16 (5): 517–536.

Gottesman, R. and R. M. Brown, eds. 1999. *Violence in America: An Encyclopedia*, vol. 3. New York: Scribner.

Hoigard, C. and L. Finstad, L. 1986. *Backstreets: Prostitution, Money and Love*. University Park: The Pennsylvania State University Press.

Inciardi, J. A. 1993. "Kingrats, Chicken Heads, Slow Necks, Freaks, and Blood Suckers: A Glimpse at the Miami Sex-for-Crack Market." In *Crack Pipe as Pimp: an Ethnographic Investigation of Sex-for-Crack Exchanges*, edited by M. Ratner, 37–68. New York: Lexington Books.

Inciardi, J. A., D. Lockwood, and A. E. Pottieger. 1993. *Women and Crack Cocaine*. New York: Macmillan.

Inciardi, J. A. and H. L. Surratt. 2001. "Drug Use, Street Crime, and Sex-Trading Among Cocaine-Dependent Women: Implications for Public Health and Criminal Justice Policy." *Journal of Psychoactive Drugs* 33 (4): 379–389.

_____. 2002. *Developing Targeted HIV and Hepatitis Interventions for Drug-Using Female Sex Workers in Miami*. Paper presented at the Fourteenth International AIDS Conference, Barcelona, Spain. July 7–12.

Inciardi, J. A., H. L. Surratt, and H. V. McCoy. 1997. "Establishing an HIV/AIDS Intervention Program for Street Drug Users in a Developing Nation." *Journal of Drug Users* 27 (Winter): 173–193.

Kennedy, L. W. and S. W. Baron. 1993. "Routine Activities and a Subculture of Violence: A Study of Violence on the Street." *Journal of Research in Crime & Delinquency* 30 (1): 88–112.

Langness, L. L. 1974. "Ritual, Power and Male Dominance." *Ethos* 2 (3): 189–212.

Latkin, C. A. 1998. "Outreach in Natural Setting: The Use of Peer Leaders for HIV Prevention Among Drug Users' Networks." *Public Health Reports* 113 (Suppl. 1): 151–159.

Levy, J. A. and S. E. Fox. 1998. "The Outreach-Assisted Model of Partner Notification with IDUs." *Public Health Reports* 113 (Suppl. 1): 160–169.

Lundsgaarde, H. P. 1977. *Murder in Space City*. New York: Oxford University Press.

Madriz, E. 1999. "Overview II." In *Violence in America: An Encyclopedia*, vol. 1, edited by R. Gottesman and R. M. Brown, 298–302. New York: Scribner.

Maher, L. 1997. "Sexed Work: Gender, Race and Resistance in a Brooklyn Drug Market." Oxford: Clarendon Press.

Merton, R. K. 1968. *Social Theory and Social Structure*. New York: Free Press.

Messner, S. F. 1983. "Regional and Racial Effect on the Urban Homicide Rate: The Subculture of Violence Revisited." *American Journal of Sociology* 88 (5): 997–1007.

Miller, E. H. 1986. *Street Woman*. Philadelphia: Temple University Press.

Montell, W. L. 1986. *Killings: Folk Justice in the Upper South*. Lexington: University Press of Kentucky.

Needle, R., N. Weatherby, B. Brown, R. Booth, M. Williams, J. Watters, et al. 1995. "The Reliability of Self-Reported HIV Risk Behaviors of Injection and Non-injection Drug Users." *Psychology of Addictive Behavior* 9: 242–250.

Nisbett, R. E. and D. Cohen. 1996. *Culture of Honor: The Psychology of Violence in the South*. Boulder, CO: Westview Press.

Northrup, G. 1985. "The Residential Treatment of Violent Youth Viewed as a Process of Acculturation." *Milieu Therapy* 4 (1): 51–59.

Ray, M. C., and E. Smith. 1991. "Black Women and Homicide: An Analysis of the Subculture of Violence Thesis." *The Western Journal of Black Studies* 15 (3): 144–153.

Shaw, C. and H. D. McKay. 1931. *Social Factors in Juvenile Delinquency.* Washington, DC: Government Printing Office.

Silbert, M. H. and A. M. Pines. 1983. "Early Sexual Exploitation as an Influence in Prostitution." *Social Work* 28: 285–289.

Sterk, C. E. and K. W. Elifson. 1990. "Drug-Related Violence and Street Prostitution." In *Drugs and Violence: Causes, Correlates, and Consequences* (NIDA Research Monograph Series #103), edited by M. De La Rosa, E. Y. Lambert, and B. Gropper, 208–221. Rockville, MD: National Institutes on Drug Abuse.

Teets, J. M. 1997. "The Incidence and Experience of Rape Among Chemically Dependent Women." *Journal of Psychoactive Drugs* 29 (4): 331–336.

Thompson, R. J. and J. Lozes. 1976. "Female Gang Delinquency." *Corrective & Social Psychiatry & Journal of Behavior Technology, Methods & Therapy* 22 (3): 1–5.

Tjaden, P. and N. Thoennes. 1998. *Prevalence, Incidence, and Consequences of Violence Against Women: Findings from the National Violence Against Women Survey.* Washington, DC: National Institute of Justice.

Walker, M. L., L. M. Schmidt, and L. Lunghofer. 1993. "Youth Gangs." In *Handbook for Screening Adolescents at Psychological Risk*, edited by M. I. Singer, L. T. Singer, and T. M. Anglin, 400–422. New York: Lexington Books/Macmillan.

Watters, J. K. and P. Biernacki, 1989. "Targeted Sampling: Options for the Study of Hidden Populations." *Social Problems* 36: 416–430.

Weatherby, N., R. Needle, H. Cesari, R. Booth, C. McCoy, J. Watters, et al. 1994. "Validity of Self-Reported Drug Use Among Injection Drug Users and Crack Cocaine Users Recruited Through Street Outreach." *Evaluation and Program Planning* 17: 347–355.

Wechsberg, W., B. MacDonald, J. Inciardi, H. Surratt, C. Leukefeld, D. Farabee, et al. 1997. *The NIDA Cooperative Agreement Standard Intervention: Protocol Changes Suggested by the Continuing HIV/AIDS Epidemic.* Bloomington, IL: Lighthouse Institute.

Weitzer, R., ed. 2000. *Sex for Sale: Prostitution, Pornography, and the Sex Industry.* New York: Routledge.

Wenzel, S. L., B. D. Leake, and L. Gelberg. 2001. "Risk Factors for Major Violence among Homeless Women." *Journal of Interpersonal Violence* 16 (8): 739–752.

Wiebel, W. W. 1990. "Identifying and Gaining Access to Hidden Populations." In *The Collection and Interpretation of Data from Hidden Populations* (NIDA Research Monograph Series #98), edited by E.Y. Lambert, 4–11. Rockville, MD: National Institutes on Drug Abuse.

_____. 1993. *The Indigenous Leader Outreach Model* (NIH Publication No. 93-3581). Rockville, MD: U.S. Department of Health and Human Services.

Wolfgang, M. E. and F. Ferracuti. 1967. *The Subculture of Violence: Towards an Integrated Theory in Criminology.* London: Tavistock.

For Discussion

1. The authors describe the benefits of using "indigenous" workers, in this instance, "active sex workers," to recruit respondents for the study. What are the benefits of this approach? Are the indigenous workers at risk by their involvement in the research? If so, what are the possible risks?

33

The Gendered Trouble with Alcohol

Young People Managing Alcohol-Related Violence

JO LINDSAY

Drug-related violence is probably more likely to occur while under the influence of alcohol than any other drug. In this Australian study, Jo Lindsay discusses alcohol-related violence and the management of these acts from the perspective of young adults in Australia. Among other issues, Lindsay focuses on the gendered dimension of domestic and public spheres in which violence occurs, and the challenges for males who wish to avoid violence while attempting to uphold their masculine identities.

Introduction

Alcohol-related violence is a disturbing element in the social lives and relationships of many young people in post-industrial societies. The development of the night-time economy where young people are encouraged to drink heavily in entertainment precincts has increased the risk of violence in recent decades and alcohol-related violence is the subject of ongoing public and professional concern and policy interventions (Babor et al. 2010). This paper analyses the drinking biography interviews of a sample of young Australians (aged 18–24) and argues that the concept of gender performance is important for understanding experiences of alcohol related violence and for developing effective policy in this domain.

As public concern about alcohol related violence has increased in Anglophile countries in the last few decades the research literature offers an increasingly sophisticated account of the complex relationship between alcohol and violence. The importance of social and situational context for understanding drinking and violence has been highlighted (Babor et al. 2010). Particular patterns of excessive drinking and violence have been linked to specific formations of gender and class.

Excessive drinking has been traditionally linked to displays of a macho version of masculine identity alongside engaging in barroom aggression and violence. Men as both perpetrators and victims continue to engage in drunken violence and suffer injuries at much higher levels than women. Young men who drink to intoxication are particularly vulnerable to experiencing violence (Hughes et al. 2008; Laslett et al. 2010; Wells and Graham 2003). Some research from Britain and Australia has found that drinking and violence is linked to working class versions of masculinity—where drunken violence

Reprinted from Jo Lindsay, 2012, "The Gendered Trouble with Alcohol: Young People Managing-Alcohol Related Violence." In *International Journal of Drug Policy* 23: 236–241. Reprinted by permission of Elsevier via Copyright Clearance Center.

becomes a protest to petty authoritarianism at venues and middle-class values of respectability (Hayward and Hobbs 2007; Tomsen 1997). Yet research from Canada and the US has found drunken aggression and violence is common amongst some middle-class groups including male university students (Graham and Wells 2003; Wells et al. 2007).

Research from the UK has also found more diverse connexions between masculinity and drinking than what the heavy drinking male stereotype would suggest (de Visser and Smith 2007; Mullen et al. 2007). In recent years there has been some recognition that female-female violence is also a serious issue—though it takes different forms to male-male violence (Day, Gough, and McFadden 2003; Forsyth and Lennox 2009).

Like public violence, intimate partner violence or domestic violence is also associated with intoxication. However, women are substantially more likely to be victims of partner violence than men (Graham et al. 2008; Hegarty et al. 2000). Intimate partner violence is recognized as a major public health issue which, despite the advances of second wave feminism, remains common and is apparently intractable (Hegarty et al. 2000). There is a substantial body of research on the links between alcohol consumption and experiences of violence (Klostermann and Fals-Stewart 2006), but research which examines the links between public and private violence is sparse.

Important explanations for alcohol-related violence include the physical and social context of public drinking venues and cultural values and expectations about the acceptability of violence (Graham and Wells 2003; Homel et al. 2004). Triggers of violence include defending honour, reputations or face saving, addressing grievances, impulsive or emotional reactions to perceived threats and fighting for excitement and enjoyment (Graham and Wells 2003).

Graham and Wells (2003) suggest that young men in Canada define themselves on a continuum from "self-proclaimed non-fighters" who avoid fights to the "recreational fighters" at the other end of the continuum who jump into fights without hesitation. There is relatively little research on the understandings of drinking and violence by the majority of drinkers at the "non-fighting" end of the continuum—those who do not engage in violence on a regular basis but work to avoid it (Mullen et al. 2007).

Policy interventions to reduce public alcohol-related violence commonly focus on public drinking venues and night-time entertainment precincts. Interventions include responsible beverage service, server violence prevention training, licensee accords, raised enforcement of licencing regulations and multi-level interventions (Brennan et al. 2011). However there is only limited evidence that these interventions work (Brennan et al. 2011). Server training courses and multi-level interventions which combine law enforcement with community mobilization and self-regulation by licensees show the most promise (Loxley et al. 2005; Warburton and Shepherd 2006).

Policy interventions targeting domestic alcohol related violence are primarily reactive rather than preventative and include the coordination of service provision and improved police responses to domestic violence (Junger et al. 2007). Broader policies aimed at enhancing pro-social development in families such as provision of early childhood services and programmes aimed at building relationship skills and parenting skills could also be seen as relevant to reducing alcohol related domestic violence. However, evaluation data from these programmes is scant (Junger et al. 2007).

This paper takes a novel approach by examining stories about violence articulated within mainstream young people's drinking biography interviews. The aim is to analyse these personal histories and contextualize alcohol related violence within the lives of young people living in Victoria, Australia, and the social landscape they inhabit and draw out the implications for alcohol policy.

Theoretical Approach

A broadly interpretive and social constructivist approach is taken in this paper where participants own interpretations of their experiences are collected and analysed. A dynamic understanding of gender relations undergirds the analysis. Masculinities and femininities are understood to be plural and socially constructed; they are linked with struggles for social power and embedded in institutional settings (Connell 2002; Tomsen 2008). In particular, a complex understanding of masculinity is important to both understand the strong association between masculinity and alcohol related violence but to also avoid essentializing violence as a "natural" expression of masculinity (Carrington, McIntosh, and Scott 2010). Masculinities are complex expressions of identity that are linked with particular socio-spatial contexts and include official masculinity, respectable masculinity, protest masculinity, threatened and queer masculinities and so on (Carrington et al. 2010). Recent research has identified mainstream types of masculinity which value a disengagement from violence which has high relevance to this paper (de Visser and Smith 2007; Tomsen 2005). In summary, this paper focuses on a sociological reading of the interview data which sees gender as a dynamic social construction.

Methodology

This study is part of a larger project entitled: "What a Great Night: The Cultural Drivers of Alcohol Consumption." The project was a tender for the provision of qualitative and quantitative research into the cultural drivers of risk taking behaviour and their affects on "low risk," "risky" and "high risk" use of alcohol amongst 14–24-year-old Australian drinkers funded by Drinkwise and the Australian Government Department of Health and Ageing. The rationale for the research was to provide nuanced information on why different groups of young people consume alcohol in high-risk, risky or low-risk ways and provide knowledge for developing effective public health interventions on youth drinking in Australia. The aim of the drinking biographies study was to (a) gather life course information about drinking to identify "low risk," "risky" and "high risk" alcohol consumption settings and contexts; and (b) examine drinking trajectories and identify cultural drivers (or triggers) of change between different patterns of drinking for experienced young drinkers in their early 20s. The project received ethics approval from the Monash University Standing Committee on Ethics for Research involving Humans (SCERH).

This study involved 60 individual, semistructured in-depth interviews with 20–24-year-olds in Melbourne (metropolitan city), Geelong (de-industrializing city) and Warrnambool (rural seaside town) in 2008. These sites were chosen to provide a sense of the range of experiences of young people living in Victoria. Our sample was purposive in that we aimed to speak to a diverse range of young people over the legal drinking age in Australia. We aimed to sample an equal number of males and females and a balance between people who study or work full time. Whilst there are many documented issues around alcohol use at university, we wanted to explore the drinking biographies of young people in a variety of contexts. We attempted to recruit people from universities, shopping centres and snowballing, asking participants to pass on our contact details to their friends.

Sixty semi-structured interviews (26 males, 34 females) were conducted. Whilst we were able to achieve a strong gender balance across our three locations, we were less successful at recruiting non-students. Most participants were recruited from universities, with fliers posted on notice boards and handouts in lectures (73% studied full-time, 20% worked full-time and 62% worked part-time). The majority of participants spoke English as their first language and were born in Australia. We did not collect more detailed data about ethnic background unless participants mentioned this in their interviews. In summary, this is a qualitative study that does not claim to be statistically representative but is large enough to provide an insight into mainstream social practices by young Victorians.

Data Collection and Analysis

A questionnaire was utilized to collect demographic data and included some multiple choice and ranking, as well as open-ended questions about alcohol consumption. The questionnaires were primarily used as a vehicle for eliciting narratives and participants were encouraged to retrospectively discuss their introduction to alcohol in their family lives growing up, throughout their time as young children, during high school, their experiences within their social groups and the role alcohol played beyond high school during their transition into University or full-time work. The interviews were conducted by either a research fellow or a research assistant at the participants' homes or at a University and lasted one to one and one-half hours. The interviewers were both female and were older than the research participants in the study (one in her 30s and one in her 40s). It is not clear to what extent the participants shaped their answers to be socially acceptable to the interviewers—we might assume that they would downplay negative aspects of their drinking and portray their current practices in a positive light yet the transcripts involve detailed descriptions of the pleasures and problems of alcohol consumption experiences over time. All participants were offered two movie tickets for their participation.

The interviews were digitally recorded, transcribed in full and coded using NVivo, qualitative analysis software. Pseudonyms are used to protect participant confidentiality. The analysis reported in this paper focuses on the ways in which alcohol related violence is represented by these young people, the way they tell their stories of past experiences and imagined futures. As the interviews were designed to gather information on young people's drinking biographies rather than specifically about violence, we can assume that violence was only salient for the people who mentioned it. Perhaps more experiences with violence may have been reported if we had asked participants to discuss specific incidents—instead we asked them to describe the place of alcohol in their social and family lives at various time periods (as a primary school child, in secondary school and since turning 18) and comment on the extent to which alcohol played a positive or negative role in each of these periods. However, when violence was mentioned the interviewers did probe further to get a full account of specific incidents and outcomes. For this paper the transcripts were read in full, and text searching and counting cases was used to identify themes. The transcripts were searched by the author for terms such as "violent," "fights," "arguments," "unhappy," and "negative experiences" and coded. Surrounding sections of the interviews were re-read in detail to contextualize the themes. Negative case analysis was then used to determine the relative strength of themes.

This qualitative study offers an insight into the experiences of alcohol related violence by "mainstream" young people and provides textured information not currently captured in available research.

Findings

Thirty-three of the 60 participants discussed alcohol related violence in their drinking biography interviews. The most common experience of violence recounted was observing violence whilst out socializing at pubs or clubs (21/60). A substantial minority discussed avoiding violence (9/60) and experiences of family violence (9/60). Less common experiences of alcohol-related violence were participating in fights (4/60 discussed this) and making efforts to stop fights (3/60).

The stories about violence and responses to it were highly gendered and also spatialized. Similar numbers of women and men talked about observing violence whilst out socializing (10 men and 11 women). However, men were more likely to discuss strategies for avoiding violence (9 men, 0 women) and being in fights (3 men, 1 woman). By contrast family violence and fights with partners were more likely to be female concerns (mentioned by 8 women and 1 man). These findings align with the literature on gendered violence in public and private domains (Graham et al. 2008; Hegarty et al. 2000).

Avoiding Violent Men in Violent Places

Most of the mainstream participants discussed their negative views of violent people and their ongoing assessment of violence prone locations. Observing public violence was reported equally by the young people living in each of the three sites—Melbourne (large metropolitan city), Geelong (deindustrializing city) and Warrnambool (a rural coastal town). Although conclusions on prevalence cannot be drawn from this small sample, the participants who lived in Geelong described the existence of a male fighting culture in that city. For example, Billy, a 23-year-old construction worker, supported the introduction of ID scanners in pubs and clubs to "make people accountable" because there were "too many fights" going on. He described how there were some men in Geelong wanting to "make a name for themselves" via fighting which is a crisp description of men in this small city struggling for social status at a time when workplace opportunities for working class men are in decline. Jim, a 20-year-old university student, spoke in similar terms about "idiots who want to fight you" in Geelong but he did not identify masculine struggles for status or reputation but instead seemed puzzled by the causes of violence and described public fighting in Geelong as "unnecessary," "senseless" and "frustrating."

Young people living in Melbourne also talked about violence around pubs and clubs in negative terms. Benn, a 22-year-old full-time university student, described how "some people get into fights when they drink" and found these outbreaks "disturbing." Catherine, a 21-year-old student, talked about violence as an irritating and banal backdrop to going out in Melbourne. She reported the need to avoid socializing with people who fight: "I don't like violent people, I hate violent people." She was sceptical of security staff and proactively called the police when fights erupted.

> CATHERINE: If I go to X Street on a Saturday night there's always a fight and that's the same like in the city as well. This place that I go [in the city] there's always some dickhead [idiot] and then the security guards always fight. And I always call the police.
>
> Q: The security guards fight each other?
>
> CATHERINE: No but it'll just be like some person gets kicked out. I can't stand security guards, they're just so violent and just crazy, so I just call the police. I hate seeing people fight, I hate seeing people hurt like just really makes me sick. And it's really sad, like people go out to look for fights, like it's just it's so unfair and then that person that gets trapped in it. And then it's probably you know have brain damage or something by the end of it and then it's just all fucked up. . . . I wouldn't hang around with violent people.

Young people living in Warrnambool also described similar instances of observing and making

efforts to avoid violence. Donald, a 20-year-old electrician, described how he saw a lot of fights at clubs and tried to stay away from them. Pete, a 20-year-old hospitality worker, talked about an area of the rural town of Warrnambool between two night clubs that has been nicknamed the "Gaza strip" because of the frequent fighting that went on there.

Two notable themes emerge from these everyday stories of observing violence whilst out socializing. Firstly, the male gender of both the perpetrators and potential victims of public violence is taken for granted. Men appear to be more active than women in assessing violence and developing detailed strategies to avoid it—this will be discussed in more detail below. Although the women dislike violence as much as the men in this study, they appear to be positioned as bystanders to it rather than potential victims. Secondly, in the accounts given in this research there is a notable social distance between these mainstream participants and the people engaging in public violence—apparently the "people who get into fights" or "dickhead at the pub" are not friends or family members or known to participants.

Performing Masculinity and Avoiding Violence

Many of the young men who discussed violence in this research spoke of the necessity of developing strategies for avoiding violence. Maintaining a masculine identity whilst desisting from violence was a complex process because one dominant expectation of masculinity involves "standing up for yourself" rather than "backing down" (Carrington et al. 2010; Tomsen 2005). According to the male participants in this research there was an ongoing threat of victimization from "dickheads at the pub" or "people trying to make a name for themselves" and assert their masculine authority. They reported that in the social settings of pubs and clubs fights were frequently initiated on some pretext or other. Some male participants suggested that a useful way of avoiding being caught in violent situations was to cultivate positive friendship networks with other men and stay close to their friends in pubs and clubs.

For Zack, a 22-year-old construction worker who lived in Warrnambool, avoiding clubs was the best strategy for avoiding violence. He described how he does not like nightclubs because there are always fights and "alcohol tips people over the edge."

John, a 24-year-old student who also lived in Warrnambool, discussed in depth strategies of self monitoring and bodily management he uses to avoid violence. John grew up in a lower socio-economic area of Melbourne which he described as "pretty rough" and he had a family history of a father who gets violent when drunk. He reported only drinking beer when he goes out "because I know I can control beer."

JOHN: Well, I learnt very quickly how not to act drunk when I was drunk, so it's your body language and stuff like that. So the way that you look at people, so when you know that you feel that you're a certain drunkness. How and when not to look at people. Where you position yourself in the room, and who you surround yourself with—like, you know, you always got to a point where you always had your back up against the wall in case you got bottled or something like that. . . .

Q: Yeah, yeah.

JOHN: So it was always, you know, the way that you carry yourself in the area or where your friends were. You always knew if your friends were over here, your friends were over there, there was one guy over there. You always knew how the crowd shifts, you know? It was just—it was pretty weird. Like I talked to a lot of friends out here and everything like that and they never had friends who got stabbed or friends who got bottled or friends who went to hospital and, you know. Yeah, it was very bizarre, it was just the way I grew up. I guess in the areas that I grew up it was pretty rough—rough areas.

As John has made a transition from his working class milieu to interacting with fellow university students he has come to recognize that his experiences of violence and the necessity for conflict avoidance skills are particular to the disadvantaged and "rough" socio-spatial context where he spent his teenage years.

Men Fighting in Public

Only four of the men in the research talked about participating in fights. Three of these men described how they were unfairly victimized by other young men who were not known to them. The examples discussed by these four men were positioned in the past—they had occurred a number of years ago suggesting perhaps that fighting is the preserve of younger men (under 20) who have not yet developed avoidance strategies.

BILLY: Me and a mate [friend] were out—this was [when we were] a bit younger—but out in town and just walking down the street and mate's about this big on me, so he's not much of a threat to anyone.

Q: A bit shorter?

BILLY: Yeah, just walk along, minding our own business, got the crap kicked out of us [beaten up] by a group of about 15 people, crossing X Street, and just all stupid stuff like that, every week, and there would always be somebody trying to beat up someone else, just because they thought they would. Geelong is the worst for that.

Q: Really?

BILLY: Everybody trying to get out there and make a name for themselves, because they think it's a small town, but I suppose you get it everywhere.

Only one man, Pete, a 22-year-old student who lived in Warrnambool, talked about asserting himself in drinking settings though he downplayed his participation in fights and emphasized that these incidents were fleeting, inconsequential and in the past. He talked about the risk of "getting clobbered" [punched] whilst out socializing but saw his own participation in fights as playful aggression.

PETE: I got the occasional one or two sort of where someone might have whacked me a bit and I'd sort of turn around and sort of whack them in the arm back or something, but . . .

Q: Nothing?

PETE: Nothing really sort of a punch up.

Q: And so it's not violence, like a bit aggression or sort of . . .

PETE: Yeah. Just a bit of stirring.

Q: Argument?

PETE: Yeah, argumentative just like oh, this one's better than this and that sort of thing.

Q: Yeah.

PETE: There was never any sort of full on pounding the hell out of someone like.

Descriptions of pride in being tough or winning fights were notably absent in the interviews. Instead the young men's descriptions of unfair victimization and necessity for avoidance strategies were more prominent in the data.

There is one contrasting example in the interviews of men being frequently engaged in violence and this is described second hand in the interview with Jessica, a 20-year-old university student from Melbourne. Jessica had little experience of violence prior to meeting her current boyfriend. She spoke about socializing with her boyfriend and his friends who she describes as unruly football players—"feral footy boys." The men frequently get into fights and the themes of male solidarity in the face of perceived threats, turf protection from rival groups and resulting confrontation with security guards and police are part and parcel of a good night out for them. Jessica can understand her boyfriend's logic of supporting his friends when fights break out but dislikes the negative outcomes for her. She particularly dislikes being "kicked out of clubs." Jessica's experiences are a vivid example of the spillover of violence onto intimate partners. Jessica had not had intimate violence directed towards her but was annoyed by having to play the role of moderating and soothing girlfriend to a man who was frequently involved in street fighting. Though she supported his masculine strategy of "standing up for your mates" in principle, her description of resentment about the interruption violence brings to her social life suggests that her patience and support for these displays of masculinity may not be ongoing. Jessica described the collective practices of masculinity by her boyfriend in the socio spatial context of being part of a local football club in an outer Melbourne suburb but these experiences stand in strong contrast to the efforts to avoid violence described by the majority of the sample.

Women Managing Male Violence in Public

In this research women were just as likely as men to observe public violence and were not always passive in the face of it. They often tried to dissuade their partners and friends from fighting and three of the women in the sample talked about actively intervening to stop alcohol-related fights. As described earlier, Catherine, from Melbourne, hates violence and takes a proactive stance by calling the police when she witnesses fights outside nightclubs. Sally, a 23-year-old student and university residence assistant in Warnambool, also reported frequently taking on the role of breaking up fights. According to her, one successful strategy is to offer alcohol as a reward—"Stop fighting and I'll buy you a beer." This strategy would dismay most public health practitioners who advocate limiting the supply of alcohol to already intoxicated patrons but for Sally it is a useful way of mollifying angry men and defusing heated exchanges.

In contrast to usual gender stereotypes Leena, a 22-year-old trainee policewoman, previously had a job breaking up fights as a bouncer at a pub.

LEENA: If anyone ever hit me, I'd smack them back. So I don't think anyone would ever dare to.

Q: But were you ever around other people who were fighting and stuff?

LEENA: Yeah but it was only at the pub. Everyone else was drunk and I was working.

Q: Oh OK. And you had to kind of deal with that did you?

LEENA: Yeah I had to get into a few fights because that was my job.

Q: Did you? Yeah. To break them up? Or to get in them?

LEENA: To get in, and break them up, and leave. I loved it.

Similar to research on UK women working as bouncers in the night time economy, Leena was happy to engage in physical violence in addition to the more traditionally feminine role of "peace-keeper" (Hobbs, O'Brien, and Westmarland 2007).

In the interviews alcohol was frequently described as a causal factor in male violence though there were no examples given of alcohol causing women to be violent. According to Mary, a 21-year-old student, "drinking brings on aggression in boys." Sexual jealousy and men fighting over women emerged as a minor theme. For example, John from Warnambool said that the key ingredients for a fight were "females and alcohol." In these instances violence is apparently a gender performance to impress women observers and frighten off potential competitors.

In other contexts the presence of women was observed to have a civilizing effect. Kate from Melbourne observed that "boys were less likely to fight" when there was a higher ratio of women to men. In the next section I examine alcohol related violence in domestic settings.

Managing Male Violence at Home

It is well established in the literature that experiences of domestic violence are mediated by gender in pronounced ways; men are the most common perpetrators and women are the most common victims. In this research family or relationship arguments and/or violence was mentioned by eight women and one man. For most of these participants avoiding violence meant steering clear of their drunken fathers and attempting to avoid antagonizing them. None of the participants described currently being in violent family situations.

Two female participants reported a long history of violence in intimate and family relationships and had taken dramatic steps to change or avoid it in the future. For example, Natalie was a 23-year-old woman from Geelong who studied full-time and worked part-time. She was in a committed relationship and planning to get married. Alcohol had played a volatile role in her family life and had led to violence and fighting and general unhappiness over the years. Natalie rarely drinks these days because of her new-found Christian faith and her negative childhood memories and her own bad experiences drinking too much a couple of years ago.

In the interview Natalie discussed her colourful upbringing in a family owned pub before her parents separated. Her family "all still drink and enjoy to drink." She recalled the distress caused by family violence and verbal abuse by her father towards her mother even after her parents had separated.

> NATALIE: It's when they step over that mark with an extra glass of scotch and coke that it turns really unhappy and in tears and violent, . . . if they're drinking they're happy and it's all good and then they turn violent, like that's the last thing that you're going to remember so . . . Yeah. I think my family just don't know when to stop drinking, like you can hit a point where you're really happy and believe you're tipsy but they just want to keep going and going and going and that's where it's stupid, like it's quite embarrassing or whatever.

Between the ages of 16 and 20 Natalie drank regularly and sometimes heavily and had a few negative experiences throwing up, passing out and almost being sexually assaulted herself. In more recent years Natalie has changed her socio-spatial context through meeting a new partner, shifting towns and now socializing with Christian friends. Alcohol now plays a very small role in her life: "My whole life has kind of transformed differently so it's not an issue at all." Her Christian faith has given her much to live for and it has allowed her to develop new social networks, "a whole new social scene," and create some distance with her family.

Kristie had also dramatically changed her socio-spatial context to avoid family violence. Kristie, age 21, lives in Geelong and has two young children, and she studies part time. She recalled lots of alcohol-related violence and trouble across most of her life. Her stepfather who she grew up with was a "violent drunk" and the children's father was also "a jerk" and would become violent when drunk. According to Kristie most men she knows "turn nasty when they drink." Kristie has turned her life around and moved interstate to escape "her drunk and violent ex" and at the time of the interview had a non-drinking partner.

It is notable that both of the women experiencing more extreme alcohol-related domestic violence had made determined efforts to avoid further family violence by dramatically changing their socio-spatial contexts; moving towns and changing their networks and socializing with non-drinkers.

Discussion and Conclusion

This research found that alcohol-related violence is problematic part of the social and family lives of many young people (about half of the sample) but is not a salient feature for all. For the participants in this research who spoke about violence, most described it as something to be observed cautiously and avoided where possible.

A gendered reading of alcohol-related violence is extremely useful in understanding patterns of victimization and avoidance in this research. Young women and men frequently socialize together in the night-time economies of industrialized countries such as the UK and Australia, and some gender convergence in drinking patterns and alcohol related harm can be observed (Babor et al. 2010). Yet the men and women in this research remain differently positioned in relation to the performance of drunk and violent expressions of masculinity by some men in both public and private spheres. Women were observers of public violence and potential victims of family violence whilst men were observers and potential victims of public violence from unknown perpetrators.

Although this research draws on a small sample, there was little evidence of adherence to or observation of a widespread culture of violence. In contrast to some research on barroom violence or violence in the night time economy there were no stories about enjoying the spectacle of fighting or masculine self-expression or pride in participating in fights (Graham and Wells 2003; Tomsen 1997). The violent contexts described in this research were to some extent socio-spatially located. The words "rough" or "tough" were sometimes used to describe working class areas and in particular participants from Geelong (a de-industrializing city) spoke about the local drinking culture there in negative terms. But looking across the data participants from each of the research sites—Geelong,

Melbourne and Warrnambool—were just as likely to report observing public fighting at clubs and pubs and the university students were as likely to have experienced public violence as the non-professional workers.

This study has a number of limitations. Violence may have been underreported because the interviews were designed to elicit drinking biographies rather than focus specifically on violence. The limited discussion of their own participation in violence and the tendency to frame incidents in the distant past rather than the present may also reflect perceptions of social desirability in the interview context resulting in violence being underreported. However the detailed interviews do offer a window to the social worlds of the mainstream where avoiding violence is a priority for both young women and men.

The key findings of this research, that alcohol-related violence is centrally about performances of masculinity and is socio-spatially contextualized, have important implications of policy development. Public violence is not fully grasped by commonly used gender neutral explanations of "young binge drinkers"—instead the targets of interventions should be particular performances of masculinity. Some men are perpetrators and most men are potential victims whilst women are usually positioned as observers rather than active agents in public alcohol related violence. The data reported here, alongside findings from other research, suggest that minority performances of masculinity are the primary problem of alcohol related violence (Tomsen 2005, 2008). Most mainstream young men, like those in this sample, actively avoid and desist from engaging in violence (de Visser and Smith 2007; Mullen et al. 2007). Masculine performance is also important for understanding violence in domestic settings. The gender-neutral term "intimate partner violence" deflects attention away from problematic performances of masculinity in domestic contexts where women are the central victims. As Tomsen has argued in his work on masculinity and crime, there is a need for education and promotion of diverse and non-violent masculinities amongst marginalized boys and men (Tomsen 2008). Interventions aimed at performances of masculinity which take social inequalities into account are potential preventative solutions to alcohol related violence in both public and domestic settings.

A focus on problematic masculinities can also assist the targeting and delivery interventions at public drinking venues. There is less need to monitor women as they are unlikely to be perpetrators or victims of public violence (at least in the Australian locations studied here). This research also suggests that to create drinking contexts where avoidance and desistance from violence are valued it would also be worth hiring bar and security staff who model peaceful rather than violent masculinities as reported by some of the participants. Currently instead of policy effectively targeting the minority expressions of violent masculinity the potential victims—mainstream men in public and women in private—must assess, manage or avoid violent socio-spatial contexts for themselves.

References

Babor, T., R. Caetano, S. Casswell, G. Edwards, N. Giesbrecht, K. Graham, et al. 2010. *Alcohol: No Ordinary Commodity*, 2nd ed. Oxford: Oxford University Press.

Brennan. I., S. C. Moore, E. Byrne, and S. Murphy. 2011. "Interventions for Disorder and Severe Intoxication in and around Licensed Premises, 1989–2009." *Addiction* 106 (4): 706–713.

Carrington, K., A. McIntosh, and J. Scott. 2010. "Globalization, Frontier Masculinities and Violence." *British Journal of Criminology* 50 (3): 393–413.

Connell, R. W. 2002. *Gender*. Cambridge: Polity Press.

Day, K., B. Gough, and M. McFadden. 2003. "Women Who Drink and Fight: A Discourse Analysis of Working-Class Women's Talk." *Feminism Psychology* 13 (2): 141–158.

De Visser, R. O., and J. A. Smith. 2007. "Alcohol Consumption and Masculine Identity among Young Men." *Psychology and Health* 22: 595–614.

Forsyth, A. J. M. and J. C. Lennox. 2010. "Gender Differences in the Choreography of Alcohol-Related Violence: An Observational Study of Aggression Within Licensed Premises." *Journal of Substance Use* 15 (2): 75–88.

Graham, K., S. Bernards, M. Munne, and C. Wilsnack, eds. 2008. *Unhappy Hours: Alcohol and Partner Aggression in the Americas*. Washington: Pan American Health Organisation.

Graham, K. and S. Wells. 2003. "Somebody's Gonna Get Their Head Kicked in Tonight: Aggression Among Young Males in Bars—A Question of Values?" *The British Journal of Criminology* 43 (3): 546–566.

Hayward. K. and D. Hobbs. 2007. "Beyond the Binge in 'Booze Britain': Market-Led Liminalisation and the Spectacle of Binge Drinking." *The British Journal of Sociology* 58 (3): 437–456.

Hegarty, K., E. Hindmarsh, and M. Gilles. 2000. "Domestic Violence in Australia: Definition, Prevalence and Nature of Presentation in Clinical Practice." *Medical Journal of Australia* 173 (7): 363–7.

Hobbs, D., K. O'Brien, and L. Westmarland. 2007. "Connecting the Gendered Door: Women, Violence and Doorwork." *British Journal of Sociology* 58 (1): 21–38.

Homel, R., R. Carvolth, M. Hauritz, G. McIlwain, and R. Teague. 2004. "Making Licensed Venues Safer for Patrons: What Environmental Factors Should Be the Focus of Interventions?" *Drug and Alcohol Review* 23 (1): 19–29.

Hughes, K., Z. Anderson, M. Morleo, and M. A. Beilis. 2008. "Alcohol, Nightlife and Violence: The Relative Contributions of Drinking Before and During Nights Out to Negative Health and Criminal Justice Outcomes." *Addiction* 103 (1): 60–65.

Junger, M., L. Feder, J. Clay, S. Côté, D. Farrington, K. Freiberg, et al. 2007. "Preventing Violence in Seven Countries: Global Convergence in Policies." *European Journal on Criminal Policy and Research* 13 (3): 327–356.

Klostermann, K. and W. Fals-Stewart. 2006. "Intimate Partner Violence and Alcohol Use: Exploring the Role of Drinking in Partner Violence and Its Implications for Intervention." *Aggression and Violent Behaviour* 11: 587–597.

Laslett, A., P. Catalano, T. Chikritzhs, C. Dale. C. Doran, J. Ferris, et al. 2010. *The Range and Magnitude of Alcohol's Harm to Others*. Deakin, ACT: Alcohol Education and Rehabilitation Foundation.

Loxley, W., D. Gray, C. Wilkinson, T. Chikritzhs, R. Midford, and D. Moore. 2005. "Alcohol Policy and Harm Reduction in Australia." *Drug and Alcohol Review* 24 (6): 559–568.

Mullen, K., J. Watson, J. Swift, and D. Black, D. 2007. "Young Men, Masculinity and Alcohol." *Drugs: Education, Prevention, and Policy* 14 (2): 151–165.

Tomsen, S. 1997. "A Top Night Out: Social Protest, Masculinity and the Culture of Drinking Violence." *British Journal of Criminology* 37: 90–102.

Tomsen, S. 2005. "Boozers and Bouncers: Masculine Conflict, Disengagement and the Contemporary Governance of Drinking-Related Violence and Disorder." *Australian & New Zealand Journal of Criminology* 38 (3): 283–297.

Tomsen, S. 2008. "Masculinities, Crime and Criminalisation." In *The Critical Criminology Companion*, edited by T. Anthony and C. Cunneen, 94–104. Sydney: Federation Press.

Warburton, A. L. and J. P. Shepherd. 2006. "Tackling Alcohol Related Violence in City Centres: Effect of Emergency Medicine and Police Intervention." *Emergency Medicine Journal* 23 (1): 12–17.

Wells, S. and K. Graham. 2003. "Aggression Involving Alcohol: Relationship to Drinking Patterns and Social Context." *Addiction* 98 (1): 33–42.

Wells, S., M. Speechley, J. J. Koval, and K. Graham. 2007. "Gender Differences in the Relationship between Heavy Episodic Drinking, Social Roles, and Alcohol-Related Aggression in a U.S. Sample of Late Adolescent and Young Adult Drinkers." *The American Journal of Drug and Alcohol Abuse* 33 (1): 21–29.

For Discussion

1. In this study, the author found that college students were just as likely as other respondents to witness fighting in clubs and bars. If you have frequented different kinds of bars, what is the extent of violence in those settings? And to what extent do males attempt to avoid fights? How are males perceived when they desist from fighting in these public places?

2. Two expected roles of bar security staff are to prevent violence from occurring in the settings, and to address it when it does occur. What are the most effective skills that bar security staff should have in order to do their jobs effectively?

34

Breakthrough in U.S. Drug Sentencing Reform

The Fair Sentencing Act and the Unfinished Reform Agenda

KARA GOTSCH

This article focuses on the Fair Sentencing Act, a piece of federal legislation that partly rectified sentencing disparities that resulted from the Anti-Drug Abuse Acts of 1986 and 1988. For over twenty years, a two-tier system created unequal parity between convictions for crack and powder cocaine. Kara Gotsch describes how possession of 5 grams of crack resulted in mandatory minimum sentences of five years in prison. In contrast, the possession of 500 grams of powder cocaine resulted in the same mandatory five-year sentence. Gotsch noted that roughly half a million people were incarcerated for a drug offense at the time that her report was written. The author argues that the legislative change partially altered the disparate sentence practice but did not eliminate it. Moreover, the disparity continues to affect a disproportionate number of African Americans.

In August 2010 U.S. President Barack Obama signed into law the Fair Sentencing Act, legislation that limits the harsh punishments that were enacted during the 1980s for low-level crack cocaine offenses. At the Oval Office signing ceremony Obama was joined by Democratic and Republican congressional leaders who had championed reform.

That day the President's press secretary, Robert Gibbs, told a reporter, "I think if you look at the people that were there at that signing, they're not of the political persuasions that either always or even part of the time agree. I think that demonstrates . . . the glaring nature of what these penalties had . . . done to people and how unfair they were."[1]

Gibbs was referring to the five- and ten-year mandatory minimum sentences prescribed under federal law for defendants caught in possession for personal use or with the intent to sell as little as five grams of crack cocaine. The drug penalties were the harshest ever adopted by Congress and were set at the height of the nation's "war on drugs," a time of significant concern—and misunderstanding—about crack cocaine.

The Fair Sentencing Act was welcomed by civil rights and community activists, but the compromise measure fell short of the changes they had sought for two decades. The new law reduces but does not eliminate a sentencing disparity that disproportionately impacts African Americans and

---

Reprinted from Kara Gotsch, 2011, *Breakthrough in U.S. Drug Sentencing Reform: The Fair Sentencing Act and the Unfinished Reform Agenda*. Washington, DC: Washington Office on Latin America.

entangles too many low-level drug offenders in the federal criminal justice system.

At the same time, the bipartisan cooperation that led to passage of the Fair Sentencing Act was historic at a time when intense partisan wrangling over a broad range of issues on Capitol Hill dominated debate and stymied action. Hopefully, the efforts to pass the Fair Sentencing Act will contribute to a broader movement to address disproportionate punishment and ensure a fairer justice system.

Mass Incarceration and Drug Sentencing

The United States leads the world in incarceration with 2.3 million people confined in federal and state prisons and local jails. This nation's "war on drugs" over the last three decades, more than any other single factor, has fueled this historic incarceration boom. The number of people behind bars for drug offenses has increased more than 12-fold since 1980. About half a million people are incarcerated for a drug offense today, compared to an estimated 41,000 in 1980.[2]

Figure 34.1 shows trends in the size of the U.S. prison population, representing state and federal prisoners, over the last 80 years. Until the late 1970s the number of prisoners had remained relatively flat for nearly a half century. Even as the country's overall population grew by 55 percent from 1940 to 1970, the number of prisoners nationwide remained around 200,000. But by the 1980s the prison population began to climb and has continued to increase ever since. What changed in the 1980s were political initiatives responding to the emergence of a new drug, crack cocaine, in urban and minority communities. Public fears, amplified by sensationalist media accounts, created a political climate that favored promises to get "tough" on drugs by stiffening drug offense penalties.

The Anti-Drug Abuse Acts of 1986 and 1988, signed by President Ronald Reagan, instituted hefty mandatory minimum sentences for drug offenses, including mandatory penalties for crack cocaine offenses that were the harshest ever adopted for low-level drug offenses. Defendants possessing as little as five grams of crack cocaine were subject to a mandatory minimum sentence of five years in prison. Defendants with at least 50 grams were subject to a ten-year mandatory minimum sentence. The severity of crack cocaine penalties was especially striking when compared to powder cocaine, a chemically similar substance. For powder cocaine, the threshold amounts to trigger the five- and ten-year

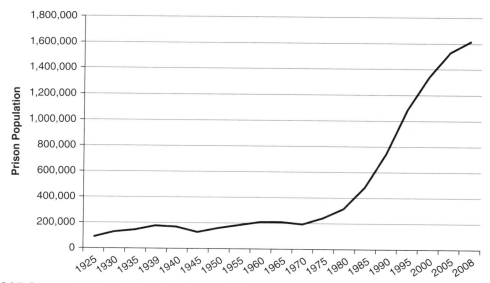

Figure 34.1 State and Federal Prison Population, 1925–2008.

Source: The Sentencing Project, at http://www.sentencingproject.org/template/page.cfm?id=107.

mandatory sentences were 100 times greater than for crack (e.g., 500 grams instead of five grams and five kilograms instead of 50 grams). This huge gap became known as the 100-to-1 sentencing disparity.

The uneven approach to federal cocaine sentencing was quickly adopted by many state governments, some of which enacted policies even more extreme than those being set at the federal level. For example, in 1989, Missouri adopted a 75-to-1 sentencing disparity between crack and powder cocaine, whereby someone convicted of selling six grams of crack cocaine faces the same prison term—a ten-year mandatory minimum—as a person who sells 450 grams of powder cocaine. In 1990 Oklahoma set a 6-to-1 quantity-based sentencing disparity that required a ten-year mandatory minimum sentence for possessing five grams of crack cocaine and 28 grams of powder cocaine.

Consequences of U.S. Drug Laws

According to Congress's legislative history, the federal drug sentences enacted during the 1980s were intended to impose stiff penalties on drug "kingpins" and high-level drug traffickers. However, research conducted by the U.S. Sentencing Commission, an independent judicial body created by Congress in 1984, found that the quantities for crack cocaine offenses were set too low to accomplish the objective of punishing high-level traffickers. Moreover, the mandatory minimum structure which took away judicial discretion at sentencing failed to differentiate between defendants' roles and culpability. In 2002 the Sentencing Commission warned that crack cocaine penalties "apply most often to offenders who perform low-level trafficking functions, wield little decision-making authority, and have limited responsibility."[3]

Figure 34.2 identifies the most common offender functions among federal crack and powder cocaine defendants sentenced in 2005. That year, low-level crack cocaine offenders, such as street-level dealers, lookouts, and couriers, comprised 61.5 percent of the 5,033 individuals charged and sentenced for crack offenses in federal court.[4]

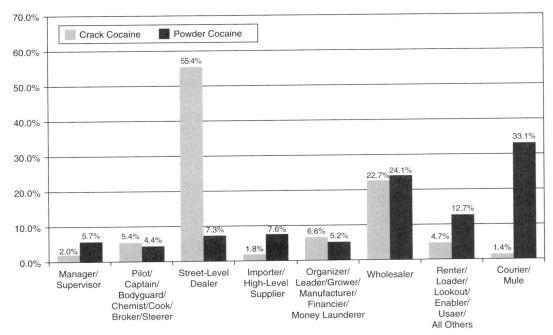

Figure 34.2 Defendant Function in Crack Cocaine vs. Powder Cocaine Cases, 2005.

Source: United States Sentencing Commission, 2005 Drug Sample.

The increased incarceration of drug offenders stemming from the 1980s policy changes represented the most significant source of growth in the federal prison system. In 1980 the 4,749 prisoners convicted of drug offenses constituted one-quarter of the federal prison population.[5] By 2009 over half of sentenced prisoners (95,205) were incarcerated for drug offenses.[6] The accompanying cost to house federal prisoners has also increased to $6 billion, up 1,700 percent since 1980.[7] Despite this enormous investment, federal prisons are operating at 35 percent above capacity.[8] Double and triple bunking is commonplace, as is the utilization of non-housing areas for sleeping quarters.

In addition to the disproportionately severe penalties associated with federal crack cocaine offenses, which tended to be low-level and nonviolent, the impact of the sentencing disparity has fallen disproportionately on African Americans. U.S. government research indicates that the prevalence of drug use is similar across racial and ethnic groups.

Drug Law's Real Life Consequences

Eugenia Jennings from Alton, Illinois, was sentenced to nearly 22 years in federal prison in 2001 for distribution of crack cocaine. U.S. District Judge G. Patrick Murphy told her at sentencing that the government had failed her. "When you were a child and you had been abused, the government wasn't there. When your stepfather abused you, the government wasn't there. When your stepbrother abused you, the government wasn't there. But, when you get a little bit of crack, the government's there."[9]

Judge Murphy's frustration stemmed from the inordinately long prison sentence he was bound to give Ms. Jennings despite her difficult and tortured childhood—she ran away from home to escape abuse but found only drug addiction to comfort her. The sentence was the result of her conviction for selling about 13 grams of crack cocaine, the weight of a few sugar packets. Her two earlier convictions for selling small quantities of crack cocaine classified her as a "career criminal," which subjected her to a stiff mandatory penalty. If her crime had involved powder cocaine rather than crack, she

might have been eligible to leave prison to care for her three young children as much as ten years earlier. Despite changes to the law to reduce sentences for low-level crack cocaine offenses, Ms. Jennings remains in federal prison today.

An estimated two-thirds of all crack cocaine users are white or Hispanic,[10] and surveys of users suggest that they generally purchase their drugs from sellers of the same racial and ethnic background.[11] Nevertheless, 79 percent of federal crack cocaine defendants in 2010 were African American.[12] Generally, African Americans are more likely to be sentenced to prison, and once there, serve more time for a drug offense, than are white drug defendants charged with comparable offenses.[13]

The obvious racial disparity associated with federal crack cocaine cases prompted the Sentencing Commission to declare in 2004 that "[r]evising the crack cocaine thresholds would better reduce the [sentencing] gap than any other single policy change, and it would dramatically improve the fairness of the federal sentencing system."[14] The significance of the racial disparity associated with crack cocaine sentencing contributed to a negative perception of the U.S. justice system in communities of color.[15] Indeed, Federal Judge Reggie Walton testified before Congress that jurors in his courtroom had refused to convict guilty defendants because "they were not prepared to put another young black man in prison knowing the disparity existed between crack and powder in those . . . cases."[16] Judge Walton believed the perceived racial injustice associated with crack cocaine sentences was ample justification for reform.

Political Context for Reform

Many factors contributed to the political atmosphere that finally enabled this long-debated sentencing reform to move forward in 2010. Most important was a convergence of views among the president, lawmakers, sentencing and legal experts, civil rights and community activists, and just about every prominent newspaper editorial board in the country, that the 100-to-1 cocaine sentencing disparity was unjust and required immediate reform.

For example, over the course of 12 years the Sentencing Commission issued four reports to

Congress on the consequences of crack cocaine sentencing policy, and each time urged reform.

After its 2007 report, the Commission proposed an amendment to the U.S. Sentencing Guidelines that would lower the recommended sentencing range for crack cocaine offenses, a guideline which judges consult when making sentencing decisions. The changes to the guidelines went into effect on November 1, 2007, thereby reducing the average crack cocaine sentence by 15 months. The mandatory minimums set by Congress did not change and judges were required to uphold the mandatory sentences unless narrow circumstances allowed for a departure.

In December 2007, after holding a hearing and receiving comments from over 30,000 individuals and organizations, the Sentencing Commission voted to make its crack cocaine sentencing guideline amendment retroactive. This proved to be very controversial among some Republican lawmakers on the Judiciary Committees in the Senate and the House of Representatives, as well as with then–Attorney General Michael Mukasey, who warned of a resulting violent crime wave if retroactivity was broadly applied. However, federal law gives the Commission the authority to make guideline reductions retroactive without requiring congressional approval, and the Commission's December 2007 vote stood. As of April 2011, 16,433 people in prison had been granted a sentence reduction (averaging 26 months). The Commission's analysis of recidivism among those released due to the 2007 retroactivity amendment shows rates of recommitments to prison after release (30.4 percent) consistent with recidivism rates for those crack cocaine offenders released prior to the availability of the sentence reduction benefit (32.6 percent).[17]

The Sentencing Commission's advocacy around crack cocaine sentencing reform was critical to emboldening Congress to finally take steps to change the harsh mandatory minimum penalties. First, the Commission's extensive research and data collection provided an important factual foundation, serving both to educate lawmakers and to provide community activists with ammunition for reform. Second, since the Commission is comprised of sentencing experts, including federal judges and lawyers, its recommendations enjoyed widespread credibility. Both Democratic and Republican lawmakers considered the Commission a reliable source of information and analysis.

In addition to the contributions of the Sentencing Commission, a committed and effective advocacy coalition had developed many years earlier to educate Congress and the public about the tragic consequences of this extreme sentencing policy. Civil rights organizations like the National Association for the Advancement of Colored People (NAACP), the American Civil Liberties Union (ACLU), and criminal justice reformers including the Sentencing Project had been calling for elimination of the sentencing disparity since the Sentencing Commission issued its first report to Congress on this topic in 1995. A reinvigorated campaign brought together a progressive constituency that employed aggressive lobbying strategies over a period of several years, including national lobby days in Washington, DC, call-in days designed to flood Capitol Hill offices with calls for reform from constituents, and ongoing media coverage featuring stories of those incarcerated under the harsh sentencing regime. Over time, the coalition broadened to also encompass legal organizations, faith-based groups (including Christian conservatives), and law enforcement.

In response to this pressure, legislation to address the crack cocaine sentencing disparity had been introduced in every congressional session for over a decade. But little progress was made. The breakthrough finally came in 2009, when Senator Dick Durbin (D-Illinois) introduced his bill to eliminate the crack cocaine sentencing disparity. As Chairman of the Senate Judiciary Committee's Subcommittee on Crime, Durbin held a hearing that featured testimony by Assistant Attorney General Lanny Breuer in favor of eliminating the sentencing disparity. Breuer's statement marked the first time since 1986 that any administration had endorsed the elimination of the disparity. This position, which was then repeated publicly numerous times by Attorney General Eric Holder, sent an important message to the Democratic Congress that sentencing reform was a priority for the Obama administration. During Obama's campaign for president he had endorsed the elimination of the disparity, and after his election the issue was highlighted on the White House website as an important civil rights priority.

After many months of negotiations in the Senate, Durbin's legislation, the Fair Sentencing Act, was brought before the Senate Judiciary Committee where a compromise version was approved. The compromise quickly passed through the Senate under unanimous consent,[18] and a few months later it was approved by voice vote[19] in the House. The resulting legislation reduced the 100-to-1 disparity to 18-to-1. The five-year mandatory minimum was now triggered when a defendant possessed for distribution at least 28 grams (1 ounce) of crack cocaine. (Previous Sentencing Commission reports had defined a mid-level operator in the drug trade as someone who sold an ounce of crack cocaine in a single transaction.) The penalty triggers for powder cocaine remained unchanged, but the legislation also increased financial penalties and raised the sentencing guidelines for cases in which a defendant uses violence or is the leader of a drug operation. Senator Jeff Sessions (R-Alabama), a longtime conservative leader, supported narrowing but not eliminating the sentencing disparity.

Senator Sessions and others on the Senate Judiciary Committee, both Republican and Democrat, refused to support legislation that treated the two forms of cocaine the same, indicating the persisting influence of long-held misconceptions about crack cocaine.

Bittersweet Victory

Passage of the Fair Sentencing Act in 2010 marked the first time in 40 years that Congress eliminated a mandatory minimum sentence. The bill struck the five-year mandatory minimum sentence for simple possession of five grams of crack cocaine, the only commonly abused drug to trigger a mandatory sentence for mere possession. Under federal law, a conviction for possession of other drugs would likely result in probation rather than a prison sentence.

The last time Congress had approved any kind of sentence reduction occurred 16 years earlier, when it created a "safety valve" that allowed judges

to avoid a mandatory minimum sentence if a defendant met certain criteria, including being charged with a non-violent offense and having a minimal criminal record. Slow progress in achieving federal sentencing reform signals how risky most politicians still consider drug and crime issues to be. By supporting a proposal to lessen penalties, many in Congress feared they would be leaving themselves vulnerable in the next election. Political cover was essential, including clear bipartisan support and avoiding a roll call vote, which would specifically identify a member of Congress with a vote in favor of the sentence reductions. Despite the political hesitance, both Republicans and Democrats spoke in favor of the Fair Sentencing Act and those who eventually sponsored the legislation in the Senate encompassed some of the more conservative and more liberal members of each party.[20]

Figure 34.3 shows the expected decline in sentencing length for crack cocaine offenses since passage of the reform. Each year an estimated 3,000 people will benefit from the sentencing changes, resulting in an average reduction of two years for those impacted. The Sentencing Commission estimates that in ten years the overall federal prison population will decline by 3,800 people as a result of the reform.[21]

The advocacy coalition that helped advance the Fair Sentencing Act had sought the complete elimination of the sentencing disparity. While most members of the coalition endorsed the compromise legislation, coalition members remain committed to ending the disparity. Despite the sentencing improvements, the new quantity triggers will still entangle people far less consequential in the drug markets than the major traffickers that the federal government claims to prioritize in its enforcement. This continued pursuit of low-level offenders absorbs resources that would be better directed at apprehending more troublesome contributors to the illegal drug trade, including large-volume operators and distribution organizations that are particularly violent, or linked to especially violent suppliers in other countries.

The reform coalition has also sought application of the new law to people sentenced under the discredited 100-to-1 disparity. The Fair Sentencing

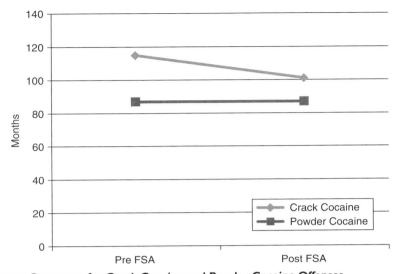

Figure 34.3 Average Sentences for Crack Cocaine and Powder Cocaine Offenses.

Source: United States Sentencing Commission, 2009 Sourcebook of Federal Sentencing Statistics and Prison Impact Model, FY2009 Datafile.

Act did not account for retroactivity, and many thousands of people in prison are still enduring excessive sentences handed down under the old law. The stories of people incarcerated weighed heavily on the reform debate. It would be cruel if their long history of injustice would now be forgotten by policymakers.

While the new law became effective in August 2010, the final sentencing guidelines that will implement the sentencing scale will take effect on November 1, 2011. At the same time, and as a result of a unanimous decision by the Sentencing Commission reached in June 2011, the new guidelines will apply to people currently incarcerated for a crack cocaine offense. The Sentencing Commission estimates that 12,000 people will benefit from a sentence reduction averaging 37 months.[22] Applications for a sentencing guideline reduction are reviewed by a federal court and the expedited releases will take place over 30 years.

Some law enforcement officials and many Republican members of the House and Senate Judiciary Committees urged the Commission to vote against retroactivity of the guidelines with claims that moving average sentences from 13 years to 10 years would result in increased crime and violence.

However, Commissioners received public comment from over 40,000 citizens and organizations in support of retroactivity. Moreover, recent data on recidivism among crack cocaine offenders found no likelihood of increased rates of reincarceration resulting from shorter prison terms. Attorney General Holder testified at a Commission hearing in June 2011 in support of retroactivity, saying "[E]nsuring a fair and effective criminal justice system . . . requires the retroactive application of [the crack cocaine] guideline amendment."[23] The Obama administration's support for retroactivity boosted public attention and interest in the Commission decision, although the Administration endorsed a more limited application than what the Commissioners eventually instituted.

Moreover, after many months of pressure from the reform community, Attorney General Holder reversed course on the Justice Department's directive to federal prosecutors on cases not yet sentenced for crack cocaine offenses committed prior to the Fair Sentencing Act's passage on August 3, 2010. For almost a year, federal prosecutors contested arguments by defense counsel and some judges that those newly sentenced crack cocaine defendants could not benefit from the mandatory minimum changes enacted by Congress if their conduct occurred prior to the Act. After numerous rulings against the Justice Department's position and with several appellate court cases pending, Holder issued a new directive in July 2011 that "pipeline" cases would now benefit from the reduced sentencing structure.

Additional options are available to better address the sentencing disparities for those incarcerated, including bipartisan legislation introduced by House members Representatives Bobby Scott (D-Virginia) and Ron Paul (R-Texas) in June 2011, the Fair Sentencing Clarification Act. This legislation would apply the new quantity triggers for the crack cocaine mandatory minimums for all conduct committed prior to the August 2010 enactment of the Fair Sentencing Act, regardless of the defendant's sentencing date. Given the strong opposition to the law by the current House Judiciary Chair, Representative Lamar Smith (R-Texas), near-term success for this legislation is unlikely. A final opportunity for retroactive relief lies with President Obama and his constitutional authority to grant prisoner commutations. But the likelihood of this option is small given that the president did not issue a single commutation in the first half of his term.

Building Momentum

In the United States, most law enforcement activity is conducted by state and local governments; only a fraction of cases are pursued at the federal level. Drug offenders constitute 18 percent of state prisoners, and overall rates of incarceration for drug offenses are at an all time high.[24] Moreover, among those incarcerated in state prison for a drug offense, six in ten persons have no history of violence or high-level drug selling activity.[25] The consequences of mass incarceration brought on by the "war on drugs" persist at all levels.

Fortunately, 2009 saw the first decline in the overall state prison population in almost 40 years. The changes at the state level are linked to new policies enacted to curb corrections growth and spending by investing in alternatives to incarceration, limiting time served in prison and enhancing reentry services to curb rates of prisoner recidivism. Progress

in stabilizing prison growth at the state level is in marked contrast to the federal prison system which has increased at 2.5 times the rate of state prisons since 2000, 4.1 percent vs. 1.5 percent.[26]

State policy reform may be a model for the federal criminal justice system, which endures many of the same crowding and budget burdens as the states. Passage of the Fair Sentencing Act was an important first step for the federal criminal justice system but it is a long way from advancing a broad agenda to significantly impact the size of its corrections population and to ensure justice for all.

Efforts are underway among the advocacy community to build upon the sentence reduction embraced by the Fair Sentencing Act and to capitalize on the reform movement that has been gaining momentum at the state level. For example, during the federal deficit debates of 2011, a letter sent to Capitol Hill—calling for sentencing reforms that would stop the growth of the federal prison system and reduce costs—was supported by 80 organizations, including the American Correctional Association, Drug Policy Alliance, United Methodist Church, National Organization for Women, and Leadership Conference on Civil and Human Rights. Reforms outlined included:

- making retroactive congressional reforms to crack cocaine sentencing;
- enhancing elderly prisoner release programs;
- expanding time credits for good behavior; and
- eliminating mandatory minimum sentences for drug offenses.

In 2011 the Obama administration proposed recalculating prisoner time credits for good behavior by increasing time off by seven days to 54 days per year. The administration also proposed a program to earn 60 days off of a prisoner's sentence for participation in rehabilitative programs. For example, prisoners working at least 180 days in the prison industries programs, which maintain government contracts to produce items like furniture, solar panels, and clothing, could receive up to 60 days per year off their sentence. Both provisions have been incorporated into bipartisan legislation that was approved by the Senate Judiciary Committee in July 2011.

With the changes in the makeup of Congress resulting from the November 2010 elections, the prospects for advancing a broader sentencing reform agenda are uncertain. Representative Lamar Smith (R-Texas) was the only Member of Congress to speak in opposition of the Fair Sentencing Act. In January 2011 he became Chairman of the House Judiciary Committee; any substantive criminal justice reform initiatives in the House of Representatives will be considered by his committee first.

At the same time, some of Representative Smith's Republican colleagues have been vocal about the need for change. For example, a prominent Subcommittee Chairman on the House Appropriations Committee, Frank Wolf (R-Virginia), has applauded state-level reform efforts to reduce incarceration levels and promote rehabilitation. Representative Wolf has also expressed interest in examining some of these efforts for federal implementation.

A new awareness of the problems that plague the American criminal justice system is clearly emerging. After taking office, President Obama's national drug policy director, a longtime police official, rejected use of the term "war on drugs." It was a promising beginning and the administration's support for reforming crack cocaine sentencing was consistent with the rhetoric. After decades of adding and escalating mandatory minimum sentences, Congress and the White House finally stepped away from the cycle of ever-harsher penalties. Given the United States' role as the principal architect and major proponent of a global drug control system that has emphasized "zero-tolerance" and criminal sanctions, the passage of the Fair Sentencing Act is a milestone not only for U.S. policy, but also for reform advocates in other countries.

Still, the drug war is deeply entrenched politically and institutionally. Achieving a more profound shift in the nation's approach to drugs will require sustained progress in reforming drug sentencing laws to ensure fair and proportionate penalties, building on the success of the Fair Sentencing Act. A more humane and effective approach to drugs will also require progress on a broader reform agenda, including:

- strengthening funding for evidence-based prevention and treatment;
- mainstreaming harm reduction interventions such as needle-exchange programs;
- re-investing in the communities that have been hardest hit by drug abuse and by the drug war;
- more selectively targeting enforcement to discourage drug market violence; and
- embracing innovative community corrections systems that can provide effective alternatives to incarceration.

How policymakers choose to respond will depend on the persuasiveness of the arguments for reform and the commitment of the advocacy community to advancing the change.

Notes

1. The White House, Office of the Press Secretary, 2010, Press briefing by Press Secretary Robert Gibbs, August 3, 2010. Retrieved from www.whitehouse.gov

2. Ryan King and Marc Mauer, 2007, *A 25-Year Quagmire: The War on Drugs and its Impact on American Society*. Washington, DC: The Sentencing Project.

3. United States Sentencing Commission, 2002, *Report to the Congress: Cocaine and Federal Sentencing Policy*, May, at http://www.ussc.gov/Legislative_and_Public_Affairs/Congressional_Testimony_and_Reports/Drug_Topics/200205_RtC_Cocaine_Sentencing_Policy/200205_Cocaine_and_Federal_Sentencing_Policy.pdf

4. United States Sentencing Commission, 2007, *Report to the Congress: Cocaine and Federal Sentencing Policy*, May, at http://www.ussc.gov/Legislative_and_Public_Affairs/Congressional_Testimony_and_Reports/Drug_Topics/200705_RtC_Cocaine_Sentencing_Policy.pdf

5. Sourcebook of Criminal Justice Statistics, 2003. "Federal prison population, and number and percent sentenced for drug offenses, United States, 1970–2004."

6. William J. Sabol and Heather C. West, 2010, *Prisoners in 2009*. Bureau of Justice Statistics, December, at http://bjs.ojp.usdoj.gov/index.cfm?ty=pbdetail&iid=2232

7. Federal Bureau of Prisons, *2011 Budget and Performance Summary: Federal Prison System*, at http://www.justice.gov/jmd/2011summary/html/fy11-bop-bud-summary.htm

8. Statement of Harley G. Lappin, Director of the Federal Bureau of Prisons, before the U.S. House of Representatives Committee on Appropriations, Subcommittee on Commerce, Justice, Science and Related Agencies, March 15, 2011, at http://appropriations.house.gov/_files/031511BOPDirectorStatement.pdf

9. Restoring Fairness to Federal Sentencing: Addressing the Crack-Powder Disparity: Hearing Before the Senate Judiciary Committee's Subcommittee on Crime and Drugs, April 29, 2009, Testimony of Cedric Parker.

10. Substance Abuse and Mental Health Services Administration, 2006, *Results from the 2005 National Survey on Drug Use and Health*, September, Detailed Table J and Table 1.43a.

11. Dorothy Lockwood, Anne E. Pottieger and James A. Inciardi, 1995, "Crack Use, Crime by Crack Users, and Ethnicity," in *Ethnicity, Race and Crime*, edited by Darnell F. Hawkins, 21. New York: State University of New York Press.

12. United States Sentencing Commission, *2010 Sourcebook of Federal Sentencing Statistics*, Table 34, at http://www.ussc.gov/Data_and_Statistics/Annual_Reports_and_Sourcebooks/2010/Table34.pdf

13. United States Sentencing Commission, 2004, *Fifteen Years of Guidelines Sentencing*, November, 122; Bureau of Justice Statistics, 1998, *Compendium of Federal Justice Statistics, 1994*, March, Table 6.11, 85; and Bureau of Justice Statistics, 2004, *Compendium of Federal Justice Statistics, 2003*, October, Table 7.16, 112.

14. U.S. Sentencing Commission, *Fifteen Years of Guidelines Sentencing.*

15. See Paul Butler, 2009, *Let's Get Free: A Hip-Hop Theory of Justice*. New York: The New Press.

16. Restoring Fairness to Federal Sentencing: Addressing the Crack-Powder Disparity: Hearing Before the Senate Judiciary Committee's Subcommittee on Crime and Drugs, April 29, 2009, Testimony of U.S. District Court Judge Reggie Walton.

17. United States Sentencing Commission, 2011, Memorandum: Recidivism Among Offenders with Sentence Modifications Made Pursuant to Retroactive Application of 2007 Crack Cocaine Amendment, May, retrieved from www.ussc.gov

18. Unanimous consent agreements permit expedited consideration of legislation, and are often used for routine or non-controversial matters, but can also be employed for sensitive issues. "A Senator may request unanimous consent on the floor to set aside a specified rule of procedure so as to expedite proceedings. If no Senator objects, the Senate permits the action, but if any one Senator objects, the request is rejected," according to the U.S. Senate's glossary of terms available at http://www.senate.gov/reference/glossary_term/unanimous_consent.htm

19. In the House of Representatives, voice votes can be conducted in which individual Members' votes are not recorded: "As many as are in favor say 'Aye.' As many as are opposed, say 'No.'" On issues that lawmakers may consider controversial, a voice vote allows legislation to move forward without linking each Member to a recorded vote. See http://thomas.loc.gov/home/lawsmade.bysec/consideration.html#voting

20. Cosponsors of the Fair Sentencing Act of 2010 included Senators Dick Durbin (D-Illinois), Patrick Leahy (D-Vermont), John Kerry (D-Massachusetts), Jeff Sessions (R-Alabama), Tom Coburn (R-Oklahoma), and Orrin Hatch (R-Utah).

21. United States Sentencing Commission, Prison Impact Model, FY2009 Datafile.

22. United States Sentencing Commission, 2011, *Analysis of the Impact of Guideline Implementation of the Fair Sentencing Act of 2010 if the Amendment Were Applied Retroactively*, May, at http://www.ussc.gov/Research/Retroactivity_Analyses/Fair_Sentencing_Act/20110520_Crack_Retroactivity_Analysis.pdf.

23. Statement of Eric H. Holder, Jr., Attorney General of the United States, before the United States Sentencing Commission, 2011, Hearing on Retroactive Application of the Proposed Amendment to the Federal Sentencing Guidelines Implementing the Fair Sentencing Act of 2010, June 1.

24. Sabol and West, *Prisoners in 2009.*

25. King and Mauer, *A 25-Year Quagmire.*

26. Sabol and West, *Prisoners in 2009.*

For Discussion

1. In a democratic nation, how did this sentence disparity continue for over twenty years?
2. Consider the material on moral panics in Part II of this book. To what extent did moral panics shape the 1986 and 1988 legislation that led to the disparity in sentences for crack and powder cocaine?

35

The New Jim Crow[1]

MICHELLE ALEXANDER

Jim Crow was not an individual but rather a derogatory caricature of an African American male. The term was widely used to refer to a system of rules and legislation that governed the behaviors of whites and African Americans. The rules were based on white supremacy. Some individuals purport that Jim Crow statutes lasted a century. Michelle Alexander argues that Jim Crow continues today and is manifested in the criminal justice system with its mass incarceration of hugely disproportionate numbers of African Americans. Alexander reviews data that suggest that mass incarceration of African Americans has been greatly influenced by convictions for drug offenses—largely possession. This article is a synopsis of Alexander's book, *The New Jim Crow: Mass Incarceration in the Age of Colorblindness*.

The subject that I intend to explore today is one that most Americans seem content to ignore. Conversations and debates about race—much less racial caste—are frequently dismissed as yesterday's news, not relevant to the current era. Media pundits and more than a few politicians insist that we, as a nation, have finally "moved beyond race." We have entered into the era of "post-racialism," it is said, the promised land of colorblindness. Not just in America, but around the world, President Obama's election has been touted as the final nail in the coffin of Jim Crow, the bookend placed on the history of racial caste in America.

This triumphant notion of post-racialism is, in my view, nothing more than fiction—a type of Orwellian doublespeak made no less sinister by virtue of the fact that the people saying it may actually believe it. Racial caste is not dead; it is alive and

---

Reprinted from Michelle Alexander, 2011, "The New Jim Crow," in *Ohio State Journal of Criminal Law* 9: 7–26. Reprinted by permission of Michelle Alexander.

well in America. The mass incarceration of poor people of color in the United States amounts to a new caste system—one specifically tailored to the political, economic, and social challenges of our time. It is the moral equivalent of Jim Crow.

I am well aware that this kind of claim may be hard for many people to swallow. Particularly if you, yourself, have never spent time in prison or been labeled a felon, the claim may seem downright absurd. I, myself, rejected the notion that something akin to a racial caste system could be functioning in the United States more than a decade ago—something that I now deeply regret.

I first encountered the idea of a new racial caste system in the mid-1990s when I was rushing to catch the bus in Oakland, California, and a bright orange poster caught my eye. It screamed in large bold print: THE DRUG WAR IS THE NEW JIM CROW. I recall pausing for a moment and skimming the text of the flyer. A radical group was holding a community meeting about police brutality, the new three-strikes law in California, the drug war, and the expansion of America's prison system. The meeting was being held at a small community church a few blocks away; it had seating capacity for no more than fifty people. I sighed and muttered to myself something like, "Yeah, the criminal justice system is racist in many ways, but it really doesn't help to make such absurd comparisons. People will just think you're crazy." I then crossed the street and hopped on the bus. I was headed to my new job, director of the Racial Justice Project for the ACLU in Northern California.

When I began my work at the ACLU, I assumed the criminal justice system had problems of racial bias, much in the same way that all major institutions in our society are plagued to some degree with problems associated with conscious and unconscious bias. As a civil rights lawyer, I had litigated numerous class-action employment discrimination cases, and I understood well the many ways in which racial stereotyping can permeate subjective decision-making processes at all levels of an organization with devastating consequences. While at the ACLU, I shifted my focus from employment discrimination to criminal justice reform, and dedicated myself to the task of working with others to identify and eliminate racial bias whenever and wherever it reared its ugly head.

By the time I left the ACLU, I had come to suspect that I was wrong about the criminal justice system. It was not just another institution infected with racial bias, but rather a different beast entirely. The activists who posted the sign on the telephone phone were not crazy; nor were the smattering of lawyers and advocates around the country who were beginning to connect the dots between our current system of mass incarceration and earlier forms of social control. Quite belatedly, I came to see that mass incarceration in the United States had, in fact, emerged as a stunningly comprehensive and well-disguised system of racialized social control that functions in a manner strikingly similar to Jim Crow.

I state my basic thesis in the introduction to my book, *The New Jim Crow*:

> What has changed since the collapse of Jim Crow has less to do with the basic structure of our society than the language we use to justify it. In the era of colorblindness, it is no longer socially permissible to use race, explicitly, as a justification for discrimination, exclusion, and social contempt. So we don't. Rather than rely on race, we use our criminal justice system to label people of color "criminals" and then engage in all the practices we supposedly left behind. Today it is perfectly legal to discriminate against criminals in nearly all the ways it was once legal to discriminate against African Americans. Once you're labeled a felon, the old forms of discrimination—employment discrimination, housing discrimination, denial of the right to vote, and exclusion from jury service—are suddenly legal. As a criminal, you have scarcely more rights, and arguably less respect, than a black man living in Alabama at the height of Jim Crow. We have not ended racial caste in America; we have merely redesigned it.[2]

I reached this conclusion reluctantly. Like many civil rights lawyers, I was inspired to attend law school by the civil rights victories of the 1950s and 1960s. Even in the face of growing social and political opposition to remedial policies such as affirmative action, I clung to the notion that the evils of Jim Crow are behind us and that, while we have a long way to go to fulfill the dream of an egalitarian, multiracial democracy, we have made real progress. I understood the problems plaguing poor communities of color, including problems associated with crime and rising incarceration rates, to be a function of poverty and lack of access to quality education—the continuing legacy of slavery and Jim Crow. I strenuously resisted the idea that a new caste system was operating in this country; I was nearly offended by the notion. But after years of working on issues of racial profiling, police brutality, drug law enforcement in poor communities of color, and attempting to assist people released from prison "re-enter" into a society that never seemed to have much use for them in the first place, I had a series of experiences that began what I call my "awakening." I began to awaken to a racial reality that is so obvious to me now that what seems odd in retrospect is that I was blind to it for so long.

Here are some facts I uncovered in the course of my work and research that you probably have not heard on the evening news:

- More African American adults are under correctional control today—in prison or jail, on probation or parole—than were enslaved in 1850, a decade before the Civil War began.[3]
- In 2007 more black men were disenfranchised than in 1870, the year the Fifteenth Amendment was ratified prohibiting laws that explicitly deny the right to vote on the basis of race.[4] During the Jim Crow era, African Americans continued to be denied access to the ballot through poll taxes and literacy tests. Those laws have been struck down, but today felon disenfranchisement laws accomplish what poll taxes and literacy tests ultimately could not.
- In many large urban areas in the United States, the majority of working-age African American men have criminal records. In fact, it was reported in 2002 that, in the Chicago area, if you take into account prisoners, the figure is nearly 80%.[5]

Those bearing criminal records and cycling in and out of our prisons today are part of a growing undercaste—not class, caste—a group of people, defined largely by race, who are relegated to a permanent second-class status by law. They can be denied the right to vote, automatically excluded from juries, and legally discriminated against in employment, housing, access to education, and public benefits, much as their grandparents and great-grandparents were during the Jim Crow era.

I find that when I tell people that mass incarceration amounts to a New Jim Crow, I am frequently met with shocked disbelief. The standard reply is: "How can you say that a racial caste system exists? Just look at Barack Obama! Just look at Oprah Winfrey! Just look at the black middle class!"

The reaction is understandable. But we ought to question our emotional reflexes. The mere fact that some African Americans have experienced great success in recent years does not mean that something akin to a caste system no longer exists. No caste system in the United States has ever governed all black people. There have always been "free blacks" and black success stories, even during slavery and Jim Crow. During slavery, there were some black slave owners—not many, but some. And during Jim Crow, there were some black lawyers and doctors—not many, but some. The unprecedented nature of black achievement in formerly white domains today certainly suggests that the old Jim Crow is dead, but it does not necessarily mean the end of racial caste. If history is any guide, it may have simply taken a different form.

Any honest observer of American racial history must acknowledge that racism is highly adaptable. The rules and reasons the legal system employs to enforce status relations of any kind evolve and change as they are challenged.[6] In the first chapter of the book, I describe the cyclical rebirths of racial caste in America. Since our nation's founding, African Americans have been repeatedly controlled through institutions, such as slavery and Jim Crow, which appear to die, but then are reborn in new form—tailored to the needs and constraints of the time.

For example, following the collapse of slavery, the system of convict leasing was instituted—a system many historians believe was worse than slavery.[7] After the Civil War, black men were arrested by the thousands for minor crimes, such as loitering and vagrancy, and sent to prison. They were then leased to plantations. It was our nation's first prison boom. The idea was that prisoners leased to plantations were supposed to earn their freedom. But the catch was they could never earn enough to pay back the plantation owner the cost of their food, clothing and shelter to the owner's satisfaction, and thus they were effectively re-enslaved, sometimes for the rest of their lives. It was a system more brutal in many respects than slavery, because plantation owners had no economic incentive to keep convicts healthy or even alive. They could always get another one.[8]

Today, I believe the criminal justice system has been used once again in a manner that effectively re-creates caste in America. Our criminal justice system functions more like a caste system than a system of crime control.

For those who find that claim difficult to swallow, consider the facts. Our prison system has quintupled for reasons that have stunningly little do with crime. In less than 30 years, the U.S. penal population exploded from around 300,000 to more than 2 million.[9] The United States now has the highest rate of incarceration in the world, dwarfing the rates of nearly every developed country, including highly repressive regimes like China and Iran.[10]

In fact, if our nation were to return to the incarceration rates of the 1970s—a time, by the way, when civil rights activists thought that imprisonment rates were egregiously high—we would have to release four out of five people who are in prison today.[11] More than a million people employed by the criminal justice system could lose their jobs.[12] That is how enormous and deeply entrenched the new system has become in a very short period of time.

As staggering as those figures are, they actually obscure the severity of the crisis in poor communities of color. Professor Loïc Wacquant has argued that the term "mass incarceration" itself is a misnomer, since it implies that nearly everyone has been subject to the new system of control.[13] But, of course that is not the case. The overwhelming majority of

the increase in imprisonment has been poor people of color, with the most astonishing rates of incarceration found among black men. It was estimated several years ago that, in Washington, D.C.—our nation's capital—three out of four young black men (and nearly all those in the poorest neighborhoods) could expect to serve time in prison.[14] Rates of incarceration nearly as shocking can be found in other communities of color across America.[15]

So what accounts for this vast new system of control? Crime rates? That is the common answer. But no, crime rates have remarkably little to do with skyrocketing incarceration rates. Crime rates have fluctuated over the past thirty years, and are currently at historical lows, but incarceration rates have consistently soared.[16] Most criminologists and sociologists today acknowledge that crime rates and incarceration rates have, for the most part, moved independently of one another.[17] Rates of imprisonment—especially black imprisonment—have soared regardless of whether crime has been rising or falling in any given community or the nation as a whole.[18]

So what does explain this vast new system of control, if not crime rates? Ironically, the activists who posted the sign on that telephone pole were right: The War on Drugs. The War on Drugs and the "get tough" movement explain the explosion in incarceration in the United States and the emergence of a vast, new racial undercaste. In fact, drug convictions alone accounted for about two-thirds of the increase in the federal system, and more than half of the increase in the state prison population between 1985 and 2000.[19] Drug convictions have increased more than 1000% since the drug war began, an increase that bears no relationship to patterns of drug use or sales.[20]

People of all races use and sell drugs at remarkably similar rates, but the enemy in this war has been racially defined.[21] The drug war has been waged almost exclusively in poor communities of color, despite the fact that studies consistently indicate that people of all races use and sell drugs at remarkably similar rates.[22] This evidence defies our basic stereotype of a drug dealer, as a black kid standing on a street corner, with his pants hanging down.[23] Drug dealing happens in the ghetto, to be sure, but it happens everywhere else in America as well. Illegal drug markets, it turns out—like American society generally—are relatively segregated by race.[24] Blacks tend to sell to blacks, whites to whites, Latinos sell to each other. University students sell to each other. People of all races use and sell drugs. A kid in rural Kansas does not drive to the 'hood to get his pot, or meth, or cocaine; he buys it from somebody down the road. In fact, the research suggests that where significant differences by race can be found, white youth are more likely to commit drug crimes than youth of color.[25]

But that is not what you would guess when entering our nation's prisons and jails, overflowing as they are with black and brown drug offenders. In the United States, those who do time for drug crime are overwhelmingly black and brown.[26] In some states, African Americans constitute 80 to 90% of all drug offenders sent to prison.[27]

I find that many people are willing to concede these racial disparities once they see the data. Even so, they tend to insist that the drug war is motivated by concern over violent crime. They say: just look at our prisons. Nearly half of the people behind bars are violent offenders. Typically this is where the discussion ends.

The problem with this abbreviated analysis is that violent crime is not responsible for the prison boom. Violent offenders tend to get longer sentences than nonviolent offenders, which is why they comprise such a large share of the prison population. One study suggests that the entire increase in imprisonment can be explained by sentence length, not increases in crime.[28] To get a sense of how large a contribution the drug war has made to mass incarceration, consider this: there are more people in prison today just for drug offenses than were incarcerated in 1980 for all reasons.[29] The reality is that the overwhelming majority of people who are swept into this system are non-violent offenders.

In this regard, it is important to keep in mind that most people who are under correctional control are not in prison or jail. As of 2008, there were approximately 2.3 million people in prisons and jails, and a staggering 5.1 million people under "community correctional supervision"—i.e., on probation or parole.[30] Millions more have felony records and spend their lives cycling in and out of prison, unable to find work or shelter, unable to vote or to serve on juries. This system depends on the prison label, not prison time. It does not matter whether you have actually spent time in prison; your second-class citizenship begins the moment you are branded a felon. It is this badge of inferiority—the criminal record—that ushers you into a parallel social universe in which discrimination is, once again, perfectly legal.

How did this extraordinary system of control, unprecedented in world history, come to pass? Most people insist upon a benign motive. They seem to believe that the War on Drugs was launched in response to rising drug crime and the emergence of crack cocaine in inner city communities. For a long time, I believed that too. But that is not the case. Drug crime was actually declining, not rising, when President Ronald Reagan officially declared the drug war in 1982.[31] President Richard Nixon was the first to coin the term a "war on drugs," but President Reagan turned the rhetorical war into a literal one. From the outset, the war had little to do with drug crime and much to do with racial politics.

The drug war was part of a grand and highly successful Republican Party strategy—often known as the Southern Strategy—of using racially coded political appeals on issues of crime and welfare to attract poor and working class white voters who were resentful of, and threatened by, desegregation, busing, and affirmative action.[32] Poor and working class whites had their world rocked by the Civil Rights Movement. White elites could send their kids to private schools and give them all of the advantages wealth has to offer. But poor and working class whites were faced with a social demotion. It was their kids who might be bused across town, and forced to compete for the first time with a new group of people they had long believed to be inferior for decent jobs and educational opportunities.[33] Affirmative action, busing, and desegregation created an understandable feeling of vulnerability, fear, and anxiety among a group already struggling for survival.

Republican party strategists found that thinly veiled promises to "get tough" on "them"—the racially defined others—could be highly successful in persuading poor and working class whites to defect from the Democratic New Deal Coalition and join the Republican Party.[34] H. R. Haldeman, President Richard Nixon's former Chief of Staff, reportedly summed up the strategy: "[T]he whole problem is really the blacks. The key is to devise a system that recognizes this while not appearing to."[35]

A couple years after the drug war was announced, crack cocaine hit the streets of inner-city communities.[36] The Reagan administration seized on this development with glee, hiring staff who were responsible for publicizing inner-city crack babies, crack mothers, the so-called "crack whores," and drug-related violence. The goal was to make inner-city crack abuse and violence a media sensation that, it was hoped, would bolster public support for the drug war and would lead Congress to devote millions of dollars in additional funding to it.[37]

The plan worked like a charm. For more than a decade, black drug dealers and users became regulars in newspaper stories and saturated the evening TV news—forever changing our conception of who the drug users and dealers are.[38] Once the enemy in the war was racially defined, a wave of punitiveness took over. Congress and state legislatures nationwide devoted billions of dollars to the drug war and passed harsh mandatory minimum sentences for drug crimes—sentences longer than murderers receive in many countries. Many black politicians joined the "get tough" bandwagon, apparently oblivious to their complicity with the emergence of a system of social control that would, in less than two decades, become unprecedented in world history.[39]

Almost immediately, Democrats began competing with Republicans to prove that they could be even tougher on "them."[40] In President Bill Clinton's boastful words, "I can be nicked on a lot, but no one can say I'm soft on crime."[41] The facts bear him out. Clinton's "'tough on crime' policies resulted in the largest increases in federal and state prison inmates of any president in American history."[42] But Clinton was not satisfied with exploding prison populations. In an effort to appeal to the "white swing voters," he and the so-called "new Democrats" championed legislation banning drug felons from public housing (no matter how minor the offense) and denying them basic public benefits, including food stamps, for life.[43] Discrimination in virtually every aspect of political, economic, and social life is now perfectly legal, once you're labeled a felon.

All of this has been justified on the grounds that getting brutally tough on "them" is the only way to root out violent offenders or drug kingpins. The media images of violence in ghetto communities—particularly when crack first hit the street—led many to believe that the drug war was focused on the most serious offenders. Yet nothing could be further from the truth. Federal funding has flowed to those state and local law enforcement agencies that increase dramatically the volume of drug arrests, not the agencies most successful in bringing down the bosses. What has been rewarded in this war is sheer numbers—the sheer volume of drug arrests.[44] To make matters worse, federal drug forfeiture laws allow state and local law enforcement agencies to keep for their own use 80% of the cash, cars, and homes seized from drug suspects, thus granting law enforcement a direct monetary interest in the profitability of the drug market itself.[45]

The results are predictable. People of color have been rounded up en masse for relatively minor, non-violent drug offenses. In 2005, for example, four out of five drug arrests were for possession, only one out of five for sales.[46] Most people in state prison for drug offenses have no history of violence or even of significant selling activity.[47] In fact, during the 1990s—the period of the most dramatic expansion of the drug war—nearly 80% of the increase in drug arrests was for marijuana possession, a drug generally considered less harmful than alcohol or tobacco and at least as prevalent in middle-class white communities as in the inner city.[48]

In this way, a new racial undercaste has been created in an astonishingly short period of time. Millions of people of color are now saddled with criminal records and legally denied the very rights that were supposedly won in the Civil Rights Movement.

The U.S. Supreme Court, for its part, has mostly turned a blind eye to race discrimination in the criminal justice system. The Court has closed the courthouse doors to claims of racial bias at every stage of the criminal justice process from stops and searches to plea bargaining and sentencing.[49] Law enforcement officials are largely free to discriminate on the basis of race today, so long as no one admits it. That's the key. In *McCleskey v. Kemp* and *United States v. Armstrong,* the Supreme Court made clear that only evidence of conscious, intentional racial bias—the sort of bias that is nearly impossible to prove these days in the absence of an admission—is deemed sufficient.[50] No matter how impressive the statistical evidence, no matter how severe the racial disparities and racial impacts might be, the Supreme Court is not interested. The Court has, as a practical matter, closed the door to claims of racial bias in the criminal justice system. It has immunized the new caste system from judicial scrutiny for racial bias, much as it once rallied to legitimate and protect slavery and Jim Crow.

In my experience, those who have been incarcerated have little difficulty recognizing the parallels between mass incarceration and Jim Crow. Many former prisoners have told me, "It's slavery on the inside; Jim Crow when you get out." Prisoners are often forced to work for little or no pay. Once released, they are denied basic civil and human rights until they die. They are treated as though they possess an incurable defect, a shameful trait that can never be fully eradicated or redeemed. In the words of one woman who is currently incarcerated:

> When I leave here it will be very difficult for me in the sense that I'm a felon. That I will always be a felon . . . it will affect my job, it will affect my education . . . custody [of my children], it can affect child support, it can affect everywhere—family, friends, housing. . . . People that are convicted of drug crimes can't even get housing anymore. . . . Yes, I did my prison time. How long are you going to punish me as a result of it?[51]

Willie Johnson, a forty-three year old African American man recently released from prison in Ohio, explained it this way:

> My felony conviction has been like a mental punishment, because of all the obstacles. . . . Every time I go to put in a [job] application—I have had three companies hire me and tell me to come to work the next day. But then the day before they will call me and tell me don't come in—because you have a felony. And that is what is devastating because you think you are about to go to work and they call you and say because of your felony we can't hire [you]. I have run into this at least a dozen times. Two times I got very depressed and sad because I couldn't take care of myself as a man. It was like I wanted to give up—because in society nobody wants to give us a helping hand.[52]

Not surprisingly, for many trapped in the undercaste, the hurt and depression gives way to anger. A black minister in Waterloo, Mississippi, put it this way:

> "Felony" is the new N-word. They don't have to call you a nigger anymore. They just say you're a felon. In every ghetto you see alarming numbers of young men with felony convictions. Once you have that felony stamp, your hope of employment, for any kind of integration into society, it begins to fade out. Today's lynching is a felony charge. Today's lynching is incarceration. Today's lynch mobs are professionals. They have a badge; they have a law degree. A felony is a modern way of saying, "I'm going to hang you up and burn you." Once you get that *F,* you're on fire.[53]

What is painfully obvious to many trapped within the system, remains largely invisible to those of us who have decent jobs and zoom around on freeways, passing by the virtual and literal prisons in which members of the undercaste live.

None of this is to say, of course, that mass incarceration and Jim Crow are the "same." There are significant differences between mass incarceration and earlier forms of racial control, to be sure—many of which are described in some detail in my book. Just as there were vast differences between slavery and Jim Crow, there are important differences between Jim Crow and mass incarceration. Yet all three (slavery, Jim Crow, and mass incarceration) have operated as tightly networked systems of laws, policies, customs, and institutions that operate collectively to ensure the subordinate status of a group defined largely by race. When we step back and view the system of mass incarceration as a whole, there is a profound sense of deja vu. There is a familiar stigma and shame. There is an elaborate system of control, complete with political disenfranchisement and legalized discrimination in every major realm of economic and social life. And there is the production of racial meaning and racial boundaries. Just consider a few of the rules, laws, and policies that apply to people branded felons today and ask yourself if they remind you of a bygone era:

- Denial of the right to vote. Forty-eight states and the District of Columbia deny prisoners the right to vote.[54] That, of course, is just the tip of the iceberg. Even after the term of punishment expires, states are free to deny people who have been labeled felons the right to vote for a period of years or their entire lives. In a few states, one in four black men have been permanently disenfranchised.[55] Nationwide, nearly one in seven black men are either temporarily or permanently disenfranchised as a result of felon disenfranchisement laws.[56]

- Exclusion from jury service. One hallmark of Jim Crow was the systematic exclusion of blacks from juries. Today, those labeled felons are automatically excluded from juries, and to make matters worse, people are routinely excluded from juries if they "have had negative experiences with law enforcement."[57] Good luck finding a person of color in a ghetto community today who has not yet had a negative experience with law enforcement. The all-white jury is no longer a thing of the past in many regions of the country, in part, because so many African Americans have been labeled felons and excluded from juries.

- Employment discrimination. Employment discrimination against felons is deemed legal and absolutely routine.[58] Regardless of whether your felony occurred three months ago or thirty-five years ago, for the rest of your life you're required to check that box on employment applications asking the dreaded question: "Have you ever been convicted of a felony?" In one survey, about 70% of employers said they would not hire a drug felon convicted for sales or possession.[59] Most states also deny a wide range of professional licenses to people labeled felons.[60] In some states, you can't even get license to be a barber if you're a felon.[61]

- Housing discrimination. Housing discrimination is perfectly legal. Public housing projects as well as private landlords are free to discriminate against criminals. In fact, those labeled felons may be barred from public housing for five years or more and legally discriminated against for the rest of their lives.[62] These laws make it difficult for former prisoners to find shelter, a basic human right.

- Public benefits. Discrimination is legal against those who have been labeled felons in public benefits. In fact, federal law renders drug offenders ineligible for food stamps for the rest of their lives.[63] Fortunately, some states have opted out of the federal ban, but it remains the case that thousands of people, including pregnant women and people with HIV/AIDS, are denied even food stamps, simply because they were once caught with drugs.[64]

- Fees and fines. What do we expect people convicted of drug felonies to do? Even if they manage to escape jail time and get nothing more than probation, they will be discriminated against in employment, denied public housing, locked out of the private housing market, and possibly denied even food stamps. Apparently what we expect them to do is to pay hundreds or thousands of dollars in fees, fines, court costs, and accumulated back child support—frequently as a condition of probation or parole.[65] And here's the kicker: Even if a former prisoner manages to get a job, up to 100% of their wages can be garnished to pay for the costs of their imprisonment, court processing fees, and back payments in child support.[66] Yes, 100% of their wages can be garnished.

What, realistically, do we expect these folks to do? What is this system designed to do? It seems designed to send them right back to prison, which is what in fact happens most of the time. About 70% of released prisoners are rearrested within three years, and the majority of those who return to prison do so within a matter of months, because the barriers to mere survival on the outside are so immense.[67]

Remarkably, as bad as all the formal barriers to political and economic inclusion are, many formerly incarcerated people tell me that is not the worst of it. The worst is the stigma that follows you for the rest of your life. It is not just the denial of the job, but the look that crosses an employer's face when he sees the "box" has been checked. It is not just the denial of public housing, but the shame of being a grown man having to ask your grandma to sleep in her basement at night. The shame associated with criminality can be so intense that people routinely try to "pass."

During the Jim Crow era, light-skinned blacks often tried to pass as white in order to avoid the stigma, shame, and discrimination associated with their race. Today, people labeled criminals lie not only to employers and housing officials, but also to their friends, acquaintances and family members. Children of prisoners lie to friends and relatives saying, "I don't know where my daddy is." Grown men who have been released from prison for years still glance down and look away when asked who they will vote for on election day, ashamed to admit they can't vote. They try to "pass" to avoid the stigma and discrimination associated with the new caste system.

An excellent ethnographic study conducted in Washington, D.C., found that even in neighborhoods hardest hit by mass incarceration—places where nearly every house has a family member behind bars or recently released from prison—people rarely "come out" fully about their own criminal history or that of their loved ones, even when speaking with relatives, friends and neighbors.[68] An eerie silence about this new system of control has befallen us, one rooted for some in shame, and for others in denial.

Yes, denial. There are two major reasons, I believe, that so many of us are in denial about the existence of racial caste in America. The first is traceable to a profound misunderstanding regarding how racial oppression actually works. If someone were to visit the United States from another country (or another planet) and ask: "Is the U.S. criminal justice system some kind of tool of racial control?," most Americans would swiftly deny it. Numerous reasons would leap to mind why that could not possibly be the case. The visitor would be told that crime rates, black culture, or bad schools were to blame. "The system is not run by a bunch of racists," the apologist would explain. They would say, "It is run by people who are trying to fight crime." Because mass incarceration is officially colorblind, and because most people today do not think of themselves as racist, it seems inconceivable that the system could function much like a racial caste system.

But more than forty-five years ago, Martin Luther King Jr. warned of the danger of precisely this kind of thinking. He insisted that blindness and indifference to racial groups is actually more important than racial hostility to the creation and maintenance of systems of racial control. Those who supported slavery and Jim Crow, he argued, typically were not bad or evil people; they were just blind.[69] Many segregationists were kind to their black shoe shiners and maids and genuinely wished them well. Even the Justices who decided the infamous Dred Scott case, which ruled "that the Negro had no rights which the white man was bound to respect," were not wicked men, he said.[70] On the whole, they were decent and dedicated men. But, he hastened to add, "They were victims of spiritual and intellectual blindness. They knew not what they did. The whole system of slavery was largely perpetuated by sincere though spiritually ignorant persons."[71]

The same is true today. People of good will—and bad—have been unwilling to see black and brown men, in their humanness, as entitled to the same care, compassion, and concern that would be extended to one's friends, neighbors, or loved ones.

After all, who among us would want a loved one struggling with drug abuse to be put in a cage, labeled a felon, and then subjected to a lifetime of discrimination, scorn and social exclusion? Most Americans would not wish that fate on anyone they cared about. But whom do we care about? In America, the answer to that question is still linked to race. Dr. King recognized that it was this indifference to the plight of African Americans that supported the institutions of slavery and Jim Crow. And this callous racial indifference supports mass incarceration today.

Another reason that we remain in deep denial is that we, as a nation, have a false picture of our racial reality. Prisoners are literally erased from the nation's economic picture. Unemployment and poverty statistics do not include people behind bars. In fact, standard reports underestimate the true jobless rates for less educated black men by as much as 24 percentage points.[72] During the much heralded economic boom of the 1990s—the Clinton years—African American men were the only group to experience a steep increase in real joblessness, a development directly traceable to the increase in the penal population.[73] During the 1990s—the best of times for the rest of America— the true jobless rates for non-college black men was a staggering 42%.[74]

Affirmative action, though, has put a happy face on this racial reality. Seeing black people graduate from Harvard and Yale and become CEOs or corporate lawyers—not to mention President of the United States—causes us all to marvel at what a long way we have come. As recent data shows, though, much of black progress is a myth.[75] In many respects, if you take into account prisoners, African Americans as a group are doing no better than they were when King was assassinated and uprisings swept inner cities across America. And that is with affirmative action!

When we pull back the curtain and take a look at what our so-called colorblind society creates without affirmative action, we see a familiar social, political and economic structure—the structure of racial caste. And the entry into this new caste system can be found at the prison gate.

So where do we go from here? What can be done to dismantle this new system of control? I spend the last chapter exploring this question in some depth. What is clear, I think, is that those of us in the civil rights community have allowed a human rights nightmare to occur on our watch.

While many of us have been fighting for affirmative action or clinging to the perceived gains of the Civil Rights Movement, millions of people have been rounded up en masse, locked in cages, and then released into a parallel social universe in which they can be discriminated against for the rest of their lives—denied the very rights our parents and grandparents fought for and some died for. The clock has been turned back on racial progress in America, yet scarcely anyone seems to notice.

What is needed, I believe, is a broad-based social movement, one that rivals in size, scope, depth, and courage the movement that was begun in the 1960s and left unfinished. It must be a multiracial, multi-ethnic movement that includes poor and working class whites—a group that has consistently been pit against poor people of color, triggering the rise of successive new systems of control.

The drug war was born with black folks in mind, but it is a hungry beast; it has caused incalculable suffering in communities of all colors. A white youth given a prison sentence rather than the drug treatment he desperately needs is suffering because of a drug war born of racial anxieties and resentments raging long before he was born. In California and throughout the Southwest, Latinos are a primary target of the drug war. And now that Wall Street executives have found they can profit from prisons, private prison companies have lobbied for punitive laws aimed at suspected illegal immigrants, in the hopes of building new immigration detention centers—the newest market for caging human beings.[76] The impulse to exploit racial fears and biases for political and economic gain is leading to a prison-building boom aimed at immigrants. If we are going to succeed in bringing this brutal system to an end, we must map the linkages between the suffering of African Americans in the drug war to the experiences of other oppressed and marginalized groups. We must connect the dots. This movement must be multi-racial and multi-ethnic, and it must have a keen sense of the racial history and racial dynamics that brought us to this moment in time.

But before this movement can even get underway, a great awakening is required. We must awaken from our colorblind slumber to the realities of race in America. And we must be willing to embrace those labeled criminals—not necessarily their behavior, but them—their humanness. For it has been the refusal and failure to fully acknowledge the humanity and dignity of *all* persons that has formed the sturdy foundation of all caste systems.

It is our task, I firmly believe, to end not just mass incarceration, but the history and cycle of caste in America.

Notes

1. This article is adapted from two speeches delivered by Professor Michelle Alexander, one at the Zocolo Public Square in Los Angeles on March 17, 2010, and another at an authors' symposium sponsored by the National Association of Criminal Defense Lawyers and the Open Society Institute on October 6, 2010.

2. Michelle Alexander, 2010, *The New Jim Crow: Mass Incarceration in the Age of Colorblindness*, 2.

3. One in eleven black adults was under correctional supervision at year end 2007, or approximately 2.4 million people. Pew Ctr. on the States, 2009, *One in 31: The Long Reach of American Corrections* (March), 5, Pew Charitable Trusts, available at http://www.pewstates.org/uploadedFiles/PSPP_1in31_report_FINAL_WEB_3-26-09.pdf online. According to the 1850 Census, approximately 1.7 million adults (ages 15 and older) were slaves. U.S. Census Bureau, 1853, *The Seventh Census of the United States: 1850*, 9, available at http://www2.census.gov/prod2/decennial/documents/1850a-01.pdf online; see also University of Virginia Library, *Historical Census Browser*, University of Virginia Library, http://mapserver.lib.virginia.edu/php/state.php (last visited July 17, 2011).

4. Contribution by Pamela S. Karlan, 2008, "Forum: Pamela S. Karlan," in Glenn C. Loury, *Race, Incarceration and American Values*, 41, 42.

5. Paul Street, 2002, *The Vicious Circle: Race, Prison, Jobs, and Community in Chicago, Illinois, and the Nation*, Chicago Urban League, 4.

6. See, e.g., Reva Siegel, 1997, "Why Equal Protection No Longer Protects: The Evolving Forms of Status-Enforcing Action," *Stan. L. Rev.* 49: 1111, 1113, 1146 (dubbing the process by which white

privilege is maintained, through the rules and rhetoric change, "preservation through transformation").

7. Douglas A. Blackmon, 2008, *Slavery by Another Name: The Re-Enslavement of Black Americans from the Civil War to World War II*; David M. Oshinsky, 1996, *Worse Than Slavery: Parchman Farm and the Ordeal of Jim Crow Justice*.

8. See Blackmon, *Slavery by Another Name*.

9. *Key Facts at a Glance: Correctional Populations*, Bureau of Justice Statistics (updated Dec. 16, 2010), available at http://bjs.ojp.usdoj.gov/content/glance/tables/corr2tab.cfm online; John Irwin, et al., 1999, *America's One Million Nonviolent Prisoners*, Justice Policy Institute, available at http://www.hawaii.edu/hivandaids/America_s_One_Million_Nonviolent_Prisoners.pdf online; Robert Longley, 2003, *U.S. Prison Population Tops 2 Million*, U.S. Government Information, http://usgovinfo.about.com/cs/censusstatistic/a/aaprisonpop.htm

10. Pew Ctr. on the States, 2008, *One in 100: Behind Bars in America 2008*, at 5 (February), http://www.pewstates.org/uploadedFiles/One%20in%20100.pdf

11. According to data provided by the Sentencing Project, in 1972, the total rate of incarceration (prison and jail) was approximately 160 per 100,000. See Mauer, *supra* note 9, at 17. Today, it is about 750 per 100,000. Lauren E. Glaze, 2010, *Correctional Populations in the United States, 2009*, Bureau of Justice Statistics, U.S. Dep't of Justice, 2, available at http://bjs.ojp.usdoj.gov/content/pub/pdf/cpus09.pdf online. A reduction of 79% would be needed to get back to the 160 figure—itself a fairly high number when judged by international standards.

12. According to a report released by the U.S. Department of Justice's Bureau of Statistics in 2006, the U.S. spent a record $185 billion for police protection, detention, judicial, and legal activities in 2003. Adjusting for inflation, these figures reflect a tripling of justice expenditures since 1982. The justice system employed almost 2.4 million people in 2003—58% of them at the local level and 31% at the state level. If four out of five people were released from prisons, far more than a million people could lose their jobs. Kristen A. Hughes, 2006, *Justice Expenditure and Employment in the United States, 2003*, Bureau

of Justice Statistics, U.S. Dep't of Justice, at 1, available at http://bjs.ojp.usdoj.gov/content/pub/pdf/jeeus03.pdf

13. See Loïc Wacquant, 2010, "Class, Race & Hyperincarceration in Revanchist America," *Daedalus* 139 (Summer): 74.

14. Donald Braman, 2004, *Doing Time on the Outside: Incarceration and Family Life in Urban America*, 3 (citing D.C. Department of Corrections 2000).

15. Eric Lotke and Jason Ziedenberg, 2005, *Tipping Point: Maryland's Overuse of Incarceration and the Impact on Community Safety* (Justice Policy Institute), 3 (reporting that in Baltimore the majority of young African American men are currently under correctional supervision). Nationwide, one in three black men will go to prison during their lifetime. See Thomas P. Boncszar, 2003, *Prevalence of Imprisonment in the U.S. Population, 1974–2001* (Bureau of Justice Statistics, U.S. Dep't of Justice), available at http://bjs.ojp.usdoj.gov/content/pub/pdf/piusp01.pdf

16. Bruce Western, 2006, *Punishment and Inequality in America* (Figure 2.1), 30.

17. See, e.g., Marc Mauer, 2006, *Race to Incarcerate*, 2nd ed., 23–35, 92–112; Michael Tonry, 2004, *Thinking About Crime: Sense and Sensibility in American Penal Culture*, 14.

18. See, e.g., Western, *Punishment and Inequality*, 35, 43.

19. Mauer, *Race to Incarcerate*, 33.

20. Marc Mauer and Ryan S. King, 2007, *A 25-Year Quagmire: The War on Drugs and Its Impact on American Society* (September), 2, 4, available at http://www.sentencingproject.org/doc/publications/dp_25yearquagmire.pdf

21. The overwhelming majority of those arrested and incarcerated for drug crimes during the past few decades have been black and brown. When the War on Drugs gained full steam in the mid-1980s, prison admissions for African Americans "skyrocketed, nearly quadrupling in three years, then increasing steadily until it reached in 2000 a level more than twenty-six times the level in 1983."
Jeremy Travis, 2002, *But They All Come Back: Facing the Challenges of Prison Reentry*, 28; see, e.g., U.S. Dep't of Health and Human Servs., Substance Abuse and Mental Health Services Administration (SAMHSA), 2001, *Summary of Findings from the 2000 National Household Survey on Drug Abuse*, 21, available at http://oas.samhsa.gov/NHSDA/2kNHSDA/chapter2.htm (reporting that 6.4 percent of whites, 6.4 percent of blacks, and 5.3 percent of Hispanics were current illegal drug users in 2000); SAMHSA, 2003, *Results from the 2002 National Survey on Drug Use and Health: National Findings*, 16, available at http://oas.samhsa.gov/nsduh/reports.htm#2k2 (revealing nearly identical rates of illegal drug use among whites and blacks, only a single percentage point between them); SAMHSA, 2003, *Results from the 2007 National Survey on Drug Use and Health: National Findings*, 25, available at http://oas.samhsa.gov/nsduh/reports.htm#2k2 (showing essentially the same findings).

22. See generally *supra*, note 21.

23. A national survey conducted in 1995 illustrated the profound and pervasive racial stereotypes associated with drug crime. Survey respondents were asked: "Would you close your eyes for a second, envision a drug user, and describe that person to me?" 95% of respondents pictured a black drug user, while only 5% imagined all other racial groups combined. Betsy Watson Burston, Dionne Jones, and Pat Robinson-Saunders, 1995, "Drug Use and African Americans: Myth Versus Reality," *J. Alcohol & Drug Educ.* 40 (Winter): 19, 20.

24. Researchers have found that drug users are most likely to report using as a main source of drugs someone who is of their own racial or ethnic background. See, e.g., K. Jack Riley, 1997, *Crack, Powder Cocaine, and Heroin: Drug Purchase and Use Patterns in Six U.S. Cities* (Office of Nat'l Drug Control Policy, Nat'l Inst. of Justice), 1; Patricia Davis and Pierre Thomas, 1997, "In Affluent Suburbs, Young Users and Sellers Abound," *Washington Post* (Dec. 14), A20.

25. The National Household Survey on Drug Abuse reported in 2000 that white youth aged 12–17 were more likely to have used and sold illegal drugs than African American youth. Neelum Arya and Ian Augarten, 2003, Critical "Condition: African-American Youth in The Justice System," table 5 (Campaign for Youth Justice), 16, 19, available at http://www.campaignforyouthjustice.org/documents/AfricanAmericanBrief.pdf online. Another study published that year revealed that white students use cocaine and heroin

at significantly higher rates than black students, while nearly identical percentages of black and white students report using marijuana. Lloyd D. Johnston et al., 2000, *National Survey Results on Drug Use, 1975–1999*, vol. 1, Secondary School Units (Nat'l Inst. on Drug Abuse, Monitoring the Future), 146, 197, available at http://monitoringthe future.org/pubs/monographs/mtf-vol1_1999.pdf online. More recent studies continue to suggest higher rates of illegal drug use and sales by white youth. See, e.g., Howard N. Snyder and Melissa Sickmund, 2006, *Juvenile Offenders and Victims: 2006 National Report* (U.S. Dep't of Justice, Nat'l Ctr. for Juvenile Justice), 81, available at http://www.ojjdp.gov/ojstatbb/nr2006/downloads/NR2006.pdf (reporting that white youth are more likely than black youth to engage in illegal drug sales); Lloyd D. Johnston et al., 2007, *National Survey Results on Drug Use, 1975–2006*, vol. II: College Students and Adults Ages 19–45 (Nat'l Inst. on Drug Abuse, Monitoring the Future), 28, available at http://www.monitoringthefuture.org/pubs/monographs/vol2_2006.pdf (stating "African-American 12th graders have consistently shown lower usage rates than White 12th graders for most drugs, both licit and illicit").

26. Although the majority of illegal drug users and dealers nationwide are white, roughly three-fourths of all people imprisoned for drug offenses since the War on Drugs began have been African American or Latino. Marc Mauer and Ryan S. King, 2004, *The Sentencing Project, Schools and Prisons: Fifty Years After* Brown v. Board of Education, 3. In recent years, rates of black imprisonment for drug offenses have dipped somewhat—declining approximately 22% from their zenith in the mid-1990s—but it remains the case that African Americans are incarcerated at grossly disproportionate rates throughout the United States. Marc Mauer, 2009, *The Sentencing Project: The Changing Racial Dynamics of the War on Drugs*, 5, available at http://www.sentencingproject.org/doc/dp_raceanddrugs.pdf

27. "Punishment and Prejudice: Racial Disparities in the War on Drugs," 2000, *Human Rights Watch* 12 (2): 19.

28. According to this study, the entire increase in the prison population between 1980 and 2001 can be explained by sentencing policy changes, not increases in crime. Mauer, *Race to Incarcerate*, 33, 36–38 (citing Warren Young and Mark Brown, 1993, "Cross-national Comparisons of Imprisonment," in *Crime and Justice: A Review of Research* 27: 33, 1–49.

29. *Unfairness in Federal Cocaine Sentencing: Is it Time to Crack the 100 to 1 Disparity?* 2009, hearing on H.R. 1459, H.R. 1466, H.R. 265, H.R. 2178 and H.R. 18 Before the H. Subcomm. On Crime, Terrorism, and Homeland Security of the H. Comm. On the Judiciary, 111th Cong. 2 (testimony of Marc Mauer, Executive Director, Sentencing Project).

30. Pew Ctr. on the States, *One in 31*, 4.

31. President Richard Nixon was the first to coin the term a "war on drugs," but the term proved largely rhetorical as he declared illegal drugs "public enemy number one" without proposing dramatic shifts in public policy. President Reagan converted the rhetorical war into a literal one, when he officially announced the War on Drugs in 1982. At the time, less than 2 percent of the American public viewed drugs as the most important issue facing the nation. See Katherine Beckett, 1997, *Making Crime Pay: Law and Order in Contemporary American Politics* 62: 163; see also Julian V. Roberts, 1992, "Public Opinion, Crime, and Criminal Justice," in *Crime and Justice: A Review of Research* 16: 99, 129–37.

32. See Beckett, *Making Crime Pay*, 31; Vesla M. Weaver, 2007, "Frontlash: Race and the Development of Punitive Crime Policy," 21 *Stud. in Am. Pol. Dev.* 21 (Fall): 230, 233, 237. See generally Robert Perkinson, 2010, *Texas Tough: The Rise of America's Prison Empire* (offering a compelling account of how the backlash against the Civil Rights Movement gave rise to mass incarceration in Texas, and, ultimately, the nation).

33. During the 1950s, the majority of Southern whites were better off than Southern blacks, but they were not affluent or well educated by any means; they were semiliterate (with less than twelve years of schooling) and typically quite poor. Only a tiny minority of whites was affluent and well educated. They stood far apart from the rest of whites and virtually all blacks. C. Arnold Anderson, 1955, "Inequalities in Schooling in the South," *Am. J. on Sociology* 60 (May): 547, 553, 557; Lani Guinier, 2004, "From Racial Liberalism to Racial

Literacy: *Brown v. Board of Education* and the Interest-Divergence Dilemma," *J. Amer. Hist.* 91 (June): 92, 103. What lower class whites did have was what W.E.B. Du Bois described as "the public and psychological wage" paid to white workers, who depended on their status and privileges as whites to compensate for their low pay and harsh working conditions. W. E. B. DuBois, 1935, "Black Reconstruction in America: An Essay Toward a History of the Part Which Black Folks Played in the Attempt to Reconstruct Democracy in America, 1860–1880," at 700. Because the Southern white elite had succeeded in persuading all whites to think in racial rather than class terms, it is hardly surprising that poor and working class whites experienced desegregation as a net loss. Derrick A. Bell, Jr., 1980, "*Brown v. Board of Education* and the Interest-Convergence Dilemma," 93 *Harv. L. Rev.* 93: 518, 525.

34. See Alexander, *The New Jim Crow*, 43–49; see, e.g., Patrick J. Buchanan, 1973 *The New Majority: President Nixon at Mid-Passage*, 60, 62; Kevin P. Phillips, 1969, *The Emerging Republican Majority*, 467–68.

35. Willard M. Oliver, 2003, *The Law & Order Presidency*, 126–27.

36. *See* Craig Reinarman and Harry G. Levine, 1995, "The Crack Attack: America's Latest Drug Scare, 1986–1992," in *Images of Issues: Typifying Contemporary Social Problems*, edited by Joel Best.

37. Reinarman and Levine, "The Crack Attack," 170–71 ("Crack was a godsend to the Right. . . . It could not have appeared at a more politically opportune moment").

38. Reinarman and Levine, "The Crack Attack"; Doris Marie Provine, 2007, *Unequal Under Law: Race in the War on Drugs*, 88.

39. Provine, *Unequal Under Law*, 117. Today the black community is divided in many respects about how best to understand and respond to mass incarceration, with some academics (and celebrities) arguing that poor education and cultural traits explain the millions of black men rotating in and out of correctional control, and others emphasizing the role of racial bias and structural inequality. See, e.g., Demico Boothe, 2007, *Why Are So Many Black Men in Prison?* (emphasizing the discriminatory nature of the prison system); Bill Cosby and Alvin F. Poussaint,

2007, *Come on People: On the Path from Victims to Victors* (arguing that poor education, as well as lack of personal responsibility and discipline, largely explain the status of black men today). The fact that many African Americans endorse aspects of the current caste system, and insist that the problems of the urban poor can be best explained by their behavior, culture, lack of education, and attitude, does not, in any meaningful way, distinguish mass incarceration from its predecessors. To the contrary, these attitudes and arguments have their roots in the struggles to end slavery and Jim Crow. As numerous scholars have observed, many black advocates during the Jim Crow era embraced a "politics of respectability" and an "uplift ideology" that led them to distance themselves from the urban poor, and to blame the least educated members of the urban poor for their own condition. See, e.g., Karen Ferguson, 2002, *Black Politics in New Deal Atlanta*, 5–11. In fact, some of the most discriminatory federal programs of the New Deal era, including the slum clearance program, received strong support from African American bureaucrats and reformers. Ferguson, *Black Politics*, 13.

40. Alexander, *The New Jim Crow*, 55–56; Beckett, *Making Crime Pay*, 61.

41. Michael Kramer, 1994, "The Political Interest Frying Them Isn't the Answer," *Time* (March 14), 32, available at http://www.time.com/time/magazine/article/0,9171,980318,00.html

42. "Clinton Crime Agenda Ignores Proven Methods for Reducing Crime," 2008, Press Release, Justice Policy Institute, April 14 (on file with the *Ohio State Journal of Criminal Law.*

43. See Alexander, *The New Jim Crow*, 56.

44. See Alexander, *The New Jim Crow*, 71–73; see Radley Balko, 2006, *Overkill: The Rise of Paramilitary Police Raids in America* (Cato Inst.), 14–15.

45. See Eric Blumenson and Eva Nilsen, 1998, "Policing for Profit: The Drug War's Hidden Economic Agenda," *U. Chi. L. Rev.* 65: 35, 44–45, 51.

46. Mauer and King, *A 25-Year Quagmire*, 3.

47. Mauer and King, *A 25-Year Quagmire*, 2.

48. Alexander, *The New Jim Crow*, 59; Ryan S. King and Marc Mauer, 2005, *The Sentencing Project, The War on Marijuana: The Transformation of the War on Drugs in the 1990s*, 1.

49. Alexander, *The New Jim Crow*, 106–16.

50. See *United States v. Armstrong*, 1996, 517 U.S. 456; *McCleskey v. Kemp*, 1987, 481 U.S. 279.

51. Jeff Manza and Christopher Uggen, 2006, *Locked Out: Felon Disenfranchisement and American Democracy*, 152.

52. Interview by Guylando A. M. Moreno with Willie Thompson, 2005, in Cincinnati, Ohio (March). See also Alexander, *The New Jim Crow*, 158–59.

53. Sasha Abramsky, 2006, *Conned: How Millions Went to Prison, Lost the Vote, and Helped Send George W. Bush to the White House*, 140.

54. American Civil Liberties Union, 2006, *Out of Step with the World: An Analysis of Felony Disenfranchisement in the U.S. and Other Democracies*, 3; The Sentencing Project, 2011, *Felony Disenfranchisement Laws in the United States*, 1.

55. Jamie Fellner and Marc Mauer, 1998, *Losing the Vote: The Impact of Felony Disenfranchisement Laws in the United States*, The Sentencing Project, 1, available at http://www.sentencingproject.org/doc/File/FVR/fd_losingthevote.pdf

56. Fellner and Mauer, *Losing the Vote*. These figures may understate the impact of felony disenfranchisement, because they do not take into account the millions of formerly incarcerated people who cannot vote in states that require people convicted of felonies to pay fines or fees before their voting rights can be restored. As legal scholar Pam Karlan has observed, "felony disenfranchisement has decimated the potential black electorate." Loury, *Race, Incarceration*, 48.

57. See Alexander, *The New Jim Crow*, 116–20 (discussing the discriminatory use of preemptory strikes against African American jurors).

58. See Devah Pager, 2007, *Marked: Race, Crime and Finding Work in an Era of Mass Incarceration*, 33; see also Legal Action Ctr., 2004, *After Prison: Roadblocks to Reentry*, 10.

59. Employers Grp. Research Servs., 2002, *Employment of Ex-Offenders: A Survey of Employers' Policies and Practices*, 6; Harry J. Holzer, Steven Raphael, and Michael A. Stoll, 2004, "Will Employers Hire Former Offenders?: Employer Preferences, Background Checks, and Their Determinants," in *Imprisoning America: The Social Effects of Mass Incarceration*, edited by Mary Pattillo, et al., 205, 209.

60. Legal Action Ctr., *After Prison*, 10.

61. Legal Action Ctr., *After Prison*; see *Ohio Rev. Code Ann.* § 4709.13 (West, Westlaw through 1991–1992 Legis. Sess.).

62. See Human Rights Watch, 2004, "No Second Chance: People with Criminal Records Denied Access to Public Housing," 33.

63. See Temporary Assistance for Needy Family Program (TANF), 2006, 21 U.S.C. § 862a(a)(2). See generally Legal Action Center, *Opting out of Federal Ban on Food Stamps and TANF*, at http://www.lac.org/toolkits/TANF/TANF.htm; Patricia Allard, 2002 *Life Sentences: Denying Welfare Benefits To Women Convicted Of Drug Offenses*, The Sentencing Project, available at http://www.sentencingproject.org/doc/publications/women_lifesentences.pdf

64. "Black Men's Jail Time Hits Entire Communities," 2010, *NPR Talk of the Nation* (August 23), http://www.npr.org/templates/story/story.php?storyId=129379700

65. Rachel L. McLean and Michael D. Thompson, 2007, "Repaying Debts," Council of State Gov'ts Justice Ctr., 7–8.

66. McLean and Thompson, "Repaying Debts," 22. See also "Out of Prison and Deep in Debt," 2007, *N.Y. Times* (October 6), A18, available at http://www.nytimes.com/2007/10/06/opinion/06sat1.html. ("People caught in this impossible predicament are less likely to seek regular employment, making them even more susceptible to criminal relapse.")

67. See Jeremy Travis, 2005, *But They All Come Back: Facing the Challenges of Prisoner Reentry*, 94.

68. See Braman, *Doing Time*, 219–20.

69. Martin Luther King, Jr., 1963, *Strength to Love*, 45 (Fortress Press, 1981).

70. King, Jr., *Strength to Love*.

71. King, Jr., *Strength to Love*.

72. Western, *Punishment and Inequality*, 91–92.

73. See Robert W. Fairlie and William A. Sundstrom, 1999 "The Emergence, Persistence, and Recent Widening of the Racial Unemployment Gap," *Indus. & Lab. Rel. Rev.* 52: 252, 257, Tables 2–3; see also Bruce Western, 2005, "Black-White Wage Inequality, Employment Rates, and Incarceration," *Am. J. Soc.* 111: 553, 557 Table 2.

74. Western, *Punishment and Inequality*, 97.

75. See The Eisenhower Foundation, 2008, *What Together We Can Do: A Forty Year Update of the*

National Advisory Commission on Civil Disorders: Preliminary Findings, available at http://www.eisenhowerfoundation.org/docs/Kerner%2040%20Year%20Update,%20Executive%20Summary.pdf

76. Laura Sullivan, 2010, "Prison Economics Help Drive Arizona Immigration Law," *National Public Radio* (October 28), http://www.npr.org/templates/story/story.php?storyId=130833741

For Discussion

1. Alexander describes how the "felon identity" remains long after one is released from prison. Discuss the restrictions in voting, social welfare and public benefits, housing, and a host of other domains that affect people who have served a prison sentence.
2. Consider the wider impact of mass incarceration on children and communities.

36

Drug Courts Are Not the Answer

Toward a Health-Centered Approach to Drug Use

DRUG POLICY ALLIANCE

Drug courts were first established over twenty years ago and continue to develop and expand in the United States and elsewhere. In this next article, the Drug Policy Alliance (DPA) considers the effectiveness of drug courts in relation to their original aims. The DPA suggests that alternative approaches need to be considered. In particular, incorporating a health-centered approach would better suit the needs of individuals in their progress toward recovery.

Introduction

Forty years after the United States embarked on a war on drugs, national surveys reveal that a large majority of Americans now believe that drug use is a health issue.[1] This social development has manifested in significant policy change. Several states have passed legislation requiring public and private health insurers to cover drug and mental health treatment on par with treatment for other chronic health conditions. On the federal level, the

Reprinted from Drug Policy Alliance, 2011, "Drug Courts Are Not the Answer: Toward a Health-Centered Approach to Drug Use." New York, 2011.

Paul Wellstone and Pete Domenici Mental Health Parity and Addiction Equity Act of 2008 and the even more expansive Affordable Care Act of 2010 promise to make drug treatment much more accessible within the mainstream health care system.

Nevertheless, U.S. policy remains dominated by a punitive approach to drug use. This legacy of punishment—and its inherent conflict with a health-centered approach—has persisted throughout the 20-year-old drug court experiment.

There is no doubt that drug courts—programs that seek to reduce drug use through mandated treatment and close judicial oversight—were created and continue to be run with unflagging dedication and concern for the health and wellbeing of individuals and communities. Nor is there any doubt that drug court judges and their staffs have helped change, even save, many lives. Most drug court judges have felt deep satisfaction in being able to help participants overcome chaos, illness and despair. There is, indeed, no shortage of success stories. Many participants have had dramatic, life-altering experiences in drug courts. Criminal justice sanctions do indeed deter some people from using drugs, and some people will stop their drug use when faced with the threat of such sanctions. These observations, however, do not end the discussion.

Most interventions help at least some people, and drug courts are no exception. But it is important to consider the full range of drug court impacts, both positive and negative, on all participants as well as on the criminal justice and other systems. It is also important to consider drug court outcomes within the larger context of potential policy options and practices to reduce drug arrests, incarceration and problematic drug use. In this light, the benefits of drug courts pale considerably.

The issue is not whether drug courts do some good—they undoubtedly do—but whether the proliferation of drug courts is good social policy as compared with other available approaches to addressing drug use. This report finds that, based on the evidence, drug courts as presently constituted provide few, if any, benefits over the incarceration model on which they seek to improve. Alternatives

to incarceration for drug possession remain essential, but better alternatives must be adopted and incarceration for drug law violations should be reduced through sentencing reform.

Sitting squarely within a framework of drug prohibition,[2] most drug courts have done a poor job of addressing participants' health needs according to health principles, and have not significantly reduced participants' chances of incarceration. They have also absorbed scarce resources that could have been better spent to treat and supervise those with more serious offenses or to bolster demonstrated health approaches, such as community-based treatment.

Most drug courts have limited their own potential to improve public safety by focusing largely on people who use drugs but have little, if any, history of more serious offenses. Many people end up in drug court because of a drug law violation—many appear to be for marijuana.[3] (The National Drug Court Institute found marijuana to be the most prevalent drug of choice among participants in at least 25 percent of drug courts surveyed nationwide in 2007.[4]) In fact, a 2008 survey of drug courts found that roughly 88 percent exclude people with any history of violent offending, and half exclude those on probation or parole or with another open criminal case.[5] Moreover, about one-third of drug court participants do not have a clinically significant substance use disorder.[6] The same survey found that 49 percent of drug courts actually exclude people with prior treatment history and almost 69 percent exclude those with both a drug and a mental health condition.

This report examines drug courts in light of the criminal justice and health issues they were designed to address. It takes as a premise that punishing people who have neither done harm to others, nor posed significant risk of doing harm (such as by driving under the influence), is inappropriate, ineffective and harmful to individuals, families and communities. The report also recognizes that, whether the chronic health issue in question is hypertension, diabetes or drug use, punishing people for straying from their treatment plans, falling short of treatment goals, or relapsing, is contrary to core health principles.

The central thesis of this report is that there is an urgent need for a non-criminal, health-centered approach to drug use. This approach must be founded on the understanding—as evidence consistently demonstrates—that the benefits of punishment-oriented treatment programs for most people whose illegal activity is limited to petty drug possession are outweighed by the negative consequences. These negative consequences include the lost opportunities of failing to dedicate criminal justice resources to more significant public safety matters and of failing to pursue effective, health-oriented policy interventions in response to drug use.

A health-centered approach would ensure that drug use or the perceived need for treatment should *never be the reason* that people enter the criminal justice system, and that the criminal justice system should *never be the primary path* for people to receive such help. Individuals' drug problems can be addressed, families and communities preserved, public health and safety improved, and money saved by providing assistance to people not only after but *before* drug use becomes problematic, *before* families fall apart, *before* disease spreads, *before* crimes are committed and *before* drug use becomes fatal.

While there is no basis in principle or evidence-based policy for bringing people into the criminal justice system (whether to jail or drug courts) solely for a drug possession offense, drug courts may be appropriate for people who have committed other offenses that require accountability, restitution and possibly incarceration. With this in mind, this report includes several relevant findings and recommendations.

The *Drug Courts and the Drug War* section of this report describes the evolution of drug courts and puts them in the context of current drug arrest practices and sentencing policies.

The next section, *Understanding Drug Courts: What the Research Shows,* provides a careful review of drug court research. It finds that claims about drug court efficacy are methodologically suspect, that the impact on incarceration is often negligible, and that costs are underestimated.

Mixing Treatment and Punishment: A Faulty Approach explores how combining principles of treatment and punishment distorts the delivery of effective legal and health services; how this distortion further enmeshes people in the criminal justice system for their drug use; and how punishment will always dominate in this arrangement.

The *Toward a Health-Centered Approach to Drug Use* section presents a framework for reducing the role of the criminal justice system in what is fundamentally a health issue and for expanding effective approaches that minimize the harms of drug use. It also includes recommendations for improving drug court practices by, among other things, focusing them away from people facing petty drug charges.

Drug Courts and the Drug War

Drug courts emerged as a direct response to the rapid escalation of the war on drugs in the 1980s and 1990s. The era saw bipartisan support for stepped-up enforcement of low-level drug laws and enhanced criminal penalties for the possession and sale of small amounts of illicit substances.[7] In turn, millions of petty cases flooded the court system and people charged with minor drug law violations received harsh sentences that drastically increased the number of people in jails and prisons.

Judges in courtrooms across the country became frustrated as the same individuals repeatedly appeared in court on petty drug charges or faced lengthy prison sentences for minor drug violations. Out of this frustration grew multiple efforts to turn the criminal courtroom into a site for therapeutic intervention, where judges aimed to reduce drug use through court-based interventions and court-supervised treatment.[8]

Drug courts are an application of therapeutic jurisprudence theories in which the judge does not ask whether the state has proven that a crime has been committed but instead whether the court can help to heal a perceived pathology.[9] Drug courts adopted the disease model[10] that posits that people struggling with drugs have a chronic disease that reduces their ability to control their behavior.[11]

Because drug courts are developed locally, they tend to vary significantly in their rules and structure. (Indeed, drug courts are better understood as a category of approaches rather than a single type.) Typically, however, drug court eligibility is limited to people arrested on a petty drug law violation or properly offense.[12] As noted previously, many of these appear to be marijuana violations. The prosecutor exercises wide discretion in determining who is actually referred to drug court. (Even where eligibility is met, about half of drug courts report rejecting eligible individuals because of capacity reasons.[13]) In most cases, participants must plead guilty as a prerequisite to entrance. Upon pleading guilty, they are mandated to treatment or other social service programs. Abstinence is monitored through frequent drug testing. Positive drug tests and other program violations are punished with sanctions, including incarceration and removal from the program.

In drug court, the traditional functions and adversarial nature of the U.S. justice system are profoundly altered. The judge—rather than lawyers—drives court processes and serves not as a neutral facilitator but as the leader of a "treatment team"[14] that generally consists of the judge, prosecutor, defense attorney, probation officer and drug treatment personnel. The judge is the ultimate arbiter of treatment and punishment decisions and holds a range of discretion unprecedented in the courtroom,[15] including the type of treatment mandated, whether methadone prescription is acceptable (and at what dosage) and how to address relapse. The defense lawyer, no longer an advocate for the participant's rights, assists the participant to comply with court rules.[16]

The expansion of drug courts and other criminal justice programs that mandate treatment in the community (as opposed to behind bars) over the last twenty years reflects a growing sentiment that incarceration is not an appropriate, effective or cost-effective response to drug use. At first glance, their expansion might suggest that U.S. policies toward drug use have become more compassionate and health-oriented; yet the dominant policy response to drug use in the U.S. remains one of criminalization and punishment.[17]

From both an international and an historical perspective, current U.S. drug laws are abnormally severe. Following President Reagan's call for a major

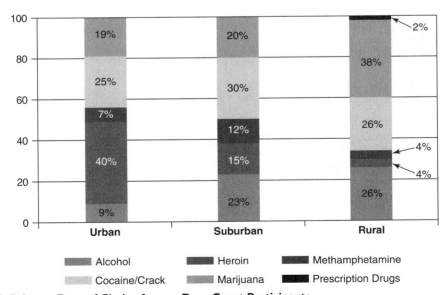

Figure 36.1 Primary Drug of Choice Among Drug Court Participants.
Percentage of Surveyed Drug Courts That Ranked Each Drug as the Leading Drug of Choice Among Participants
Source: Huddleston, West, Doug Marlowe and Rachel Casebolt. 2008. "Painting the Current Picture: A National Report Card on Drug Courts and Other Problem-Solving Court Programs in the United States." *National Drug Court Institute* 2 (1).

escalation of the war on drugs in 1982, annual drug arrests tripled to more than 1.8 million in 2007[18] (before declining to 1.6 million in 2009[19]). This increase primarily involved not serious drug trafficking or sales, but possession; 79 percent of the growth in drug arrests during the 1990s was for marijuana possession alone.[20] The number of people incarcerated for drug law violations has increased 1,100 percent since 1980.[21] Today, nearly 6 in 10 people in a state prison for drug law violations have no history of violence or high-level drug sales.[22]

The U.S. locks up hundreds of thousands of people annually for drug law violations that would not warrant imprisonment in many European and Latin American countries, where incarceration for drug possession alone is comparatively rare.[23] Even for drug law violations that warrant imprisonment in Europe, sentences are generally longer in the U.S.[24] For example, a large-scale trafficking offense in Sweden (considered to be one of the strictest European countries with respect to drugs) merits a *maximum* prison sentence of 10 years.[25] In the U.S., by comparison, for over two decades until 2010, distribution of just 50 grams of crack cocaine (the weight of one candy bar) triggered a federal mandatory *minimum* prison sentence of 10 years.[26] Even after the 2010 federal crack sentencing reform, distribution of just 28 grams of crack cocaine triggers a mandatory minimum sentence of 5 years.[27]

In the U.S., the consequences of a criminal conviction, particularly for a drug law violation, are severe and life-long. People convicted of a felony, whether or not they are ever incarcerated, face significantly diminished employment opportunities and much lower lifetime earnings. They may be prevented from voting and/or prohibited from accessing student loans, food stamps or other public assistance.

Criminal justice policies have not only limited the freedoms and opportunities of people convicted of low-level drug violations, but have also determined *who gains access* to limited publicly funded treatment resources.

The country's treatment system has not expanded proportionately to meet the growth in criminal justice referrals to treatment, which accounted for about 38 percent of participants in publicly funded programs by 2007—

including 162,000 people ordered to treatment for marijuana that year.[28] As a result, treatment access for people seeking treatment voluntarily outside of the criminal justice system has diminished.[29] The proportion of treatment capacity available to the hundreds of thousands of people who seek treatment voluntarily each year (on their own volition or on the recommendation of a loved one, health provider, employer or other non-criminal justice source) fell from 65.1 percent in 1997 to 62.5 percent in 2007.[30]

According to a 2007 Substance Abuse and Mental Health Services Administration (SAMHSA) study, treatment spending fell from 2.1 percent to 1.3 percent of all health spending between 1987 and 2003. During that time, private insurance payments for treatment declined by 24 percent, while public spending on treatment increased 7.5 percent annually (more slowly than other health spending), likely to pay for treatment mandated by the criminal justice system.[31]

> In addition to capacity limitations that lead to lengthy waiting lists, many people seeking treatment voluntarily (i.e., without a criminal justice mandate) face significant barriers. Federal government data find that 37 percent of people who want but do not receive treatment simply cannot afford it, while another 15 percent don't know how to access it.[32] This suggests that people with more resources are better able to get treatment when they want it, while those with fewer resources have fewer treatment opportunities outside of the criminal justice system.

Stopgap Approaches to Systemic Problems

Drug courts have flourished at the expense of support services that are more accessible and that are more effective at improving health and reducing crime.[33] The focus on drug courts has distracted attention from the real, systemic issues that drive the scale and cost of incarceration for drug law violations[34]—primarily aggressive policing strategies and draconian sentencing laws.[35]

For people with few resources, the criminal justice system has become a primary avenue to treatment programs. Nonetheless, many who enter the criminal justice system do not actually receive such services. People who are in prison and have a history of regular drug use are today less than *half as likely* to receive treatment while incarcerated as in 1991.[36] The criminal justice system may ultimately provide the least help to the people with the greatest need.

The country's more than 2,100 drug courts were estimated to have roughly 55,000 participants in 2008,[37] representing a tiny fraction of the more than 1.6 million people arrested on drug charges every year.[38] That is, there is one drug court for every 26 drug court participants—and, for every one drug court participant, there are 29 other people arrested for a drug law violation who are not in a drug court.

Although drug courts tend to describe their participants as "drug-involved," this tends to obscure the reality that an overwhelming number of drug court participants wind up there for a drug law violation—often petty possession. Most drug courts continue to exclude even the lowest-level sellers and the vast majority of courts exclude people with any prior conviction or current charge for a violent offense (due partly to an ill-advised federal funding requirement).[39]

With drug court completion rates ranging widely from 30 percent to 70 percent,[40] it is probably optimistic to assume that even 25,000 people will complete a drug court program each year.* The rest are deemed to have "failed." Even if drug courts were dramatically expanded to scale to cover all people arrested for drug possession, between 500,000 and 1 million people would still be ejected from a drug court and sentenced conventionally every year.[41] As this report discusses, however, drug courts should not focus their resources on those arrested for simple drug possession.

Absent policies to stem the flow of people into (and retention within) the criminal justice system for petty drug law violations, drug courts and other criminal justice-based treatment programs will not meaningfully reduce the imprisonment of people who use drugs.[42]

---

*According to the Government Accountability Office (GAO), drug court completion rates are not directly comparable because "drug court programs have different program completion requirements, the rates were measured over varying rime periods, and study designs can affect the completion measures." There is thus no single average rate of completion.

Disparate Impacts on People of Color

Drug law enforcement practices and sentencing policies have had profound, disparate impacts on people and communities of color. By 2003, African Americans were arrested for drug law violations at a rate 238 percent higher than whites[43] and African Americans and Latinos comprised two-thirds of people incarcerated for drug law violations[44]—even though they use and sell drugs at rates comparable to whites.[45]

Mass arrests and incarceration of people of color—largely due to drug law violations[46]—have hobbled families and communities by stigmatizing and removing substantial numbers of men and women. In the late 1990s, nearly one in three African-American men aged 20–29 were under criminal justice supervision,[47] while more than two out of five had been incarcerated—substantially more than had been incarcerated a decade earlier and orders of magnitudes higher than that for the general population.[48] Today, 1 in 15 African-American children and 1 in 42 Latino children have a parent in prison, compared to 1 in 111 white children.[49] In some areas, a large majority of African-American men—55 percent in Chicago, for example[50]—are labeled felons for life, and, as a result, may be prevented from voting and accessing public housing, student loans and other public assistance.

Unfortunately, drug courts may actually exacerbate existing racial disparities in the criminal justice system. First, drug courts may increase the number of people of color brought into the criminal justice system. An increase in drug arrests (an effect called net-widening) has been documented following the establishment of drug courts.[51] Second, the number of people of color incarcerated may increase; net-widening brings in many people who do not meet narrow drug court eligibility criteria.[52] Third, African Americans have been at least 30 percent more likely than whites to be expelled from drug court[53] due in part to a lack of culturally appropriate treatment programs,[54] few counselors of color in some programs[55] and socioeconomic disadvantages.[56] Finally, people who do not complete drug court are often given a sentence that is significantly longer—in one drug court, even two to five times longer—than if they were conventionally sentenced in the first place (often, because they have forfeited the opportunity to plead to a lesser charge).[57]

Understanding Drug Courts: What the Research Shows

Drug courts are some of the most-studied criminal justice programs in recent years. Unfortunately, most of the existing research suffers major methodological shortcomings that render oft-cited drug court data unreliable and misleading. Attempts to generalize the findings of numerous drug court evaluations—in studies called meta-analyses—have been hamstrung by the lack of credible data in the original research. Moreover, drug court evaluations, which are often conducted by program developers (rather than independent researchers), largely focus on identifying best practices and improving outcomes rather than fundamental policy questions, such as whether a particular drug court reduces crime, incarceration and costs and, if so, whether the drug court does so better than other policy options.

As one researcher testified at congressional hearing in 2010, "Over half of the criminal justice programs designated as 'evidence-based' programs in the National Registry of Evidence Based Programs include the program developer as evaluator. The consequence is that we continue to spend large sums of money on ineffective programs (programs that do no good, and in certain circumstances actually do harm). It also means that many jurisdictions become complacent about searching for alternative programs that really do work."[58]

This appears to be true of drug courts. A close analysis of the most reliable research studies finds that on the whole drug courts, as currently devised, may provide little or no benefit over the wholly punitive system they intend to improve upon. Although many individuals will benefit from drug courts each year, many others will ultimately be worse off than if they had received health services outside the criminal justice system, had been left alone, or even been conventionally sentenced.

Finding: Drug Court Research Is Often Unreliable

Despite the large number of studies on drug courts, the poor quality of that research has led many to conclude that there is insufficient evidence to demonstrate that drug courts reduce crime and drug use. As John Roman, senior researcher at the Urban Institute, put it: "The central criticism is that they employ convenience samples or compare drug court participants with drug court failures, in effect stacking the deck to ensure that the study finds a positive effect of drug court."[59] Meta-analyses (i.e., studies that aggregate and analyze data from multiple drug court evaluations) have been conducted in an attempt to provide more generalized and reliable data; however, meta-analyses' output is ultimately limited by the quality of the data that went in.

A 2006 meta-analysis report oft-cited by drug court supporters as conclusive evidence that drug courts reduce recidivism, for example, warns that "The overall findings tentatively suggest that drug offenders participating in a drug court are less likely to reoffend than similar offenders sentenced to traditional correctional options. The equivocation of this conclusion stems from the generally weak methodological nature [of] the research in this area."[60] Of the 38 studies included in the meta-analysis, only four used "random assignment to conditions" in order to protect against bias. A separate 2006 meta-analysis also frequently relied upon by drug court proponents as proof of drug courts' efficacy found that the studies it depended on for its analysis had measured recidivism rates only for drug court participants who successfully completed the program—a group that accounted, on average, for only 50 percent of those who originally enrolled.[61]

The poor quality of the research has led federal Government Accountability Office (GAO) analysts and other researchers to conclude that the drug court research lacks critical insight into what happens to participants once they are expelled or graduate, and provides limited evidence as to whether drug courts change behavior and lessen recidivism and re-arrest.[62]

In an attempt to produce more reliable findings on drug court outcomes, the National Institute of Justice funded a five-year, national drug court study—the Multi-Site Adult Drug Court

Evaluation (MADCE)—that aims to address many of the shortcomings of existing drug court research. Preliminary results of MADCE, which appears to be better designed than previous studies, were released in 2009 and 2010, and are considered in this report.

Finding: Drug Court Outcomes Are Not Markedly Better Than Probation

Unsound drug court studies have repeatedly claimed that drug courts reduce drug use and criminal behavior, but significant methodological shortcomings call their positive findings into question. Indeed, preliminary results of the lengthiest and largest study so far, the MADCE, find that drug court participation did not lead to a statistically significant reduction in re-arrests.[63]

Drug court evaluations that have reached more positive conclusions than the MADCE study have, in most cases, failed to account for the practice of "cherry-picking," tend to use improper comparison groups, and frequently fail to include follow-up data. Ultimately, most drug court studies are so poorly designed that they reveal only the obvious: that the successes succeed and the failures fail.[64]

Cherry-picking is the selection of people deemed more likely to succeed. Many drug courts cherry-pick participants for at least two reasons. First, prosecutors and judges may cherry-pick defendants because of the limited capacity of the drug court combined with the political importance of achieving high success rates. Second, some drug courts may opt to knowingly enroll persons who do not need treatment, but for whom drug court participation is seen as the only way to avoid a criminal record for a petty drug law violation. This may not be an insignificant occurrence. As mentioned previously, about one-third of drug court participants do not have a clinically significant substance use disorder.[65]

As a result of cherry-picking, people who suffer from more serious drug problems are often denied access to drug court.[66] This, in turn, gives rise to misleading data because it yields drug court participants who are, on the whole, more likely to succeed than a comparison group of conventionally sentenced people who meet drug court eligibility criteria but who are not accepted into the drug court.

The use of non-equivalent treatment and comparison groups may be the most prevalent and serious flaw in drug court research. For example, many studies use a treatment group comprised either of graduates only or of graduates and those still in drug court, electing not to count the many who have dropped out or been ejected from the program. That treatment group is then compared with either a group that was ineligible for drug court, that was eligible but opted for conventional sentencing, or that was expelled from or dropped out of drug court.[67] Although these biases can be mitigated to some extent by statistically accounting for people's background and risk factors, including motivation and drug use severity, most drug court evaluations do not account for these biases.[68]

A 2005 Government Accountability Office (GAO) analysis of drug court research attempted to extract conclusions based on studies that met *very basic* reliability standards. The GAO's review found some positive drug court impacts on recidivism while participants remained in the program (in comparison with conventional sentencing), limited evidence that reductions in recidivism endure after program participation, and no evidence that specific drug court components (including incarceration sanctions) affect recidivism or program completion. The GAO concluded that drug courts' impacts on drug use are mixed.[69]

Three U.S. drug court program evaluations have used more reliable, controlled designs: Maryland's Baltimore Drug Court, Arizona's Maricopa County Drug Court and New Mexico's Las Cruces DWI Court. These three programs randomly assigned people either to drug court or conventional probation. The studies of these three programs are the most rigorous drug court evaluations available. Importantly, even these studies fall far short of establishing the efficacy of drug courts under controlled conditions. Nor do they come close to illustrating that drug courts are typically effective in practice.

For example, Baltimore's drug court participants were less likely to be re-arrested than the control group of probationers during the first two years after the initial arrest.[70] After three years, however, this difference became statistically insignificant, with a stunning 78 percent of drug court participants being re-arrested.[71] Overall, drug court participants averaged 2.3 re-arrests, compared with 3.4 for the control group[72]—a difference that is statistically significant but which may not warrant the substantial resources invested.

Maricopa County's drug court did not reduce recidivism or drug use after 12 months.[73] A 36-month follow up study (which unfortunately excluded nearly 20 percent of original study participants) found that, although Maricopa County drug court participants were less likely to be re-arrested than the control group, there was no difference in the average number of re-arrests between the groups—probably because a portion of drug court participants had a higher number of re-arrests.[74]

Las Cruces' DWI court found no difference in traffic offense reconviction rates, although DWI court participants' reconviction rates for alcohol-related or serious offenses (including simple and aggravated DWI) were slightly lower than for probationers.[75] Researchers cautioned that their sample sizes were small, and that enhanced DWI sanctions implemented in the state prior to the study may have "yielded the same or very similar results as a very expensive individual and group treatment program."[76]

Because virtually no drug court collects or maintains good data, it is unknown whether the Baltimore, Maricopa County and Las Cruces findings are representative. But what is certain is that any reliable data for one court cannot be assumed to apply to another (even if they admit similar types of people) because drug courts differ widely with respect to a host of relevant factors—including their use of drug testing, sanctions, incentives, hearings, treatment and social services, and judicial demeanor and experience.[77]

Ultimately, the most sound studies, including preliminary findings from MADCE, suggest that despite a cosmetically more health-centered approach most drug courts produce remarkably similar outcomes to the conventional, wholly punitive approach that such courts seek to improve upon.

Finding: Incarceration Sanctions Do Not Improve Outcomes

To manage drug court participant compliance, the National Association of Drug Court Professionals (NADCP) encourages the use of rewards and sanctions, including incarceration and program expulsion.[78] Rewards might include praise from the bench, reduced frequency of drug testing, reduced fees or gift certificates. Sanctions, which grow more severe (or "graduated") with subsequent transgressions—including continued drug use or drug relapse—might include warnings from the bench, increased frequency of drug testing, increased fees and incarceration in jail for days or weeks.

Research on the impact of "graduated sanctions" on compliance suffers from many of the same problems as drug court studies in general: a lack of data, site-specific findings that cannot be generalized to other courts, and selection bias, where drug court participants may be more likely to comply with court directives than those not accepted into the drug court.[79] Moreover, research has failed to tackle critical questions about sanctioning practices, including whether *incarceration* sanctions in particular (i.e., jail time) add value over a graduated sanctions framework that does not include incarceration. (The multi-year, multi-site MADCE study also does not address incarceration sanctions separately from other sanctions.)

As the California Society of Addiction Medicine has noted, not a single study has shown that incarceration sanctions improve substance use treatment outcomes.[80] Research also suggests no benefit in reduced re-arrests. According to one major study from the Washington State Institute for Public Policy, for example, adult drug courts reported a reduction in recidivism of 8.7 percent—significantly less than reductions recorded in probation-supervised treatment programs (18 percent) and on par with the reduction recorded by programs offering community-based drug treatment (8.3 percent), neither of which use incarceration as a sanction.[81]

California's experience, too, calls these sanctions into question. Since 2001, that state's landmark probation-supervised treatment program, which does not allow incarceration sanctions, has produced completion rates similar to those of drug courts (See Sidebar: Proposition 36).

Despite this lack of evidence, the power of drug court judges to order the incarceration of people who do not abstain from drug use or who commit minor program violations (including missing a meeting or being obstinate) is thought by many drug court proponents to be a critical component of drug court success. Incarceration sanctions are standard in drug courts and are even recommended by the NADCP.[82] In at least some jurisdictions, incarceration is the single most widely utilized sanction despite the range of sanctions available to judges.[83] Each court determines its own policies for who is incarcerated, for what reason, and for how long. For drug court participants, this sanction can be severe.

Incarceration sanctions have been associated with a higher likelihood of re-arrest and a lower probability of program completion.[84] A person's sense of autonomy and motivation—integral to progress in treatment—can be undermined if they feel they are sanctioned unfairly.[85] Moreover, for days or weeks at a time, an incarceration sanction places a person who may be struggling with drugs into a stressful, violent and humiliating environment, where drugs are often available (and clean syringes almost never), where sexual violence is common (and condoms rare), where HIV, hepatitis C, tuberculosis and other communicable diseases are prevalent, where medical care is often substandard, and where drug treatment is largely nonexistent.

In drug court, incarceration for a drug relapse or a positive drug test often interrupts the treatment process, disrupts a person's attempts to maintain employment and stable social bonds, and reinforces the notion that the person is deviant. The pain, deprivation and atypical, dehumanizing routines that people experience while incarcerated can create long-term negative consequences.[86]

As noted by the National Association of Counties, people with mental illness—at least one in six of the prison population[87]—are severely traumatized by incarceration.[88] Although only 30 percent of drug courts knowingly accept people with co-occurring mental health and substance use disorders,[89] the imposition of incarceration sanctions on these—and on undiagnosed—individuals is counterproductive and creates lasting harm.

Incarceration, when used to punish continued drug use or relapse, is fundamentally at odds with a health approach to drug use. In a treatment setting, relapse is met with more intensive services. In drug court, relapse is often met with temporary or permanent removal of treatment services.

Finding: Drug Courts Limit Access to Proven Treatments

Drug courts agree to provide participants with the services they need to address their drug issues in exchange for compliance with the court's conditions.[90] However, drug courts often fail to live up to their end of the bargain.

Drug courts often inadequately assess people's needs and, as a result, place them in inappropriate treatment. Overcrowded court dockets leave judges unable to effectively manage participant cases.[91] Insufficiently trained court staff often send participants to services irrespective of their specific needs.[92] Some courts use a "shotgun" approach in which they subject participants to several programs with incompatible philosophies.[93] In many cases, referrals to treatment are made not because the program is appropriate for the participant but because a drug court-approved treatment provider has an opening.[94]

Moreover, abstinence-only ideology continues to obstruct appropriate treatment placement, particularly with respect to opioid addiction. According to the National Academy of Sciences' Institute of Medicine, "methadone maintenance has been the most rigorously studied [treatment] modality and has yielded the most incontrovertibly positive results."[95] Methadone and other opioid-maintenance treatments effectively prevent withdrawal symptoms, decrease cravings and overdose, and allow patients to maintain employment.[96] Maintenance treatments are well-documented to reduce crime and disease[97] while saving between $4[98] and $37[99] per dollar invested.

Despite endorsements by Centers for Disease Control and Prevention, the Institute of Medicine, SAMHSA, the National Institute on Alcohol Abuse and Alcoholism, the National Institute on Drug Abuse, the World Health Organization, and even the National Association of Drug Court Professionals, most, drug courts continue to prohibit methadone treatment or other maintenance therapies because of an ideological preference for abstinence.[100] This denial of a highly successful treatment for opioid dependence nearly guarantees that most opioid-dependent individuals will fail in drug court.

To be sure, some treatment quality issues are not unique to drug courts but are endemic to the larger publicly funded treatment system.[101] The lack of diverse, high-quality treatment options is particularly detrimental for people of color, women and young people. Programs are predominantly staffed by counselors who lack the training, skills and experience to treat the diverse populations they encounter.[102] African-American men and women with heroin or cocaine problems, for example, are asked to succeed in programs that were originally designed for white men struggling with alcohol problems.[103]

As a National Institute of Justice report concludes, some drug court treatment session attendance problems may not be caused by intractable participants, but rather by the placement of participants in inappropriate or low-quality programs.[104] People who are harmed more than helped by a treatment program—or treated in a manner insensitive to their race, socioeconomic status, gender, sexuality or, ironically, the severity of their drug problem—are left without recourse and ultimately punished by a system that short-changes them. In the end, struggling drug court participants are often blamed for the inadequacies of the treatment system.

Finding: Drug Courts May Not Improve Public Safety

The claim that drug courts intend to reduce crime among "drug-involved offenders" is misleading. As previously mentioned, many drug court participants are not guilty of a crime against person or property but of a petty drug law violation—many of them apparently involving marijuana. Few drug court participants have long or varied histories of offending. Moreover, as previously noted, roughly one-third of drug court participants do not have clinically significant substance use disorders.[105] That is, the "criminal conduct" that drug courts are currently positioned to address is drug use, a behavior that for many participants is not compulsive.

Even when it comes to drug law violations, the majority of drug courts exclude all but those convicted of low-level drug possession. Even addicted persons who are caught selling petty amounts of drugs simply to support their own addictions are typically barred from drug court. As a result, most drug courts cater to those who are least likely to be jailed or imprisoned and who generally pose little threat to the safety of person or property. Only a handful of drug courts nationwide admit individuals with any previous serious or violent conviction, no matter how long ago the conviction occurred.[106]

Moreover, when drug court participants are arrested, it is typically for a drug law violation, not for a crime against person or property. Early findings of the Multi-Site Adult Drug Court Evaluation (MADCE), for example, show that arrests for "violent, weapons-related or public order offenses" were "rare" for both the drug court participants and those in the comparison group.[107]

As long as drug courts focus on people who use drugs (rather than on people who commit serious or violent crime), the programs are unlikely to provide worthwhile benefit over other policy approaches to drug use. Indeed, research consistently supports changing the population of drug court participants, because "drug courts work better for those who are at an inherently higher risk for future criminal behavior."[108] Given who they accept, it is no surprise that drug courts on the whole have not produced significant reductions in serious or violent crime.

Finding: Drug Courts May Not Reduce Incarceration

While drug courts do often reduce pre-trial detention, the extent to which they reduce incarceration overall is questionable. This conclusion is supported by the preliminary results of the five-year Multi-Site Adult Drug Court Evaluation (MADCE), which found no statistically significant reduction in incarceration for drug court participants over the comparison group after 18 months.[109] Several factors contribute to these apparently counterintuitive findings.

First, drug courts may actually increase the number of people incarcerated for drug law violations due to net-widening, a process by which the introduction or expansion of a drug court (or other diversion program) is followed by an increase in drug arrests.[110] Many of these newly arrested people will face incarceration rather than drug court because of drug court capacity constraints and strict eligibility criteria.

This phenomenon has been dramatic in Denver, where the number of people imprisoned for drug law violations doubled soon after the city established drug courts.[111] Net-widening may happen because law enforcement and other criminal justice practitioners believe people will finally "get help" within the system. Unfortunately, as in the Denver example, the number of people arrested for eligible offenses prior to the establishment of the drug courts had already far exceeded what the drug court could absorb.[112]

Second, people who do not complete drug court may actually face longer sentences—up to two to five times longer, according to one study—than if they had been conventionally sentenced in the first place.[113] Since somewhere between 30 and 70 percent of all drug court participants will complete the program,[114] the number of people ejected and facing potentially longer jail or prison sentences as a result of having participated in a drug court (partly for having forfeited their opportunity to plead to a lesser charge) is substantial.

Third, drug courts' use of incarceration sanctions results in a significant total number of days spent behind bars.[115] Indeed, data from a Baltimore drug court suggested that participants were incarcerated *more often* and for the *same amount of total days as* a control group of probationers, generally for program violations, not even including the incarceration later experienced by the 45 percent of people expelled from the program.[116]

Drug courts, as currently constituted, may ultimately serve not as an alternative but as an *adjunct* to incarceration.[117]

Drug Courts As Adjunct—Not Alternative—to Incarceration

Three years into a study of Baltimore's drug court, 31 percent of participants had graduated after spending an average of nearly 22 months in the program. Another 11 percent were still participating, while 45 percent had been terminated after an average of almost 17 months in the program.[118] In other words, nearly half of participants were deemed "failures" even though they had attempted to adhere to rigorous drug court requirements for nearly a year and a half—a period longer than what their conventional sentences may have been.

In a community-based program, improvements made during those 17 months could very well have been indicators of success, meriting further supports to maintain participants' progress. In the drug court, however, 17 months of attempted adherence was eventually deemed insufficient, at which point the participants were removed from the program to begin serving day one of their original sentence.

Baltimore's misdemeanor drug court participants spent more than twice as many days incarcerated as their misdemeanor control counterparts and almost as many days as felony drug court participants.[119] The drug court thus punished participants with misdemeanor charges as if they had been convicted of a felony.

Finding: Drug Courts May Not Cut Costs

Claims that drug courts save many thousands of dollars per participant, or millions of dollars annually per drug court, are misleading. Not a single cost analysis has looked at the full range of costs of a U.S. drug court. Moreover, preliminary results from MADCE show that the average net cost benefit to society is not statistically significant.[120]

Most studies calculate drug court savings based on assumed reductions in pre-trial detention and recidivism.[121] However, as illustrated above, it is unclear to what extent, if at all, drug courts actually reduce incarceration.[122] Even if drug courts do create some savings in pre-trial detention and recidivism, those savings are likely to disappear when program costs are accounted for—costs that are almost always overlooked. Such costs include drug tests, the not uncommon use of incarceration for detoxification,[123] net-widening,[124] incarceration sanctions,[125] and the cost of harsher sentences on expelled drug court participants.[126]

Additionally, drug court cost-savings assertions are often inflated by inaccurately assuming that all drug court participants are bound for jail or prison. Because most drug courts exclude people with more serious offenses or histories,[127] it is inappropriate to compare the cost of a one-to-three year drug court program against the cost of a one-to-three year period of incarceration. Given who is actually in most drug courts, the cost of drug court is more accurately compared with a jail term of a few weeks or months followed by one-to-three years of probation—an issue overlooked in nearly every drug court cost analysis.[128]

Finally, it must also be asked whether drug courts save money not only in comparison with conventional sentencing of those who possess small amounts of drugs, but also in comparison with a non-criminal justice approach. Such a comparison would uncover significantly different outcomes, costs and savings for an entirely different set of investments. For example, drug treatment has consistently been associated with net benefits and savings, ranging from $1.33 to $23.33 saved per dollar invested.[129]

Although some may suggest that drug courts reduce "society costs" by reducing criminal behavior, this—even if true—is hardly unique to drug courts. Drug treatment itself is associated with significant reductions in illegal activity, particularly reduced drug use and reduced drug sales, as well as minor property offenses associated with drug-procurement behavior.[130] According to one recent analysis by the Washington State Institute for Public Policy, drug courts produced $2 in benefits for every dollar spent. By contrast, drug treatment in the community produced $21 in benefits to victims and taxpayers in terms of reduced crime for every dollar spent—or ten times the benefit produced by drug courts.[131]

Mixing Treatment and Punishment: A Faulty Approach

The fundamental tension that exists between the goals of treatment and punishment—and the predominance of punishment over treatment in any criminal justice-based program—means that drug courts cannot hope to substantially reduce the number of people incarcerated for drug use as long as drug use is criminalized. Indeed, it means that drug courts are apt to incarcerate those who could most benefit from treatment.

Fundamental Paradox of Drug Courts

Drug courts are grounded in two contradictory models. The disease model assumes that people with an addiction disorder use drugs compulsively—that is, despite negative consequences.[132] The rational actor model, which underlies principles of punishment, assumes that people weigh the benefits of their actions against the potential consequences of those actions.[133]

These dueling models result in people being "treated" through a medical lens while the symptoms of their condition—chiefly, the inability to maintain abstinence—are addressed through a penal one. The person admitted into drug court is regarded as not fully rational and only partially responsible for their drug use; yet the same person is considered sufficiently rational and responsible to respond to the "carrots and sticks" (i.e., rewards and sanctions) of drug court.[134]

Under this approach, those suffering more serious drug problems are most likely to "fail" drug court and be punished.[135] In the end, the person who has the greatest ability to control his or her own drug use will be much more likely to complete treatment and be deemed a "success."

In blending two incompatible philosophies,[136] a drug court (or any other criminal justice-based program) cannot adhere to both approaches and faithfully embody either one. This incongruity results in thousands of drug court participants being punished or dropped from programs each year for failing to overcome addictions in a setting not conducive to their success.

Abstinence-Only and the Predominance of Punishment over Treatment

A health-centered response to drug use assesses improvement by many measures—not simply by people's drug use levels, but also by their personal health, employment status, social relationships and general well-being. "Success" in the criminal justice context, by contrast, boils down to the single measure of abstinence—because any drug use is deemed illegal behavior. Both approaches already exist in the U.S. today; the wealthy often benefit from one, while people of less means are by and large subject to the other.

Rehabilitative regimes that rely on criminal justice coercion have historically devolved into increasingly punitive systems.[137] Drug courts' attempts to meld treatment and punishment ultimately succumb to the dominance of punishment over therapeutic principles. Though a judge may provide leniency to those who make important strides, drug court participants will eventually be labeled "failures" and sanctioned unless they achieve and maintain abstinence for a period of time that the judge deems reasonable. Duty-bound to penal codes that criminalize drug use, drug courts' ultimate demand is complete abstinence from drugs. Meanwhile, the many other medical and social indicators of wellbeing become secondary or tertiary.

No form of treatment—court-mandated or otherwise—can guarantee long-term abstinence from drug use. Moreover, lapses in treatment compliance are a predictable feature of substance use disorders, just as they are with other chronic conditions, including diabetes and hypertension. But drug courts make it difficult for people whose only "crime" is their drug use to extricate themselves from the criminal justice system. The court, bound to the benchmark of abstinence, and rooted in principles of deterrence, retribution and incapacitation,[138] equates drug relapse with criminal recidivism and punishes it as such.

Drug court adaptations in Canada, Australia and the United Kingdom have expanded measures of success to include decreased drug use and crime, while broadly allowing opioid-maintenance therapy (such as methadone) and, in some circumstances, tolerating cannabis use.[139] In the U.S., too, a handful of drug courts have adopted similar harm reduction measures, suggesting that some pragmatic reforms are feasible even absent a major shift in domestic drug policies.

Toward a Health-Centered Approach to Drug Use

Twenty years of evidence clearly demonstrates that drug courts cannot effectively reduce the burden on the criminal justice system created by 1.6 million annual drug arrests and that they cannot provide health-oriented treatment within a punitive structure. Indeed, it appears that, on a policy level, they may be making matters worse by absorbing resources and momentum that could be focused on developing non-criminal justice responses to drug use and by preserving criminal justice resources for addressing crimes against people and property.

Stopgap measures to address the drug arrest epidemic within the criminal justice system have failed. It is time for a new approach to drug use— one focused on health. A health paradigm recognizes that the criminalization of drug use does more harm than good; that prevention, treatment and other social supports are often more appropriate and cost-effective than criminal justice involvement; and that, similar to alcohol consumption, drug use does not always impede a person's functioning or ability to be successful, and therefore not everyone who uses a drug needs treatment.

Moving from the criminal paradigm to this new health paradigm entails improving and standardizing drug court practices, working toward the

Proposition 36: Better But Not Health-Centered

California provides an important case study in how treatment within the criminal justice system will always come second to that system's primary missions of deterrence, retribution and incapacitation.

Passed by 61 percent of voters in 2000, Proposition 36 permanently changed the state's sentencing law to require probation and treatment rather than incarceration for a first and second low-level drug law violation. The Drug Policy Alliance, with support from many others, designed Prop. 36 and spearheaded the campaign to pass the law. Its intent is to provide universal access to treatment for eligible candidates while prohibiting their incarceration (including incarceration sanctions), to prevent cherry-picking of participants, to allow drug testing for treatment (but not punitive) purposes, and to empower health providers—not judges—to make treatment decisions.[140]

Prop. 36 represents a positive modification of drug courts, taken to scale. From 2001–2006, when Prop. 36 was funded at $120 million a year, 36,000 people were enrolled annually[141] (nearly ten times the number of people enrolled in all of California's drug courts and nearly two-thirds the number of people participating in all drug courts nationwide),[142] completion rates were comparable to those of other criminal justice programs,[143] and the number of

people in California prisons for drug possession dropped by more than 27 percent.[144] An estimated $2,861 was saved per participant, or $2.50 for every dollar invested,[145] and there were no adverse effects on crime trends.[146]

Prop. 36 is instructive in that its participants' completion rates are comparable to drug courts', but Prop. 36 participants were not cherry-picked and were not subject to incarceration sanctions.[147]

Nevertheless, Prop. 36 remains—like drug courts—squarely within the criminal Justice system. Admission to the program follows conviction (similar to most drug courts), participants appear to have displaced voluntary clients in cash-strapped publicly funded programs (even though Prop. 36 funding helped establish nearly 700 new program sites),[148] and failure to maintain abstinence ultimately results in expulsion from the program and imposition of conventional sentencing.[149]

Despite Prop. 36's demonstrated cost savings and public safety record, funding decisions ten years later confirm that treatment in California remains secondary to punishment. Over a four-year period, California entirely eliminated treatment funding for Prop. 36—from a high of $145 million in 2007–08 to nothing in 2010–11.

---

removal of criminal penalties for drug use, and shifting investments into public health programs that include harm reduction and other interventions and treatments.

Recommendation: Reserve Drug Courts for Serious Offenses and Improve Practices

As this report emphasizes, drug courts are bound by the rules of the criminal justice system in which they exist. As policy makers and advocates work to improve that larger system, however, there are things that drug courts themselves—and those who dispense drug court funding—can do immediately to improve and standardize practices to

more effectively and cost-effectively apply their limited resources.

Numerous scholars and researchers who have looked closely at drug courts have proposed a series of reforms and best practices to improve drug courts, including:

- Focus drug court resources on people facing lengthy prison terms to ensure that drug court is actually a diversion from incarceration and not more restrictive than the conventional sentence;[150]
- Adopt objective admission criteria and reduce the prosecutor's role as gate-keeper;[151]
- Use a pre-plea rather than a post-plea model;[152]

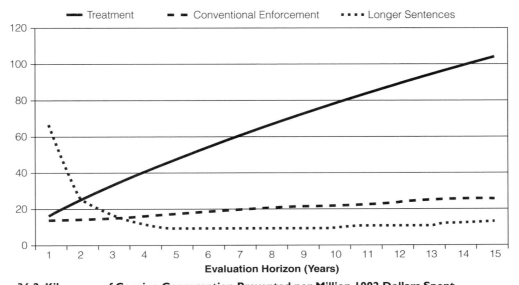

Figure 36.2 Kilograms of Cocaine Consumption Prevented per Million 1992 Dollars Spent.

Source: Caulkins, Jonathan P., et al., 1997, *Mandatory Minimum Drug Sentences; Throwing Away the Key or the Taxpayers' Money.* RAND Corporation.

- Ensure due process protections and enhance the role of defense counsel;[153] and
- Improve data collection, research rigor, and implementation of demonstrated best practices.[154]

To this list, the Drug Policy Alliance recommends adding the following:

- Prohibit the use of incarceration sanctions for drug law violations and provide a treatment response instead;
- Incorporate health measures—not simply abstinence—into program goals;
- Improve overall treatment quality and employ opioid maintenance treatments and other evidence-based therapies;
- Work to ensure that drug courts are more health-oriented than punitive;
- Use drug tests as a treatment tool, not as punishment;
- Empower treatment professionals in decision-making;
- Reduce turnover of trained and experienced court, probation and treatment staff to improve program continuity and consistency;

- Ensure that punishment for "failing" the program is not worse than the original penalty for the offense; and
- Work to establish other local alternatives outside the drug court for those who want and need access to treatment but do not warrant intensive court resources (e.g., probation-supervised treatment).

While these short-term fixes would help improve the functioning, transparency and accountability of drug courts, policymakers must also ask what other interventions might be equally or more successful with different populations. After all, there will not be one policy solution to the issues of drug use or public safety. Rather, U.S. drug policy will benefit when a range of options is available and when robust research drives policy decisions.

Recommendation: Work Toward Removing Criminal Penalties for Drug Use

Even as drug courts continue to proliferate, the federal government and some states are seeking out more systemic changes to address the dual burdens of mass drug arrests and incarceration.

Many of these measures aim to reduce the number of people going to prison for a petty drug offense, shorten the length of time served for drug law violations, or reduce probation and parole revocations for drug use.[155]

To limit the number of people going to prison for a petty drug law violation, several states have implemented alternative-to-incarceration programs and others are moving in that direction. Several years ago, for example, Texas successfully opted for alternatives to incarceration rather than build a new prison.[156] New York adopted major reforms of its 36-year-old Rockefeller Drug Laws in 2009, including alternatives to incarceration for petty drug possession and sales offenses.[157] As this report was published, California was considering ending prison sentences for most petty drug offenses. South Carolina was aiming to reduce its prison population by handling more low-level drug and other offenses outside of prison walls.[158] And an Oklahoma legislator had promised to introduce his own plan to divert thousands of people convicted of petty offenses from prison.[159]

Programs that provide alternatives to incarceration for a substantial portion of people convicted of a petty drug law violation improve the utilization of limited resources and allow the criminal justice system to focus on matters of greater public safety. As some states are already learning, reducing penalties is an even more effective way to reduce costs while preserving public safety. In 2010, Colorado reduced penalties for some low-level possession offenses and New Jersey restored judges' discretion to waive mandatory minimum sentences for certain low-level drug law violations that take place in "drug-free zones." In late 2010, Indiana's Criminal Code Evaluation Commission advised the state to shorten sentences for drug possession and some low-level sales offenses.[160] And at the federal level, landmark legislation in 2010 dramatically reduced disproportionate sentencing for crack cocaine, and repealed a mandatory minimum drug sentence for the first time since the 1970s (what had been a five-year sentence for possession of five grams of crack cocaine—the weight of two sugar packets).[161]

As Some States Are Already Learning, Reducing Penalties Is an Even More Effective Way to Reduce Costs While Preserving Public Safety

These are all important steps toward reducing the incarceration of people for drug use. But they do not reduce (and may run the risk of increasing through net-widening) the number of *drug arrests* that absorb huge amounts of law enforcement and court personnel time and overwhelm alternative-to-incarceration programs. As a result, some states and local authorities are pursuing programs aimed at reducing drug arrests.

At the state level, spending can be reprioritized in order to focus resources on preventing people from entering the criminal justice system—and hastening their exit from it. In 2009, for example, California spent $90 million in federal Byrne Justice Assistance Grants on drug treatment and intensive probation supervision instead of on the state's "buy-bust" programs that result in thousands of low-level drug arrests annually.[162] In so doing, the state generated about $200 million in cost savings rather than the additional costs (of as much as $900 million) that would have been associated with new court cases and incarceration.[163]

At the local level, too, resource allocation is being rethought and some jurisdictions are working to implement changes in arrest practices. For example, a collaborative effort in Seattle, which includes law enforcement, defense attorneys and social services among others, expects to roll out in 2011 a pre-booking diversion program called Law Enforcement Assisted Diversion (LEAD) that aims to reduce the number of people entering the criminal justice system for a low-level drug law violation by providing linkages to community-based treatment and support services.[164] In San Diego, the police department has calculated significant cost savings to the local government through its Serial Inebriate Program (SIP), which provides treatment and housing to the city's most costly individuals suffering from alcoholism and chronic homelessness.[165]

These changes are steps in the right direction. However, they fall short of what is ultimately necessary to reduce the role of the criminal justice system in this health issue: a removal of criminal penalties for drug use absent harm—or substantial risk of harm, such as driving under the influence—to others. As long as more than 1.6 million people are arrested every year for drug law violations and hundreds of thousands more are sanctioned for drug-related violations of parole or probation,[166] drug cases will continue to swamp the criminal justice system and have a negative impact on individuals and communities.

Nationally, 46 percent of all drug arrests are for marijuana possession.[167] Ending criminal penalties for marijuana use would represent a significant advancement toward a health approach. Lawmakers and voters in numerous states considered bills and ballot measures to eliminate or reduce penalties for marijuana possession in 2010 and many are expected to do so again in 2012. With recent polls showing nearly half the country in favor of taxing and regulating marijuana, there is currently unprecedented momentum for major policy reforms.

In recent years, other countries have taken even broader steps toward ending the criminalization of drug use. In 2008, a Brazilian appeals court ruled that based on the constitutional principles of harm, privacy and equality, the law criminalizing drug possession for personal use is unconstitutional. In 2009, Mexico, Argentina and the Czech Republic all made possession of small quantities of drugs non-criminal offenses. Though these reforms were made absent a larger health-centered agenda, they reflect an increasing awareness that prohibitionist policies are counterproductive—at least with respect to drug possession.

Portugal presents the most significant and successful example of a post-criminalization, health-centered drug policy. In 2001, Portuguese legislators decriminalized low-level drug possession and reclassified it as an administrative violation. At the heart of this policy change was the recognition that the criminalization of drug use was not justifiable and that it was actually a barrier to more effective responses to drug use.[168]

Portugal's Post-Criminalization Policy Success

Portugal's move to decriminalize all low-level drug possession in 2001 was not simply a legal change but a comprehensive paradigm shift toward expanded access to prevention, treatment, harm reduction and social reintegration services.[169] The explicit aim of the policy shift was to adopt an approach to drugs based not on dogmatic moralism and prejudice but on science and evidence. The criminalization of drug use was deemed a barrier to more effective, health-centered responses and at odds with the principle that people who use drugs deserve to be treated with dignity and respect.[170]

Portugal's legal and policy changes altered the role of police officers, who now issue citations—but do not arrest—people found in possession of small amounts of illicit substances. Cited persons are ordered to appear at a "dissuasion commission," an administrative panel that operates outside of the criminal justice system. The panel, with two health practitioners and one legal practitioner, examines the individual's needs and circumstances, and determines whether to make referrals to treatment or other services, and/or to impose fines or other non-criminal penalties.

By decreasing the stigma around drug use, decriminalization allowed for the discussion of previously taboo issues and optimum policy responses, including whether to create supervised injection facilities and to introduce sterile syringe exchange programs in prisons.[171] Further, the administrative, community-based "dissuasion commissions" have provided earlier intervention for drug users, a broader range of responses, an increased emphasis on prevention for occasional users, and increased provision of treatment and harm reduction services.[172]

A decade later, Portugal's paradigm change from a punitive approach to a health-centered one has proved enormously popular. It has not created a haven for "drug tourists" nor has it led to increased drug use rates, which continue to be among the lowest in the European Union.[173] Rather, fatal overdose from opiates has been cut nearly in half,[174] new HIV/AIDS infections in people who inject drugs fell by two-thirds,[175] the number of people in treatment increased[176] and the number of people on opioid maintenance treatments more than doubled.[177] Portugal's paradigm shift has facilitated better uptake of prevention, treatment, harm reduction and social reintegration services and, ultimately, a more realistic approach to drug use driven by experience and evidence.[178]

The failure of U.S. stopgap measures and the success of the Portuguese model challenge advocates and policymakers in the U.S. to focus on building the political will to work toward removing criminal penalties for drug use and implement instead a comprehensive and effective health-centered approach.

Recommendation: Invest in Public Health, Including Harm Reduction and Treatment

Public health interventions are wise, necessary long-term investments. They reduce the harms associated with drug use, prevent crimes against people and property, and cut associated costs. These approaches must not begin and end with abstinence-only programs. While treatments aimed at supporting people who desire to cease drug use must be made much more widely available, strategies to prevent overdose deaths and reduce the spread of communicable disease are also critical and must be expanded.

A 2006 analysis found that every dollar invested in drug treatment saves $7 due to increased employment earnings and reduced medical care, mental health services, social service supports, and crime.[179] A 1994 RAND study commissioned by the U.S. Army and the White House Office of National Drug Control Policy found treatment to be seven times more effective at reducing cocaine consumption than domestic law enforcement, ten times more effective than drug interdiction, and 23 times more effective than trying to eradicate drugs at their source.[180] A 1997 SAMHSA study found that treatment reduces drug selling by 78 percent, shoplifting by almost 82 percent, and assaults by 78 percent.[181]

Despite the health and fiscal benefits of drug treatment, too many people lack access to it. Federal health care legislation, signed by President Obama in 2010, takes a promising step forward by expanding eligibility for private and public insurance and by requiring all insurers to provide coverage for substance use and mental health service benefits on par with coverage for other chronic conditions. This parity requirement will help to reduce two significant barriers to treatment—cost and stigma—by promising to make treatment accessible through public and private health insurance and through more doctors' offices.

Significantly, under the new health care legislation, all nonelderly adults with income up to 133 percent of the federal poverty level will become eligible for Medicaid in 2014.[182] This will capture many currently uninsured people, including many in the criminal justice system. Medicaid eligibility will not translate into real access to treatment, however, unless states work to preserve, and then expand, their addiction treatment systems. As adults become able to access drug treatment through Medicaid, it will make even less sense to invest in resource-intensive drug courts that focus on people whose illegal activity is largely limited to drug use. These new dollars, too, must not be devoted solely to abstinence-only approaches, such as those mandated by drug courts, but to a wide range of services that focus on improving people's health.

Bringing drug treatment into the primary care setting is essential, but it is not enough. Programs designed for people who do not routinely access the mainstream health care system are also needed. For example, syringe exchange programs and safe injection facilities—which focus on empowering individuals to make healthier choices—have proven to be safe, effective opportunities for more marginalized people to engage help and services.[183]

Just as public health principles support the use of condoms, contraceptives, cigarette filters and seat belts to reduce health risks, drug policies must seek to reduce the harms and risks associated with drug use. As Portuguese policymakers learned, an overemphasis on abstinence can obstruct efforts to successfully mitigate drug-related harms.[184] Programs that focus on reducing drug-related harms and risks result in better individual and public health than criminal justice interventions—including drug courts—and, by any measure, deliver more bang for the buck. Failing to invest in such programs is expensive in terms of both lives and dollars.

Drug overdose is now the second leading cause of accidental death, trailing only motor vehicle fatalities.[185] According to the National Institute on Drug Abuse, injection drug use is responsible for one-third of adult and adolescent HIV/AIDS cases, while more than one-half of HIV/AIDS cases at birth are the result of a parent contracting HIV through injection drug use. Hepatitis B and C are prevalent in 65 percent and 75 percent, respectively, of people who have injected drugs for six years or less. People who use drugs, either intravenously or otherwise, are two to six times more likely than others to contract tuberculosis. The geographic distribution of syphilis and gonorrhea infections reflects the distribution of crack cocaine use.[186]

Overdose deaths and the spread of HIV/AIDS, hepatitis, tuberculosis, syphilis and gonorrhea are *largely preventable*. Good Samaritan policies, which encourage people to call for help in the case of a suspected drug overdose, may help reduce fatalities. Proven public health measures, such as syringe exchange programs, have consistently been shown to substantially reduce the rate of HIV/AIDS transmission among people who inject drugs without increasing injection drug use.[187] Facilities that allow supervised, on-site injection of drugs reduce vein damage, disease transmission[188] and fatal overdose[189] as well as public disorder, improper syringe disposal and public drug use.[190] Additionally, the provision of naloxone (an FDA-approved overdose antidote) to people who use opioids—either as prescription analgesics for pain (such as phentanyl, oxycodone, hydromorphone and methadone) or as a result of opioid dependence—can greatly reduce fatal overdose.[191]

Moreover, non-judgmental services such as syringe exchanges reach people turned off by or excluded from abstinence-only programs. In 2005, more than 85 percent of roughly 160 syringe exchange programs in the U.S. regularly made treatment referrals.[192] Many referrals were for people who do not inject drugs, illustrating that such programs deliver important health services for a larger community beyond their primary syringe-exchanging clients.[193] In 2009, the federal government removed a significant hurdle when it ended the ban on federal dollars going to life-saving syringe exchange programs. Much more is needed in the way of direct investment—and these costs could easily be covered by reduced investment in arrests and incarceration for drug law violations.

Similarly, many people struggling with drugs may benefit from a variety of support services before—or in lieu of—formal treatment services. It is well-documented that stable social and financial circumstances help prevent relapse both during and after treatment, regardless of whether a person is mandated to treatment by the courts.[194] Efforts to aid people with drug problems might therefore involve addressing other needs entirely, such as access to physical and mental health services, housing, employment or education.

Conclusion

There are several reasons why now is the time to rethink our drug policies, including drug courts. The hysteria of the 1980s drug war is now a distant memory, and states and the federal government are seeking cost-effective ways to achieve better results. The Obama Administration's commitment to a greater public health approach than its predecessors has already resulted in significant policy reform, with the inclusion of drug treatment in the 2010 health care laws. At the same time, the federal crack cocaine sentencing reform of 2010 illustrates that bipartisan consensus is possible on drug policy. Moreover, the evidence from abroad regarding the health and fiscal benefits of harm reduction strategies and non-punitive approaches has grown dramatically. And here at home, harm reduction programs once regarded as inconceivable in some parts of the U.S. are now standard. Finally, the criminalization-focused approach to drug policy, including drug courts, continues to fail to demonstrate its efficacy or cost-efficacy.

Let's be clear: drug court programs have saved lives. People correctly perceive them as having benefits. Drug court proponents deserve to take pride in their accomplishments. However, we all, including drug court supporters, have an obligation to step outside the drug court paradigm to consider other approaches that might work better and whether the particular modalities of the drug court are best directed at people other than those whose only offense is drug use or drug possession. This will not be easy.

People have a vested interest in defending and promoting that which they have given so many years of their lives. Drug courts have developed substantial political rapport, which risks providing them immunity from honest, critical analyses.

Looking forward, however, we should strive toward a world where drug courts focus primarily on more serious offenses and where drug use absent harm to others is no longer regarded as a criminal justice matter.

Notes

1. Lake Research Partners, 2009, "New Poll Shows Majority of Americans Support Efforts to Make Alcohol and Drug Addiction Treatment More Accessible, Affordable," June, www.facesand voicesofrecovery.org/pdf/OSI_Lake Research_2009.pdf; Substance Abuse and Mental Health Services Administration (SAMHSA), 2008, "New National Poll Reveals Public Attitudes on Substance Abuse, Treatment and the Prospects of Recovery," September, www .guidetofeelingbetter.org/GuideToFeelingBetter/ SAMHSA%20Attitude%20Surveys%20Results .pdf; Rasinski, K. A., and D. R. Gerstein. and R. D. Lee, n.d., "Public Support for Substance Abuse Treatment Coverage: Results of a National Survey." Unpublished, <http://www.rwjf.org/ reports/grr/041644.htm#FINDINGS>. See also: *Faces and Voices of Recovery*, "Resources," <http:// www.facesandvoicesofrecovery.org/resources/ other_research.php>.

2. Boldt, Richard, 2009, "A Circumspect Look at Problem-Solving Courts," in *Problem-Solving Courts: Justice for the Twenty-First Century?*, eds. Paul C. Higgens and Mitchell B. MacKinem (Santa Barbara: ABC-CLIO).

3. Bhati, Avi, John Roman, and Aaron Chalfin, 2008, *To Treat or Not to Treat: Evidence on the Effects of Expanding Treatment to Drug-Involved Offenders*, Washington DC: The Urban Institute, 2008.

4. Huddleston, West, Doug Marlowe and Rachel Casebolt, 2008, "Painting the Current Picture: A National Report Card on Drug Courts and Other Problem-Solving Court Programs in the United States." *National Drug Court Institute* 2 (1).

5. Huddleston, Marlowe, and Casebolt, "Painting the Current Picture."

6. DeMatteo, David S., Douglas B. Marlowe, and David S. Festinger, 2006, "Secondary Prevention Services for Clients Who Are Low Risk in Drug Court: A Conceptual Model," *Crime and Delinquency* 52 (1): 114–134.

7. Boldt, Richard, 1998, "Rehabilitative Punishment and the Drug Treatment Court Movement," *Washington University Law Quarterly* 76: 1205–1306.

8. National Association of Criminal Defense Lawyers (NACDL), 2009, *America's Problem-Solving Courts: The Criminal Costs of Treatment and the Case for Reform,* Washington DC: NACDL.

9. Hoffman, Morris B., 2002, "Therapeutic Jurisprudence, Neo-Rehabilitationism, and Judicial Collectivism: The Least Dangerous Branch Becomes the Most Dangerous," *Fordham Urban Law Journal* 29 (5): 2063–2098.

10. Hoffman, "Therapeutic Jurisprudence"; Hoffman, Morris B., 2000, "The Drug Court Scandal," *North Carolina Law Review* 78 (5): 1437–534; Miller, Eric J., 2004, "Embracing Addiction: Drug Courts and the False Promise of Judicial Interventionism," *Ohio State Law Review* 65: 1479–1576.

11. Miller, "Embracing Addiction."

12. Bhati, Roman, and Chalfin, *To Treat or Not to Treat.*

13. Bhati, Roman, and Chalfin, *To Treat or Not to Treat.*

14. Boldt, "A Circumspect Look."

15. Boldt, "A Circumspect Look."

16. NACDL, *America's Problem-Solving Courts.*

17. Stevens, Alex, 2008, "Alternatives to What? Drug Treatment Alternatives as a Response to Prison Expansion and Overcrowding," Paper presented at the Second Annual Conference of the International Society for the Study of Drug Policy, Lisbon, Portugal, April 3–4 2008 <http://issdp .org/lisbon2008_public/alternatives%20to%20 what_stevens.pdf>.

18. Mauer, Marc, and Ryan S. King, 2007, *A 25-Year Quagmire: The War on Drugs and Its Impacts on American Society* (Washington DC: The Sentencing Project), September <http://www.sentencing project.org/doc/publications/dp_25yearquagmire .pdf>.

19. Federal Bureau of Investigation, "Crime in the United States 2009" <http://www2.fbi.gov/ucr/ cius2009/data/table_29.html>.

20. Mauer and King, *A 25-Year Quagmire.*

21. Mauer and King, *A 25-Year Quagmire*.

22. Mauer and King, *A 25-Year Quagmire*. See also Boynum D., and P. Reuter, 2005, *An Analytic Assessment of US Drug Policy* (Washington DC: The AEI Press); Rossman et al., 2008, *A Portrait of Adult Drug Courts* (Washington DC: The Urban Institute); and Pollack, Harold, Peter Reuter and Eric Sevigny, 2010, "If Drug Treatment Works So Well, Why Are So Many Drug Users in Prison?" Paper presented at the National Bureau of Economic Research Conference on Economical Crime Control, January 15–16, <http://www.nber.org/confer/2010/CRIs10/Reuter.pdf>.

23. Stevens, "Alternatives to What?"

24. Stevens, "Alternatives to What?"

25. European Legal Database on Drugs, 2008, "Illegal Possession of Drugs," <http://eldd. emcdda .europa.eu/html.cfm/index5749EN.html>.

26. United States Sentencing Commission, *Federal Sentencing Guidelines Manual (2010)* §2D1.1

27. United States Sentencing Commission, *Federal Sentencing Guidelines Manual (2010)* §2D1.1.

28. SAMHSA, Office of Applied Studies, 2009, *Treatment Episode Data Set (TEDS). Highlights: 2007 National Admissions to Substance Abuse Treatment Services*, DASIS Series: S-45, DHHS Publication No. (SMA) 09-4360, Rockville, MD, Table A1 <http://wwwdasis.samhsa.gov/teds07/tedshigh2k7 .pdf>; SAMHSA, Office of Applied Studies, 2009, *The TEDS Report: Substance Abuse Treatment Admissions Referred by the Criminal Justice System*, Rockville, MD, August <http://www.oas.samhsa .gov/2k9/211/211CJadmits2k9.pdf>.

29. Hser, Yih-Ing, et al., 2007, "Impact of California's Proposition 36 on the Drug Treatment System: Treatment Capacity and Displacement," *American Journal of Public Health* 97 (1): 104–109. This trend has also occurred in the UK. Finch, Emily, et al., 2003, "Sentenced to Treatment: Early Experience of Drug Treatment and Testing Orders in England," *European Addiction Research* 9 (3): 131–137; and in Canada, Rush, Brian R., and T. Cameron Wild, "Substance Abuse Treatment and Pressures from the Criminal Justice System: Data From a Provincial Client Monitoring System," *Addiction* 98 (8): 1119–1128.

30. SAMHSA, *Treatment Episode Data Set (TEDS)*, Table 4; 1997 data from <http://wwwdasis .samhsa.gov/teds97/id77.htm>.

31. Mark, Tami L., et al., 2007, "Trends in Spending for Substance Abuse Treatment, 1986–2003," *Health Affairs* 26 (4): 1118–1128.

32. SAMHSA, Office of Applied Studies, 2009, *2008 Survey on Drug Use & Health: National Findings*, NSDUH Series H-36, HHS Publication No. SMA 09-4434, Rockville, MD, September, Table 5.54B <http://www.oas.samhsa.gov/nsduh/ 2k8nsduh/2k8Results.pdf>.

33. Stevens, "Alternatives to What?"

34. Stevens, Alex, Tim McSweeney, Marianne van Ooyen and Ambros Uchtenhagen, 2005, "On Coercion," *International Journal of Drug Policy* 16: 207–209.

35. Levine, Harry G., and Deborah Peterson Small, 2008, *Marijuana Arrest Crusade: Racial Bias and Police Policy in New York City, 1997–2007* (New York: New York Civil Liberties Union), April, <http://www.nyclu.org/files/MARIJUANA-ARREST-CRUSADE_Final.pdf>; Bewley-Taylor, Dave, Chris Hallam, and Rob Allen, 2009, *The Incarceration of Drug Offenders: An Overview* (London: The Beckley Foundation Drug Policy Programme), <http://www.beckleyfoundation .org/pdf/BF_Report_16.pdf>; Mauer, Marc, 2009, *The Changing Racial Dynamics on the War on Drugs* (Washington DC: The Sentencing Project) <http://www.sentencingproject.org/doc/ dp_raceanddrugs.pdf>.

36. Mauer and King, *A 25-Year Quagmire*.

37. Bhati, Roman, and Chalfin, *To Treat or Not to Treat*.

38. Federal Bureau of Investigation, "Crime in the United States 2009."

39. King, Ryan S. and Jill Pasquarella, 2009, *Drug Courts: A Review of the Evidence* (Washington DC: The Sentencing Project).

40. United States General Accounting Office, 2005, *Adult Drug Courts: Evidence Indicates Recidivism Reductions and Mixed Results from Other Outcomes* (Washington DC: GPO).

41. These drug court failure estimates are based on 1.4 million people who were arrested for drug possession in 2007. See U.S. Department of Justice, *Estimated Arrests for Drug Abuse Violations by Age Group, 1970–2007.*

42. Bhati, Roman, and Chalfin, *To Treat or Not to Treat*; Stevens, "Alternatives to What?"; Pollack, Reuter, and Sevigny, "If Drug Treatment Works So Well"; See also Austin, James and Barry Krisberg, 1982,

"The Unmet Promise of Alternatives to Incarceration," *Crime and Delinquency* 28 (3): 374–409.

43. King, Ryan S., 2008, *Disparity by Geography: The War on Drugs in America's Cities,* (Washington DC: The Sentencing Project) <http://www .sentencingproject.org/doc/publications/ dp_drugarrestreport.pdf>.

44. Mauer, *The Changing Racial Dynamics.*

45. Mauer and King, *A 25-Year Quagmire*; Mauer, *The Changing Racial Dynamics.*

46. Mauer, Marc, and Tracy Huling, 1995, *Young Black Americans and the Criminal Justice System: Five Years Later* (Washington DC: The Sentencing Project) <http://www.sentencingproject.org/doc/ publications/rd_youngblack_5yrslater.pdf>.

47. Mauer and Huling, *Young Black Americans.*

48. Uggen, Christopher, Sara Wakefield, and Bruce Western, 2005, "Work and Family Perspectives on Reentry," in *Prisoner Reentry and Crime in America,* eds. Jeremy Travis and Christy Visher (Cambridge: Cambridge University Press).

49. Schirmer, Sarah, Ashley Nellis, and Marc Mauer, 2009, *Incarcerated Parents and Their Children* (Washington DC: The Sentencing Project) <http:// www.sentencingproject.org/doc/publications/ publications/inc_incarceratedparents.pdf>.

50. Street, Paul, 2002, *The Vicious Circle: Race, Prison, Jobs, and Community in Chicago, Illinois, and the Nation,* Chicago Urban League. <http://www .thechicagourbanleague.org/cms/lib07/ IL07000264/Centricity/Domain/76/_Files/ theviciouscircle.pdf>.

51. Hoffman, "The Drug Court Scandal"; NACDL, *America's Problem-Solving Courts.*

52. O'Hear, Michael, 2009, "Rethinking Drug Courts: Restorative Justice as a Response to Racial Injustice," *Stanford Law & Policy Review* 20: 101–137.

53. Belenko, Steven R., 2001, *Research on Drug Courts: A Critical Review (2001 Update),* (New York: National Center on Addiction and Substance Abuse at Columbia University). See also Bowers, Josh, 2008, "Contraindicated Drug Courts," *UCLA Law Review* 55.

54. Lutze, Faith E., and Jacqueline G. van Wormer, 2007, "The Nexus Between Drug and Alcohol Treatment Program Integrity and Drug Court Effectiveness: Policy Recommendations for Pursuing Success," *Criminal Justice Policy Review* 18 (3): 226–245.

55. Anspach, Donald F. and Andrew S. Ferguson, 2003, *Assessing the Efficacy of Treatment Modalities in the Context of Adult Drug Courts: Final Report* (Portland, ME: University of Southern Maine).

56. Bowers, "Contraindicated Drug Courts."

57. Gottfredson, Denise C., and M. Lyn Exum, 2002, "The Baltimore City Drug Treatment Courts: One-Year Results from a Randomized Study," *Journal of Research on Crime and Delinquency* 39: 337–356; Gottfredson, Denise C., et al., 2006, "Long-Term Effects of Participation in the Baltimore City Drug Treatment Court: Results from an Experimental Study," *Journal of Experimental Criminology* 2 (1): 67–98; Bowers, Josh, "Contraindicated Drug Courts"; O'Hear, Michael, "Rethinking Drug Courts."

58. Hawken, Angela, 2010, "Quitting Hard Habits: Efforts to Expand and Improve Alternatives to Incarceration for Drug-Involved Offenders." Testimony to U.S. House of Representatives Committee on Oversight and Government Reform Subcommittee on Domestic Policy Hearing, July 22.

59. Roman, John K., 2010, "Quitting Hard Habits: Efforts to Expand and Improve Alternatives to Incarceration for Drug-Involved Offenders." Testimony to U.S. House of Representatives Committee on Oversight and Government Reform Subcommittee on Domestic Policy Hearing, July 22.

60. Wilson, D. B., O. Mitchell, and D. L. MacKenzie, 2006, "A Systematic Review of Drug Court Effects on Recidivism," *Journal of Experimental Criminology* 2: 459–487.

61. Latimer, J., K. Morton-Bourgon, and J. Chretien, 2006, *A Meta-Analytic Examination of Drug Treatment Courts: Do They Reduce Recidivism?* Canada Dept. of Justice, Research & Statistics Division.

62. Fischer, B., 2003, "Doing Good with a Vengeance: A Critical Assessment of the Practices, Effects and Implications of Drug Treatment Courts in North America," *Criminal Justice* 3 (3): 227–248; United States General Accounting Office, 1997, *Drug Courts: Overview of Growth, Characteristics, and Results* (Washington DC: GPO); United States General Accounting Office, *Adult Drug Courts.*

63. Roman, John K., "Quitting Hard Habits."

64. Goldkamp, J. S., M. D. White, and J. B. Robinson, "Do Drug Courts Work? Getting Inside the Drug Court Black Box," *Journal of Drug Issues* 31 (1): 32.

65. DeMatteo, Marlowe, and Festinger, "Secondary Prevention Services."

66. Goldkamp, J., 2000, "The Drug Court Response: Issues and Implications for Justice Change," *Albany Review* 63: 923–961; Fischer, B., "Doing Good with a Vengeance"; NACDL, *America's Problem-Solving Courts.*

67. United States General Accounting Office, *Drug Courts: Overview of Growth, Characteristics, and Results*; United States General Accounting Office, *Adult Drug Courts*; Belenko, Stephen R., 1998, "Research on Drug Courts: A Critical Review," *National Court Institute Review* 1 (1): 1–42; Belenko, 1999, "Research on Drug Courts: A Critical Review (1999 Update)," *National Drug Court Institute Review* 1 (2): 1–59; Belenko, *Research on Drug Courts: A Critical Review (2001 Update)*; Fischer, B., "Doing Good with a Vengeance."

68. United States General Accounting Office, *Drug Courts: Overview of Growth, Characteristics, and Results*; United States General Accounting Office, 2002, *Drug Courts: Better DOJ Data Collections and Evaluation Efforts Needed to Measure Impact of Drug Court Programs* (Washington DC: GPO); United States General Accounting Office, *Adult Drug Courts.*

69. United States General Accounting Office, *Adult Drug Courts.*

70. Gottfredson and Exum, "The Baltimore City Drug Treatment Courts"; Gottfredson, Denise C., Stacy S. Najaka, and Brook Kearley, 2003, "Effectiveness of Drug Treatment Courts: Evidence from a Randomized Trial," *Criminology and Public Policy* 2: 171–196.

71. Gottfredson et al., "Long-Term Effects of Participation."

72. Gottfredson et al., "Long-Term Effects of Participation."

73. Deschenes, Elizabeth Piper, et al., 1996, *An Experimental Evaluation of Drug Testing and Treatment Interventions for Probationers in Maricopa County, Arizona* (Santa Monica, CA: RAND), <http://www.rand.org/pubs/drafts/2008/DRU1387.pdf>.

74. Turner, Susan et al., 1999, "Perceptions of Drug Court: How Offenders View Ease of Program Completion, Strengths and Weaknesses, and the Impact on Their Lives," *National Drug Court Institute Review* 2: 61–85.

75. Breckenridge, J. F. et al., 2000, "Drunk Drivers, DWI 'Drug Court' Treatment, and Recidivism: Who Fails?" *Justice Research and Policy* 2 (1): 87–105.

76. Breckenridge et al., "Drunk Drivers," 103.

77. Goldkamp et al., "Do Drug Courts Work?"

78. The National Association of Drug Court Professionals, 1997, *Defining Drug Courts: The Key Components.*

79. King and Pasquarella, *Drug Courts*; Harrell, Adele and John Roman, 2001, "Reducing Drug Use and Crime among Offenders: The Impact of Graduated Sanctions," *Journal of Drug Issues* 31 (1): 207–232.

80. California Society of Addiction Medicine, "Proposition 36 Revisited" <http://www. csam-asam .org/prop36article.vp.html>; See also Goldkamp et al., "Do Drug Courts Work?"; Hepburn, John R., and Angela Harvey, 2007, "The Effect of the Threat of Legal Sanction on Program Retention and Completion: Is That Why They Stay in Drug Court?" *Crime and Delinquency* 53 (2): 255–280.

81. Drake, Elizabeth, Steve Aos, and Marna G. Miller, 2009, "Evidence-Based Public Policy Options to Reduce Crime and Criminal Justice Costs: Implications in Washington State," *Victims and Offenders* 4:170–196 <www.wsipp.wa.gov/rptfiles/09-00-1201.pdf>.

82. The National Association of Drug Court Professionals, *Defining Drug Courts.*

83. Rempel, Michael et al., 2003, *The New York State Adult Drug Court Evaluation: Policies, Participants, and Impacts*, Center for Court Innovation, 68.

84. Goldkamp et al., "Do Drug Courts Work?"

85. Longshore, Douglas et al., 2007, *Evaluation of the Substance Abuse and Crime Prevention Act: Final Report* (Los Angeles, CA: UCLA Substance Abuse Programs).

86. Haney, Craig, 2002, "The Psychological Impact of Incarceration: Implications for Post-Prison Adjustment," presented at "From Prison to Home: The Effect of Incarceration and Reentry on Children, Families and Communities," January 30–31, 2002 <http://aspe.hhs.gov/hsp/prison2home02/haney.pdf>.

87. Beck, Allen J., and Laura M. Maruschak, 2001, *Mental Health Treatment in State Prisons, 2000*, Special Report, NCJ 188215 (Washington DC: Department of Justice, Bureau of Justice Statistics), 1–8; Haney, "The Psychological Impact of Incarceration," estimates that this figure may be more than 20 percent.

88. Rosado, Edwin, 2002, *Diverting the Mentally Ill from Jail* (National Association of Counties Legislative Department).

89. Bhati, Roman, and Chalfin, *To Treat or Not to Treat*.

90. Lutze and van Wormer, "The Nexus Between Drug and Alcohol Treatment Program Integrity and Drug Court Effectiveness."

91. Hoffman, "The Drug Court Scandal"; Lutze and van Wormer, "The Nexus Between Drug and Alcohol Treatment Program Integrity and Drug Court Effectiveness."

92. Anspach and Ferguson, *Assessing the Efficacy of Treatment Modalities*.

93. Anspach and Ferguson, *Assessing the Efficacy of Treatment Modalities*; Lutze and van Wormer, "The Nexus Between Drug and Alcohol Treatment Program Integrity and Drug Court Effectiveness."

94. Boldt, "Rehabilitative Punishment."

95. Institute of Medicine, 1990, *Treating Drug Problems, Volume I: A Study of the Evolution, Effectiveness, and Financing of Public and Private Drug Treatment Systems* (Washington DC: National Academy Press), 187.

96. Kleber, Herbert D., MD, "Methadone Maintenance Four Decades Later: Thousands of Lives Saved But Still Controversial," *Journal of the American Medical Association* 300 (19): 2303–2305.

97. Amato, Laura et al., 2005, "An Overview of Systematic Reviews of the Effectiveness of Opiate Maintenance Therapies: Available Evidence to Inform Clinical Practice and Research," *Journal of Substance Abuse Treatment* 28: 321–330; Kleber, "Methadone Maintenance."

98. Gerstein, D.R. et al., 1994, *Evaluating Recovery Services: The California Drug and Alcohol Treatment Assessment (CALDATA) General Report*, State of California Department of Alcohol and Drug Problems, 61–90.

99. Zarkin, Gary A. et al., 2005, "Benefits and Costs of Methadone Treatment: Results from a Lifetime Simulation Model," *Health Economics* 14: 1133–1150.

100. O'Donnell, Colleen, and Marcia Trick, 2006, *Methadone Maintenance Treatment and the Criminal Justice System* (Washington DC: National Association of State Alcohol and Drug Abuse Directors, Inc.); California Society of Addiction Medicine, 2002, "California Drug Courts Denying Methadone," *CSAM News* 28 (1).

101. Anspach and Ferguson, *Assessing the Efficacy of Treatment Modalities*.

102. Anspach and Ferguson, *Assessing the Efficacy of Treatment Modalities*.

103. Lutze and van Wormer, "The Nexus Between Drug and Alcohol Treatment Program Integrity and Drug Court Effectiveness."

104. Anspach and Ferguson, *Assessing the Efficacy of Treatment Modalities*; King and Pasquarella, *Drug Courts*.

105. DeMatteo, Marlowe, and Festinger, "Secondary Prevention Services."

106. Bhati, Roman, and Chalfin, *To Treat or Not to Treat*.

107. Roman, "Quitting Hard Habits."

108. Rempel, Michael et al., 2010, "The Impact on Criminal Behavior and Participant Attitudes: Results from NIJ's Multi-Site Adult Drug Court Evaluation, Part 2," presented at NADCP 16th Annual Training Conference, Boston, MA, June 4, http://www. urban.org/UploadedPDF/412141-the-impact-on-criminal.pdf>.

109. Rempel, Michael, and Mia Green, 2009, "Do Drug Courts Reduce Crime and Produce Psychosocial Benefits? Methodology and Results from NIJ's Multi-Site Adult Drug Court Evaluation (MADCE)," presented at American Society of Criminology Conference, Philadelphia, PA, November 5, <http://www.urban.org/UploadedPDF/412043_do_drug_courts.pdf>.

110. Hoffman, "The Drug Court Scandal"; see also King and Pasquarella, *Drug Courts*; and NACDL, *America's Problem Solving Courts*.

111. Hoffman, "The Drug Court Scandal."

112. Hoffman, "The Drug Court Scandal."

113. O'Hear, "Rethinking Drug Courts"; see also Fluellen, Reginald, and Jennifer Trone, 2000, *Do Drug Courts Save Jail and Prison Beds?* (New York: Vera Institute of Justice).

114. United States General Accounting Office, *Adult Drug Courts*.

115. See Goldkamp, J., "The Drug Court Response"; Gottfredson et al., "The Effectiveness of Drug

Treatment Courts"; Harrell, Adele, 2003, "Judging Drug Courts: Balancing the Evidence," *Criminology and Public Policy* 2 (2): 207–212; and Gottfredson et al., "Long-Term Effects of Participation."

116. Gottfredson et al., "Long-Term Effects of Participation."

117. Harrell, "Judging Drug Courts."

118. Gottfredson et al., "Long-Term Effects of Participation."

119. Gottfredson et al., "Long-Term Effects of Participation."

120. Roman, "Quitting Hard Habits."

121. Belenko, "Research on Drug Courts: A Critical Review."

122. Belenko, "Research on Drug Courts: A Critical Review"; United States General Accounting Office, *Drug Courts: Overview of Growth, Characteristics, and Results*; United States General Accounting Office, *Adult Drug Courts.*

123. United States General Accounting Office, *Drug Courts: Overview of Growth, Characteristics, and Results.*

124. Hoffman, "The Drug Court Scandal"; King and Pasquarella, *Drug Courts*; NACDL, *America's Problem Solving Courts.*

125. Goldkamp, "The Drug Court Response"; Gottfredson et al., "Effectiveness of Drug Treatment Courts."

126. Fluellen and Trone, *Do Drug Courts Save Jail?*; Gottfredson and Exum, "The Baltimore City Drug Treatment Courts"; O'Hear, "Rethinking Drug Courts."

127. Miller, "Embracing Addiction"; Bhati, Roman, and Chalfin, *To Treat or Not to Treat*; Rossman et al., *A Portrait of Adult Drug Courts*, Washington DC: The Urban Institute, 2008; Pollack et. al., "If Drug Treatment Works So Well, Why Are So Many Drug Users in Prison?"

128. Fluellen and Trone, *Do Drug Courts Save Jail?*

129. Ettner, Susan L. et al., 2006, "Benefit-Cost in the California Treatment Outcome Project: Does Substance Abuse Treatment Pay for Itself?" *Health Services Research* 41 (1): 192–213.

130. SAMHSA, 1997, *The National Treatment Improvement Evaluation Study (NTIES), Final Report.*

131. Drake, Aos, and Miller, "Evidence-Based Public Policy Options."

132. See generally Boldt, "Rehabilitative Punishment"; Hoffman, "Therapeutic Jurisprudence"; Miller, "Embracing Addiction."

133. Miller: Ibid.

134. Bowers, "Contraindicated Drug Courts." Ethnographic descriptions of how this paradox manifests in practice are provided by study of a juvenile drug court in Whiteacre, Kevin, 2007, "Strange Bedfellows: The Tension of Coerced Treatment," *Criminal Justice Policy Review* 18 (3): 260–273: "Staff members experienced personal ambivalence over the efficacy of sanctions as a therapeutic tool, particularly when faced with some juveniles' continued noncompliance despite the sanctions. Staff neutralized this tension by attributing noncompliance to the juveniles' lack of motivation, concluding coerced treatment only works for those who are "ready" for treatment. This would appear to pose a paradox for coerced treatment, which is meant to induce compliance specifically among those who are not motivated." See also Whiteacre, K. (2008). "Drug Court Justice: Experiences in a Juvenile Drug Court." New York: Peter Lang Publishing.

135. Hoffman, "Therapeutic Jurisprudence."

136. Boldt, "Rehabilitative Punishment."

137. Boldt, "Rehabilitative Punishment"; Boldt, "A Circumspect Look."

138. Boldt, "A Circumspect Look."

139. Bakht, Natasha and Paul Bentley, 2004, *Problem Solving Courts as Agents of Change* (Ottawa: National Judicial Institute); see also Nolan, James L. Jr., 2009, *Legal Accents, Legal Borrowing: The International Problem-Solving Court Movement* (Princeton, NJ: Princeton University Press).

140. California Department of Alcohol and Drug Programs, "Proposition 36 Ballot Initiative (2000 General Election)" <http://www.adp.ca.gov/SACPA/Proposition_36_text.shtml>. http://www.adp.ca.gov/sacpa/Proposition_36_text.shtml

141. Longshore, Douglas et al., 2004, *Evaluation of the Substance Abuse and Crime Prevention Act: 2003 Report* (Los Angeles, CA: UCLA Integrated Substance Abuse Programs).

142. California Department of Alcohol and Drug Programs and Judicial Council of California, 2002, Administrative Office of the Courts, *Drug Court Partnership Act of 1998, Chapter 1007, Statutes 1998—Technical Report.*

143. Longshore et al., 2007, *Evaluation of the Substance Abuse and Crime Prevention Act: Final Report.*

144. Ehlers, Scott and Jason Ziedenberg, *Proposition 36: Five Years Later,* Washington DC: Justice Policy Institute, April 2006.

145. Longshore et al., 2006, *SACPA Cost-Analysis Report (First and Second Years)* (Los Angeles, CA: UCLA Integrated Substance Abuse Programs).

146. Ehlers and Ziedenberg, *Proposition 36: Five Years Later.*

147. Longshore et al., *Evaluation of the Substance Abuse and Crime Prevention Act: 2005 Report,* Los Angeles, CA: UCLA Integrated Substance Abuse Programs.

148. Hser et al., "Impact of California's Proposition 36."

149. California Department of Alcohol and Drug Programs, 2005, *Substance Abuse and Crime Prevention Act of 2000 (SACPA—Proposition 36): Fourth Annual Report to the Legislature,* October 2005.

150. Stevens et al., "On Coercion"; NACDL, *America's Problem-Solving Courts.*

151. NACDL, *America's Problem-Solving Courts.*

152. NACDL, *America's Problem-Solving Courts.*

153. Boldt, "Rehabilitative Punishment"; Miller, "Embracing Addiction"; NACDL, *America's Problem-Solving Courts.*

154. Belenko, "Research on Drug Courts: A Critical Review"; Belenko, *Research on Drug Courts: A Critical Review (2001 Update)*; Fischer, B., "Doing Good with a Vengeance"; United States General Accounting Office, *Drug Courts: Overview of Growth, Characteristics, and Results;* United States General Accounting Office, *Drug Courts: Better DOJ Data Collections;* King and Pasquarella, *Drug Courts*; NACDL, *America's Problem-Solving Courts.*

155. For a summary of drug law and penalty changes in 2010, see Porter, Nicole D., 2011, *The State of Sentencing 2010: Developments in Policy and Practice* (Washington DC: The Sentencing Project).

156. The Pew Center on the States, 2010, *Prison Count 2010: State Population Declines for the First Time in 38 Years*, Washington DC, April <http://www.pewstates.org/uploadedFiles/Prison_Count_2010.pdf?n=880>.

157. Drug Policy Alliance, 2009, *New York's Rockefeller Drug Laws: Explaining the Reforms of 2009*, New York, <http://www.drugpolicy.org/docUploads/Explaining_the_RDL_reforms_of_2009_FINAL.pdf>.

158. Murphy, Sean, 2011, "GOP Lawmakers Paying Price for Tough-on-Crime Laws," *Associated Press*, January 31, http://blog.al.com/wire/2011/02/gop_lawmakers_paying_price_for.html

159. Murphy, "GOP Lawmakers Paying Price."

160. Murphy, "GOP Lawmakers Paying Price."

161. Baker, Peter, 2010, "Obama Signs Law Narrowing Cocaine Sentencing Disparities," *New York Times*, August 3, <http://thecaucus.blogs.nytimes.com/2010/08/03/obama-signs-law-narrowing-cocaine-sentencing-disparities/?nl=us&emc=politicsemailema3>.

162. California Emergency Management Agency, 2010, *Joint Legislative Budget Committee Report*, Table B, January. See also US Government Accountability Office, *Department of Justice Could Better Assess Justice Assistance Grant Program Impact.* October <http://www.gao.gov/new.items/d11187.pdf>.

163. Drug Policy Alliance, 2010, "$90 Million in Federal Funds Going to California Counties for Drug Treatment & Probation," March 8, http://www.drugpolicy.org/news/2010/03/90-million-federal-funds-going-california-counties-drug-treatment-probation

164. The Defender Association-Racial Disparity Project, 2010, "Law Enforcement Assisted Diversion (LEAD): A Pre-Booking Diversion Model for Low-Level Drug Offenses." Seattle, WA, <http://www.law.seattleu.edu/Documents/cle/archive/2010/032610%20Restorative%20Justice/215pm%20LEAD%20concept%20paper.pdf>.

165. San Diego Police Department, *Serial Inebriate Program* <http://www.sandiego.gov/sip/>.

166. Federal Bureau of Investigation, "Crime in the United States 2009."

167. Federal Bureau of Investigation, "Crime in the United States 2009."

168. Hughes, Caitlin Elizabeth, and Alex Stevens, 2010, "What Can We Learn from the Portuguese Decriminalization of Illicit Drugs?" *British Journal of Criminology* 50 (5).

169. Hughes and Stevens, "What Can We Learn?"

170. Hughes and Stevens, "What Can We Learn?"; Hughes, Caitlin Elizabeth, 2006, "Overcoming

Obstacles to Reform?: Making and Shaping Drug Policy in Contemporary Portugal and Australia (Ph.D. thesis, The University of Melbourne).

171. Hughes and Stevens, "What Can We Learn?"

172. Hughes and Stevens, "What Can We Learn?"

173. Greenwald, Glenn, 2009, *Drug Decriminalization in Portugal: Lessons for Creating Fair and Successful Drug Policies*, Washington DC: Cato Institute; Hughes and Stevens, "What Can We Learn?"

174. Hughes and Stevens, "What Can We Learn?"

175. Instituto da Droga e da Toxicodependência, 2009, *Relatório Anual 2008: A Situação do País em Matéria de Drogas e Toxicodependências*, Portugal, 2009.

176. Hughes and Stevens, "What Can We Learn?"

177. Instituto da Droga e da Toxicodependência, *Relatório Anual 2008*.

178. Hughes and Stevens, "What Can We Learn?"

179. Ettner et al., "Benefit-Cost in the California Treatment Outcome Project."

180. Rydell, Peter C. and Susan S. Everingham, 1994, *Controlling Cocaine: Supply Versus Demand Programs*, Santa Monica, CA: RAND.

181. SAMHSA, *The National Treatment Improvement Evaluation Study (NTIES)*.

182. CNN, 2010, "Timeline: When Health Care Reform Will Affect You," March 26, <http://www.cnn.com/2010/POLITICS/03/23/health.care.timeline/index.html>.

183. Heimer, Robert, 1998, "Can Syringe Exchange Serve as a Conduit to Substance Abuse Treatment?" *Journal of Substance Abuse Treatment* 15 (3): 183–191; MacPherson, Donald, 2001, *A Framework for Action: A Four-Pillar Approach to Drug Problems in Vancouver*, City of Vancouver, April; Broadhead, Robert et al., 2002, "Safer Injection Facilities in North America: Their Place in Public Policy and Health Initiatives," *Journal of Drug Issues* 32 (1): 329–356; Wood et al., 2006, "Attendance at Supervised Injection Facilities and Use of Detoxification Services," *New England Journal of Medicine* 354: 2512–2514.

184. Hughes and Stevens, "What Can We Learn?"

185. Paulozzi, Leonard J., "Trends in Unintentional Drug Overdose Deaths," statement made before the Senate Judiciary Subcommittee on Crime and Drugs, March 12, 2008 <http://www.hhs.gov/asl/testify/2008/03/t20080312b.html>.

186. National Institute on Drug Abuse, 1999, "Infectious Diseases and Drug Abuse," *NIDA Notes* 14 (2).

187. World Health Organization, 2004, *Policy Brief: Provision of Sterile Injecting Equipment to Reduce HIV Transmission*, Geneva: WHO.

188. Gibson, David R., Neil M. Flynn, and Daniel Perales, 2001, "Effectiveness of Syringe Exchange Programs in Reducing HIV Risk Behavior and HIV Seroconversion among Injecting Drug Users," *AIDS* 15: 1329–1341.

189. Kerr et al., 2006, "Drug-Related Overdoes Within a Medically Supervised Safer Injection Facility," *International Journal of Drug Policy* 17: 436–441.

190. Wood et al., 2004, "Changes in Public Order After the Opening of a Medically Supervised Safer Injecting Facility for Illicit Injection Drug Users," *Canadian Medical Association Journal* 171 (7): 731–734.

191. Maxwell, S. Bigg, D. Stanczykiewicz, K. Carlberg-Racich, 2006, "Prescribing Naloxone to Actively Injecting Heroin Users: A Program to Reduce Heroin Overdose Deaths," *Journal of Addictive Diseases* 25 (3): 89–96.

192. Centers for Disease Control and Prevention, 2007, "Syringe Exchange Programs: United States, 2005," *Morbidity and Mortality Weekly Report* 56 (44): 1164–1167.

193. Heimer, "Can Syringe Exchange Serve?"

194. Sung, Hung-en, and Steven Belenko, 2005, "Failure After Success: Correlates of Recidivism Among Individuals Who Successfully Completed Coerced Drug Treatment," *Journal of Offender Rehabilitation* 42 (1): 75–97; SAMHSA, Office of Applied Studies, *Employment Status and Substance Abuse Treatment Admissions: 2006*.

For Discussion

1. Review the website material of the National Association of Drug Court Professionals. Find out the number of drug courts in the United States, and the ways that drug courts have expanded, for example, veterans' courts.

2. Should we criminalize drug use or treat it as health problem? Why?

Policy Considerations

The federal approach to drug use and drug control has included a number of avenues for reducing both the supply of and the demand for illicit drugs. Historically, the supply-and-demand reduction strategies were grounded in the classic deterrence model: (1) through legislation and criminal penalties, individuals would be discouraged from using drugs, and (2) by making an example of traffickers, the government would force potential dealers to seek out other economic pursuits. In time, other components were added: treatment for the user, education and prevention for the would-be user, and research to determine how to best develop and implement plans for treatment, education, and prevention.

By the early 1970s, when it appeared that the War on Drugs had won few if any battles, new avenues for supply-and-demand reduction were added. Federal interdiction initiatives involved charging Coast Guard, Customs, and Drug Enforcement Administration operatives with intercepting drug shipments coming to the United States from foreign ports, and in the international sector there were attempts to eradicate drug-yielding crops at their source. On the surface, none of these strategies seemed to have much effect, and illicit drug use continued to spread.

The problems were many. Legislation and enforcement alone were not enough, and early education programs of the "scare" variety quickly lost their credibility. Moreover, for most social scientists and clinicians, treating problem drug use as a medical problem seemed to be the logical solution. However, for several reasons, treatment programs did not seem to be working very effectively. First, the course of treatment was often of insufficient length to have any significant impact (length of stay in treatment is a critical factor for producing positive outcomes). Second, several treatment initiatives were characterized by structural or program barriers that contributed to high treatment dropout rates (barriers reflected *high threshold* when people tried to access treatment, and *low tolerance* once people commenced treatment). Third, programs often failed to recognize that treatment had to be matched to client needs; a "one size, fits all" approach was ineffective for several clients. Fourth, a comprehensive treatment program that incorporated ancillary supports (e.g., addressing accommodation problems) and aftercare was not usually available.

Given the perceived inadequacy of the traditional approaches to drug control, federal authorities in the late 1970s began drawing plans for a more concerted assault on drugs, both legislative and technological. It began with the RICO (Racketeer-Influenced and Corrupt Organizations) and CCE (Continuing Criminal Enterprise) statutes. What RICO and CCE accomplished was the forfeiture of the fruits of criminal activities by eliminating the rights of traffickers to their personal assets, whether these be cash, bank accounts, real estate, automobiles, jewelry and art, equity in businesses, directorships in companies, or any kind of goods or entitlements obtained in or used for a criminal enterprise.

The new, evolving federal drug strategy considered it crucial to include the U.S. military in its war on drugs. In 1982, the Department of Defense Authorization Act was signed into law, making the entire war chest of U.S. military power available to law enforcement—for training, intelligence gathering, and detection. Beginning in 1982, the war on drugs had a new look. Put into force was the Bell 209 assault helicopter, more popularly known as the Cobra. None in the military arsenal were faster, and in its gun-ship mode it could destroy a tank. In addition, there was the awesome Sikorsky Black Hawk assault helicopter, assigned for operation by US Customs Service pilots. Customs also had the Cessna Citation, a jet aircraft equipped with radar originally designed for F-16 fighters. There was the Navy's EC-2, an aircraft equipped with a radar disk capable of detecting other aircraft from as far as 300 miles away. There were "Fat Albert" and his pals—aerostat surveillance balloons 175 feet in length equipped with sophisticated radar and listening devices. Fat Albert not only could pick up communications from Cuba but also could detect traffic in "Smugglers' Alley," a wide band of Caribbean sky that is virtually invisible to land-based radar

systems. There were NASA satellites to spy on drug operations as far apart as California and Colombia, airborne infrared sensing and imaging equipment that could detect human body heat in the thickest underbrush of Florida's Everglades, plus a host of other devices—deemed to be high-tech during that era. In all, drug enforcement appeared well equipped for battle.

The final component added to the drug war armamentarium was "zero tolerance," a 1988 White House antidrug policy based on a number of premises: (1) that if there were no drug "abusers," there would be no drug problem; (2) that the market for drugs is created not only by availability but also by demand; (3) that drug use starts with a willful act; (4) that the perception that drug users are powerless to act against the influences of drug availability and peer pressure is an erroneous one; (5) that most individuals who use illegal drugs can choose to stop their drug-taking behaviors and must be held accountable if they do not; (6) that individual freedom does not include the right to self- and societal destruction; and (7) that public tolerance for drug use must be reduced to zero. As such, the zero tolerance policy expanded the war on drugs from suppliers and dealers to users as well—especially casual users—and meant that planes, vessels, and vehicles could be confiscated for carrying even the smallest amount of a controlled substance.

By the late 1980s, well after the newest "war on drugs" had been declared and put into operation, it had already been decided by numerous long-time observers that the more than 70 years of federal prohibition since the passage of the Harrison Act of 1914 were not only a costly and abject failure but represented a totally doomed effort as well. It was argued that drug laws and drug enforcement had served mainly to create enormous profits for drug dealers and traffickers, greatly contributed to overcrowded jails, created conditions for police and other government corruption, damaged foreign relations, and contributed to predatory street crime conducted in the pursuit of funds deemed to be needed to purchase illicit drugs.

Several years later, advances in surveillance technology have contributed greatly to increases in drug seizures by state and federal law enforcement.

Moreover, technology has made it easier and quicker for law enforcement to share information across global networks. Despite these major developments, data from the United States, Europe, and Australia show that the purity of heroin, cocaine, and cannabis has *increased* and street prices for illicit drugs have generally *declined* despite an escalation in the quantity of drugs seized (Werb et al. 2013). This pattern is inconsistent with "supply and demand" assumptions. That is, the street price of illicit drugs should increase if fewer supplies are reaching drug markets. However, drug markets have expanded to include a host of new synthetic psychoactive drugs. This change might have worked to maintain or reduce prices of more established street drugs (e.g., marijuana, cocaine) because of increasing competition to attract buyers who now have access to a greater variety of psychoactive substances and through alternative markets.

Prohibition of several drugs has been a key feature of US domestic drug policies. The late 1980s marked the onset of renewed calls for the decriminalization, if not the outright legalization, of some, most, or all illicit drugs. This perspective has continued to gain support with proponents of legalization who focus on a number of points. First, advocates of legalization argue that drug laws create evils far worse than the drugs themselves—corruption, violence, street crime, and disrespect for the law. Second, legislation that was intended to control drugs often fails to reduce demand. Third, an activity that a significant segment of the population of any society is committed to doing should not be made illegal. A social system simply cannot arrest, prosecute, and punish such large numbers of people, particularly in a democracy. And specifically in this regard, liberal democracies should not interfere with personal behavior if liberty is to be maintained. Finally, if marijuana, cocaine, crack, heroin, and other drugs were legalized, a number of positive things would happen:

1. Drug prices would fall and subsequently so would crime committed for the purpose of obtaining funds with which to support expensive drug habits.

2. Users could obtain their drugs at low, government-regulated prices and would no longer be forced to engage in sex work and street crime to support their drug use.

3. Declines in the levels of drug-related crime would reduce overcrowding in jails and prisons and provide more resources for law enforcement personnel to focus their energies on the "real criminals" in society.

4. Drug production, distribution, and sale would be removed from the criminal arena, and the violence associated with drug distribution rivalries would be eliminated.

5. Government corruption and intimidation by traffickers, as well as drug-based foreign policies, would be effectively reduced, if not eliminated entirely.

6. The often draconian measures undertaken by police to enforce the drug laws would be curtailed, thus restoring to the American public many of its hard-won civil liberties.

In contrast, those who oppose drug legalization argue that legalizing heroin, cocaine, and other illicit drugs would increase their availability, and in turn create a public health problem of massive proportions.

The decriminalization and legalization debates continue, but major changes in marijuana legislation occurred in 2012. Approximately 55% of voters in Colorado and Washington passed ballot measures that provide for the legal regulation of marijuana for use among individuals aged 21 and older. The new legislation allows for the production and distribution of marijuana via private enterprises that are licensed by the State. Additionally, the Colorado law allows adults to grow a maximum of six cannabis plants and authorizes them to give the product to others, although *sales* from one individual to another are prohibited—legal purchases must be made from one of the state-licensed businesses. Businesses are not permitted to keep records of buyers' identities but are allowed to request proof of age.

In Washington, growers and sellers need to be licensed by the state and a prior criminal record can reduce the likelihood of obtaining a license. Individuals aged 21 and older can possess a maximum of one ounce of marijuana, and higher amounts of marijuana-infused products. Individuals are not permitted to grow marijuana unless they fall within the scheme of the State's *medical marijuana* legislation. Otherwise, home cultivation for non-medical use remains illegal. The possession and sale of marijuana still violate federal statutes; however, in August 2013, the federal government announced that it will not prosecute individuals who violate federal marijuana laws but who are in compliance with marijuana laws in the two states. The federal government has also issued several exemptions to this policy, including that federal prosecution will commence against individuals who are involved in the diversion of marijuana across state borders or who possess marijuana on federal property.

The potential benefits and consequences of these two legislative changes are yet unknown. However, the changes are likely to raise considerable revenue for the two states, and they have the potential to reduce stigma, and jail and prison populations. Some media commentary in the United States has suggested that the new marijuana laws are unprecedented, and that governments in other countries will be interested in the outcomes. The laws are "unprecedented" in *contemporary* US society, but more accurately reflect a return to legal tolerance that was in place up until the early twentieth century. Moreover, drug laws in Portugal were altered drastically in 2001 when that country decriminalized a host of drugs, including cocaine and heroin. Although possession is still illegal in Portugal, the act is handled under administrative rather than criminal law (drug trafficking remains a criminal offense). Interested readers are encouraged to review the debate over the results of Portugal's wide-scale decriminalization (see Hughes and Stevens 2012). Recent changes in Colombia have resulted in the decriminalization of small amounts of cocaine and marijuana for personal use. In Ecuador, the possession of drugs for personal use has been decriminalized and lighter sentences are now imposed for traffickers who supply small amounts of drugs. Although Uruguay has never criminalized possession of drugs when intended for personal use, proposed legislation in that country would allow for the government to authorize licenses for marijuana farms and to regulate the sales of marijuana through pharmacies. Consumers would need to be registered with the government before they can purchase state-regulated marijuana. The presidential plan is to sell marijuana that is both cheaper and of higher quality than illicit sources. Tourists from other countries will not be permitted to participate in the scheme. In the Netherlands, drug use remains illegal, although possessing small amounts is generally overlooked by law enforcement. That policy is likely to continue in Amsterdam, where coffee shops are a huge boost for tourism in the city. Globally, small yet instrumental changes in drug laws quite possibly could pave the way for additional reforms.

Foreign Policy and the US War on Drugs

The United States and the vast majority of other member states of the United Nations are signatories to or have ratified three UN treaties that relate to international drug control. The 1961 Single Convention on Narcotic[1] Drugs (and its amended protocols) describes 119 psychoactive substances over which domestic and international controls are warranted. The 1961 Convention also mandates control over several precursors, that is, chemicals or natural products that are used to produce or manufacture illicit substances. These precursors include safrole (used to manufacture MDMA), ephedrine (used to produce methamphetamine), and other substances. International drug control was expanded through the 1971 Convention on Psychotropic Substances, which broadened the list of psychoactive substances to include amphetamines, barbiturates, and some hallucinogens. The 1988 Convention Against Illicit Traffic in Narcotic Drugs and Psychotropic Substances emphasizes the role of law enforcement and international cooperation that focuses on anti-trafficking initiatives. The 1988 Convention addresses issues such as money laundering and asset forfeiture.

The Obama Administration requested approximately $25 billion for its federal drug control programs in fiscal year 2014. Approximately one-fifth of the funds will be spent on international and interdiction programs. Crop eradication is a major international initiative and refers to the planned destruction of plants that are known to produce psychoactive effects. These plants are considered to be the primary sources of supply of illicit drugs that are available in the United States. As a tool of contemporary US international drug policy, crop eradication is aimed at coca and opium poppies, although during the late 1960s, US-sponsored crop eradication focused on cannabis grown in Mexico. The assumption is that the use of heroin and cocaine will decline if opium poppies and coca are eradicated. Crop destruction occurs through the spraying of toxic chemicals (i.e., herbicides) or through uprooting the plants by machine or manually. Although led and funded by the United States, crop eradication usually requires the support of a foreign government. In Colombia, coca eradication commenced in 1994 with the provision of additional US funds beginning in 2000 in support of an initiative known as Plan Colombia. Other US funding has supported crop eradication in Colombia, the Andean region and Mexico. Eradication is often conducted by US defense contractors and the herbicides have been provided by US-based companies (e.g., Monsanto).

US-sponsored eradication of illicit crops is highly controversial. The US government has long argued that it is cheaper to destroy crops at the source rather than spend funds on anti-trafficking efforts designed to stop the flow of illicit drugs into the United States. In other words, officials have argued that is cheaper to destroy a field of coca than to detect and confiscate cocaine powder that the field would likely produce. Opponents of crop eradication have emphasized its implications for people's health and incomes, particularly for peasant farmers and their families.

Aerial eradication involves the spraying of harmful pesticides that can negatively impact on the health of area residents and can destroy animal and other plant life. Although the US government has claimed that the pesticides cause minimal harm, the World Wildlife Fund has referred to the spraying as "ecocide." In recent years, aerial fumigation has occurred only in Colombia. However, in 2011, large numbers of Colombian peasant farmers engaged in protest by blocking roads, arguing that crop eradication caused damage to people's health, polluted water supplies, and killed domestic animals and other crops. Manual and machine

eradication take considerably more time than aerial fumigation, but they are believed to be safer than aerial spraying. Bolivia uses machines and manual labor to destroy coca fields, although under the leadership of President Evo Morales (a former coca farmer), approximately two-thirds of Bolivia's coca are legal and utilized for purposes other than for the manufacture of coca paste and cocaine hydrochloride. The US Drug Enforcement Administration once had a field office in Bolivia; however, Morales ended this relationship in 2008. Still, the conflict between government eradication programs and local residents continues; in 2013, coca farmers in Bolivia shot two police officers who were involved in the manual destruction of coca fields. Similar violence has occurred in Afghanistan during eradication of poppy plants. In 2009, the US government ended its direct role in eradication but continues to support eradication by providing funds to the Afghan Ministry of Counter Narcotics. Additionally, the US Embassy in Kabul reported in 2013 that $18.2 million was provided by the United States to Afghanistan's Good Performers' Initiative. This initiative provides funds to Afghan provinces that are reportedly "poppy-free" or that have reduced poppy growing by 10% from the previous year. The direct economic benefits of US funds to farmers is unclear.

The United States also has funded "alternative development" initiatives. These strategies have sought to encourage farmers to switch from illicit to licit crops. US funds have been used to train farmers in the techniques required for new crop production. Alternative development initiatives are usually accompanied by fiscal encouragement, and they can also provide finances to improve infrastructure such as roads. In theory, alternative development is a progressive strategy which considers the economic consequences to farmers whose crops may be subjected to forced eradication. In practice, the programs are difficult to implement. For example, the alternative crop is not usually as profitable as coca or opium poppy. Moreover, peasant farmers often lack trust in US-sponsored anti-drug initiatives. In 2003, a US pilot and Colombian military officer were killed after the Revolutionary Armed Forces of Colombia (FARC) shot down their plane.

US defense contractors who survived the crash were held hostage for nearly five years.

US officials argue that coca eradication in Colombia has reduced the supply of cocaine from that country. However, recent evidence suggests that the price of cocaine has declined and the purity has increased in the United States, Australia, and western Europe (Werb et al. 2013). On the surface then, coca eradication does not appear to have had a major impact on the availability of cocaine in the United States. If it had, we would expect the price of cocaine to increase and purity levels to decline (although several other factors can affect drug markets). The benefits and harm of crop eradication as well as other US policies on foreign soil have been widely debated. The Latin American Commission on Drugs and Democracy consists of individuals in high-level leadership positions in South and Central American countries. A report by the Commission (2009) called for strong consideration of alternative drug control strategies and a re-think of US-style drug prohibition:

> It is imperative to review critically the deficiencies of the prohibitionist strategy adopted by the United States and the benefits and drawbacks of the harm reduction strategy followed by the European Union. (2009, 3)

In Mexico, drug-related violence has escalated substantially in recent years. At least 60,000 people have been killed (including bystanders and others who have not been directly involved in the illicit drug trades), although the accuracy of official estimates has not been validated. It is believed that several drug-related fatalities are not included in the estimates, and large numbers of individuals are missing. The violence has spilled over into neighboring regions. In 2011, for example, twenty-seven people were killed by decapitation, their bodies discovered on private property in Guatemala. The attack was conducted by members of one Mexican cartel. Much of the violence relates to drug trafficking and competition among drug cartels. Mexico is a major supplier of black-tar heroin into the United States, and most of the cocaine that is available in the United States comes from South America via Mexico. Additionally,

clandestine labs in Mexico are believed to produce most of the methamphetamine in the United States that originates from outside the United States. Mexico has long been a major source of marijuana in the United States, although domestically grown marijuana has increased dramatically over the last two decades. Given this background, there is a tendency to blame Mexico for some of the drug problems in the United States. In fact, demand by US consumers fuels the drug supply from foreign sources. Moreover, in 2010 and 2011, the majority of guns discovered from crime scenes in Mexico originated in the United States.

Shirk (2011) argues the importance of US intervention in the Mexican drug war. The land border between Mexico and the United States runs some 2,000 miles, and Shirk reminds us of the yearly $300 billion that results from cross-border legitimate trade as well as "the everyday interactions of more than 14 million people" (2011, 5) who live adjacent to the US-Mexico border. According to Shirk, a weakened Mexican government increases the likelihood of "spillover violence," illegal immigrants, drugs, and weaponry into the United States (2011, 4). US intervention, however, needs to be carefully implemented. Clashes between the two governments have focused on the new Mexican president's concern that US intervention is far too invasive. Aerial surveillance by US spy planes in Mexico territory has been reduced substantially—at the request of the new Mexican government. Some $2 billion in US aid (the Mérida strategy)—allegedly destined to assist Mexico in fighting its drug war—was delayed after Senator Patrick Leahy (Vermont) requested detailed information as to what the funds would accomplish. US foreign policy has the potential to control international drug markets. However, policies can also contribute to the expansion of drug markets. The articles in this section address domestic and foreign policies that relate to the US War on Drugs.

Notes

1. Narcotics refer to opioids, although the list of drugs described in the Treaty include a host of non-opioid drugs, for example, cannabis, cocaine.

References

Hughes, C. E. and A. Stevens. 2012. "A Resounding Success or a Disastrous Failure: Re-Examining the Interpretation of Evidence on the Portuguese De-criminalisation of Illicit Drugs." *Drug and Alcohol Review* 31 (1): 101–113.

Latin American Commission on Drugs and Democracy. 2009. *Drugs and Democracy: Toward a Paradigm Shift. Statement by the Latin American Commission on Drugs and Democracy.* New York: Open Society Institute; São Paulo: Instituto Fernando Henrique Cardoso; Rio de Janeiro: Viva Rio; Rio de Janeiro: Centro Edelstein de Pesquisas Sociais.

Shirk, D. A. 2011. *The Drug War in Mexico: Confronting a Shared Threat.* New York: Council on Foreign Relations.

Werb, D., T. Kerr, B. Nosyk, S. Strathdee, J. Montaner, and E. Wood. 2013. "The Temporal Relationship Between Drug Supply Indicators: An Audit of International Government Surveillance Systems." *British Medical Journal*, Open Access, 3:e003077.

37

Blurred Boundaries

The Therapeutics and Politics of Medical Marijuana

J. MICHAEL BOSTWICK

Despite the legal (but regulated) availability of medical marijuana in several states, debates continue to surface around this intervention. In this article, J. Michael Bostwick uses the concept of "blurred boundaries" to refer to the legal, medical, or social ambiguities between "recreational" versus medical, benefit versus harm of use, laboratory research and pharmacologic application versus federal restrictions, and state versus federal law.

Very few drugs, if any, have such a tangled history as a medicine. In fact, prejudice, superstition, emotionalism, and even ideology have managed to lead cannabis to ups and downs concerning both its therapeutic properties and its toxicological and dependence-inducing effects.

(E. A. CARLINI[1])

Marijuana is unique among illegal drugs in its political symbolism, its safety, and its wide use.

(G. J. ANNAS[2])

Little about the therapeutics or politics of medical marijuana seems straightforward. Despite marijuana's current classification as a Schedule I agent under the federal Controlled Substances Act, a designation declaring it to have high abuse potential and "no currently accepted medical use,"[3] physicians and the general public alike are in broad agreement that *Cannabis sativa* shows promise in combating diverse medical ills. As with opium poppies before it, study of a drug-containing plant has resulted in the discovery of an endogenous control system at the center of neurobiological function whose manipulation has significant implications for the development of novel pharmacotherapies.[4]

As recreational use continues to be endemic in the United States and medical use of smoked cannabis burgeons, it becomes increasingly clear that the two are not discreet from each other, with implications medically for both seasoned and naive users. Even as proponents of legalization contend that smoked marijuana is a harmless natural substance that improves quality of life, a growing body of evidence links it in a small but significant number of users to addiction and the induction or aggravation of psychosis. As laboratory and clinical investigation exposes more of the workings of the recently discovered endocannabinoid system and potential pharmacologic applications show increasing promise, federal law puts a damper on almost any research. As an increasing number of states legalize marijuana's medical use, the federal government maintains its resolute stance that its use for any reason is criminal, a stance that renders prescribers simultaneously law-abiding healers and defiant scofflaws. In what has been called "medicine by popular vote,"[5] the states formulate medical marijuana statutes based not on scientific evidence but on political ideology and gamesmanship.

In each of these respects—recreational versus medical use, benefit versus harm of use, laboratory research and pharmacologic application versus federal restrictions, and state versus federal law— boundaries blur. Contradictions and paradoxes emerge. This article explores each of these areas, with the intent of educating physicians so that they can decide for themselves whether marijuana is a panacea, a scourge, or both. PubMed searches were conducted using the following keywords: *medical marijuana*, *medical cannabis*, *endocannabinoid system*, *CB1 receptors*, *CB2 receptors*, *THC*, *cannabidiol*, *nabilone*, *dronabinol*, *nabiximols*, *rimonabant*, *marijuana legislation*, *marijuana abuse*, *marijuana dependence*, and *marijuana and schizophrenia*. Bibliographies were hand searched for additional references relevant to clarifying the relationships between medical and recreational marijuana use and abuse.

What Is Medical Marijuana?

For 5 millennia, *Cannabis sativa* has been used throughout the world medically, recreationally, and spiritually.[6] As a folk medicine marijuana has been "used to treat an endless variety of human miseries," although typically under the aegis of strict cultural controls, according to DuPont.[7] The first medical use probably occurred in Central Asia and later spread to China and India. The Chinese emperor Shen-Nung is known to have prescribed it nearly 5 millennia ago. Between 2000 and 1400 BC, it traveled to India and from there to Egypt, Persia, and Syria. Greeks and Romans valued the plant for its ropelike qualities as hemp, although it also had

medical applications. The medieval physician Avicenna included it in his formulary, and Europeans of the same epoch ate its nutritional seeds and made its fibers into paper, a practice that continued for centuries. Indeed, the American Declaration of Independence was purported to have been drafted on hemp-based paper.[8,9]

Traditional Eastern medicine met Western medicine when W. B. O'Shaughnessy, an Irish physician working in Calcutta in the 1830s, wrote a paper extolling "Indian hemp."[10] The list of indications for which he recommended cannabis—pain, vomiting, convulsions, and spasticity—strikingly resembles the conditions for which modern medical marijuana proponents extol its virtues. As of 1854, the medical use of cannabis received official legitimacy by its listing in the US Dispensatory.[11] The black leather bags of 19th-century US physicians commonly contained (among many other plant-based medicaments) cannabis tinctures and extracts for ailments ranging from insomnia and headaches to anorexia and sexual dysfunction in both sexes.[12]

Cannabis-containing remedies were also used for pain, whooping cough, asthma, and insomnia and were compounded into extracts, tinctures, cigarettes, and plasters.[13,14] More recently, the Institute of Medicine issued a report based on a summary of the peer-reviewed literature addressing the efficacy of therapeutic marijuana use. The 1999 study found at least some benefit for smoked marijuana in stimulating appetite, particularly in AIDS-related wasting syndrome, and in combating chemotherapy-induced nausea and vomiting, severe pain, and some forms of spasticity.[15,16]

Contemporary Americans who eschew mainstream medical treatments while embracing herbal remedies perpetuate this 19th-century tradition of cannabis use. Even if cannabis use lacks the scientific legitimacy endowed by the randomized controlled trials that underpin modern evidence-based medicine, these individuals assert that the smoked herb is highly effective against "a vast array of diseases that are refractory to all other medications"[17] and requires no further study to prove its medical worth. Americans who shun prescription drugs but stock up on "natural" compounds in the vitamin section of their local grocery store are prime candidates for this long-established folk nostrum, an "organic" means of self-medication.

With gardening sections in bookstores displaying robust selections of manuals for cannabis cultivation, an uninformed shopper might conclude that growing marijuana is as legitimate in the United States as cultivating roses or zinnias. Anyone with a credit card has ready access to blueprints for marijuana propagation and culture. The concentration of δ-9-tetrahydrocannabinol (THC), the psychoactive ingredient in cannabis, ranges from less than 0.2% in fiber-type hemp (so-called ditch weed) to 30% in the flower buds of highly hybridized sinsemilla.[18] With the goal of achieving better, more intense highs, cannabis cultivators have crossed and recrossed diverse strains with the result that an average THC content of 2% in 1980 became 4.5% in 1997 and 8.55% by 2006.[19,20]

The term *medical marijuana* is ambiguous in that it can refer to 2 of the 3 forms in which cannabinoids occur.[18,21] These include (1) endocannabinoids, arachidonic acid derivatives such as anandamide produced in human tissue like any other endogenous neurotransmitters; (2) phytocannabinoids, the hundreds of compounds in the *C. sativa* plant, including the 2 most medically relevant ones, THC and cannabidiol; and (3) synthetic cannabinoids, laboratory-produced congeners of THC and cannabidiol that form the foundation of the pharmaceutical industry in cannabinoid-related products.[21] For purposes of this review, *medical marijuana* will be synonymous with *botanical cannabis*, the second option, as distinct from the third option, *pharmaceutical cannabinoids*, which are synthetic cannabinoid-based medications in use or under development.

Botanical cannabis attracts the notoriety and controversy. Given the far-flung influence of endocannabinoids throughout the body, it is not surprising that botanical cannabis has traditionally been used to combat so many ills. In modern times, it has become an option of last resort for those for whom available pharmaceuticals have proven ineffective, including individuals with intractable nausea and vomiting with cancer chemotherapy or anorexia in human immunodeficiency virus

disease. This is the same substance, of course, that delights recreational users, blurring the boundary between health care and pleasure.

Recreational Use Blends Into Medical Use

For recreational users, access to marijuana has always been about getting intoxicated. In the 21st century, cannabis is the most widely used illicit drug in the world,[22] with the United Nations estimating that up to 190 million people consumed cannabis in 2007.[23–25] Alice B. Toklas's legendary brownies notwithstanding, smoke inhalation is the preferred method of ingestion.[20] Unlike eaten botanical cannabis, smoked botanical cannabis affords high bioavailability, rapid and predictable onset, and easy titration that allows the smoker to maximize desired psychotropic effects and minimize negative ones.[26,27] In what Russo calls an "entourage effect," other cannabinoid constituents of the smoke besides THC may enhance the high[28] or reduce the toxic effects of unopposed THC.[29] Under the influence of the inhaled drug, most users experience "mild euphoria, relaxation, and perceptual alterations, including time distortion and intensification of ordinary experiences such as eating, watching films, listening to music, and engaging in sex."[20] A few experience dysphoria, anxiety, even frank paranoia—symptoms that can also trouble medical users.[30] As cannabis strains are bred that amplify THC content and diminish counteracting cannabidiol, highs become more intense but so do degrees of anxiety that can rise to the level of panic and psychosis, particularly in naive users and unfamiliar stressful situations.[31–33]

Marijuana is touted as a kind of social lubricant, helping users relax and feel more expansive and less self-conscious. Effects that can limit use in a medical setting (short-term memory disruption, a sense of slowed time, increased body awareness, reduced ability to focus, incoordination, and sleepiness) are exactly the sensations recreational users prize.[21,34] Cohen[35] sums it up thus: "Can the recreational use of marijuana cause cognitive impairment? The most obvious answer is 'yes'—after all, this is the basic reason for its recreational use."

Whereas the psychoactive properties of cannabis were first recognized thousands of years ago, these mind-transcending qualities were valued primarily as religious adjuncts. In the West before the mid-20th century, recreational cannabis use was restricted to such fringe or marginalized groups as European intellectuals, rural Brazilian blacks and fishermen, and impoverished Mexicans for whom it was "the opium of the poor." Use became increasingly popular in African American and immigrant Hispanic neighborhoods before 1950. The "explosion of its consumption for hedonistic purposes" to the point that up to two-thirds of US young adults, transcending social class and race, had tried cannabis did not occur until the 1970s and 1980s.[12] This explosion happened not only among those getting high for fun but also in those seeking to treat protean medical conditions.

Medical and recreational users differ in how they use the drug. The amount used and goals of ingestion diverge.[36] The fundamental motivation (symptom relief) of the former does not match the goal (getting high) of the latter.[25] Nonetheless, several studies have demonstrated significant overlap between medical users and recreational users. In a Canadian study of 104 human immunodeficiency virus–positive adults, 43% reported botanical cannabis use in the previous year. Although two-thirds endorsed medical indications, ranging from appetite stimulation and sleep induction to antiemesis and anxiolysis, a full 80% of this group also used it recreationally.[37] Another team of Canadian investigators interviewed 50 self-identified medical cannabis users, finding that "typically medical cannabis use followed recreational use and the majority of those interviewed were long-term and sometimes heavy recreational users." Most medical users continued their recreational use.[38] One of the "protean" medical indications is even drug dependence itself. Although there is no research to support a substitution strategy, addicts attempting to reduce negative outcomes from alcohol, prescription drugs, or illicit drugs, such as opiates, may have switched to medical cannabis, regarded as a safer option than the substances on which they were formerly dependent.[39,40]

Blurring the boundary between medical and recreational use still further, interviews with more than 4100 Californians revealed that the medically ill prefer inhaling their medication. When taken in pill form, drug effects are harder to control and more likely to prove noxious or excessively prolonged.[26] Unlike smoked cannabis, swallowed cannabis undergoes first-pass hepatic metabolism, leading to variable and unpredictable amounts of active agent reaching target tissues. Absorption is more erratic and peak concentrations lower.[11] Smoked cannabis offers both rapid response and easy titration[35] based on the number of inhalations. In the manner of patient-controlled analgesia (the bedside narcotics pumps used in medical settings), smokers can dose themselves repeatedly throughout the day, inhaling enough THC to get analgesic benefit but not enough to sustain motor or psychoactive adverse effects that will dissipate rapidly, if they occur at all.[27,41] Medical users may actually consume less than recreational users, inhaling doses sufficient only to produce desired clinical effects for only as long as needed.[35] Vaporizers that heat cannabis enough to release cannabinoids but not the smoke and toxins generated with combustion have the potential to reduce respiratory symptoms and decrease negative effects on pulmonary function associated with burning the drug.[42,43]

Medical users have the added benefit of breathing in such other marijuana components as cannabidiol, purported to act synergistically with THC in both increasing benefits and reducing adverse effects.[44] THC-induced euphoria may also work synergistically with the drug's analgesic effects.[21] In contrast to the usual medical model, the patient rather than physician determines the correct dose. The physician's instructions to the patient may be as vague as telling him or her to smoke as much as needed.[45]

As with the Canadian studies, the California study found that medical use often "occurred within a context of chronic use." That is, those who favored smoked cannabis for medical purposes were kindly disposed toward the drug from previous recreational experience with it and were typically unperturbed by cognitive and euphoric adverse effects. Indeed, the combination of physical and emotional relief botanical cannabis provides may motivate the medically ill to continue using it.[26] Further confirming this relationship were the demographics that emerged from an English study of botanical cannabis use in individuals with chronic pain, multiple sclerosis, depression, arthritis, and neuropathy. Botanical cannabis users were significantly more likely to be young, male, and recreationally familiar with the drug ($P < .001$).[46] A recent California study of patrons of medical marijuana clinics found similar demographics: a sample that was three-fourths male, three-fifths white, and overwhelmingly familiar with cannabis from recreational use. Although men, whites, and African Americans were overrepresented, women, Latinos, and Asian Americans had disproportionately low representation.[47]

Botanical cannabis is clearly not for everyone. Multiple observers report that patients without recreational experience have difficulty tolerating its psychoactive adverse effects and ultimately refuse to continue using it.[28] Elikkottil et al.[21] caution about drawing conclusions that botanical cannabis is only for "potheads," however, given that randomized controlled trials of botanical cannabis in inexperienced users have not been performed.

The Relationship Between Psychosis and Marijuana

Marijuana continues to have the reputation among the general public as being benign, non–habit-forming, and incapable of inducing true addiction.[39,48] For most users this may be so. Experimentation with marijuana has become an adolescent rite of passage, with the prevalence of use peaking in the late teens and early 20s, then decreasing significantly as youths settle into the adult business of establishing careers and families. With a lifetime dependence risk of 9% in marijuana users versus 32% for nicotine, 23% for heroin, 17% for cocaine, and 15% for alcohol,[23] the addiction risk with marijuana is not as high as that for other drugs of abuse. Unlike cocaine dependence, which develops explosively after first use, marijuana dependence comes on insidiously.[49] Marijuana use typically starts at a younger age than cocaine use (18 versus 20 years of age). The risk for new-onset dependence is essentially zero after the age of 25 years, whereas cocaine dependence continues to accrue until the age of 45 years. Likewise, the average age at first alcohol use is the same as for marijuana, but alcohol users will keep on making the transition from social use to dependence for decades after first use.[49]

One in 11 users—1 in 6 for those starting in their early teens—is hardly an inconsequential percentage, however.[30] Like all addictive drugs, marijuana exerts its influence through the midbrain reward center, triggering dopamine release in the prefrontal cortex.[51] Although its existence was questioned until recently, a withdrawal syndrome is increasingly appreciated, characterized by irritability, anxiety, anorexia and weight loss, restlessness, disturbed sleep, and craving.[52]

DuPont[7] writes that "marijuana makes users stupid and lazy," citing an extreme amotivational syndrome characterized by listlessness and apathy in heavy smokers, not just when using the drug but all the time. The befuddled, endearingly dissolute stereotype, parodied in "stoner" movies like Cheech and Chong's *Up in Smoke*, is not what happens to most occasional users who experience only temporary mild perceptual changes accompanying a general sense of well-being and ease with the world. The disputed amotivational syndrome of heavy use resembles the negative symptom complex of schizophrenia.[53,54]

Using hospitalization as a proxy for serious psychiatric illness, Schubart et al.[55] identified a dose-response relationship, with incidental users having 1.6 times the chance of hospitalization and heavy users 6.2 times the risk. "The association of cannabis use with psychiatric inpatient treatment is a clear indication of the association of cannabis use with mental illness," they wrote. More specifically and more ominously, those with a psychotic predisposition may respond to marijuana with more marked perceptual changes into which they have little insight, accompanied by elevations in hostility and paranoia.[56] Schizophrenia has been posited as a hypercannabinoid condition because schizophrenic patients have significantly elevated cerebrospinal fluid levels of anandamide, the most important endogenous cannabinoid.[57] Cannabis use has been implicated as a potential cause, aggravator, or masker of major psychiatric symptoms, including psychotic, depressive, and anxiety disorders, particularly in young people.[30,58,59] In underscoring the potential for psychosis, a longitudinal study of more than 50,000 Swedish conscripts has been influential. During a 27-year follow-up period, the more cannabis individuals had used in adolescence, the more likely they were to develop schizophrenia, with those who had used cannabis on more than 50 occasions nearly 7 times more likely to manifest the disease than those who had never used cannabis.[60]

This association between cannabis and psychosis notwithstanding, the question of whether cannabis causes psychosis remains unresolved, even as evidence mounts that its use worsens the course of psychotic illness. In an Australian cohort, Degenhardt et al.[61] tested 4 hypotheses regarding the association between cannabis use and schizophrenia, including that cannabis use (1) may cause schizophrenia in some patients, (2) may precipitate psychosis in vulnerable individuals, (3) may exacerbate symptoms of schizophrenia, or (4) may be more likely in individuals with schizophrenia. They noted that during the last 3 decades of the 20th century, cannabis use had significantly increased in Australia without a corresponding increase in schizophrenia prevalence, an observation that gravitated against a simple cause-and-effect relationship between the two. However, they also found that cannabis use precipitated the onset of the disease in the vulnerable and exacerbated the course of the illness in those who already had it.

In a 2007 meta-analysis pooling 35 longitudinal, population-based studies, Moore et al.[59] found an elevated odds ratio (OR) of 1.41 (95% confidence interval [CI], 1.20-1.65) for psychosis in individuals who had ever used cannabis. They also demonstrated a dose-response effect, with the OR increasing to 2.09 (95% CI, 1.54–2.84) for more frequent users, defined—depending on the study—as daily, weekly, or more than 50 times in their lives. A Dutch study[62] shows how this association plays out in actual numbers. For 3 years, van Os et al. followed up 3964 psychosis-free individuals, 312 of whom used cannabis. During the observation period, 8 of the 312 (2.2%) developed psychotic symptoms, with 7 of the 8 (88%) having severe enough symptoms to justify receiving a full-fledged diagnosis. Of the 3652 nonusers, 30 (0.8%) developed symptoms, with only 3 of the 30 (10%)

meeting criteria for a psychotic disorder. The risk was small in both groups but impressively elevated in users versus nonusers.

For individuals already diagnosed as having a schizophrenic spectrum disorder, ongoing cannabis use predicts a rockier course. Comparing 24 abusing and 69 nonabusing schizophrenic patients who were otherwise clinically indistinguishable, Linszen et al.[63] found 42% of abusers versus only 17% of nonabusers experiencing psychotic relapse during the year-long study period ($P = .03$). Moreover, when they compared heavy users (>1 marijuana cigarette per day) with mild users (≤ 1 cigarette per day), they found an even more robust correlation, with 61% of the heavy users versus 18% of the mild users experiencing relapse ($P = .002$). The longer the period of cannabis use, the higher the risk of relapse. In a 10-year follow-up of 229 patients after first hospitalization for schizophrenia, Foti et al.[64] demonstrated that the 10% to 18% who continued to use cannabis throughout the study period had a more severe course as measured by the intensity of positive psychotic symptoms. The association was bidirectional: cannabis smokers had worse psychosis, and the more intensely psychotic individuals were more likely to smoke cannabis.

Van Os et al. hypothesize that cannabis may exert its negative influence through causing dysregulation in the endogenous cannabinoid system that (among many other interactions) modulates dopamine and other neurotransmitter systems within the brain. They posit a "preexisting vulnerability to dysregulation" that accounts for why some individuals and not others respond to cannabis with psychosis.[62] Using contemporary epigenetic terminology, Henquet et al.[65] attribute the greater psychosis risk in certain cannabis users to a synergy between gene (inborn susceptibility) and environment (exogenous trigger). Moreover, increasing evidence implicates a vulnerable developmental period—peripuberty—when cannabis use is more likely to cause trouble.

Dangers of Early Use

Whereas adult users appear comparatively immune to cannabis-induced behavioral and brain morphologic changes, the same cannot be said of individuals initiating use during their early teens, when effects are both more severe and more long-lasting than in adults.[66] During puberty, a period characterized by significant cerebral reorganization, particularly of the frontal lobes implicated in behavior, the brain is especially vulnerable to adverse effects from exogenous cannabinoids.[58,67] How they interfere with this remodeling process during what Schneider[67] calls a "sensitive period" is unknown, although Bossong and Niesink[68] propose that exogenous cannabis use can induce schizophrenia during late brain maturation through physiologic disruption of the endogenous cannabinoid system that modulates glutamate and γ-aminobutyric acid release in prefrontal neurocircuitry, an iteration of the hypothesis of van Os et al. Furthermore, in keeping with the epigenetic hypothesis of Henquet et al., carriers of a specific polymorphism of the catechol oxidase methyltransferase gene (*COMT* valine 158 allele) are especially likely to develop psychotic symptoms or full-blown schizophrenia, an effect attenuated or eliminated if cannabis use is delayed until after brain maturity.[69]

Short of full-blown schizophrenia, many other persistent effects have been observed in heavy (defined as weekly or more often) pubertal users, including working memory deficits, reduced attention, reduced processing speed, anhedonia, abnormal social behavior, susceptibility to mood and anxiety disorders, and greater likelihood of dependence.[67,70] Kuepper et al.[71] posit that ongoing cannabis use may increase psychotic disorder risk by making transient psychotic experiences in adolescent users persist to the point of becoming permanent.

A study from 6 European countries comparing the health and legal implications of cannabis initiation before the age of 16 years found it associated with higher levels of abuse not only of cannabis but also of other illicit drugs, higher rates of both physical injuries and psychosomatic symptoms, academic failure, and delinquency.[72] Poor academic achievement, deviant childhood and adolescent behavior, rebelliousness, and parental histories of substance abuse characterize those at highest risk of dependence.[20,73] Those who started using marijuana before the age of 12 years had nearly 5 times the hospitalization rate of those starting in their later teens. Moderate use after the age of 18 years was not associated

with increased rates of mental illness, concluded Schubart et al.[55] Protective against dependence is adult age of initiation and low-to-moderate use, particularly when marijuana is ingested for therapeutic rather than recreational purposes.[66]

With regard to cannabis as a "gateway" drug, its regular or heavy use in adolescence is clearly associated with increased risk for both abuse and dependence on other illicit drugs.[44] Neither causality nor directionality has been proven, however. Cannabis use may simply be a marker for deviant behavior, with the tendency to advance to harder drugs the result of their simply being available.[39,44,74] In what has been called a "reverse gateway," cannabis use weekly or more often predisposes adolescent users to more than 8 times the risk of eventual tobacco use and progression to nicotine dependence.[75]

Schneider[66] reminds us that most adolescents who use cannabis do not experience harmful outcomes. Concerning psychosis specifically, Luzi et al.[76] emphasize that only 3% of heavy users actually develop schizophrenia. Nonetheless, reducing or delaying cannabis use could postpone or even prevent 1 in 6 cases of new-onset psychosis.[60,77]

Adolescent cannabis use is also associated with depressive and anxiety disorders that emerge later in life.[44] In a cohort of Australian girls followed up for 7 years from the ages of 14 to 15 years, 60% had used cannabis by the end of the study and 7% were daily users. Although the presence of current depression and anxiety did not predict cannabis use, gravitating against a self-medication hypothesis, Patton et al.[50] observed a dose-related risk of eventual depression and anxiety. Weekly use was associated with nearly double the risk (OR, 1.9; 95% CI, 1.1–3.3) of subjects later reporting anxiety or depression, and daily use corresponded with an OR of 5.6 (95% CI, 2.6–12). The authors were reluctant to attribute the increased risk to cannabis alone, observing that social consequences of frequent use, including educational failure, unemployment, and crime, could account—at least in part—for the psychopathology.

Even as Patton et al.[50] did not find that depression or anxiety drove teens to smoke marijuana, some recreational users appear to use it in a manner suggestive of antidepressant or anxiolytic medications.

Teens using cannabis to decrease anxiety frequently meet criteria for anxiety disorders before their cannabis dependence begins.[32] Bottorff et al.[78] reported on 20 adolescents who used marijuana regularly, finding that these adolescents distinguished themselves from recreational users in that they smoked marijuana not primarily for enjoyment but rather for its capacity to relieve anxiety and lift mood, reduce stress, facilitate sleep, and lessen pain. They titrated their intake, often using several times a day and beginning and ending the day with smoking, and frequently using alone. "Unlike the spontaneity typically involved in recreational use," Bottorff et al. write, "these youth were thoughtful and prescriptive with their marijuana use, carefully monitoring and titrating their use to optimize its therapeutic effect." "Unmet health needs" for them included access to legitimate treatment for depression, insomnia, and anxiety. The paradox of marijuana both inducing and relieving anxiety is reconciled by understanding that effects on anxiety levels are dose dependent.[32] Although deliberate self-medication bears little resemblance to getting high for the pleasure—and occasionally panic—of it, it brings its own dangers. Individuals with anxiety disorders who use marijuana, alcohol, or other drugs in this way are up to 5 times more likely to develop substance dependence than anxious individuals who do not self-medicate.[3]

In sum, marijuana offers the recreational substance abuse version of caveat emptor. Although cannabis is an enjoyable diversion for most, it is linked to self-medication, addiction, or mental illness in a few, particularly those who start young.[3]

Dangers of Medical Marijuana

Those skeptical of botanical cannabis do not argue that it is necessarily bad. Rather they contend that the benefits of cannabis—particularly when smoked—remain scientifically unproven, not only on its own merits but also compared with other available treatments. They contend that the usual standards for evaluating pharmacotherapies have been largely side-stepped.[17] They want legitimate research. In a 2008 position paper, the American College of Physicians trod a middle ground between praising and demonizing botanical cannabis,

stating it is "neither devoid of potentially harmful effects nor universally effective" and calling for "sound scientific study" and "dispassionate scientific analysis" to find the appropriate balance.[79]

Critics of botanical cannabis are less sanguine than the American College of Physicians. They assert that garden-grown cannabis is neither pure nor refined, standards Americans have come to expect in their medications. DuPont calls it "a crude drug, a complex chemical slush," composed of well more than 400 different chemicals from 18 different chemical families, with the smoke containing more than 2000 chemical compounds.[7] In the short term, cannabis can cause increased heart rate, vasodilation with decreased blood pressure (as outwardly manifested by bloodshot eyes), and dizziness.[4] Although the use of vaporizers can minimize toxic exposure,[42,43] cannabis smoke contains many of the same toxins found in tobacco smoke, a concern not for palliative use in the terminally ill but for long-term smokers who put themselves at risk for pharyngitis, rhinitis, asthma, bronchitis, emphysema, and lung cancer.[11,80,81] "The increasing cries for the release of smoked marijuana to treat a variety of medical problems [are] rich in anecdotal testimonies and lacking scientific validation," Schwartz and Voth[82] state, adding that "a wonder drug it isn't." Yet jurisdiction after jurisdiction has permitted the voters rather than researchers following standard US Food and Drug Administration (FDA) protocols to endorse its medical use. "Medicolegal and political issues tend to overshadow the science and the medicine of marijuana use."[83]

So what is already known about the therapeutic potential of cannabis and where might research go were there no proscriptions against studying the plant?

The Endocannabinoid System

Although cannabis has been part of the world's herbal pharmacopoeia for millennia, next to nothing about its mechanisms of action was known until the last half century. As with all folk medicines, practitioners established the therapeutic benefits and risks of their plant-derived remedies through careful observation. In this respect, the cannabis story mirrors that of the Oriental poppy,

Papaver somniferum, the source of opium, which was appreciated both as a renowned painkiller and a tantalizing drug of abuse for thousands of years before its active agent, morphine, was identified in modern times along with opioid receptors, endogenous opioids, and an internal opioid system. "In both instances," write Baker et al.,[4] "studies into drug-producing plants led to the discovery of an endogenous control system with a central role in neurobiology."

Modern scientific study of cannabis commenced with the isolation and structural elucidation of THC in 1964.[51] Not until 1990 was the cannabinoid receptor with which THC interacts, CB1, cloned,[84] and it was 1992 before anandamide, the endogenous ligand corresponding to THC and binding to CB1 receptors, was discovered.[85] Since then, an additional cannabinoid receptor, CB2, has been identified, and the 2 receptors have been found to have disparate distributions and functions in an endocannabinoid system that extends far and wide within the body as a physiologic modulator not only of the central nervous system but also of the autonomic nervous system, immune system, gastrointestinal tract, reproductive system, cardiovascular system, and endocrine network.[30,86]

Described as a "ubiquitous network in the nervous system"[87] that regulates synaptic neurotransmission in both excitatory and inhibitory circuits,[4] the endocannabinoid system is a finely tuned physiologic modulator, an "integral part of the [body's] central homeostatic modulatory system"[10] acting to regulate neurotransmitter release at the level of the synapse.[88] It functions in parallel and in conjunction with adrenergic, cholinergic, and dopaminergic systems in both the central and autonomic nervous systems, with influence on functions as disparate as blood pressure and bone growth.[30,51,84,88] In a specific organ system such as the gut, in which the endocannabinoid system is increasingly understood to have a complex and ubiquitous presence, regional variation in receptor distribution and organ-specific actions can influence functions as diverse as regulation of food intake, visceral sensation, gastrointestinal motility, gastric secretion, intestinal inflammation, and cell proliferation, to list only some.[89] CB1 receptors with their psychoactive

potential are found in the central nervous system and widely distributed throughout the gut.[89] CB2 receptors essentially reside only in the periphery, where their activity is intrinsic to cellular and humoral responses related to neuroinflammation and pain,[86] as well as the critical gastrointestinal functions of digestion and host defense.[89]

The most common G protein–coupled receptors in the central nervous system (CB1 receptors) concentrate in specific brain areas that govern pleasure, movement, learning and memory, and pain, including the frontal cortex, basal ganglia, hippocampus, and cerebellum.[76] In the mesolimbic reward center, they reinforce pleasurable activities via anandamide, the endogenous cannabinoid that subtly regulates dopamine release. Exogenous plant-derived THC is a sledgehammer compared with anandamide's delicate chisel, the former causing marked disruption of neuronal signaling and circuit dynamics in the finely tuned endogenous system[56,88] and inducing addiction in the susceptible.[51] The presence of CB1 receptors in the cerebellum and basal ganglia explains both positive and negative influences of cannabinoids on motor tone and coordinated movement, including THC-induced discoordination or clumsiness in recreational users on the one hand and amelioration of spasticity in upper motor neuron diseases such as multiple sclerosis on the other.[87,88] Through their actions in the hippocampus, CB1 receptors modulate mood, and through activity in both the hippocampus and prefrontal cortex, they influence many elements of cognition, including concentration, short-term memory processing, attention, and tracking behavior.[20,73,87] They influence vegetative functions at the hypothalamic level; "the munchies," to which recreational marijuana smokers are prone and for which medical marijuana is prescribed, result from THC stimulation of CB1 receptors that govern food intake.[89] Nociception is modulated via spinal cord dorsal primary afferent tracts, central components of pain pathways whose manipulation by THC gives rise to its vaunted analgesic capacities. CB1 receptors modulate the activity of dopaminergic neurons that project to the prefrontal cortex from the brainstem reward center, thereby factoring in susceptible individuals into cannabis abuse and dependence.[90] Of note, due to the near absence of brainstem CB1 receptors, the drug spares the autonomic nervous system, no matter how much is ingested, with the result that a lethal overdose in humans has never been reported.[4,87] They are distributed so widely, however, that activating for one purpose can cause indiscriminate activation and a host of unwanted adverse effects throughout the body, a major challenge for pharmaceutical development.[84]

Promising Pharmaceutical Applications

In the rapidly growing field of endocannabinoid pharmacology, the potential for designing pharmacologic interventions is as broad as the endocannabinoid system's bodily distribution.[91] "Perhaps no other signaling system discovered during the past 15 years is raising as many expectations for the development of new therapeutic drugs, encompassing such a wide range of potential strategies for treatments," Di Marzo[92] writes. Describing the endocannabinoid system as "having pleiotropic homeostatic function," he asserts that salutary effects will come from many strategies, including drugs engineered to act as agonists or antagonists through both direct and indirect means, as well as agents to increase synthesis, reduce reuptake, or decrease degradation of endocannabinoids in neuronal synapses.[30] Medications active as analgesics, muscle relaxants, immunosuppressants, anti-inflammatories, appetite modulators, antidepressants, antiemetics, bronchodilators, neuroleptics, antineoplastics, and antiallergens are all possible as a consequence of this "pleiotropic" endocannabinoid system lending itself to manipulation through so many pathways.[92] Di Marzo conceptualizes the overarching pharmaceutical goal as "increasing or decreasing the tone of the endocannabinoid system while keeping side effects at bay."

More recently, researchers have stated that the power of new pharmacologic products will obviate the need for botanical cannabis. Izzo and Camilleri[93] envision "selective modulation of the endocannabinoid system in humans using modern pharmacological principles." Whereas botanical cannabis may be justifiable for experienced users with terminal illness and a tolerance for its psychoactive effects, particularly while awaiting these new drugs, Kalant[28] argues that future advances will result from developing highly selective, pure pharmaceuticals taken orally to bypass the health consequences of smoke exposure.[17,28]

Examples of specific strategies include using cannabinoid receptor agonists to increase gut motility in conditions such as ileus and using antagonists to decrease motility in inflammatory bowel disease.[93,94] Cannabinoid receptor agonists could also reduce inflammation peripherally through CB2 agonist activity.[95] Although mechanisms are poorly understood, cannabinoid agonists have shown promise in the laboratory as antineoplastic agents, with demonstrated antitumor effects including decreased angiogenesis, decreased metastasis through interference with cell migration, inhibited carcinogenesis, and attenuated inflammation.[94] Cannabinoid receptor antagonists could reverse the low blood pressure found in hemorrhagic shock, septic shock, and cirrhotic liver failure.[84]

The relationship between cannabis use and psychotic illness remains unsettled, even as hypothesized dysregulation of the endocannabinoid system in a number of psychiatric disorders has implications for developing treatments capable of manipulating relevant brain regions.[61,90,96] Given the increased density of CB1 receptors in the prefrontal cortex of schizophrenic patients[90] and the potential role of central CB1 receptor agonists such as THC in the production of schizophreniform illnesses,[30] the experimental CB1 receptor antagonist SR141716 has shown potent antipsychotic activity acting like an atypical antipsychotic.[54] Cannabidiol has also demonstrated antipsychotic properties without extrapyramidal adverse effects through poorly understood actions on both cannabinoid and noncannabinoid receptors.[30,91] In the cases of both SR141716 and cannabidiol, it is unclear whether they exert their influence directly via the CB1 receptor or indirectly through CB1 modulation of the dopaminergic and glutaminergic systems believed to be involved in the cognitive and behavioral impairments of schizophrenia. Regardless, each shows promise as a novel agent for treating psychotic disorders.[54]

Speaking to the broad promise of cannabinoid-based pharmaceuticals, Ben Amar[11] writes that "for each pathology it remains to be determined what type of cannabinoid and what route of administration are most suitable to maximize the beneficial effect of each preparation and minimize the incidence of undesirable reactions." Further understanding of the workings of the endocannabinoid system will continue to shed new light on disease processes.[21] The goals of research should be to identify the best strategies for exploiting the endocannabinoid system's physiologic and pathophysiologic effects and fashion pharmaceuticals accordingly.[5]

Currently Available Pharmaceuticals

To date, only 4 pharmaceutical cannabinoids have been marketed. The first and second (dronabinol and nabilone) have been available in the United States since 1985 and a third one (nabiximols) in Canada since 2005.[36] A fourth (rimonabant) has shown promise treating nicotine dependence and reducing appetite in obese individuals. Available in Europe since 2006, the FDA failed to approve its release in the United States over concerns it can induce depression and suicidal behavior.[56,84,90]

The 2 US agents are CB1 receptor agonists, based on cannabis' primary psychoactive component, THC. FDA approved since 1985,[97] dronabinol (Marinol), a Schedule III controlled substance, is synthetic THC indicated for treating chemotherapy-induced nausea and vomiting and AIDS-related anorexia and wasting. With similar indications, nabilone (Cesamet) is a synthetic analog of THC. Dronabinol's therapeutic effect unfolds gradually for 30 to 60 minutes and lasts up to 6 hours. At 60 to 90 minutes, nabilone takes longer to act but persists as long as 12 hours.[14]

Even though the antiemetic efficacy of both dronabinol and nabilone equals or exceeds that of phenothiazines, their use is limited by the narrow gap between effective therapeutic doses and doses that cause such adverse effects as euphoria, dysphoria, cognitive clouding, drowsiness, and dizziness that are particularly problematic in naive users, whether smoking marijuana or taking oral pharmaceuticals.[11,44,88,98] The irony, of course, is that the "high" for one class of users is the "acute toxic effect" for another.[30] Moreover, because of variable absorption and first-pass kinetics, pharmaceutical cannabinoids achieve unpredictable blood levels, delaying both onset and cessation of therapeutic action while making the elusive therapeutic but nontoxic blood level that much harder to achieve. Interest in these agents has waned for arresting nausea and emesis with the advent of 5-HT_3 receptor antagonists like ondansetron that have greater potency, minimal psychotropic effects, and intravenous capabilities.[11]

Playing the devil's advocate, Ware and St. Arnaud-Trempe[99] question why dronabinol or nabilone would ever be preferable to inhaled THC, given their adverse effects and delayed onset of action and botanical cannabis' lower cost and readier availability. Although the delayed onset is problematic when treating acute nausea, these pharmaceutical cannabinoids may have a therapeutic edge over other oral agents in managing delayed nausea and vomiting or preventing it altogether.[17,21,29,100] Wilkins[27] and Turcotte et al.[14] emphasize that pharmaceutical cannabinoids should not be first-line therapies when better tolerated and more effective agents exist. For an indication such as emesis, dronabinol or nabilone is best reserved for cases resistant to standard therapies.[14]

Cannabidiol, the other important component found in botanical cannabis, is distinguished by its multiple peripheral mechanisms, including interaction with vanilloid receptors, modulation of adenosine signaling, interference with proinflammatory cytokines, and both immunosuppressant and antioxidant activity.[33] Cannabidiol lacks psychoactivity and may mitigate the anxiety and paranoia THC can induce, particularly in naive users. Mounting evidence suggests that the 2 cannabinoids work synergistically through an "entourage effect," with their interaction reducing the noxious effects of unopposed THC.[29,90] Moreover, through nonreceptor actions, cannabidiol has shown promise in its own right in the central nervous system as a possible anxiolytic and antipsychotic agent, as well as an anticonvulsant and neuroprotective agent.[56,76,91]

In Canada, an additional agent not yet available in the United States (but currently in phase 3 trials) more closely approximates the beneficial delivery method of smoked cannabis absent some of the risks, including tolerance, withdrawal, and high abuse potential.[21,25] With indications for cancer pain and neuropathic pain in multiple sclerosis, nabiximols (Sativex) is a mouth spray that contains both THC and cannabidiol in liquid form to take advantage of the modulatory interaction between the two.[10,29] Administered as an oromucosal spray, nabiximols uses a novel delivery method, absorption through the buccal mucosa, with the rapid-onset advantage of inhaled cannabis and the obvious benefit of controlled and regulated delivery but without such deleterious effects of smoking as sedation and memory impairment.[101]

Rapid uptake notwithstanding, a clinically significant difference between botanical cannabis and nabiximols is the latter's reduced bioavailability. With peak plasma THC concentrations nearly 20 times lower than with smoked cannabis, nabiximols flattens the steep-slope pharmacokinetic profile found in botanical cannabis, with corresponding reductions in adverse psychotropic effects.[25,29] It is this pharmacokinetic divergence from botanical cannabis that reduces the likelihood of nabiximols inducing dependence.[14,25] The nabiximols story underscores how a pharmaceutical that contains the same active ingredient as smoked cannabis can have disparate therapeutic effects stemming from divergent modes of administration and dissimilar amounts of absorbed THC and cannabidiol.[14,36]

Federal Barriers to Cannabis Research

For nearly a century, cannabis was a part of the American pharmacopeia,[83] but by the 1930s, its days as a legitimate treatment were numbered. The flames of popular fear had been fanned for decades by the popular press[102] and by the likes of such high-camp films as the 1936 *Reefer Madness*, which hysterically portrayed "marihuana" as a threat to Western civilization through its purported capacity to induce user insanity and incite societal mayhem. In a standoff foreshadowing the current medical-political gridlock, the Federal Bureau of Narcotics over the objection of the American Medical Association pushed for the congressional passage of the 1937 Marihuana [sic] Tax Act that taxed cannabis at $1 an ounce when taken medicinally, $100 an ounce when used for unapproved purposes.[11] Musto[102]

contends that the law was actually meant to placate xenophobic law enforcement officials and legislators from southwestern and western states who associated marijuana's use with "degenerate Mexicans and migrant workers," feared as a locus of crime and "deviant behavior." Pharmaceutical companies opposed any regulation.[102] In 1942, its removal from the US Dispensatory after nearly a century stripped it of any remaining therapeutic legitimacy.[47]

Not until 1970, however, citing marijuana's potential for abuse and addiction, did the US Congress finally declare it to have no medical value, rendering illegal a plant that had been used medicinally throughout the world for thousands of years.[51,83] Ironically, given the recent hue and cry over medical marijuana having been legalized without scientific input, the US Congress had failed to follow its usual review process dictated by the Controlled Substances Act that requires scientific evaluation and testimony before legislative action. It declared cannabis illegal in the absence of such evidence.[15]

With cannabis declared to have "no currently accepted medical use," the FDA designated it a Schedule I drug, a categorization reserved for street drugs with high abuse potential, such as heroin, Quaaludes, lysergic acid diethylamide, and 3,4-methylenedioxymethamphetamine.[3] This designation has resulted in a near-cessation of scientific research on cannabis in the United States, particularly because the only federally authorized source of cannabis is a strain grown at the University of Mississippi and accessible to researchers only by applying to the National Institute on Drug Abuse,[103] which is reluctant to support medical research and has historically focused its efforts (almost) exclusively on demonstrating the drug's harmful effects.[14] According to Ware et al.,[46,81,99] most cannabis research in the United States occurs "under a paradigm of prohibition and the study of risk is not yet balanced by much-needed research on benefits."

In challenging the one-sided devaluation of cannabis as a dangerous substance, Cohen[35] emphasizes that medical decision making is not based on risk alone. "The linchpin for medical decision-making is not *risk*—for no treatment is without risk—but the *balancing of risks and benefits*." Any rational consideration of legalizing medical marijuana should thus include both sides of the equation. Martin[17] writes that the "basic principles of medicine should take precedence over political expediency in the development of a rational strategy for any therapeutic agent, even one as controversial as marijuana." Marijuana being relegated to Schedule I status appears especially irrational when precedence exists for assigning potential drugs of abuse Schedule II status when they also possess manifest medical benefits. Opioids, including morphine, are derived from the sap of *P somniferum*, the opium poppy. Widely abused in forms ranging from intravenous heroin to oral oxycodone, opioids nonetheless remain in other forms the most potent painkillers in the legitimate pharmacologic armamentarium. Cocaine, a product of the leaves of the *Erythroxylum coca* plant, likewise has ongoing utility as a topical anesthetic and vasoconstrictor. Closely related structurally to methamphetamine, a scourge among drug abusers in broad swaths of rural America,[104] psychostimulants such as methylphenidate and dextroamphetamine are treatment mainstays for attention-deficit/hyperactivity disorder. All these drug classes, plus barbiturates and sedative-hypnotics such as benzodiazepines, have high abuse potential but also important legitimate medical roles. "Their addicting liability alone has not automatically been allowed to contraindicate their use," states Cohen.[35] Readily available for laboratory scrutiny, the medically active ingredients have been isolated and purified so that physicians can prescribe them "free of a hodgepodge of inactive and potentially harmful substances."[7]

The involvement of an alphabet soup of federal agencies with divergent missions creates a series of potential barriers because several have the power to veto proposed initiatives.[105] The FDA, for example, authorizes research to proceed on safety and efficacy, the National Institute on Drug Abuse provides the research material, and the Drug Enforcement Agency grants the investigator the actual license to perform the research. Any one of these agencies has the power to halt an initiative in its tracks.[15] As described earlier in this article, the political climate at the federal level has essentially quashed the type of research that is routine before commercial introduction of new drugs. Ironically what Cohen[15] calls "federal intransigence" toward cannabis continues, even as knowledge about the substance—most generated in research laboratories outside the United States in countries, such as Canada, that legalized medical botanical cannabis in 2006—has advanced to the point that the drug and its interactions with the endocannabinoid system can actually be studied biochemically.[11,77] Moreover, the intransigence perpetuates what Aggarwal et al.[10] label a "translational gap" between "patient-centered medicine" as manifested in the public's wide support and use of botanical cannabis and the research-driven scientific knowledge that cannot accrue until federal prohibitions on research are lifted. Ill-informed practitioners are thus left to make do with anecdotal testimony and case reports—the least rigorous form of evidence—to guide their prescribing.[10] The current catch-22 is that the cannabis that should be studied—diverse strains hybridized by entrepreneurial drug dealers—is illegal and the cannabis that can be legally studied—the decades-old Mississippi strain—is essentially kept off-limits.

It is a judicial fluke that the National Institute on Drug Abuse has provided medical marijuana to a handful of patients (never more than 32, currently 4 surviving) as the outcome of the settlement in a lawsuit pressed in 1976 by a man with cannabis-responsive glaucoma. That settlement became the basis for the FDA's Compassionate Investigational New Drug Study program for patients with marijuana-responsive conditions. No patient has been enrolled since 1992, when the George H. W. Bush administration suspended new registration in reaction to a large influx of applications from AIDS patients.[106,107]

States' Defiance of Federal Law

Meanwhile, in the legal arena, the federal government pits itself against increasing numbers of states—16 plus the District of Columbia—with regulations permitting botanical cannabis use for certain chronically or critically ill patients that contradict federal law.[10] A consequence of the discrepancies between federal and state statutes is that users and purveyors of botanical cannabis for any purpose can be arrested and charged with federal crimes, even in states where possessing small quantities or growing one's own stash for medical use is legal. In the absence of an overarching federal approach, these states lack consensus on what constitutes physician authorization, which patients qualify for treatment, and how they can acquire their botanical cannabis, creating what is essentially a "regulatory vacuum."[3,15] Possession limits, for example, range from 1 oz and 6 plants in Alaska and Montana to 24 oz and 24 plants in Oregon.[108] Some state laws are remarkably lax. For example, when California became the first American state to legalize botanical cannabis in 1996, it allowed wide latitude for its use, permitting physicians to prescribe it not only for serious medical illnesses but also "for any other illness for which marijuana provides relief," including such emotional conditions as depression and anxiety, a state of affairs that has "maximally broaden(ed) the range of allowable indications."[26] Moreover, no provision of the law defines what constitutes a bona fide patient-physician relationship.[15] An estimated 250,000 to 300,000 Californians have garnered physician approval, a number that belies botanical cannabis being provided only to the seriously ill and dying. A new industry has arisen around cultivating and dispensing medical marijuana to the hundreds of thousands of individuals authorized to use it.

Organized medicine continuing to condemn the federal government for its stance toward medical marijuana drives the ongoing legislative and scientific chaos. The American Medical Association, the Institute of Medicine, and the American College of Physicians contend that the "patchwork of state laws" do little to "establish clinical standards for marijuana use"[3] and have called for reclassification of cannabis as a Schedule II controlled substance so researchers can follow "the principles that are used to evaluate all other pharmacotherapies [that] have largely been ignored for medical marijuana." These principles include pharmaceutical companies petitioning the FDA for the right to put new compounds through a battery of tests in animals and humans that ensure that the drug's benefits outweigh its risks,[79] determining precise dosing regimens, seeking FDA approval for the proposed new drug, and manufacturing unadulterated active drug to high standards. Until this change occurs, a redesignation that would acknowledge not only its abuse risks but also its therapeutic benefits, the "rigorous scientific evaluation" that underpins pharmaceutical regulation in the United States cannot proceed.[3]

Conclusions

Given cannabis' worldwide use for thousands of years for medical and spiritual purposes, the contemporary American tumult over medical marijuana seems peculiar and misguided. Despite cannabis being part of the US pharmacopeia through much of the 19th and early 20th centuries, a federal government deeply suspicious of mind-altering substances began imposing restrictions on its prescription in the late 1930s, culminating in 1970 when the US Congress classified it as a Schedule I substance, illegal, without redeeming qualities.

Despite its illegality, cannabis has in the latter half of the 20th century become the most abused illicit substance in the United States. For most individuals, recreational cannabis use is essentially harmless, a rite of passage ending as young people settle into careers and adult intimate relationships.[20,109,110] For 10%, however, the drug becomes addictive, its relaxing properties transforming into a constant need that interferes with interpersonal and occupational advancement. For an even smaller proportion—those with a predisposition toward psychotic illness—it may abet the earlier emergence of psychosis and a rockier illness course if use persists.

Prohibition notwithstanding, cannabis' recognized medical uses never went out of favor in alternative medicine circles. Its therapeutic properties have been particularly favored by former recreational users familiar with its psychoactive effects, some of whom blur boundaries by continuing to use it recreationally. In the 1980s, it was found effective for treating severe nausea induced by cancer chemotherapy and cachexia in AIDS patients. The first cannabinoid-based pharmaceuticals—dronabinol and nabilone—came into medical use in 1985. Without an understanding of how these medications worked, they were prescribed empirically. As the mysteries of the endocannabinoid system were unraveled during ensuing decades, however, a rationale for both its recreational and sweeping medical effects has emerged.

The natural next step—pharmaceutical development—has been thwarted by the federal government's seeming unwillingness to have new scientific discovery supplant long-standing ideology. Bureaucratic hurdles not erected for other potential pharmaceuticals continue to interfere with legitimate cannabis research. The federal government instituted its 1970 ban in the absence of scientific evidence supporting its position. It maintains the ban, despite scientific evidence suggesting that cannabis could have positive effects on the many organ systems endocannabinoid activity modulates.

Although remaining at risk of arrest on federal charges, medical users have increasing latitude as more and more states endorse botanical cannabis. In defiance of a federal ban that appears increasingly irrational, 16 states and the District of Columbia have legalized botanical cannabis' medical use. Without a federal umbrella, regulations lack any state-to-state uniformity about what constitutes acceptable indications, appropriate prescriber-patient relationships, or legitimate means of acquiring botanical cannabis. In such states, physicians who prescribe medical marijuana are susceptible to prosecution under the same statutes as drug dealers.[111] Public approval and political expediency rather than scientific data drive the continued implementation of these state laws.

Like alcohol imbibers during the Prohibition era in the United States, recreational users continue to smoke cannabis illicitly, as they have always done. Because of this modern-day prohibition, opportunities to further study marijuana's risks and benefits and develop new pharmacotherapies are squandered. In passing their own regulations endorsing medical marijuana use, states defy the federal government. In each of these instances, boundaries among the legal, social, and medical realms blur. Depending on context, marijuana can thus be panacea, scourge, or both.

It is high time for the federal government to acknowledge and accept this "both-ness" by reclassifying marijuana so that it has the same status as certain opiates and stimulants. The Schedule II classification of these pharmaceuticals countenances not only a healthy respect for their addictive potential but also a robust appreciation for their medicinal value.[112] By forcing marijuana to languish as a Schedule I drug with a "high potential for abuse, no accepted medical use, and no accepted safety for use in medically supervised treatment,"[104] the federal government thumbs an illogical nose at contemporary public sentiment, recent scientific discoveries, and potentially head-to-toe therapeutic breakthroughs. This reclassification would be a first step toward reconciling federal and state law and permitting long-stifled research into a potential trove of therapeutic applications to commence.

References

1. Carlini, E. A. 2004. "The Good and the Bad Effects of (-) Trans-Delta-9-Tetrahydrocannabinol (Δ19-THC) on Humans." *Toxicon* 44 (4): 461–467.
2. Annas, G. J. 1997. "Reefer Madness: The Federal Response to California's Medical-Marijuana Law." *New Engl J Med* 337 (6): 435–439.
3. Hoffmann, D. E. and E. Weber. 2010. "Medical Marijuana and the Law." *N Engl J Med* 362 (16): 1453–1457.
4. Baker, D., G. Pryce, G. Giovannoni, and A. J. Thompson. 2003. "The Therapeutic Potential of Cannabis." *Lancet Neurol* 2 (5): 291–298.
5. Voth, E. A. 2001. "Guidelines for Prescribing Medical Marijuana." *West J Med* 175 (5): 305–306.
6. Pertwee, R. G. 2006. "Cannabinoid Pharmacology: The First 66 Years." *Br J Pharmacol* 147 (suppl 1): S163–S171.
7. DuPont, R. L. 2000. *The Selfish Brain: Learning from Addiction.* Center City, MN: Hazelden.
8. Herer, J. n.d. "The Emperor Wears No Clothes." http://www.electricemperor.com/eecdrom/ <HTML/EMP/02/ECH02_03.HTM>. Accessed September 12, 2011.
9. U.S. Constitution Online. n.d. Answers From the FAQ, Page 8:Q145. "What Kind of Paper Was the Constitution Written On?" <http://www.usconstitution.net/constfaq_a8.html. Accessed September 12, 2011>.

10. Aggarwal, S. K., G. T. Carter, M. D. Sullivan, C. ZumBrunnen, R. Morrill, and J. D. Mayer. 2009. "Medicinal Use of Cannabis in the United States: Historical Perspectives, Current Trends, and Future Directions." *J Opioid Manag* 5 (3): 153–168.

11. Ben Amar, M. 2006. "Cannabinoids in Medicine: A Review of Their Therapeutic Potential." *J Ethnopharmacol* 105 (1–2): 1–25.

12. Zuardi, A. W. 2006. "History of Cannabis as a Medicine: A Review." *Rev Bras Psiquiatr* 28 (2): 153–157.

13. Fisar, Z. 2009. "Phytocannabinoids and Endocannabinoids." *Curr Drug Abuse Rev* 2 (1): 51–75.

14. Turcotte, D., J. A. Le Dorze, F. Esfahani, E. Frost, A. Gomori, and M. Namaka. 2010. "Examining the Roles of Cannabinoids in Pain and Other Therapeutic Indications: A Review." *Expert Opin Pharmacother* 11 (1): 17–31.

15. Cohen, P. J. 2010. "Medical Marijuana 2010: It's Time to Fix the Regulatory Vacuum." *J Law Med Ethics* 38 (3): 654–666.

16. Watson, S. J., J. A. Benson Jr., and J. E. Joy. 2000. "Marijuana and Medicine: Assessing the Science Base: A Summary of the 1999 Institute of Medicine Report." *Arch Gen Psychiatry* 57 (6): 547–552.

17. Martin, B. R. 2002. "Medical Marijuana: Moving Beyond the Smoke." *Lancet* 360 (9326): 4–5.

18. Grotenhermen, F. 2005. "Cannabinoids." *Curr Drug Targets CNS Neurol Disord* 4 (5): 507–530.

19. Ashton, C. H. 1999. "Adverse Effects of Cannabis and Cannabinoids." *Br J Anaesth* 83 (4): 637–649.

20. Hall, W. and L. Degenhardt. 2009. "Adverse Health Effects of Non-medical Cannabis Use." *Lancet* 374 (9698): 1383–1391.

21. Elikkottil, J., P. Gupta, and K. Gupta. 2009. "The Analgesic Potential of Cannabinoids." *J Opioid Manag* 5 (6): 341–357.

22. Di Forti, M., P. D. Morrison, A. Butt, and R. M. Murray. 2007. "Cannabis Use and Psychiatric and Cognitive Disorders: The Chicken or the Egg?" *Curr Opin Psychiatry* 20 (3): 228–234.

23. Ben Amar, M. and S. Potvin. 2007. "Cannabis and Psychosis: What Is the Link?" *J Psychoactive Drugs* 39 (2): 131–142.

24. Robson, P. 2001. "Therapeutic Aspects of Cannabis and Cannabinoids." *Br J Psychiatry* 178: 107–115.

25. Robson, P. 2011. "Abuse Potential and Psychoactive Effects of Δ-9-Tetrahydrocannabinol and Cannabidiol Oromucosal Spray (Sativex), a New Cannabinoid Medicine." *Expert Opin Drug Saf* 10 (5): 675–685.

26. O'Connell, T. J. and C. B. Bou-Matar. 2007. "Long Term Marijuana Users Seeking Medical Cannabis in California (2001–2007): Demographics, Social Characteristics, Patterns of Cannabis and Other Drug Use of 4117 Applicants." *Harm Reduct J* 4: 16.

27. Wilkins, M. R. 2006. "Cannabis and Cannabis-Based Medicines: Potential Benefits and Risks to Health." *Clin Med* 6 (1): 16–18.

28. Kalant, H. 2008. "Smoked Marijuana as Medicine: Not Much Future." *Clin Pharmacol Ther* 83 (4): 517–519.

29. Russo, E. and G. W. Guy. 2006. "A Tale of Two Cannabinoids: the Therapeutic Rationale for Combining Tetrahydrocannabinol and Cannabidiol." *Med Hypotheses* 66 (2): 234–246.

30. Gerra, G., A. Zaimovic, M. L. Gerra, et al. 2010. "Pharmacology and Toxicology of Cannabis Derivatives and Endocannabinoid Agonists." *Recent Pat CNS Drug Discov* 5 (1): 46–52.

31. Burgdorf, J. R., B. Kilmer, and R. L. Pacula. 2011. "Heterogeneity in the Composition of Marijuana Seized in California." *Drug Alcohol Depend* 117 (1): 59–61.

32. Crippa, J. A., A. W. Zuardi, R. Martin-Santos, et al. 2009. "Cannabis and Anxiety: A Critical Review of the Evidence." *Hum Psychopharmacol* 24 (7): 515–523.

33. Zuardi, A. W. 2008. "Cannabidiol: From an Inactive Cannabinoid to a Drug with Wide Spectrum of Action." *Rev Bras Psiquiatr* 30 (3): 271–280.

34. Campbell, F. A., M. R. Tramer, D. Carroll, D. J. Reynolds, R. A. Moore, and H. J. McQuay. 2001. "Are Cannabinoids an Effective and Safe Treatment Option in the Management of Pain? A Qualitative Systematic Review." *BMJ* 323 (7303): 13–16.

35. Cohen, P. J. 2009. "Medical Marijuana: The Conflict Between Scientific Evidence and Political Ideology. Part One of Two." *J Pain Palliat Care Pharmacother* 23 (1): 4–25.

36. Wang, T., J. P. Collet, S. Shapiro, and M. A. Ware. 2008. "Adverse Effects of Medical Cannabinoids: A Systematic Review." *CMAJ* 178 (13): 1669–1678.

37. Furler, M. D., T. R. Einarson, M. Millson, S. Walmsley, and R. Bendayan. 2004. "Medicinal

and Recreational Marijuana Use by Patients Infected with HIV." *AIDS Patient Care STDS* 18 (4): 215–228.

38. Ogborne, A. C., R. G. Smart, T. Weber, C. Birchmore-Timney. 2000. "Who Is Using Cannabis as a Medicine and Why: An Exploratory Study." *J Psychoactive Drugs* 32 (4): 435–443.

39. Raphael, B., S. Wooding, G. Stevens, and J. Connor. 2005. "Comorbidity: Cannabis and Complexity." *J Psychiatr Pract* 11 (3): 161–176.

40. Reiman, A. 2009. "Cannabis as a Substitute for Alcohol and Other Drugs." *Harm Reduct J* 6: 35–39.

41. Marmor, J. B. 1998. "Medical Marijuana." *West J Med* 168 (6): 540–543.

42. Earleywine, M. and S. S. Barnwell. 2007. "Decreased Respiratory Symptoms in Cannabis Users Who Vaporize." *Harm Reduct J* 4: 11.

43. Van Dam, N. T. and M. Earleywine. 2010. "Pulmonary Function in Cannabis Users: Support for a Clinical Trial of the Vaporizer." *Int J Drug Policy* 21 (6): 511–513.

44. Hall, W. and L. Degenhardt. 2007. "Prevalence and Correlates of Cannabis Use in Developed and Developing Countries." *Curr Opin Psychiatry* 20 (4): 393–397.

45. Nierengarten, M. B. 2007. "Guidelines Needed for Medical Use of Marijuana." *Lancet Oncol* 8 (11): 965.

46. Ware, M. A., H. Adams, G. W. Guy. 2005. "The Medicinal Use of Cannabis in the UK: Results of a Nationwide Survey." *Int J Clin Pract* 59 (3): 291–295.

47. Reinarman, C., H. Nunberg, F. Lanthier, and T. Heddleston. 2011. "Who Are Medical Marijuana Patients? Population Characteristics from Nine California Assessment Clinics." *J Psychoactive Drugs* 43 (2): 128–135.

48. Johns, A. 2001. "Psychiatric Effects of Cannabis." *Br J Psychiatry* 178: 116–122.

49. Wagner, F. A., J. C. Anthony. 2002. "From First Drug Use to Drug Dependence; Developmental Periods of Risk for Dependence Upon Marijuana, Cocaine, and Alcohol." *Neuropsychopharmacology* 26 (4): 479–488.

50. Patton, G. C., C. Coffey, J. B. Carlin, L. Degenhardt, M. Lynskey, and W. Hall. 2002. "Cannabis Use and Mental Health in Young People: Cohort Study." *BMJ* 325 (7374): 1195–1198.

51. Kogan, N. M. and R. Mechoulam. 2007. "Cannabinoids in Health and Disease." *Dialogues Clin Neurosci* 9 (4): 413–430.

52. Cooper, Z. D. and M. Haney. 2009. "Actions of Delta-9-Tetrahydrocannabinol in Cannabis: Relation to Use, Abuse, Dependence." *Int Rev Psychiatry* 21 (2): 104–112.

53. Lynskey, M. and W. Hall. 2000. "The Effects of Adolescent Cannabis Use On Educational Attainment: A Review." *Addiction* 95 (11): 1621–1630.

54. Roser, P., F. X. Vollenweider, and W. Kawohl. 2010. "Potential Antipsychotic Properties of Central Cannabinoid (CB1) Receptor Antagonists." *World J Biol Psychiatry* 11 (2, pt 2): 208–219.

55. Schubart, C. D., M. P. Boks, E. J. Breetvelt, et al. 2011. "Association Between Cannabis and Psychiatric Hospitalization." *Acta Psychiatr Scand* 123 (5): 368–375.

56. Murray, R. M., P. D. Morrison, C. Henquet, and M. Di Forti. 2007. "Cannabis, the Mind and Society: The Hash Realities." *Nat Rev Neurosci.* 8 (11): 885–895.

57. Leweke, F. M., A. Giuffrida, U. Wurster, H. M. Emrich, and D. Piomelli. 1999. "Elevated Endogenous Cannabinoids in Schizophrenia." *Neuroreport* 10 (8): 1665–1669.

58. Malone, D.T., M. N. Hill, and T. Rubino. 2010. "Adolescent Cannabis Use and Psychosis: Epidemiology and Neurodevelopmental Models." *Br J Pharmacol* 160 (3): 511–522.

59. Moore, T. H., S. Zammit, A. Lingford-Hughes, et al. 2007. "Cannabis Use and Risk of Psychotic or Affective Mental Health Outcomes: A Systematic Review." *Lancet* 370 (9584): 319–328.

60. Zammit, S., P. Allebeck, S. Andreasson, I. Lundberg, and G. Lewis. 2002. "Self Reported Cannabis Use as a Risk Factor for Schizophrenia in Swedish Conscripts of 1969: Historical Cohort Study." *BMJ* 325 (7374): 1199.

61. Degenhardt, L., W. Hall, and M. Lynskey. 2003. "Testing Hypotheses About the Relationship Between Cannabis Use and Psychosis." *Drug Alcohol Depend* 71 (1): 37–48.

62. van Os, J., M. Bak, M. Hanssen, R. V. Bijl, R. de Graaf, and H. Verdoux. 2002. "Cannabis Use and Psychosis: a Longitudinal Population-Based Study." *Am J Epidemiol* 156 (4): 319–327.

63. Linszen, D. H., P. M. Dingemans, and M. E. Lenior. 1994. "Cannabis Abuse and the Course of

Recent-Onset Schizophrenic Disorders." *Arch Gen Psychiatry* 51 (4): 273–279.

64. Foti, D. J., R. Kotov, L. T. Guey, and E. J. Bromet. 2010. "Cannabis Use and the Course of Schizophrenia: 10-Year Follow-Up After First Hospitalization." *Am J Psychiatry* 167 (8): 987–993.

65. Henquet, C., R. Murray, D. Linszen, and J. van Os. 2005. "The Environment and Schizophrenia: The Role of Cannabis Use." *Schizophr Bull* 31 (3): 608–612.

66. Grotenherrnen, F. 2007. "The Toxicology of Cannabis and Cannabis Prohibition." *Chem Biodivers* 4 (8): 1744–1769.

67. Schneider, M. 2008. "Puberty as a Highly Vulnerable Developmental Period for the Consequences of Cannabis Exposure." *Addict Biol* 13 (2): 253–263.

68. Bossong, M. G. and R. J. Niesink. 2010. "Adolescent Brain Maturation, the Endogenous Cannabinoid System and the Neurobiology of Cannabis-Induced Schizophrenia." *Prog Neurobiol* 92 (3): 370–385.

69. Caspi, A., T. E. Moffitt, M. Cannon, et al. 2005. "Moderation of the Effect of Adolescent-Onset Cannabis Use On Adult Psychosis by a Functional Polymorphism in the Catechol-O-Methyltransferase Gene: Longitudinal Evidence of a Gene X Environment Interaction." *Biol Psychiatry* 57 (10): 1117–1127.

70. Jacobus, J., S. Bava, M. Cohen-Zion, O. Mahmood, and S. F. Tapert. 2009. "Functional Consequences of Marijuana Use in Adolescents." *Pharmacol Biochem Behav* 92 (4): 559–565.

71. Kuepper, R., J. van Os, R. Lieb, H. U. Wittchen, M. Höfler, and C. Henquet. 2011. "Continued Cannabis Use and Risk of Incidence and Persistence of Psychotic Symptoms: 10 Year Follow-Up Cohort Study." *BMJ* 342: d738.

72. Kokkevi, A., S. Nic Gabhainn, and M. Spyropoulou. 2006. "Early Initiation of Cannabis Use: A Cross-National European Perspective." *J Adolesc Health* 39 (5): 712–719.

73. Hall, W. and M. Lynskey. 2009. "The Challenges in Developing a Rational Cannabis Policy." *Curr Opin Psychiatry* 22 (3): 258–262.

74. Fergusson, D. M., J. M. Boden, and L. J. Horwood. 2006. "Cannabis Use and Other Illicit Drug Use: Testing the Cannabis Gateway Hypothesis." *Addiction* 101 (4): 556–569.

75. Patton, G. C., C. Coffey, J. B. Carlin, S. M. Sawyer, and M. Lynskey. 2005. "Reverse Gateways? Frequent Cannabis Use as a Predictor of Tobacco Initiation and Nicotine Dependence." *Addiction* 100 (10): 1518–1525.

76. Luzi, S., P. D. Morrison, J. Powell, M. di Forti, and R. M. Murray. 2008. "What Is the Mechanism Whereby Cannabis Use Increases Risk of Psychosis?" *Neurotox Res* 14 (2–3): 105–112.

77. Large, M., S. Sharma, M. T. Compton, T. Slade, and O. Nielssen. 2011. "Cannabis Use and Earlier Onset of Psychosis: A Systematic Meta-Analysis." *Arch Gen Psychiatry* 68 (6): 555–561.

78. Bottorff, J. L., J. L. Johnson, B. M. Moffat, and T. Mulvogue. 2009. "Relief-Oriented Use of Marijuana by Teens." *Subst Abuse Treat Prev Policy* 4: 7.

79. Cohen, P. J. 2009. "Medical Marijuana: The Conflict Between Scientific Evidence and Political Ideology. Part Two of Two." *J Pain Palliat Care Pharmacother* 23 (2): 120–140.

80. Kahan, M. and A. Srivastava. 2007. "Is There a Role for Marijuana in Medical Practice? No." *Can Fam Physician* 53 (1): 22–25.

81. Ware, M. A. 2007. "Is There a Role for Marijuana in Medical Practice? Yes." *Can Fam Physician* 53 (1): 22–25.

82. Schwartz, R. H. and E. A. Voth. 1995. "Marijuana as Medicine: Making a Silk Purse Out of a Sow's Ear." *J Addict Dis* 14 (1): 15–21.

83. MacDonald, J. 2009. "Medical Marijuana: Informational Resources for Family Physicians." *Am Fam Physician* 80 (8): 779.

84. Marx, J. 2006. "Drug Development; Drugs Inspired by a Drug." *Science* 311 (5759): 322–325.

85. Ashton, C. H. 2001. "Pharmacology and Effects of Cannabis: A Brief Review." *Br J Psychiatry* 178: 101–106.

86. Di Marzo, V. and L. D. Petrocellis. 2006. "Plant, Synthetic, and Endogenous Cannabinoids in Medicine." *Annu Rev Med* 57: 553–574.

87. Carter, G. T. and V. Ugalde. 2004. "Medical Marijuana: Emerging Applications for the Management of Neurologic Disorders." *Phys Med Rehabil Clin N Am* 15 (4): 943–954, ix.

88. Iversen, L. 2003. "Cannabis and the Brain." *Brain* 126 (pt 6): 1252–1270.

89. Izzo, A. A. and K. A. Sharkey. 2010. "Cannabinoids and the Gut: New Developments and Emerging Concepts." *Pharmacol Ther* 126 (1): 21–38.

90. Breivogel, C. S. and L. J. Sim-Selley. 2009. "Basic Neuroanatomy and Neuropharmacology of Cannabinoids." *Int Rev Psychiatry* 21 (2): 113–121.

91. Scuderi, C., D. D. Filippis, T. Iuvone, A. Blasio, A. Steardo, and G. Esposito. 2009. "Cannabidiol in Medicine: A Review of Its Therapeutic Potential in CNS Disorders." *Phytother Res* 23 (5): 597–602.

92. Di Marzo, V. 2008. "Targeting the Endocannabinoid System: to Enhance or Reduce?" *Nat Rev Drug Discov* 7 (5): 438–455.

93. Izzo, A. A. and M. Camilleri. 2008. "Emerging Role of Cannabinoids in Gastrointestinal and Liver Diseases: Basic and Clinical Aspects." *Gut* 57 (8): 1140–1155.

94. Oesch, S. and J. Gertsch. 2009. "Cannabinoid Receptor Ligands as Potential Anticancer Agents: High Hopes for New Therapies?" *J Pharm Pharmacol* 61 (7): 839–853.

95. Di Marzo, V. and F. Piscitelli. 2011. "Gut Feelings About the Endocannabinoid System." *Neurogastroenterol Motil* 23 (5): 391–398.

96. Parolaro, D., N. Realini, D. Vigano, C. Guidali, and T. Rubino. 2010. "The Endocannabinoid System and Psychiatric Disorders." *Exp Neurol* 224 (1): 3–14.

97. "Medical Marijuana." 2010. *Med Lett Drugs Ther* 52 (1330): 5–6.

98. Lupica, C. R., A. C. Riegel, A. F. Hoffman. 2004. "Marijuana and Cannabinoid Regulation of Brain Reward Circuits." *Br J Pharmacol* 143 (2): 227–234.

99. Ware, M. A. and E. St. Arnaud-Trempe. 2010. "The Abuse Potential of the Synthetic Cannabinoid Nabilone." *Addiction* 105 (3): 494–503.

100. Kalant, H. 2004. "Adverse Effects of Cannabis on Health: An Update of the Literature Since 1996." *Prog Neuropsychopharmacol Biol Psychiatry* 28 (5): 849–863.

101. Perez, J. and M. V. Ribera. 2008. "Managing Neuropathic Pain with Sativex: A Review of Its Pros and Cons." *Expert Opin Pharmacother* 9 (7): 1189–1195.

102. Musto, D. F. 1972. "The Marihuana Tax Act of 1937." *Arch Gen Psychiatry* 26 (2): 101–108.

103. Harris, G. 2010. "Researchers Find Study of Medical Marijuana Discouraged." *New York Times*. Available at: http://www.nytimes.com/2010/01/19/health/policy/19marijuana.html?scp=1&sq=Researchers%20find%20study%20of%20medical%20marijuana%20discouraged&st=cse. Accessed January 5, 2011.

104. Lineberry, T. W. and J. M. Bostwick. 2006. "Methamphetamine Abuse: A Perfect Storm of Complications." *Mayo Clin Proc* 81 (1): 77–84.

105. Gostin, L. O. 2005. "Medical Marijuana, American Federalism, and the Supreme Court." *JAMA* 294 (7): 842–844.

106. Duara, N. 2011. "4 Americans Get Pot from US Government." 2011. http://www.13abc.com/story/15565279/4-americans-getpot-from-us-government?clientty. Accessed October 8, 2011.

107. Seamon, M. J. 2006. "The Legal Status of Medical Marijuana." *Ann Pharmacother* 40 (12): 2211–2215.

108. Medical Marijuana—ProCon.org. 2011. "16 Legal Medical Marijuana States and DC: Laws, Fees, and Possession Limits." http://medicalmarijuana.procon.org/view.resource.php?resourceID=000881. Accessed August 20, 2011.

109. Chen, K. and D. B. Kandel. 1998. "Predictors of Cessation of Marijuana Use: An Event History Analysis." *Drug Alcohol Depend* 50 (2): 109–121.

110. Duncan, G. J., B. Wilkerson, and P. England. 2006. "Cleaning Up Their Act: The Effects of Marriage and Cohabitation on Licit and Illicit Drug Use." *Demography* 43 (4): 691–710.

111. Dresser, R. 2009. "Irrational Basis: The Legal Status of Medical Marijuana." *Hostings Cent Rep* 39 (6): 7–8.

112. Steinbrook, R. 2004. "Medical Marijuana, Physician-Assisted Suicide, and the Controlled Substances Act." *N Engl J Med* 351 (14): 1380–1383.

For Discussion

1. Review the website material of Medical Marijuana Canada (http://medicalmarijuana.ca) and compare differences with California's policies relating to medical marijuana.

2. How do you think the contradictions between state and federal laws (concerning medical marijuana) will be resolved?

38

Rethinking U.S. Drug Policy

PETER HAKIM

Peter Hakim suggests that US drug policy is at a critical juncture in its contemporary history. The demand for drugs remains high, supply continues, purity has increased, and price has declined over the past several years. Moreover, Hakim notes the subtle change in attitudes among the American public (but also a "silent tolerance") and the critical view of US drug policies by government leaders in other countries. Hakim argues that now is the time for a crucial debate over US policies. The author offers several government initiatives that would foster reconsideration of US policies and possibly pave the way for change.

Three out of four Americans now believe that the United States' forty year "war against drugs" has failed. That view, reported in a 2008 Zogby International survey carried out in collaboration with the Inter-American Dialogue, reveals the profound disappointment of US citizens with their government's anti-drug policies. It suggests that a new US strategy for dealing with illicit drugs is needed and could generate substantial public support.

There is no fully objective way to judge the success or failure of current US drug policy. We simply cannot know what results a different strategy would have produced. The outcomes might well have been a lot worse. However, the available evidence suggests that in the past two decades, US anti-drug policies—focused on prohibiting drug production, trade, and consumption, and punishing those involved—have done little to diminish the problems they were designed to address. They have neither curbed the supply nor reduced the consumption of illegal substances in the United States. In countries across the globe, drug-related problems, such as organized crime, violence, and corruption have worsened as a result. In some countries these issues threaten the political and social stability of the state.

In recent years, some modest changes have been introduced into US drug laws and regulations, and changing public attitudes in the United States and elsewhere may now be opening the way for more substantial reform. The Obama White House has gone further than any previous administration in acknowledging the deficiencies of Washington's drug strategy. It has taken steps toward developing a policy approach that regards drug use and addiction more as health concerns than as criminal activities, and shifts the emphasis from law enforcement toward prevention and treatment. Some in Congress are also pressing for careful review of current drug legislation and a systematic consideration of alternatives. Several state governments have already revised their drug laws and practices and many

Reprinted from Peter Hakim, 2011, *Rethinking US Drug Policy*. Oxford: Beckley Foundation. Reprinted by permission.

others are contemplating changes. Marijuana is now sold lawfully as medicine in more than a dozen states, although, in a referendum last November, California voters rejected legislation that would have fully legalized cannabis sales.

More than ever before, opportunities are emerging for a serious rethinking of US drug policies. Yet, debate and discussion on drug policies is still muted at the national level, and there remains a considerable political discomfort and resistance to engaging with the issues involved. A central roadblock to drug policy reform is the silent tolerance of ineffective, even socially damaging, laws and policies because no specific alternative strategy has yet gathered much public or political support.

What is most needed now is a serious and far-reaching national debate on (1) the effectiveness and multiple costs (social, political, and economic) of current US drug policies and (2) an intense, open-minded search for alternative approaches that could reduce the risks and damage of drug trafficking and abuse.

> The way forward lies in acknowledging the insufficient results of current policies . . . and launching a broad debate about alternative strategies. . . . Each country must face the challenge of opening up a large public debate about the seriousness of the problems and the search for policies consistent with its history and culture.

That was the conclusion of a highly regarded report[1] released last year by a commission of distinguished Latin American leaders, headed by three of the region's most respected former presidents, Fernando Henrique Cardoso of Brazil, Ernesto Zedillo of Mexico, and César Gaviria of Colombia (who also served as secretary general of the Organization of American States). The report *Drugs and Democracy: Toward a Paradigm Shift,* also sets out a framework for an alternative strategy that promises to improve US-Latin American anti-drug cooperation and merits careful consideration in Washington.

What, then, will it take to generate the much needed policy debate and review of US drug policy? We are proposing six US government initiatives, which are discussed further below, that would set the stage for a rethinking of the US approach to illicit drugs. And because the United States exerts

such an enormous influence on global policy worldwide, changes in US laws and policies would profoundly affect the approaches of other governments and multilateral institutions.

1. Support recent Congressional initiatives in the House and Senate to establish commissions to review US anti-drug strategy and related policies, and develop alternative domestic and international approaches. Make sure that all US government agencies cooperate fully in these reviews.

2. Join with other key nations to organize an inter-governmental task force on narcotics strategy that would review and appraise global policy efforts on drugs. The purpose is to assess the costs and effectiveness of bilateral policies and programs and those of multilateral agencies; how they can be made more effective; and how cooperative initiatives can be strengthened.

3. Press for a comprehensive review of existing treaties and obligations that provide the legal underpinnings of the international narcotics regime. Instead of continuing to rigidly support these UN treaties, which have guided global activities for the past two decades, but are now outdated, the US government should be at the forefront of efforts to renew and reform them.

4. Substantially expand data collection and analysis on all important aspects of the drug problem, and the policies and programs designed to address them. Encourage other governments and multilateral agencies similarly to develop better data and statistics on drug-related issues.

5. Finance a range of research and analysis of multiple aspects of the problem—and encourage other countries to do likewise, and make the efforts comparable. Some of this research should be physiological and health related, to better understand the varied effects of drugs—in the short and longer term—and possible ways to reduce addiction and negative side effects. Others should be on the economic, social, and criminal aspects of drug use.

6. Identify drug programs and initiatives at the community, state, and federal levels that promise real benefits in such areas as reducing drug addiction and the health risks of addicts, increasing prospects of training and rehabilitation for those convicted of drug offenses, and decreasing drug related crimes. These initiatives and others should be systematically monitored and evaluated to determine whether they should be scaled up and extended. Other countries should be encouraged to identify and carefully study especially promising anti-drug efforts.

The War on Drugs at an Impasse

Although statistics on drug use in the United States are not fully reliable, the numbers available indicate that US consumption of cocaine and marijuana has been essentially stable for many years—although considerably reduced from its peak in the 1970s and 1980s. The data also show that, today, the United States consumes illegal substances at a rate some three times that of Europe—although the use of drugs in the EU continues to grow rapidly and a few countries actually consume more per capita than the United States. In both the United States and Europe, the wholesale and street prices of cannabis and cocaine have declined in the past several years, although reportedly their potency has increased and demand remains steady. Across the world, illicit drugs appear to be available at stable or declining prices, a recent EU Commission study concluded that global drug production and use remained largely unchanged during the period from 1998 through 2007.

The two pillars of the US battle to keep drugs out of the United States—eradication of source crops and interdiction of illegal narcotics shipments—have lost much of their credibility. They are increasingly judged to be ineffective in reducing the supply of drugs in the United States and other international markets (although it is uncertain what the consequences would be if the United States were to terminate these supply side efforts). From time to time, individual countries have achieved some significant declines in the cultivation, production, or transit of illegal drugs, but these have invariably been offset by increases in other countries—the

so-called "balloon effect." Extensive eradication led to dramatically diminished coca leaf production in Peru and Bolivia in the 1990s, but this, in turn, resulted in a rapid expansion of cultivation in Colombia. When Colombia began to massively spray coca plants, production shifted to other areas of the country. The United States' notable success in closing down drug transit routes through the Caribbean in the early 1990s led to the rerouting of cocaine shipments through Mexico and Central America.

The harm done by the production and trade in illegal drugs, combined with the increasingly well-documented collateral damage from anti-drug efforts, has now extended throughout the Americas. Illicit drugs and associated criminal activity are today critical problems for nearly every nation in the hemisphere.

Latin American and Caribbean countries of the region are no longer merely producers or transit points. Many of them have also become major consumers of drugs, although still at far lower per capita rates than the United States and Europe. No country is safe. Virtually everywhere in the Americas, delinquency, violence, and corruption are fueled by illegal drugs. In some countries, democratic stability is threatened. In many places, ordinary citizens point to exploding criminality and street violence as their nation's single most serious problem.

It is not surprising that Latin American and Caribbean governments have become more and more critical of US anti-drug policies. US drug consumption has long been blamed for crime and violence in the region. Now, increasingly, Washington's anti-drug policies are seen not only as ineffectual, but as actually compounding these problems. This point of view was carefully discussed in the previously mentioned report of the Latin American Commission.

Over the years, US drug policies have regularly provoked tensions between Washington and Latin America. Governments increasingly resent Washington's inflexible approach to fighting drugs and its persistent efforts to impose that approach on the rest of the hemisphere. However, most Latin American governments welcome US cooperation to help confront crime and violence associated with the drug trade.

They are, however, puzzled and frustrated that US government officials and political leaders are unwilling to question Washington's long-standing policies and begin to consider alternative approaches—despite the mounting evidence that US anti-drug programs are ineffective, and in many situations, counterproductive. Latin Americans know that, given the size of the US drug market and Washington's dominant role in shaping international anti-drug policies, no initiative to revise global strategies and put new approaches in place can succeed without US support and leadership. Without a change in US policy, there is little room for most countries to shift their own policies.

No Politically Acceptable Alternatives Yet

US anti-drug policies have not diminished the production or consumption of drugs either in the United States or overseas (although it is hard to rebut the argument that production and use would be much higher in the absence of US efforts). Nor have US initiatives succeeded in reducing the damage associated with the drug trade. In some places, the policies themselves are complicating the problems and creating international ill-will for Washington. Why then have alternative approaches been so staunchly resisted? Why do they remain so politically unpalatable?

Part of the answer is that no existing policy option offers a solution to the problem. No serious analyst suggests that drug consumption can actually be eliminated or even reduced very much. The alternative framework that has gotten greatest attention is not even aimed at curbing drug use. The so-called "harm reduction" approach is, instead, directed toward identifying and putting in place policies, laws, and practices that can diminish the damage that drugs and anti-drug measures do to individuals and their families, communities, and nations. Many advocates of this policy change acknowledge that efforts to lessen the harm that drugs inflict on people and society may actually lead to higher rates of consumption.

Alternatives that do not constrain consumption (and may even lead to greater use) have little appeal to parents who want to keep drugs away from their children—and even less to those who

view drug use through a moral lens, and favor the "no tolerance" approaches that have long shaped US policies. Strategies like harm reduction are complex to explain and do not inspire much enthusiasm. On the contrary, they are easy targets for criticism, and often provoke fervent opposition. They appear nakedly pragmatic, short on principles, and a sign of resignation. They require trade-offs and choices that people do not want to make. Politically, there is not much to be gained by advocating them. Yet they are currently the best available.

Another major hurdle to change is the political and bureaucratic interests in the US government that have developed and hardened over the years, and which today staunchly defend the status quo and consistently resist any fundamental policy shift. Washington's powerful anti-drug agencies have been largely impervious to new ideas.

For a decade or more, policy debates and discussions on the issues and approaches have been muted, and US programs have not been rigorously scrutinized or evaluated. The basic data and information needed to assess the problem and measure policy results has not been routinely collected, analyzed, and made public.

So, What Can Be Done?

Despite the drawbacks, there is a growing convergence among drug policy experts on the core elements of an alternative strategy for addressing the problems associated with illicit drugs. Intellectually, the ground appears increasingly set. Partisan differences are not a major factor. Conservative and liberal analysts have mostly come to the same conclusions. Reflecting this emerging consensus, the Latin American Commission report, entitled *Drugs and Democracy: Toward a Paradigm Shift*, sets out the essential framework and guidelines for developing new, more effective drug policies in the Americas.

- On the demand side of the equation, the Commission calls for policies aimed at reducing the harm associated with the use of illicit drugs. Efforts to eliminate drug consumption are largely futile and often end up increasing the damage to individuals and their families and communities. Evidence drawn from many different countries under very diverse drug control regimes suggests that consumption is just not affected very much by government policies or programs. The elimination or even a significant decrease of drug use is probably not a feasible policy objective in most places.

- The Commission recommends that substance abuse be managed as a long-term health problem, not as a criminal activity. Arresting and imprisoning drug users does little, if anything to reduce consumption, and may cause more harm to the individual and society than the drug use itself. Treatment, not punishment, is the right way to deal with drug addicts and abusers. Although efforts at treatment and rehabilitation so far have had only limited success, some promising approaches have been identified.

- According to the Commission, governments should consider decriminalizing or depenalizing the use and possession of marijuana, the most widely used and least addictive drug. The argument for treating marijuana differently than other illicit drugs is straightforward. Putting an end to the criminal sanctions on marijuana also eliminates most of its harmful consequences—including the crime and violence associated with its production, distribution, and sale; the damage done to the careers and lives of the many young people arrested and imprisoned; the health dangers from unregulated marijuana markets; and the huge financial burdens associated with enforcement (overstretched police and overcrowded prisons and courts, for example). Whether legalization will increase the number of users is uncertain, but what evidence there is suggests the effect will be modest. Several countries in Latin America—and the number is growing steadily—have already stopped punishing marijuana consumption. Although in international forums Washington strongly opposes decriminalizing marijuana, the trend is also beginning to take hold in the United States. By legalizing marijuana for medical purposes, California and a growing number of other states have gone a long way toward making the drug legally accessible to those who want it and signaled the widening tolerance of its use. And Californians will soon have the opportunity to vote on whether to make all marijuana use lawful.

- There is wide agreement that eradication and interdiction have not been effective in curbing the supply of illicit drugs, and have often proven costly and counterproductive. To be sure, they have, at times, succeeded in sharply curtailing the cultivation and transport of illegal drugs. In nearly every case, however, drug activity has simply shifted elsewhere, either within the same country or to other nations. The consensus, however, is weaker when it comes to alternative strategies for restricting drug supplies. Rising incomes in rural areas appear to have been a factor in declining drug crop cultivation in some areas. But rural or alternative development schemes have so far not shown much success in curbing drug planting and harvest. Multiple reasons are offered for their failure—inadequate funding and training of farmers; poor transport and other infrastructure; low and/or volatile prices for alternative crops; and little or no safety nets when there is a poor harvest. In most places where they are grown, no other crop can effectively and consistently compete with coca leaves or cannabis. National development that reaches rural areas and leads to increasing incomes and nonfarm employment may be the only sustainable path to reducing crop production.

- The drug trade is rightfully considered the greatest danger to security and safety in many countries of Latin America and the Caribbean—because of the extreme violence and widespread corruption that is associated with the production, sale, and export of drugs. Indeed, most Latin American governments consider the control of crime and violence—not the elimination of the drug trade—to be their main goal. The Commission endorses the view that national governments need to sustain their battle against drug criminals and cartel leaders in order to provide minimal levels of citizen security and check the growing influence of organized, transnational crime. But the fight against criminal activity, however necessary, has not significantly diminished drug activity anywhere. Colombia succeeded in destroying the huge cartels that once dominated the country's drug business—but it was then taken over by guerillas, paramilitary forces, and new gangs of narco-traffickers. Most estimates suggest that the quantity of drugs produced and shipped overseas has remained largely unchanged.

This widening consensus notwithstanding, the political resistance to changes in US national drug policy is formidable. Even though most Americans believe their country's anti-drug efforts have failed, and the fact that the Obama administration has begun to promote alternative approaches, public discussion and debate on drug policy has been largely muted in the United States. The issue was hardly mentioned in the 2008 presidential campaign, and most politicians today want to avoid taking a stand on the matter.

The main challenge for US drug policy is getting the relevant issues and choices onto the political agenda, and subjecting them to serious scrutiny and debate. Although most Latin American governments would welcome changes in US policy, the central purpose of a new strategy would be to serve the interests of the American people—to enable the United States to deal with its drug problems in ways that are less harmful to its citizens and communities, and allow Washington to work more cooperatively and effectively with other nations to address a critical regional and global problem. A more intelligent drug policy could help remove a major irritant in US relations in the hemisphere: the widespread perception in Latin America that the countries of the region are paying a huge price in violent crime and insecurity because of the US appetite for drugs.

Changing US Views and Attitudes

Evolving public attitudes and a changing US political context—along with changes in Europe and Latin America—may be setting the stage for a shift in US drug policy. Prospects are better today than at any time in living memory for consideration of alternative policy proposals. But still, there are no debates or discussions of these issues.

An increasing number of Americans support major change in US polices. Recent polls suggest that nearly half of all Americans favor legalizing the possession of small amounts of marijuana for personal use—although less than a third favors full legalization.[2] According to a 2008 Zogby poll, some 27 percent of Americans believe that legalizing some drugs is the best way to combat both the international and domestic drug trade. This is more than twice the number who advocate stopping the cultivation of drug crops overseas.

These shifting views appear more and more to be influencing state-level policies in the United States. By allowing marijuana to be prescribed and sold for medical purposes, California has essentially made its use and possession free of criminal penalties—and other states are following suit. Indeed, there are now few places in the United States that actively prosecute possession of small quantities of any drug. Relatively few Americans today are imprisoned for simply using drugs; the great majority of those behind bars have been caught selling or transporting narcotics and have agreed to plead guilty to the lesser crime of possession in exchange for a shorter sentence.

The past two years of economic recession have brought home to many Americans the immense financial and human costs of punitive drug policies. No other country keeps a larger fraction of its population in jail—the consequence of a US anti-drug policy that calls for the long-term incarceration of those involved in narcotics activity. That has now become too expensive, even if it keeps US drug consumption lower than it might be (and there is no reliable evidence that it does). The large and growing public expenditure needed to pay for prisons, and the resulting fiscal drain on states and localities are only part of the price. There is also the disruption of individual lives, the grave damage to families, vastly overburdened courts and police in community after community, and the nation's diminished image abroad.

Economic shortfalls are compelling state and federal officials to consider alternatives to long-term imprisonment. An increasing number of states are establishing special courts to deal in a more targeted way with drug offenders; the exceptionally harsh sentences established for crack cocaine are being eliminated; and parole and treatment options are getting more attention. The trend toward de facto decriminalization of marijuana use may be also linked to the high cost of penalizing it.

Another factor causing Americans to reconsider their drug policies is the relentless brutality of Mexico's drug related violence—and the enormous media attention it has received.

Events in Mexico have made US officials and the general public painfully aware of the catastrophic consequences in Latin America of the massive US demand for drugs. It has also made clear how dangerous and destructive the spillover of that violence could be for US border communities and states.

Latin Americans are troubled about US drug policies and how they affect the region—and increasingly, they are making their views known and acting on them. Although few governments have directly challenged Washington on its drug strategy, they are, more and more, adopting the alternative menu of approaches offered by the Latin American Commission report. Even as the Mexican government fiercely battles powerful drug cartels, it has this year legalized possession of small quantities of narcotics. Several other governments in the region (including Colombia, Peru, Uruguay, and Venezuela) have adopted similar laws, and Argentina's Supreme Court recently decided that personal use should not be prosecuted.

Perhaps, most importantly, the Obama White House, more than any previous US administration, is critical of past drug policies and programs and open to new strategies for dealing with drugs and associated problems. Although proposed expenditures on anti-drug measures have not shifted much so far, the president has rejected the outworn "war on drugs" label for US strategy. In May 2010, he announced a revised national policy[3] that would, as recommended by the Latin American Commission report, treat drug use more as a public health issue, not just a criminal matter, and focus on prevention and treatment.

Getting Drug Policy on Washington's Agenda

Still, the shifting attitudes and emerging trends notwithstanding, core US policies, although widely recognized to be failing in their objectives, remain unchanged. They appear stuck on autopilot. Reform of US drug laws and policies is still barely a visible item on the Obama administration's agenda. So far, the changes announced by the White House are mostly of tone and emphasis rather than of policies, programs, and budgets. Drug policy largely remains a marginal matter for Congress.

Fear of illicit drugs—as a source of crime and violence and, even more, as a magnetic temptation for children and teens—is still a powerful deterrent to any public support for relaxation of hard-line, punitive anti-drug policies. The arguments favoring change, moreover, appear to many to be defeatist and unprincipled. They indicate a willingness to tolerate activities that we know to be harmful, dangerous, and immoral.

It will be difficult to persuade Americans and their elected officials to seriously consider the policies of tolerance and accommodation, which are counterintuitive and frightening to many. The first challenge is to generate an honest, well-informed, and wide-ranging exploration and debate on alternative drug policies across the Americas. Such a debate might at least systematically expose the US public and lawmakers to the growing evidence that suggests that alternative policies could reduce the risks and damage of drug trafficking and substance abuse—both in the United States and in neighboring countries.

Some ideas and recommendations for the US government that would help to encourage the much needed debate and reconsideration of US drug policies are:

Better Data and Information

One substantial impediment to informed debate—as well as credible research and ultimately better policies—is the dismal state of data and information on virtually all aspects of the drug problem. The poor quality and inconsistency of basic data frustrates efforts to accurately assess existing policies and programs, compare results across countries, and devise and estimate the impact of new approaches. What information is produced is often not fully accessible, or it comes from agencies that employ different definitions and methodologies, yielding conflicting and confusing results. Moreover, the data and information are mostly gathered and interpreted by agencies committed to the status quo.

According to a recent European Commission report, "There remains a dearth of data or indicators for comparing how one country's drug problem compares to another, for describing how a country's problem has changed over time, or for assessing how drug policy has contributed to observed changes in national drug problems.

Data collection across countries and over time is particularly suspect because of incomparable definitions (for instance of what constitutes a drug offense or a drug-related death) and repeated changes in methodology. Serious policy studies, competent evaluations, and robust debate all require a huge effort to improve and expand the data and statistics on all dimensions of drug activity."[4]

It will never be easy to collect and interpret data or to compile reliable statistics on illegal, underground activities. But much more can be done to fill in basic gaps and remedy the incomplete, inadequate, incomparable, and often contradictory data on drugs. Some areas in which improvements are essential include (1) the number of users of each of the major illicit drugs, the frequency of use, the quantities consumed, and even a rough sense of the effects of use; (2) the charges levied against drug offenders, their treatment by police, courts, and in prison, and what happens to them after release; (3) the quality and prices of illegal drugs in different locations in the United States and worldwide; and (4) the extent of drug cultivation and production in different countries (reconciling the vastly different estimates by UN and US surveys).

In short, data on drug use and addiction needs to be brought up to the standards expected for other major health and medical problems confronting the United States and other nations.

Careful Review and Evaluation of Programs

Like health measures and medical treatments, drug policies and programs should be designed and implemented to assure that the results can be thoroughly reviewed and evaluated. The agencies responsible for collecting and disseminating the data and information, and conducting evaluations, should be independent of those responsible for carrying out these programs. In the short term, it would be helpful for the US government, based on what evidence is available, to do what it can to single out the most promising anti-drug initiatives at the community, state, and federal levels in such critical areas as reducing drug addiction and lowering health risks to addicts, increasing opportunities for training convicted drug offenders, and diminishing drug related crimes. Efforts to intensely monitor and evaluate these initiatives should be quickly put in place, and a few especially strong programs should be scaled up so they can be tested among wider populations. Washington should also be encouraging (and increasing support for) international agencies, foreign governments, and academic analysts to carefully study the costs and effects of policy changes in other countries—for example, Portugal's decriminalization of the use and possession of small quantities of drugs, and Colombia's efforts to promote alternative rural development schemes in areas of intense coca growing.

We need to better understand the effects of the drug problem on individuals and communities, the impact of different responses, and to identify new ways to treat and mitigate harm. Substantially more attention should be given to understanding the multiple issues involved in battling criminal organizations and the violence, corruption, and other damage they perpetrate—and to developing strategies, both national and multilateral, for dealing with them.

US Congressional Commissions

Although President Obama appears ready to consider new approaches to drugs and drug-related issues, so far his administration has mostly continued the anti-drug policies of his predecessors. There has been little public discussion of the issues or choices outside the context of US programs to assist Mexico and Colombia (and more modestly Central America and the Caribbean) to address drug-related crime and violence. And regardless of the administration's preferences, it will be no surprise if the White House, with an already overly ambitious agenda, decides to postpone addressing the politically sensitive issue of narcotics.

Still, the administration should support and encourage the approval of proposed legislation to establish commissions in both the House and Senate to review US anti-drug policies and develop alternative domestic and international strategies. The White House should make sure that all US government agencies are fully forthcoming and cooperative with these congressional inquiries.

An International or Regional Task Force on Drug Policy

The Latin American Commission report has brought much needed attention to the failures of US anti-drug policies, and to the urgency of developing more effective policy approaches to regional and global drug problems. Governments, in this hemisphere and beyond, should recognize the valuable contribution that the report has made to debate and discussion of the issues, and consider how best to draw on that effort, and seek together to develop and mobilize support for new narcotics strategies.

One idea, for example, would be for the US government to promote the organization of an international task force on drugs (that could either be sponsored by the UN or organized as an independent body by a smaller group of governments) to review global policy efforts on drugs. The purpose would be to assess the effectiveness of current guidelines, policies, and programs of multilateral agencies and bilateral programs; how they can be made more effective; and how cooperation can be strengthened.[5]

Important emphasis should be given to scrutinizing the UN resolutions that set the legal underpinnings of the international narcotics regime. These have guided global activities—particularly those of the UN and other multilateral agencies—for nearly 20 years, and need to be revised and updated, taking into account the growing demand for alternative approaches to narcotics control.

A Hemispheric Effort

There is also a strong argument for a hemispheric initiative, perhaps managed by the OAS, given the deepening urgency of drug related problems in Latin America and the Caribbean and the growing thought and attention that governments are now giving to alternative strategies. The Latin American Commission report provides the rationale and needed direction for new policy approaches across the region.

There are several immediate measures that Washington could pursue in support of the report's recommendations. These would be welcomed in Latin America and contribute to stronger regional anti-drug efforts, One important step would be to reorient law enforcement initiatives in the hemisphere so they are less US-centric. Instead, Washington should be actively developing and pursuing cooperative approaches with Latin American governments—not only at a technical and bureaucratic level, but in formulating policies and strategies. To date, these have been mostly drawn up in Washington, with US agencies taking the lead in devising plans for implementing them. Latin American governments should be encouraged to develop their own approaches and cooperate among themselves, as well as with the United States, on drug matters. The hub-and-spoke model, with Washington at the center, needs to be replaced.

The US government might also consider encouraging the OAS to extend its drug activities beyond the solid professional work done by the Inter-American Drug Abuse Commission (CICAD) in the assessment of the anti-narcotics efforts of member countries, and begin systematic efforts to evaluate the policy frameworks for dealing with drug problems in the hemisphere. CICAD can and should play a broader role in regional and national policy development.

Washington should certainly relinquish its dominant, sometimes stifling, role in shaping regional counternarcotics efforts and genuinely cooperate with Latin American governments in developing fresh ideas and strategies.

Notes

1. *Drugs and Democracy: Toward a Paradigm Shift.* Statement by the Latin American Commission on Drugs and Democracy. http://www.drogas edemocracia.org/Arquivos/declaracao_ingles_site.pdf

2. ABC News/Washington Post Poll, April 21–24, 2009; CBS News Poll, March 12–16. 2009.

3. Office of the President of the United States, 2010, *The 2010 National Drug Control Strategy,* http://www.contexto.org/pdfs/USantidrogasres2.pdf

4. Trimbos Institute and RAND, 2009, *A Report on Global Illicit Drugs Markets 1998–2007*, European Communities. http://ec.europa.eu/justice_home/doc_centre/drugs/studies/doc/report_short_10_03_09_en.pdf

5. The ideas for international cooperation put forth by Eduardo Posada in a recent Inter-American Dialogue paper "Reshaping Drug Policy in the Americas: In Search of a Multilateral Approach" are worth exploring. https://www.thedialogue.org/uploads/Documents_and_PDFs/Posada_Paper_September_2008.pdf

For Discussion

1. Hakim argues that "most politicians today want to avoid taking a stand on" US drug policies. Why have politicians avoided the debate?
2. Consider how domestic drug policies in the United States affect other countries.

39

The U.S. "War on Drugs" in Afghanistan

Reality or Pretext?

JULIEN MERCILLE

The US government has used two claims to justify its role in Afghanistan: US involvement is needed to destabilize the Taliban and to reduce the availability of illegal drugs (namely opioids) in the United States and elsewhere. Julien Mercille uses several illustrations to critically examine these claims. He suggests that joint US/NATO strategies in Afghanistan work to maintain the illicit drug trade, and that US military operations in Afghanistan are justified under the guise of the War on Drugs.

Reprinted from Julien Mercille, 2011, "The U.S. 'War on Drugs' in Afghanistan: Reality or Pretext?" In *Critical Asian Studies* 43: 285–309. Reprinted by permission of Taylor & Francis via Copyright Clearance Center.

Mainstream commentary asserts that the United States is conducting a war on drugs in Afghanistan in order to reduce drug consumption in the West and Afghanistan and weaken the Taliban, the alleged culprits behind the trade. In contrast, this article argues that Washington is not conducting a real war on drugs in Afghanistan. This is demonstrated by considering a number of aspects of the war on drugs that show that, up to this day, Washington has consistently supported or tolerated the drug trade. After outlining the components of the conventional interpretation and discussing the writings of selected critical authors, this article's argument will be explained and illustrated through reference to the situation in Afghanistan since 2001. The official war on drugs is systematically contrary to what a real war would entail because it is only those individuals and groups who have links with the insurgency who are targeted, whereas U.S. allies involved in drugs are not. It is therefore asserted that the war on drugs is a pretext to suppress the insurgency, not a real attempt at reducing drug production and consumption.

In recent years, Afghanistan has produced up to 7,700 metric tons of raw opium annually, accounting for 90 percent of global production and valued at about $3 billion in Afghanistan and $60 billion on the streets worldwide (Fig. 39.1).[1] Raw opium and heroin are trafficked out of the country to consumer markets—the most lucrative one being Europe—via three main routes (see Fig. 39.2): through Iran to Turkey and Western Europe; through Pakistan to Africa, Asia, the Middle East, and Iran; and through Central Asia to the Russian Federation. A relatively small amount of Afghan heroin reaches the United States; America's main suppliers are Mexico and Colombia.[2] Afghanistan is also thought to have become the world's leading producer of hashish, of which an estimated 1,500 to 3,500 tons is exported each year. The total export value is unknown, but it is likely to be substantially less than for opiates (about 15 percent according to some estimates). This article is restricted to opiates since our knowledge of the hashish industry is relatively limited.[3]

The Conventional Interpretation

The conventional view of the so-called war on drugs has been presented by a number of current and former U.S. government officials, in particular by assistant secretaries for International Narcotics and Law Enforcement Affairs in the U.S. Department of State and Drug Enforcement Administration officials, and as well in various congressional reports. International drug control institutions such as the United Nations Office on Drugs and

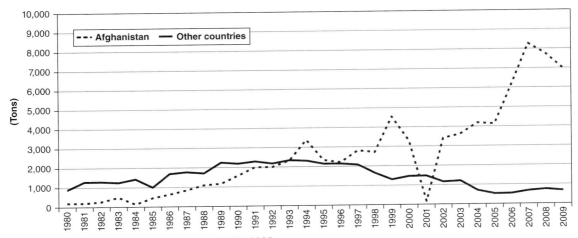

Figure 39.1 Global Opium Production, 1980–2009.
Source: Unodc 2009 [Addiction], 10.

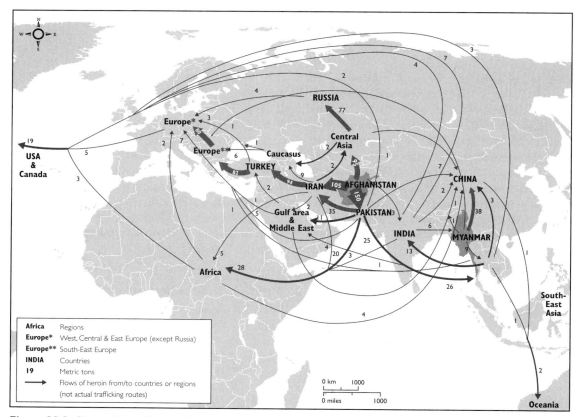

Figure 39.2 Global Asian Heroin Flows.
Raw opium and heroin are trafficked out of the country to consumer markets through Iran to Turkey and Western Europe; through Pakistan to Africa, Asia, the Middle East, and Iran; and through Central Asia to the Russian Federation. A relatively small amount of Afghan heroin reaches the United States; America's main suppliers are Mexico and Colombia. Source: Unodc 2009 [Addiction], 14.

Crime (Unodc) have more or less followed this view, as have a number of scholars and journalists.[4]

Although differences are evident among them, the conventional views essentially make the following points:

- The United States and NATO are conducting a drug war in Afghanistan.
- The Taliban are the driving force behind the Afghan drug industry, while drugs fuel the insurgency by providing significant financial resources.
- The fact that poppy cultivation is concentrated in the south and west of Afghanistan,

regions where the Taliban are most active, suggests that insurgents are responsible for skyrocketing narcotics production.

- The Taliban have recently become involved in the chemical precursors business, giving them an additional source of profits. (Precursors are chemicals that are shipped illegally into Afghanistan and that are used to transform opium into morphine and heroin).
- The Taliban and traffickers launder their drug money using the informal *hawala* financial system, so prevention is difficult.[5]
- Heroin is the world's deadliest drug, adding to the urgency of reducing supply.

- Corrupt Afghan government officials and police are also involved in drugs and benefit financially from it.
- The solution to this problem combines eradication of poppy fields in Afghanistan, arrests of Afghan drug traffickers, and support for "alternative development" to shift farmers away from poppy cultivation and toward other crops or occupations.

Thus, the conventional view holds that the U.S. government and military are concerned about drugs because they are dangerous and harmful substances linked to crime and insurgency. This explains why they conduct operations in Afghanistan to reduce opium and heroin production, a goal they attempt to reach in conjunction with the overarching objective of defeating the Taliban and bringing "stability" to Afghanistan. Because the Taliban are important players in the drug trade—perhaps even the most important ones according to some authors—insurgency and drugs reinforce one another: the Taliban encourage poppy cultivation, and in turn, drug trafficking finances their operations.

Therefore, reducing drug supply will weaken the insurgency, while eliminating militants will lead to a drop in poppy cultivation. The significance of this drug-insurgency nexus is sometimes demonstrated by maps showing that the Taliban are located in the geographical areas where the poppies are cultivated, mostly in the south and west. The problem is compounded by the fact that the Taliban are now involved in the precursor trade from which they draw additional profits. Drug profits are laundered by the informal hawala system, which makes it even more difficult to freeze drug money and trace the traffickers who recycle dirty funds.

Analysts recognize that Afghan government officials and the police derive profits from the drug business, but tend to blame this on corruption, giving the impression that what is needed is to clean up the "bad apples" as opposed to any radical reorientation of U.S. policy. Finally, drug warriors are keen to emphasize operations in supplier countries like eradication, crop substitution, and alternative development.

Proponents of this conventional view are many, but some representative examples will suffice as illustrations. General David Petraeus, then commander of U.S. Central Command and now commander of U.S. and ISAF (International Security Assistance Force) forces in Afghanistan, spoke for many when he told the U.S. Senate Armed Services Committee in March 2010, "Another major component of our strategy is to disrupt narcotics trafficking, which provides significant funding to the Taliban insurgency. This drug money has been the oxygen in the air that allows these groups to operate."[6] Gretchen Peters, in her book *Seeds of Terror: How Heroin Is Bankrolling the Taliban and al Qaeda*, argues: "The union of narco-traffickers, terrorist groups, and the international criminal underworld is the new axis of evil. It doesn't stop at Afghanistan's porous borders." Further, "In terms of market share, this coalition [of Taliban insurgents and drug traffickers] has quickly become dominant: opium produced in southern provinces where the insurgency reaps financial benefits accounted for roughly 80 percent of global supply in 2008."[7] Likewise, the U.S. State Department maintains,

> The connection between poppy cultivation, the narcotics trade, and insurgency groups became more evident in 2009; nearly all significant poppy cultivation now occurs in areas with active insurgent elements. Cultivation was largely confined to six provinces in the south and west of the country. Narcotics traffickers provide revenue and material support, such as vehicles, weapons, and shelter, to the insurgents, who, in exchange, provide protection to growers and traffickers and promise to prevent the Afghan government from interfering with their activities.[8]

A recent *National Geographic Magazine* article entitled "Opium Wars" also adopts the same reasoning.[9] It describes and illustrates with pictures how the Taliban are involved in the drug trade while Americans and U.S. Marines work hard to bring agricultural development to the country to wean farmers away from poppy cultivation.

Mainstream commentators disagree among themselves about tactics, asking, for instance, should we prioritize eradication or "interdiction" and the fostering of "alternative livelihoods"? But as is often the case, debates among mainstream analysts reflect those within government circles—in this case between the Bush administration's call for eradication and Obama's preference for interdiction and development. Thomas Schweich, for example, appointed in 2007 by President George W. Bush as coordinator for Counter-narcotics and Justice Reform in Afghanistan, argued strongly in favor of eradication, while a number of (mostly liberal) researchers have contested this method and supported alternative development to wean farmers away from growing poppies.[10] Nevertheless, the mainstream analysts all put the spotlight on "insurgents" and "terrorists" and neglect to examine the U.S. and NATO roles. Vanda Felbab-Brown, a political scientist at the Brookings Institution, favors interdiction and alternative livelihoods to fight drug production because such methods do not increase the insurgents' "political capital" (i.e., the popular support they have).[11] But her sight is still squarely focused on "the nexus of drugs and insurgency in Afghanistan," and the point of her book is to advise "governments under attack, such as those of Afghanistan and Colombia" on how to "ultimately prevail over both insurgent forces and the illicit economies from which the insurgents derive much of their strength." Peasants and farmers in Colombia and Afghanistan, repeatedly attacked by their own governments and their allies—warlords, paramilitaries, NATO and U.S. troops—might have a different view of the nature of the situation, to say the least. But for Felbab-Brown, the fact that such governments and their allies are directly involved in and benefit from the drug trade is incidental.[12]

A Critical Interpretation

The remainder of this article presents an alternative interpretation of the war on drugs in Afghanistan, arguing that it is not real and suggesting that it is mostly a rhetorical device used by the U.S. government and elites as a pretext for intervention against groups that challenge U.S. hegemony abroad. Other authors have hinted at this interpretation or developed it in regard to other times and places and this paper may be seen as complementing their work.[13]

In this article, U.S. foreign policy is thought to be shaped primarily by American elites' global political economic interests. These consist in expanding markets and investment opportunities, supporting and protecting friendly governments, and fundamentally preserving a "healthy" global economic and political climate conducive to the implementation of those goals, as articulated decades ago in "NSC-68," the document produced in 1950 that outlines U.S. cold war global strategy. Geopolitics is also relevant, as when control is sought over strategic territories in Eurasia to counteract Russia's and China's influence over the continent. Another important U.S. need is to maintain "credibility," a process whereby American officials signal to would-be challengers that defying U.S. hegemony will not be tolerated: failing to respond decisively (which sometimes means militarily) even to isolated instances of independence or defiance could embolden challenges elsewhere. The diplomatic record (declassified and public) of postwar U.S. foreign policy contains many references to such concerns on the part of policy-makers, articulated metaphorically in terms of "falling dominos," "apples in a barrel infected by one rotten one," or a growing "cancer"—all references to perceived threats posed by countries or social movements that pursue an independent course of economic and political development. Such threats need to be checked effectively to prevent further "infection" in other places. In short, interventions by U.S. elites to secure their global interests require pretexts, and I maintain that the war on drugs is one of those.[14]

In order to better explain this article's perspective, the remainder of this section compares and contrasts its argument with those of two important analysts: Alfred McCoy, because his writings on the relationship of the drug trade and U.S. foreign policy have been very influential, and Peter Dale Scott, because his own thesis about this relationship is ambitious and challenging, a thesis that argues a high degree of responsibility on the part of the U.S. government in supporting the global drug trade. It is important to preface the discussion by noting that the interpretation presented in this article has much in common with McCoy's and Scott's and has itself been influenced by their work.

As such, it should be seen as complementing and building on it rather than as entirely distinct and different.

Alfred McCoy has documented extensively the nature of the relationship between the CIA and drug proxies around the globe. He has illustrated clearly the CIA's complicity in the global drug trade since World War II through support for local drug lords who were useful in carrying out U.S. global strategy during and after the Cold War in a number of countries. One point of difference arises, however, with regards to the meaning and uses of Washington's drug wars. This article emphasizes that the United States is not conducting a real war on drugs internationally, only using it rhetorically in order to repress groups or individuals that challenge American power, like the Taliban. In contrast, McCoy accepts that U.S. presidents since Richard Nixon have been waging actual wars on drugs, but he argues that the process has been ineffective and self-defeating because those interventions have resulted in an increased global supply by stimulating production worldwide. For instance, McCoy writes that in the early 1970s, "Nixon had won a total victory in the first of America's four drug wars . . . by applying the full coercive resources of the United States government to eradicate narcotics production at its source," but that unfortunately this victory "unleashed market forces that would ultimately expand the drug trade on five continents," including "Europe and Australia—continents that had been heroin-free for decades."[15] McCoy summarizes nicely his conceptualization of the war on drugs by stating that "the U.S. and UN have persisted, for over fifty years, in a Quixotic, self-defeating strategy that defies the dynamics of the global drug market." He compares the leaders of America's drug wars since the 1970s as being "rather like Mickey Mouse in the animated Disney film *Fantasia*—a 'sorcerer's apprentice' frantic to stem rising waters by attacking the bucket-carrying brooms with an ax, only to have the chips resurrect as full-grown brooms and the flood turn into a torrent."[16]

In contrast, I maintain that the United States has not "persisted for over fifty years" nor "applied its full coercive resources" to fight drugs. There cannot possibly be a war on drugs when Washington has long supported drug traffickers and pursued a number of other policies supporting or tolerating the global drug trade. In sum, whereas McCoy sees a U.S. policy "clash between prohibition and protection during the cold war," I find no evidence of a clash and assert that the ideas of "prohibition" and "drug wars" are simply used as pretexts to carry out policies aimed at maintaining American elites' global hegemony. Therefore, the "war on drugs" works hand in hand with "protection": they both are part of the same process of maintaining elite power.[17]

Peter Dale Scott has been a prolific writer on U.S. politics and drugs and has presented ambitious arguments on the subject, raising a number of key issues, such as the role of Western banks in laundering drug money. This article's main difference with Scott is its interpretation of U.S. foreign policy and its relationship with drugs. Scott tends to conceive of U.S. foreign policy as significantly influenced by secretive groups—see his references to a "global CIA-drug connection," a pragmatic alliance between intelligence services and drug proxies.[18] This leads him to suggest that the U.S. government may have intervened to stimulate the drug trade, perhaps because of lobbying by interested groups, giving rise to a "sustained pattern of [U.S.] intervention in support of drug economies." He observes, "The global drug traffic itself will continue to benefit from the protracted conflict. . . . in Afghanistan, and some of the beneficiaries may have been secretly lobbying for it."[19] Likewise, he wonders whether Washington intervened in Afghanistan in 2001 or elsewhere previously to protect the drug industry in order to stimulate the American economy: "The consistent U.S. recourse to actions that have built up the global drug traffic raises an analogous question: Did the United States seek to maintain control over the global drug economy to ensure that its riches would strengthen the U.S. economy and to deny them to communist enemies?" Suggestively he points to the fact that "the U.S. military intervention in Afghanistan in 2001 was accompanied by restoration of opium for the world market" because the Taliban had successfully eliminated poppy cultivation on the eve of the 2001 U.S. invasion of Afghanistan through a ban on cultivation starting in 2000.[20]

I contend that available evidence does not support such arguments—as Scott himself concedes when he writes: "I have no evidence that the U.S. government intervened militarily as a conscious means of maintaining control over the global drug traffic."[21] This article emphasizes that U.S. foreign policy is shaped by broad political economic imperatives and it is unlikely that particular groups like the CIA or drug traffickers would be able to push government policies in directions that depart fundamentally from the elite interests that are predominant. Thus, although it will take some time before we have access to the internal records outlining Bush administration thinking on the attack on Afghanistan, I argue that the United States intervened in Afghanistan for the same reasons it has intervened overseas for decades, namely, to maintain credibility by attacking al-Qaeda after 9/11 to show the world and other would-be challengers that defiance will not be tolerated. Further, Afghanistan's location is of great geostrategic value—as the Carter Doctrine made explicit in 1980—near the Persian Gulf's energy reserves, while providing the U.S./NATO with a foothold in Eurasia, with opportunities to challenge the consolidation of the Shanghai Cooperation Organization, led by Russia and China, on the continent.[22]

It is also unlikely that U.S. officials would have been so worried about the Taliban cultivation ban as to wish to intervene to repeal it. As well-informed observers have noted, it was doubtful that the Taliban could have maintained their ban for long because it cut off a vital means of survival for farmers in the countryside—it was effectively "an act of economic suicide" that created popular resentment against the Taliban regime, which is one reason why it imploded rapidly after the United States attacked. David Macdonald, who has worked for years with Unodc in Afghanistan and the Ministry of Counter Narcotics in Kabul, reported that the ban "was initiated by the Taliban in the knowledge, at least by some ranking Talib, that it could be no more than a temporary, and unsustainable, measure"; the ban put many farmers in debt, and "if the Taliban had continued with the ban they would have run the risk of a revolt from many of the farming communities left more debt-ridden because of the ban."[23]

Finally, even if the Taliban had been able to wipe out all drug production in Afghanistan permanently, new production would most probably have emerged in other countries to meet world demand for narcotics, preserving the global drug trade.

The remainder of this article argues that Washington is not conducting a real war on drugs in Afghanistan, because in so many cases, U.S./NATO policies are exactly the opposite of what such a war would entail, and their efforts have even led to increases in opium production in Afghanistan, which skyrocketed from 185 tons in 2001 to 6,900 tons in 2009.[24] This will be discussed through the cases of the respective roles played by the Taliban and local U.S. allies in drug trafficking; the geographical fallacy of focusing almost exclusively on poppy cultivation while neglecting drug money; the sources of chemical precursors used to make heroin; drug money laundering; U.S./Western support for the world's most lethal drugs, tobacco and alcohol; and the emphasis on drug control policies that are ineffective (enforcement and overseas operations) while neglecting those that have been proven to work (treatment and prevention). As will be seen, mainstream commentary glosses over Washington's large share of responsibility for the dramatic expansion in opiate production since 2001, while magnifying the Taliban's role, which available data indicate is minor. Also, identifying drugs as a main cause behind the growth of the insurgency absolves the U.S./NATO of their own responsibility in fomenting it: the very presence of foreign troops in the country as well as their destructive attacks on civilians are significant factors behind increases in popular support for or tolerance of the Taliban, or at least opposition to foreign troops. In fact, as a recent Unodc report notes, reducing drug production would have only a "minimal impact on the insurgency's strategic threat," because the Taliban receive "significant funding from private donors all over the world," a contribution that "dwarfs" drug money.[25]

The Taliban's Role

A Unodc report published in 2009 gives a good example of the conventional view on the Taliban's role in the Afghan drug industry. The report claims that the Taliban draw some $125 million annually from narcotics, resulting in the "perfect storm" of drugs and terrorism heading toward Central Asia and endangering its significant energy resources. Unodc maintains that a decade ago the Taliban earned $85 million per year from drugs, but since 2005 this figure has jumped to $125 million. Although this is presented as a significant increase, the Taliban play a more minor role in the opium economy than the report would have us believe and drug money is likely a secondary source of funding for them. Indeed, Unodc itself estimates that only 10 to 15 percent of Taliban funding is drawn from drugs and 85 percent comes from "non-opium sources" such as private donations.[26]

The total revenue generated by opiates within Afghanistan is about $3 billion per year. According to Unodc, the Taliban get only 4 percent of this sum. Farmers selling their opium harvest to traffickers get 21 percent. And the remaining 75 percent? Al-Qaeda? No: the report specifies that al-Qaeda "does not appear to have a direct role in the Afghan opiates trade," although it may participate in "low-level drugs and/or arms smuggling" along the Pakistani border.[27] Instead, the remaining 75 percent is captured by government officials, the police, local and regional power brokers, and traffickers—in short, many of the groups now supported (or tolerated) by the United States and NATO are important actors in the drug trade. Therefore, claims that "Taliban insurgents are earning astonishingly large profits off the opium trade" are misleading.[28] Nevertheless, Unodc insists on the Taliban-drugs connection but pays less attention to individuals and groups supported by Washington. The agency seems to be acting as an enabler of U.S./NATO policies in Afghanistan: when asked what percentage of total drug income in Afghanistan is captured by government officials, the Unodc official who supervised the above report quickly replied: "We don't do that, I don't know."[29]

The precise share of total drug money in Afghanistan captured by the various actors involved in the trade can only be roughly estimated.[30] One reason is the lack of data due to the illicit nature of this economic activity; another is the difficulty in defining who exactly is a Taliban among all groups opposed to foreign troops. In addition, many players fit in more than one category. For example, a number of traffickers are also police officers: should they be classified as "traffickers" or "government actors"? Similarly, many traffickers are simultaneously allied with the insurgents, government-backed militias, and the police: should they be considered on the government's side or the Taliban's? Answers to such questions determine how drug money captured by the insurgents' allies and the U.S./NATO–backed government is apportioned. Further, other militants tap into the drug trade, in particular, the Haqqani network and the group led by Gulbuddin Hekmatyar. The 2009 Unodc report considered neither one of these groups; had they been included, the total amount of drug money captured by insurgents would perhaps be larger. But perhaps not: because those groups are based partly in Pakistan a portion of their drug money income would not be taken out of the $3 billion Afghan drug trade, but rather out of the $1 billion Pakistani drug trade. This factor would need to be included in the equation, along with the proportion of drug money taken by Pakistani officials, who are U.S. allies.[31]

In short, the Taliban appear to be, in relative terms, minor actors in the drug trade in terms of the income they derive from it. However, this does not necessarily mean that the groups actively supported by the U.S./NATO capture all the money not appropriated by the Taliban, as more or less independent traffickers, militias, warlords, and strongmen capture a portion of the funds. Nevertheless, U.S./NATO forces do not target such groups to the same extent as the insurgents, or at all. But no matter the exact share of drug money captured by the various warring groups, it may be appropriate to conclude this section with one of Gretchen Peters's findings—buried deep in her book, since it contradicts her central thesis: "The Taliban and their allies may be earning hundreds of millions from the drug trade, but one thing almost everyone interviewed for this project agreed on was that crooked members of Hamid Karzai's administration are earning even more."[32] This assessment is corroborated by the fieldwork of David Mansfield, who reports that among Afghans, "there is a growing belief in the south that those working for the government are more actively involved in the trade in narcotics than the Taliban . . . farmers in some of the most rural areas often claim that it is only those in positions of power in their area that can trade illegal drugs."[33]

The U.S. Role

Beyond the numbers just discussed, the broader role of U.S. foreign policy in Afghanistan in supporting the drug trade must be examined. The problem is not that a number of bad apples in the Afghan government and police take part in the narcotics industry, but that the U.S./NATO share a significant part of responsibility in the dramatic expansion of opiates production since 2001 (and since the 1980s).[34] The United States attacked Afghanistan in 2001, in alliance with Northern Alliance warlords and drug lords and showered them with weapons, millions of dollars, and diplomatic support. The empowerment and enrichment of those warlords enabled them to tax and protect opium traffickers, leading to the quick resumption of narcotics production after the hiatus of the 2000–2001 Taliban ban, as many observers have documented.[35]

Therefore, to blame "corruption" and "criminals" for the current state of affairs is to ignore the direct and predictable effects of U.S. policies, which have followed a historical pattern of toleration and empowerment of strongmen involved in drugs. Such local warlords were on the American side during its cold war with China and the Soviet Union and their participation in narco-trafficking enabled them to raise funds and strengthen their position, as numerous researchers have shown. For example, in the 1950s, Washington supported KMT troops stationed in Burma against Communist China; during the Vietnam War, the CIA allied itself with Hmong drug lords in Laos against local communists (the Pathet Lao), and even helped transport Hmong opium with Air America, the CIA carrier. In the 1980s, the U.S.-backed Contras were involved in drug operations to support their fight against the leftist Sandinista government in Nicaragua. In Afghanistan, the United States armed and financed mujahideen fighters against the Soviet invaders in the 1980s. The mujahideen were involved in the opiates trade, with American protection and diplomatic

support, and this helps explain why Afghanistan rose from a minor narcotics producer to the world's main opium supplier (see Fig. 39.1 above).[36]

Impunity and support for drug lords and warlords continues. An August 2009 U.S. Senate report noted that no major traffickers had been arrested in Afghanistan since 2006, and that successful prosecutions of significant traffickers are often overturned by a simple bribe or protection from higher officials, revealing counter-narcotics efforts to be deficient at best—notwithstanding the allocation of $383 million since 2005 to "rule of law" and "justice reform" in Afghanistan by the United States.[37]

True, important figures such as Haji Bashir Noorzai have been arrested, but such arrests are exceptions. Before his arrest in New York in 2005, Noorzai, nicknamed the "Pablo Escobar of Afghanistan" by DEA (Drug Enforcement Administration) agents, had collaborated with the U.S. government, serving as an asset to U.S. agents, even if they were aware of his record as a drug dealer. Why was he eventually taken into custody? In 2004, poppy production was booming in Afghanistan and the United States had to demonstrate it was doing something against drugs. Because the Americans and British and the Karzai administration could not decide on one counter-narcotics policy, they came up with a target everybody could agree on: according to a then U.S. embassy official in Afghanistan, "Zal [Zalmay Khalilzad, former U.S. ambassador in Afghanistan] wanted to find a superficial solution that was high-profile and made everyone happy. . . . That ended up being the arrest of Haji Bashir Noorzai."[38] So much for a real concern with drugs on Washington's part.

Afghan governors and customs and police officials are known to be making large amounts of money by offering protection to drug traffickers. This is why positions like police chief in certain districts can be auctioned off to the highest bidder: a six-month appointment to such a privileged position can go for as much as $100,000. As an official in the Afghan Finance Ministry recently declared: "We all eat corruption and drug money, albeit in different quantities."[39]

Drug control policy is generally overridden by more important foreign policy objectives, as in

2005 when the DEA found nine tons of opiates in the offices of the governor of Helmand, Sher Mohammed Akhundzada. President Karzai removed him from the governorship but soon after appointed him Member of Parliament, where he still sits today. Akhundzada's case has never been investigated, and he has never faced charges. The *New York Times* reported that the DEA had been "thwarted in their attempts to stem drug corruption" by American officials and had been "blocked from taking any action against the governor, who had close ties to American and British military, intelligence and diplomatic officials." Moreover, in 2007 Hamid Karzai appointed Izzatullah Wasifi as anticorruption chief, with responsibility for drugs, even if he had earlier been convicted for attempting to sell heroin worth $2 million on the streets to an undercover agent in Las Vegas, an act for which he served nearly four years in prison in the United States.[40]

More recently, the *New York Times* revealed that Ahmed Wali Karzai, President Hamid Karzai's brother, had long been on the CIA payroll, notwithstanding his probable shady dealings in drugs. But this is only the tip of the iceberg: a former CIA officer asserted, "Virtually every significant Afghan figure has had brushes with the drug trade." Wali Karzai has been tied to narcotics in a number of U.S. intelligence reports. In 2004, large amounts of heroin were reportedly found near Kandahar but Wali Karzai and an aide to President Hamid Karzai made phone calls to officials for the drugs not to be impounded. In 2006, 110 pounds of heroin were found near Kabul, and U.S. officials had clues that the shipment was linked to an intermediary of Wali Karzai's—and yet those events were not investigated further.[41]

NATO forces also contribute to the expansion of the drug industry by sponsoring some of its leading traffickers. A recent New York University report noted that in Badakhshan Province, General Nazri Mahmad, a warlord who "control[s] a significant portion of the province's lucrative opium industry," had the contract to provide security for the German Provincial Reconstruction Team. Another ISAF ally is Colonel Abdul Razik, the leader of a tribal militia and police force on the Afghanistan/Pakistan border that extends across Kandahar and Helmand provinces. ISAF is allied with Razik because he provides security, but he is also involved in narcotics. Finally, NATO's mission is to support the Afghan government, but a 2005 report charged that the parliament included seventeen drug traffickers, in addition to a number of members of criminal gangs and commanders.[42]

Geographical Fallacy

Poppy cultivation has in recent years been concentrated in Afghanistan's south, where the Taliban presence is most extensive. This geographical correlation between cultivation and insurgency is clearly highlighted in mainstream accounts such as Unodc reports, which state that 98 percent of opium poppy cultivation takes place in southern and western Afghanistan, the least secure regions. Maps are often used to illustrate graphically how drugs and insurgency coincide spatially by pointing to the superimposition of areas of cultivation and areas of insecurity—and how this contrasts with the "poppy-free" areas of the north, where there is less militant activity.[43]

It is true that cultivation is concentrated in the south, but there is plenty of drug money in the north and elsewhere—regions over which the Afghan government and foreign troops have more control. Geographically, the fact that drug money and trafficking have spread in almost all areas of Afghanistan can be seen from a map of drug trading centers, literally scattered all over the country (Fig. 39.4).[44] For instance, Balkh Province may be "poppy-free," but its center, Mazar-i Sharif, is awash in drug money. Nangarhar was poppy-free in 2008, although it still remains a province where a large amount of opiates is trafficked. As Afghanistan expert Barnett Rubin noted, some Western officials imply that political elites in northern Afghanistan are engaging in successful counter-narcotics while the southern drug economy expands. But the fact is that, although the commanders who control northern Afghanistan today may have eliminated cultivation, few if any have moved against trafficking. Most of them, it is widely believed, continue to profit from it, and some are believed to have become millionaires.[45]

Precursors

Precursors are the chemicals used to transform opium into morphine and heroin, the most important of which is acetic anhydride. Some commentators have pointed to the possible involvement of Taliban networks in the precursor trade, a claim reinforcing the view that insurgents dominate the drug industry.[46] This claim needs to be put in perspective, however. Although the Taliban surely take a cut out of the precursor trade, Western countries and some of their allies are also involved. For instance, "Europe, China, and the Russian Federation" are "major acetic anhydride sources for Afghanistan."[47] Unodc reported that 220 liters of acetic anhydride were intercepted in 2009 at Kabul airport, apparently originating from France, while Afghan authorities reported that some precursors in morphine laboratories were from South Korea.[48] As such, the International Narcotics Control Board (INCB) stated in its 2009 report on precursors that "control measures applied to internal trade in the European Union appear to be insufficient to prevent the diversion of the substance [acetic anhydride]."[49]

The total value of the Afghan trade in chemical precursors is unclear, but available data suggest the retail value of acetic anhydride alone was about $450 million in 2009.[50] Part of that money returns to Western chemical corporations in the form of profits, but Western businesses do not receive much criticism compared to the Taliban, nor are their factories and labs raided—indicating again that Washington's prime concern is not with drugs, but with the insurgency.

Money Laundering

The conventional view notes that the informal banking network operating in Afghanistan and neighboring countries, called hawala, makes it easy for insurgents to launder their criminal proceeds. For example, Peters argues that we need to bring "transparency" to the unregulated hawala.[51] However, the need to regulate and clean up the formal Western banking system of drug money is much greater, at least for those truly concerned with reducing the size of the drug trade. Indeed, of the annual $65 billion global market for opiates, only 5 to 10 percent ($3 to 5 billion) is estimated to be laundered by informal banking systems, while legal trade activities and the formal banking system launder about 90 percent of global narcotics funds. Furthermore, former Unodc chief Antonio Maria Costa asserted that drug money may have recently rescued some failing banks: "Interbank loans were funded by money that originated from drug trade and other illegal activities," he said, and there are "signs that some banks were rescued in that way." "At a time of major bank failures, *money doesn't smell,* bankers seem to believe," Costa wrote in the 2009 *World Drug Report.*[52]

There is nothing new in this state of affairs. In 1979, the U.S. government launched Operation Greenback to investigate U.S. banks' drug money laundering, but it failed, as President Reagan eased rather than tightened financial regulations and froze the hiring of inspectors, while George H. W. Bush, who led the antidrug effort, "wasn't really too interested in financial prosecution," according to Charles Blau, the chief prosecutor in Operation Greenback at the time.[53] Closer to Afghanistan, the Bank of Credit and Commerce International (BCCI), which ceased its operations in 1991, had shady links with the underworld, including drug traffickers in Pakistan who laundered their drug proceeds through it, while the CIA had its own accounts with the bank for its covert operations. Some have pointed to such ties to explain why New York prosecutor Robert Morgenthau complained that the U.S. Justice Department hindered investigations into the bank's activities. Morgenthau said, "We have had no cooperation from the Justice Department since we first asked for records in March 1990. In fact they are impeding our investigation, and Justice Department representatives are asking witnesses not to cooperate with us." Moreover, as one U.S. intelligence officer observed, "If B.C.C.I. is such an embarrassment to the U.S. that forthright investigations are not being pursued, it has a lot to do with the blind eye the U.S. turned to the heroin trafficking in Pakistan."[54] Clearly, U.S. concern with drug money laundering is highly selective.

Heroin, the World's Deadliest Drug?

Drug warriors point to the fact that heroin is "the world's deadliest drug," causing up to 100,000 deaths

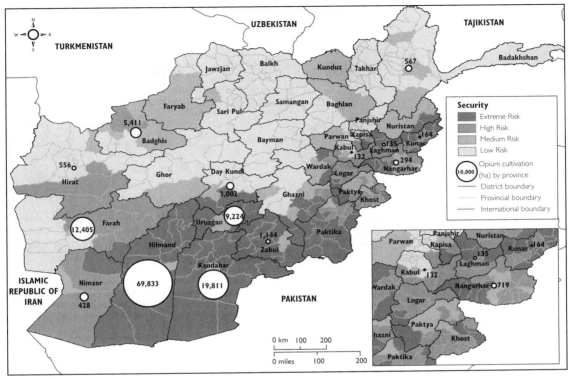

Figure 39.3 Security and Opium Poppy Cultivation, 2009.
Source: Unodc 2009 [Addiction], 107.

per year.[55] Illegal drugs can certainly be dangerous—altogether they kill about 200,000 people every year (including deaths due to HIV/AIDS transmission through needles). However, a real war on drugs should certainly target tobacco and alcohol, the record holders in terms of deaths. According to the WHO (World Health Organization), tobacco kills about 5.4 million people every year—one in ten adult deaths worldwide—and alcohol accounts for 1.8 million additional ones. In the twentieth century, the tobacco epidemic killed 100 million people and the WHO estimates that if present consumption patterns continue, the annual number of deaths will increase to 10 million by the year 2020. Some 70 percent of these will be in developing countries, which are the main target of the tobacco industry's marketing efforts.[56]

Western governments benefit in significant ways from the tobacco industry, as they collect $110 billion in tobacco taxes each year—but they only spend 0.3 percent of it on tobacco control.[57] U.S. companies manufacture 500 billion cigarettes a year and export 100 billion annually. Furthermore, the U.S. government has a record of assisting U.S. firms in breaking import restrictions in developing countries to increase market share. In the 1980s, the Reagan administration pressured Asian countries to open their borders, leading to increases in smoking rates where American companies captured larger portions of markets like South Korea. More recently, researchers have noted that "virtually all trade liberalisation agreements promote trade in tobacco products without consideration of public health concerns," leading to higher consumption through lower prices and increased advertising. This is why tobacco companies like Philip Morris have stated in internal discussions that "Philip Morris strongly supports NAFTA and also supports

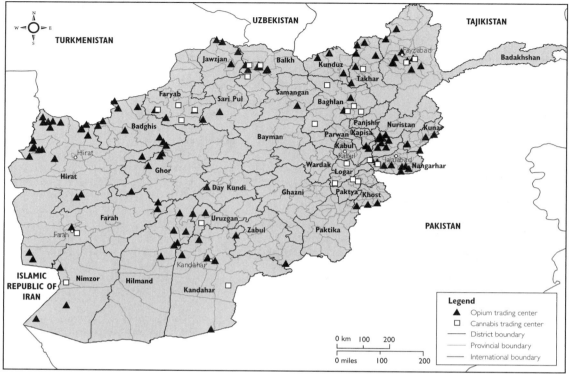

Figure 39.4 Drug Trading Centers in Afghanistan, 2009.
Source: Unodc 2010 (Cannabis), 36.

the Uruguay Round process [to establish the WTO]. . . . The removal of trade barriers will provide us with expanded market opportunities . . . both the NAFTA and the Uruguay Round [are] real 'winners' as far as Philip Morris is concerned."[58]

International Monetary Fund (IMF) policies, shaped by the West, also contribute to spreading tobacco use. The IMF has pushed for tobacco tax and tariff reductions and privatization of state-owned tobacco companies, which has meant massive marketing campaigns that target young people and women, who in many developing countries had traditionally not smoked. The result has been marked increases in smoking and attacks against tobacco control measures by the transnational tobacco companies that have bought the state-owned enterprises.[59]

EU countries also grow tobacco and work to expand tobacco firms' markets. For example, researchers have argued that the UK played a "central

role" in abetting British American Tobacco's campaign to influence EU policy to make it more favorable to its corporate interests by providing "crucial political legitimacy to BAT's campaign for regulatory reform."[60] Moreover, the EU is currently involved in attempting to negotiate a Free Trade Agreement with Thailand in which "the EU insists on covering all areas of trade, while Thailand wants alcohol and tobacco excluded from the talks" for health reasons—a familiar pattern in which profits trump health concerns.[61]

Effective vs. Ineffective Drug Control

Mainstream authors emphasize drug control operations in supplier countries (and incarceration at home) as the way to tackle the narcotics problem. There are tactical debates, in particular between proponents of eradication and alternative livelihoods, but the spotlight remains on overseas producers.

The problem is that drug policy research has consistently found that in order to reduce drug consumption in the West, overseas intervention and incarceration/enforcement at home are the least effective methods. In fact, researchers widely agree that the four most popular methods to control drugs should be ranked as follows, from most to least effective: (1) treatment of addicts (e.g., methadone, counseling); (2) prevention (e.g., school-based campaigns); (3) enforcement (e.g., incarceration); and (4) overseas operations in producer countries (e.g., eradication, crop substitution).

For example, a widely cited 1994 RAND report calculated that "treatment" for addicts domestically was the most effective method for reducing cocaine consumption in the United States; targeting "source countries" overseas was assessed to be twenty-three times less cost effective, "interdiction" eleven times less cost effective, and "domestic enforcement" seven times less cost effective.[62] More recently, a survey of existing drug control research by twelve leading authors corroborated those findings by concluding that "If a society is committed to 'doing something' about its drug problem, a substantial expansion of [treatment] services, particularly for people dependent on opiates, is likely to produce the broadest range of benefits . . . yet . . . most societies invest in these services at a low level, resulting in limited access and inadequate quality." Moreover, "efforts by wealthy countries to curtail cultivation of drug-producing plants in poor countries have not reduced aggregate drug supply or use in downstream markets, and probably never will . . . it will fail even if current efforts are multiplied many times over."[63]

The problem is that the West (and countries elsewhere) has consistently emphasized, over several decades, the strategies that have been shown not to work or for which there is almost no evidence of effectiveness (enforcement and overseas operations), but have neglected those that have been proven to work (treatment and prevention)—another demonstration that drug warriors are not truly committed to combating the drug trade. Europe, the largest consumer of Afghan opiates, has improved its drug policy record over the last two decades by bringing "harm reduction" and

treatment strategies into the mainstream of drug policy, but there is still room for improvement. For example, although opioid substitution treatment and needle and syringe exchange programs now reach more addicts, "important differences between [European] countries continue to exist in scale and coverage"; in particular, "Overall provision of substitution treatment in the Baltic States and the central and south-east European regions, except in Slovenia, remains low despite some recent increases."[64] Leading specialists Peter Reuter and Alex Stevens report that in Britain (whose government was put in charge of counter-narcotics in Afghanistan), "Despite rhetorical commitments to the rebalancing of drug policy spending towards treatment . . . the bulk of public expenditure continues to be devoted to criminal justice measures," so much that "the prison population has increased rapidly in the past decade [and] the use of imprisonment has increased even more rapidly for drug offenders than other offenders. . . . These increases have contributed significantly to the current prison-overcrowding crisis in the United Kingdom."[65]

In short, several decades of drug policy research have shown conclusively that treatment and prevention are the most effective methods to address the drug epidemic, but drug warriors still emphasize the tough, but least effective, methods. Overseas, these methods allow elites to intervene militarily in the pursuit of fundamental foreign policy objectives as seen above. Domestically, although this argument is outside the scope of this article, the war on drugs has often served as a means of social control, for instance, by incarcerating minorities and the underclass.[66]

Conclusion

This article has sought to demonstrate that the U.S. has not been conducting a real war on drugs in Afghanistan because its drug control policies are systematically contrary to what should be done to reduce narcotics production and consumption. It has been suggested that talk of a war on drugs has acted in effect as one more justification for intervention in Afghanistan, in addition to the "war on terror," human rights, and Afghan women's liberation. Indeed, one recurring feature of the official drug war is that U.S. officials use it to arrest or attack only individuals thought to have links with the insurgency, while U.S. allies involved in drugs are tolerated and supported. Therefore, in practice, the war on drugs is not used to target drugs but to target those who oppose U.S. policies in Afghanistan. It is in this sense that the drug war can be interpreted as a device that facilitates the U.S. intervention and counterinsurgency campaign in Afghanistan. The fact that only insurgents are targeted but not drugs has even become official and explicit policy under the Obama administration: his administration has recently elaborated a target list of fifty "major drug traffickers *who help finance the insurgency*" to be killed or captured by the military.[67] This policy is explicitly not against drugs per se because the target is not poppies, heroin or drug labs—it is the insurgency. If traffickers help the Taliban, they will be targeted—but if they support government forces, apparently, they will be tolerated, or even supported.

The policy is being applied on the ground, where U.S. military forces have become closely associated with counter-narcotics operations. For example, in Afghanistan, the DEA is usually focused on prosecuting up to twenty "high value targets," i.e., individuals who are the most wanted drug traffickers in the country from the DEA's point of view. As stated by Michael Braun, a former senior DEA official still involved in operations in Afghanistan, among those twenty individuals, "most, if not all, are members of the Taliban. Those who aren't Taliban are closely linked to the Taliban." The result is that raids end up targeting insurgents. A Senate report noted, "The DEA took down twenty-five heroin processing labs in fiscal year 2009—all of which had ties to the Taliban." Also, in October 2009, the DEA and U.S. military Special Forces, together with the Counter Narcotics Police of Afghanistan and Afghan Army Commandos, raided a major heroin laboratory in Southern Afghanistan where they killed 16 Taliban while seizing almost two tons of opium and heroin. Joint U.S. military-DEA raids like this "are now taking place weekly" in Afghanistan, according to Braun. "Robust military support" is provided to counter-narcotics operations, which "are jointly planned, coordinated, de-conflicted and executed"

by U.S. military and drug control personnel: in short, "U.S. Military Special Forces operators are working shoulder-to-shoulder with law enforcement agents [creating] a counter-insurgency capability that is second-to-none."[68]

Moreover, as the U.S. Senate Caucus on International Narcotics Control noted, "corrupt [Afghan] public officials have rendered many aspects of the counter-narcotics program useless, including using the eradication program as a means of extortion and by robbing alternative livelihood programs of resources intended for the Afghan farmer."[69] Similarly, U.S. government officials told the U.S. Office of the Inspector General, "There is a persistent impression that Afghan Government–led eradication of poppy is highly selective, usually avoiding action against farmers who are politically connected."[70] Therefore, counter-narcotics money also contributes to supporting U.S. allies in the Afghan government who use drug control funds to strengthen their position vis-à-vis their rivals and/or the Afghan population.

Finally, although one can only speculate as to the exact motives that have led the Bush and Obama administrations to gradually increase the intensity of the war on drugs in Afghanistan from 2005 onwards, culminating recently with significantly more engagement on the part of the U.S. military, the fact that this has corresponded with the return of the Taliban insurgency and their gradual involvement in drugs would also seem to suggest that the drug war is invoked when it is useful in justifying the fight against those who oppose U.S. policies. Indeed, until 2005, Washington was simply not concerned with narcotics. The Pentagon thought that eradicating poppy crops would upset farmers and hurt attempts to win Afghan popular support. Also, many Afghan allies drew money and power from the drug industry and therefore, destroying drug labs and poppy fields would have dealt a direct blow to American operations. As a Kabul diplomat conceded in 2003, "Without money from drugs, our friendly warlords can't pay their militias. It's as simple as that." Thus, as James Risen has suggested, the Pentagon and the White House refused to bomb the twenty-five or so drug facilities that the CIA had identified on its maps in 2001 for fear of alienating U.S.-backed warlords involved in drugs who were useful in the U.S. military campaign. Similarly, in 2005, the Pentagon denied all but three of twenty-six DEA requests for airlifts. Barnett Rubin summarized the U.S. attitude well when he wrote in 2004, "When he visits Afghanistan, Defense Secretary Donald Rumsfeld meets military commanders whom Afghans know as the godfathers of drug trafficking. The message has been clear: Help fight the Taliban and no one will interfere with your trafficking."[71] However, in 2005, the United States developed its first counter-narcotics strategy for Afghanistan and drugs moved up slightly on the official agenda. As Vanda Felbab-Brown noted, the intensification of counter-narcotics policies from 2004 onwards "took place against the backdrop of an upsurge in armed opposition to the NATO- and U.S.-backed Afghan national government." In other words, whereas in the years immediately after 2001, it was mostly U.S.-backed warlords who benefited from the drug trade because the Taliban had been routed by the invasion, "since 2005 the Taliban has been able to tap into the drug trade."[72] It would seem it then became useful politically for the U.S./NATO to talk of a "war on drugs" as a reason to fight the Taliban, on top of the "war on terrorism" pretext.

Notes

1. However, total opium production in 2010 is estimated at 3,600 metric tons, a 48 percent decrease from 2009, due in part to diseases that affected opium fields: Unodc 2010 (Survey), 7. Unodc 2010 (Report), 37. On the importance of narcotics to the Afghan economy, see Ward and Byrd 2004.
2. U.S. Department of State 2010, 104. Unodc 2010 (Report), 41–42.
3. On hashish in Afghanistan, see Clarke 2010; Mercille 2010; Unodc 2010 (Cannabis).
4. Beers 2002; Braun 2009; Charles 2004; Davids 2002; Ehrenfeld 2005; Peters 2009 (Seeds); Peters 2009 (Taliban); U.S. Senate, Committee on Foreign Relations 2009.
5. The hawala system is an informal financial transfer system used in Afghanistan in parallel with the formal banking sector. The hawala system handles financial transfers, currency exchange, and often, drug money Under the Taliban regime

(1996–2001), the hawala markets fully replaced the formal banking sector. See Thompson 2006.
6. Cited in U.S. Senate, Caucus on International Narcotics Control 2010, 23.
7. Peters 2009 (Seeds), 22; and Peters 2009 (Taliban), 7.
8. U.S. Department of State 2010, 99.
9. Draper 2011.
10. Schweich 2008.
11. Felbab-Brown 2010.
12. Felbab-Brown 2010, 9, 179.
13. For example, Chien, Connors, and Fox 2000; Chomsky 1992; Chomsky 2000, 62–81; Reinerman and Levine, eds. 1997; Stokes 2005.
14. On NSC-68, see Block 1980. On geopolitics, see Brzezinski 1988. On the need to maintain credibility, see McMahon 1991; and Chomsky 1989, chap. 3.
15. McCoy 2004, 47–48. McCoy develops the same argument in a number of publications: McCoy 2003; McCoy 2000; McCoy 1992.
16. McCoy 2003, 456, 387.
17. McCoy 2003, 459. For an argument similar to this article's on Nixon's drug war, see Kuzmarov 2009.
18. Those secretive forces may even have been responsible for orchestrating events like 9/11, according to Scott, who writes: "As I shall argue, America's major foreign wars are typically preceded by deep events like the Tonkin Gulf incidents, 9/11, or the 2001 anthrax attacks. This suggests that what I call the war machine in Washington (including but not restricted to elements in the Pentagon and the CIA) may have been behind them." Scott 2010 (War), 4; see also Scott 2003 (CIA); Scott 2010 (War); Scott 2007; Scott 2010 (Kyrgyzstan); Scott 2010 (Triumph); Scott 2009.
19. Scott 2010 (War), 237, 232–33.
20. Scott 2003 (Drugs), 28, 33. See also similar comments in Scott 2010 (War), 237, 232–33. Michel Chossudovsky argues a similar point. See Chossudovsky 2004.
21. Scott 2003 (Drugs), 43.
22. For an influential analysis of the importance of Eurasia predating 9/11, see Brzezinski 1998; see also Kolhatkar and Ingalls 2006, chap. 7; Klare 2008.
23. McCoy 2010; Macdonald 2007, 84; Chouvy 2009, 151.
24. Unodc 2010 (Survey).
25. Unodc 2009 (Addiction), 113–14.

26. Unodc 2009 (Addiction) 3, 113.
27. Unodc 2009 (Addiction), 102.
28. Peters 2009 (Taliban), 19.
29. Interview by the author, November 2, 2009.
30. For an excellent account of the structure of the Afghan drug industry, see Shaw 2006.
31. Unodc 2009 (Addiction), 3.
32. Peters 2009 (Seeds), 133–34.
33. Mansfield 2010, 22–23.
34. There are, obviously, other domestic and local factors, but nevertheless, Western intervention has acted as an important stimulus.
35. Chandra 2006, 64–92; Corti and Swain 2009; Rashid 2008; Rubin 2004.
36. Cockburn and St. Clair 1998; McCoy 2003; Scott and Marshall 1998.
37. U.S. Senate 2009; GAO 2010.
38. Peters 2009 (Seeds), 202; embassy official quoted on p. 193.
39. Rashid 2008, 328; IRIN 2010.
40. Risen 2007. See also Pennington 2007; Rubin 2009.
41. Filkins, Mazzetti, and Risen 2009; Risen 2008.
42. Sherman and DiDomenico 2009; Aikins 2005; Wider 2005.
43. Unodc 2009 (Addiction), 106.
44. Unodc 2010 (Cannabis), 36.
45. Rubin 2007.
46. See for instance Unodc 2009 (Addiction).
47. Unodc 2009 (Addiction), 75; see also U.S. Department of State 2010, 79, which reaches similar conclusions.
48. Unodc 2009 (Addiction), 70; Unodc 2008, 156.
49. INCB 2010, 17.
50. Author's calculations from data reported in Unodc 2009 (Addiction).
51. Peters 2009 (Seeds), 231.
52. Unodc 2009 (Addiction), 7; Reuters 2009; Unodc 2009 (Report), 3 (emphasis in original). See also Reuter and Truman 2004.
53. Morley 1989.
54. Quoted in Beaty et al. 1991; see also Cooley 2002, 90–94; Scott and Marshall 1998, xv–xvii.
55. Unodc 2009 (Addiction), 9.
56. WHO 2002; WHO 2008; WHO 2009; WHO n.d.
57. WHO n.d.
58. Shaffer, Brenner, and Houston 2005, 14: ii19–ii25, ii24; the Philip Morris quote is from the text of a discussion document used at a top management

meeting, March 29, 1985, quoted on p. ii23. See also McKee 2009; Zeigler 2006, 25.
59. Gilmore, Fooks, and McKee 2009.
60. Smith et al. 2010.
61. "Thai–EU FTA talks stuck over alcohol, tobacco," *The Nation* (Bangkok), 16 September 2010; Arunmas 2010.
62. Rydell and Everingham 1994.
63. Babor et al. 2010, 255, 254. Nevertheless some good accounts illustrate what drug control in Afghanistan could look like. See, for example Caulkins, Kleiman, and Kulick 2010; Jelsma and Kramer 2009; Mansfield and Pain 2008.
64. Hedrich, Pirona, and Wiessing 2008, 506–7.
65. Reuter and Stevens 2008, 467, 470.
66. For more on the war on drugs as a form of social control, see, for example, footnote 13.
67. U.S. Senate 2009, 1 (emphasis added). See also Risen 2009.
68. Braun 2009, 3–5; U.S. Senate 2010, 2.
69. U.S. Senate 2010, 39.
70. U.S. Department of State and the Broadcasting Board of Governors Office of Inspector General 2009, 22.
71. McGirk 2003; Risen 2006, 154; Meyer 2006; Rubin 2004.
72. Felbab-Brown 2010, 147, 150.

References

Aikins, Matthieu. 2009. "The Master of Spin Boldak." *Harper's*, December. www.harpers.org/archive/2009/12/0082754 (accessed March 2, 2011).

Arunmas, Phusadee. 2010. "Activists Boycott Hearings." *Bangkok Post,* September 30.

Babor, Thomas, et al. 2010. *Drug Policy and the Public Good.* Oxford: Oxford University Press.

Beaty, Jonathan and S. C. Gwynne. 1991. "B.C.C.I.: the Dirtiest Bank of All." *Time,* July 29, www.time.com/time/magazine/article/0,9171,973481,00.html (accessed 2 March 2011).

Beers, Rand. 2003. *Narco-Terror: The Worldwide Connection Between Drugs and Terrorism.* Hearing before the U.S. Senate Judiciary Committee, Subcommittee on Technology, Terrorism, and Government Information. March 13, 2002. Washington, DC: Government Printing Office.

Block, Fred. 1980. "Economic Instability and Military Strength: the Paradoxes of the 1950 Rearmament Decision." *Politics & Society* 10 (1): 35–58.

Braun, Michael. 2009. Statement for the record before the U.S. Senate Caucus on International Narcotics Control regarding "U.S. counternarcotics strategy in Afghanistan." October 21. (accessed June 14, 2010). http://www.drugcaucus.senate.gov/Braun-Statement-10-21-09.pdf

Brzezinski, Zbigniew. 1998. *The Grand Chessboard*. New York: Basic Books.

Caulkins, Jonathan, Mark Kleiman, and Jonathan Kulick. 2010. *Drug Production and Trafficking, Counterdrug Policies, and Security and Governance in Afghanistan*. New York: New York University, Center on International Cooperation. June.

Chandra, Vishal. 2006. "Warlords, Drugs and the 'War on Terror' in Afghanistan: The Paradoxes." *Strategic Analysis* 30, no. 1 (January–March): 64–92.

Charles, Robert. 2004. *U.S. Policy and Colombia*. Testimony before the House Committee on Government Reform. June 17. merln.ndu.edu/archivepdf/colombia/State/33663.pdf (accessed 2 March 2011).

Chien, Arnold, Margaret Connors, and Kenneth Fox. 2000. "The Drug War in Perspective." In *Dying for Growth*, edited by Jim Yong Kim et al. Monroe, ME: Common Courage, 293–327.

Chomsky, Noam. 1989. *Necessary Illusions*. Cambridge, MA: South End Press.

———. 1992. *Deterring Democracy*. New York: Hill and Wang. 107–38.

———. 2000. *Rogue States: The Rule of Force in World Affairs*. Cambridge, MA: South End Press.

Chossudovsky, Michel. 2004. "The Spoils of War: Afghanistan's Multibillion Heroin Trade." April 5. www.globalresearch.ca/articles/CHO404A.html (accessed July 16, 2009).

Chouvy, Pierre-Arnaud. 2009. *Opium: Uncovering the Politics of the Poppy*. London: I. B. Tauris.

Clarke, Robert. 2010. *Hashish!*, 2nd ed. Los Angeles: Red Eye Press.

Cockburn, Alexander, and Jeffrey St. Clair. 1998. *Whiteout: The CIA, drugs and the Press*. London: Verso.

Cooley, John. 2002. *Unholy Wars*. 3rd ed. London: Pluto.

Corti, Daniela, and Ashok Swain 2009. "War On Drugs and War on Terror: Case of Afghanistan." *Peace & Conflict Review* 3 (2): 41–53. Spring.

Davids, Douglas J. 2002. *Narco Terrorism: A Unified Strategy to Fight a Growing Terrorist Menace*. Ardsley, NY: Transnational Publishers.

Draper, Robert. 2011. "Opium Wars." Photographs by David Guttenfelder. *National Geographic Magazine* 219 (2): 58–83.

Ehrenfeld, Rachel. 2005. *Funding Evil: How Terrorism Is Financed—and How to Stop It*. Expanded ed. Chicago and Los Angeles: Bonus Books.

Felbab-Brown, Vanda. 2010. *Shooting Up: Counterinsurgency and the War On Drugs*. Washington, DC: Brookings Institution Press.

Filkins, Dexter, Mark Mazzetti, and James Risen. 2009. "Brother of Afghan Leader Said to Be Paid by CIA." *New York Times*, October 27.

GAO. 2010. *Afghanistan Drug Control*. Washington, DC: U.S. Government Accountability Office. March.

Gilmore, Anna, Gary Fooks, and Martin McKee. 2009. "The International Monetary Fund and Tobacco: a Product Like Any Other?" *International Journal of Health Services* 39 (4): 789–93.

Hedrich, Dagmar, Alessandro Pirona, and Lucas Wiessing. 2008. "From Margin to Mainstream: The Evolution of Harm Reduction Responses to Problem Drug Use in Europe." *Drugs: Education, Prevention and Policy* 15, no. 6 (December): 503–17.

INCB. 2010. *Precursors and Chemicals Frequently Used in the Illicit Manufacture of Narcotic Drugs and Psychotropic Substances 2009*. New York: United Nations Publication.

IRIN. 2010. "Afghanistan: Running on Drugs, Corruption and Aid." May 10. www.irinnews.org/Report.aspx?ReportID=89078 (accessed March 2, 2011).

Jelsma, Martin, and Tom Kramer. 2009. "Redefining Targets: Towards a Realistic Afghan Drug Control Strategy." *Drug Policy Briefing*, no. 30. Amsterdam: Transnational Institute. December.

Klare, Michael. 2008. *Rising Powers, Shrinking Planet: The New Geopolitics of Energy*. New York: Metropolitan Books.

Kolhatkar, Sonali, and James Ingalls. 2006. *Bleeding Afghanistan: Washington, Warlords, and the Propaganda of Silence*. Cambridge, MA: South End Press.

Kuzmarov, Jeremy. 2009. *The Myth of the Addicted Army*. Amherst: University of Massachusetts Press.

Macdonald, David. 2007. *Drugs in Afghanistan: Opium, Outlaws and Scorpion Tales*. London: Pluto.

Mansfield, David. 2010. "Where Have All the Flowers Gone? Assessing the Sustainability of Current Reductions in Opium Production in Afghanistan." Kabul: AREU. May 1.

Mansfield, David, and Adam Pain. 2008. "Counter-Narcotics in Afghanistan: The Failure of Success?" Kabul: AREU.

McCoy, Alfred. 1992. "Heroin as a Global Commodity: A History of Southeast Asia's Opium Trade." In *War on Drugs: Studies in the Failure of U.S. Narcotics Policy*, edited by Alfred W. McCoy and Alan A. Block. Boulder: Westview Press, 237–79.

———. 2000. "From Free Trade to Prohibition: A Critical History of the Modern Asian Opium Trade." *Fordham Urban Law Journal* 28: 307–49.

———. 2003. *The Politics of Heroin: CIA Complicity in the Global Drug Trade*. Rev. ed. Chicago: Lawrence Hill Books.

———. 2004. "The Stimulus of Prohibition: A Critical History of the Global Narcotics Trade." In *Dangerous Harvest: Drug Plants and the Transformation of Indigenous Landscapes*, edited by Michael K. Steinberg, Joseph J. Hobbs, and Kent Mathewson. Oxford: Oxford University Press, 24–114.

———. 2010. "Can Anyone Pacify the World's Number One Narco-State?" *TomDispatch.com*, March 30. www.tomdispatch.com/blog/175225/alfred_mccoy_afghanistan_as_a_drug_war (accessed March 2, 2011).

McGirk, Tim. 2003. "Drugs? What Drugs?" *Time*, August 18.

McKee, Martin. 2009. "Opium, Tobacco and Alcohol: The Evolving Legitimacy of International Action." *Clinical Medicine* 9 (4): 338–41.

McMahon, Robert. 1991. "Credibility and World Power: Exploring the Psychological Dimension in Postwar American Diplomacy." *Diplomatic History* 15 (4): 455–71.

Mercille, Julien. 2010. "Afghan Hash at an All-Time High." *Asia Times online*. April 20, www.atimes .com/atimes/South_Asia/LD20Df02.html (accessed 2 March 2011).

Meyer, Josh. 2006. "Pentagon Doing Little in Afghan Drug Fight." *Los Angeles Times*, 5 December.

Morley, Jefferson. 1989. "Contradictions of Cocaine Capitalism." *The Nation*, October 2. 341–47.

Pennington, Matthew. 2007. "Afghan Anti-Corruption Chief Is a Convicted Heroin Trafficker." *Associated Press*, 9 March.

Peters, Gretchen. 2009 (Seeds). *Seeds of Terror: How Heroin Is Bankrolling the Taliban and Al Qaeda*. New York: St. Martin's Press.

———. 2009 (Taliban). "The Taliban and the Opium Trade." In *Decoding the New Taliban*, edited by Antonio Giustozzi. London: Hurst and Co., 7–22.

Rashid, Ahmed. 2008. *Descent into Chaos*. London: Allen Lane.

Reinerman, Craig, and Harry G. Levine, eds. 1997. *Crack in America: Demon Drugs and Social Justice*. Berkeley and Los Angeles: University of California Press.

Reuter, Peter, and Alex Stevens. 2008. "Assessing UK Drug Policy from a Crime Control Perspective." *Criminology and Criminal Justice* 8 (4): 461–82.

Reuter, Peter, and Edwin Truman. 2004. *Chasing Dirty Money*. Washington, DC: Institute for International Economics.

Reuters. 2009. "UN Crime Chief Says Drug Money Flowed into Banks." January 25.

Risen, James. 2006. *State of War*. London: The Free Press.

———. 2007. "Poppy Fields Are Now a Front Line in Afghanistan's War." *New York Times*, May 16.

———. 2008. "Reports Link Karzai's Brother to Afghanistan Heroin Trade." *New York Times*, October 4.

———. 2009. "Drug Chieftains Tied to Taliban Are U.S. Targets." *New York Times*, August 10.

Rubin, Barnett. 2004. "Afghanistan's Fatal Addiction." *International Herald Tribune*, October 28.

———. 2004. *Road to Ruin: Afghanistan's Booming Opium Industry*. New York: New York University, Center on International Cooperation.

———. 2007. "Counter-narcotics in Afghanistan: First Installment." icga.blogspot.com/2007/08/counter-narcotics-in-afghanistan-first.html (accessed March 2, 2011). August 24.

Rubin, Elizabeth. 2009. "Karzai in His Labyrinth." *New York Times*, August 4.

Rydell, Peter, and Susan S. Everingham. 1994. *Controlling Cocaine: Supply Versus Demand Programs*. Santa Monica, CA: RAND.

Schweich, Thomas. 2008. "Is Afghanistan a Narco-State?" *New York Times Magazine.* July 27.

Scott, Peter Dale, and Jonathan Marshall. 1998. *Cocaine Politics.* Berkeley and Los Angeles: University of California Press.

Scott, Peter Dale. 2003 (CIA). "The CIA's Secret Powers." *Critical Asian Studies* 35 (2): 233–58.

———. 2003 (Drugs). *Drugs, Oil, and War: the United States in Afghanistan, Colombia, and Indochina.* Lanham, MD: Rowman and Littlefield.

———. 2007. *The Road to 9/11: Wealth, Empire, and the Future of America.* Berkeley and Los Angeles: University of California Press.

———. 2009. "America's Afghanistan: the National Security and a Heroin-Ravaged State." *The Asia-Pacific Journal* 20 (3). May 17. www.japanfocus.org/-Peter_Dale-Scott/3145 (accessed March 2, 2011).

———. 2010 (Kyrgyzstan). "Kyrgyzstan, the U.S. and the Global Drug Problem: Deep Forces and the Syndrome of Coups, Drugs, and Terror." *The Asia-Pacific Journal* 28 (3). July 12. www.japanfocus.org/-Peter_Dale-Scott/3384 (accessed March 2, 2011).

———. 2010 (Triumph). "Can the U.S. Triumph in the Drug-Addicted War in Afghanistan? Opium, the CIA and the Karzai Administration." *The Asia-Pacific Journal* 14 (5). April 5. www.japanfocus.org/-Peter_Dale-Scott/3340 (accessed March 2, 2011).

———. 2010 (War). *American War Machine: Deep Politics: the CIA Global Drug Connection, and the Road to Afghanistan.* Lanham, MD: Rowman and Littlefield.

Shaffer, E. R., J. E. Brenner, and T. E. Houston. 2005. "International Trade Agreements: A Threat to Tobacco Control Policy." *Tobacco Control* 14: ii19–ii25.

Shaw, Mark. 2006. "Drug Trafficking and the Development of Organized Crime in Post-Taliban Afghanistan." In *Afghanistan's Drug Industry*, edited by Doris Buddenberg and William Byrd. Geneva: Unodc; Washington, DC: World Bank, 189–214.

Sherman, Jake, and Victoria DiDomenico. 2009. *The Public Cost of Private Security.* Center on International Cooperation, New York University, September 2009.

Smith, Katherine E., et al. 2010. "'Working the System.' British American Tobacco's Influence on the European Union Treaty and Its Implications for Policy: An Analysis of Internal Tobacco Industry Documents." *PLoS Medicine* 7, no. 1 (January): 1–17.

Stokes, Doug. 2005. *America's Other War: Terrorizing Colombia.* London: Zed Books.

Thompson, Edwina. 2006. "The Nexus of Drug Trafficking and Hawala in Afghanistan." In *Afghanistan's Drug Industry*, edited by Doris Buddenberg and William Byrd. Vien: Unodc; Washington, DC: World Bank, 155–88.

Unodc (United Nations Office on Drugs and Crime). 2008. *Afghanistan Opium Survey 2008.* Vienna: Unodc.

———. 2009 (Addiction). *Addiction, Crime and Insurgency: the Transnational Threat of Afghan Opium.* Vienna: Unodc.

———. 2009 (Report). *World Drug Report 2009.* Vienna: Unodc.

———. 2010 (Cannabis). *Afghanistan Cannabis Survey 2009.* Vienna: Unodc.

———. 2010 (Report). *World Drug Report 2010.* Vienna: Unodc.

———. 2010 (Survey). *Afghanistan Opium Survey 2010.* Vienna: Unodc.

U.S. Department of State. 2010. *International Narcotics Control Strategy Report 2010.* www.state.gov/p/inl/rls/nrcrpt/2010/index.htm (accessed March 2, 2011).

U.S. Department of State and the Broadcasting Board of Governors Office of Inspector General. 2009. *Status of the Bureau of International Narcotics and Law Enforcement Affairs Counter Narcotics Programs in Afghanistan Performance Audit.* Arlington, VA: Office of the Inspector General. December.

U.S. Senate, Caucus on International Narcotics Control. 2010. *U.S. Counternarcotics Strategy in Afghanistan.* July, drugcaucus.senate.gov (accessed March 2, 2011).

U.S. Senate, Committee on Foreign Relations. 2009. "Afghanistan's Narco War: Breaking the Link Between Drug Traffickers and Insurgents." August 10. Washington, DC: GPO.

Ward, Christopher, and William Byrd. 2004. *Afghanistan's Opium Drug Economy.* Washington, DC: World Bank. December.

WHO. n.d. "Why Is Tobacco a Public Health Priority?" www.who.int/tobacco/health_priority/en/index.html. (accessed March 2, 2011).

———. 2002. *World Health Report 2002*. Geneva: World Health Organization.

———. 2008. *Report on the Global Tobacco Epidemic, 2008*. Geneva: World Health Organization.

———. 2009. *Report on the Global Tobacco Epidemic, 2009*. Geneva: World Health Organization.

Wilder, Andrew. 2005. *A House Divided? Analysing the 2005 Afghan Elections*. Kabul: AREU.

Zeigler, Donald. 2006. "International Trade Agreements Challenge Tobacco and Alcohol Control Policies." *Drug and Alcohol Review* 25 (November): 567–79.

For Discussion

1. A "drug-terror nexus" refers to the links between the War on Drugs and the War on Terrorism. What are these links?

2. In late 2013, the United Nations reported a 50 percent increase in opium poppy cultivation from the previous year and the largest land use of opium poppy cultivation that had ever been recorded in Afghanistan. Consider these claims in light of Mercille's arguments.